Street by Street

HAMPSHIRE

Enlarged areas ALDERSHOT, ANDOVER, BASINGSTOKE, BOURNEMOUTH, FAREHAM, FARNHAM, GOSPORT, HAVANT, NEWBURY, PORTSMOUTH, SOUTHAMPTON, WINCHESTER

Plus Camberley, Canford Heath, Christchurch, Ferndown, Haslemere, North Tidworth, Poole, Sandhurst, Thatcham, Verwood, Wimborne Minster

2nd edition June 2005

© Automobile Association Developments Limited 2005

Original edition printed May 2001

Ordnance Survey® This product includes map data licensed from Ordnance Survey® with the permission of the Controller of Her Majesty's Stationery Office. © Crown copyright 2005. All rights reserved. Licence number 399221.

Published by AA Publishing, a trading name of Automobile Association Developments Limited, whose registered office (from 1st October 2005) will be Fanum House, Basing View, Basingstoke, Hampshire RG21 4EA.
Registered number 1878835.

Mapping produced by the Cartography Department of The Automobile Association. (A02256)

A CIP Catalogue record for this book is available from the British Library.

Printed and bound by Leo, China

The contents of this atlas are believed to be correct at the time of the latest revision. However, the publishers cannot be held responsible or liable for any loss or damage occasioned to any person acting or refraining from action as a result of any use or reliance on any material in this atlas, nor for any errors, omissions or changes in such material. This does not affect your statutory rights. The publishers would welcome information to correct any errors or omissions and to keep this atlas up to date. Please write to Publishing, The Automobile Association, Fanum House (FH17), Basing View, Basingstoke, Hampshire, RG21 4EA.

Ref: MX08z

Key to map pages	ii-iii
Key to map symbols	iv-1
Map pages - 1:10,000	2-25
Map pages - 1:17,500	26-237
Map pages - 1:25,000	238-357
Index – towns & villages	358-359
Index – streets	360-403
Index – featured places	403-410
Acknowledgements	410

ii

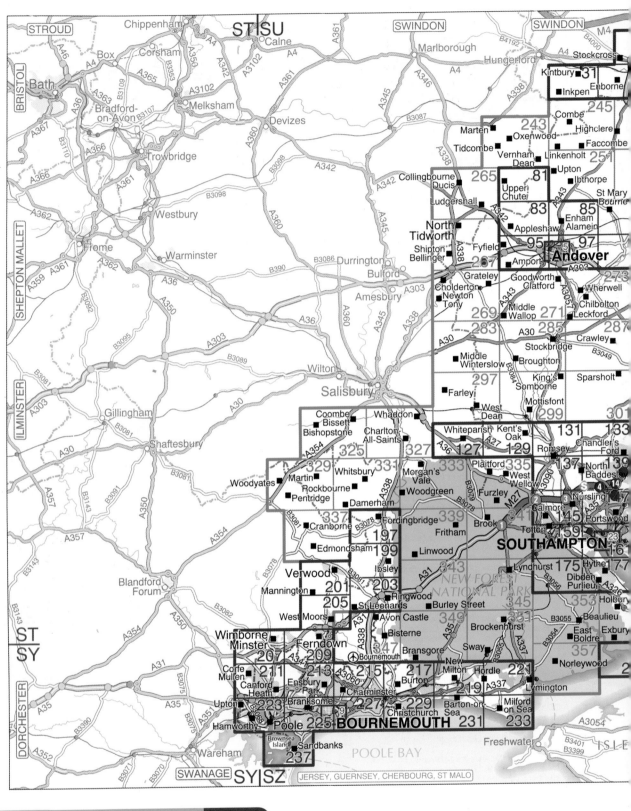

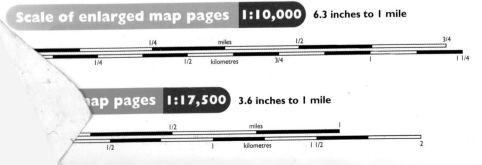

Scale of enlarged map pages **1:10,000** 6.3 inches to 1 mile

map pages **1:17,500** 3.6 inches to 1 mile

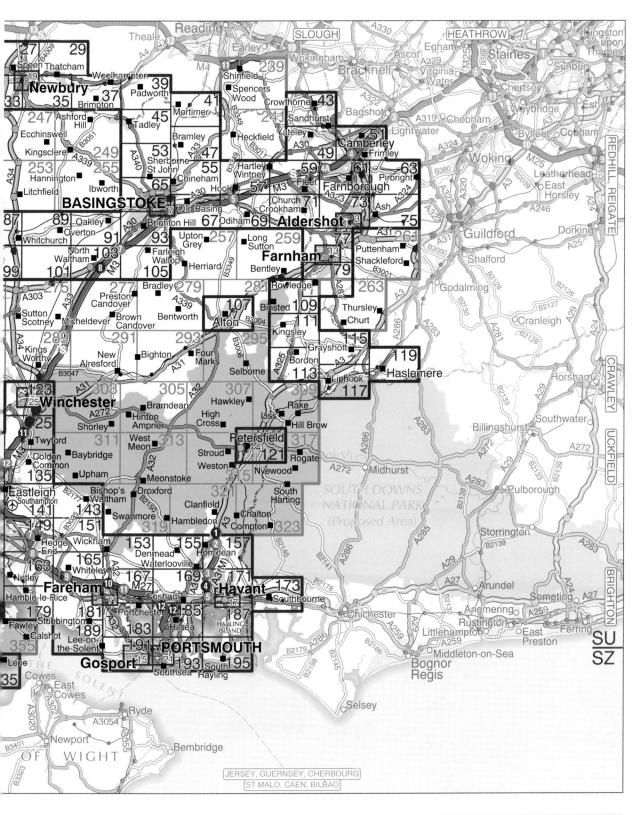

National Grid references are shown on the map frame of each page.
Red figures denote the 100 km square and the blue figures the 1km square.

Example, page 107 : Treloar College 473 141

The reference can also be written using the National Grid two-letter prefix shown on this page, where 4 and 1 are replaced by SU to give SU7341

2.5 inches to 1 mile **Scale of map pages** 1:25,000

Junction 9	Motorway & junction
Services	Motorway service area
	Primary road single/dual carriageway
Services	Primary road service area
	A road single/dual carriageway
	B road single/dual carriageway
	Other road single/dual carriageway
	Minor/private road, access may be restricted
← ←	One-way street
	Pedestrian area
	Track or footpath
	Road under construction
	Road tunnel
P	Parking
P+	Park & Ride
	Bus/coach station
	Railway & main railway station
	Railway & minor railway station
⊖	Underground station

⊖	Light railway & station
++++++++++	Preserved private railway
LC	Level crossing
●—●—●—●	Tramway
------------	Ferry route
....	Airport runway
— · — · — · —	County, administrative boundary
285	Page continuation 1:25,000
93	Page continuation 1:17,500
7	Page continuation to enlarged scale 1:10,000
	River/canal, lake
	Aqueduct, lock, weir
465 ▲ Winter Hill	Peak (with height in metres)
	Beach
	Woodland
	Park
	Cemetery
	Built-up area
	Featured building
⌐⌐⌐⌐⌐⌐	City wall

A&E	Hospital with 24-hour A&E department		⚔	Castle
PO	Post Office		🏛	Historic house or building
📖	Public library		Wakehurst Place NT	National Trust property
_i_	Tourist Information Centre		M	Museum or art gallery
_i_	Seasonal Tourist Information Centre		♟	Roman antiquity
⛽ ⛽	Petrol station, 24 hour Major suppliers only		⚑	Ancient site, battlefield or monument
†	Church/chapel		🏭	Industrial interest
🚻	Public toilets		❀	Garden
♿	Toilet with disabled facilities		◉	Garden Centre Garden Centre Association Member
PH	Public house AA recommended		🌷	Garden Centre Wyevale Garden Centre
🍴	Restaurant AA inspected		🌲	Arboretum
Madeira Hotel ▄▄	Hotel AA inspected		🐖	Farm or animal centre
🎭	Theatre or performing arts centre		🦌	Zoological or wildlife collection
🎥	Cinema		🐦	Bird collection
⚑	Golf course		🦆	Nature reserve
▲	Camping AA inspected		🐟	Aquarium
🚐	Caravan site AA inspected		V	Visitor or heritage centre
▲🚐	Camping & caravan site AA inspected		⛲	Country park
⚓	Theme park		⌒	Cave
⛪	Abbey, cathedral or priory		✻	Windmill
			🛢	Distillery, brewery or vineyard

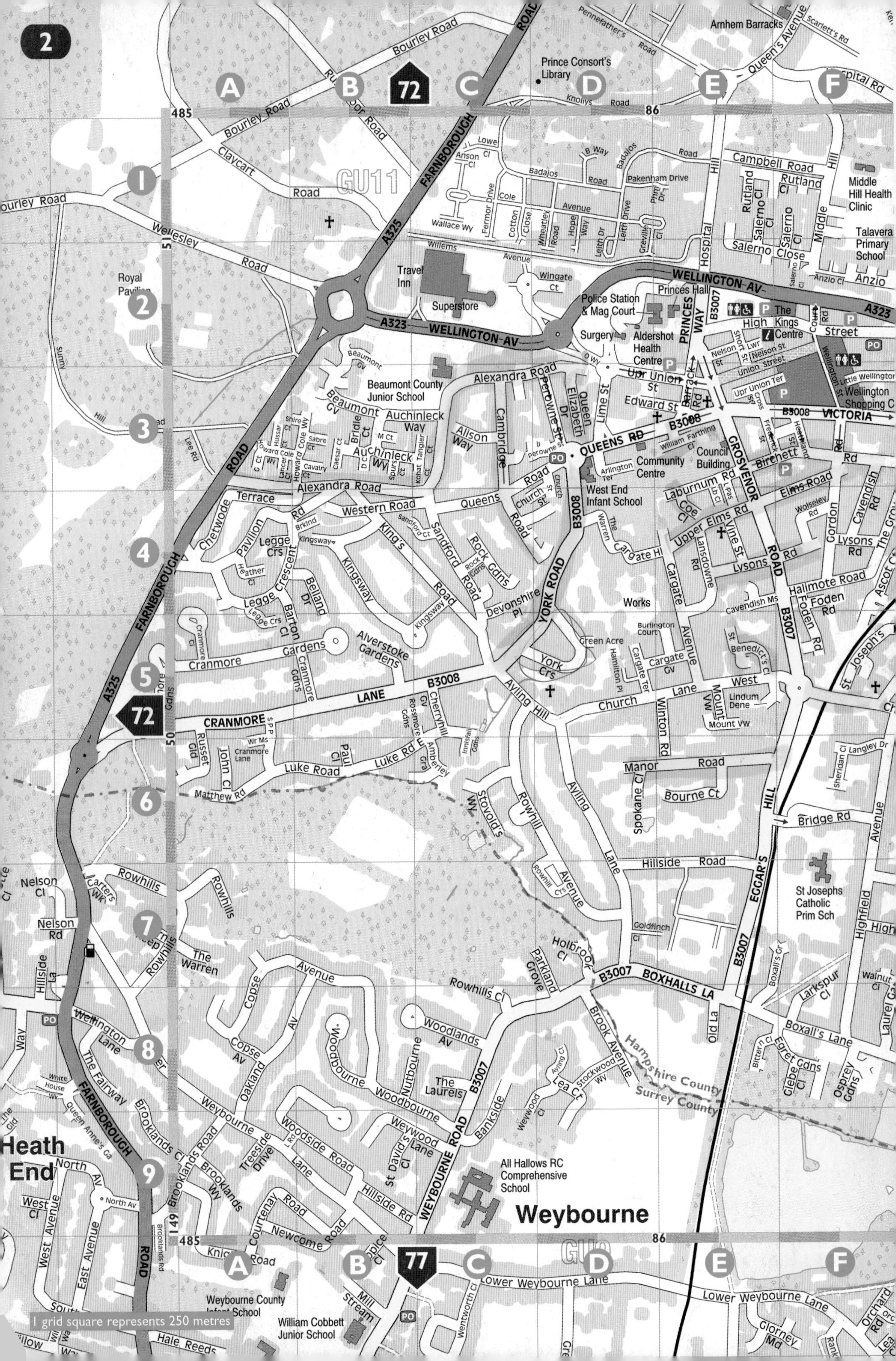
2
72
77
A
B
C
D
E
F
1
2
3
4
5
6
7
8
9
485
86
51
50
149
GU11
GU9
Bourley Road
Rushmoor Road
Claycart Road
Wellesley Road
Royal Pavilion
Sunny Hill Road
Lee Rd
Farnborough Road
A325
A323
Wellington Av
Travel Inn
Superstore
Willems Avenue
Wingate Ct
Pennefather's Road
Arnhem Barracks
Scarlett's Rd
Queen's Avenue
Hospital Rd
Prince Consort's Library
Knollys Road
Lowe Cl
Anson Cl
B Way
Badajos Road
Pakenham Drive
Campbell Road
Rutland Cl
Rutland Cl
Salerno Cl
Salerno Close
Middle Hill
Middle Hill Health Clinic
Talavera Primary School
Anzio Cl
Fermor Drive
Cole Avenue
Cotton Close
Wheatley Road
Hope Way
Leith Dr
Leith Drive
Greville Cl
Wallace Wy
Hospital Hill
Police Station & Mag Court
Princes Hall
Princes Way
Surgery
Aldershot Health Centre
The Kings Centre
High Street
Court Rd
Nelson St
Short St
Union Street
Upr Union St
Upr Union Ter
Cross St
Barrack Rd
Wellington St
Little Wellington
Wellington Shopping Centre
B3008
Victoria
Edward St
Queens Rd
William Farthing Cl
Community Centre
Council Building
Arlington Ter
West End Infant School
Grosvenor Road
Frederick St
Heathland St
Birchett Rd
Laburnum Rd
Elms Road
Upper Elms Rd
Vine St
Lansdowne Rd
Coe Cl
Wolseley Rd
Cavendish Rd
Gordon Rd
Lysons Rd
Lysons Road
Halimote Road
Foden Rd
Cavendish Ms
Ascot Cl
St Joseph's Rd
Beaumont Gv
Beaumont County Junior School
Alexandra Road
Perowne St
Queen Elizabeth Dr
Lime St
Auchinleck Way
Alison Way
Cambridge Road
Bridle Ct
Caesar Ct
Cavalry Ct
Hussar Ct
Shire Ct
Sabre Ct
Lancer Ct
Howard Cole Wy
M Ct
Tangier Ct
Kohat Ct
Spurs Ct
Terrace Rd
Western Road
Queens Road
Church St
Sandford Ct
Sandford Road
Rock Gdns
Kingsway
King's Road
Pavilion Rd
Chetwode Terrace
Legge Crs
Legge Crescent
Heather Cl
Belland Dr
Barton Cl
Devonshire Pl
York Road
York Crs
B3008
The Warren
Cargate Hl
Cargate Avenue
Cargate Gv
Cargate Ter
Works
Burlington Court
Green Acre
Hamilton Pl
St Benedict's Cl
Cranmore Gardens
Cranmore Gdns
Cranmore Cl
Alverstoke Gardens
Cranmore Lane
Russet Gld
John Cl
Wr Ms
Paul Cl
Luke Road
Luke Rd
Cherryhill Gv
Rossmore Gdns
Amberley Gra
Innisfail Gdns
Matthew Rd
Ayling Hill
Ayling Lane
Church Lane West
Winton Rd
Mount Vw
Lindum Dene
Manor Road
Spokane Cl
Bourne Ct
Bridge Rd
Langley Dr
Sheridan Cl
Stovold's Wy
Rowhill Avenue
Rowhill Crs
Hillside Road
Eggar's Hill
B3007
St Josephs Catholic Prim Sch
Highfield Avenue
Goldfinch Cl
Holbrook Cl
Parkland Grove
Boxhalls La
Boxall's Gr
Boxall's Lane
Larkspur Cl
Walnut Cl
Laurel Gdns
Old La
Bittern Cl
Egret Gdns
Glebe Cl
Osprey Gdns
Nelson Cl
Nelson Rd
Carter's Wk
Rowhills
The Warren
Hillside La
Rowhills Cl
Wellington Lane
The Fairway
White House Wk
Queen Anne's Ga
Brooklands Cl
Brooklands Road
Brooklands Wy
Brooklands Rd
Copse Av
Copse Avenue
Oakland Av
Woodbourne
Nutbourne
Woodlands Av
The Laurels
Bankside
Weybourne Road
Weybourne Lane
Weywood Lane
Weywood Cl
Woodside Road
St David's Cl
Hillside Rd
Treeside Drive
Courtenay Road
Newcome Road
Spice Cl
Brook Avenue
Lea Ct
Stockwood Wy
Ayling Ct
Hampshire County
Surrey County
All Hallows RC Comprehensive School
Weybourne
Heath End
North Av
West Cl
West Avenue
East Avenue
Knights Road
Weybourne County Infant School
William Cobbett Junior School
Mill Stream
Wentworth Cl
Lower Weybourne Lane
Glorney Md
Orchard Rd
Hale Reeds
1 grid square represents 250 metres

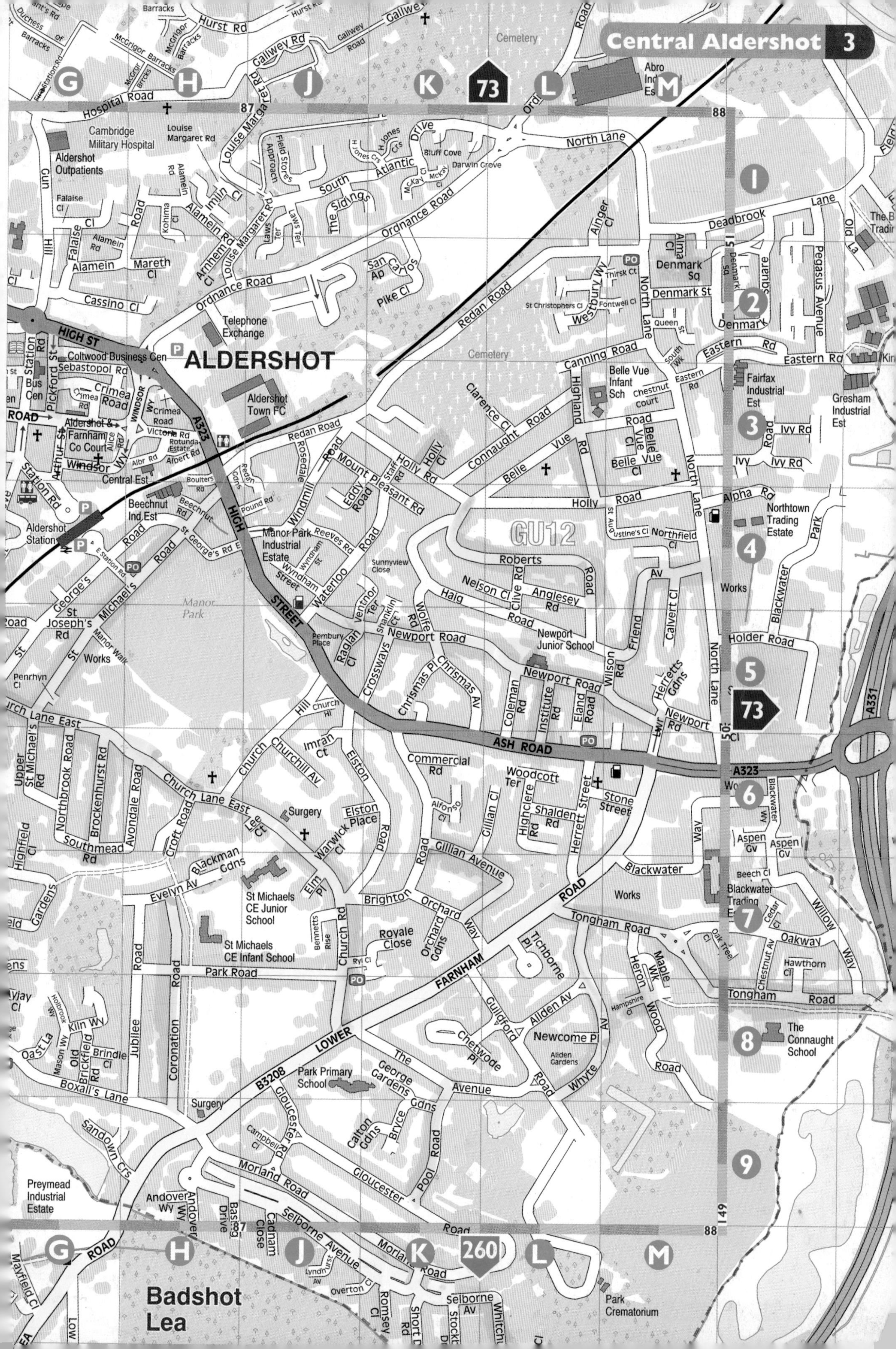
ALDERSHOT
GU12
Badshot Lea
Cemetery
Abro Industrial Est
Cambridge Military Hospital
Aldershot Outpatients
Hospital Road
Louise Margaret Rd
Telephone Exchange
Coltwood Business Cen
Aldershot Town FC
Aldershot & Farnham Co Court
Central Est
Beechnut Ind Est
Aldershot Station
Manor Park Industrial Estate
Manor Park
Sunnyview Close
Belle Vue Infant Sch
Fairfax Industrial Est
Gresham Industrial Est
Northtown Trading Estate
Works
Newport Junior School
Blackwater Trading Est
The Connaught School
St Michaels CE Junior School
St Michaels CE Infant School
Surgery
Park Primary School
Preymead Industrial Estate
Park Crematorium
HIGH ST
HIGH STREET
A323
ASH ROAD
A331
B3208
LOWER FARNHAM ROAD
North Lane
Ordnance Road
Redan Road
Canning Road
Connaught Road
Belle Vue Rd
Holly Road
Eastern Rd
Denmark St
Denmark Sq
Pegasus Avenue
Deadbrook Lane
Blackwater Park
Holder Road
Newport Road
Church Lane East
Tongham Road
Gallwey Rd
Hurst Rd
South Atlantic Drive
Alamein Rd
Cassino Cl
Station Rd
Windsor Wy
Crimea Road
St George's Road
St Michael's Road
Wyndham Street
Waterloo Road
Mount Pleasant Rd
Windmill Road
Haig Road
Roberts Road
Anglesey Rd
Friend Av
Calvert Cl
Wilson Rd
Herretts Gdns
Commercial Rd
Gillian Avenue
Brighton Road
Orchard Way
Church Rd
Park Road
Coronation Road
Jubilee Road
Boxall's Lane
Elston Road
Guildford Road
Allden Av
Newcome Pl
The Avenue
Gloucester Road
Morland Road
Selborne Avenue
Pool Road
Whyte Av
Hampshire Cl
Heron Wood Road
Oakway
Willow Way
Tongham Road
73
260
87
88
149
150
151
G
H
J
K
L
M
1
2
3
4
5
6
7
8
9

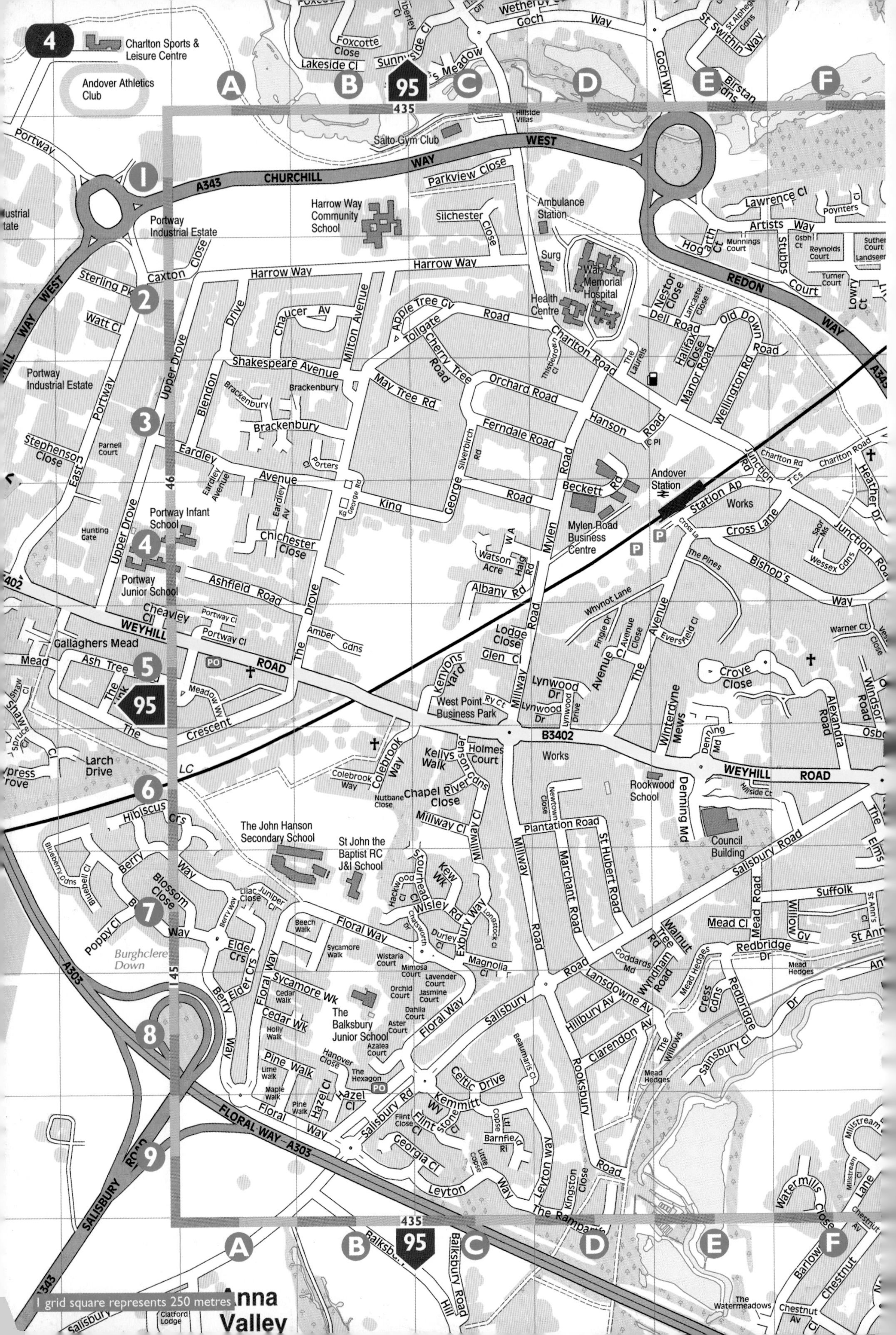

4
Charlton Sports & Leisure Centre
Andover Athletics Club
95
435
Salto Gym Club
Churchill Way West
A343
Portway Industrial Estate
Harrow Way Community School
Parkview Close
Silchester Close
Ambulance Station
War Memorial Hospital
Health Centre
Harrow Way
Caxton Close
Sterling Pk
Watt Cl
Upper Drove
Blendon Drive
Chaucer Av
Milton Avenue
Apple Tree Gv
Tollgate Road
Cherry Tree Road
Charlton Road
Shakespeare Avenue
May Tree Rd
Orchard Road
Brackenbury
Ferndale Road
Hanson Road
Eardley Avenue
King George Road
Mylen Road
Beckett Rd
Andover Station
Station Ap
Mylen Road Business Centre
Portway Infant School
Portway Junior School
Chichester Close
Ashfield Road
Watson Acre
Haig Rd
Albany Rd
Weyhill Road
Gallaghers Mead
Ash Tree
The Link
The Crescent
Portway Cl
Meadow Wy
The Drove
Amber Gdns
Lodge Close
Glen Cl
Lynwood Dr
Kenyons Yard
West Point Business Park
B3402
Works
Colebrook Way
Kellys Walk
Jenson Gdns
Holmes Court
Chapel River Close
Millway Cl
Millway Road
Rookwood School
Denning Md
Council Building
Plantation Road
Marchant Road
St Hubert Road
Salisbury Road
Suffolk
Mead Cl
Redbridge Dr
The John Hanson Secondary School
St John the Baptist RC J&I School
Hibiscus Crs
Berry Way
Blossom Close
Elder Crs
Floral Way
Sycamore Wk
Cedar Wk
Pine Walk
Hazel Cl
The Balksbury Junior School
The Hexagon
Lansdowne Av
Clarendon Av
Rooksbury Road
Celtic Drive
Kemmitt Wy
Georgia Cl
Leyton Way
Kingston Close
The Ramparts
Burghclere Down
Floral Way A303
Salisbury Road
Larch Drive
Redon Way
Lawrence Cl
Artists Way
Bishop's Way
Junction Road
Cross Lane
The Avenue
Avenue Close
Winterdyne Mews
Croye Close
Alexandra Road
Windsor Road
Weyhill Road
Wellington Rd
Old Down Road
Manor Road
Halifax Close
Dell Road
Nestor Close
Hogarth Ct
Stubbs Court
Watermills Close
Millstream Lane
Chestnut
Barlow
The Watermeadows
Balksbury Hill
Balksbury Road
Anna Valley
Clatford Lodge
A343
1 grid square represents 250 metres

G
H
J
K
96
L
M
36
37
46
145
1
2
3
4
5
6
7
8
9
ANDOVER
SP10
ENHAM ARCH ROUNDABOUT
FOLLY ROUNDABOUT
WALWORTH ROUNDABOUT
A3057 NORTHERN AVENUE
A3093 CHURCHILL WAY
A343
NEWBURY ST
NEW ST
A3057 NEW STREET
EAST ST
EASTERN AVENUE
A3057 WESTERN AVENUE
WESTERN AV
WESTERN AVE
WESTERN ROAD
A3057 WINCHESTER ROAD
WINCHESTER ROAD
A303
Camelot Close
Galahad Close
Greenwich Way
Meridian Pk
Works
West March Business Centre
River Way
Superstore
Cusden Dr
Ward Cl
Artists Wy
Moore Cl
Moore Close
Hepworth Cl
Constable Court
Watery Lane
Colenzo Drive
Majorca Av
Toledo Gv
Madrid Road
Vigo Road
Granada Place
March Cl
Main
Barcelona Close
Valencia Way
Corunna
Seville Crs
Household Waste Disposal Centre
Spring Lane
Surg
Pellican Ct
Dances Cl
College Mews
Shepherds
Charlton Road
Cricklade Coll
Cricklade Theatre
Mag Ct
Andover Leisure Centre
Marlborough St
Chantry St
West St
Portland Grove
The Chantry Centre
Bus Stn
County Court
Guildhall
King's Yd
High St
Hlth Cen
Surgery
Andover Museum & The Museum of the Iron Age
St John's Rd
Weavers Cl
Recreation Road
Acre Path
Borsberry Close
Sports Centre
Batchelors Barn Road
Vigo J&I School
Norman Gate School
The Mark Way School
London Road
Stiles Drive
Pearman Drive
Winton Cha
Springfield Close
Harvey Place
Admirals Way
Adelaide Rd
Beale's Close
Eastfield Road
Eastfield Rd
Acre Ct
Rack Cl
Woodlands Close
Tyrells Croft
Sheep Fair Cl
Sidmouth Rd
Walled Meadow
Andover CE Primary Sch
Fire Stn
Clover Mews
Kings Mdw
East St
London Street
Bell Road
Wool Grove
Pen Cl
Highlands Road
Highlands Rd
Shepherds Row
Micheldever Road
Cummins Cl
Beech Gdns
Greenhaven Close
Wolversdene Road
Wolversdene Close
Wolversdene Gdns
Wolversdene Rd
Quality Hotel
Bridge Street
Pol Stn
CAB
Borden Gates
Savoy Cl
Dene Rd
Dene Road
Vincent Drive
Wolverdene School
Love Lane
Heath V
Southview Gdns
Leigh Gdns
Leigh Road
Leigh Cl
Bere Hill Crs
Dene Path
Farrs Avenue
Belmont Road
Belle Vue Road
Hedge End Road
Hedge End Rd
Charnwood Close
Dunmow Road
Winton Road
Old Winton Garages
Ashlawn Gdns
The Mews
Cornfields
End Road
Herons Ri
South Neville Close
Bere Hill Fm
Junction Road
Balmoral Road
Bingo Hall
Leicester Pl
The Broadway
Bentall Pl
Anton Trading Estate
Mill Road
Anton Mill Road
Westview Gardens
South Street
Elm Bank Road
Oak Bank
Humberstone Rd
Croft Av
Winchester Gdns
Coachways
Pitts Lane
Barlows Lane
Anton Road
Anton Junior School
Anton County Infant School
Croft Gardens
Wellesley Rd
Andover Golf Club
Golf Course
Cricketers Way
Swallowfields
Pilgrims Way
Walworth Road
Walworth Rd
North Way
West Way
Humber Court
Mersey Court
Lune Court
Itchen Court
Trent Court
Thames Court
Spey Court
Tyne Court
Wye
Clyde Ct
Forth Ct
Hamble Court
Helford Ct
Medway Ct
Marshall Sq
Jardine Sq
Laker Sq
Graveney Square
Edrich Square
Martin Wy
Dove Cl
Robin Wy
Cricketers Wy
Nelson Walk
Napier Walk
Rodney Ct
Jervis Court
Admirals Court
Somerville Court
Mountbatten Court
Drake Court
Colling Walk
Byng Walk
Beatty Court
Surg
PO

6
65
463
93
A
B
C
D
E
F
1
2
3
4
5
6
7
8
9
53
52
51
RINGWAY NORTH
Priestley Road
Works
Playing Field
Sherborne Road
Upton Crescent
Maple Crs
Oakridge West Community Centre
Oakridge
Oakridge Infant School
Oakridge Junior School
Sutton Rd
Dove House School
Aldermaston Rd S
Tempus Business Centre
Hubbard Road
Millard Close
Osborne Close
Edison Road
Hamilton Close
Houndmills
Telford Road
Knights Park Road
Joule Road
Joule Rd
Hillary Road
Maple Ridge School
St Thomas' Cl
The Vyne Community School
Darlington Road
South View
Gower Cl
Arlott Dr
Merton Road
Lancaster Rd
Lancaster Road
Richmond Road
Queen
Kingsclere Road
Cromwell Road
Vyne Road
Weale Court
Fencott Place
Norden Cl
Lyford Road
Brunel Road
Burgess Road
Soper Grove
Phoenix Pk Terrace
Houndmills Road
Stephenson Rd
Cemetery
Holy Ghost Chapel Ruins
Chapel Hill
Pelton Road
BASINGSTOKE
Basingstoke Station
Clifton Ter
Bunnian Pl
Alencon Link
Winterthur Way
Provident Way
A340
The Malls Shopping Centre
VICTORY ROUNDABOUT
The Anvil Concert Hall
CHURCHILL WAY
CHURCHILL WAY WEST
A3010
Basingstoke Sports Centre
Bus Station
Church Plaza
Millennium Court
Deep La
College Rd
Lower Brook Street
Queen's Road
Brookvale Hall
Welton Ct
Victory Park
University College Winchester (Chute House)
Festival Place Shopping Centre
Ster Century Cinema
THORNYCROFT ROUNDABOUT
WAY WEST
Southend Rd
Essex Rd
Glebe Gardens
Church Cottage
Elbow Cnr
Church St
George Street
Alexandra Rd
Rochford Rd
Rayleigh Rd
Flaxfield Ct
Flaxfield Court
Church Sq
Council Building
King George V Playing Field
Deep Lane
Wilton Place
Basingstoke College of Technology
Hackwood Med Centre
Timberlake Rd
Flaxfield Road
Cross St
Wote St
Superstore
Worting Road
Sarum Hill
Mosque
Seal Rd
Red Lion Hotel
Thornycroft Industrial Est
Kings School
Trinity Church Hall
Haymarket Thtr
Feathers La
Willis Mus
Davy Close
Morse Road
Grafton
Worting Rd
Surgery
Amazon Close
Antar Cl
Attwood Cl
Westdeane Ct
Townsend Cl
Downsland Rd
Roundmead Rd
Winchcombe Rd
Fabian Close
Bramblys Drive
Church Grange & Bramblys Grange Health Cen
Winton Square
Winchester St
Old Mkt Sq
Mkt Pl
London St
Anchor Yard
Victoria Street
New Road
DSS
South Ham Road
RINGWAY WEST
Knight St
Goodman Cl
Knight Street
Stukeley Cl
Fletcher Cl
Longmoor Rd
Bowyer Close
Hamelyn Road
Penrith Road
Chester Pl
Winchester Road
Deane's Almhouses
Southern Road
Aldworth
Sandys Crs
Cemetery
Hamelyn Close
Hardy La
Devonshire Place
Frances Rd
Bounty Road
Beaconsfield Road
Kings Furlong
RG22
Packenham Rd
Mosscrop Court
Bounty Rise
Irish Centre
Fairfields Prim Sch & Arts Centre
Padwick Cl
Hawkfield Lane
Carnival Hall
Fairfields Road
Paul's Rd
Bolton Crs
Elizabeth Road
Packenham Road
Allen Close
Infant School
Kings Furlong Junior School
Pittard Rd
Frescade Crescent
Blair Rd
Hammond Road
Sylvia Close
May's Bounty (Basingstoke & North Hants Cricket Club)
Fairfields Recreation Ground
Montague Place
Castle Road
Council Rd
Cliddesden Rd
Wallis Road
Kimberley Rd
Kings Furlong Centre
Cordale Road
Charles Richards Cl
Portacre Rise
Upr Chestnut Drive
Lwr Chestnut Drive
Kings Furlong Drive
Kingsvale Ct
Wessex Close
Cordale Rd
SOUTH RINGWAY
Diana Cl
South Ham
Culver Road
Queen Marys College
WINCHESTER ROAD ROUNDABOUT
Kipling Walk
St Johns CE Primary School
Cranbourne Secondary School
King's Road
Patrick's Road
Kelvin Hill
Tennyson Way
View Road
Austen Grove
Cobbett Green
A30
Frithmead Close
Schroeder Close
Cliddesden Court
Winchester Road Industrial Estate
Kimbell Road
Lister Road
Wella Road
Cranbourne
Midlane Close
Cranbourne Ct
Horwood Gdns
Hanover Gdns
Anstey Cl
Kingsmill Road
Foyle Park
Coombehurst Drive
Neville Close
1 grid square represents 250 metres
Superstore

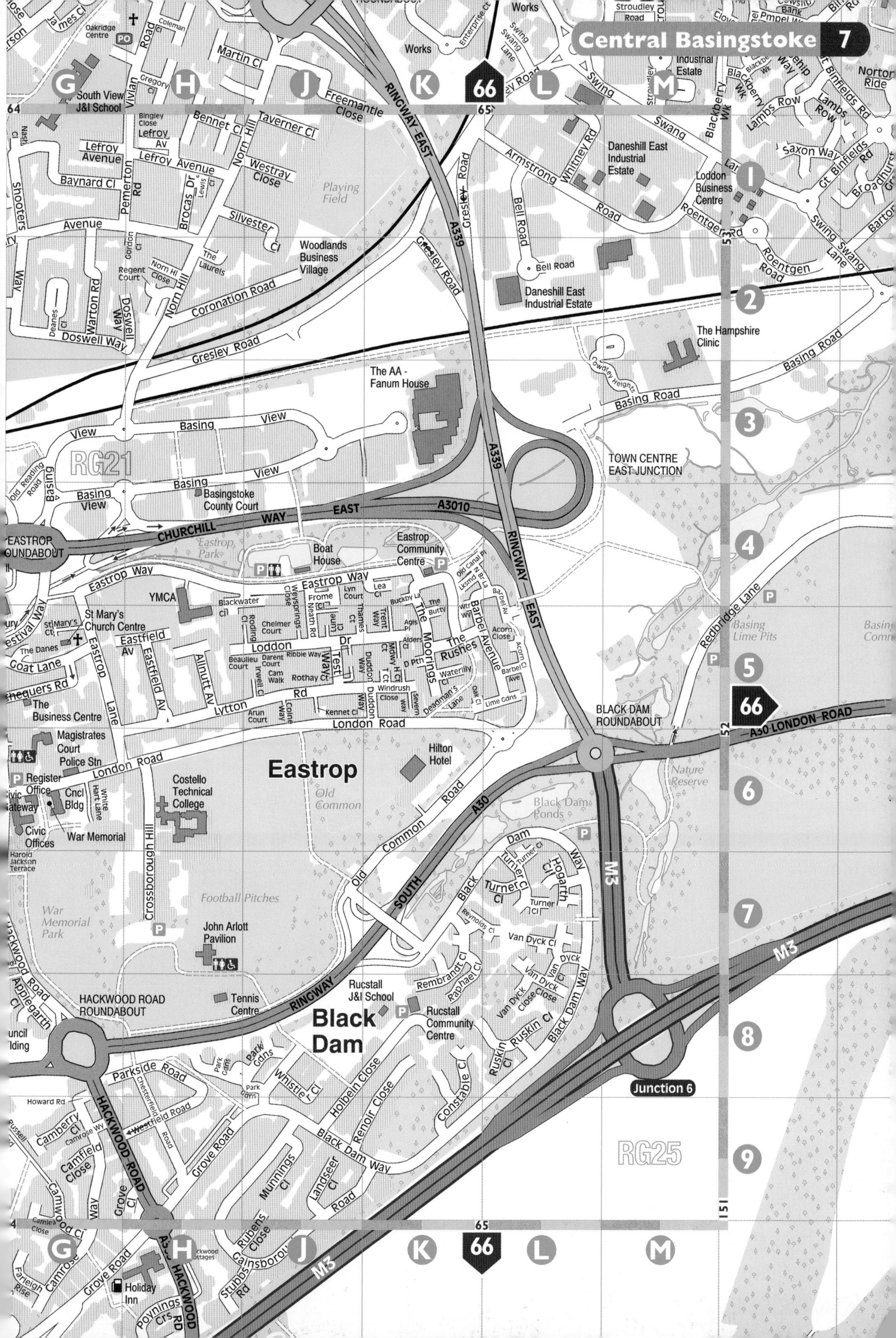
Central Basingstoke
7
66
G
H
J
K
L
M
South View J&I School
Oakridge Centre
Martin Cl
Freemantle Close
Works
Industrial Estate
Stroudley Road
Norton Ride
Lambs Row
Saxon Way
Gt. Binfields Rd
Broadhurst
Swing Swang Lane
Swang
Daneshill East Industrial Estate
Loddon Business Centre
Roentgen Rd
Roentgen Road
Bell Road
Armstrong Road
Whitney Rd
Gresley Road
RINGWAY EAST
A339
Bennet Cl
Taverner Cl
Lefroy Avenue
Lefroy Av
Westray Close
Playing Field
Baynard Cl
Pemerton Rd
Brocas Dr
Silvester Cl
Avenue
Shooters Way
Woodlands Business Village
Regent Court
Norn Hill
Coronation Road
Warton Rd
Doswell Way
Deanes Cl
Gresley Road
Daneshill East Industrial Estate
The Hampshire Clinic
Basing Road
Cowdrey Heights
The AA - Fanum House
Basing View
RG21
Old Reading Road
Basingstoke County Court
CHURCHILL WAY EAST
A3010
TOWN CENTRE EAST JUNCTION
EASTROP ROUNDABOUT
Eastrop Park
Boat House
Eastrop Community Centre
Eastrop Way
YMCA
Festival Way
St Mary's Church Centre
The Danes
Goat Lane
Chequers Rd
Eastfield Av
Eastrop Lane
Loddon Dr
The Moorings
The Rushes
Barbel Avenue
Allnutt Av
Lytton Rd
London Road
Redbridge Lane
Basing Lime Pits
BLACK DAM ROUNDABOUT
A30 LONDON ROAD
The Business Centre
Magistrates Court
Police Stn
Register Office
Civic Gateway
Cncl Bldg
Civic Offices
War Memorial
Eastrop
Hilton Hotel
Costello Technical College
Old Common
Old Common Road
Nature Reserve
Black Dam Ponds
Black Dam Way
Crossborough Hill
Football Pitches
War Memorial Park
John Arlott Pavilion
RINGWAY SOUTH
A30
Turner Cl
Hogarth Cl
Van Dyck Cl
M3
Tennis Centre
Rucstall J&I School
Rucstall Community Centre
Black Dam
Rembrandt Cl
Raphael Cl
Ruskin Cl
HACKWOOD ROAD ROUNDABOUT
Hackwood Road
Applegarth
Parkside Road
Park Gdns
Whistler Cl
Holbein Close
Renoir Close
Constable Cl
Junction 6
Westfield Road
Camberry Cl
Camfield Close
Grove Road
Munnings Cl
Landseer Cl
Black Dam Way
RG25
HACKWOOD ROAD
Rubens Close
Gainsborough
Stubbs Rd
Holiday Inn
Poynings Crs
Grove Road
Farleigh Rise
64
65
51
52
53
1
2
3
4
5
6
7
8
9

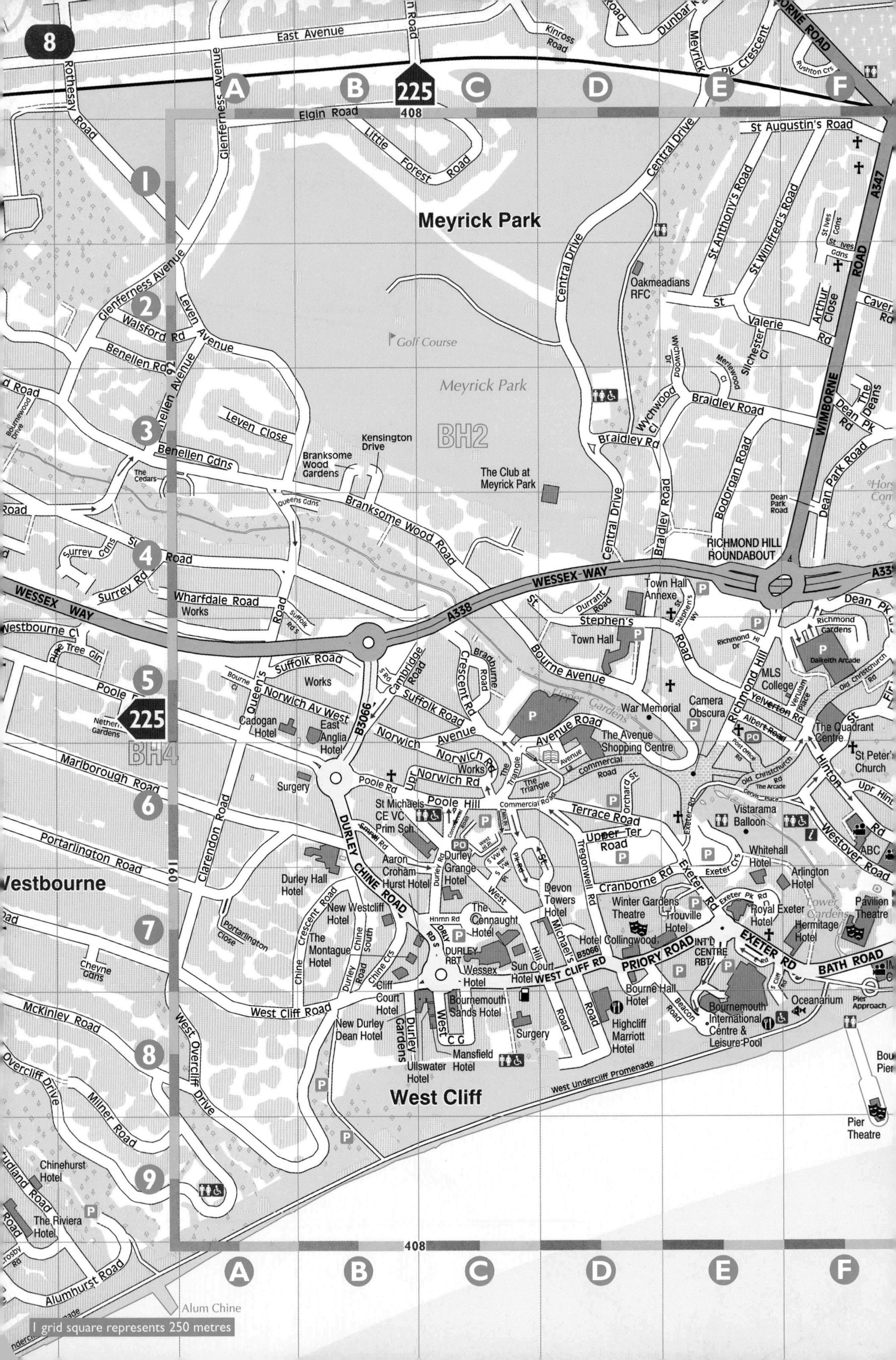

225
A
B
C
D
E
F
1
2
3
4
5
6
7
8
9
408
160
East Avenue
Kinross Road
Dunbar Rd
Meyrick Pk Crescent
Rushton Crs
Rothesay Road
Glenferness Avenue
Elgin Road
Little Forest Road
St Augustin's Road
Central Drive
St Anthony's Road
St Winifred's Road
St Ives Gdns
A347
Meyrick Park
Oakmeadians RFC
St Valerie Rd
Arthur Close
Silchester Cl
Wychwood Dr
Merlewood Cl
Golf Course
Walsford Rd
Benellen Rd
Leven Avenue
Benellen Avenue
Bournewood Drive
Leven Close
Kensington Drive
BH2
Braidley Road
Braidley Rd
Wychwood Cl
WIMBORNE ROAD
Dean Pk Rd
The Deans
Dean Park Road
Dean Park Road
Benellen Gdns
The Cedars
Branksome Wood Gardens
The Club at Meyrick Park
Queens Gdns
Branksome Wood Road
Bodorgan Road
RICHMOND HILL ROUNDABOUT
Surrey Gdns
Surrey Rd
WESSEX WAY
A338
Wharfdale Road
Works
Suffolk Rd's
Town Hall Annexe
Durrant Road
St Stephen's Road
St Stephen's Wy
Town Hall
Dean Pk Cr
Richmond Gardens
Richmond Hl Dr
Westbourne Cl
Pine Tree Gln
Suffolk Road
Bradburne Road
Crescent Rd
Bourne Avenue
Richmond Hill
Daikeith Arcade
Old Christchurch Rd
Bourne Cl
Queen's Road
Cambridge Road
Suffolk Road
Poole Rd
Netherall Gardens
Norwich Av West
B3066
Upper Gardens
War Memorial
Camera Obscura
MLS College
Verulam Place
Yelverton Rd
Cadogan Hotel
East Anglia Hotel
Norwich Avenue
Avenue Road
The Avenue Shopping Centre
Albert Road
Post Office Rd
The Quadrant Centre
St Peter's Church
BH4
Marlborough Road
Surgery
Upr Norwich Rd
Works
The Triangle
Avenue La
Commercial Road
Orchard St
Old Christchurch Rd
The Arcade
Gervis Place
Hinton Rd
Upr Hinton Rd
Poole Hill
St Michaels CE VC Prim Sch
Commercial Road
Terrace Road
Exeter Rd
Vistarama Balloon
Westover Road
Portarlington Road
Clarendon Road
DURLEY CHINE ROAD
Durley Rd
Durley Grange Hotel
Aaron Croham Hurst Hotel
Upper Ter Road
Whitehall Hotel
Arlington Hotel
ABC
Westbourne
Durley Hall Hotel
West Hill Rd
Devon Towers Hotel
Tregonwell Road
Cranborne Rd
Exeter Crs
Exeter Pk Rd
Royal Exeter Hotel
Lower Gardens
Pavilion Theatre
New Westcliff Hotel
Crescent Road
Portarlington Close
The Connaught Hotel
Winter Gardens Theatre
Trouville Hotel
Hermitage Hotel
Cheyne Gdns
The Montague Hotel
Chine Crs
DURLEY RBT
Hotel Collingwood
St Michael's Road
B3066
INT'L CENTRE RBT
EXETER RD
BATH ROAD
Chine
Durley Road
Cliff Court Hotel
Wessex Hotel
Sun Court Hotel
WEST CLIFF RD
PRIORY ROAD
Bourne Hall Hotel
Beacon Road
Bournemouth International Centre & Leisure Pool
Oceanarium
Pier Approach
McKinley Road
West Cliff Road
New Durley Dean Hotel
Durley Gardens
West Cliff Gdns
Bournemouth Sands Hotel
Surgery
Highcliff Marriott Hotel
Overcliff Drive
Milner Road
West Overcliff Drive
Mansfield Hotel
Ullswater Hotel
West Undercliff Promenade
West Cliff
Pier Theatre
Chinehurst Hotel
Studland Road
The Riviera Hotel
Crosby Rd
Alumhurst Road
Alum Chine
Undercliff Promenade
1 grid square represents 250 metres

BOURNEMOUTH
Springbourne
Poole Bay
WESSEX WAY
A338
LANSDOWNE ROAD
HOLDENHURST RD
ST PAULS RD A35
ST SWITHUN'S RD S
CHRISTCHURCH ROAD
A35
GERVIS ROAD
BATH ROAD
East Overcliff Drive
Undercliff Drive
ST PAULS ROUNDABOUT
BOURNEMOUTH STATION ROUNDABOUT
THE LANSDOWNE ROUNDABOUT
ST PETERS ROUNDABOUT
Bournemouth Station
Travel Interchange
Dean Park Cricket Ground
The Bournemouth Nuffield Hospital
Bournemouth University
Bournemouth & Poole College
Bournemouth College
Russell Cotes Art Gallery & Museum
Langtry Manor Lovenest of a King Hotel
Malmesbury Park CP School
St Clements CE Infant School
Bethany CE Junior School
Parkway Retail Park
BH1
226

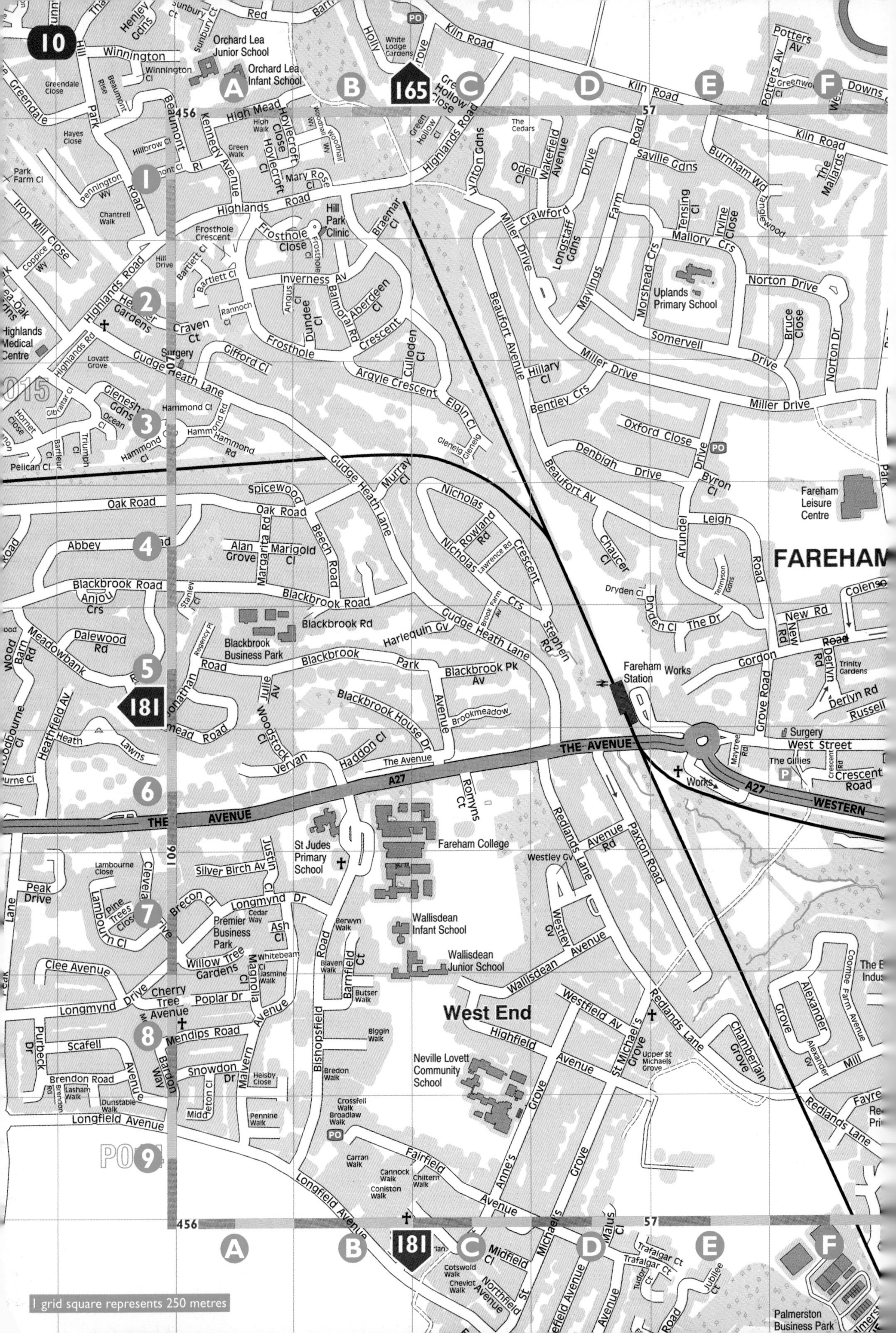
10
165
181
FAREHAM
West End
Orchard Lea Junior School
Orchard Lea Infant School
Uplands Primary School
Hill Park Clinic
Highlands Medical Centre
Fareham Leisure Centre
Fareham Station
Blackbrook Business Park
Fareham College
St Judes Primary School
Wallisdean Infant School
Wallisdean Junior School
Neville Lovett Community School
Premier Business Park
Palmerston Business Park
Kiln Road
Highlands Road
Gudge Heath Lane
Miller Drive
Beaufort Avenue
Oak Road
Blackbrook Road
Blackbrook Park Avenue
THE AVENUE
A27
WESTERN
West Street
Gordon Road
Redlands Lane
Paxton Road
Wallisdean Avenue
Highfield Avenue
Longfield Avenue
Longmynd Drive
Bishopsfield Road
Mendips Road
Fairfield Avenue
Somervell Drive
Norton Drive
Arundel Drive
Denbigh Drive
Frosthole Crescent
Argyle Crescent
Nicholas Crescent
456
57
1 grid square represents 250 metres

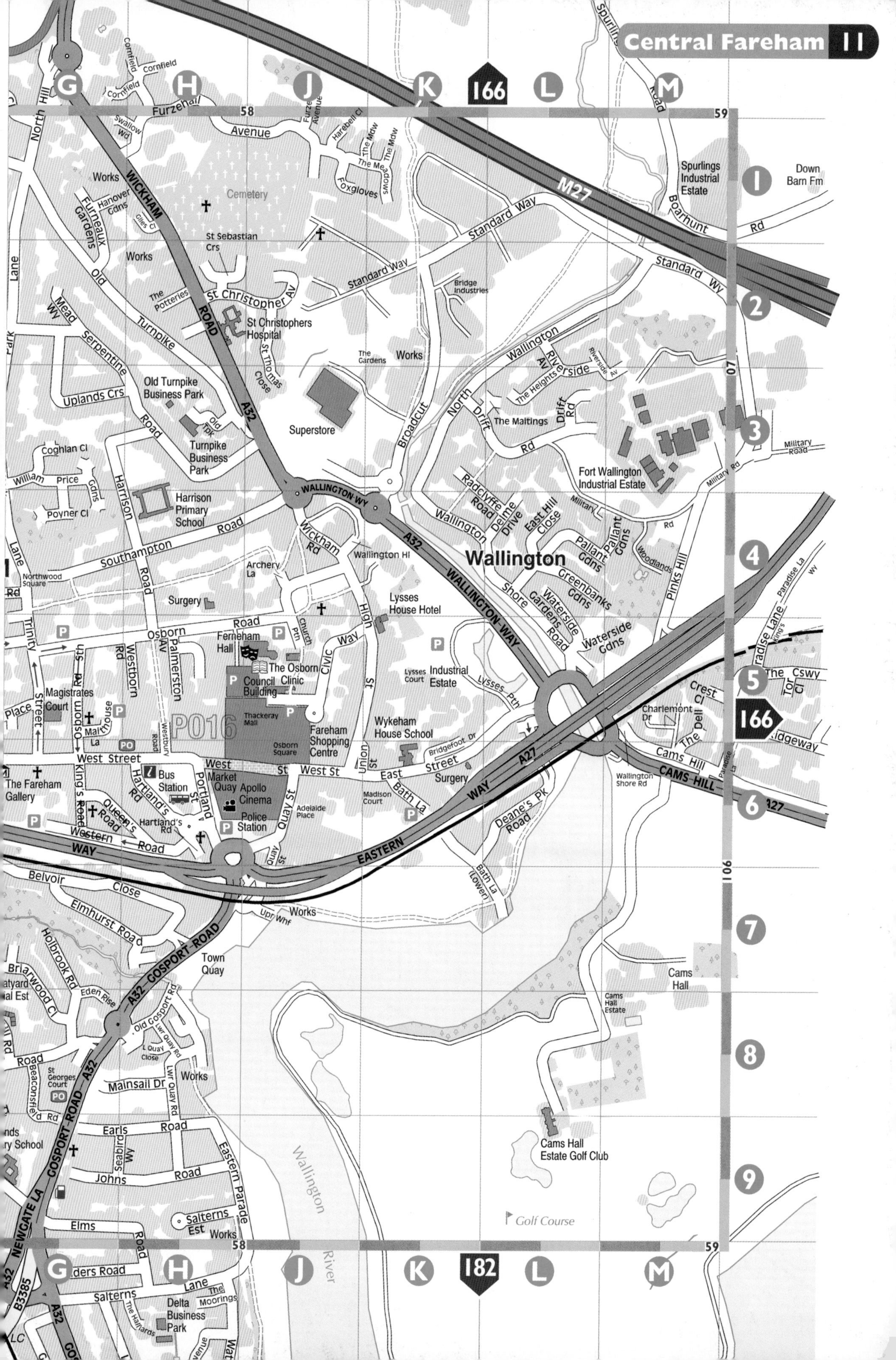
G
H
J
K
166
L
M
58
59
Cornfield
Furzehall
Avenue
Harebell Cl
The Mdw
The Meadows
Foxgloves
Cemetery
Works
Hanover Gdns
Furneaux Gardens
WICKHAM ROAD
A32
St Sebastian Crs
St Christopher Av
St Christophers Hospital
St Thomas Close
Standard Way
Bridge Industries
Spurlings Industrial Estate
Boarhunt Rd
Down Barn Fm
M27
Standard Wy
The Gardens
Superstore
Broadcut
Wallington
Riverside Av
The Heights
North Drift
The Maltings
Drift Rd
Fort Wallington Industrial Estate
Military Road
Military Rd
Old Turnpike Business Park
Turnpike Business Park
Uplands Crs
Serpentine Road
Coghlan Cl
William Price Gdns
Poyner Cl
Harrison Road
Harrison Primary School
Southampton Road
WALLINGTON WY
Wickham Rd
Wallington Hl
Archery La
Radclyffe Road
Delme Drive
East Hill Close
Pallant Gdns
Woodlands
Pinks Hill
Wallington
Greenbanks Gdns
Waterside Gardens
Shore Road
Waterside Gdns
Paradise Lane
Northwood Square
Surgery
Lysses House Hotel
High St
Osborn Road
Ferneham Hall
The Osborn Clinic
Council Building
Civic Way
Church Pth
Lysses Court
Industrial Estate
Lysses Pth
Magistrates Court
Thackeray Mall
Osborn Square
Fareham Shopping Centre
Wykeham House School
Bridgefoot Dr
PO16
Westborn Rd
Palmerston Av
Westbury Road
Malthouse La
Trinity Street
West Street
West St
East Street
Union St
Bus Station
Market Quay
Apollo Cinema
Police Station
Portland St
Quay St
Adelaide Place
Madison Court
Bath La
Deane's Pk Road
The Fareham Gallery
Queen's Road
King's Road
Hartland's Rd
Western Road
WAY
EASTERN WAY
A27
The Cswy
Tor Cl
Crest Cl
Charlemont Dr
The Dell
166
Ridgeway
Cams Hill
CAMS HILL
Wallington Shore Rd
Bath La (Lower)
Belvoir Close
Elmhurst Road
Holbrook Rd
Upr Whf
Works
Town Quay
A32 GOSPORT ROAD
Briarwood Cl
Eden Rise
Old Gosport Rd
Lwr Quay Rd
Quay Close
Cams Hall
Cams Hall Estate
St Georges Court
Beaconsfield Rd
Mainsail Dr
Earls Road
Seabird Wy
Johns Road
Eastern Parade
Elms Road
Salterns Est
Cams Hall Estate Golf Club
Golf Course
Wallington River
NEWCATE LA
B3385
Salterns Lane
The Moorings
Delta Business Park
The Halyards
182
ders Road
1
2
3
4
5
6
7
8
9
07
106

76
78
FARNHAM
GU9
Farnham Park Golf Club
The Grange
Old Park Lane
Farnham Castle Keep
CASTLE HILL
CASTLE ST
A287
Three Stiles Road
Larkfield Rd
Crondall Lane
Beavers Hill
Byworth Road
Tor Road
Tor Rd
Hill View Road
Waynflete Lane
Marston Rd
Hazell Road
The Chantrys
Coxbridge Mdw
West End Grove
Parfitts Cl
Mt Pleasant
Beavers Road
Potters Gate CE Primary School
Potters Gate
Falkner Road
Surrey Institute of Art and Design
Friars Field
Castle Field
Lion & Lamb Yard Shopping Centre
Lowndes Buildings
Long Garden Place
Superstore
Works
Bishop's Table Hotel
St Andrews CE Infant School
Farnham Museum
Adult Education Centre
Mead Lane
Brookmead Court
Meadow Bank
Crosby Way
Middle Church Lane
Vicarage La
WEST STREET
A325
Cemetery
River Wey
Weydon Ml Lane
Weydon La
Farnham Business Park
The Hop Kiln
The Pilgrims Way Primary School
FARNHAM BY-PASS
A31
ALTON ROAD
Runwick Ho
Works
The Hatches
WRECCLESHAM ROAD
Weydon Lane
Talbot Road
Upper Way
Pilgrims Cl
Baldreys
Green Lane
Chestnut Avenue
Bardsley Dr
Selborne Gdns
Middlefield
Lynton Cl
Greenfield Road
Grove End Road
Brambleton Avenue
Hillary Rd
Hillary Cl
The Drive
St Johns Gv
River Row
River Lane
Yatesbury Close
Weydon County Secondary School
Grovebell Industrial Est
Riverdale
Beldham Road
Greenhill Way
Firfield Rd
Highlands Cl
Aveley Lane
B3384
1 grid square represents 250 metres

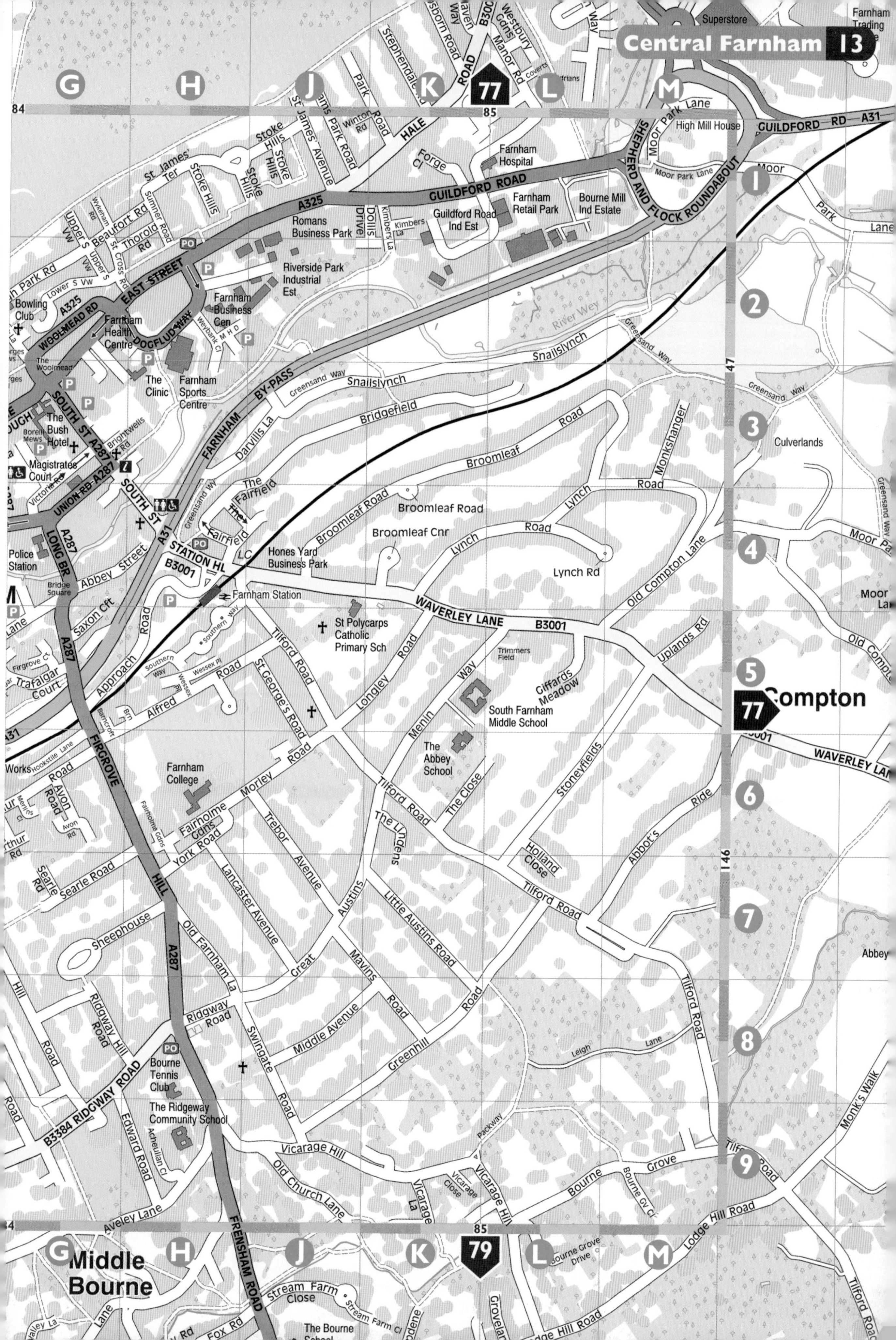

Superstore
Farnham Trading
G
H
J
K
77
L
M
84
85
HALE ROAD
GUILDFORD ROAD
A325
GUILDFORD RD A31
High Mill House
Moor Park Lane
SHEPHERD AND FLOCK ROUNDABOUT
Farnham Hospital
Farnham Retail Park
Bourne Mill Ind Estate
Guildford Road Ind Est
Romans Business Park
Riverside Park Industrial Est
Farnham Business Cen
EAST STREET
WOOLMEAD RD
DOGFLUD WAY
Bowling Club
Farnham Health Centre
The Clinic
Farnham Sports Centre
FARNHAM BY-PASS
River Wey
Snailslynch
Greensand Way
Bridgefield
Broomleaf Road
Broomleaf Cnr
Lynch Road
Lynch Rd
Monkshanger
Culverlands
Moor Park Lane
The Bush Hotel
Magistrates Court
SOUTH ST
UNION RD A287
LONG BR
Police Station
STATION HL
B3001
Hones Yard Business Park
Farnham Station
WAVERLEY LANE
St Polycarps Catholic Primary Sch
Old Compton Lane
Uplands Rd
Trimmers Field
Giffards Meadow
South Farnham Middle School
The Abbey School
Compton
77
Tilford Road
St George's Road
Longley Road
Menin Way
The Close
Stoneyfields
Abbot's Ride
Holland Close
Farnham College
Morley Road
Fairholme Gdns
York Road
Searle Road
Trebor Avenue
Lancaster Avenue
The Lindens
Little Austins Road
Great Austins
Mavins Road
FIRGROVE HILL
A287
Sheephouse
Old Farnham La
Ridgway Road
Ridgway Hill Road
Middle Avenue
Greenhill Road
Swingate Road
Leigh Lane
B3384 RIDGWAY ROAD
Bourne Tennis Club
The Ridgeway Community School
Edward Road
Vicarage Hill
Old Church Lane
Packway
Bourne Grove
Lodge Hill Road
Monk's Walk
Aveley Lane
FRENSHAM ROAD
Middle Bourne
79
Bourne Grove Drive
Stream Farm Close
The Bourne School
1
2
3
4
5
6
7
8
9
47
146

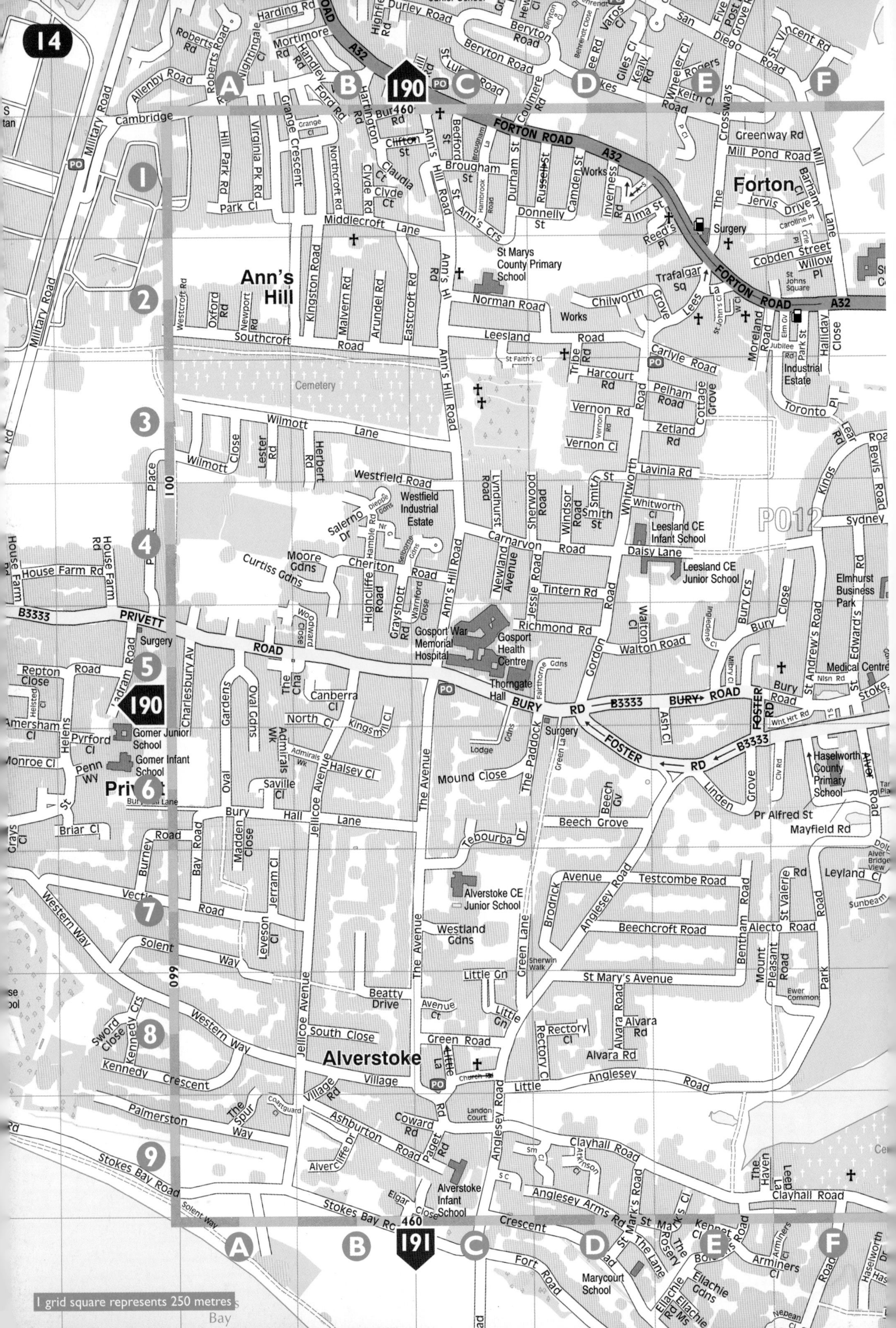
Forton
Ann's Hill
Privett
Alverstoke
PO12
Forton Road
Privett Road
Bury Road
Foster Rd
Stokes Bay Road
Gosport War Memorial Hospital
Gosport Health Centre
St Marys County Primary School
Leesland CE Infant School
Leesland CE Junior School
Gomer Junior School
Gomer Infant School
Alverstoke CE Junior School
Alverstoke Infant School
Haselworth County Primary School
Marycourt School
Westfield Industrial Estate
Elmhurst Business Park
Cemetery
190
191

1 grid square represents 250 metres

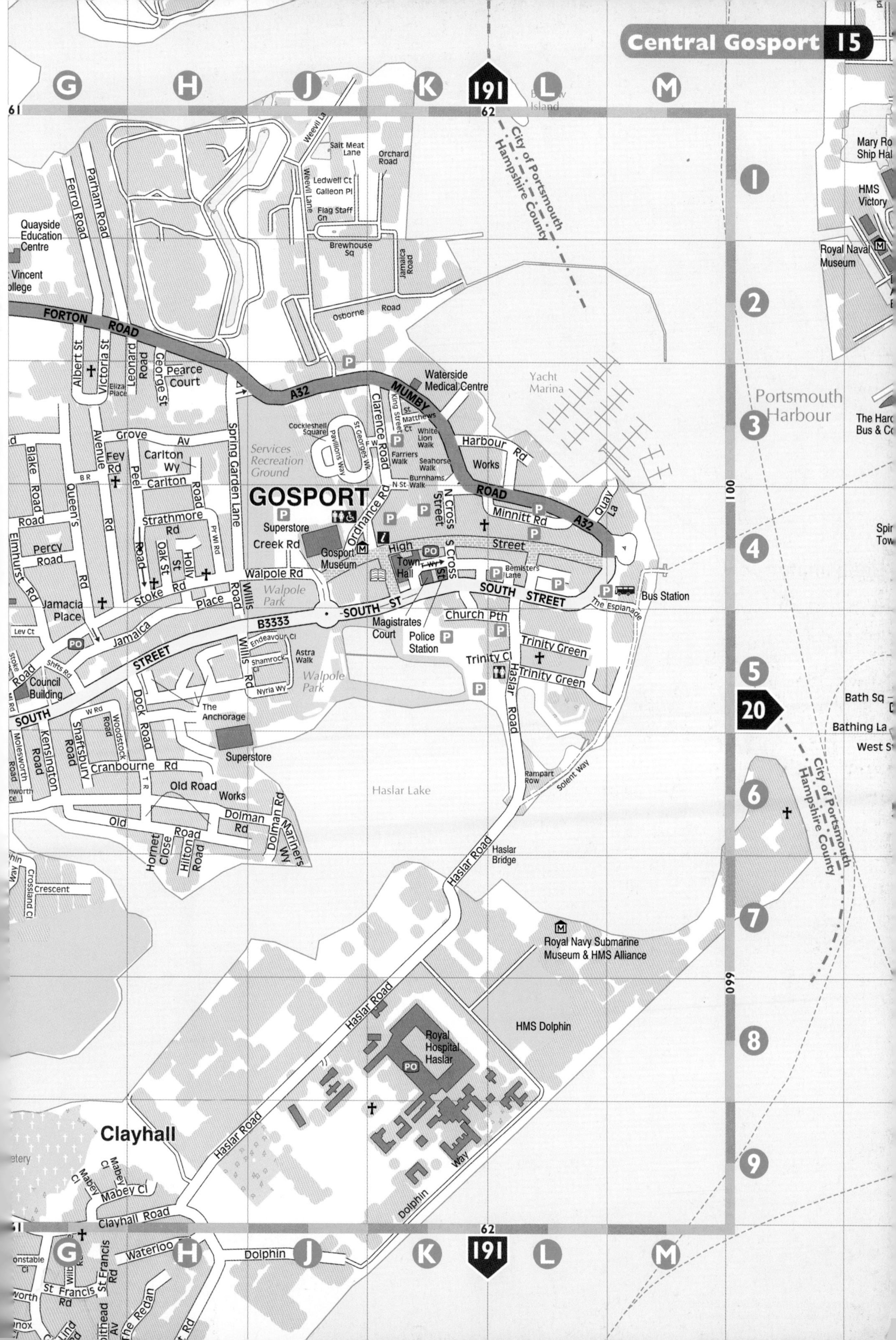

191
62

I

City of Portsmouth
Hampshire County

Mary Ro
Ship Hal

HMS
Victory

Royal Naval
Museum

2

Quayside
Education
Centre

St Vincent
College

FORTON   ROAD

A32

MUMBY

Waterside
Medical Centre

Yacht
Marina

Portsmouth
Harbour

3

The Hard
Bus & Co

Albert St
Victoria St
Leonard Road
George St
Eliza Place
Pearce Court

Parham Road
Ferrol Road

Spring Garden Lane

Weevil La

Salt Meat
Lane

Ledwell Ct
Galleon Pl

Weevil Lane

Flag Staff
Gn

Orchard
Road

Brewhouse
Sq

Jamaica Road

Osborne   Road

Clarence Road
Ordnance Rd

Cockleshell
Square

Pavilions Way

St Georges Wk

King Street

St St
Matthews
Ct

White
Lion
Walk

Farriers
Walk

Seahorse
Walk

Burnhams

N St Walk

Harbour
Works

Harbour   Rd

ROAD

A32

Quay La

100

4

Spir
Tow

Grove   Av

Blake Road
Queen's   Road

Fey
Rd

Peel

B R

Carlton
Wy

Carlton   Road

Strathmore
Rd

Pr Wl Rd

Holly   St

Oak St

Stoke   Rd

GOSPORT

Superstore

Creek Rd

Gosport
Museum

High
Town
Hall

PO

Minnitt Rd

Street

Bemisters
Lane

The Esplanade

Bus Station

Elmhurst   Rd
Percy
Road

Jamaica
Place

Lev Ct

PO

Walpole Rd

Walpole
Park

Jamaica   STREET

B3333

SOUTH   ST

Wills   Rd

Willis   Rd

Endeavour Cl

Shamrock
Cl

Astra
Walk

Nyria Wy

Magistrates
Court

Police
Station

Church Pth

Trinity Cl

Church   Pth

South   Street

SOUTH   STREET

Trinity Green

Trinity Green

Haslar   Road

5

20

Bath Sq

Bathing La

West S

SOUTH   Road

Council
Building

Shaftsbury   Road

Kensington   Road

Molesworth   Road

Dock   Road

W Rd

Woodstock
Road

Cranbourne   Rd

T R

Old Road

Old   Road
Works

The Anchorage

Superstore

Dolman   Rd

Dolman
Rd

Mariners   Wy

Haslar Lake

Rampart
Row

Solent Way

6

7

Hornet
Close

Hilton
Road

Old   Road

Crossland Cl

Crescent

Haslar Road

Haslar
Bridge

Royal Navy Submarine
Museum & HMS Alliance

660

Clayhall

Haslar Road

HMS Dolphin

8

Royal
Hospital
Haslar

PO

9

Cemetery

Mabey
Cl

Mabey Cl

Mabey Cl

Clayhall Road

Dolphin   Way

Constable
Cl

St Francis
Rd

St Francis   Rd

Waterloo

Dolphin

Smithead Rd

The Redan

Willi   Rd

Lenox

61

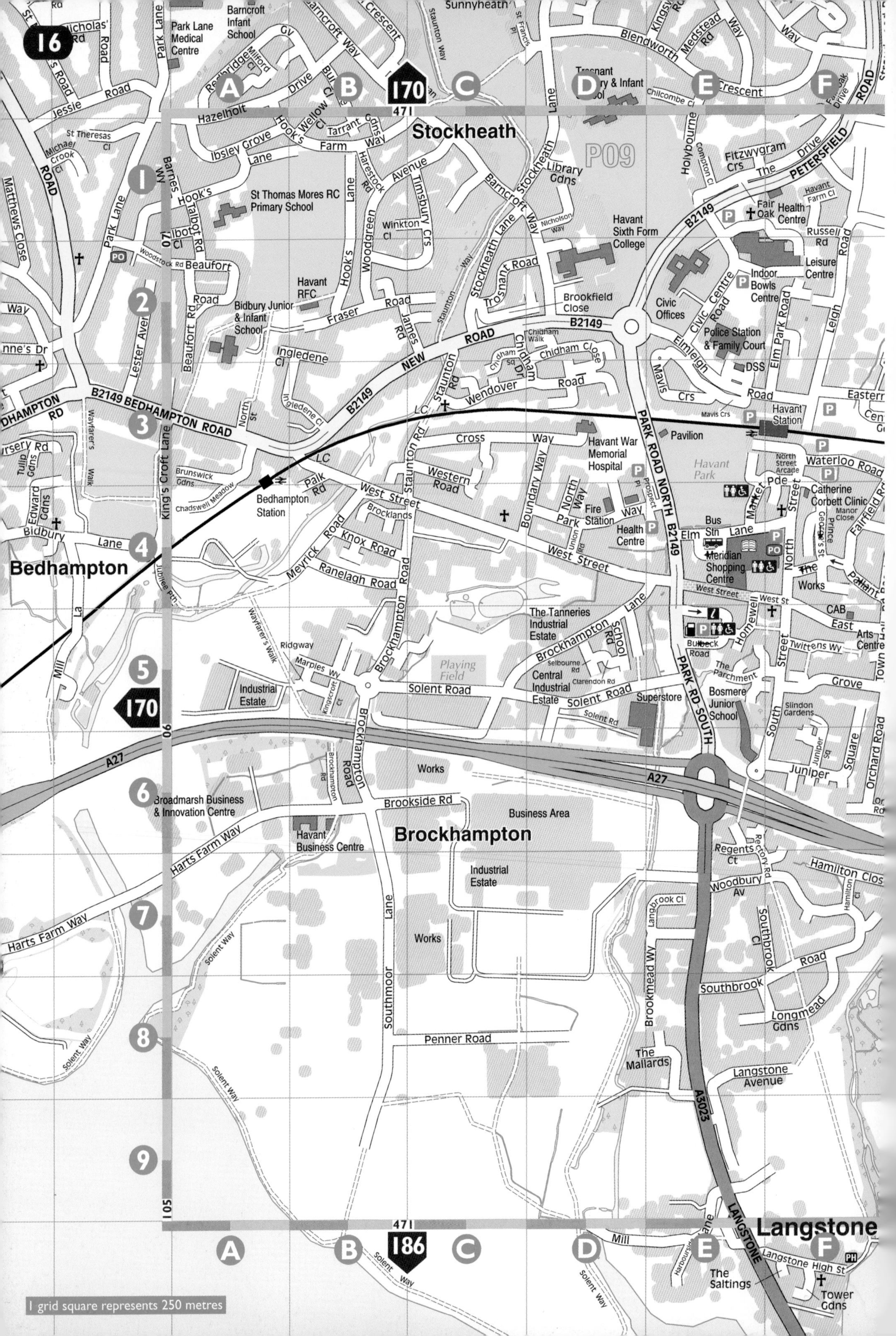

16

Park Lane Medical Centre
Barncroft Infant School

170 471

Stockheath

St Thomas Mores RC Primary School

Havant RFC

Bidbury Junior & Infant School

Ingledene Cl

B2149 BEDHAMPTON ROAD

Brunswick Gdns

Chadswell Meadow

Bedhampton Station

Bedhampton

Brocklands

170

A27

Industrial Estate

Broadmarsh Business & Innovation Centre

Havant Business Centre

Harts Farm Way

Harts Farm Way

Solent Way

Solent Way

Solent Way

171

P09

Havant Sixth Form College

Brookfield Close

B2149

Havant War Memorial Hospital

Fire Station

Health Centre

Western Road

West Street

Knox Road

Ranelagh Road

Marples Wy

Ridgway

Wayfarer's Walk

The Tanneries Industrial Estate

Playing Field

Central Industrial Estate

Selbourne Rd

Clarendon Rd

Solent Road

Solent Rd

Brockhampton Road

Solent Road

West Street

Brockhampton

Brookside Rd

Business Area

Industrial Estate

Works

Works

Southmoor Lane

Penner Road

Blendworth

Petersfield Road

The Drive

Fitzwygram Crs

Fair Oak

Health Centre

Russell Rd

Leisure Centre

Indoor Bowls Centre

Civic Offices

Police Station & Family Court

DSS

Civic Centre Road

Elmleigh Road

Mavis Crs

Mavis Crs

Pavilion

Havant Park

Havant Station

Waterloo Road

North Street Arcade

Catherine Corbett Clinic

George's St

Manor Close

Bus Stn

Market Pde

North Street

Meridian Shopping Centre

PO

The Works

West Street

West St

CAB

East

Arts Centre

Twittens Wy

The Parchment

Grove

Superstore

Bosmere Junior School

Slindon Gardens

Juniper Sq

Juniper Square

Orchard Road

PARK RD SOUTH

A27

Regents Ct

Hamilton Clos

Woodbury Av

Southbrook Ct

Southbrook Road

Longmead Gdns

Brookmead Wy

The Mallards

Langstone Avenue

A3023

471 186

Langstone

Mill

Langstone High St

The Saltings

Tower Gdns

PH

1 grid square represents 250 metres

A   B   **170** 471   C   D   E   F

I

2

3

4

5

6

7

8

9

A   B   **186** 471   C   D   E   F

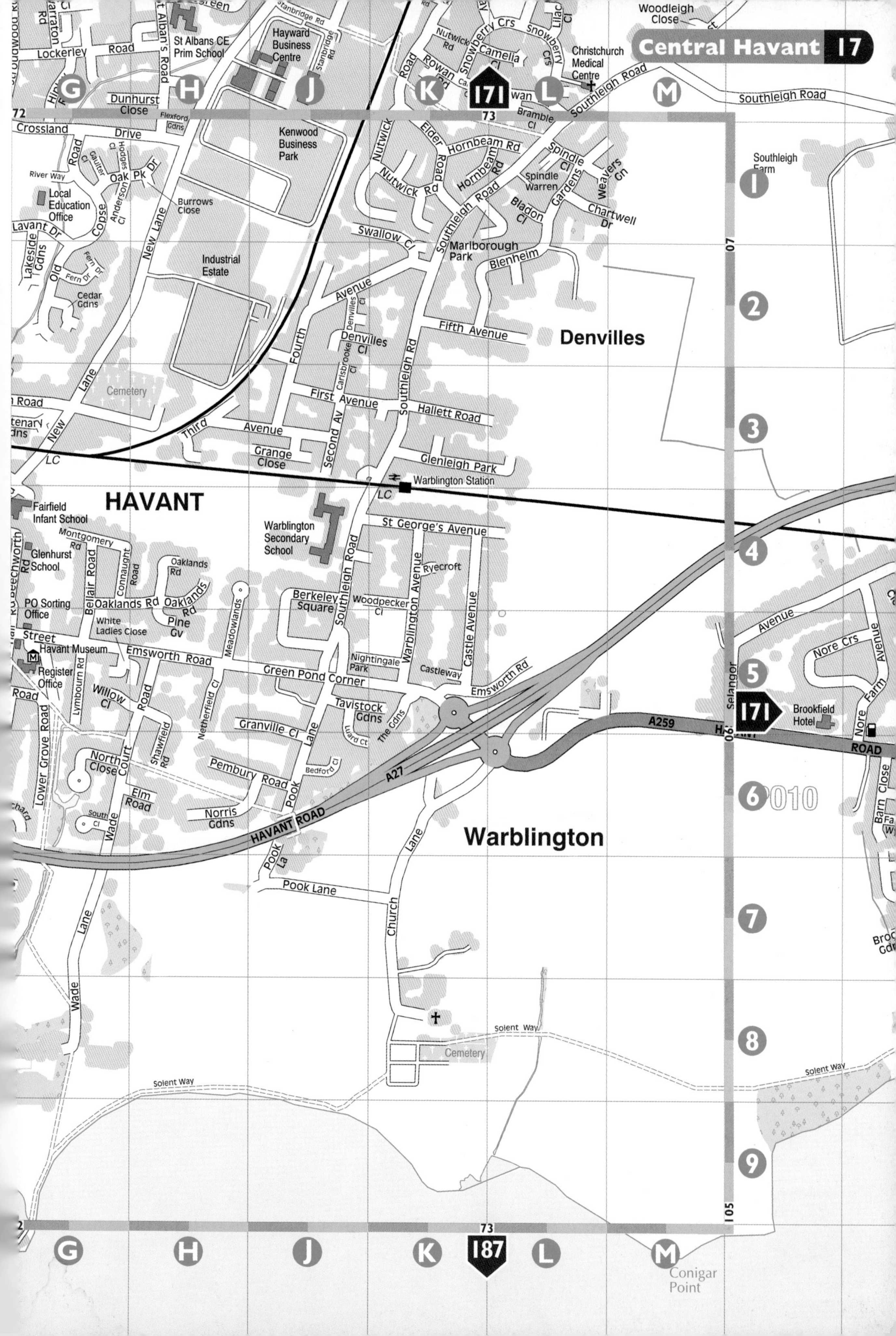
HAVANT
Denvilles
Warblington
Woodleigh Close
Christchurch Medical Centre
Southleigh Road
Southleigh Farm
St Albans CE Prim School
Hayward Business Centre
Kenwood Business Park
Industrial Estate
Lockerley Road
Dunhurst Close
Crossland Drive
Flexford Gdns
Local Education Office
River Way
Oak Pk Dr
Burrows Close
Lavant Dr
Lakeside Gdns
Fern Dr
Cedar Gdns
Copse
Anderson Cl
New Lane
Cemetery
Stanbridge Rd
Nutwick Rd
Snowberry Crs
Camellia Cl
Rowan Rd
Lilac Cl
Bramble Cl
Elder Road
Hornbeam Rd
Spindle Cl
Spindle Warren
Weavers Gn
Gardens
Bladon Cl
Chartwell Dr
Swallow Cl
Marlborough Park
Blenheim
Fourth Avenue
Denvilles Cl
Carisbrooke Cl
Fifth Avenue
First Avenue
Second Av
Third Avenue
Grange Close
Hallett Road
Glenleigh Park
Southleigh Rd
Warblington Station
LC
Fairfield Infant School
Glenhurst School
Montgomery Rd
Beechworth Rd
Bellair Road
Connaught Road
Oaklands Rd
Oaklands Rd
Pine Gv
Meadowlands
PO Sorting Office
White Ladies Close
Havant Museum
Register Office
Street
Emsworth Road
Warblington Secondary School
St George's Avenue
Berkeley Square
Southleigh Road
Woodpecker Cl
Warblington Avenue
Ryecroft
Castle Avenue
Nightingale Park
Castleway
Green Pond Corner
Emsworth Rd
Lymbourn Rd
Willow Cl
Road
Netherfield Cl
Tavistock Gdns
Granville Cl
The Gdns
Lodge Cl
Shawfield Rd
Lower Grove Road
North Close
Court
Elm Road
Pembury Road
Bedford Cl
Pook Lane
South Cl
Wade
Norris Gdns
A27
HAVANT ROAD
Pook La
Pook Lane
Church Lane
Wade Lane
Solent Way
Cemetery
Selangor
A259
ROAD
Avenue
Nore Crs
Nore Farm Avenue
Brookfield Hotel
Barn Close
Conigar Point
171
187
G H J K L M
1 2 3 4 5 6 7 8 9
72 73 07 06 05

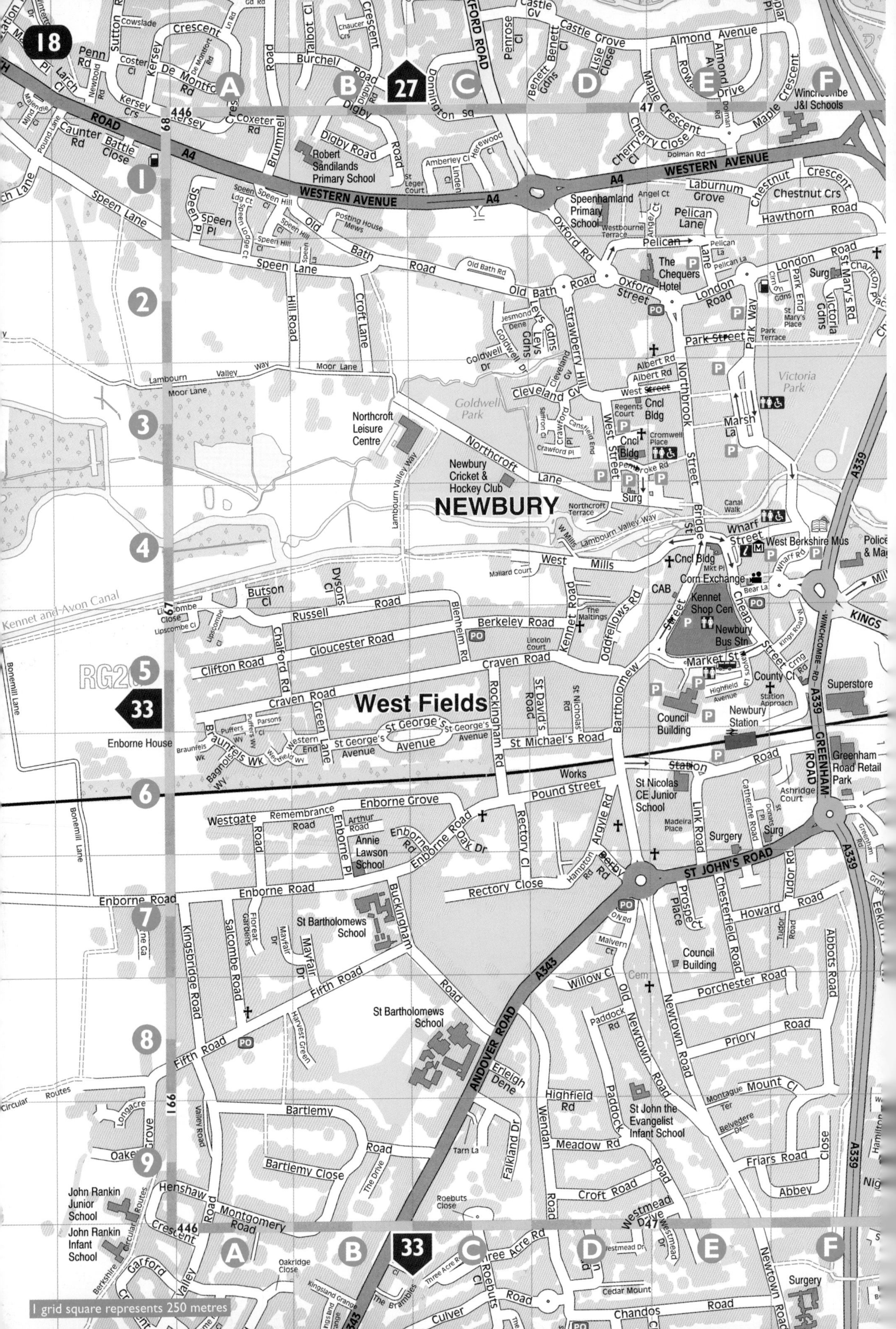

18
27
33
33
A
B
C
D
E
F
A
B
C
D
E
F
1
2
3
4
5
6
7
8
9
446
47
446
47
68
67
66
RG20
NEWBURY
West Fields
WESTERN AVENUE
A4
ROAD
OXFORD ROAD
Castle Gv
Castle Grove
Almond Avenue
Almond Drive
Maple Crescent
Maple Crescent
Winchcombe J&I Schools
Cherry Close
Cherry Cl
Dolman Rd
Penrose Cl
Benett Cl
Benett Gdns
Lisle Close
Donnington Sq
Digby Road
Burchell Road
Talbot Cl
Chaucer Crs
Crescent
Robert Sandilands Primary School
Herewood Cl
Amberley Cl
Linden Cl
St Leger Court
Cowslade
Sutton Rd
Penn Rd
Kersey Crs
Kersey Crescent
De Montfort Rd
Coster Cl
Newbold Rd
Larch Cl
Coxeter Rd
Brummell Road
Counter Rd
Battle Close
Pound Lane
Speen Lane
Speen Pl
Speen Lodge Ct
Speen Hill
Old Bath Road
Posting House Mews
Old Bath Rd
Hill Road
Croft Lane
Moor Lane
Lambourn Valley Way
Laburnum Grove
Chestnut Crescent
Chestnut Crs
Hawthorn Road
Speenhamland Primary School
Angel Ct
Pelican Lane
Pelican La
Westbourne Terrace
Oxford Rd
Oxford Street
The Chequers Hotel
London Road
Park Way
Park End
St Mary's Place
St Mary's Rd
Victoria Gdns
Park Terrace
Park Street
Victoria Park
Charlton Place
Surg
Jesmond Dene
Leys Gdns
Goldwell Dr
Strawberry Hill
Cleveland Gv
Northbrook Street
Albert Rd
West Street
Regents Court
Cncl Bldg
Cromwell Place
Crawford Pl
Saffron Cl
Cansfield End
Marsh La
Goldwell Park
Northcroft Leisure Centre
Northcroft Lane
Newbury Cricket & Hockey Club
Pembroke Rd
Northcroft Terrace
Canal Walk
Lambourn Valley Way
W Mills
West Mills
Bridge St
Wharf Street
Wharf Rd
West Berkshire Mus
Police & Mag
Mkt Pl
Corn Exchange
Bear La
CAB
Kennet Shop Cen
Newbury Bus Stn
Cheap Street
Market St
Mayors La
Kings Road W
KINGS
Mallard Court
Kennet Road
The Maltings
Oddfellows Rd
Kennet and Avon Canal
Butson Cl
Dysons Cl
Russell Road
Blenheim Rd
Berkeley Road
Lincoln Court
Lipscombe Close
Lipscombe Cl
Chalford Rd
Gloucester Road
Clifton Road
Craven Road
Bonemill Lane
Enborne House
Puffers Wy
Parsons
Braunfels Wk
Bagnols Wy
Western End
Green Lane
St George's Avenue
Rockingham Rd
St David's Road
St Nicholas' Rd
St Michael's Road
Bartholomew
County Cl
Highfield Avenue
Station Approach
Council Building
Newbury Station
Superstore
WINCHCOMBE RD
A339
GREENHAM ROAD
Greenham Road Retail Park
Ashridge Court
Station Road
Works
Pound Street
St Nicolas CE Junior School
Madeira Place
Link Road
Catherine Road
St Donats Pl
Surgery
Westgate Road
Remembrance Road
Enborne Grove
Arthur Road
Enborne Pl
Annie Lawson School
Enborne Road
Oak Dr
Rectory Cl
Rectory Close
Argyle Rd
Hampton Rd
Derby Rd
ST JOHN'S ROAD
Prospect Place
Chesterfield Road
Tudor Rd
Howard Road
Abbots Road
Enborne Road
Kingsbridge Road
Salcombe Road
Floreat Gardens
Mayfair Dr
St Bartholomews School
Buckingham Road
Fifth Road
Harvest Green
Malvern Ct
Willow Cl
Council Building
Porchester Road
Cem
Old Newtown Road
Newtown Road
Paddock Rd
Priory Road
ANDOVER ROAD
A343
Erleigh Dene
Highfield Rd
Paddock Road
St John the Evangelist Infant School
Montague Ter
Mount Cl
Belvedere Dr
Friars Road
Close
Abbey
Circular Routes
Longacre
Grove
Oaken
Valley Road
Bartlemy Road
Bartlemy Close
The Drive
Tarn La
Falkland Dr
Wendan Road
Meadow Rd
Croft Road
Roebuts Close
Westmead Drive
Westmead Dr
John Rankin Junior School
John Rankin Infant School
Henshaw Crescent
Montgomery Road
Garford Crescent
Oakridge Close
Kingsland Grange
The Brambles
Three Acre Rd
Roebuts Cl
Cedar Mount
Road
Chandos Road
Culver Road
Newtown Road
Surgery
A343
1 grid square represents 250 metres

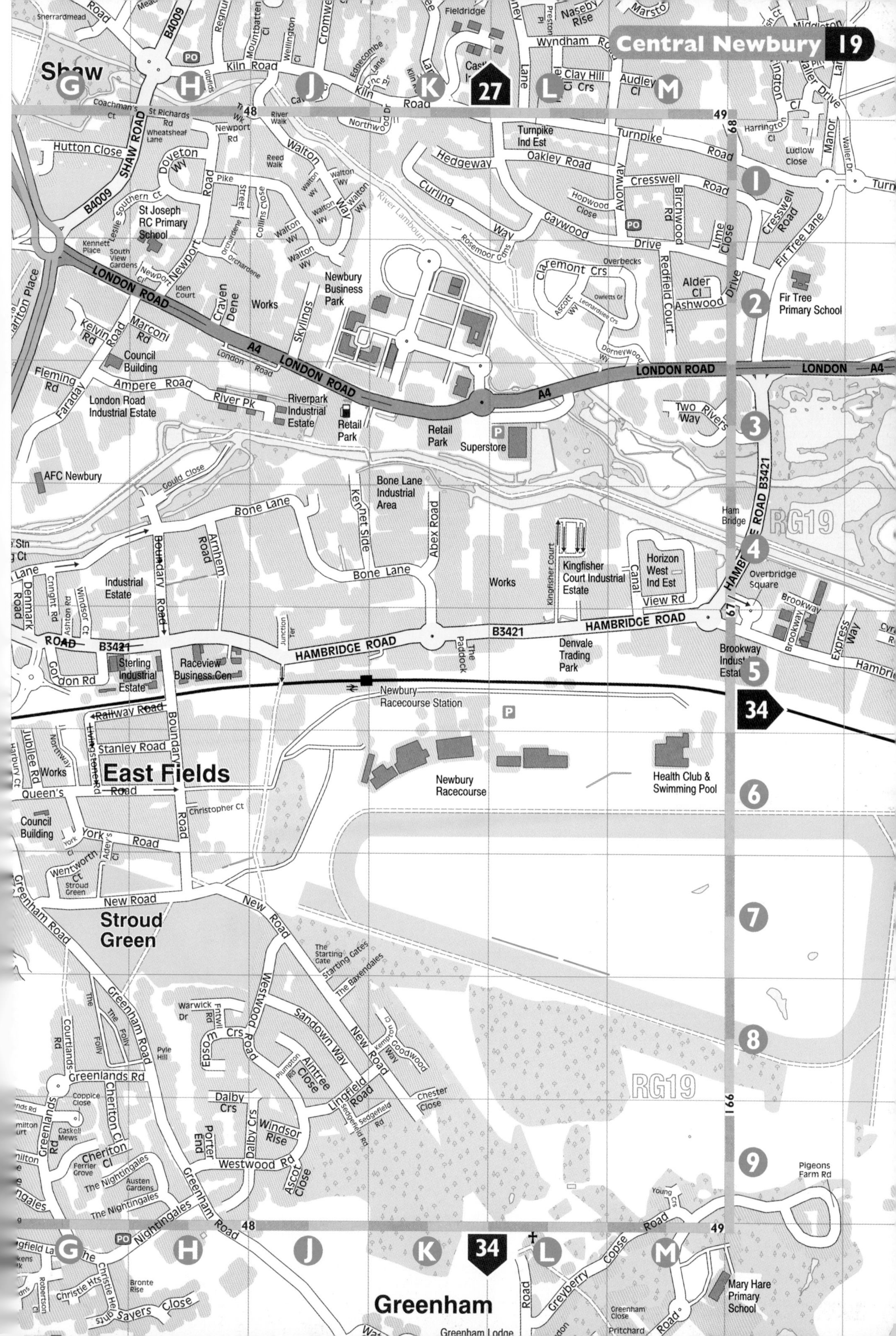
Shaw
Stroud Green
East Fields
Greenham
LONDON ROAD
HAMBRIDGE ROAD
Newbury Racecourse
Newbury Business Park
Newbury Racecourse Station
Bone Lane Industrial Area
London Road Industrial Estate
Riverpark Industrial Estate
Retail Park
Superstore
AFC Newbury
Fir Tree Primary School
St Joseph RC Primary School
Mary Hare Primary School
Health Club & Swimming Pool
Kingfisher Court Industrial Estate
Horizon West Ind Est
Denvale Trading Park
Sterling Industrial Estate
Raceview Business Cen
Turnpike Ind Est
Council Building
RG19
27
34

PORTSMOUTH
Old Portsmouth
Portsea
Portsmouth Harbour
HM Naval Base
Mary Rose Ship Hall
HMS Victory
Royal Naval Museum
Dockyard Apprentice Exhibition
Mary Rose Exhibition
Action Stations! Exhibition
Ticket Office
HMS Warrior
The Hard Interchange Bus & Coach Station
Portsmouth Harbour Station
Spinnaker Tower
Gunwharf Quays Retail & Leisure Park
St Georges Business Centre
United Services Sports Ground
HMS Temeraire
Victoria Stadium
Grammar School
University of Portsmouth
HMS Nelson
Cathedral Discovery Centre
St Johns RC Cathedral
Victoria Park Swimming Centre
New Theatre Royal
Land Registry
United Services RFC
Nuffield Centre University of Portsmouth
Indoor Tennis Centre
Portsmouth Grammar Jun Sch
Council Building
City Museum & Records Office
KINGS ROAD ROUNDABOUT
St Judes CE (Controlled) Prim School
Holiday Inn
Portsmouth Natural Health Centre
Isle of Wight Car Ferry Terminal
Fish Market
Camber Place
Cathedral Church of St Thomas of Canterbury
Round Tower
Town Walls
Square Tower
Battery Row
The Long Curtain (Old Town Defences)
Gordon Road
Clarence Pier & Amusement Centre
Clarence Esplanade
Hovercraft Terminal
Southsea Common
Royal Navy Memorial
Bus Station
Royal Navy Submarine Museum & HMS Alliance
City of Portsmouth
Hampshire County
Register Office
Portsea Clinic
University of Portsmouth
North Street Treadgolds Museum
John Pounds Community Centre
St Georges CE Primary School
Univ of Portsmouth
Portsmouth High Sch GDST
A B C D E F
1 2 3 4 5 6 7 8 9
191
15
463
100
099
1 grid square represents 250 metres

Fratton
Fratton Station
Southsea
Cascades Shopping Centre
The Bridge Shopping Centre
Portsmouth & Southsea Stn
Guildhall
Civic Offices
Victory Business Centre
Kings Theatre
Natural History Museum & Butterfly House
St Johns College
Priory College
Wimbledon Park Sports Cen
Mayville High School
Winston Churchill Avenue A2030
Victoria Road North
Victoria Road South
Holbrook Road A2030
Albert Road B2154
Elm Grove
Goldsmith Avenue
Clarence Parade
St Helen's Parade
Fratton Road A2047
Commercial Rd
Marketway
Station Street
Arundel Street
Lake Road
P05

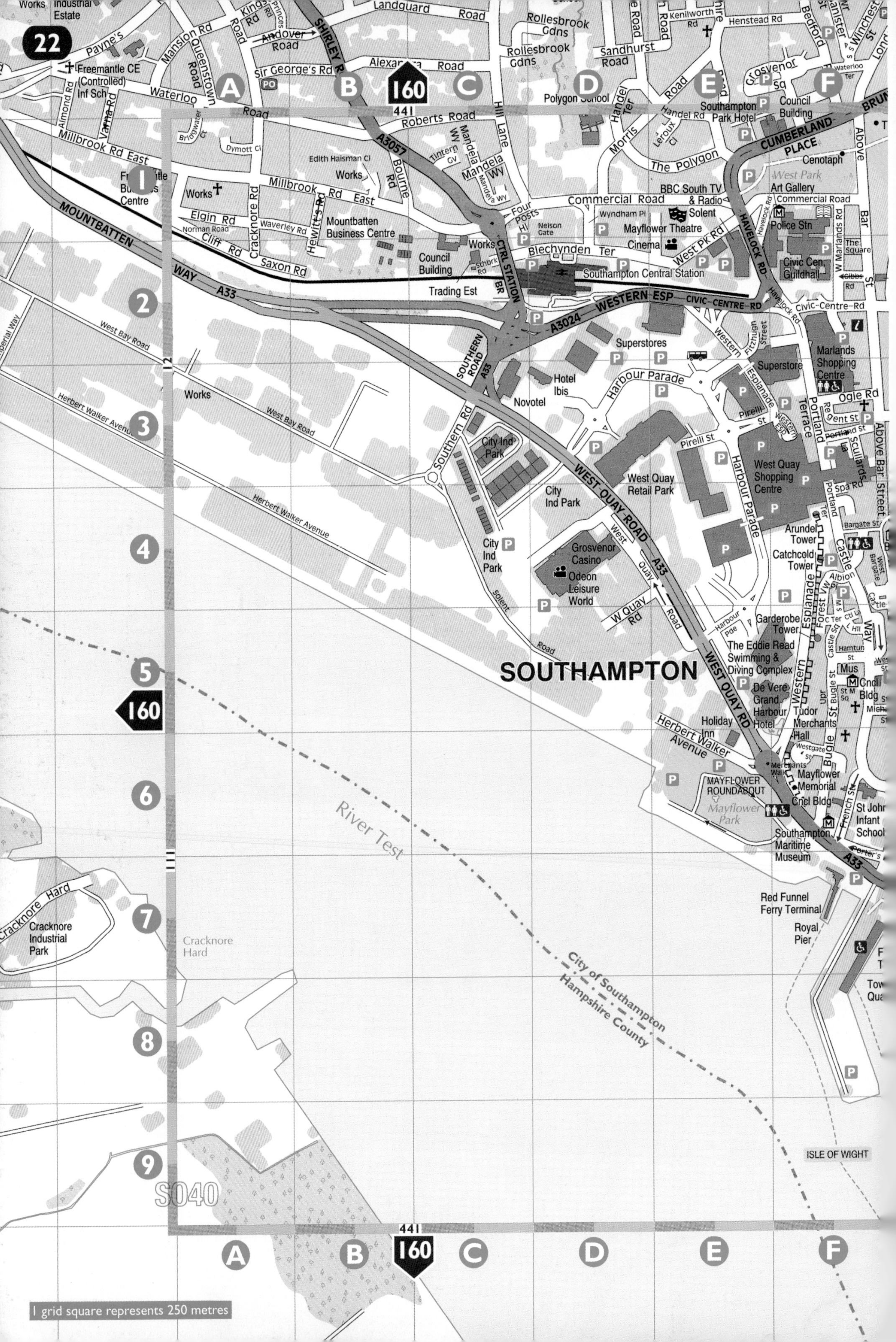
SOUTHAMPTON
River Test
City of Southampton
Hampshire County
MOUNTBATTEN WAY
A33
WEST QUAY ROAD
WEST QUAY RD
A3024 WESTERN ESP
CIVIC CENTRE RD
SHIRLEY RD
A3057
CUMBERLAND PLACE
Southampton Central Station
West Quay Shopping Centre
West Quay Retail Park
Marlands Shopping Centre
Mayflower Theatre
Police Stn
Civic Cen. Guildhall
Art Gallery
Cenotaph
BBC South TV & Radio Solent
Polygon School
Southampton Park Hotel
Council Building
Novotel
Hotel Ibis
Superstores
Superstore
Grosvenor Casino
Odeon Leisure World
City Ind Park
Trading Est
Mountbatten Business Centre
Freemantle CE (Controlled) Inf Sch
The Eddie Read Swimming & Diving Complex
De Vere Grand Harbour Hotel
Holiday Inn
Tudor Merchants Hall
Mayflower Memorial
Mayflower Park
MAYFLOWER ROUNDABOUT
Southampton Maritime Museum
Red Funnel Ferry Terminal
Royal Pier
Arundel Tower
Catchcold Tower
Garderobe Tower
St John's Infant School
ISLE OF WIGHT
Cracknore Industrial Park
Cracknore Hard
West Bay Road
Herbert Walker Avenue
Harbour Parade
Commercial Road
Blechynden Ter
Millbrook Rd East
Waterloo Road
Landguard Road
Alexandra Road
Roberts Road
Hill Lane
The Polygon
Southern Road
Portland Terrace
Above Bar Street
Bugle St
Castle Way
French St
SO40
160
441
1 grid square represents 250 metres

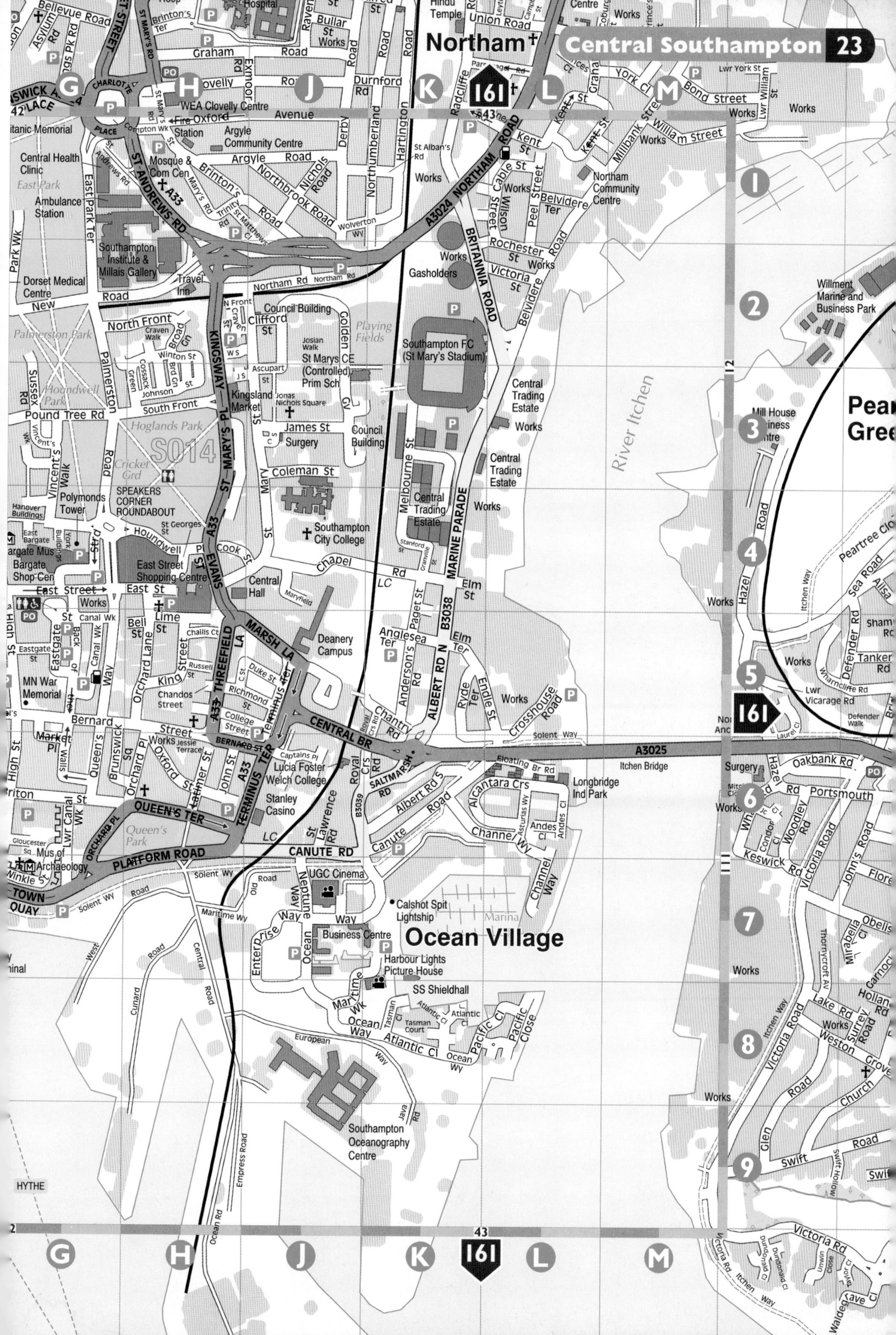
Northam
Ocean Village
River Itchen
Southampton FC (St Mary's Stadium)
Southampton Oceanography Centre
Itchen Bridge
A3025
A3024 Northam Road
Central Trading Estate
Hoglands Park
SO14
Speakers Corner Roundabout
East Street Shopping Centre
Southampton City College
Southampton Institute & Millais Gallery
Central Health Clinic
Ambulance Station
Dorset Medical Centre
Palmerston Park
Houndwell Park
Queen's Park
Platform Road
Canute Rd
Town Quay
Mus of Archaeology
MN War Memorial
Polymonds Tower
Deanery Campus
Lucia Foster Welch College
Stanley Casino
UGC Cinema
Calshot Spit Lightship
Harbour Lights Picture House
SS Shieldhall
Business Centre
Longbridge Ind Park
Willment Marine and Business Park
Mill House Business Centre
Gasholders
Northam Community Centre
Council Building
St Marys CE (Controlled) Prim Sch
Kingsland Market
WEA Clovelly Centre
Argyle Community Centre
Mosque & Com Cen
Fire Station
Hindu Temple
HYTHE
G
H
J
K
L
M
161
43
12
1
2
3
4
5
6
7
8
9

Weeke
Fulflood
Sleepers' Hill
Stanmore
Weeke CP School
Winchester Lawn Tennis Club
Peter Symonds College
Nethercliffe Preparatory School
Andover Rd Retail Park
Lankhills School
The Westgate School
Western Primary School
Winchester Station
Hampshire Records Office
Police HQ
HM Prison
University College Winchester
Royal Hampshire County Hospital
Sarum Road Hospital
The Plague Monument
The Guard Room
The Westgate
The Great Hall
Reg Mus
Gurkha Museum
Law Courts
Royal Hampshire Regiment Museum & Memorial Garden
Hotel du Vin
Council Building
Christ's Hospital
Cemetery
Oram's Arbour
Garden Centre
Sleepers Delle Gardens
Stockbridge Road
Bereweeke Road
Chilbolton Avenue
Romsey Road
Andover Road
St Cross Road
Sarum Road
Stoney Lane
Park Road
Cheriton Road
Airlie Road
Sleepers' Hill
Christchurch Road
Edgar Road
Stanmore Lane
1 grid square represents 250 metres

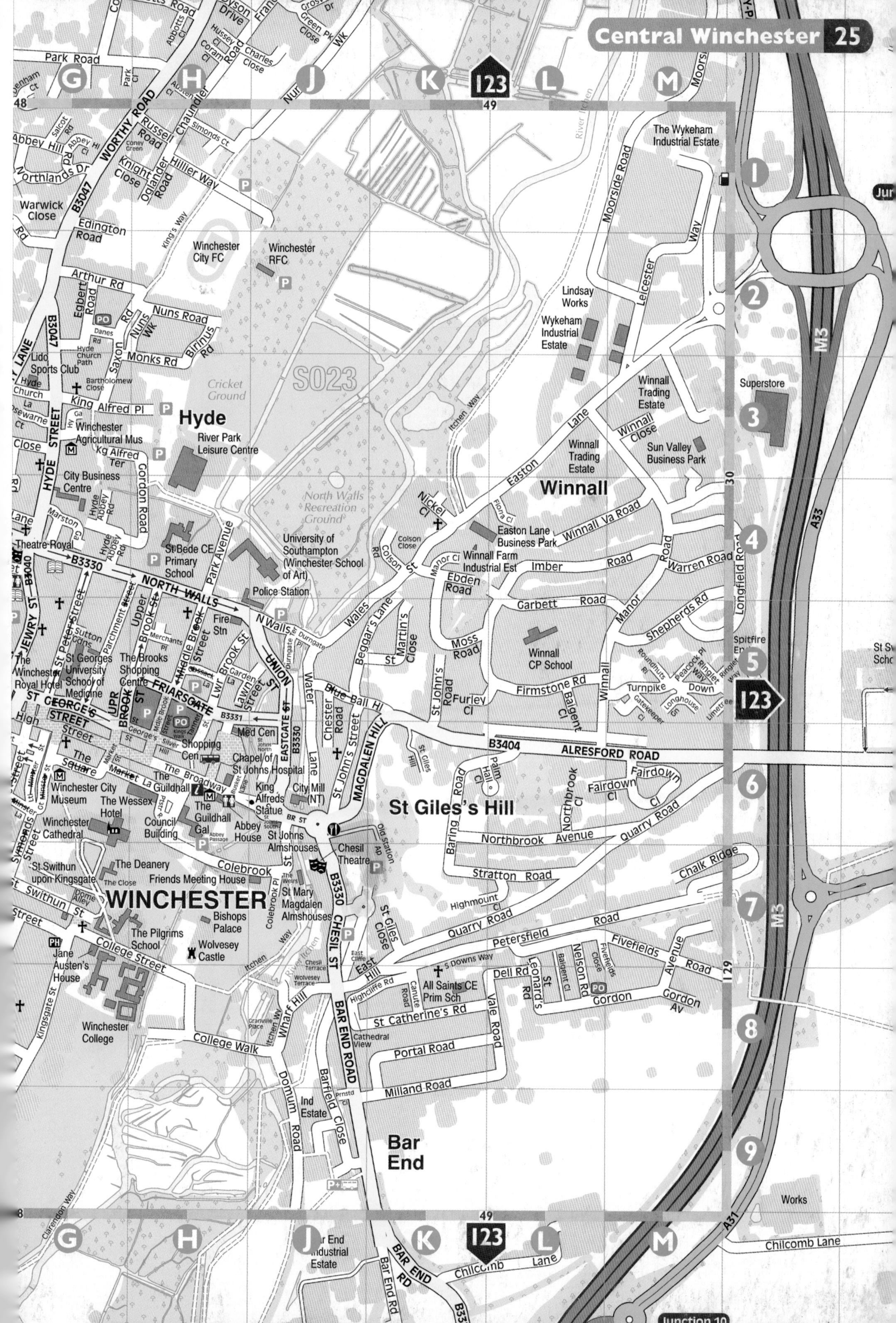
G
H
J
K
123
L
M
48
49
1
2
3
4
5
6
7
8
9
30
29
Abbotts Road
Dyson Drive
Park Road
Worthy Road
B3047
Chaundler
Russell Road
Hillier Way
Knight Close
Oglander Road
Abbey Hill
Northlands Dr
Warwick Close
Edington Road
Winchester City FC
Winchester RFC
Arthur Rd
Egbert Road
Nuns Road
Saxon Rd
Monks Rd
Birinus Rd
Lido Sports Club
Hyde Church
King Alfred Pl
Cricket Ground
Hyde
Winchester Agricultural Mus
Kg Alfred Ter
River Park Leisure Centre
City Business Centre
Gordon Road
Hyde Street
Theatre Royal
B3330
North Walls
St Bede CE Primary School
Park Avenue
North Walls Recreation Ground
University of Southampton (Winchester School of Art)
Police Station
S023
Itchen Way
River Itchen
The Wykeham Industrial Estate
Moorside Road
Leicester Way
Lindsay Works
Wykeham Industrial Estate
Winnall Trading Estate
Winnall Close
Sun Valley Business Park
Superstore
M3
A33
Easton Lane
Winnall
Nickel Cl
Easton Lane Business Park
Winnall Va Road
Winnall Farm Industrial Est
Imber Road
Warren Road
Longfield Road
Ebden Road
Garbett Road
Manor Road
Shepherds Rd
Moss Road
Winnall CP School
Spitfire End
Firmstone Rd
Furley Cl
Baigent Cl
Turnpike Down
Colson Rd
Wales St
Beggar's Lane
St Martin's Close
Water Lane
Chester Road
St John's Street
Magdalen Hill
Jewry St
St Peter Street
Parchment Street
Upper Brook St
Middle Brook Street
Lwr Brook St
Union St
Eastgate St
B3330
The Brooks Shopping Centre
St Georges University School of Medicine
The Winchester Royal Hotel
Friarsgate
B3331
Med Cen
St George's Street
High Street
Upr Brook St
Shopping Cen
Chapel of St Johns Hospital
The Broadway
The Square
Market La
The Guildhall
Winchester City Museum
The Wessex Hotel
Winchester Cathedral
Council Building
The Guildhall Gal
Abbey House
King Alfreds Statue
City Mill (NT)
St Johns Almshouses
Chesil Theatre
St Giles's Hill
B3404
Alresford Road
Baring Road
Palm Hall Cl
Northbrook Cl
Fairdown Cl
Northbrook Avenue
Quarry Road
Stratton Road
Chalk Ridge
Highmount Cl
Colebrook St
Friends Meeting House
The Deanery
St Swithun upon Kingsgate
St Swithun St
WINCHESTER
St Mary Magdalen Almshouses
Bishops Palace
B3330 Chesil St
St Giles Close
Petersfield Road
Fivefields Road
Avenue
The Pilgrims School
Wolvesey Castle
College Street
Jane Austen's House
Winchester College
East Hill
S Downs Way
All Saints CE Prim Sch
Dell Rd
St Leonard's Rd
Nelson Rd
Gordon Road
Gordon Av
Highcliffe Rd
Canute Road
St Catherine's Rd
Vale Road
Wharf Hill
College Walk
Cathedral View
Portal Road
Milland Road
Bar End Road
Barfield Close
Domum Road
Ind Estate
Bar End
Works
Clarendon Way
Kingsgate St
Bar End Industrial Estate
Bar End Rd
Chilcomb Lane
A31
Junction 10

Boxford
School Lane
Winterbourne Road
Winterbourne Holt
Boxford Common
Snelsmore Common Country Park
Honeybottom
Lambourn Valley Way
River Lambourn
Copse Barn
Hunt's Green
Huntsgreen Farm
Bagnor
Woodspeen
Woodspeen Farm
Watermill Theatre
PH
Snake Lane
Dairy Farm
Donnington
Chapel Road
Rookswood
Cricketers
Stockcross Primary School
PO
Church Road
Glebe Lane
Stockcross
The Vineyard at Stockcross
Deanwood Farm
B4000
A34
Lambourn Road
The Sydings
Speen
Station Rd
Winterton Dr
Manor Pl
Penn Road
Sutton Road
Larch Cl
BATH ROAD
Speen House
Benham Chase
GRAVEL HILL
A4
Benham Park
Elmore House
Church La
Battle Cl
Pound St
1 grid square represents 500 metres

33

Speen 27
Hill House
B4494
G
H
J
K
L
M
Home Farm
46
47
48
49
Arlington Grange Farm
Oaklands
Curridge Road
Snelsmore East Common
The Mary Hare School for the Deaf
Woodside
Grange Farm
A34
A339
Snelsmore House
Donnington Valley Golf Club
Shaw Dene House
Golf Course
Donnington Valley Hotel
Donnington Holt
High Wood
Brickkiln Wood
Red Farm
Donnington Castle
Shaw Farm
LONG LANE
28
Mousefield Farm
Stone Copse
The Castle Special School
Castle Lane
Shop Lane
OXFORD ROAD
Shaw Cum Donnington Prim Sch
Yew Gate
The Priory
Love Lane
Donnington Pk
B4009
Kingsley Close
Owen Rd
Lamp Acres
Cemetery
Sycamore Rise
Stoney Lane
Stable Ct
Dene Way
Battlesite 1644
Trinity School & Performing Arts College
Shaw Hill
Regnum Drive
Cromwell Road
Orchard Cl
Pear Tree Lane
Wansey Gdns
Fleetwood Cl
Road
Chaucer Crs
Brummell Rd
Talbot Cl
Burchell Rd
Kersey Crs
RG14
Poplar Pl
Church Rd
Well Meadow
Castle Gv
Almond Avenue
Penrose Cl
Rowan Drive
Maple Crs
Shaw
Edgecombe La
Kiln Rd
Castle Ind Park
Wyndham Rd
Sorrel Cl
Audley Cl
Naseby Ri
Marsh Dr
Harrington Close
Turnpike Ind Est
Turnpike Road
Robert Sandilands Primary Sch
Winchcombe
18
19
WESTERN AVENUE
A4
Chestnut Crs
Hutton Close
SHAW ROAD
Newport Rd
Walton Way
Hedgeway
Oakley Road
Hopwood Cl
Cresswell Road
Curling Way
Gaywood Drive
Hawthorn Rd
Speenhamland Primary School
Old Bath Road
Speen Lane
Hill Road
Croft Lane
Pelican
London Road
St Joseph RC Prim Sch
Pike St
LONDON ROAD
Newbury Business Park
Redfield Ct
Ashwood Cl
The Chequers Htl
Strawberry Hl
Northbrook St
Park Wy
Craven Dene
Marconi Cncl Bldg
Works
Skyllings
Kelvin Rd
Fir Tree Lane
Moor Lane
Ampere Rd
River Pk
Northcroft Leisure Centre
Northcroft Lane
Newbury Cricket & Hockey Club
Cncl Bldgs
34
Riverpark Industrial Estate
Retail Park
Superstore
Two Rivers Wy
AFC Newbury
Bone Lane Ind Area
NEWBURY
Police Stn & Mag Ct
BRIDGE ROAD
Ham Bridge
Victoria Park
Cncl Bldg
I
2
3
4
5
6
7
8
71
70
69
68

28
27
35
Longlane
Ashmore Green
Cold Ash
THATCHAM
Bucklebury Alle
Downe House School
Cold Ash Farm
Fisher's Farm
Craven Farm
Rookery Farm
Layleys Garden
Westrop Farm
Thirtover
Cold Ash St Marks CE Primary School
Ridge House Pre-Preparatory School
St Finians RC Primary School
Hatchgate Farm
Regency Park Hotel
Henwick Manor
Lower Henwick Farm
Stone Copse
Fir Tree Primary School
West Berkshire Community Hospital
Whitelands Park Primary School
St Marys CE Junior Sch
Dunston Park Infant Sch
Council Building
Thatcham Bowling Club
Kingsland Centre
Long Lane
B4009
Fisher's Lane
Stoney Lane
Hermitage Road
Drove Lane
The Ridge
Cold Ash Hill
Ashmore Green Road
Bowling Green Rd
Heath Lane
Westfield Road
Turnpike Rd
Benham Hill
Bath Road
A4
Lower Way
1 grid square represents 500 metres

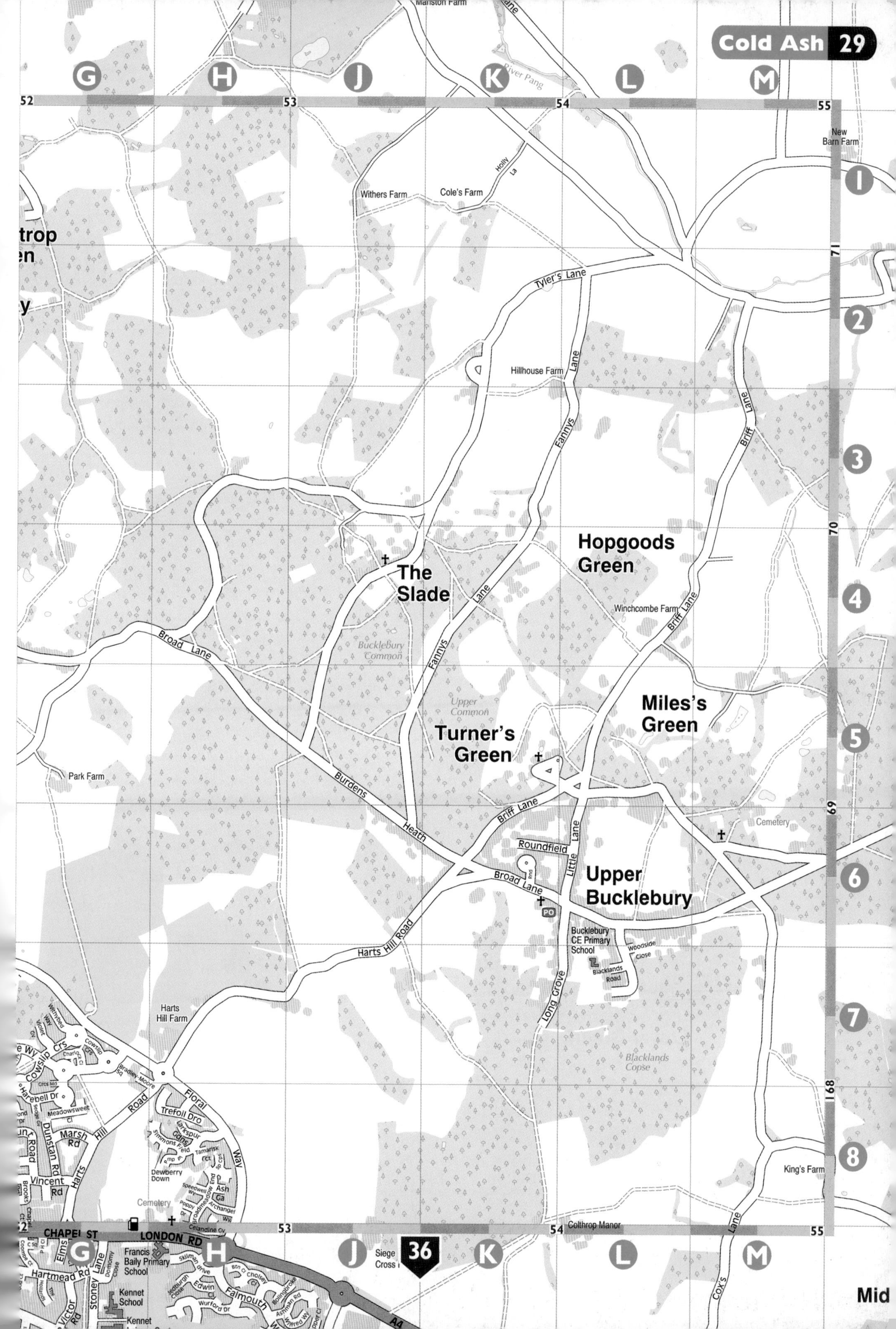

G   H   J   K   L   M

52   53   54   55

New Barn Farm

I

Marston Farm

River Pang

Holly La

Withers Farm   Cole's Farm

71

Tyler's Lane

2

Hillhouse Farm

Fannys Lane

Brif Lane

3

70

Hopgoods
Green

† The
Slade

4

Winchcombe Farm

Brif Lane

Fannys Lane

Broad   Lane

Bucklebury
Common

Upper
Common

Miles's
Green

5

Turner's
Green

69

†

Burdens

Brif Lane

Heath

Little Lane

Cemetery

†

Roundfield

6

Broad   Lane

Upper
Bucklebury

Park Farm

† PO

Harts Hill Road

Bucklebury
CE Primary
School

Woodside
Close

Blacklands
Road

Long Grove

7

Harts
Hill Farm

Blacklands
Copse

168

Whitmers Way

Cowslip CR's

Charq

Chapel

Bradley Moore
Rd

Floral

8

Harebell Dr

Meadowsweet

Trefoil Dro

King's Farm

Marsh
Rd

Harts Hill

Road

Way

Larkspur

Tamarisk

Dewberry
Down

Ash
Ga

Vincent
Rd

Cemetery

†

Celandine Cv

Francis
Baily Primary
School

Kennet School

Siege
Cross

36

Colthrop Manor

Cox's Lane

Kennet

A4

Mid

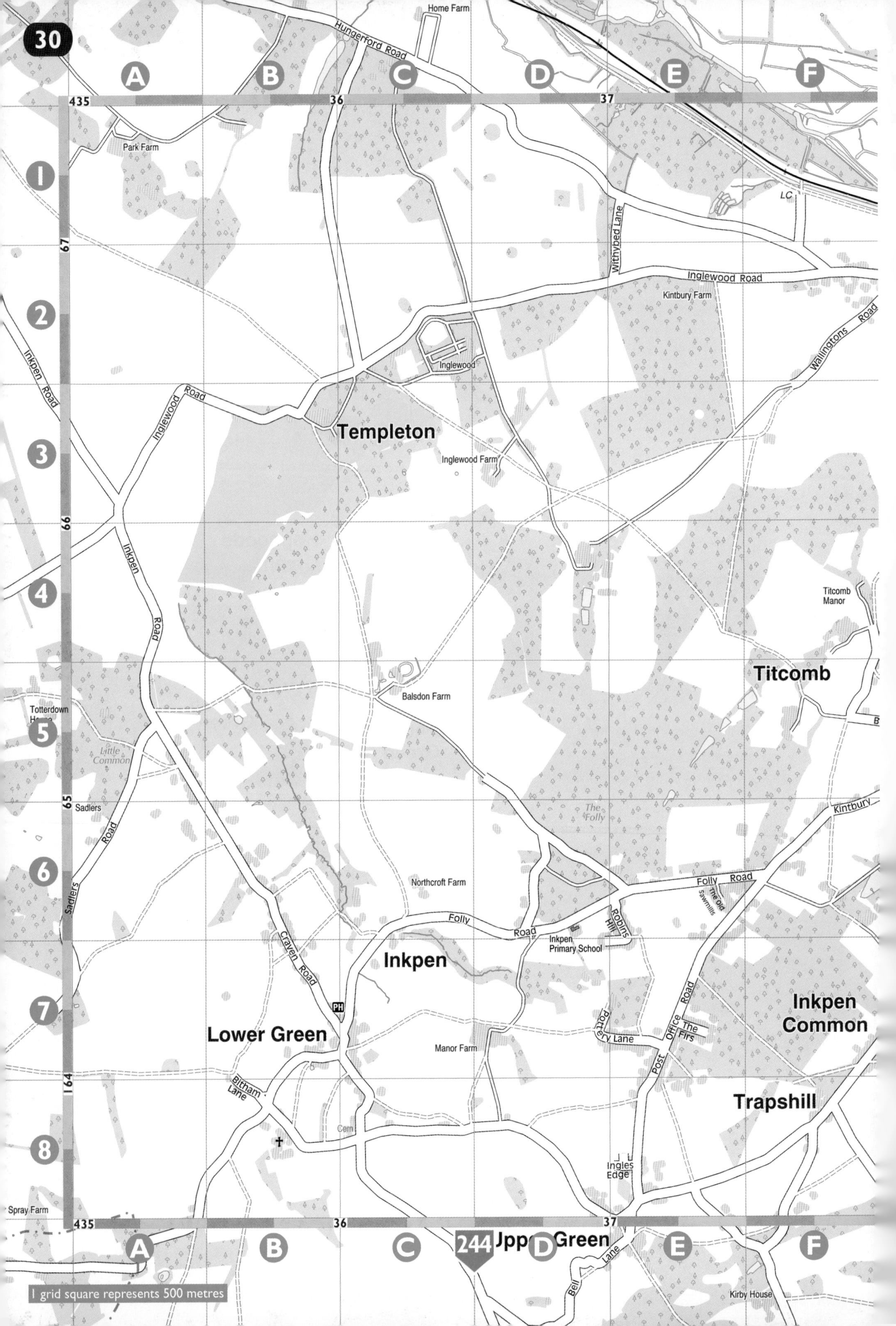

A   B   C   D   E   F

435   36   37

Home Farm

Hungerford Road

Park Farm

I

67

Withybed Lane

Inglewood Road

LC

2

Inkpen Road

Kintbury Farm

Wallingtons Road

Inglewood Road

Inglewood

3

66

Inglewood Road

Templeton

Inglewood Farm

Titcomb
Manor

4

Inkpen Road

Titcomb

Totterdown
House

Balsdon Farm

5

65

*Little
Common*

Sadlers

Kintbury

*The
Folly*

6

Sadlers Road

Northcroft Farm

Folly   Road

The Old
Sawmills

Folly   Road

Robins Hill

Inkpen
Primary School

7

64

Craven Road

PH

Inkpen

Post Office Road

The
Firs

**Inkpen
Common**

Lower Green

Pottery Lane

Manor Farm

Bitham
Lane

Cern

Trapshill

8

†

Ingles
Edge

Spray Farm

435   36   37

A   B   C   D   E   F

Bell Lane

Kirby House

1 grid square represents 500 metres

Barton Court
River Kennet
G
H
J
K
L
M
38
39
40
41
The Wilderness
High Street
Kintbury Station
LC
LC
PH
Kennet & Avon Canal
Mill Bank
The Croft
Church Street
Forge Cl
PO
Kintbury St Marys CE Primary Sch
Harold Road
Newbury St
Irish Hill Road
Titcombe Way
Holt
The Pentlands
Gainsborough Av
Burtons Hill
Lawrence Mead
Long Cl
Craven Wy
Queen's Way
Road
Kintbury
The Haven
Inkpen Road
Dunn Crs
Green
Craven Close
The Green
Layland's Green
Layland's Green
Hamstead Holt Farm
Old Lane
Illwills Border
Kintbury Holt Farm
Hightree Copse
Wergs Copse
Hill
Pebble
Hamstead Mar
32
Great Holt Copse
Lane
Road
Cemetery
Forbury Lane
Forbury House
KINTBURY CROSS WAYS
Holt Lodge
New Mill
Rooksnest Lane
Burgess Lane
Holt Manor Farm
Waterman's Farm
Heads Lane
Hell Corner
Nature Reserve
Watery Lane
Malt House
Hazelby House
8
245
West Woodhay
Fishponds Farm
1
2
3
4
5
6
7
8
67
66
65
164

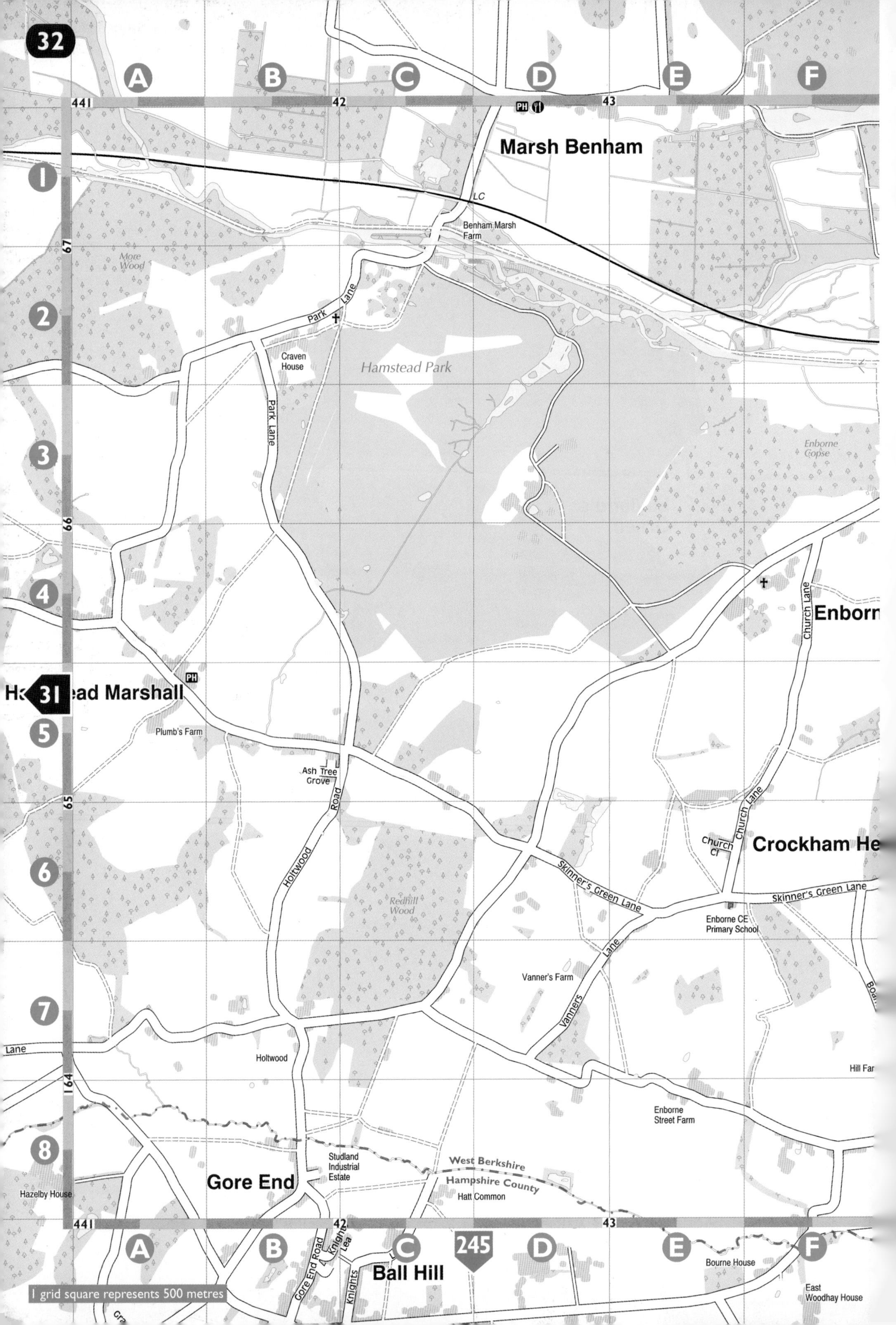

A
B
C
D
E
F
441
42
43
Marsh Benham
LC
Benham Marsh Farm
More Wood
Park Lane
Craven House
Hamstead Park
Park Lane
Enborne Copse
Church Lane
Enborn
31
ead Marshall
Plumb's Farm
Ash Tree Grove
Road
Holtwood
Church Lane
Church Cl
Crockham He
Skinner's Green Lane
Skinner's Green Lane
Redhill Wood
Enborne CE Primary School
Vanner's Farm
Vanners Lane
Lane
Holtwood
Hill Far
Enborne Street Farm
Studland Industrial Estate
Gore End
West Berkshire
Hampshire County
Hatt Common
Hazelby House
245
Gore End Road
Knights Lea
Knights
Ball Hill
Bourne House
East Woodhay House
1 grid square represents 500 metres
1
2
3
4
5
6
7
8
67
66
65
164

NEWBURY
West Fields
Skinners Green
Wash Common
Enborne Row
Wash Water
Benham Park
Elmore House
Church La
Western Avenue
Primary Sch
Old Bath Road
Speen Lane
Croft Lane
Moor Lane
Northcroft Lane
Northcroft Leisure Centre
Newbury Cricket & Hockey Club
The Chequers Htl
Strawberry Hl
Northbrook St
London Rd
Park Wy
Albert Rd
Cncl Bldgs
Marsh La
River Kennet
Kennet and Avon Canal
West Mills
Mallard Court
CAB
Kennet Shop Cen
Corn Ex
Market St
Newbury Station
Council Building
Station Rd
Russell Rd
Berkeley Road
Clifton Rd
Gloucester Road
Craven Road
St George's Av
St Michael's Rd
Rockingham Rd
Kennet Rd
Bartholomew St
Enborne House
Braunfels Wk
Bonemill Lane
Enborne Gv
Pound St
Rectory Cl
Hampton Rd
St Nicolas CE Junior School
Link Road
St John's Rd
Chesterfield Road
Enborne Road
Annie Lawson School
Kingsbridge Rd
Salcombe Road
Floreat Gdns
Mayfair Dr
St Bartholomews School
Buckingham Road
Fifth Road
Fifth Rd
Green Lane
Enborne Gate
Skinner's Green Lane
A34
Newtown Road
Paddock Road
Highfield Rd
St John the Evangelist Infant School
Meadow Rd
Wendan Road
Bartlemy Cl
Bartlemy Rd
The Drive
Tarn Lane
Oaken Grove
Valley Rd
Montgomery Rd
John Rankin Junior School
John Rankin Infant School
Berkshire Circular Routes
Henshaw Crescent
Three Acre Rd
Roebuts Cl
Bruan Rd
Chandos Road
Sandleford
Rupert Road
Robins Cl
Byron Cl
Tydehams
Heather Gdns
Monks Lane
Newbury College
Sidestrand Road
Woodside
Middle Cl
Avenue
Battlesite 1643
Cope Hall Lane
Pond Cl
Elizabeth Av
Hill Cl
Falkland Garth
Barn Crs
Wood Rdg
Andover Road
A343
Foxgrove
Wash Common Farm
Essex St
Cary Cl
Battle Rd
Stuart Road
Charles St
Falkland Rd
Falkland Memorial
Surgery
Newbury RFC
Dormer Cl
Battery End
Wheatlands Lane
Falkland Primary School
Park House School
Spencer Rd
Warren Road
Warren Lodge
Stapleton Cl
Skippons Cl
Hampdens
Villiers Wy
Gilroy Cl
Balfour Crs
Meyrick Drive
Mansell Dr
Gorselands
The Gabriels
Round End
Kendrick Rd
Enborne Ldg La
Enborne St
Bell Holt
Chiltern Cl
Cheviot
Glendale Av
The Hollies
Normay Rise
Holborne Cl
Ladwell Cl
Willowmead Cl
Conifer Crest
The Grange
Garden Close
Badgers Rdg
Lane
Smallridge
Sandpit Hill
Boame's Farm
The Cedars
Enborne Street
Andover Drove
West Berkshire
Hampshire County
River Enborne
Falkland Farm
Station Rd
G
H
J
K
L
M
1
2
3
4
5
6
7
8
44
45
46
47
65
67
164
26
18
34
246

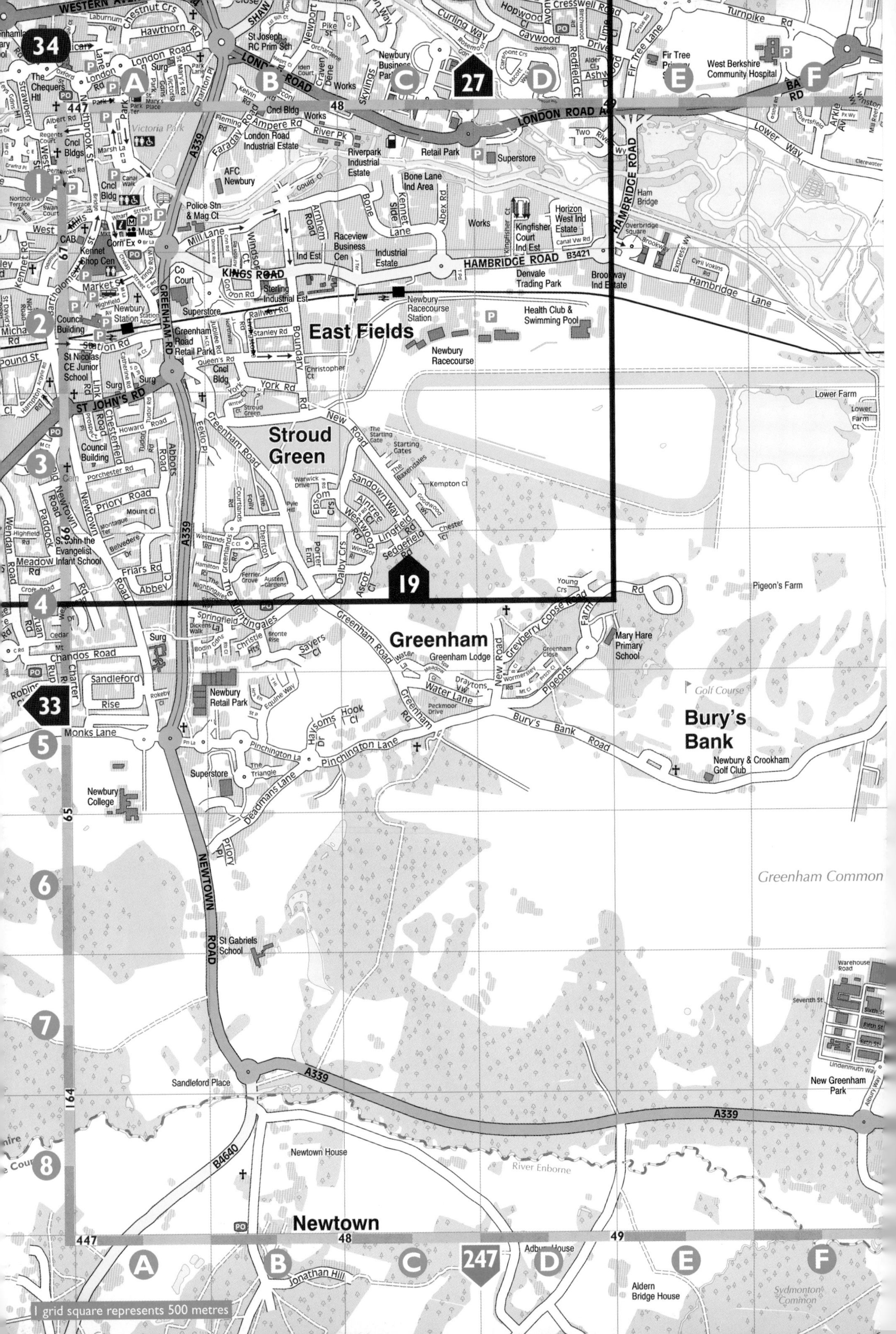
34
27
33
19
247
East Fields
Stroud Green
Greenham
Bury's Bank
Newtown
Greenham Common
Victoria Park
London Road Industrial Estate
Riverpark Industrial Estate
Retail Park
Superstore
Newbury Racecourse
Newbury Racecourse Station
Health Club & Swimming Pool
West Berkshire Community Hospital
Newbury Retail Park
Newbury College
St Gabriels School
Sandleford Place
Newtown House
River Enborne
New Greenham Park
Newbury & Crookham Golf Club
Mary Hare Primary School
Greenham Lodge
Pigeon's Farm
Lower Farm
Aldern Bridge House
Sydmonton Common
A339
HAMBRIDGE ROAD
LONDON ROAD
GREENHAM RD
NEWTOWN ROAD
ST JOHN'S RD
KINGS ROAD
1 grid square represents 500 metres

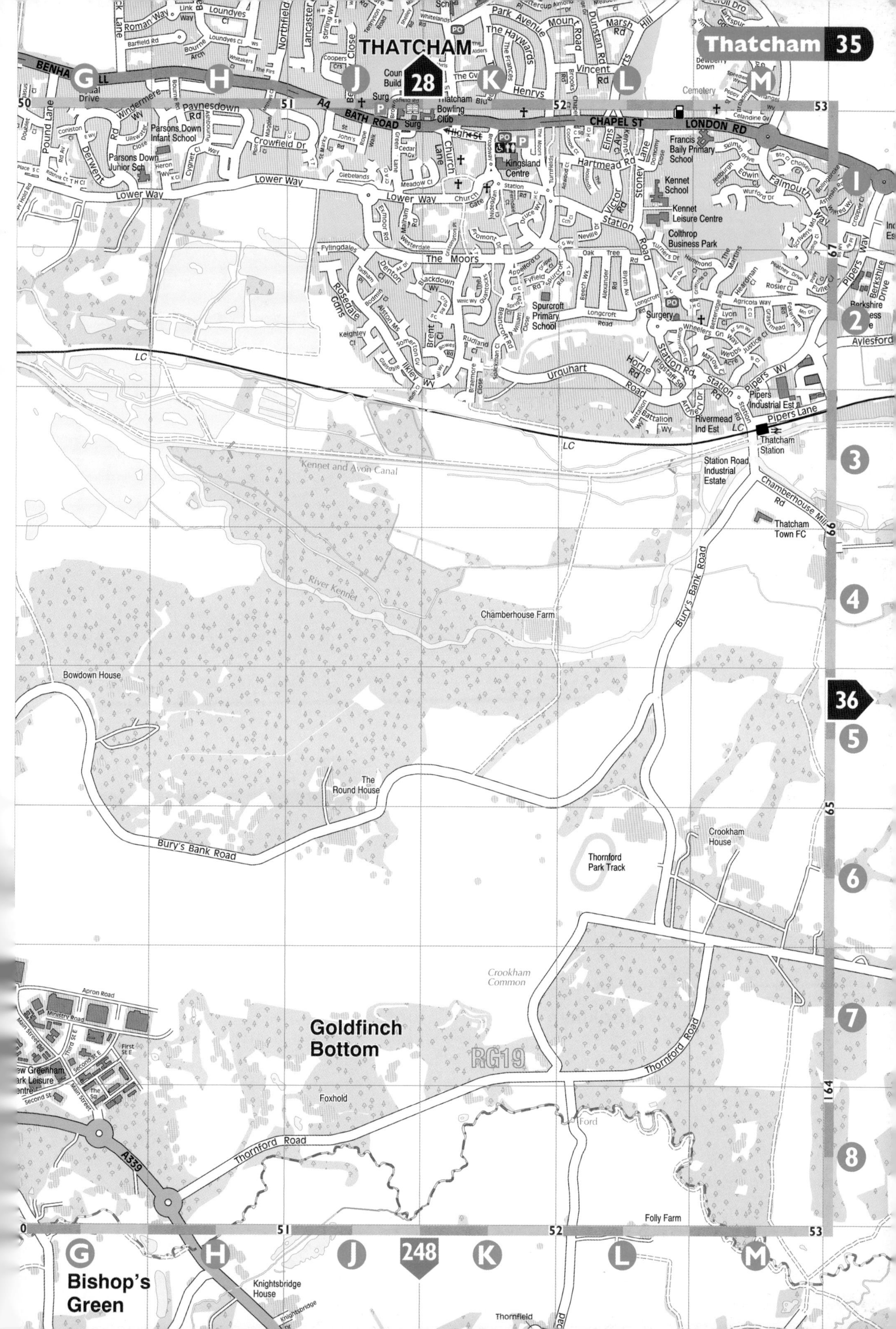

THATCHAM

28

Bishop's Green

Goldfinch Bottom

RG19

248

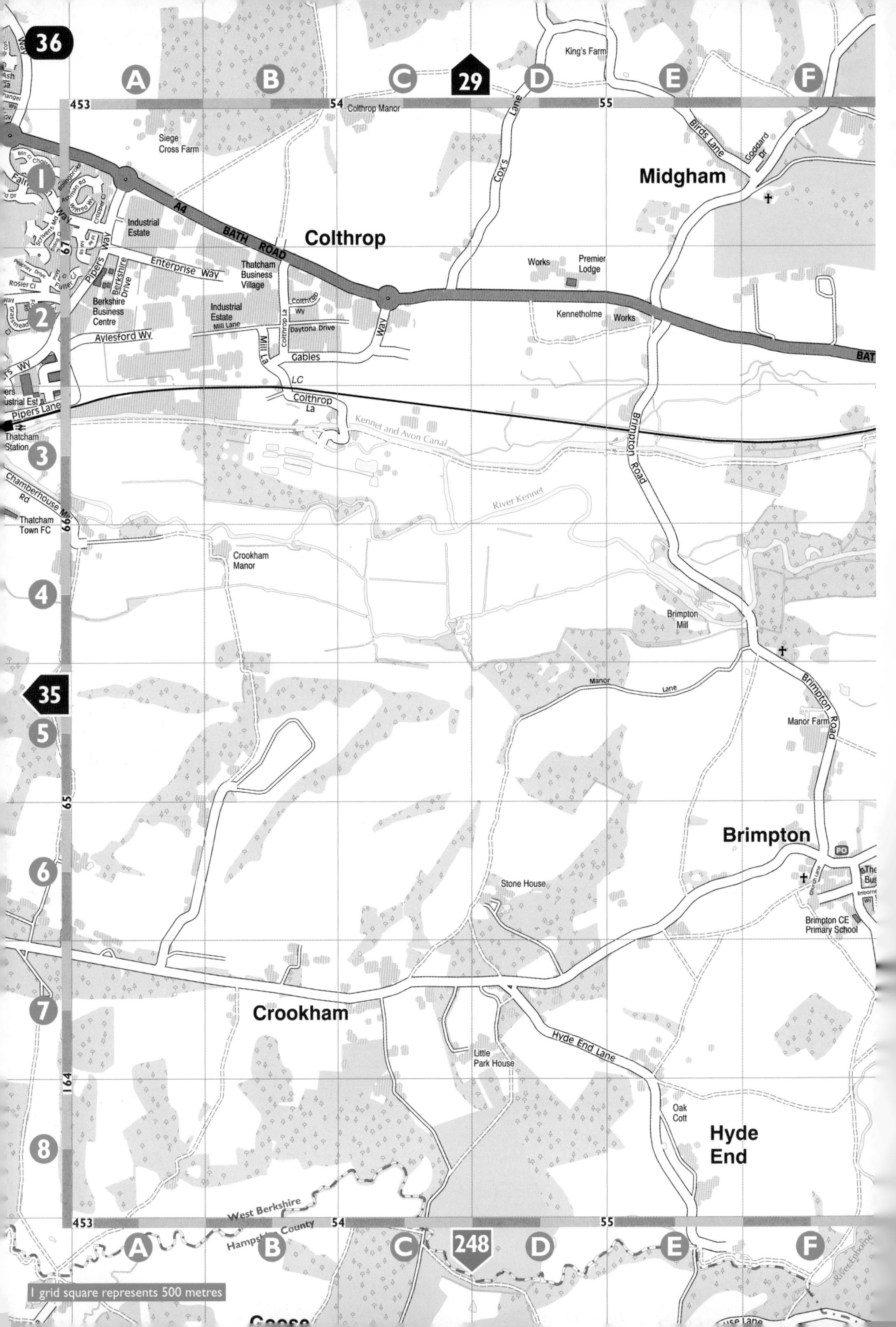

A   B   C   29   D   E   F

453   54   Colthrop Manor   55

Siege
Cross Farm

Midgham

King's Farm

Birds Lane

Goddard Dr

Cox's Lane

1

Fairm

Ash

Cholsey

Bun

Cippenham Rd

Crossel Cl

Pivett Wy

Industrial
Estate

A4   BATH   ROAD

Colthrop

Pipers Way

Berkshire
Drive

Enterprise Way

Thatcham
Business Village

Works

Premier
Lodge

2

Rosier Cl

Grassmead

Way

Berkshire
Business
Centre

Aylesford Wy.

Industrial
Estate
Mill Lane

Colthrop La

Colthrop
Wy

Daytona Drive

Gables

Mill La

Way

Kennetholme   Works

BAT

Fuller Cl

3

rs Wy

ustrial Est

Pipers Lane

Thatcham
Station

LC

Colthrop
La

Kennet and Avon Canal

Brimpton Road

4

Chamberhouse Mill Rd

Thatcham
Town FC

River Kennet

Crookham
Manor

Brimpton
Mill

35

65

5

Manor   Lane

Manor Farm

Brimpton Road

Brimpton

6

PO

Church Lane

Brimpton CE
Primary School

Endmore

aThe
Bus

Stone House

7

Crookham

Hyde End Lane

Little
Park House

8

164

Oak
Cott

Hyde
End

453   54   West Berkshire   55

Hampshire County

A   B   C   248   D   E   F

Rivar Enborne

Goose

Upper Woolhampton
Woolhampton CE Primary School
Carbinswood Lane
Wessex Downs Golf Club
Place Farm
Midgham House
Hallcourt Farm
Midgham Park
The Court
Elstree School
Home Farm School
New Road Hill
Woolhampton
Victor Pl
Woolhampton Hill
Orchard Close
Midgham Station
Station Rd
Angel Mead
LC
BATH ROAD
A4
Railside
Frouds Lane
Old Mill
BASINGSTOKE
River Enborne
A340
Aldermaston CE Primary School
Wasing Lane
Wasing Lower Farm
Aldermaston
The Street
Congreve Close
Shalford Farm
Back Lane
Wasing Park
Wasing
Wasing Farm
Youngs Industrial Estate
Boot Farm
PAICES HILL
Wasing Wood
Blacknest Farm
38
249

A   B   C   D   E   F

459   60   BATH ROAD A4   61

Hall Place Farm

Knott Lane

Beenham Grange

Courtyard by Marriott

The Crescent

River Kennet

Berkshire Circular Route

Oak End Wy

1

67

Aldermaston Station

A340

Wharfside

Berkshire Circular Routes

Mallard Way

Heron Wy

Lower

Swan Drive

Aldermaston Wharf

Padworth Lane

BASINGSTOKE ROAD

Orchard Dene Dr

Mill Lane

Alderbridge School

Lodge Farm

2

A340

Froud's Lane

Old Mill

Berkshire Circular Routes

Padworth College

Padworth

The Ark School

School Road

3

66

BASINGSTOKE ROAD

†

4

A340

Fisherman's Lane

Upper Church Farm

The Old Rectory

Aldermaston Primary

37

PO

PH

The Street

Cedars School

Berkshire Circular Routes

Rectory Road

Hatch Farm House

5

THE ST

Congreve Close

Church Road

Spring Lane

6

65

A340

Portland House

†

Raghill

Court Farm

Raghill Farm

Pa

7

164

HILL

Red Lane

Reading Road

Chapel Lane

Youngs Industrial Estate

Little Heath

Soke Rd

8

PAICES

Ald Sok

459   60   61

A   B   C   44   D   E   F

Deco Pond

I grid square represents 500 metres

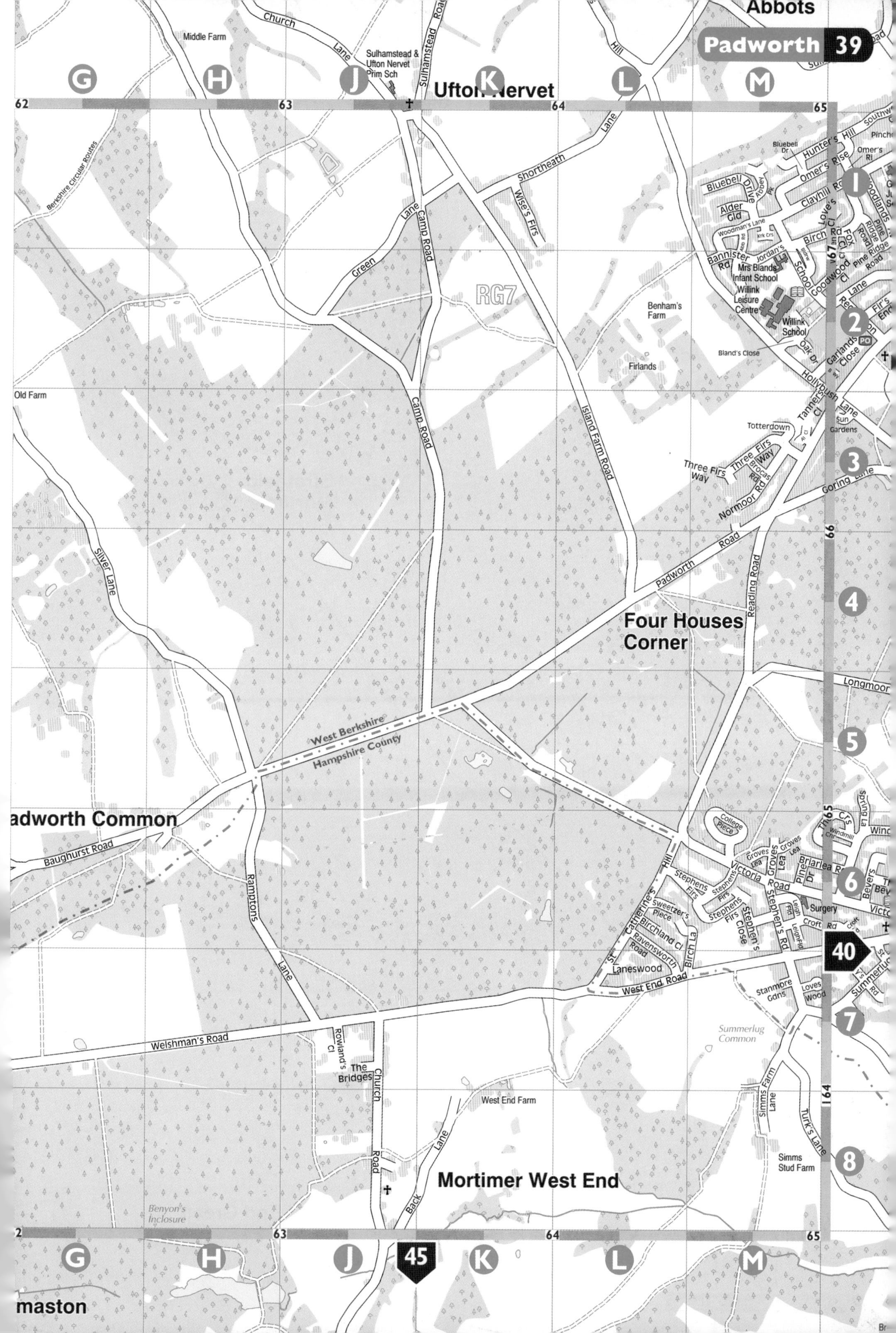

G   H   J   K   L   M

62   63   64   65

Church Lane

Middle Farm

Sulhamstead &
Ufton Nervet
Prim Sch

Ufton Nervet

Shortheath

Wise's Firs

RG7

Green Lane

Camp Road

Island Farm Road

Benham's
Farm

Firlands

Bland's Close

Berkshire Circular Routes

Old Farm

Silver Lane

Ramptons Lane

West Berkshire
Hampshire County

Padworth Common

Baughurst Road

Welshman's Road

Rowland's Cl

The Bridges

Church Road

Back Lane

Benyon's
Inclosure

Mortimer West End

West End Farm

West End Road

Laneswood

Ravensworth
Road

Birchland Cl

Sweetzer's Piece

Catherine St

Birch La

Stephen's Close

Stephen's Firs

Stephens Firs

St Stephens
Hill

Victoria Road

College
Piece

Groves Lea

Groves Lea

Briarlea Rd

Surgery

Croft Rd

Leigh Field

Stanmore
Gdns

Loves
Wood

Summerlug
Common

Simms Farm
Lane

Turk's Lane

Simms
Stud Farm

Four Houses
Corner

Padworth Road

Reading Road

Longmoor

Normoor Rd

Three Firs
Way

Three Firs Way

Totterdown

Goring Lane

Tamsett Cl

Hollybush Lane

Garlands Close

Sun
Gardens

PO

Oak Dr

Bluebell
Drive

Alder
Cld

Birch Cl

Bannister
Rd

Mrs Bland's
Infant School

Willink
Leisure
Centre

Willink
School

Woodman's Lane

Jordan's Lane

Goodwood

Clayhill Rd

Love's

Hunter's Hill

Omer's Rise

Bluebell
Dr

Omer's Rl

Pinch

Woodlands

Pine Ridge
Road

Fir's
Cl

Spring La

Windmill

Beyers

Victo

I

2

3

4

5

6

40

7

8

A   B   C   D   E   F

465   66   67

Longmoor Lane

Warennes Wood

Sawyers Ley

Wokefield Park Golf Club

Mortimer Park

Golf Course

I

65

Mortimer Common

Berkshire Circular Routes

Brewery Common

Mann's Farm

Mortimer House

Nightingale Lane

Windmill Road

Windmill Clr

The Bevers

The Bevers

Briarlea Rd

Groves Lea

Groves

St Stephen's Rd

Leigh Fld

Surgery

Victoria Road

King Street

Hammonds Heath

Wheat's Farm

Berkshire Circular Routes

2

Mortimer

PO

St Mary's Rd

Summerlug Rd

St John's Rd

Garth Rd

Croft

Loves Wood

Crft

Mortimer St John's Infant School

The Orchard Road

The Avenue

Berkshire Circular Routes

Street

Monktons Lane

Gordon Palmer Close

The Street

Grazeley Road

39

Stanmore Gdns

The Avenue

The Avenue

Kiln Lane

Mortimer Lodge

Mortimer St Marys CE Junior School

Church Farm Barns

**Stratfield
†Mortimer**

Mortimer Station

Station Road

3

64

Simms Farm Lane

Turk's Lane

The Avenue

Drury Lane

Berkshire Circular Routes

Pitfield Lane

The For

4

Farm

5

63

Brocas Lands Farm

Berkshire Circular Routes

Littl Par

Sheepgrove Farm

6

Butlers Lands

West Berkshire

Wigmore Farm

45

Hampshire County

Park Lane

7

I 62

North Copse

Green Lane

8

Clappers Farm Rd

Brickledon's Farm

Lavell's Farm

Lavell's Lane

The Springs

Mortimer Lane

West End Green

Fair Oak Lane

Herriot's Far

465   66   67

A   B   C   D   E   F

I grid square represents 500 metres

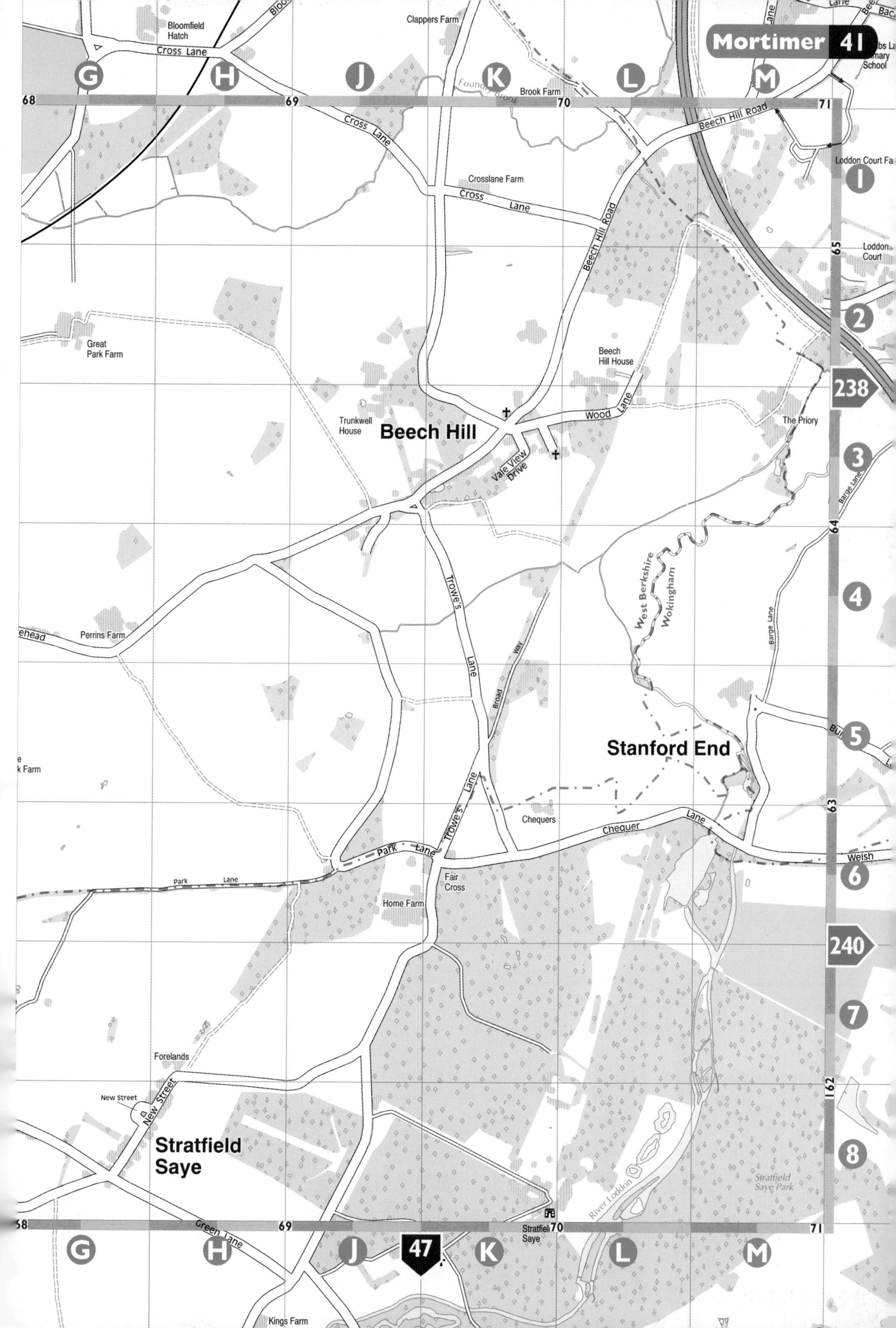

G H J K L M

68 69 70 71

Bloomfield Hatch

Cross Lane

Clappers Farm

Founds Brook

Brook Farm

Beech Hill Road

Loddon Court Fa

I

65 Loddon Court

Crosslane Farm

Cross Lane

Beech Hill Road

2

238

Great Park Farm

Beech Hill House

Trunkwell House

Beech Hill

Wood Lane

The Priory

3

Vale View Drive

64

West Berkshire Wokingham

Barge Lane

4

ehead Perrins Farm

Trowes Lane

Broad Way

Stanford End

Burt Lane

5

k Farm

Trowes Lane

Chequers

Chequer Lane

63 Welsh

6

Park Lane

Fair Cross

Home Farm

240

Park Lane

7

Forelands

162

New Street

New Street

8

Stratfield Saye

Stratfield Saye Park

River Loddon

58 Green Lane 69 70 71

G H J **47** K L M

Stratfield Saye

Kings Farm

Wick
Hill

The Ridges

Wellingtonia Avenue
(Arboretum)

Wellingtonia Avenue

North
Court

East
Court

Finchampstead
Sports Club

THE VILLAGE

Primary
School

Burnmoor
Meadow

Ridge Farm

Warren
Lodge

Rectory Farm

Lower Sandhurst Road

Moor
Green Farm

Hall Farm

Blackwater River

Wokingham
Hampshire County

Mill Farm

Eversley
CC

Eversley
Cross

Eversley
Cen

California Chalet
Touring Park

Gorse Ride
Junior School

King's
Mere

Queen's
Mere

Brooklands

Thames castles path

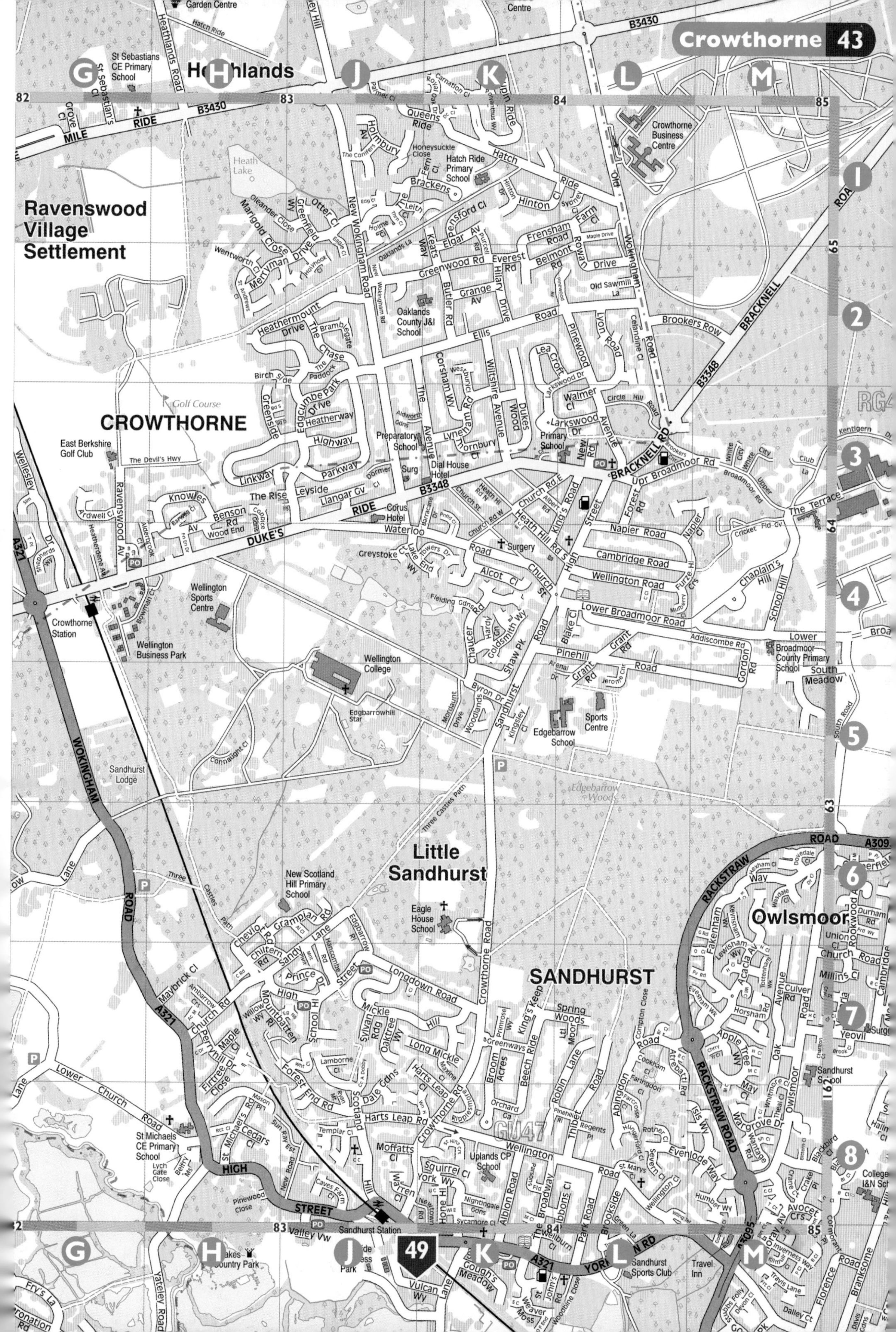
Crowthorne 43
Heathlands
Garden Centre
Hatch Ride
St Sebastians CE Primary School
Mile Ride
B3430
Ravenswood Village Settlement
Heath Lake
Queens Ride
Holmbury Av
Honeysuckle Close
Hatch Ride Primary School
Crowthorne Business Centre
Brackens
Hinton Rd
Pensford Cl
Elgar Av
Keats Way
Frensham Road
Belmont Rd
Rowan Drive
Farm Cl
Old Sawmill La
Greenwood Rd
Everest Rd
Hilary Drive
Grange Av
Butler Rd
New Wokingham Road
Wokingham Road
Oakland's County J&I School
Marigold Close
Merryman Drive
Greenfield Wy
Otter Cl
Wentworth Cl
Heathermount Drive
The Chase
Bramblegate
Ellis Road
Brookers Row
Bracknell
B3348
Pinewood
Lyon Road
Lea Croft
Larkswood Dr
Walmer Cl
Circle Hill Road
Corsham Wy
Lyneham Rd
Wiltshire Avenue
Dukes Wood
Thornbury Cl
Edgcumbe Park Drive
Heatherway
Highway
Parkway
Linkway
Greenside
Birch Side
Golf Course
CROWTHORNE
East Berkshire Golf Club
The Devil's Hwy
Ravenswood Av
Preparatory School
Surg
Dial House Hotel
Primary School
Bracknell Rd
Upr Broadmoor Rd
Broadmoor Rd
White City
Club La
The Terrace
Knowles Av
Benson Rd
Wood End
The Rise
Leyside
Llangar Gv
Dormer Cl
Corus Hotel
Duke's Ride
Waterloo Road
Church St
Heath Hill Rd
King's Road
High Street
Forest Rd
Napier Road
Napier Cl
Cricket Fld Gv
Cambridge Road
Wellington Road
Furze Hl Crs
Chaplain's Hill
School Hill
Lower Broadmoor Road
Addiscombe Rd
Lower Broadmoor Rd
Broadmoor County Primary School
South Meadow
South Road
Surgery
Greystoke Ct
Lake End Wy
Alcot Cl
Wellesley Dr
Shepherds Wy
Heatherdene Av
Crowthorne Station
Wellington Sports Centre
Wellington Business Park
Bowman Cl
Fielding Gdns
Chaucer Rd
Hardy Gn
Goldsmith Wy
Shaw Pk
Blake Cl
Pinehill Road
Grant Rd
Jerome Cnr
Gordon Rd
Wellington College
Edgbarrowhill Star
Byron Dr
Mordaunt Drive
Woodlands
Sandhurst Road
Kingsley Cl
Edgebarrow School
Sports Centre
Edgebarrow Woods
Connaught Cl
Sandhurst Lodge
Three Castles Path
Little Sandhurst
Wokingham Road
A321
Rackstraw Road
A3095
A309
Owlsmoor
New Scotland Hill Primary School
Eagle House School
Cheviot Rd
Grampian Rd
Chiltern Rd
Sandy Lane
Prince Dr
Edgbarrow Ri
Longdown Road
Crowthorne Road
SANDHURST
Maybrick Cl
Ambarrow Crs
Church Rd
Perryhill Dr
Maple Cl
Firtree Close
Mountbatten Ri
Willow Wy
School Hl
Mickle Hill
Sylvan Rdg
Oaktree Wy
Long Mickle
Lamborne Cl
Forest End Rd
Dale Gdns
Harts Leap Cl
Harts Leap Rd
Scotland Hill
Broom Acres
Beech Ride
Kings Keep
Spring Woods
Robin Lane
Thibet Road
Regents Pl
Abingdon Road
Cookham Cl
Faringdon Cl
Atrebatti Rd
Isis Wy
Evenlode Way
Humber Wy
Wellington Cl
Lower Church Road
St Michaels CE Primary School
Lych Gate Close
Berry Ms
St Michael's Rd
Cedars
High Street
Pinewood Close
Caves Farm Cl
Moffatts Cl
Templar Cl
Squirrel Cl
York Wy
Warren Cl
Uplands CP School
Nightingale Gdns
Sycamore Cl
Albion Road
The Broadway
Gibbons Cl
Park Road
Brookside
Wellington Road
St Marys Cl
GU47
Sandhurst Station
Valley Vw
Yorktown Rd
Sandhurst Sports Club
Travel Inn
Gough's Meadow
Vulcan Wy
Weaver Moss
Wellburn Cl
Sandhurst School
Yeovil Rd
Owlsmoor Rd
Wargrove Dr
Apple Tree Wy
May Cl
Avocet Crs
Inverness Way
Travis Lane
Florence Road
Branksome
Dalley Ct
Cormorant Pl
Blackbird Cl
College Town I&N Sch
Rookwood Av
Durham Rd
Union Cl
Church Road
Millins Cl
Culver Rd
Horsham Rd
Lewisham Wy
Acacia Av
Fakenham Wy
Hexham Cl
Dovedale Cl
Yateley Road
Fry's La
Coronation Rd
Yateley Country Park
Lakes Country Park
Kentigern Dr
RG47
49
G H J K L M
1 2 3 4 5 6 7 8
82 83 84 85
61 62 63 64 65

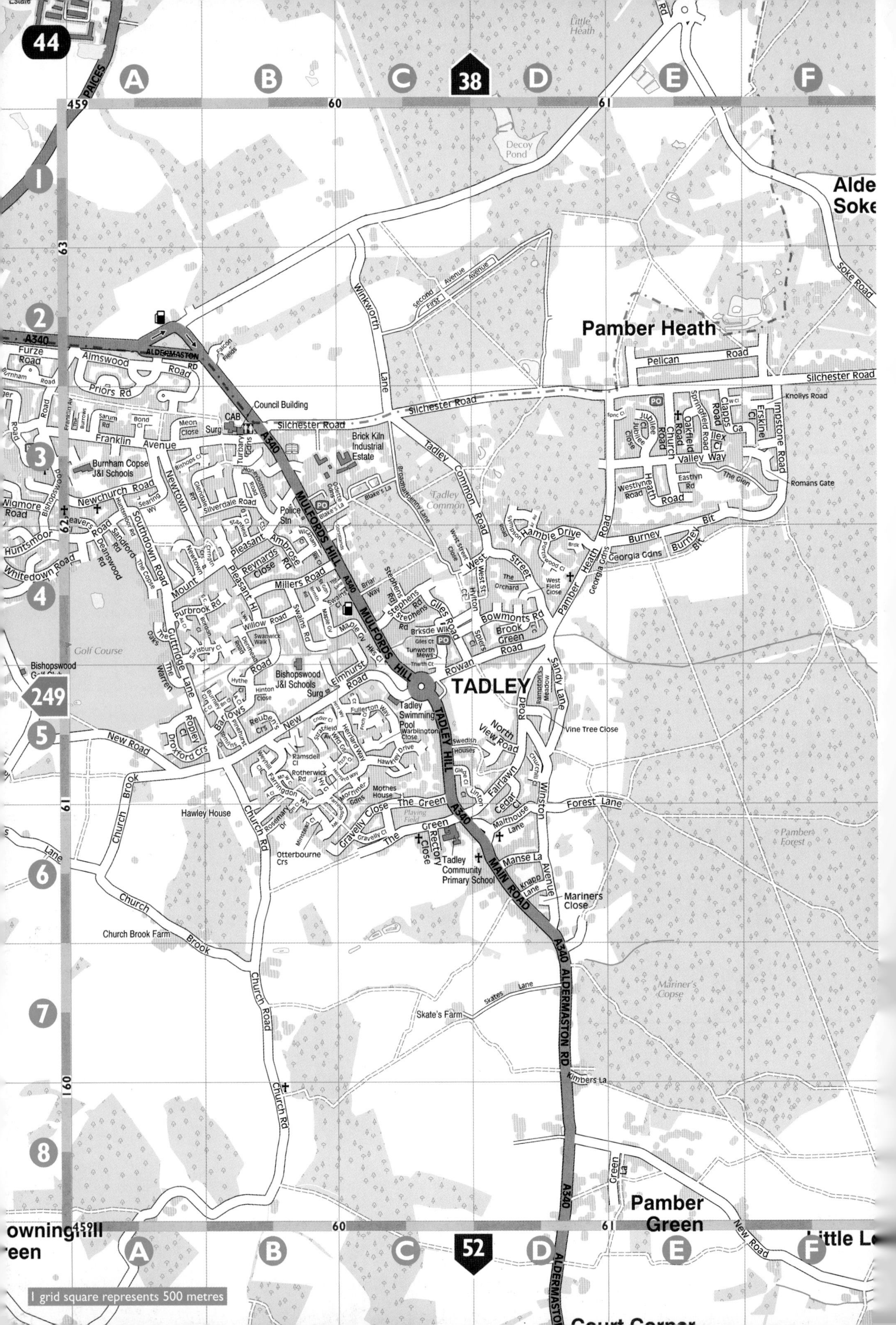
44
38
52
249
A
B
C
D
E
F
1
2
3
4
5
6
7
8
TADLEY
Pamber Heath
Pamber Green
Little Heath
Decoy Pond
Tadley Common
Pamber Forest
Mariner's Copse
Golf Course
A340
MULFORDS HILL
TADLEY HILL
MAIN ROAD
ALDERMASTON RD
Silchester Road
Franklin Avenue
Newchurch Road
Church Road
Church Brook
New Road
Forest Lane
Soke Road
Pelican Road
Council Building
Brick Kiln Industrial Estate
Burnham Copse J&I Schools
Bishopswood J&I Schools
Tadley Swimming Pool
Tadley Community Primary School
Hawley House
Church Brook Farm
Skate's Farm
Mothes House
Otterbourne Crs
Vine Tree Close
Mariners Close
Romans Gate
Knollys Road
1 grid square represents 500 metres

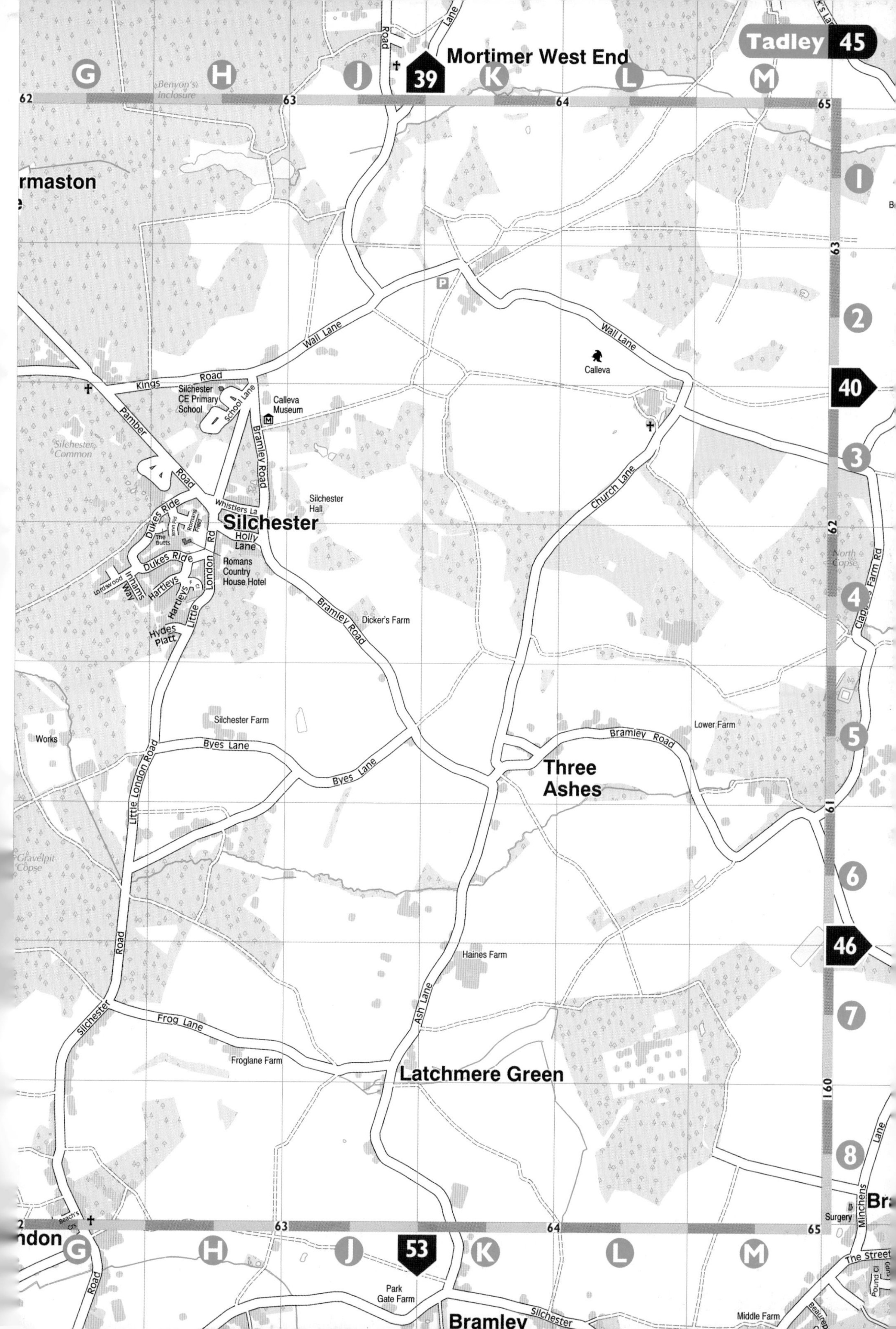

G   H   J   **39** Mortimer West End   K   L   M

62   63   64   65

I

2

40

3

Benyon's
Inclosure

...rmaston
...e

Wall Lane

Calleva

Wall Lane

Kings   Road

Pamber

Silchester
CE Primary
School

School Lane

Calleva
Museum

Church Lane

Clappers Farm Rd

North
Copse

62

Silchester
Common

Bramley Road

Whistlers La

Silchester
Hall

Silchester

Holly
Lane

Dukes Ride

The Butts

Romans Field

London Rd

Lordswood

Dukes Ride

Hartleys

Little London

Inhams Way

Hydes
Platt

Romans Country
House Hotel

Bramley Road

Dicker's Farm

4

Silchester Farm

Works

Byes Lane

Little London Road

Byes Lane

Lower Farm

Bramley   Road

**Three
Ashes**

5

161

Gravelpit
Copse

6

46

Haines Farm

7

Silchester Road

Frog Lane

Ash Lane

160

Minchens Lane

Froglane Farm

Latchmere Green

8

Surgery

Br...

...ndon

...each's Cits

G   H   J   **53**   K   L   M

The Street

Pound Cl

62   63   64   65

Park
Gate Farm

Silchester

Middle Farm

Bramley

46
40
45
53
54
Bramley
West End Green
Fair Oak Green
Bramley Green
Barefoot House
Holly Cross
Oliver's Farm
Folly Farm
Southend Farm
Lillymill Farm
Herriot's Farm
Lavell's
Green Lane
Stratfield Saye Road
Folly Lane
Mill Lane
Oliver's Lane
Minchens Lane
Sherfield Road
Lane End
German Road
Officers Row
Campbell Court Industrial Estate
Bramley CE J&I School
Bramley Station
Strawberry Fields
Surgery
The Street
Coopers Lane
Moat Close
Bromelia Close
Longbridge Rd
The Smithy
Farriers Cl
Watford Copse
Bow Brook
Baker's Farm
Dixon Road
Reading Road
Bramley Road
Greenway
Sherfield on Loddon CC
River Loddon
Rags Copse
1 grid square represents 500 metres

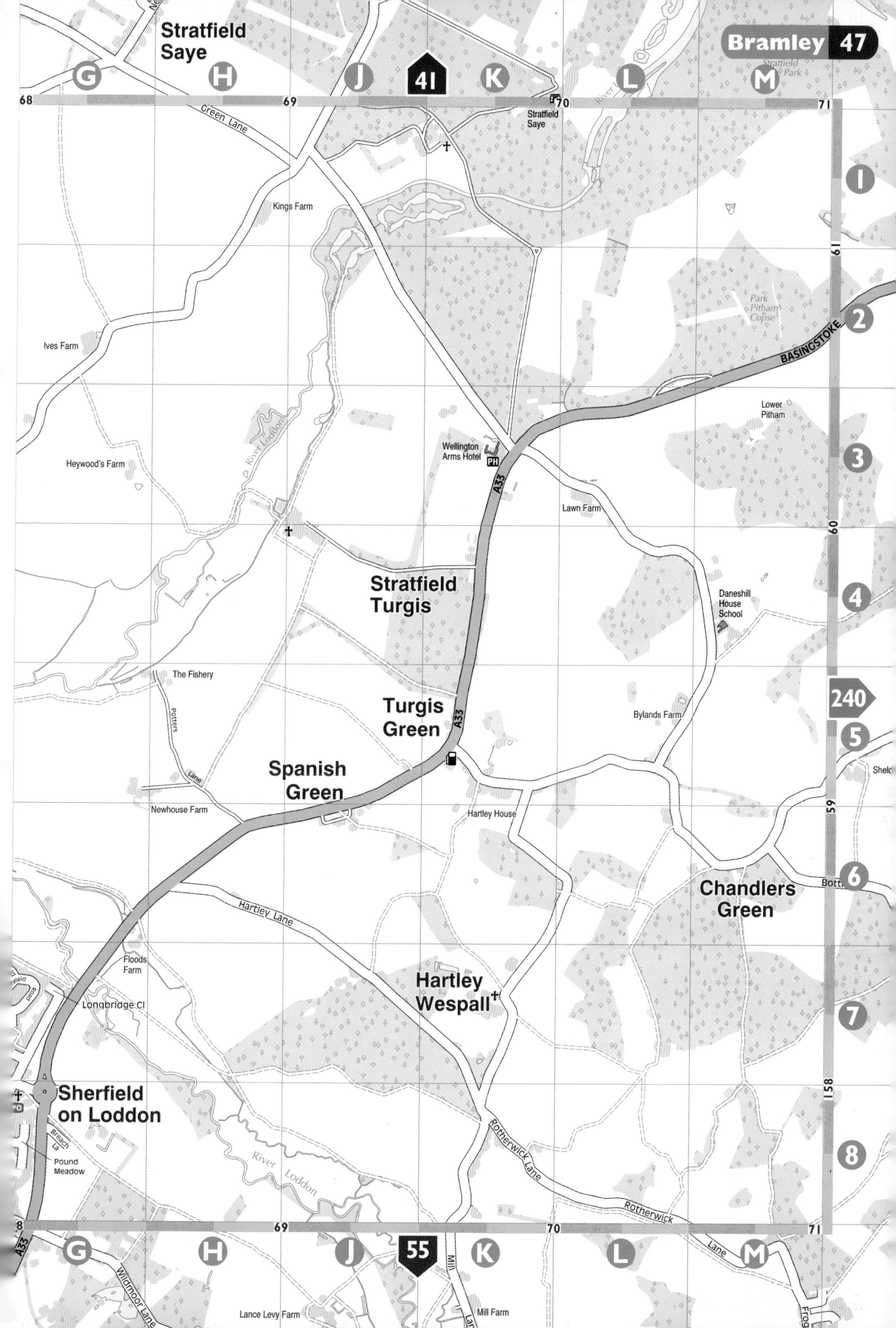
Stratfield Saye
G
H
J
41
K
L
M
Stratfield Park
68
69
70
71
Green Lane
Stratfield Saye
River
1
Kings Farm
61
Park Pitham Copse
2
BASINGSTOKE
Ives Farm
Lower Pitham
Wellington Arms Hotel
PH
3
Heywood's Farm
River Loddon
A33
Lawn Farm
60
Stratfield Turgis
Daneshill House School
4
The Fishery
240
Turgis Green
A33
Bylands Farm
Potters
5
Spanish Green
Lane
Sheld
Newhouse Farm
Hartley House
59
6
Chandlers Green
Both
Hartley Lane
Floods Farm
Hartley Wespall
Longbridge Cl
7
Sherfield on Loddon
158
Breach La
Rotherwick Lane
8
Pound Meadow
River Loddon
Rotherwick
A33
G
H
J
55
K
L
Lane
M
Wildmoor Lane
Mill
Lance Levy Farm
Mill Farm
Frog

48
42
41
59
A
B
C
D
E
F
1
2
3
4
5
6
7
8
479
80
81
61
60
59
158
Eversley CC
Eversley Cross
Eversley
PH
PO
Mayfield Ct
Jarvis Cl
Paul's Fld
Road
The Fielders
Yeomans
Sherlock Lea
Hollybush Lane
Hollybush Ln
Northwick
New Rd
Chequers Lane
B3016
Marsh Lane
Fox Lane
B3272
Canberra Close
Three Castles Path
Mayflower Dr
Crosby Gdns
Reading Road
Blaire Pk
Copse La
Moulsham La
River Rd
Coombe Rd
Moulsham Lane
Ives Cl
Brooklands
Castor Ct
West Green
Green La
Frensham Cl
Celandine Ct
Fallowfield
Vicarage Road
The Link
Crondall End
Chandlers
Vicarage Lane
Croft Lane
The Gallop
Village Way
Firglen Drive
Bridge Wk
Mill Lane
The Crs
W Fryerne
Stable Vw
Broome Cl
Lane
Preparatory School
Yateley Green
Up Green
Firgrove Road
Cooper's Hill
Hill
Clover La
Bracken La
Ilex Cl
Robins Gv Crs
Firgrove Road
Bramling Av
Aylesham Way
Blakes Ride
Colwyn Cl
Selwyn Dr
Southwark Cl
Partridge Av
Swallow Cl
Kingfisher Dr
Connaught Cl
School Lane
Firgrove Manor
Rokes Pl
Tesimond Dr
Monteagle La
Dunsmore Gdns
Rywes Av
Oldcorne Hollow
Huddington Gld
Throgmorton Road
Carnet Fld
Catesby Gdns
Westfields Primary School
Yateley School & 6th Form Centre
Kits Croft
Old School La
Macrae Rd
Calcott Pk
Hall Lane
Wistaria La
Lawford Crescent
Cranford Park Drive
GU46
Health Centre
YATE
St Peter's CE Jun School
Yateley Infant School
Home Park Rd
Farm View
Winton Crs
Drive
Hall Farm Crescent
Manor Park
Maple Gdns
Lucas Cl
Handford Lane
The Dell
Byways
Lymington Av
Hilltop Vw
Vigo La
Patten Av
Cullen Cl
Dickens Wy
Limecroft
Monteagle La
Greenhaven
Shelley Wk
Monteagle Lane
The Sett
Wordsworth
Cornfields
Cibbs Way
Keats Wy
Hardy Avenue
Newlands CP School
Dungells La
Hangerfield Cl
Mistletoe Rd
The Oaks
Newlands Cl
Christie Walk
Wildwood Gdns
Herriot Court
Blackbushe Business Park
Gorselands
Stookes Way
Harvest Close
Wordsworth Av
Betjeman Walk
Little Vigo
Vigo Lane
Freshwood Dr
Whitley Road
Barton's Drive
Birchview Cl
Tudor Drive
Woodlands
Mims Cl
Walnut Cl
Handford Lane
Works
Eversley Common
Works
Blackbushe Airport
A30
Hartford Bridge Flats
A327
B3013
Cricket
West Minley Farm
Yateley Heath Wood
Blackbushes Road
Minley Wood
Blackbushe
1 grid square represents 500 metres

Frogmore
Darby Green
Cricket Hill
Blackwater
Sandhurst Station
Trilakes Country Park
Yateley Common Country Park
Yateley Common
Hawley Common
Hornley Common
Hawley Lake
Minley Manor
Home Farm
Hill Farm
Cemetery
Bracknell Forest
Hampshire County
Blackwater River
Frogmore Community School
Potley Hill County Primary School
Frogmore Junior School
Frogmore County Infant School
Sandhurst Sports Club
Travel Inn
White Hart Industrial Estate
Pinewood Infant School
Lakeside Business Park
Uplands CP School
St Michaels CE Primary School
READING ROAD
B3272
A30
A321
A327
MINLEY ROAD
YORKTOWN RD
MARSHALL ROAD
A3095
GU17
GU47
43
50
60

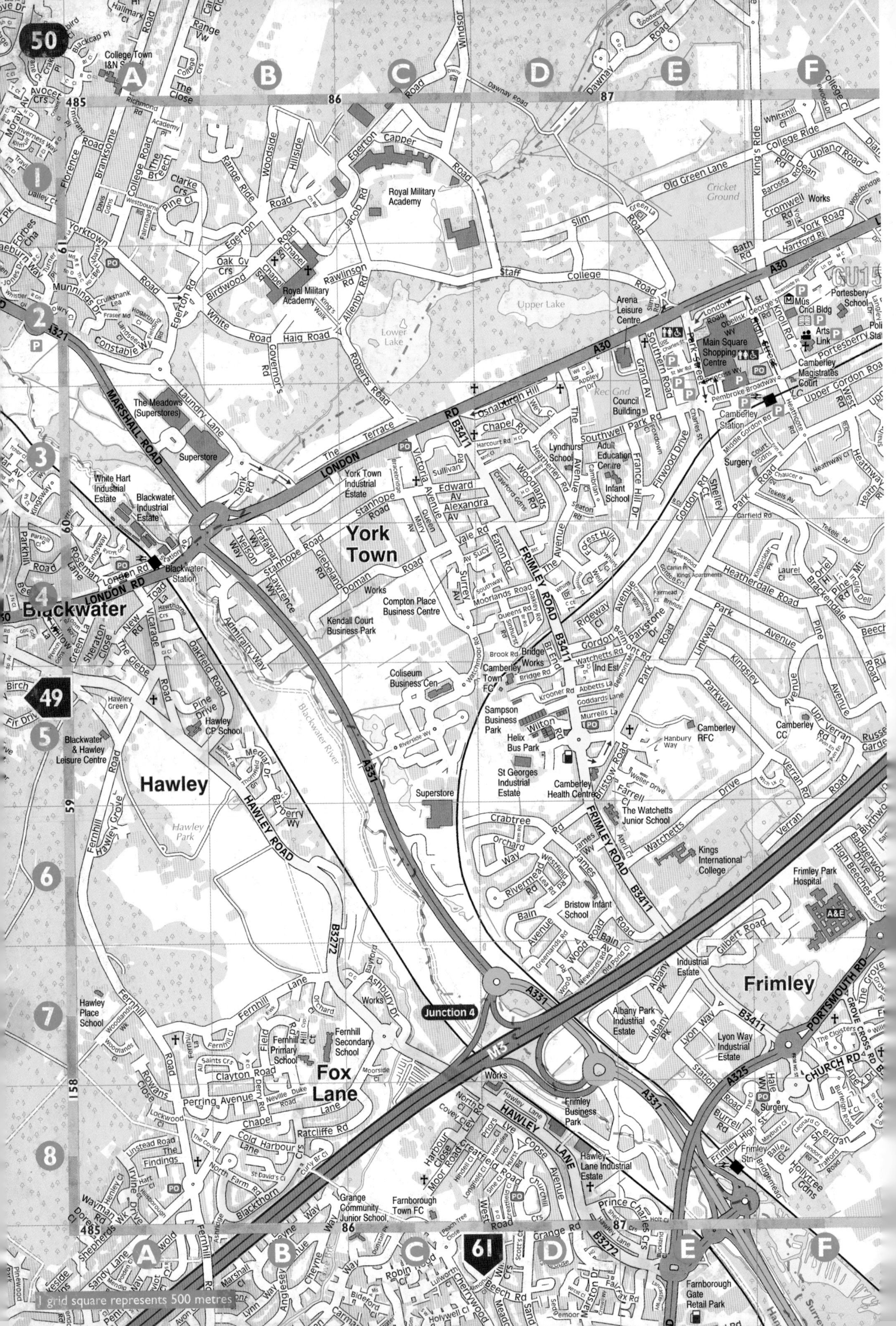
50
A
B
C
D
E
F
485
86
87
1
2
3
4
5
6
7
8
61
60
59
158
49
61
College Town I&N S
Richmond Rd
Florence Road
Branksome
College Road
The Beech
Academy
Range Ride
Woodside
Hillside
Egerton
Capper
Road
Windsor
Dawnay Road
Dawnay
Royal Military Academy
Old Green Lane
King's Ride
College Ride
Upland Road
Old Dean Rd
Cricket Ground
Cromwell
Works
York Road
Hartford Ri
Bath Rd
Slim
Green La
Clarke Crs
Pine Cl
Yorktown
Westbourne
Fairmead
Egerton Rd
Oak Cv Crs
Birdwood
Chapel
Jacob Rd
Rawlinson Rd
Allenby Rd
Staff
College
Road
Upper Lake
Lower Lake
Arena Leisure Centre
Munnings Dr
Cruikshank Lea
Fraser Md
Hogarth
Landseer
Constable Wy
White
Road
Haig Road
Governor's Rd
Roberts Road
A321
A30
GU15
Portesbery School
Mus
Cncl Bldg
Arts Link
Camberley Magistrates Court
Portesbery
Upper Gordon Road
Main Square Shopping Centre
London Road
Obelisk Wy
Park St
High St
Knoll Rd
Princess Wy
Pembroke Broadway
Camberley Station
Middle Gordon Rd
Southern Road
Grand Av
Council Building
Rec Gnd
Osnaburgh Hill
Appley Dr
The Terrace
London
Rd
B3411
Chapel Rd
The Avenue
Southwell Park Rd
Lyndhurst School
Adult Education Centre
Infant School
France Hill Dr
Firwood Drive
Charles St
Surgery
Court Gdns
Chaucer
Heathway Cl
Heathway
Tekels Av
Garfield Rd
MARSHALL ROAD
The Meadows (Superstores)
Laundry Lane
Superstore
White Hart Industrial Estate
Blackwater Industrial Estate
Tank Rd
York Town Industrial Estate
Victoria
Avenue
Sullivan
Edward Av
Alexandra Av
Crawford Gdns
Woodlands Rd
Heatherley Rd
Seaton Rd
Stannhope Road
Kingsway
Parkhill Rd
Rosemary Lane
Park Road
Blackwater Station
London Rd
LONDON RD
Blackwater
Station Ap
Nelson Way
Trafalgar Wy
Stanhope Road
Glebeland Rd
Doman Road
Mary Queen
York Town
Vale Rd
Eaton Rd
FRIMLEY ROAD
Forest Hills
Gordon Rd
Shelley
Park
Heatherdale Road
Laurel Cl
Brackendale
Pine Mt
Oriel
Avenue
Parkstone Dr
Rideway Cl
Linkway
Kingsley
Parkway
Kings Apartments
Beech
Vicarage Road
New Rd
Sheraton Close
Green La
The Glebe
Oakfield Road
Lawrence Wy
Admiralty Way
Works
Compton Place Business Centre
Kendall Court Business Park
Surrey Av
Moorlands Road
Queens Rd
Southway
Watchmoor Rd
Brook Rd
Bridge Works
Bridge Rd
Gordon
Watchetts Rd
Ind Est
Abbetts La
Goddards Lane
Krooner Rd
Murrells La
Belmont Rd
Birch
Fir Drive
Hawley Green
Pine Drive
Hawley CP School
Blackwater & Hawley Leisure Centre
Coliseum Business Cen
Camberley Town FC
Sampson Business Park
Helix Bus Park
Wilton Rd
Hanbury Way
Camberley RFC
Camberley CC
Upr Verran Rd
Verran Rd
Russell Gardens
Hawley
Medlar Dr
Thornfield Gn
Barberry Wy
HAWLEY ROAD
Blackwater River
Riverside Wy
A331
Superstore
St Georges Industrial Estate
Camberley Health Centre
Bristow Road
Weller Drive
Farrell Cl
The Watchetts Junior School
Drive
Verran
Road
Hawley Park
Fernhill Road
Hawley Grove
Crabtree
Orchard Way
Rd
James Wy
Westfield Rd
Rivermead Rd
Bristow Infant School
Bain Avenue
Watchetts
Kings International College
Frimley Park Hospital
A&E
Badgerwood Drive
High Beeches
Blythwood
B3272
Bayford Cl
Ashbury Dr
Works
Greenlands Rd
Wood Road
Bain Av
Newlands Rd
Old Pond Cl
Gilbert Road
Industrial Estate
Albany Pk
Frimley
PORTSMOUTH RD
The Grove
Hawley Place School
Fernhill Lane
Woodlands Wk
Woodlands
Fernhill Cl
Field
Fernhill Primary School
Fernhill Secondary School
Orchard Cl
Junction 4
Albany Park Industrial Estate
B3411
Lyon Way
Lyon Way Industrial Estate
The Cloisters
Grove Cross Rd
CHURCH RD
Apex Dr
Saints Crs
Clayton Road
Derry Rd
Neville Duke Road
Fox Lane
Moorside Cl
M3
Works
Station
A325
Hale Wy
Surgery
Burleigh Road
Sheridan
Rowans Close
Perring Avenue
Chapel Lane
Lockwood Cl
Cold Harbour Lane
Ratcliffe Rd
North Cl
Covey Cl
Hawley Lane
HAWLEY LANE
Copse Avenue
Frimley Business Park
A331
Burrell Rd
Frimley High St
Bailey Cl
Hollytree Gdns
Trafford Road
Unstead Road
The Findings
The Covert
North Farm Rd
St David's Cl
Blackthorn
Curly Br Cl
Harbour Close
Moor Road
Creatfield Road
Priors
Lye
Churchill
Avenue
Hawley Lane Industrial Estate
Frimley Stn
Bridgemead
Irvine Drive
Hart Cl
Wayman Rd
Doreen Cl
Shepherds Wk
Grange Community Junior School
Farnborough Town FC
West Rd
Prince Charles Crs
Holt Cl
Grange Rd
B3272
Sandy Lane
Marshall
Lynn Way
Anglesey
Cheyne
Way
Robin Cl
Bideford
Cherrywood
Holywell Cl
Beech Rd
Marston Dr
Fairfax Rd
Farnborough Gate Retail Park
1 grid square represents 500 metres

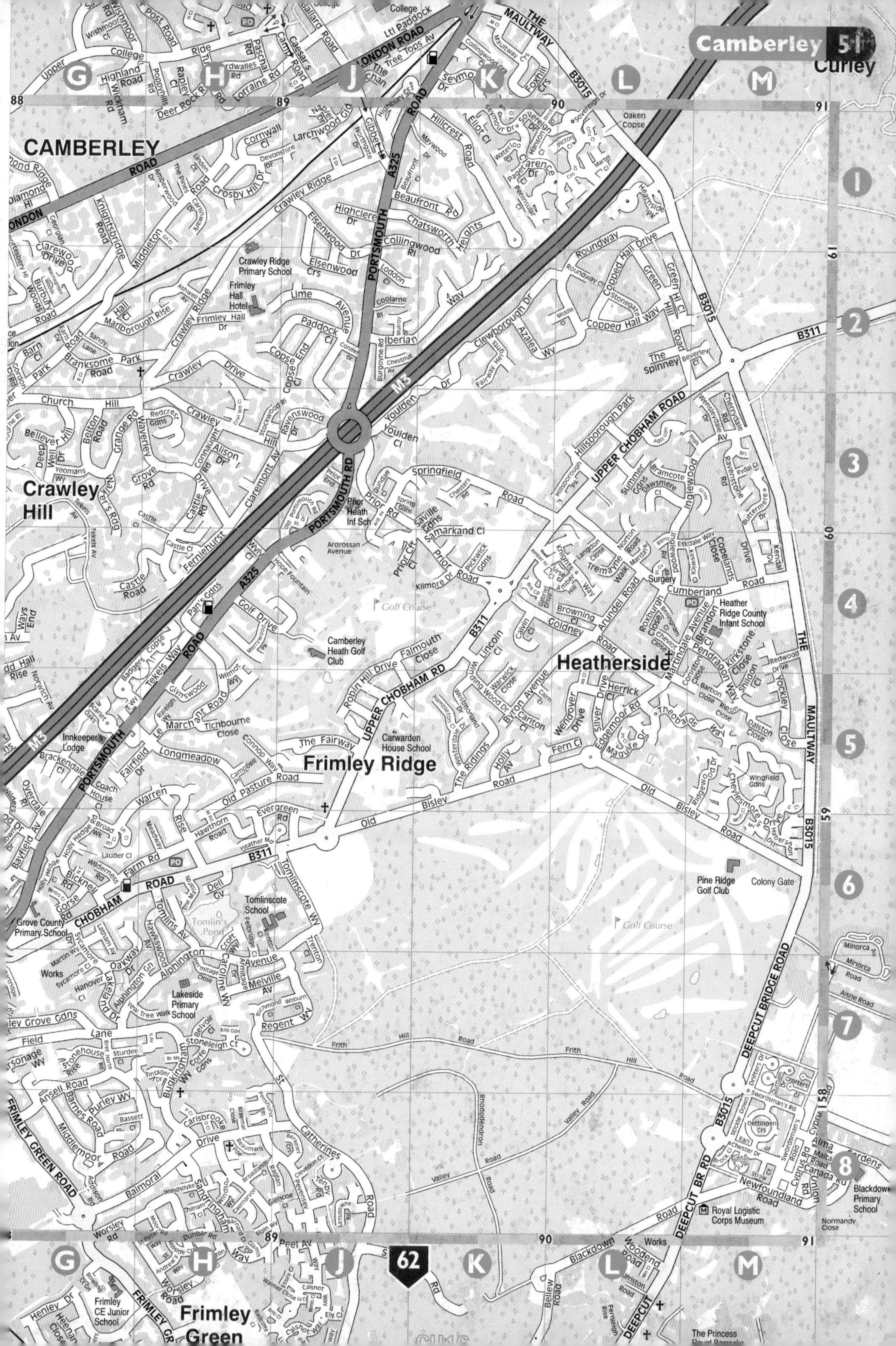
Curley
CAMBERLEY
Crawley Hill
Heatherside
Frimley Ridge
Frimley Green
LONDON ROAD
THE MAULTWAY
B3015
B311
M3
A325
PORTSMOUTH ROAD
UPPER CHOBHAM ROAD
CHOBHAM ROAD
DEEPCUT BRIDGE ROAD
FRIMLEY GREEN ROAD
Oaken Copse
Crawley Ridge Primary School
Frimley Hall Hotel
Prior Heath Inf Sch
Ardrossan Avenue
Golf Course
Camberley Heath Golf Club
Carwarden House School
Heather Ridge County Infant School
Surgery
Innkeeper's Lodge
Tomlinscote School
Tomlin's Pond
Grove County Primary School
Lakeside Primary School
Works
Pine Ridge Golf Club
Colony Gate
Royal Logistic Corps Museum
Blackdown Primary School
Normandy Close
Frimley CE Junior School
The Princess Royal Barracks
Frith Hill Road
Valley Road
Rhododendron Road
Old Bisley Road
Crawley Ridge
Crawley Drive
Church Hill
Knightsbridge Road
Middleton Rd
Marlborough Rise
Branksome Park Road
Copped Hall Drive
Copped Hall Way
Clewborough Dr
Azalea Wy
Youlden Dr
Youlden Cl
Springfield Road
Hillsborough Park
Cumberland Road
Arundel Road
Coldney Road
Martindale Avenue
Pendragon Way
Edgemoor Rd
Silver Drive
Wendover Drive
Fern Cl
Holly Av
The Ridings
Robin Hill Drive
Falmouth Close
The Fairway
Old Pasture Road
Longmeadow
Le Marchant Road
Tekels Way
Golf Drive
Evergreen Rd
Hawthorn Road
Warren Rise
Farm Rd
Dell Gv
Tomlinscote Wy
Alphington Avenue
Melville Av
Regent Wy
Field Lane
Stoneleigh Ct
Buckingham Wy
Balmoral Drive
Sandringham Wy
Carisbrooke Drive
Ansell Road
Barnes Road
Middlemoor Road
Worsley Rd
Peel Av
Dunbar Rd
Blackdown Road
Woodend Road
Bellew Road
Newfoundland Road
Cyprus Rd
Canada Rd
Alma Gardens
Minorca Road
Aisne Road
Swordsman's Rd
Dettingen Crs
Hillcrest Road
Beaufront Rd
Chatsworth Heights
Highclere Dr
Elsenwood Dr
Collingwood Rl
Lime Avenue
Paddock Cl
Copse End
Ravenswood Dr
Alison Dr
Castle Road
Fernlehurst
Claremont Av
Prior Rd
Samarkand Cl
Pickwick Gdns
Klimore Dr
Lincoln Cl
Winding Wood Dr
Byron Avenue
Ravenstone Rd
Kendal Gv
Kirkstone Close
Yockley Close
Dalston Close
Wingfield Gdns
Chevelsmore Drive
Copelands Close
Cherrydale Rd
Inglewood Av
G
H
J
K
L
M
1
2
3
4
5
6
7
8
88
89
90
91
61
60
59
58

62

44
A
B
C
D
E
F
459
60
61
owninghill
reen
Pamber
Green
Little Lo
New Road
Green
La
A340
ALDERMASTON ROAD
Court Corner
Wyeford Farm
Ramsdell Road
Bramley
Road
Pamber End
West
Heath
Old Vyne
Lane
bush Lane
The Priory
Primary
School
Priory
Farm
Salters Heat
White Hart
Lane
PH
Sherborne
Road
Charter
Alley
Tubb's
Lane
Rawlins Farm
Trading
Estate
Beal's Pightle
255
Ramsdell
RG26
Sheepwash Lane
Salters Heath Road
Privett
Copse
Monk Sherborne
The Cl
Kiln
Lane
Kiln
Green
Basingstoke Road
Lower Farm
Salters
Heath Road
West
End
Weybrook Ct
Manor
Farm
64
59
58
57
156
1
2
3
4
5
6
7
8
1 grid square represents 500 metres
Field Barn Farm

G
H
J
45
K
L
M
62
63
64
65
Surgery
Minchens
The Street
Pound Cl
Beaurepaire Cl
Middle Farm
Church Lands
The Street
Park Gate Farm
Bramley Corner
Silchester Road
Boar's Bridge
Silchester Road
Tudor Cl
Pamber Farm
Locksbridge Lane
46
Beaurepaire House
Vyne Road
Hill End Farm
Baker's Farm
Beaurepaire Farm
Vyne Lodge Farm
Cranes Copse
Morgaston Road
Morgaston Wood
Vyne Park
The Vyne (NT)
Vyne Farm
Vyne Road
54
Cu
Cranesfield
Cem
Vyne Meadow
Sherborne St John CE Primary
Cranes Bourne Fld
Vyne Road
Mari's Lane
Spier's Copse
Crockford
Chineham Business Park
Manor Rd
Tyfield
Elm Road
Dark La
Dancers Meadow
Kiln Road
PO
65
Lime
59
58
57
156
2
3
4
5
6
7
8

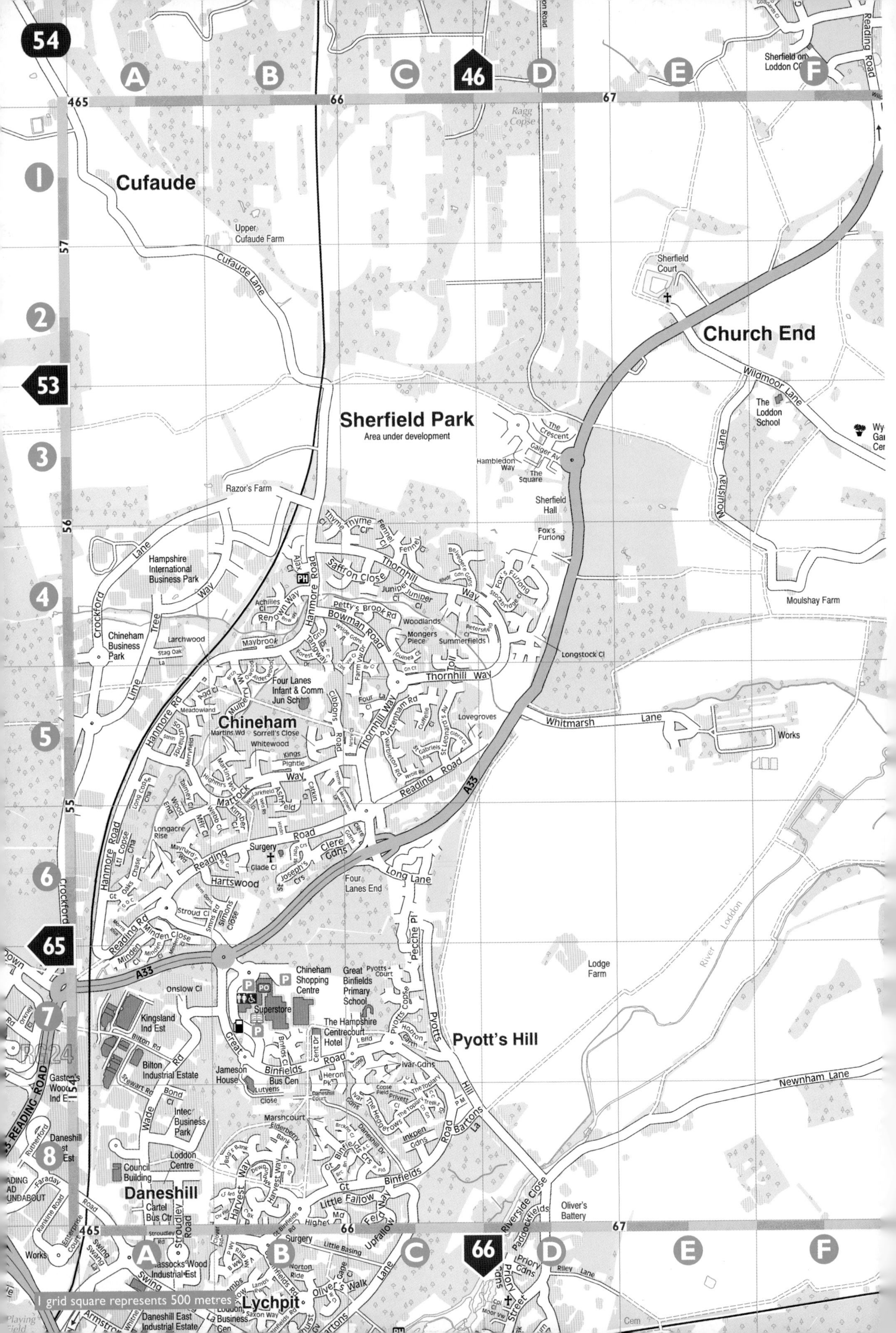
54
53
65
46
66
Cufaude
Upper Cufaude Farm
Cufaude Lane
Ragg Copse
Sherfield on Loddon
Reading Road
Sherfield Court
Church End
Wildmoor Lane
The Loddon School
Moulshay Lane
Moulshay Farm
Sherfield Park
Area under development
The Crescent
Galger Av
Hambledon Way
The Square
Sherfield Hall
Fox's Furlong
Razor's Farm
Hampshire International Business Park
Crockford Lane
Chineham Business Park
Tree Way
Larchwood
Stag Oak La
Lime
Hanmore Road
Saffron Close
Thornhill Way
Juniper Cl
Petty's Brook Rd
Bowman Road
Woodlands
Mongers Piece
Summerfields
Longstock Cl
Maybrook
Four Lanes Infant & Comm Jun Sch
Thornhill Way
Whitmarsh Lane
Works
Chineham
Martins Wd
Sorrell's Close
Whitewood
Kings Pightle
Lovegroves
Reading Road
A33
Surgery
Glade Cl
Hartswood
Reading Rd
Minden Close
Stroud Cl
Four Lanes End
Long Lane
Pecche Pl
Lodge Farm
River Loddon
Onslow Cl
Kingsland Ind Est
Bilton Rd
Bilton Industrial Estate
Chineham Shopping Centre
Superstore
Great Binfields Primary School
Pyotts Court
The Hampshire Centrecourt Hotel
Pyotts Copse
Pyotts Hill
Pyott's Hill
Newnham Lane
Jameson House
Binfields Road
Bus Cen
Lutyens Close
Intec Business Park
Wade Rd
Bond Cl
Gaston's Wood Ind Est
Daneshill East Est
Council Building
Loddon Centre
Daneshill
Cartel Bus Ctr
Stroudley Road
Harvest Way
Marshcourt
Elderberry Bank
Inkpen Gdns
Bartons La
Little Fallow
Riverside Close
Paddockfields
Oliver's Battery
Works
Tassocks Wood Industrial Est
Lychpit
Daneshill East Industrial Estate
Oliver's Walk
Priory Gdns
Priory Street
Riley Lane
Cem
1 grid square represents 500 metres

Pound Meadow
River Loddon
47
Rotherwick Lane
Wildmoor Lane
Lance Levy Farm
Mill Lane
Mill Farm
Frog Lane
Lyde G
Mill Lane
Whitewa CE Prim School
Summerstead Farm
Wildmoor
Wildmoor Lane
Ellis Farm
Lyde River
B3349
The Old House
Tylney Park Golf Club
Golf Course
56
Tylney Hall Hotel
Blackland's Farm
Ridge Lane
Tylney Lane
Hale Farm
Deanlands Farm
Newnham Lane
Manor Farm
Ridge Lane
Newnham
Poors Farm Road
Poors Farm
Pot Lane
Gold's Farm
Crown Lane
Newnham Road
Water End Lane
67
Nately Scures
Water End Park (Mobile Home Park)
Crown La
A30
LONDON
A33
G H J K L M
1 2 3 4 5 6 7 8
68 69 70 71
57 56 55 54

Mattingley
Bottle Lane
240
Lyde Green
Frog Lane
Black Wood
RG27
River Whitewater
Wedman's Lane
Cowfold Farm
Lampards Cl
Cowfold Lane
Rotherwick
Street End Copse
Whitewater CE Primary School
The Street
Readon Pond
Hook Road
Bunker's Hill Farm
Post Horn Lane
Borough Court
Golf Club
Golf Course
Searl's Lane
B3349
55
Tylney Hall Hotel
Ridge Lane
Griffin Way North
Hook House Hotel
Coppice
Reading Road
London Road A30
Hook J&I School
Hook Com Cen
Griffin Way South
Holt Way
Holt Lane
Holt
Hook
Hook Bowling Club
Owen's Farm
Station Road
Bramshott Drive
Superstore
Bartley Wood Business Park (West)
Hook Station
Newnham
Newnham Road
Rectory Road
Osborn Way
Industrial Estate
Bartley Way
Bartley Wood Business Park (East)
Scotland Farm
Old School Rd
Morris Street
Foster Business Park
68
Hook Common
A287
M3
Bartley Heath
Works
1 grid square represents 500 metres

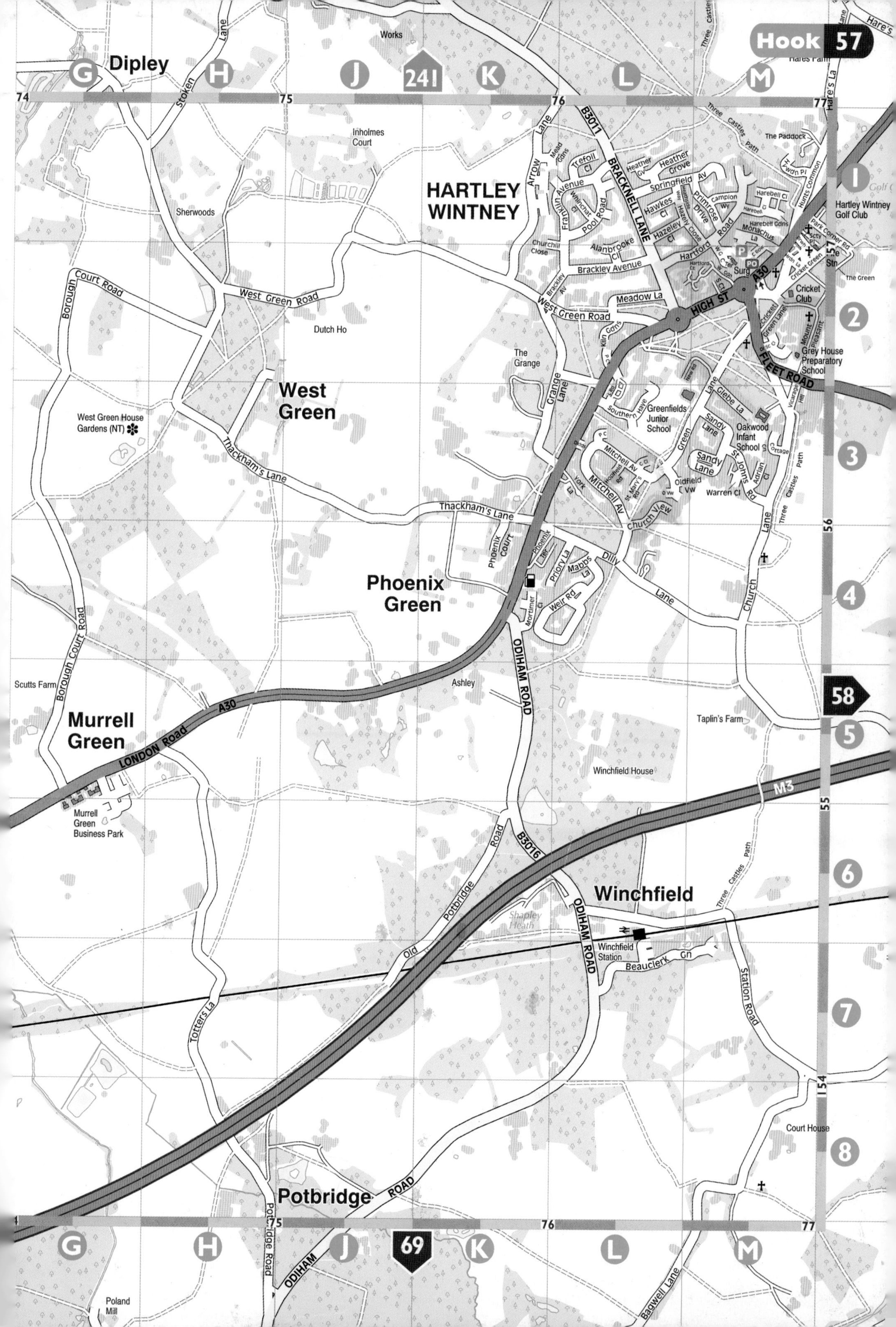
Dipley
Works
241
HARTLEY
WINTNEY
West
Green
Phoenix
Green
Murrell
Green
Winchfield
Potbridge
Inholmes
Court
Sherwoods
Dutch Ho
The
Grange
West Green House
Gardens (NT)
Scutts Farm
Ashley
Murrell
Green
Business Park
Winchfield House
Taplin's Farm
Shapley
Heath
Winchfield
Station
Court House
Poland
Mill
Hartley Wintney
Golf Club
Greenfields
Junior
School
Oakwood
Infant
School
Grey House
Preparatory
School
Cricket
Club
The Green
The Paddock
Hares Farm
Stoken Lane
Borough Court Road
West Green Road
Thackham's Lane
LONDON Road
A30
HIGH ST
FLEET ROAD
BRACKNELL LANE
B3011
B3016
ODIHAM ROAD
Old Potbridge Road
Totters La
Potbridge Road
Station Road
Bagwell Lane
Church Lane
Dilly Lane
Three Castles Path
Arrow Lane
Brackley Avenue
Meadow La
Grange Lane
Mitchell Av
Church View
Mortimer Cl
Weir Rd
Mabbs La
Priory La
Phoenix Court
Beauclerk Gn
M3
58
69

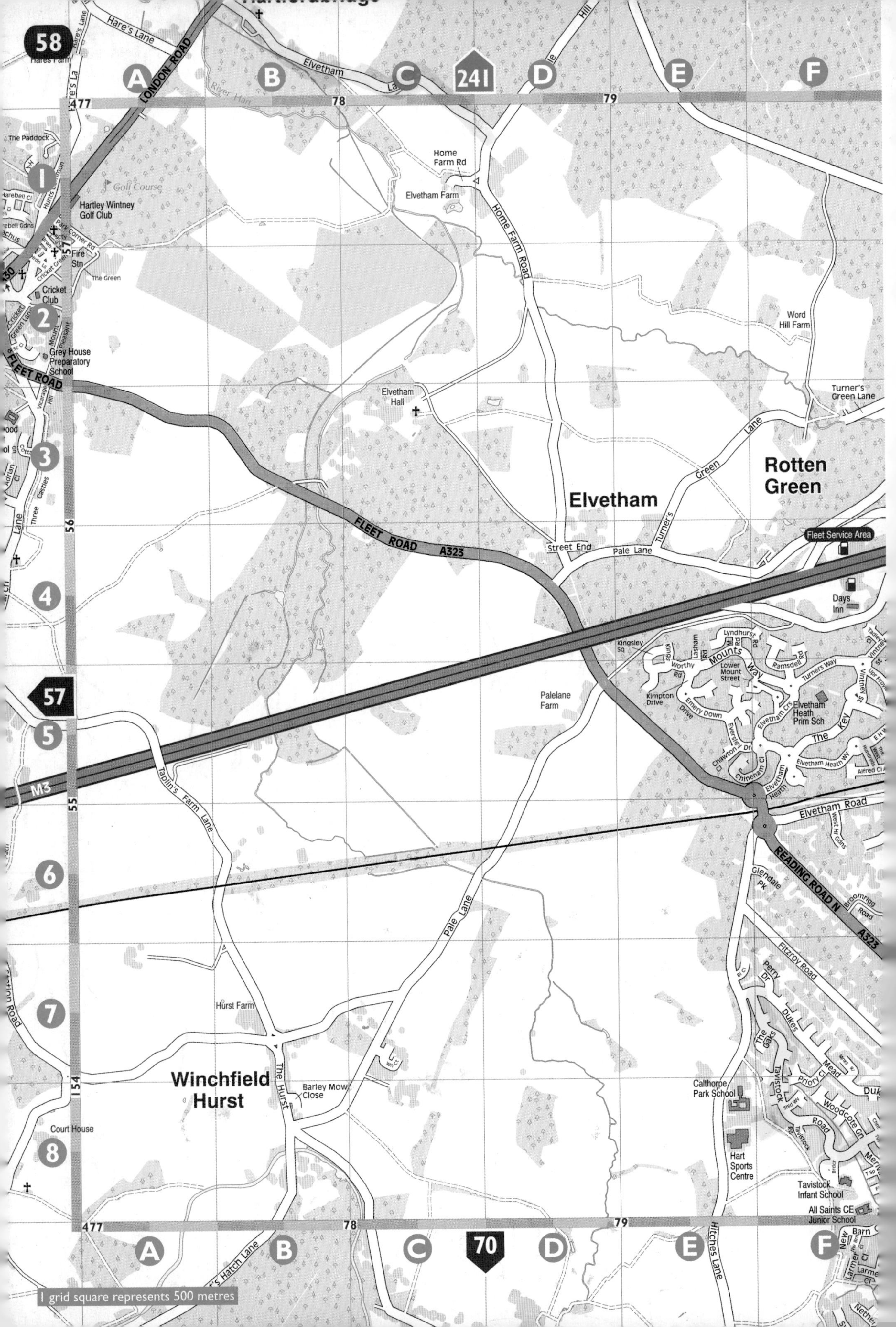
58
241
57
70
Elvetham
Rotten Green
Winchfield Hurst
FLEET ROAD A323
LONDON ROAD
READING ROAD N A323
M3
Hartley Wintney Golf Club
Golf Course
Elvetham Farm
Home Farm Rd
Home Farm Road
Elvetham Hall
Word Hill Farm
Turner's Green Lane
Fleet Service Area
Days Inn
Street End
Pale Lane
Palelane Farm
Elvetham Heath Prim Sch
Taplin's Farm Lane
Hurst Farm
The Hurst
Barley Mow Close
Court House
Calthorpe Park School
Hart Sports Centre
Tavistock Infant School
All Saints CE Junior School
Hitches Lane
Elvetham Road
Fitzroy Road
Grey House Preparatory School
Cricket Club
The Green
The Paddock
Hare's Lane
Elvetham Lane
River Hart
1 grid square represents 500 metres

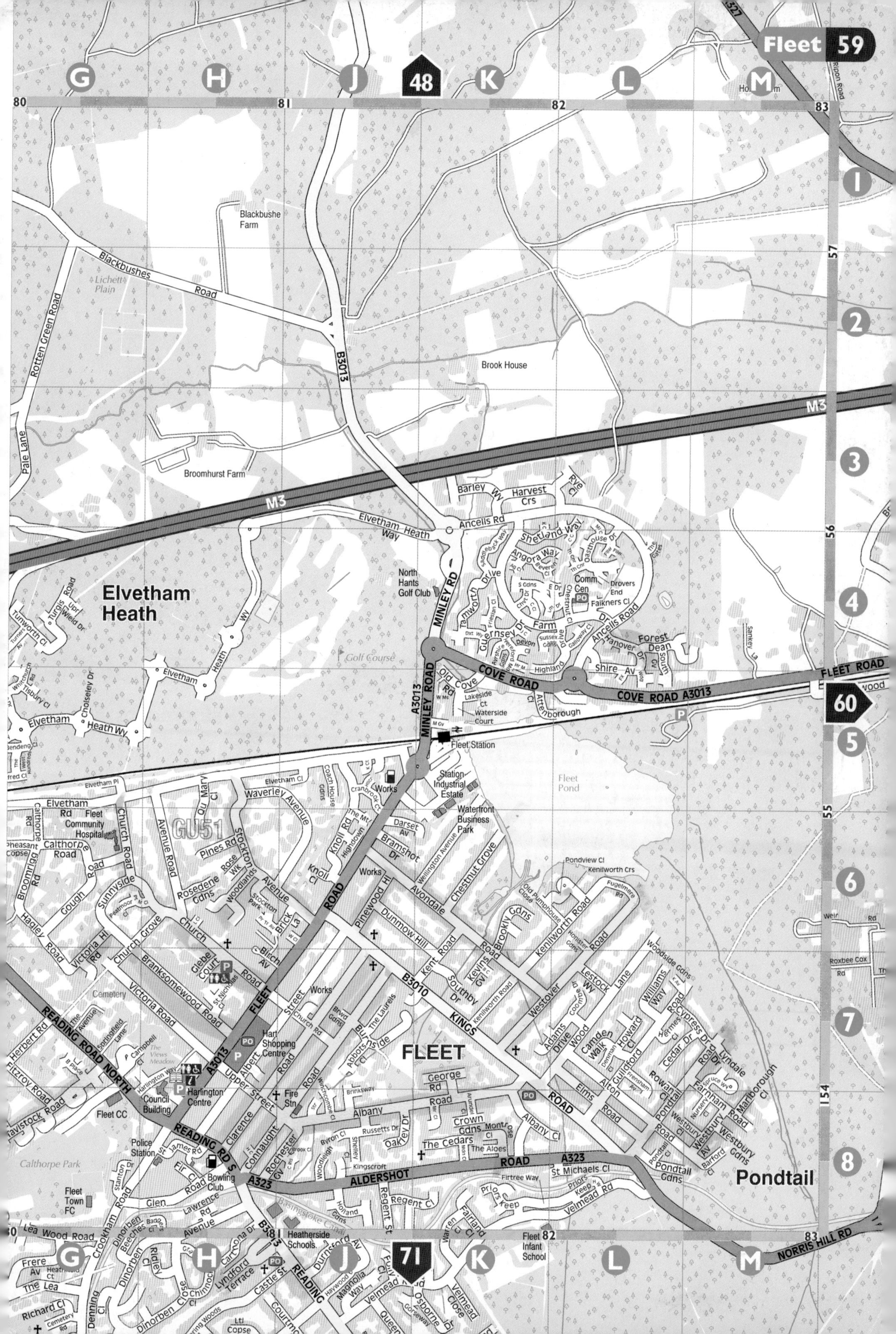
Elvetham Heath
FLEET
Pondtail
Fleet Pond
Blackbushe Farm
Brook House
Broomhurst Farm
North Hants Golf Club
Fleet Station
Station Industrial Estate
Waterfront Business Park
Hart Shopping Centre
Harlington Centre
Council Building
Fleet Community Hospital
Police Station
Bowling Club
Fleet CC
Fleet Town FC
Calthorpe Park
Heatherside Schools
Fleet Infant School
M3
B3013
A3013
MINLEY ROAD
COVE ROAD A3013
FLEET ROAD
READING ROAD NORTH
READING RD S
ALDERSHOT ROAD A323
KINGS ROAD B3010
NORRIS HILL RD
GU51
48
60
71

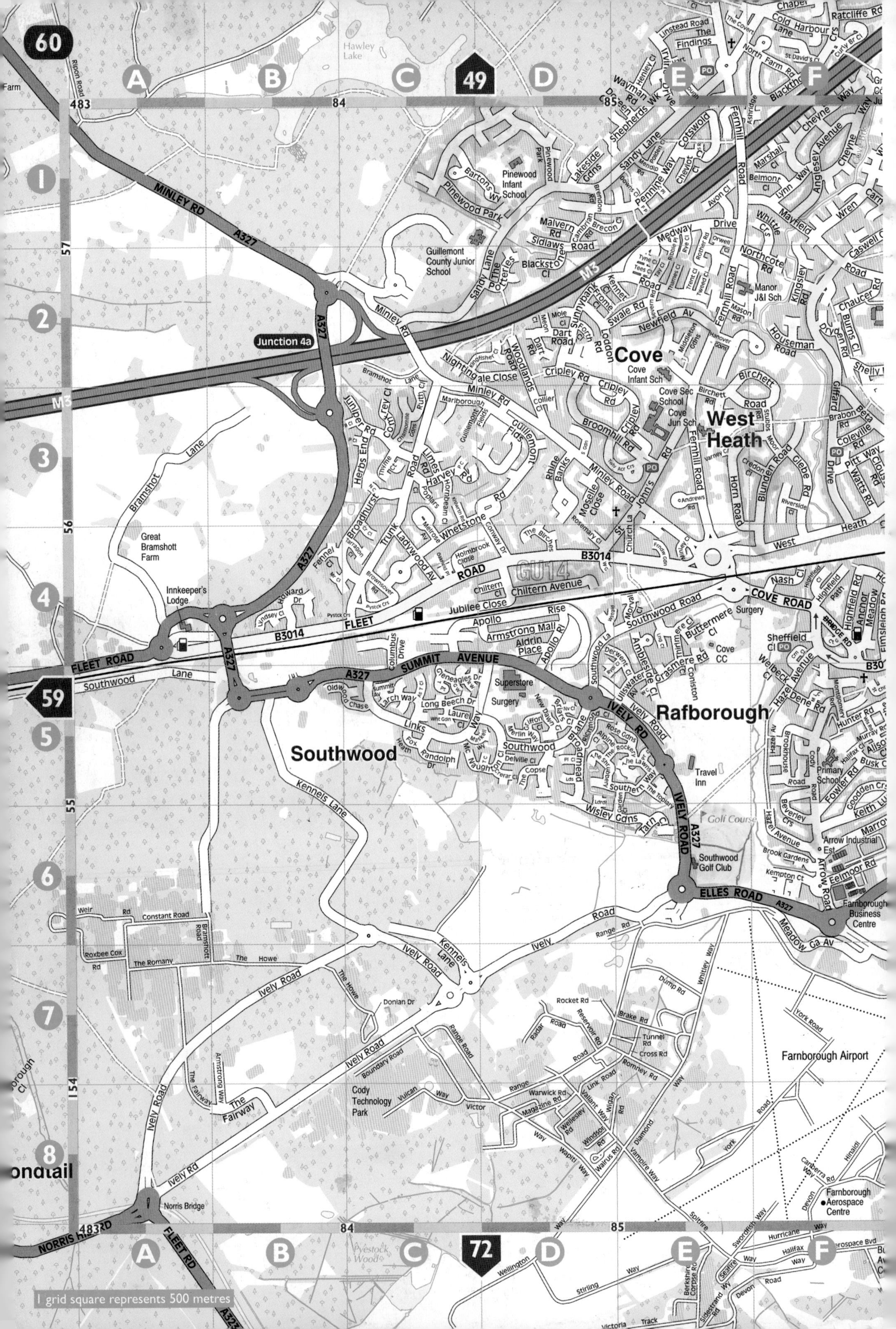

A
B
C
49
D
E
F
483
84
85
1
2
3
4
5
6
7
8
57
56
55
154
Hawley Lake
Farm
Ripon Road
MINLEY RD
A327
Junction 4a
M3
Bramshot Lane
Great Bramshott Farm
Innkeeper's Lodge
FLEET ROAD
59
Southwood Lane
B3014
FLEET ROAD
Pinewood Infant School
Pinewood Park
Bartons Wy
Guillemont County Junior School
Sandy Lane
The Potteries
Minley Rd
Malvern Rd
Sidlaws Road
Blackstone Cl
Lakeside Gdns
Shepherds Wk
Wayman Rd
Irving Drive
The Findings
Linstead Road
Cotswold Cl
Pennine Way
Cheviot Cl
Fernhill Road
Cold Harbour Lane
Chapel
Ratcliffe Rd
North Farm Rd
Blackthorn
Ashridge
Marshall Cl
Belmont Cl
Lynn Way
Anglesey Avenue
Cheyne Way
Mayfield
Wren
Caswell Cl
Whittle Crs
Northcote Rd
Manor J&I Sch
Kingsley
Chaucer
Drive
Medway
Avon Cl
Newfield Av
Swale Rd
Sunnybank
Frome Cl
Kennet Rd
Dart Road
Loddon Rd
Woodlands Road
Nightingale Close
Cove
Cove Infant Sch
Cripley Rd
Broomhill Rd
Cove Sec School
Cove Jun Sch
West Heath
Birchett Road
Houseman Road
Dryden Rd
Burns Cl
Shelly
Giffard Drive
Brabon Rd
Coleville Rd
Pitt Way
Watts Rd
Blunden Road
Glebe Rd
Horn Road
Fernhill Rd
St John's Rd
Minley Road
Moselle Close
Rhine Banks
Bramshot Lane
Juniper Rd
Herbs End
Limes Rd
Harvey Rd
Guillemont Flds
Marlborough
Whetstone Rd
Ladywood Av
Broadhurst
Trunk Road
Conway Dr
Holmbrook Close
Chiltern Avenue
Chiltern Cl
Jubilee Close
Howard Dr
GU14
The Birches
West Heath
Nash Cl
COVE ROAD
Highfield Rd
Highfield Path
Anchor Meadow
Southwood Road
Surgery
Buttermere Cl
Thirlmere Cl
Cove CC
Grasmere Rd
Coniston
Ambleside Cl
Ullswater
Derwent Cl
Apollo Rise
Armstrong Mall
Aldrin Place
Apollo Rl
Columbus Drive
SUMMIT AVENUE
Superstore
Surgery
Gleneagles Dr
Larch Way
Long Beech Dr
Laurel Cl
Links Way
Oldwood Chase
Fox Heath
Randolph Dr
Southwood
Mc Naughton Cl
Delville Cl
The Copse
Broadmead
IVELY RD
Ively Road
Rafborough
Travel Inn
Golf Course
Southwood Golf Club
Wisley Gdns
Sheffield Cl
Welbeck Avenue
Hazel Dene Rd
Hunter Rd
Murray Rd
Busk Cl
Primary School
Fowler Rd
Gooden Crs
Keith Lu
Brookhouse Road
Cody Road
Beverley Crs
Hazel Avenue
Brook Gardens
Arrow Industrial Est
Arrow Road
Eelmoor Rd
Kempton Ct
ELLES ROAD
Farnborough Business Centre
Meadow Ga Av
Kennels Lane
Weir Rd
Constant Road
Bramshott Road
Roxbee Cox Rd
The Romany
The Howe
Ively Road
Range Rd
Whitley Way
Donlan Dr
Rocket Rd
Dump Rd
Reservoir Rd
Brake Rd
Tunnel Rd
Cross Rd
Radar Road
Romney Rd
Range Road
Boundary Road
Cody Technology Park
Vulcan Way
Victor Way
Warwick Rd
Magazine Rd
Link Road
Valiant Way
Wellesley Rd
Windsor Rd
Wapiti Way
Walrus Rd
Vampire Way
Diamond Way
Armstrong Way
The Fairway
York Road
York
Farnborough Airport
Canberra Way
Hinaidi
Farnborough Aerospace Centre
Devon Rd
Ively Rd
Norris Bridge
NORRIS HILL RD
FLEET RD
A323
Pyestock Wood
72
Wellington
Stirling Way
Berkshire Copse Rd
Sidestrand Rd
Victoria Track
Seafire Way
Swordfish Way
Hurricane Way
Halifax Way
Aerospace Bvd
Spitfire
ondtail
1 grid square represents 500 metres

Farnborough
61
50
62
73
Hawley Lane
Frimley Green
Farnborough Green
Farnborough Street
FARNBOROUGH
Farnborough Park
Mytchett
South Farnborough
Farnborough Main Station
Farnborough North Stn
Frimley Stn
North Camp Station
Farnborough Gate Retail Park
Princes Mead Shopping Centre
Kingsmead Shopping Centre
Farnborough College of Technology
Queen Elizabeth Park
Kingsgrove Industrial Est
Linsford Business Park
Holly Lodge Primary School
The Jigsaw School
Mytchett Primary School
Frimley CE Junior School
Cross Farm Infant School
Frimley Green Medical Centre
Henry Tyndale School
Farnborough Hill School
North Farnborough County Infant School
St Michaels Abbey
Salesian College
South Farnborough County Junior School
South Farnborough Infant School
St Marks CE Primary School
The Wavell Technology College
The Samuel Cody School
Marlborough County Infant School
Aldershot Military
The Sixth Form College
Cherry Wood Primary School
Oak Farm Community School
St Bernadettes County Primary School
Farnborough RFC
Farnborough Town FC
Hawley Lane Industrial Estate
Eelmoor Road Depot Trading Est
Camp Road Industrial Est
Enterprise Industrial Est
Community Centre
Council Building
Recreation Centre
Police Station
FARNBOROUGH ROAD
ALEXANDRA ROAD
LYNCHFORD RD
MYTCHETT ROAD
FRIMLEY GREEN RD
FRIMLEY ROAD
STURT ROAD
MEUDON AV
VICTORIA RD
A325
A331
A3011
A327
B3411
B3012
B3014
B3272
B3403
B3165
B3166
Hampshire County
Surrey County
G
H
J
K
L
M
86
87
88
89
54
55
56
57
1
2
3
4
5
6
7
8

62
51
61
74
Deepcut
Mytchett Place
The Princess Royal Barracks
Blackdown Barracks
Brunswick Road
Lake Road
St Cross Rd
Blackdown Road
Bellew Road
Woodend Road
Alfriston Road
DEEPCUT
B3015
Lakeside International Hotel
Lakeside Country Club
Basingstoke Canal
Clewborough House School at Cheswycks
B3012 GUILDFORD ROAD
Old Guildford Road
GAPEMOUTH ROAD
Deepcut Place
Mytchett Heath
Mytchett Place Road
Keogh Close
Barnsley Cl
Army Medical Services Museum
Keogh Barracks
Mytchett Lake
Mytchett Lake Road
Grayswood Drive
MYTCHETT ROAD
B3411
Romping Downs
Royal Logistic Corps Museum
Newfoundland Road
Alma Gardens
Blackdown Primary School
Normandy Close
Frimley Green Medical Centre
Mytchett Primary School
Rorkes Drift
Salisbury Grove
Lynwood Dr
Jubilee Road
Hazel Rd
Drake Av
Holly Lodge Primary School
Carrington La
FRIMLEY ROAD
Homeleigh Crescent
Rosemary Avenue
Nexus Park
LYSONS AV
STRATFORD RD B3165
B3166
Works
Station Ap
Ash Vale Station
Enterprise Industrial Est
Station Rd East
Greatbottom Flash
GU16
A B C D E F
1 2 3 4 5 6 7 8
489 90 91
57 56 55 54
1 grid square represents 500 metres

Bisley Camp
Pirbright Camp
Alexander Barracks
Elizabeth Barracks
Army Training Regiment
Brunswick Road
Basingstoke Canal
B3012 GOLE ROAD
Goal Farm Golf Club
Golf Course
Pirbright Common
Dawney's Hill
DAWNEY HILL
A324
CONNAUGHT
Brookwood
Curzon Bridge
STANLEY HILL
Stanley Pool
Mazamboni Farm
GRANGE ROAD
B3405 SCHOOL LANE
Pirbright Primary School
Knowl Hill School
Surgery
Church Lane
Thompsons Close
Works
Pirbright
GUILDFORD ROAD
Mill Lane
Pirbright Lodge
Duchies
Rails Farm
Stream Farm
ALDERSHOT ROAD
Upper Stanford Road
Stanford Brook
Stanford Common
Henley Gate
Henleypark Lake
Cobbett Hill
75

52
A
B
C
D
E
F
459
60
61
Manor Farm
Field Barn Farm
Basingstoke Road
55
A339
KINGSCLERE ROAD
ALDERMASTON ROAD A340
Elm Bottom C
Golf Course
Weybrook Park Golf Club
Parklands Hospital
The Donald Burrell Cent
Rooksdown Lane
Whitedown
54
KINGSCLERE
ROAD
Saxon Wood School
Surgery
Gander Dr
Rooksdown Av
Mill Rd
Julius Cl
Vespasian Gdns
Balsan Cl
Kingsclere Rd
Wellington Terrace
Napoleon Dr
Augustus Dr
Waterloo Av
Dunsford Crs
Rose Hodson Pl
Tiberius Cl
Beech Way
Hazelwood Dr
Hazelwood Cl
Arundel Gdns
Oaklands Way
Roman Rd
Firs Wy
Elmwood Wy
Hawthorn
Willow Wy
Sycamore Wy
Cedar Way
Laburnum Wy
Blackthorn Way
Fort Hill Community School
Restormel Cl
Carlisle Cl
Kenilworth Rd
Pendennis Cl
Tintagel Cl
Warwick Rd
Winklebury
Winklebury J&I School
Roman Road
Carisbrooke Cl
Coppice Ms
Bury Rd
Willoughby Wy
Woolford Way
Dover Cl
Surgery
Winklebury Medical Centre
Winklebury Centre
Castle Hill Infant School
Winklebury Way
Playing Fields
Ludlow Gdns
Ludlow Cl
Harlech Close
Forum Cl
Dudley Cl
Pembroke Rd
Tiverton Rd
Hereford Rd
Wayside Rd
Vue Cinema
Euskirchen Way
Basingstoke Leisure Par
Basingstoke Planet Ice
Basingstoke Aquadrome
Travel Inn
B3400 CHURCH
255
PO
Wootton St Lawrence
53
Worting Wood Farm
Worting
Roman Way
Roman Road
Tiverton
Dorchester Cl
Hastings Cl
West Ham
Bowlplex
Beckett Cl
Wykeham Drive
Glebe Lane
Aylings Cl
Monton Trading Estate
West Ham Lane
B3400 WORTING ROAD
Mercer Cl
Fiske Cl
W Ham Cl
Fire Stn
Worting Rd
Old Worting Road
Worting House
Church La
152
B3400
WORTING
ROAD
WORTING
Worting County Infant School
Buckskin
Cotswold Cl
Mourne Cl
Tweeds
Campsie Cl
Cairngorm Cl
Butler Cl
Bardwell Cl
Peter's
St Nicholas
Road
Woburn Gardens
Peveral
Hampshire
Kempshott
Brewer Cl
Branton Cl
Claythorpe Rd
Chivers Cl
Cheviot
Allston
Dibley
Michael's Road
Bishop Challoner RC School
Challoner Cl
Dartmouth Walk
South Ham
St Annes
The Ridgeway
92
1 grid square represents 500 metres

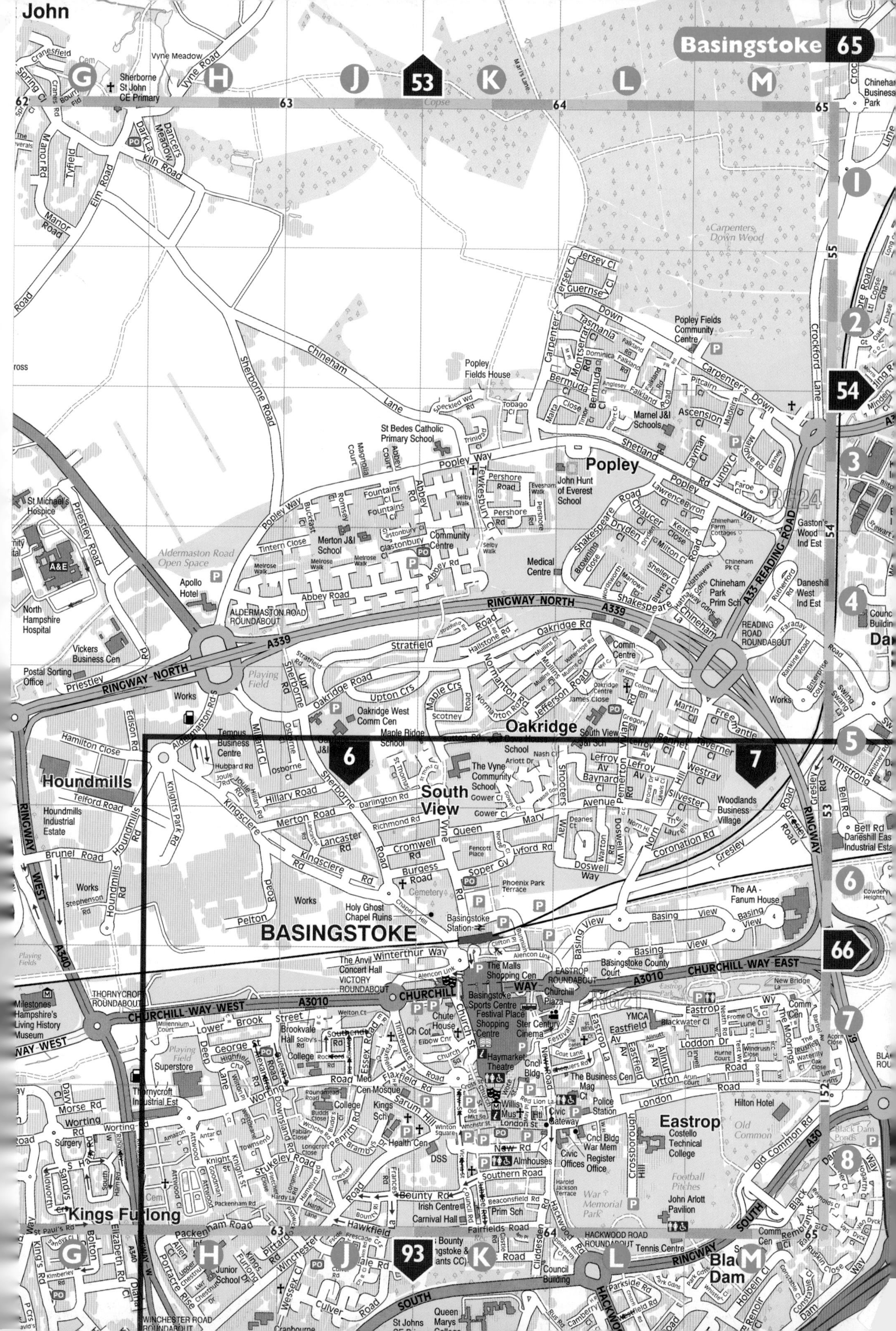
Basingstoke 65
John
Sherborne St John CE Primary
Vyne Meadow
Vyne Road
Kiln Road
Manor Rd
Elm Road
Chineham Lane
Sherborne Road
Carpenters Down Wood
Popley Fields Community Centre
Popley Fields House
St Bedes Catholic Primary School
Popley
Popley Way
John Hunt of Everest School
Marnel J&I Schools
Merton J&I School
Community Centre
Aldermaston Road Open Space
Medical Centre
Chineham Park Prim Sch
Apollo Hotel
St Michael's Hospice
North Hampshire Hospital
Vickers Business Cen
Postal Sorting Office
Aldermaston Road Roundabout
Ringway North
A339
A33 Reading Road
Reading Road Roundabout
Gaston's Wood Ind Est
Daneshill West Ind Est
Oakridge
Oakridge Road
Oakridge West Comm Cen
Maple Ridge School
Tempus Business Centre
Houndmills
Houndmills Industrial Estate
The Vyne Community School
South View
Woodlands Business Village
Coronation Rd
Holy Ghost Chapel Ruins
Basingstoke Station
BASINGSTOKE
The AA Fanum House
The Anvil Concert Hall
Victory Roundabout
Winterthur Way
The Malls Shopping Cen
Eastrop Roundabout
Basingstoke County Court
Churchill Way East
A3010
Churchill Way West
Thornycroft Roundabout
Milestones Hampshire's Living History Museum
Basingstoke Sports Centre
Festival Place Shopping Centre
Haymarket Theatre
Chute House
Superstore
Thornycroft Industrial Est
Kings Furlong
Worting Rd
Eastrop
Costello Technical College
Hilton Hotel
Old Common
Council Offices
Register Office
War Memorial Park
John Arlott Pavilion
Hackwood Road Roundabout
Winchester Road Roundabout
Ringway South
Black Dam
Ringway West
A340
A30
53
54
66
93
6
7

Old Basing
Lychpit
Hatch
Daneshill
London Road
M3
Junction 6
Basing House
Basingstoke Common
Huish Lane
Polecat Corner
Hackwood Farm
Roundtown
Huish House
Moorhams Farm
Hodd's Fm
Home Farm
Hackwood House
Tunworth House
1 grid square represents 500 metres

66
54
7
65
93
256

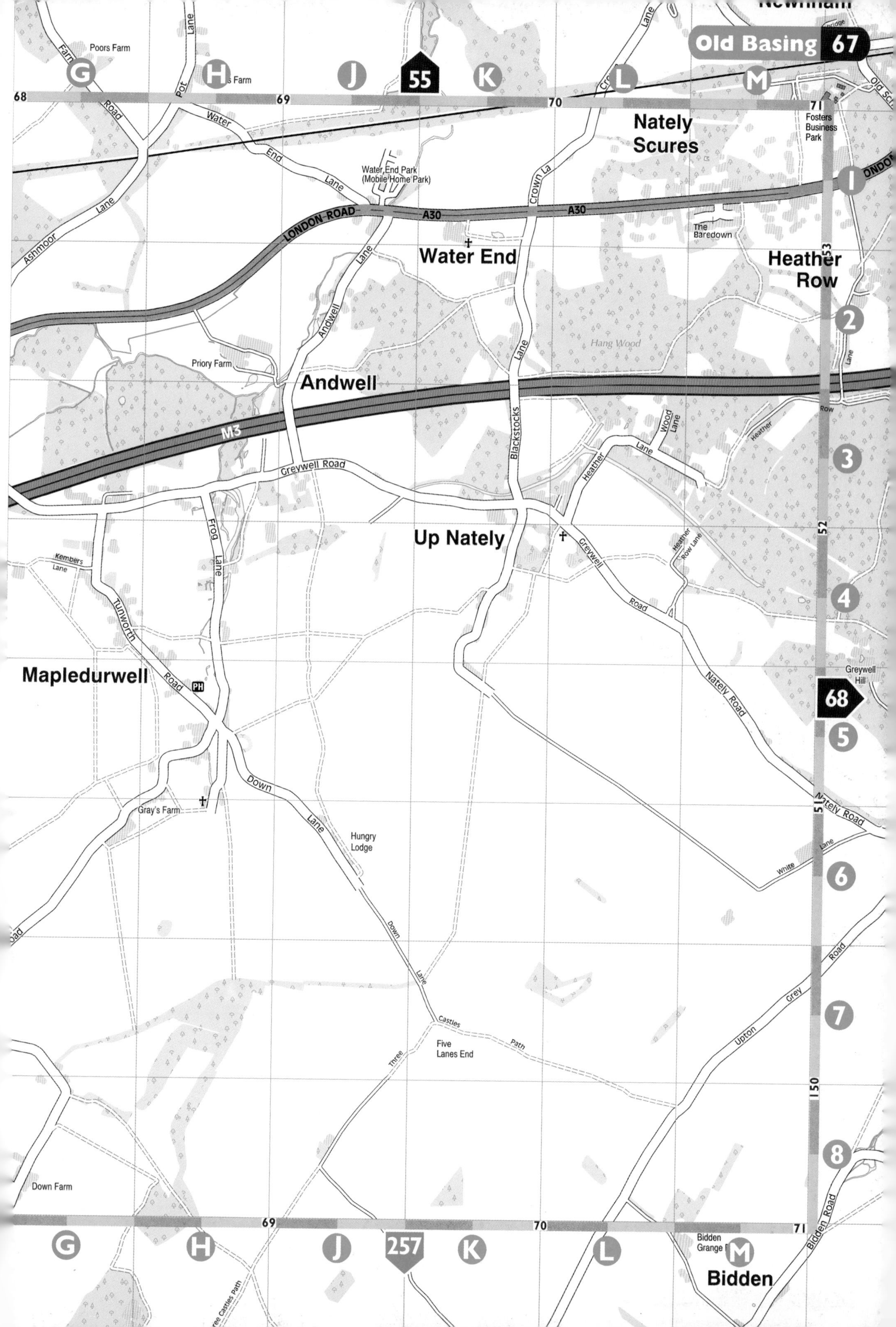

Old Basing 67
55
68
257
Nately Scures
Water End
Heather Row
Andwell
Up Nately
Mapledurwell
Bidden
Poors Farm
Priory Farm
Water End Park (Mobile Home Park)
Fosters Business Park
The Baredown
Hang Wood
Gray's Farm
Hungry Lodge
Five Lanes End
Down Farm
Bidden Grange
Greywell Hill
London Road
A30
M3
Water End Lane
Andwell Lane
Crown Lane
Blackstocks Lane
Greywell Road
Heather Lane
Wood Lane
Heather Row Lane
Nately Road
White Lane
Upton Grey Road
Bidden Road
Tunworth Road
Frog Lane
Kembers Lane
Down Lane
Three Castles Path
Ashmoor Lane
Farm Road
Pot Lane
PH

Newnham
68
56
Heather Row
Works
Hook Common
Junction 5
M3
A287
B3349
Warnborough Green
Odiham Castle
North Warnborough
Greywell
Greywell Hill
67
Butter Wood
Three Castles Path
Deptford Lane
Hook Road
Bidden Road
Robert Mays School
Odiham Firs
Chosley Farm
Ford Farm
Lodge Farm
The Odiham Health Centre
ALTON ROAD
DUNLEY'S HILL
BRIDGE ROAD
HOOK ROAD
Odiham Airfield
257
1 grid square represents 500 metres

Court House
Potbridge
57
Potbridge Road
ODIHAM
Bagwell Lane
Poland Mill
Swan's Farm
Basingstoke Canal
B3016
Whitehall
Poland Lane
Poland Farm
Sprat's Hatch Farm
Sprat's Hatch Lane
Odiham Common
Three Castles Path
LONDON ROAD
A287
Basingstoke Canal
Broad Oak
Broad Oak Lane
Dogmersfield Lake
Great Park
Dogmersfield Park
Colt Hill
Linden Av
Road
Farnham Road
Hatchwood House
Farnham Road
Farnham Rd
70
The George Hotel
Archery Flds
Archery Fields
Mildmay Court
Cemetery
Mayhill Junior School
Buryfields
Odiham Cottage Hospital
Buryfields Infant School
Cemetery Hill
ODIHAM
Hillside
A287
FARNHAM ROAD
Works
Bullock's Farm
Hillside Road
Roke Lane
Buttridge
Long Lane
Snatchangers Farm
Readon Farm House
258
Roke Lane
Roke Farm
G
H
J
K
L
M
74
75
76
77
1
2
3
4
5
6
7
8
53
52
51
150

Court House
58
A
B
C
D
E
F
477
78
79
Hart Sports Centre
All Saints CE Junior School
Sprat's Hatch Lane
Hitches Lane
Dogmersfield CE Primary School
Dogmersfield
Pilcot Road
Crookham Village
Grove Farm
Tundry Pond
The Street
Veronica Drive
Stroud Lane
Ormersfield Farm
Levignen Cl
Camus Cl
Velmead Community Centre
Dogmersfield Park
Chalky Lane
69
Coxmoor Wood
Crondall Road
Hancock's Farm
Bowenhurst La
Coxmoor Farm Light Industrial Estate
Small Acres Farm
A287
FARNHAM ROAD
Works
Rye Common
Finns Industrial Park
Bowenhurst La
Mill Lane
Downsland House
Marsh Farm Business Centre
Bowling Alley
Hannam's Copse
Eastbridge
Lefroy's Fld
Hyde Lane
Redlands La
Surgery
Home Farm
259
1
2
3
4
5
6
7
8
53
52
51
150
1 grid square represents 500 metres

Church Crookham
Ewshot
Aldershot Road
Reading Road South
Beacon Hill Road
Odiham Road
Bourley Road
Sandy Lane
Ewshot Lane
Dare's Lane
Redfields Lane
Watery Lane
Gally Hill Road
Crookham Road
Norris Hill Rd
Church Lane
Heath Lane
Fleet Business Park
Redfields Business Park
Stillers Farm
Dares Farm
Lea Farm
Tennis Club
St Nicholas School
Court Moor School
Heatherside Schools
Fleet Infant School
Church Crookham Junior School
Tweseldown Infant School
Crookham CE Infant School
Leipzig Road
Leipzig Barracks
Wakefords Copse
Tadpole Lane
Badger Way
Fox Way
Velmead Farm
Redlands
Warren Corner
Chestnut Copse
Works
Potters Ind. Park
Ayesgarth
Conifer Close
Calthorpe Park
GU52
A323
A287
B3013
59
72
76
G H J K L M
80 81 82 83
1 2 3 4 5 6 7 8
53 52 51 150

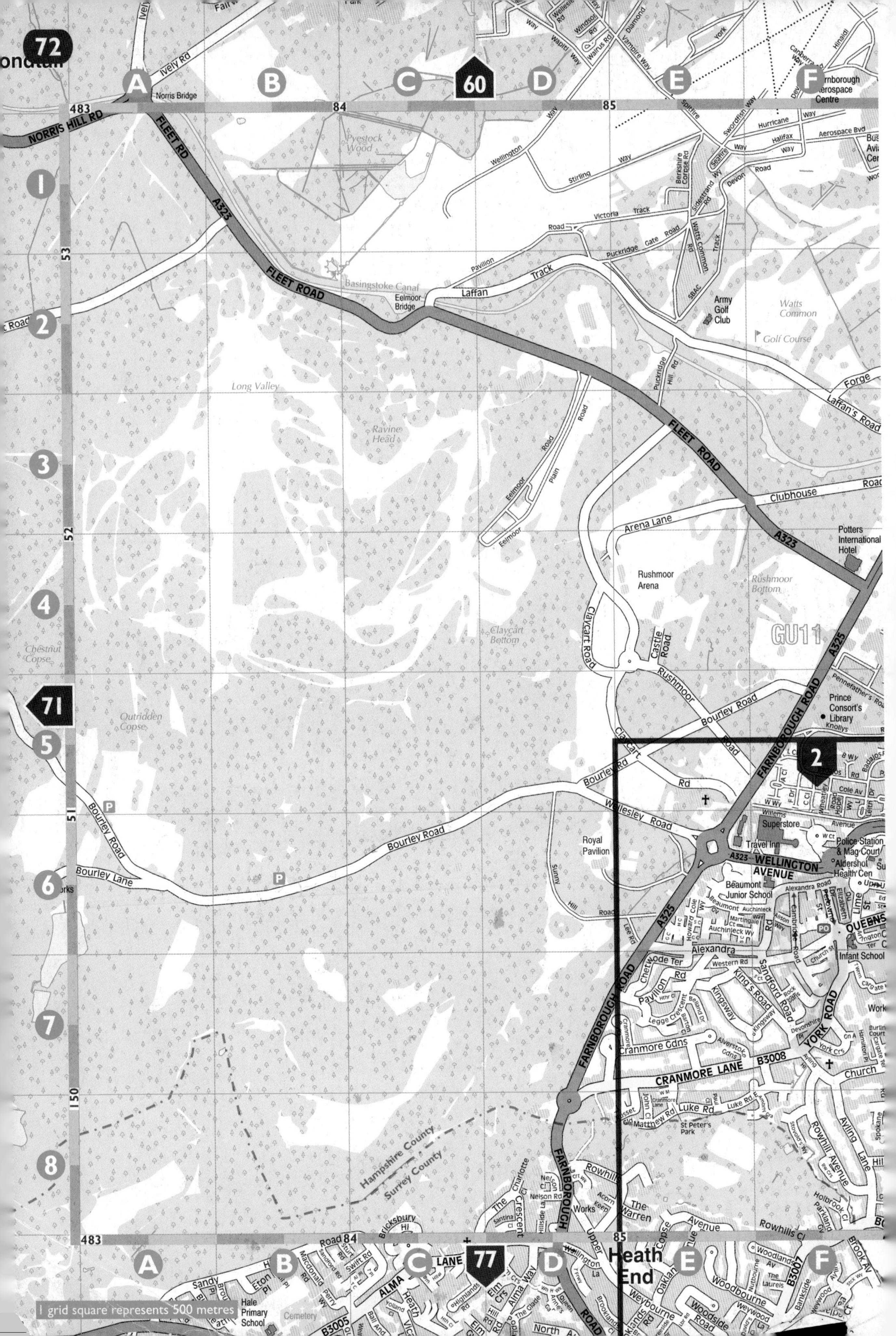
72
60
71
77
2
A
B
C
D
E
F
1
2
3
4
5
6
7
8
483
84
85
53
52
51
150
NORRIS HILL RD
FLEET RD
A323
FLEET ROAD
Ively Rd
Norris Bridge
Pyestock Wood
Basingstoke Canal
Eelmoor Bridge
Laffan Track
Pavilion Road
Victoria Track
Puckridge Gate Road
Watts Common Rd
Wellington Way
Stirling Way
Berkshire Copse Rd
Sidestrand Rd
Devon Road
Farnborough Aerospace Centre
Aerospace Bvd
Army Golf Club
Watts Common
Golf Course
Forge
Laffan's Road
Long Valley
Ravine Head
Eelmoor Road
Plain Road
Clubhouse Road
Arena Lane
Rushmoor Arena
Potters International Hotel
Rushmoor Bottom
Claycart Bottom
Claycart Road
Castle Road
Rushmoor Road
GU11
Chestnut Copse
Outridden Copse
Bourley Road
Bourley Lane
Bourley Rd
Wellesley Road
Royal Pavilion
Sunny Hill Road
FARNBOROUGH ROAD
A325
Prince Consort's Library
Superstore
Travel Inn
A323 WELLINGTON AVENUE
Police Station & Mag Court
Aldershot Health Cen
Beaumont Junior School
Alexandra Road
Auchinleck Way
Cambridge Road
Sandford Road
King's Road
Kingsway
Pavilion Rd
Legge Crescent
Cranmore Gdns
CRANMORE LANE B3008
YORK ROAD
Infant School
Church
Luke Rd
Matthew Rd
St Peter's Park
Rowhill Avenue
Ayling Lane
Holbrook Parkland
Hampshire County
Surrey County
The Crescent
Nelson Rd
Works
The Warren
Avenue
Rowhills Cl
Bricksbury Hill
ALMA LANE
Heath End
Woodbourne
Weybourne Rd
Woodside Road
Hale Primary School
Cemetery
B3005
B3007
Upper Wellington La
North
1 grid square represents 500 metres

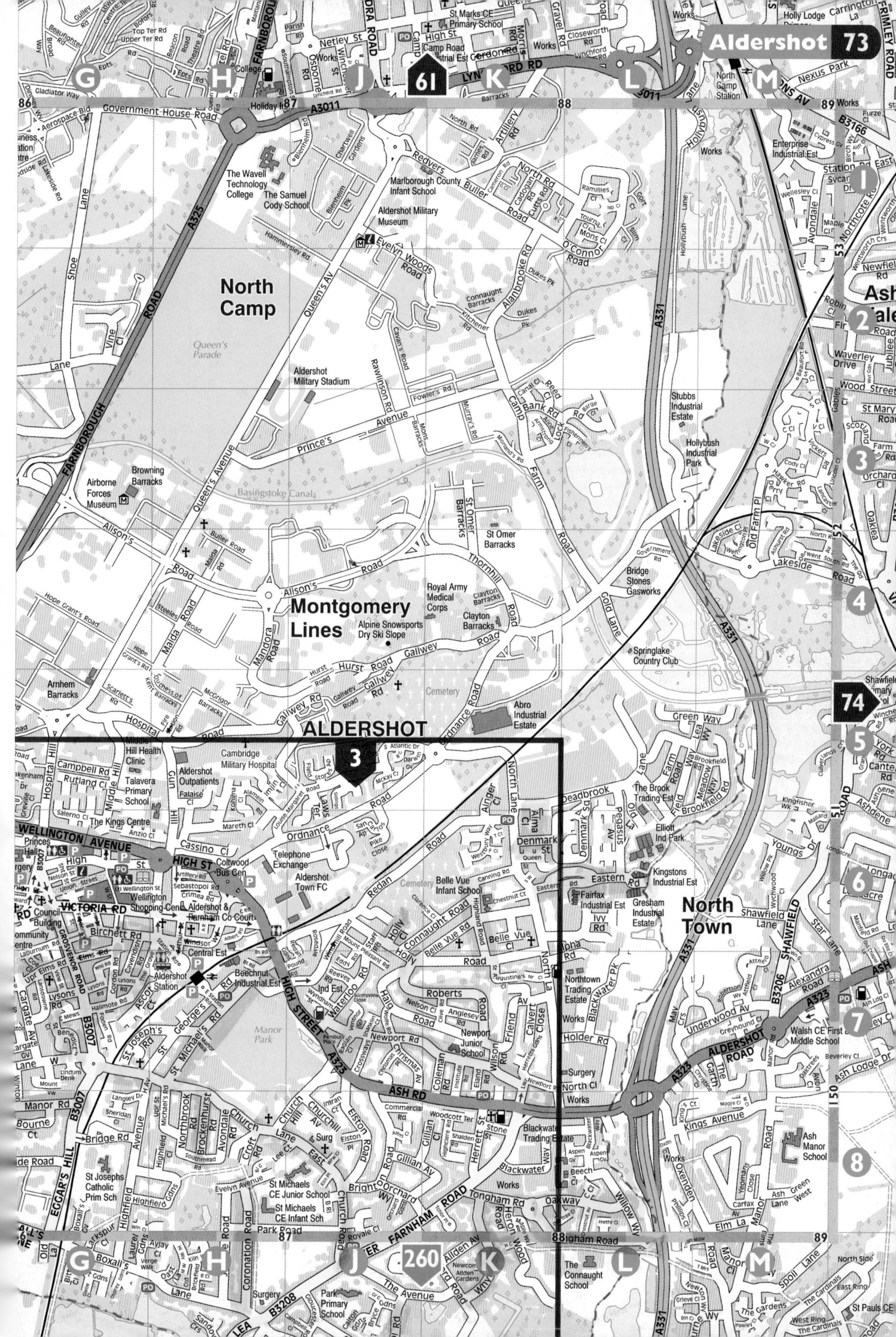
North Camp
Queen's Parade
Montgomery Lines
ALDERSHOT
North Town
The Wavell Technology College
The Samuel Cody School
Marlborough County Infant School
Aldershot Military Museum
Aldershot Military Stadium
Airborne Forces Museum
Browning Barracks
Basingstoke Canal
St Omer Barracks
Royal Army Medical Corps
Clayton Barracks
Alpine Snowsports Dry Ski Slope
Arnhem Barracks
Cemetery
Abro Industrial Estate
Bridge Stones Gasworks
Springlake Country Club
Stubbs Industrial Estate
Hollybush Industrial Park
Enterprise Industrial Est
North Camp Station
Cambridge Military Hospital
Aldershot Outpatients
Middle Hill Health Clinic
Talavera Primary School
The Kings Centre
Telephone Exchange
Aldershot Town FC
Coltwood Bus Cen
Wellington Shopping Cen
Aldershot & Farnham Co Court
Council Building
Community Centre
Central Est
Aldershot Station
Beechnut Industrial Est
Ind Est
Manor Park
Belle Vue Infant School
Newport Junior School
Northtown Trading Estate
Fairfax Industrial Est
Gresham Industrial Estate
Kingstons Industrial Est
Elliott Ind Park
The Brook Trading Est
Blackwater Trading Estate
Walsh CE First & Middle School
Ash Manor School
St Josephs Catholic Prim Sch
St Michaels CE Junior School
St Michaels CE Infant Sch
The Connaught School
Park Primary School
Holly Lodge Primary
St Marks CE Primary School
Camp Road Industrial Est
Holiday Inn
College
Government House Road
Queen's Avenue
Alison's Road
Hospital Road
Gallwey Road
Ordnance Road
Wellington Avenue
High St
High Street
Victoria Rd
Grosvenor Road
Ash Rd
Aldershot Road
Farnham Road
Lynchford Rd
Farnborough Road
Eggar's Hill
Shawfield Road
Gold Lane
Camp Farm Road
Prince's Avenue
A325
A3011
A331
A323
B3007
B3208
B3206
B3166
61
74
3
260
86
87
88
89
50
51
52
53
G
H
J
K
L
M
1
2
3
4
5
6
7
8

74
62
73
260
A
B
C
D
E
F
1
2
3
4
5
6
7
8
489
90
91
53
52
51
150
Ash Vale
Ash
Ash Green
Wy
GU12
Ash Common
Wyke Common
Greatbottom Flash
Downs
Holly Lodge Primary School
Carrington La
Frimley Road
Homeleigh Crescent
Rosemary Avenue
Nexus Park
Tysons Av
Station Vw
Furze Cl
B3166
Station Ap
Ash Vale Station
Enterprise Industrial Est
Cypress Gv
Birch Wy
Station Rd East
Chart House Rd
Sycamore Dr
Northcote Rd
Avondale
Wentworth Close
Wentworth Crs
Vale Rd
Horseshoe Lane
Newfield Rd
Rowcroft Cl
Pine Cl
Heathvale Br Rd
Robin Cl
Fir Acre Road
Cuthbert Rd
Hutton Road
Chambers Rd
Waverley Drive
Jubilee Drive
Wood Street
Gables Cl
St Mary's Road
Scotland Farm Rd
Scotland Cl
Springfield Rd
Prospect Road
Enfield Rd
Orchard Cl
Elleray Cl
Gorselands Cl
Crescent Lane
Oaklea
B3411
Foxhurst Rd
Chandlers Rd
Ash Vale Health Cen
Newlands Dr
Vickers
Hawker Rd
Lakeside
Road
Burrwood Gdns
Wharf Road
Grenadier Rd
Woollards Road
Vale Rd
Balmoral Road
B3411
Ash Hill Road
Shawfield Primary School
Grove Rd
College
Hillside Road
Winchester Rd
York Rd
Canterbury Rd
Exeter Rd
Murrell Rd
Beeching Cl
Heathcote Rd
Fairview Road
Elm Vw
Miles Rd
Wren Ct
Ash Hl Rd
Fox Hills Lane
Ashbourne Close
Ravenscroft Close
Upr Pinewood Road
Nightingale Rd
Pinewood Rd
Kirriemuir Gdns
Brackendene
Guildford Road
A323
Dene Cl
Pirbright Road
School Lane
Wyke CP School
Wyke Avenue
Wyke Lane
Ashdene Crs
Ashdene Rd
Salisbury Rd
York Road
Ash Grange CP School
Cem
Potters Crs
Chester Rd
Ash Station
Kingfisher Wk
Youngs Dr
Longacre
Church View
Ewins Cl
Britten Cl
Ash Church Rd
Longfield Road
Collins Gdns
Church La
St Peters Md
Foreman Pk
Old Rectory Dr
Grange Road
Foreman Road
Harper's Road
East Wyke Farm
Shawfield
Star Lane
Alexandra Road
B3206
Ash Street
Southlands Cl
Lodden Way
Southlands Rd
South Lane
Willow Flds
Whitethorn Cl
The Briars
Wey Cl
CE First & Middle School
Ash Lodge Dr
Kennet Cl
Beverley Cl
Ash Green Road
Drovers Way
White Lane
Pound Farm Lane
Pound Farm
Green Lane West
Ash Green La East
Old Farm Wk
Cross Tree Wy
Hazel Road
Ash Manor School
Ash Green Lane West
Manor Rd
North Side
East Ring
Spoil Lane
The Cardinals
West Ring
Poyle Farm
1 grid square represents 500 metres

Henley Gate
63
G
H
J
K
L
M
92
93
94
95
Cobbett Hill Road
PIRBRIGHT ROAD
A324
Works
Henleypark Farm
Henley Park
A323
Whipley Manor
ALDERSHOT ROAD
Longerend Farm
Hunts Hill Road
Normandy
Anchor Close
Normandy Common La
Well Lane
GUILDFORD ROAD
Normandy Common
Mariners Drive
Sandy Lane
Willey Green
Frog Grove Lane
Surgery
Glaziers Lane
Balles Lane
GU3
Walden Cottages
Westwood Lane
Russellplace Farm
White Hart
Wood Street Vi
Westwood Place
Wanborough Station
Broads
The Paddocks
Beech Lane
Orchard Way
Orchard Close
Szabo Crs
Christmaspie Av
Cull's Road
Laureldene
Willow Drive
Flexford
Wanborough Youth House
Flexford Road
Christmaspie
Green Lane East
West Flexford Lane
Wildfiel
261
Greencut Copse
Wanborough Wood
1
2
3
4
5
6
7
8
53
52
51
150

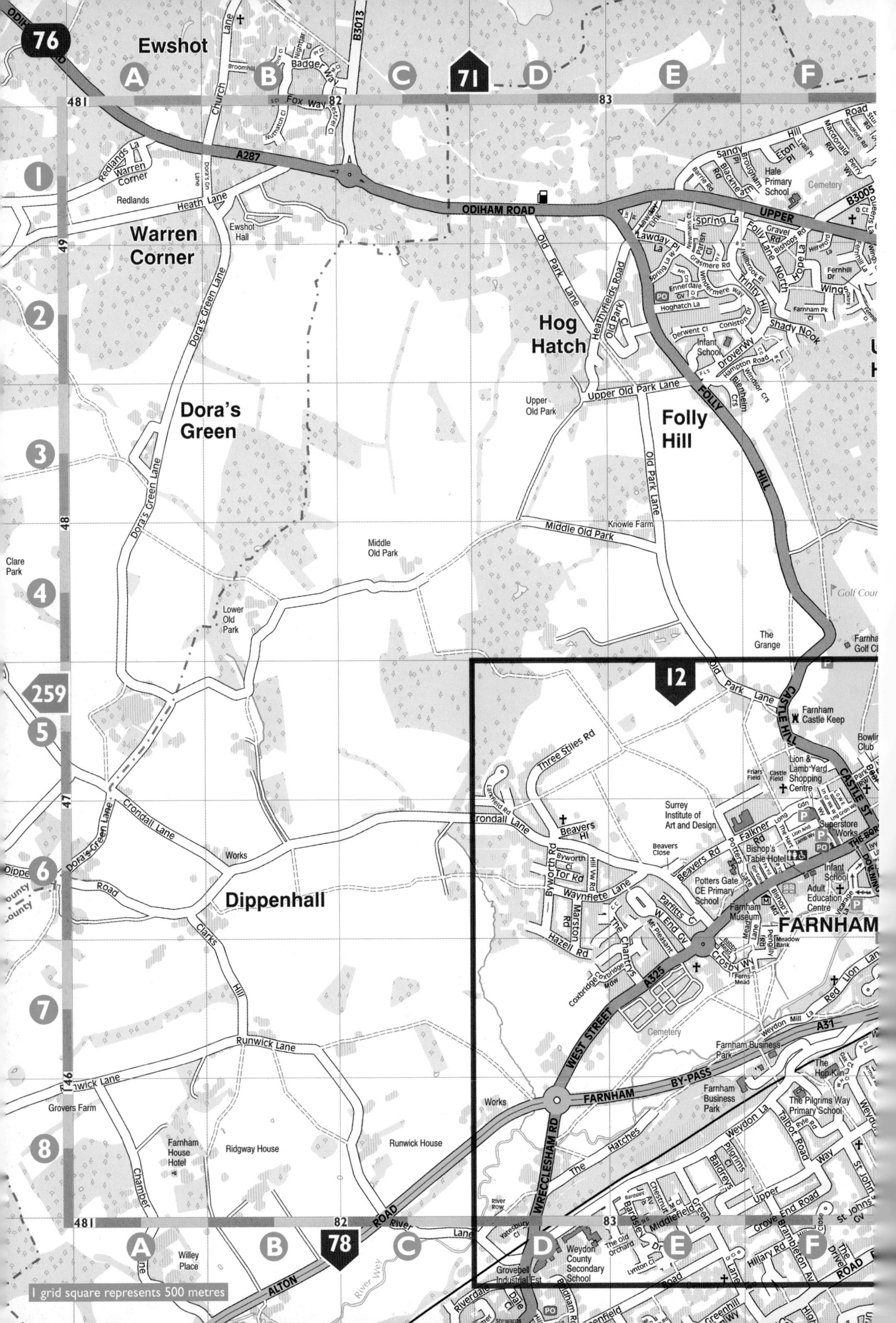

76
71
12
259
78
Ewshot
Warren Corner
Redlands
Ewshot Hall
Dora's Green
Hog Hatch
Folly Hill
Upper Old Park
Middle Old Park
Lower Old Park
Knowle Farm
Clare Park
The Grange
Farnham Castle Keep
Surrey Institute of Art and Design
Dippenhall
FARNHAM
Works
Grovers Farm
Farnham House Hotel
Ridgway House
Runwick House
Willey Place
Farnham Business Park
The Pilgrims Way Primary School
Weydon County Secondary School
Grovebell Industrial Est
Hale Primary School
Cemetery
A287
ODIHAM ROAD
B3013
B3005
UPPER
FOLLY HILL
CASTLE HILL
CASTLE ST
A325
WEST STREET
WRECCLESHAM RD
FARNHAM BY-PASS
A31
ALTON ROAD
Heath Lane
Dora's Green Lane
Old Park Lane
Heathyfields Road
Upper Old Park Lane
Middle Old Park
Crondall Lane
Three Stiles Rd
Beavers Rd
Falkner Rd
Clarks Hill
Runwick Lane
Chamber Lane
The Hatches
Weydon La
Red Lion La
Weydon Mill La
Talbot Road
Upper Way
Middlefield
Green Lane
River Lane
River Wey
1 grid square represents 500 metres

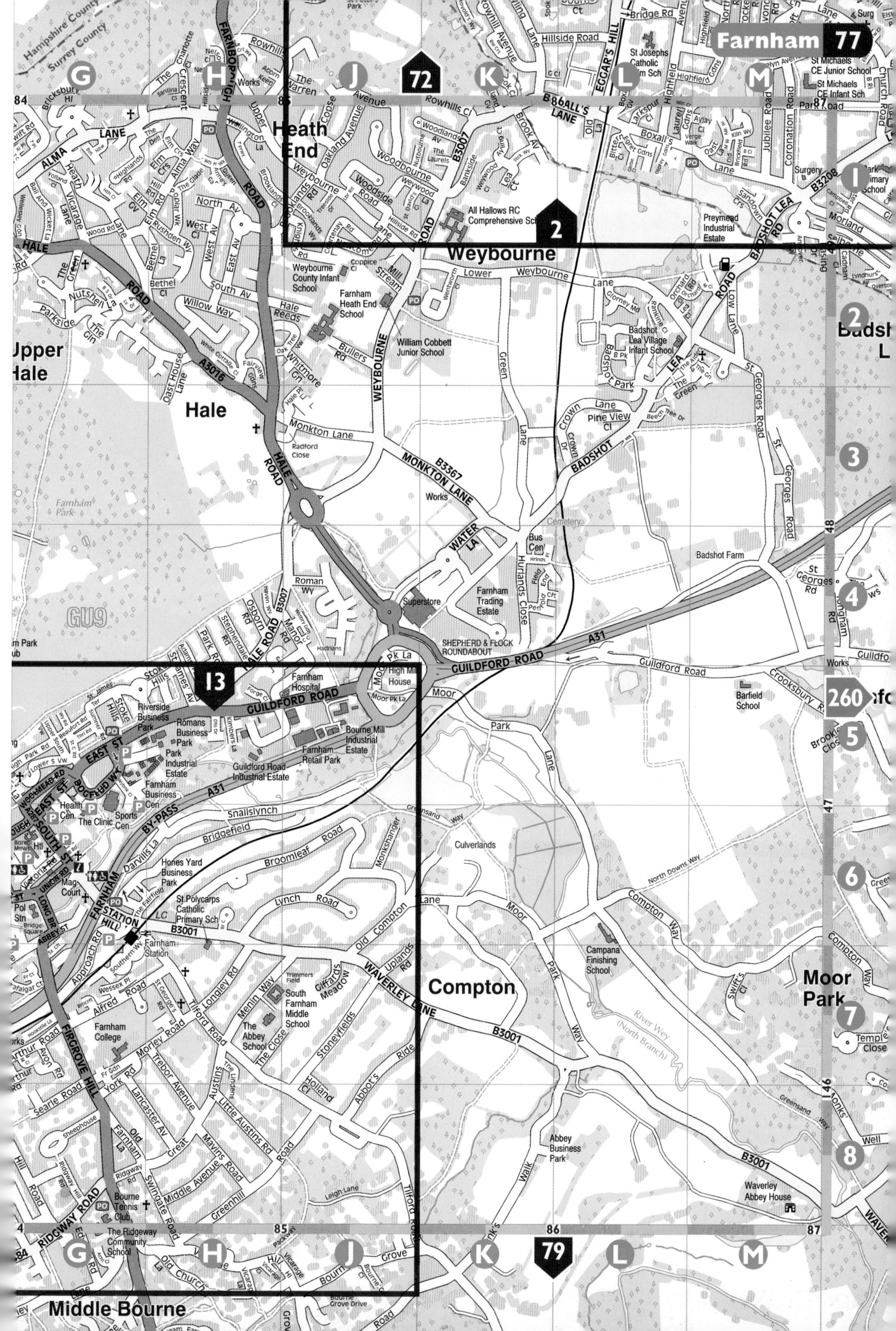
Heath End
Weybourne
Upper Hale
Hale
Compton
Moor Park
Middle Bourne
Badshot Farm
Farnham Park
GU9
72
2
13
260
79
All Hallows RC Comprehensive Sch
Weybourne County Infant School
Farnham Heath End School
William Cobbett Junior School
Badshot Lea Village Infant School
St Josephs Catholic Prim Sch
St Michaels CE Junior School
St Michaels CE Infant Sch
Preymead Industrial Estate
Farnham Trading Estate
Superstore
Shepherd & Flock Roundabout
Farnham Hospital
Riverside Business Park
Romans Business Park
Park Industrial Estate
Farnham Business Cen
Bourne Mill Industrial Estate
Farnham Retail Park
Guildford Road Industrial Estate
Hones Yard Business Park
St Polycarps Catholic Primary Sch
Farnham Station
South Farnham Middle School
The Abbey School
Farnham College
Bourne Tennis Club
The Ridgeway Community School
Culverlands
Campana Finishing School
Abbey Business Park
Waverley Abbey House
Barfield School
Guildford Road
Monkton Lane
Weybourne Road
Hale Road
Farnborough Road
Waverley Lane
Firgrove Hill
Ridgway Road
Crooksbury Road
Badshot Lea Road
Moor Park Lane
Compton Way
North Downs Way
Greensand Way
River Wey (North Branch)
A31
A3016
B3007
B3001
B3367
B3208
84
85
86
87
48
47
146

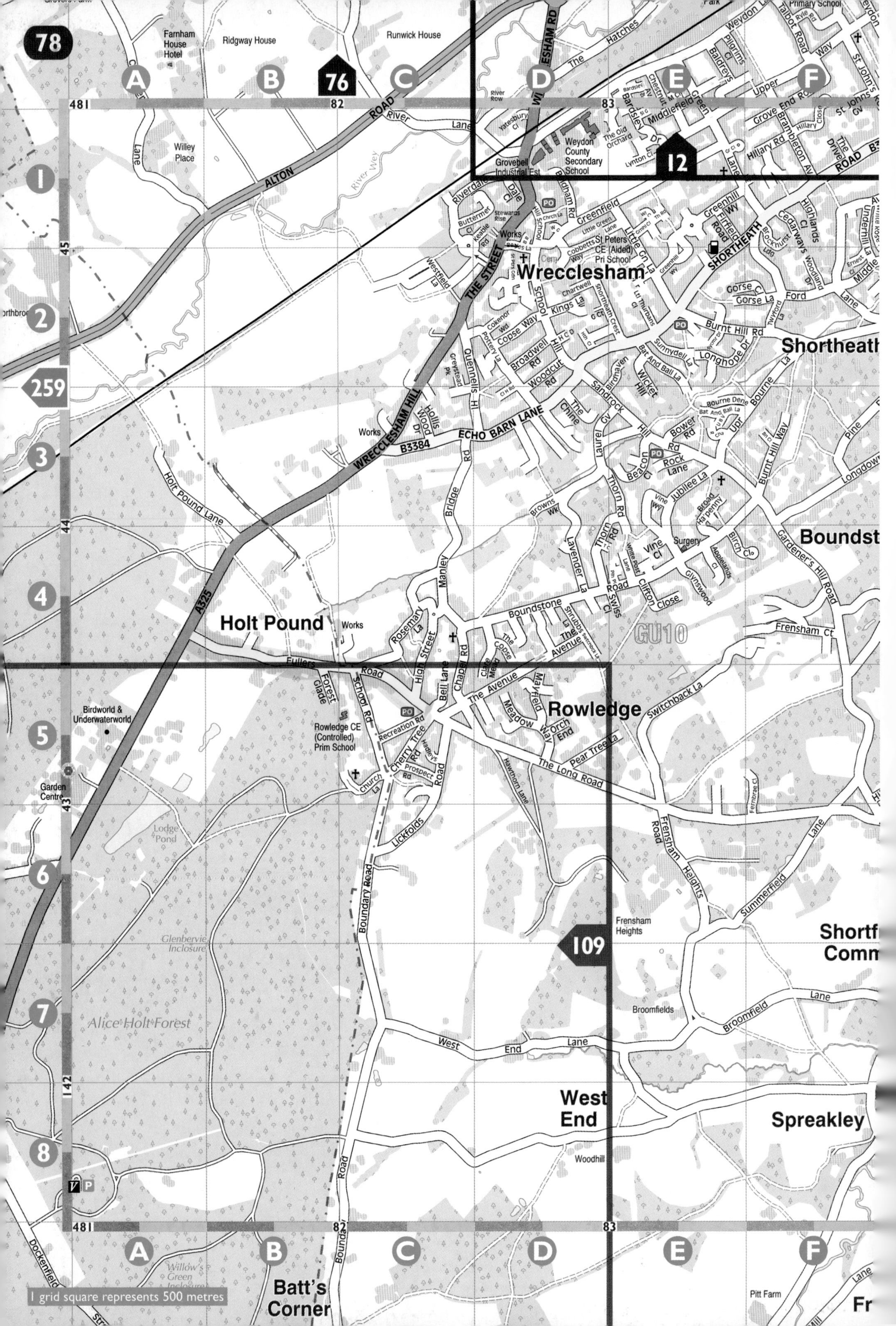
Farnham House Hotel
Ridgway House
Runwick House
76
12
259
109
Willey Place
ALTON ROAD
River Lane
River Wey
WRECCLESHAM RD
The Hatches
Weydon County Secondary School
Grovebell Industrial Est
Wrecclesham
THE STREET
WRECCLESHAM HILL
ECHO BARN LANE
B3384
Shortheath
SHORTHEATH
Boundstone
Holt Pound
Holt Pound Lane
A325
Works
GU10
Fullers Road
Rowledge
Rowledge CE (Controlled) Prim School
Birdworld & Underwaterworld
Garden Centre
Lodge Pond
The Long Road
Frensham Heights
Frensham Heights Road
Glenbervie Inclosure
Alice Holt Forest
Boundary Road
West End Lane
Broomfields
Broomfield Lane
West End
Spreakley
Woodhill
Willow's Green Inclosure
Batt's Corner
Pitt Farm
Dockenfield
Summerfield Lane
Switchback La
Gardener's Hill Road
Burnt Hill Rd
Boundstone Rd
Manley Bridge Rd
High Street
Bell Lane
Chapel Rd
School Rd
Lickfolds Road
Shortf
Comm
A B C D E F
1 2 3 4 5 6 7 8
481 82 83
45 44 43 142
1 grid square represents 500 metres

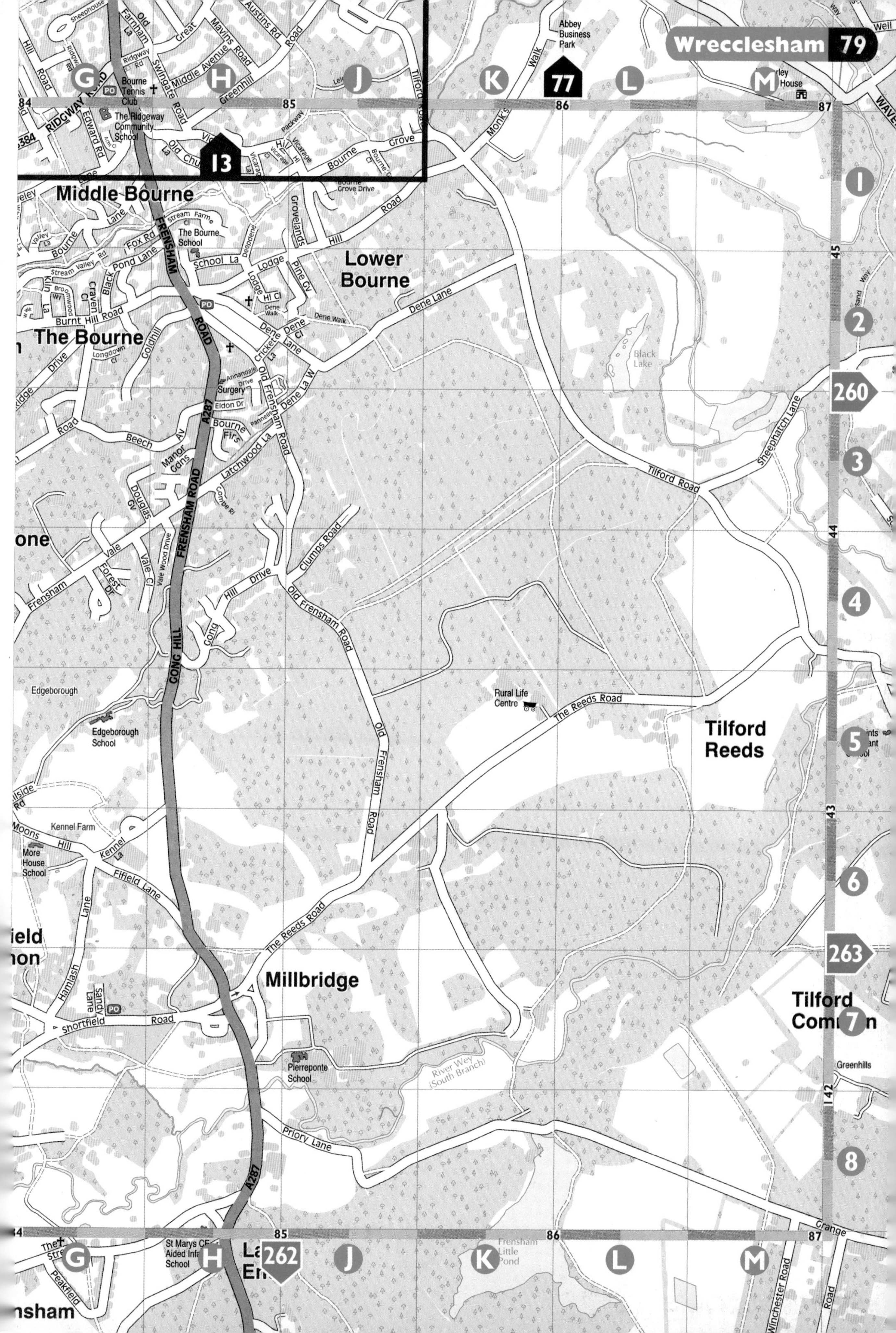
Middle Bourne
Lower Bourne
The Bourne
Tilford Reeds
Millbridge
Tilford Common
Abbey Business Park
77
13
260
263
262
Bourne Tennis Club
The Ridgeway Community School
The Bourne School
Surgery
Edgeborough
Edgeborough School
Kennel Farm
More House School
Rural Life Centre
Pierreponte School
River Wey (South Branch)
Black Lake
Frensham Little Pond
St Marys CE Aided Infant School
Greenhills
Frensham Road
Gong Hill
A287
Ridgeway Road
Old Farnham La
Great Austins
Mavins Road
Middle Avenue
Austins Rd
Swingate Road
Greenhill
Tilford Road
Monk's Walk
Bourne Grove
Bourne Grove Drive
Grovelands
Hill Road
Dene Lane
Dene Walk
Dene Cl
Cricketers La
Old Frensham Road
Dene La W
Annandale Drive
Eldon Dr
Pannells
Bourne Firs
Latchwood La
Combe Rl
Beech Av
Manor Gdns
Douglas Gv
Vale Cl
Vale Wood Drive
Forest Dr
Clumps Road
Gong Hill Drive
School La
Lodge Hl Cl
Pine Gv
Stream Farm Cl
Fox Rd
Black Pond Lane
Stream Valley Rd
Bourne Lane
Valley La
Craven Cl
Burnt Hill Road
Goldhill
Longdown Cl
The Reeds Road
Sheephatch Lane
Fifield Lane
Kennel La
Moons Hill
Hamlash Lane
Sandy Lane
Shortfield Road
Priory Lane
Grange
Winchester Road
Peakfield
The Street
Edward Rd
Packway
Vicarage Hl
Vicarage La
Old Church La
Mollison Rd
Sheephouse
Ridgway Rd
Hill Road
G
H
J
K
L
M
1
2
3
4
5
6
7
8
84
85
86
87
45
44
43
42

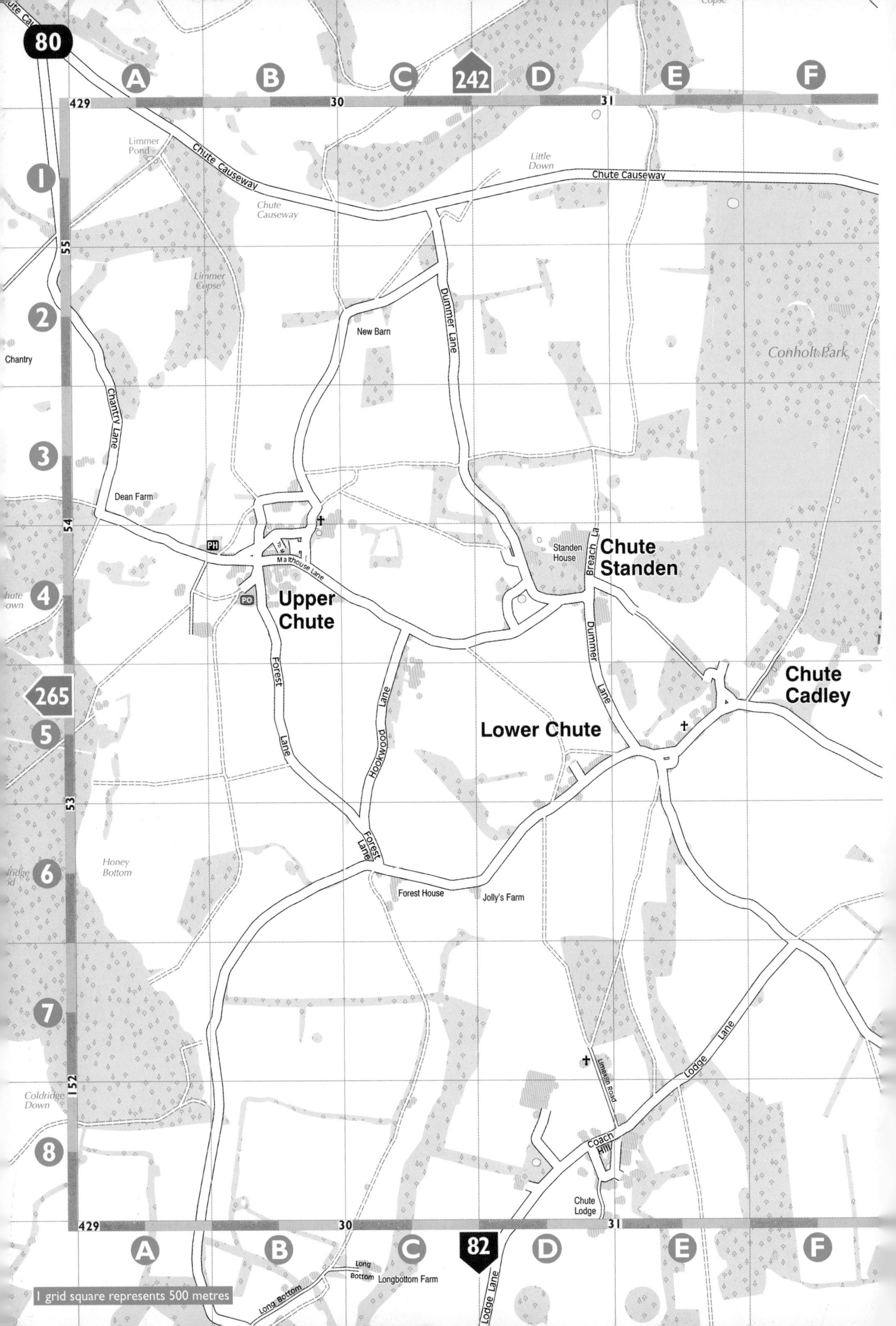
80
242
265
82
A
B
C
D
E
F
1
2
3
4
5
6
7
8
429
30
31
55
54
53
152
Limmer Pond
Chute Causeway
Chute Causeway
Little Down
Chute Causeway
Limmer Copse
New Barn
Dummer Lane
Conholt Park
Chantry
Chantry Lane
Dean Farm
PH
Malthouse Lane
PO
Upper Chute
Standen House
Breach La
Chute Standen
Dummer Lane
Forest Lane
Hookwood Lane
Chute Cadley
Lower Chute
Forest Lane
Honey Bottom
Forest House
Jolly's Farm
Lodge Lane
Limekiln Road
Coach Hill
Chute Lodge
Coldridge Down
Long Bottom
Longbottom Farm
Long Bottom
Lodge Lane
1 grid square represents 500 metres

Ankers Farm
G
H
J
243
K
L
M
Conholt Hill
Conholt Lane
Middle
Conholt Farm
Conholt House
Hungerford Lane
Wiltshire County
Hampshire County
Hampshire
Gate
Cathanger
Wood
Rushmore
Down
Holt Lane
Dowlands Farm
250
Tangley
Bottom
Clark
Lane
Tangley
Farm
Tangley
Hungerford Lane
PH
83
32
33
34
35
55
54
53
152
1
2
3
4
5
6
7
8

80
A
B
C
D
E
F
429
30
31
Coach Hill
Chute Lodge
Long Bottom
Longbottom Farm
Lodge Lane
Biddesden House
Biddesden Lane
265
Wiltshire County
Hampshire County
Redenham Dro
Redenham Drove
Flinty Cott
Redenham
Redenham House
Privet La
Privet Lane
New House Lane
Tilly Down
St Peters CE Primary School
Back Lane
Ragged Appleshaw
Appleshaw
PO
PH
West Park
A342
267
Barncroft
Ramridge House
Ramridge Cott
94
ANDOVER
Lane
1
2
3
4
5
6
7
8
51
50
49
148
1 grid square represents 500 metres

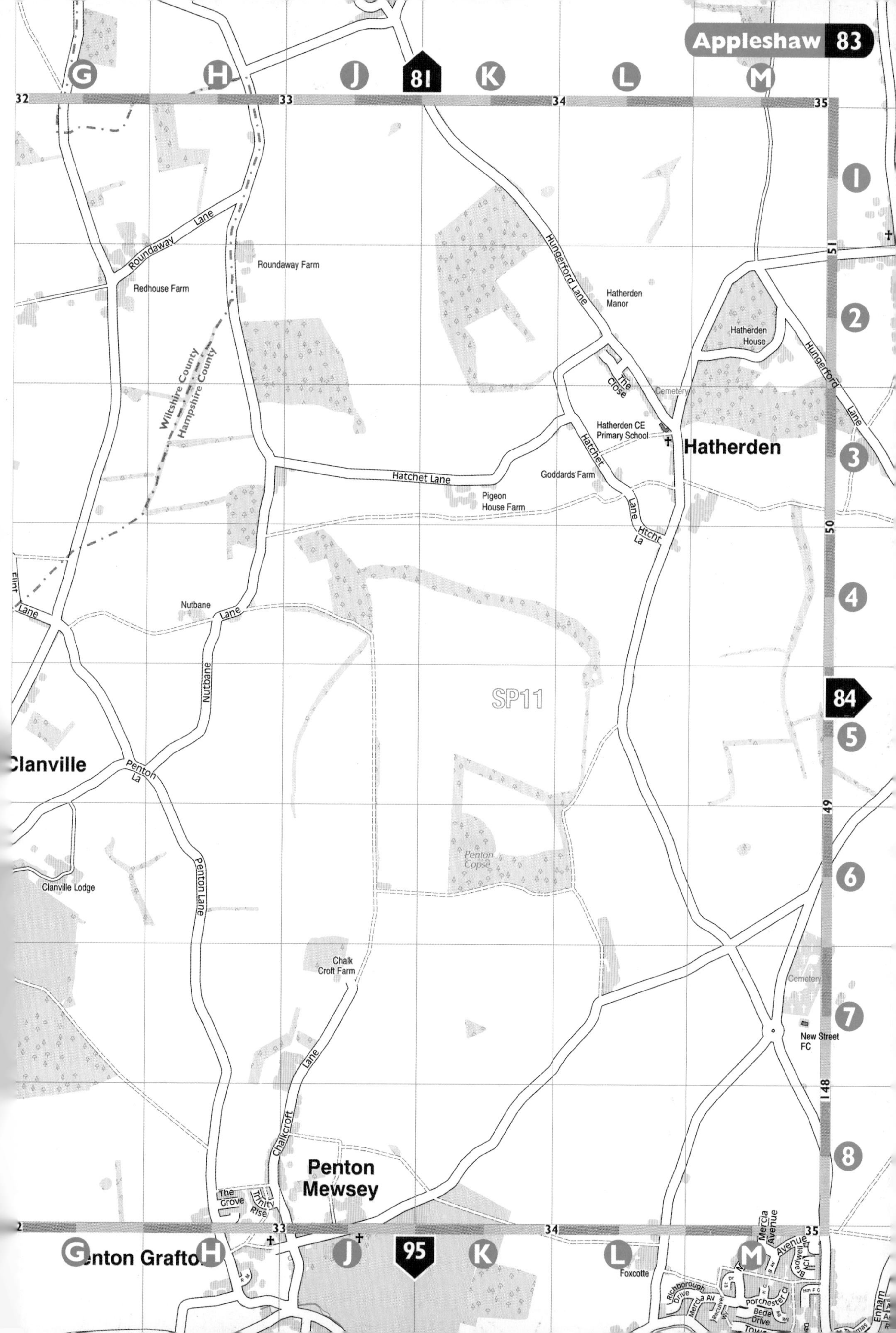

G   H   J   81   K   L   M

32   33   34   35

I

Roundaway Lane

Roundaway Farm

Redhouse Farm

Hungerford Lane

Hatherden Manor

Hatherden House

2

Wiltshire County

Hampshire County

The Close

Cemetery

Hatherden CE Primary School

Hatherden

3

Hatchet Lane

Goddards Farm

Pigeon House Farm

Hatchet La

Htcht La

Hungerford Lane

50

4

Flint Lane

Nutbane Lane

Nutbane Lane

SP11

84

5

Clanville

Penton La

Clanville Lodge

Penton Lane

Penton Copse

49

6

Chalk Croft Farm

Cemetery

7

New Street FC

148

Chalkcroft Lane

8

The Grove

Trinity Rise

Penton Mewsey

G   Penton Grafton   H   J   95   K   L   M

2   33   34   35

Foxcotte

Mercia Avenue

Richborough Drive

Mercia Av

Bede Drive

Porchester C

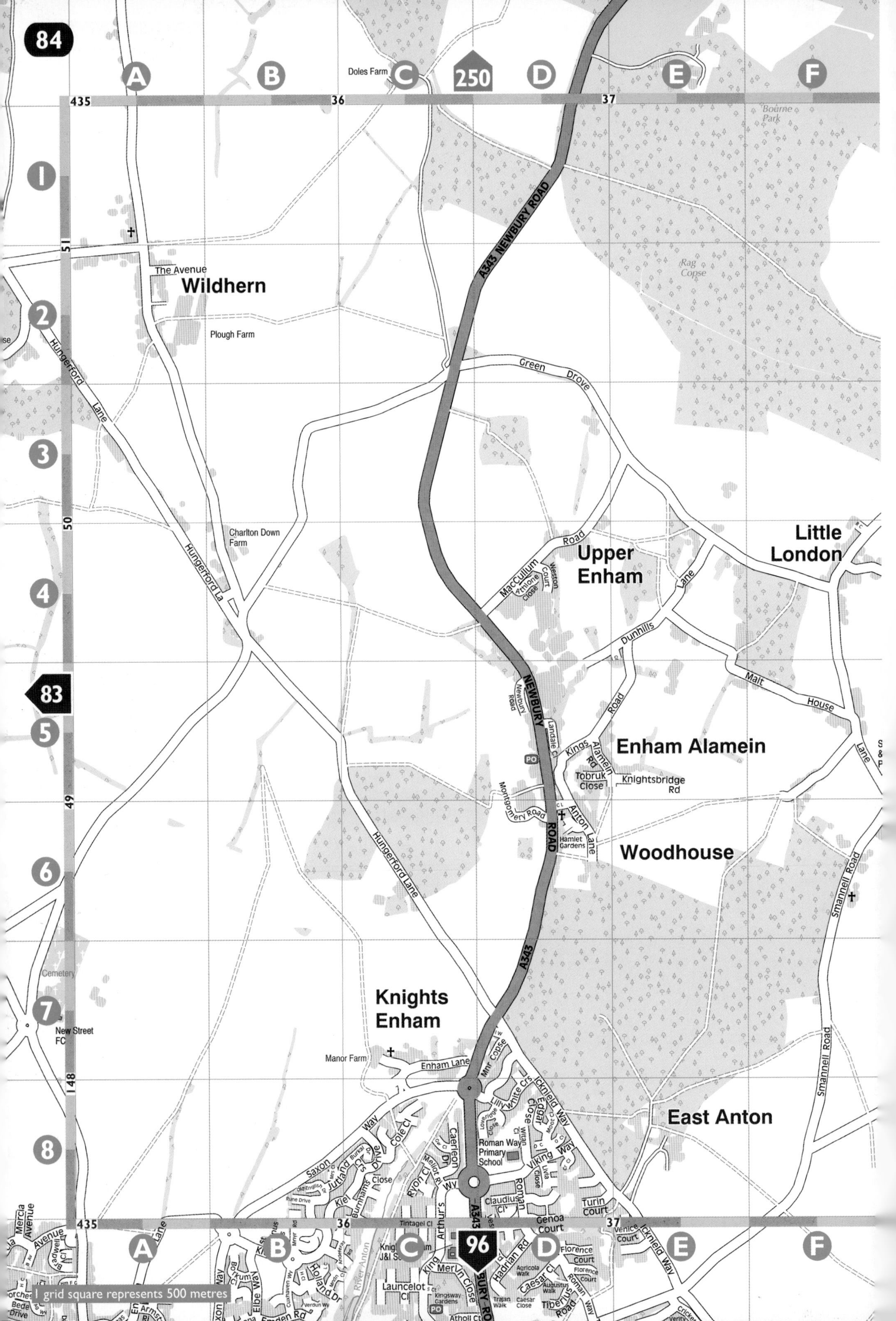
250
A
B
C
D
E
F
435
36
37
Doles Farm
Bourne Park
A343 NEWBURY ROAD
Rag Copse
The Avenue
Wildhern
Plough Farm
Hungerford Lane
Green Drove
Charlton Down Farm
Hungerford La
MacCullum Road
Weston Court
Athlone Close
Upper Enham
Little London
Dunhills Lane
Malt House Lane
NEWBURY ROAD
Newbury Road
Landale Cl
Kings Road
Alamein Rd
Enham Alamein
Tobruk Close
Knightsbridge Rd
Montgomery Road
Anton Lane
Hamlet Gardens
Woodhouse
Smannell Road
Hungerford Lane
A343
Cemetery
New Street FC
Knights Enham
Manor Farm
Enham Lane
Mnr Copse
Lilly White Crs
Icknield Way
Edgar Close
East Anton
Saxon Way
Cole Cl
Jutland Drive
Caerleon Dr
Roman Way Primary School
Viking Way
Burnhams Close
Kiel
Ryon Cl
Mellor Rd
Wy
Roman
Claudius Cl
Turin Court
Genoa Court
Arthur's
A343
Tintagel Cl
Venice Court
Icknield Way
Mercia Avenue
Avenue
Knights Enham J&I Sch
King
Merlin Close
Hadrian Rd
Florence Court
Agricola Walk
Caesar Cl
Augustus Walk
Roman Way
Tiberius Road
Launcelot Cl
Kingsway Gardens
Trajan Walk
Caesar Close
Holland Dr
Elbe Way
Borkum Cl
Emden Rd
Atholl Ct
River Anton
I
2
3
4
5
6
7
8
51
50
49
148
83
96
1 grid square represents 500 metres

Stoke
W. Bottom
G
H
J
250
K
L
M
38
39
40
41
Stokehill Farm
Frenches Farm
Stoke Hill
Gangbridge
B3048
1
51
2
Test
Oak Tree Farm
Stoke Road
3
Upper
Wyke
50
Ridges
Copse
Stoke Road
4
Hackwood
Copse
Middle
Wyke Farm
86
5
Smannell
Enham CE
Primary School
Stoke Road
Finkley Road
Test Way
Smannell
49
Lower
Wyke Farm
6
Malt House La
Finkley
House
Finkley Road
7
Finckley Manor
Farm
148
8
Walworth Road
39
40
41
G
H
J
97
K
L
M
Faulkner
Down F
Finkley Down
Farm Park
PO
Ox Drove
Rise

A   B   C   251   D   E   F   Egbury Castle

441   42   Cold Harbour   43

1

Wakeswood

Gangbridge   Lane

148   Swampton

51

Baptist Hill   Spring   Hill   Lane   Wadwick Bottom

2   Test Way   Batsford

St Mary Bourne   Primary School

PO   Hilst Copse   Egbury   Road   Jamaica Farm

PH   Stevens Green

Bourne Meadow   † St Mary Bourne

3   B3048   Bourne Court

50

Derry Down   Health Clinic   Test Way

PH

4   South Vw   Ter

Middle   Derrydown   Farm   New

85   e Farm   Barn Farm

5   B3048   Harroway

49   Test Way

er   Farm

6   Chapmansford Farm

Bourne Rivulet

7

148   Harroway

8   Apsley Farm

The Common

441   42   98   43

A   B   C   D   E   F

Far   Do   m   B3048

I grid square represents 500 metres

252
Cooper's in the Wood Farm
Cole Henley Manor Farm
Cole Henley
Cole Henley Farm
Larks Barrow Hill
Newbarn Down Copse
Hogdigging Copse
RG28
Harroway
Newbury Road
Down Farm
Dirty Corner
Bloswood Lane
A34
88
Gowdown Copse
Whitchurch Station
Works
Station Rd
Fairfield
Council Building
Kingsley Pk
Evingar Road
Evingar Gdns
Ardglen Industrial Estate
Oakland Rd
Bellevue
Firsway
Kings Wk
Lynch Hill
WHITCHURCH
Manor Farm
Bloswood Drive
Ardglen Road
Lwr Evingar Road
Newbury St
London St
Town Mill Lane
The Green
Hillside
The Mansion
Bell Street
Med Cen
Fairclose
Church Street
Fire Stn
Silk Mill
Winchester Street
Test Road
Lynch Hill
Whitchurch CE Primary School
Hurstbourne Park
Cemetery
Wells's Lane
Works
McFauld Way
Daniel Rd
Broadway
Testbourne Community School
Micheldever Road
99
The Weir
Winchester Road
Webbs Farm Cl
Charlcot Farm
Charlcot Cl
Micheldever Cl

A
B
C
D
E
F
253
Whitnal
447
48
49
New Barn
Peak House Farm
La Bresse
Cole Henley
Cole Henley Farm
Twinley Lane
Square Oaks
RG28
Wooldings Farm
Wooldings Vineyard
The Orchards
50
Harroway
Priory Lane
Twinley Lane
87
S Vw Cottages
Home Farm
Laverstoke Ho
Priory Farm
Freefolk
PH
Laverstoke Mill (Engineering Works)
LONDON ROAD
ROTTEN HILL
Laverstoke
B3400
Colne Valley Way
Laverstoke Lane
Park
LONDON ROAD
Hillside
The Green
The Gables
Florence Portal Cl
River Test
148
Wheeler
Brooks Cl
100
Spring Pond Farm
I grid square represents 500 metres

254
101
90
Foxdown
Quidhampton
Lynch
Southington
OVERTON
Overton Station
Works
Polhampton Farm
Overton CE Primary School
Court Farm
Court Drove
B3051
KINGSCLERE ROAD B3051
Hilltop Road
Elm Rd
Beech Cl
Copse Road
Station Hill
Hill Meadow
Foxdown
North Fld
Lordsfield Gdns
Church Road
Glebe Meadow
Silk Mill Lane
The Lynch
Bridge St
Overton Rec Grnd
Waltham Rd
Riverside Close
Station Road
Surg
Turnpike Cottages
LONDON ROAD B3400
Comm Cen
HIGH ST
Southington Close
Southington La
Vinns Lane
B3400
ROTTEN HILL
Harveys Fld
Woodlands
Oak Cl
Red Lion Lane
Lion Cl
Poyntz Rd
Winchester Street
The Orchard
Battens Avenue
The Green
Two Gate Lane
Nightingale Rise
Sprents Lane
Papermakers
Greyhound La
Alexander Road
Dellands Lane
Dellands
Crawts Road
Charledown Road
Poultons Road
Pond Close
Sapley Lane
Winchester St
Highfields
Mede Close
Pound Road
Waltham Road
Hazelcombe
Berrydown Lane
Berrydown Court
Berrydown Farm
Source of the Test
Turrill Hill Farm
Sapley Farm House
Waltham Lane
Bramdown Copse
Lower White Cottages
Courts Fld
Two Ga Mw
Trims Court

Ashe Warren Ho
254
Little Deane Wood
Wayfarer's Walk
Deane Down Farm
Harrow Way
Cl
Polhampton Farm
Wayfarer's Walk
ANDOVER ROAD B3400
Deane
Ashe
Source of the River Test
ANDOVER ROAD
PH
B3400
Cheesedown Farm
89
Ashe Park
Burley Wood
Burley Lane
Waltham Lane
Steventon
Waltham Lane
Bramdown Copse
Basset's Farm
Stubb's Copse
102
West Wood
1 grid square represents 500 metres

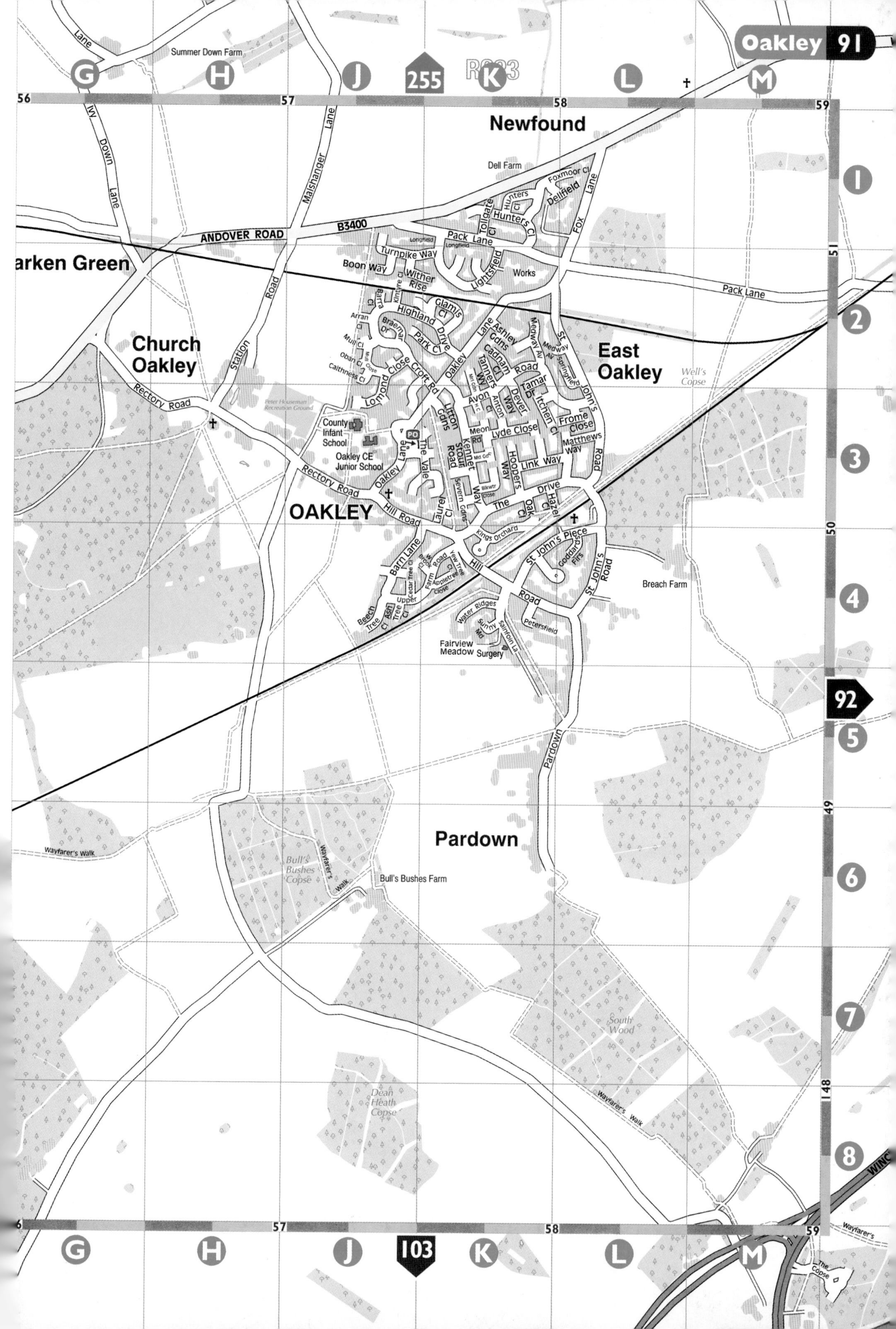
Newfound
Church Oakley
East Oakley
OAKLEY
Pardown
Summer Down Farm
Dell Farm
Works
Breach Farm
Bull's Bushes Farm
Fairview Meadow
Surgery
County Infant School
Oakley CE Junior School
Peter Houseman Recreation Ground
Well's Copse
Bull's Bushes Copse
South Wood
Dean Heath Copse
Wayfarer's Walk
ANDOVER ROAD
B3400
Pack Lane
Rectory Road
Station Road
Malshanger Lane
Ivy Down Lane
Fox Lane
St John's Road
Hill Road
Pardown
Barn Lane
Oakley Lane
The Vale
Highland Drive
Kennet Road
Hoopers Way
Link Way
Lyde Close
Frome Close
Matthews Way
St John's Piece
Goddards Firs
Kings Orchard
Petersfield
Water Ridges
Sunny Md
Sainfoin La
Turnpike Way
Boon Way
Wither Rise
Lightsfield
Tollgate Cl
Hunters Cl
Dellfield
Foxmoor Cl
Glamis Cl
Park Cl
Croft Rd
Lomond Close
Caithness Cl
Oban Cl
Mull Cl
Arran Cl
Barra Cl
Braemar Dr
Kintyre Cl
Ashley Gdns
Cadnam Cl
Tanners Wy
Avon Ct
Anton Cl
Meon Rd
Dever Way
Tamar Dr
Itchen Cl
Medway Av
Litton Gdns
Stour Road
Severn Gdns
The Drive
Oak Cl
Hazel Cl
Laurel Cl
Farm Close
Appletree Close
Yew Tree Cl
Cedar Tree Cl
Upper Ash Tree Cl
Beech Tree Cl
Longfield
arken Green
G H J K L M
56 57 58 59
51 50 49 148
1 2 3 4 5 6 7 8
255
103
92

92
WORTING ROAD
64
Kempshott
Battledown Farm
Pack Lane
Stratton Park
Basingstoke RFC
Down Grange Athletics Track
The Hawthorns School
South Ham
Bishop Challoner RC School
St Annes Catholic Primary School
Aldworth Science College
Park View Infant Sch
Park View Junior School
South Ham Medical Centre
The Ridgeway Centre
Limington House School
Brighton Hill Community College
WINCHESTER ROAD
A30
RG22
Kempshott Infant School
Kempshott Junior School
Beech Down Prim School
Gillies Health Centre
Hatch Warren Primary School
91
Hatch Warren
Hatch Warren Retail Park
Superstore
St Marks Primary School
Woodland Park
Beggarwood Surgery
Basingstoke Golf Club
Golf Course
Kempshott Park
Broadmere
104
1 grid square represents 500 metres

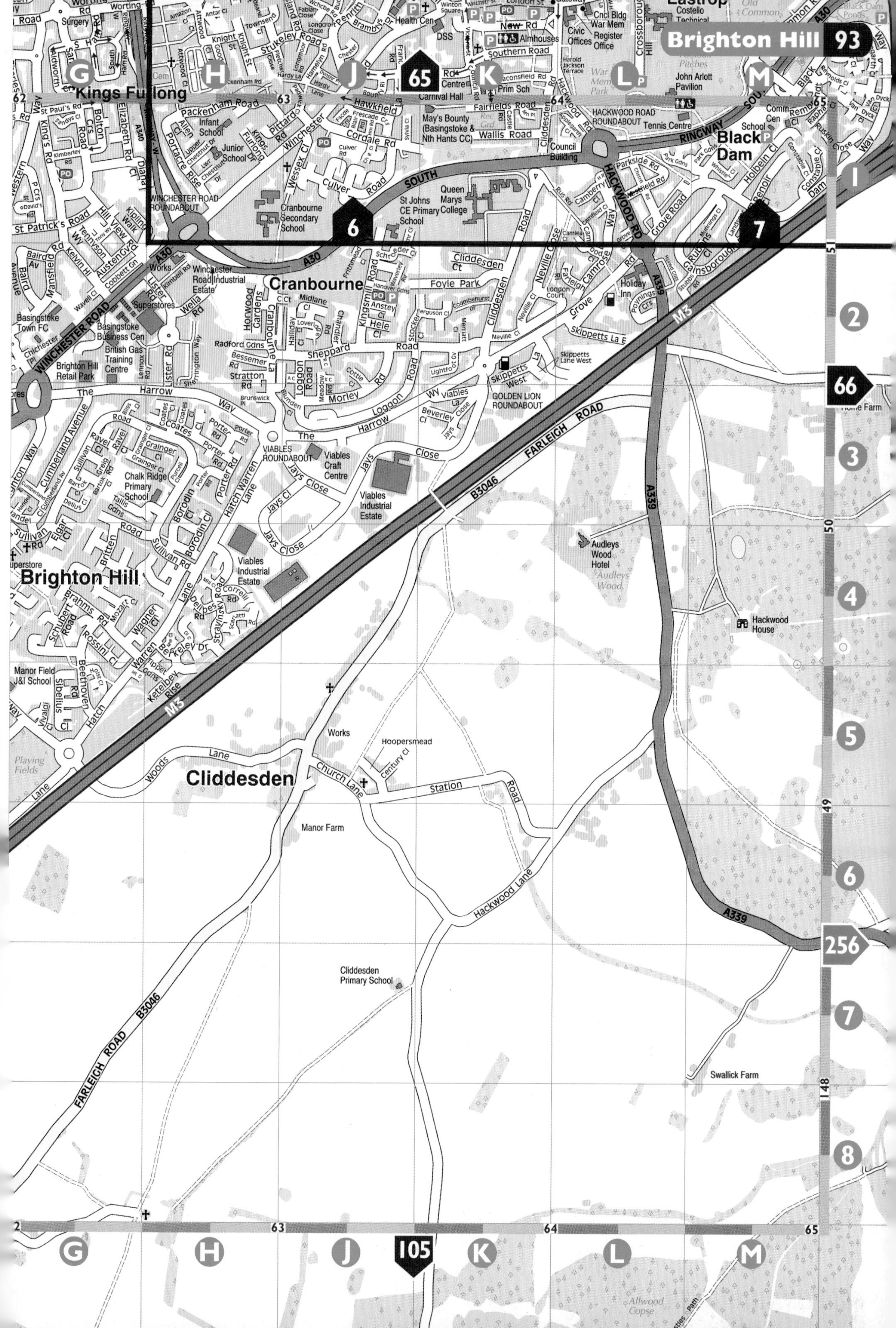

Kings Furlong
Cranbourne
Brighton Hill
Cliddesden
Black Dam
Eastrop
65
66
105
256
6
7
G
H
J
K
L
M
1
2
3
4
5
6
7
8
62
63
64
65
51
50
49
148
A30
A339
M3
A340
B3046
WINCHESTER ROAD
FARLEIGH ROAD
HACKWOOD RD
RINGWAY SOUTH
WINCHESTER ROAD ROUNDABOUT
HACKWOOD ROAD ROUNDABOUT
GOLDEN LION ROUNDABOUT
VIABLES ROUNDABOUT
The Harrow Way
Cumberland Avenue
Packenham Road
Winchester Rd
Cordale Rd
Culver Road
Hawkfield La
Southern Road
New Rd
Fairfields Road
Wallis Road
Cliddesden Road
Cliddesden Ct
Foyle Park
Kingsmill Road
Sheppard Road
Stocker Cl
Loggon Road
Morley Rd
Skippetts La E
Skippetts Lane West
Neville Cl
Camrose Way
Grove Road
Gainsborough Rd
Jays Close
Sullivan Rd
Borodin Cl
Brahms Rd
Mozart Cl
Wagner Cl
Beethoven Rd
Rossini Cl
Warren Way
Keteibey Rise
Hatch Warren Lane
Woods Lane
Church Lane
Station Road
Hackwood Lane
St Patrick's Road
Hill View Rd
Kipling Walk
Tennyson Wy
Austen Gv
Baird Av
Mansfield Rd
Kelvin Hl
Lister Rd
Wella Rd
Harrow Way
Horwood Gardens
Cranbourne La
Radford Gdns
Stratton Rd
Basingstoke Town FC
Basingstoke Business Cen
British Gas Training Centre
Brighton Hill Retail Park
Superstores
Winchester Road Industrial Estate
Works
Cranbourne Secondary School
St Johns CE Primary School
Queen Marys College
Infant School
Junior School
Council Building
Civic Offices
Register Office
Cncl Bldg War Mem
Almshouses
Health Cen
DSS
Carnival Hall
May's Bounty (Basingstoke & Nth Hants CC)
War Mem Park
John Arlott Pavilion
Tennis Centre
Comm Cen
School
Holiday Inn
Costello Technical
Viables Craft Centre
Viables Industrial Estate
Chalk Ridge Primary School
Manor Field J&I School
Playing Fields
Audleys Wood Hotel
Audleys Wood
Hackwood House
Home Farm
Hoopersmead
Manor Farm
Cliddesden Primary School
Swallick Farm
Allwood Copse
Old Common
Black Dam Ponds

Ramridge House
Ramridge Cott
82
Privet Lane
ANDOVER ROAD A342
Fyfield Lane
Dauntsey Drove
Fyfield Road
Fyfield Road
Mayfield Avenue Ind Park
Weyhill Business Park
Fairways
Tittymouse Lane
Rectory Pl
The Fairground
Rectory Place
Weyhill
Lodge Drive
Weyhill Gardens
Fyfield
Duncan's Close
Grange Cl
Michaelmas Drove
Dauntsey Lane
Amesbury Road
A303
Mullenspond
Elm Cl
Stanbury Cl
Lambourne Cl
Lambourne Way
Stanbury Road
Beech Close
Halcyon Dr
PO
The Hawk Conservancy
267
Pillhill Brook
Sarson Lane
Bush Farm
East Cholderton
Wiremead La
Wiremead Lane
Sarson
Sarson Cl
Chapel Cl
Pillhill Brook
Monxton
Amport
Hay Down Lane
Furzedown Lane
Amport House
Amport CE J&I School
Keeper's Hill
Green Lane
Abbotts Ann Road
Chalkpit Lane
Fox Farm
270
Broad Road
Drove
1 grid square represents 500 metres

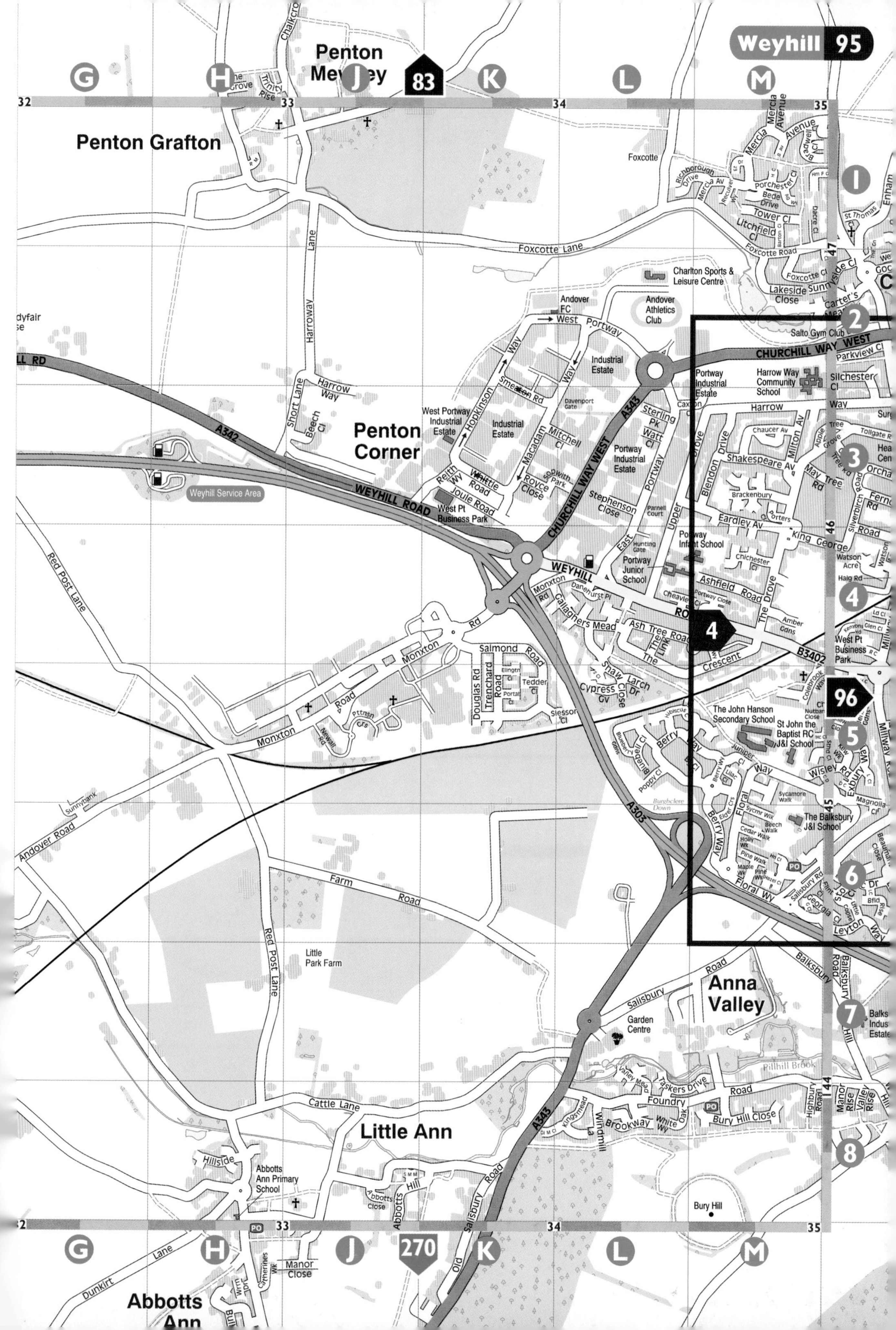
Penton Mewsey
Penton Grafton
Foxcotte
Foxcotte Lane
Charlton Sports & Leisure Centre
Andover FC
Andover Athletics Club
Salto Gym Club
CHURCHILL WAY WEST
Industrial Estate
Portway Industrial Estate
Harrow Way Community School
West Portway Industrial Estate
Penton Corner
Weyhill Service Area
WEYHILL ROAD
A342
A343
A303
B3402
West Pt Business Park
Portway Infant School
Portway Junior School
The John Hanson Secondary School
St John the Baptist RC J&I School
The Balksbury J&I School
Red Post Lane
Andover Road
Monxton Road
Farm Road
Little Park Farm
Salisbury Road
Anna Valley
Garden Centre
Pillhill Brook
Cattle Lane
Little Ann
Abbotts Ann Primary School
Bury Hill
Abbotts Ann
Dunkirt Lane
Manor Close
83
4
96
270

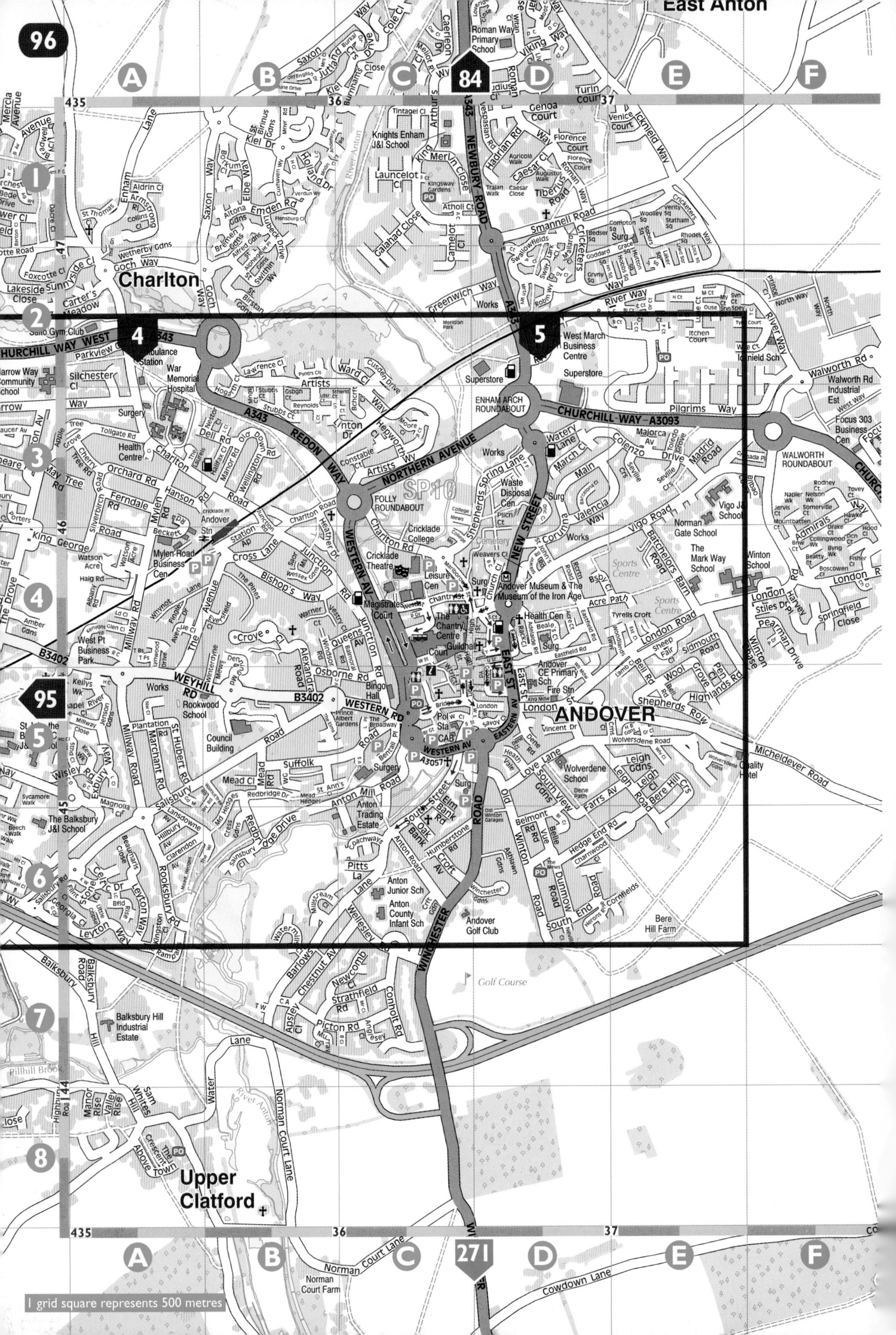

96
East Anton
A
B
C
84
D
E
F
Roman Way Primary School
Saxon Way
Jutland Cres
Burnhams Close
Carleon Dr
Viking Way
Turin Court
Genoa Court
Venice Court
Icknield Way
Tintagel Cl
Knights Enham J&I School
King Arthur's Way
Merlin Close
Launcelot Cl
Kingsway Gardens
Atholl Ct
Galahad Close
Camelot Cl
NEWBURY ROAD
A343
Vespasian Rd
Hadrian Rd
Florence Court
Caesar Cl
Tiberius Road
Roman Way
Crickleters
Smannell Road
Goddard Sq
Rhodes Way
Kiel Dr
Holland Dr
Emden Rd
Elbe Way
Saxon Way
Altona Gdns
Bremen Gdns
Lubeck Drive
Swithin Wy
River Anton
Enham Lane
Aldrin Cl
Armstrong Cl
Collins Cl
St Thomas
Wetherby Gdns
Goch Way
Charlton
Foxcotte Cl
Foxcotte Road
Sunnyside Cl
Lakeside Close
Carter's Meadow
Mercia Avenue
Bedwell Avenue
Bede Drive
Dacre Cl
Greenwich Way
Works
River Way
North Way
Itchen Court
Prince Cl
Salto Gym Club
CHURCHILL WAY WEST
A343
4
Ambulance Station
Parkview Gdns
War Memorial Hospital
Lawrence Cl
Ward Cl
Cusden Drive
Artists Way
Pyntrs Cls
Stubbs Ct
Reynolds Ct
Linton Dr
Hogarth Cl
Superstore
5
West March Business Centre
Superstore
Icknield Sch
Walworth Rd
Walworth Rd Industrial Est
West Way
Focus 303 Business Cen
ENHAM ARCH ROUNDABOUT
CHURCHILL WAY-A3093
Pilgrims Way
WALWORTH ROUNDABOUT
Harrow Way Community School
Silchester Cl
Surgery
A343
REDON WAY
NORTHERN AVENUE
Henworth Cl
Moore Cl
Constable Cl
Artists Wy
Tollgate Rd
Health Centre
Charlton Road
Nestor Dell
Old Down Rd
Manor Rd
Wellington Rd
May Tree Rd
Orchard Rd
Cherry Tree Rd
Silverbirch Road
Ferndale Rd
Hanson Rd
Mylen Rd
Watery Lane
March Cl
Main Crs
Majorca Av
Colenzo Drive
Madrid Road
Toledo Grove
Seville Crs
Works
Waste Disposal Cen
Shepherds Spring Lane
New Street
FOLLY ROUNDABOUT
SP10
Charlton Road
Heather Dr
Cricklade College
Andover Stn
Station Ap
Beckett Rd
Mylen Road Business Cen
King George Road
Watson Acre
Porters
Cross Lane
Junction Rd
Bishop's Way
Wessex Gdns
Cricklade Theatre
Leisure Cen
Cemetery
Weavers Cl
Corunna
Valencia Way
Works
Vigo Road
Batchelors Barn Road
Norman Gate School
The Mark Way School
Vigo Jr School
Sports Centre
Admirals Way
Winton School
London Rd
Haig Rd
Albany Rd
The Drove
Amber Gdns
Millway Rd
Whynot Lane
The Avenue
The Pines
Magistrates Court
Andover Museum & The Museum of the Iron Age
Acre Path
Health Cen
Tyrells Croft
London Road
Stiles Dr
Springfield Close
Pearman Drive
Harvey Rd
Kenyons Glen Cl
West Pt Business Park
B3402
Crove Cl
Warner Ct
Queens Av
Windsor Rd
WESTERN AV
Junction Rd
The Chantry Centre
Guildhall
Court
EAST ST
Andover CE Primary Sch
Fire Stn
Eastfield Rd
Sheep Fair
Sidmouth Road
Wool Grove
Pen Cl
Highlands Rd
Shepherds Row
Winton Chase
95
Kellys Wk
Works
WEYHILL RD
Rookwood School
B3402
Osborne Rd
Bingo Hall
WESTERN RD
Prince Albert Gardens
The Broadway
London St
Eastern Av
Dene Rd
ANDOVER
Vincent Dr
Wolversdene Road
Micheldever Road
Quality Hotel
Plantation Rd
Marchant Rd
St Hubert Rd
Millway Road
Council Building
Suffolk
WESTERN AV
A3057
Savoy Cl
CAB
Surgery
Mead Hedges
Mead Cl
Redbridge Dr
St Ann's Cl
Anton Mill Road
Anton Trading Estate
Love Lane
Wolverdene School
South View Gdns
Farrs Av
Leigh Gdns
Leigh Road
Bere Hill Crs
Sycamore Walk
The Balksbury J&I School
Exbury Rd
Magnolia Cl
Salisbury Rd
Lansdowne Av
Hillbury Av
Clarendon Av
Rooksbury Rd
Redbridge Drive
Coachways
South Street
Elm Bank Rd
Oak Bank
Humberstone Rd
Croft Av
Old Winton Rd
Belmont Rd
Vue Rd
Hedge End Rd
Charnwood Cl
Pitts La
Anton Road
Anton Junior Sch
Anton County Infant Sch
Winchester Gdns
Ashlawn Gdns
Dunmow Road
South End Road
Cornfields
Bere Hill Farm
Andover Golf Club
Georgia Cl
Leyton Way
Flint Cl
Little Cl
Millstream Cl
Watermills Cl
Wellesley Rd
Barlows La
Chestnut Av
Newcomb Cl
Strathfield Rd
Conholt Rd
Apsley Cl
Picton Rd
Anglesey Cl
WINCHESTER ROAD
Golf Course
Balksbury Road
Balksbury Hill
Balksbury Hill Industrial Estate
Pillhill Brook
Lane
Water Lane
River Anton
Norman Court Lane
Manor Rise
Valley Rise
Sam Whites Hill
Above Town
The Crescent
Upper Clatford
Highbury Road
435
36
37
47
46
45
44
1
2
3
4
5
6
7
8
271
Norman Court Lane
Norman Court Farm
Cowdown Lane
1 grid square represents 500 metres

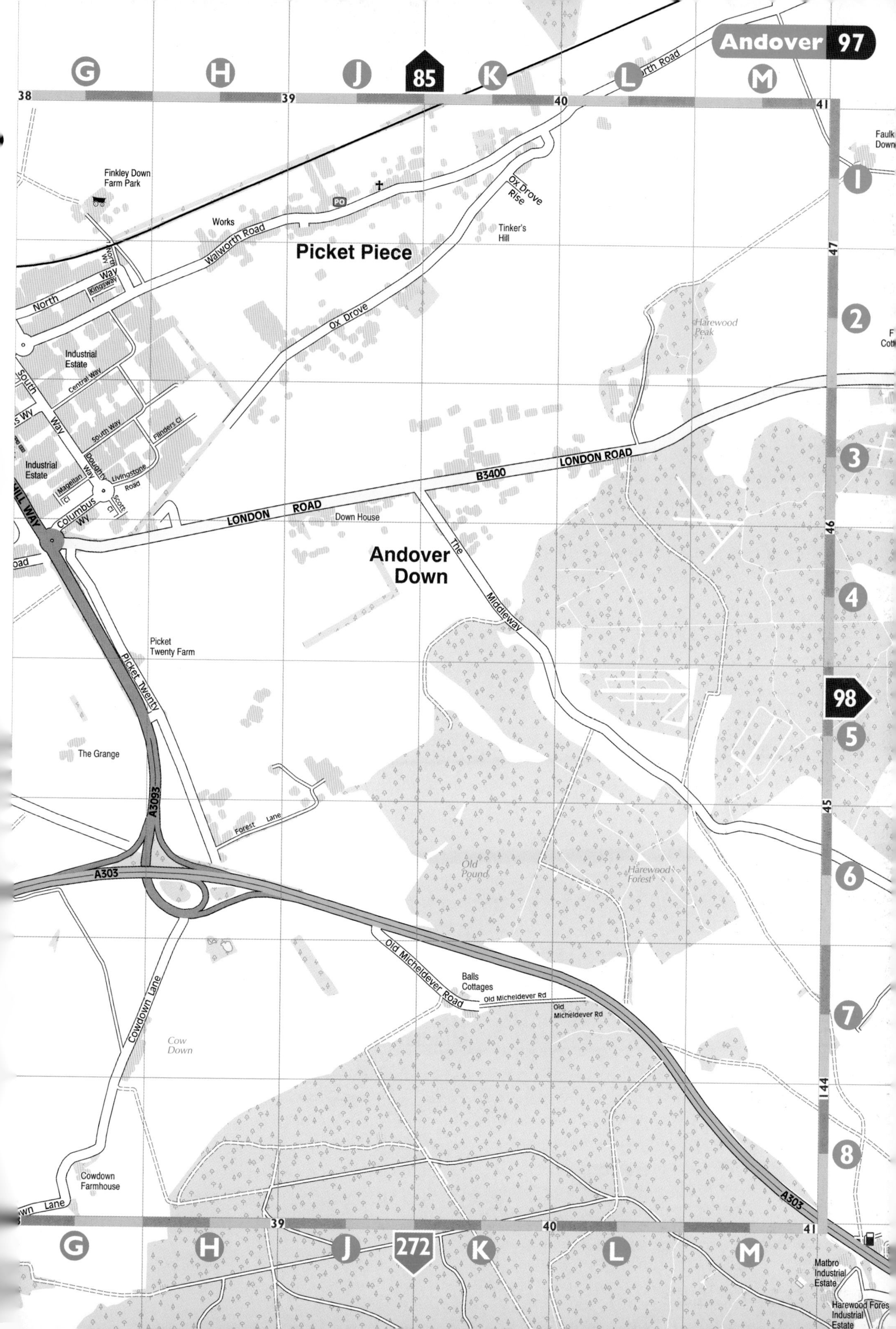

Faulk
Down

Harewood
Peak

F
Cott

Finkley Down
Farm Park

Works

Ox Drove
Rise

North
Way

Kingsway

Walworth Road

PO

†

Picket Piece

Tinker's
Hill

Ox Drove

North
Way

South
Way

Central Way

Industrial
Estate

South Way

Flinders Cl

Livingstone
Road

Magellan
Cl

Boughts
Way

Scott

Columbus
Wy

Industrial
Estate

HILL WAY

oad

B3400

LONDON ROAD

LONDON   ROAD

Down House

The Middleway

**Andover
Down**

Harewood
Peak

Harewood
Forest

Picket
Twenty Farm

Picket Twenty

A3093

The Grange

Forest   Lane

Old
Pound

Harewood
Forest

A303

Cowdown Lane

Cow
Down

Old Micheldever Road

Balls
Cottages

Old Micheldever Rd

Old
Micheldever Rd

A303

Cowdown
Farmhouse

wn   Lane

98

Matbro
Industrial
Estate

Harewood Fores
Industrial
Estate

98
86
97
273
A
B
C
D
E
F
1
2
3
4
5
6
7
8
441
42
43
47
46
45
144
Faulkner's Down Farm
Fox Cottages
Test Way
B3400
The Common
B3048
Hurstbourne Priors
LONGPARISH ROAD
Budgett Farm
Drury Cl
Tracy's Dell
Longparish House
PO
Longparish
Middleton Farm
Lower Mill
Mill Lane
The Middleway
Middleton
PH
Southside Road
Longparish School
Southside Farm
Forton
A303
B3048
The Avenue
Matbro Industrial Estate
Industrial Estate
Monier Williams Rd
1 grid square represents 500 metres

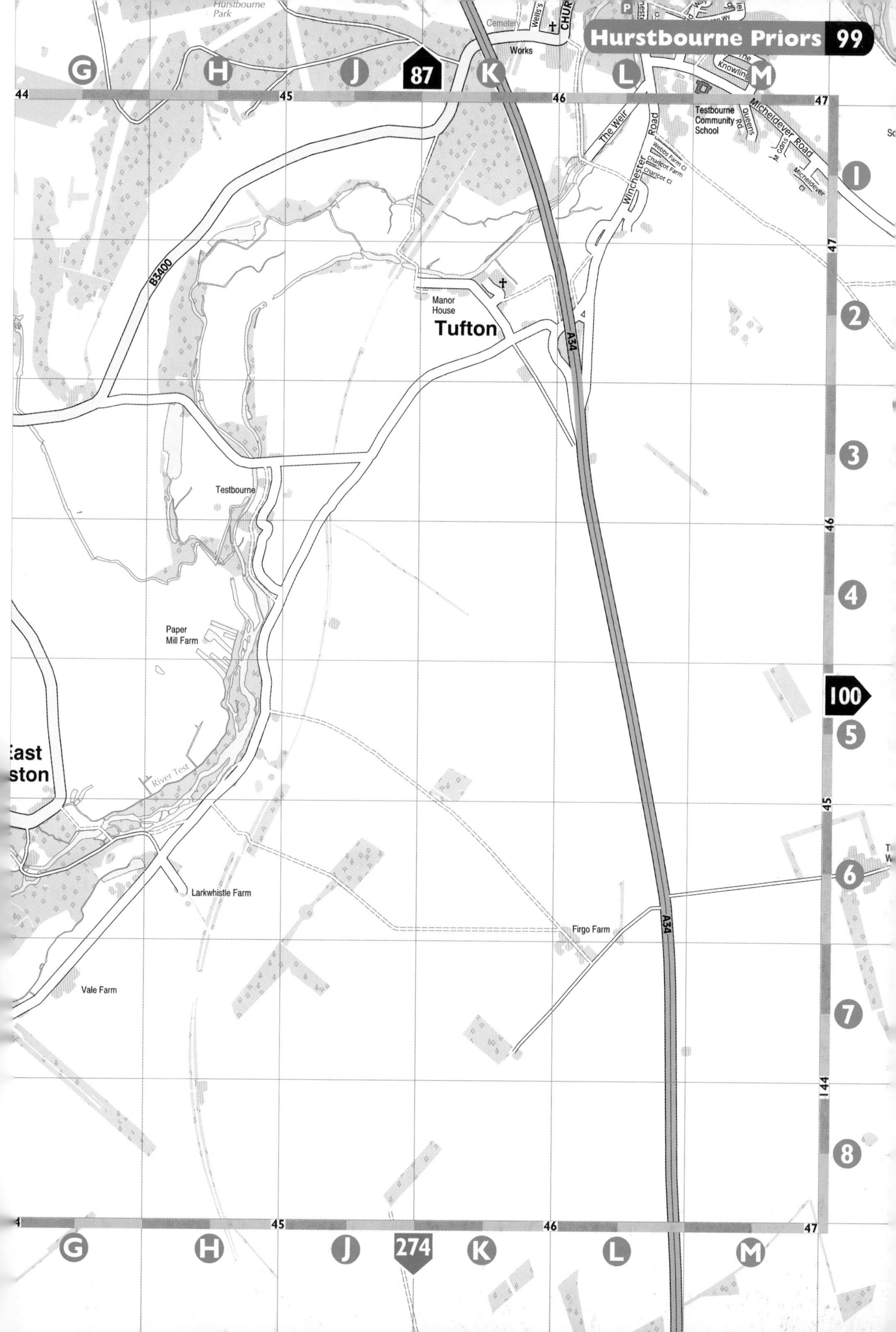

G H J 87 K L M

44 45 46 47

Hurstbourne
Park

Cemetery
Wells'
CHUR

Works

P

The
Knowling

The Weir

Testbourne
Community
School

Queen's
Rd

Micheldever Road

Winchester Road

Webbs Farm Cl

Charldot Farm

Charldot Cl

Micheldever
Cl

B3400

Manor
House

Tufton

A34

Testbourne

Paper
Mill Farm

East
...ston

River Test

Larkwhistle Farm

Firgo Farm

A34

Vale Farm

I

2

3

4

100

5

6

7

144

8

47

46

45

G H J 274 K L M

4 45 46 47

A   B   C   **88**   D   E   F

447   48   49

Wheeler
Brooks
Cl

Micheldever Road

Southfield Farm

Spring
Pond Farm

I   47

Jever

M Cars

Knowle
Hassock

New Barn
Cotts

Laverstoke
Grange Farm

2

3   46

Laverstoke Lane

New
Barn Farm

Micheldever Road

4

Brickkilns
Wood

99   45

5

Tufton
Warren Farm

Freefolk
Wood

6

7   144

Blind
End
Copse

8

447   48   49

A   B   C   **274**   D   E   F

1 grid square represents 500 metres

G   H   J   89   K   L   M

50   51   52   53

Copse

1

Lower
Whitehill
Cottages

2

Southley Farm

3

Upper
Whitehill Farm

Burley Lane

47

46

Pilgrim's Farm

4

Laverstoke
Wood

Test Valley
Golf Club   Golf Course

102

5

45

Roundwood Farm

6

Cobley
Wood

Bellevue
Plantation

7

Popham
Beacons

Popham
Airfield

144

8

Works

G   H   J   275   K   L   M

51   52   53

102

Bramber Copse

Stubb's Copse

Waltham Lane

A   B   C   **90**   D   E   F

453   54   55

Bassett...

West Wood

✝

1

2   Waltham   Manor Farm

Lane

Folly Farm

3

Burley Lane   46

4

Steventon Warren Farm

101

5   Basingstoke Crematorium

Waltham Trinleys

6

Bellevue Plantation

7   West Farm

A303   144

Popham Airfield   A33

8   Popham Court Farm

453   54   55

A   B   C   **276**   D   E   F

1 grid square represents 500 metres

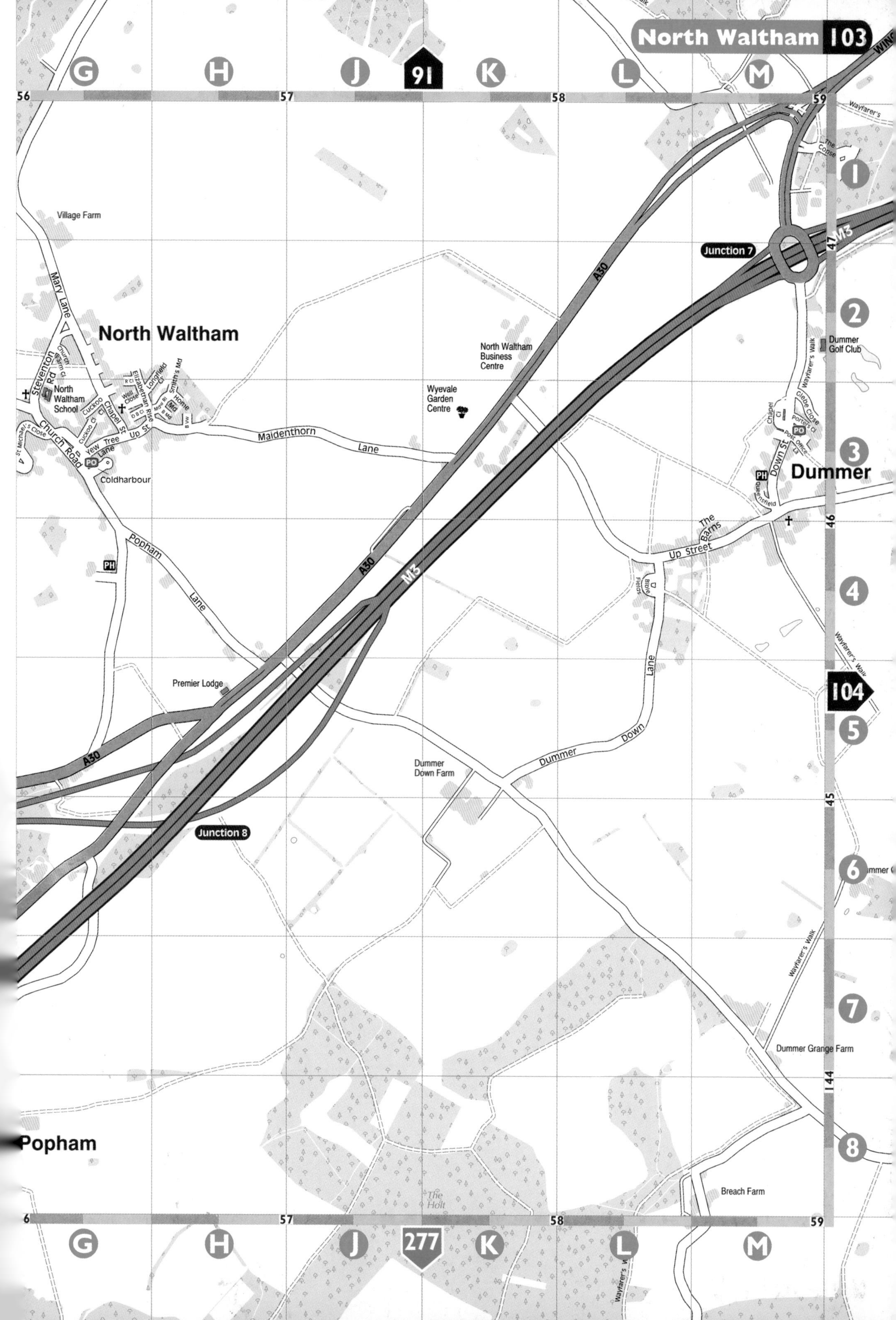

North Waltham

Village Farm

Mary Lane

Steventon Rd

Church Cl

North Waltham School

St Michael's Close

Church Road

Elizabethan Walk

Longfield

Well Close

Chapel St

Cuckoo Cl

Yew Tree Lane

Smith's Mdw

Home Mdw

Up St

Maidenthorn Lane

Coldharbour

Popham Lane

PH

PH

Premier Lodge

A30

A30

A30

M3

Junction 8

Junction 7

47 M3

46

45

144

North Waltham Business Centre

Wyevale Garden Centre

Dummer Down Farm

Dummer Down Lane

Up Street

The Barns

Blake Fields

Dummer

PH

Down St

PO

Chapel Cl

Porters Cl

Glebe Close

Queensfield

Dummer Golf Club

Wayfarer's Walk

Wayfarer's Walk

Wayfarer's Walk

The Copse

Wayfarer's Walk

Dummer Grange Farm

Breach Farm

The Holt

Popham

104

277

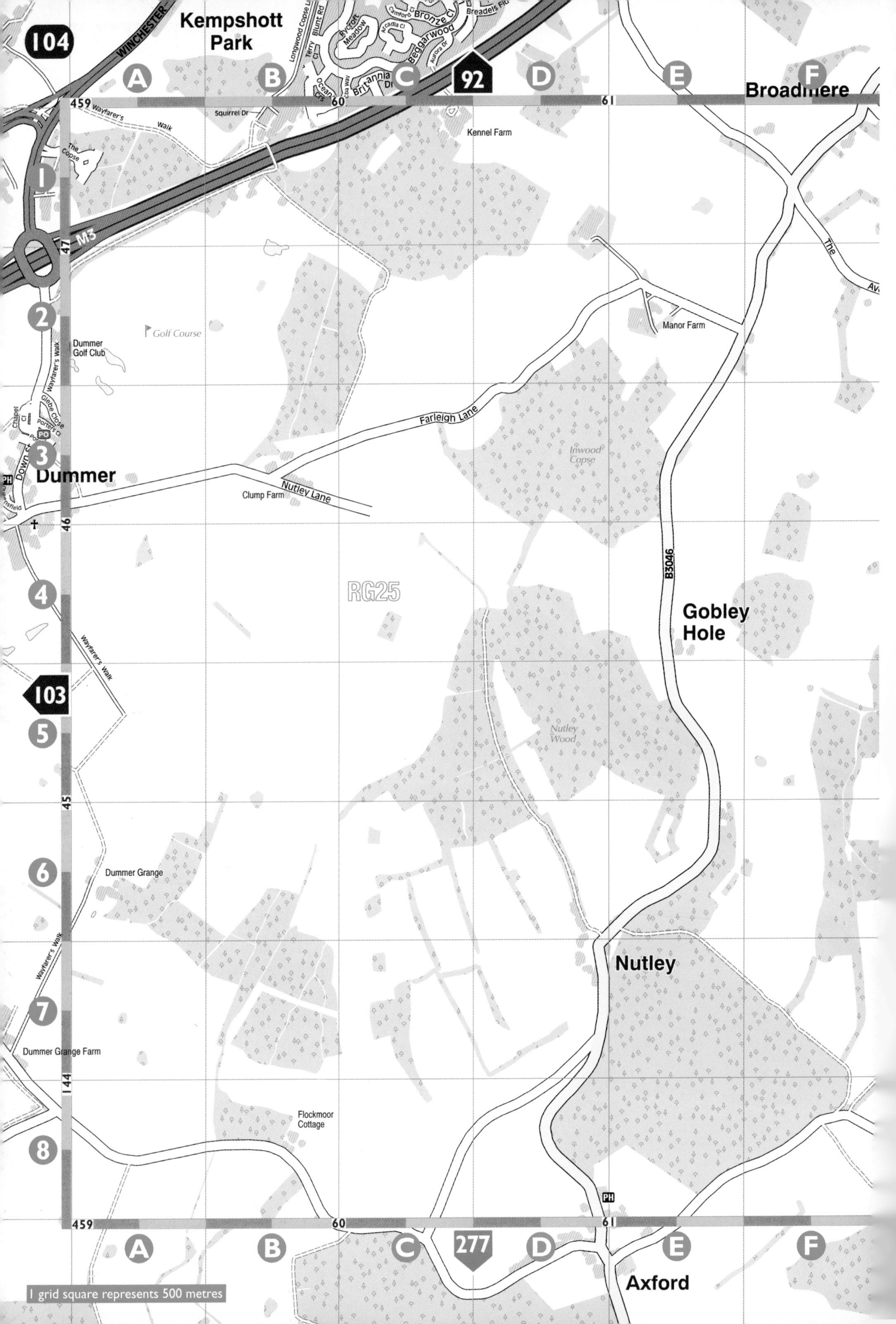
104
Kempshott
Park
92
Broadmere
Kennel Farm
Manor Farm
Golf Course
Dummer
Golf Club
Dummer
Farleigh Lane
Clump Farm
Nutley Lane
Inwood
Copse
RG25
B3046
Gobley
Hole
103
Nutley
Wood
Dummer Grange
Nutley
Dummer Grange Farm
Flockmoor
Cottage
277
Axford
1 grid square represents 500 metres

G
H
J
93
K
L
M
62
63
64
65
Allwood Copse
Three Castles Path
Farleigh Wallop
Grammarsham Lane
Bedlam Bottom
Northgate Farm
Northgate Lane
Great Wood
Church Lane
Ellisfield
Ellisfield Manor
Green Lane
Farrier's Field
Norton's Wood
Furzen Lane
Three Castles Path
Merritts Farm
256
Upper Common
Bell Lane
College Farm
Lower Common
College Lane
Three Castles Path
Nutley Down
High Wood
Berrydown Lane
Berrydown Farm
Preston Oak Hills
Red Lane
Moundsmere Manor
278
47
46
45
144
1
2
3
4
5
6
7
8

Shalden
280
279
294
Alton
Newtown
The Butts
Beech
Chawton
Basingstoke Road
New Odiham Road
Old Odiham Road
Southwood Road
Brick Kiln Lane
Whitedown Lane
Selborne Road
Winchester Road
Chawton Park Road
Mounters Lane
Wolf's Lane
Snode Hill
Medstead Road
Wellhouse Road
Anstey Lane
Southwood Farm
Warren Farm
Greenwood Farm
Will Hall Farm
Wyards Farm
Chawton Park Farm
Lumbry Farm
Amery Wood
Thedden Copse
Ackender Wood
Alton College
Alton Community Hospital
Alton Sports Centre
Jane Austen's House
Curtis Museum
Brewery
Wootey Primary School
Amery Hill Sec School
Anstey County Junior School
St Lawrence CE (Controlled) Primary Sch
The Butts County Prim Sch
Whitedown Special School
Fire Station
Salvation Army
Superstore
Cemetery
A339
A31
B3349
1 grid square represents 500 metres

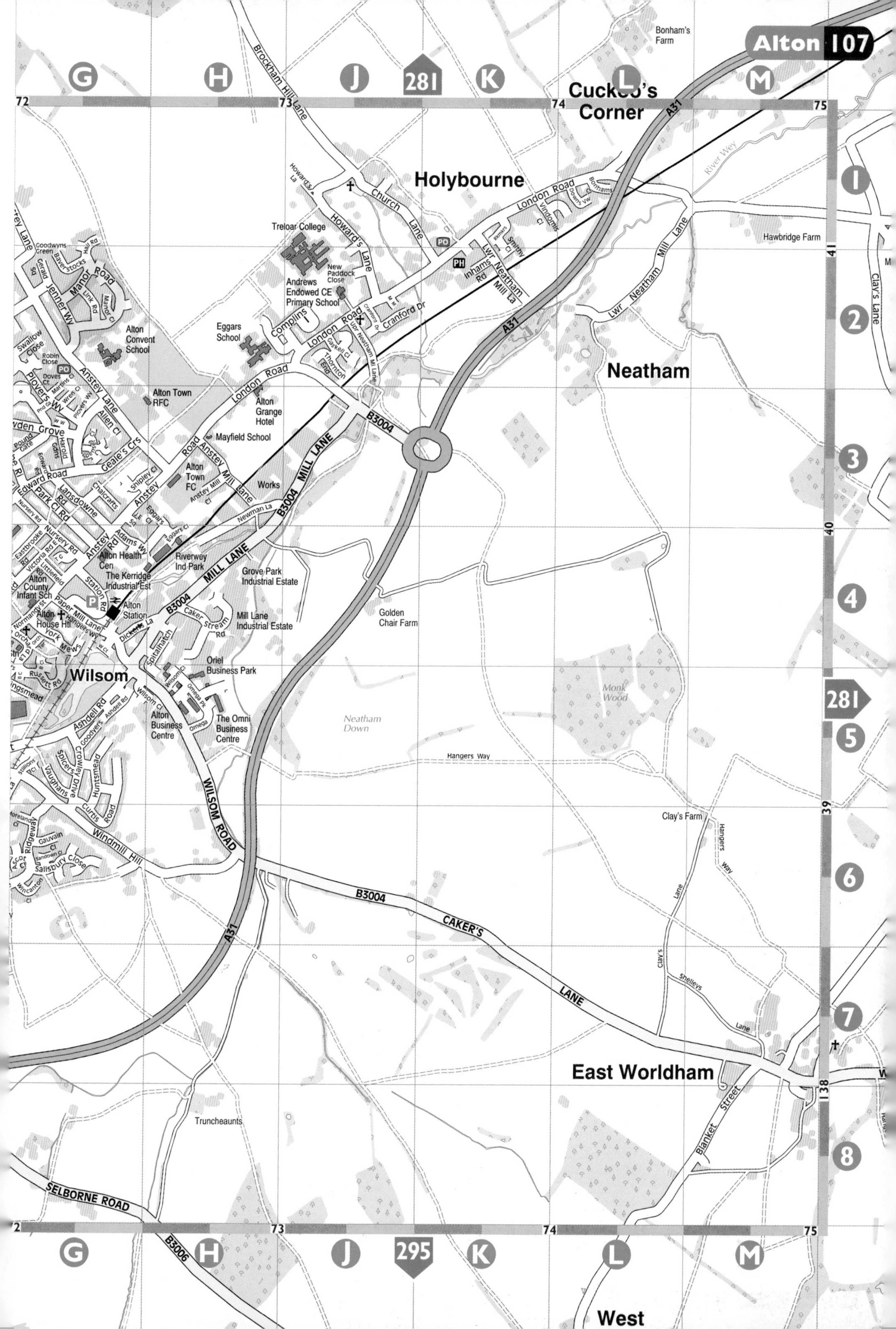

Cuckoo's Corner
Holybourne
Neatham
Wilsom
East Worldham
West
Bonham's Farm
Hawbridge Farm
Clay's Lane
Treloar College
Andrews Endowed CE Primary School
New Paddock Close
Eggars School
Alton Convent School
Alton Town RFC
Alton Grange Hotel
Mayfield School
Alton Town FC
Works
Riverwey Ind Park
Grove Park Industrial Estate
Alton Health Cen
The Kerridge Industrial Est
Alton County Infant Sch
Alton Station
Alton House Htl
Mill Lane Industrial Estate
Oriel Business Park
The Omni Business Centre
Alton Business Centre
Golden Chair Farm
Neatham Down
Monk Wood
Hangers Way
Clay's Farm
Truncheaunts
Brockham Hill Lane
Church Lane
Howard's Lane
London Road
Lwr Neatham Mill La
Lwr Neatham Mill Lane
Upr Neatham Mill Lane
Cranford Dr
Complins
Inhams Rd
Manor Road
Jenner Wy
Anstey Lane
Anstey Road
Anstey Mill Lane
Geale's Crs
Edward Road
Park Cl Rd
Lansdowne Rd
Nursery Rd
Station Rd
Paper Mill Lane
Newman La
B3004 MILL LANE
Caker Stream Rd
Dickens La
Spitalhatch
Wilsom Cl
Ashdell Rd
Crowley Drive
Huntsmead
Curtis Road
Windmill Hill
Salisbury Close
WILSOM ROAD
B3004 CAKER'S LANE
Clay's Lane
Shelleys Lane
Blanket Street
SELBORNE ROAD
B3006
A31
River Wey
G H J K L M
281
295
72 73 74 75
41 40 39 38
1 2 3 4 5 6 7 8

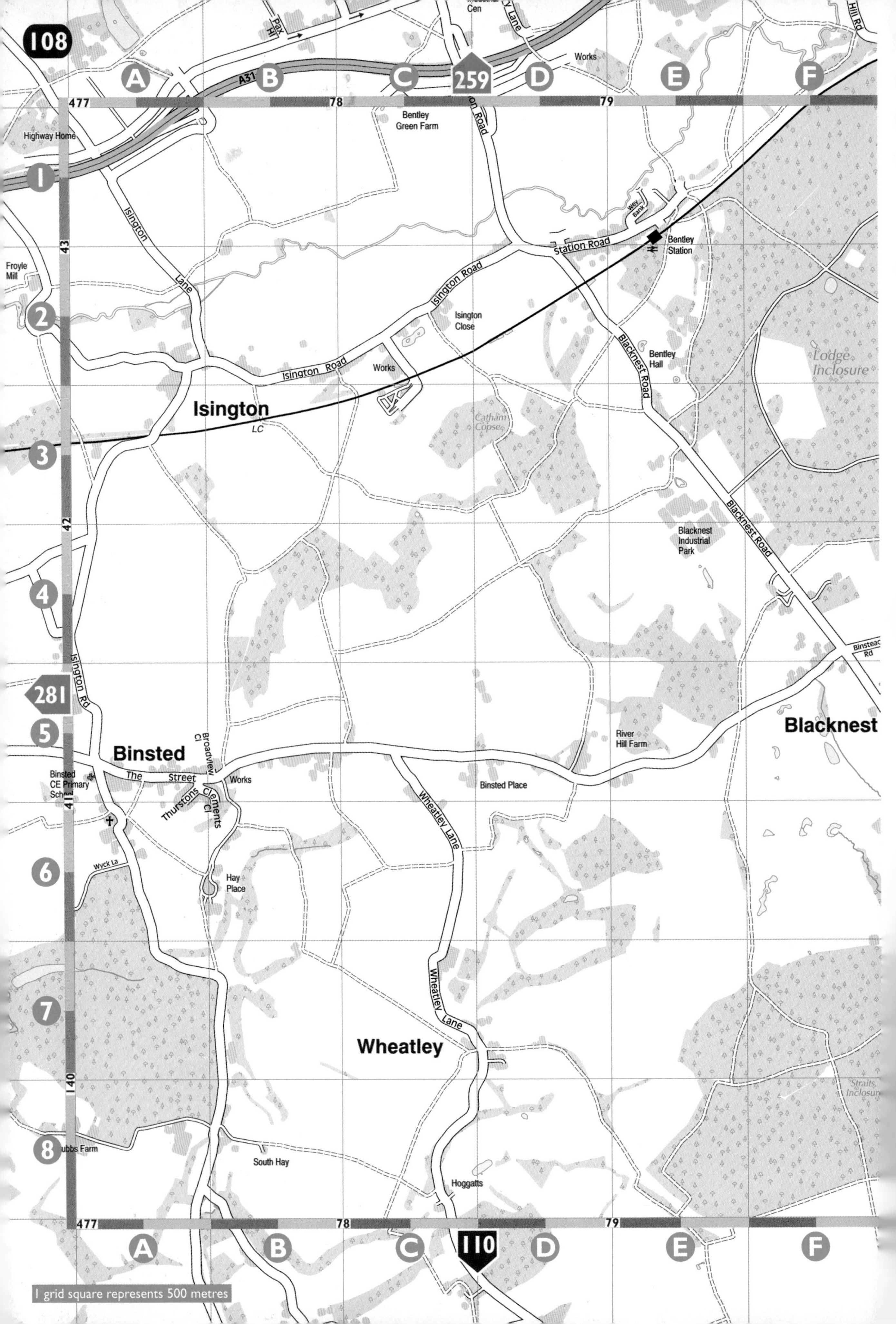

A   B   C   259   D   E   F

477   78   79

A31

Highway Home

Froyle
Mill

I

43

2

Isington Lane

Bentley
Green Farm

Station Road

Well
Bank

Bentley
Station

Isington Road

Isington
Close

Blacknest Road

Bentley
Hall

3

42

Isington

LC

Isington Road

Works

Catham
Copses

4

281

5

Binsted

Isington Rd

41

Binsted
CE Primary
School

The Street

Broadview Cl

Thurstons

Clements Cl

Works

Blacknest
Industrial
Park

River
Hill Farm

Binsted Place

Blacknest

Binstead
Rd

6

Wyck La

Hay
Place

Wheatley Lane

7

140

Wheatley Lane

Wheatley

Straits
Inclosure

8

Stubbs Farm

South Hay

Wheatley Lane

Hoggatts

477   78   79

A   B   C   110   D   E   F

Lodge
Inclosure

I grid square represents 500 metres

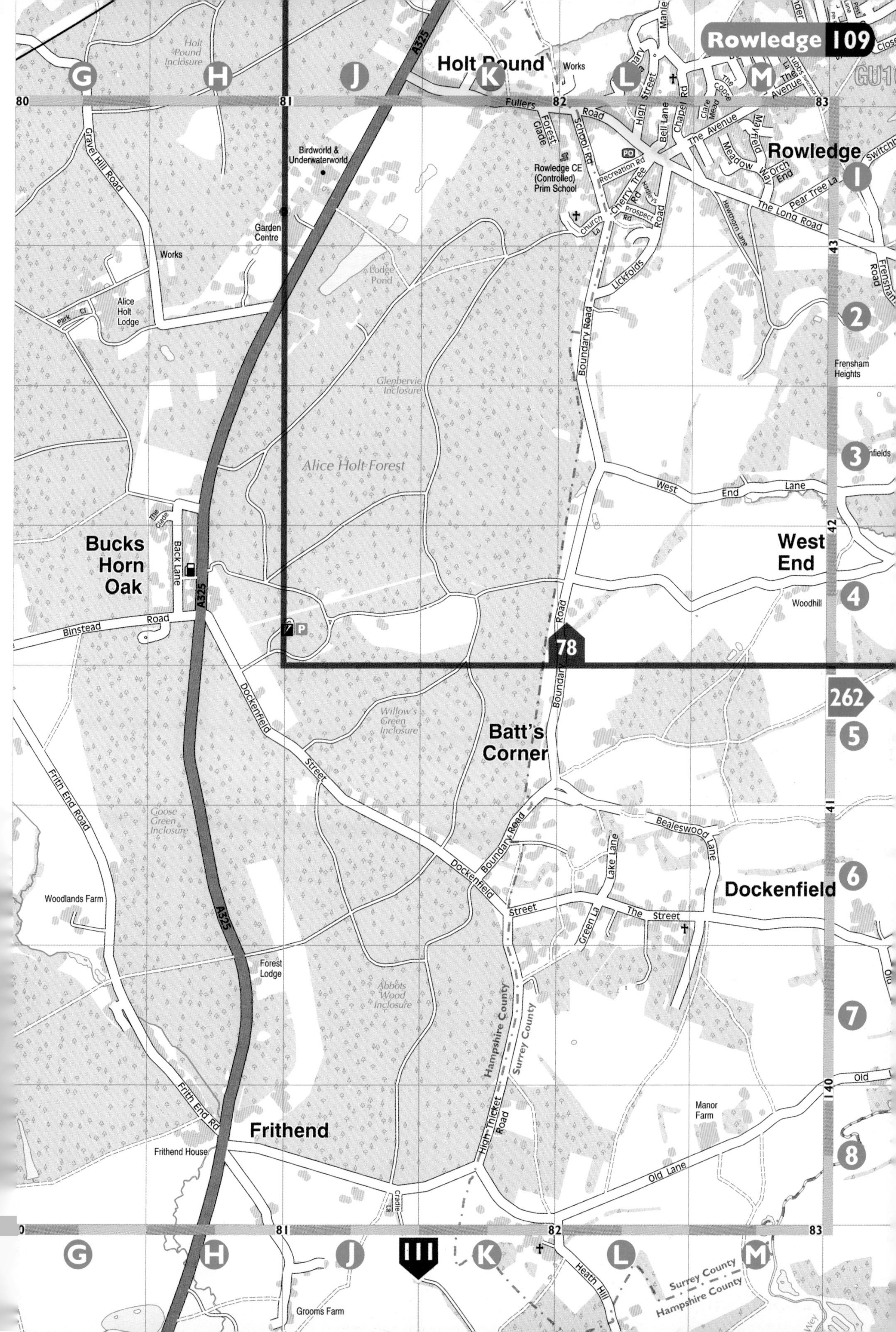
Holt Pound
Holt Pound Inclosure
Works
Fullers
Forest Glade
School Rd
Road
High Street
Bell Lane
Chapel Rd
The Avenue
Clare Mead
The Copse
Mayfield
Meadow Way
Orch End
Rowledge
Switchback
Pear Tree La
The Long Road
Hawthorn Lane
Frensham Road
Birdworld & Underwaterworld
Rowledge CE (Controlled) Prim School
Recreation Rd
Cherry Tree Rd
Hadleys
Prospect Rd
Road
Church La
Lickfolds
Gravel Hill Road
Garden Centre
Works
Lodge Pond
Alice Holt Lodge
Park Cl
Boundary Road
Frensham Heights
Glenbervie Inclosure
Alice Holt Forest
West End Lane
West End
Woodhill
The Glade
Back Lane
Bucks Horn Oak
A325
Binstead Road
78
262
Dockenfield Street
Willow's Green Inclosure
Batt's Corner
Boundary Road
Bealeswood Lane
Goose Green Inclosure
Frith End Road
Lake Lane
Dockenfield
Woodlands Farm
Street
Green La
The Street
Forest Lodge
Abbots Wood Inclosure
Hampshire County
Surrey County
High Thicket Road
Old
Manor Farm
Frith End Rd
Frithend
Frithend House
Old Lane
Cradle La
80
81
82
83
43
42
41
40
G
H
J
K
L
M
1
2
3
4
5
6
7
8
111
Heath Hill
Surrey County
Hampshire County
Grooms Farm
Wey

A   B   C   108   D   E   F

477   78   79

1

39

2

281

3

Kingsley

38

STREET   FORGE ROAD   B3004   Dean Farm Golf Club

4

Lode Farm

Golf Course

Oxney Stream

5

Rookery Farm

Oxney Farm

Oxney Pool

6

Shortheath Common

295

Shortheath

Western Rd   Amherst Road   Louisburg Road   Eastern Road   FARNHAM RD

North   Central   Parade   Road

Stable   Road   Southern Road   B3002

STATION ROAD

7

Gibbs Lane

Old Station Way   Bolley Av   Cem   Ladysmith Pl   CAMP ROAD

Bordon Trading Est   Oakhanger Road   B3002

Haweswater Cl   Rydal   Kildare Rd   A325

Bordon Infant School

8

Lions Fld

136

Slab   Hogmoor Road   BUDDS LANE

477   78   79

A   B   C   112   D   E   F

The Warren

Moor Cl

1 grid square represents 500 metres

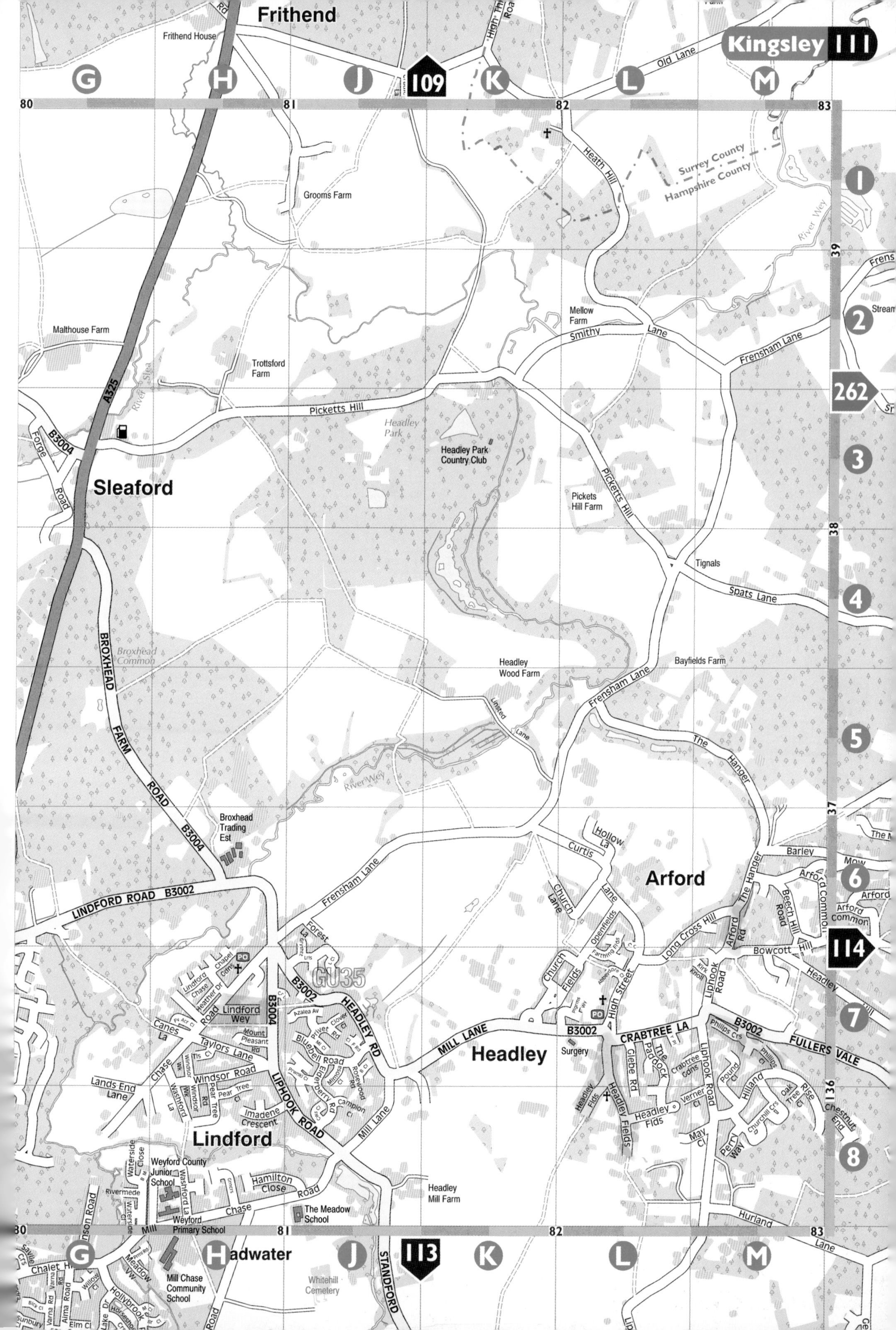

Frithend
Frithend House
Kingsley 111
109
Old Lane
G
H
J
K
L
M
80
81
82
83
Heath Hill
Surrey County
Hampshire County
Grooms Farm
River Wey
Frensham Lane
Mellow Farm
Smithy Lane
Malthouse Farm
Trottsford Farm
A325
River Slea
Picketts Hill
262
B3004
Forge Road
Headley Park
Headley Park Country Club
Sleaford
Pickets Hill Farm
Picketts Hill
Tignals
Spats Lane
Broxhead Common
BROXHEAD FARM ROAD B3004
Headley Wood Farm
Bayfields Farm
Frensham Lane
Linsted Lane
The Hanger
River Wey
Broxhead Trading Est
Hollow La
Curtis Lane
Barley Mow
Arford
Arford Common
Arford Rd
Beech Hill Road
LINDFORD ROAD B3002
Frensham Lane
Church Lane
Long Cross Hill
Forest La
Openfields
Farthing Flds
Bowcott Hill
114
Headley Hill
GU35
Church Fields
High Street
Kirk Knoll
Liphook Road
Lindford Chase
Heather Dr
Chapel Gdns
B3002 HEADLEY RD
B3004
Lindford Wey
Azalea Av
Privet Rd
Clover Cl
MILL LANE
B3002
CRABTREE LA
B3002
FULLERS VALE
Phillips Crs
Canes La
Taylors Lane
Mount Pleasant Rd
Bluebell Road
Headley
Surgery
Glebe Rd
The Paddock
Crabtree Gdns
Liphook Road
Pound Cl
Phillips Cl
Windsor Road
Elderberry Rd
Mimosa Cl
Rosewood Rd
Lands End Lane
Chase La
Washford La
Pear Tree Rd
Pear Tree Cl
Campion Cl
Headley Flds
Headley Fields
Verner Cl
Hilland
Oak Tree Cl
Rise
Churchill Crs
Chestnut End
Imadene Crescent
LIPHOOK ROAD
Mill Lane
May Cl
Perry Way
Lindford
Waterside Close
Weyford County Junior School
Washford La
Hamilton Close
Headley Mill Farm
Rivermede
Chase Road
The Meadow School
Weyford Primary School
Hurland Lane
Mill
Hadwater
113
STANDFORD
Chalet Hill
Meadow Vw
Mill Chase Community School
Whitehill Cemetery
Alma Road
Hollybrook
Elm Cl
1
2
3
4
5
6
7
8
36
37
38
39

110
Blackmoor
Whitehill
Hogmoor Inclosure
Golf Course
The Warren
Blackmoor Golf Club
Albury Farm
Blackmoor House
Brockbridge Farm
Benhams Farm
Benhams Lane
Sotherington Lane
Blackmoor Road
Drift Road
Firgrove Road
Liphook Road
Walldown Rd
PETERSFIELD ROAD
A325
A325 WOOLMER ROAD
HIGH STREET
BUDDS LANE
Woolmer Way
Hogmoor Rd
Golf Lane
The Links
The Fairway
Fir Grove
Plantation Way
Bracken Lane
Eveley Cl
Heather Cl
Champney Cl
Sutton Field
New Road
Lemon Grove
Princes Cl
Oak Tree Rd
Conifer Close
Forest Road
The Woodlands
Pelham Cl
Woodlea Primary School
Chase Community Hosp
Conde Way
Malmsbury Road
South Hurst
Alpine Rd
Athol Rd
Stubbington Av
Dudley Cl
Cornwall Rd
Kent Rd
York Cl
Argyle Cl
Wellington Av
Woodpecker Cl
Jacaranda Rd
Lilac Cl
Surgery
Surg
Moor Cl
Spruce Avenue
Cypress Rd
Mornington Rd
Juniper Cl
Selborne Way
Warren Close
Bramley Wk
St Andrews Rd
The Sands
Broomfield Rd
Fernlea
Cranmer Bottom
Woolmer Pond
Snap
477
78
79
35
34
33
132
295
308
A3
1 grid square represents 500 metres

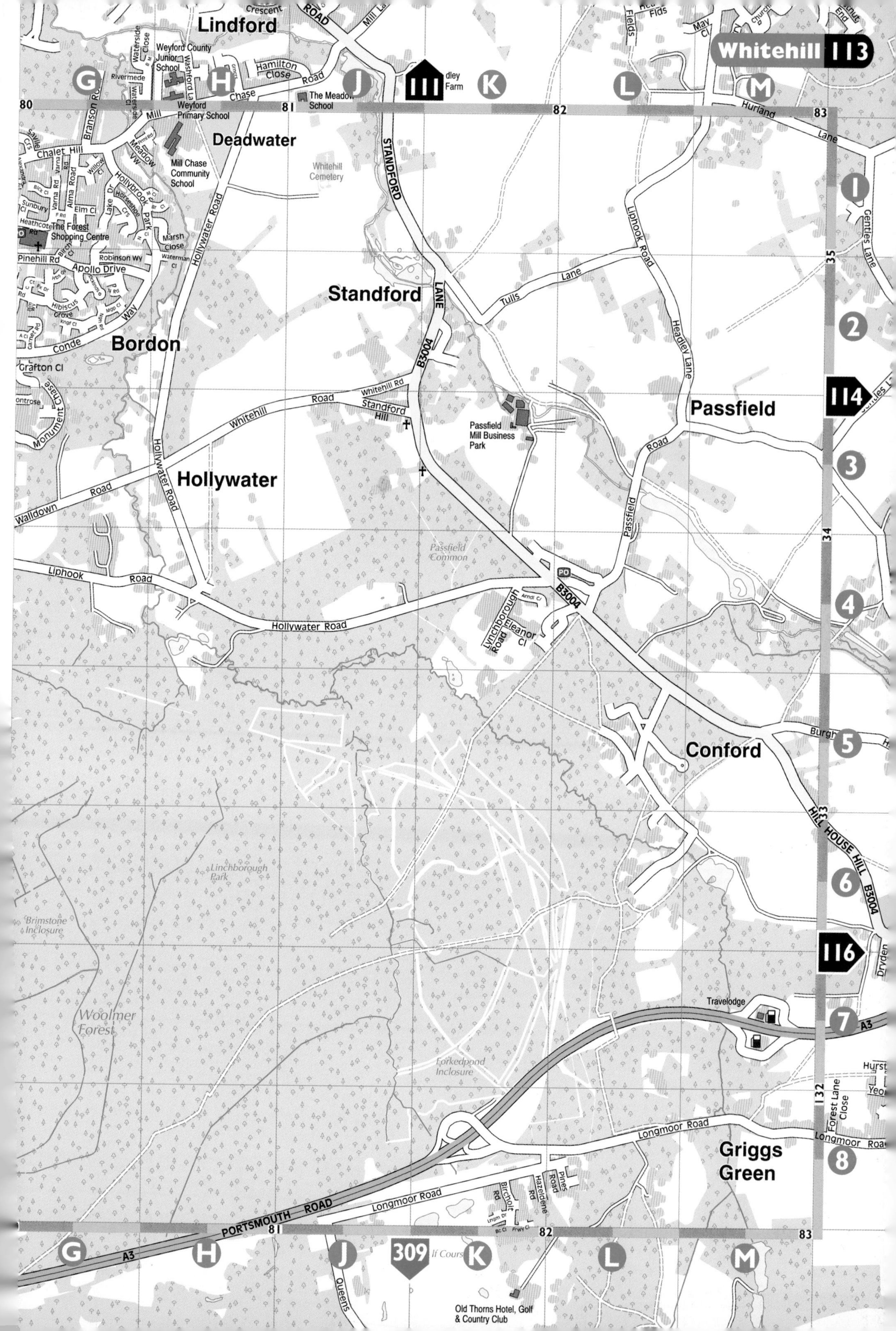

Whitehill 113
Lindford
Weyford County Junior School
Hamilton Close
Chase Road
The Meadow School
Weyford Primary School
Deadwater
Mill Chase Community School
Whitehill Cemetery
STANDFORD LANE
Hurland Lane
Chalet Hill
Alma Road
Elm Cl
Sunbury
The Forest Shopping Centre
Robinson Wy
Pinehill Rd
Apollo Drive
Marsh Close
Hibiscus Grove
Hollybrook Park
Hollywater Road
Liphook Road
Tulls Lane
Gentles Lane
Standford
Bordon
Conde Way
Grafton Cl
Monument Chase
B3004
Whitehill Rd
Whitehill Road
Standford Hill
Passfield Mill Business Park
Headley Lane
Passfield
Passfield Road
Hollywater
Walldown Road
Passfield Common
Lynchborough Road
Eleanor Cl
Hollywater Road
Conford
Burgh
HILL HOUSE HILL B3004
Linchborough Park
Brimstone Inclosure
Woolmer Forest
Forkedpond Inclosure
Travelodge
A3
Forest Lane Close
Longmoor Road
Griggs Green
Bircholt Rd
Hazelbene Rd
Pines Road
PORTSMOUTH ROAD
Queens
Old Thorns Hotel, Golf & Country Club
114
116
111
309
G H J K L M
1 2 3 4 5 6 7 8
80 81 82 83
132 33 34 35

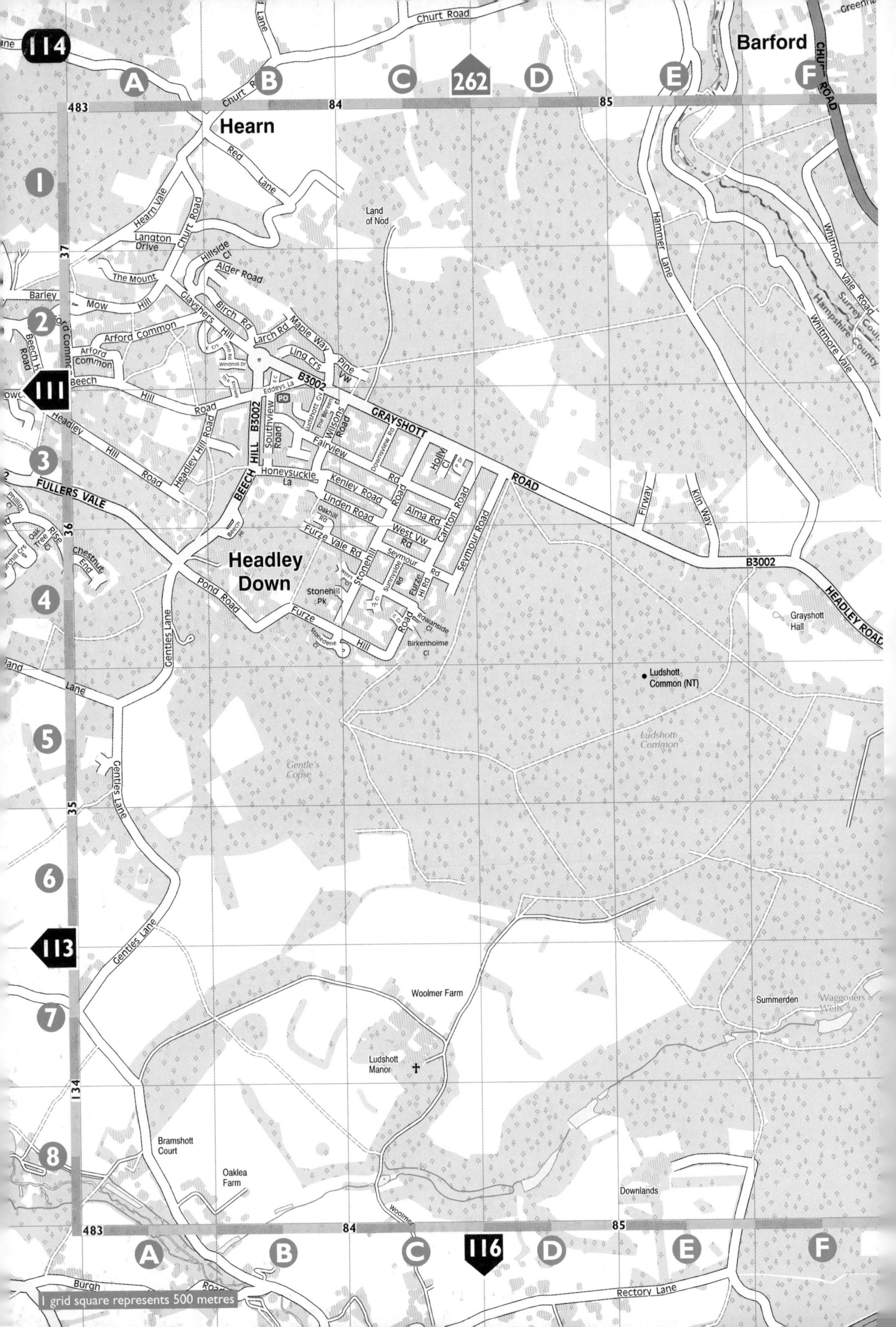
114
262
111
113
116
Barford
Hearn
Headley
Down
Land of Nod
Churt Road
Red Lane
Hearn Vale
Langton Drive
The Mount
Hillside Cl
Alder Road
Barley Mow Hill
Arford Common
Beech Hill Road
Headley Hill Road
Fullers Vale
Pond Road
Gentles Lane
Grayshott Road
B3002
Hammer Lane
Firway
Kiln Way
Whitmoor Vale Road
Headley Road
Grayshott Hall
Ludshott Common (NT)
Ludshott Common
Gentle's Copse
Woolmer Farm
Ludshott Manor
Summerden
Waggoners Wells
Bramshott Court
Oaklea Farm
Downlands
Rectory Lane
1 grid square represents 500 metres

G
H
J
263
K
L
M
86
87
88
89
Golf Course
Highcombe Bottom
1
Beacon Hill
Eight Acres
Heath Close
Churt Wynde
Linkside North
Linkside East
Linkside West
Sandheath Rd
Clovelly Road
Linkside South
Glen Rd
Glen Cl
Glen Rd
Hill Road
Grove Road
Beacon Hill Road
Tilford Road
Cricket Close
Hindhead Golf Club
CHURT ROAD
Steepways
Golf Links Av
Fairways
Corry Rd
Beacon Hill County Primary School
Parsons Lane
Beacon Hill Court
Wood Road
Downview Cl
Trimmers Wd
A287
2
The Beacon
Hillgarth
Ridge Moor Cl
Tilford Road
3
TILFORD ROAD
Tower Road
Mead Road
36
GU26
Pine Bank
Tower Road
Highfield Crs
Glenville Gdns
Moorlands Cl
Huntingdon Ho Dr
Hindhead
A287
4
PH
Heather Way
Tyndalls
Greensand Way
A3 PORTSMOUTH RD
Whitmore Vale Road
Vale Wood Lane
Grayshott Clinic
The Spinney
Waggoners Wy
Saddlers Scarp
Waggoners
Wheelwrights La
Horseshoe Bend
Bridle Cl
Halters End
Beech La
School Rd
Beech Hanger End
Grayshott CE Primary School
Chestnut Cl
Vicarage Gdns
Church La
Avenue Rd
Glen Rd
Glen Rd
Hurstmere Cl
Tarn Rd
HEADLEY ROAD
B3002
Grayshott
Hill Road
Jubilee La
Crossways Road
Oakhurst
The Avenue
Council Building
Surgery
Forestdale
Boundary Rd
St Edmunds School
5
HINDHEAD ROAD A287
Waggoners Wells Road
Ladygate Drive
Hunters Moon
Stoney Bottom
Kingswood Firs
Kingswood Firs
Cypress Wy
Tudor Cl
Hazel Gv
35
6
Greensand Way
Nutcombe
Mount Alvernia
Kingswood Lane
High Pitfold
Hazel Grove
Sandy Lane
118
High Pitfold
A3
Lane
Amesbury School
Nutcombe Lane
7
High Pitfold Farm
Glenlea
Lion Lane
Farnham Lane
Glenlea Hollow
134
Bramshott Chase
Hammer Lane
HINDHEAD ROAD A287
Lion Lane
8
Bramshott Common
Knockhundred Lane
The Edge Sports Centre
Woolmer Hill Athletics Track
Braeside Cl
Tree Av
Cherry Tree Avenue
The Paddock
Stoatley
PORTSMOUTH ROAD
Woolmer Hill Road
Sandy Lane
117
Tennis Centre
Woolmer Hill Technology College
Woolmer Hill
Critchmere
Critchmere Hill
Holy Cross Hospital
Chiltcroft Rd
Shottermill Infant School
The Avenue
The Woodlands Lane
Underwood Rd
Farnham

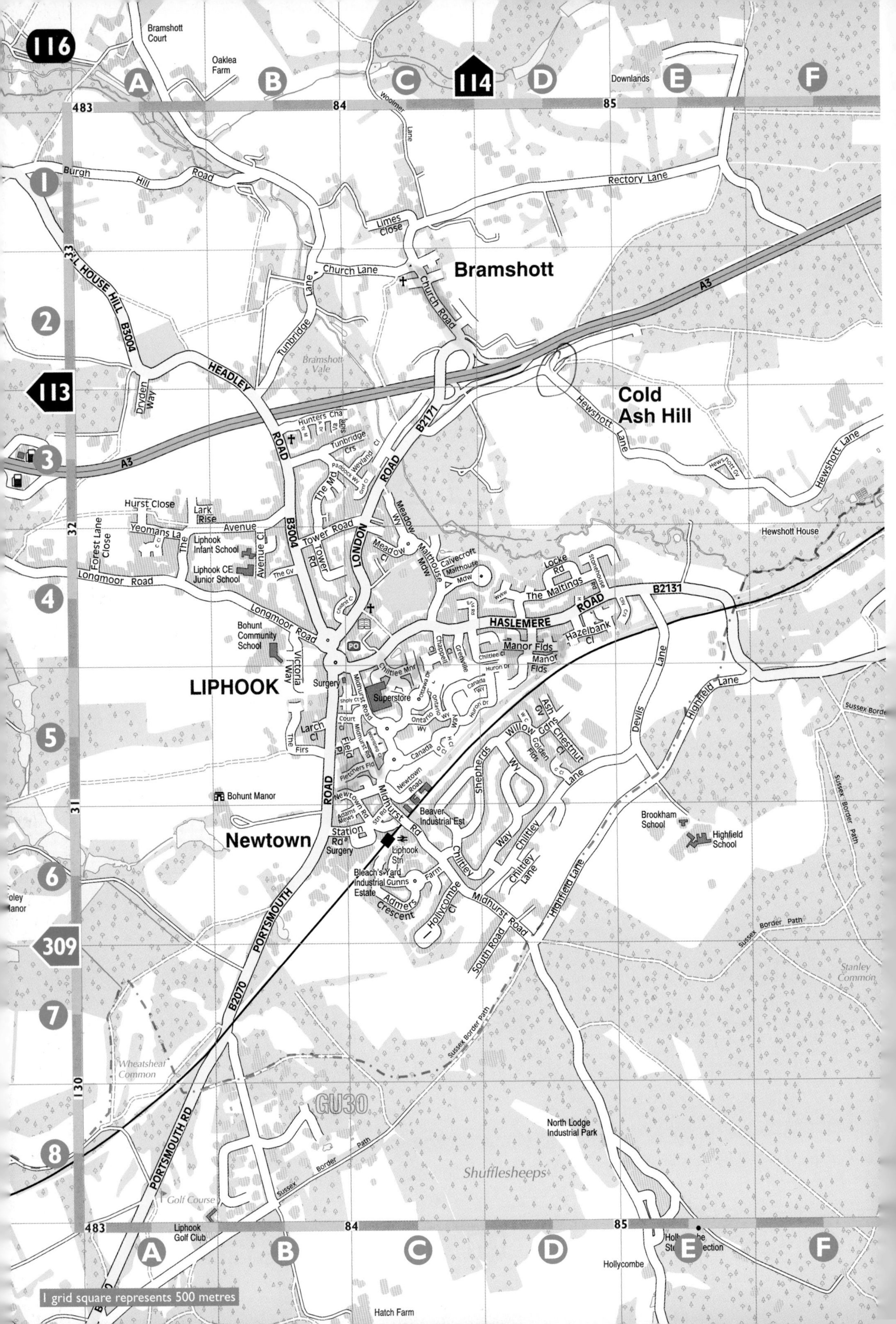

116
114
113
309
A
B
C
D
E
F
1
2
3
4
5
6
7
8
483
84
85
33
32
31
130
Bramshott Court
Oaklea Farm
Downlands
Woolmer Lane
Burgh Hill Road
Rectory Lane
Limes Close
Church Lane
Church Road
Bramshott
A3
Tunbridge Lane
Bramshott Vale
Headley Road
B3004
Dryden Way
Cold Ash Hill
Hewshott Lane
Hunters Cha
Tunbridge Crs
Weyland Cl
The Md
B2171
London Road
Hurst Close
Lark Rise
Avenue
Yeomans La
The Avenue
Avenue Cl
Forest Lane Close
Liphook Infant School
Liphook CE Junior School
Longmoor Road
Tower Road
Tower Rd
Meadow Wy
Meadow Cl
Malthouse Mdw
Calvecroft
Locke Rd
The Maltings
Stonehouse Rd
B2131
Hewshott House
Haslemere Road
Hazelbank Cl
Manor Flds
Bohunt Community School
Victoria Way
LIPHOOK
Surgery
Superstore
Chiltlee Mnr
Midhurst Road
Canada Wy
Ontario Wy
Huron Dr
Chappell Cl
Grenville Cl
Devils Lane
Highfield Lane
Sussex Border Path
Larch Cl
The Firs
Field Pl
Fletchers Fld
Ash Gv
Willow Gdns
Golden Flds
Chestnut Cl
Lane
Shepherds Way
Chiltley Way
Chiltley Lane
Newtown Road
Newtown Rd
Adams Mews
Beaver Industrial Est
Midhurst Rd
Bohunt Manor
Newtown
Station Rd
Surgery
Liphook Stn
Bleach's Yard Industrial Estate
Gunns Farm
Admers Crescent
Hollycombe Cl
Midhurst Road
South Road
Brookham School
Highfield School
Stanley Common
Foley Manor
Portsmouth Road
B2070
Wheatsheaf Common
GU30
North Lodge Industrial Park
Shufflesheeps
Portsmouth Rd
Golf Course
Liphook Golf Club
Hollycombe
Hatch Farm
1 grid square represents 500 metres

Bramshott Common
115
The Edge Leisure Centre
Woolmer Hill Athletics Track
PORTSMOUTH ROAD
Knockhundred Lane
Woolmer Hill Road
Sandy Lane
Tennis Centre
Woolmer Hill Technology College
Woolmer Hill
Critchmere
Holy Cross Hospital
Shottermill Infant School
Shottermill
HINDHEAD RD
B2131
LIPHOOK RD
Hatchetts Drive
Lower Hanger
Woolmer Hill Rd
Fir Tree Avenue
Sunvale Av
Oak Tree Lane
Border Rd
Cemetery
Pitfold Av
Critchmere Lane
Hammer Lane
Hampshire County
West Sussex County
Hammer Bottom
Moor Rd
Copse Road
Heath Rd
Hammer
LINCHMERE ROAD
The Millstream
The Herons Swimming & Fitness
Kings Road Industrial Est
Superstore
Vicarage Lane Clinic
Camelsdale County First School
CAMELSDALE RD
New Rd
School Rd
Springfarm Rd
Hillside Rd
Marley Lane
Marley Combe Road
The Old Quarry
Penwith Drive
Gillham's Lane
LIPHOOK ROAD
Hammer Hill
Linchmere Road
Linchmere Common
Marley Common
Sussex Border Path
Danley Lane
Linchmere
Marley House
Cognor Wood
Marley Heights
Stanley Farm
Greenhill Wood
Parkgate Rough
Oakreeds
118

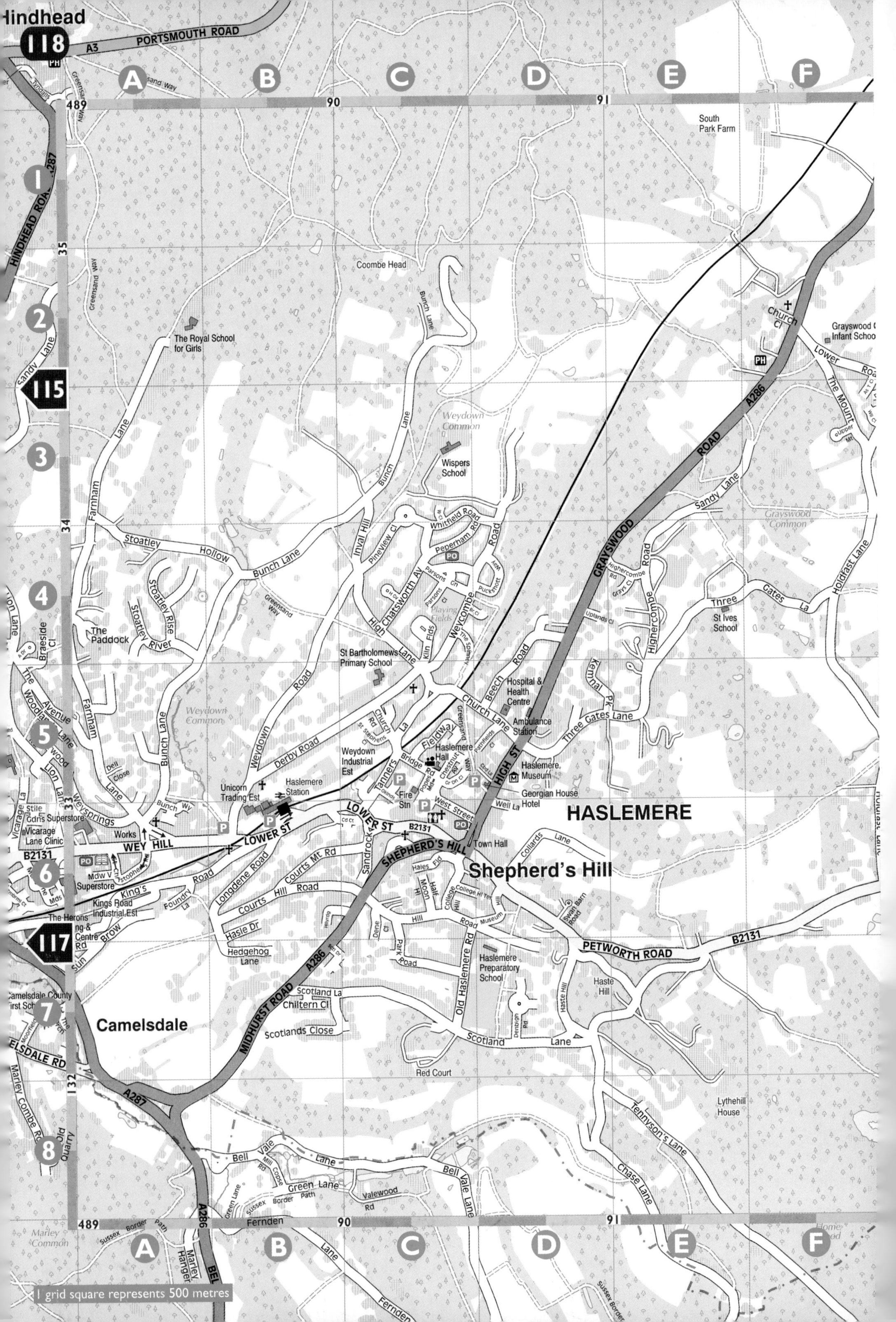

Hindhead
118
PORTSMOUTH ROAD
A3
A
B
C
D
E
F
489
90
91
South Park Farm
1
HINDHEAD ROAD
A287
35
2
Coombe Head
Bunch Lane
The Royal School for Girls
Greensand Way
115
Sandy Lane
Church Cl
Grayswood C of E Infant School
Lower Road
The Mount
Weydown Common
3
Farnham Lane
Wispers School
GRAYSWOOD ROAD
A286
Sandy Lane
Grayswood Common
34
Stoatley Hollow
Bunch Lane
Inval Hill
Pineview Cl
Whitfield Road
Peperham Rd
Chatsworth Av
Weycombe Road
Highercombe Road
Holdfast Lane
4
Stoatley Rise
Parsons Gn
Playing Fields
Three Gates La
Uplands Cl
St Ives School
The Paddock
Stoatley River
High Lane
Kiln Flds
The Spinney
Beech Road
Kemnal Pk
Braeside Cl
St Bartholomews Primary School
Hospital & Health Centre
The Avenue
Woodland Lane
Weydown Common
Weydown Road
Church Lane
Ambulance Station
Three Gates Lane
5
Farnham Lane
Derby Road
Church Rd
Fieldway
Haslemere Hall
Weydown Industrial Est
Haslemere Museum
Lion Lane
Dell Close
Bunch Lane
Unicorn Trading Est
Haslemere Station
Tanners La
Bridge Rd
Chestnut Av
Georgian House Hotel
HIGH ST
Vicarage La
33
Weysprings
Bunch Wy
Fire Stn
West Street
Well La
HASLEMERE
Superstore
Vicarage Lane Clinic
Works
WEY HILL
LOWER ST
B2131
Town Hall
Collards Lane
6
SHEPHERD'S HILL
Sandrock
Courts Mt Rd
Shepherd's Hill
Superstore
King's Road
Longdene Road
Courts Hill Road
Hales Fld
Half Moon Hl
College Hill
The Herons
Kings Road Industrial Est
Foundry La
Hill Road
Swan Barn Road
Hasle Dr
Dene Cl
Museum
117
Sun Brow
Hedgehog Lane
Park Road
Old Haslemere Rd
PETWORTH ROAD
B2131
Haslemere Preparatory School
Haste Hill
Camelsdale County First Sch
7
MIDHURST ROAD
A286
Scotland La
Chiltern Cl
Camelsdale
Scotlands Close
Scotland Lane
Denbigh Rd
Haste Hill
ELSDALE RD
Red Court
132
A287
Lythehill House
Marley Combe Rd
Old Quarry
8
Tennyson's Lane
Bell Vale Lane
Mill Copse Rd
Green Lane
Sussex Border Path
Valewood Rd
Bell Vale Lane
Chase Lane
Green Lane
489
Fernden
90
91
Marley Common
Sussex Border Path
Marley Hanger
A286
Fernden Lane
Sussex Border
Home Wood
1 grid square represents 500 metres

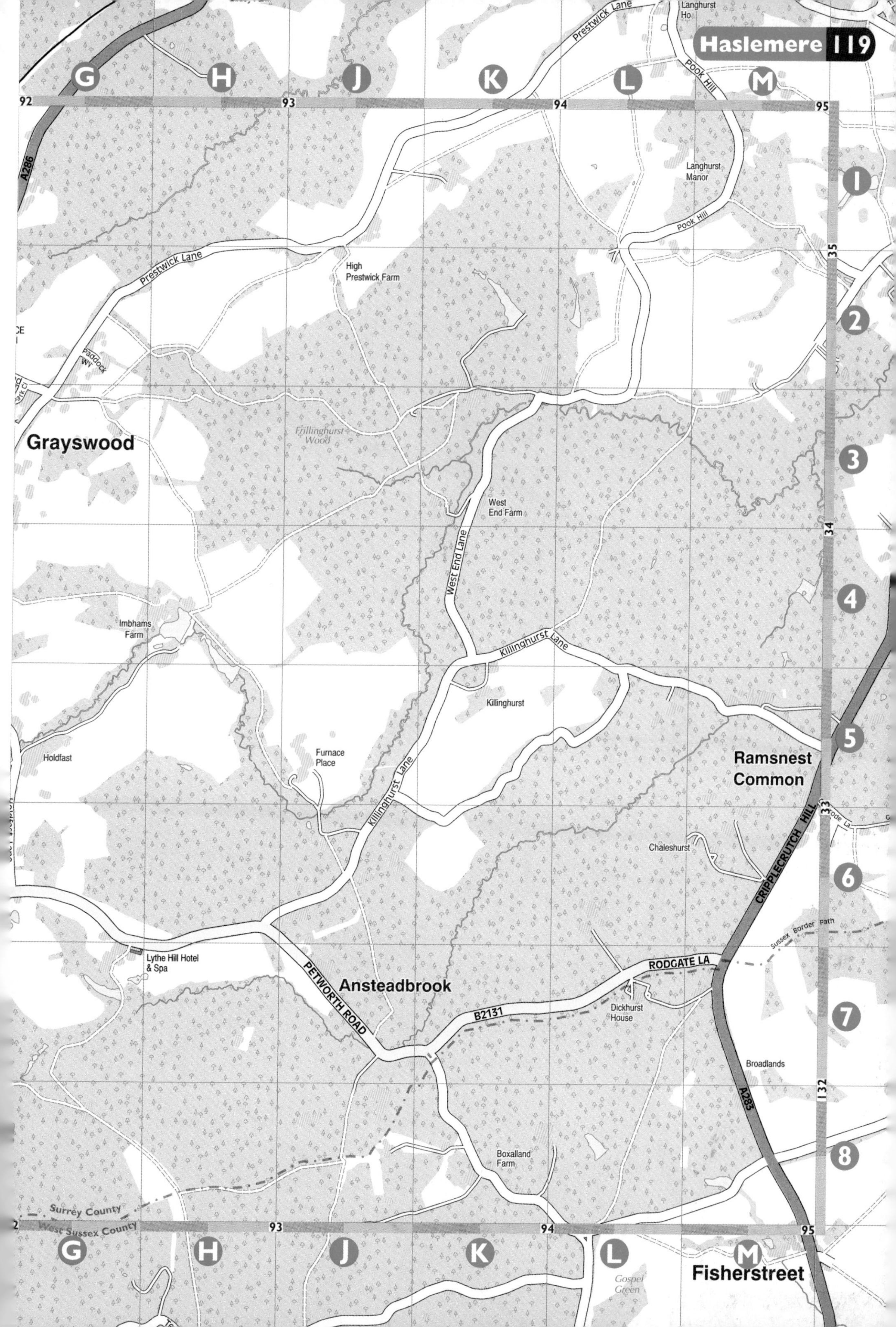

G H J K L M

92 93 94 95

1

2

3

34

4

35

5

6

33

7

132

8

Prestwick Lane

Langhurst
Ho

Pook Hill

Langhurst
Manor

Pook La

Prestwick Lane

High
Prestwick Farm

Grayswood

Paddock
Wy

Frillinghurst
Wood

West
End Farm

West End Lane

Killinghurst Lane

Killinghurst

Imbhams
Farm

Holdfast

Furnace
Place

Killinghurst Lane

**Ramsnest
Common**

Chaleshurst

CRIPPLECRUTCH HILL

Sussex Border Path

Lythe Hill Hotel
& Spa

RODGATE LA

PETWORTH ROAD

Ansteadbrook

B2131

Dickhurst
House

Broadlands

A283

Boxalland
Farm

Surrey County

West Sussex County

G H J K L M

93 94 95

Gospel
Green

Fisherstreet

A286

Marsh
Marsh Farm
Brickyards Ind Estate
Ashford Chace
307
Church Common
Island
Steep
Steep School
Steep Farm
Mill Lane
Church Road
Hangers Way
Stonerwood Park
Bedales School
Ridge Common Lane
Harrow Lane
Waterworks Road
Farnham Road
A3
Dunhurst (Bedales Junior School)
Collyers
Lord's Farm
Sheet City Primary School
Mill Lane
School Lane
Sheet
Village St
Long Road
A272
Bell Hill
Reservoir Lane
Whitehouse Gdns
Coxes Meadow
Ridge Common
Sandsbury Lane
Aldersnapp Farm
Monks Orchard
Monks Wood
The Purrocks
Tilmore Road
Stafford Rd
Selborne Cl
Kingsfernsden Lane
Town Lane
Inmans Lane
Portland's
Woodbury Av
Bell Hl Rdg
Bell Hill
Shear Hill
Cemetery
Buckmore Avenue
Highfield Rd
Kimbers
Hogarth Close
B2070
Ramshill
Churchers College
Churchfield Road
Merryfield Rd
Hazelbank Close
Pulens Lane
Love Lane
315
Stroud Farm
Beckham Lane
Stoneham Cl
Stoneham Pk
Winchester Road
Winchester Road
A272
Lynton Road
Stanton Road
Oaklands Road
Station Road
Madeline Road
North Rd
Balmoral Wy
Woolner Avenue
Sandringham Rd
Petersfield Town FC
The Herne Junior School
Long Down
Upper Wardown
Dukes Cl
Kings Road
Princes Road
Queens Road
Rushes Road
Frenchmans Road
Meon Cl
Penns Rd
Osborne Road
Station Rd
College St
Grenehurst Way
Tor Wy
Love Lane
Readon Cl
The Herne Farm Leisure Centre
Lwr Wardown
Noreuil Rd
Petersfield Station
Chapel St
Windsor Road
Winton Rd
Lyndum Cl
George Av
Barham Rd
Upr Heyshott
Lwr Heyshott
Moggs Mead
Hanger Way
PETERSFIELD
Lavant St
Charles St
Park Rd
Folly Lane
Bepton Down
Marden Way
Cundles
Harting Down
Holt Down
Great Hanger
Lower Mead
Gloucester Close
Vauxhall Way
Drum Mead
Council Building
Amey Ind Est
Swan St
Surg
The Square
High St
The Clyd
Petersfield Swimming Pool
Wetherdown
Head Down
Heath Road
York Cl
Buckingham Road
Bedford Road
A3
The Spain
Sheep St
St Peter's Rd
Dragon Street
Herne Rd
Marden Wy
Petersfield Business Park
Borough Hill
Petersfield Community Hospital
Petersfield Inf Sch
Hylton Rd
The Maltings
The Avenue
Weston Road
Borough Road
Churchers College Junior Department
Superstore
Fore Br
Sussex Gdns
Heath Road West
Heath Pond
Torberry Drive
Heath Road East
B2199
The Mead
Grange Road
Borough Grove
The Petersfield School
The Causeway
Cranford Road
B2146
Sussex Road
Paddock Way
Larcombe Road
Itchen Cl
Aron Cl
Stour Cl
Orwell Rd
Kennet Rd
Test Cl
Avon Cl
Arun Cl
The Causeway
Causeway
Russell Way
Petersfield Golf Club (old course)
Golf Course
Wylds Lane
The Causeway
Stanbridge Farm
A B C D E F
1 2 3 4 5 6 7 8
473 74 75
26 25 24 23 22
1 grid square represents 500 metres

308
316
Bowyer's Common
Stodham Park
Clayton Court
Tankerdale Lane
Petersfield Golf Club
Golf Course
Stodham Lane
Sussex Border Path
Durford Wood
Upper Adhurst Farm
LONDON ROAD
B2070
Adhurst St Mary
A272
Hampshire County
West Sussex County
Westmark Farm
River Rother
Rother Close
Copse Close
Pulens Cr
Geddes Way
Tilmore Brook
Petersfield RFC
Durleighmarsh Farm
Wenham Manor Farm
Durleighmarsh
Barnfield Road
Heathfield Road
Taro Leisure Centre
Council Building
Penns Place
Durford Abbey Farm
Eastlake Cl
Clare Gdns
Durford Road
Fern Close
Sandy Close
Woodlark Gdns
Harrier Way
Bramble Road
Rival Moor Road
Ryefield Close
Gorse Road
Teazle Cl
Moor Road
Ryefield
Rival Lodge
West Heath Common
Down Park Farm
GU31

122
288
301
124
24
A
B
C
D
E
F
1
2
3
4
5
6
7
8
445
46
47
31
30
29
128
Harestock
Weeke
Fulflood
Sleepers' Hill
Stanmore
Pitt
Oliver's Battery
St Cross
S022
Henry Beaufort School
Harestock Primary School
Barton Farm
Winchester Lawn Tennis Club
Peter Symonds College
Lankhills School
Nethercliffe School
Andover Road Retail Park
The Westgate School
Western Primary Sch
Winchester Station
Rec Office
Theatre Royal
Police HQ
HM Prison
University College Winchester
Garden Centre
Royal Hampshire County Hospital
A&E
Cemetery
Sarum Road Hospital
Royal Winchester Golf Club
Teg Down
Golf Course
Kings School
St Peters School
Stanmore Primary School
St Faiths Primary School
Hospital of St Cross
South Winchester Golf Club
Surgery
Superstore
Olivers Battery School
The Great Hall
Law Courts
Reg Mus
Hotel du Vin
Cinema
Cncl Bldgs
Mus
Deane Down Drove
Andover Road
B3420
B3049
B3041
B3040
B3335
A3090
Stockbridge Rd
Bereweeke Road
Chilbolton Avenue
Romsey Road
Sarum Road
St James' Lane
Milnthorpe Lane
Sleepers' Hill
Cromwell Road
Stanmore Lane
Badger Farm Road
Christchurch Road
Edgar Road
St Cross Road
Kingsgate
Dean Lane
Teg Down Meads
Kilham Lane
Stoney Lane
Westman Road
Taplings Road
Rowlings Road
Vernham Road
Lynford Av
Cheriton Road
Fordington Road
Milverton Road
Greenhill Road
Byron Avenue
Airlie Road
Ranelagh Road
Wavell Way
Ridgeway
Whiteshute Lane
Grange Road
Clarendon Way
1 grid square represents 500 metres

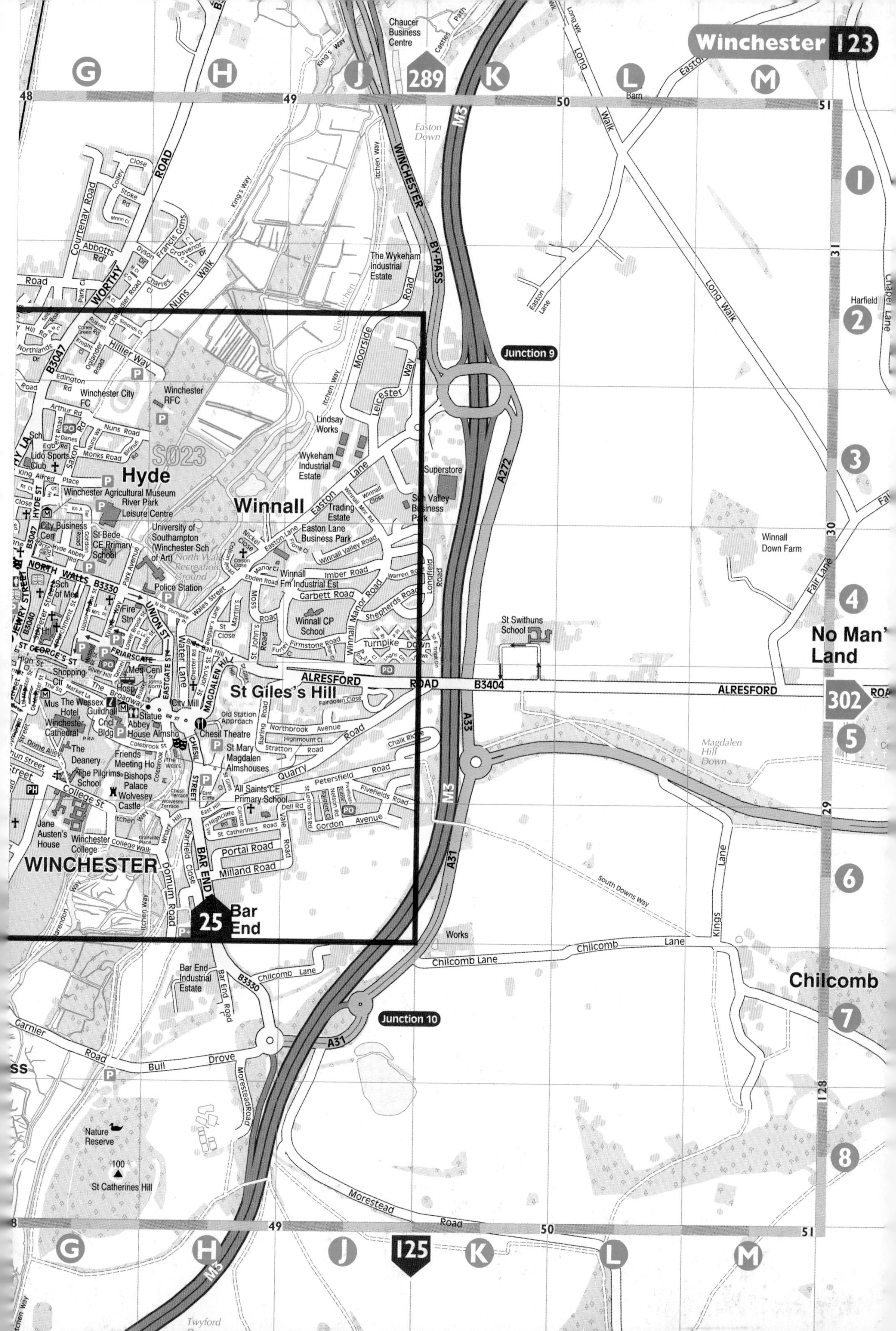
G
H
J
K
L
M
289
Chaucer
Business
Centre
King's Way
Long Walk
Easton Down
WINCHESTER BY-PASS
M3
Itchen Way
ROAD
Courtenay Road
Abbotts Rd
WORTHY
Francis Gdns
Grosvenor Dr
Nuns Walk
The Wykeham Industrial Estate
Easton Lane
Harfield
Chapel Lane
Junction 9
Hillier Way
Moorside
Leicester Way
Lindsay Works
B3047
Edington Rd
Winchester City FC
Winchester RFC
Nuns Road
Monks Road
SO23
Hyde
Lido Sports Club
Wykeham Industrial Estate
Superstore
A272
Winchester Agricultural Museum
River Park Leisure Centre
Winnall
Trading Estate
Son Valley Business Park
Winnall Down Farm
Fair Lane
City Business Cen
St Bede CE Primary School
University of Southampton (Winchester Sch of Art)
North Walls Recreation Ground
Easton Lane Business Park
Winnall Valley Road
NORTH WALLS B3330
Police Station
Winnall Fm Industrial Est
Imber Road
Garbett Road
Longfield Road
St Swithuns School
No Man's Land
Winnall CP School
Winnall Manor Road
Shepherds Road
Wales Street
St John's Road
Moss Road
Firmstone Road
Turnpike Down
UNION ST
EASTGATE ST
Water Lane
MAGDALEN HILL
ST GEORGE'S ST
FRIARSGATE
Shopping Ctr
ALRESFORD ROAD B3404
ALRESFORD ROAD
302
St Giles's Hill
City Mill
The Wessex Hotel
Guildhall
Statue
Abbey House
Almshouses
Old Station Approach
Chesil Theatre
Northbrook Avenue
Quarry Road
Chalk Ridge
Winchester Cathedral
The Deanery
Friends Meeting Ho
St Mary Magdalen Almshouses
Magdalen Hill Down
A33
The Pilgrims School
Bishops Palace
Wolvesey Castle
College St
CHESIL STREET
All Saints CE Primary School
Petersfield Road
Fivefields Road
Gordon Avenue
Jane Austen's House
Winchester College
St Catherine's Road
Vale Road
Portal Road
Milland Road
WINCHESTER
Domum Road
BAR END
25 Bar End
South Downs Way
Kings Lane
A31
Works
Chilcomb Lane
Chilcomb
Bar End Industrial Estate
B3330
Junction 10
Garnier Road
Bull Drove
Morestead Road
Nature Reserve
100
St Catherines Hill
Morestead Road
48
49
50
51
31
30
29
128
1
2
3
4
5
6
7
8
125
Twyford

124
122
301
133
134
Oliver's Battery
Compton End
Compton Down
Compton
Shawford
South Down
Otterbourne
Junction 11
BADGER FARM ROAD
A3090
HOCKLEY LINK
B3335
ST CROSS ROAD
M3
Hospital of St Cross
Olivers Battery Primary School
Compton CE Primary School
Shepherds Down Special School
Twyford St Mary's CE Primary School
Shawford Station
Shawford House
Four Dell Farm
Freemantles Copse
Richmond Park
River Itchen
Itchen Way
Monarch's Way
Silkstead Lane
Shepherds Lane
Hurdle Way
Compton Street
Otterbourne Road
Poles Lane
Grove Road
Southdown Road
Fairfield Road
Cross Way
Bridge Lane
Shawford Road
Cliff Way
Field Close
Clease Way
Carmans Lane
Place Lane
Attwoods Drove
Martins Fields
Sparrowgrove
Waterworks Road
Oakwood Close
Highways Road
Tilden Rd
Grange Road
Five Bridges Road
Texas Drive
Oliver's Battery Road
Momford Road
Sunnydown Road
1 grid square represents 500 metres

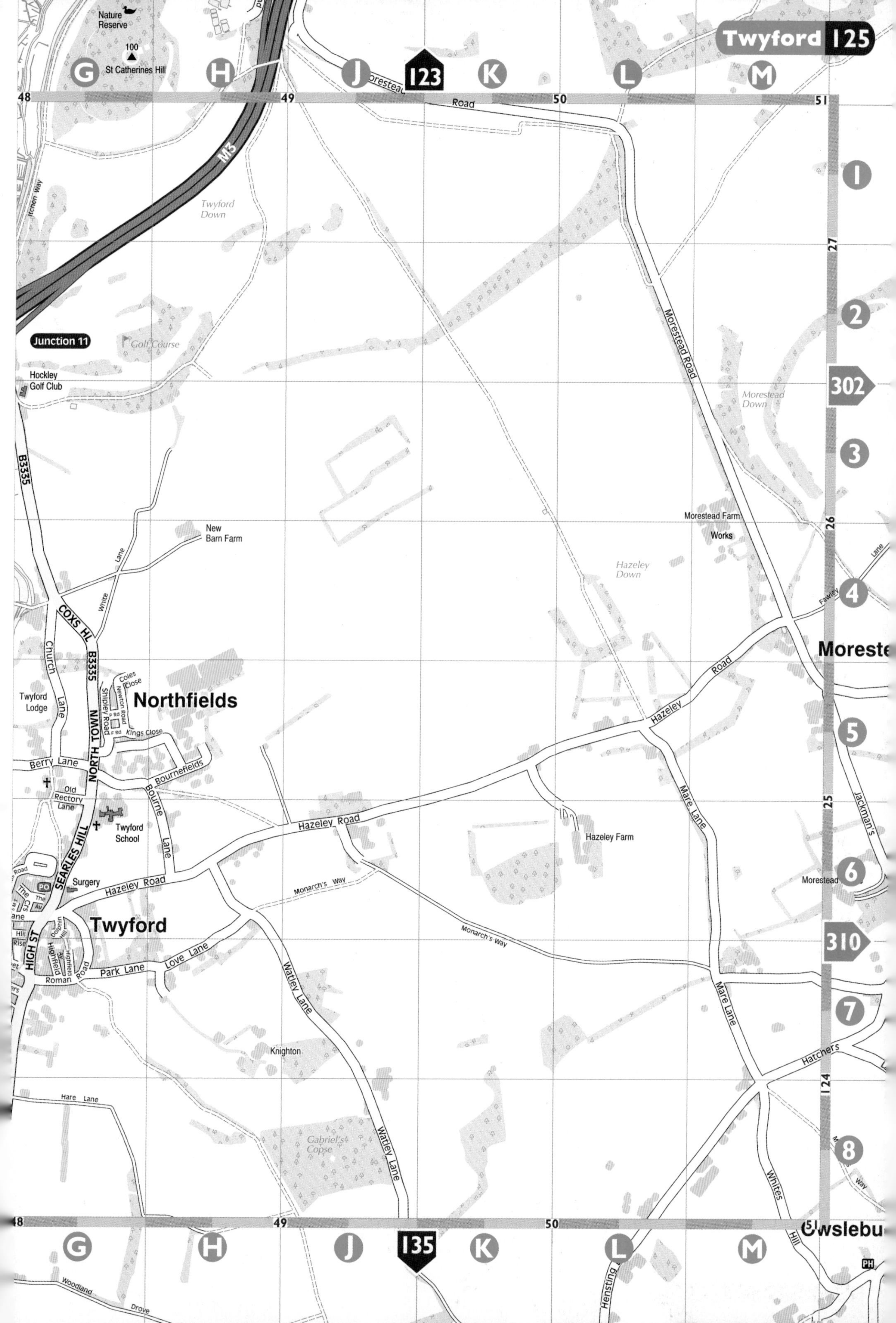

Nature Reserve
100
St Catherines Hill
G
H
J
123
K
L
M
Morestead Road
M3
Itchen Way
Twyford Down
Junction 11
Golf Course
Hockley Golf Club
Morestead Road
Morestead Down
302
Morestead Farm
Works
New Barn Farm
White Lane
B3335
COXS HL
Hazeley Down
Fawley Lane
Moreste
Church Lane
Twyford Lodge
Coles Close
Shipley Road
Newton Road
Northfields
Kings Close
Berry Lane
Bournefields
NORTH TOWN
Hazeley Road
Old Rectory Lane
Bourne Lane
Twyford School
Hazeley Road
Mare Lane
Jackman's
Hazeley Farm
SEARLES HILL
Surgery
Hazeley Road
Monarch's Way
Morestead
Twyford
Monarch's Way
310
HIGH ST
Highfield
Dolphin Hill
Roman Road
Park Lane
Love Lane
Watley Lane
Mare Lane
Knighton
Hatchers
Hare Lane
Gabriel's Copse
Watley Lane
Whites Hill
1
2
3
4
5
6
7
8
27
26
25
124
48
49
50
51
135
Owslebu
Hensting
Woodland Drove
PH

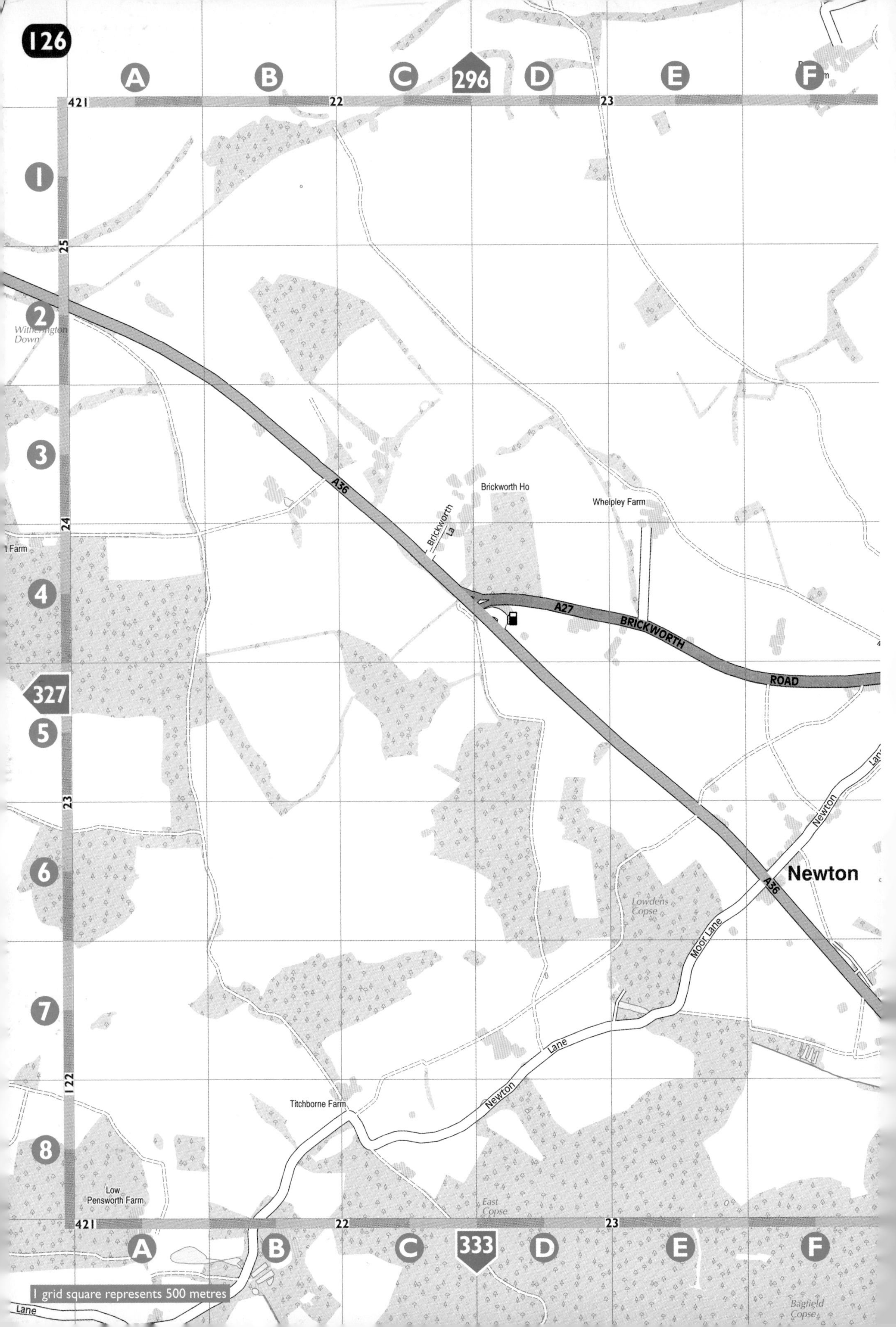
A
B
C
296
D
E
F
421
22
23
1
25
2
Witherington Down
3
A36
Brickworth Ho
Whelpley Farm
Brickworth La
24
Farm
4
A27
BRICKWORTH
ROAD
327
5
23
Newton
6
Lowdens Copse
Moor Lane
Newton
Lane
7
Lane
Newton
Titchborne Farm
122
8
Low Pensworth Farm
East Copse
421
22
23
A
B
C
333
D
E
F
1 grid square represents 500 metres
Lane
Bagfield Copse

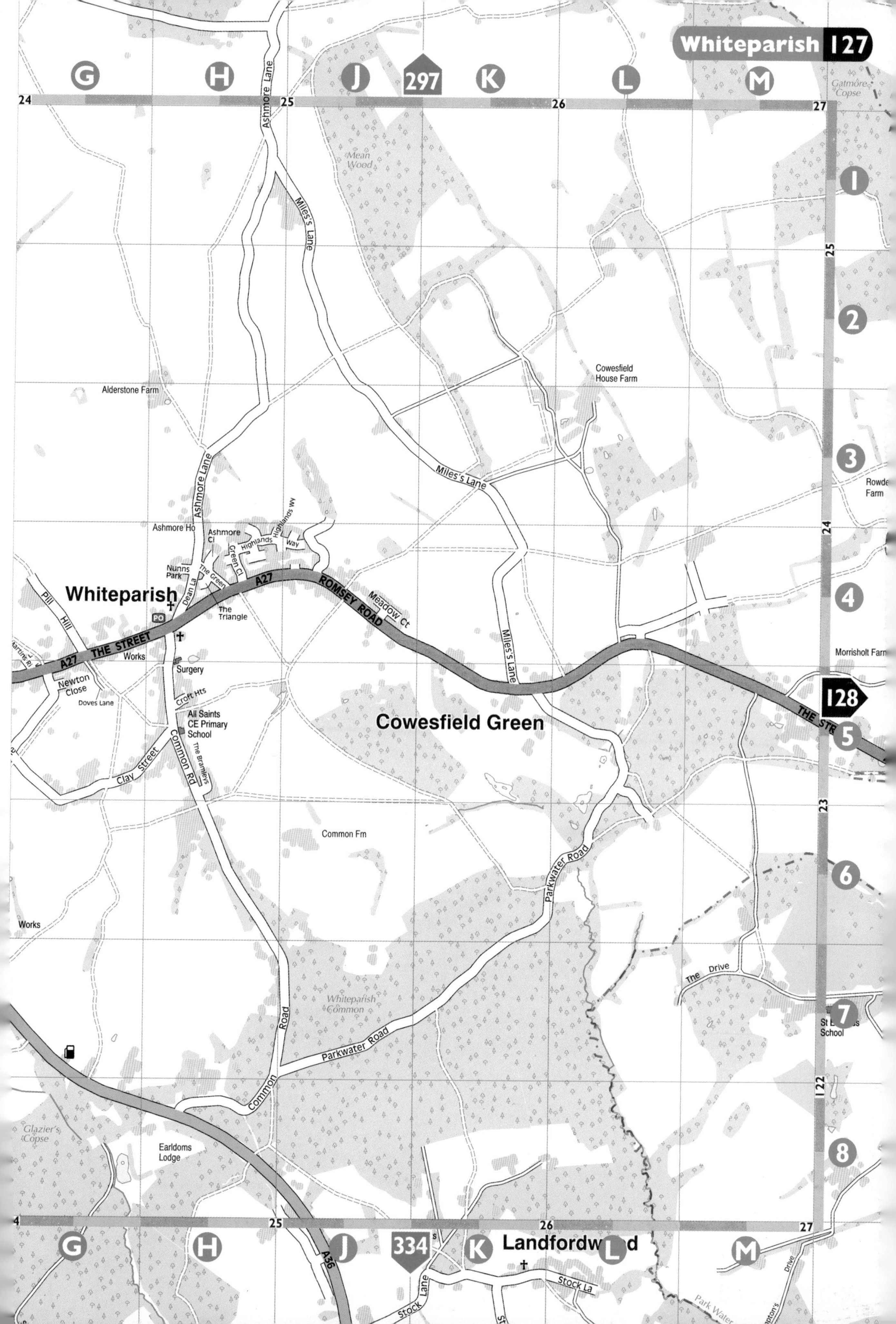

G H Ashmore Lane J 297 K L M

24 25 26 27

1

2

3 Rowde Farm

4

Morrisholt Farm

I28 THE STR

5

23

6

I22

7 St E s School

8

Gatmore Copse

Mean Wood

Cowesfield House Farm

Alderstone Farm

Miles's Lane

Miles's Lane

Miles's Lane

Ashmore Lane

Ashmore Ho
Ashmore Cl
Highlands
Highlands Wy
Way
Green Cl
The Green
Nunns Park
Dean La
Whiteparish
PO
The Triangle
A27
A27 THE STREET
Works
Martins Rd
Pill Hill
Newton Close
Doves Lane
Surgery
Croft Hts
Clay Street
Common Rd
The Bramleys
All Saints CE Primary School

ROMSEY ROAD
Meadow Ct

Cowesfield Green

Common Fm

Whiteparish Common

Parkwater Road

Common Road

Parkwater Road

Works

Glazier's Copse

Earldoms Lodge

The Drive

Drive

ton's

Park Water

G H J A36 334 s K L **Landfordw d** M

4 25 26 27

Glazier's Copse

Stock Lane

St

Stock La

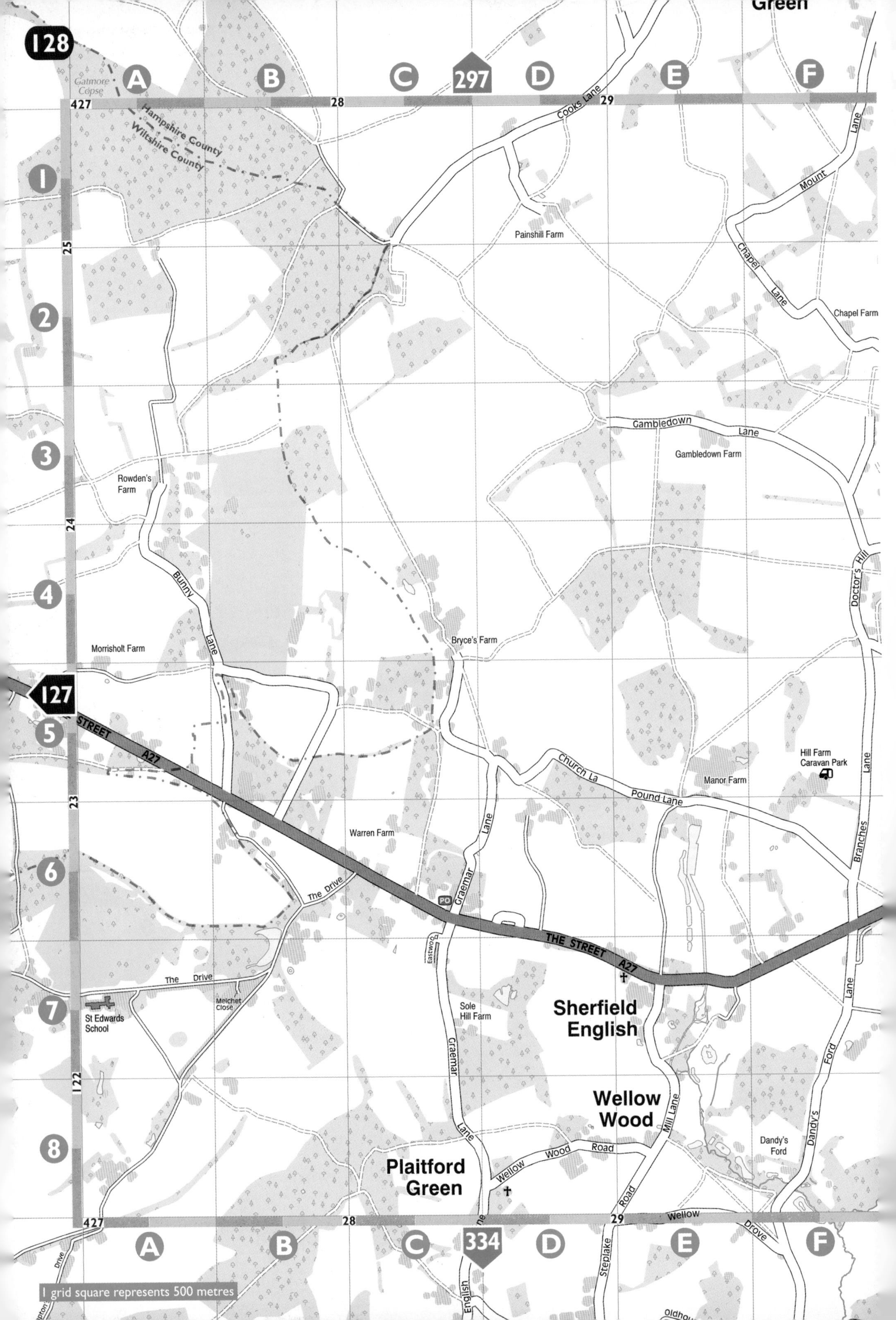
128
297
127
334
Green
Gatmore Copse
Hampshire County
Wiltshire County
Cooks Lane
Painshill Farm
Mount Lane
Chapel Lane
Chapel Farm
Gambledown Lane
Gambledown Farm
Rowden's Farm
Bunny Lane
Morrisholt Farm
Bryce's Farm
Doctor's Hill
Branches Lane
Hill Farm Caravan Park
Manor Farm
Church La
Pound Lane
Warren Farm
Graemar Lane
THE STREET A27
STREET A27
The Drive
Eastwood
St Edwards School
Melchet Close
Sole Hill Farm
Sherfield English
Wellow Wood
Mill Lane
Dandy's Ford
Dandy's Ford Lane
Wellow Wood Road
Plaitford Green
Steplake Road
Wellow Drove
English
Drive
Oldhou
A B C D E F
1 2 3 4 5 6 7 8
427 28 29
25 24 23 122
1 grid square represents 500 metres

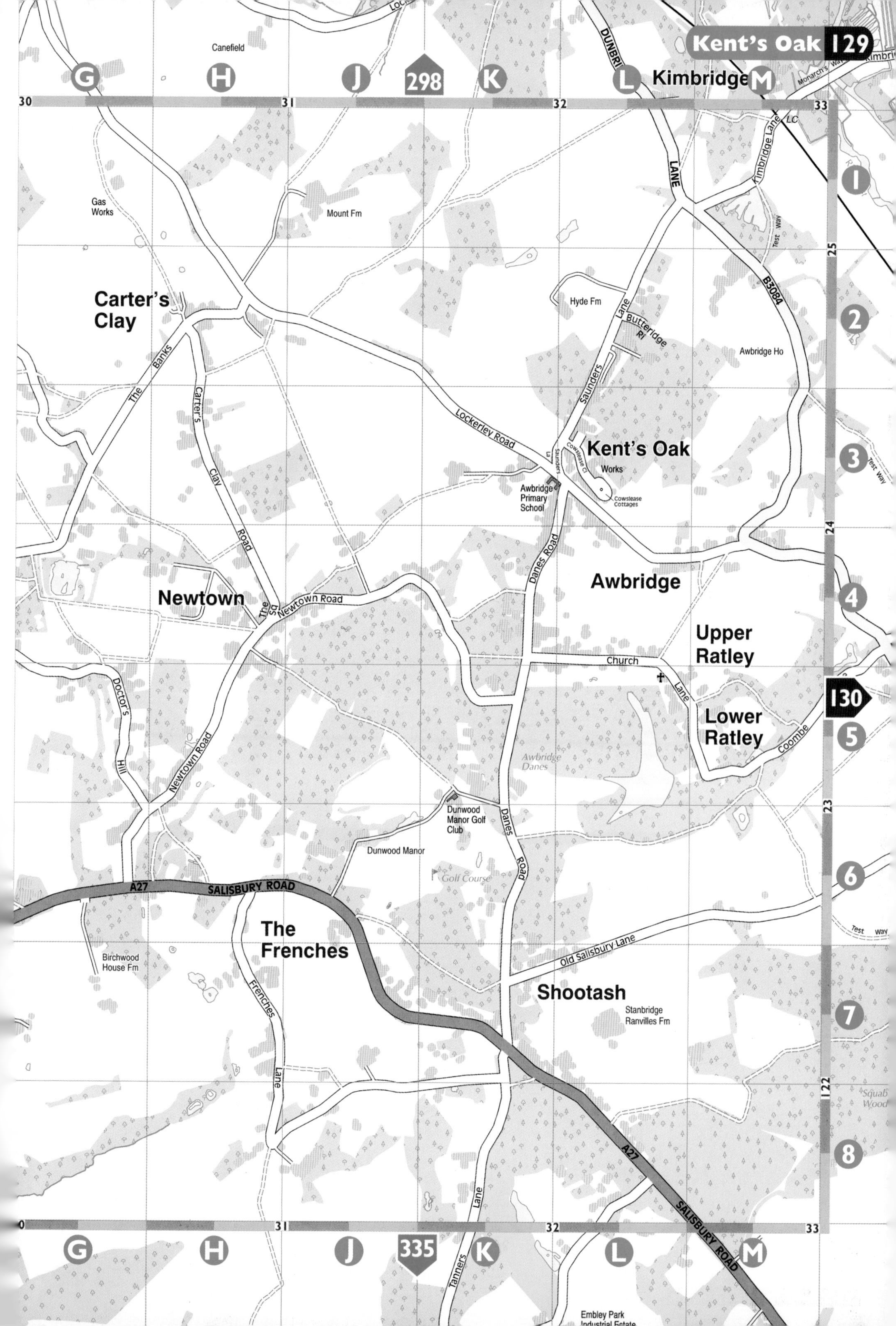

Canefield

Gas
Works

Mount Fm

**Carter's
Clay**

The Banks

Carter's

Lockerley Road

Hyde Fm

Saunders Lane

Butteridge Rd

Awbridge Ho

Clay Road

Kent's Oak

Works

Awbridge
Primary
School

Cowslease Cl

Saunders Ln

Cowslease
Cottages

Awbridge

Danes Road

Newtown

The Sq

Newtown Road

Church

**Upper
Ratley**

Lane

130

Awbridge
Danes

**Lower
Ratley**

Coombe

Doctor's Hill

Newtown Road

Dunwood
Manor Golf
Club

Danes Road

Dunwood Manor

Golf Course

A27 SALISBURY ROAD

**The
Frenches**

Birchwood
House Fm

Frenches Lane

Old Salisbury Lane

Shootash

Stanbridge
Ranvilles Fm

Test way

Squab
Wood

A27

Lane

SALISBURY ROAD

Tanners Lane

Embley Park
Industrial Estate

Kimbridge

DUNBRI

LANE

Kimbridge Lane

Test Way

B3084

LC

130
299
129
136
A
B
C
D
E
F
1
2
3
4
5
6
7
8
433
34
35
25
24
23
122
Timsbury
Romsey
STOCKBRIDGE ROAD
A3057
GREATBRIDGE ROAD
B3084
STANBRIDGE LANE
Cooks Lane
Heron Lane
Yokesford Hill
Jinny Lane
Rudd Lane
Kimbridge Lane
Monarch's Way
Hill View Road
New Road
Mannyngham Way
Chapel La
Test Way
River Test
Linhay Meads
Cottages Waterworks
House Waterworks
Hunts Fm
Old Redland Tile Works
Casbrook Common
Timsbury Manor
Brook Fm
Works
Wynford Farm Industrial Est
Belbins
Stanbridge Earls School
South Drive
Roke Manor Fm
Roke Manor
Squabb Wood
SO51
Greatbridge Ho
Great Bridge
Greatbridge Business Park
Budds Lane
Budds Lane Trading Est
Frobisher Industrial Cen
Romsey Industrial Est
Hampshire Brewery
Romsey Industrial Estate
Fishlake Meadows
Priestlands
DUTTONS RD
MALMESBURY RD
Station Rd
Romsey Station
The Romsey School
CHERVILLE ST
Hollman Dr
Princes Rd
Duttons Rd
Romsey Abbey CE (A) Prim Sch
The White Horse Hotel
Town Hall
Clinic
Bus Station
THE HUNDRED
ALMA RD
Plaza Theatre
Romsey Infant Sch
Millstream Rise
Surg
1 grid square represents 500 metres

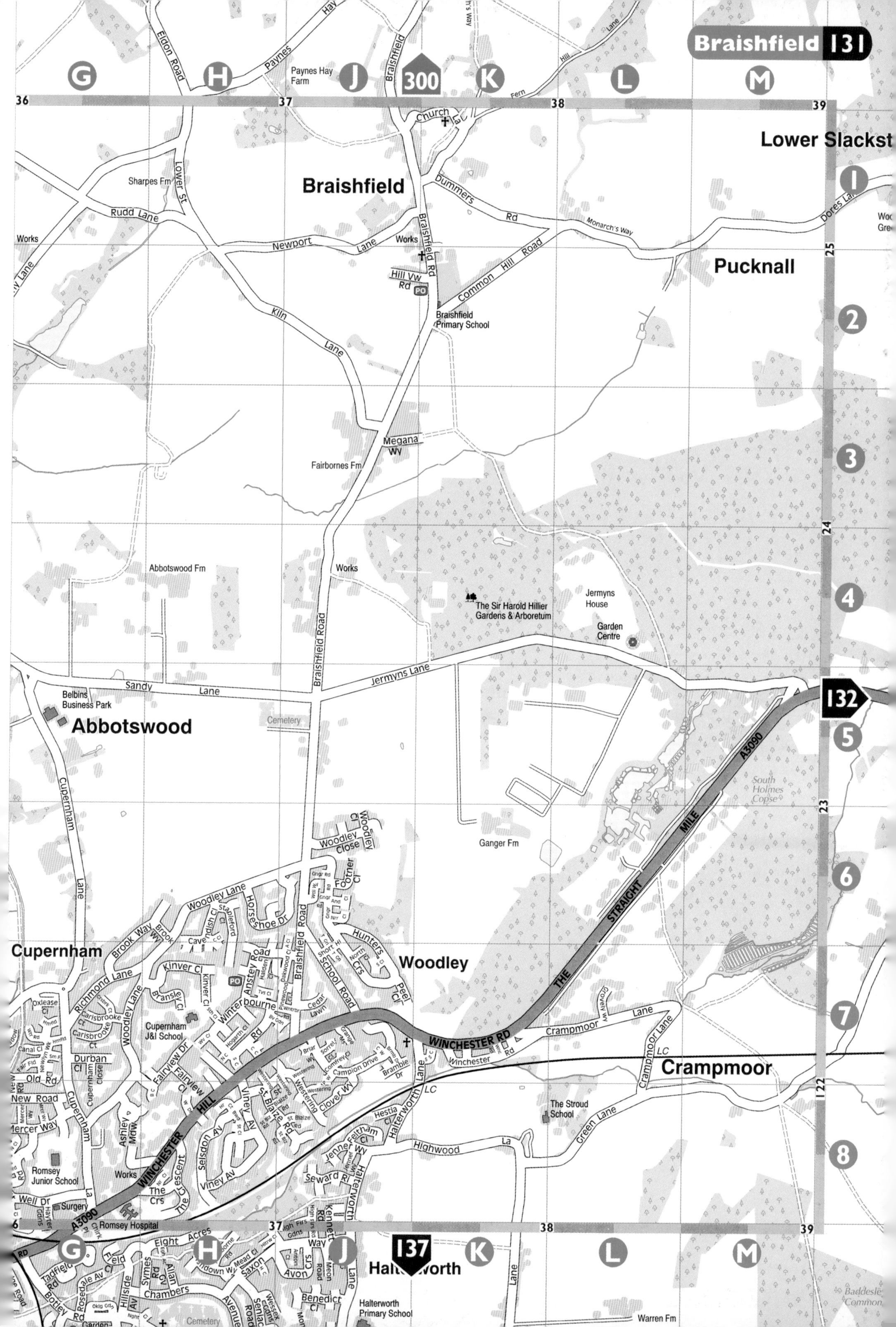
G
H
J
300
K
L
M
Paynes Hay Farm
Braishfield
Lower Slackst
Sharpes Fm
Works
Rudd Lane
Newport Lane
Dummers Rd
Monarch's Way
Common Hill Road
Braishfield Rd
Hill Vw Rd
Braishfield Primary School
Pucknall
Kiln Lane
Megana Wy
Fairbornes Fm
Abbotswood Fm
Works
The Sir Harold Hillier Gardens & Arboretum
Jermyns House
Garden Centre
Sandy Lane
Jermyns Lane
Braishfield Road
Belbins Business Park
Abbotswood
Cemetery
132
South Holmes Copse
Cupernham Lane
Ganger Fm
THE STRAIGHT MILE
A3090
Woodley Close
Woodley Lane
Cupernham
Woodley
Brook Way
Richmond Lane
Kinver Cl
Cupernham J&I School
Winterbourne Rd
School Road
Hunters Crs
Peel Cl
WINCHESTER RD
Crampmoor Lane
Crampmoor
Durban Cl
Old Rd
New Road
Mercer Way
Fairview Dr
WINCHESTER HILL
Campion Drive
Bramble Dr
Halterworth Lane
The Stroud School
Green Lane
Highwood La
Romsey Junior School
Works
The Crs
The Crescent
Viney Av
Selsdon Av
Seward Ri
Well Dr
Surgery
Romsey Hospital
Eight Acres
Avon Crs
Halterworth
137
Halterworth Primary School
Chambers
Cemetery
Warren Fm
Baddesley Common
36
37
38
39
25
24
23
22
1
2
3
4
5
6
7
8

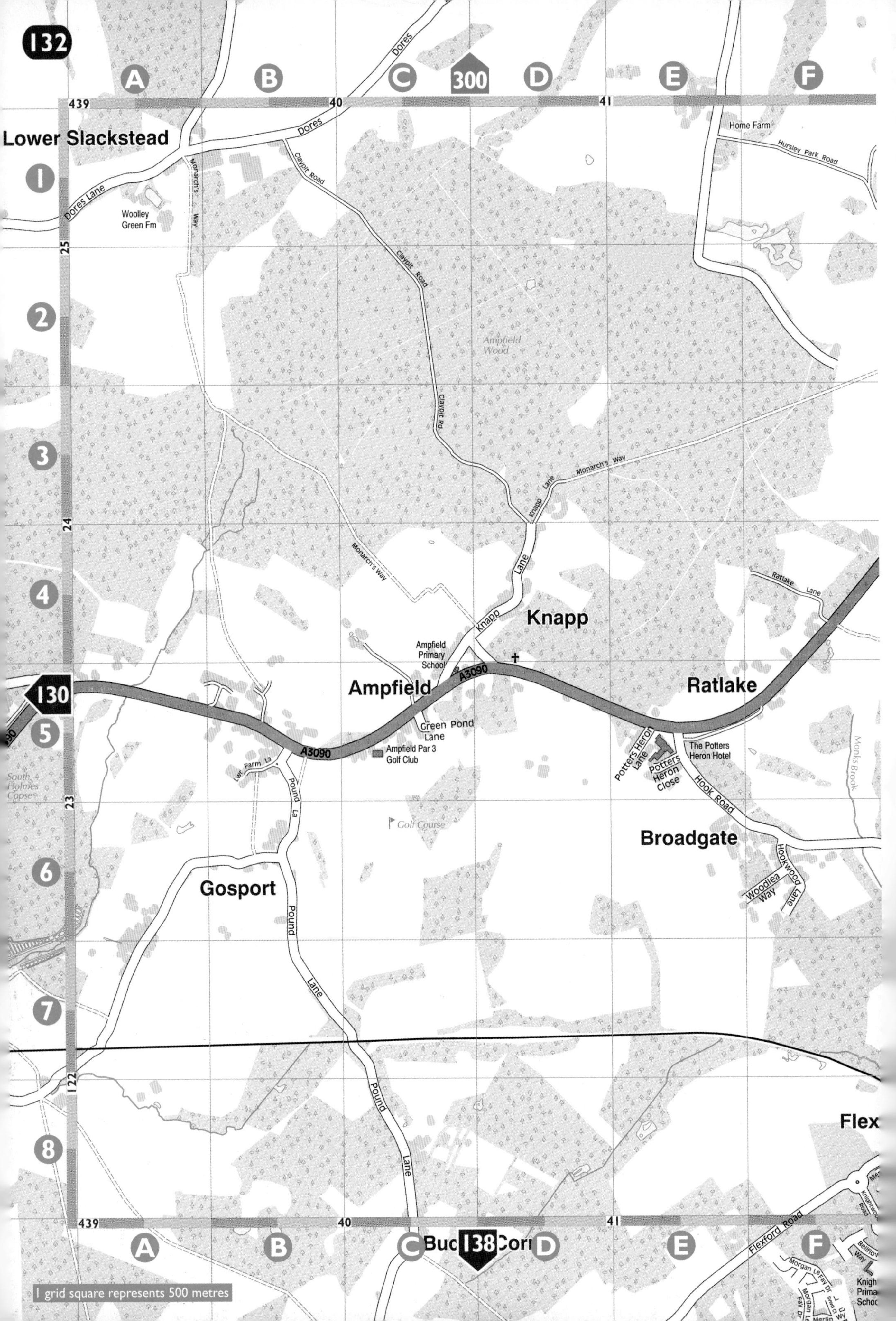

A
B
C
300
D
E
F
439
40
41
Lower Slackstead
Dores
Dores Lane
Monarch's Way
Claypit Road
Woolley Green Fm
Home Farm
Hursley Park Road
1
25
2
Ampfield Wood
Claypit Rd
3
Monarch's Way
Knapp Lane
24
Monarch's Way
4
Ratlake Lane
Knapp
Ampfield Primary School
Ampfield
A3090
Ratlake
130
5
Green Pond Lane
A3090
Ampfield Par 3 Golf Club
Lwr Farm La
Pound La
Potters Heron Lane
Potters Heron Close
The Potters Heron Hotel
Hook Road
Monks Brook
South Holmes Copse
23
Golf Course
Broadgate
6
Gosport
Pound Lane
Hookwood Lane
Woodlea Way
7
122
Flex
8
439
40
41
A
B
C
Bu
138
Cor
D
E
F
Flexford Road
Knightwood Road
Morgan Le Fay Dr
Merlin Way
Knigh Prima Schoo
1 grid square represents 500 metres

Hursley
Bunstead
Silkstead
Ladwell
Hocombe
Hiltingbury
Chandler's Ford
Hursley Park
Cemetery
Monarch's Way
Shawlands Farm
Keble Memorial Primary School
Field House
Hawstead Farm
Home Farm
Cranbury House
Cranbury Park
Freemantles Copse
Hiltingbury County J & I School
Leigh House Hospital
Sherbourne House School
Thornden School
Pitmore School
Wessex Nuffield Hospital
Merdon Junior School
Scantabout Primary School
Hocombe Road
Hursley Road
Hiltingbury Road
Poles Lane
Collins Lane
Bunstead Lane
Silkstead Lane
Winchester Road
Kingsway
Lakewood Road
Common Road
Valley Road
A3090
B3043
301
124
134
139
SO53

134
124
133
139
140
A
B
C
D
E
F
1
2
3
4
5
6
7
8
445
46
47
23
22
21
120
Otterbourne
Sparrowgrove
Waterworks Road
Richmond Park
Regent Close
Copse Close
Poles Lane
Norlands Drive
Bourne Close
Oakwood Close
Oakwood Avenue
Greenacres Drive
Greenacres Dr
Brooklyn Cl
Old Parsonage Ct
Coles Mede
Cranbourne Drive
Cranbury Close
Main Road
Works
Twyford Moors
River Itchen
Itchen Way
B3335
B3354
HIGHBRIDGE ROAD
Otterbourne CE Primary School
Kiln Lane
Otterbourne Hill
M3
Boyatt La
Chapel Lane
Boyatt Lane
Park Lane
Lincolns Rise
Boyatt Crescent
Wessex Nuffield Hospital
Junction 12
Thornden School
A335
ALLBROOK WAY
Pitmore Close
Pitmore Road
The Itchen Navigation
Brambridge House
Brambridge
Highbridge
Wardle Road
Lordswood
Church Lane
Bishopstoke Lane
Fleming Pl
Orchard Close
New Road
Moors Close
Lower Moors Road
Spring Lane
Spring
Surgery
PO
St Vigor Way
Colden Common Primary School
Upper Moors
Burr Close
Brickmakers
Setters Close
Pallet Close
Callowing Close
Tess Farm Road
Piping Road
Crays Close
Valley Close
Church
Pantheon Road
Doric Close
Oakfields
Porchester Rise
Highclere Drive
Walmer Close
Allbrook Knoll
Knowle Hill
Broom Hill Way
ALLBROOK HILL
Allbrook
Bosville
Birch Grove
Penshurst Way
Woburn Close
Torre Close
Sovereign Way
Saddlers Close
Windsor Gate
Woodside Avenue
Kenilworth Drive
Arundel Road
Loughwood Close
Travelodge
Chatsworth Road
Rufford Close
Harewood Close
Buckland Close
Broadlands Avenue
TWYFORD ROAD
The Haven
Rosebery Crescent
Consort Cl
Itchen Way
Stoke Common
Surbiton Road
Victoria Road
Consort Road
Boyatt Wood
Crestwood College
Royston Avenue
Oak Tree Way
St Catherine's Road
Ruskin Rd
The Recess
Lawn Road
The Nook
Albert Road
St Catherines Rd Junior Sch
Surgery
Boyatt Shopping Cen
Inf Sch
Shakespeare Road
Winston Cl
Whyteways
Selbourne Dr
Beaulieu Rd
St Lawrence Rd
Darwin Rd
St John's Rd
Shakespeare Business Centre
TWYFORD RD
Mount View
Mottisfont Rd
Parham Dr
Byron Rd
Archers
The Crescent
Newtown Rd
Cemetery
Boyatt Wood Industrial Estate
EASTLEIGH
Dutton Lane
Works
Church Road
Bishops Court
Stoke Common Road
Pendula Way
Wilmot Close
Darlington Road
Jockey Lane
The Mount Hospital
Edward Av
Longmead Av
St Mary's Rd
Nelson Rd
Drake Road
Rogers Cl
Rogers Road
Sydney Rd
St Margarets Rd
Stoke Park Road
Stoke Park Rd
West Dr
Underwood Rd
Asford Gv
Church
Stoke Park Farm
Industrial Est
Laburnum Gv
The Crescent Prim School
Police Stn
Council Building
Health
Eastleigh RFC
Itchen Way
Surgery
Portal Road
Riverside
Sedgewick Rd
Escombe Rd
Hamilton Rd
East Dr
Underwood
Cotton Close
Shears Rd
BISHOPSTOKE ROAD
ROMSEY ROAD
STATION
1 grid square represents 500 metres

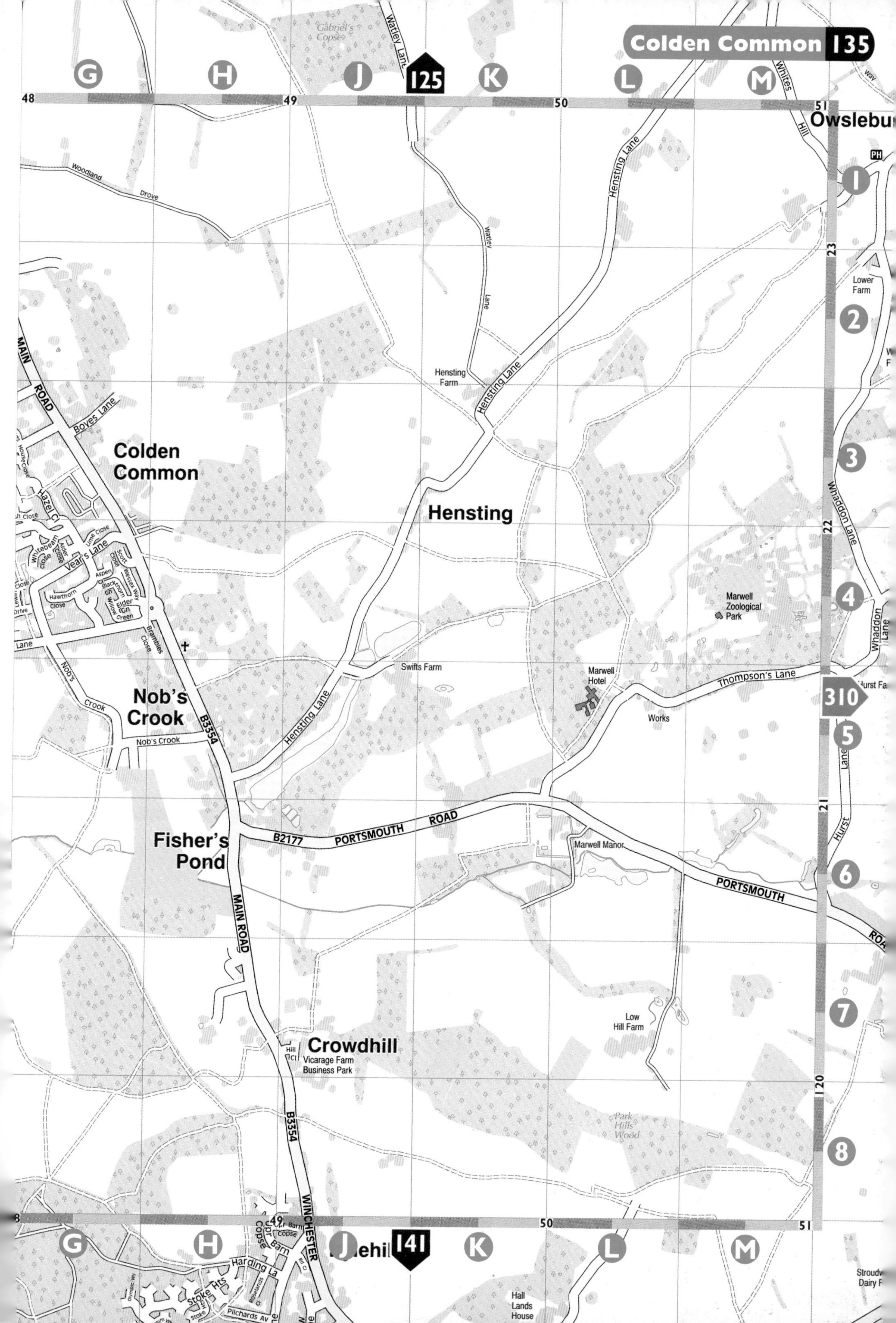
G
H
J
125
K
L
M
48
49
50
51
Gabriel's Copse
Watley Lane
Whites Hill
Owslebu
PH
1
23
Lower Farm
2
3
Whaddon Lane
22
4
Woodland Drove
Hensting Lane
Watley Lane
Hensting Farm
Colden Common
Hensting
MAIN ROAD
Boyes Lane
Hazel Cl
Lime Close
Whitebeam Close
Alder Close
Vear's Lane
Scott Close
Wessex Way
Aspen
Hawthorn Close
Elder Gn
Drive
Lane
Brambles Close
Nob's Crook
Swifts Farm
Marwell Zoological Park
Marwell Hotel
Thompson's Lane
310
Hurst Fa
Works
5
Nob's Crook
B3354
21
Hurst Lane
B2177 PORTSMOUTH ROAD
Fisher's Pond
Marwell Manor
PORTSMOUTH ROAD
6
MAIN ROAD
7
Low Hill Farm
Crowdhill
Vicarage Farm Business Park
120
Park Hills Wood
B3354
8
WINCHESTER
141
Harding La
Stoke Hts
Pilchards Av
Hall Lands House
Stroudw Dairy F

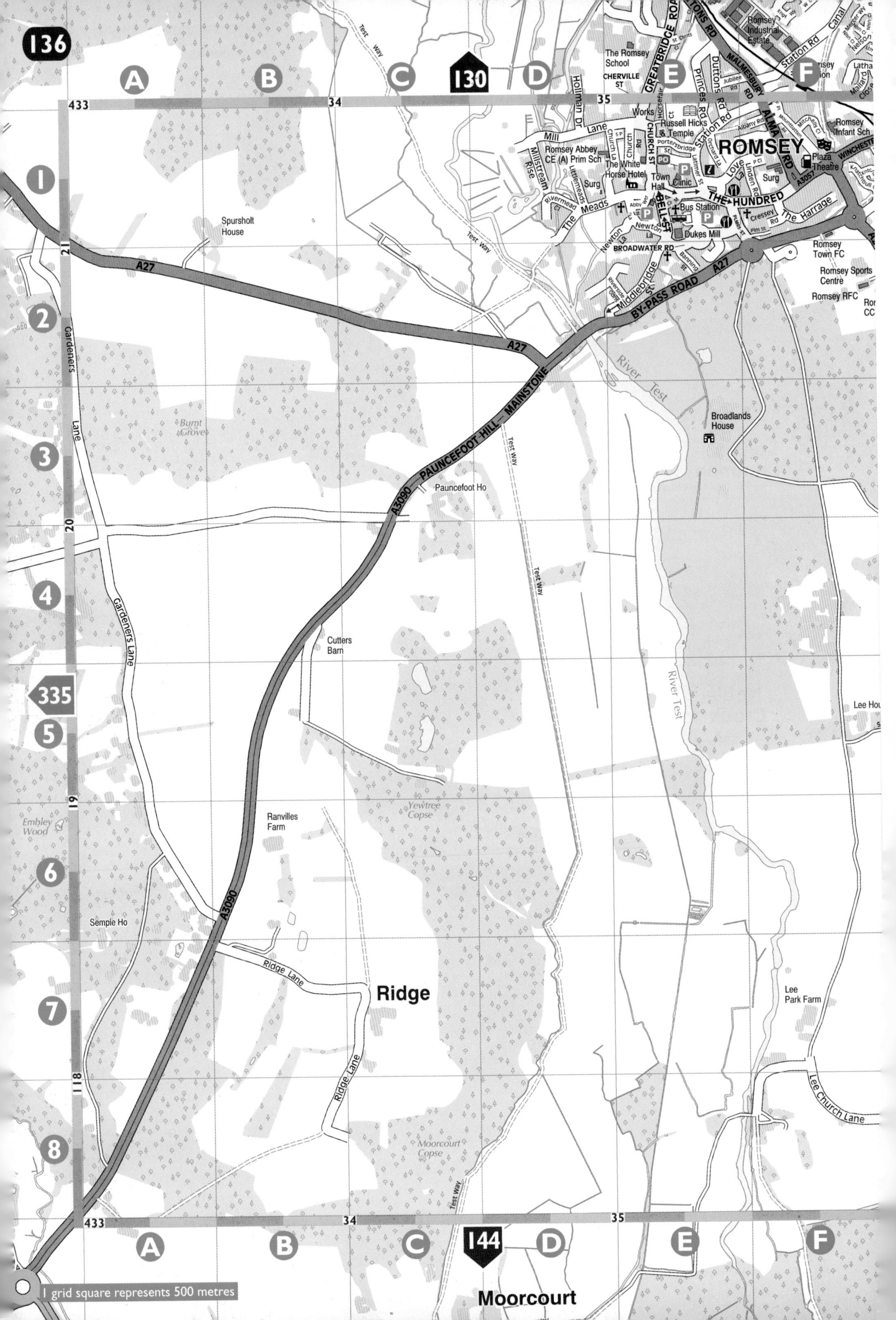

130
144
335
A
B
C
D
E
F
1
2
3
4
5
6
7
8
433
34
35
21
20
19
118
ROMSEY
Romsey Industrial Estate
The Romsey School
CHERVILLE ST
GREATBRIDGE RD
MALMESBURY RD
ALMA RD
Station Rd
Canal
Romsey Infant Sch
Hollman Dr
Mill Lane
Works
Russell Hicks & Temple
Romsey Abbey CE (A) Prim Sch
The White Horse Hotel
Millstream Rise
Surg
Town Hall
Clinic
THE HUNDRED
Plaza Theatre
A3057
WINCHESTER
The Meads
Bus Station
Dukes Mill
Newton La
BROADWATER RD
BELL ST
CHURCH ST
The Harrage
Cressey Rd
Romsey Town FC
Romsey Sports Centre
Romsey RFC
BY-PASS ROAD
Middlebridge St
A27
Spursholt House
Test Way
River Test
Broadlands House
Burnt Grove
PAUNCEFOOT HILL - MAINSTONE
A3090
Pauncefoot Ho
Gardeners Lane
Cutters Barn
Lee Hou
Embley Wood
Ranvilles Farm
Yewtree Copse
Semple Ho
Ridge Lane
Ridge
Lee Park Farm
Lee Church Lane
Moorcourt Copse
Moorcourt
1 grid square represents 500 metres

Halterworth
Whitenap
Halterworth Primary School
Mountbatten School
Romsey Hospital
Romsey Junior Sch
Garden Centre
Cemetery
Warren Fm
Botley Road
BOTLEY ROAD A27
LUZBOROUGH LANE
SOUTHAMPTON ROAD
A3090
A3057
A27
Premier Works Way
Ashfield
Hoe Farm
Hoe Lane
Telegraph Wood
Toothill
Toothill Road
Upper Toothill Road
Nightingale Wood
Greenhill Lane
Rownhams Lane
Packridge Lane
Lee Drove
Lee Lane
Lee
Coldharbour Lane
Travel Inn
Rownhams Service Area
M27
Romsey Golf Club
Upton
Golf Course
131
138
145

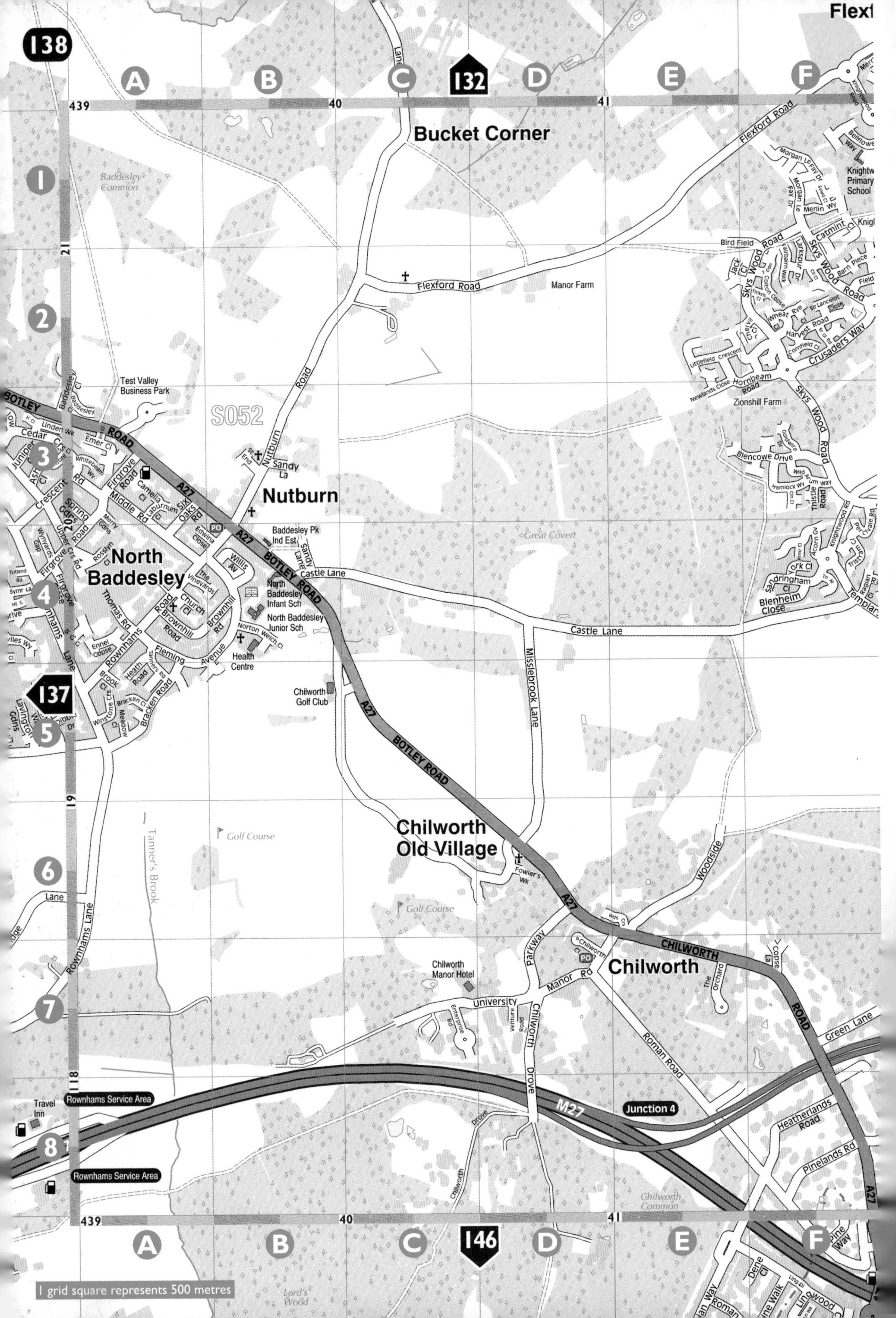
138
132
137
146
Flext
Bucket Corner
Flexford Road
Manor Farm
Baddesley Common
Test Valley Business Park
S052
Nutburn
Nutburn Road
Sandy La
North Baddesley
Baddesley Pk Ind Est
Castle Lane
BOTLEY ROAD
A27
North Baddesley Infant Sch
North Baddesley Junior Sch
Health Centre
Chilworth Golf Club
Great Covert
Misslebrook Lane
Chilworth Old Village
Golf Course
Tanner's Brook
Rownhams Lane
Woodside
Chilworth
CHILWORTH ROAD
Chilworth Manor Hotel
University
Chilworth Drove
Roman Road
Green Lane
M27
Junction 4
Rownhams Service Area
Travel Inn
Heatherlands Road
Pinelands Rd
Chilworth Common
Lord's Wood
Knightwood Primary School
Skys Wood Road
Crusaders Way
Hornbeam Road
Zionshill Farm
Blencowe Drive
Sandringham Cl
Blenheim Close
York Cl
Templars
1 grid square represents 500 metres

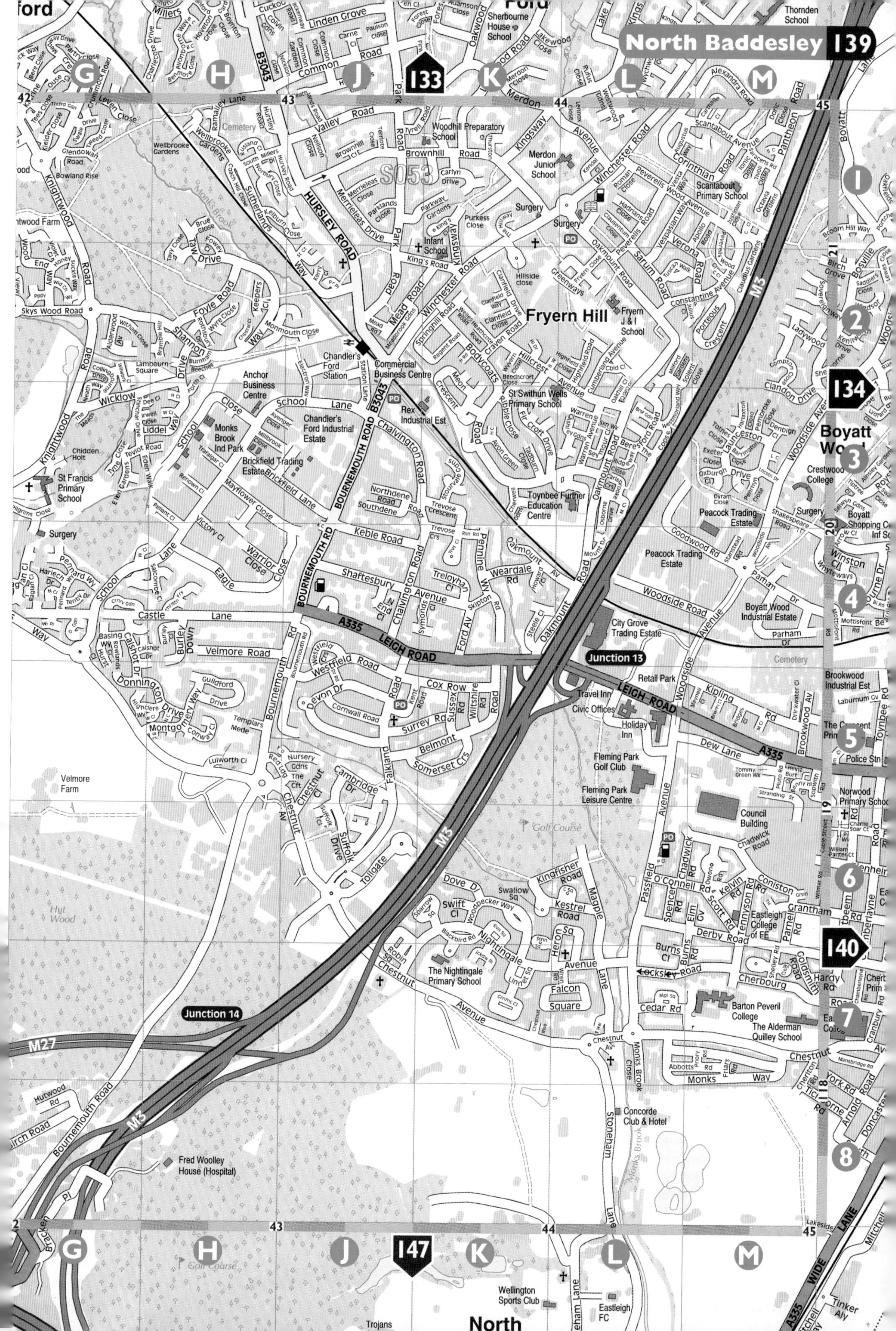

North Baddesley
139
133
134
140
147
G
H
J
K
L
M
42
43
44
45
I
2
3
4
5
6
7
8
21
20
19
18
Thornden School
Sherbourne House School
Linden Grove
Common Road
Common Gardens
Oakwood
Merdon
Ramalley Lane
Leven Close
Cemetery
Wellbrooke Gardens
Valley Road
Woodhill Preparatory School
Brownhill Road
S053
Merdon Junior School
Kingsway
Winchester Road
Scantabout Avenue
Scantabout Primary School
Corinthian Road
Pantheon Road
Alexandra Road
Boyatt
Knightwood Road
Glendowan Road
Bowland Rise
Sutherlands
Hursley Road
HURSLEY ROAD
B3043
Merrieleas Drive
Parkway Gardens
Carlyn Drive
Purkess Close
Surgery
Infant School
King's Road
Monks Brook
Brue Close
Taw Drive
Foyle Road
Keepers Cl
Skys Wood Road
Shannon Drive
Monmouth Close
Lambourn Square
Wicklow
Liddel Way
Chandler's Ford Station
Commercial Business Centre
Station Lane
Anchor Business Centre
School Lane
Monks Brook Ind Park
Chandler's Ford Industrial Estate
Rex Industrial Est
Brickfield Trading Estate
Brickfield Lane
Chidden Holt
St Francis Primary School
Mayflower Close
Victory Cl
Warrior Close
Eagle Close
BOURNEMOUTH ROAD
BOURNEMOUTH RD
Chalvington Road
Northdene Road
Southdene
Keble Road
Trevose Crescent
Shaftesbury Avenue
Treloyhan Cl
Pennine Way
Weardale Rd
Oakmount Av
Mead Road
Springhill Road
Bodycoats Road
Craven Road
Clanfield Drive
Hillcrest Avenue
St Swithun Wells Primary School
Meon Crescent
Ribble Close
Fir Croft Drive
Avon Green
Fryern Hill
Fryern J & I School
Hillside Close
Greenways
Oakmount Road
Sarum Road
Peverells Road
Peverells Wood Avenue
Verona Road
Constantine Avenue
Porteous Crescent
Cumberland Avenue
Warren Avenue
Beresford Road
The Copse
Toynbee Further Education Centre
M3
Ladywood
Clandon Drive
Boyatt Wood
Crestwood College
Launceston Drive
Woodside Avenue
Peacock Trading Estate
Shakespeare Road
Goodwood Rd
Boyatt Shopping Centre
Winston Cl
Woodside Road
Boyatt Wood Industrial Estate
Parham Dr
Mottisfont Rd
Cemetery
City Grove Trading Estate
Junction 13
Retail Park
A335
LEIGH ROAD
Castle Lane
Velmore Road
Calshot Dr
Burley Down
School Lane
Westfield Road
Cox Row
Devon Dr
Cornwall Road
Surrey Rd
Sussex Rd
Wiltshire Rd
Belmont
Somerset Crs
Guildford Drive
Donnington Drive
Montgomery Way
Templars Mede
Lulworth Cl
Nursery Gdns
Chestnut Av
Cambridge Dr
Suffolk Drive
Falkland Road
Tollgate
Velmore Farm
Hut Wood
Travel Inn
Civic Offices
Holiday Inn
Kipling Rd
Brookwood Av
Brookwood Industrial Est
Dew Lane
Fleming Park Golf Club
Fleming Park Leisure Centre
Golf Course
Council Building
Chadwick Road
Police Stn
Norwood Primary School
Passfield Avenue
O'Connell Rd
Coniston Rd
Kingfisher Road
Dove Dr
Swallow Sq
Swift Cl
Woodpecker Way
Kestrel Road
Magpie Lane
Heron Sq
Nightingale Avenue
The Nightingale Primary School
Falcon Square
Robin Sq
Chestnut Avenue
Junction 14
M27
Eastleigh College of FE
Derby Road
Burns Cl
Lockslеy Road
Cherbourg Rd
Cedar Rd
Barton Peveril College
The Alderman Quilley School
Abbotts Rd
Monks Way
Friars Rd
Monks Brook Close
Chestnut Av
Stoneham Lane
Concorde Club & Hotel
York Rd
Arnold Road
Doncaster
Hutwood Rd
Birch Road
Bournemouth Road
Fred Woolley House (Hospital)
Bracken Pl
Wellington Sports Club
Eastleigh FC
Trojans
North
Lakeside
WIDE LANE
Tinker Aly
Mitchell

140
134
139
147
148
A
B
C
D
E
F
1
2
3
4
5
6
7
8
445
46
47
EASTLEIGH
Bishopstoke
Moorgreen
Shakespeare Business Centre
Brookwood Industrial Est
The Crescent Prim School
Police Stn
Council Building
Health Centre
ROMSEY ROAD
BISHOPSTOKE ROAD
FAIROAK ROAD
ALAN DRAYTON WAY
SOUTHAMPTON RD
STATION HILL
TWYFORD
WIDE LANE
Eastleigh Station
Eastleigh RFC
Norwood Primary School
Eastleigh Museum
Swan Centre
Eastleigh College
Cherbourg Prim Sch
Quilley School
Phoenix Industrial Park
Deacon Trading Estate
Tower Industrial Estate
Tower Lane
Chickenhall Lane
Campbell Road
Works
Barton River
Itchen Navigation
Itchen Way
River Itchen
Surgery
Devine Gdns
Stoke Park Wood
Stoke Park Rd
Stoke Park Infant School
Stoke Park Junior School
Oakgrove Road
S050
West Horton Farm
Allington Manor Business Centre
Allington Manor Farm
Allington Manor School
Hogwood Lane
Allington Lane
Itchen Valley Country Park
Decoy Covert
Southampton International Airport
Spitfire Loop
Mitchell Way
Tinker Aly
Lakeside
Oaklands House
Winslowe House
Moorgreen Farm
Mans Bridge
BRIDGE ROAD
Garden Centre
Cemetery
The Kings
M27
A27
A335
B3037
1 grid square represents 500 metres

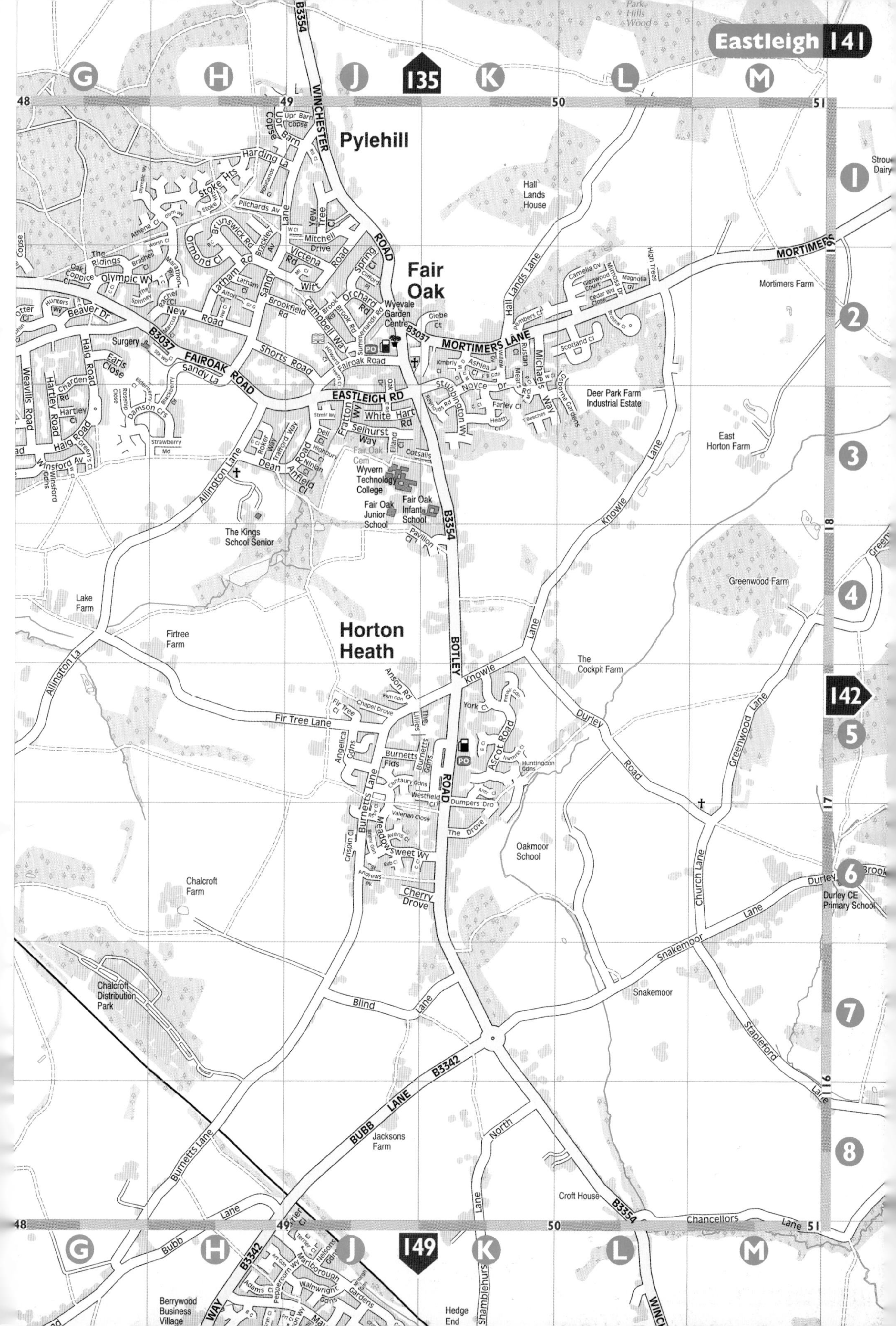

135

Park
Hills
Wood

G   H   J   **135**   K   L   M

48   49   WINCHESTER   50   51

Strou
Dairy

I

Pylehill

Upr Barn
Copse
Upr
Barn

MORTIMERS RD

Harding La

Stoke
Hts

MORTIMERS

Pilchards Av

Mortimers Farm

2

Hall
Lands
House

The
Ridings

Olympic Wy

Oak
Coppice
Cl

Brunswick Rd
Blackley Av

Ormond Cl

Mitchell
Drive

Victena
Rd

Spring
Rd

Yew
Tree
La

W Cl

**Fair
Oak**

Camelia Gv
Glenwood
Court
Cedar Wd
Close
Magnolia
Gv

High Trees

East
Horton Farm

3

Hunters
Wy

Beaver Dr

New   Road

Latham
Rd

Campbell Way

Orchard
Rd

Clifford

Wyevale
Garden
Centre

Glebe
Ct

Pembers Cl

Michaels Way

Scotland Cl

Deer Park Farm
Industrial Estate

B3037

B3037   FAIROAK   ROAD

Surgery

Earls
Close

Sandy La

Brookfield
Rd

Shorts   Road

Fairoak Road

B3037

MORTIMERS LANE

Kmbrly
Cl

Ashlea

Noyce
Dr

Farley Cl

Rustan

Osborne Gardens

Knowle

Weavills Road

Hartley Road

Halg Road

Chardens
Rd

Sandy La

Damson Crs

EASTLEIGH RD

White Hart
Rd

Selhurst
Way

Stmfr
Wd

Cotsalls

Stubbington Wy

Heath

Beeches

Lane

Greenwood
Farm

4

Winsford Av
Winsford
Gdns

Halg Road

Strawberry
Md

Allington Lane

Dell

Anfield
Cl

Dean

Fratton
Wy

Cem
**Wyvern
Technology
College**

Fair Oak
Junior
School

**Fair Oak
Infant
School**

B3354

Pavilion
Cl

The Cockpit Farm

Greenwood Lane

142

**The Kings
School Senior**

Lake
Farm

**Horton
Heath**

BOTLEY

Knowle

The Cockpit Farm

Durley

Road

†

142

5

Allington La

Firtree
Farm

Fir Tree Lane

Anson Rd
Chapel Drove

Fir Tree
Cl

Exm Gdn

The
Lillies

Burnetts

York
Cl

Knowle
Cl

Intel Gdn

Huntingdon
Gdns

Nwmr

ROAD

Ascot Road

Durley
Road

Church Lane

6

Durley
Brook

Durley CE
Primary School

Angelica
Gdns

Burnetts
Flds

Centaury Gdns

Crispin Cl

Westfield
Cl

Valerian Close

Avens Cl

The   Drove

Evb Cl

Dumpers Dro

Oakmoor
School

Snakemoor

Chalcroft
Farm

Sweet Wy

Andrews
Pk

Cherry
Drove

Burnetts Lane

Blind   Lane

Snakemoor

Stapleford Lane

7

Chalcroft
Distribution
Park

Bubb Lane

BUBB   LANE

Jacksons
Farm

B3342

North   Lane

Croft House

B3354

Chancellors   Lane

8

48   49   50   51

G   H   J   **149**   K   L   M

Bubb

B3342

Warnborough

Nelson

Wainwright

Pepper

Gardens

Shamblehurst La

WINCHESTER

Berrywood
Business
Village

WAY

Adams Cl

Hedge
End

142
310
Lower Upham
PORTSMOUTH ROAD
A
B
C
D
E
F
451
52
53
PO
B3037
B2177
Stroudwood
Stroudwood Dairy Farm
MORTIMERS LANE
Mortimers Farm
WINCHESTER ROAD
Woolstreet Farm
King's Way
Stakes Lane
Stakes La
Stakes Farm
1
2
3
4
5
6
7
8
Alma Lane
Scivier's Lane
Durley Hall Lane
Durley Hall Farm
Wintershill Hall
Wintershill
Greenwood Lane
Winters Hill
Durley Street
Newt
The Drove
Manor Road
Durley Manor Farm
Tangier Farm
141
18
17
16
Durley Brook Road
Durley CE Primary School
Durley
Parsonage Lane
Kytes Lane
Lower Farm
Brown Heath
Mincingfield Farm
Mincingfield Lane
White Gates
The Sawmills
Heathen Street
Gregory Lane
Stapleford Farm
River Hamble
150
Durley Mill
Mill La
Calcot
Calcot La
Hill Farm
Harfields Farm
1 grid square represents 500 metres

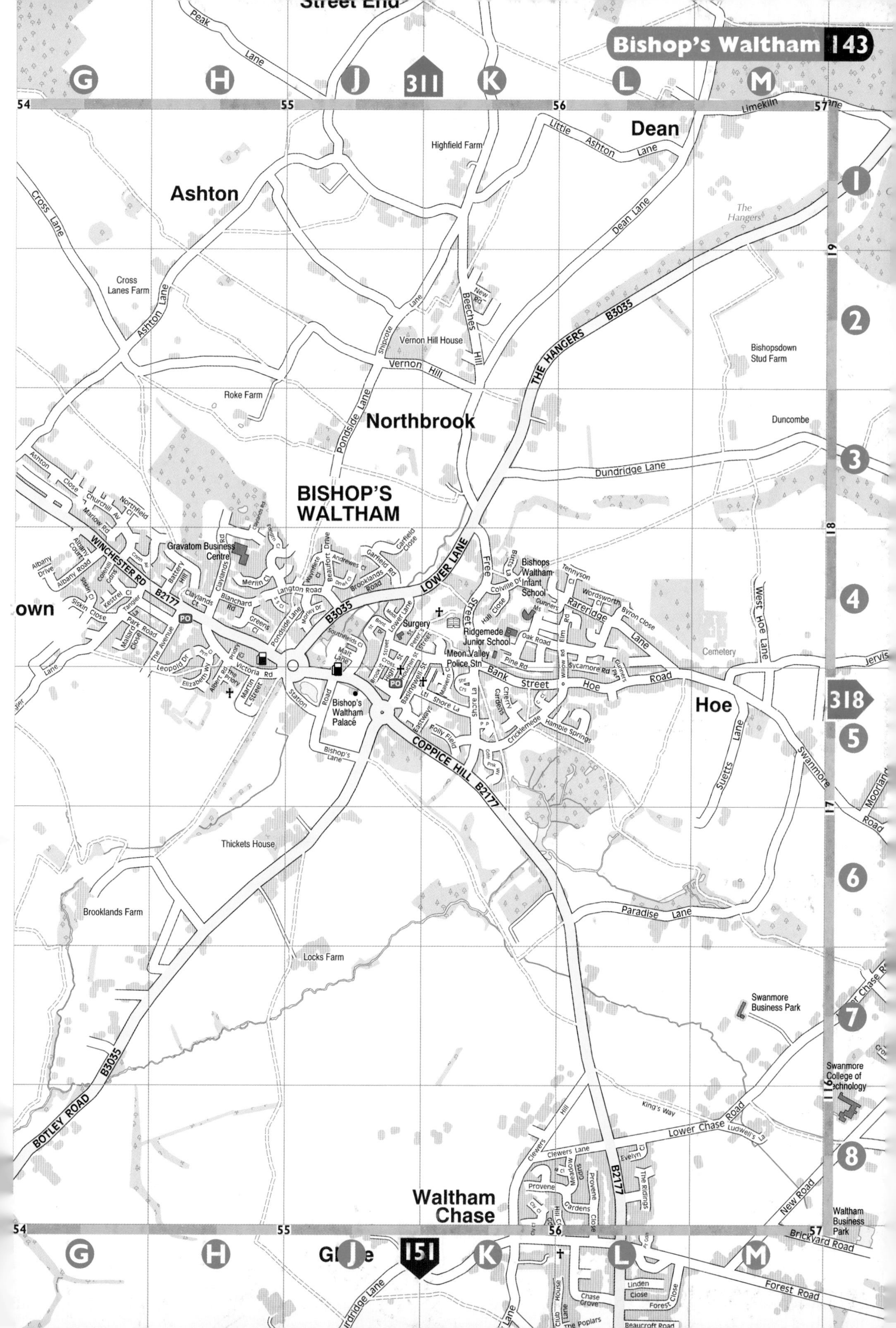

Street End
Peak Lane
G
H
J
311
K
L
M
54
55
56
57
Limekiln Lane
Dean
Little Ashton Lane
Highfield Farm
Ashton
Cross Lane
The Hangers
Dean Lane
Cross Lanes Farm
Ashton Lane
Shipcote Lane
New Rd
Beeches Hill
Vernon Hill House
Vernon Hill
THE HANGERS
B3035
Bishopsdown Stud Farm
Roke Farm
Pondside Lane
Northbrook
Duncombe
Dundridge Lane
BISHOP'S WALTHAM
Northfield Cl
Churchill Av
Marlow Rd
Ashton Close
WINCHESTER RD
Albany Court
Albany Drive
Albany Road
Gravatom Business Centre
Claylands Rd
Battery Hill
B2177
Merlin Cl
Langton Road
Wayneflete Cl
Beaufort Drive
Andrewes Cl
Garfield Rd
Garfield Close
Brooklands Road
LOWER LANE
Free Street
Colville Dr
Bishops Waltham Infant School
Tennyson Cl
Wordsworth Cl
Rareridge
Byron Close
own
Siskin Close
Kestrel Cl
Tangier La
Park Road
Mallard Close
The Avenue
Claylands Ct
Blanchard Rd
Greens Cl
Morley Dr
B3035
Lower Lane
Surgery
Hall Close
Gunners Ms
Ridgemede Junior School
Oak Road
Elm Rd
Lane
West Hoe Lane
Cemetery
Jervis
Leopold Dr
Elizabeth Wy
Albert Rd
The Priory
Victoria Rd
Martin Street
Southfields Cl
Malt Lane
Brook St
Cross St
High St
Houchin St
Basingwell St
Meon Valley Police Stn
Pine Rd
Sycamore Rd
Willow Rd
Gunners Pk
Bank Street
Hoe Road
Hoe
318
Station Road
Bishop's Waltham Palace
Eastways
Shore La
Malvern Cl
Folly Field
Cherry Gardens
Cricklemede
Hamble Springs
Suetts Lane
Swanmore Road
Moorland
Bishop's Lane
COPPICE HILL B2177
Thickets House
Paradise Lane
Brooklands Farm
Locks Farm
Swanmore Business Park
Swanmore College of Technology
King's Way
Lower Chase Road
Ludwell's La
Clewers Hill
Clewers Lane
Evelyn Cl
B2177
The Ridings
Meadow Gdns
Provene Gardens
Provene Close
New Road
BOTLEY ROAD
B3035
Waltham Chase
Waltham Business Park
Brickyard Road
Forest Road
151
Linden Close
Forest Close
Chase Grove
Club House Lane
The Poplars
Beaucroft Road
Dundridge Lane
1
2
3
4
5
6
7
8
19
18
17
116

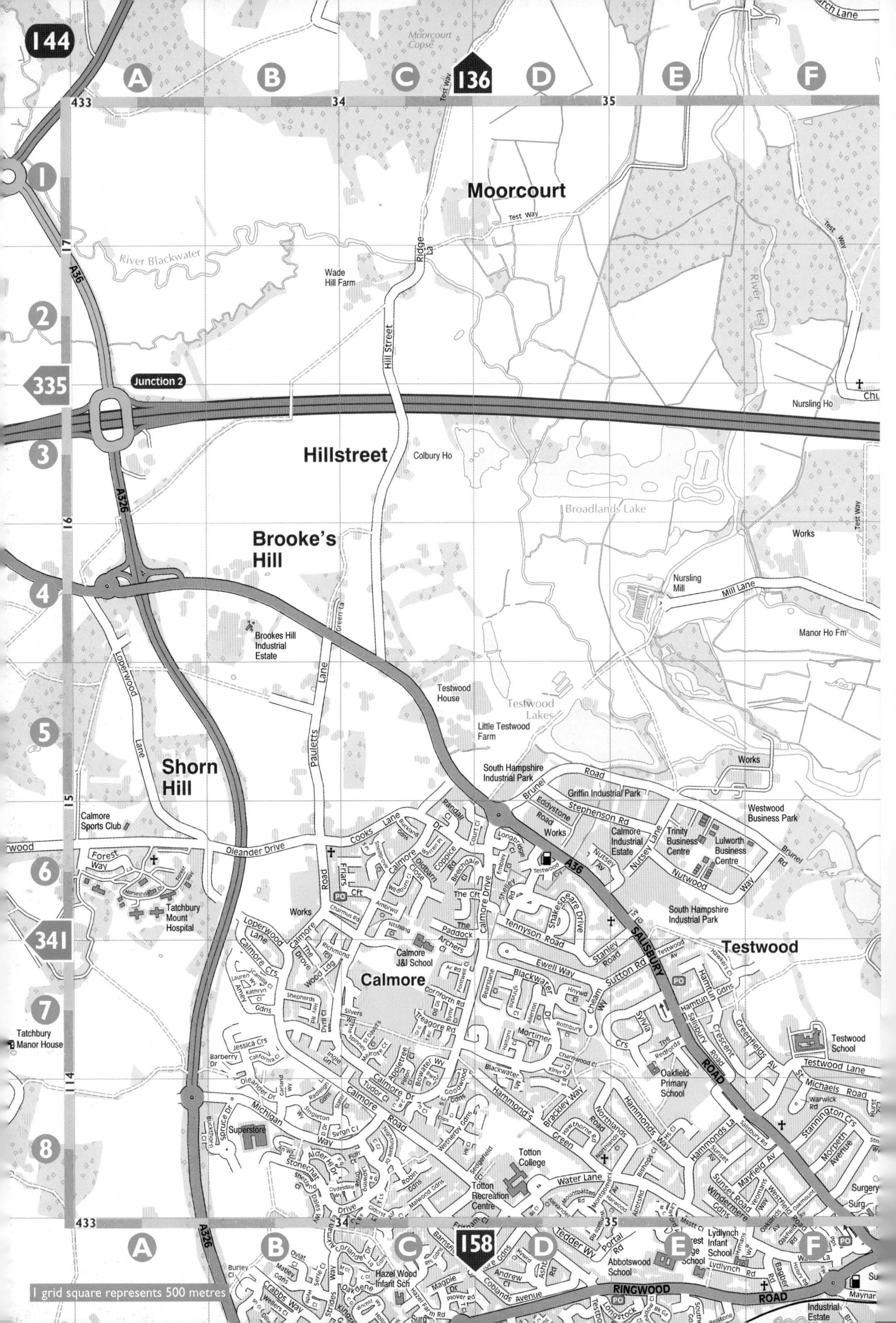
144
136
335
341
158
A
B
C
D
E
F
1
2
3
4
5
6
7
8
433
34
35
17
16
15
14
Moorcourt Copse
Moorcourt
Test Way
River Blackwater
Wade Hill Farm
Ridge La
Hill Street
River Test
Junction 2
Nursling Ho
Hillstreet
Colbury Ho
Broadlands Lake
Brooke's Hill
Works
Nursling Mill
Mill Lane
Manor Ho Fm
Brookes Hill Industrial Estate
Green La
Loperwood Lane
Pauletts Lane
Testwood House
Testwood Lakes
Little Testwood Farm
Shorn Hill
South Hampshire Industrial Park
Brunel Road
Griffin Industrial Park
Westwood Business Park
Stephenson Rd
Eddystone Road
Calmore Industrial Estate
Trinity Business Centre
Lulworth Business Centre
Nutsey Lane
Nutwood Way
Calmore Sports Club
Oleander Drive
Cooks Lane
Forest Way
Tatchbury Mount Hospital
Testwood
Calmore
Calmore J&I School
Tennyson Road
Shakespeare Drive
Stanley Road
Ewell Way
Sutton Rd
Blackwater Dr
Salisbury Road
Hamtun Gdns
Hamtun Crescent
Greenfields Av
Testwood School
Testwood Lane
St Michaels Road
Tatchbury Manor House
Oakfield Primary School
Hammond's Green
Hammonds Way
Michigan Way
Superstore
Calmore Road
Totton College
Water Lane
Totton Recreation Centre
Stanningtons Crs
Morpeth Avenue
Surgery
Abbotswood School
Lydlynch Infant School
Lydlynch Rd
Ringwood Road
Hazel Wood Infant Sch
Coblands Avenue
Industrial Estate
A36
A326
1 grid square represents 500 metres

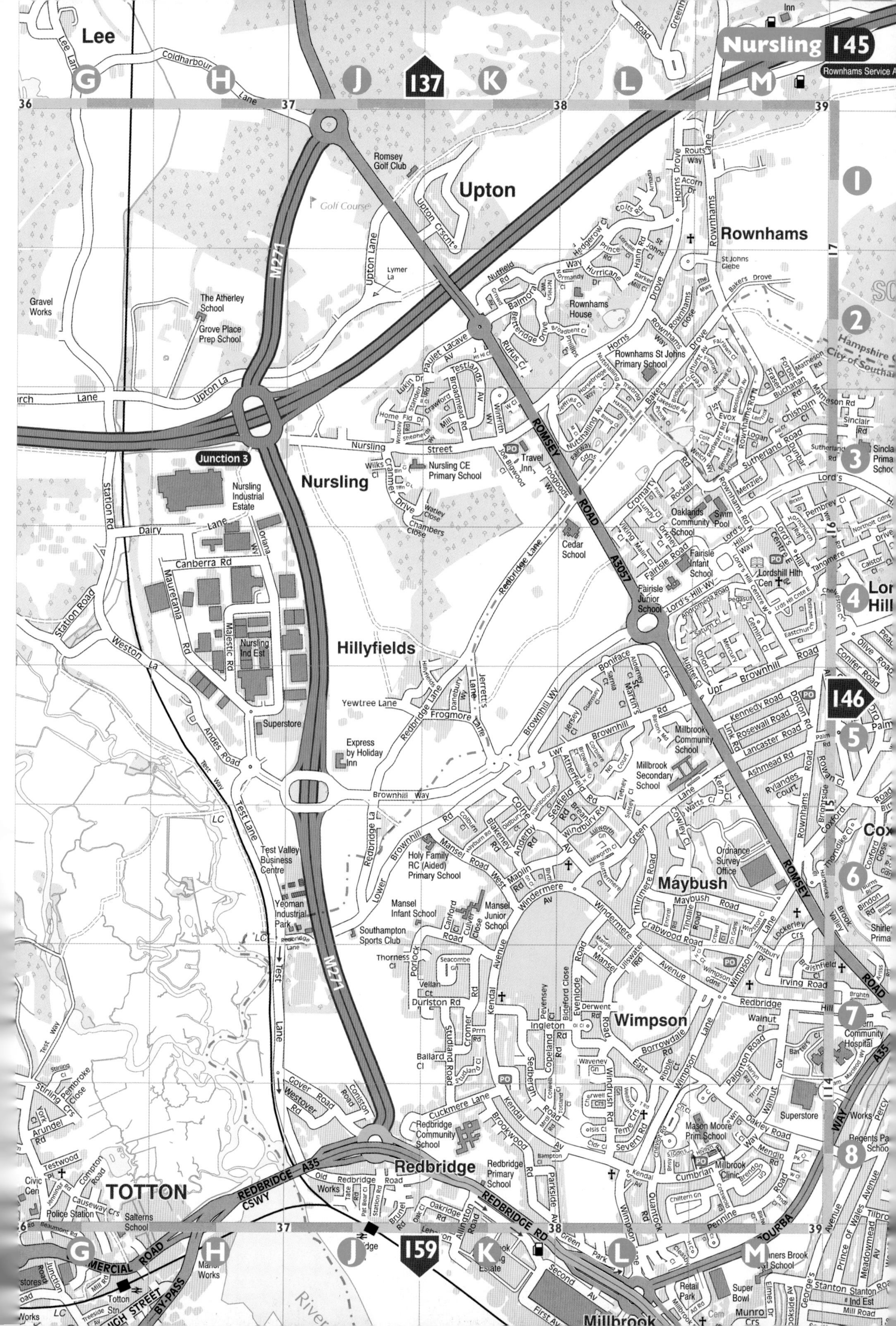
Nursling 145
Rownhams Service Area
137
146
159
Lee
Lee Lane
Coldharbour Lane
G
H
J
K
L
M
36
37
38
39
Upton
Romsey Golf Club
Golf Course
Upton Crscnt
Upton Lane
Lymer La
Rownhams
St Johns Glebe
Bakers Drove
Horns Drove
Routs Way
Acorn Dr
Hedgerow Cl
Hurricane Dr
Normandy Cl
Rownhams House
Nutfield Rd
Balmoral Cl
Betteridge Drive
Rufus Cl
Paulet Lacave Av
Testlands Av
Broadmead Rd
Winfrith Way
Home Fld Dr
Crawford Cl
Lukin Dr
Rownhams St Johns Primary School
Nutshalling Av
Hampshire
City of Southampton
The Atherley School
Grove Place Prep School
Gravel Works
M271
Upton La
Church Lane
Junction 3
Station Rd
Nursling Industrial Estate
Dairy Lane
Canberra Rd
Mauretania Rd
Majestic Rd
Nursling Ind Est
Oriana Wy
Weston La
Station Road
Superstore
Andes Road
Test Way
Test Lane
Nursling
Nursling Street
Nursling CE Primary School
Travel Inn
Joe Bigwood Cl
Chambers Close
Cranmer Drive
Watley Close
Wilks Cl
ROMSEY ROAD
A3057
Cedar School
Redbridge Lane
Rownhams Way
Rownhams Close
Rownhams Rd
Fraser Cl
Buchanan Rd
Matheson Rd
Sinclair Rd
Chisholm Cl
Sutherland Road
Logan Cl
Menzies Cl
Dunbar Cl
Lord's Hill Way
Fairisle Road
Fairisle Infant School
Fairisle Junior School
Oaklands Community School
Swim Pool
Cromarty Rd
Lundy Cl
Orkney Cl
Viking Cl
Rockall Cl
Lordshill Hlth Cen
Lord's Hill Centre E
Lords Hill Centre W
Pembrey Cl
Tangmere Dr
Andromeda Road
Saturn Cl
Gemini Cl
Mercury Cl
Orion Cl
Jupiter Cl
Upr Brownhill Rd
Brownhill Road
Olive Rd
Conifer Road
Eastchurch Cl
Lor Hill
Hillyfields
Yewtree Lane
Frogmore Lane
Jerretts Lane
Danebury Wy
Express by Holiday Inn
Brownhill Wy
Boniface Crs
St Martin's Cl
Jersey Cl
Lwr Brownhill Rd
Millbrook Community School
Millbrook Secondary School
Kennedy Road
Rosewall Road
Lancaster Road
Dorton Rd
Link Rd
Ashmead Rd
Rylandes Court
Rowan Cl
Brightside
Coxford Road
Brownhill Way
Redbridge La
Lower Brownhill Rd
Holy Family RC (Aided) Primary School
Mansel Road West
Mansel Infant School
Mansel Junior School
Bakeney Rd
Colne Av
Anderby Rd
Seafield Rd
Windbury Rd
Lulworth Cl
Green Lane
Cowley Cl
Watts Cl
Thirlmere Road
Ordnance Survey Office
Maybush
Maybush Road
Crabwood Road
Windermere Av
Windermere Avenue
Lockerley Crs
Irving Road
Brookvalley
Shirley Primary
Test Valley Business Centre
Yeoman Industrial Park
Southampton Sports Club
Redbridge Lane
Thorness Cl
Porlock Rd
Canford Cl
Culver Close
Seacombe Gn
Vellan Ct
Durlston Rd
Kendal Avenue
Cromer Rd
Studland Road
Ballard Cl
Pevensey Cl
Bideford Close
Evenlode Road
Derwent Rd
Ingleton Rd
Copeland Rd
Sedbergh Rd
Wimpson
Wimpson Lane
Borrowdale Rd
Windrush Rd
Ribble Cl
Redbridge Hill
Walnut Cl
Paignton Road
Oakley Road
Mendip Rd
Superstore
Community Hospital
Mason Moore Prim School
Millbrook Clinic
Cumbrian Way
Chiltern Gn
Pennine Rd
Quantock Rd
Severn Rd
Teme Crs
Cuckmere Lane
Redbridge Community School
Brookwood Rd
Kendal Av
Parkside Av
Redbridge Primary School
Redbridge
Gover Road
Westover Rd
Coniston Road
Old Redbridge Road
Works
Tate Rd
Station Rd
Brunel Rd
Oakridge Road
Allington Road
REDBRIDGE RD
REDBRIDGE A35 CSWY
TOTTON
Testwood Pl
Compton Road
Stirling Crs
Pembroke Close
York Cl
Arundel Rd
Civic Cen
Causeway Crs
Police Station
Salterns School
Beaumont Rd
COMMERCIAL ROAD
BY-PASS
HIGH STREET
Mill Rd
Totton Stn
Junction Rd
Works
Green Park Rd
Second Av
First Av
Millbrook
Retail Park
Super Bowl
Munro Crs
Prince of Wales Avenue
Meadowmead Av
Stanton Road
Ind Est
Mill Road
Regents Park School
TOURBA WAY
A35
River
LC
1
2
3
4
5
6
7
8
15
16
17
14

146
Rownhams Services
138
Junction 4
Heatherlands Road
Pinelands Rd
Chilworth Common
Lord's Wood
SO16
Hampshire County
City of Southampton
Southampton Municipal Golf Course
Golf Course
Bassett Row
Golf Course Road
Bassett Heath Av
Saxholm Way
Oakwood Infant School
Oakwood Junior School
Sinclair Primary School
Lord's Hill Way
Council Building
Southampton Sports Centre
Lordswood
Lord's Hill
Aldermoor
Aldermoor Health Centre
Bradbury Centre & Rosewood School
Vermont School
Red Lodge School
Winchester Road
Bassett Avenue
The Phoenix Cinema
Boldrewood Centre
145
Princess Anne Hospital
Hollybrook Cemetery
Hollybrook Infant School
Hollybrook Junior School
Southampton General Hospital
Coxford
Shirley Warren
Wordsworth House
Northbrook Industrial Estate
Malvern Business Centre
Upper Shirley
Bellemoor Secondary School
Health Clinic
Shirley Warren Primary School
Shirley J&I School
Old Shirley
Southampton Common
Western Community Hospital
Wordsworth Inf Sch
Council Building
Tauntons College
King Edward VI School
Superstore
Regents Park Girls School
Southampton Cemetery
Shirley High St
Police Stn
Foundry Lane Primary Sch
Shirley
160
Shirley Health Cen
Tanners Brook J&I School
St Marks CE Junior School
Elizabeth House Htl
The Avenue
1 grid square represents 500 metres

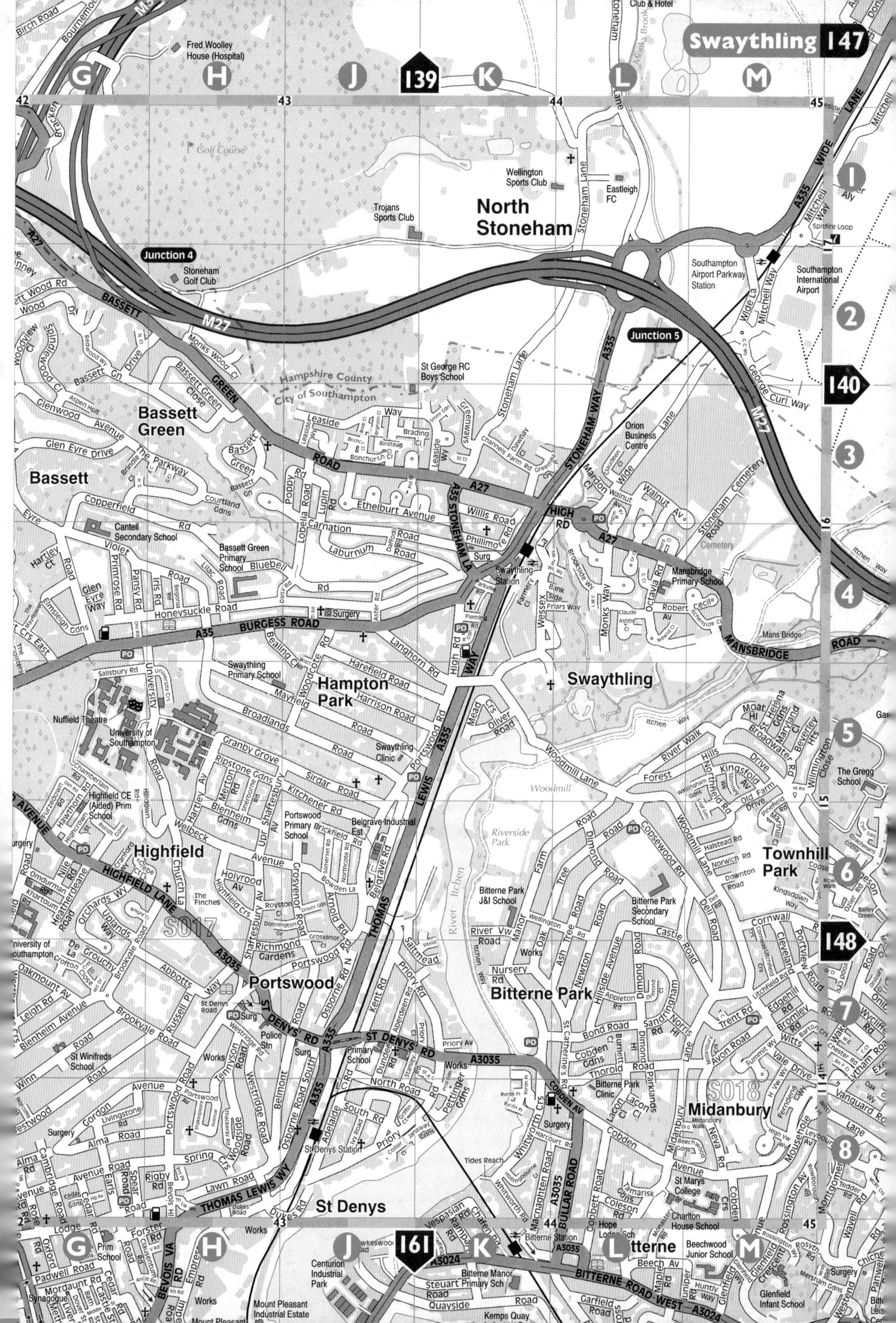
North Stoneham
Bassett Green
Bassett
Hampton Park
Swaythling
Highfield
Portswood
Bitterne Park
Townhill Park
Midanbury
St Denys
Southampton International Airport
Southampton Airport Parkway Station
Swaythling Station
St Denys Station
Bitterne Station
University of Southampton
Junction 4
Junction 5
Hampshire County
City of Southampton
SO17
SO18
139
140
148
161

148
147
161
140
162
A
B
C
D
E
F
1
2
3
4
5
6
7
8
445
46
47
Mans Bridge
BRIDGE ROAD
M27
A27
Moorgreen
Winslowe House
Moorgreen Farm
Garden Centre
Cemetery
The Kings Primary School
The Gregg School
Townhill Park
Townhill Junior School
Townhill Infant School
Townhill Park Health Clinic
Hatch Bottom
St James CE Primary School
Moorgreen Hospital
Monarch Way
B3035
HIGH STREET
Surgery
Express by Holiday Inn
West End
Hampshire CCC (The Rose Bowl)
Tennis & Health Club
Hickley Farm
SWAYTHLING ROAD
CHURCH HILL
MOORHILL ROAD
Moorlands Infant School
West End Road
Westend Road
Harefield Junior School
Harefield Infant School
Woodlands Community School
Harefield
Council Building
Thornhill Park
CHARLES WATTS WAY A334
Junction 7
THORNHILL PK RD
BITTERNE ROAD EAST A334
MAYBRAY KING WY
BURSLEDON ROAD A3024
Bitterne Leisure Centre
Health Cen
Harefield Clinic
AMF Bowling
Bitterne CE (Controlled) Junior Sch
Police Station
Kanes Hill Primary School
KANES HILL
Upper Northam Drive
Thornhill Primary School
Thornhill Clinic
Thornhill
Itchen College
Sholing Common
Sholing J&I School
Sholing Technology College
Sholing
SO19
Hightown Primary School
Hightown
Weston Common
St Monica Junior Sch
Solent Peoples Theatre
BURSLEDON ROAD
Botley Road
A27 WEST END
1 grid square represents 500 metres

Jacksons Farm
141
Croft House
Chancellors Lane
Burnetts Lane
Bubb Lane
Berrywood Business Village
Hedge End Station
Shamblehurst Lane
Winchester Road
Botley Park Hotel, Golf & Country Club
Golf Course
Boorley Green
Dowd's Farm
Tollbar Way
Solent Industrial Estate
Nelson Industrial Park
Hedge End Business Centre
Waterloo Industrial Estate
Flanders Industrial Park
Wellington Pk
Botley Road
Drummond Rd
Berrywood Primary School
Long Common
Grange Rd
Missenden Acres
Botleigh Grange Hotel
Garden Centre
Woodhouse Lane
Retail Park
Shamblehurst Prim Sch
Wildern Secondary School
Clinic
Wildern
Charles Watts Way
Hedge End Retail Park
HEDGE END
Broadoak
Broad Oak
Holmesland
Botley CE Primary School
Woodhill Preparatory School
High Street
150
Lwr Northam Rd
Upper Northam Road
Strawberry Fields
Police Station
Freegrounds County J&I School
Kings Copse Avenue
Brook Lane
Kings Copse Prim School
St John's Road
Heathhouse Lane
Tanhouse Lane
Manor Farm
Boundary Acre
Peewit Hill Cl
Pyland's Lane
Dodwell Lane
163
Junction 8
M27

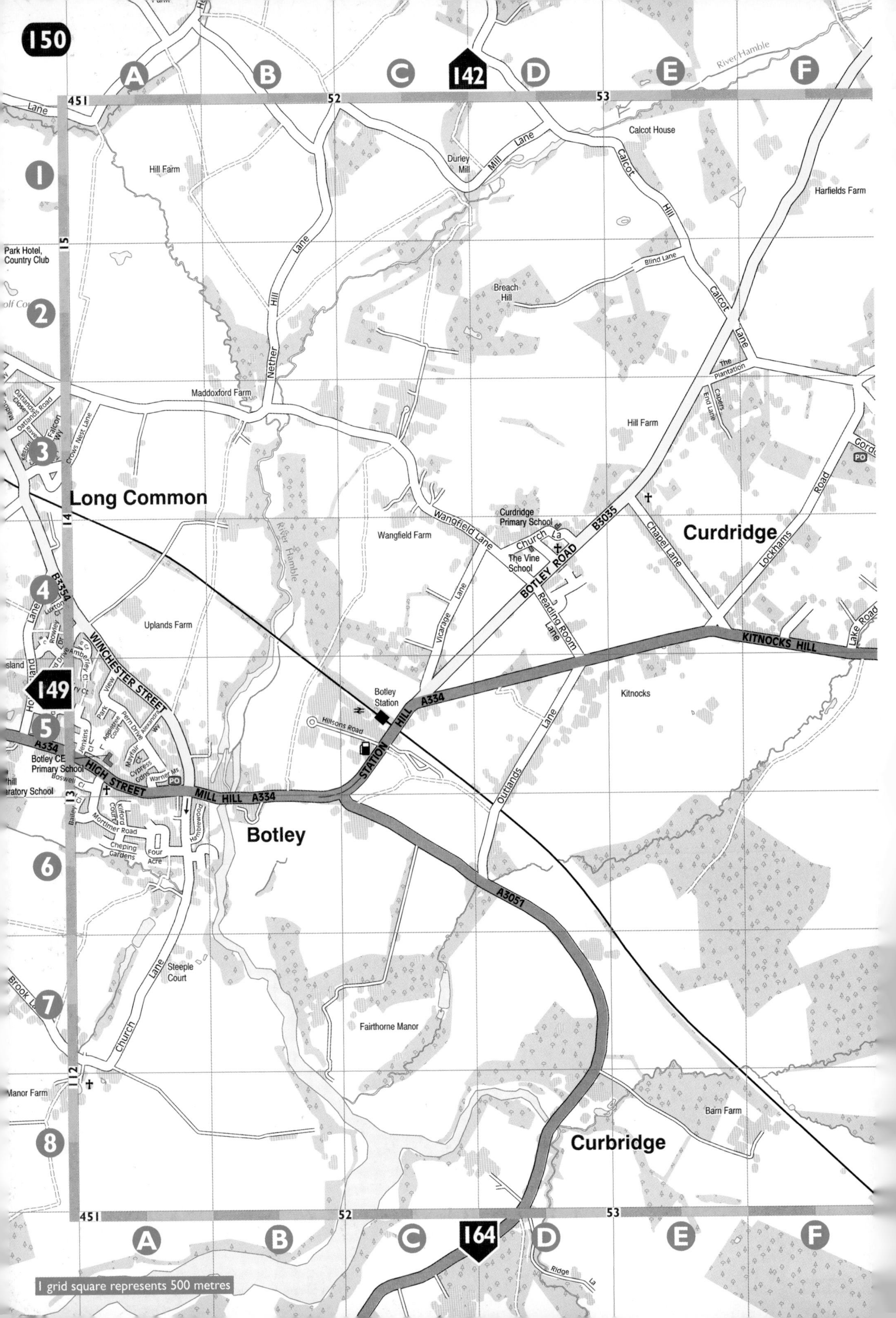

A
B
C
142
D
E
F
River Hamble
451
52
53
Lane
Hill Farm
Durley Mill
Mill Lane
Calcot House
Calcot Hill
Harfields Farm
1
15
Park Hotel, Country Club
Nether Hill Lane
Blind Lane
Breach Hill
2
Calcot Lane
The Plantation
Capers End Lane
Maddoxford Farm
Hill Farm
Oatlands Close
Oatlands Road
Falcon Wy
Crows Nest Lane
3
PO
Long Common
Curdridge Primary School
Church La
B3035
Curdridge
Wangfield Farm
Wangfield Lane
The Vine School
BOTLEY ROAD
Chapel Lane
Lockhams Road
14
River Hamble
4
B3354
Luxton Cl
Rowley Dr
Vicarage Lane
Reading Room Lane
Uplands Farm
KITNOCKS HILL
Lake Road
Amberley Ct
WINCHESTER STREET
149
View
Park
Botley Station
A334
Kitnocks
Hillsons Road
5
Jenkins Ct
Appletree Court
Fern Drive
Alexandra Wy
STATION HILL
Outlands Lane
A334
Botley CE Primary School
Mayfair Ct
Cypress Gdns
Warner Ms
PO
HIGH STREET
MILL HILL A334
Boswell Cl
aratory School
13
Bailey Cl
Kilford Court
Mortimer Road
Hamblewood
Botley
Cheping Gardens
Four Acre
6
A3051
Steeple Court
Church Lane
Brook La
7
Fairthorne Manor
112
Manor Farm
Barn Farm
Curbridge
8
451
52
53
A
B
C
164
D
E
F
Ridge La
1 grid square represents 500 metres

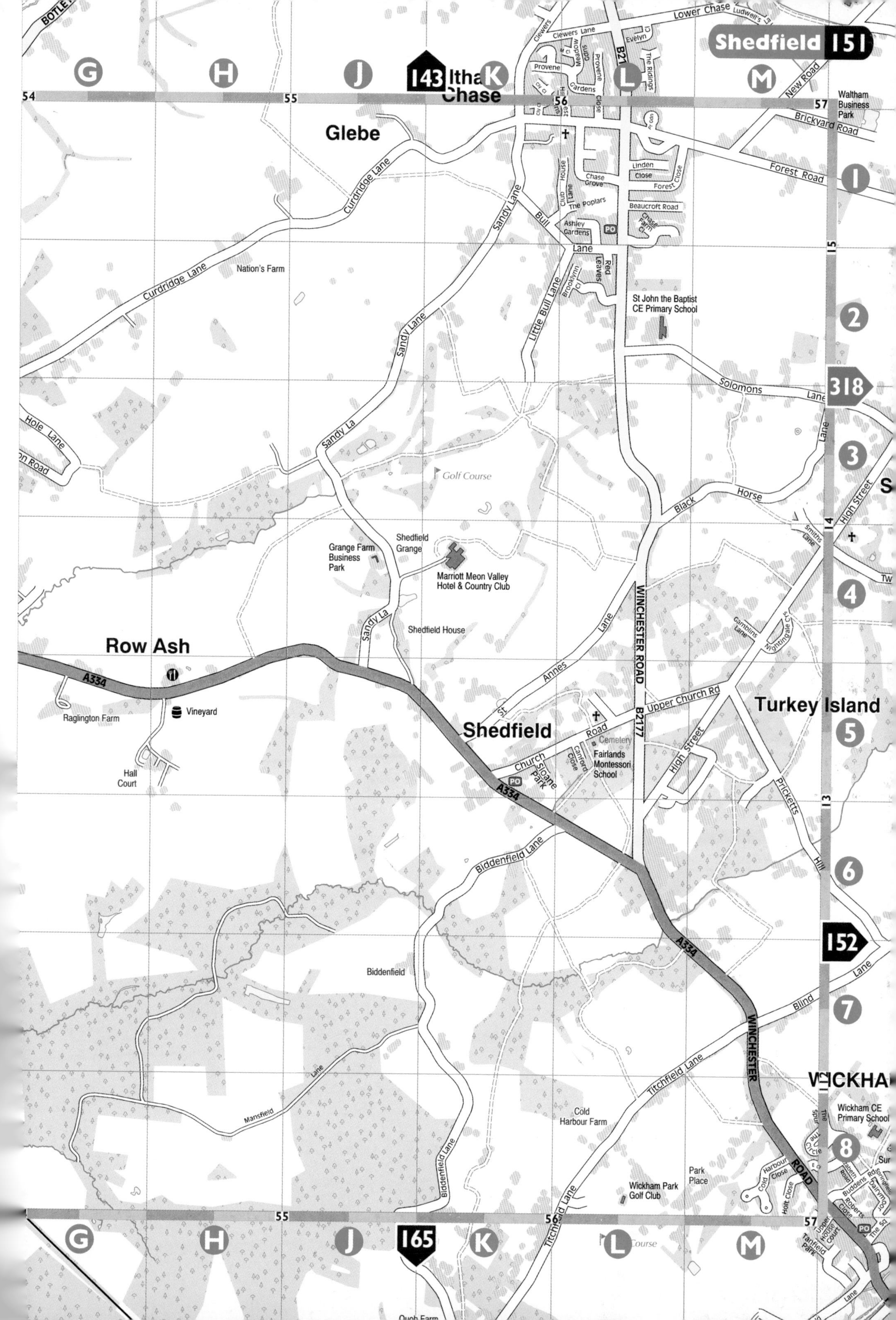

Glebe
Row Ash
Shedfield
Turkey Island
Curdridge Lane
Sandy Lane
Nation's Farm
Little Bull Lane
Bull Lane
St John the Baptist CE Primary School
Solomons Lane
Black Horse Lane
High Street
Golf Course
Grange Farm Business Park
Shedfield Grange
Marriott Meon Valley Hotel & Country Club
Shedfield House
Winchester Road
B2177
A334
St Annes Lane
Upper Church Rd
Church Road
Cemetery
Fairlands Montessori School
Sloane Park
Vineyard
Raglington Farm
Hall Court
Biddenfield Lane
Biddenfield
Mansfield Lane
Titchfield Lane
Cold Harbour Farm
Blind Lane
Wickham Park Golf Club
Park Place
Wickham CE Primary School
Prickets Hill
Gamblins Lane
Nightingale Cres
Smiths Lane
Forest Road
Brickyard Road
New Road
Waltham Business Park
Lower Chase
Clewers Lane
Linden Close
Forest Close
Chase Grove
Beaucroft Road
Chase Farm Cl
The Poplars
Ashley Gardens
Red Leaves
Brooklynn Cl
Club House Lane
Provene Gardens
Provene Close
Hole Lane
Cold Harbour Close
Holt Close
Budden's Road
Roberts Road
Tanfield Park
Upper Crescent
143
318
152
165

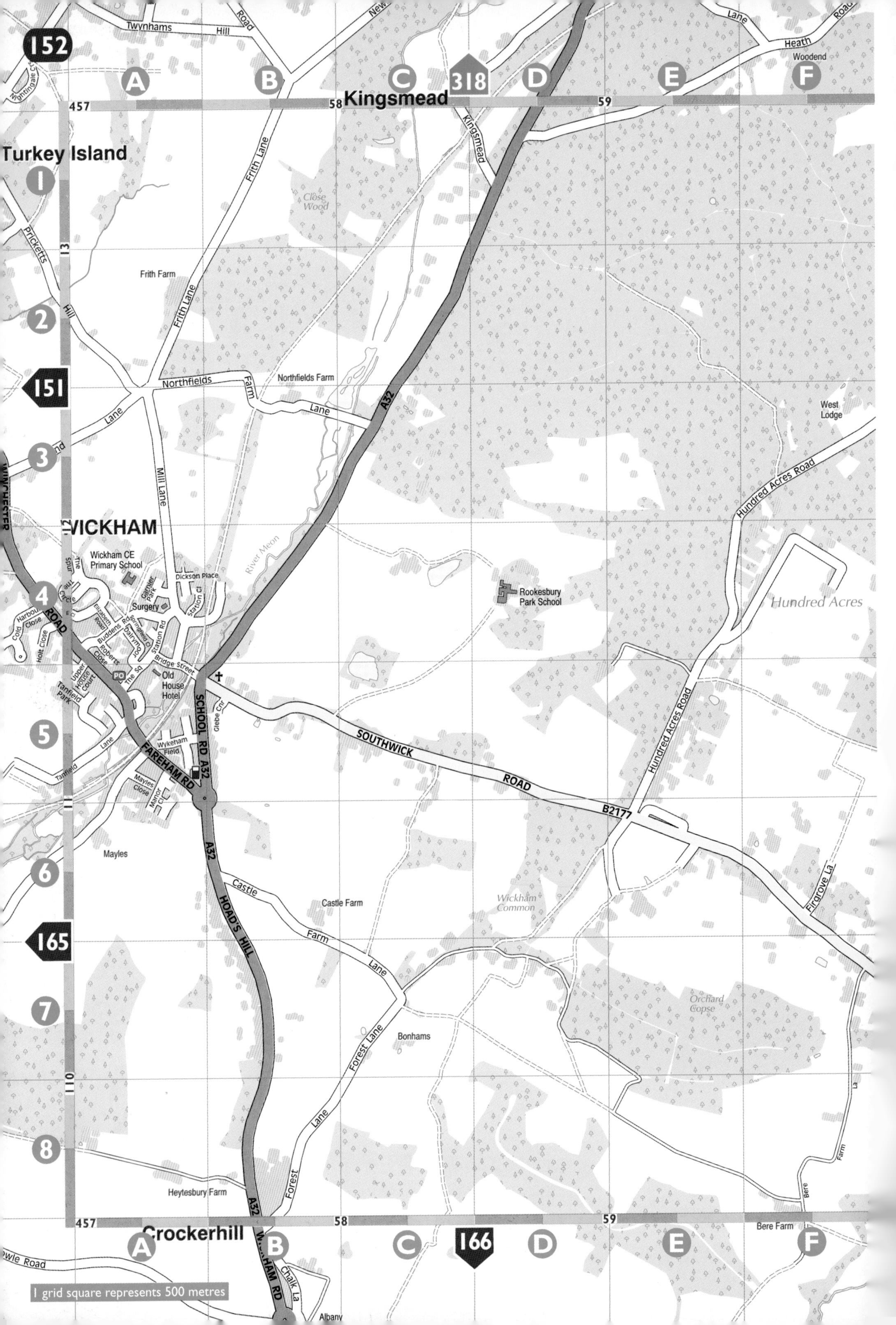
152
151
165
318
166
Kingsmead
Turkey Island
WICKHAM
Crockerhill
Twynhams Hill
Frith Lane
Frith Farm
Close Wood
Northfields Farm
Northfields Lane
Farm Lane
Mill Lane
Prickettts Hill
Wickham CE Primary School
Surgery
Dickson Place
Station Cl
Station Rd
Bridge Street
The Sq
Old House Hotel
River Meon
Rookesbury Park School
SOUTHWICK ROAD
B2177
A32
SCHOOL RD A32
FAREHAM RD
HOAD'S HILL
Glebe Cnr
Tanfield Lane
Tanfield Park
Upper House Court
Holt Close
Roberts Close
Buddens Rd
Wykeham Field
Mayles Close
Manor Cl
Mayles
Castle Farm Lane
Castle Farm
Wickham Common
Forest Lane
Bonhams
Orchard Copse
Heytesbury Farm
Hundred Acres
Hundred Acres Road
West Lodge
Firgrove La
Bere Farm Lane
Bere Farm
Heath Road
Woodend
Chalk La
Albany
A B C D E F
1 2 3 4 5 6 7 8
457 58 59
13 12 11 110
1 grid square represents 500 metres

Liberty
Road
Kiln Hill
Dradfield Lane
Southend Lane
Southend
319
Mensiands Lane
Huntbourn
Church Road
Ingoldfield Lane
Newtown
Hoe Gate
Bent Farm
Hoe Street
Rudley Mill
Hundred Acres Road
Newtown Soberton Infant School
St Martin's Corner
Hoe Moor Farm
Bunns Lane
King's Way
Worlds E
Forest Fm
Trampers Lane
Goathouse Fm
Kiln Lane
Hipley
Forest R
Apless Lane
Little Forest
154
Green Lane
Shoot Hill
North Boarhunt
Hipley Copse
Beckford Lane
Lower Beckford
Quagg Fm
Ashlands
Common Lane
Trampers Lane
South Hants Country Club
Blackhouse Lane
B2177
PO17
Staple Cross
Mitchelland
Lodge Farm
King's Way
Walton Heath
167
G
H
J
K
L
M
60
61
62
63
1
2
3
4
5
6
7
8
13
12
11
110

154
319
168
153
A
B
C
D
E
F
1
2
3
4
5
6
7
8
463
64
65
13
12
11
110
Hoe Gate
Worlds End
Forest Gate
Anthill Common
Furzeley Corner
Forest of Bere
Creech Woods
Place Wood
Bittles Fm
Pithill Fm
Rookwood Fm
Bent Farm
Great Ervills Farm
Crabbick Farm
Inhams
Glasspool
Denmead Health Centre
Park Road
Works
Bunkers Hill
The Smithy
The Orchard
The Spinney
Paddock End
Parklands Business Park
Furzeley Golf Club
Golf Course
Lower Beckford
Lovelocks
Creech Farm
Belney Farm
Mitchelland
Closewood
Sheepwash Farm
Wanstead Farm
King's Way
Mensiands Lane
HAMBLEDON ROAD
B2150
Rushmere Lane
Wayfarer's Walk
Kidmore Lane
Uplands Road
Broad Lane
Upr Crabbick La
Thompsons Lane
Anthill Cl
School Lane
Inhams Lane
Lower Crabbick Lane
Forest Road
Apless Lane
Beckford Lane
Harvest Road
Green Lane
Southwick Road
Hawthorn Rd
Yew Tree Gdns
Lowland Rd
Woodrow
Roman Gn
Creech View
The Willows
The Meadow
Home Mead
Pond Piece
Cottage Cl
Ashling Cl
Ashling Park Road
Fairfield
Ashling Gdns
Chestnut Cl
Bere Road
Field Wy
Brookside Cl
The Spring
Forest Md
Kilnside
Cemetery La
Cem
Furzeley Road
Sheepwash Lane
Newlands
Belney Lane
Pitt
Hill
Denmead Junior School
P07
1 grid square represents 500 metres

G
H
J
K
L
M
320
169
156
66
67
68
69
1
2
3
4
5
6
7
8
12
13
10
Lovedean
Eastland Gate
DENMEAD
Anmore
Wecock
Soake
Cowplain
WATERLOOVILLE
The Crossways
Broadway Fm
Shrover
Meadowlands Junior School
Meadowlands Infant School
Woodlands Education Centre
Rachel Madocks School
Denmead Infant School
Byngs Business Park
Old Park Farm
Sundridge School
Hart Plain Infant School
Hart Plain Junior School
Cowplain Community School
Waterlooville Health Centre
Churchill Yard Industrial Est
Jubilee Business Cen
Brambles Fm Industrial Estate
Pipers Wood Ind Park
Superstore
Works
Waterloo School
Cemetery
Old Mill Lane
Broadway Lane
Day Lane
Coldhill Lane
Lovedean Lane
New Road
White Horse Lane
Edneys Lane
Anmore Lane
Anmore Road
Soake Road
Closewood Road
Newlands Lane
HAMBLEDON ROAD
B2150
LONDON ROAD
A3
MAUREPAS WAY
Hart Plain Avenue
Milton Road
Sunnymead Drive
Haslar Crescent
Windsor Road
Charlesworth Drive
Andrew Crescent
Tennyson Crs
Queen's Road
Highfield Avenue
Rowlands Av
Jubilee Road
Aston Rd
Hulbert Rd
Monarch's Way
Wayfarer's Walk

321
170
155
HORNDEAN
Blendworth
Causeway
Cowplain
Enterprise Industrial Estate
Enterprise Rd
Highcroft Industrial Estate
Horndean FC
Horndean Technology College
Junior School
Infant School
Westfield Industrial Estate
George Gale & Co Ltd Brewery
Horndean Health Centre
Cadlington Ho
Industrial Estate
Superstore
Junction 2
DELL PIECE WEST
DELL PIECE EAST
PORTSMOUTH ROAD
HAVANT ROAD
LONDON ROAD
A3(M)
A3
B2149
Blendworth Common
Golf Course
Padnell Infant School
Padnell Junior School
Waterlooville Golf Club
The Queen's Inclosure
Queens Inclosure Primary School
Surgery
Bell's Copse
Havant Thicket
Staunton Country Park
Dunsbury Hill Fm
Pyle Fm
Hockham Court
Warren Pk Prim Sch
Monarch's Way
Lovedean Lane
Padnell Road
Park Lane
Castle Road
Rowlands
Horndean Road
Five Heads Road
Catherington Lane
Victory Avenue
Crouch Lane
Lovedean Lane
Hazleton Way
Greenfield Crescent
Padnell Avenue
Tempest Avenue
Hulbert Road
1 grid square represents 500 metres

G   H   J   322   K   L   M

72   73   74   75

I

13

2

South
Holt Fm

Old
Idsworth

Wick Fm

Idsworth Ho

Woodhouse Lane

Road

Road

Treadwheel   Road

Woodhouse

Ashcroft
Lane

Finchdean

Dean
Lane

Sussex Border Path

Finchdean Rd

3

12

**Deanlane
End**

Wa
Do

Magpie Rd

Woodhouse Lane

Drews
Farm

4

Monarch's Way

The
Holt

Wellsworth

Sussex Border Path

Finchdean Rd

5

Stan

Monarch's Way

Links Lane

Holt Gdns

Bowes

Wellsworth La

Wellswood
Gdns

Meadowlands

Broad Ct

Uplands Road

Greatfield
Way

The Peak

Hill

Path

The Peak

The Fairway

Surgery

Golf Course

Links

PH   PO   PH

Lane

Finchdean   Road

Rowland's
Castle Station

6

11

Sussex Border Path

Monarch's Way

**Rowland's
Castle**

B2149

Kings Cl

Castle

Royal Gdns

Castle   Road

**Red
Hill**

Rednill Road

Nightingale Cl

Kingfisher Cl

Blackbird Rd

Brambling
Rd

Mallard
Road

Hazeldean Dr

Hill Brow Cl

The
Drift

College Cl

Sandstead Cl

Tanglea

Glen Dr

Glen Dr

Woodberry
La

Horsepasture
Farm

Sussex

Border

Path

7

10

MANOR LODGE ROAD

Durrants

St Johns Primary
School Rowlands
Castle

Sussex   Border   Path

Holme
Farm

8

B2149

DURRANTS ROAD

WHICHERS GATE ROAD

B2148

Durrants
Gdns

Whichers
Cl

Innkeeper's
Lodge Hotel

LC

Stubbe

72   73   74   75

G   H   **171**   K   L   M

Staunton Way

Staunton Park

COMLEY

West Sussex County
Hampshire County

Woodberry Lane

Path

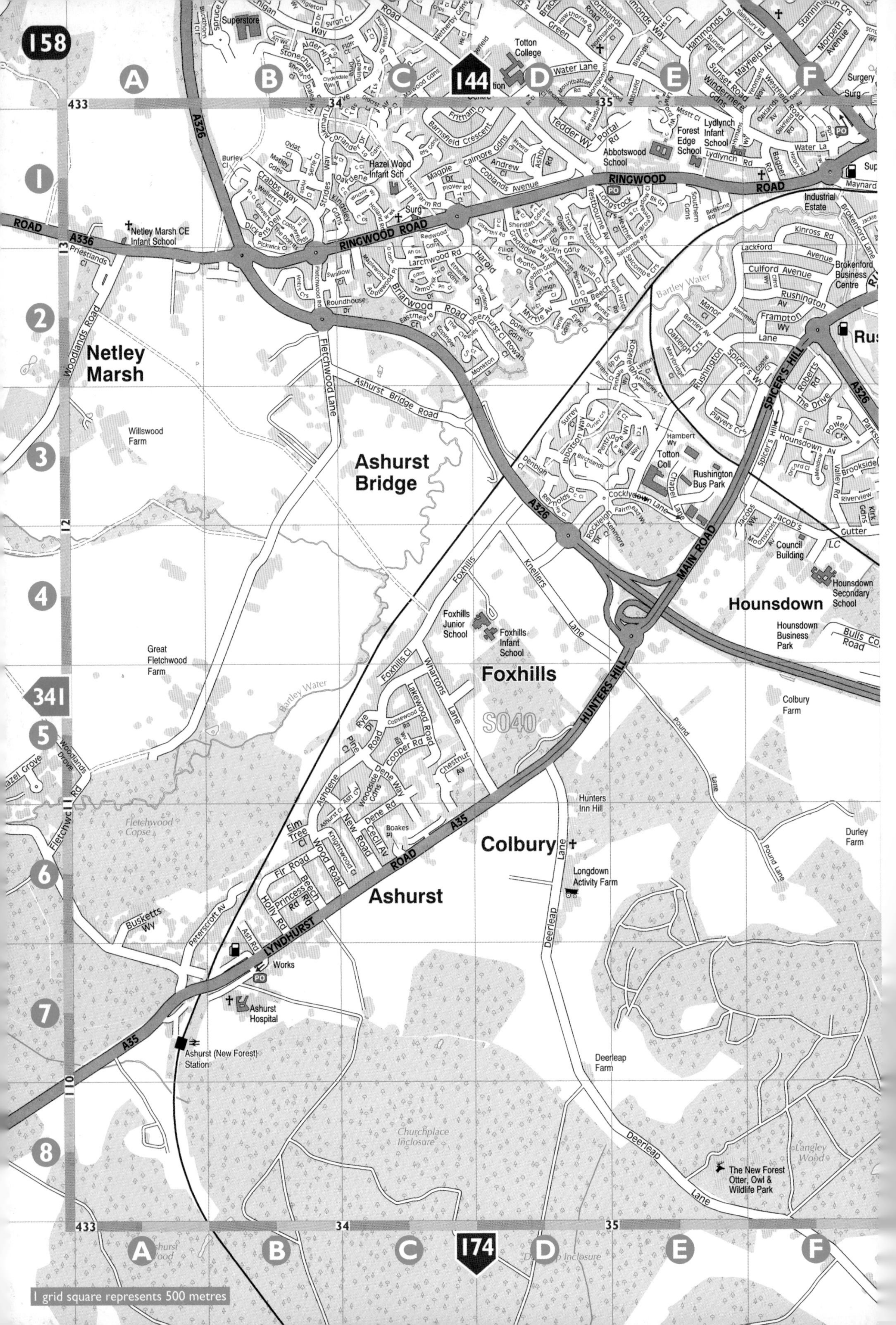
158
144
341
174
A
B
C
D
E
F
1
2
3
4
5
6
7
8
433
34
35
13
12
11
110
Netley Marsh
Ashurst Bridge
Foxhills
Colbury
Ashurst
Hounsdown
Totton College
Hazel Wood Infant Sch
Netley Marsh CE Infant School
Forest Edge School
Abbotswood School
Lydlynch Infant School
Industrial Estate
Brokenford Business Centre
Totton Coll
Rushington Bus Park
Council Building
Hounsdown Secondary School
Hounsdown Business Park
Foxhills Junior School
Foxhills Infant School
Willswood Farm
Great Fletchwood Farm
Colbury Farm
Durley Farm
Hunters Inn Hill
Longdown Activity Farm
Deerleap Farm
Ashurst Hospital
Ashurst (New Forest) Station
Works
Churchplace Inclosure
Fletchwood Copse
Langley Wood
The New Forest Otter, Owl & Wildlife Park
Superstore
Surgery
RINGWOOD ROAD
A336
A326
A35
LYNDHURST ROAD
MAIN ROAD
SPICER'S HILL
HUNTERS HILL
Fletchwood Lane
Ashurst Bridge Road
Woodlands Road
Deerleap Lane
Pound Lane
Kneller's Lane
Bartley Water
SO40
1 grid square represents 500 metres

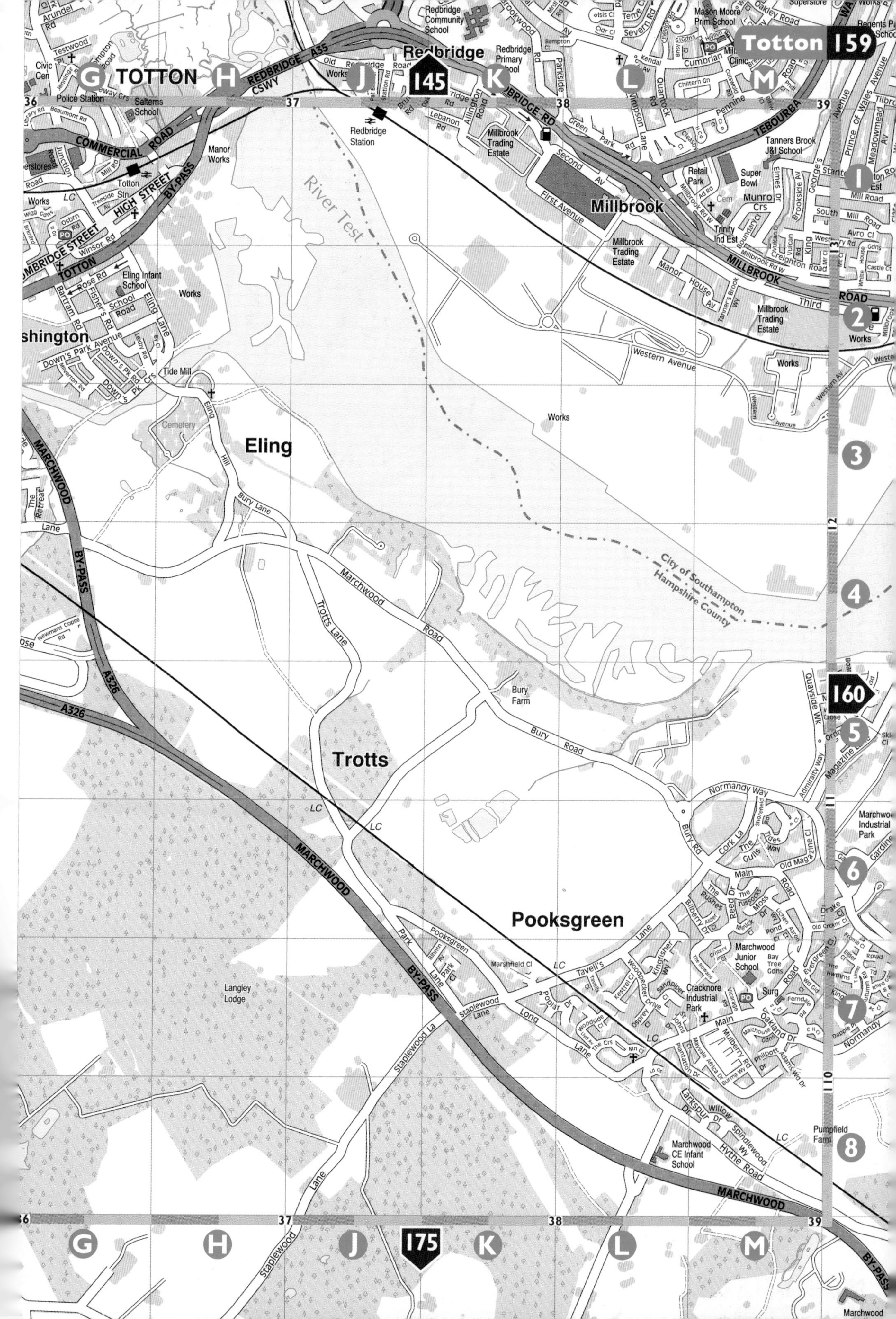
TOTTON
Redbridge
Millbrook
Eling
Trotts
Pooksgreen
145
160
175
G
H
J
K
L
M
1
2
3
4
5
6
7
8
36
37
38
39
13
12
11
110
Redbridge Community School
Redbridge Primary School
Mason Moore Prim School
Civic Cen
Police Station
Salterns School
Testwood
Arundel Rd
REDBRIDGE CSWY
A35
COMMERCIAL ROAD
HIGH STREET
BY-PASS
Totton Stn
Manor Works
Redbridge Station
River Test
Millbrook Trading Estate
Second Av
First Avenue
REDBRIDGE RD
Green Park Rd
Simpson Lane
Quantock Rd
Pennine Rd
Severn Rd
Kendal
Cumbrian
Oakley Road
TEBOURBA
Tanners Brook J&I School
Retail Park
Super Bowl
Munro Crs
Trinity Ind Est
Cem
Prince of Wales Avenue
Meadowmead Av
Mill Road
South Mill Road
Avro Cl
Creighton Road
MILLBROOK ROAD
Third
Manor House Av
Tanner's Brook Wy
Works
Western Avenue
Western Av
Eling Infant School
School Road
Eling Lane
Rose Rd
Bartram Rd
Fisher's Rd
Down's Park Avenue
Down's Pk Rd
Down's Pk Crs
Tide Mill
Cemetery
Eling Hill
Bury Lane
Marchwood Road
Trotts Lane
City of Southampton
Hampshire County
MARCHWOOD BY-PASS
A326
The Retreat
Newmans Copse Rd
Bury Farm
Bury Road
Normandy Way
Bury Rd
Cork La
The Gulls
Tides Way
Old Magazine Cl
Main Road
Admiralty Way
Quayside Wk
Magazine Lane
Marchwood Industrial Park
Pooksgreen
Park Lane
Park Cl
Marshfield Cl
Tavell's Lane
Kingfisher Wy
Woodpecker Drive
Kestrel Cl
Osprey
Sandpiper
Poplar Dr
Woodside Cl
The Crs
Long Lane
Staplewood Lane
Staplewood La
Langley Lodge
Marchwood Junior School
Bay Tree Gdns
Cracknore Industrial Park
Surg
Main Rd
Oakland Dr
Mulberry Rd
Africa Dr
Plantation Dr
Philpott Dr
Adams Wd Dr
Larkspur Dr
Willow Dr
Spindlewood Wy
Hythe Road
Marchwood CE Infant School
Pumpfield Farm
MARCHWOOD
LC
Evergreen Cl
Drake
Normandy
Marchwood

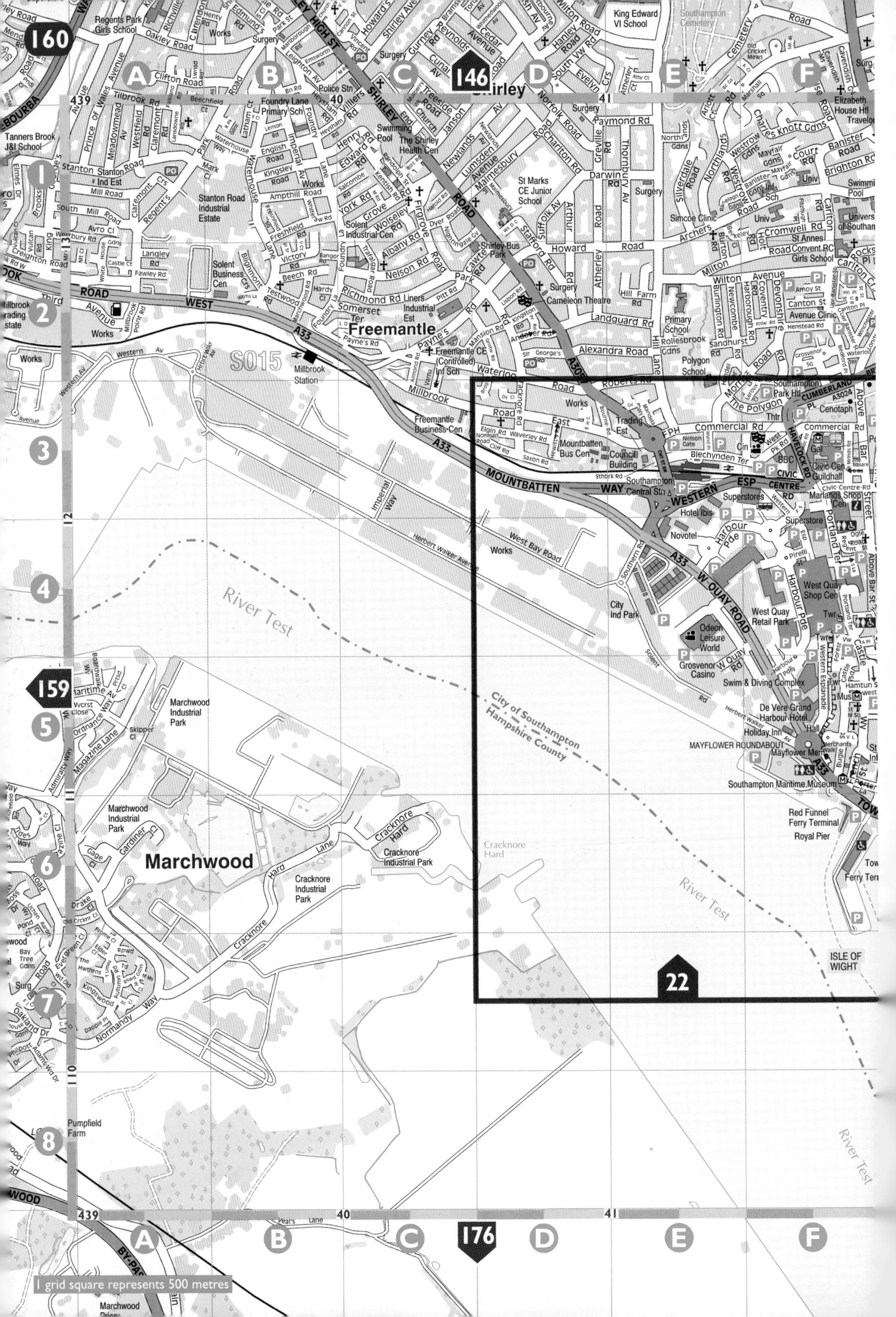
160
146
159
22
176
A
B
C
D
E
F
1
2
3
4
5
6
7
8
439
40
41
112
111
110
113
Regents Park Girls School
Oakley Road
Clifton Road
Tilbrook Rd
Foundry Lane Primary Sch
Police Stn
Shirley
Shirley High St
Howard's
Shirley Av
Surgery
King Edward VI School
Southampton Cemetery
Cemetery Road
Elizabeth House Htl
Tanners Brook J&I School
Stanton Road
Stanton Ind Est
Mill Road
Stanton Road Industrial Estate
Prince of Wales Avenue
Meadowmead
Westfield
Claremont Rd
English Road
Kingsley Road
Ampthill Road
Imperial Av
Swimming Pool
The Shirley Health Cen
Newlands
Lumsden Avenue
Malmesbury
St Marks CE Junior School
Paymond Rd
Darwin Rd
Thornbury Av
Greville Rd
Surgery
Northlands Road
Silverdale Road
Charles Knott Gdns
Banister Road
Brighton Rd
Univ
Swimming Pool
Archers Road
Simcoe Clinic
Cromwell Rd
St Annes Road Convent RC Girls School
Howard Road
Suffolk Av
Arthur Rd
Stafford Rd
Shirley Bus Park
Solent Industrial Cen
Nelson Rd
Victory Rd
Beech Rd
Richmond Rd
Liners Industrial Est
Solent Business Cen
Langley Rd
Fawley Rd
Avro Cl
Creighton Road
West Road
Third Avenue
Millbrook Trading Estate
Works
Western Av
Millbrook Station
SO15
A33
Freemantle
Somerset Ter
Payne's Rd
Freemantle CE (Controlled) Inf Sch
Waterloo Road
Millbrook
Freemantle Business Cen
Cameleon Theatre
Hill Farm Rd
Landguard Rd
Alexandra Road
Primary School
Rollesbrook Gdns
Polygon School
Wilton Avenue
Milton Road
Canton St
Avenue Clinic
Southampton Park Htl
The Polygon
Cumberland Pl
A3024
Cenotaph
Above Bar
Commercial Rd
Blechynden Ter
Nelson Gate
Cin
BBC
Civic Cen
Guildhall
Havelock Rd
Civic Centre Rd
Marlands Shop Cen
Mountbatten Bus Cen
Council Building
Trading Est
Cracknore Rd
Elgin Rd
Waverley Rd
Cliff Rd
Saxon Rd
Mountbatten Way
Southampton Central Stn
Western Esp
Superstores
Hotel Ibis
Novotel
Harbour Pde
Superstore
Portland Ter
West Quay Shop Cen
West Quay Retail Park
Southern Rd
City Ind Park
Odeon Leisure World
Grosvenor Casino
W Quay Rd
Swim & Diving Complex
De Vere Grand Harbour Hotel
Holiday Inn
Mayflower Roundabout
Mayflower Mem
Southampton Maritime Museum
Red Funnel Ferry Terminal
Royal Pier
Town Ferry Terminal
Isle of Wight
West Quay Road
West Bay Road
Imperial Way
Herbert Walker Avenue
Works
River Test
City of Southampton
Hampshire County
Cracknore Hard
Marchwood Industrial Park
Marchwood Industrial Park
Marchwood
Gardiner Cl
Gage Cl
Magazine Lane
Ordnance Way
Maritime Av
Skipper Cl
Admiralty Way
Cracknore Hard Lane
Cracknore Industrial Park
Cracknore Industrial Park
Cracknore Road
Kingswood
Normandy Way
Evergreen Cl
Oakland Dr
Pumpfield Farm
Veal's Lane
By-Pass
Marchwood Priory
Surg
1 grid square represents 500 metres

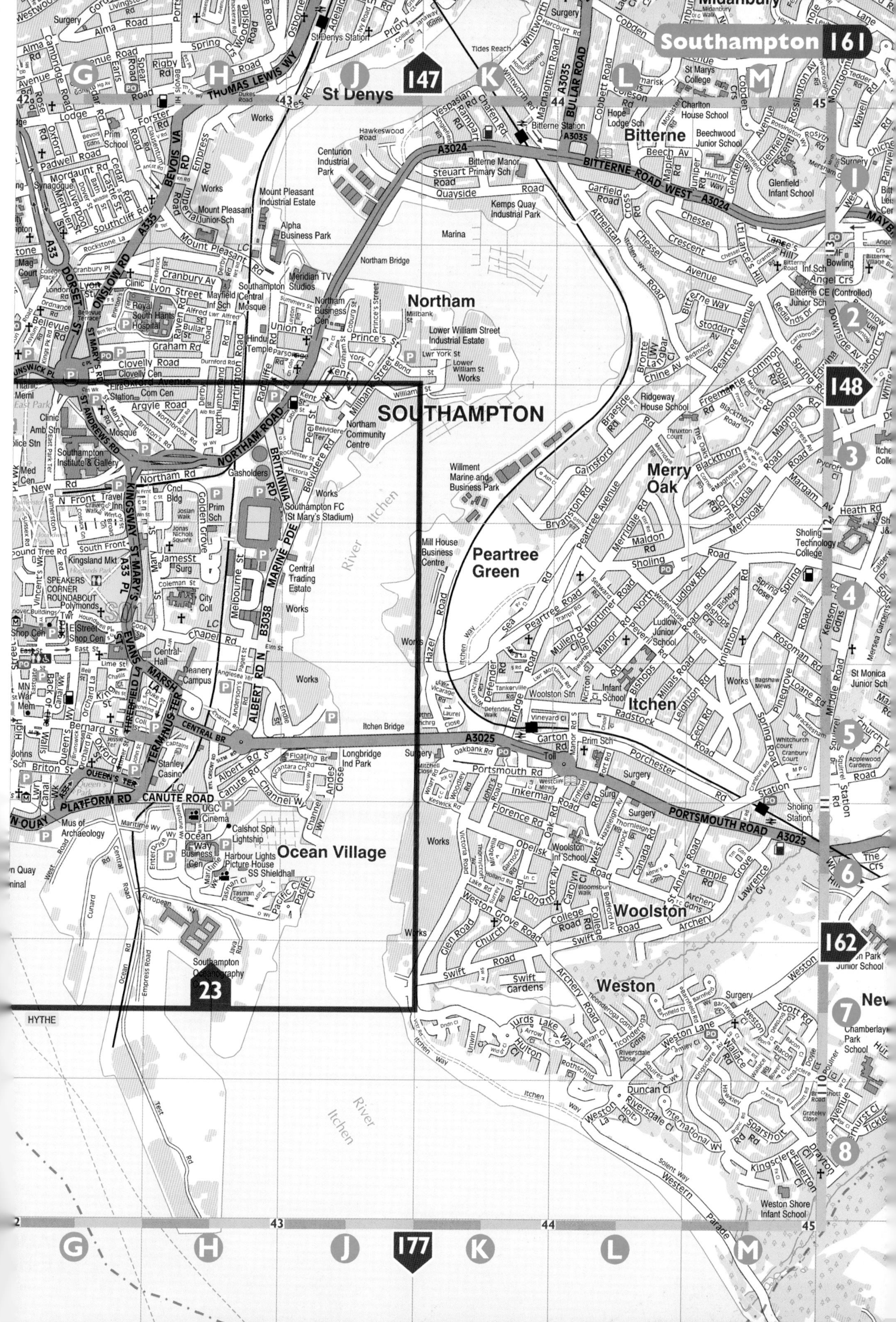

Southampton 161
St Denys
Bitterne
Northam
SOUTHAMPTON
Merry Oak
Peartree Green
Itchen
Ocean Village
Woolston
Weston
River Itchen
HYTHE
147
148
162
177
23
BITTERNE ROAD WEST
BULLAR ROAD
THOMAS LEWIS WY
BEVOIS VA
DORSET ST
ONSLOW RD
NORTHAM ROAD
BRITANNIA RD
MARINE PDE
ALBERT RD N
CENTRAL BR
KINGSWAY
ST MARY'S PL
EVANS ST
TERMINUS TER
PLATFORM RD
CANUTE ROAD
PORTSMOUTH ROAD
Southampton FC (St Mary's Stadium)
Southampton Oceanography Centre
Southampton Institute & Gallery
Royal South Hants Hospital
Mus of Archaeology
Calshot Spit Lightship
Harbour Lights Picture House
SS Shieldhall
Mount Pleasant Industrial Estate
Centurion Industrial Park
Alpha Business Park
Kemps Quay Industrial Park
Meridian TV Studios
Willment Marine and Business Park
Mill House Business Centre
Central Trading Estate
Longbridge Ind Park
Sholing Technology College
Sholing Station
Woolston Stn
Bitterne Station
St Denys Station
Itchen Bridge
G
H
J
K
L
M
1
2
3
4
5
6
7
8

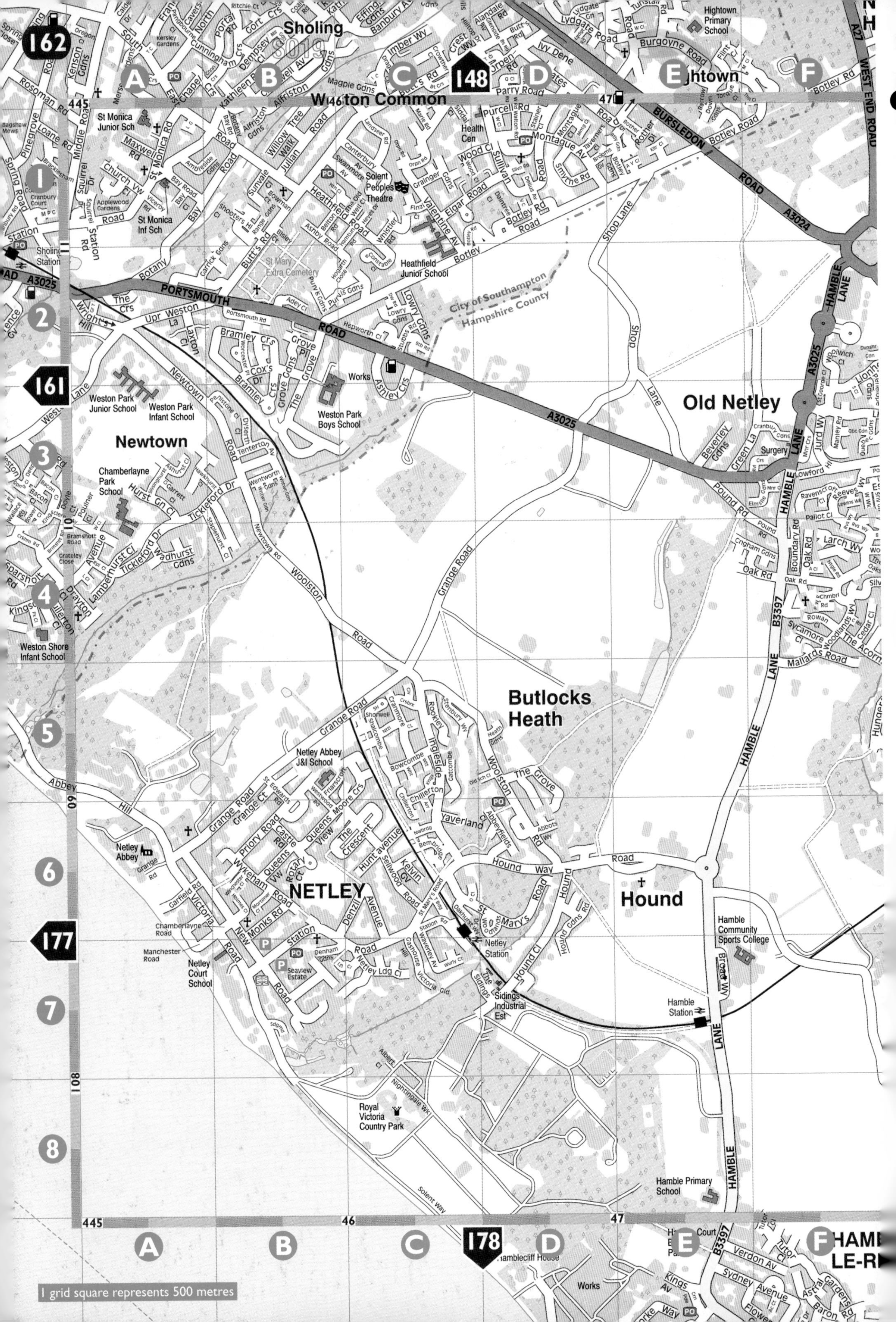
162
148
161
177
178
Sholing
SO19
Weston Common
Bitterne (partial, cut off): "ghtown"
Hightown Primary School
Newtown
Old Netley
Butlocks Heath
NETLEY
Hound
St Monica Junior Sch
St Monica Inf Sch
Sholing Station
Solent Peoples Theatre
Heathfield Junior School
St Mary Extra Cemetery
Health Cen
Weston Park Junior School
Weston Park Infant School
Weston Park Boys School
Works
Chamberlayne Park School
Weston Shore Infant School
Netley Abbey J&I School
Netley Abbey
Netley Court School
Netley Station
Sidings Industrial Est
Royal Victoria Country Park
Hamble Community Sports College
Hamble Station
Hamble Primary School
Hamblecliff House
City of Southampton
Hampshire County
PORTSMOUTH ROAD
A3025
A3024
A27
BURSLEDON ROAD
WEST END ROAD
HAMBLE LANE
B3397
Botley Road
Grange Road
Woolston Road
Newtown Road
Hound Road
Shop Lane
Pound Rd
Solent Way
Victoria Road
Station Road
Upr Weston La
Spring Road
Middle Road
Kathleen Rd
Manchester Road
Chamberlayne Road
Surgery
A B C D E F
1 2 3 4 5 6 7 8
445 46 47
110 109 108
1 grid square represents 500 metres

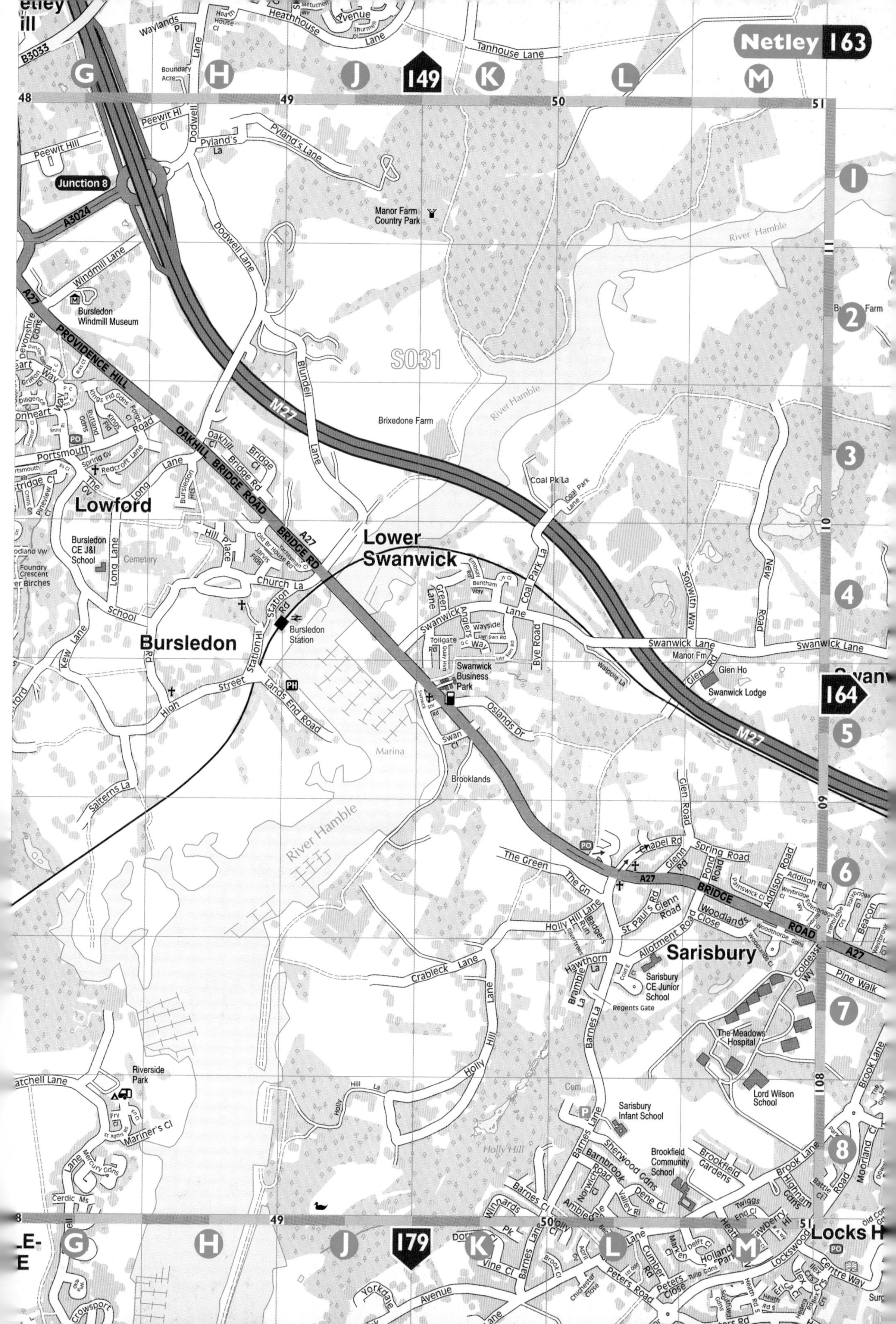
149
164
179
Lowford
Bursledon
Lower Swanwick
Sarisbury
Locks H
Junction 8
A3024
B3033
A27
M27
PROVIDENCE HILL
OAKHILL BRIDGE ROAD
BRIDGE RD
BRIDGE ROAD
Peewit Hill
Peewit Hl Cl
Waylands Pl
Heathhouse Lane
Tanhouse Lane
Boundary Acre
Dodwell Lane
Pyland's La
Pyland's Lane
Manor Farm Country Park
River Hamble
Windmill Lane
Bursledon Windmill Museum
SO31
Blundell Lane
Brixedone Farm
Coal Pk La
Coal Park Lane
Coal Park La
Portsmouth Road
Redcroft Lane
Long Lane
Oakhill
Bridge Rd
Bridge Cl
Bursledon Hts
Hill Place
Cemetery
Bursledon CE J&I School
Church La
School Lane
Station Rd
Station Hl
Bursledon Station
High Street
Lands End Road
Kew Lane
Salterns La
Green Lane
Bentham Way
Swanwick Lane
Anglers Way
Wayside
Tollgate
Swanwick Business Park
Oslands Dr
Swan Cl
Brooklands
Marina
Bye Road
Walpole La
Sopwith Way
New Road
Manor Fm
Glen Rd
Glen Ho
Swanwick Lodge
Glen Road
Chapel Rd
Spring Road
Glenn Rd
Pond Road
Addison Road
Addison Rd
The Green
The Gn
Holly Hill Lane
St Paul's Rd
Glenn Road
Woodlands Close
Allotment Road
Hawthorn La
Bramble La
Barnes La
Regents Gate
Sarisbury CE Junior School
The Meadows Hospital
Lord Wilson School
Crableck Lane
Holly Hill Lane
Holly Hill La
Holly Hill
Riverside Park
Mariner's Cl
Mercury Gdns
Cerdic Ms
Sarisbury Infant School
Brookfield Community School
Brookfield Gardens
Sherwood Gdns
Barnbrook Road
Norwich Cl
Dene Cl
Barnes Cl
Brook Lane
Highnam Gdns
Pine Walk
Coldeast Wy
Beacon
Moorland Cl
Battle Cl
Twiggs End Cl
Vine Cl
Peters Road
Peters Close
Holland Park
Lockswood
Centre Way
Yorkdale
Crowsport
Avenue
Cem
Bursledon
Swanwick
Swanwick Lane

164
150
163
180
Curbridge
Burridge
Whiteley
Swanwick
Park Gate
Titchfield Park
Locks Heath
Barn Farm
Bury Farm
Ridge Farm
Burridge Farm
Burridge Social & Sports Club
Eyers Down Farm
Ridge La
Burridge Road
BOTLEY ROAD
A3051
Whiteley Lane
Green Lane
Swanwick Lane
New Road
Bluebell Wy
Thyme Avenue
Saffron Way
Rookery Avenue
Yew Tree Drive
Whiteley Way
Parkway
Solent Hotel & Spa
Whiteley Primary School
Park Gate Business Cen
Swanwick Stn
Chandlers Way
Junction 9
M27
A27
BRIDGE RD
SOUTHAMPTON RD
Station Rd
Pine Walk
Brook Lane
Barratt Ind Park
Apple Industrial Est
Council Building
Park Gate Primary School
Travel Inn
Segensworth Road
Witherbed Lane
Barnes Way
Wallis Road
Brunel Way
Concorde Way
Betty's Drive
Lady Betty's Drive
Mollison Ri
Skylark Meadows
Park Farm
Lee Ground Coppice
Talisman Business Centre
Lord Wilson School
Hunts Pond Road
Lockswood
Church Road
Segensworth
Works
1 grid square represents 500 metres

Whiteley 165
151
152
166
181
Tapnage
Knowle Village
Funtley
Lee Ground
Hill Park
Titchfield Lane
Biddenfield Lane
Mayles Lane
Knowle Road
Fontley Road
River Lane
Funtley Road
Ironmill Lane
Springles Lane
Lavey's Lane
River Meon
M27
Quob Farm
Webbs Land
Cold Harbour Farm
Wickham Park Golf Club
Golf Course
Park Place
Dimmock's Moor
Botley Wood
Flagpond Copse
Fiddlers Green
Cemetery
Knowle Farm
Mayles Corner
Great Funtley Farm
Pegham Industrial Park
Lakeside
The Waters
Kneller Court
Dean Farm Estate
Ashlyn Farm
Garden Centre
Honey Lane
Orchard Lea Infant School
Orchard Lea Junior School
Oak Meadow Primary School
Henry Cort Community
Hill Park Clinic
Red Barn Lane
Kiln Road
Highlands Rd
Mayles
Tanfield
Lechlade Gdns
Kingston Gdns
Thames Dr
High Mead
Funtley Hill
Knowle Gate
Charity View
Osborne Place
Victoria Mews
North Square
Central Square
Greater Horseshoe Wy
Lesser Horseshoe Cl
Fareham Pk
Whinchat Cl
Wynton Way
Hillson
Frostshole Cl
Mallory Crs
Maylings Farm Road
Miller Dr
Crawford Dr

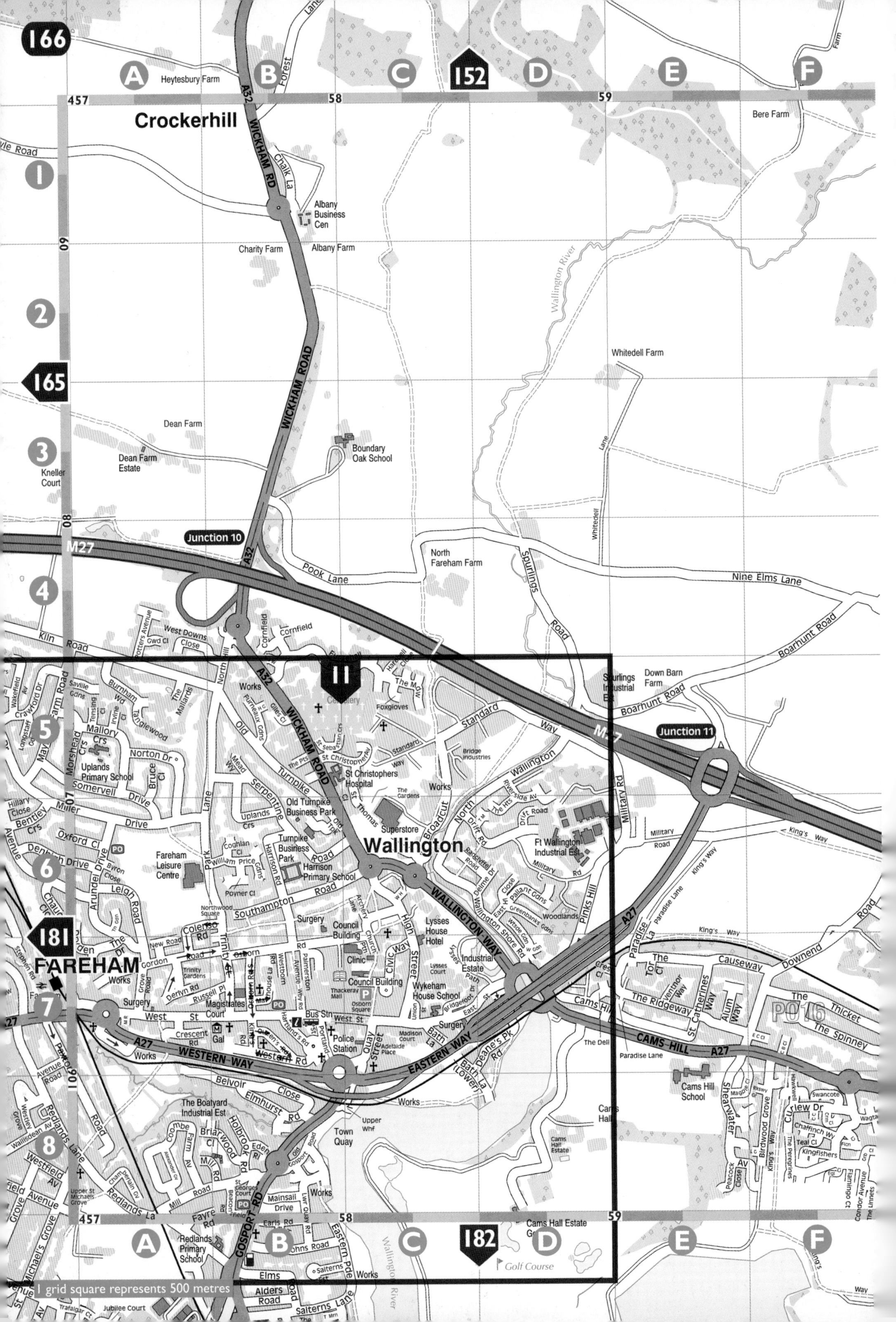
166
152
165
181
182
11
Crockerhill
Wallington
FAREHAM
Junction 10
Junction 11
WICKHAM ROAD
WALLINGTON WAY
WESTERN WAY
EASTERN WAY
CAMS HILL
GOSPORT RD
Heytesbury Farm
Albany Farm
Charity Farm
Dean Farm
Dean Farm Estate
Boundary Oak School
Whitedell Farm
North Fareham Farm
Bere Farm
Spurlings Industrial Est
Down Barn Farm
Pook Lane
Nine Elms Lane
Boarhunt Road
Kiln Road
Fareham Leisure Centre
Uplands Primary School
Harrison Primary School
St Christophers Hospital
Old Turnpike Business Park
Ft Wallington Industrial Est
Council Building
Lysses House Hotel
Wykeham House School
Police Station
Town Quay
The Boatyard Industrial Est
Cams Hill School
Cams Hall Estate
Redlands Primary School
Golf Course
Wallington River
1 grid square represents 500 metres

Mitchelland
B2177
King's Way
153
G
H
J
K
L
M
60
61
62
63
Walton Heath
Blackhouse
Common Lane
Portchester Lane
Bridge St
Back Lane
West Street
Norton Rd
Castle Rd
Norton Cl
North
West Road
Boulter
Main Rd
West Drive
Pins
Fareham Road
Surgery
High St
Southwick
Golf Cour
Manor Farm
Boarhunt
Ashley Down Farm
Boarhunt Road
Offwell Farm
Drove Road
Swivelton Lane
Monument Lane
Portchester Lane
Crooked Walk Lane
168
Royal Armouries Fort Nelson
National Museum of Artillery
Portsdown Hill Road
Nelson Lane
Downend Road
Fort Southwick
Skew Road
M27
Ports Down
Hillsley Road
Kingscote Rd
Almondsbury Road
Tintern Cl
Longdean Cl
Dore Avenue
Waltham Cl
Kilmiston Dr
Weyhill Cl
Rogate Gdns
Skew Road
Portchester Hts
Hill Road
Anson Grove
Carlton Road
Browning Avenue
Keats Av
Chaucer Av
Shelley Av
Dryden Av
Coleridge Rd
Wordsworth Av
Masefield Av
Macaulay Av
Bridges Av
Bude Cl
Falmouth Road
Pentland Rise
Southwick Av
Edward Gv
Seaview Av
Lancaster Cl
Danes Rd
Merlin Gdns
Jute Cl
High Vw
Harting Gdns
Froxfield Gdns
Nyewood Av
Burrton Close
Northern County J&I School
Laverock Lea
Red Barn Rise
Richmond Rise
Hill View Rd
Leith Avenue
Raymond Rd
Newbolt Road
Hillside Crs
Truro Rd
Mousehole Rd
Pendennis Rd
Helston Rd
Camelot Crs
Solent Vw
Hawthorn Cl
Portsview Gdns
Colinton Av
Morningside Av
Mountview Av
Portchester Crematorium
Linden Lea
Portsview Avenue
Jubilee Avenue
Sedgefield Close
Allaway Avenue
Beverston
Deerh
The Pines
The Thicket
Tamar Cl
Winnham Drive
Redwood Dr
Simpson Cl
Red Barn County Primary School
The Hillway
Kelvin Grove
Junior School
Saxon Shore Infant Sch
King Richard Secondary School
Rockingham Wy
A27 PORTCHESTER RD
Ashtead Cl
The Crossway
Portchester Station
New Town
Portsdown Rd
Parry Cl
Neelands Gv
Sullivan Cl
Coltsmead
Beach Dr
Shorehaven
Farm
Romsey Avenue
Quintrell Av
Queensway
The Close
The Kingsway
The Fairway
The Downsway
St Helena Wy
The Leaway
St James Wy
Station Rd
A27
SOUTHAMPTON ROAD
Wicor County Primary School
PORTCHESTER
Portchester Health Centre
Hamilton Rd
City of Portsmouth
Hampshire County
Castle Trading Estate
183
Brenchley Cl
Cornaway La
Westlands Gv
Medical Centre
Vincent Gv
Frobisher Gv
Marlborough Gv
Wellington Gv
Portchester Community School
Sunningdale Rd
Castle Street
Myrtle Avenue
The Keep
Port Solent
Lock View
Council Building
Orchard Grove
White Hart Lane
Cranleigh Rd
Sennen Pl

Mitchelland
154
Place Wood
Wanstead Farm
Belney Lane
Sheepwash Farm
Wayfarer's Walk
Boulter La
Wood Lane
West
Main
West Drive
North
Road E
South Rd
Priory Rd
East Road
Pinsley
Drive
Southwick Park
Naval Recreation Centre
Golf Course
Southwick Park Lake
Pitymoor Lane
Comphouse Farm
Hookheath Farm
Mill Lane
Broomfield House
Purbrook
Potwell
Drove Road
B2177
New Barns
167
Pigeon House Lane
Pigeon House Farm
Fort Southwick
Workshop
North Rd
The Circus Road
Pound Road
Eastfield Rd
Link Road
Hilltop Rd
South Rd
Aerial Rd
South Sp
Hampshire County
City of Portsmouth
James Callaghan Dr
SOUTHWICK ROAD B2177
Widley Walk
Fort Widley
Ports Down
Butterfly Drive
Rockrose Wy
Chalkpit Road
Lime Gv
PORTSDOWN HILL ROAD
B2177 SOUTHWICK HILL ROAD
Leominster Road
Blakemere Crescent
Meadowsweet Way
Harleston Rd
Mablethorpe Road
Lowestoft Rd
Dormington Rd
Bredenbury Crs
Peterborough Rd
Queen Alexandra Hospital
A&E
Cavell Dr
Orkney Rd
Kintyre Rd
Winchcombe Road
Woofferton Road
Deerhurst Crescent
Beverston Road
Collington Crs
Ludlow
Abbeydore Rd
Credenhill Rd
Bromyard Crs
Washbrook Road
Braintree Road
Colchester Rd
Hythe Road
Wymering
Birdlip Rd
Colesbourne Rd
Hempsted Rd
Council Building
Allaway Av
Allaway Avenue
Sudbury Rd
Clacton Rd
Whitstable Rd
Sevenoaks Rd
Portsdown Primary School
Council Building
Paulsgrove
St Pauls Catholic VA Primary School
Paulsgrove Primary School
Cheltenham Rd
Rochford Rd
Westerham Cl
Sundridge Cl
King Richard Secondary School
SOUTHAMPTON ROAD
M27
A3
NORTHERN RD
LONDON RD
Farmlea Rd
Paulsgrove Industrial Centre
A27 SOUTHAMPTON ROAD
Halstead Rd
Bell Rd
Ashurst Rd
Travel Inn
Binnacle Wy
Medina Road
Acorn Business Centre
Freshwater Rd
Surgery
Wayte St
Albert Rd
463
64
65
184
Superstore
Portsmouth Marriott Hotel
WESTERN ROAD
Medina Primary School
Gurnard Rd
Cosham Health Centre
Magdala Rd
Port Way
Newlyn Wy
Port Solent
1 grid square represents 500 metres
Junction 12
Works

WATERLOOVILLE
155
Pipers Wood Ind Park
Elettra Av
Silverthorne Wy
Relay Rd
Works
Aysgarth Road
Winifred Rd
Superstore
Maurepas Way
Hulbert Rd
Spur Rd
Warfield Avenue
Warfield Crs
Waterloo School
Cemetery
Cavendish Dr
Ferndale
Royal Wy
Tempest
Hulbert Rd
Forest End
Norton Cl
Windrush Gdns
Plant Farm
Rockville Dr
Surg
London Road
A3
Hunters Ride
Broadlands Av
Stakes Hill
Elmwood Av
Beechwood Av
Maralyn Avenue
Hurstville Dr
Stakes Hill Infant School
Hulbert Junior School
Laburnum Road
Farm La Cl
Brightside
Waite End Prim School
Mill Rd
Gordon Rd
Cunningham Rd
Beresford Cl
Bell Crs
Walton Cl
Anne Crs
Elizabeth Rd
Springwood Av
Frendstaple
Mountbatten Dr
Corbett Road
Montgomery Wk
Philip Road
Purcell Cl
Elizabeth Wy
Durham Gdns
Lombardy Ri
St Peters Primary School
Oaklands Catholic School
Newlands Farm
Newlands Lane
Southwick House
Purbrook
Purbrook J&I School
Woodlands Gv
Bursledon Rd
Newlands Rd
Purbrook Gdns
Marrels Wd
Heath Road
Purbrook Heath Road
Purbrook CC
Widley Walk
Wayfarer's Wk
Stakes Road
Aldermoor Road
Westbrook Gv
Queens Gv
Shaftesbury Av
Sullivan Way
Britten Wy
Kennedy Close
Holst Wy
Place Crs
Stakes Hill Road
The Crookhorn Community School
Ladybridge Road
Park Farm Rd
Stakes Road
Claremont Gdns
Purbrook Way
Scratchface Ln
Riverside School
Park Avenue
Alameda Wy
Alameda Road
Greenacre Gdns
Morelands Road
Shillinglee
Park Road
St John's Av
Frances Road
Sandy Brow
Fir Copse Rd
Privett Road
Crown Cl
Surgery
Zeus La
Tor Close
Lind Close
Apollo Dr
College Road
170
Serpentine Rd
Lone Valley
Deverell Pl
Highbank Av
Bushy Mead
Widley Gdns
The Thicket
Sovereign La
Farthings Ga
Trojan Wy
Athena Av
Crookhorn Lane
Perseus Place
Atlantis Av
Widley Farm
Victoria Av
Geoffrey Avenue
Applewood Gv
Valley Cl
Widley
Purbrook Park School
Liddiards Way
Oracle Dr
Lily Av
Hillside Av
Parker Gardens
The Crest
The Dale
The Rise
Underdown Av
Morelands Primary School
Portsmouth Golf Club
Jason Pl
College Rd
Icarus Pl
Meadow Edge
The Brow
Golf Course
New Down Lane
Hilltop Crs
Boundary Way
Crest Pth
B2177
Hoylake Rd
Fort Purbrook
Ashley Rd
Peter
Hampshire County
City of Portsmouth
Portsdown Hill Road
Troon Crs
Birkdale Av
Farlington Av
Burnham Road
Ainsdale Rd
Gillman Road
Drayton Lane
Down End Road
Moortown Av
Blake Road
London Road
Chalkridge Road
Cranborne Road
Courtmount Gv
Colville Rd
Widley Road
Carmarthen Avenue
Brecon Avenue
Merthyr Avenue
Aberdare Av
Uplands Road
Portsdown Avenue
Sea View Road
Highlands Rd
Woodfield Avenue
Fortunes Way
Penk Ridge
Grant Road
Solent Infant School
Galt Road
Old Rectory Road
Evelegh Road
Rectory Av
Westways
Auriol
Southdown Rd
Lam Av
Penarth Av
Penrhyn Av
Solent Road
Futcher School
Drayton
Solent Junior School
Dene Hollow
Havant Road
A2030
Farlington
Broad Gdns
Cosham
Havant Road
Medical Cen
Surgery
Aldsworth Cl
Manor Ms
Chilgrove Rd
Havant Rd
Lower Farlington Rd
Waterworks Road
First Avenue
Second Avenue
Almond Cl
Hampshire County
City of Portsmouth
Mulberry La
Court Cl
Carshalton Av
Racton Av
Waverley Rd
Laburnum Av
Station Road
Lealand Road
Copsey Gv
Grove Road
Fitzherbert Rd
Old Farm Way
Shearwater Dr
Binness Way
The Saltings
Hilary Av
J&I School
Mansvid Av
Stuart Avenue
Beaconsfield Avenue
Gofton Av
Braemar Av
Invergordon Av
Lower Drayton Lane
Homefield Rd
Kirton Rd
Springfield School
185
South Road
Zetland Rd
Knight Gdns
Warrior Business Centre
Lonsdale Avenue
Court Lane
Old Manor Way
G
H
J
K
L
M
66
67
68
69
1
2
3
4
5
6
7
8
06
07
08
09

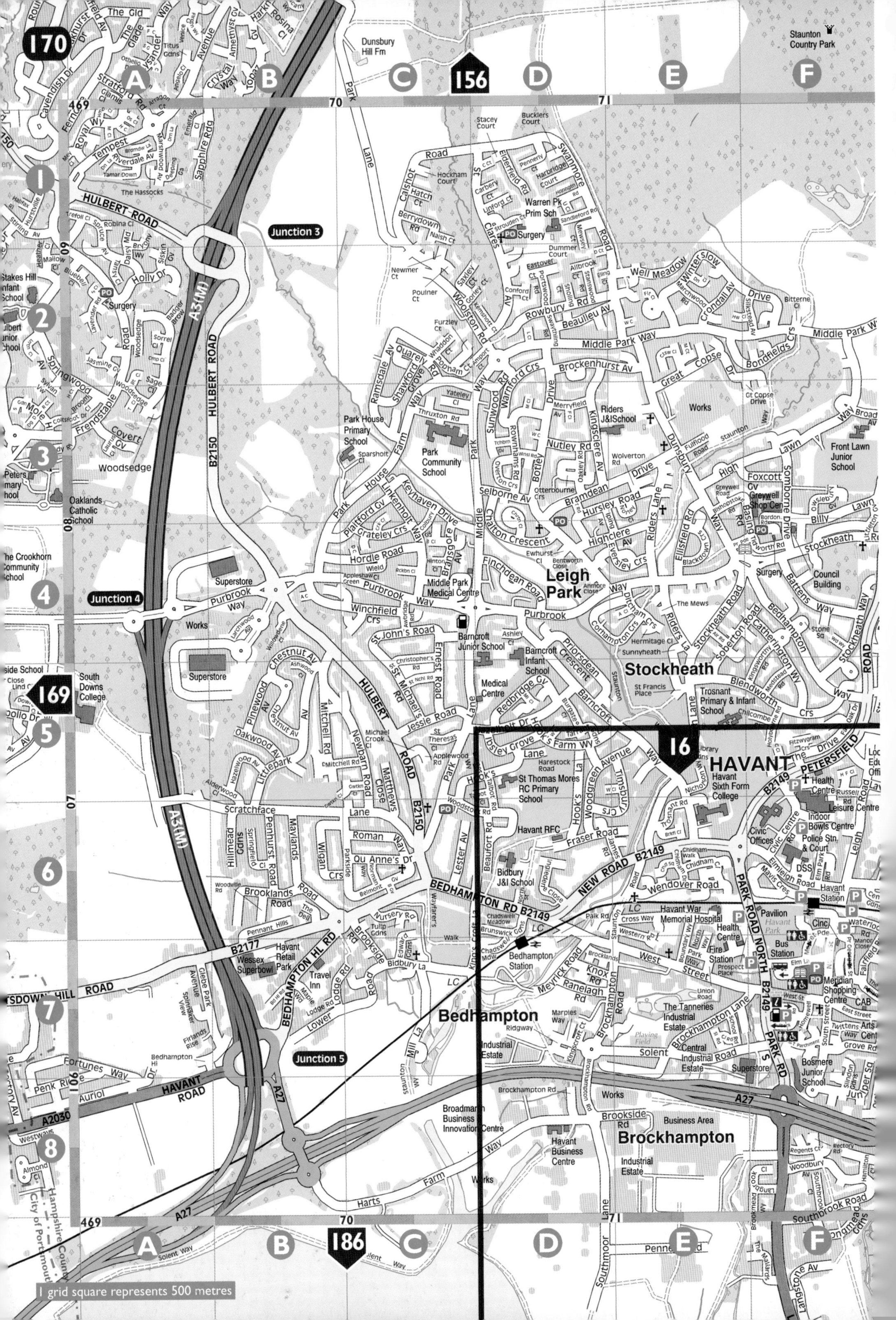

170
156
169
16
186
A
B
C
D
E
F
1
2
3
4
5
6
7
8
469
70
71
Dunsbury Hill Fm
Staunton Country Park
Junction 3
Junction 4
Junction 5
HULBERT ROAD
B2150 HULBERT ROAD
A3(M)
Park Lane
Stacey Court
Bucklers Court
Hockham Court
Calshot Ct
Hatch Ct
Berrydown Rd
Naish Ct
Newmer Ct
Poulner Ct
Warren Pk Prim Sch
Surgery
Dummer Court
Swanmore Road
Well Meadow
Wintershow
Crondall Av
Bitterne Cl
Middle Park Way
Rowbury Rd
Beaulieu Av
Brockenhurst Av
Great Copse Dr
Bondfields Crs
Works
Ct Copse Drive
Riders J&I School
Front Lawn Junior School
Broad Way
Park House Primary School
Park Community School
Thruxton Rd
Yateley Cl
Ramsdale Av
Shawford Grove
Quarely Rd
Sunwood Rd
Warnford Crs
Merryfield Av
Kingsclere Av
Nutley Rd
Botley Dr
Wolverton Rd
Bramdean Drive
Dunsbury Way
Staunton Road
High Lawn Way
Foxcott Gv
Greywell Shop Cen
Sombome Drive
Billy Lawn
Stockheath Rd
Council Building
Battens Way
Chalton Crescent
Selborne Av
Hursley Road
Highclere Av
Eversley Crs
Riders Lane
Ellisfield Rd
Blackdown Crs
Leigh Park
Finchdean Road
Purbrook Way
The Mews
Ditcham Crs
Cornampton Crs
Stockheath
Stockheath Road
Soberton Road
Catherington Wy
Bedhampton Way
Blendworth Crs
Trosnant Primary & Infant School
St Francis Place
Hermitage Cl
Sunnyheath
Stockheath Way
Keyhaven Drive
Linkenholt Way
Plaitford Gv
Grateley Crs
Hordle Road
Bransgore Av
Middle Park Medical Centre
Winchfield Crs
St John's Road
Barncroft Junior School
Barncroft Infant School
Ashley Cl
Priorsdean Crescent
Medical Centre
Redbridge Gv
Ernest Road
Superstore
Works
South Downs College
Chestnut Av
Pinewood Av
Oakwood Av
Mitchell Rd
Newbarn Road
Matthews Close
HULBERT ROAD B2150
Jessie Road
St Theresas Cl
Applewood Rd
Little Park
Hook's Farm Wy
Harestock Road
St Thomas Mores RC Primary School
Woodgreen Avenue
Timsbury Crs
Havant RFC
Fraser Road
HAVANT
Havant Sixth Form College
Trosnant Rd
Nicholson Wy
PETERSFIELD RD B2149
Health Centre
Leisure Centre
Civic Offices
Civic Centre Rd
Indoor Bowls Centre
Police Stn. & Court
DSS
Elm Park Rd
Emlelgh Road
Leigh Road
Scratchface Lane
Penhurst Road
Maylands
Hillmead Gdns
Wigan Crs
Roman Way
Qu Anne's Dr
Brooklands Road
Lester Av
Beaufort Rd
Bidbury J&I School
NEW ROAD B2149
Wendover Road
BEDHAMPTON RD B2149
Chadswell Meadow
Brunswick Gdns
Bedhampton Station
Havant War Memorial Hospital
Health Centre
Fire Station
Prospect Place
West Street
Havant Station
Pavilion
Havant Park
Bus Station
Meridian Shopping Centre
CAB
East Street
Arts Cent
South Street
Twittens Way
Grove Rd
Bosmere Junior School
PARK ROAD NORTH
B2149 PARK RD S
Pennant Hills
B2177
Havant Retail Park
Wessex Superbowl
Travel Inn
BEDHAMPTON HL RD
Brookside Rd
Nursery Rd
Bidbury La
Lower Lodge Rd
Mill La
Bedhampton
Ridgway
Industrial Estate
Meyrick Road
Knox Rd
Ranelagh Rd
Brockhampton Road
The Tanneries Industrial Estate
Playing Field
Brockhampton Lane
Central Industrial Estate
Solent Road
Superstore
Union Road
Woodsedge
Oaklands Catholic School
The Crookhorn Community School
Stakes Hill Infant School
Springwood Av
Frendstaple
Covert Gv
Mole Hl
Tempest Av
Riverdale Av
The Hassocks
Tamar Down
Sapphire Rdg
Stratford Rd
Cavendish Dr
The Glade
Crystal Way
Avenue
Holly Dr
Badger Brow
HULBERT ROAD
PORTSDOWN HILL ROAD
Glebe Park Avenue
Firlands Rise
Bedhampton Hl
Fortunes Way
Penk Ridge
Auriol
HAVANT ROAD
A2030
A27
Almond Cl
Hampshire County
City of Portsmouth
Broadmarsh Business Innovation Centre
Havant Business Centre
Brockhampton Rd
Works
Brookside Rd
Business Area
Brockhampton
Industrial Estate
Harts Farm Way
Solent Way
Southmoor Lane
Penner Rd
The Mallards
Langbrook Cl
Woodbury Av
Southbrook Road
Rectory Rd
Regents Ct
Langstone Av
1 grid square represents 500 metres

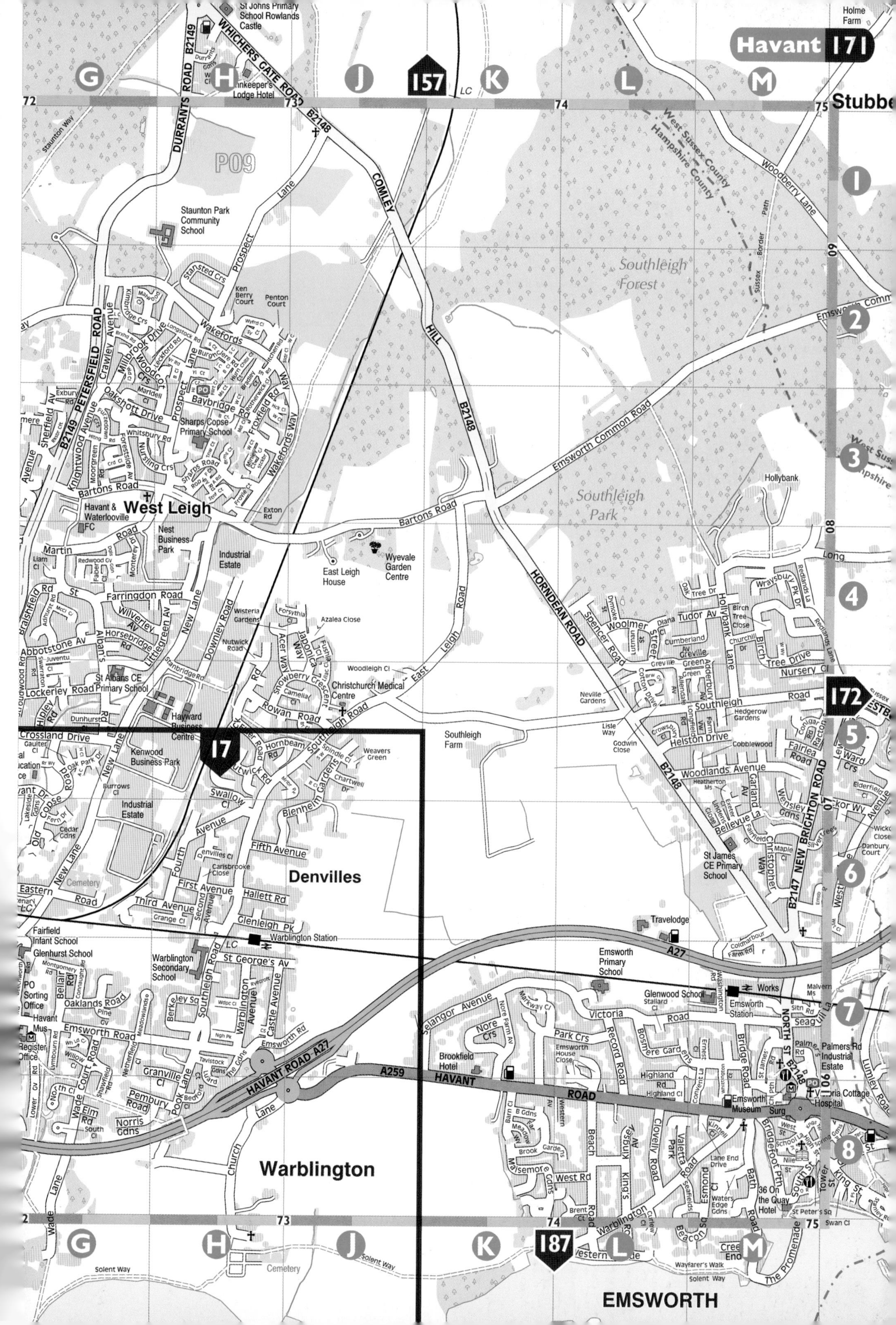

West Leigh
Denvilles
Warblington
EMSWORTH
Southleigh Forest
Southleigh Park
Stubbe
Staunton Park Community School
Sharps Copse Primary School
Havant & Waterlooville FC
Nest Business Park
Industrial Estate
East Leigh House
Wyevale Garden Centre
Christchurch Medical Centre
St Albans CE Primary School
Hayward Business Centre
Kenwood Business Park
Southleigh Farm
St James CE Primary School
Travelodge
Emsworth Primary School
Glenwood School
Emsworth Station
Warblington Station
Warblington Secondary School
Fairfield Infant School
Glenhurst School
Brookfield Hotel
Emsworth Museum
Victoria Cottage Hospital
36 On the Quay Hotel
Palmers Rd Industrial Estate
Innkeeper's Lodge Hotel
St Johns Primary School Rowlands Castle
Hollybank
Holme Farm
West Sussex County
Hampshire County
PETERSFIELD ROAD
HORNDEAN ROAD
COMLEY HILL
Emsworth Common Road
Bartons Road
HAVANT ROAD A27
A259 HAVANT ROAD
NEW BRIGHTON ROAD
NORTH ST
Solent Way
157
17
172
187

172
171
187
A
B
C
D
E
F
1
2
3
4
5
6
7
8
475
76
77
08
06
105
Westbourne
New Brighton
Lumley
Hermitage
Breach
Southbourne
Prinsted
Woodmanc
Nutbo
Aldsworth
Monk's Farm
Hollybank
West Sussex County
Hampshire County
Commonside
Westbourne County Primary School
Cemetery
Cemetery Lane
FOXBURY LANE
B2147
Common Road
Woodmancote Lane
Duffield Lane
Walnut Tree Dr
South La
Long Copse Lane
School Lane
River Street
North St
Mill Road
Edgell Rd
Kingfisher Drive
Mallard Wy
Church Rd
WESTBOURNE ROAD
NEW BRIGHTON ROAD
Sussex Border Path
River Ems
Surgery
Whitechimney Rw
Old Farm Lane
A27
P010
Mill Lane
Lumley Road
Stein Rd
South Lane
Hither Gn
Fraser Gdns
Lauder Cl
Breach Avenue
Haslemere Road
Bourne Vw Cl
East Fld Cl
Kelsey Av
Glenwood Rd
Works
Bourne Community College
Park Road
Clovelly Road
Mountwood Road
Smallcutts Av
Hartland Ct
St John's Rd
Manor Road
Manor Gdns
Manor Way
Priors Cl
Furnston Gv
Cooks Lane
Priors Leaze Lane
Hurstwood Av
Guildford Cl
Southbourne Station
Lodgebury Close
Southbourne County J&I School
Goodwood Court
Inlands Road
LC
First Av
Second Av
Longlands Road
The Drive
Garsons Road
Alfrey Cl
Mosdell Rd
New Rd
MAIN ROAD
A259
The Crescent
Church Rd
Frarydene
Prinsted Lane
Ham La
School La
Farm La
Tuppenny Lane
Penny Lane
Southbourne Av
Apple Grove
Gordon Road
Thorney Road
Woodfield Pk Rd
Bramley Gdns
Orchard La
Sadlers Walk
The Rookery
Pagham Cl
Slipper Road
Roundhouse Meadow
Mill Quay
Heron Quay
Osprey Quay
Thornham Lane
Palmers Rd Industrial Estate
Victoria Cottage Hospital
Queen St
King St
South St
West St
The Promenade
36 On the Quay Hotel
St Peter's Sq
Swan Cl
Malvern Ms
Lewis Road
Ward Crs
Elderfield Cl
Wickor Wy
Wickor Close
Danbury Court
Westbourne Avenue
Oakmeadow Cl
Christopher Way
Maple Cl
Wensley Gdns
Racton Rd
Redlands Lane
Thorney Road
Nature Reserve
Chidham Point
Prinsted Point

1 grid square represents 500 metres

Funtington
Hambrook
Stanes Fm
Lynch Down
Haresfoot Cl
Five Acres
B2146
Common Road
Admirals Walk
Dukes Meadow
Church La
Watery Lane
Marlpit Lane
Hambrook Business Centre
Cheesemans La
Northbrook Farm
Balsam's Farm
Woodmancote Lane
W Ashling Rd
Hambrook Hill (North)
Nightingale Lane
Devils Copse
Mill Rd
Down Street
Funtington County Primary School
Heather Cl
School Dell
Mill Road
Mill Pond La
West Ashling Road
A27
Hambrook House
Scant Road
Scant Road (East)
Scant Road (West)
Newells Lane
Southbrook Road
SOUTHBROOK
Broad Road
Hambrook Hl (South)
Aviary Cl
Waterloo Farm
B2146 RATHAM LANE
Conifer Dr
The Avenue
Priors Leaze Lane
Priors Leaze
Oak Tree Farm
Ratham Mill
Yeomans Fld
Drift Lane
Broad Rd
Nutbourne Station
LC
Flatt Road
Flatt Rd
Mudberry Lane
Green La
Pottery La
A259
MAIN A259 ROAD
A259 MAIN ROAD
Maybush Drive
Ivydene Crescent
Cot Lane
STATION RD
Broadbridge Business Centre
Broadbridge Ct
Broadbridge Farm
Hamstead Meadow
Chidham Lane
Chidham Parochial Primary School
Southfields Industrial Estate
Delling La
Delling Close
Eastfield Fm
Elm Pk
Green La
Bosham FC
Marcuse Flds
Westbrook Fld
Critchfield Rd
Brook Av
Lane
Fairfield Rd
Westward La
Leander Rd
Bosham Church
Steels Lane
The Millstream
G H J K L M
78 79 80 81
1 2 3 4 5 6 7 8
105e

Churchplace Inclosure
158
Deerleap Lane
The New Forest Otter, Owl & Wildlife Park
Langley Wood
A
B
C
D
E
F
433
34
35
Ashurst Wood
Deerleap Inclosure
1
09
Ashurst Lodge
2
River
Longdown Inclosure
3
08
Matley Wood
Matley Heath
4
344
5
Matley Passage
07
Decoy Pond Farm
Black Down
6
7
Beaulieu Road Station
Beaulieu Hotel
106
Denny Wood
8
Denny Lodge
New Forest
BEAULIEU ROAD
352
1 grid square represents 500 metres

Pumpfield

G   H   Lane   J   **159**   K   L   MARCHWOOD   M

36   37   38   39

Staplewood Lane

1
Marchwood
Priory
Hospital

Arters   Lawn   Twiggs Lane

2

60

Lane   End

Twiggs   Lane   Beaulieu Road   Birchlands Farm

3

Twiggs

Foxhill Farm   Carter's Lane

80

Ipley
Inclosure   **4** App

Marchwood
Inclosure

176

5

07

Ipley
Manor

Yew
Tree
Heath

6

Beaulieu River

7

06

Ferny
Crofts   **8**

King's
Hat
Inclosure

36   37   38   39

G   H   J   **353**   K   L   M

176
160
175
353
Pumpfield Farm
River Test
Veal's Lane
Marchwood Priory Hospital
Main Road
Church Farm Close
BY-PASS
A326
Gdn City
Church Farm
Lock's Farm
Dibden
The Old Manor
Manor Road
Main Road
LC
Dibden Golf Centre
Golf Course
PO
Southampton Road
Beaumaris Gdns
Mountfield
Clayfields Sports Centre
Depedene
Applemore
Marchwood Inclosure
HYTHE BY-PASS
Lower Mullin's Lane
Upper Mullin's Lane
Douglas Wy
Malwood
West Road
Roberts Rd
Hollybank
Solent Drive
Fairway Road
Dale Road
Ferry Rd
Widecombe Dr
Tamar Gv
Laurel Cl
Copsewood Rd
Hillview Road
Fern Road
The Mead
Glenside
The Vale
Sunningdale
Whittington Close
Fairview
Sizer Way
Hawkhill
Rowhill Dr
Claypits
Claypits La
Challenger Wy
Corsair Dr
Cheviot Dr
Cumberland Way
Cabot Dr
Cygnus Gdns
Canterbury Dr
Cambria Dr
Caledonia Dr
Cordelia Cl
Corinna Gdns
Brecon Cl
Kiln Cl
Orchard Infant School
Superstore
Applemore Recreation Centre
Oak Lodge School
Applemore Coll
Redwood Cl
Alder Cl
Beechwood Wy
Oakenbrow
Fernlea Wy
Pennine Gdns
Kensington Flds
Challenger Way
Noadswood Comprehensive School
Water Lane
Peartree Rd
Orchard Wy
Braehead
Mullin's Lane
Overbrook
Armada Dr
Golden Hind Pk
Beaulieu Rd
Highlands Wy
Hythe Medical Cen
Roman Rd
Buchan Ct
Lewis Cl
Huxley Ct
Milne Cl
Oaklands Way
Cleveland Dr
North Road
Lime Walk
Lime Cl
Pine Cl
Squirrels Wk
Badgers Wk
Valleydene
Whitewater Ri
Foxtail Drive
Bullrush
Partridge Road
Nash Road
Nash Cl
Noads Way
Ranfurly Gdns
Amberslade Wk
Dibden Purlieu
Roman Way
Wellington Cl
West Road
Talbot Rd
Oak Cl
Oak Road
Haynes Way
Beaulieu
Woodlands Cl
Wildground Infant School
Wildground Cl
Wildground Junior School
Roman Road
A326
Mansell Cl
Merriefield
Whinfield Rd
Watermans La
Crete Lane
Crete Road
Armitage Av
Heatherstone Av
Armwood Av
Hayley Cl
Surgery
Lunedale Rd
Solent Rd
Monks Wk
Villiers Rd
Beverley Road
Forest Front
Butts Ash Lane
HYTHE
The Noads
Dibden Inclosure
King's Hat Inclosure
Fawley Inclosure
Crabhat
1 grid square represents 500 metres

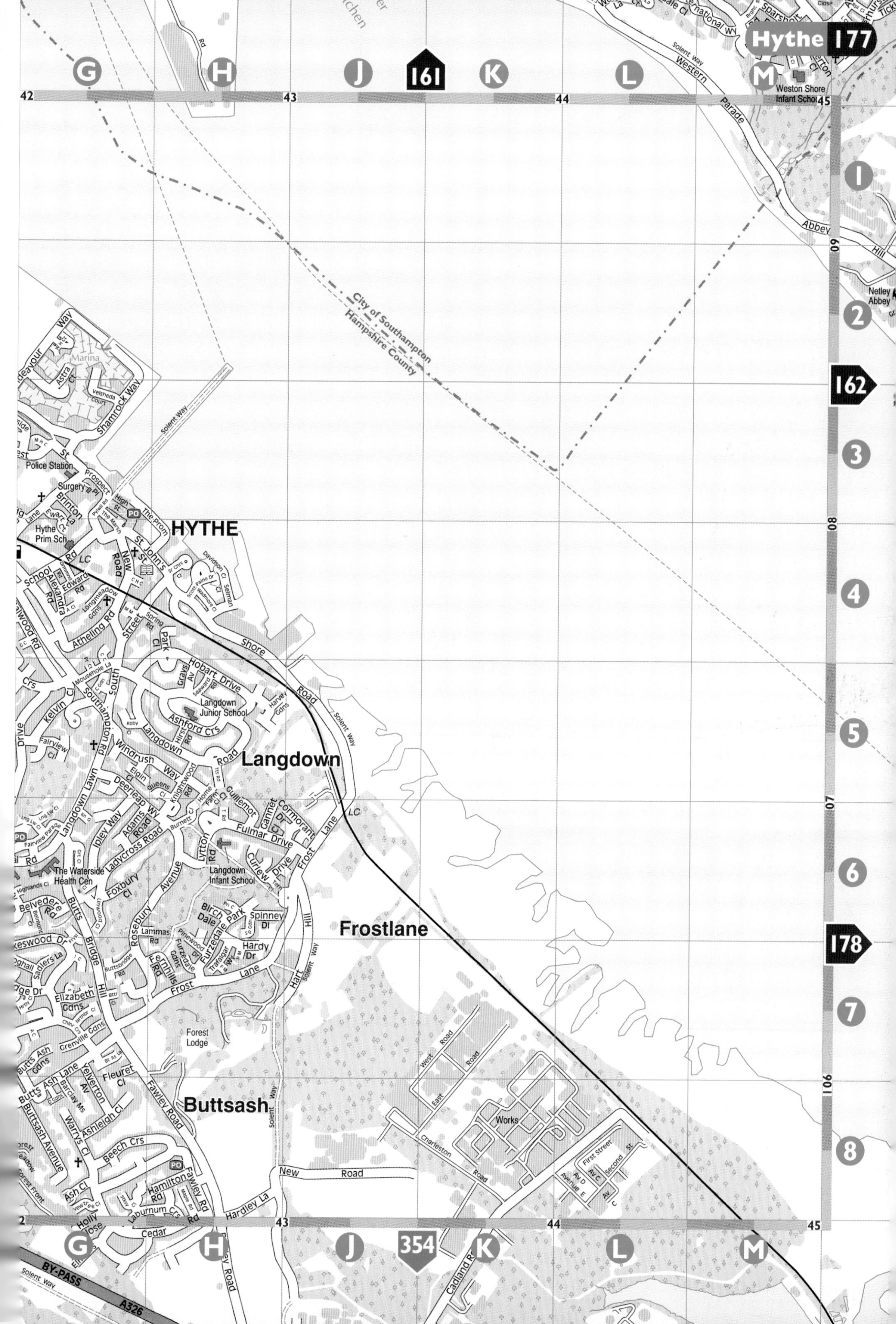
161
162
178
354
HYTHE
Langdown
Frostlane
Buttsash
City of Southampton
Hampshire County
Weston Shore Infant School
Netley Abbey
Western Parade
Abbey Hill
Solent Way
Marina
Shamrock Way
Police Station
Surgery
Hythe Prim Sch
Langdown Junior School
Langdown Infant School
The Waterside Health Cen
Forest Lodge
Works
Shore Road
Hobart Drive
Ashford Crs
Langdown Road
Windrush Way
Southampton Rd
South Street
New Road
St John's St
Frost Lane
Fulmar Drive
Curlew Drive
Cormorant Dr
Guillemot Cl
Ladycross Road
Foxbury Cl
Rosebury Avenue
Butts Bridge Hill
Fawley Road
Hardley La
New Road
Charleston Road
West Road
East Road
First Street
Second St
Beech Crs
Hamilton Rd
Laburnum Crs
Cedar Rd
Holly Close
BY-PASS
A326
Cadland Rd
Butts Ash Lane
Buttsash Avenue
Ashleigh Cl
Yelverton Av
Fleuret Cl
Grenville Gdns
Elizabeth Gdns
Keswood Dr
Belvedere Rd
Kelvin Cl
Atheling Rd
Alexandra Rd
Edward Rd
School Rd
Langdown Lawn
Ipley Way
Adams Road
Deerleap Wy
Birch Dale
Spinney Dl
Hardy Dr
Lammas Rd
Fernhills Rd
Furzedale Gdns
Pinewood Dr
Lytton Rd
Gannet Cl
Hart Hill
Hirst Rd
Graysl Av
Harvey Gdns
Davidson Cl
Selman
Astra Ct
Velsheda Court
Prospect Pl
High St
The Prom
Brinton La
Spring Cl
Park Cl
Elgin Cl
Queens Cl
Knightwood Rd
Home Farm Cl
Burnett Cl
42
43
44
45
G
H
J
K
L
M
1
2
3
4
5
6
7
8
09
08
07
106

Victoria Country Park
162
Hamble Court Business Park
Hamblecliff House
Works
HAMB LE-RI
B3397
Verdon Av
Sydney Avenue
Kings Av
Yorke Way
Chalmers Wy
Cliffe Av
Coach Road
Grantham Av
Flowers Cl
Astral Gardens
Baron Rd
Barton Dr
Spitfire Way
Cirrus Gdns
Beech Gdns
Beech Cl
Westfield Cl
South Ct
Ensign Way
Ensign Wy
Solent Way
Works
Southampton Water
177
Cadland Creek
J Av
Avenue
354
Foreshore
North
South
North Trestle Road
P.L.P.H.
Rd
E Avenue
Burmah Road South
Burmah Road N
Jetty Road
South Trestle Road
Cadland Road
Old Agwi Road
Agitor Road
Road
Seps
Flume Rd
2nd St
4th Street
3rd Street
1st Street
Marsh Lane
Salterns La
Marsh Ln
Rye Paddock La
Copthorne Lane
Copthorne Lane
Ashlett
Ashlett Road
Ashlett Cl
Clinic
Church
Orchard Cl
Woodville Rd
School Rd
Infant School
Fawley
Ashlett Cr
PO
I grid square represents 500 metres
A B C D E F
1 2 3 4 5 6 7 8
445 46 47
07 06 05 104

163

180

Warsash

Newtown

Hook

Hook
Park

Fleetend

Locks H

River Hamble

Hamble
Common

Hamble
Spit

Marina

Hook with
Warsash
CE Primary
School

COWES
ISLE OF WIGHT

180
164
179
188
Titchfield Park
Locks Heath
Fleetend
Abshot
Titchfield Common
Titchfield
Little Posbrook
Meon
Southampton Road A27
Warsash Road
Hunts Pond Road
Hook Lane
Brownwich Lane
Posbrook Lane
Common Lane
Segensworth Road
Church Road
Locksheath Park Road
Brownwich Farm
Hookgate Coppice
Singledge
Chilling
Solent Court
Solent Way
Triangle Lane
Occupation Lane
St Margarets Lane
West Street
Coach Hill
Holiday Inn
Travel Inn
Works
West Hill Park School
St Anthonys Catholic Prim Sch
St John the Baptist CE Prim Sch
Locks Heath J&I School
Titchfield Primary School
Park Farm
1 grid square represents 500 metres

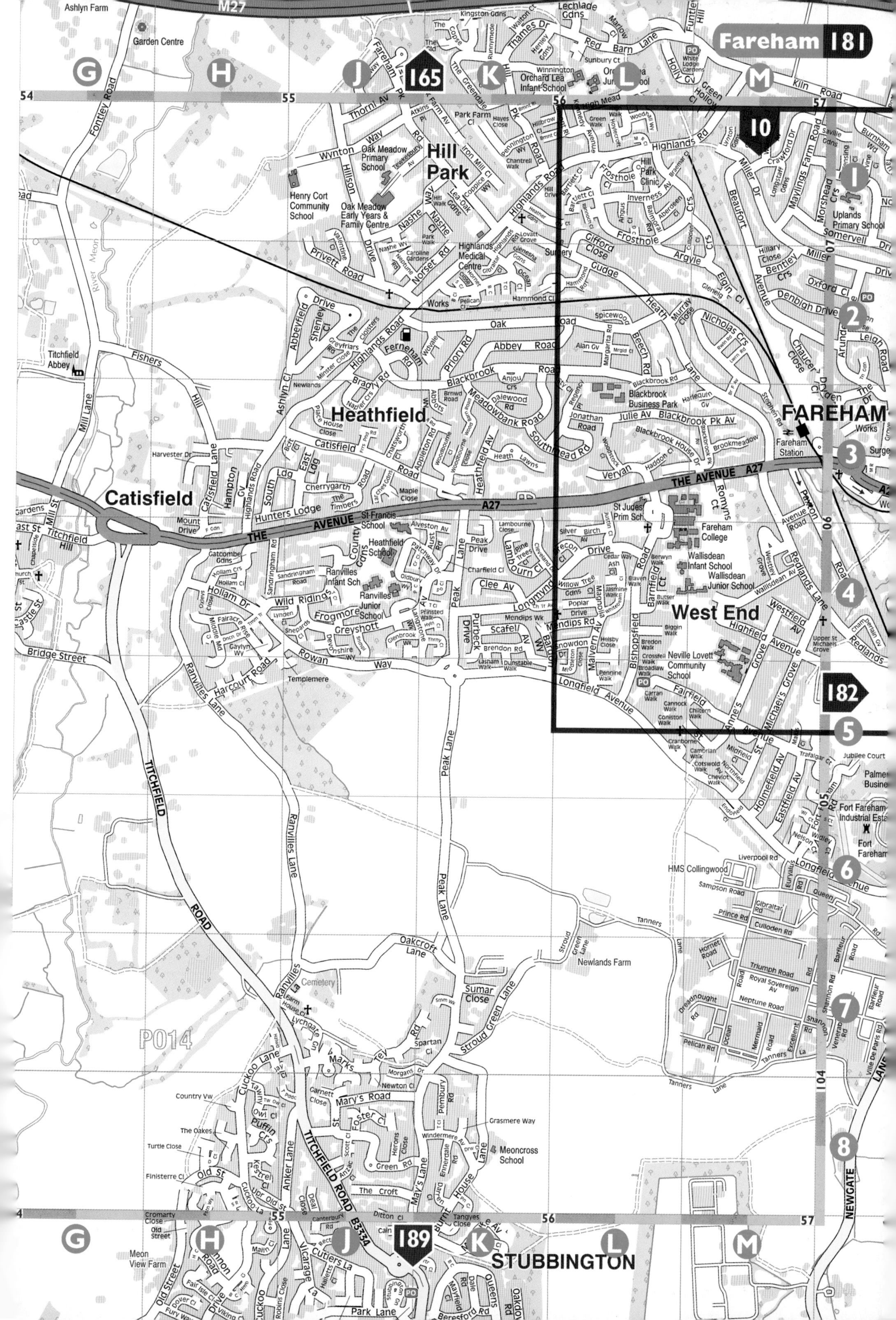

Fareham 181
M27
Ashlyn Farm
Garden Centre
G
H
J
K
L
M
165
10
182
189
54
55
56
57
Fontley Road
Hill Park
Heathfield
Catisfield
FAREHAM
West End
STUBBINGTON
Titchfield Abbey
Fishers Hill
Mill Lane
Henry Cort Community School
Oak Meadow Primary School
Oak Meadow Early Years & Family Centre
Highlands Medical Centre
Orchard Lea Infant School
Hill Park Clinic
Uplands Primary School
Blackbrook Business Park
Fareham Station
Fareham College
Wallisdean Infant School
Wallisdean Junior School
Neville Lovett Community School
St Francis School
Heathfield School
Ranvilles Infant Sch
Ranvilles Junior School
St Judes Prim Sch
Meoncross School
Highlands Road
Oak Road
Abbey Road
Blackbrook Road
Catisfield Road
THE AVENUE A27
Longfield Avenue
Rowan Way
Bridge Street
Titchfield Hill
Ranvilles Lane
TITCHFIELD ROAD
Peak Lane
Oakcroft Lane
Stroud Green Lane
Tanners Lane
Newlands Farm
Cemetery
HMS Collingwood
Fort Fareham Industrial Estate
Fort Fareham
Templemere
Harcourt Road
Hollam Dr
Wild Ridings
Frogmore
Greyshott
Mendips Rd
Highfield Avenue
Westfield Av
Redlands Lane
Gudge Heath Lane
Frostholе Av
Argyle Crs
Miller Dr
Beaufort Avenue
Denbigh Drive
Sumar Close
Mary's Road
Anker Lane
Cuckoo Lane
Old St
Meon View Farm
Park Lane
Vicarage La
NEWGATE LANE
B3334
P014
Kiln Road
Red Barn Lane
Privett Road
Hillson Drive
Wynton Way
Thorni Av
Hunters Lodge
Mount Drive
Heathfield Av
Meadowbank Road
Southmead Rd
Jonathan Road
Julie Av
Blackbrook Pk Av
Veryan
Bishopsfield Road
Fairfield Avenue
Holmefield Av
Eastfield Av
Liverpool Rd
Sampson Road
Prince Rd
Culloden Rd
Triumph Road
Royal Sovereign Av
Neptune Road
Pelican Rd
Dreadnought Rd
Shannon Rd
Queens Rd

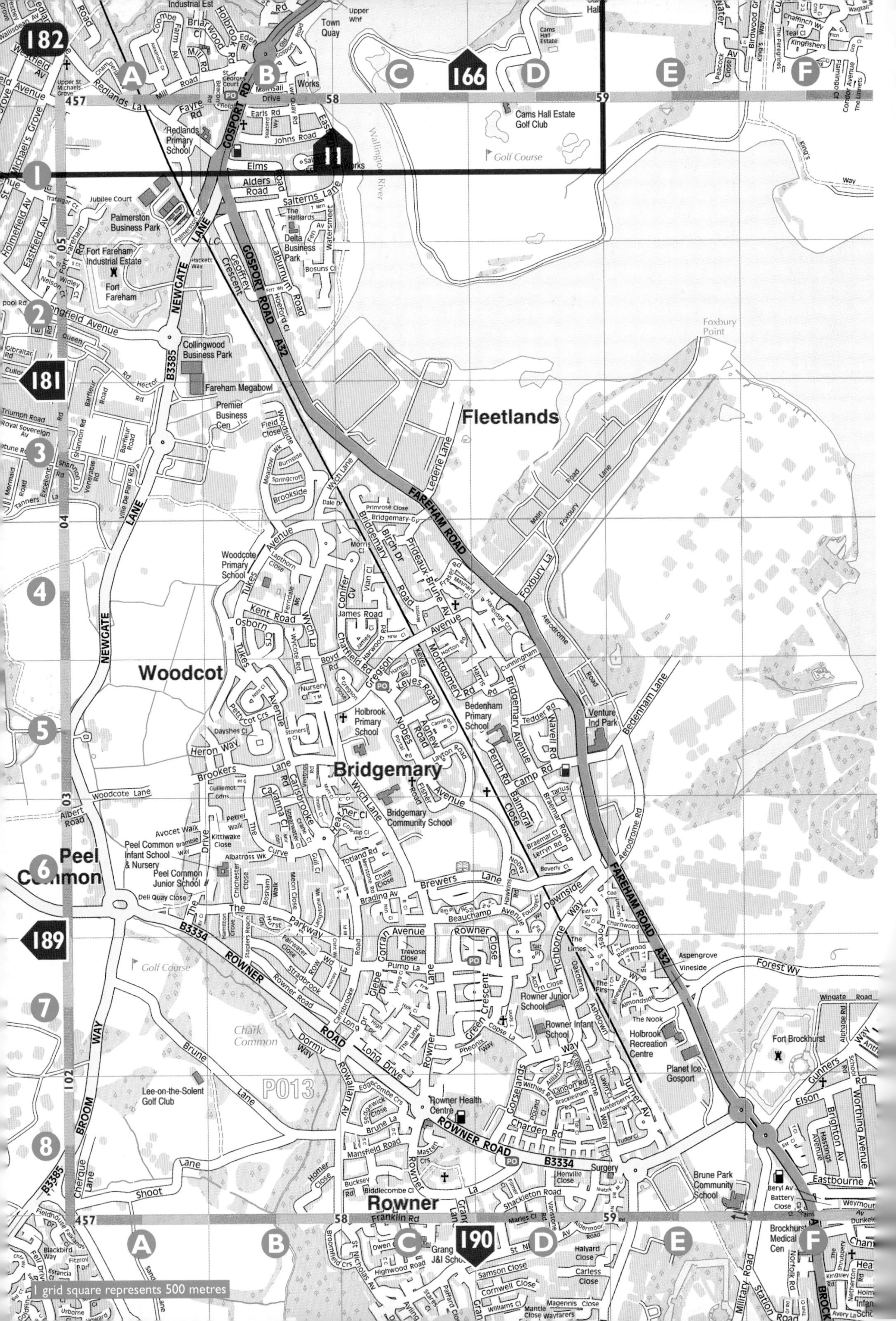

182
166
11
181
189
190
A
B
C
D
E
F
1
2
3
4
5
6
7
8
457
58
59
05
04
03
102
Industrial Est
Upper Whf
Town Quay
Cams Hall Estate
Cams Hall Estate Golf Club
Golf Course
Wallington River
Redlands Lane
Fayre Rd
Redlands Primary School
GOSPORT RD
Mill Road
Mainsail Drive
Earls Rd
Johns Road
Elms
Alders Road
Salterns Lane
Jubilee Court
Palmerston Business Park
Fort Fareham Industrial Estate
Fort Fareham
Delta Business Park
Laburnum Road
Bosuns Cl
GOSPORT ROAD A32
Geoffrey Crescent
NEWGATE LANE
B3385
Longfield Avenue
Queen
Collingwood Business Park
Fareham Megabowl
Premier Business Cen
Hector Rd
Barfleur Rd
Triumph Road
Royal Sovereign Av
Shannon Rd
Venerable Rd
Villa De Paris Rd
Tanners La
Foxbury Point
Fleetlands
Lederle Lane
Main Road
Foxbury Lane
Foxbury La
Aerodrome Road
FAREHAM ROAD
Wych Lane
Field Close
Woodside Avenue
Meadow Wk
Burnside
Springcroft
Brookside
Dale Dr
Primrose Close
Bridgemary Gv
Bridgemary Road
Birch Dr
Prideaux-Brune Av
Woodcote Primary School
Tukes Avenue
Lapthorn Close
Kent Road
Osborn Crs
Conifer Gv
Vian Cl
James Road
Chatfield Rd
Harwood Rd
Montgomery Rd
Harris Rd
Cunningham Dr
Bridgemary Avenue
Woodcot
Boyd Rd
Gregson Avenue
Keyes Road
Nursery Cl
Pettycot Crs
Holbrook Primary School
Bedenham Primary School
Tedder Rd
Wavell Rd
Venture Ind Park
Bedenham Lane
Dayshes Cl
Heron Way
Stoners Cl
Nobes Avenue
Agnew Road
Layton Road
Perth Rd
Camp Rd
Brookers Lane
Woodcote Lane
Albert Road
Bridgemary
Carisbrooke Rd
Wych Lane
Fisher Road
Heather Cl
Bridgemary Community School
Balmoral Close
Braemar Road
Aerodrome Rd
Avocet Walk
Peel Common Infant School & Nursery
Kittiwake Close
Albatross Wk
Peel Common Junior School
The Drive
The Curve
Totland Rd
Chale Close
Brewers Lane
Beverly Cl
Downside
Peel Common
Deli Quay Close
Chichester Close
Bosham Walk
Meon Close
Brading Av
Beauchamp Avenue
Hawkins Rd
The Parkway
Hamilton Grove
Staplers Reach
B3334
ROWNER ROAD
Fairwater Close
Stradbrook
Corran Avenue
Trevose Close
Rowner Close
Tichborne Way
Forest Way
Charnwood
Rosewood
A32
Aspengrove
Vineside
Forest Wy
Golf Course
Pump La
Glebe Dr
Green Crescent
Acorn Close
Oakdene
The Limes
The Firs
Almondside
The Nook
Wingate Road
Rowner Junior School
Rowner Infant School
Holbrook Recreation Centre
Fort Brockhurst
Gunners Way
Planet Ice Gosport
Elson Rd
Chark Common
Brune Lane
Dormy Way
Long Drive
The Links
Rowner Lane
Pheonix Way
Copse La
Ashdown
Gorselands
Withies Rd
Landon Rd
Turner Av
Worthing Avenue
Brighton Av
Hastings Avenue
Lee-on-the-Solent Golf Club
PO13
Rowallan Av
Edgecombe Crs
Sedgewick Close
Rowner Health Centre
ROWNER ROAD
Brune La
Charden Rd
Tudor Cl
Eastbourne Av
Mansfield Road
Masten Crs
B3334
Surgery
Henville Close
Brune Park Community School
Beryl Av
Battery Close
Weymouth Av
BROOM WAY
B3385
Cherque Lane
Shoot Lane
Homer Close
Bucksey Rd
Biddlecombe Cl
Rowner
Shackleton Road
Vanstone Rd
Grange Lane
Franklin Rd
Marles Cl
Aldermoor Road
Dunkeld Rd
Fieldhouse Dr
Blackbird Way
Fitzroy Dr
Estancia
Fell Drive
Broomfield Crs
St Nicholas Av
Owen Cl
Grange J&I School
Highwood Road
Halyard Close
Carless Close
Samson Close
Cornwell Close
Williams Cl
Magennis Close
Mantle Close
Wayfarers
Military Road
Station Road
Brockhurst Medical Cen
Norfolk Rd
Avery La
BROCKHURST
1 grid square represents 500 metres

PORTCHESTER
Portchester Station
A27 SOUTHAMPTON ROAD
Pewit Island
Portsmouth Harbour
Portchester Castle
Cemetery
Castle County Primary School
Portchester Community School
Westlands Medical Centre
Council Building
Wicor County Primary School
King Richard Secondary School
Port Solent
Elson
Elson County Infant School
Elson County Junior School
Goodway Sea School
Hardway
Priddy's Hard
Explosion! Museum of Naval Firepower
St Johns CE
167
184
191

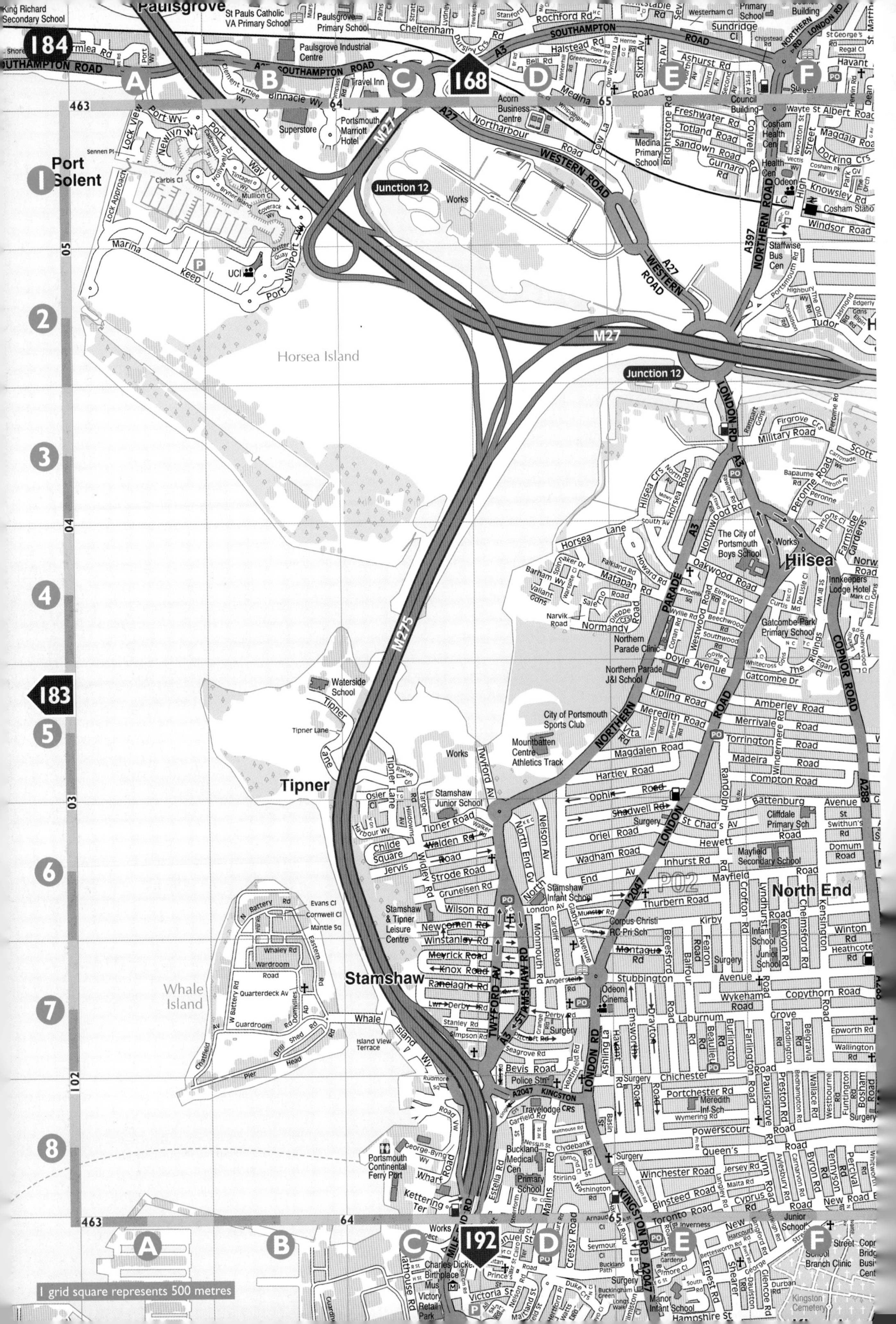
184
168
183
192
A
B
C
D
E
F
1
2
3
4
5
6
7
8
463
64
65
05
04
03
102
Paulsgrove
King Richard Secondary School
St Pauls Catholic VA Primary School
Paulsgrove Primary School
Paulsgrove Industrial Centre
SOUTHAMPTON ROAD
Travel Inn
Binnacle Wy
Superstore
Portsmouth Marriott Hotel
Port Solent
Lock View
Port Wy
Newlyn Wy
Lock Approach
Marina Keep
UCI
Junction 12
Works
Acorn Business Centre
Northarbour Road
WESTERN ROAD
A27
M27
M275
A3
A397
A2047
A288
Medina Primary School
Cosham Health Cen
Cosham Station
Staffwise Bus Cen
Council Building
Horsea Island
Military Road
Hilsea
The City of Portsmouth Boys School
Innkeepers Lodge Hotel
Gatcombe Park Primary School
COPNOR ROAD
NORTHERN PARADE
Northern Parade Clinic
Northern Parade J&I School
City of Portsmouth Sports Club
Mountbatten Centre Athletics Track
Waterside School
Tipner
Tipner Lane
Stamshaw Junior School
Stamshaw
Stamshaw & Tipner Leisure Centre
Stamshaw Infant School
Corpus Christi RC Pri Sch
Whale Island
Cliffdale Primary Sch
Mayfield Secondary School
North End
PO2
LONDON RD
Odeon Cinema
KINGSTON RD
Police Stn
Travelodge
Buckland Medical Cen
Primary School
Portsmouth Continental Ferry Port
Meredith Inf Sch
Charles Dickens Birthplace Mus
Victory Retail Park
Manor Infant School
Kingston Cemetery
1 grid square represents 500 metres

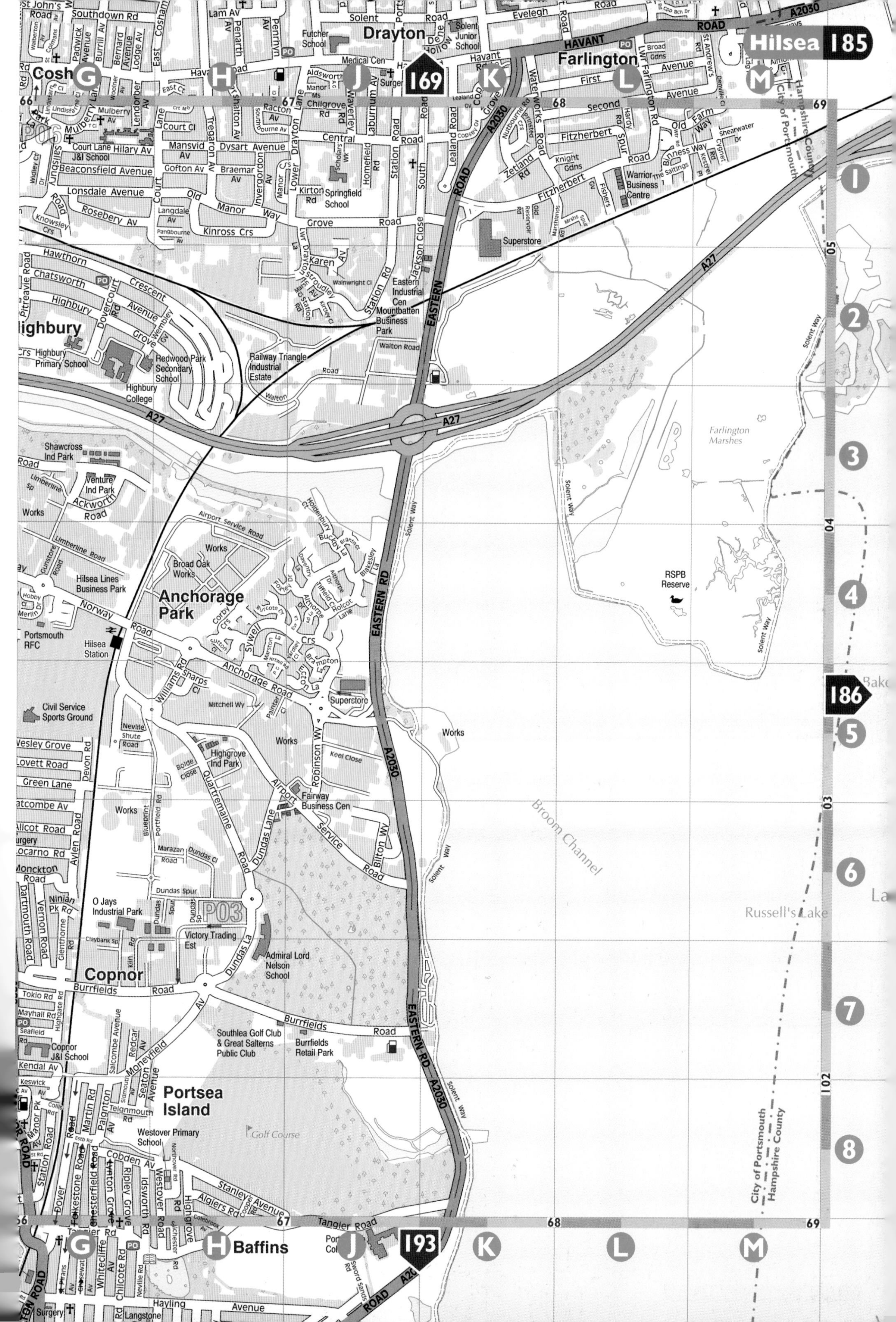

Hilsea 185
169
186
193
Drayton
Farlington
Cosham
Highbury
Anchorage Park
Copnor
Portsea Island
Baffins
Farlington Marshes
RSPB Reserve
Broom Channel
Russell's Lake
EASTERN RD
A2030
A27
HAVANT ROAD
Solent Way
Hilsea Station
Superstore
Works
City of Portsmouth
Hampshire County
Golf Course
Southlea Golf Club & Great Salterns Public Club
Burrfields Retail Park
Admiral Lord Nelson School
Victory Trading Est
O Jays Industrial Park
Highgrove Ind Park
Fairway Business Cen
Hilsea Lines Business Park
Portsmouth RFC
Civil Service Sports Ground
Shawcross Ind Park
Venture Ind Park
Broad Oak Works
Railway Triangle Industrial Estate
Eastern Industrial Cen
Mountbatten Business Park
Highbury College
Redwood Park Secondary School
Highbury Primary School
Springfield School
Warrior Business Centre
Futcher School
Solent Junior School
Westover Primary School
Copnor J&I School
Court Lane J&I School
PO3
PO6
G H J K L M
1 2 3 4 5 6 7 8
66 67 68 69

A2030
Westway
Almor
City of Portsmouth

A

B

C

Broadmarsh
Business
Innovation Centre

Farm
Works

Havant
Business
Centre

D

Brookside
Rd

Business Area

Brockhampton

Industrial
Estate

Regents Ct

Woodbury

E

Cl

F

Rectory
Rd

A27

Harts

Way

Solent Way

469

70

Southmoor Lane

71

Penner Road

Southbrook Road

Longmead

Langstone Av

The Mallards

Langbrook Cl

I

469

A27

Solent Way

Solent Way

Solent Way

Mill

Langstone High St

Langstone

16

Langstone

Harbourside Lane

St Cuns
Tower

PH

LANGSTONE

Langstone High

ROAD

P

05

2

Solent Way

North Binness
Island

Broad Lake

3

04

Solent Way

Long
Island

4

Solent Way

Baker's Island

Havant Road

New

185

5

03

South Binness
Island

Avenue

Meadow
Cl

Rogers

Victoria

6

Langstone Harbour

Mill
Close

HAVANT
RD

ussell's Lake

7

102

City of Portsmouth
Hampshire County

8

West Lane

469

70

71

A

B

C

D

E

Daw

F

Langstone Channel

Havant Billy Coastal Path

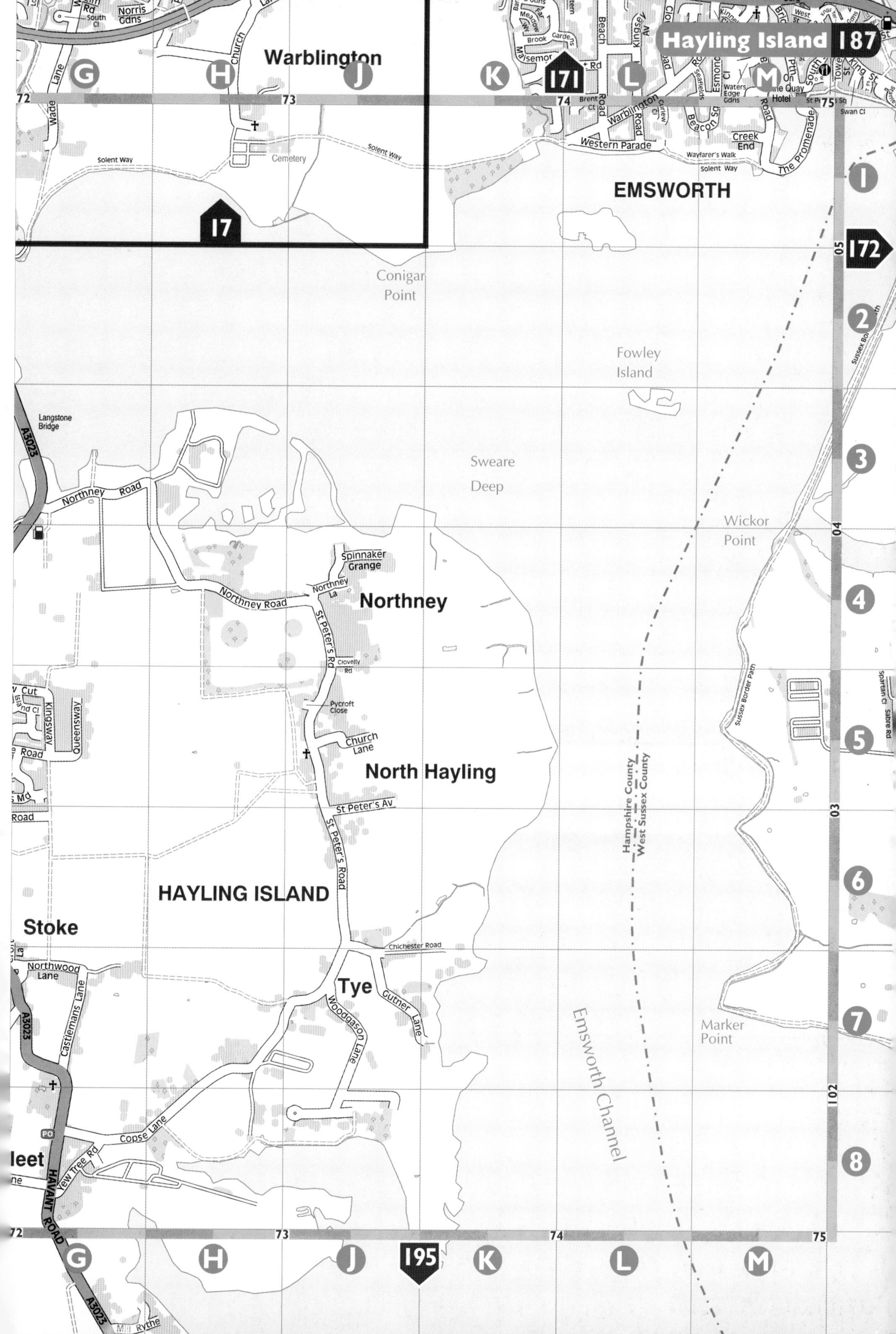

Warblington

EMSWORTH

G H J K L M

I

17

172

Norris Gdns

Church Lane

Cemetery

Solent Way

Conigar Point

Fowley Island

Sweare Deep

Wickor Point

Langstone Bridge

Northney Road

Spinnaker Grange

Northney La

Northney

St Peter's Rd

Clovelly Rd

Pycroft Close

Church Lane

North Hayling

St Peter's Av

St Peter's Road

Queensway

Kingsway

HAYLING ISLAND

Stoke

Northwood Lane

Castlemans Lane

Chichester Road

Tye

Woodgason Lane

Gutner Lane

Copse Lane

View Tree Rd

HAVANT ROAD

PO

leet

Mill Rythe

A3023

Hampshire County
West Sussex County

Sussex Border Path

Spartan Cl

Sabre Rd

Marker Point

Emsworth Channel

Western Parade

Beacon Sq

Solent Way

Wayfarer's Walk

Creek End

The Promenade

Warblington Road

Kingsley Rd

Brent Ct

Waters Edge Gdns

Quay Hotel

Swan Cl

Sussex Bdy

05

04

03

102

G 72 H 73 J K 74 L M 75

1

2

3

4

5

6

7

8

195

Solent Way

Brownwich Fa...

180

Meon

River Meon

Titchfield
Haven

Knights
Bank
Haven Cl...

Cliff

Hill H

Road

A B C D E F

451 52 53

I
2
3
4
5
6
7
8

03
02
01
00

451 52 53

A B C D E F

1 grid square represents 500 metres

STUBBINGTON

The Solent

Gosport Airfield

HMS Daedalus

LEE-ON-THE-SOLENT

190
189
182
Rowner
Rowner Road
B3334
Brune Park Community School
Brockhurst Medical Cen
Brockhurst Road
A32
Grange J&I School
Sandhill Lane
St Nicholas Av
Brockhurst
HMS Sultan
Siskin J&I Sch
Rowner Swimming Centre
Military Road
Grange Road
Ann's Hill
Cemetery
Lee-on-the-Solent Junior School
Elmore Avenue
Gosport Road
Portsmouth Road B3333
Privett Road
B3333
Privett
Gomer J&I School
Browndown
Browndown Road
Browndown Point
Bay House School
Alverstoke
Stokes Bay Road
Stokes Bay
Solent Way
River Alver
The Solent
457
58
59
A
B
C
D
E
F
1
2
3
4
5
6
7
8
101
100
99
098
1 grid square represents 500 metres

Elson
Hardway
Priddy's Hard
Forton
Newtown
GOSPORT
Clayhall
183
14
15
20
192
Elson County Infant School
Elson County Junior School
Explosion! Museum of Naval Firepower
St Johns CE Primary School
City of Portsmouth
Hampshire County
Burrow Island
Quayside Education Centre
St Vincent College
St Marys County Prim Sch
Industrial Estate
Waterside Medical Centre
Yacht Marina
Portsmouth Harbour
Leesland CE Infant School
Leesland CE Junior School
Business Park
Medical Cen
Council Building
Superstore
Museum
Town Hall
Bus Station
The Esplanade
Haslar Lake
Haslar Bridge
Royal Navy Submarine Museum & HMS Alliance
HMS Dolphin
Education Other Than At School (EOTAS)
Royal Hospital Haslar
Haselworth County Primary Sch
Alverstoke CE Junior School
Alverstoke Infant School
Marycourt School
Cemetery
Gosport & Stokes Bay Golf Club
Golf Course
Fort Monckton
Gilkicker Point
ISLE OF WIGHT
Mary Rose Ship Hall
HMS Victory
Portsmouth Historic Dockyard
Royal Naval Museum
Action Stations! Exhibition
Dockyard Apprentice Exhibition
Mary Rose Exhibition
Flagship Portsmouth
Ticket Office & Warrior Exhibition
HMS Warrior
Portsmouth Harbour Station
Spinnaker Tower
Isle of Wight Car Ferry Terminal
Fish Market
Round Tower
Square Tower
Cathedral Church of St Thomas Canterbury
FORTON RD
A32
MUMBY RD
SOUTH ST
BURY RD
FOSTER RD
B3333
Haslar Road
Clayhall Road
Dolphin Way
Fort Road
Military Road
Solent Way
Anglesey Road
Little Anglesey Road
Mayfield Road
Jamaica Pl
Stoke Rd
Walpole Rd
Leesland Road
Norman Rd
Carnarvon Rd
Richmond Rd
Gordon Road
St Andrew's Road
Sydney Road
Kings Rd
Grove Av
Ferrol Road
Parham Road
Mill Pond Rd
Cobden St
Toronto Pl
Palmyra Rd
Amberley Rd
Reeds Rd
Welch Rd
Melville Road
Fieldmore Rd
San Diego Rd
Dukes Rd
Beryton Road
Priddy's Hard
Heritage Way
Britannia Way
Beech Gv
Testcombe Road
Beechcroft Road
St Mary's Avenue
Green Rd
Westfield Ind Est
Health Centre
War Mem Hospital
Thorngate Hall
Lodge Gardens
Surgery
Works
P012
G
H
J
K
L
M
60
61
62
63
0
1
2
3
4
5
6
7
8
099
098
100
101

192
184
191
20
21
PORTSMOUTH
Portsea
Somers Town
Fratton
Kingston
Old Portsmouth
Southsea
HM Naval Base
Portsmouth Continental Ferry Port
Charles Dickens' Birthplace Mus
Victory Retail Park
CHURCH STREET ROUNDABOUT
MILE END RD
MARKETWAY
Highbury College
Cathedral Discovery Centre
HMS Nelson
St Johns Cath
Shopping Centre
Victoria Park Swimming Centre
Portsmouth & Southsea Stn
Guildhall
Civic Off
St Edmunds Catholic Sec Sch
St Johns Catholic Prim Sch
Canal Wk
Greetham St School
Somers Park Prim Sch
Fire Station
WINSTON CHURCHILL AV A2030
Priory College
Cumberland Business Cen
Fratton Station
The Pompey Centre (Retail Park)
KINGSTON RD A2047
FRATTON RD
LAKE RD
HOLBROOK RD
A2030 HOLBROOK RD
VICTORIA RD NORTH
ANGLESEA RD
CAMBRIDGE RD
ST MICHAEL'S RD
HAMPSHIRE TERRACE
LANDPORT TERRACE
KING'S TERRACE
JUBILEE TER
MUSEUM RD
KINGS RD ROUNDABOUT
HIGH ST A3
ST GEORGE'S RD
KING'S RD
B2154 ELM GROVE
Univ of Portsmouth
United Services Sports Ground
Victoria Stadium
HMS Temeraire
Gunwharf Quays Retail & Leisure Park
Spinnaker Tower
Fish Market
Portsmouth Grammar Jun Sch
City Mus
St Judes CE (Controlled) Pri Sch
Cathedral Church of St Thomas of Canterbury
Round Tower
Square Tower
The Long Curtain (Old Town Defences)
Clarence Pier & Amusement Centre
Hovercraft Terminal
Southsea Common
Queen's Hotel
Royal Naval Memorial
PIER ROAD
SOUTHSEA TER
BELLEVUE TERR
WESTERN PDE
CLARENCE PDE A288
Portsmouth High Sch
St Johns College
Kings Theatre
Goldsmith Infant Sch
Fernhurst Junior School
Devonshire Infant Sch
University of Portsmouth
ALBERT RD
WAVERLEY RD
St Swithuns RC (Aided) Prim Sch
EASTERN PARADE
ST HELENS PARADE
SOUTH PDE
CLARENDON RD
Natural History Museum & Butterfly House
Royal Beach Hotel
South Parade Pier
Skate Park
Seacrest Hotel
Clarence Esplanade
D-Day Museum & Overlord Embroidery
Sea Life Centre
Southsea Castle
The Pyramids Leisure Centre
JERSEY, GUERNSEY, ST MALO, CHERBOURG, CAEN, BILBAO
ISLE OF WIGHT
Spitbank Fort
HM Prison
A B C D E F
1 2 3 4 5 6 7 8
463
64
65
100
99
098
1 grid square represents 500 metres

Island

Golf Course

Westover Primary School

185

Tangier Road

Portsmouth College

Baffins

Tangier Road

Baffins Road

Milton Road

Langstone Junior School

Hayling Avenue

Jenkins Grove

Cedar Gv

Ebery Grove

Marina Gv

Myrtle Gv

Tamworth Rd

Avenue

Maydman Sq

Walsall Road

Cheslyn Rd

Langstone

St Marys Hosp

Priorsdean Av

Road

Petworth

Romsey Rd

Eastern Rd

East Shore School

Moorings Way Infant School

Moorings

Godwit

Schooner Way

Way

Miltoncross Secondary School

Cemetery

A2030 VELDER AV

Bonchurch Rd

Edgeware Rd

Warren Avenue Industrial Est

The Hvn

Milebush Rd

Siskin Cl

Whimbrel Ct

Sanderling Rd

Durlin Ct

Furze Lane

Cluster Industrial Estate

St Georges Ind Est

Road

Speck's Rd

Carisbrooke Rd

Surgery

Church Vw

Meon

St James Hospital

Mayles Rd

Crofton Rd

Shelford Rd

Holland

Warren

Junior School

Milton

Locksway Road

Longshore Way

Solent Way

Broom Cl

SMITH AV A2030

Milton Park

Priory

Meon Infant Sch

Hollam

Posbrooke Rd

Cansfield Rd

Weston

Locksway Rd

Rosetta

Pleasant Rd

Trevis Rd

Seaway

Wimborne Road

Woodmancote Rd

Teddington Rd

Middlesex Rd

Gurney Rd

Perth Rd

Dunbar Rd

Kingsley

Yeo Ct

Road

Horse Sands Ck

Works

Ferry Road

Hampshire County City of Portsmouth

University of Portsmouth

Fe

100

194

Wimbourne J&I Sch

Glasgow Road

PO4

Surgery

Albert Rd

Suffolk Rd

Avenue

Bransbury Road

Eastney Beam Engine House

Ferry Road

Fort Cumberland

Westfield

Eastfield

Devonshire

Winter

Maxwell Road

Cumberland Infant Sch

Reginald Road

Landguard Road

Methuen

Ringwood Rd

Minstead

Henderson Road

Dunn

Cockleshell Gdns

Finch Rd

Gibraltar Rd

Fort Cumberland

Gibraltar Road

Centurion Gs

Fort Cumberland Road

HIGHLAND RD

B2154

Eastney Health Cen

Lidlard Gdns

Flinders Gdns

Hopkins Court

Churchill Court Square

Eastney

Halliday Crescent

Melville

Esplanade Gdns

Driftwood Gdns

Eastney Swimming Baths

CROMWELL RD

Kimberley Rd

Collins Road

Lindley Av

Tokar St

Grove

Mountbatten Square

The Royal Marines Mus

Esplanade

West Winner

Burbidge Gv

Brading Av

Selsey Av

ST GEORGE'S RD

A288

Solent Way

East

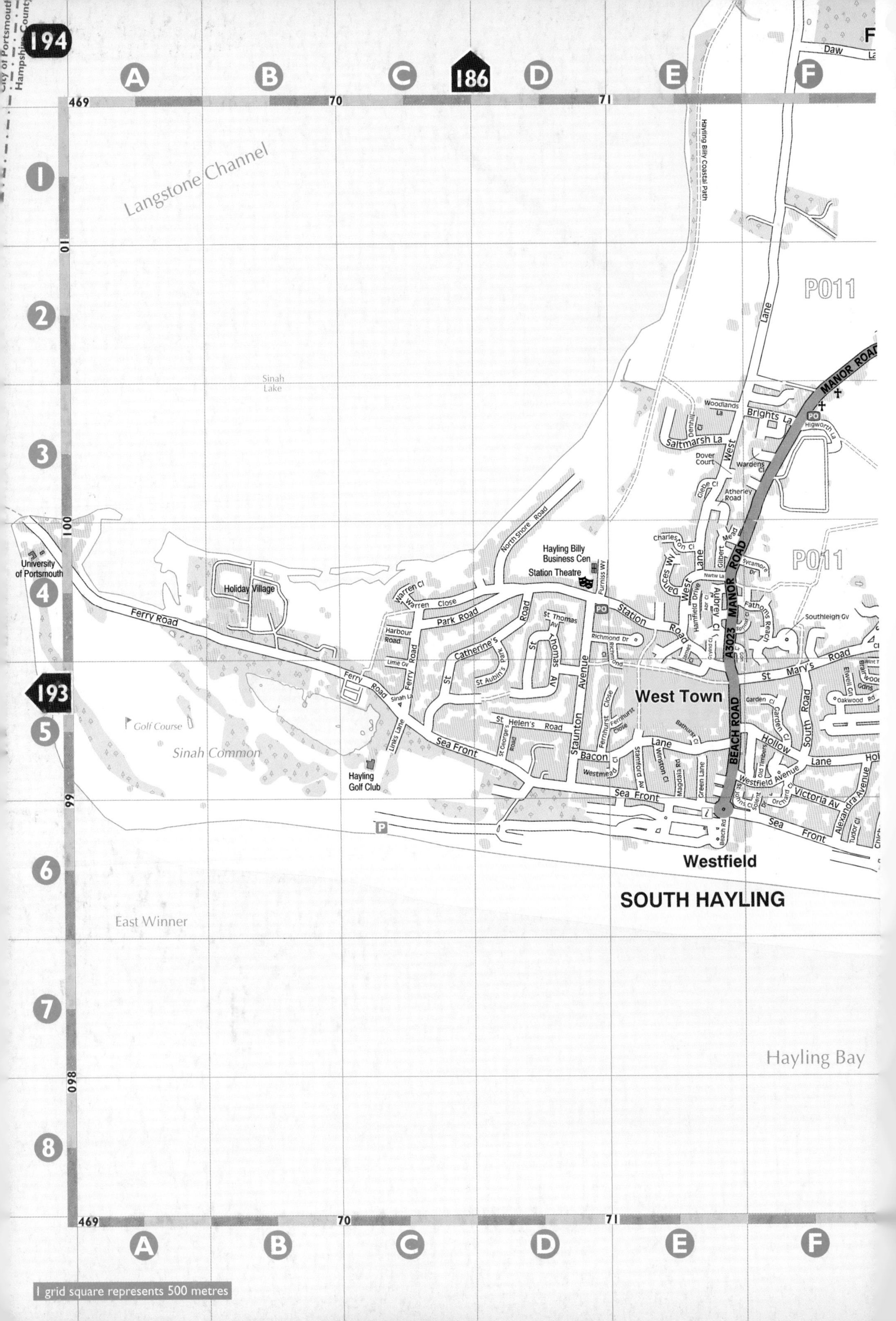

186
193
A B C D E F
1 2 3 4 5 6 7 8
469
70
71
10
100
99
098
Langstone Channel
Sinah Lake
University of Portsmouth
Holiday Village
Ferry Road
Golf Course
Sinah Common
Hayling Golf Club
East Winner
Hayling Billy Coastal Path
Hayling Billy Business Cen
Station Theatre
North Shore Road
Warren Cl
Warren Close
Park Road
Harbour Road
Ferry Road
Sinah La
Links Lane
Sea Front
St Catherine's Road
St Aubin's Park
St Thomas Av
St Helen's Road
St George's Road
Staunton Avenue
Station Road
Richmond Dr
Fernhurst Close
Bacon Lane
Westmead Cl
Stamford Av
Winston Cl
Green Lane
West Town
Westfield
SOUTH HAYLING
Hayling Bay
West Lane
Saltmarsh La
Woodlands La
Brights La
Dover Court
Wardens Cl
Atherley Road
Glebe Cl
Charleston Cl
Gilbert Mead
Aubrey Cl
Hamfield Drive
MANOR ROAD
A3023
BEACH ROAD
Sycamore Dr
Fathoms Reach
Southleigh Gv
St Mary's Road
Garden Cl
South Road
Hollow Lane
Westfield Avenue
Victoria Av
Alexandra Avenue
Sea Front
Oakwood Rd
Higworth La
Daw La
PO11
PO

leet

G H J 187 K L M

72 73 74 75

Copse La
PO
View Tree Rd
HAVANT ROAD
A3023

Mill Rythe La

Manor House

Holiday Centre

Mill Rythe J&I School

A3023

Mill Rithe

Rest-A-Wyle Av
Pound Lea

Road

Kings Road

Lulworth Cl

Katrina Gdns

The Hayling School

Dundonald Cl
Eastwood Cl

Works
Church

Tournerbury
Lane

Laburnum Grove
Beech Grove
Poplar Grove
Hawthorne Gv

Legion Rd

Road

Mengham Infant School

St Mary's

Palmerston Rd

Mengham Junior School

Cherrywood Gdns
Elm
Gr
Astwood Gr

St Leonard's
Avenue

Hayling Island Health Centre

PO

Willow Lane

Mengham Rd

Selsmore

Ramsey Rd
Lyndhurst Rd

Webster Avenue
Sea Grove Av

Manor Wy

Mengham Avenue

Mengham
Lane

Mengham Rd

Road

Bound Lane

North Crs

Webb La
Grand Pde
Webb Cl

Orchard Rd

Tsnoring

Wyborn Cl

St Andrew's Road

Old School Dr

Norman Rd

Silversands

Harold Road

St Hermans Rd

Old School Dr
PO

Fishery La

Foreland Ct

Marshall

Sea Front

Sea Front
P

Southwood

The Glade

Bembridge Drive

Meath Cl
St

The Strand

Culver Rd

Road

Winsor Cl

Simmons ton
Salterns Cl
Lane

Salterns

Blackthorn Dr
Blackthorn Rd
Ilex Walk
Kingfisher Cl

Mengham Salterns

Marine

Seaview

Walk
Seaview Cl

Road

Selsmore Avenue

Astrid

Burdale

Selsmore
Lane

Mengham

Selsmore

Eastoke

Eastoke
Avenue

Rowan Cl
Eastoke Close

Creek

Birgess Cl
West Haye Road

Eastoke
Road

Sandy

Wheatlands

Southwood Road

Birdham Rd
Haven Road

Point
Coronation

Avenue
Treloar Rd

Haven Road

Bosmere Rd

Fishermans Wk

Earnley

Haslemere Gdns
Sidlesham Cl

Pagham Rd

Selsey Cl
Itchenor Rd

Road
Bracklesham

Road

Treloar Road

100
99
898

1
2
3
4
5
6
7
8

Black Poir

Bracklesham Rd

Eastoke

A
B
C
330
D
E
F
Sandleheath
Alderholt
Camel Green
Ashf
Bleak Hill
Sandle Dairy Farm
Puddleslosh Lane
Mari Lane
Forres Sandle Manor School
Industrial Estate
Old Brickyard Rd
Elms Cl
Tanners Lane
Lower Court Wood
Wilkins's Coomb
Sandle Manor
Station Road
Marbrean Close
Elmwood Av
Downwood Cl
Brympton Cl
Mayfield Rd
Sandle Copse
Manor Farm Rd
Jubilee Rd
Fordingbridge Business Park
Works
Ashford Close
Victoria Rd
Victoria Gdns
Beechwood
Ashford Works Industrial Estate
Ashford
Ashford Water
Alderholt Road
Alderholt Mill Farm
Hampshire County
Dorset County
Sandleheath Road
Home Farm
Alderholt Park
High Wood
BOWERWOOD ROAD
FORDINGBRIDGE ROAD
337
Midgham Farm
Highwood Close
Station Road
STATION ROAD
Station Yd
B3078
Churchill Cl
Blackwater Gv
Blackwater Cl
Charing Cross
Attwood Close
Apple Tree Rd
Lime Tree Cl
Pear Tree Cl
Alder Dr
Earlswood Dr
Oak Road
Pine Rd
Broomfield Dr
Fern Cl
Hazel Close
Birchwood Drive
Park Lane
St James CE First School
Coppers Cl
Hayters Way
Down Lodge Cl
Windsor Wy
Camel Green Road
Fir Tree Hill
Gilbert Close
Wren Gdns
Kestrel Way
Saxon Way
Tudor Cl
Bramble Close
Ashtell's Wy
South Hill
Hillbury Road
Drove End Farm
Ringwood Road
North End Lane
Lomer Lane
Harbridge Drove
Warren Park Farm
Alderholt Common
198
411
12
13
1
2
3
4
5
6
7
8
15
14
13
112
1 grid square represents 500 metres

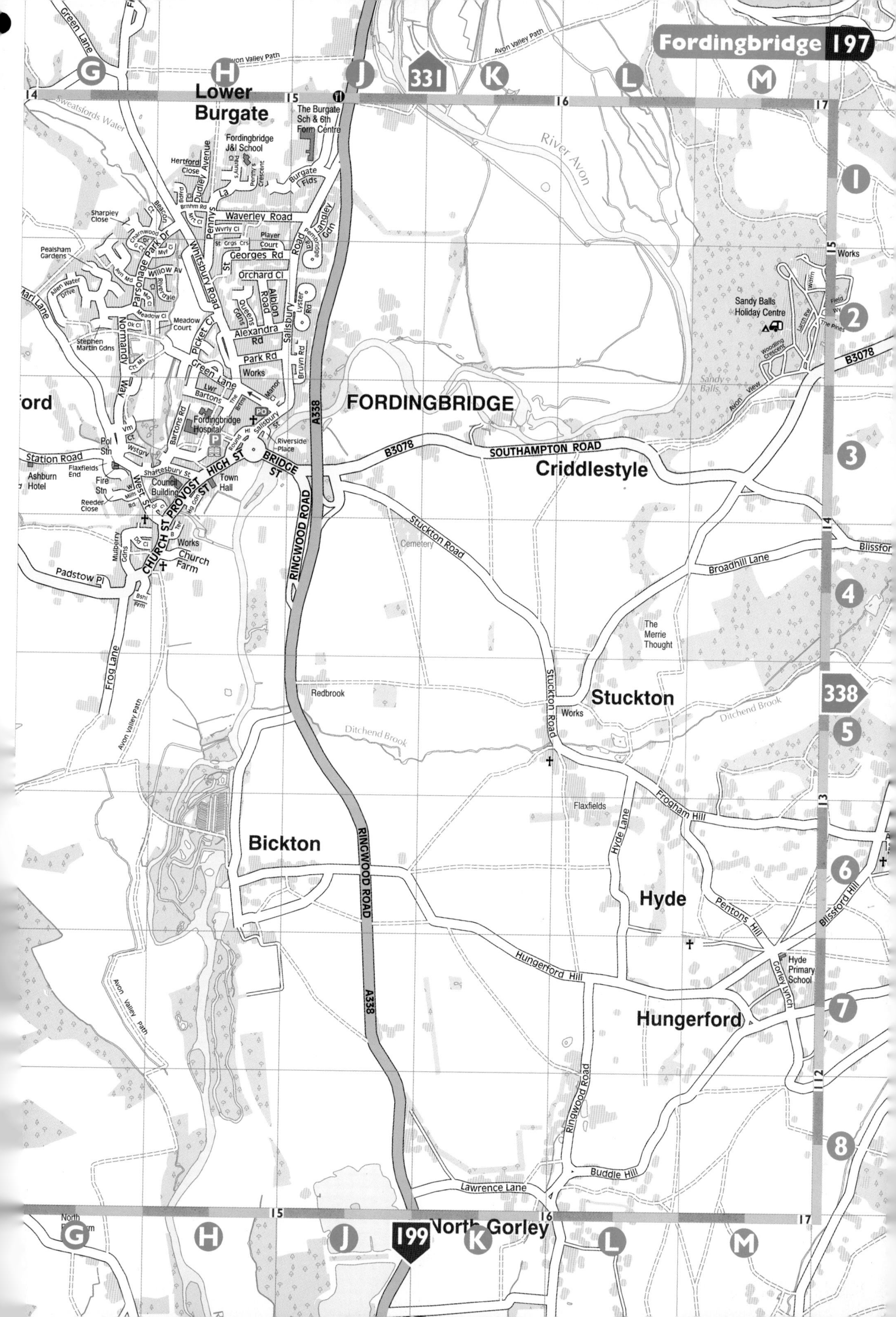
Lower Burgate
The Burgate Sch & 6th Form Centre
Fordingbridge J&I School
FORDINGBRIDGE
Criddlestyle
Southampton Road
Sandy Balls Holiday Centre
Stuckton
Bickton
Hyde
Hungerford
Hyde Primary School
The Merrie Thought
Redbrook
Flaxfields
Cemetery
Ringwood Road
Stuckton Road
Frogham Hill
Hungerford Hill
Buddle Hill
Lawrence Lane
Broadhill Lane
Hyde Lane
Pentons Hill
Gorley Lynch
Blissford Hill
Ditchend Brook
River Avon
Avon Valley Path
Station Road
Fordingbridge Hospital
Council Building
Town Hall
Ashburn Hotel
Waverley Road
Whitsbury Road
Alexandra Rd
Park Rd
Green Lane
Frog Lane
Padstow Pl
Church Farm
High St
Provost St
Church St
Bridge St
Salisbury Rd
Riverside Place
North Gorley
331
338
199

196
A
B
C
D
E
F
411
12
13
Warren Park Farm
Alderholt Common
Harbridge Drove
Lomer Lane
North End Lane
Bleak Hill
Harbridge
Whitefield Bottom
Sleep Brook
Dorset County
Hampshire County
North Plumley Farm
Harbour Brook
Turmer
Harbridge School
Plumley Farm
Lower Turmer
Plumley Wood
Harefield Plantation
Turmer Brook
Home Farm
Shepherds Lane
Shepherds Hill
Chestnut Avenue
Nea Drive
Ellingham Drive
Ringwood Forest
Somerley Park
Somerley
Ashley Drive
Ebblake
Parkland Cl
B3081
1
2
3
4
5
6
7
8
11
10
09
08
337
201
202
1 grid square represents 500 metres

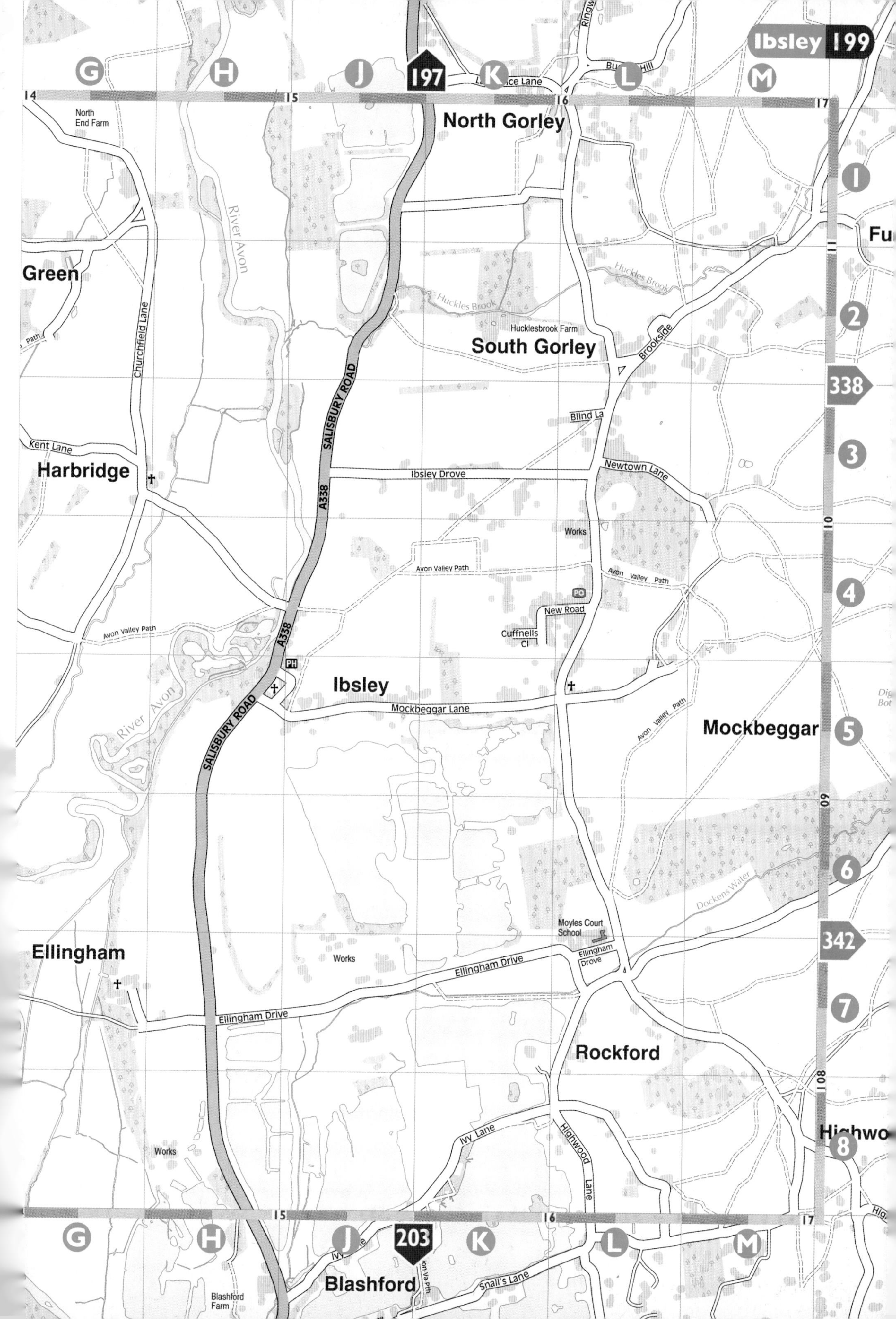

G   H   J   **197**   K   L   M

14   15   16   17

North Gorley

Lawrence Lane

Burley Hill

Rushy

1

Green

River Avon

North
End Farm

Huckles Brook

Huckles Brook

Fu

Churchfield Lane

Path

Hucklesbrook Farm

South Gorley

Brookside

2

338

Kent Lane

Blind Lane

Newtown Lane

3

Harbridge

Ibsley Drove

Works

4

A338

SALISBURY ROAD

Avon Valley Path

Avon Valley Path

PO

Avon Valley Path

New Road

Cuffnells
Cl

Avon Valley Path

PH

A338

Ibsley

Mockbeggar Lane

Mockbeggar

5

Dig
Bot

River Avon

SALISBURY ROAD

Avon Valley Path

60

Dockens Water

6

Moyles Court
School

342

Ellingham

Ellingham
Drove

Works

Ellingham Drive

7

Ellingham Drive

Rockford

08

Ivy Lane

Highwood Lane

Highwo

Works

High

8

G   H   J   **203**   K   L   M

15   16   17

Ivy Lane

Snail's Lane

Avon Valley Path

Blashford

Blashford
Farm

Ⓐ Ⓑ Ⓒ ⬥336 Ⓓ B3081 Ⓔ Ⓕ

405 06 07

Sutton Holms

River Crane

Works

Romford

Boys Wood

STATION ROAD

Station Rd

Ⓘ **Woodlands**

60

Chapel Lane

Brook Lane

Whitmore La

Verwood Road

Church

Crane Valley Golf Club

Golf Course

Albion Way

Jessica Av

Pine Vw Rd

Road

West Close

Little Dewlands

Old St

† †

Whitmore

New Rd

Hillside

Burgess Fld

Park Lane

Dewlands

stagswood

⓶

Woodlands Common

Mount Pleasant Farm

Haywar

⓷

Woodland
anor Far

Woodlands Park

80

Dewlands Common

Horton Way

Margards

⓸

Bridge Farm

⓸

Gravel Works

⓹

07

Knob's Crook

Monmouth's Ash

Slough Lane

Horton Common

⓺

Holt Lodge Farm

⓺

Ⓖ01

Horton Heath

Ⓞ7

Clump Hill

†

Horton Road

Ringwood Road

©

Holt Road

Mannington

Burt's Lane

Lower Mannington

405 06 07

Ⓐ Ⓑ **Crooked Withies** Ⓒ ⬥**204** Ⓓ Ⓔ Ⓕ

Road

1 grid square represents 500 metres

G H J 337 K L M

08 09 10 11

BH31

Trinity CE VA First Schl

Stephen's Castle

Hillside First School

Police Station

RINGWOOD ROAD

St Stephens La

Starlight Farm Close

VERWOOD

Strathmore Dr

Compton Close

Acorn Wy

Crescent Rd

Black Hill

Sherwood

Noon Hill Road

Shard Cl

Ind Est

Sandy Lane

Raymond Cl

B3081

The Cha

The Oaks

Eastworth Road

Coronation Road

Moorlands Road

Manor Wy

Howard Rd

B3072

MANOR ROAD

Chiltern Drive

Pennine Way

Verwood Leisure Centre

Buggens La

Burnbake

Foxes Close

Owls Road

New Meadow

Lake Road

Aspen Drive

The Chase

Hunters Cl

198

The Forestside

3

Howe Lane

The Emmanuel CE VA Middle School

Verwood CE First School

Spring Close

Summer Flds

St Michaels Road

Newtown Road

Lake Road

Woodlinken Drive

Fairwood Rd

Lavender Close

Roseberry Close

Enterprise Park

RINGWOOD ROAD

Ebblake

Cemetery

River Crane

Surgery

Bingham Rd

Brook Drive

Hazelwood Drive

Woodlinken Dr

Magnolia

Acacia Av

Wisteria Dr

Brunel Cl

Parkway

Forest Close

Ebblake Ind Est

Bessemer Ct

4

River Crane

Potterne Way

Liederbach Dr

Kiln Way

Ebblake Close

5

Manor Farm

B3072

MANOR ROAD

202

Crab Orchard Way

Crab Orchard

ROAD

Sandy Lane

VERWOOD

6

7

Lower Common

Church

Three Legged Cross First School

Surgery

Camellia Close

Ball Close

Joys Rd

Evergreen Close

Furzelands Road

Moors Valley Golf Club

Golf Course

8

Three Legged Cross

RINGWOOD ROAD

Fern Bank

Long Meadow Industrial Estate

Magpies Sports Club

Works

Golf V P

Moors Valley Country Park

G H J 205 K L M

09 10 11

Woolsbridge

Ringwood Road

Ashley Heath Industrial Estate

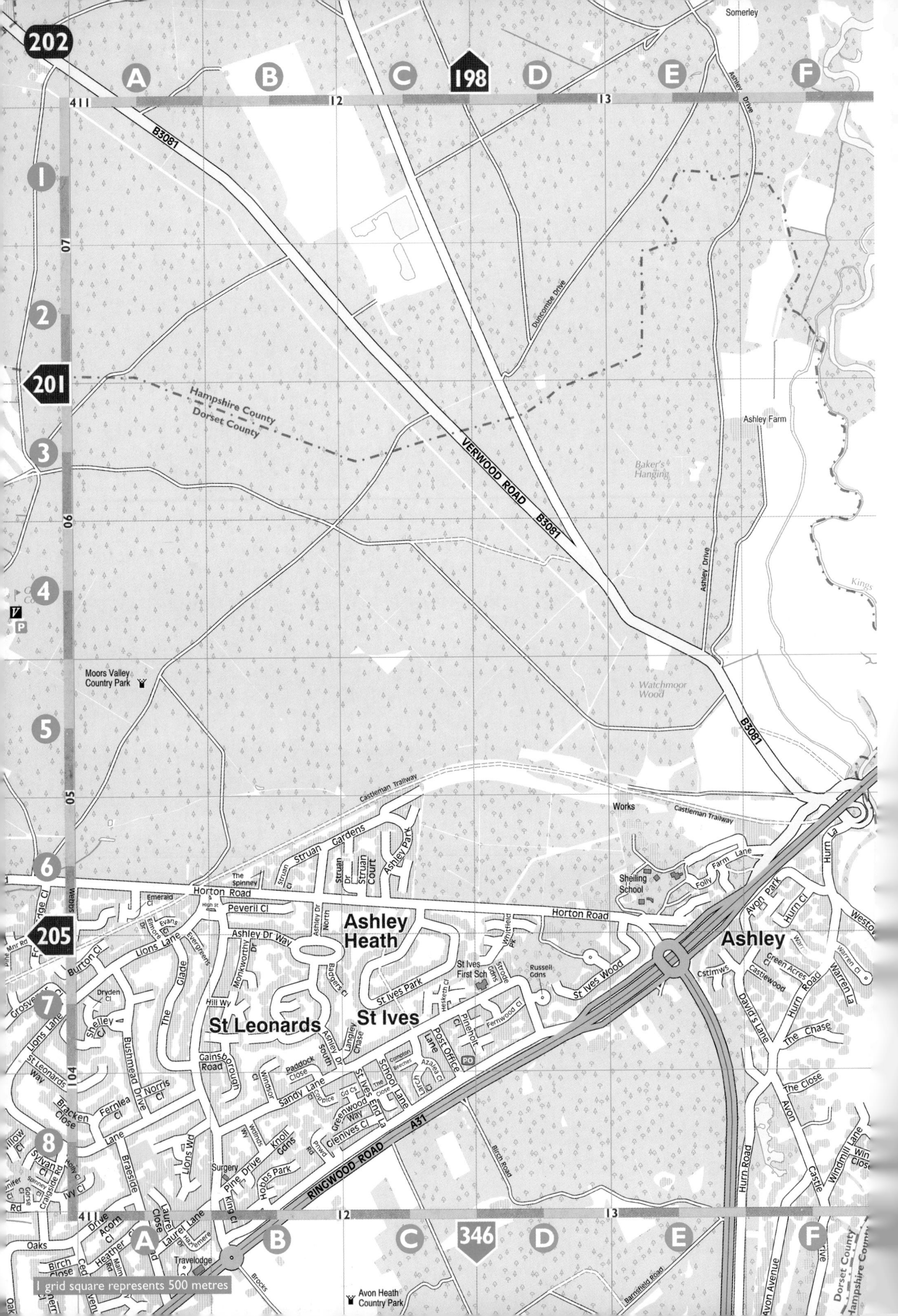

A　　B　　C　198　D　　E　　F

411

12

13

Somerley

Ashley Drive

B3081

1

07

2

201

Hampshire County

Dorset County

VERWOOD ROAD B3081

Ashley Farm

Baker's
Hanging

3

06

Duncombe Drive

4

P

Moors Valley
Country Park

Watchmoor
Wood

Kings

5

05

B3081

Castleman Trailway

Works

Castleman Trailway

6

Ashley

The Spinney

Struan Gardens

Struan Dr

Struan Court

Ashley Park

Horton Road

Sheiling
School

Folly Farm Lane

Avon Park

Hurn Cl

Weston

High St

Emerald Cl

Peveril Cl

Ashley Dr

Ashley Dr Way

Horton Road

Green Acres

Castlewood

Hurn Cl

205

Evans Cl

Monkworthy Dr

Ashley Heath

Whitfield Pk

Cstlmws

Warren La

Pine Mnr Rd

Burton Cl

Lions Lane

The Glade

Badgers Cl

St Ives Park

St Ives
First Sch

Russell Gdns

St Ives Wood

Hurn Road

David's Lane

Hurn Road

Castlewood

Warren Cl

7

Grosvenor Cl

Dryden Cl

Shelley Cl

Hill Wy

St Leonards

St Ives

Hesketh Cl

Strode

Ferntheath Cl

The Chase

Fernhill Cl

Bushmead Drive

Gainsborough
Road

Langley Chase

Compton Beeches

Pinehurst

Post Office PO

Azalea Ct

The Close

Avon

104

St Leonards
Way

Norris Cl

Fernlea Cl

Paddock
Close

Sandy Lane

Windsor Cl

Ashley Dr South

St Ives End Lane

School Lane

Compton

Larch Cl

Birch Road

Windmill Lane

Castle

8

Bracken Close

Lions Wd

Knoll Gdns

Greenwood Way

Glenives Cl

RINGWOOD ROAD A31

Barnsfield Road

Avon Avenue

Sylvan Cl

Spinney Cl

Craigside Rd

Surgery

Pine Drive

Hoobs Park

King Cl

Oaks

Birch

411

12

13

A　　B　346　C　D　　E　　F

Travelodge

Avon Heath
Country Park

1 grid square represents 500 metres

G   H   J   199   K   L   M

14   15   16   17

Ivy Lane

Highw

Highwood Lane

Works

I

Blashford

Snail's Lane

Highwood Lane

1

Snail's Lane

North
Poulner

Blashford
Farm

Cowpitts

2

Avon Vly Path

Works

Highwood Lane

Corley Road

Old Farm
Close

Lane

Works

Woolmer Lane

Works

Headlands
Business Park

Waterside
Close

North Poulner Road

Poulner J&I Sch

Lin Brook

Forestside
Gdns

Shaw
Rd

Lawren

3

Gouldings
Farm

Hurst
Rd

Northfield Road

Morant Road

Northfield Road

Kingfisher Way

Pilgrim Pk

Fairlie

Dene Cl

Holm

P Rd

Denholm

River Avon

Salisbury Road

A338

Salisbury Road

Pound La

Gravel Lane

Highfield Avenue

Highfield Drive

Broadshard

Seymour
Close

Wanstead

Fairlie

Works

Parker
Cl

Corley

Ptlnr
Pk

Chester Rd

Drake

Narrow

Grn

Linford

4

RINGWOOD

Farm
La

Orchard Ct

Manor
Ct

Highfield Rd

Meadow Road

Avonlea
School

Hampton
Drive

Middleton

Mdw

Meadow Wy

Oak La

Lumby
Dr Pk

Lumby Dr

Beechcroft

Gypsy La

Southampton Road

Headlands
Business
Park

Eastfields

Chic

Frobisher

Anson Cl

Somerv

Cook

Beatty Cl

Hds

Raleigh

Poulner

The Mount

Narrow
La

A31

Kestrel
Ct

Southampton Rd

Lilac Cl

Winston

Wessex
Est

Wessex Rd

Jubilee Cl

Pipers
Ash

Audemer
Ct

POULNER HILL

5

342

Shopping
Centre

Stallards
La

Gravel La

P

P

Parsonage

Ringwood Secondary
School

Green La

Barn La

Keppel
Cl

Spittlefields

Eastfield
Cl

Back Down Lane

Notable Lane

Market
PO

Strides La

Centre

Mtng Pl

West St

High St

PO

Carvers
Trading
Est

Collins La

Top La

Ringwood
CE Infant
School

Manor Rd

Clough's

Road

Cadogan
Ct

Poplar

Crs

Lane

Redwood
Cl

East View

Old Barn
Cl

Pleasant

Lane

Ash Gv

Hightown

6

The
Bridges

MANSFIELD RD

Christchurch Rd

Kings Arms La

Kings
Arms
Row

Surg

Works

School La

College Rd

Ringwood
Recreation
Centre

Kingsfield

Poplar

Hilton
Rd

Westbury

Gardner

Woodford
Close

Old Stacks
Gdns

The
Cloisters

Hightown Road

Hightown Hill

Riverside

Ynes La

Kings Arms La

Bickerley Rd

Quomo

Woodcot

CHRISTCHURCH RD

Nsry

Cemetery

Ringwood
Junior
School

Hightown Road

Addison
Square

Way

Euston

Embankment Wy

Gov

Gardner

Old Barn

Brks

Hightown Gdns

Lakeside

Lakeview Dr

Ashley Rd

Forestlake Av

Ashburn
Garth

Forest
Court
Hills

Council
Building

Cxstn

Ringwood
Trading Est

Ctr Gdns

Castleman

Crow

Hightown
Industrial
Est

Lych Gate
Court

Pelican Rd

Swan Md

Linnet

Watership Dr

Duck Island
La

Parkside

Candlesticks Inn

Stchfld

Mc

Stchfld

New St

Police
Station

Pullman
Way

Arch Lane

Crow Arch

Lane

Crow

7

Millstream
Trading
Est

Ringwood
Brewery

Crow Arch Lane
Industrial Est

Wood End Rd

Ft Edge

Westover Farm

River Avon

Avon Valley

Avon Valley
Path

Moorland
Gate

Willow Dr

Stag
Business
Park

Moortown
Lodge
Hotel

CHRISTCHURCH ROAD

Moortown

Moortown

Lane

104

Crow

Lane

8

Lane

Lane

Strides Cl

Hampshire Hatches
Lane

Long Lane

Streets Lane

Barrack

G   H   J   347   K   L   M

14   15   16   17

Green

Upper K
Farm

204
Mannington
Ringwood Road
200
Lower Mannington
A
B
C
D
E
F
405
06
07
Crooked Withies
Haddons Dr
Holt Heath
Newman's Farm
National Nature Reserve
Holt Heath
Newman's Lane
WEST MOORS ROAD
Gulliver's Farm
Woodside Road
Bond Avenue
Denewood Road
STATION
St Mary's CE First School
Heston Wy
Castleman Trailway
Riverside Road
Surgery
Farm Road
Birch Grove
Pennington Road
Queens
White Sheet Plantation
Uddens Water
Ferndown Stour and Forest Trail
Ferndown Forest Golf Club
Golf Course
Ameysford
Dorset Police Eastern Division HQ
Forest Links Rd
Garden Copse Farm
Uddens Plantation
A31
Cobham Road
Ameysford Road
Leeson Drive
Kingsway
Redwood Drive
Cedar Wy
Pine Glen Avenue
Maple Drive
Hazel Drive
Bedborough Farm
Uddens Drive
Telford Rd
Lancaster Road
Maple Business Park
Ferndown Business Park
Ferndown Industrial Estate
209
Hilltop Road
Larks Rise
Ryan Cl
Pinewood
Haviland Road
Cobham
Johnson Road
Nimrod Way
Heather Dr
High Trees Wk
1
2
3
4
5
6
7
8
05
04
03
02
1 grid square represents 500 metres

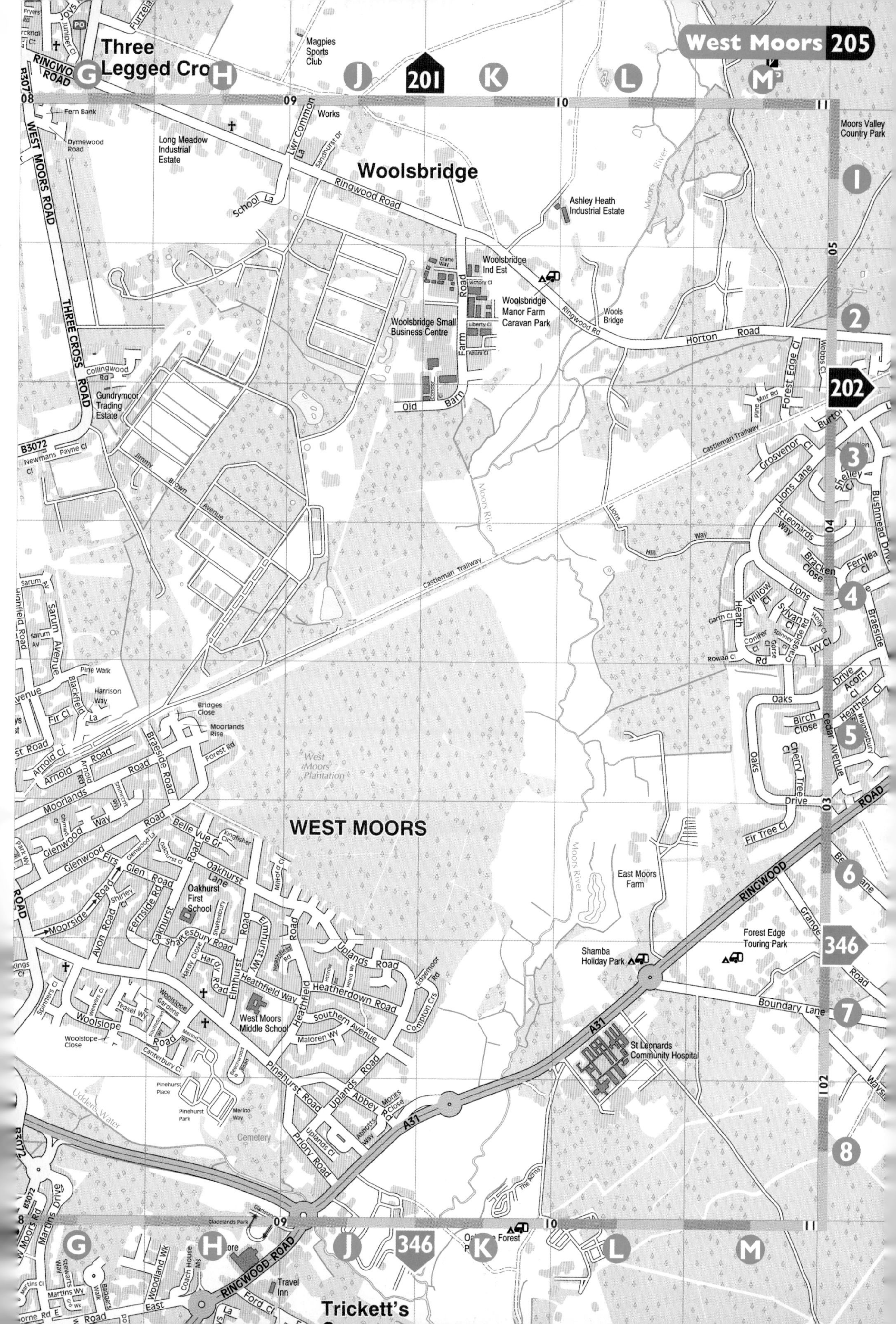
Three Legged Cross
Magpies Sports Club
201
Woolsbridge
Long Meadow Industrial Estate
Lwr Common La
Works
Ringwood Road
School La
Ashley Heath Industrial Estate
Moors River
Moors Valley Country Park
Woolsbridge Ind Est
Woolsbridge Manor Farm Caravan Park
Woolsbridge Small Business Centre
Farm Road
Old Barn
Wools Bridge
Horton Road
Forest Edge Cl
202
WEST MOORS ROAD
THREE CROSS ROAD
Fern Bank
Dymewood Road
Collingwood Rd
Gundrymoor Trading Estate
B3072
Newmans Cl
Payne Cl
Jimmy Brown Avenue
Castleman Trailway
Lions Lane
Grosvenor Cl
St Leonards Way
Hill Way
Bracken Close
Fernlea Cl
Bushmead Drive
Heath Rd
Willow Cl
Sylvan Cl
Craigside Rd
Ivy Cl
Braeside
Rowan Cl
Garth Cl
Conifer Cl
Oaks Drive
Acorn Cl
Heather Cl
Birch Close
Cedar Avenue
Cherry Tree Cl
Drive
Fir Tree Cl
Sarum Avenue
Pine Walk
Blackfield La
Harrison Way
Fir Cl
Bridges Close
Moorlands Rise
Forest Rd
Braeside Road
Arnold Cl
Arnold Road
Moorlands Road
West Moors Plantation
WEST MOORS
Glenwood Road
Glenwood Way
Belle Vue Gr
Kingfisher
Oakhurst Lane
Firs Glen Road
Moorside Road
Avon Road
Shirley Cl
Fernside Rd
Oakhurst First School
Shaftesbury Road
Hardy Close
Hardy Road
Elmhurst Road
Elmhurst Way
Milford Cl
Heathfield Way
Uplands Road
Heatherdown Road
Edgemoor Rd
West Moors Middle School
Southern Avenue
Maloren Wy
Compton Crs
Woolslope Road
Woolslope Gardens
Woolslope Close
Teasel Wy
Spinners Cl
Weavers Cl
Canterbury Cl
Merino Wy
Pinehurst Road
Pinehurst Place
Pinehurst Park
Abbey Road
Monks Close
Abbotts Way
Uplands Cl
Priory Road
Cemetery
Udden's Water
East Moors Farm
RINGWOOD ROAD
A31
Shamba Holiday Park
Forest Edge Touring Park
346
Grange Road
Boundary Lane
St Leonards Community Hospital
Gladelands Park
The Acorns
Oakdene Forest Park
Travel Inn
Ford Cl
Coach House Ms
Woodland Wk
Martins Drive
Martins Wy
Stewarts Way
Badgers Walk
East
Trickett's

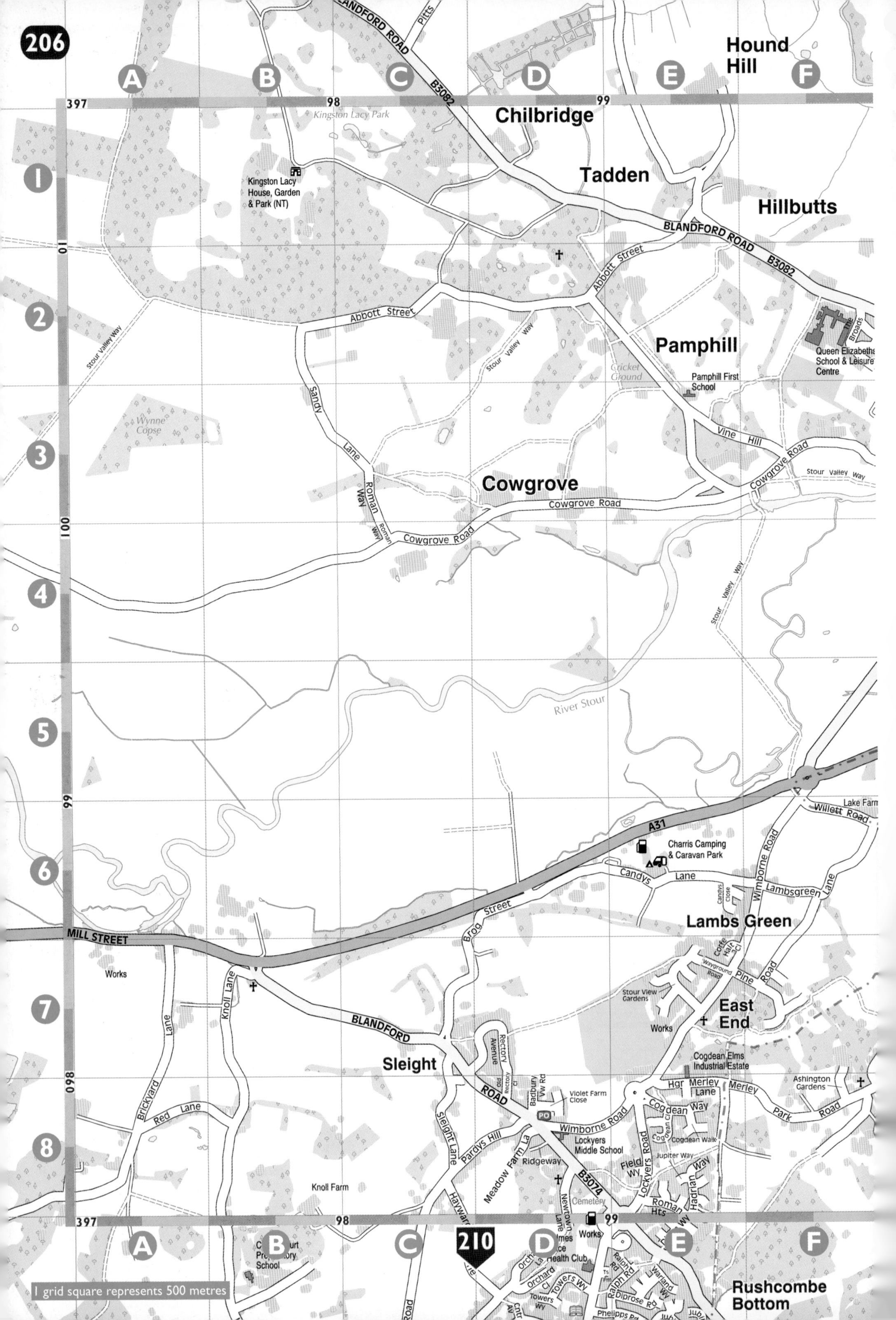

Hound Hill
Chilbridge
Kingston Lacy Park
Tadden
Hillbutts
Kingston Lacy House, Garden & Park (NT)
BLANDFORD ROAD
B3082
Abbott Street
Pamphill
Queen Elizabeths School & Leisure Centre
The Broads
Pamphill First School
Cricket Ground
Stour Valley Way
Sandy Lane
Wynne Copse
Vine Hill
Cowgrove Road
Cowgrove
Roman Way
River Stour
A31
Charris Camping & Caravan Park
Lake Farm
Willett Road
Candys Lane
Candys Close
Wimborne Road
Lambsgreen Lane
Lambs Green
Brog Street
MILL STREET
Works
Knoll Lane
Corfe Hall Cl
Wayground Road
Pine Road
Stour View Gardens
East End
BLANDFORD ROAD
Sleight
Rectory Avenue
Cogdean Elms Industrial Estate
Hgr Merley Lane
Merley Park Road
Ashington Gardens
Brickyard Lane
Red Lane
Violet Farm Close
Cogdean Way
Cogdean Walk
Sleight Lane
Pardys Hill
Lockyers Middle School
Jupiter Way
Ridgeway
Meadow Farm La
Field Wy
Lockyers Road
Hadrian Way
Knoll Farm
B3074
Cemetery
Roman Hts
Newtown Lane
Works
Rushcombe Bottom
1 grid square represents 500 metres

210

Field Hill

Colehill

G H J K L M

400 01 02 03

Wilksworth Farm

Wilksworth Farm Caravan Park

Long Lane Farm

St Michaels CE Middle School

Beaucroft Foundation School

WIMBORNE MINSTER

Wimborne Hospital

Tivoli Theatre

Wimborne Town FC

Priest's House Mus & Garden

Wimborne Minster

Beechleas Hotel

Grammar School Lane

Deans Court

Leigh

Wimborne RFC

Dorset County

Poole

Trinity Industrial Estate

Brook Park Estate

208

Ashington

Merley Court Touring Park

Merley House

Oakley

Merley First School

Oakley Shopping Centre

Merley

Rose Lawn Coppice

G H J K L M

00 01 02 03

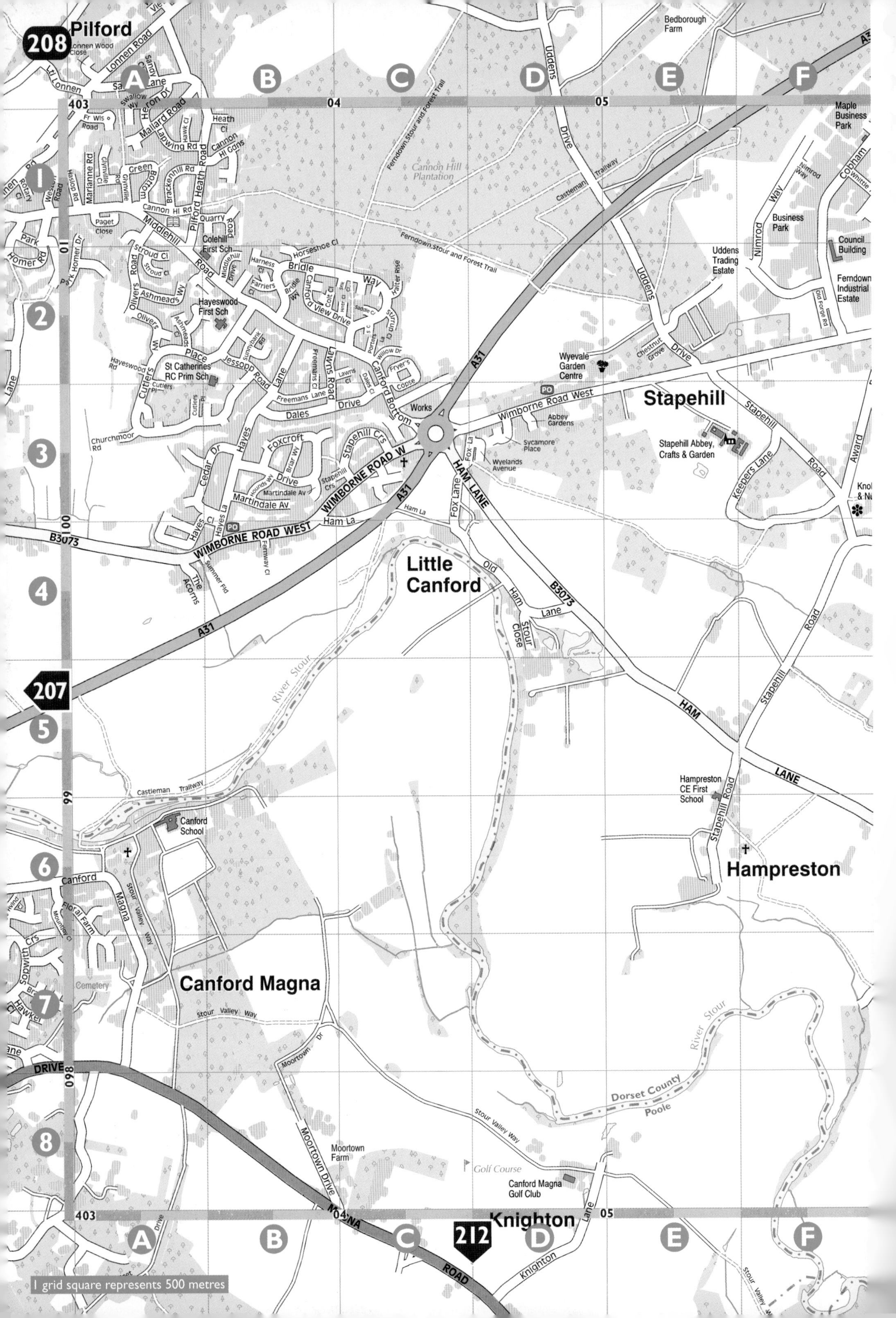

Lonnen Wood
Close

Lonnen Road

Sandy
Lane

Heron Dr

403

Fr Wls
Road

Weston Rd

Lonnen
Rotary
Park

Swallow
Way

Sa Lane

A

Mallard Road

Clynville
Gardens

Marianne Rd

Green
Bottom

Clynville
Road

Lapwing Rd

Heath
Road

Cannon
Hi Gdns

B

04

Cannon Heath Cl

Horseshoe Cl

Ferndown,Stour and Forest Trail

Cannon Hill
Plantation

C

Bedborough
Farm

Uddens

Drive

05

A31

D

Castleman Trailway

E

Maple
Business
Park

Nimrod
Way

Nimrod Way

Cobham

Whittle

Business
Park

F

Council
Building

Ferndown
Industrial
Estate

I

Homer Rd

010

Homer Dr

Middlehill

Paget
Close

Cannon Hi Rd

Brackenhill Rd

Pilford Heath Road

Quarry
Road

Colehill
First Sch

Middlehill
Drive

Harness

Farriers

Bridle
Wk

Bridle
Way

Carter Rise

2

Park

Lane

Stroud Cl

Oliver's
Road

Ashmead's

Stroud Cl

Oliver's

Ashmead's Wy

Cutler's

Cutlers
Pl

Hayeswood
Rd

St Catherines
RC Prim Sch

Hayeswood
First Sch

Place

Jessopp Road

Freemans Lane

Dales

Lawns
Cl

Canford View Drive

Colt Cl

Saddle Cl

Portals
Cl

Freemans Cl

Lawns Road

Willow Dr

Canford Bottom

Fryer's
Copse

Works

Wimborne Road West

PO

Abbey
Gardens

Uddens
Trading
Estate

Chestnut
Grove

Uddens

Drive

Wyevale
Garden
Centre

Stapehill

3

Churchmoor
Rd

Cedar
Dr

Hayes
Drive

Foxcroft

Briar Wy

Hounds Wy

Hayes Cl

Martindale Av

Stapehill
Crs

Stapehill Crs

Martindale Av

A31

PO

WIMBORNE ROAD WEST

Ham La

Fox La

Ham La

HAM LANE

Fox Lane

Sycamore
Place

Wyelands
Avenue

Stapehill Abbey,
Crafts & Garden

Stapehill Abbey,
Crafts & Garden

Keepers Lane

Stapehill

Road

Award

Knoll
& Nu

B3073

Summer Fld

Fernway Cl

The
Acorns

WIMBORNE ROAD WEST

A31

**Little
Canford**

Old

Ham
Close

Stour

Lane

B3073

4

River Stour

HAM

207

5

LANE

Stapehill Road

99

Castleman Trailway

Canford
School

Hampreston
CE First
School

Hampreston

6

Canford

Magna

Stour Valley Way

Floral Farm

Moortown Cl

Canford

Hampreston

Sopwith
Crs

Cemetery

Canford Magna

Stour Valley Way

River Stour

7

Hawker Cl

Lane

DRIVE

080

Moortown Dr

Moortown Drive

Moortown Farm

Stour Valley Way

Dorset County
Poole

8

M04NA

403

A

B

04

B

Golf Course

Canford Magna
Golf Club

C

212

Knighton

Knighton

Lane

05

D

Knighton

ROAD

E

Stour Valley Way

F

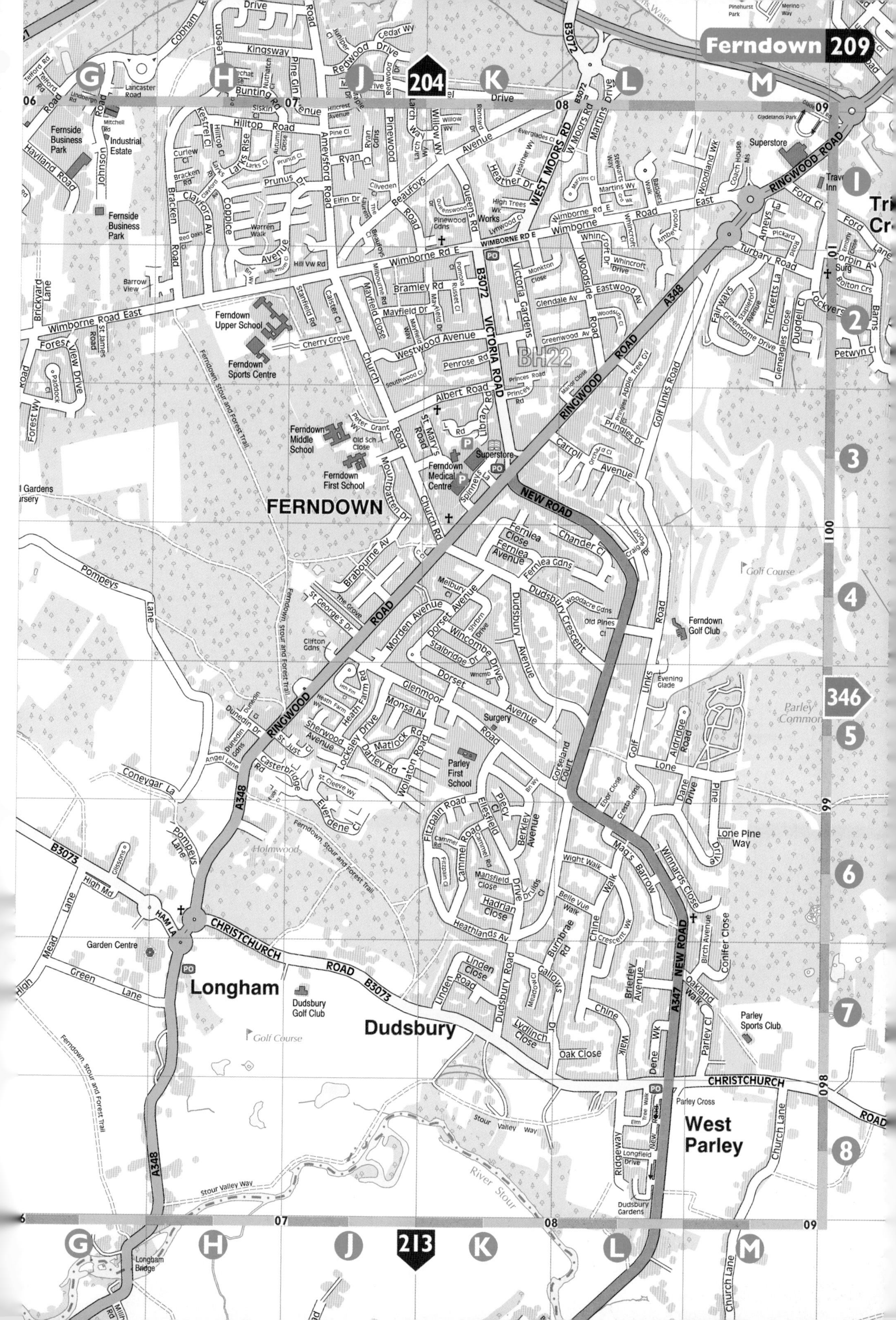

Ferndown 209
204
213
346
FERNDOWN
Longham
Dudsbury
West Parley
BH22
Ferndown Upper School
Ferndown Sports Centre
Ferndown Middle School
Ferndown First School
Ferndown Medical Centre
Superstore
Fernside Business Park
Industrial Estate
Ferndown Golf Club
Parley First School
Surgery
Garden Centre
Dudsbury Golf Club
Golf Course
Parley Sports Club
Parley Common
Parley Cross
Dudsbury Gardens
Longham Bridge
River Stour
Stour Valley Way
Ferndown Stour and Forest Trail
Wimborne Road East
Ringwood Road
New Road
Victoria Road
West Moors Rd
Christchurch Road
Church Road
Golf Links Road
Dorset Avenue
Dudsbury Avenue
Pompeys Lane
Green Lane
Mead Lane

210
206
222
Corfe Mullen
Hill View
Rushcombe Bottom
Beacon Hill
Upton
Upton Heath
Poor Common
Knoll Farm
Castle Court Preparatory School
Lockyers Middle School
Holmes Place Health Club
Henbury View First School
Rushcombe First School
Springdale First School
Corfe Hills School
Upton Health Cen
Birchwood Medical Cen
Beacon Hill Touring Park
Works
Surgery
Cemetery
HIGHER BLANDFORD ROAD
B3074
BLANDFORD RD N
A35
A350
UPTON ROAD
POOLE RD
Wareham Road
Old Wareham Road
Rushall Lane
Waterloo Road
Broadmoor Road
Knoll Lane
Brook Lane
Springdale Road
Corfe Lodge Road
Abbotsbury Road
Roman Road
Hanham Road
Albert Road
Blythe Road
Central Av
South Rd
Wimborne Road
Castleman Trailway
Dorset County
Poole
Longmeadow Lane
Broadstone Way
Beacon Road
Corfe Way
Upton Way
Clarendon Road
Redwood Road
1 grid square represents 500 metres

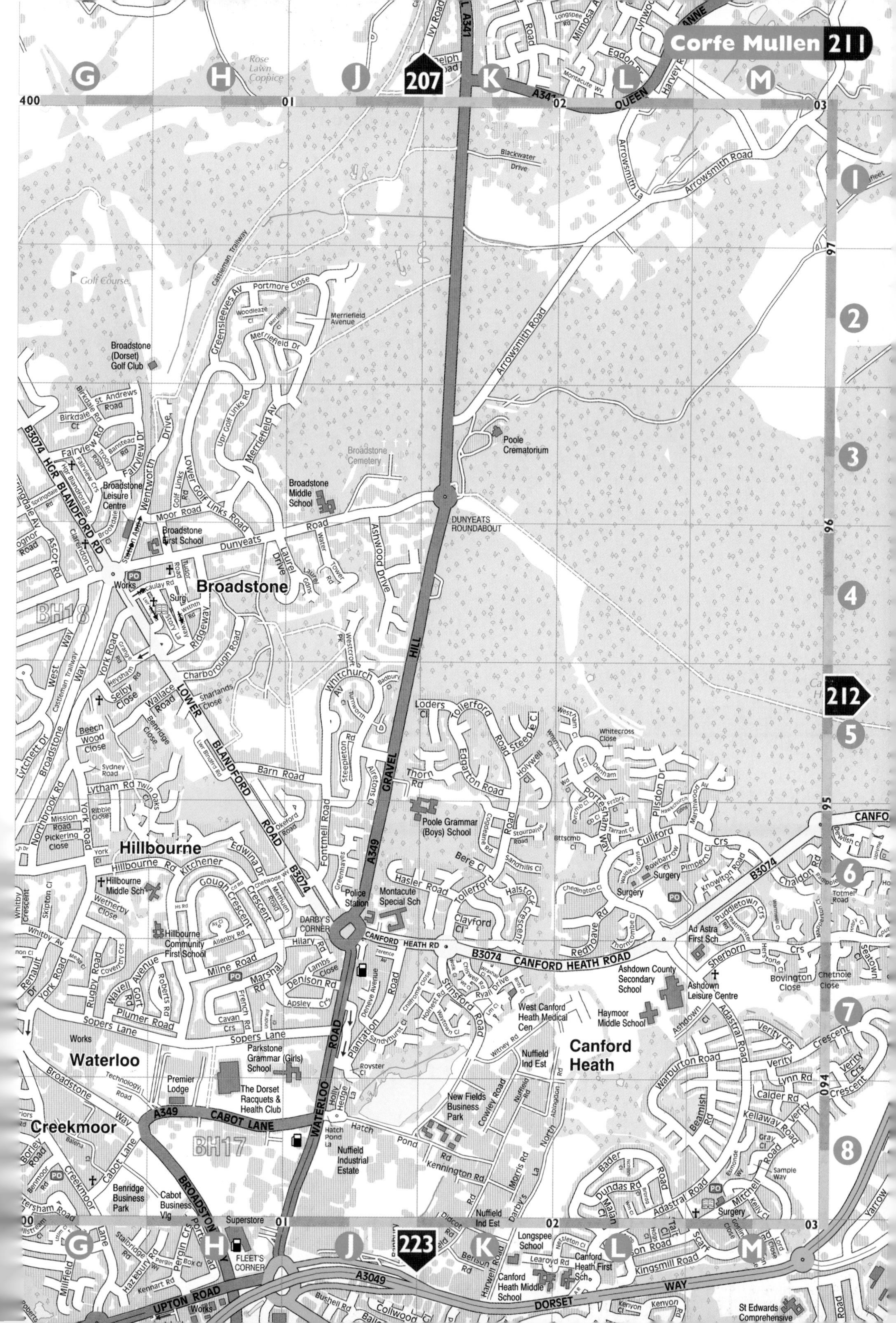
G
H
J
K
L
M
207
212
223
Rose Lawn Coppice
Ivy Road
A341
Longspee
Mimosa
Egdon Dr
Montacute Wy
QUEEN ANNE
Harvey Rd
400
01
02
03
Blackwater Drive
Arrowsmith La
Arrowsmith Road
Castleman Trailway
Golf Course
Portmore Close
Greensleeves Av
Woodleaze Cl
Merriefield Cl
Merriefield Dr
Merriefield Avenue
Broadstone (Dorset) Golf Club
St Andrews Road
Birkdale Rd
Birkdale Ct
Banstead Rd
Troon Road
Fairview Road
Fairview Dr
Fairview Crs
Wentworth Drive
Upr Golf Links Rd
Lower Golf Links Road
Golf Links Rd
Merriefield Av
Broadstone Cemetery
Poole Crematorium
B3074 HGR BLANDFORD RD
Broadstone Leisure Centre
Moor Road
Broadstone First School
Broadstone Middle School
Dunyeats Road
DUNYEATS ROUNDABOUT
Laurel Drive
Laurel Gdns
Water Tower Rd
Ashwood Drive
Springdale Rd
Clarendon Cl
Ascot Rd
Tudor Road
Macaulay Rd
Works
Broadstone
Surg
Victory La
Ridgeway
BH18
Charborough Road
West Way
Castleman Trailway
York Road
Grange Rd
Heysham Rd
Selby Close
Wallace Road
Sharlands Close
LOWER BLANDFORD ROAD
Lwr Blandford Rd
Westcroft Pk
Whitchurch Av
Badbury
Turnworth Cl
GRAVEL HILL
A349
Loders Cl
Tollerford Road
Steeple Cl
Whitecross Close
Beech Wood Close
Benridge Close
Sydney Road
Lytchett Dr
Broadstone
Northbrook Rd
Barn Road
Steepleton Rd
Thorn Rd
Eggardon Road
Holwell Cl
Denham
Portesham Way
Pilsdon Dr
Marshwood Av
Hawkchurch Gdns
Lytham Rd
Twin Oaks
Mission Road
Ribble Close
Pickering Close
York Road
Okeford Road
Fontmell Road
Poole Grammar (Boys) School
Stourpaine Road
Tarrant Cl
Culliford Crs
Hillbourne
Hillbourne Rd
Kitchener Cres
Edwina Dr
B3074
Greenhayes
Coppleane Rd
Bere Cl
Sandhills Cl
Rowbarrow Cl
Surgery
Pimpern Cl
Knowlton Road
B3074
CANFORD
Chaldon Rd
Totmel Road
Hillbourne Middle Sch
Gough Crescent
Crescent
Methuen Road
Police Station
Montacute Special Sch
Hasler Road
Tollerford
Halstock Crescent
Chedington Cl
Surgery
Redhoave Rd
Thorncombe Cl
Puddletown Crs
Whitby Crescent
Skipton Cl
Wetherby Close
DARBY'S CORNER
Clayford Cl
Ad Astra First Sch
Whitby Av
Hillbourne Community First School
Allenby Rd
Hilary Rd
CANFORD HEATH RD
B3074 CANFORD HEATH ROAD
Sherborn Crs
Renault Dr
York Road
Rugby Road
Coventry Crs
Wavell Avenue
Roberts Rd
Milne Road
Marshal Rd
Lambs Close
Denison Rd
Deneve Avenue
Ryall Drive
Ashdown County Secondary School
Ashdown Leisure Centre
Bovington Close
Chetnole Close
Seatown Cl
Court Rd
Plumer Road
French Rd
Cavan Crs
Apsley Crs
Chilfrome Close
Holnest Rd
Stinsford Road
West Canford Heath Medical Cen
Haymoor Middle School
Ashdown
Adastral Road
Verity Crs
Crescent
Sopers Lane
Sopers Lane
Works
Waterloo
Parkstone Grammar (Girls) School
WATERLOO ROAD
Plantation
Sandyhurst Cl
Witney Rd
Nuffield Ind Est
Canford Heath
Royster Cl
Warburton Road
Verity
Lynn Rd
Verity Crs
Crescent
Calder Rd
Broadstone Technology Road
Premier Lodge
The Dorset Racquets & Health Club
Holly Hedge La
Cowley Road
Nuffield Rd
North Abingdon Rd
New Fields Business Park
Beamish Rd
Kellaway Road
Verity
A349 CABOT LANE
Creekmoor
Way
Hatch Pond La
Hatch Pond Rd
Nuffield Industrial Estate
Kennington Rd
Morris Rd
Darby's La
Gray Cl
Sample Way
Borley Road
Benmoor Rd
Creekmoor
Cabot Lane
BH17
Benridge Business Park
Cabot Business Vlg
BROADSTONE WAY
Bader Rd
Dundas Rd
Malan Cl
Adastral Road
Mitchell Road
Surgery
Superstore
Nuffield Ind Est
Longspee School
Canford Heath First Sch
Learoyd Rd
Kingsmill Road
FLEET'S CORNER
Millfield
Hazelbury Rd
Kennart Rd
Pergin Crs
Stanbridge Rd
UPTON ROAD
Works
A3049
DORSET WAY
Bushell Rd
Colwood
Berlson Rd
Harwell Road
Canford Heath Middle School
Kenyon Rd
St Edwards Comprehensive
Yarrow
1
2
3
4
5
6
7
8
97
96
95
094

212
208
211
224
Knighton
Bear
West Howe
Alderney
Turbary Common
Newtown
Rossmore
BH11
BH12
Magna Road
A341
Ringwood Road
A348
Canford Heath Road
Canford Way
A3049
Wallisdown Road
B3068 Ringwood Road
Bearwood County Primary School
Eastlands Farm
Bearwood Medical Cen
Oakmead School College
Knighton Heath Golf Club
Golf Course
Turbary Retail Park
Francis Avenue Industrial Est
Ringwood Road Retail Park
Knighton Heath Industrial Estate
West Howe Industrial Estate
Drewitts Industrial Estate
Police Station
Council Building
Superstore
Tower Park
Megabowl
UCI Cinema
Acorn Business Centre
Mannings Heath Retail Park
Alderney Community Hospital
Winchelsea Special Sch
Alderney Middle Sch
Rossmore Community College
Kemp Welch Leisure Centre
Trinidad First Sch
Newtown Bus Pk
Chalwyn Industrial
Rosemary Medical Cen
St Josephs RC Combined
Moortown Farm
Canford Magna Golf Club
Stour Valley Way
Poole
1 grid square represents 500 metres

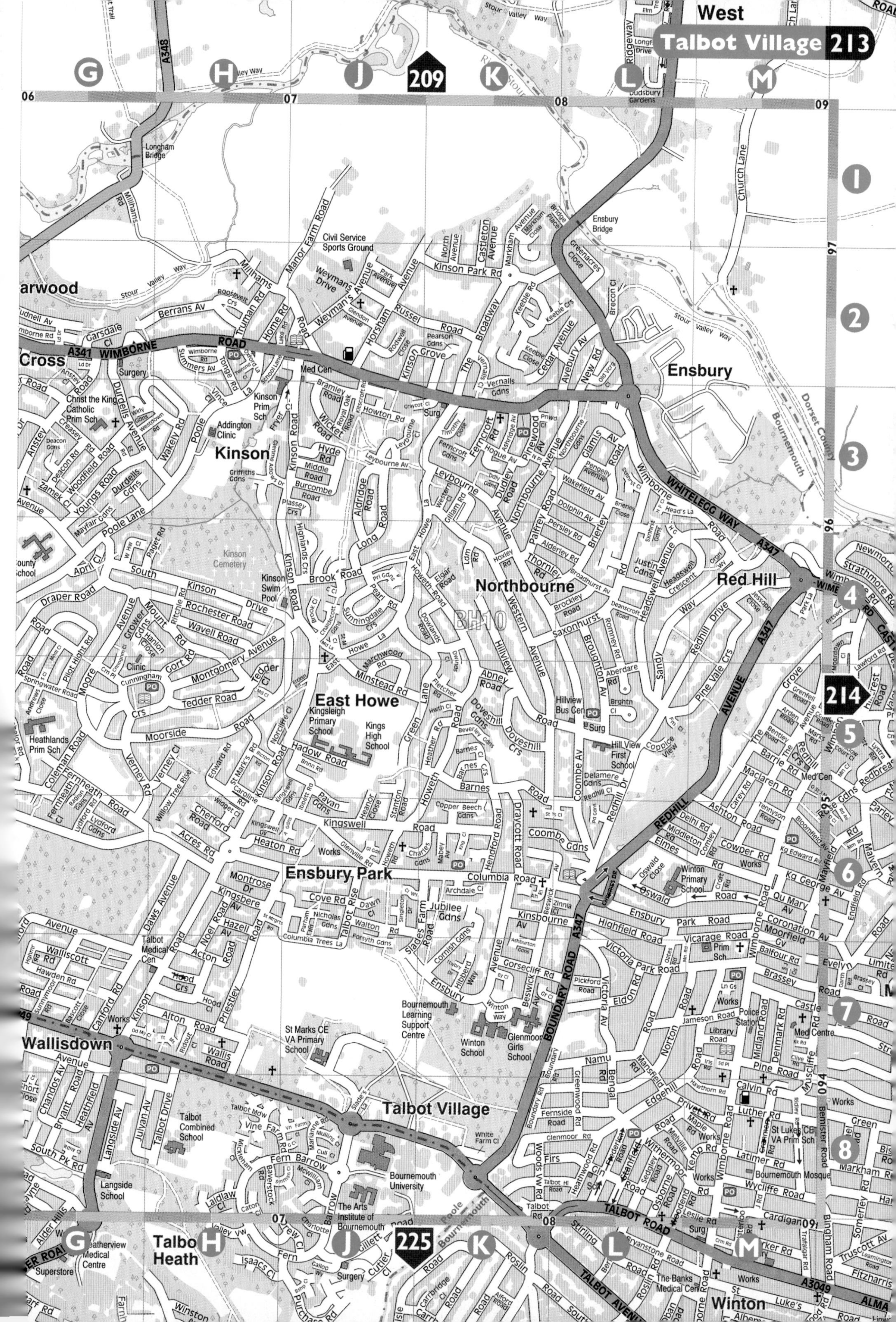
West
209
Dudsbury Gardens
Longham Bridge
Ensbury Bridge
Civil Service Sports Ground
Stour Valley Way
Church Lane
Ensbury
Kinson
Addington Clinic
Christ the King Catholic Prim Sch
Kinson Prim Sch
Kinson Cemetery
Kinson Swim Pool
Northbourne
Red Hill
BH10
East Howe
Kingsleigh Primary School
Kings High School
Heathlands Prim Sch
Hillview Bus Cen
Hill View First School
214
Winton Primary School
Ensbury Park
Talbot Medical Cen
Bournemouth Learning Support Centre
Winton School
Glenmoor Girls School
St Marks CE VA Primary School
Wallisdown
Talbot Village
Talbot Combined School
Bournemouth University
The Arts Institute of Bournemouth
Langside School
St Lukes CE VA Prim Sch
Bournemouth Mosque
Med Centre
Police Station
Library
The Banks Medical Cen
Talbot Heath
Heatherview Medical Centre
Superstore
225
Winton
A341 WIMBORNE ROAD
WHITELEGG WAY A347
REDHILL AVENUE A347
BOUNDARY ROAD A347
TALBOT ROAD
TALBOT AVENUE
A3049
Dorset County
Bournemouth
Kinson Road
Poole Lane
Moorside Road
Columbia Road
Wimborne Road
Castle Road
Talbot Drive

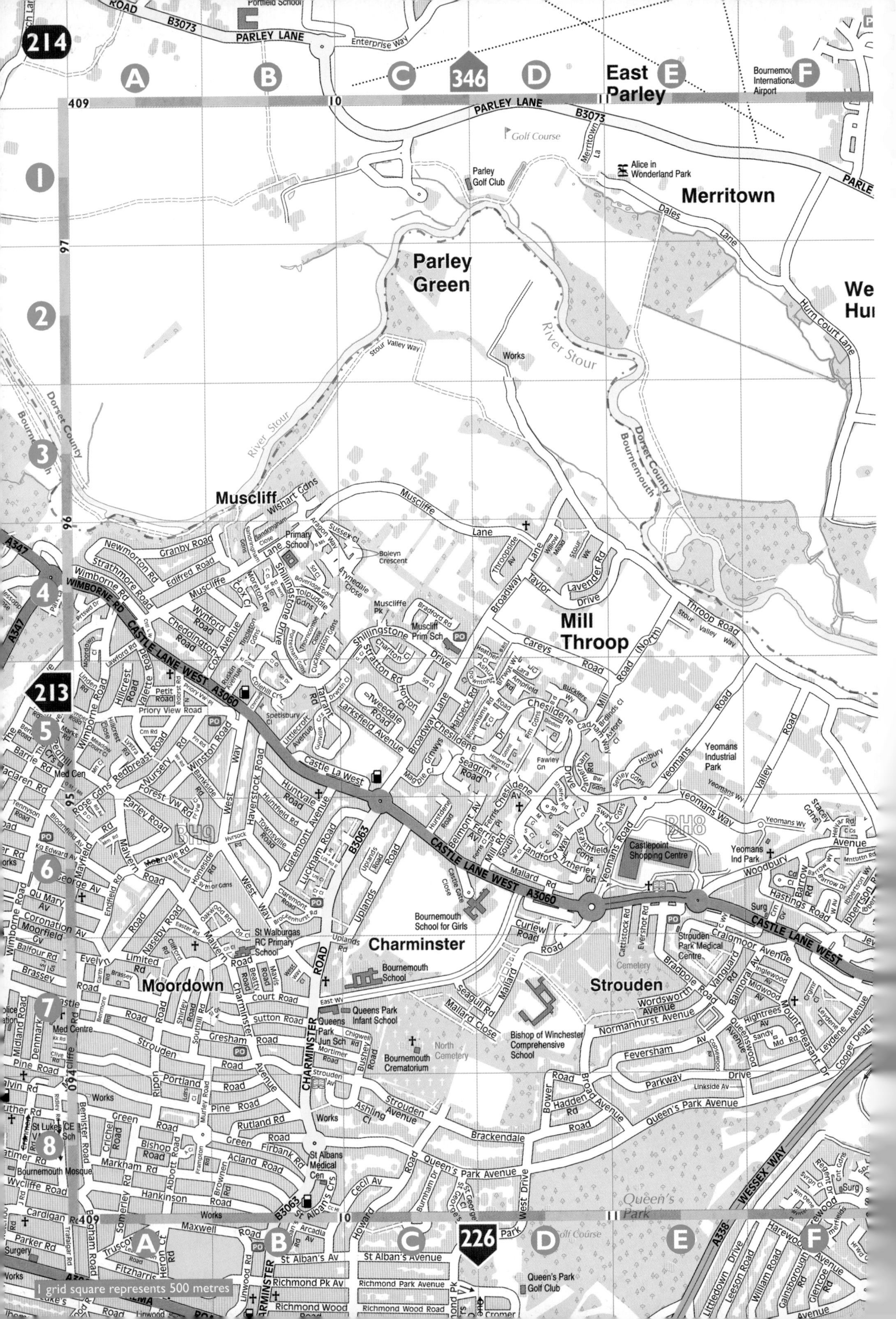

214
346
213
226
A
B
C
D
E
F
1
2
3
4
5
6
7
8
409
10
97
96
95
094
Portfield School
PARLEY LANE
B3073
Enterprise Way
East Parley
Bournemouth International Airport
Golf Course
Parley Golf Club
Alice in Wonderland Park
Merritown
Merritown La
Dales Lane
Parley Green
Stour Valley Way
River Stour
Works
Hurn Court Lane
Dorset County
Bournemouth
Muscliff
Muscliffe Lane
Wishart Gdns
Primary School
Boleyn Crescent
Newmorton Road
Granby Road
Strathmore Road
Edifred Road
Wimborne Rd
WIMBORNE RD
CASTLE LANE WEST A3060
Muscliffe Road
Wynford Road
Cheddington Road
Cox Avenue
Shillingstone Drive
Muscliffe Pk
Muscliff Prim Sch
Throopside Av
Broadway Lane
Taylor Drive
Lavender Rd
Mill Throop
Throop Road
Stour Valley Way
Careys Road
Mill Road (North)
Yeomans Road
Valley Road
Yeomans Industrial Park
Yeomans Way
Yeomans Ind Park
BH8
Castlepoint Shopping Centre
Woodbury Avenue
Hastings Road
Barrow Rd
Stacey Gdns
Hillcrest Road
Valette Road
Petit Road
Priory View Road
Redbreast Road
Nursery Road
Winston Road
Bankside Road
West Way
Haverstock Road
Huntvale Road
Huntfield Rd
Townsville Road
Claremont Avenue
Luckham Road
Uplands Road
Tarrant Rd
Tweedale Road
Larksfield Avenue
Stratton Rd
Horton Cl
Chesildene Avenue
Seagrim Road
Harbeck Rd
Castle La West
Fawley Gn
Holbury Cl
Castle Gate Close
Belmont Av
Hurstdene Road
Ferris Av
Mill Rd South
Landford Way
Brashfield Road
Mallard Rd
Tytherley Gn
Bournemouth School for Girls
Charminster
BH9
Rose Gdns
Parley Road
Malvern Road
Moorvale Rd
Homeside Rd
Mayfield Rd
Endfield Rd
George Av
Qu Mary Av
Coronation Av
Moorfield Gv
Balfour Rd
Brassey Road
Evelyn Road
Limited Rd
Naseby Road
Malvern Road
St Walburgas RC Primary School
Beatty Road
Mavis Road
Charminster Road
Moordown
Bournemouth School
Court Road
Sutton Road
Queens Park Infant School
Queens Park Jun Sch
Mortimer Road
Bournemouth Crematorium
North Cemetery
Curlew Road
Seagull Rd
Mallard Close
Bishop of Winchester Comprehensive School
Cattistock Rd
Evershot Rd
Strouden Park Medical Centre
Craigmoor Avenue
Cemetery
Strouden
Bradpole Road
Vanguard Road
Wordsworth Avenue
Normanhurst Avenue
Feversham Av
Parkway Drive
Linksidе Av
Balmoral Av
Midwood Av
Hightrees Av
Mount Pleasant Dr
Leydene Avenue
Cooper Dean
Queen's Park Avenue
Brackendale Road
Bower Road
Hadden Rd
Broad Avenue
Med Cen
Tennyson Road
Bloomfield Av
Kg Edward Av
Wimborne Road
Midland Road
Denmark Road
Med Centre
Strouden Road
Gresham Road
Portland Road
Pine Road
Ripon Road
Pine Road
Rutland Rd
Green Road
Firbank Rd
Acland Road
St Albans Medical Cen
Ashling Cl
Strouden Avenue
Works
Green Road
Crichel Road
Bishop Road
Abbott Road
Markham Rd
Hankinson Road
Bemister Road
Pine Road
St Lukes CE VA Sch
Bournemouth Mosque
Wycliffe Road
Cardigan Rd
Parker Rd
Surgery
Trafalgar Rd
Somerley Road
Bengham Road
Maxwell Road
Linwood Rd
Heron Ct Rd
Fitzharris
Charminster Road
B3063
St Alban's Crs
Arcadia Av
Cecil Av
Howard Road
Burnham Dr
St George's Av
West Drive
Park
Queen's Park
Golf Course
Queen's Park Golf Club
St Alban's Av
St Alban's Avenue
Richmond Pk Av
Richmond Park Avenue
Richmond Wood Road
Cromer
WESSEX WAY
A338
Littledown Drive
Leeson Road
William Road
Gainsborough Rd
Glencoe Rd
Harewood Avenue
Surg
1 grid square represents 500 metres

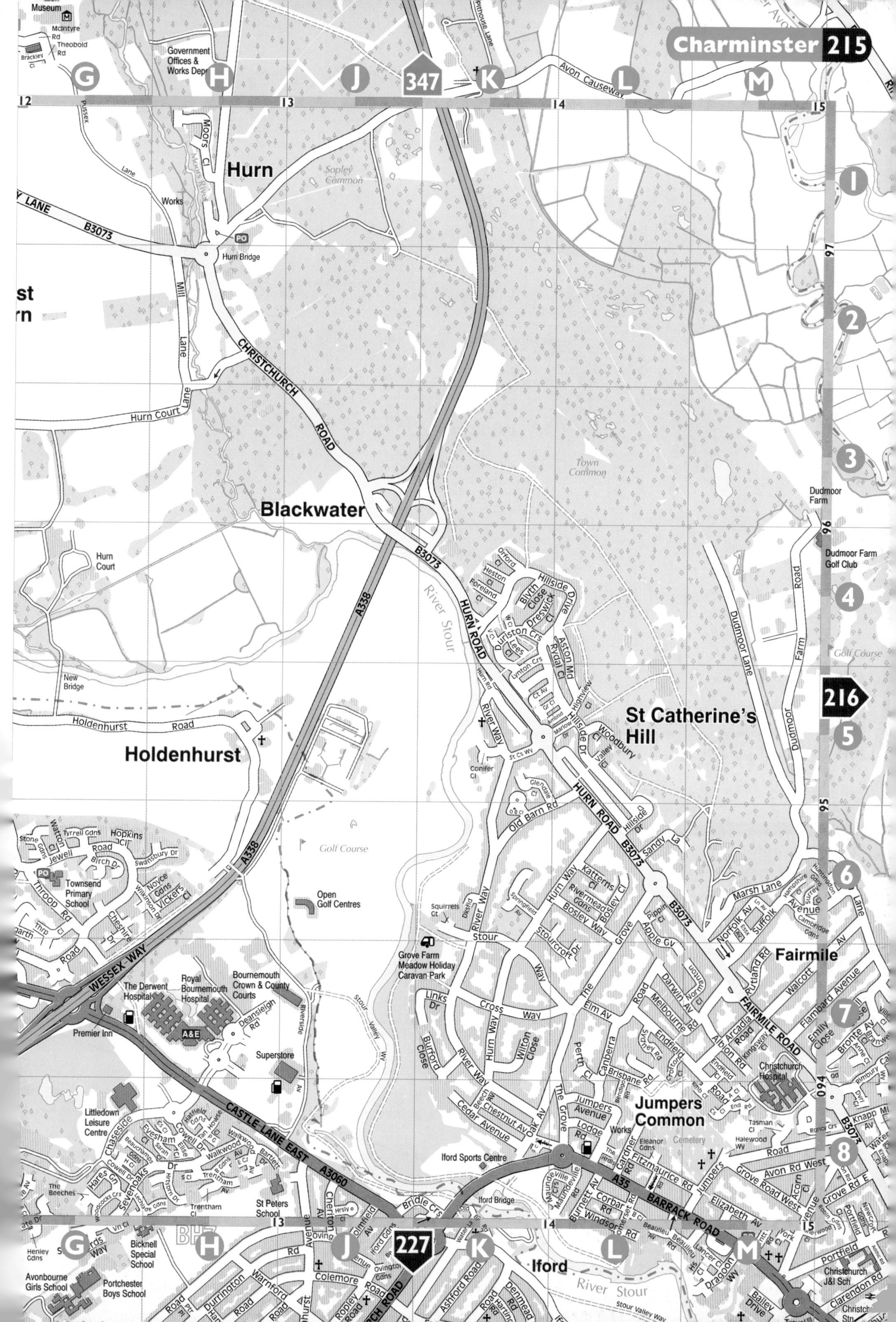
Charminster 215
347
216
227
Museum
McIntyre Rd
Theobold Rd
Brackley Cl
Government Offices & Works Dept
Pithouse Lane
Avon Causeway
Hurn
Moors Cl
Moors River
Sopley Common
Works
B3073
PO
Hurn Bridge
Mill Lane
CHRISTCHURCH ROAD
Hurn Court Lane
Blackwater
Town Common
Dudmoor Farm
Dudmoor Farm Golf Club
Golf Course
Hurn Court
New Bridge
River Stour
HURN ROAD
A338
Holdenhurst Road
Holdenhurst
St Catherine's Hill
Dudmoor Lane
Dudmoor Farm Road
Hillside Drive
Blyth Close
Dreswick Cl
Heston Cl
Foreland Cl
Dunston Crs
Lees Cl
Lynton Crs
Aston Md
Rydal Cl
Highview Cl
Woodbury
Valley Cl
Hillside Dr
River Way
St Cs Wy
Conifer Cl
Glendale Cl
Old Barn Rd
Sandy La
Golf Course
Open Golf Centres
Wessex Way
Tyrrell Gdns
Hopkins Cl
Watton Cl
Jewell Rd
Birch Dr
Swansbury Dr
Townsend Primary School
Throop Rd
Noyce Gdns
Vickers Cl
Cheshire Dr
The Derwent Hospital
Royal Bournemouth Hospital
Bournemouth Crown & County Courts
A&E
Premier Inn
Deansleigh Rd
Riverside Av
Superstore
Stour Valley Wy
Grove Farm Meadow Holiday Caravan Park
Squirrels Ct
Stour Rd
Links Dr
Cross Way
Hurn Way
Katterns Cl
Rivermead Gdns
Bosley Way
Bosley Cl
Stourcroft Dr
Grove Rd
Pippin Cl
Apple Gv
Marsh Lane
Norfolk Av
Suffolk Avenue
Fairmile
FAIRMILE ROAD
Rutland Rd
Walcott Av
Flambard Avenue
Emily Close
Bronte Av
Christchurch Hospital
Burford Close
Wilton Close
Elm Av
Canberra Rd
Melbourne Rd
Darwin Av
Endfield Rd
Brisbane Rd
Perth Cl
Albion Rd
Arcadia Road
Kingsway Cl
Jumpers Common
Cemetery
Jumpers Avenue
Lodge Rd
Works
Cedar Avenue
Chestnut Av
Oak Av
The Grove
Littledown Leisure Centre
Chaseside
Evesham Cl
Cowell Dr
Walkwood Av
Sevenoaks Dr
Trentham Av
Trentham Cl
The Beeches
CASTLE LANE EAST
A3060
St Peters School
Iford Sports Centre
Iford Bridge
Bridle Crs
Maundeville Rd
Corbar Rd
Windsor Rd
Fitzmaurice Rd
A35 BARRACK ROAD
Elizabeth Av
Grove Road West
Avon Rd West
Grove Rd E
Portfield Rd
Henley Gdns
Bicknell Special School
Avonbourne Girls School
Portchester Boys School
Durrington Rd
Warnford Road
Colemore Road
Ropley Road
Ashford Road
Iford
River Stour
Dragoon Wy
Bailey Drive
Christchurch J&I Sch
Clarendon Rd
Stour Valley Way
BH7
G
H
J
K
L
M
1
2
3
4
5
6
7
8
12
13
14
15
97
96
95
094

216
347
215
228
Sopley
Winkton
North Bockhampton
Middle Bockham
South Bockhampton
Burton
Fairmile
Somerford
BH23
Hampshire County
Dorset County
Moorlands College
Sopley Park
Homefield Preparatory School
Homefield School
Burton CE Primary School
Burton Medical Cen
Dudmoor Farm
Dudmoor Farm Golf Club
Golf Course
Winkton Common
Christchurch Hospital
River Avon
Avon Trading Park
Southern Electric Museum
The Grange Comprehensive School
Somerford Pri & Comm Sch
Lr Clockhouse Farm
Salisbury Road
Stony Lane
Burley Road
Bockhampton Road
Hawthorn Road
Waterditch Road
Lyndhurst Road
Preston Lane
Hill Lane
Derritt Lane
Priest Lane
Harpway Lane
Avon Valley Path
Christchurch By-Pass
Purewell Cross
Fairmile Road
Marsh Lane
Whitehayes Rd
Summers Lane
Ambury Lane
1 grid square represents 500 metres

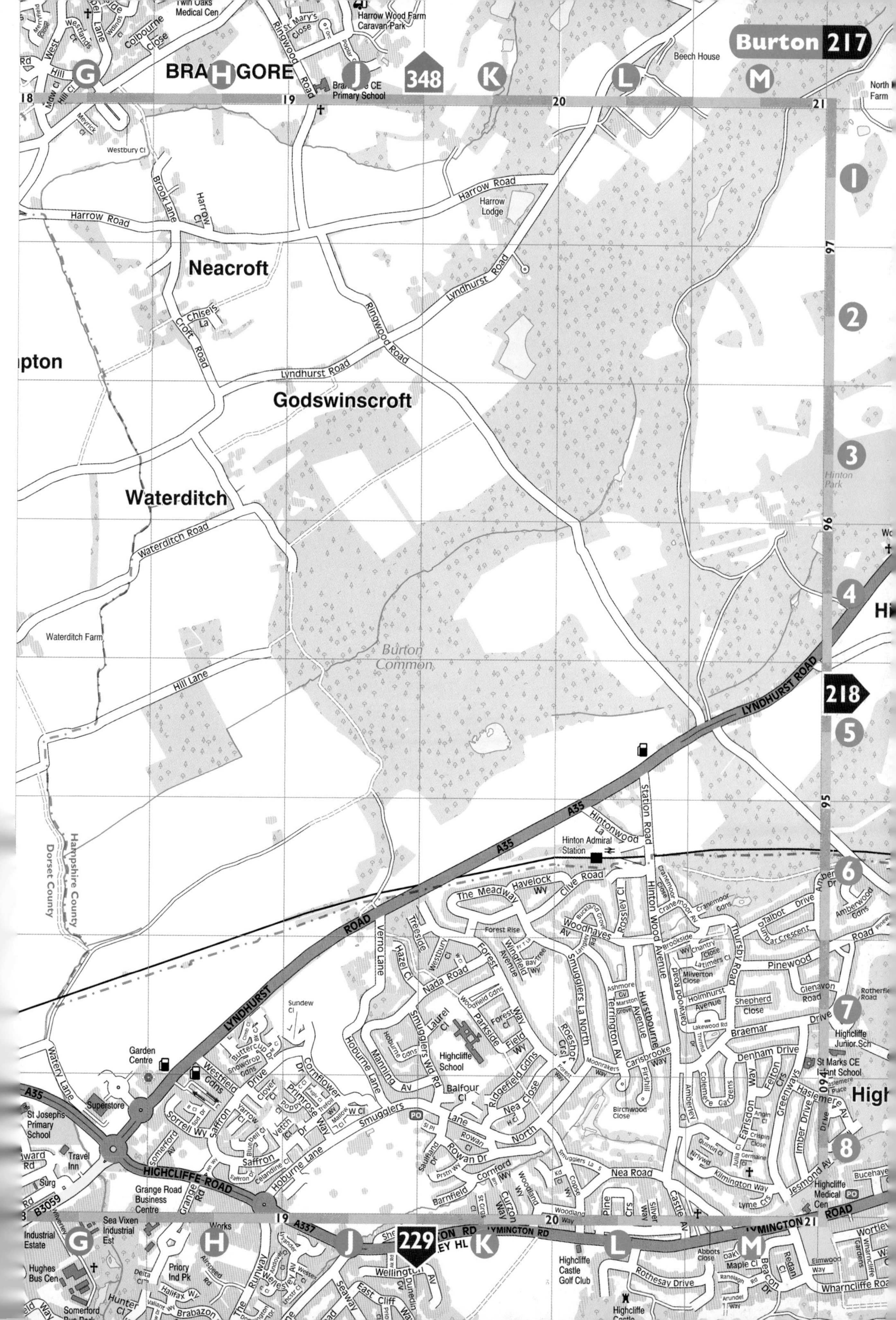

Bransgore
Neacroft
Godswinscroft
Waterditch
Burton Common
Hinton Park
Harrow Road
Harrow Lodge
Lyndhurst Road
Ringwood Road
Croft Road
Chisels La
Brook Lane
Harrow Cl
Westbury Cl
Waterditch Road
Waterditch Farm
Hill Lane
Watery Lane
Beech House
North Farm
Harrow Wood Farm Caravan Park
Bransgore CE Primary School
Hampshire County
Dorset County
Hinton Admiral Station
Station Road
Hintonwood La
Clive Road
The Meadway
Havelock Wy
Hinton Wood Avenue
Cranemoor Av
Thursby Road
Pinewood Road
Glenavon Road
Braemar Drive
Highcliffe Junior Sch
St Marks CE Infant School
Highcliffe School
Smugglers Lane
Hoburne Lane
Verno Lane
Forest Rise
Nea Road
Nea Close
Highcliffe Road
Lymington Rd
Highcliffe Medical Cen
Highcliffe Castle Golf Club
Rothesay Drive
Garden Centre
Superstore
St Josephs Primary School
Travel Inn
Grange Road Business Centre
Sea Vixen Industrial Est
Priory Ind Pk
Hughes Bus Cen
348
218
229

218
349
217
230
Beckley
Hinton
New Milton
Walkford
Highcliffe
Old Milton
Ossemsley Manor
Beckley Farm
Hinton House
Hinton Park
Works
Dark Lane
B3055
BASHLEY CROSS ROAD
Stem Lane
Walkford Lane
New Lane
Smithy Lane
North Drive
South Drive
Holm Hill Lane
Birch Av
Forest View
Robin Crs
Lawn View
Sammy Miller Motorcycle Museum
Bashley Manor Farm
Walkford Brook
Velvet Lawn Road
Doe Copse Way
Hazelwood Avenue
Beechwood Av
Rosewood Gardens
Kennard Road
Marryat Road
Cabot Lwy
Avenue
Marley Av
Chatsworth Way
Arundel Cl
Queensway
Trading Estate
Drake Close
Nelson Close
Hardy Close
Brownsea Cl
Carisbrooke
Gore Road Ind Est
Hamilton Bus Pk
Wick 1 Ind Est
Wick 2 Ind Est
Williams Ind Park
Milton Bus Cen
Gore Road
Gore Road Industrial Est
Fawcett Road
Pleasance Way
Albert Road
Davis Fld
New Milton Recreation Centre
The Arnewood School
Culver Rd
Milton Md
Well Cl
Cemetery
Works
Church La
OLD MILTON GN
Golf Course
Dorset County
Hampshire County
Chewton Glen Hotel
A337
CHRISTCHURCH ROAD
Christchurch Rd
Chiltern Drive
Parkland Drive
Moorland Av
Southern La
Heathy Close
Barton Way
Arnolds Close
Eldon Av
Wavendon Avenue
Hengistbury Road
Seafield Road
Three Acre Dr
Sea Road
Byron Road
Barton Lane
Western Avenue
Knighton Park
Seacroft Av
Pine Cl
Carlton
Glen Cl
Studley Court
Field Pl
The Crescent
Hurst Cl
Chewton Farm Road
Walkford Road
Avenue Road
Seaview Rd
Chewton Common Road
Chewton Way
Highland Av
Elphinstone Road
Jacobean Close
Arran Way
Bracken Way
Heath Road
Southwood Av
Glenville Road
Plantation Dr
Amberwood Dr
Amberwood Gdns
Talbot Drive
Dunbar Crescent
Pinewood Road
Glenavon Road
Rotherfield Road
Walkford Way
Wyndham Rd
Solent Rd
Hurst Cl
Holly Lane
Highcliffe Junior Sch
St Marks CE Infant School
Haslemere Place
Haslemere Av
Greenways
Jesmond Av
Gordon Rd
Seaton Road
Stanley Road
Holme Rd
Pol Stn
Stuart Road
Jay's Court
Montagu Road
Chewton Lodge
Mill Lane
Loraine Avenue
Abingdon Drive
Studley Close
The Dell
Glendrive
Bartonside Rd
Bute Drive
Waterford Road
Waterford Place
Wortley Road
Highcliffe Medical Cen
LYMINGTON ROAD
Elmwood Way
Redan Cl
Chewton Bunny
Island View Road
Island Vw Rd
Naish Road
Cleveland Cl
Powerscourt Rd
Purbeck Rd
Marine Drive West
Cliffe Rd
Barton Rd
Fairfield Road
Seaward Avenue
Keysworth Avenue
Beach Avenue
Barton Wd
421
22
23
97
96
95
1 grid square represents 500 metres

New Milton 219
350
220
231
G
H
J
K
L
M
24
25
26
27
97
96
95
094
2
3
4
5
6
7
8
Tiptoe
Bashley
Bashley Park
Hoburne Bashley
Bashley Drive
Marlpit Lane
Middle Road
Danehurst New Road
School
Wootton
Crabbswood Lane
St Johns
Road
Northover Lane
ARNEWOOD
Vaggs Lane
B3055
SWAY ROAD
BASHLEY ROAD
Mark's Lane
FERNHILL LA
B3058
BH25
Ballard College
Hordle Grange
Silver Street
Surgery
Earlswood Park
Frampton Close
Park Rd
Park Close
Brockhills Lane
Cullwood Lane
Oakwood Av
Otters Walk
Cull Lane
Hollands Wood
Keswick Rd
Marston Rd
Charles Crs
Hilton Rd
Ferndale Rd
Winchester Road
Ashley Common Road
Holly La
Miller Close
Franklin Road
Bertram Rd
Yew La
Gainsborough Av
Winton Wy
Violet Lane
Palmer Pl
Linford Close
Barrs Wood Drive
Barrs Avenue
Wood Road
Brook Avenue
Meadow Road
Manor Road
Grove Road
Fernhill Road
Leigh Road
Pond Cl
Avenue Road
Ballard College
New Milton Station
Surg
Osborne Road
Warwick Av
Ashley Road
Lyon Avenue
York Av
Herbert Road
Spencer Road
Whitefield Road
Peckham Avenue
Council Building
Old Milton Rd
Elm Av
STATION ROAD
Compton Road
Pol Stn
Wessex Avenue
Crossmead Avenue
Waverley Road
Copse Av
Hale Av
Fir Avenue
South Av
Mendip Cl
Milton Gv
Haven Gdns
Newlands Road
Ashington Pk
Eastlands
Aysha Cl
Caird Avenue
Superstore
Ashdown Walk
Canada House Business Centre
Works
Carrick Way
Brecon
Benmore Cl
Spring Lane
Andrew
Glen Spey
Ashley Road
Lower
Pitts Pl
Ridge
High
Crescent
Willowdene Cl
Ashley Junior School
New Milton Sports Club
Ashley
Golden Hill
Ashley Infant School
Hare Lane
Ashley Lane
Ashley La
Blenheim Crs
Stoneleigh Av
Pinewood Road
Lavender Rd
Heath Road
Danecrest Rd
Dudley Av
Stopples Lane
Everton Rd
Hordl
Hordle Lane
Dilly Lane
Dane's Stream
ROAD
LYMINGTON
LYMINGTON ROAD
A337
Ashley Manor Farm
Angel Lane
Ashley Clinton House
CHRISTCHURCH ROAD
Downton
MILFORD ROAD
Barton-on-Sea
Golf Course
Barton Common Road
Solent Drive
Meadow Wy
Becton
Mitchell Cl
Maple Cl
The Martells
Silverdale
Barton Common Lane
Durlston Court School
Greenacre
Highlands Road
Friars Walk
Farm Lane N
Chestnut Avenue
Uplands Av
Ashmore
Green La
Newton Rd
Fenleigh Cl
Haysoms Close
Cowper Av
Orchard Grove
New Milton J&I School
Barton Court Road
Furze Cft
Norris Gdns
Aspen Place

Mead End Road
Arnewood Manor
Avon Water
B3055
South Sway Lane
350
Lane
Pauls Lane
Mount Pleasant Lane
Kings Lane
King's Farm
Mount P
North Common Lane
Mill Lane
ROAD
BRIDGE
WOOD
Linnies Lane
Agars Lane
Barrows Lane
Little Arnewood House
Flexford Lane
Hazelhurst Farm
South Sway Lane
Arnewood Court
Bowling Green
Hannah Way
Sway Road
Works
Gordleton Industrial Estate
Gordleton Industrial Park
The Mill at Gordleton Hotel
Gordleton Farm
Ramley Road
Ramley
Agar's Lane
Silver Street
Lane
Hordle
Cottagers
Sheldrake Gdns
Woodcock Lane
White Barn Crs
Slade Cl
Mallard Cl
Everton Road
Sycamore Rd
Stopples Lane
219
Heather Close
Everton Rd
Hordle CE Prim Sch
Arnewood House
Batchley Farm
Upr Common Rd
Wainsford House
Hordle Lane
Vicarage Lane
Elizabeth Crs
Longfield Road
Pegasus Av
Sylvan Cl
Sky End La
Dudley Av
Everton Road
Wainsford Road
Efford House
Greenmead Avenue
Buckstone Cl
Everton
Manor Ho
Honeysuckle Gardens
Everlea Cl
Frys Lane
Golden Crs
Beacon Cl
Harts Wy
Fox Fld
Centre Lane
East La
Firmount Cl
Yeatton Ho
Shepherds Wy
Farmers Walk
Crossways
Old Christchurch Road
Works
Roberts Cl
MILFORD ROAD
The Grange
Leagreen
CHRISTCHURCH RD
A337
Ash Grove
Lime Grove
Grange Close
Hordle Lane
LYMINGTON ROAD
Lymore Lane
Barnes Lane
Braxton Gardens
CHRISTCHURCH ROAD
232
Newlands Manor
Lytton Lawn Touring Park
I grid square represents 500 metres

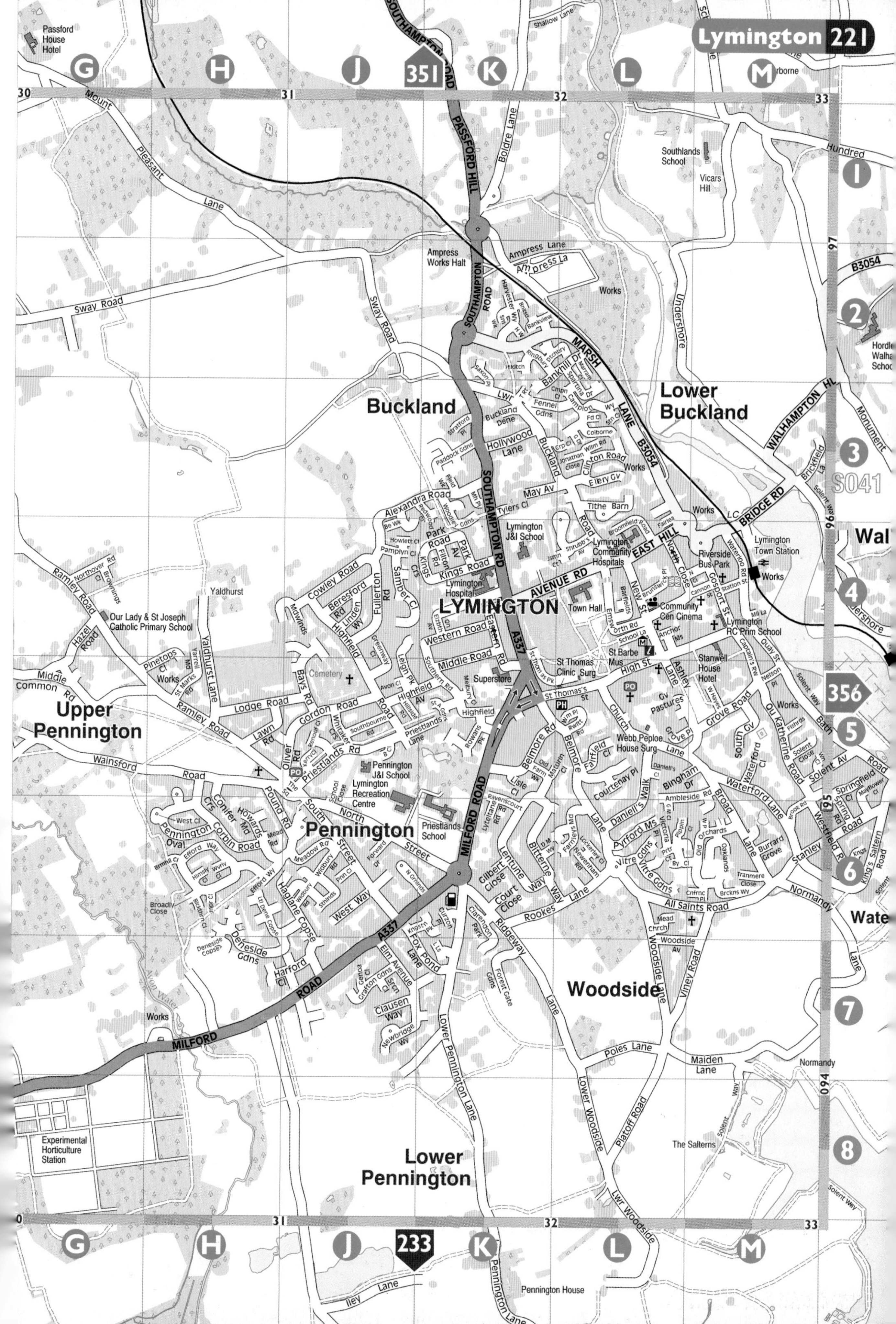
Passford House Hotel
G
H
J
351
K
L
M
30
31
32
33
Mount Pleasant Lane
PASSFORD HILL
Boldre Lane
Southlands School
Vicars Hill
Hundred
B3054
Ampress Works Halt
Ampress Lane
Ampress La
Works
Sway Road
SOUTHAMPTON ROAD
Undershore
MARSH LANE
Buckland
Lower Buckland
WALHAMPTON HL
Monument
Hollywood Lane
Clinton Road
May Av
Tithe Barn
Alexandra Road
Tyiers Cl
Lymington J&I School
Lymington Community Hospitals
EAST HILL
BRIDGE RD
LC
Riverside Bus Park
Lymington Town Station
Works
SO41
SOUTHAMPTON RD
Kings Road
Lymington Hospital
AVENUE RD
LYMINGTON
Town Hall
Community Cen Cinema
Lymington RC Prim School
Cowley Road
Beresford Rd
Linden Wy
Fullerton Rd
Samber Cl
Highfield
Yaldhurst
Our Lady & St Joseph Catholic Primary School
Ramley Road
Northover Rd
Hazel Road
Pinetops Cl
Yaldhurst Lane
Western Road
Middle Road
Cemetery
Superstore
St Thomas Clinic Surg
St Barbe Mus
High St
St Thomas's St
Stanwell House Hotel
Quay St
Bath Road
356
Middle Common Rd
Upper Pennington
Lodge Road
Gordon Road
Priestlands Rd
Wainsford Road
Belmore Rd
Church Lane
Webb Peploe House Surg
Grove Road
Waterford Lane
Solent Av
Springfield Cl
Pennington J&I School
Lymington Recreation Centre
Priestlands School
Pennington
North Street
South Street
MILFORD ROAD
Pennington Oval
Corbin Road
Courtenay Pl
Bingham Dr
Daniell's Walk
Pyrford Ms
Vitre Gdns
Broad Lane
Burrard Grove
Stanley Rd
Westfield Rd
Kings Saltern Road
Normandy Lane
West Way
Hagiane Copse
Deneside Gdns
Harford Cl
A337
ROAD
Fox Pond Lane
Elm Avenue
Clausen Way
Gilbert Close
Court Close
Rookes Lane
Ridgeway Lane
All Saints Road
Woodside Lane
Viney Road
Woodside
Works
MILFORD
Poles Lane
Maiden Lane
Normandy
Lower Pennington Lane
Lower Woodside
Platoff Road
Experimental Horticulture Station
The Salterns
Lower Pennington
Lwr Woodside
Solent Way
0
31
32
33
G
H
J
233
K
L
M
Pennington House
Iley Lane
Pennington Lane
1
2
3
4
5
6
7
8
97
96
95
094

210
A
B
C
D
E
F
1
2
3
4
5
6
7
8
397
98
99
93
92
91
090
A35
A350
UPTON ROAD
POOLE RD
DORCHESTER ROAD
BLANDFORD RD N
BLANDFORD ROAD
B3068
Upton
Turlin Moor
Hamworthy
Lake
BH15
Hickory Close
Redwood Road
Beacon Rd
Marsh La
Holly Close
French's Farm Rd
Poppy Close
Greenway Crs
Sea View Road
Pinewood Rd
Upton Infant Sch
Upton Junior Sch
Moorland Way
Yarrells Preparatory School
Upton Health Cen
Douglas Cl
Meadows Close
Warbler Close
Heights Road
Meadows Dr
Dacombe Drive
Palmerston Road
Gorse La
Upton Heath Estate
Martingale Cl
Poole Road
Old Kiln Road
Factory Road
Upton House
Upton Country Park
Pergins Island
Sandy Lane
Beach Rd
Otter Close
Slough Lane
Saltings Rd
Lytchett Way
Furzey Rd
Shore La
Border Dr
Border Road
Pine Vw Cl
Peters Close
Allens Lane
Allens Road
Willow Close
Ind Est
Works
Lytchett Bay
Dorset County
Poole
Rice Gardens
Turlin Moor Middle School
Turlin Moor Community First School
Keysworth Road
Turlin Road
Egmont Road
Foreland Road
Fitzworth Avenue
Junction Road
Hamworthy Station
Carters Avenue
Calloway Rd
Symes Road
Hewitt Road
Falconer Dr
Harkwood Drive
Inglesham Way
Dawkins Road
Freshwater Drive
Almer Rd
Dawkins Bus Cen
Carisbrooke Crescent
Upwey Av
Winspit Close
Beckhampton Road
Hamworthy Community Clinic
Woodlands Avenue
Woodlands Crescent
Hoyal Road
Hercules Rd
Samson Road
Goliath Road
Delilah Road
Hamilton Road
Hamilton Crs
Lake Crs
Fort Cumberland Close
Normandy Way
David Way
Jacobs Rd
Lake Road
Lake Drive
Lake Av
Coles Avenue
Legion Road
Rockley Road
Hounslow Close
Superstore
Carter Community Sports College
Hinchliffe Rd
Hamworthy First Sch
Hamworthy Middle Sch
Tuckers La
Ashmore Av
Blandford Close
Moorings Close
Lulworth Avenue
Branksea Avenue
Purbeck Avenue
Birchwood Medical Cen
Martin Close
Nuthatch Close
Swallow Cl
Woodpecker Drive
Pinetree Wk
Petersham Rd
Castleman Trailway
Holton Point
Rockley Viaduct
Rockley Park
Walcheren Place
Napier Road
Rockley Sands
Wood Bar Looe
Wareham Channel
WAREHAM
Gold Point
Gold Point Heath
1 grid square represents 500 metres

Creekmoor
Stanley Green
Oakdale
Longfleet
Sterte
POOLE
Lower Hamworthy
Holes Bay
Parkstone Bay
Poole Harbour
Poole Park
Poole High School
Poole Stadium (Speedway Track & Football Stadium)
Poole Hospital
Poole Station
Oakdale Middle School
St Edwards Comprehensive School
Canford Heath Middle School
Canford Heath First Sch
Longspee School
Stanley Green First Sch
St Marys Catholic Combined School
Longfleet CE Combined School
Dorset Magistrates Court
Bournemouth & Poole College
Jellicoe Theatre
The Dolphin Shop Cen & Sports Cen
Dolphin Swimming Pool
The Seldown Lane Lighthouse
Council Building
County Court Offices
Civic Ce Annexe
Arndale Court Hotel
Express by Holiday Inn
Mansion House Hotel
Guildhall
Old Town First School
Coastguard Office
Custom House
Waterfront Museum
Lifeboat Museum
Poole Pottery
Purbeck Pottery
New Harbour Road South
Freight Ferry Terminal
Passenger Ferry Terminal
Sterte Industrial Estate
Stanley Green Ind Est
Fleetspoint Bus Cen
Sovereign Bus Cen
Sovereign Bus Park
Wessex Gate Retail Park
Fleetsbridge Business Cen
Benridge Business Park
Cabot Business Vlg
Nuffield Industrial Estate
Nuffield Ind Est
Kinson Pottery Industrial Estate
FLEET'S CORNER
A35
A350
A3049
A349
B3068
B3093
BH17
BH15
CABOT LANE
UPTON ROAD
DORSET WAY
BROADSTONE WAY
WIMBORNE ROAD
FERNSIDE ROAD
LONGFLEET RD
PARKSTONE ROAD
COMMERCIAL ROAD
RINGWOOD
HOLES BAY ROAD
WEST QUAY RD
WEST STREET
TOWNGATE BRIDGE
KINGLAND RD
MOUNT PLEASANT RD
BRIDGE AP
WAREHAM
Poole
Dorset County
211
224
236
G H J K L M
1 2 3 4 5 6 7 8
400 01 02 03
93 92 91 090

224
212
223
237
A
B
C
D
E
F
1
2
3
4
5
6
7
8
403
04
05
93
92
91
090
Newtown
Rossmore
Branksome
Parkstone
Branksome Park
Lilliput
Canford Cliffs
Rossmore Community College
Kemp Welch Leisure Centre
Mannings Heath Retail Park
Works
Newtown Bus Pk
Chalwyn Industrial Estate
Rosemary Medical Cen
Yys Business Park
Branksome Cemetery
Branksome Heath Middle School
Sylvan First School
Seaview Bus Cen
Kinson Pottery Industrial Estate
St Josephs RC Combined School
Heatherlands First School
Health Centre
Police Station
Courthill First School
Superstore
The Victoria School
John Neame Swim Pool
Parkstone Stn
Cncl Bldg
Baden Powell & St Peters CE Mid Sch
Uplands School
Penn Hill Clinic
Parkstone Golf Club
Golf Course
Luscombe Valley
Parkstone Cemetery
Lilliput CE First Sch
Salterns Harbourside Hotel
Compton Acres Gardens
Bournemouth & Poole College
Jellicoe Theatre
Surgery
Wareham Road
Kimmeridge Av
Herbert Avenue
Turbary Close
Cranborne Crs
Melbury Avenue
Arne Avenue
Rossmore Road
Livingstone Road
Ringwood Road
Sea View Rd B3061
Ashley Road
Alder Road A3049
Bournemouth Rd Castle Hill A35
Bournemouth Road A35
Commercial Road
Poole Road
Parkstone Avenue
Penn Hill Avenue
Sandbanks Road
Elgin Road
Compton Avenue
Canford Cliffs Road
Western Road
Lilliput Road
B3369 Sandbanks Road
Haven Road
Western Road
Spencer Road
Martello Road
Links Road
Kings Avenue
Bingham Avenue
Archway Road
B3065
BH14
1 grid square represents 500 metres

Talbot Village
213
226
8
Talbot Heath
Bourne Valley
Talbot Woods
Winton
Meyrick Park
Westbourne
West Cliff
Alum Chine
Branksome Chine
Poole Bay
BH2
BH3
BH4
BH13
Talbot Combined School
Langside School
The Arts Institute of Bournemouth
Heatherview Medical Centre
Superstore
St Aldhelms CE Combined School
Gas Works
Bourne Valley Business Park
Talbot Heath School
Oakmeadians RFC
The Club at Meyrick Park
Golf Course
Branksome Stn
Medical Centre
Town Hall
Town Hall Annexe
RICHMOND HILL ROUNDABOUT
The Avenue Shop Cen
Camera Obscura
Cadogan Hotel
East Anglia Hotel
Durley Hall Hotel
New Durley Dean Hotel
Ullswater Hotel
Mansfield Hotel
Bournemouth Sands Hotel
Highcliff Marriott Htl
International Centre & Leisure Pool
Oceanarium
Bournemouth Pier
Pier Theatre
Pavilion Theatre
BATH HILL RBT
Herbert Day Hospital
Chinehurst Hotel
The Riviera Hotel
St Martins School
The Banks Medical Cen
Bournemouth Mosque
Dean Park Cricket Ground
Pavilion
TALBOT ROAD
TALBOT AVENUE A347
WIMBORNE ROAD A347
WESSEX WAY A338
A35
B3065
B3066
ALDER ROAD
LANSDOWNE RD
BATH RD
EXETER ROAD
W CLIFF RD
PRIORY RD
THE AVENUE
B3065 PINECLIFF ROAD
East Avenue
Alyth Road
Glenferness Avenue
Surrey Road
Poole Road
Westbourne Cl
Princess Road
Portarlington Rd
Marlborough Rd
Alumhurst Road
Western Road
West Overcliff Drive
Durley Chine
Central Drive
Cavendish Rd
St Stephen's Road
Leven Avenue
Branksome Wood Road
Winston Avenue
Bourne Valley Rd
Promenade
West Undercliff Promenade
G H J K L M
06 07 08 09
2 3 4 5 6 7 8
93 92 91 090

226
214
225
9
A
B
C
D
E
F
1
2
3
4
5
6
7
8
409
10
11
93
92
090
Springbourne
Boscombe
BOURNEMOUTH
Poole Bay
Queen's Park
King's Park
BH1
A3049
A338
A347
A35
B3063
WESSEX WAY
ALMA ROAD
RICHMOND PK RD
CHARMINSTER RD
HOLDENHURST RD
ASHLEY ROAD
WIMBORNE ROAD
LANSDOWNE ROAD
ST PAULS RD
ST SWITHUN'S RD
CHRISTCHURCH ROAD
BATH ROAD
GERVIS RD
PT RD
Queen's Park Golf Club
AFC Bournemouth (Fitness First Stadium)
King's Park Athletics Centre
Kings Park Primary School
The Park School
St Albans Medical Cen
Linwood School
St Martins School
Richmond Court Business Cen
Malmesbury Park CP School
The Bournemouth Nuffield Hospital
Dean Park Cricket Ground
Pavilion
Parkway Retail Park
Bournemouth Station
Superstore
BOURNEMOUTH STN RBT
Bournemouth College
Elstead Hotel
Langtry Manor Lovenest of King Hotel
Carrington House Hotel
Bournemouth University
Bus Centre
Pol Stn & Courts
Synagogue & Day School
Russell-Cotes Art Gal & Museum
De Vere Royal Bath Htl
Pavilion Theatre
Oceanarium
Bournemouth Pier
Pier Theatre
Boscombe Pier
Chine Hotel
Fircroft Hotel
Shelley Museum
Boscombe Manor Medical Centre
Bethany CE Junior School
St Clements CE Infant Sch
Bournemouth Mosque
Menzies East Cliff Court Htl
Cumberland Hotel
Bay View Court Hotel
Ocean View Hotel
Cliffeside Hotel
Heathlands Htl
Queens Hotel
Quality Hotel
Belvedere Hotel
Marsham Court Hotel
Miramar Hotel
Menzies Carlton Hotel
Piccadilly Hotel
Burley Court Hotel
Menzies Anglo-Swiss Htl
Suncliff Htl
Grosvenor Hotel
Russell Court Hotel
Pavilion Hotel
IMAX
ABC
Odeon
ST PETERS RBT
BATH HILL RBT
Undercliff Drive
Overcliff Drive
Christchurch Road
Holdenhurst Rd
Boscombe Cliff Road
The Marina
St John's Road
1 grid square represents 500 metres

215
228
Iford Sports Centre
Littledown
Avonbourne Girls School
Portchester Boys School
Bicknell Special School
BH7
Iford
River Stour
Stour Valley Way
Christchurch Road
A35
Barrack Road
Tuckton
Portcastrian RFC
Stourfield J&I Sch
West Southbourne
Pokesdown
Pokesdown Station
Pokesdown Prim Sch
Wessex Complementary Medical Cen
Spectrum Sports Club
Southbourne Grove
Southbourne Rd
Parkwood Road
Wentworth College
St Peters School
Southbourne
Belle Vue
Overcliff Drive
Southbourne Coast Road
BH5
BH6
Poole Bay
G
H
J
K
L
M
1
2
3
4
5
6
7
8
13
14
15

228
216
227
A
B
C
D
E
F
1
2
3
4
5
6
7
8
415
16
17
93
91
090
CHRISTCHURCH
Purewell
Somerford
Stanpit
Wick
BH6
CHRISTCHURCH BY-PASS
A35
B3073
B3059
BARGATES B3073
STOUR ROAD
PUREWELL CROSS RD
SOMERFORD
ROAD
Purewell
Avon Trading Park
Briar Park Business Centre
Christchurch J&I Sch
Christchurch Stn
Travel Inn
Police Station
Saxon Centre
Saxon Square Shop Cen
The Regent Centre
Twynham School
The Priory CE VA Prim Sch
Christchurch Castle & Norman House
Christchurch Priory
Red House Mus & Gardens
Southern Electric Museum
Civic Offices
Two Riversmeet Leisure Centre
The Grange Comprehensive School
Somerford Pri & Comm Sch
Christchurch Medical Centre
Silver Bus Park
Groveley Bus Cen
Mudeford Infant Sch
Mudeford Junior Sch
Airfield Ind Est
St Katharines CE VA Prim Sch
St Peters School
Club House Rowing
Stanpit Marsh
Shermin's Bank
Coastguard Way
Rushford Warren
Waterside
Christchurch Harbour
Dorset County
Bournemouth
River Avon
River Stour
Stour Valley Way
Broadway
Southbourne Coast Road
Hengistbury Head
1 grid square represents 500 metres

St Josephs Primary School
Travel Inn
Edward Rd
HIGHCLIFFE
Sorrell Wy
Saffron
Somerford Av
Hoburne Lane
Smugglers
Rowan Dr
North
Nea Road
Castle Av
Jesmond
Highcliffe Medical Cen
LYMINGTON ROAD
Grange Road Business Centre
Grange Rd
Sea Vixen Industrial Est
Industrial Estate
Works
Hughes Bus Cen
Somerford Bus Park
Priory Ind Pk
Airspeed Rd
The Runway
Wellesley Av
Shelley Cl
LYMINGTON RD
SHELLEY HL
A337
Wellington Av
Highcliffe Castle Golf Club
Highcliffe Castle
Rothesay Drive
Abbots Close
Oakley Way
Maple Cl
Beacon Dr
Redan Cl
Golf Course
Beaver Ind Est
Ambassador Ind Est
Brabazon Dr
Viscount Dr
Seaway
East Cliff Way
Dunedin Gv
Seafield Road
Hynesbury Road
Avenue
Southcliffe Road
Bure Lane
Friars Cliff
Bure Homage Lane
Waterford Lodge Hotel
Bure Cl
Bure Rd
Rook Hill Rd
Friars Road
Vecta Cl
Cliff Dr
Seaway Av
Havilland Way
Charlotte Cl
Ricardo Crs
Bure Hvn Drive
Sheldrake Road
Peregrine Rd
Mudeford
Merlin Wy
Falcon Dr
Island View Av
Avon Run Cl
Run Road
Avon
Raven Way
Kingfisher Wy
Osprey Cl
Farm La
Fulmar Rd
Wren Cl
Highcliffe Medical Centre
Robins Wy
Capesthorne
The Avonmouth Hotel
Mudeford
Viking Way
Stour Valley Way
217
230
G
H
J
K
L
M
19
20
21
93
92
91
090
2
3
4
5
6
7
8

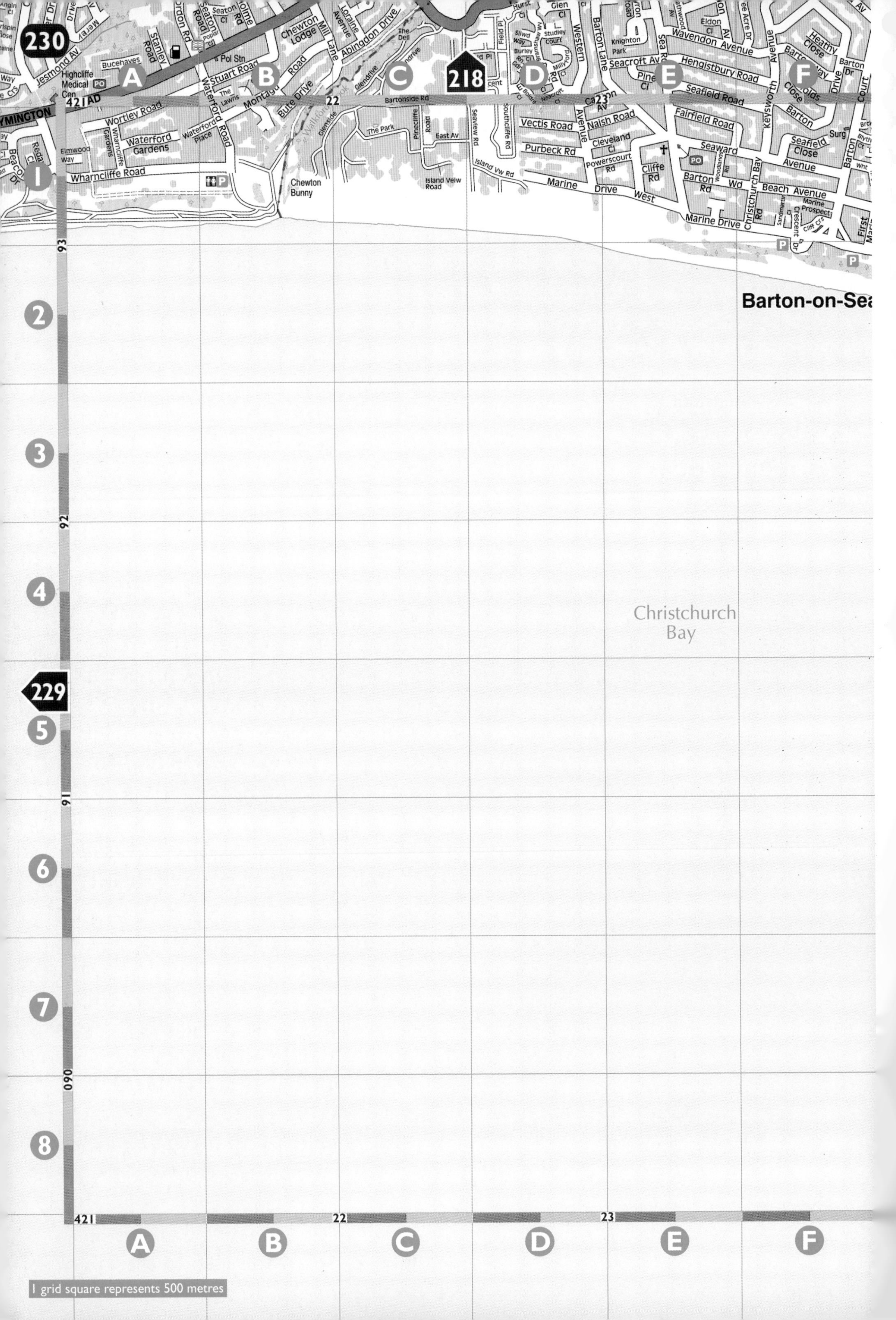
230
218
229
A
B
C
D
E
F
1
2
3
4
5
6
7
8
421
22
23
93
92
91
090
Highcliffe Medical Cen
Jesmond Av
Bucehayes
Stanley Road
Pol Stn
Stuart Road
Chewton Lodge
Mill Lane
Abingdon Drive
The Dell
Montagu Road
Bute Drive
Bartonside Rd
Wortley Road
Wharncliffe Gardens
Waterford Gardens
Waterford Place
Waterford Road
Wharncliffe Road
Elmwood Way
Glenside
The Park
Pinecliffe Road
East Av
Seaview Rd
Chewton Bunny
Island Vw Rd
Island Veiw Road
Southcliffe Rd
Vectis Road
Purbeck Rd
Naish Road
Cleveland Cl
Powerscourt Rd
Barton Lane
Western Avenue
Knighton Park
Seacroft Av
Pine Cl
Sea Rd
Wavendon Avenue
Hengistbury Road
Seafield Road
Fairfield Road
Keysworth Avenue
Heathy Close
Barton Dr
Seafield Close
Seaward Avenue
Cliffe Rd
Barton Wd Rd
Beach Avenue
Marine Prospect
Marine Drive
Marine Drive West
Christchurch Bay Rd
Barton-on-Sea
Christchurch Bay
1 grid square represents 500 metres

G H J 219 K L M

24 25 A337 26 CHRISTCHURCH ROAD 27

Highlands Road
Summerfield
Avenue
Dilly
Greenacre
Durlston Court School
Common Lane
The Willows
Silverdale
The Martells
The Fairway
Maple
Newton Rd
Royston Place
B3058
Solent Drive
Mitchell Cl
Meadow Wy
Barton
Willow Wk
Grove Road
Marine Drive East
Common Road
Golf Course
Barton-on-Sea Golf Club
MILFORD ROAD

Downton

Taddiford Farm

Danes Stream

B3058

Hordle House School

Ashley

93
Shorefield Rd Seabr
Dane Rd
1
2
3
92
4
232
5
91
6
7
090
8

24 25 26 27

G H J K L M

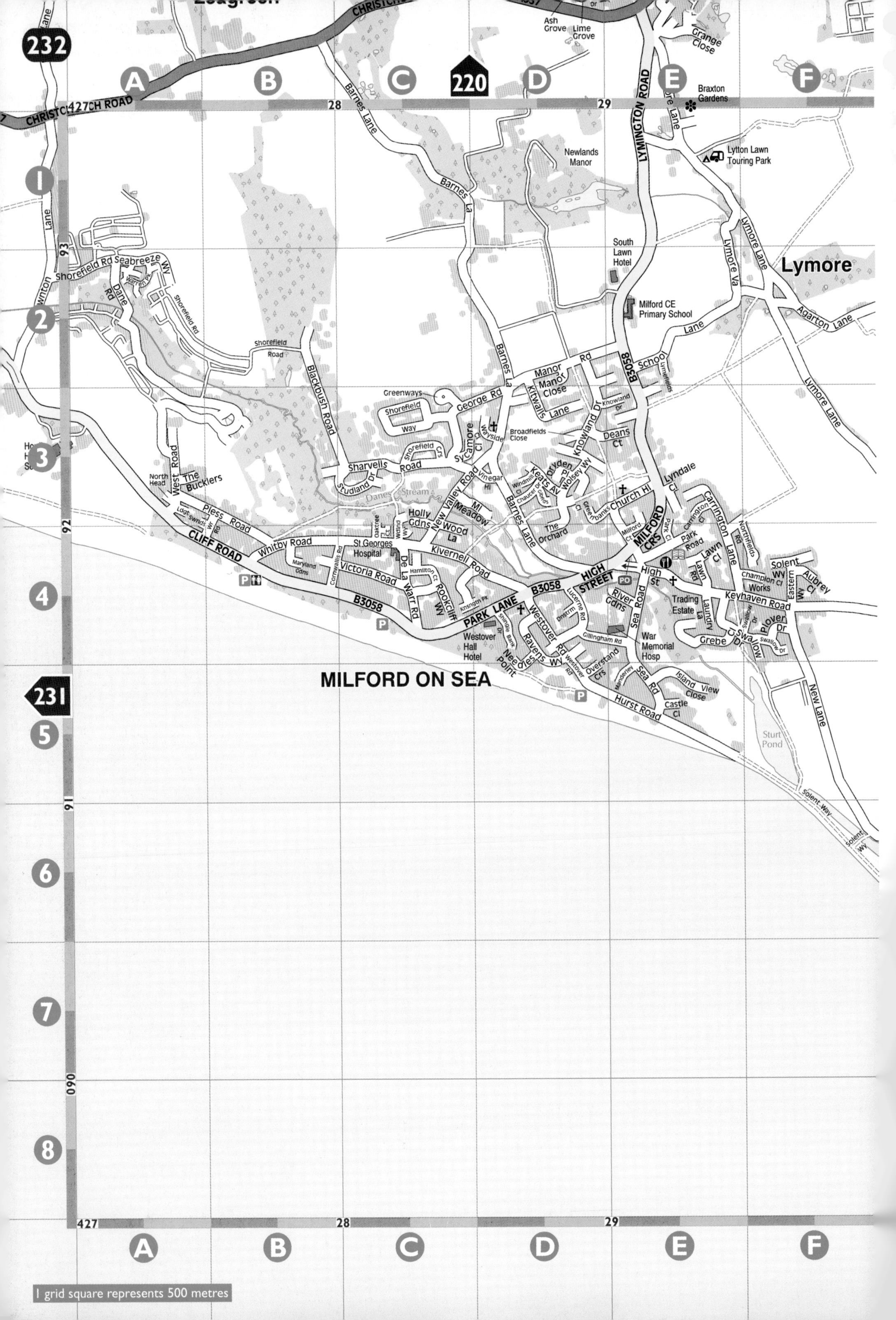
232
220
231
Lymore
MILFORD ON SEA
Lymington Road
Christchurch Road
Barnes Lane
Newlands Manor
South Lawn Hotel
Milford CE Primary School
Braxton Gardens
Lytton Lawn Touring Park
Shorefield Rd
Seabreeze Wy
Dane Rd
Shorefield Road
Blackbush Road
Greenways
Shorefield Way
George Rd
Manor Rd
Manor Close
Kitwalls Lane
Knowland Dr
Deans Ct
School Lane
Lymore Va
Lymore Lane
Agarton Lane
Sharvells Road
Studland Dr
Sycamore Cl
Vinegar Hl
Broadfields Close
Keats Av
Dryden Pl
Wolsey Wy
Church Hl
Lyndale Cl
Carrington Lane
North Head
West Road
The Bucklers
Pless Road
Cliff Road
Whitby Road
St Georges Hospital
Holly Gdns
New Valley Road
Wood La
Mill Meadow
Kivernell Road
Victoria Road
De La Warr Rd
Rookcliff Wy
Park Lane
B3058
High Street
Milford Crs
The Orchard
Park Road
Lawn Cl
Keyhaven Road
Solent Wy
Aubrey Cl
Champion Cl Works
Trading Estate
River Gdns
Sea Road
Westover Rd
Westover Hall Hotel
Ravens Wy
Needles Point
Overstand Crs
War Memorial Hosp
Grebe Cl
Swallow Dr
Plover Dr
Sea Rd
Island View Close
Castle Cl
Hurst Road
Sturt Pond
New Lane
Solent Way
1 grid square represents 500 metres

G   H   J   K   L   M

Lower
Pennington
221

30   31   32   33

Experimental
Horticulture
Station

Iley Lane

Lwr Pennington Lane

Pennington House

Woodside

Platoff R.

Solent Way

93

Pennington
Marshes

Solent Way

92

Agarton Lane

Avon Water

Van Farm

Keyhaven
Marshes

Lymore
Lane

Keyhaven

Harewood
Green

Aubrey House

New Rd

Road

Keyhaven

Salt
Grass

Saltgrass Lane

Solent Way

Solent Way

91

Solent Way

90

Hurst
Beach

Solent Way

Solent Way

Hurst Castle

I
2
3
4
5
6
7
8

234

354

A B C D E F

441 42 43

1

Salternshill Copse

Salternshill

2

rokes

Lower
Exbury

Inchmery House

Gins

3

Gins Lane

Beaulieu River

98

Gins House

rren Lane

4

Needs
Ore Point

357

5

Warren Farm

Warren Lane

The Solent

97

6

7

096

8

441 42 43

A B C D E F

I grid square represents 500 metres

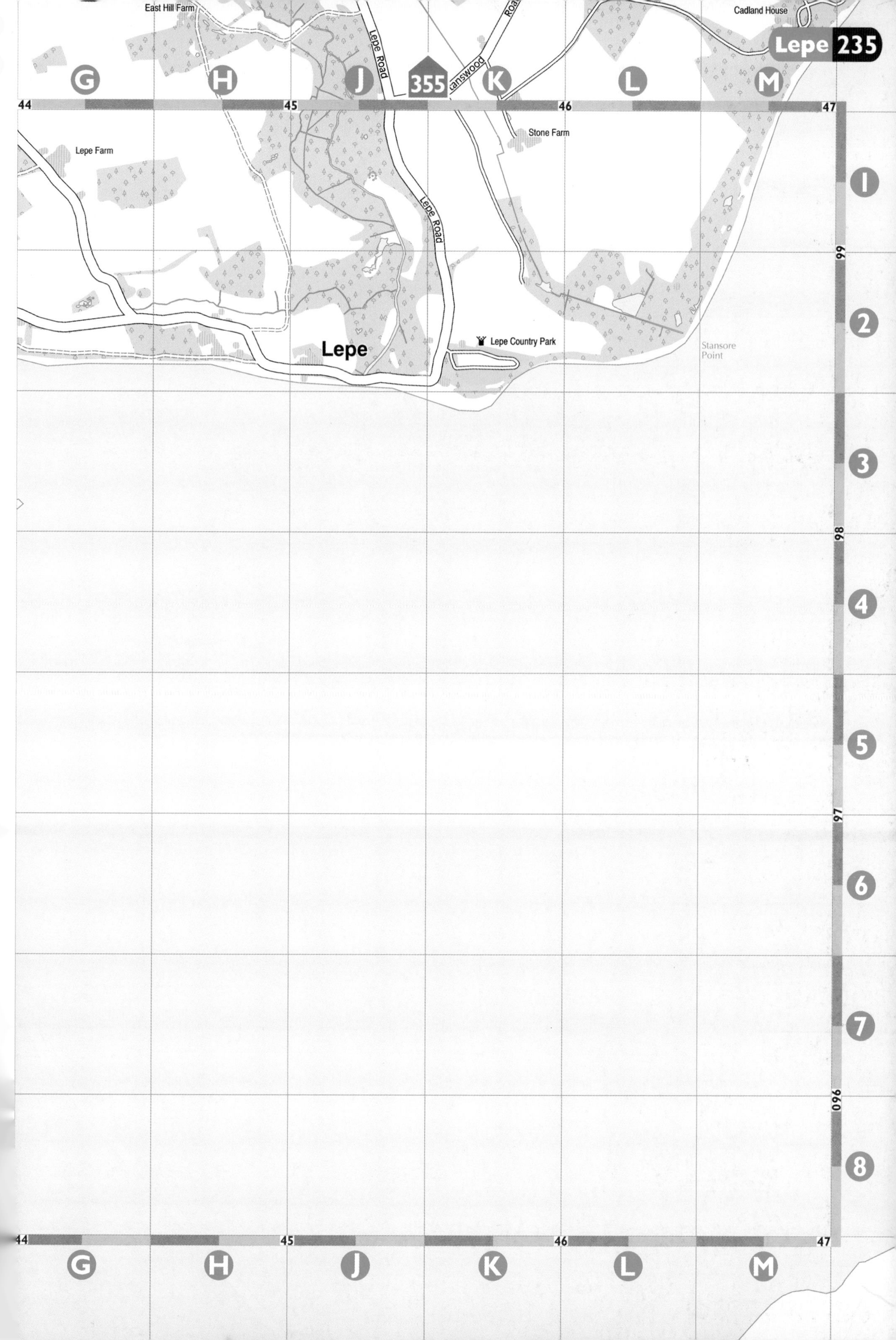

East Hill Farm

Cadland House

G
H
J
K
L
M

Lepe Road
Stanswood Road

355

44
45
46
47

Lepe Farm

Stone Farm

Lepe Road

I

99

Lepe

Lepe Country Park

Stansore Point

2

98

3

4

97

5

6

96

7

8

44
45
46
47

G
H
J
K
L
M

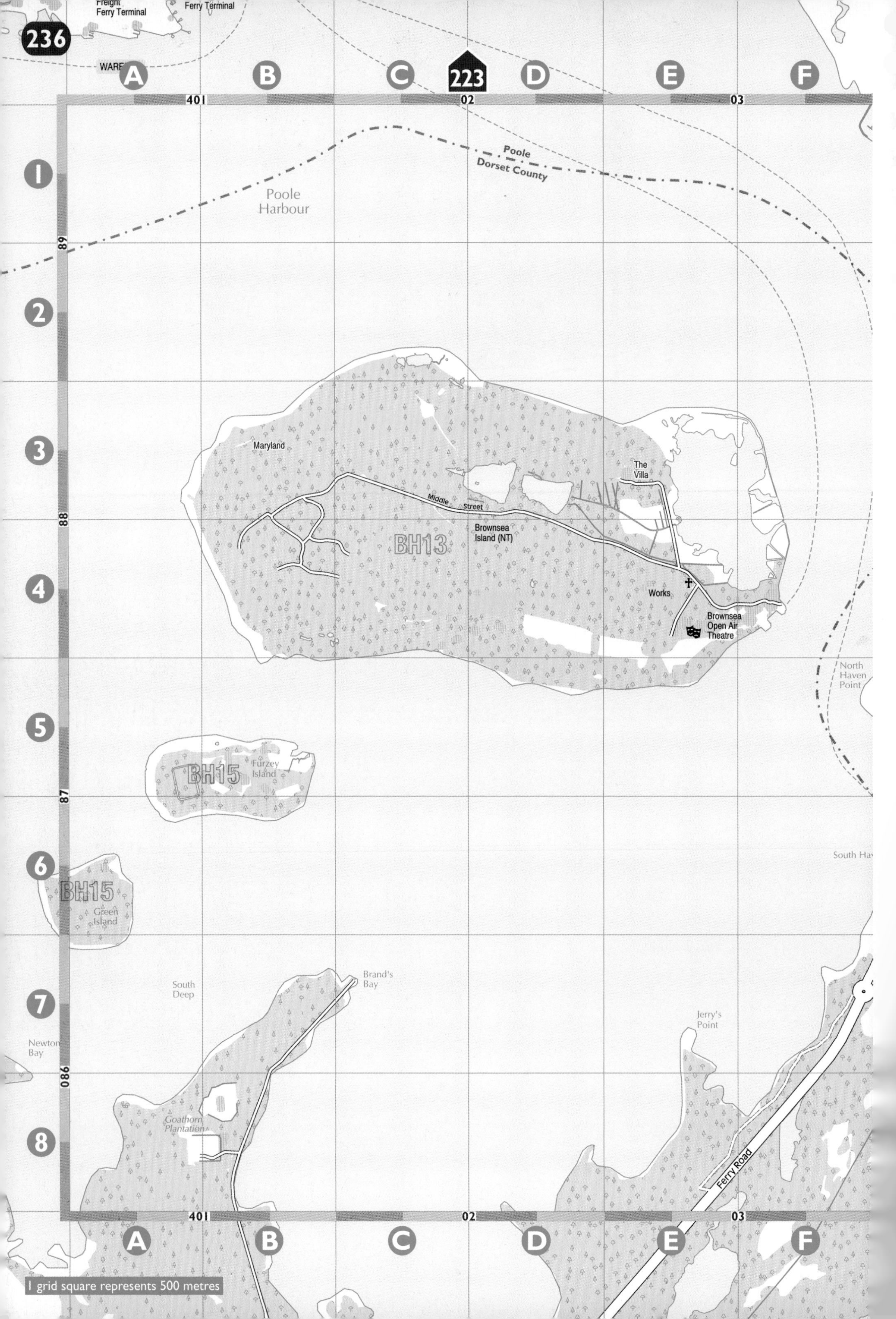

Freight Ferry Terminal

Ferry Terminal

WARF

A   B   C   D   E   F

401   02   03

89

Poole
Dorset County

Poole
Harbour

Maryland

The
Villa

Middle   Street

BH13

Brownsea
Island (NT)

Works

Brownsea
Open Air
Theatre

North
Haven
Point

BH15   Furzey
Island

South Hav

BH15
Green
Island

Brand's
Bay

South
Deep

Jerry's
Point

Newton
Bay

980

Goathorn
Plantation

Ferry Road

A   B   C   D   E   F

401   02   03

88

87

1 grid square represents 500 metres

G H J **224** K L M

Salterns
Harbourside
Hotel

Marina

Lilliput

Lilliput Road

Dorset Lake Av

B3369 SANDBANKS

Crichel Mount
Road

Gulliver Close

Lagado

Bingham Avenue

Lilliput Road

Compton
Acres Gardens

Canford Cliffs Road

De Mauley Road

Newton Rd

Oratory
Garden

Mrflds
Rd

Chcr
Rd

Elmstead
Rd

PO

Branksome

CLIFF ROAD

HAVEN ROAD   WESTERN   PO   B3065

ROAD

**Canford
Cliffs**

Minterne
Road

Mount
Grace
Drive

Alington
Road

Alington
Close

Alington

Brudenell Av

Dornie Rd

Nairn Road

Canford Crs

B3065

Imbrecourt

Norfolk
Lodge
Hotel

Bessborough Road

Mcndr
Rd

Bodley
Road

Beaumont

Flaghead Road

St Clair Rd

Cliff Dr

Maxwell
Road

Esplanade

Meriden
Close

Martello
Park

I

89

SHORE ROAD

Brudenell
Road

B3369

HAVEN ROAD

Crosby
Pines

Flaghead Chine

Chaddesley
Glen

Rd

Cliff Drive

Promenade

Canford
Cliffs Chine

2

Main
Channel

Harbour
Heights
Hotel

St Anns
Hospital

Flag Head
Chine

3

88

Shore Road

Chddsly
Rd

Sandbanks
Hotel

Poole Head

4

BANKS ROAD

B3369

Coastguard
Road

PO   P

PANORAMA ROAD

Sandbanks

B3369

BANKS ROAD

Grasmere
Rd

Salter Road

Seacombe
Road

Brownsea Road

Sandbanks
Business
Centre

FERRY WAY

Ferry Wy

Haven
Hotel

5

87

ven Point

6

Shell
Bay

CHERBOURG

7

986

GUERNSEY
JERSEY
ST MALO
SUMMER ONLY

8

South   West   Coast   Path

04   05   06

G H J K L M

Studland Bay

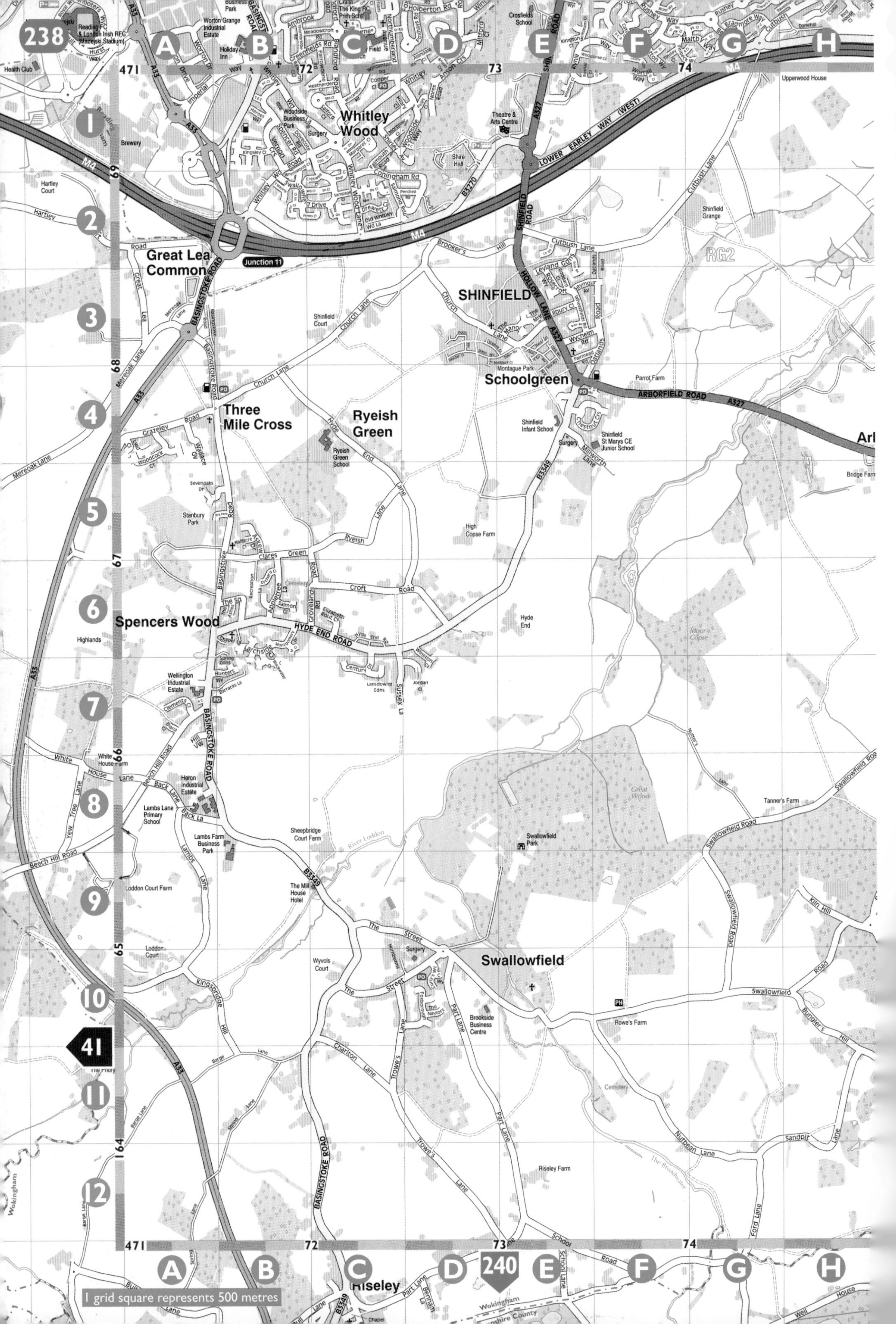
238
A
B
C
D
E
F
G
H
Reading FC & London Irish RFC (Madejski Stadium)
Health Club
Worton Grange Industrial Estate
Holiday Inn
Crosfields School
Whitley Wood
Woodside Business Park
Surgery
Brewery
Theatre & Arts Centre
Shire Hall
LOWER EARLEY WAY (WEST)
Upperwood House
M4
A33
A327
B3270
Hartley Court
Shinfield Grange
RG2
Great Lea Common
Junction 11
BASINGSTOKE ROAD
SHINFIELD
Shinfield Court
Church Lane
Cutbush Lane
Brooker's Hill
HOLLOW LANE
Schoolgreen
Montague Park
Parrot Farm
ARBORFIELD ROAD
Three Mile Cross
Ryeish Green
Ryeish Green School
Shinfield Infant School
Shinfield St Marys CE Junior School
Mereoak Lane
Grazeley Road
Bridge Farm
Sevenoaks Dr
Stanbury Park
High Copse Farm
Clares Green
Croft Road
Hyde End Lane
B3349
Spencers Wood
HYDE END ROAD
Highlands
Hyde End
Moor Copse
Wellington Industrial Estate
White House Farm
Heron Industrial Estate
Lambs Lane Primary School
Lambs Farm Business Park
Beech Hill Road
Yew Tree Lane
Sheepbridge Court Farm
River Loddon
Great Wood
Swallowfield Park
Tanner's Farm
Swallowfield Road
Loddon Court Farm
The Mill House Hotel
Kiln Hill
Loddon Court
Wyvols Court
The Street
Surgery
Swallowfield
Kingsbridge Hill
Brookside Business Centre
Part Lane
Rowe's Farm
Bunglers Hill
41
Barge Lane
The Priory
Chariton Lane
Trowe's Lane
Cemetery
Nutbean Lane
Sandpit Lane
Riseley Farm
The Broadwater
Wokingham
Ford Lane
School Road
School Lane
Riseley
240
71
72
73
74
64
65
66
67
68
69
1
2
3
4
5
6
7
8
9
10
11
12
1 grid square represents 500 metres

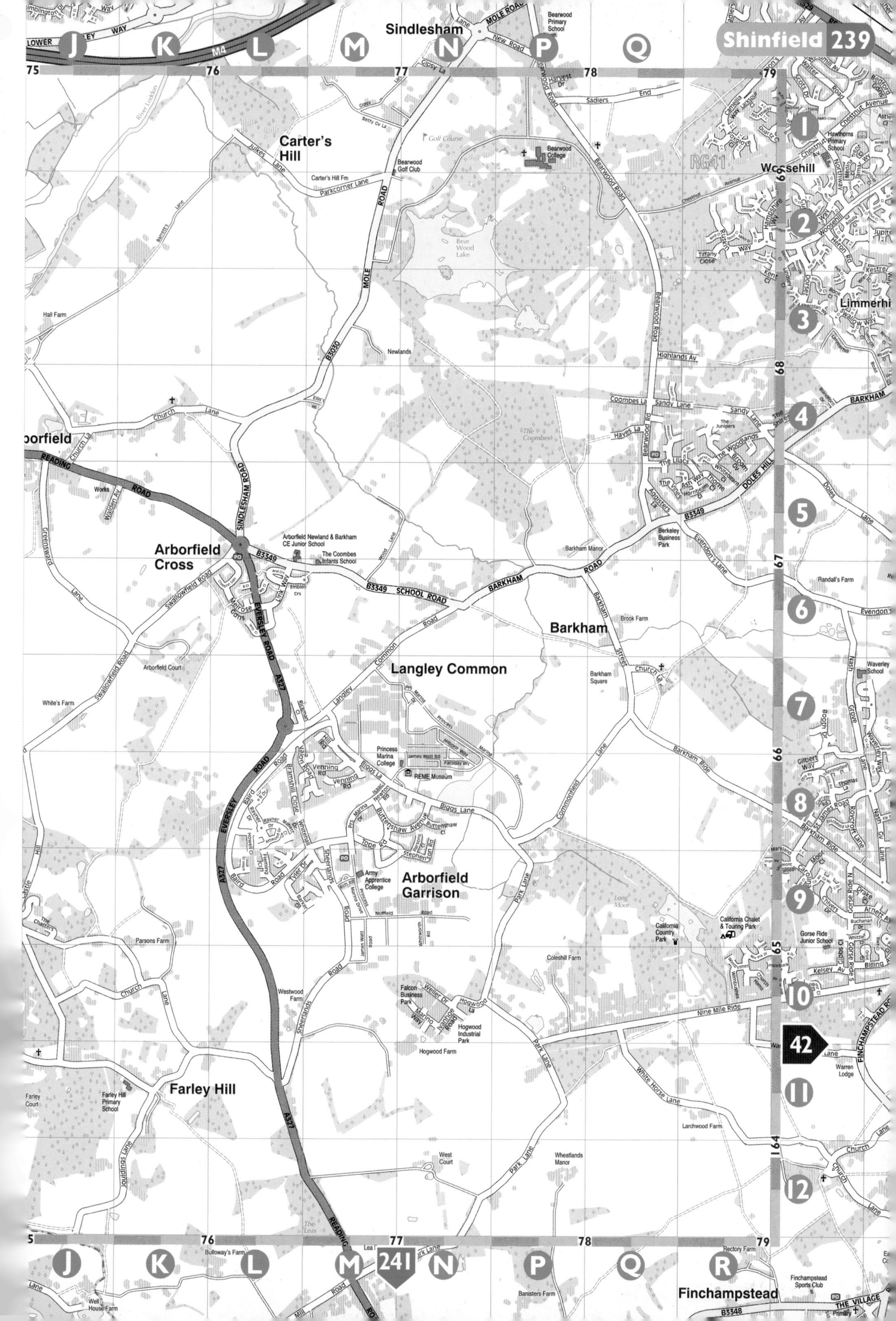
Sindlesham
Carter's Hill
Woosehill
Limmerhill
Arborfield
Arborfield Cross
Barkham
Langley Common
Arborfield Garrison
Farley Hill
Finchampstead
Bear Wood Lake
Bearwood College
Bearwood Golf Club
Princess Marina College
REME Museum
Army Apprentice College
California Country Park
Falcon Business Park
Hogwood Industrial Park
Berkeley Business Park
MOLE ROAD
SINDLESHAM ROAD
READING ROAD
EVERSLEY ROAD
BARKHAM ROAD
SCHOOL ROAD
DOLES HILL
Bearwood Road
Nine Mile Ride
Park Lane
Commonfield Lane
White Horse Lane
Barkham Ride
Barkham Street
Swallowfield Road
A327
B3349
B3030
M4

42
241

A　B　C　D　238　E　F　G　H

1

63

2

◀ 41

3

62

4

5

61

6

7

60

8

◀ 47

9

59

10

158

11

12

A　B　C　D　56　E　F　G　H

Wokingham

Bull Lane
Serval Lane

Riseley

B3349

Bull Lane

Sun La

Welsh Lane

B3349

Park Corner

Bull Lane

Norton Rd
Chapel La
Poachy La

Part Lane

Benham La

Odiham Road

Wokingham
Hampshire County

Part Lane

School Lane

Road

Riseley Farm

Well House

Cordery's Farm

Wellington
Country Park

Wellington
Country Park

Riseley
Mill

Hall's Farm

Ford Lane

Springwater Farm

Stratfield
Saye Park

Wellington
Monument

Heckfield
Heath House

Heckfield
Heath

The Causeway

River Whitewater

Park Farm

A33

Heckfield
Place

Copse Lane

Bramshill

Park Pitfield
Copse

BASINGSTOKE ROAD

Heckfield

Church Lane

B3349

B3011

Lower
Pitham

Highfield
House

Great
Danmoor
Copse

Holdshott Farm

New
Inn

Laundry Lane

Laundry La

Daneshill
House School

Home Farm

Alder
Moor
Copse

Lane

Plough

Hazeley Lea

Hazeley

Sheldons Farm

Hudsons
Meadow

Hound Green

Hound Gn

ds Farm

Chandlers
Green

Bottle

Lane

Vicarage Lane

Thackham's Farm

B3349

Reading Road

B3011

Red Hill

Blue
House Farm

Warwick Lane

Bottle Lane

Mattingley

PH

Dipley

Sherwoods

Stovel Lane

RG27

1 grid square represents 500 metres

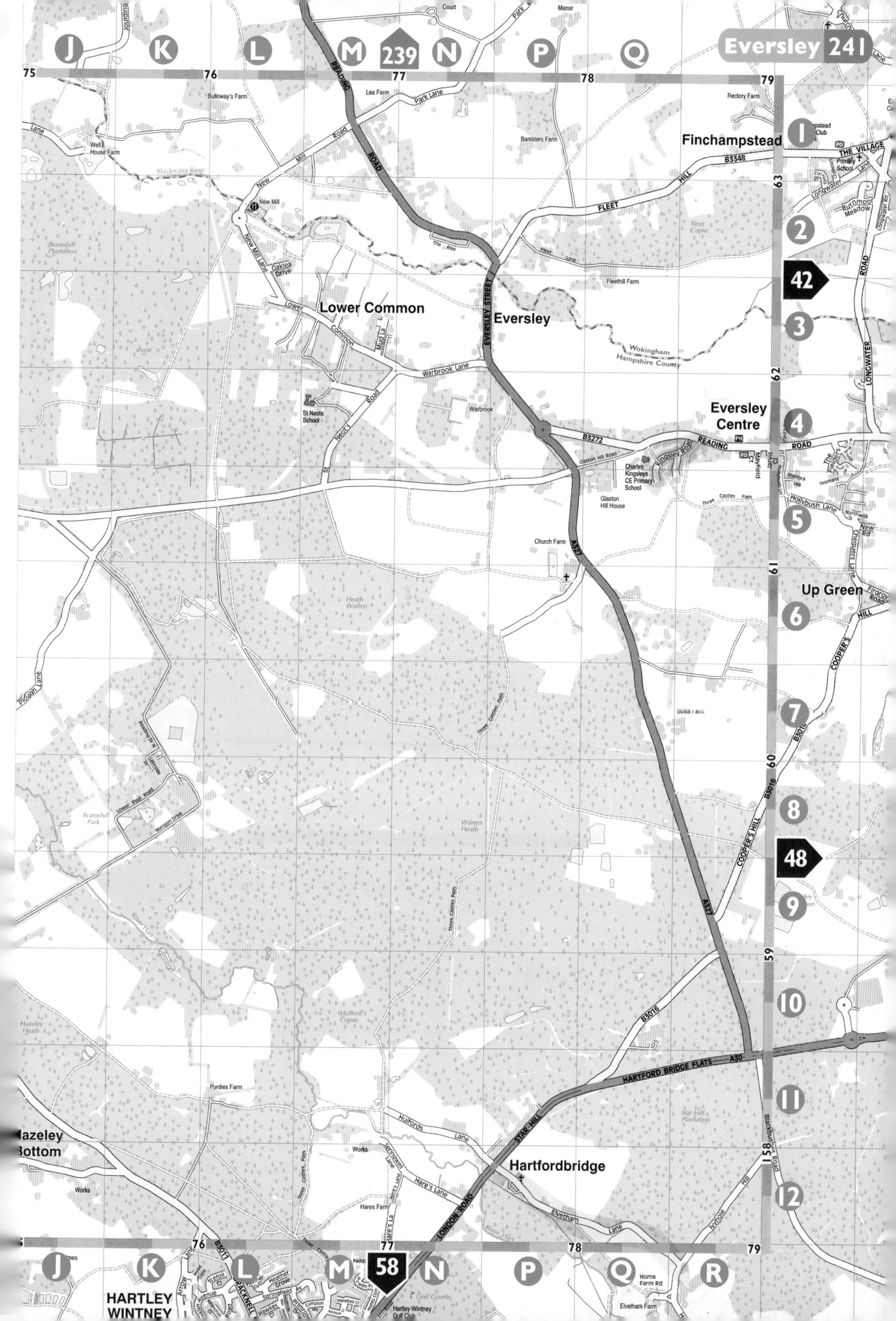

J
K
L
M
239
N
P
Q
75
76
77
78
79
READING ROAD
Lea Farm
Park Lane
Bulloway's Farm
Rectory Farm
Well House Farm
Blackwater River
New Mill Road
Banisters Farm
Finchampstead
THE VILLAGE
B3348
FLEET HILL
New Mill
Bramshill Plantation
New Mill Lane
Oaklea Drive
The Rise
Fleet Lane
Fleet Copse
Fleethill Farm
Longwater Lane
Burnmoor Meadow
Lower Common
EVERSLEY STREET
Eversley
Mud La
Wokingham
Hampshire County
Warbrook Lane
St Neots School
St Neot's Road
Warbrook
Eversley Centre
B3272
READING ROAD
Glaston Hill Road
Kingsley Road
Charles Kingsleys CE Primary School
Glaston Hill House
Mayfield Ct
Hollybush Lane
Three Castles Path
Church Farm
A327
Up Green
COOPER'S HILL
Heath Warren
Three Castles Path
B3016
Warren Heath
Bramshill Park
Lower Pool Road
Mansion Drive
River Hart
Hazeley Heath
Hulford's Copse
HARTFORD BRIDGE FLATS
A30
Star Hill Plantation
STAR HILL
Purdies Farm
Hulfords Lane
Hazeley Bottom
Works
Hartfordbridge
Hare's Lane
Hares Farm
LONDON ROAD
Elvetham Lane
Ivyhole Hill
Blackbushe Road
Home Farm Rd
Elvetham Farm
58
R
HARTLEY WINTNEY
B3011
Hartley Wintney Golf Club
1
2
42
3
4
5
6
7
8
48
9
10
11
12
63
62
61
60
59
58

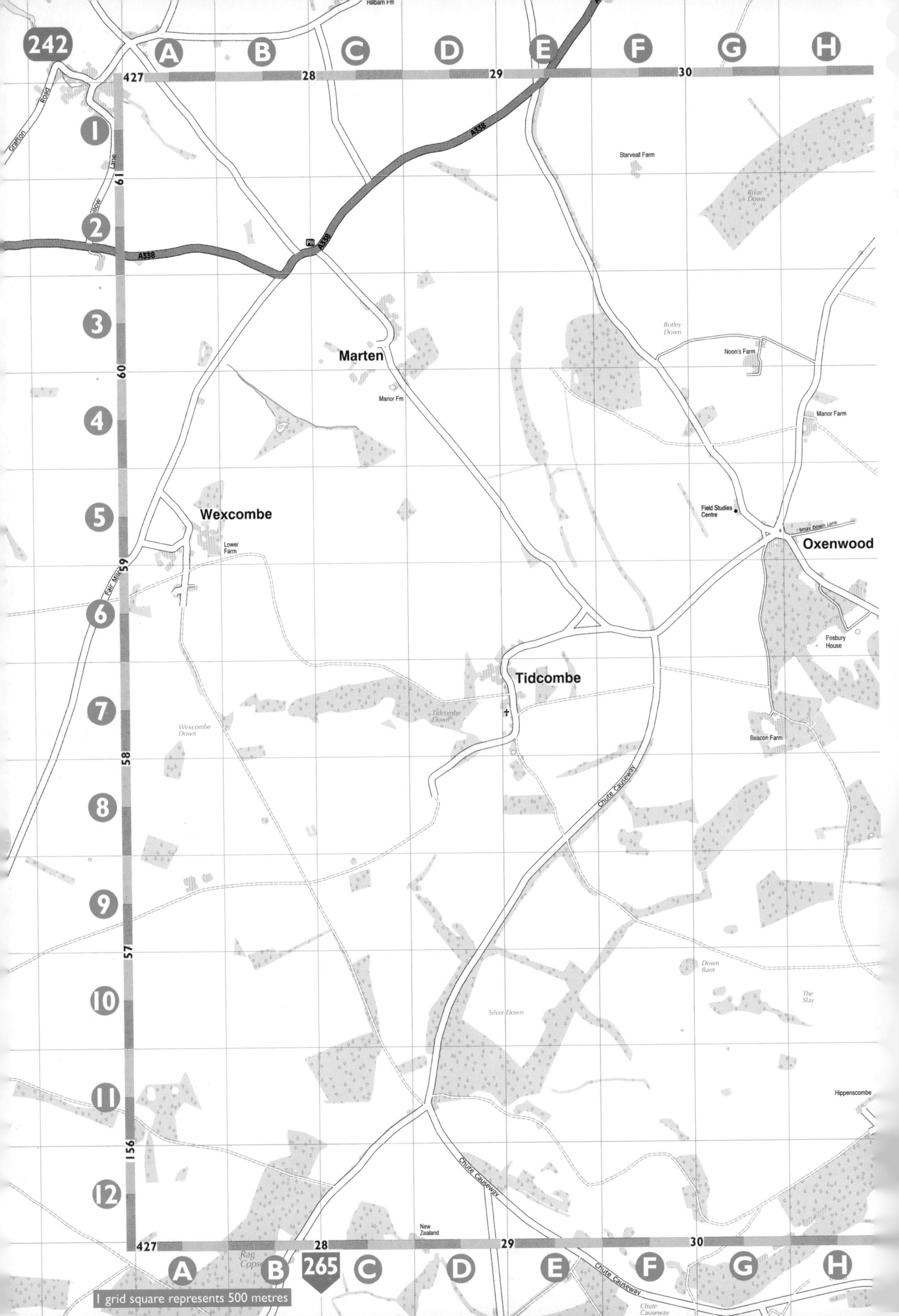

242

427 · 28 · 29 · 30

A · B · C · D · E · F · G · H

Grafton Road

Willow Lane

61

Hilbarn Fm

A338

PH

A338

Marten

Manor Fm

Starveall Farm

Botley Down

Noon's Farm

River Down

Manor Farm

Wexcombe

Lower Farm

60

Fair Mile

59

Field Studies Centre

Smay Down Lane

Oxenwood

Fosbury House

Tidcombe

Tidcombe Down

Wexcombe Down

58

Chute Causeway

Beacon Farm

Silver Down

57

Down Barn

The Slay

156

Hippenscombe

Rag Cops

New Zealand

Chute Causeway

Chute Causeway

1 · 2 · 3 · 4 · 5 · 6 · 7 · 8 · 9 · 10 · 11 · 12

427 · 28 · 29 · 30

A · B · 265 · C · D · E · F · G · H

1 grid square represents 500 metres

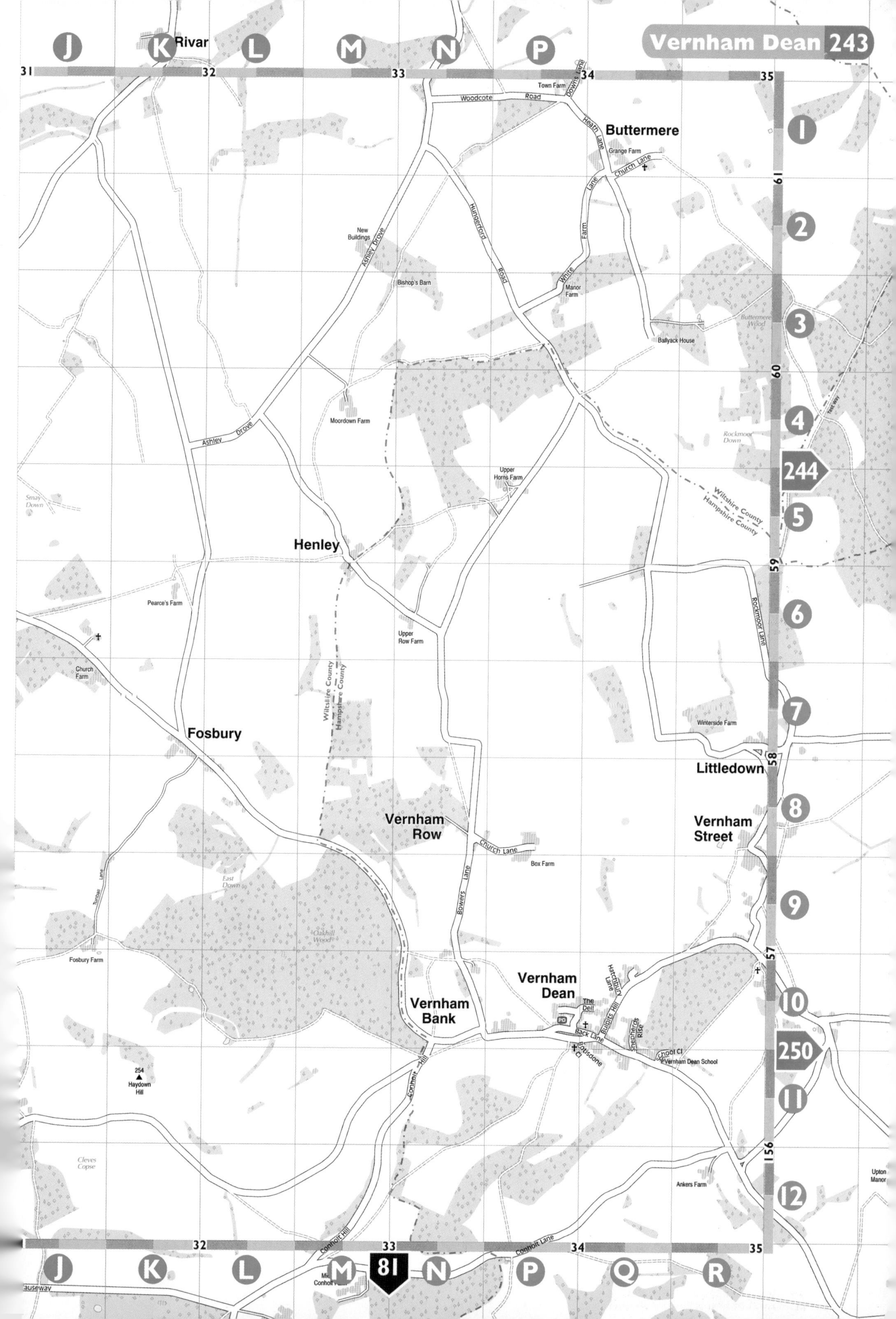

J K **Rivar** L M N P

Buttermere

Town Farm
Woodcote Road
Heath Lane
Grange Farm
Church Lane
White Farm Lane
Manor Farm
New Buildings
Bishop's Barn
Ballyack House
Buttermere Wood

Ashley Drove
Moordown Farm
Upper Horns Farm

Ashley Drove
Henley
Pearce's Farm
Upper Row Farm

Church Farm

Fosbury

Wiltshire County
Hampshire County

Rockmoor Down
Rockmoor Lane

Winterside Farm

Littledown

Vernham Row
Church Lane
Box Farm
Bowers Lane

Vernham Street

East Down
Oakhill Wood

Turnpike Lane

Vernham Dean
Hatchbury Lane
The Dell
PO
Back Lane
Coldstone
Shepherds Rise
Bublic Hill
School Cl
Vernham Dean School

Vernham Bank

Conholt Hill

254 Haydown Hill

Fosbury Farm

Cleves Copse

Ankers Farm

Upton Manor

J K L M N P Q R

81

Conholt Hill
Conholt Lane
Causeway
Mr Conholt

244
250

35
61
60
59
58
57
56

244
A
B
C
D
30
E
F
G
H
West Berkshire
Wiltshire County
Lower Spray Farm
Spray Road
435
36
37
38
Upper Green
Bell Lane
Kirby House
Park House
63
62
61
60
59
58
1
2
3
4
5
6
7
8
9
10
11
12
Combe Gibbet
Test Way
West Woodhay Down
Walbury Hill
Wright's Farm
Wayfarer's Walk
High
Lower Farm
Combe
Manor Farm
Church Lane
Eastwick
Ballyack House
Hogs Hole
Combe Wood
243
West Berkshire
Hampshire County
Wiltshire
Hampshire
Rockmoor Lane
Hart Hill Down
Winterside Farm
Manor House
Linkenholt
PO
Manor Farm
Faccombe
Netherton
Littledown
Vernham Street
250
1 grid square represents 500 metres

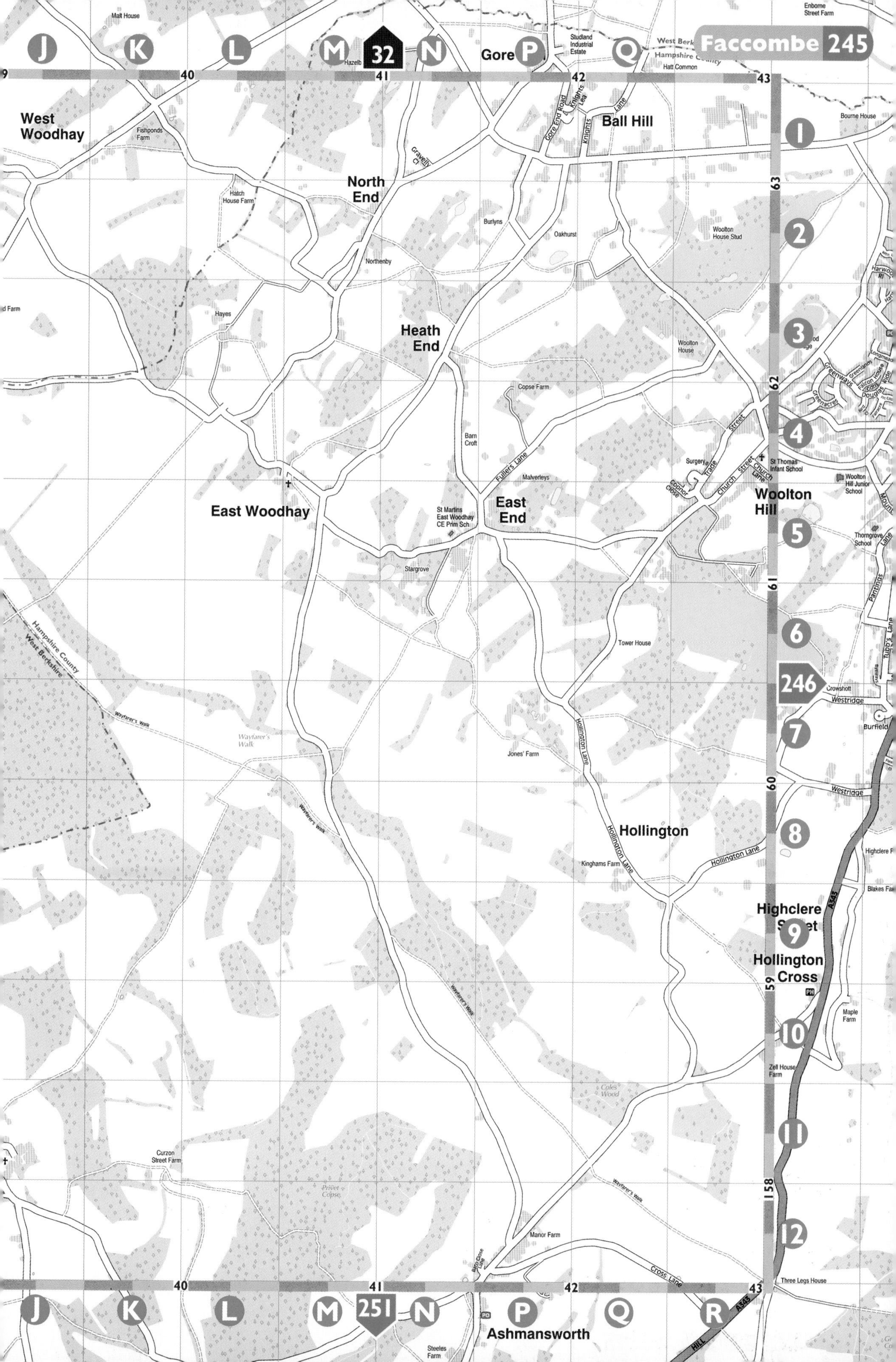
West Woodhay
Fishponds Farm
Malt House
Hatch House Farm
North End
Gravelly Cl
Gore
Studland Industrial Estate
Hatt Common
West Berkshire
Hampshire County
Enborne Street Farm
Gore End Road
Knights Lea
Knights Lane
Ball Hill
Bourne House
Burlyns
Oakhurst
Woolton House Stud
Northenby
Hayes
Heath End
Woolton House
Copse Farm
Barn Croft
Fullers Lane
Malverleys
Surgery
Trade Street
Church Street
Church Lane
Coppice Close
St Thomas Infant School
Woolton Hill
Woolton Hill Junior School
Greenways
Greenacres
Douglas Ride
Longmead
Harwood Rise
East Woodhay
St Martins East Woodhay CE Prim Sch
East End
Stargrove
Thorngrove School
Pantings
Tubb's Lane
Tower House
Crowshott
Westridge
Burfield
Hampshire County
West Berkshire
Wayfarer's Walk
Jones' Farm
Hollington Lane
Hollington
Kinghams Farm
Highclere Farm
Blakes Farm
A343
Highclere Street
Hollington Cross
PH
Maple Farm
Zell House Farm
Coles Wood
Curzon Street Farm
Privet Copse
Manor Farm
Barn Close Lane
Cross Lane
Three Legs House
Ashmansworth
PO
Steeles Farm
HILL
32
246
251
J K L M N P Q R
40 41 42 43
63 62 61 60 59 158
1 2 3 4 5 6 7 8 9 10 11 12

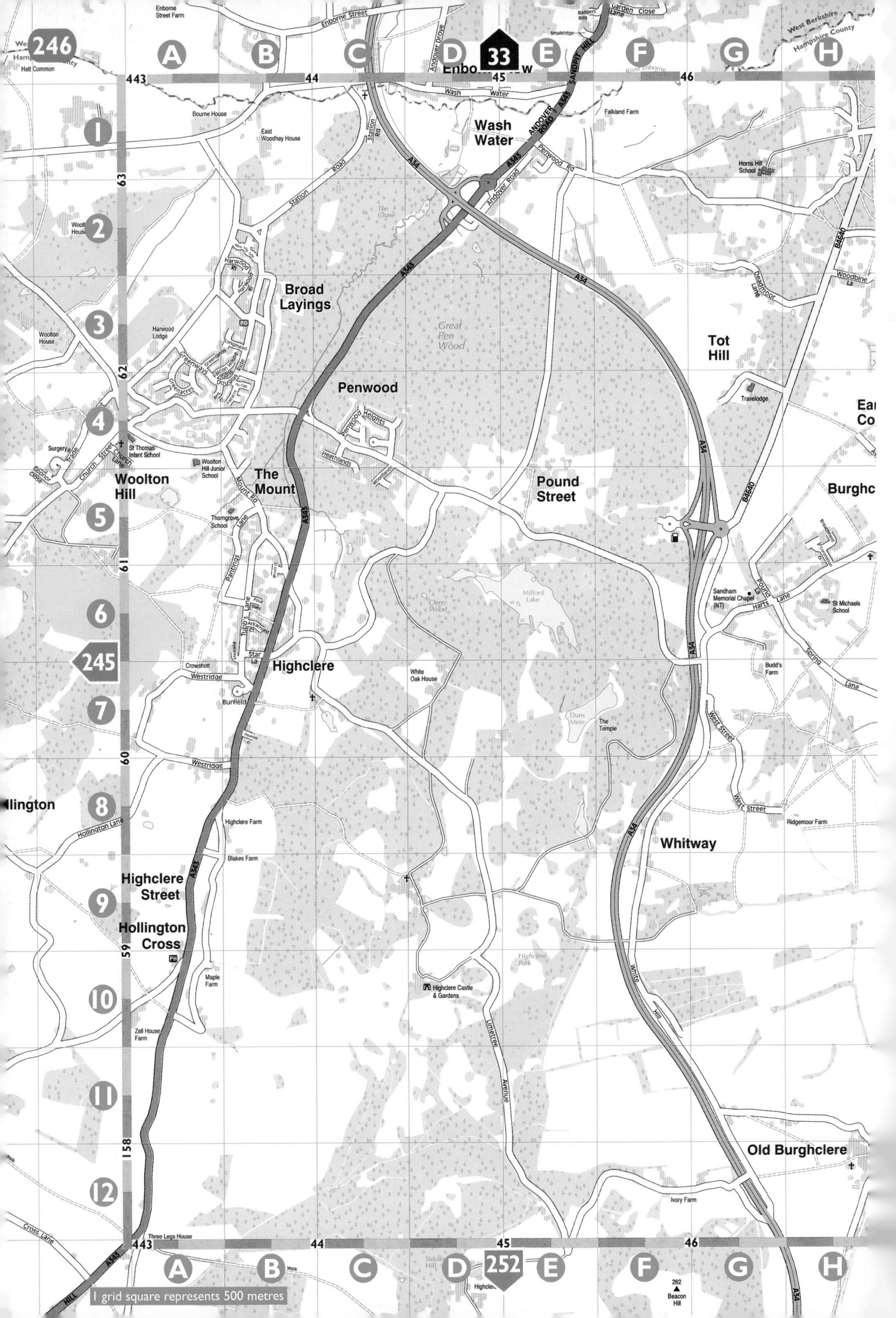

246
33
245
252
A
B
C
D
E
F
G
H
443
44
45
46
63
62
61
60
59
158
1
2
3
4
5
6
7
8
9
10
11
12
Enborne Street Farm
Enborne Street
Garden Close
Hatt Common
West Berkshire
Hampshire County
River Enborne
Wash Water
Bourne House
East Woodhay House
Station Rd
Station Road
Andover Drove
Andover Road
Sandpit Hill
A343
A34
Penwood Rd
Falkland Farm
Horris Hill School
B4640
Woodbine La
Deadmoor Lane
Wash
Water
Harwood Rd
Broad Layings
The Chase
Great Pen Wood
Tot Hill
Travelodge
Woolton House
Harwood Lodge
Longmead
Greenways
Greenacres
Penwood
Penwood Heights
Heathlands
Woodlands
Surgery
Trade
Church Street
Church Lane
St Thomas Infant School
Woolton Hill Junior School
Woolton Hill
The Mount
Mount Rd
Pound Street
Burghclere
Thorngrove School
Pantings Lane
Milford Lake
Sandham Memorial Chapel (NT)
Pound La
Harts Lane
St Michaels School
Tubb's Lane
Arkwright Cl
Star La
Crowshott
Westridge
Highclere
Burfield
White Oak House
Budd's Farm
Spring Lane
West Street
Duns Mere
The Temple
llington
Highclere Farm
Hollington Lane
Ridgemoor Farm
Whitway
Blakes Farm
Highclere Street
Hollington Cross
Maple Farm
Highclere Park
Highclere Castle & Gardens
White Hill
Zell House Farm
Limetree Avenue
Old Burghclere
Ivory Farm
Three Legs House
Cross Lane
HILL
Walk
262
Beacon Hill
1 grid square represents 500 metres

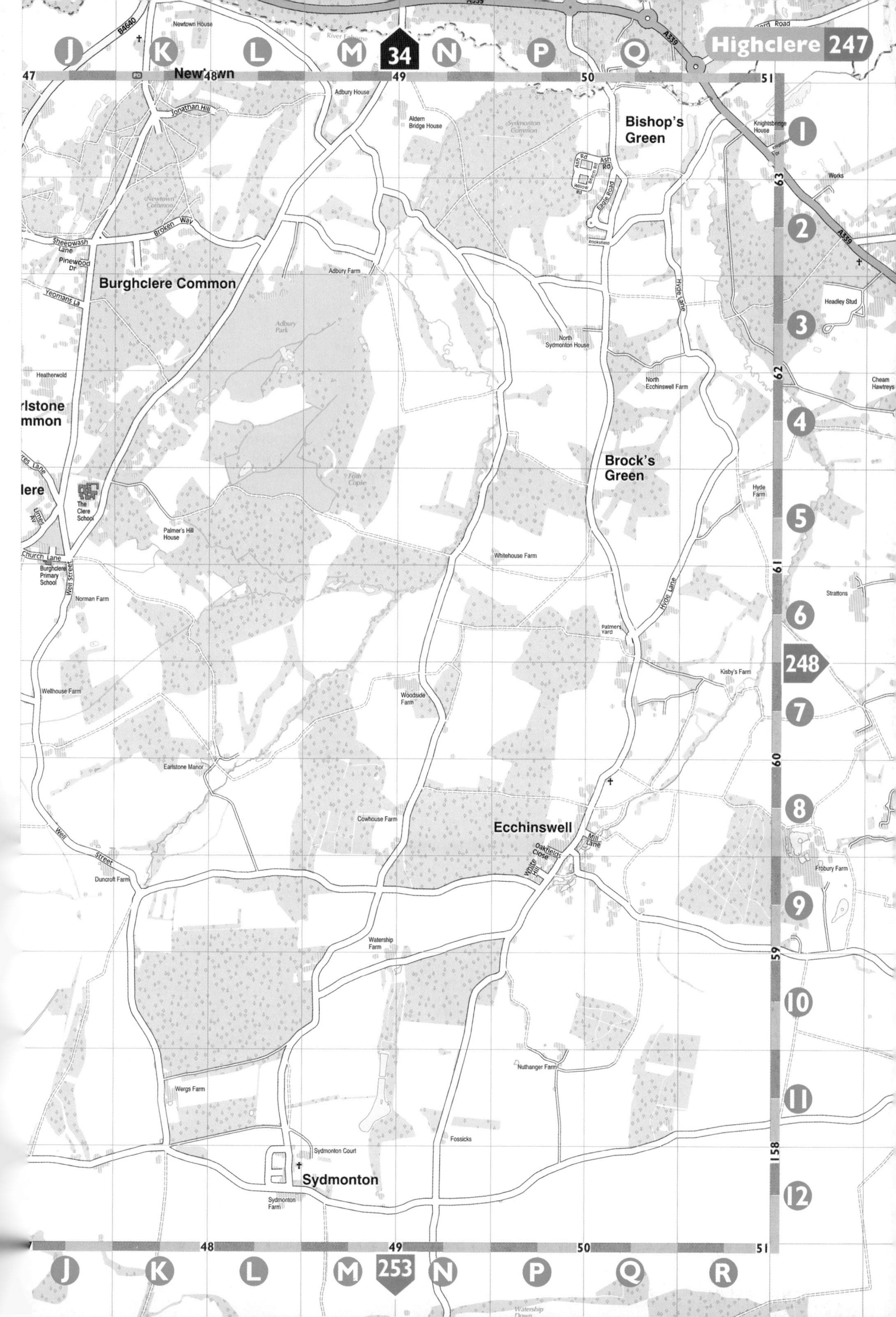

J K L M **34** N P Q

47 New'48wn 49 50 51

Newtown House

River Enborne

Adbury House

Aldern Bridge House

Sydmonton Common

Bishop's Green

Knightsbridge House

Works

I

2

Headley Stud

3

Cheam Hawtreys

4

Jonathan Hill

Newtown Common

Broken Way

Sheepwash Lane

Pinewood Dr

Yeomans La

Burghclere Common

Adbury Farm

Adbury Park

Ash Rd
Birch Rd
Ash Rd
Willow
Brookfield

Lane Road

North Sydmonton House

North Ecchinswell Farm

Hyde Lane

Heatherwold

Frith Copse

Palmer's Hill House

arlstone ommon

lere

The Clere School

Little Av

Church Lane

Burghclere Primary School

Well Street

Norman Farm

Wellhouse Farm

Whitehouse Farm

Palmers Yard

Brock's Green

Hyde Farm

5

Strattons

6

248

Kisby's Farm

7

Earlstone Manor

Woodside Farm

8

Frobury Farm

Duncroft Farm

Cowhouse Farm

Ecchinswell

Oakfields Close

White Hill

Mill Lane

9

Watership Farm

10

Wergs Farm

Nuthanger Farm

11

Sydmonton Court

Fossicks

58

12

Sydmonton Farm

Sydmonton

Watership

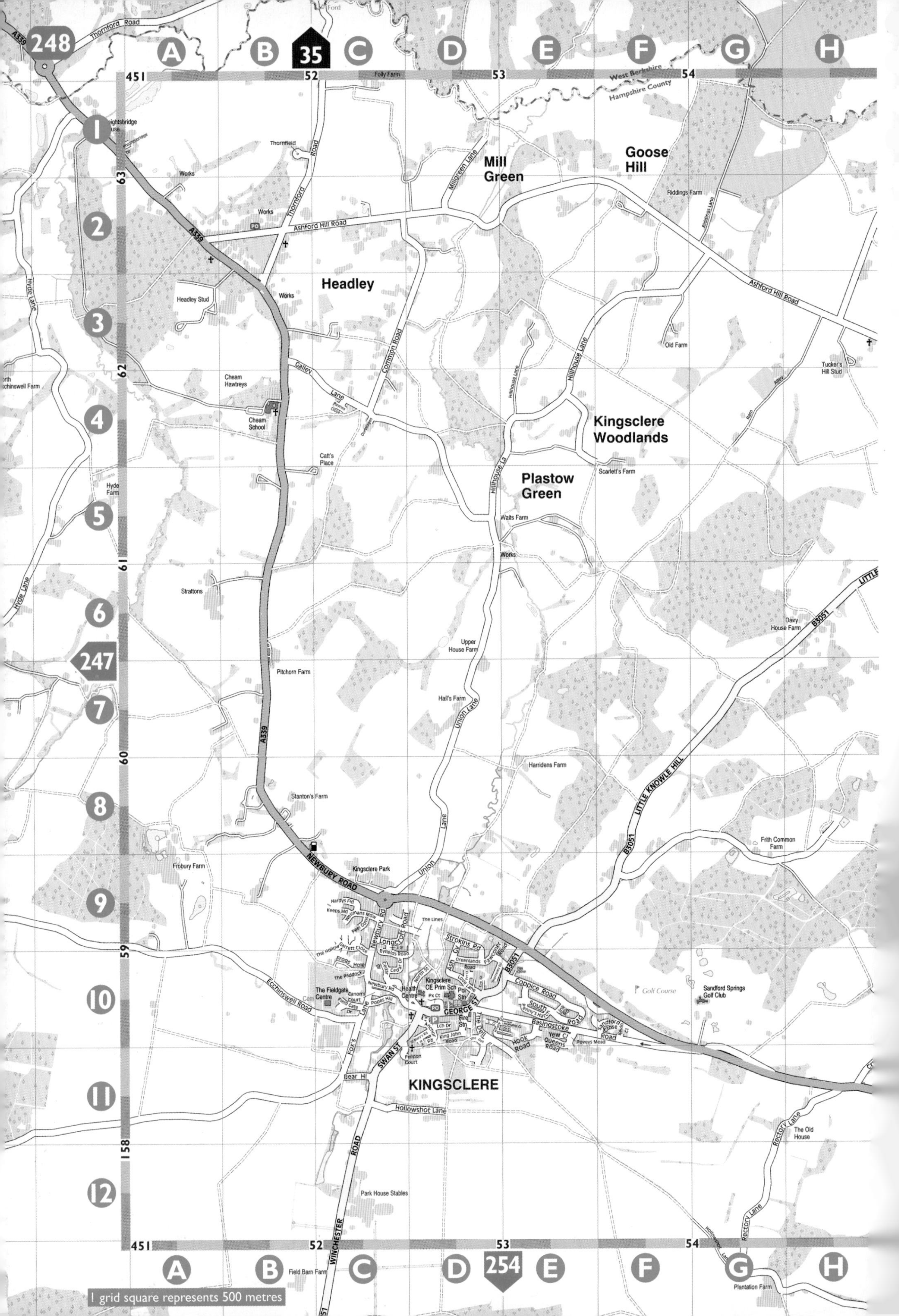

248
35
A
B
C
D
E
F
G
H
451
52
53
54
Folly Farm
West Berkshire
Hampshire County
Thornford Road
A339
Ford
Knightsbridge House
Thornfield
Thornford Road
Works
Mill Green
Millgreen Lane
Goose Hill
Riddings Farm
Riddings Lane
Ashford Hill Road
Headley
Headley Stud
Hyde Lane
North Ecchinswell Farm
Galley Lane
Common Road
Cheam Hawtreys
Cheam School
Catt's Place
Hyde Farm
Old Farm
Tucker's Hill Stud
Kingsclere Woodlands
Hillhouse Lane
Hillhouse La
Plastow Green
Scarlett's Farm
Watts Farm
Strattons
Dairy House Farm
B3051
LITTLE KNOWLE HILL
Upper House Farm
Pitchorn Farm
Hall's Farm
Union Lane
Harridens Farm
Stanton's Farm
Frith Common Farm
Frobury Farm
NEWBURY ROAD
Kingsclere Park
Union Lane
The Lines
Strokins Rd
Greenlands Road
Coppice Road
Ecchinswell Road
The Fieldgate Centre
Kingsclere CE Prim Sch
Health Centre
GEORGE ST
Basingstoke Road
Hook Road
Yew C
Queens Road
Poveys Mead
Golf Course
Sandford Springs Golf Club
Fox's Lane
SWAN ST
Bear Hl
KINGSCLERE
Hollowshot Lane
WINCHESTER ROAD
Rectory Lane
The Old House
Park House Stables
Field Barn Farm
254
Plantation Farm
1
2
3
4
5
6
7
8
9
10
11
12
63
62
61
60
59
158
247
1 grid square represents 500 metres

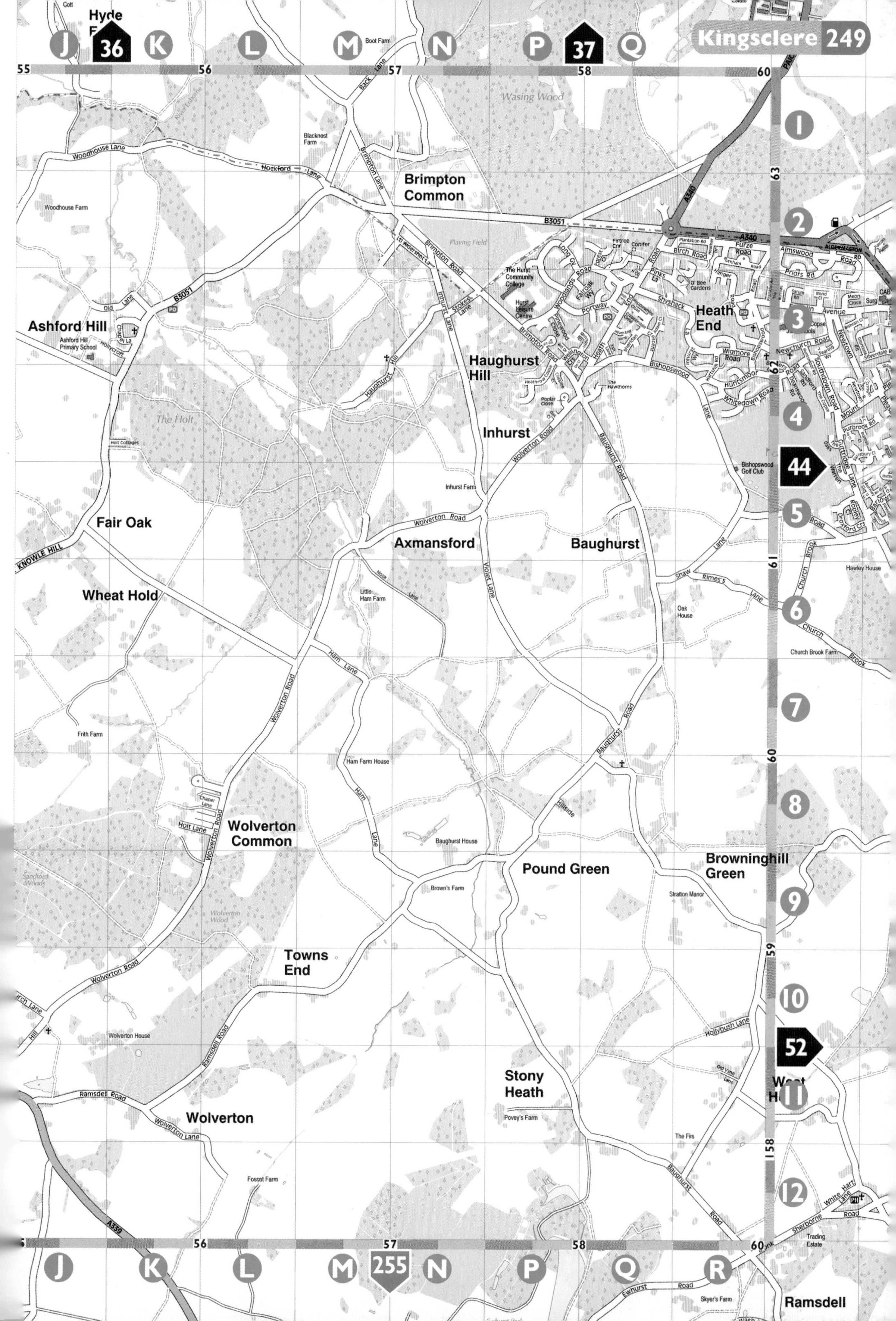

Kingsclere 249
Hyde
36
37
Boot Farm
Back Lane
Wasing Wood
Blacknest Farm
Woodhouse Lane
Hockford Lane
Brimpton Lane
Brimpton Common
Woodhouse Farm
B3051
A340
Playing Field
Brimpton Road
The Hurst Community College
Hurst Leisure Centre
Firtree Cnr
Conifer Cl
Birch Road
Furze Road
Almswood Road
Priors Rd
Aldermaston
Pinks La
Portway
Fairoak Wy
Woodlands Road
Shyshack La
O' Bee Gardens
Heath End
Avenue
Newchurch Road
Newtown
Wigmore Road
Huntsmoor
Whitedown Road
Bishopswood Road
Bishopswood Lane
Southdown Road
Silverdale Rd
Ashford Hill
Ashford Hill Primary School
Old Lane
Chapel La
Hollycroft
Haughurst Hill
Inhurst Lane
Stokes Lane
Heathrow Copse
Poplar Close
The Hawthorns
The Holt
Holt Cottages
Inhurst
Wolverton Road
Baughurst Road
Bishopswood Golf Club
44
Purbrook Rd
Cuttridge Lane
Inhurst Farm
Fair Oak
Axmansford
Baughurst
Knowle Hill
Hook Lane
Little Ham Farm
Violet Lane
Shaw Lane
Rimes's Lane
Oak House
Church Brook
Hawley House
Church Brook Farm
Wheat Hold
Ham Lane
Frith Farm
Ham Farm House
Chapel Lane
Holt Lane
Wolverton Common
Baughurst House
Hillside
Pound Green
Browninghill Green
Brown's Farm
Stratton Manor
Sandford Woods
Wolverton Wood
Towns End
Hollybush Lane
52
Old Vine Lane
Church Lane
Wolverton House
Ramsdell Road
Stony Heath
Povey's Farm
West Heath
Wolverton
Wolverton Lane
The Firs
Foscot Farm
A339
White Hart Lane
Sherborne Road
Trading Estate
255
Ewhurst Road
Skyer's Farm
Ramsdell

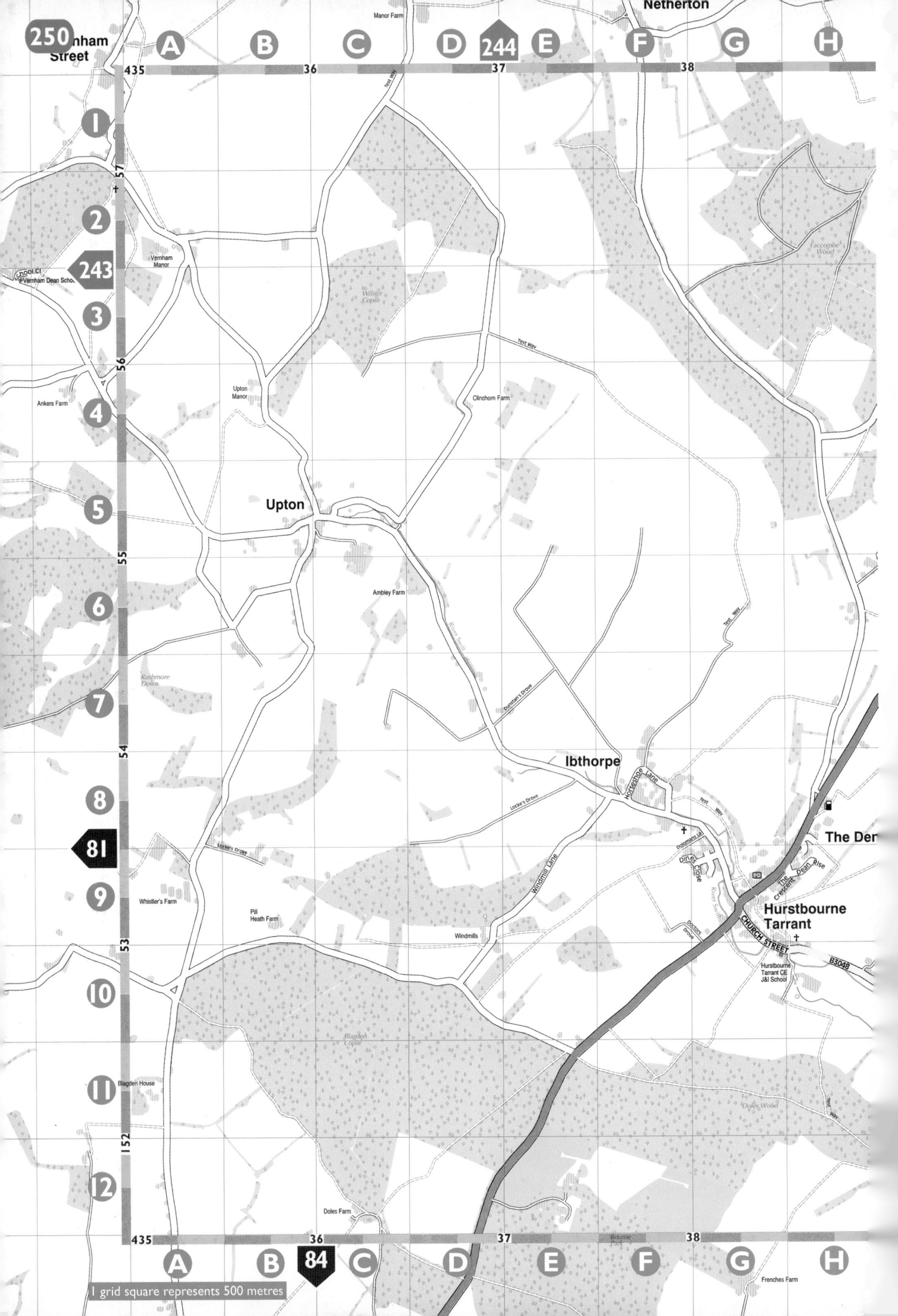

250
nham
Street
Netherton
Manor Farm
244
A
B
C
D
E
F
G
H
435
36
37
38
57
56
55
54
53
152
1
2
3
4
5
6
7
8
9
10
11
12
243
81
84
Test Way
Vernham Manor
Vernham Dean School
Ankers Farm
Wilster Copse
Upton Manor
Clinchorn Farm
Faccombe Wood
Upton
Ambley Farm
River Swift
Rushmore Down
Dunstan's Drove
Ibthorpe
Horseshoe Lane
Locke's Drove
Windmill Lane
Dolomans La
Dines Close
The Crescent
Dean Rise
The Den
PO
Whistler's Farm
Pill Heath Farm
Windmills
Doctors Drove
Hurstbourne Tarrant
CHURCH STREET
B3048
Hurstbourne Tarrant CE J&I School
Blagden Copse
Blagden House
Doles Wood
Doles Farm
Frenches Farm
1 grid square represents 500 metres

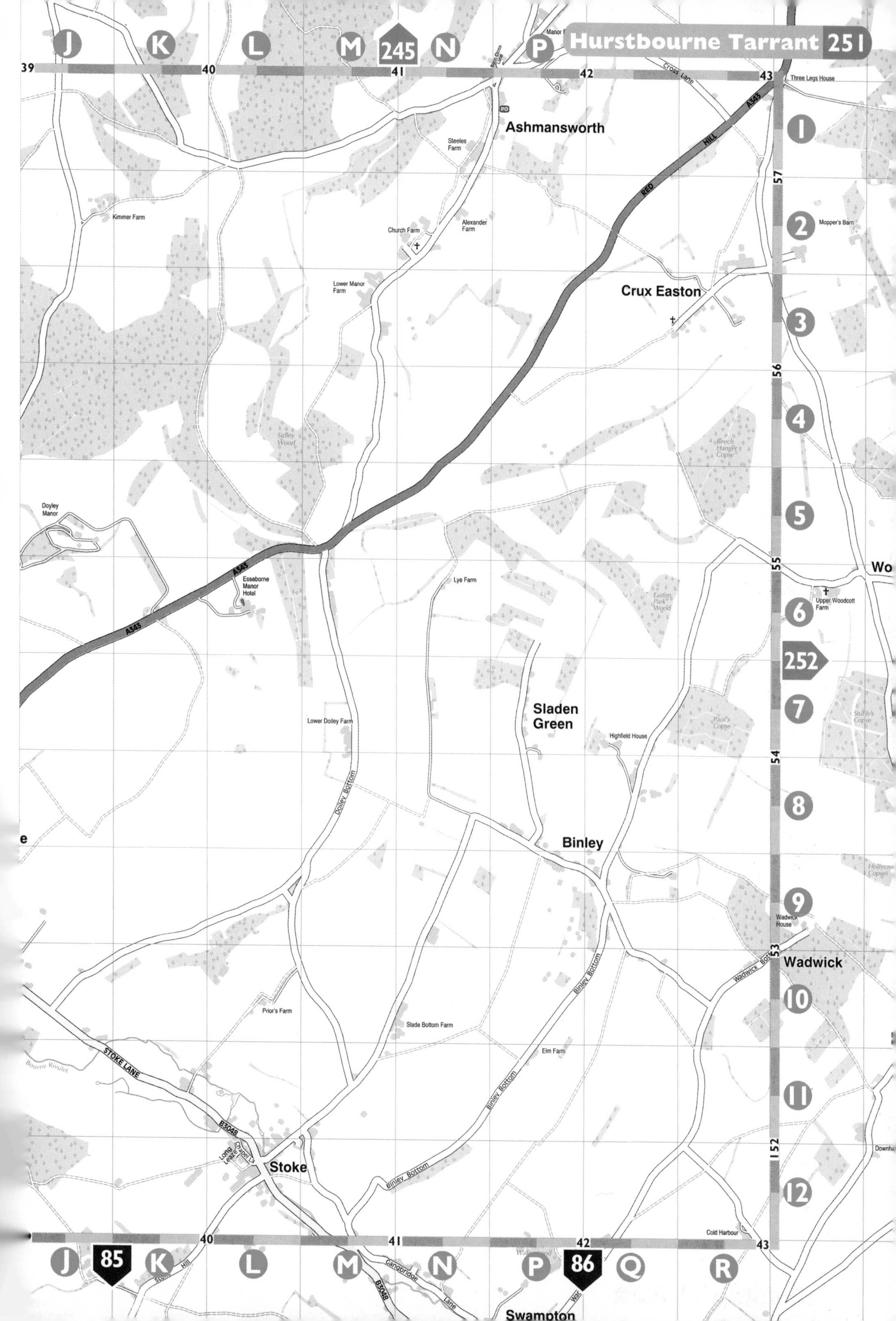

Three Legs House

Manor

1

Mopper's Barn

2

Ashmansworth

Steeles
Farm

Church Farm

Alexander
Farm

Crux Easton

3

Kimmer Farm

Lower Manor
Farm

4

Sidley Wood

Beech
Hanger
Copse

5

Doyley
Manor

Wo

A343

Esseborne
Manor
Hotel

Lye Farm

Upper Woodcott
Farm

6

Easton
Park
Wood

252

7

Stubb's
Copse

Lower Dolley Farm

Sladen
Green

Paul's
Copse

Highfield House

8

Dolley Bottom

Binley

Hollyern
Copse

9

Wadwick
House

Prior's Farm

Binley Bottom

Slade Bottom Farm

Wadwick Road

Wadwick

10

STOKE LANE

Elm Farm

11

Bourne Rivulet

B3048

Long
Lees

Stoke

Binley Bottom

12

Downha

Cold Harbour

Swampton

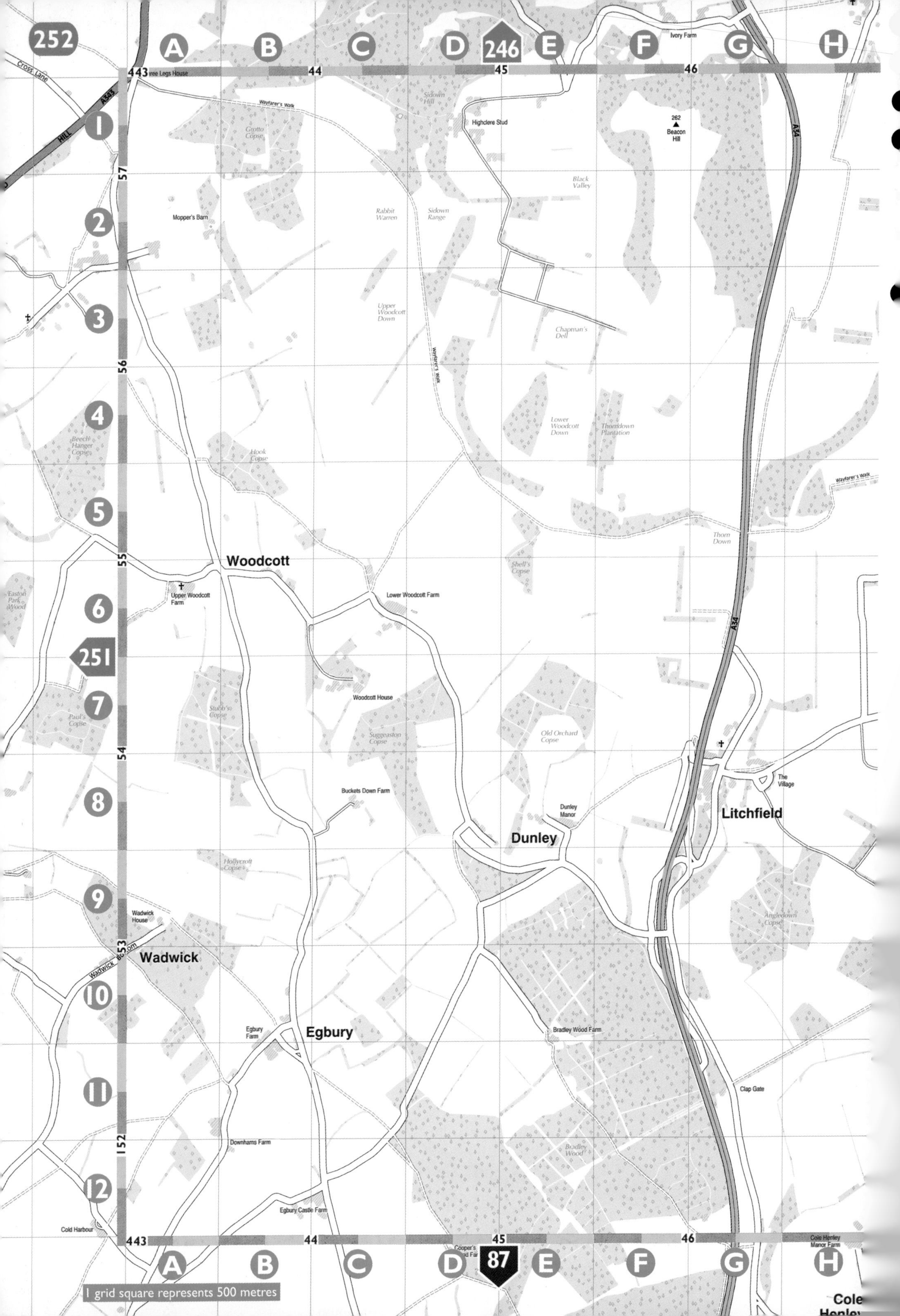
252
246
251
87
A
B
C
D
E
F
G
H
1
2
3
4
5
6
7
8
9
10
11
12
443
44
45
46
57
56
55
54
53
152
Cross Lane
A343
HILL
Three Legs House
Wayfarer's Walk
Grotto Copse
Sidown Hill
Highclere Stud
Ivory Farm
262
Beacon Hill
A34
Mopper's Barn
Rabbit Warren
Sidown Range
Black Valley
Upper Woodcott Down
Chapman's Dell
Beech Hanger Copse
Hook Copse
Lower Woodcott Down
Thorndown Plantation
Thorn Down
Shell's Copse
Woodcott
Upper Woodcott Farm
Lower Woodcott Farm
Easton Park Wood
Woodcott House
Stubb's Copse
Paul's Copse
Suggeaston Copse
Old Orchard Copse
Buckets Down Farm
Dunley Manor
Dunley
The Village
Litchfield
Hollycroft Copse
Angledown Copse
Wadwick House
Wadwick
Wadwick Bottom
Egbury Farm
Egbury
Bradley Wood Farm
Clap Gate
Downhams Farm
Bradley Wood
Egbury Castle Farm
Cold Harbour
Cole Henley Manor Farm
1 grid square represents 500 metres

Sydmonton
Sydmonton Farm
247
Watership Down
Barton Copse
234
Ladle Hill
Ladle Hill (Unfinished Hill Fort)
Wayfarer's Walk
Cannon Heath Down
Hare Warren Down
Ashley Warren Down
Great Litchfield Down
Ashley Warren Farm
Cannon Heath Farm
Hare Warren Farm
Robley Belt
254
Little Down
Hare Warren Copse
Down Farm
Caesar's Belt
Litchfield Down
Roman Road
Ridgeway Copse
Ridgeway Farm
Streetley Copse
Furze Copse
Willesley Warren Farm
Paul's Wood
Twinley Manor
Twinley Lane
Whitnal
Peak House Farm
La Bresse
New Barn
88
B3051
Frost Hi
Meadro
Stud

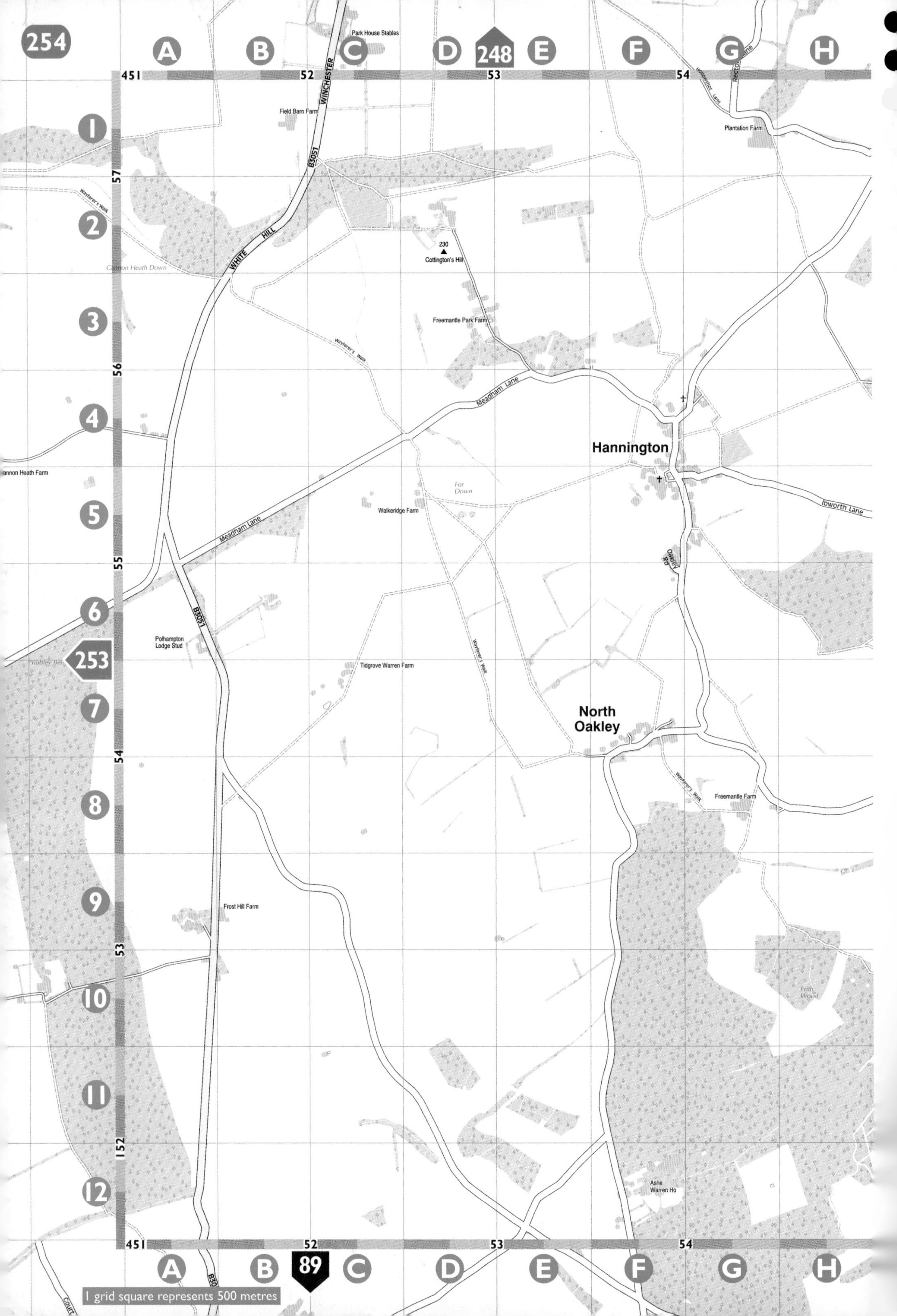

A
B
C
D
248
E
F
G
H
451
52
53
54
Park House Stables
Field Barn Farm
WINCHESTER
B3051
WHITE HILL
Plantation Farm
Rectory Lane
Wayfarer's Walk
Cannon Heath Down
230
Cottington's Hill
Freemantle Park Farm
Meadham Lane
Hannington
Cannon Heath Farm
For Down
Walkeridge Farm
Ibworth Lane
Oakley Rd
Polhampton Lodge Stud
Tidgrove Warren Farm
253
North Oakley
Freemantle Farm
Frost Hill Farm
Frith Wood
Ashe Warren Ho
1
2
3
4
5
6
7
8
9
10
11
12
57
56
55
54
53
152
89
1 grid square represents 500 metres

55 56 57 58 60

Foscot Farm

Ewhurst Park

Home Farm

✝ Ewhurst House

Dorrel Wood

Pitt Hall Fm

Folly Dairy

Balstone Farm

Ibworth

Warren Bottom Copse

Hay Wood

White Lane

Shear Down Farm

Great Deane Wood

Malshangar House

Summer Down Farm

Summer Down Lane

Hook Lane

Lloyd's Lane

A339

A339

Ewhurst Road

Skyer's Farm

Skyer's Wood

Woodgarston Farm

Upper Wootton

✝ Whitedown

Tangier

Wootton St Lawrence

KINGSCLERE ROAD

RG23

Trading Estate

1 Ramsdell

2

52

3 Farm

4

5

6

7

8

64 PO

9

10

11

12 WORTING ROAD

B3400

Sherbo...
Monk...
Bandhu...
Sheepwash Lane
Basingstoke Road

57 56 55 54 53 52

55 56 57 58 60

Deane Down Farm

Newfound

Foxmoor...
Bellfield Lane
Hunters...

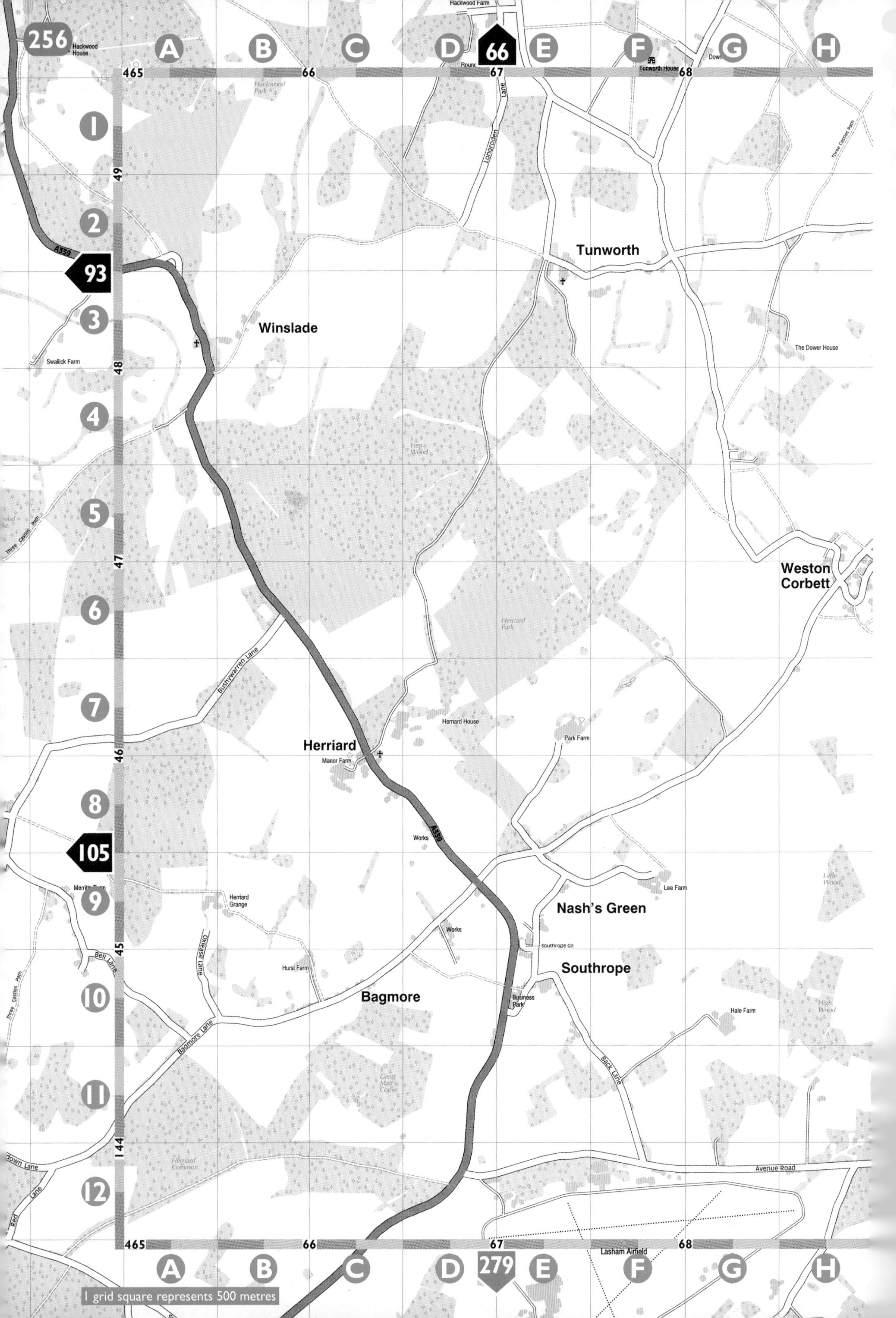

A   B   C   D   66   E   F   G   H
465   66   67   68

1
49
2
93
3
48
Winslade
Swallick Farm
4
5
47
6
7
46
Busarywarren Lane
Herriard
Manor Farm
8
105
9
Merritts Farm
Herriard Grange
10
45
Bell Lane
Bagmore Lane
11
144
Red Lane
Crown Lane
Herriard Common
12
465   66   67   68
A   B   C   279   E   F   G   H

Hackwood Farm
Hackwood Park
Round
Longrodden Lane
Tunworth
Tunworth House
Down
Three Castles Path
The Dower House
Weston Corbett
Herriard Park
Heys Wood
Herriard House
Park Farm
Lee Farm
Little Wood
Nash's Green
Works
Southrope Gn
Southrope
Works
Hurst Farm
Business Park
Hale Farm
High Wood
Great Mats Copse
Back Lane
Avenue Road
Lasham Airfield
A339

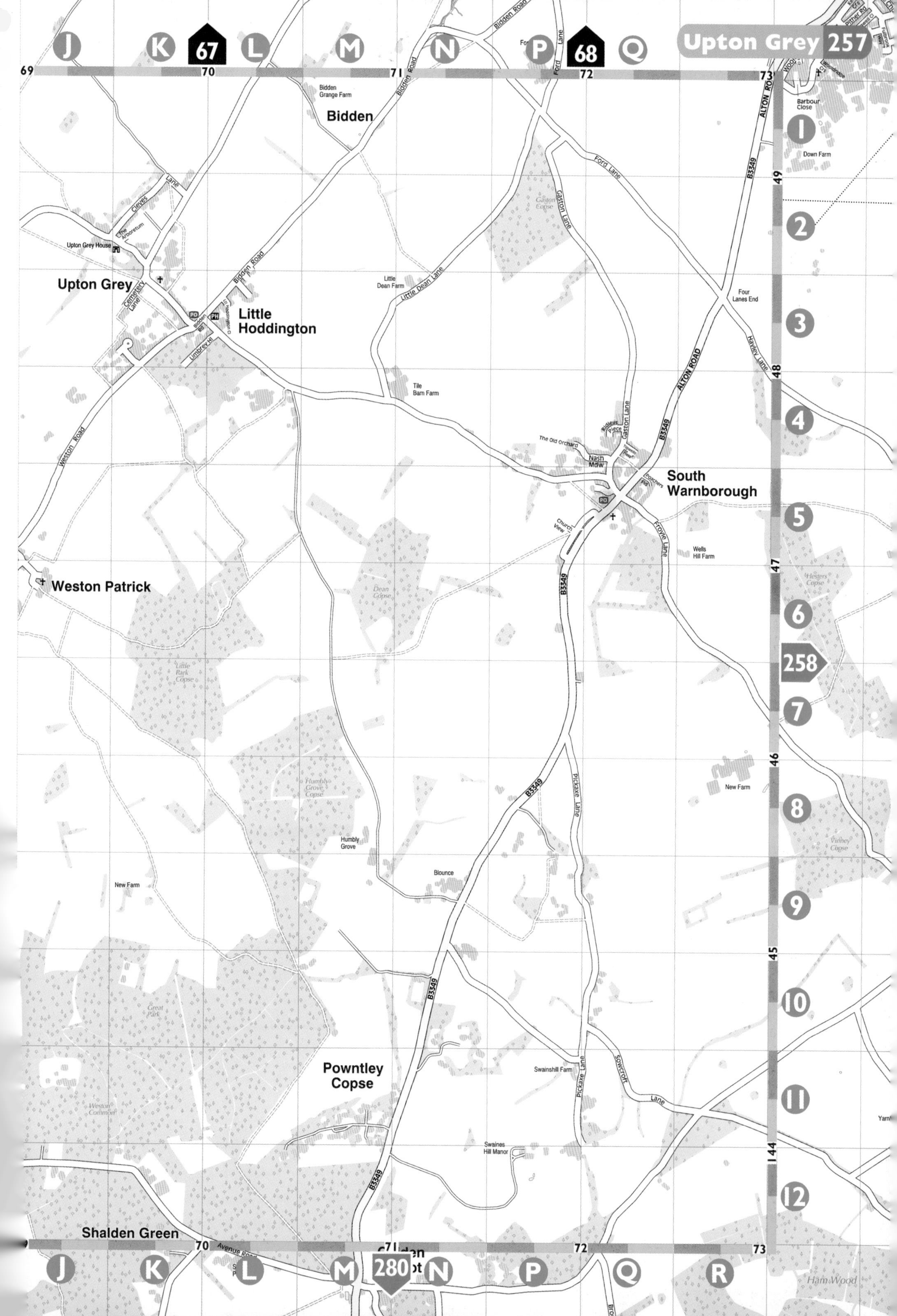

J 69 **K** **67** 70 **L** **M** 71 **N** **P** **68** 72 **Q** 73

49 **48** **47** **46** **45** **44**

1 **2** **3** **4** **5** **6** **258** **7** **8** **9** **10** **11** **12**

Bidden Road

Bidden Grange Farm

Bidden

Little Dean Farm

Little Dean Lane

Ford Lane

Gaston Lane

Gaston Copse

Four Lanes End

Harley Lane

ALTON ROAD

B3349

Down Farm

Barbour Close

Cleves Lane

The Arboretum

Upton Grey House

Upton Grey

Bidden Road

PO PH

Little Hoddington

Limbrey Ln.

Weston Road

Tile Barn Farm

Dean Copse

The Old Orchard

Nash Maw

PO

Gaston Lane

South Warnborough

Hook Lane

Church View

B3349

Wells Hill Farm

Hester's Copse

Weston Patrick

Little Park Copse

Howe Lane

New Farm

B3349

Humbly Grove Copse

Humbly Grove

Blounce

Pickaxe Lane

New Farm

Finney Copse

New Farm

Great Park

Weston Common

Powntley Copse

B3349

Swainshill Farm

Sowcroft

Pickaxe Lane

Lane

Yarn...

Swaines Hill Manor

Ham Wood

Shalden Green

Avenue Road

Shalden

J 69 **K** 70 **L** **M** 71 **N** **280** **P** 72 **Q** **R** 73

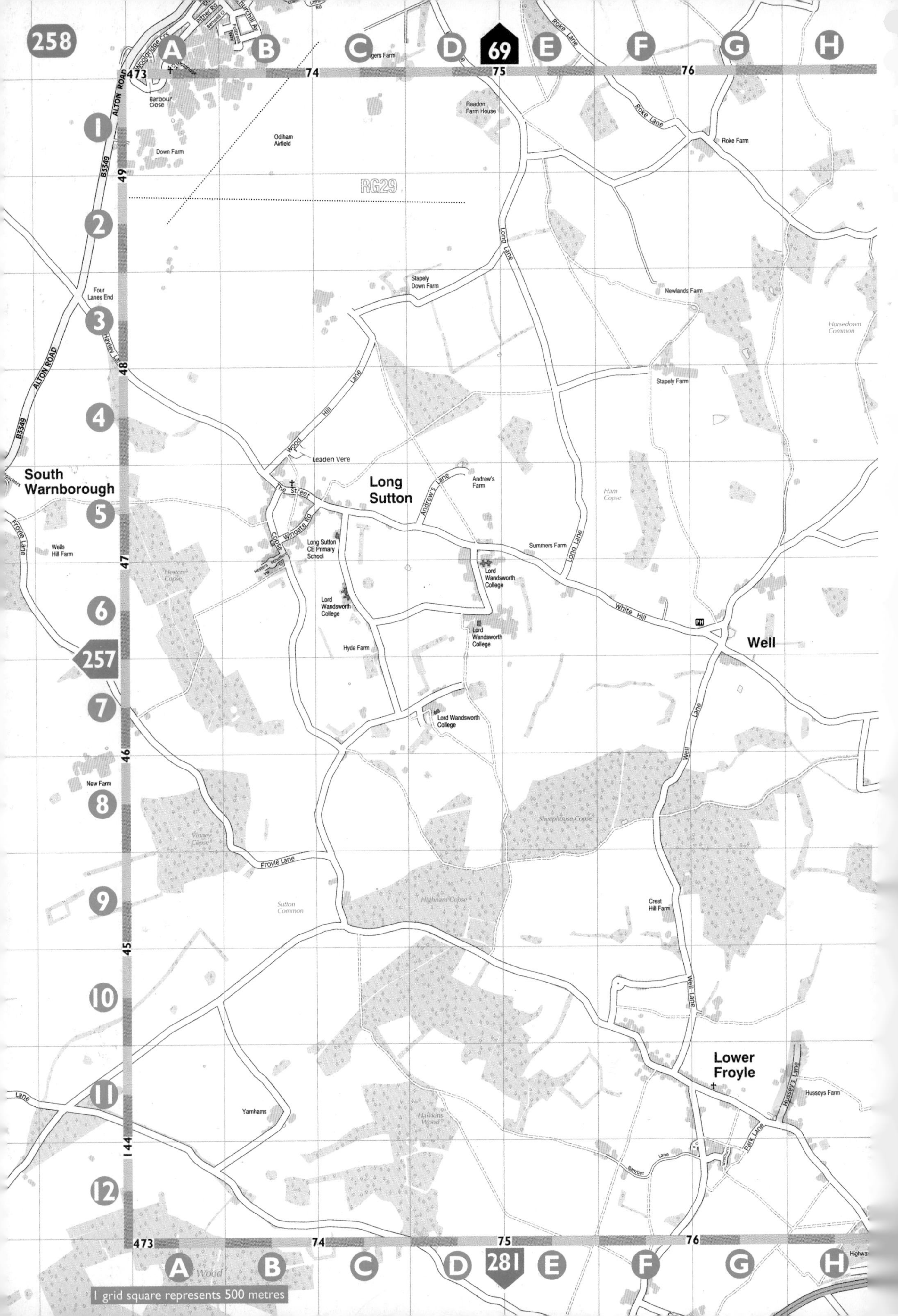

A B C D 69 E F G H

473 74 75 76

49

I

48

2

3

4

South
Warnborough

47

5

6

257

7

46

8

9

45

10

11

44

12

473 74 75 281 76

A B C D E F G H

Pither Rd
Thornhill Av
Roke Lane
ALTON ROAD
B3349
Barbour Close
Down Farm
Odiham Airfield
RG29
Readon Farm House
Roke Lane
Roke Farm
Four Lanes End
Stapely Down Farm
Long Lane
Newlands Farm
Horsedown Common
Harvey Lane
Wood Hill Lane
Leaden Vere
Long Sutton
Andrew's Farm
Andrew's Lane
Stapely Farm
Ham Copse
Wells Hill Farm
The Street
Wingate Rd
Long Sutton CE Primary School
Lord Wandsworth College
Summers Farm
Long Lane
Hester's Copse
Hyde Farm
Lord Wandsworth College
White Hill
PH
Well
New Farm
Vinney Copse
Lord Wandsworth College
Well Lane
Sheephouse Copse
Froyle Lane
Froyle Lane
Sutton Common
Highnam Copse
Crest Hill Farm
Well Lane
Lower Froyle
Hussey's Lane
Hussey's Farm
Lane
Yarnhams
Hawkins Wood
Park Lane
Bambers Lane
Highway

ALTON ROAD
B3349
Froyle Lane

I grid square represents 500 metres

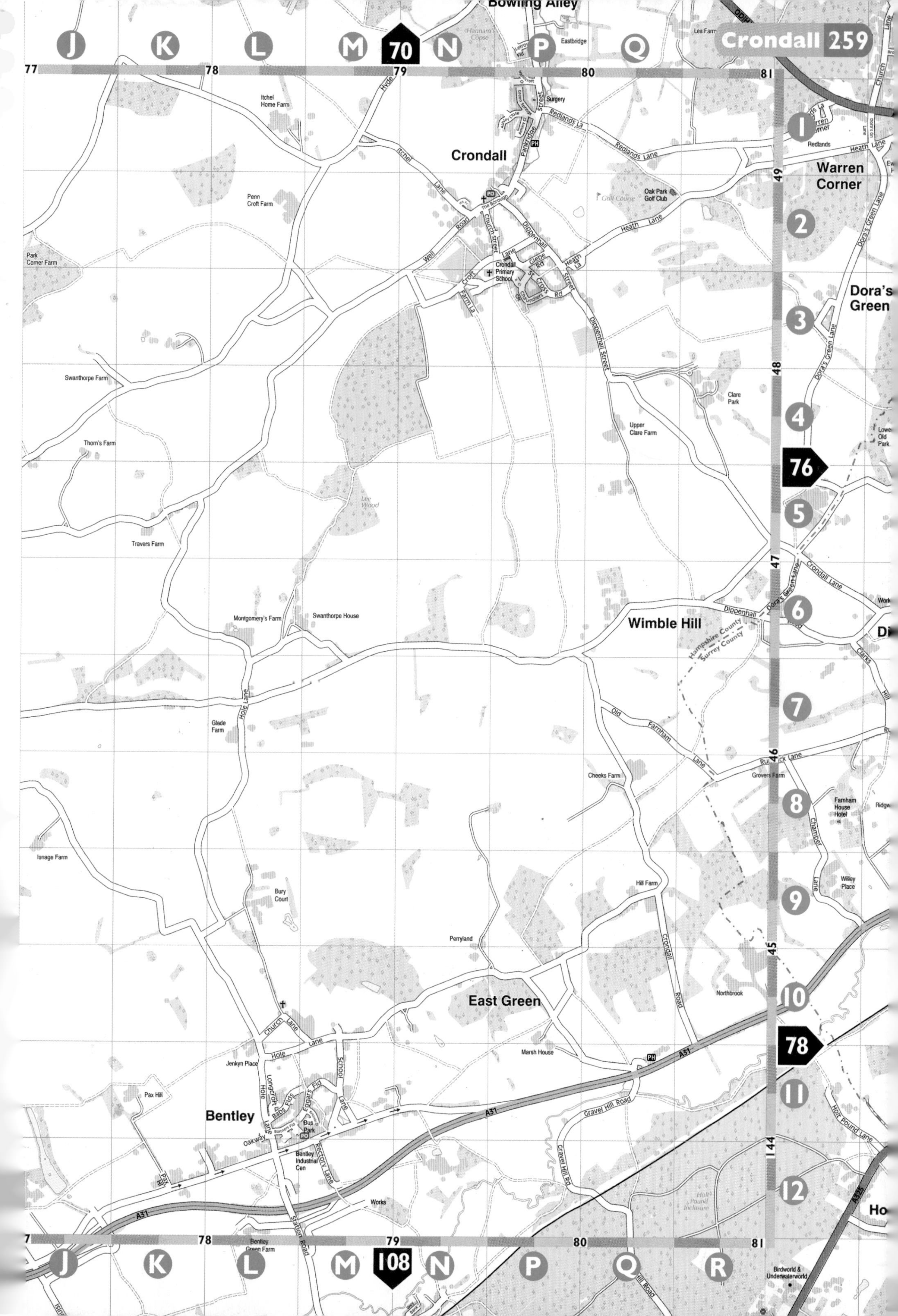
Bowling Alley
70
76
78
108
Crondall
Warren Corner
Dora's Green
Wimble Hill
East Green
Bentley
Itchel Home Farm
Penn Croft Farm
Park Corner Farm
Swanthorpe Farm
Thorn's Farm
Travers Farm
Montgomery's Farm
Swanthorpe House
Glade Farm
Isnage Farm
Bury Court
Perryland
Jenkyn Place
Pax Hill
Bentley Industrial Cen
Works
Bentley Green Farm
Marsh House
Hill Farm
Cheeks Farm
Upper Clare Farm
Clare Park
Oak Park Golf Club
Golf Course
Crondall Primary School
Surgery
Eastbridge
Lea Farm
Redlands
Northbrook
Grovers Farm
Farnham House Hotel
Willey Place
Holt Pound Inclosure
Birdworld & Underwaterworld
Lee Wood
Hannam's Copse
Hampshire County
Surrey County
Redlands Lane
Heath Lane
Dippenhall Street
Dora's Green Lane
Crondall Lane
Old Farnham Lane
Runwick Lane
Chamber Lane
Crondall Road
Gravel Hill Road
Holt Pound Lane
Hole Lane
Church Lane
School Lane
Longcroft
Rectory Lane
Oakway
Babs Fld
Edgars Fld
Bus Park
Pax Hill
Well Road
Itchel Lane
Hyde Lane
Church Street
The Borough
Pankridge Street
Croft Lane
Farm La
Glebe Rd
St Cross Rd
Chandlers La
Heath La
A31
A325
J K L M N P Q R
77 78 79 80 81
49 48 47 46 45 144
1 2 3 4 5 6 7 8 9 10 11 12

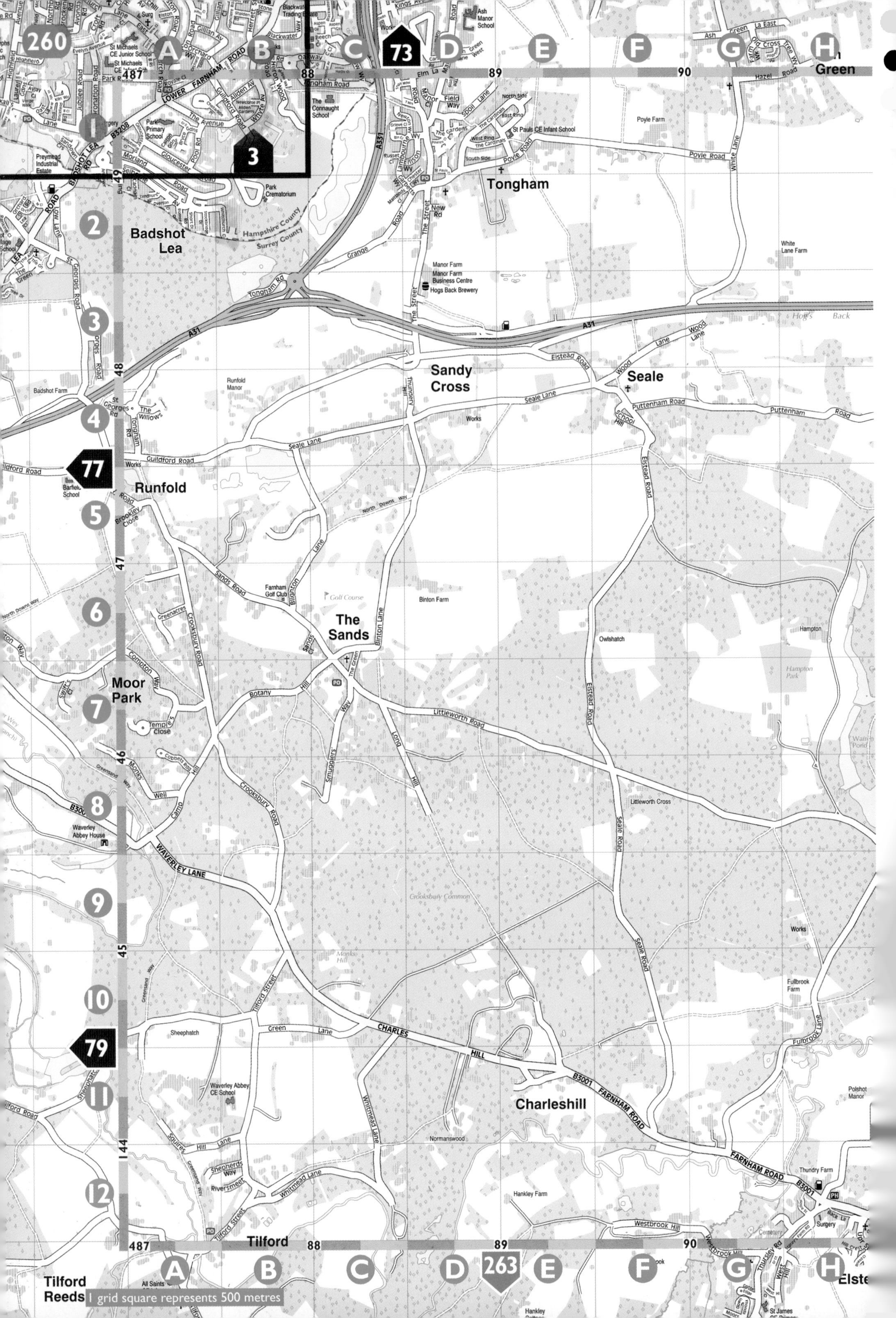

260
73
77
79
3
263
A
B
C
D
E
F
G
H
1
2
3
4
5
6
7
8
9
10
11
12
487
88
89
90
49
48
47
46
45
144
Tongham
Badshot Lea
Sandy Cross
Seale
Runfold
The Sands
Moor Park
Charleshill
Tilford
Tilford Reeds
Green
Elste
Park Crematorium
Hampshire County
Surrey County
Manor Farm
Manor Farm Business Centre
Hogs Back Brewery
Poyle Farm
White Lane Farm
Hog's Back
Badshot Farm
Runfold Manor
Farnham Golf Club
Golf Course
Binton Farm
Owlshatch
Hampton
Hampton Park
Littleworth Cross
Crooksbury Common
Monks Hill
Waverley Abbey House
Sheephatch
Waverley Abbey CE School
Normanswood
Hankley Farm
Fullbrook Farm
Polshot Manor
Thundry Farm
Works
Seale Lane
Elstead Road
Puttenham Road
Guildford Road
Sands Road
Crooksbury Road
Littleworth Road
Seale Road
Botany Hill
Binton Lane
Charles Hill
B3001 Farnham Road
Waverley Lane
Tilford Street
Green Lane
Whitmead Lane
Westbrook Hill
Poyle Road
White Lane
Hazel Road
Elm La
Tongham Road
Lower Farnham Road
The Street
Grange Road
A31
A331
B3208
St Pauls CE Infant School
The Connaught School
Park Primary School
Preymead Industrial Estate
North Downs Way
Greensand Way
Fulbrook Lane
1 grid square represents 500 metres

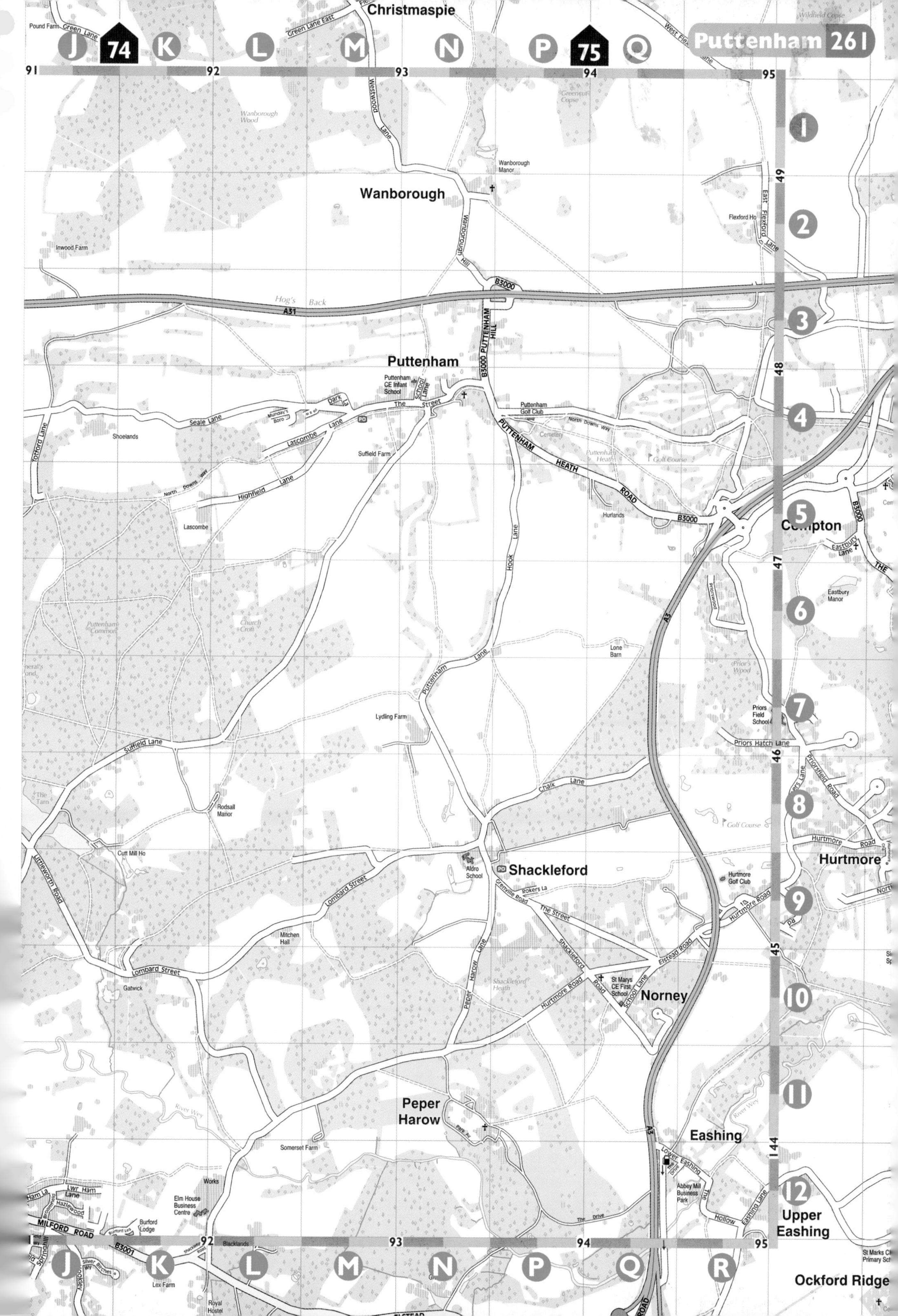
Christmaspie
Wanborough
Wanborough Wood
Wanborough Manor
Westwood Lane
Wanborough Hill
Inwood Farm
Pound Farm
Green Lane
Green Lane East
Flexford Ho
East Flexford Lane
Hog's Back
A31
B3000
B3000 PUTTENHAM HILL
Puttenham
Puttenham CE Infant School
School Lane
The Street
Dark Lane
Seale Lane
Lascombe Lane
Shoelands
Suffield Farm
Puttenham Golf Club
North Downs Way
Cemetery
Puttenham Heath
Golf Course
PUTTENHAM HEATH ROAD
Hurlands
Highfield Lane
Lascombe
Totford Lane
Compton
Eastbury Lane
Eastbury Manor
Hook Lane
A3
Puttenham Common
Church Croft
Lone Barn
Priors Wood
Priors Field School
Priors Hatch Lane
Priorsfield Road
Puttenham Lane
Lydling Farm
Suffield Lane
Chalk Lane
The Tarn
Rodsall Manor
Cutt Mill Ho
Littleworth Road
Hurtmore
Hurtmore Road
Hurtmore Golf Club
Aldro School
Shackleford
Rokers La
Grenville Road
The Street
Lombard Street
Mitchen Hall
Shackleford Road
Elstead Road
St Marys CE First School
School Lane
Norney
Peper Harow Lane
Shackleford Heath
Hurtmore Road
Gatwick
River Wey
Peper Harow
Park Av
Somerset Farm
Eashing
Lower Eashing
The Drive
Abbey Mill Business Park
The Hollow
Eashing Lane
Upper Eashing
Works
Elm House Business Centre
Burford Lodge
Ham La
Lwr Ham Lane
Hazlewood
MILFORD ROAD
B3001
Blacklands
Lex Farm
Royal Hostel
Ockford Ridge
St Marks CE Primary Sch
J 74 K L M N P 75 Q R
91 92 93 94 95
1 2 3 4 5 6 7 8 9 10 11 12
49 48 47 46 45 144

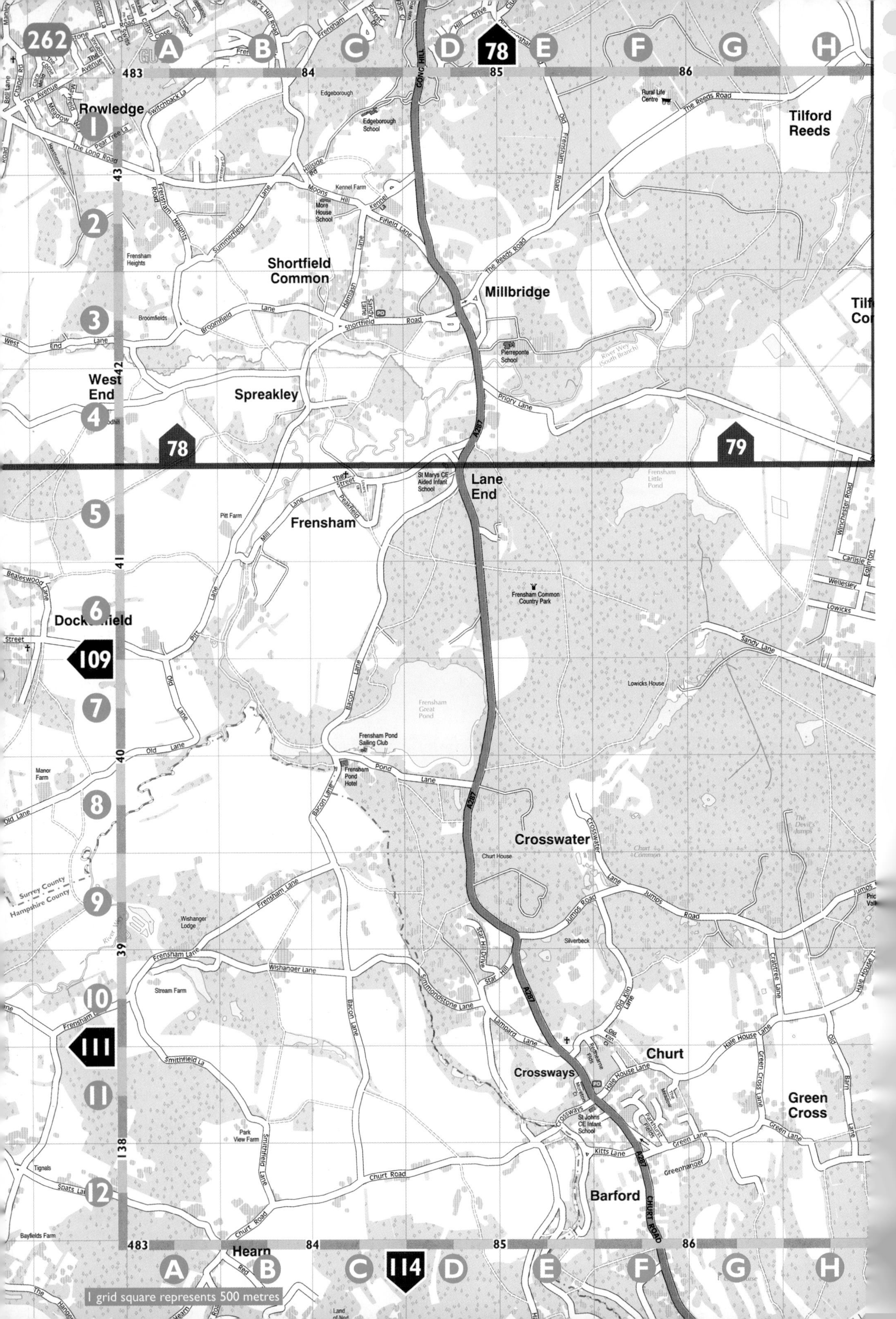

Rowledge
Tilford Reeds
Shortfield Common
Millbridge
West End
Spreakley
Lane End
Frensham
Dockenfield
Crosswater
Churt
Crossways
Green Cross
Barford
Hearn
Frensham Heights
Broomfields
Edgeborough
Edgeborough School
Kennel Farm
More House School
Rural Life Centre
Pierrepont School
St Marys CE Aided Infant School
Pitt Farm
Frensham Common Country Park
Frensham Little Pond
Frensham Great Pond
Frensham Pond Sailing Club
Frensham Pond Hotel
Lowicks House
Manor Farm
Churt House
Silverbeck
Wishanger Lodge
Stream Farm
Park View Farm
St Johns CE Infant School
Tignals
Bayfields Farm
Surrey County
Hampshire County
GONG HILL
A287
CHURT ROAD
The Reeds Road
Frensham Road
Priory Lane
Pond Lane
Bacon Lane
Jumps Road
Frensham Lane
Wishanger Lane
Simmondstone Lane
Churt Road
Smithfield Lane
Sandy Lane
Old Lane
Pitt Lane
Mill Lane
Green Lane
Kitts Lane
Hale House Lane
Crabtree Lane
Green Cross Lane
Old Barn Lane
Crosswater Lane
Star Hill
Old Kiln Lane
Lampard Lane
Shortfield Road
Broomfield Lane
West End Lane
Moons Hill
Fifield Lane
Switchback Lane
The Long Road
Pear Tree La
Sandy Lane
Winchester Road
Wellesley
Lowicks
1 grid square represents 500 metres

78 79 109 111 114

Tilford
Elstead
Pot Common
Rushmoor
Thursley
Pitch Place
Bowlhead Green
Hankley Common Golf Club
Tilford Road
Thursley Road
Woolfords Lane
Houndown Lane
Dyehouse Road
Portsmouth Road
Highfield Lane
Hyde Lane
Salops Lane
Westbrook Hill
Whitmead Lane
Tilford Street
Milford Road
Greensand Way
Hankley Farm
Hankley Cottage
Tadmoor Cottage
Woolford's Farm
Red House Farm
Truxford
Dye House
Smallbrook
Churt Place
Hyde Farm
Ridgeway Farm
Marchants Farm
Stock Farm
Green Farm
Pitlands Farm
Lower Highfield Farm
Bedford Farm
Emley Farm
Abbot's Lodge
The Grange
Greenhills
Thundry Farm
Westbrook
St James CE Primary School
All Saints CE Infant School
Elstead Common
Ockley Common
Thursley Common
Hankley Common
Houndown
Pudmore Pond
The Moat
Stockbridge Pool
French Lane
Cosford Road
Rutton Hill Road
Park Lane
Begley Farm
Beacon Hill
260
115

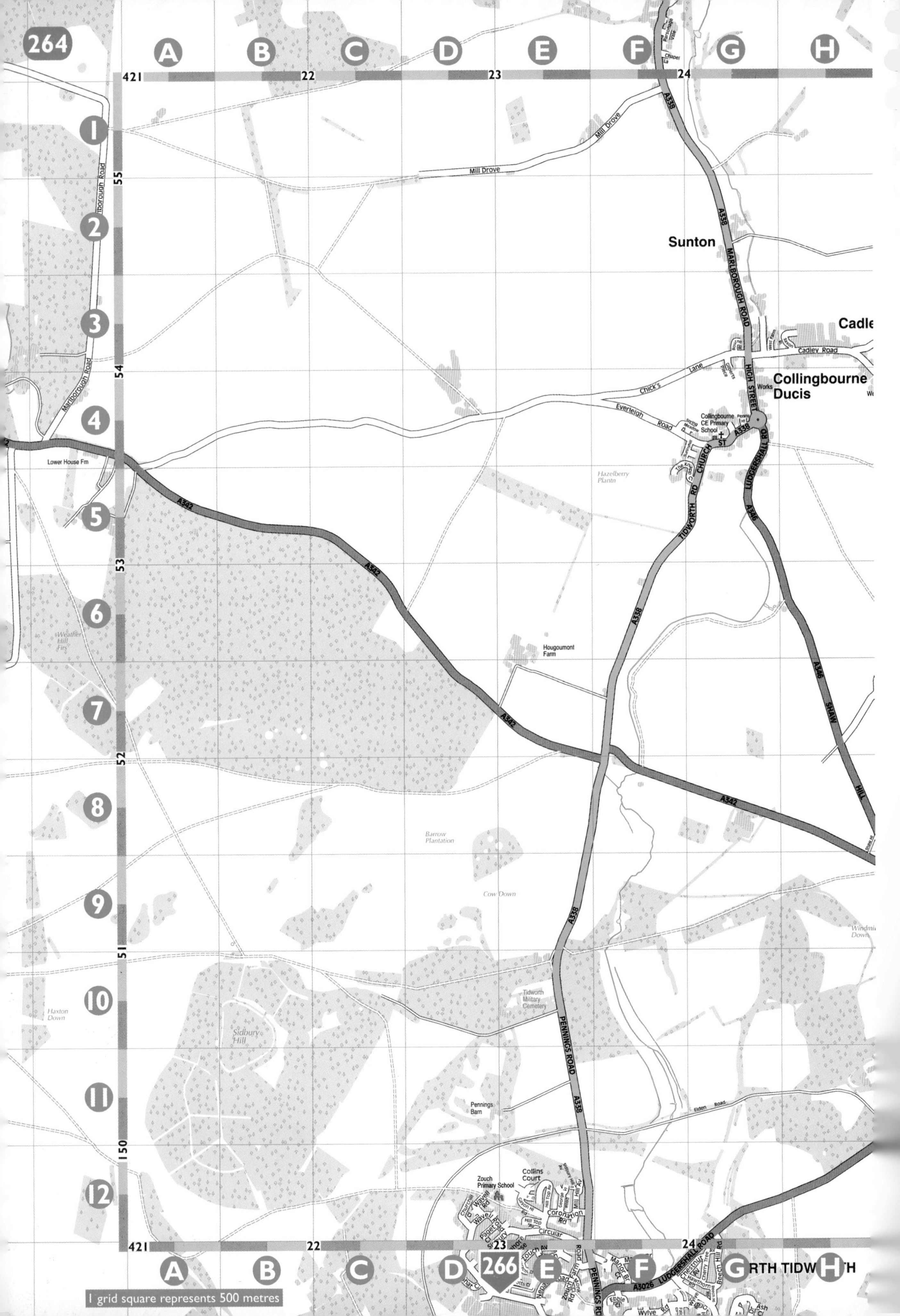

A B C D E F G H

421 22 23 24

Mill Drove

Mill Drove

Sunton

Cadle

Cadley Road

Collingbourne
Ducis

Chick's Lane

Everleigh Road

Collingbourne
CE Primary
School

Hazelberry
Plantn

Lower House Fm

A342

Weather
Mill Firs

Hougoumont
Farm

A342

Barrow
Plantation

Cow Down

Tidworth
Military
Cemetery

Haxton
Down

Sidbury
Hill

Pennings
Barn

Elden Road

Collins
Court

Zouch
Primary School

Coronation

Circular

Windmill
Down

421 22 23 24

A B C D 266 E F G RTH TIDW H TH

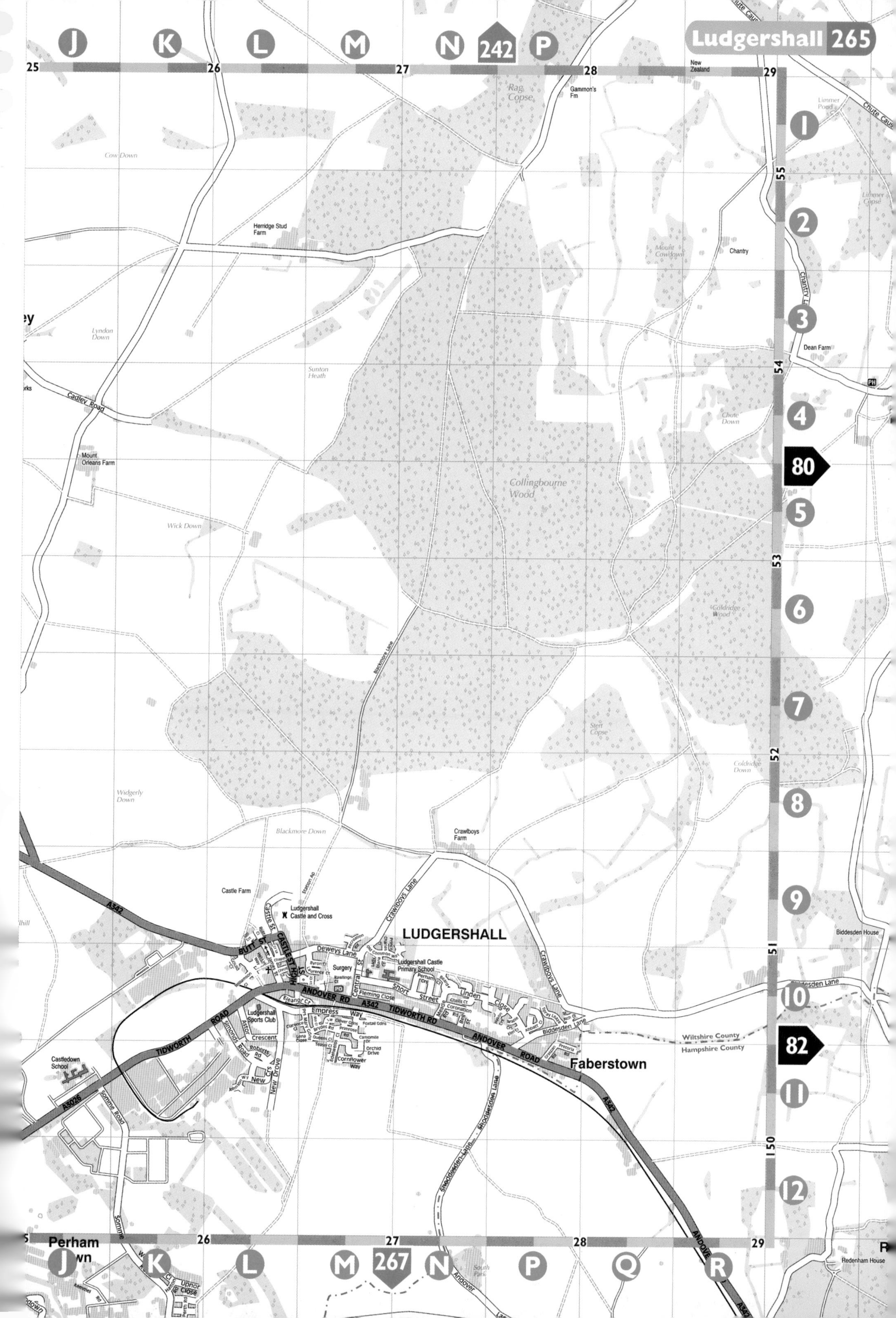

242
80
82
267
LUDGERSHALL
Faberstown
Perham
Rag Copse
Gammon's Fm
New Zealand
Limmer Pond
Chute Causeway
Cow Down
Herridge Stud Farm
Mount Cowdown
Chantry
Chantry Lane
Dean Farm
Lyndon Down
Sunton Heath
Cadley Road
Chute Down
Mount Orleans Farm
Collingbourne Wood
Wick Down
Coldridge Wood
Blackmore Lane
Stert Copse
Coldridge Down
Widgerly Down
Blackmore Down
Crawlboys Farm
Castle Farm
Ludgershall Castle and Cross
Crawlboys Lane
Biddesden House
Biddesden Lane
Deweys Lane
Surgery
Ludgershall Castle Primary School
Butt St
Castle St
High St
Andover Rd
Tidworth Rd
Tidworth Road
Andover Road
Empress Way
Short Street
Linden Close
Coronation Rd
Ludgershall Sports Club
Astor Crescent
Simonds Road
Roberts Rd
New Drove
Cornflower Way
Orchid Drive
Pretoria
Wiltshire County
Hampshire County
Castledown School
Somme Road
Shoddesden Lane
Upnor Close
South Park
Redenham House
A342
A3026

A B C D 264 E F G H

421 22 24

NORTH TIDWORTH

1

2

3

4

5

6

7

8

9

10

11

12

South Tidworth

Shipton Bellinger

421 22 23 24

I grid square represents 500 metres

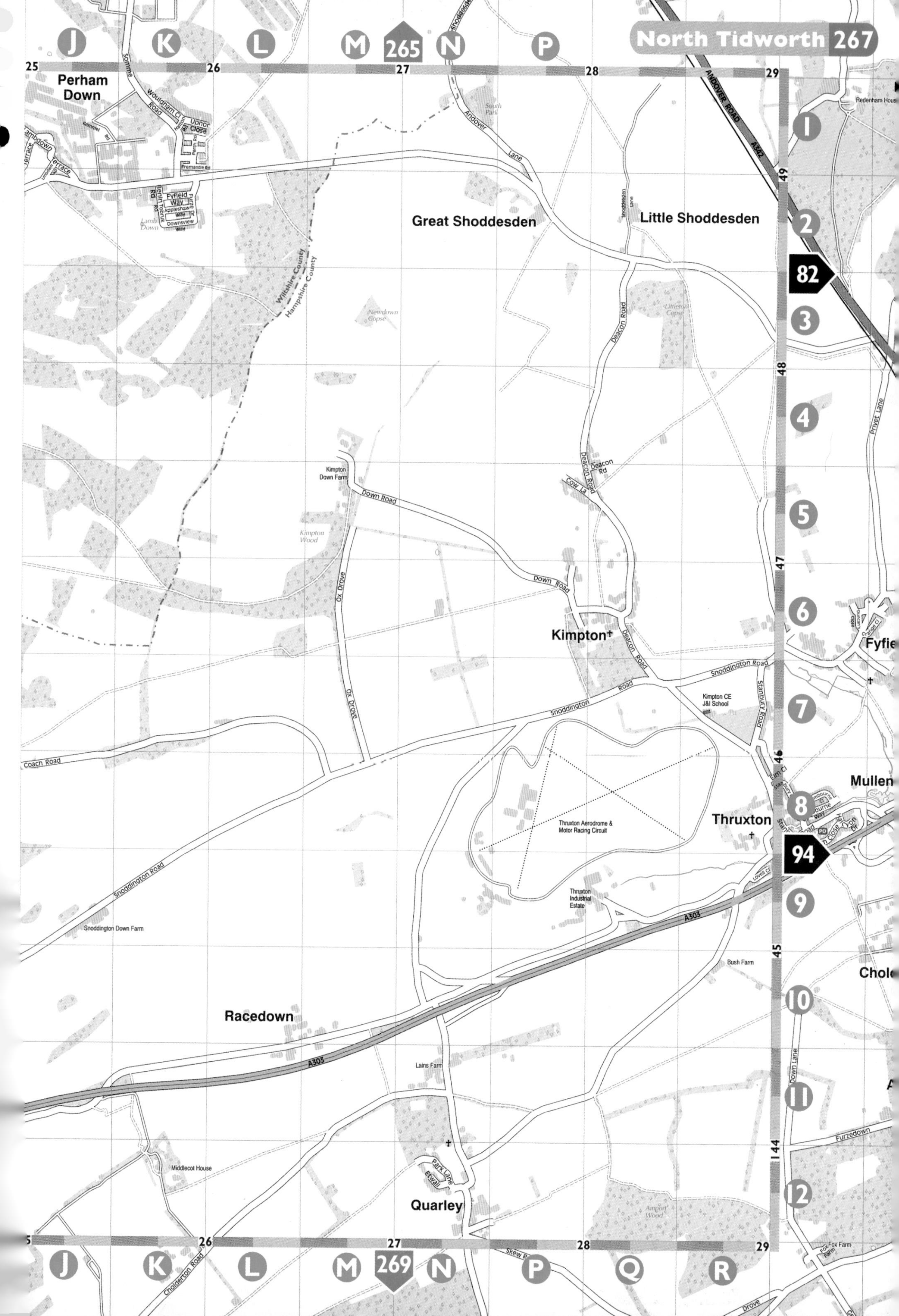

J K L M 265 N P
25 26 27 28 29
Perham Down
Great Shoddesden
Little Shoddesden
Wiltshire County
Hampshire County
Newdown Copse
Littleton Copse
Andover Lane
Andover Road
A342
Deacon Road
Kimpton Down Farm
Down Road
Kimpton Wood
Ox Drove
Kimpton
Cow La
Deacon Rd
Snoddington Road
Kimpton CE J&I School
Stanbury Road
Coach Road
Thruxton Aerodrome & Motor Racing Circuit
Thruxton
Thruxton Industrial Estate
Snoddington Down Farm
A303
Bush Farm
Racedown
Lains Farm
Middlecot House
Quarley
Park Lane
Amport Wood
Down Lane
Furzedown
Fox Farm
Cholderton Road
Skew Road
Privet Lane
Redenham House
Fyfield
Mullen
82
94
1 2 3 4 5 6 7 8 9 10 11 12
49 48 47 46 45 144
J K L M 269 N P Q R

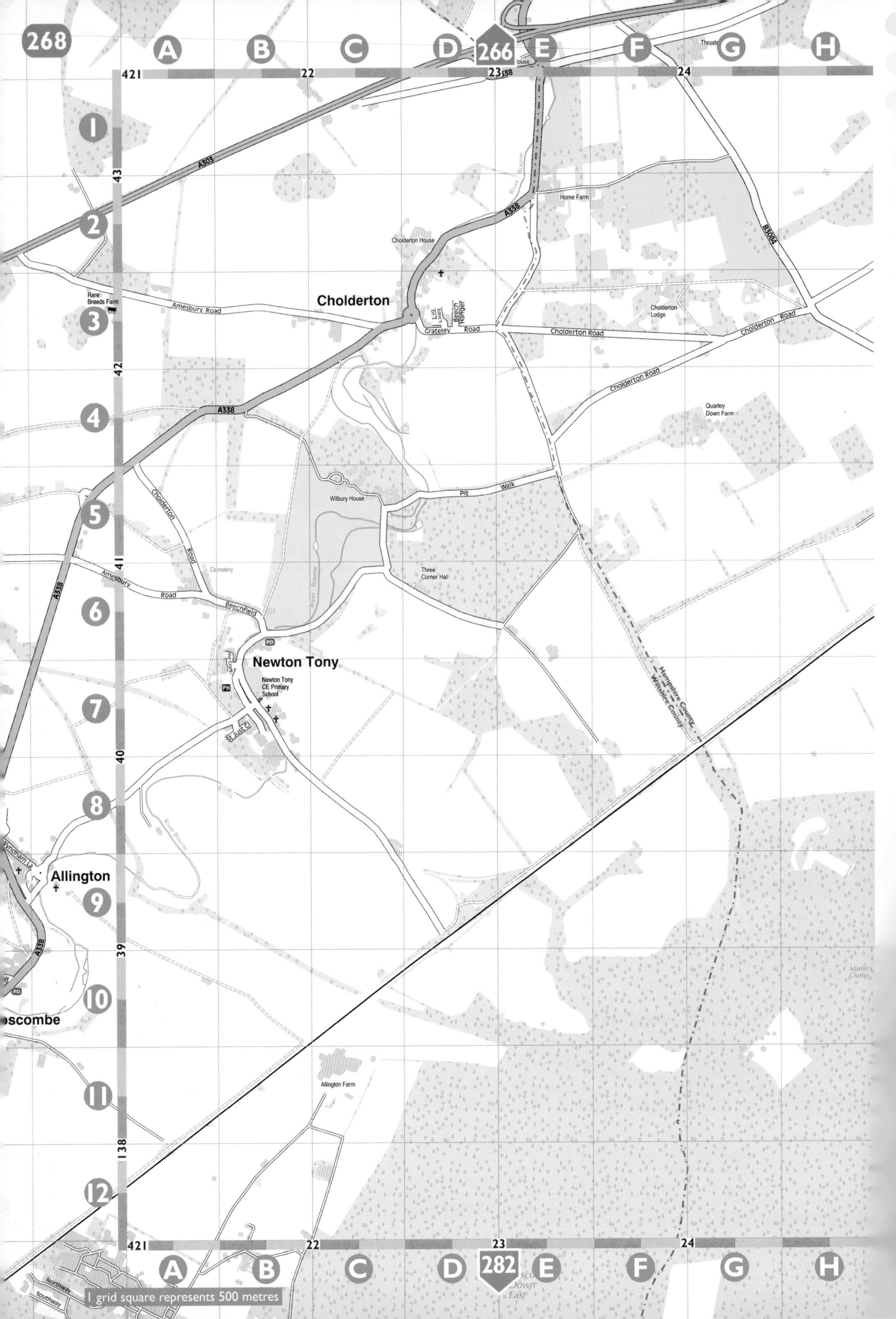

266
A
B
C
D
E
F
G
H
421
22
23
24
A303
A338
B3084
Home Farm
Cholderton House
Cholderton
Rare Breeds Farm
Amesbury Road
Grateley Road
Beech Hanger
Cholderton Road
Cholderton Lodge
Quarley Down Farm
Pit Walk
Wilbury House
Three Corner Hat
Cholderton Road
Amesbury Road
Cemetery
Beechfield
River Bourne
Newton Tony
Newton Tony CE Primary School
The Croft
St Just Cl
Hampshire County
Wiltshire County
Allington
Wyndham La
oscombe
Allington Farm
Martin's Clump
Northway
Southway
Boscombe Down East
43
42
41
40
39
138
1
2
3
4
5
6
7
8
9
10
11
12
282

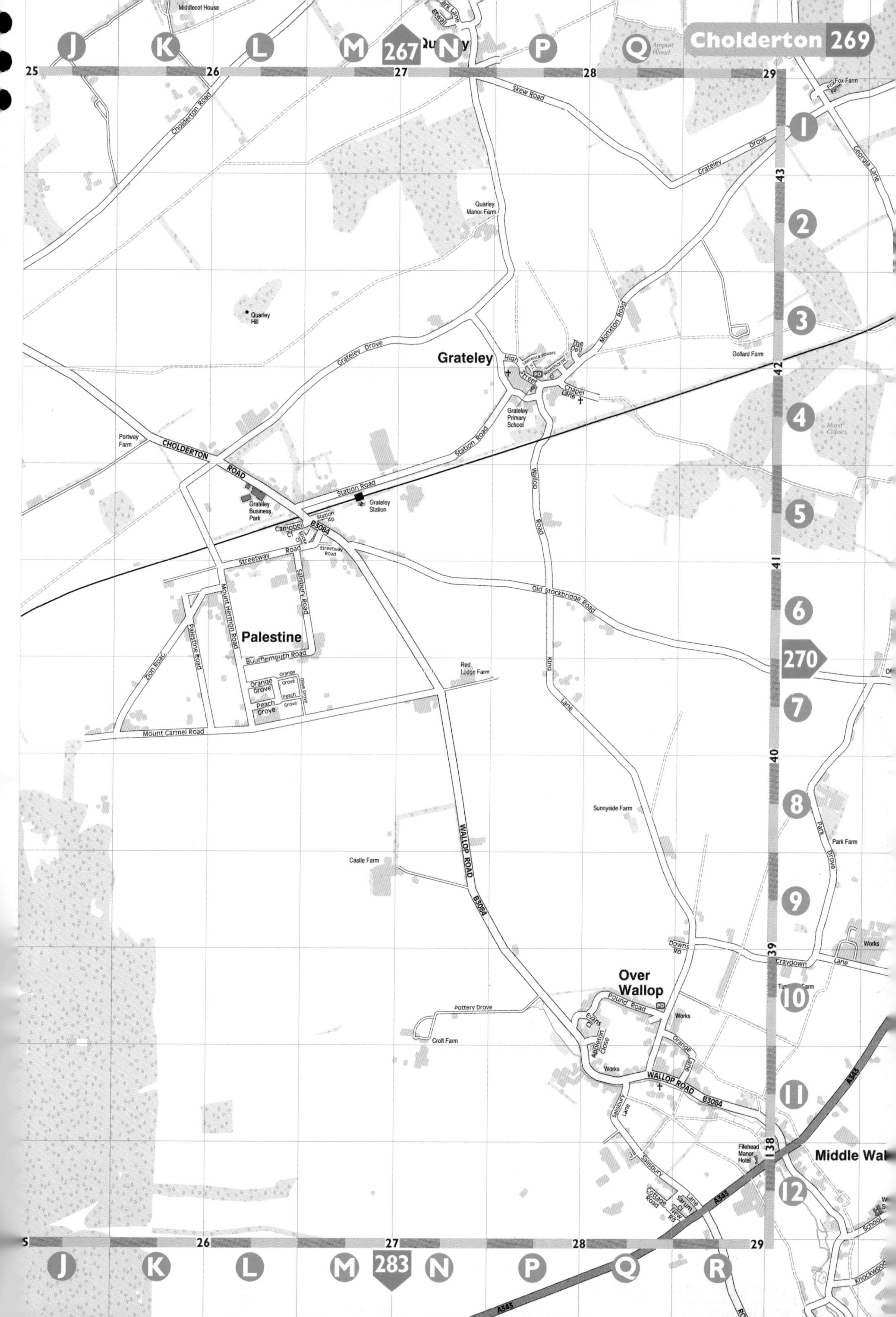
Middlecot House
Cholderton Road
Skew Road
Grateley Drove
Georgia Lane
Fox Farm
Amport Wood
Quarley Manor Farm
Quarley Hill
Grateley Drove
Grateley
High Street
Laurence Houses
Hawthorne Cl
The Dell
Monxton Road
Chapel Lane
Gollard Farm
Grateley Primary School
Hurst Copses
Portway Farm
CHOLDERTON ROAD
Station Road
Grateley Business Park
Grateley Station
Station Ap
Campbell Cl
B3084
Streetway Road
Wallop Road
Salisbury Road
Old Stockbridge Road
Mount Hermon Road
Palestine
Palestine Road
Zion Road
Bournemouth Road
Orange Grove
Peach Grove
Olive Grove
Red Lodge Farm
Mount Carmel Road
King Lane
Sunnyside Farm
Park Drove
Park Farm
WALLOP ROAD
B3084
Castle Farm
Downs Rd
Craydown Lane
Works
Over Wallop
Pound Road
Evans Cl
Appleton Close
Orange Lane
Pottery Drove
Croft Farm
Works
WALLOP ROAD
B3084
A343
Salisbury Lane
Fifehead Manor Hotel
Middle Wal
Salisbury Lane
Cottage Road
Sarum
New Rd
School
Knockwood
A343
25 26 27 28 29
43 42 41 40 39 138
J K L M N P Q R
1 2 3 4 5 6 7 8 9 10 11 12
267
270
283

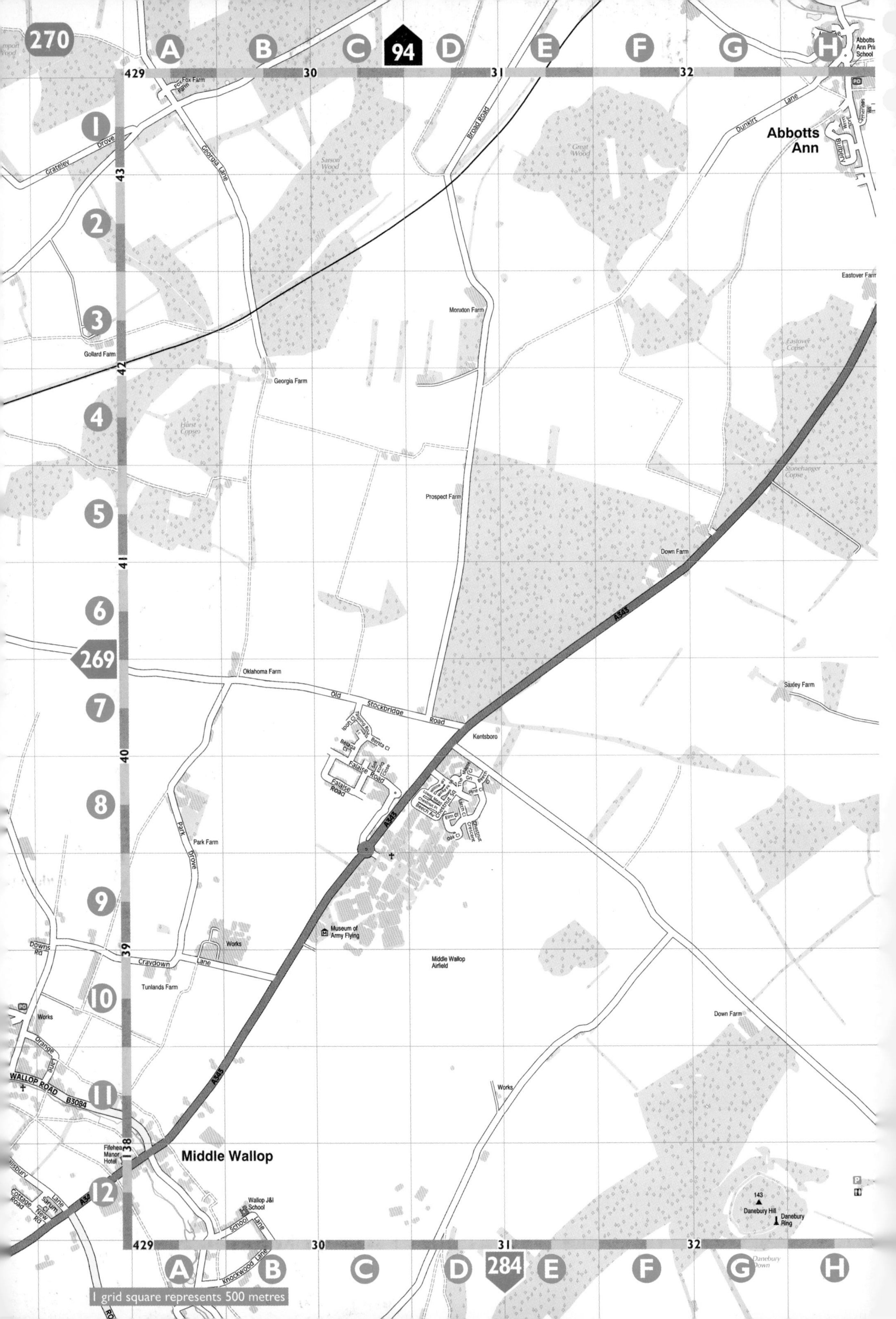

94

Abbotts
Ann Pri
School

**Abbotts
Ann**

Eastover Farm

A   B   C   D   E   F   G   H

429   30   31   32

I   Grateley   Fox Farm   Georgia Lane   Sarson Wood   Broad Road   Great Wood   Dunkirt Lane   PO

43

2

Monxton Farm

3   Gollard Farm

42   Georgia Farm

4   Hurst Copse   Prospect Farm   Stonehanger Copse

Eastover Copse

5   Down Farm

41   A343

6

269   Old Stockbridge Road   Oklahoma Farm   Saxley Farm

7   Kentsboro   Benta Cl   Falaise Road

40   Beech Cl   Elm Cl   Oak Cl   Chestnut Crescent

8   Park Farm   Park Grove

9   Museum of Army Flying   Works

39   Downs Rd   Craydown Lane   Tunlands Farm   Middle Wallop Airfield   Down Farm

10   PO   Works

Orange Lane

11   WALLOP ROAD   B3094

138   Fifehead Manor Hotel   Works

12   **Middle Wallop**   Wallop J&i School   Daneburyy Hill   Danebury Ring   143   Danebury Down

429   30   31   32

A   B   C   D   E   F   G   H

284

Little Ann

J K **95** L M N Upper Clatford P **96**

Cowdown Lane

Norman Court Lane

Green Meadows Lane

Hampshire Golf Club

Golf Course

St John's Cross

Fullerton Road

Salisbury Road

Red Rice Road

Home Farm

Goodworth Clatford

Clatford CE J&I School

St Annes C of E

Red Rice

Farleigh School

Barrow Hill

Stockbridge Road

Fullerton Road

WINCHESTER ROAD

ROMSEY ROAD

Dipden Bottom

Flint Farm

Westover Farm

River Anton

272

Longstock Road

Rowbury Farm

Fullerton Road

Fullerton Road

Fullerton Manor

Fullerton

Clatford Oakcuts

Stockbridge Road

Longstock Road

Hazel Down

Charity Down Farm

Hazeldown Farm

The Turret

J K L M **285** N P Q R

Church Road

Church Road

Church Road

Cemetery

LECKFORD LANE

Leckfi

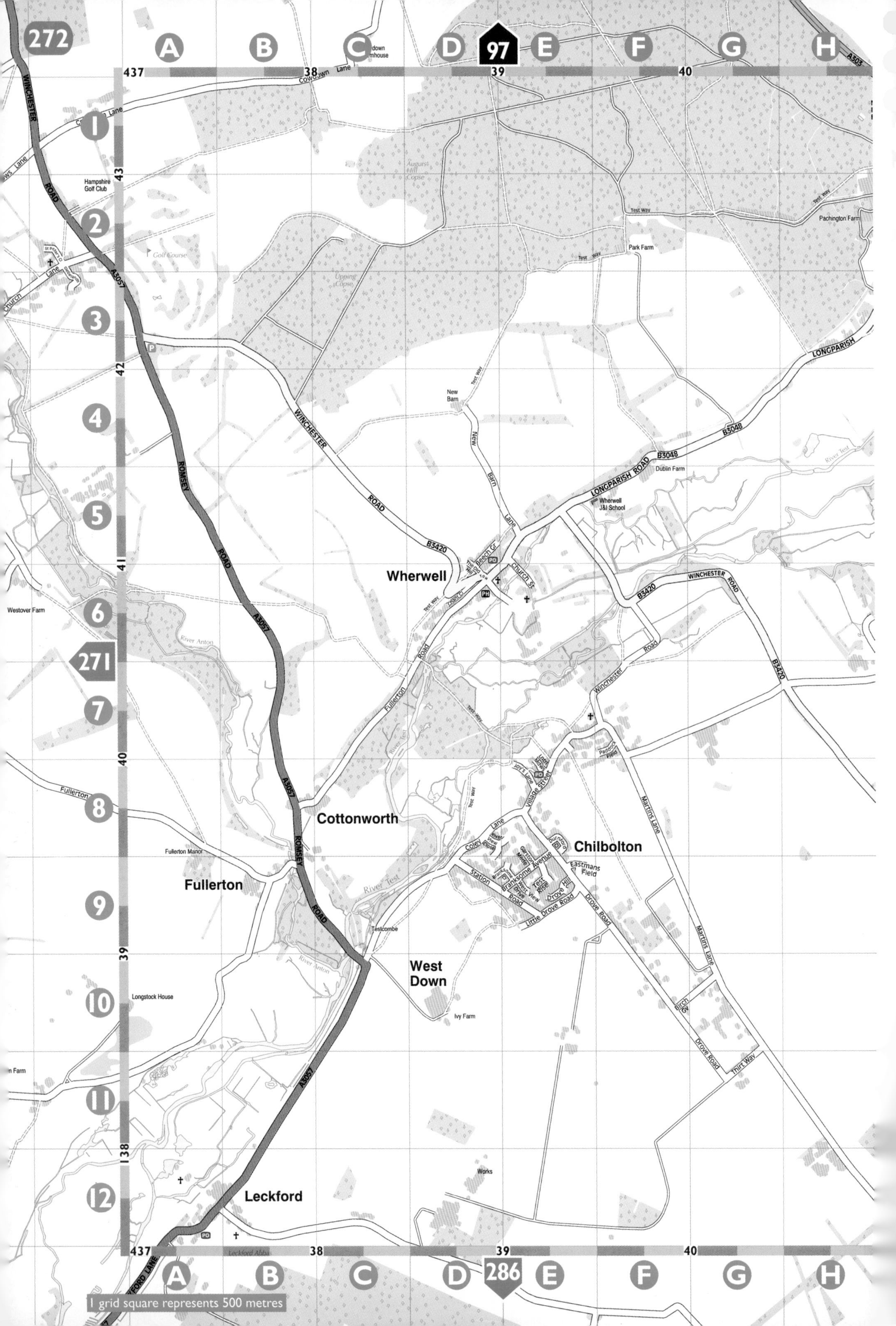

97

A B C D E F G H

437 38 39 40

1

Cowdown Lane

Hampshire Golf Club

2

St Peter's Church
Church Lane

Golf Course

3

Upping Copse

4

WINCHESTER ROAD

New Barn

Test Way

Test Way

LONGPARISH

Park Farm

Pachington Farm

5

ROMSEY ROAD

B3420

Beacon Gr

Dublin Farm

B3048

B3048

Wherwell J&I School

LONGPARISH ROAD

River Anton

6

Wherwell

PO

PH

Church St

WINCHESTER ROAD

B3420

7

Westover Farm

Fullerton Road

Test Way

B3420

8

Fullerton

Fullerton Manor

ROMSEY ROAD

Cottonworth

River Test

Martins Lane

Chilbolton

Eastmans Field

9

Testcombe

West Down

Station Road
Joys Lane
Village Street
Branksome Avenue
Little Drove Road
Drove Hill
Drove Road

Martins Lane

10

Longstock House

Ivy Farm

11

River Anton

A3057

12

Leckford

Works

Leckford Abbas

A B C D E F G H

437 38 39 40

1 grid square represents 500 metres

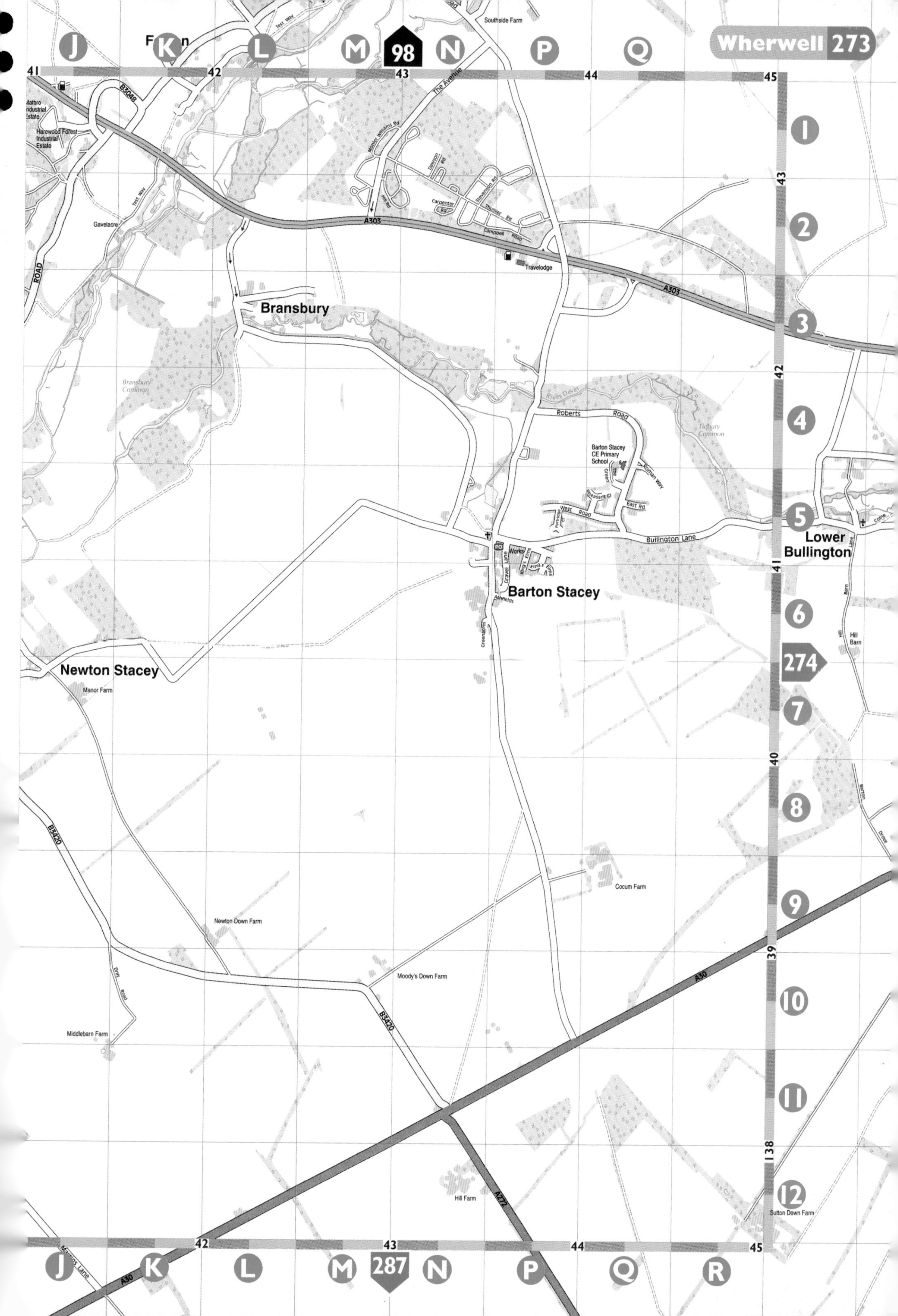
Southside Farm
Test Way
B3048
Matbro Industrial Estate
Harewood Forest Industrial Estate
The Avenue
Monxton Williams Rd
Dawson Rd
Stevenson Rd
Carpenter Rd
Hill Rd
Thurlow Rd
Campbell Road
A303
Travelodge
Gavelacre
ROAD
Bransbury
Bransbury Common
River Dever
Roberts Road
Tidbury Common
Barton Stacey CE Primary School
Roman Way
Pleasant Cl
East Rd
West Road
Bullington Lane
Works
Gravel Lane
King's Elms
Ashfields
Barton Stacey
Greenacres
Lower Bullington
Hill Barn
Barton Drove
Newton Stacey
Manor Farm
B3420
Cocum Farm
Newton Down Farm
Moody's Down Farm
Drift Road
Middlebarn Farm
A30
Hill Farm
A272
Sutton Down Farm
Marlins Lane
274
98
287

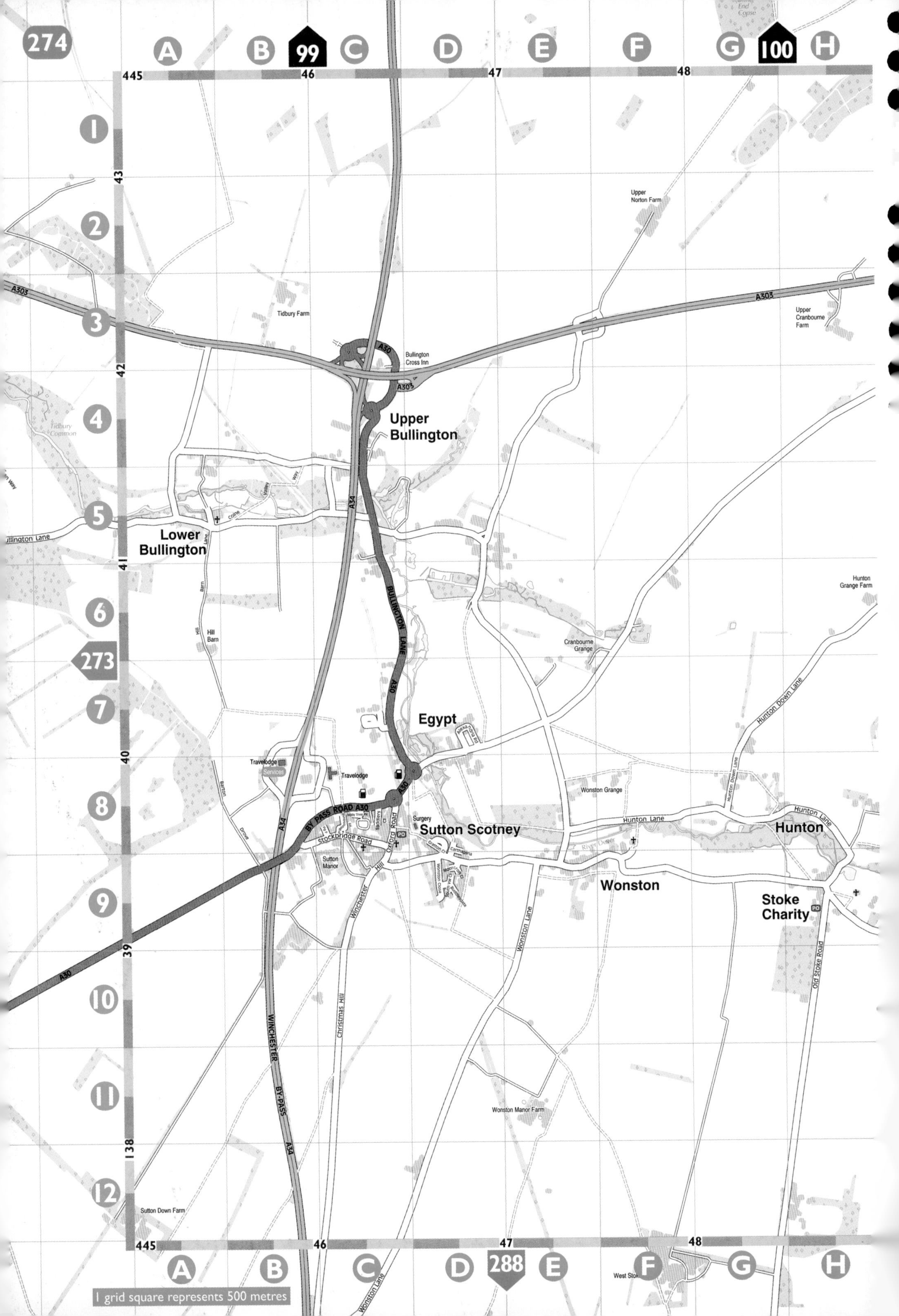

A B **99** C D E F G **100** H

445 46 47 48

I

43

2

42

3

Tidbury Farm

Bullington Cross Inn

A303

Upper Norton Farm

Upper Cranbourne Farm

4

Tidbury Common

Upper Bullington

Colne

Valley Way

5

41

Lower Bullington

Bullington Lane

Barn Lane

A34

Hill Barn

Hunton Grange Farm

6

Hill Drove

273

Cranbourne Grange

Hunton Down Lane

7

40

BULLINGTON LANE A30

Egypt

Travelodge

Services

A30

Wonston Grange

8

Barton Drove

A34

Travelodge

Stockbridge Road

BY PASS ROAD A30

Sutton Manor

Surgery

PO

Sutton Scotney

Hunton Lane

River Dever

Hunton Lane

Hunton

9

39

A30

Winchester Hill

Christmas Hill

Oxford Drove Road

Wonston

Wonston Lane

Stoke Charity

PO

Old Stoke Road

10

WINCHESTER BY-PASS A34

11

38

Wonston Manor Farm

12

Sutton Down Farm

445 46 47 48

A B C D **288** E F G H

J K L M 101 N P

49 50 51 52 53

Works

Brush
New
Road

Andover Road

Overton Road

Micheldever Station

Micheldever Station

Warren Farm

Northbrook Farm

Larkwhistle Farm Road

Hunton Down Farm

Weston Down Road

Northbrook House

276

West Stratton

Norsebury House

Northbrook

Weston Colley

River Dever

River Dever

Borough Farm

Cowdown Farm

PO Brook Lane

Micheldever Primary School

Micheldever

Duke Street

PH

Winchester Road

I 1
2
3
4
5
6
7
8
9
10
11
12

43

42

41

40

39

I 38

A B C D E F G H

453 54 55 56

1
2
3
4
5
6
7
8
9
10
11
12

43
42
41
40
39
38

Popham

Woodmancott

Larewhistle Farm Road

Black Wood

Bradley Farm

M3

Rownest Wood

College Wood

Works

Emble Wood

Lone Farm

Parkhill Farm

A33

Whiteway Farm

Stratton House

Candover Copse

West Stratton

PO

Thorny Down Wood

Foxhill

Church Bank Road

PH

East Stratton

Baring Close

Wey Farm Road

Coose Lane

Cowdown Farm

New Farm

Dodsley Wood

Burcot Farm

Stratton Lane

Micheldever Wood

Northington Down Farm

Northington

453 54 55 56

A B C D E F G H

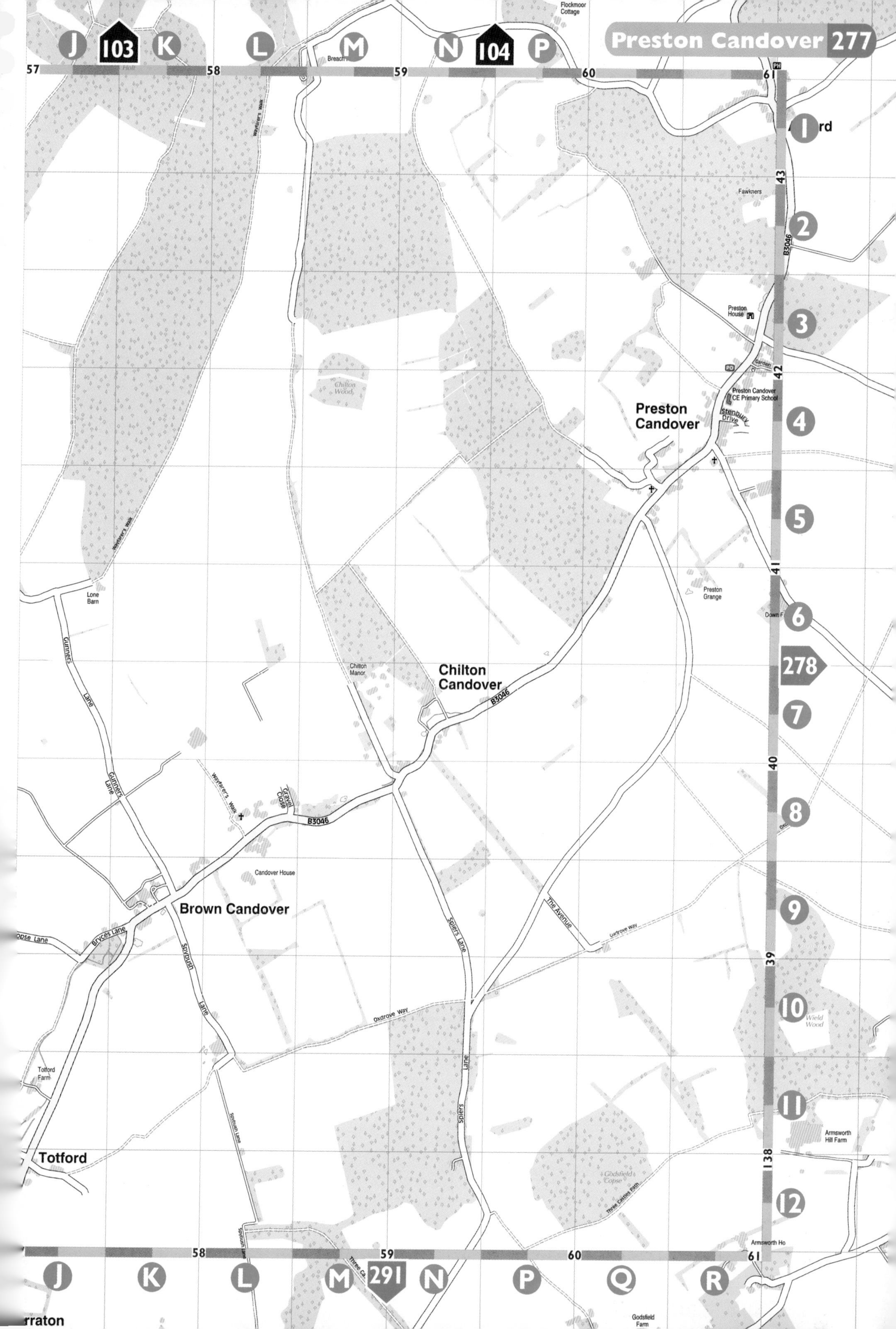

103
104
J
K
L
M
N
P
Q
R
57
58
59
60
61
43
42
41
40
39
138
1
2
3
4
5
6
7
8
9
10
11
12
278
291
Flockmoor Cottage
Wayfarer's Walk
Fawkners
Preston House
Garden
Preston Candover CE Primary School
Preston Candover
Stenbury Drive
Chilton Wood
B3046
Preston Grange
Lone Barn
Gunners Lane
Chilton Manor
Chilton Candover
Gravel Close
Candover House
Brown Candover
Bryces Lane
Spybush Lane
Spiers Lane
The Avenue
Oxdrove Way
Wield Wood
Armsworth Hill Farm
Totford Farm
Totford
Godsfield Copse
Three Castles Path
Armsworth Ho
Godsfield Farm

105

A   B   C   D   E   F   G   H

461   62   63   64

Axford

1

Fawkners

2

Preston
Ho
3

PO

Preston Candover
CE Primary School

Preston
Candover
4

Preston
Down

Bradley

Preston
Grange
5

Down Farm
6

277

Three Castles Path

Lower
Wield

7

Ashley Farm

8

9

Upper Wield

10

Wield
Wood

PO

Home Close

Pound

11

Armsworth
Hill Farm

Barton
Copse

Three Castles Path

Wield Road

Red
Barn Farm

Barton Industrial
Estate

Newmer Farm

12

Ferney Lane

Armsworth Ho

461   62   63   64

Ferney   Lane

A   B   C   D   **292**   E   F   G   Ha ley

Heath
Green

Hattingley Road

1 grid square represents 500 metres

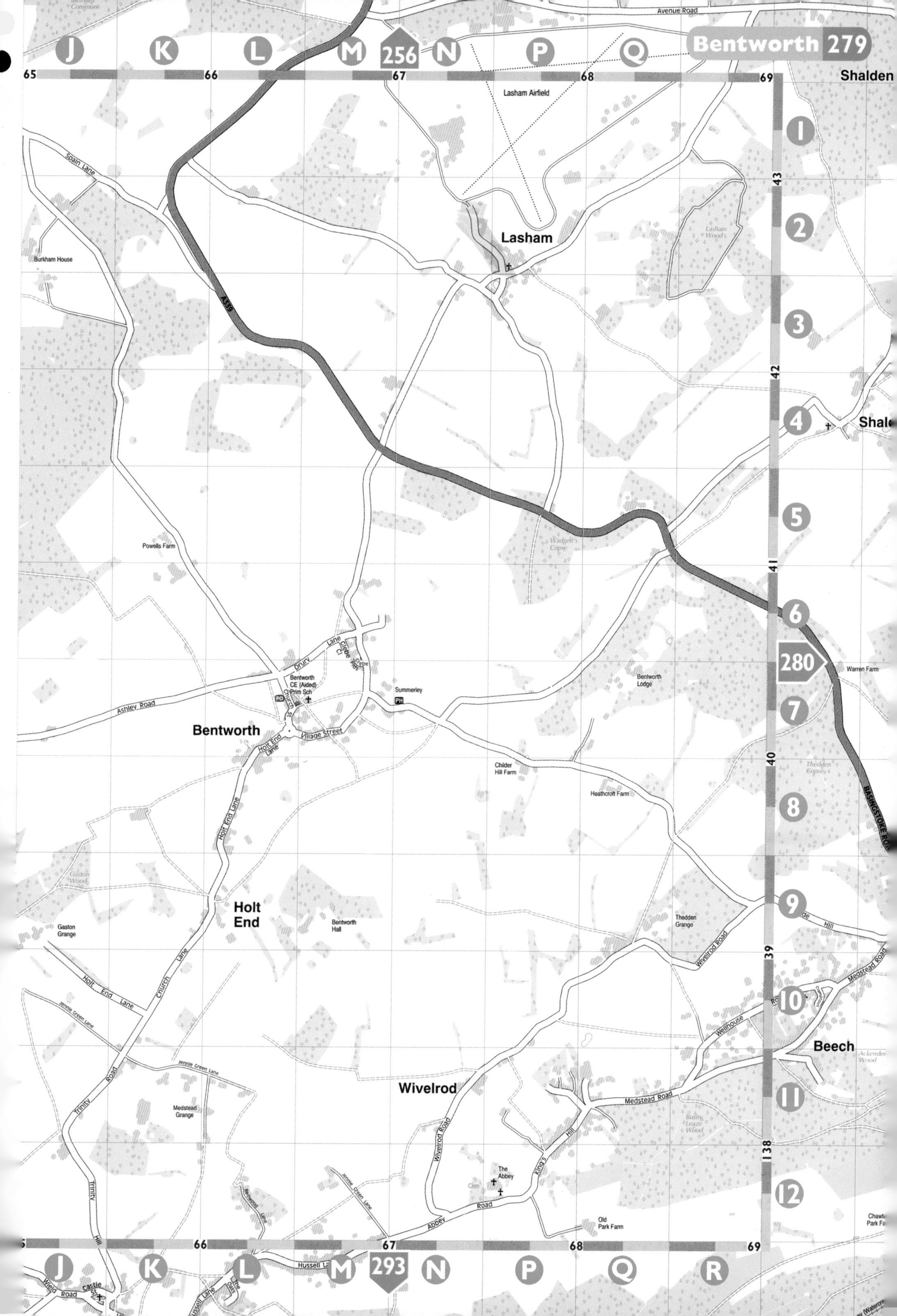

J K L M 256 N P Q Q

65 66 67 68 69 Shalden

1

Avenue Road

Lasham Airfield

2

Lasham Wood

43

Lasham
†

3

42

Burkham House

4 † Shale

Soain Lane

41

Powells Farm

5

A339

Wadgett's Copse

6

Lane
Drury
Lane
Close View

280 Warren Farm

Bentworth
CE (Aided)
Prim Sch

Summerley

Bentworth
Lodge

7

PO PH

Ashley Road

Bentworth
Village Street

Childer
Hill Farm

40

Thedden
Copse

Holt End Lane

Heathcroft Farm

8

Church Lane

Gaston
Wood

**Holt
End**

Bentworth
Hall

9 e Hill

Gaston
Grange

Wivelrod Road

Thedden
Grange

Medstead Road

39

Wellhouse

10

Holt End Lane

Jennie Green Lane

Jennie Green Lane

Beech

Ackender
Wood

Trinity

Medstead
Grange

Wivelrod

Knock Road

Medstead Road

11

Bushy
Leaze
Wood

138

Trinity Hill

The Abbey
Cem
† †

12

Old
Park Farm

Chawt
Park Fa

66 67 68 69

J K L M 293 N P Q R

Wood Road Castle

Hussell Lane

Hussell La

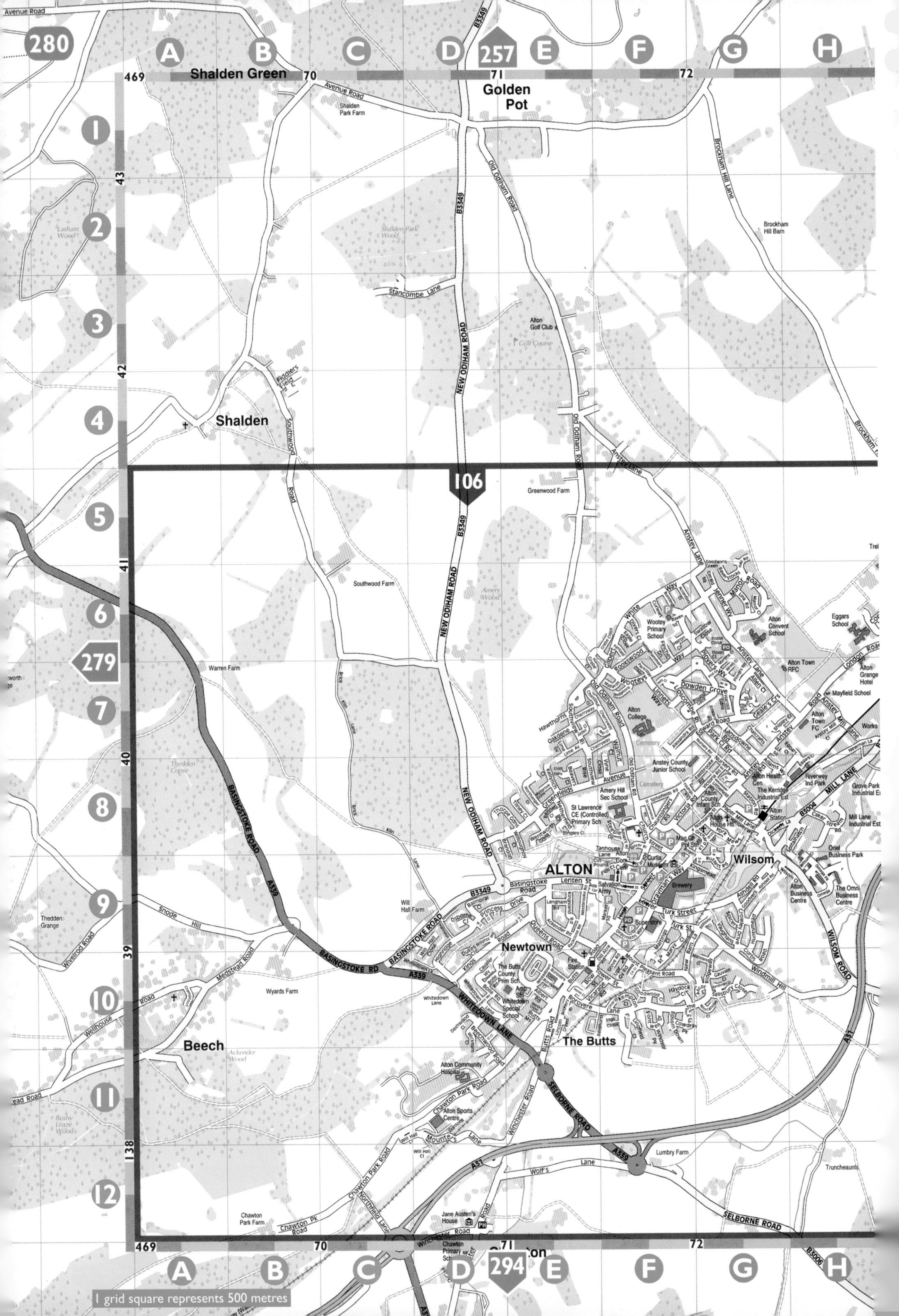

A B C D 257 E F G H

Shalden Green

Avenue Road

Golden Pot

469 70 71 72

Brockham Hill Lane

1

'Lasham Wood'

43

2

Shalden Park Farm

Shalden Park Wood

Brockham Hill Barn

3

42

Stancombe Lane

Alton Golf Club

Golf Course

4

Shalden

Fiddlers Field

New Odiham Road

Old Odiham Road

Anstey Lane

106

Greenwood Farm

5

Southwood Road

41

Southwood Farm

Amery Wood

Goodwins Green

White Way

Wootey Primary School

Alton Convent School

Eggars School

London Road

6

279

Warren Farm

Basingstoke Road

A339

New Odiham Road

Alton College

Dowden Grove

Alton Town RFC

Alton Grange Hotel

Mayfield School

7

40

Thedden Copse

Anstey County Junior School

Alton Town FC

Amery

Mill Lane

Works

8

Kiln

Cemetery

Anstey County Infant Sch

St Lawrence CE (Controlled) Primary Sch

Alton Health Cen

The Kerridge Industrial Est

Grove Park Industrial Es

9

39

Snode Hill

Medstead Road

Thedden Grange

Will Hall Farm

Basingstoke Road

Tanhouse Lane

Curtis Museum

ALTON

Lenten St

Turk Street

Salvation Army

Brewery

Wilsom

Alton Business Centre

The Omni Business Centre

10

38

Wellhouse

Wiveliscombe Road

Wyards Farm

Whitedown Lane

A339

Whitedown Special School

Newtown

The Butts County Prim Sch

Fire Station

Superstore

Oriel Business Park

11

Beech

Ackender Wood

Chawton Park Road

Alton Community Hospital

Butts Road

The Butts

Windmill Hill Road

Wilsom Road

Selborne Road

Bushy Leaze Woods

12

Chawton Park Farm

Chawton Pk Road

Mounters Lane

Will Hall Cl

Northfield Lane

A31

Wolf's Lane

A339

Selborne Road

Lumbry Farm

Truncheaunts

B3006

469 70 71 72

A B C D 294 E F G H

Jane Austen's House

Chawton Primary School

Winchester Road

J K L M N P Q
258
73 74 75 76 77
Ham Wood
Spollycombe Copse
Holybourne Down
Upper Froyle
Treloar Trust
Treloar School
Highway Home
Old Lane
Froyle Mill
Isington Lane
Isingt
River Wey
A31
Bonham's Farm
Mill Court
Cuckoo's Corner
107
108
Holybourne
London Road
Church Lane
Howard's Lane
New Paddock Close
Andrews Endowed CE Primary School
Cranford Dr
Inhams Rd
Lwr Neatham Mill La
Neatham Mill Lane
Lwr Neatham
Neatham
Hawbridge Farm
Styne Farm
Malms Farm
West Court
Binsted
Binsted CE Primary School
The Street
Thurstons Cl
Clements Cl
Broadview Cl
Isington Rd
Hay Place
Clay's Lane
B3004
MILL LANE
Golden Chair Farm
Wyck Lane
Wyck
Stubbs Farm
Wyck Place
Monk Wood
Neatham Down
Hangers Way
Clay's Farm
Clay's Lane
Shelleys Lane
Wyck Lane
Pookles Lane
B3004 CAKER'S LANE
East Worldham
Blanket Street
WORLDHAM HILL
GREEN STREET
Oaklands Farm
Kingsley Stream
Hangers Way
110
1 2 3 4 5 6 7 8 9 10 11 12
43 42 41 40 39 138
74 75 76 77
J K L M N P Q R
295
West Worldham
Binswood
Rookery Farm

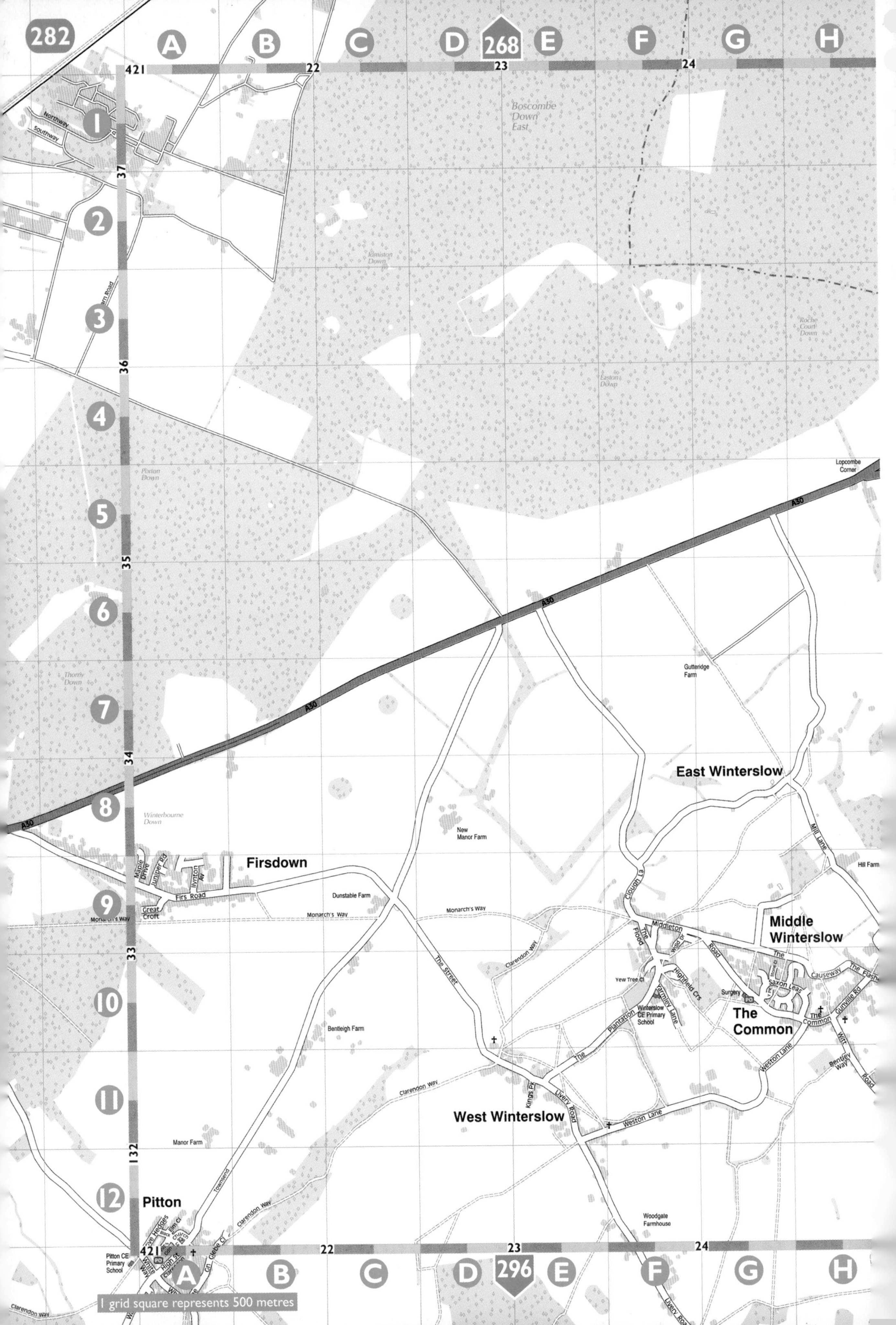

282

A B C D 268 E F G H

421
22
23
24

Northway
Southway

1

37

2

3

36

4

Porton
Down

5

35

6

Thorny
Down

7

34

A30

8

Winterbourne
Down

9

Monarch's Way

Middle
Drive
Lippert Rd
Tinton Av
Firs Road
Great
Croft

Firsdown

Dunstable Farm
Monarch's Way

Monarch's Way

New
Manor Farm

Clarendon Way

The Street

East Winterslow

Clough La

Middleton
The Flood

Middle
Winterslow

Highfield Cres

Yew Tree Cl

Winterslow
CE Primary
School

Surgery

Saxon Leas

The
Common

The Causeway

The Flash

Gutteridge
Farm

Hill Farm

Mill Lane

Gunville Rd

The Common

33

10

Bentleigh Farm

The Plantation

Weston Lane

Bentley Way

Will Rd

11

132

Manor Farm

Clarendon Way

Kings Pl

Lively Road

West Winterslow

Weston Lane

12

Pitton

Townsend

Clarendon Way

Woodgate
Farmhouse

Lively Road

Pitton CE
Primary
School

421

High St

A B C D 296 E F G H
22
23
24

Clarendon Way

Lopcombe
Corner

A30

Boscombe
Down
East

Idmiston
Down

Easton
Down

Roche
Court
Down

1 grid square represents 500 metres

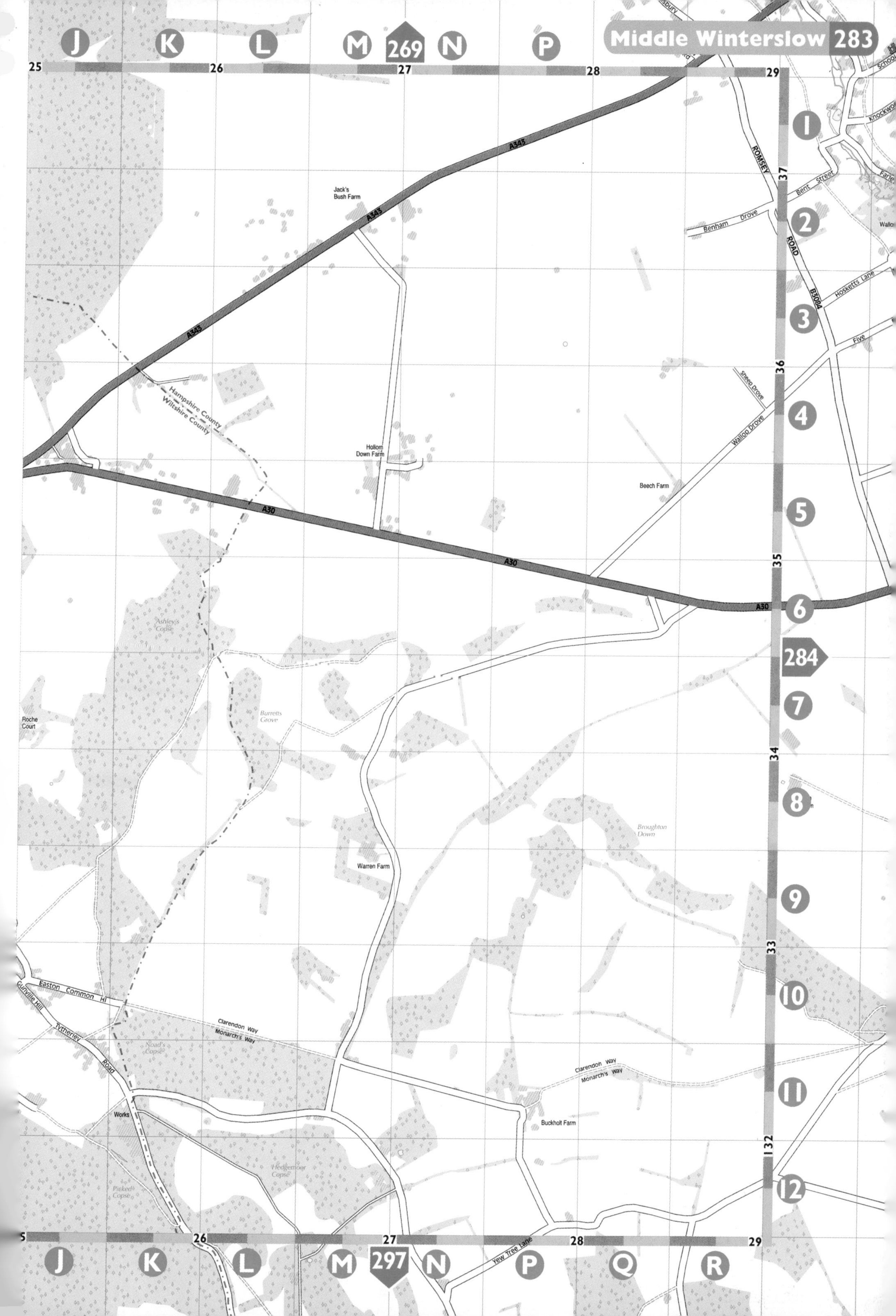
J
K
L
M
269
N
P
25
26
27
28
29
A343
Jack's Bush Farm
ROMSEY
ROAD
B3084
Benham Drove
Bent Street
Hosketts Lane
Five
Sheep Drove
Wallop Drove
Hampshire County
Wiltshire County
Hollom Down Farm
Beech Farm
A30
Ashley's Copse
Roche Court
Burretts Grove
Warren Farm
Broughton Down
Easton Common Hl
Gunville Hill
Tytherley Road
Clarendon Way
Monarch's Way
Noad's Copse
Works
Buckholt Farm
Hedgemoor Copse
Picked Copse
Yew Tree Lane
1
2
3
4
5
6
284
7
8
9
10
11
12
37
36
35
34
33
132
297
Q
R

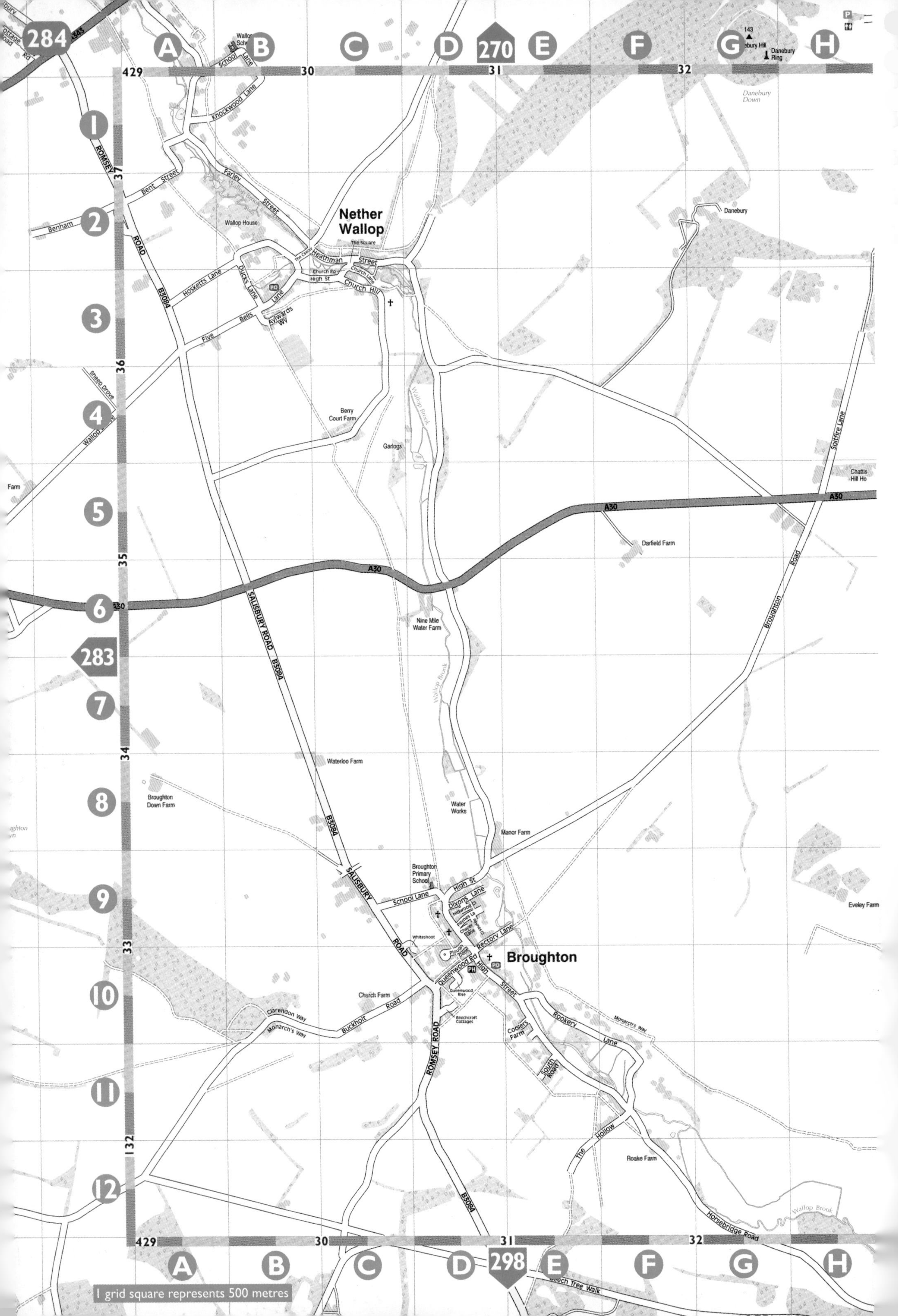

A B C D **270** E F G H

429   30   31   32

1

2 Benham

Nether Wallop

Wallop House

The Square

3

4 Berry Court Farm

Garlogs

5 A30

Darfield Farm

Chattis Hill Ho

6 A30

Nine Mile Water Farm

283

7

Waterloo Farm

8 Broughton Down Farm

Water Works

Manor Farm

Eveley Farm

9

Broughton Primary School

Dixons Lane

Broughton

10 Church Farm

Clarendon Way

Monarch's Way

Beechcroft Cottages

Coolers Farm

Rookery Lane

Monarch's Way

11

The Hollow

Roake Farm

Wallop Brook

12

Horsebridge Road

429   30   31   32

A B C D **298** E F G H

Beech Tree Walk

1 grid square represents 500 metres

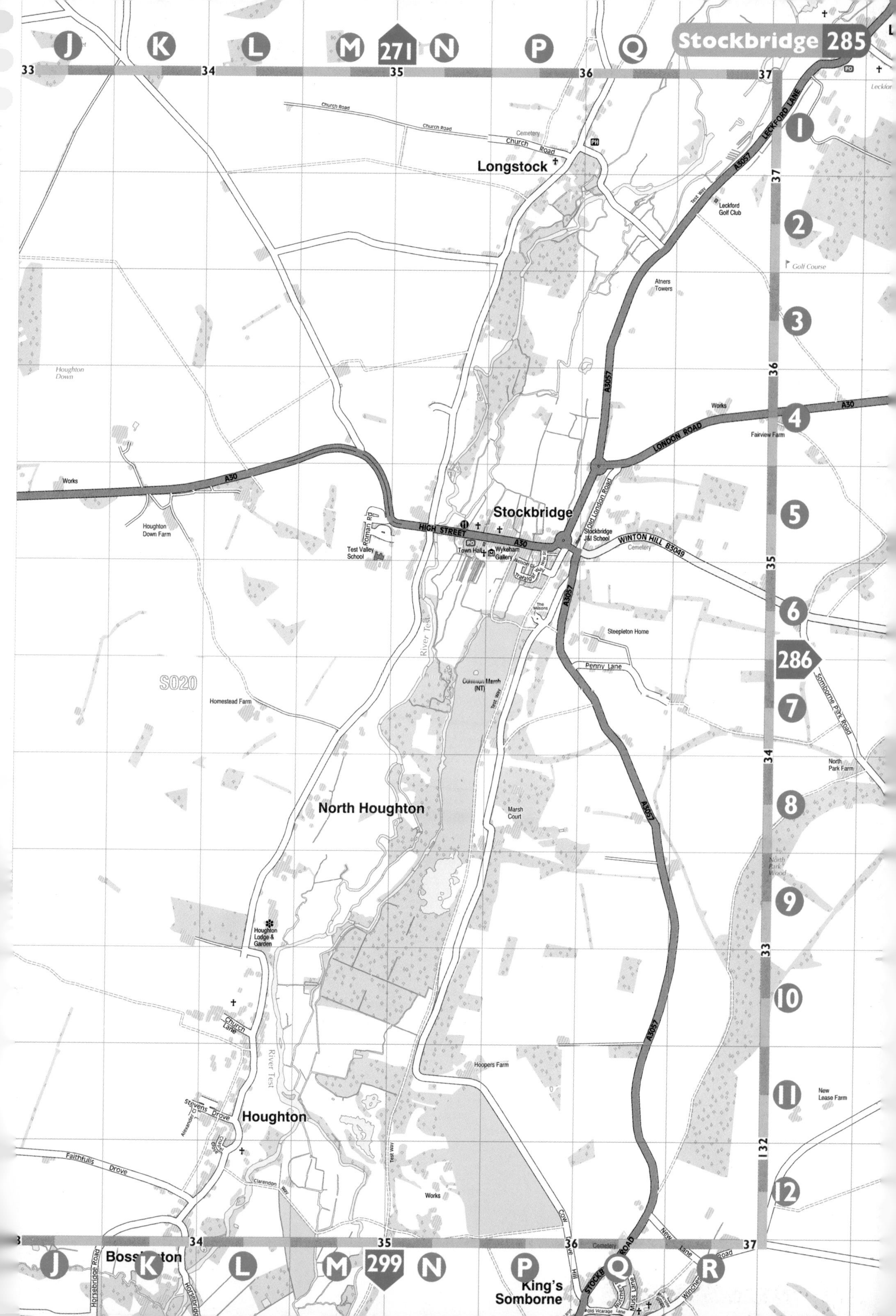

Stockbridge 285
271
299
286
J
K
L
M
N
P
Q
R
33
34
35
36
37
1
2
3
4
5
6
7
8
9
10
11
12
132
Longstock
Stockbridge
North Houghton
Houghton
King's Somborne
Bossington
Church Road
Cemetery
Leckford Lane
A3057
Test Way
Leckford Golf Club
Golf Course
Atners Towers
Houghton Down
Works
London Road
A30
Fairview Farm
Houghton Down Farm
High Street
Roman Rd
Test Valley School
Town Hall
Wykeham Gallery
Stockbridge J&I School
Old London Road
Winton Hill B3049
The Mitsons
Steepleton Home
Penny Lane
Somborne Park Road
River Test
SO20
Homestead Farm
Common Marsh (NT)
North Park Farm
Marsh Court
North Park Wood
Houghton Lodge & Garden
Church Lane
Hoopers Farm
New Lease Farm
Stevens Drove
Faithfulls Drove
Clarendon Way
Cow Drove Hill
Stockbridge Road
New Lane
Horsebridge Road
Old Vicarage Lane
Muss Lane

286

A   B   C   D   272   E   F   G   H

Leckford

Works

437   38   39   40

Leckford Abbas

1

LECKFORD LANE

A3057

Test Way

PO

37

Leckford
Golf Club

2

Atners
Towers

Golf Course

3

36

Works

4   A30

LONDON ROAD

Fairview Farm

New Farm

Sandydown Farm   Heath House

Juniper's Oak

5

HILL B3049

35

Stockbridge
Down

6   B3049

285   B3049

Bushy
Copse

7

34

North
Park Farm

Somborne Park Road

Winter
Down
Copse

8

A3057

9

North
Park
Wood

33

Little
Somborne House

Rookley
Manor

10

Somborne Pk Rd

Whitenall Road

Whitenall Road

Court Lane

A3057

Little
Somborne

Up Somborne

11

New
Lease Farm

32

Chalk Hill

12

New
Lane

Winchester Road

437   38   39   40

Chalk Vale

Chalk Vale
Farm

A   B   C   D   300   E   F   G   H

1 grid square represents 500 metres

Ashley

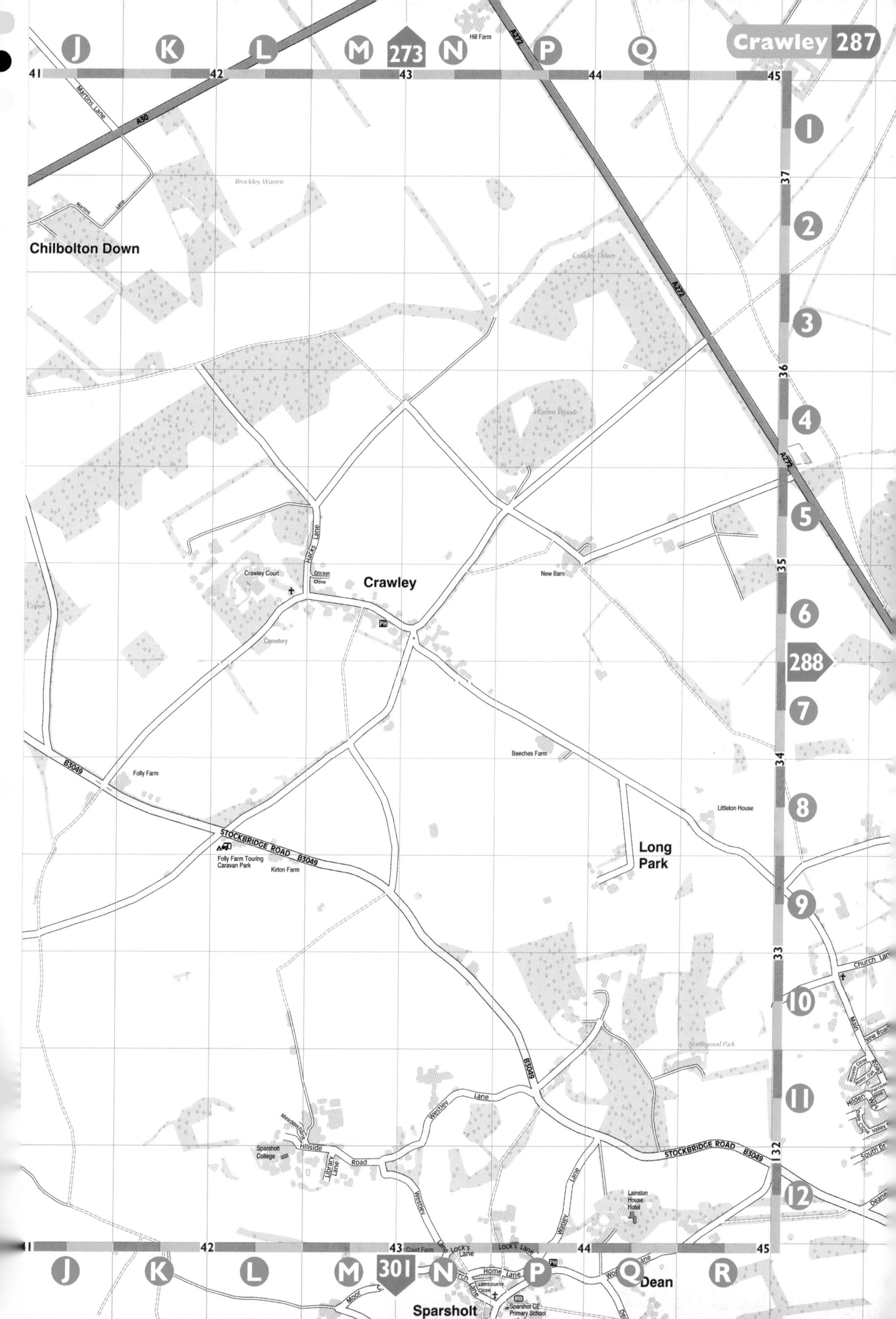

Crawley 287
273
Hill Farm
A272
A30
Martins Lane
Brockley Warren
Chilbolton Down
Crawley Down
Warren Wood
Hacks Lane
Crawley Court
Cricket Close
Crawley
PH
Cemetery
New Barn
Copse
288
B3049
Folly Farm
Beeches Farm
Littleton House
STOCKBRIDGE ROAD B3049
Folly Farm Touring Caravan Park
Kirton Farm
Long Park
Church Lane
Main
New Road
Northwood Park
Westley Lane
Meadowbank
Hillside Road
Sparsholt College
Library Lane
Westley Lane
Watley Lane
Lainston House Hotel
STOCKBRIDGE ROAD B3049
South Dr
Court Farm
Lock's Lane
Home Lane
Lambourne Close
Sparsholt CE Primary School
Dean
Sparsholt
301
41
42
43
44
45
37
36
35
34
33
32
J
K
L
M
N
P
Q
R
1
2
3
4
5
6
7
8
9
10
11
12

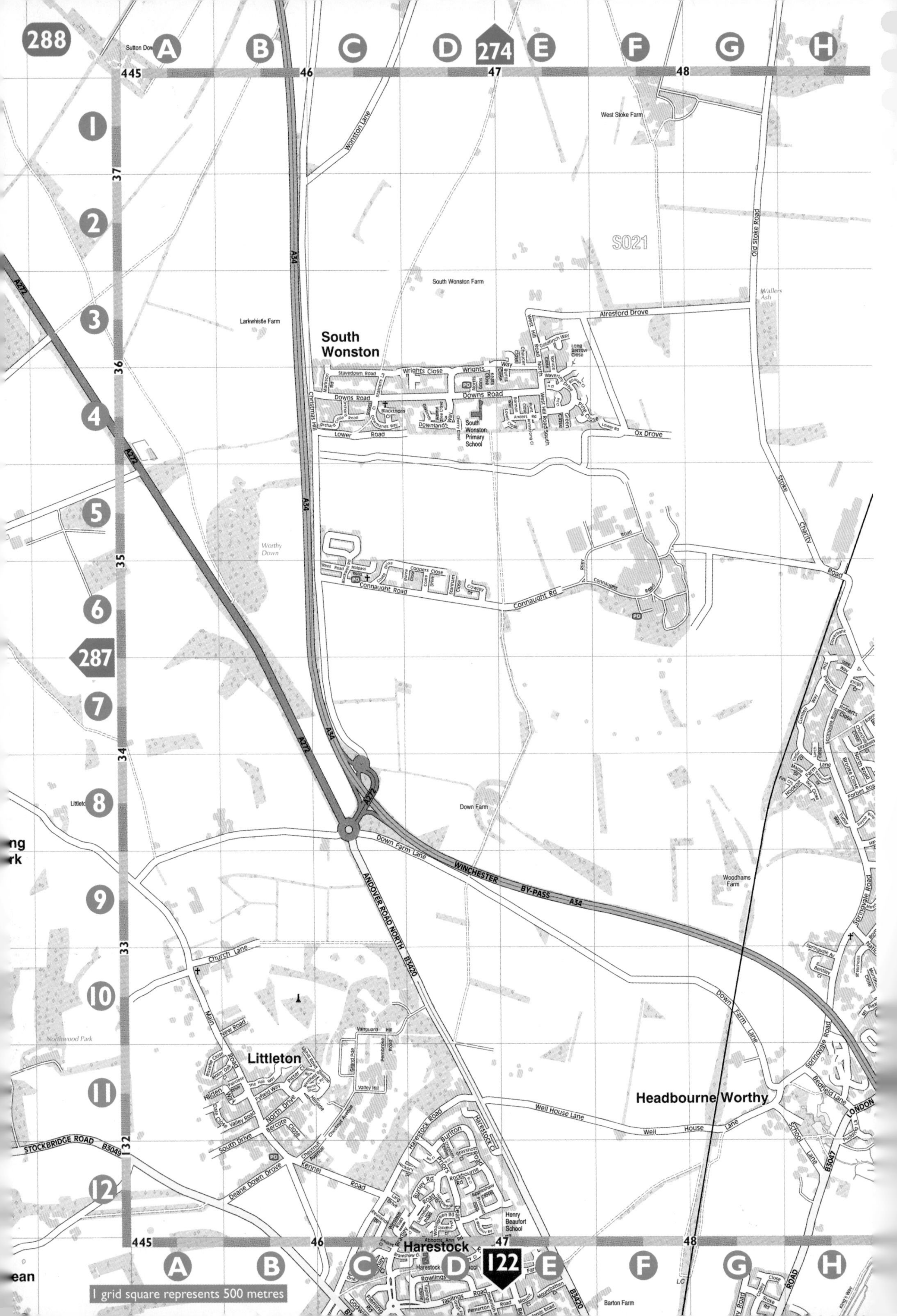

274

287

122

South
Wonston

Littleton

Harestock

Headbourne Worthy

I grid square represents 500 metres

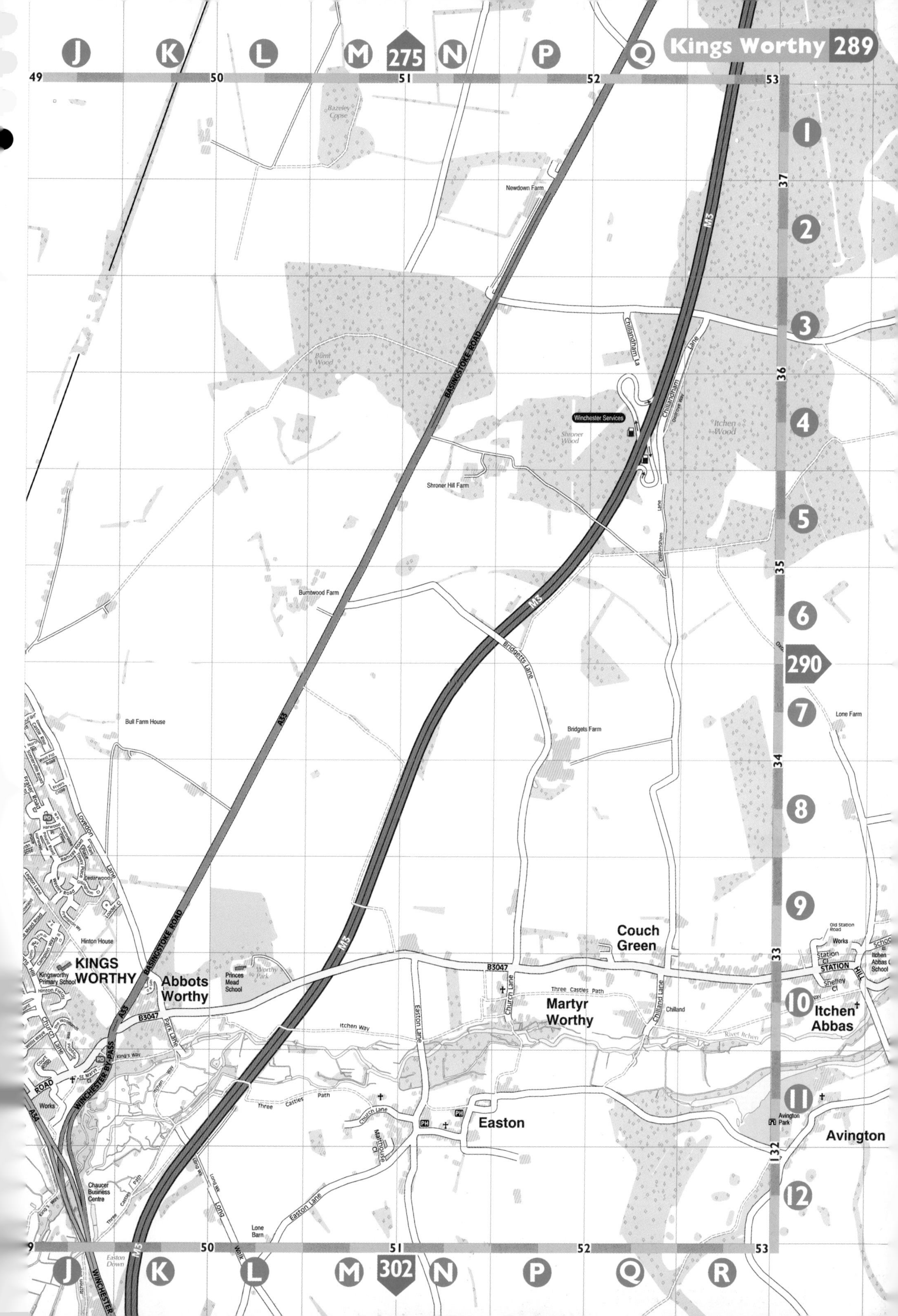
275
302
290
Bazeley Copse
Newdown Farm
M3
Chillandham La
Chillandham Lane
BASINGSTOKE ROAD
Burnt Wood
Winchester Services
Shroner Wood
Itchen Wood
Shroner Hill Farm
Burntwood Farm
Bridgetts Lane
Bull Farm House
Bridgets Farm
Lone Farm
A33
Loveden Lane
Hinton House
KINGS WORTHY
Kingsworthy Primary School
Abbots Worthy
Princes Mead School
Worthy Park
Couch Green
B3047
Church Lane
Three Castles Path
Martyr Worthy
Chilland Lane
Chilland
Itchen Way
River Itchen
Easton Lane
Old Station Road
Works
Station Cl
STATION HILL
Shelley Cl
Itchen Abbas School
Itchen Abbas
Avington Park
Avington
WINCHESTER BY-PASS
ROAD
A34
Works
Three Castles Path
Church Lane
Malthouse Cl
Easton
Chaucer Business Centre
Long Walk
Lone Barn
Easton Down
WINCHESTER

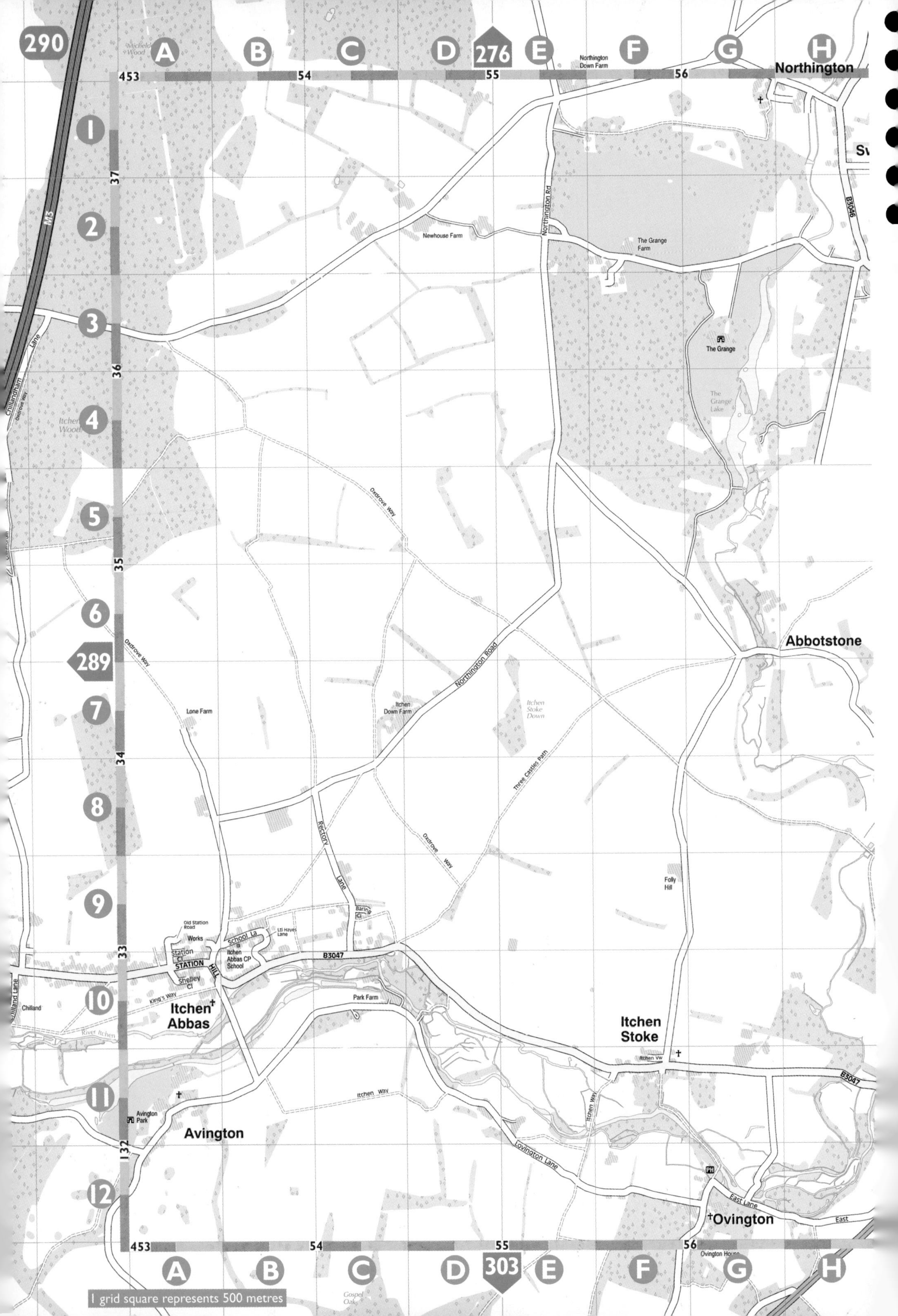

290
276
289
303
Northington
Northington Down Farm
Newhouse Farm
The Grange Farm
The Grange
The Grange Lake
Northington Rd
B3046
Oxdrove Way
Itchen Wood
Chillandham Lane
M3
Abbotstone
Northington Road
Lone Farm
Itchen Down Farm
Itchen Stoke Down
Three Castles Path
Rectory Lane
Folly Hill
Baring Cl
Old Station Road
Works
Station Cl
STATION HILL
Shelley Cl
School La
Itchen Abbas CP School
Ltl Hayes Lane
B3047
King's Way
Chilland
Chilland Lane
Itchen Abbas
River Itchen
Park Farm
Itchen Stoke
Itchen Vw
Itchen Way
Avington Park
Avington
Ovington Lane
East Lane
East
Ovington
Ovington House
PH
Gospel Oak
1 grid square represents 500 metres

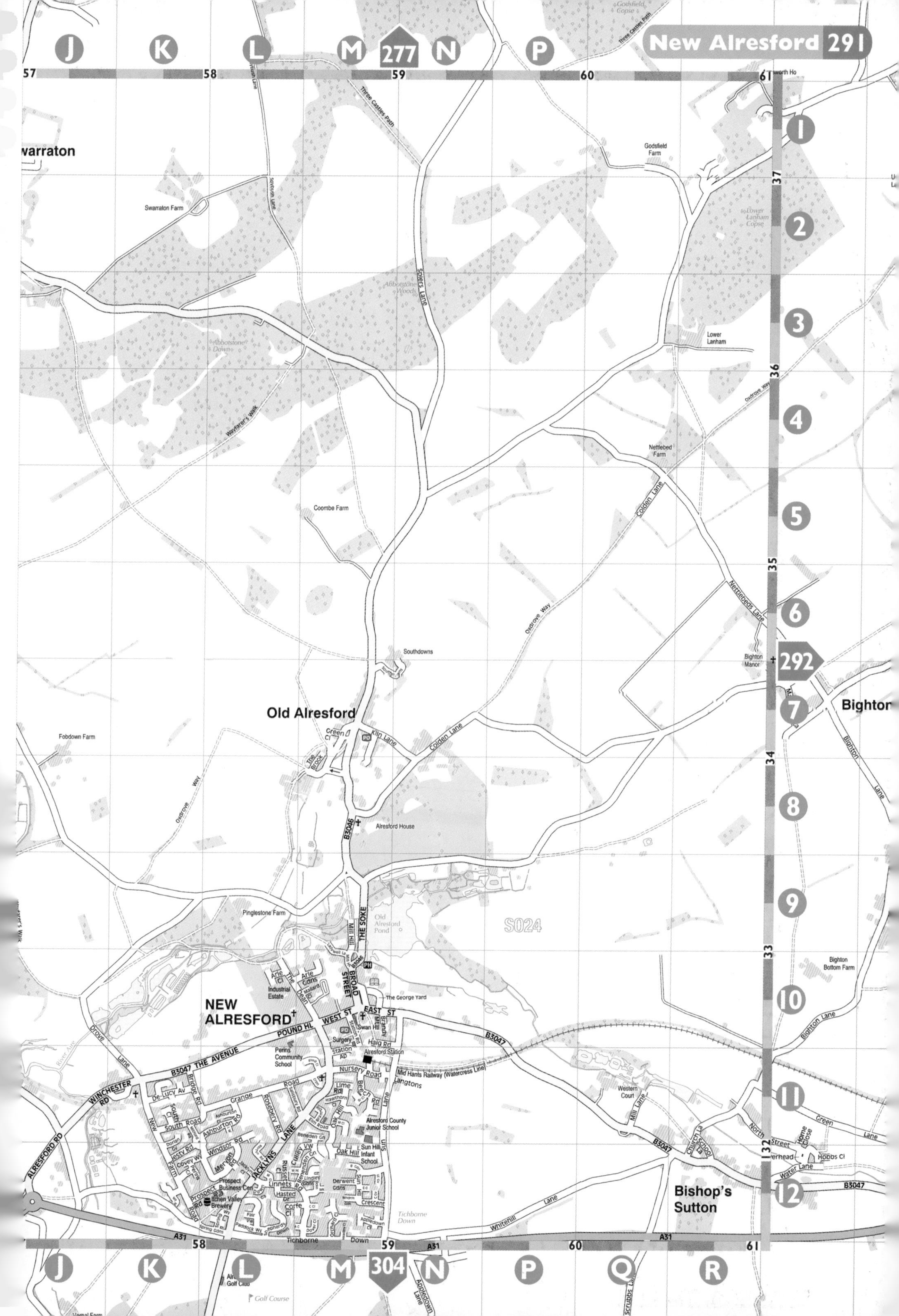
J
K
L
M
277
N
P
57
58
59
60
61
1
2
3
4
5
6
7
8
9
10
11
12
37
36
35
34
33
132
292
304
Q
R
Godsfield Copse
Three Castles Path
Godsfield Farm
Lower Lanham Copse
Lower Lanham
Swarraton
Swarraton Farm
Abbotstone Down
Abbotstone Woods
Spiers Lane
Wayfarer's Walk
Oxdrove Way
Nettlebed Farm
Colden Lane
Coombe Farm
Nettlebeds Lane
Bighton Manor
Bighton
Bighton Lane
Southdowns
Old Alresford
Kiln Lane
Fobdown Farm
Alresford House
B3046
Pinglestone Farm
THE SOKE
Mill Hill
BROAD STREET
Old Alresford Pond
SO24
Bighton Bottom Farm
Industrial Estate
NEW ALRESFORD
The George Yard
EAST ST
WEST ST
POUND HL
B3047 THE AVENUE
Drove Lane
Perins Community School
Alresford Station
Mid Hants Railway (Watercress Line)
Nursery Road
Langtons
WINCHESTER RD
Grange Road
Jacklyns Lane
Alresford County Junior School
Sun Hill Infant School
Western Court
Mill Lane
Church La
School La
North Street
Green Lane
Hobbs Cl
Water Lane
B3047
Bishop's Sutton
ALRESFORD RD
Prospect Business Cen
Itchen Valley Brewery
Tichborne Down
Whitehill Lane
A31
Golf Club
Golf Course
Appledown Lane
Scrubbs Lane

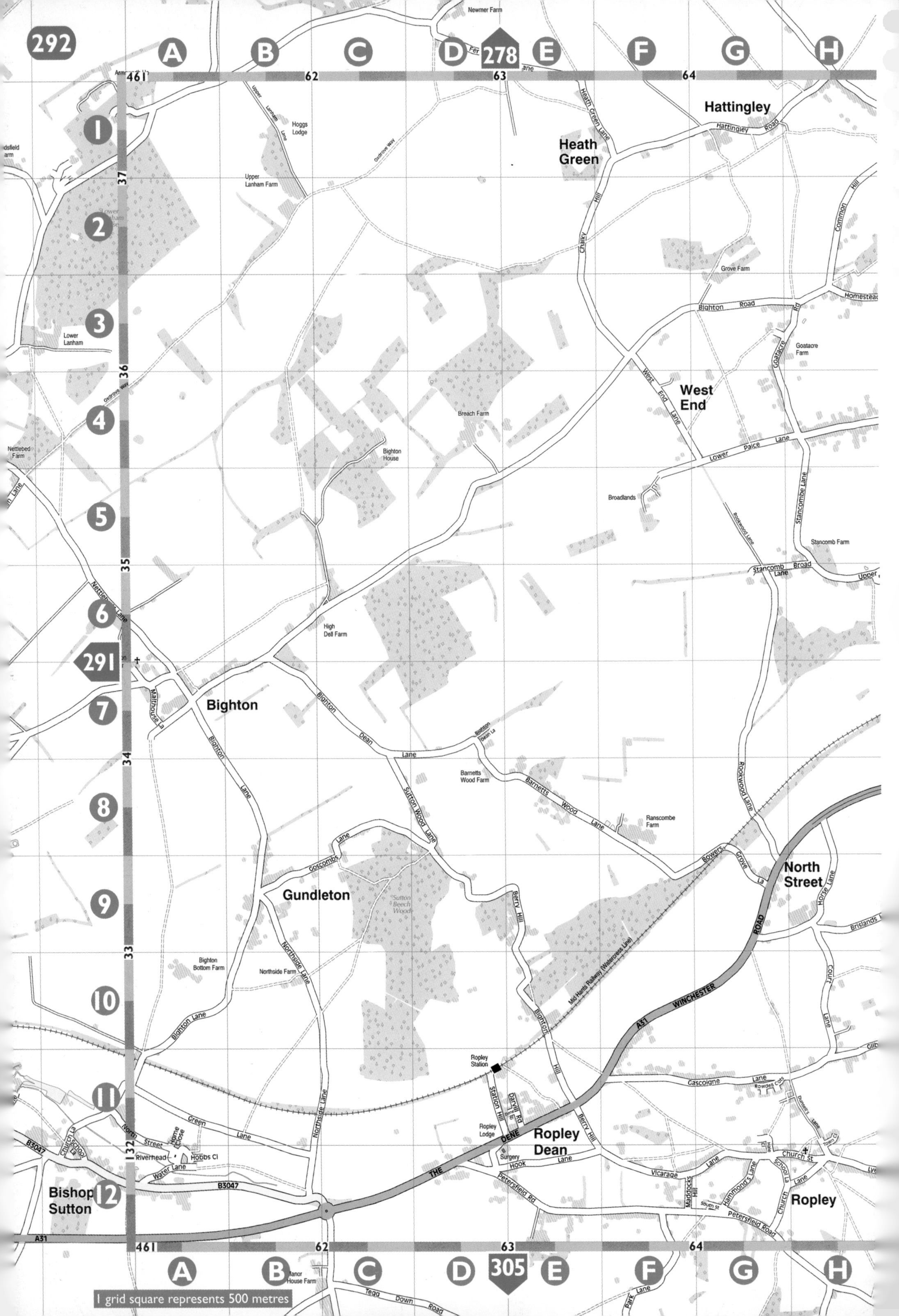

A B C D 278 E F G H

1
2
3
4
5
6
291
7
8
9
10
11
12

37
36
35
34
33
32

461 62 63 64

Newmer Farm

Arm...

Upper Lanham Lane

Hoggs Lodge

Upper Lanham Farm

Oxdrove Way

Hattingley

Heath Green

Hattingley Road

Heath Green Lane

Chalky Hill

Grove Farm

Bighton Road

Goatacre Rd

Goatacre Farm

Homestead

West End

West End Lane

Lower Paice Lane

Stancombe Lane

Breach Farm

Bighton House

Broadlands

Rosewood Lane

Stancomb Farm

Stancomb Lane Broad

Upper

Lower Lanham

Nettlebed Farm

...dsfield Farm

Nettlebed Lane

High Dell Farm

Bighton

Bighton Lane

Malthouse La

Bighton Dean Lane

Sutton Wood Lane

Bighton Dean La

Barnetts Wood Farm

Barnetts Wood Lane

Ranscombe Farm

Rookwood Lane

North Street

Gundleton

Goscombs Lane

Sutton Beech Wood

Berry Hill

Bowers Grove La

Horse Lane

Brislands

Court Lane

Bighton Bottom Farm

Northside Farm

Northside Lane

Bighton Lane

Mid Hants Railway (Watercress Line)

A31 WINCHESTER ROAD

Gascoigne Lane

Rowden Cas

Dessey Lane

Ropley Station

Ropley Lodge

Station Hill

THE DENE

Ropley Dean

Surgery

Hook

Petersfield Rd

Berry Rd

Berry Hill

Bighton Hill

Vicarage Lane

Maddocks Lane

Hammond's Lane

South St

Church Lane

School St

Lye

Ropley

Petersfield road

Bishop Sutton

B3047

French St

North Street

Home Close

Riverhead

Hobbs Cl

Water Lane

Green Lane

Northside Lane

B3047

A31

461 62 63 64

A B C D 305 E F G H

1 grid square represents 500 metres

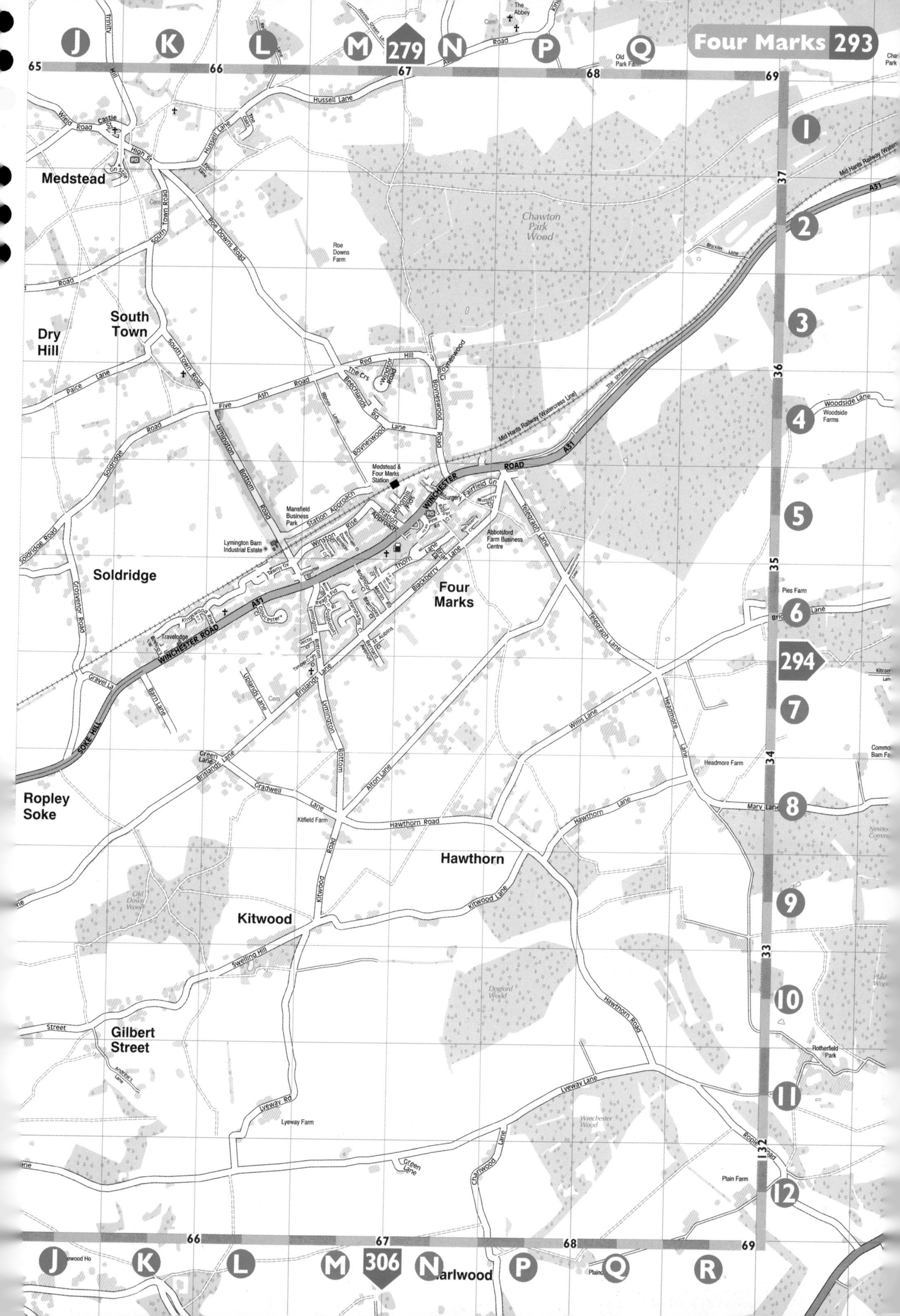

J K L M 279 N P Q

65   66   67   68   69

I
2
3
4
5
6
294
7
8
9
10
11
12

Medstead

Dry Hill

South Town

Soldridge

Ropley Soke

Chawton Park Wood

Roe Downs Farm

Medstead & Four Marks Station

Mansfield Business Park

Lymington Barn Industrial Estate

WINCHESTER ROAD

Travelodge

A31

Four Marks

SOKE HILL

Kitwood

Gilbert Street

Hawthorn

Woodside Lane
Woodside Farms

Pies Farm

Headmore Farm

Mary Lane

Rotherfield Park

Old Down Wood

Swelling Hill

Dogford Wood

Winchester Wood

Plain Farm

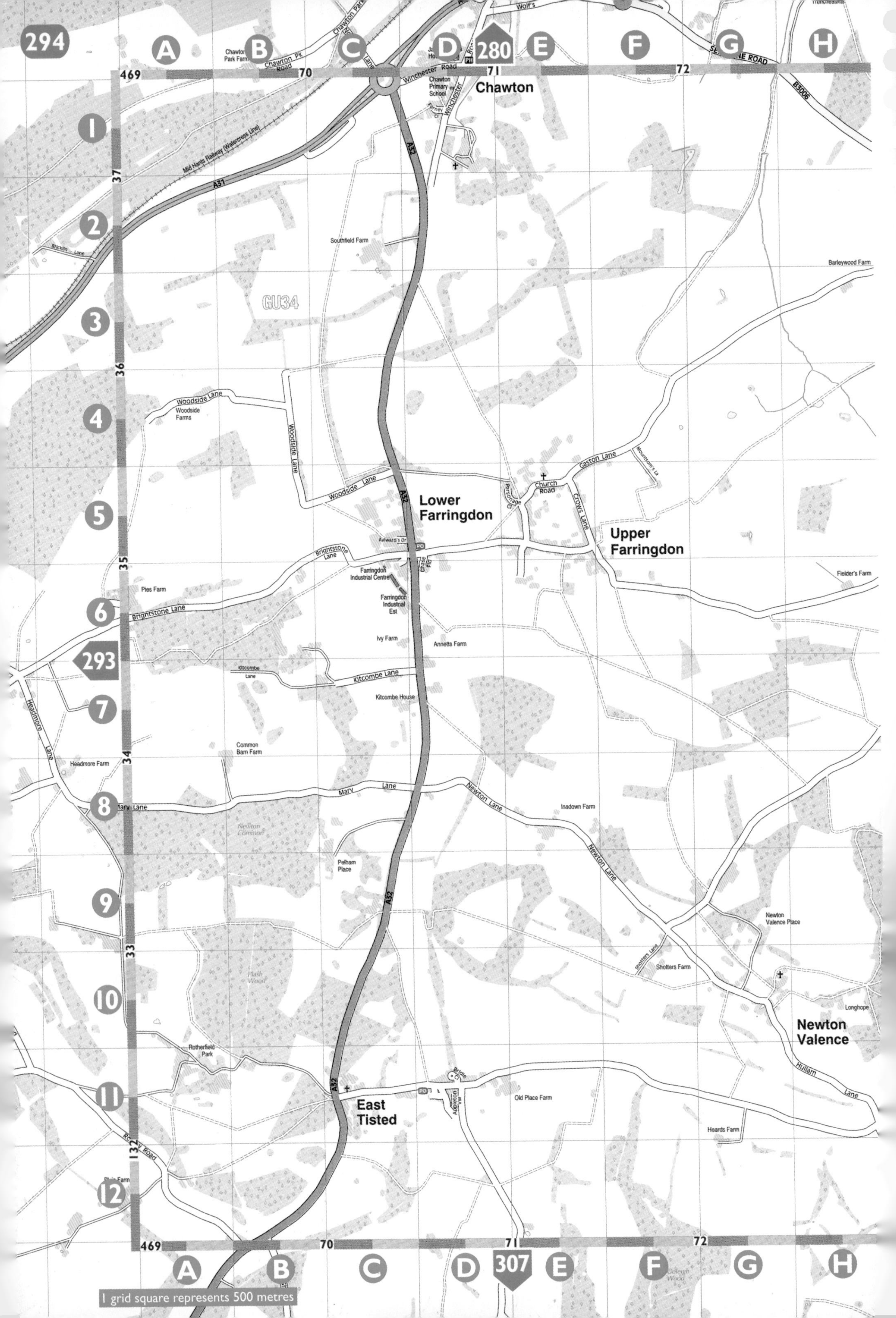

294

A   B   C   D   280   E   F   G   H

469   70   71   72

Chawton Pk Road

Chawton Pk Farm

Winchester Road

Chawton Primary School

Chawton

SELBORNE ROAD

B3006

1

37

Mid Hants Railway (Watercress Line)

A31

Bricklin Lane

2

Southfield Farm

GU34

Barleywood Farm

3

36

Woodside Lane

Woodside Farms

4

Woodside Lane

Gaston Lane

Mountain La

Church Road

Lower Farringdon

Parsonage

Crows Lane

Upper Farringdon

5

35

Brightstone Lane

Aylward's Dr

The Chase

Chase Rd

Fielder's Farm

Pies Farm

Farringdon Industrial Centre

Farringdon Industrial Est

6

Brightstone Lane

293

Ivy Farm

Annetts Farm

Kitcombe Lane

Kitcombe Lane

7

34

Headmore Lane

Headmore Farm

Kitcombe House

Common Barn Farm

8

Mary Lane

Mary Lane

Newton Lane

Inadown Farm

Newton Common

Newton Lane

9

33

Pelham Place

Newton Valence Place

10

Plash Wood

Bottom Lane

Shotters Farm

Newton Valence

Longhope

11

32

Rotherfield Park

Rce Road

East Tisted

Alginton's Vw

Old Place Farm

Hollam Lane

Heards Farm

12

Pin Farm

469   70   71   307   72

A   B   C   D   E   F   G   H

Leigh Wood

1 grid square represents 500 metres

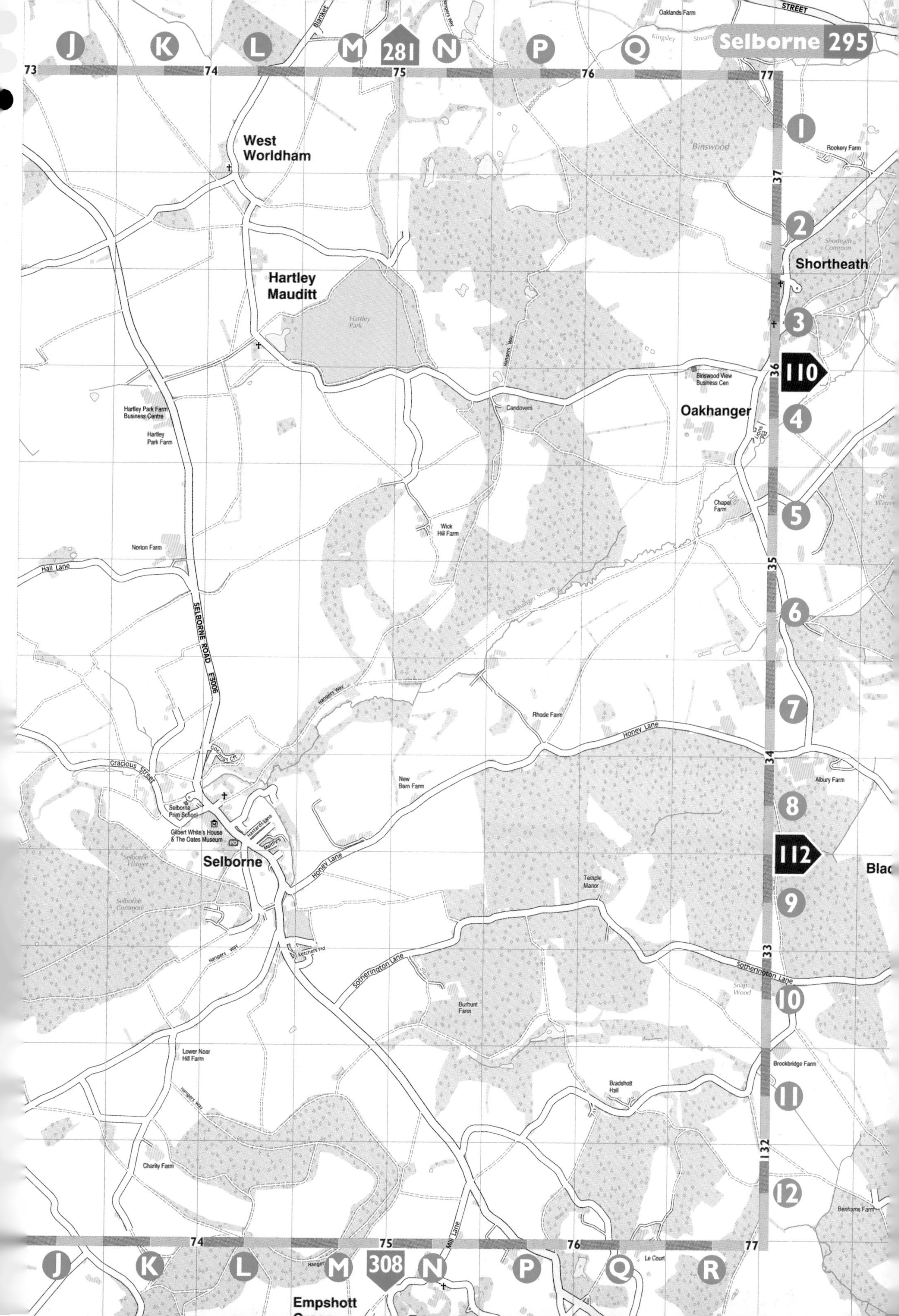

281

West
Worldham

Hartley
Mauditt

*Hartley
Park*

Hartley Park Farm
Business Centre

*Hartley
Park Farm*

Norton Farm

Hall Lane

SELBORNE ROAD B3006

Gracious Street

Selborne
Prim School

Gilbert White's House
& The Oates Museum

Selborne

*Selborne
Hanger*

*Selborne
Common*

Hangers Way

Ketcher's End

Lower Noar
Hill Farm

Charity Farm

Hangers Way

Cowslips Cnr

Candovers

Hangers Way

*Wick
Hill Farm*

Rhode Farm

New
Barn Farm

Honey Lane

Sotherington Lane

Burhunt
Farm

Honey Lane

Temple
Manor

Bradshott
Hall

Oakhanger Stream

Binswood

Oaklands Farm

Kingsley   Stream

STREET

Rookery Farm

2

Shortheath

3

110

4

*Binswood View
Business Cen*

Oakhanger

*Chapel
Farm*

5

*The
Warre*

6

7

8

Albury Farm

112

Blac

9

Sotherington Lane

*Snap
Wood*

10

Brockbridge Farm

11

I32

12

Benhams Farm

37

36

35

34

33

Le Court

308

Empshott

Pitton

A B C D E F G H

282

Pitton CE
Primary
School

Pitton
Lodge

All Saints
CE Primary
School

Farley

Hound
Wood

The Livery

Park Lane

Blackmoor
Copse

Bainridge
Copse

Lucewood Lane

Penny's Lane

The Street

Ben Lane

Nightwood
Copse

Keepers Cott

Hawks
Grove

Coachworks

East
Grimstead

Whitehouse Farm

Manor Farm

Works

Walden
House

River Dunn

Dean Road

Dean Road

Crockford Road

Greenfields

West Dean Farm

West
Grimstead

Windswhistle Lane

Dean
Hill Farm

A B C D E F G H

1 grid square represents 500 metres

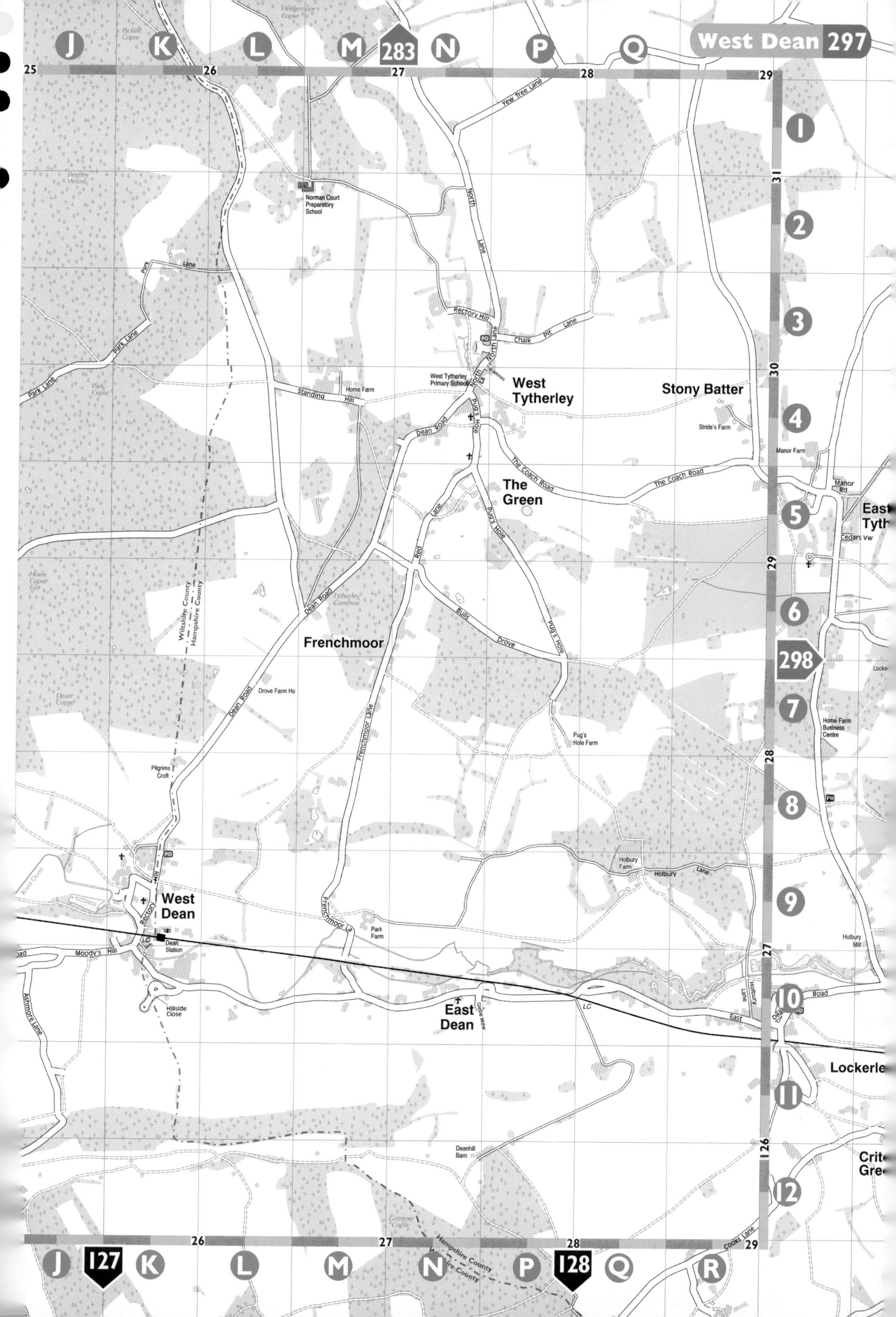

J K L M 283 N P Q

25 26 27 28 29

I
2
3
4
5
6
298
7
8
9
10
11
12

31
30
29
28
27
126

Hedgemoor Copse
Pickett Copse

Bentley Wood

Norman Court
Preparatory
School

Yew Tree Lane

North Lane

Rectory Hill
Chalk Pit Lane

Park Lane
Park Lane
Park Copse

Standing Hill
Home Farm

West Tytherley
Primary School

West Tytherley

Stony Batter

Stride's Farm

Manor Farm

Manor Rd

**East
Tyth**

Cedars vw

PO

Dean Road

The Coach Road
The Coach Road

The Green

Pug's Hole

Red Lane

Howe Copse East

Dean Road

Wiltshire County
Hampshire County

Tytherley Common

Frenchmoor

Drove Farm Ho

Bulls Drove

Pug's Hole

Pug's Hole Farm

Home Farm
Business
Centre

PH

Dean Copse

Frenchmoor Lane

Pilgrims Croft

Holbury Lane
Holbury Farm
Holbury

Holbury Mill

River Dunn

Moody's Hill

West Dean

Dean Station

Hillside Close

Frenchmoor La

Park Farm

East Dean

LC

Lockerley
Road

East Dean Road

Lockerle

Ashmore Lane

Deanhill Barn

Catmore Copse

Hampshire County
shire County

Crit
Gre

J 127 K L M N P 128 Q R

26 27 28 29

Cooks Lane

298
284
297
129
A
B
C
D
E
F
G
H
1
2
3
4
5
6
7
8
9
10
11
12
429
30
31
32
Horsebridge Road
Beech Tree Walk
Queenwood Farm
Crown Farm
Stony Batter
Stride's Farm
Manor Farm
The Coach Road
Manor Rd
East Tytherley
Cedars Vw
Bentley Farms
B3084
Pittleworth Farm
Lockerley Hall
Laine Copse
Back Lane
Home Farm Business Centre
Spearywell Wood
PH
Cadbury Fm
Holbury Lane
Spearywell
Holbury Mill
Lockerley Water Farm
Mottisfont Abbey & Garden (NT)
Oakley Rd
Keepers Lane
Benger's Lane
Mottisfont Club House
East Dean Road
River Dun
Hatt Lane
Church Lane
Mottisfont
Hatt Hill
Lockerley
Lockerley CE J&I School
Lockerley Rd
Dunbridge Station
Dunbridge
Butt's Green
Cooks Lane
Oval Rd
Works
Critchell's Green
Mill Rise
Lockerley Road
Canefield
DUNBRIDGE LANE
Kimbridge
Gas Works
Mount Fm
1 grid square represents 500 metres

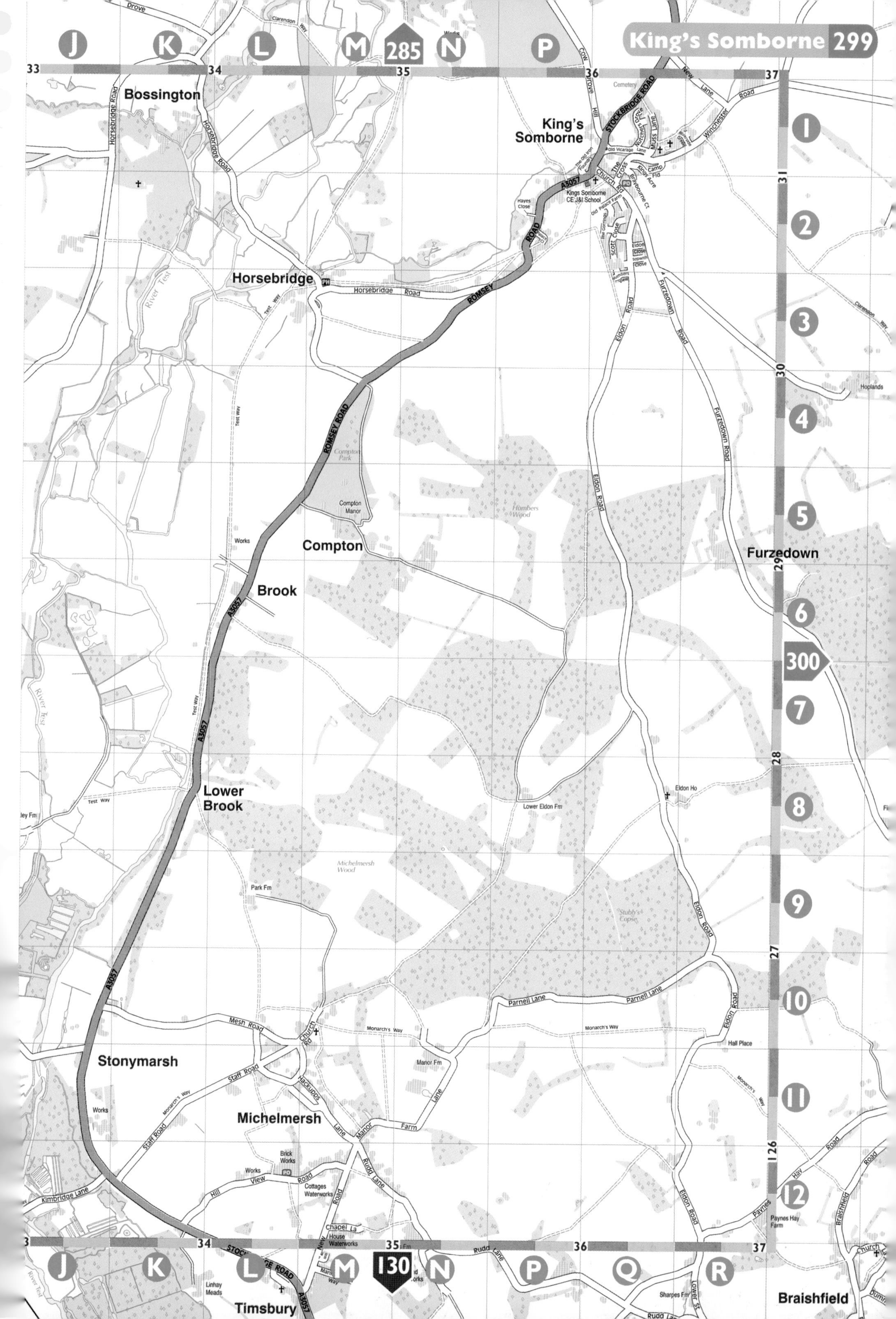

285
130
300
J
K
L
M
N
P
Q
R
33
34
35
36
37
1
2
3
4
5
6
7
8
9
10
11
12
Bossington
Horsebridge Road
Horsebridge Road
Drove
Clarendon Way
Cow Drove Hill
Cemetery
STOCKBRIDGE ROAD
New Lane
Winchester Road
King's Somborne
Old Vicarage Lane
Muss Lane
The Cross
Church Rd
Kings Acre
Camp Fld
Braybourne Ct
Kings Somborne CE J&I School
Old Palace Farm
Hayes Close
Scott Close
Eldon Close
Romsey Road
A3057
Horsebridge
Horsebridge Road
River Test
Test Way
Furzedown Road
Eldon Road
Clarendon Way
Hoplands
ROMSEY ROAD
Compton Park
Compton Manor
Hombers Wood
Compton
Works
Brook
Furzedown
Eldon Ho
Lower Eldon Fm
Lower Brook
Michelmersh Wood
Park Fm
Stubb's Copse
Parnell Lane
Mesh Road
Church Rd
Monarch's Way
Hall Place
Stonymarsh
Staff Road
Manor Fm
Hackupps Lane
Works
Michelmersh
Manor Farm Lane
Brick Works
Rudd Lane
Hill View Road
Cottages
Waterworks
Kimbridge Lane
Chapel La
House
Waterworks
New Lane
Paynes Hay Road
Paynes Hay Farm
Braishfield Road
Lower St
Sharpes Fm
STOCKBRIDGE ROAD
Linhay Meads
Timsbury
Braishfield
Church

286

299

A · B · C · D · 286 · E · F · G · H

437 · 38 · 39 · 40

Chalk Vale
Chalk Farm

Ashley

Ashley's Wood

Great Up Samborne Wood

Ashley Down

Forest of Bere Farm

Clarendon Way

Clarendon Way

Clarendon Way

Furzedown Road

Hoplands

Clarendon Way

Luke Copse

Mount Down

Furzedown

Parnholt Wood

Farley Down

Bailey's Down

Farley Fm

Eldon Ho

Fishponds Fm

Berrydown Farm

Eldon Road

Farley Ho

Farley Lane

Oakfield

Dores Lane

Dores Lane

Hall Place

Furzedown Road

Gudge Copse

Eldon Road

Kings Somborne Road

Pitt Fm

Farley Lane

Upper Slackstead

Dores Lane

Paynes Hay Farm

Braishfield Road

Church

Lower Slackstead

Dores Lane

Eldon Road

Sharpes Fm

Woolley

1 grid square represents 500 metres

A · B · 131 · C · D · E · F · G · H

437 · 38 · 39 · 40

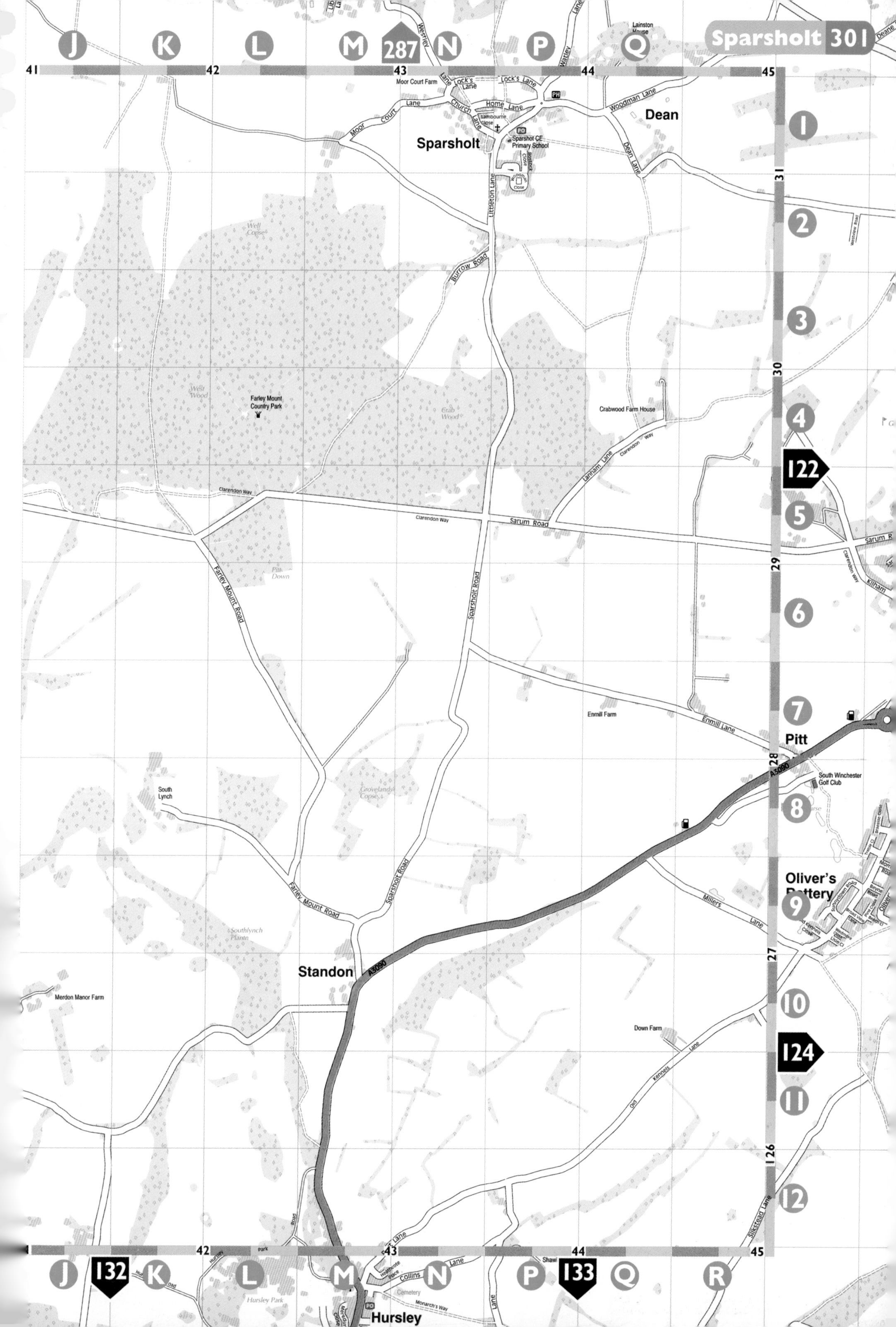

287
122
124
132
133
Sparsholt
Dean
Moor Court Farm
Moor Court Lane
Lock's Lane
Church Lane
Home Lane
Woodman Lane
Dean Lane
Lambourne Close
Sparsholt CE Primary School
Littleton Lane
Burrow Road
Well Copse
West Wood
Farley Mount Country Park
Crab Wood
Crabwood Farm House
Clarendon Way
Lanham Lane
Sarum Road
Farley Mount Road
Pitt Down
Sparsholt Road
Enmill Farm
Enmill Lane
Pitt
A3090
South Winchester Golf Club
South Lynch
Grovelands Copse
Oliver's Battery
Millers Lane
Southlynch Plantn
Standon
Merdon Manor Farm
Down Farm
Old Kennels Lane
Silkstead Lane
Killham
Hursley Park
Collins Lane
Cemetery
Monarch's Way
Hursley

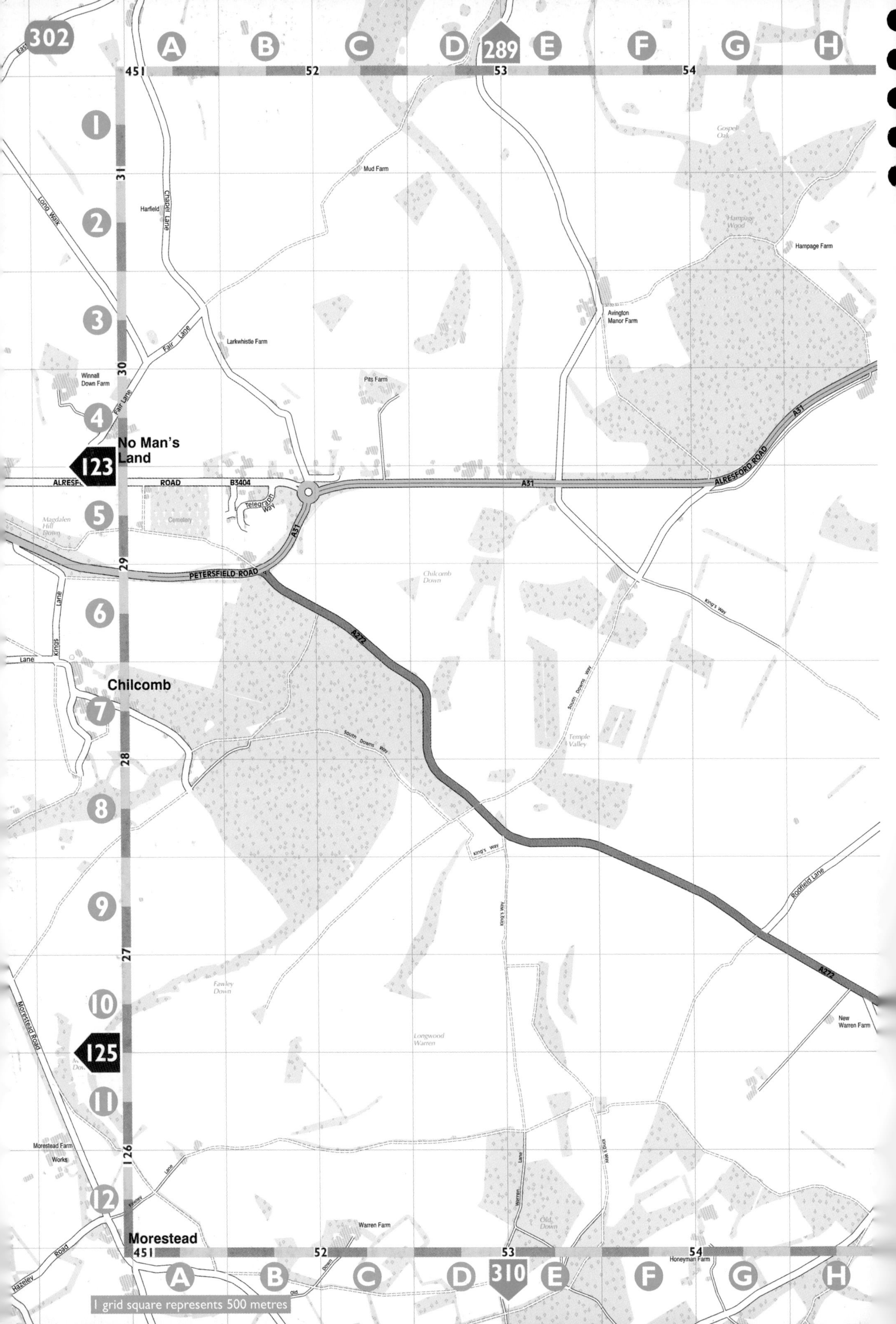
A
B
C
D
289
E
F
G
H
451
52
53
54
Gospel Oak
Mud Farm
Harfield
Chapel Lane
Long Walk
Hampage Wood
Hampage Farm
Avington Manor Farm
Larkwhistle Farm
Fair Lane
Winnall Down Farm
Pits Farm
No Man's Land
123
ALRESF
ROAD
B3404
A31
ALRESFORD ROAD
Telegraph Way
Cemetery
Magdalen Hill Down
PETERSFIELD ROAD
Chilcomb Down
King's Way
Kings Lane
Lane
A272
Chilcomb
South Downs Way
Temple Valley
King's Way
Roofield Lane
Fawley Down
Morestead Road
125
New Warren Farm
Longwood Warren
Morestead Farm
Works
Fawley Lane
Warren Lane
Old Down
Warren Farm
Morestead
Hazeley Road
Honeyman Farm
Down
Old
310
1 grid square represents 500 metres

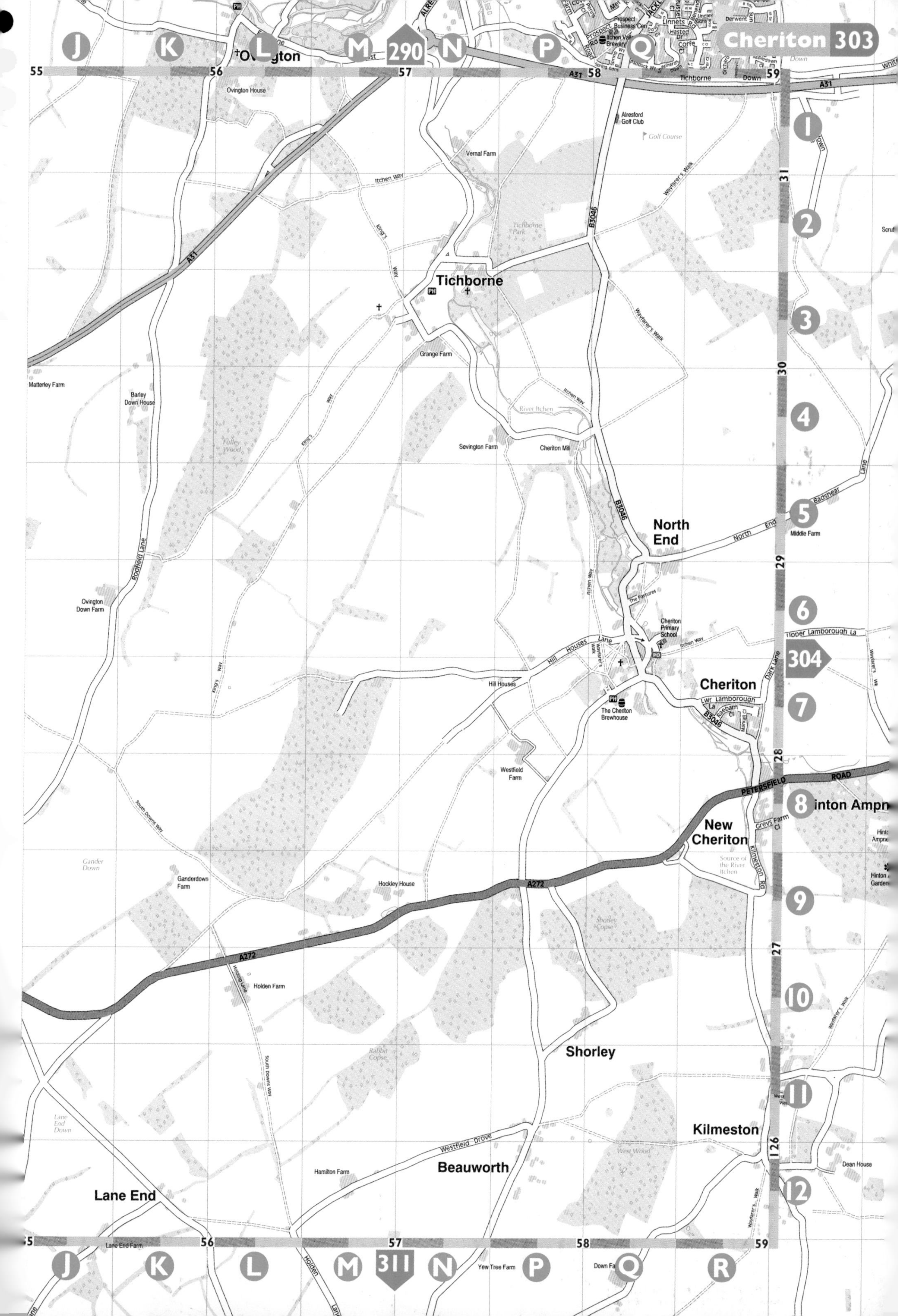

Ovington
Ovington House
Tichborne
Vernal Farm
Alresford Golf Club
Golf Course
Itchen Way
King's Way
Wayfarer's Walk
Tichborne Park
Grange Farm
Matterley Farm
Barley Down House
Fulley Wood
River Itchen
Sevington Farm
Cheriton Mill
North End
Badshear Lane
Middle Farm
Rodfield Lane
Ovington Down Farm
The Pastures
Cheriton Primary School
Hill Houses Lane
Hill Houses
Upper Lamborough La
Cheriton
Lwr Lamborough La
Raebarn Cl
Markall Cl
Dark Lane
The Cheriton Brewhouse
Westfield Farm
South Downs Way
Petersfield Road
Greys Farm Cl
New Cheriton
Source of the River Itchen
Kilmeston Rd
Gander Down
Ganderdown Farm
Hockley House
Shorley Copse
Holden Farm
Holden Lane
Rabbit Copse
Shorley
Lane End Down
Kilmeston
West Wood
Westfield Drove
Hamilton Farm
Beauworth
Lane End
Dean House
Lane End Farm
Yew Tree Farm
Down Fa
Tichborne Down
Prospect Business Cen
Itchen Valley Brewery
Linnets Rd
Hasted Dr
Corfe
A31
A272
B3046
290
304
311

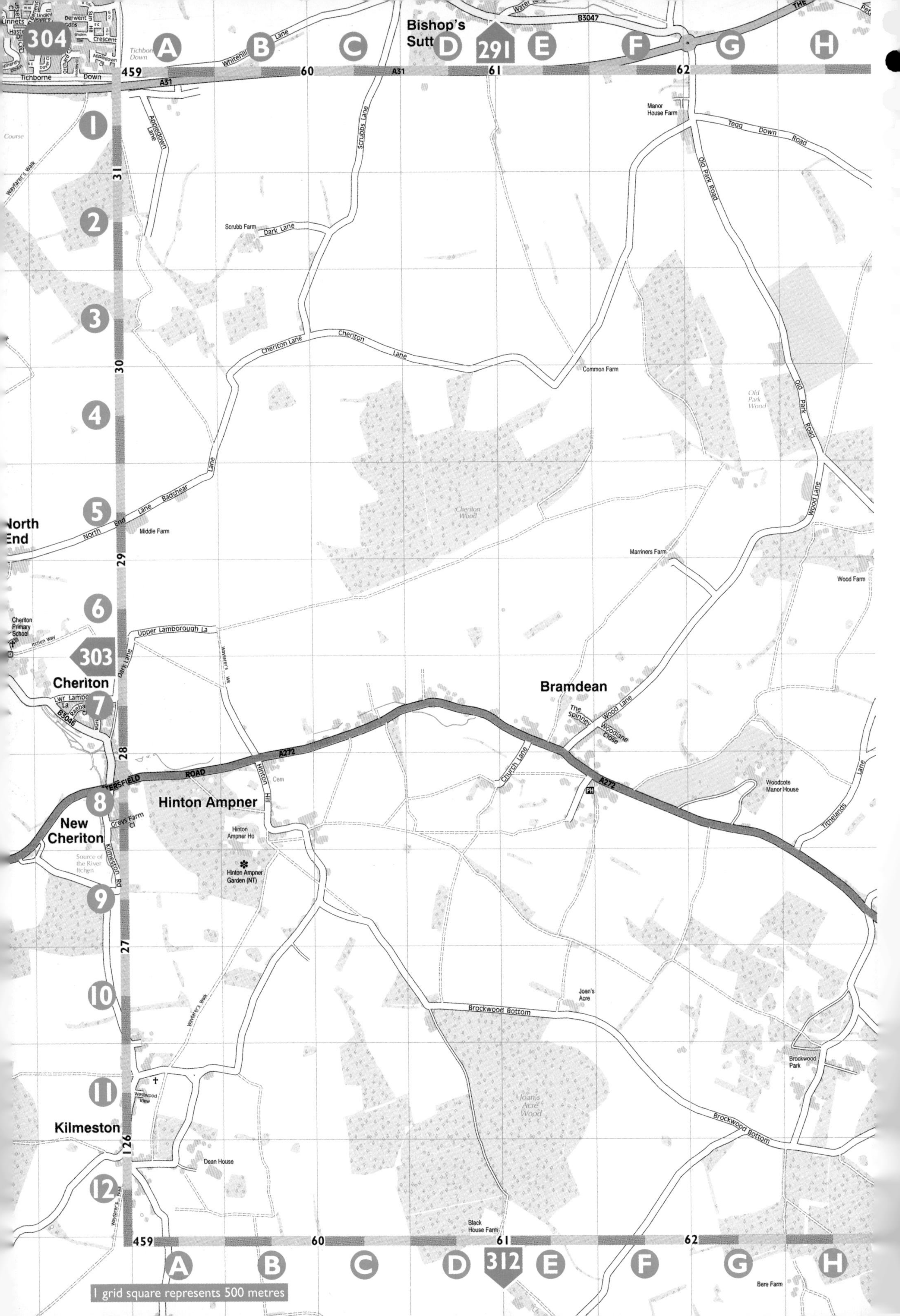

304
291
312
303
Bishop's Sutt
Tichborne Down
Whitehill Lane
B3047
A31
Manor House Farm
Tegg Down Road
Old Park Road
Applesdown Lane
Scrubbs Lane
Scrubb Farm
Dark Lane
Wayfarer's Walk
Cheriton Lane
Common Farm
Old Park Wood
Badshear Lane
North End Lane
Middle Farm
North End
Cheriton Wood
Wood Lane
Marriners Farm
Wood Farm
Cheriton Primary School
Itchen Way
Upper Lamborough La
Dark Lane
Cheriton
B3046
Bramdean
The Spinney
Woodlane Close
A272
Church Lane
PH
Woodcote Manor House
Tithelands Lane
Hinton Hill
Cem
Hinton Ampner
Hinton Ampner Ho
Hinton Ampner Garden (NT)
New Cheriton
Greys Farm Cl
Source of the River Itchen
Kilmeston Rd
Joan's Acre
Brockwood Bottom
Brockwood Park
Joan's Acre Wood
Westwood View
Kilmeston
Dean House
Black House Farm
Bere Farm
1 grid square represents 500 metres

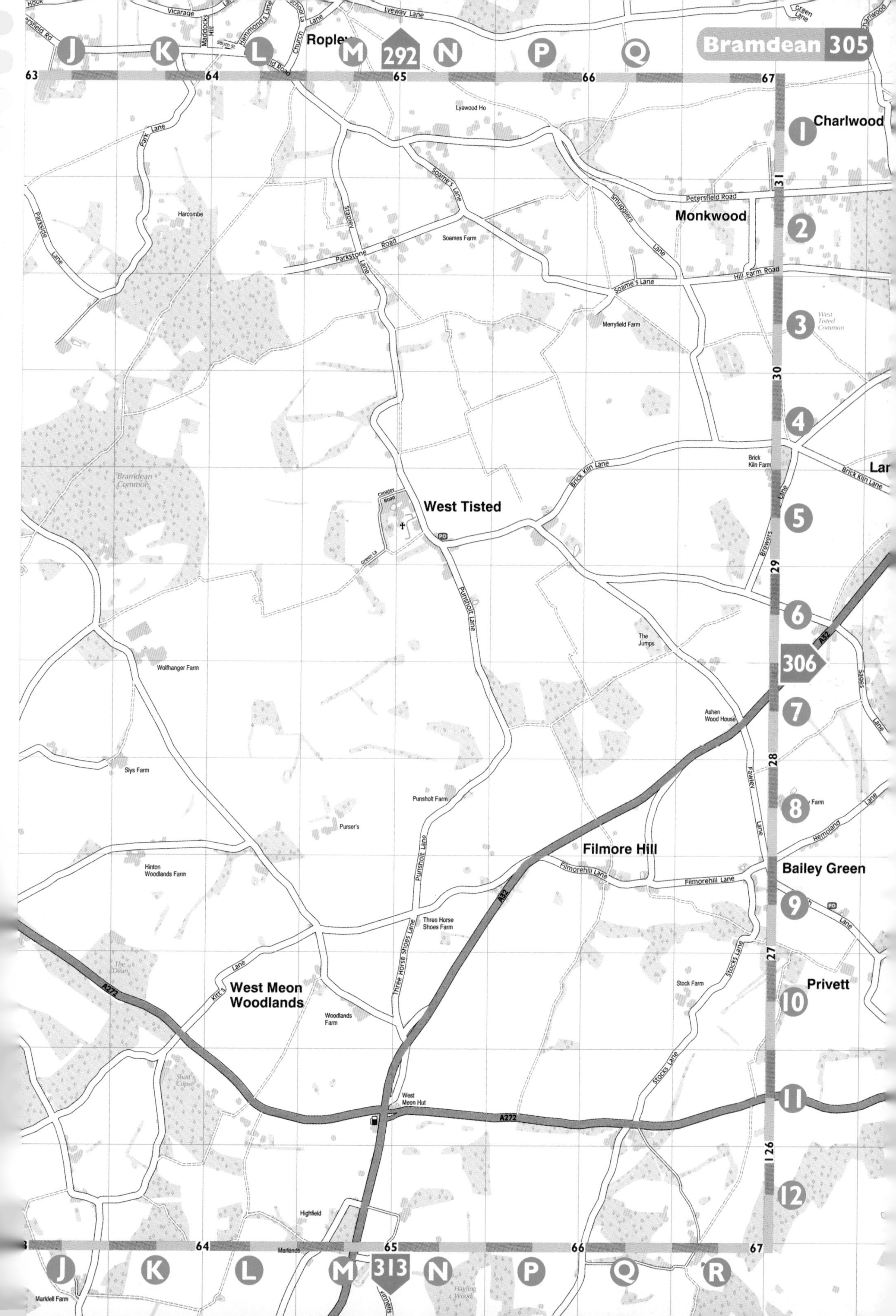

Ropley
292
Vicarage
Maddocks Hill
Hammond's Lane
School La
Church Lane
South St
Lyeway Lane
J
K
L
M
N
P
Q
63
64
65
66
67
Lyewood Ho
Charlwood
Park Lane
Soame's Lane
Snugglers Lane
Petersfield Road
Monkwood
Harcombe
Parkside Lane
Stapley Lane
Parkstone Road
Soames Farm
Soame's Lane
Hill Farm Road
Merryfield Farm
West Tisted Common
Bramdean Common
Brick Kiln Lane
Brick Kiln Farm
Brick Kiln Lane
Clinkley Road
West Tisted
Green La
Brewers Lane
Punsholt Lane
The Jumps
306
A32
Wolfhanger Farm
Ashen Wood House
Sages Lane
Slys Farm
Fawley Lane
Punsholt Farm
Purser's
Farm
Hempland Lane
Punsholt Lane
Filmore Hill
Hinton Woodlands Farm
Filmorehill Lane
Filmorehill Lane
Bailey Green
A32
Three Horse Shoes Farm
Three Horse Shoes Lane
Lane
The Dean
A272
Kitt's Lane
West Meon Woodlands
Stocks Lane
Stock Farm
Privett
Woodlands Farm
Shutt's Copse
Stocks Lane
West Meon Hut
A272
Highfield
Marlands
Hayling Wood
Mardell Farm
313
R
1
2
3
4
5
6
7
8
9
10
11
12
31
30
29
28
27
26

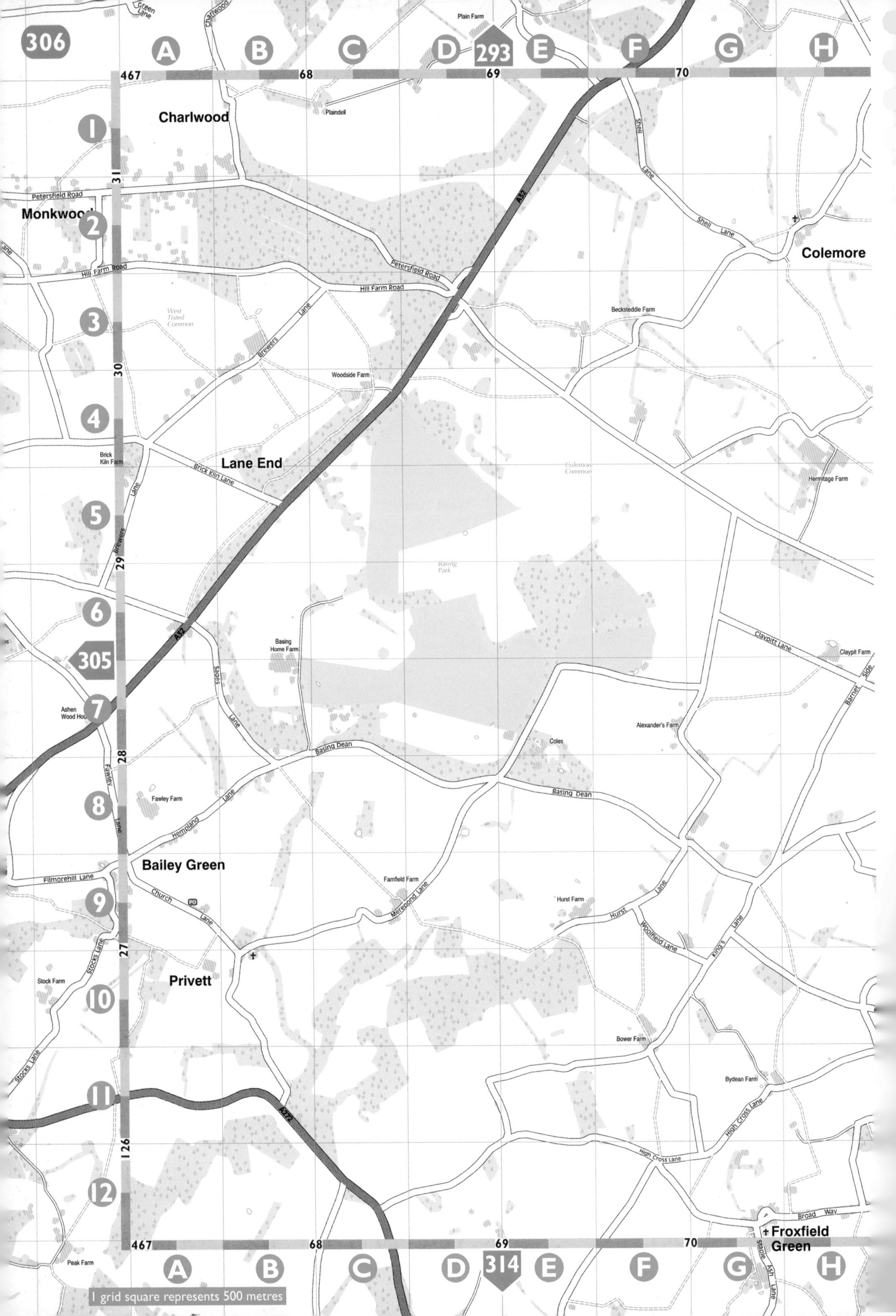
306
293
305
314
A B C D E F G H
1 2 3 4 5 6 7 8 9 10 11 12
467 68 69 70
31 30 29 28 27 126
Charlwood
Monkwood
Colemore
Lane End
Bailey Green
Privett
Froxfield Green
Plain Farm
Plaindell
Green Lane
Charlwood
Petersfield Road
Hill Farm Road
Hill Farm Road
Petersfield Road
West Tisted Common
Brewers Lane
Woodside Farm
Shell Lane
Shell Lane
Becksteddle Farm
A32
Brick Kiln Farm
Brick Kiln Lane
Colemore Common
Hermitage Farm
Brewers Lane
Basing Park
Basing Home Farm
Claypitt Lane
Claypit Farm
Barnet Side
Ashen Wood House
Sages Lane
Alexander's Farm
Coles
Basing Dean
Basing Dean
Fawley Lane
Fawley Farm
Hempland Lane
Filmorehill Lane
Church Lane
Farnfield Farm
Merepond Lane
Hurst Farm
Hurst Lane
Woolfield Lane
King's Lane
Stock Farm
Stocks Lane
Stocks Lane
Bower Farm
Bydean Farm
A272
High Cross Lane
High Cross Lane
Broad Way
Stable Ash Lane
Peak Farm
1 grid square represents 500 metres

Empshott Green
Empshott
Goleigh Farm
Keyham Farm
Vann Farm
Lythanger
Hawkley Hurst
Slade Farm
Church Farm
Field Farm
Manor House
Lowergreen Farm
Hawkley
Five Ash Farm
Pococks Lane
Hawkley Road
Warren Farm
Cheesecombe Farm Lane
Barnet Side
Oakshott Farm
Ragmore Lane
Green Lane
Warren Lane
Warren Corner
King's Lane
Oakshott
Hill Farm
Cottage Lane
Ivyhouse Lane
Blackmore Lane
Ivyhouse Farm
Bensgreen Farm
Honeycritch Lane
Old Litten Lane
Wheatham Farm
Ringsgreen Lane
The Slade
High Cross Lane
Cockshott Lane
Week Green Farm
Wyke Green Farm
High Cross
Froxfield Endowed Infant School
Hangers Way
Ashford Chace
Mill Lane
Bushy Hill
Steep Marsh Farm
Brickyards Ind Estate
Soalwood Lane
Stoner Hill
Broadhanger
King Lane
Broad Way
Island
Church Common
Steep
Steep School
Steep Farm
Stonerwood Park
Bedales

294
308
315
120

308
295
307
316
120
121
Empshott Green
Empshott
Greatham
Liss Forest
Burgates
West Liss
The Mint
Hill Side
East Liss
LISS
Prince's Marsh
Steep Marsh
Selborne Road
B3006
A3
A325 Woolmer Road
Farnham Road
Station Road
Hill Brow Road
Hawkley Road
Snailing Lane
Church Lane
Mill Lane
Forest Road
Warren Road
Stodham Lane
Tankerdale Lane
Le Court
Lythanger
Hawkley Hurst
Mill Farm
Greatham Primary School
Goleigh Farm House
Park Lands Farm
Scotland Farm
Barefoots Farm
Lyss Place
Wheatham Farm
Flexcombe
Coldhayes
Garden Centre
Bowyer's Common
Petersfield Golf Club
Brickyards Ind Estate
Steep Marsh Farm
Benhams Farm
GU33
1 grid square represents 500 metres

PORTSMI ROAD

Longmoor Road

Griggs Green

LIPHO

Longmoor Road

Liphook CE Junior School

Longmoor Road

Queens Road

Old Thorns Hotel, Golf & Country Club

Golf Course

Foley Manor

Ne

116

Wheatsheaf Common

PORTSMOUTH RD

Weavers Down

Forest Mere

B2070

Golf Course

Liphook Golf Club

Longmoor Inclosure

Home Park

Sussex Border Path

Ripsley House

The Wylds

Langley

Sussex Border Path

Langley Court

Chapel Common

Mangers

Reeds Lane

Reeds Lane

Palmers

Brewells Lane

Milland House

Road

Hampshire County West Sussex County

Rake Firs

Ciddy Hall

St Patrick's Lane

St Patrick's Lane

Rake Business Park

Rake CE First School

Maysleith

Maysleith Wood

Rake

B2070

Bull Hill

Hatch Lane

Sandy Lane

Princess

Canhouse Lane

Hampshire County West Sussex County

B2070

Sussex Border Path

Goldring

Hill Brow

Canhouse Lane

Great Trippetts Farm

Rake Road

Chorley Common

Milland

New Barn Farm

Harting Combe

Cook's Pond Road

Bobbolds Farm

Border Wood

Tullecombe

Trotten Marsh

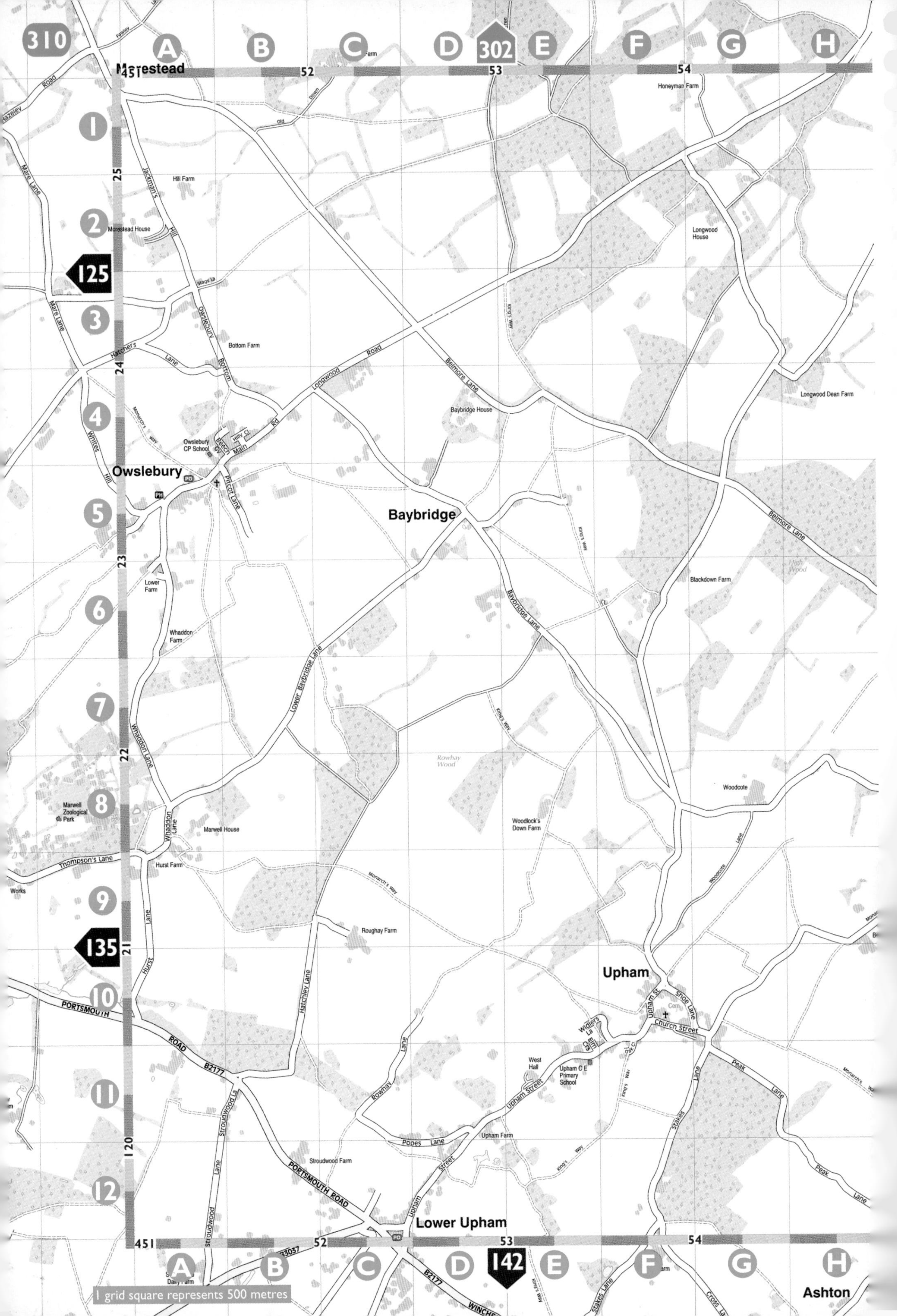

310

A   B   C   D   302   E   F   G   H

Morestead

52   53   54

1

25

Hill Farm

2

Morestead House

125

3

24

Bottom Farm

Owslebury
CP School

Owslebury

PO

PH

5

23

Lower
Farm

Baybridge House

Baybridge

6

Whaddon
Farm

Longwood
House

Honeyman Farm

Longwood Dean Farm

Blackdown Farm

High
Wood

Belmore Lane

7

22

Rowhay
Wood

8

Marwell
Zoological
Park

Marwell House

Woodcote

Woodlock's
Down Farm

9

Thompson's Lane

Hurst Farm

Works

135

21

Roughay Farm

Upham

10

PORTSMOUTH

ROAD

B2177

Cem

Church Street

West
Hall

Upham C E
Primary
School

11

20

Popes Lane

Upham Farm

Stroudwood Farm

12

PORTSMOUTH ROAD

Lower Upham

PO

451   52   53   142   54

A   B   B3037   C   D   E   F   G   H

WINCHE

Ashton

1 grid square represents 500 metres

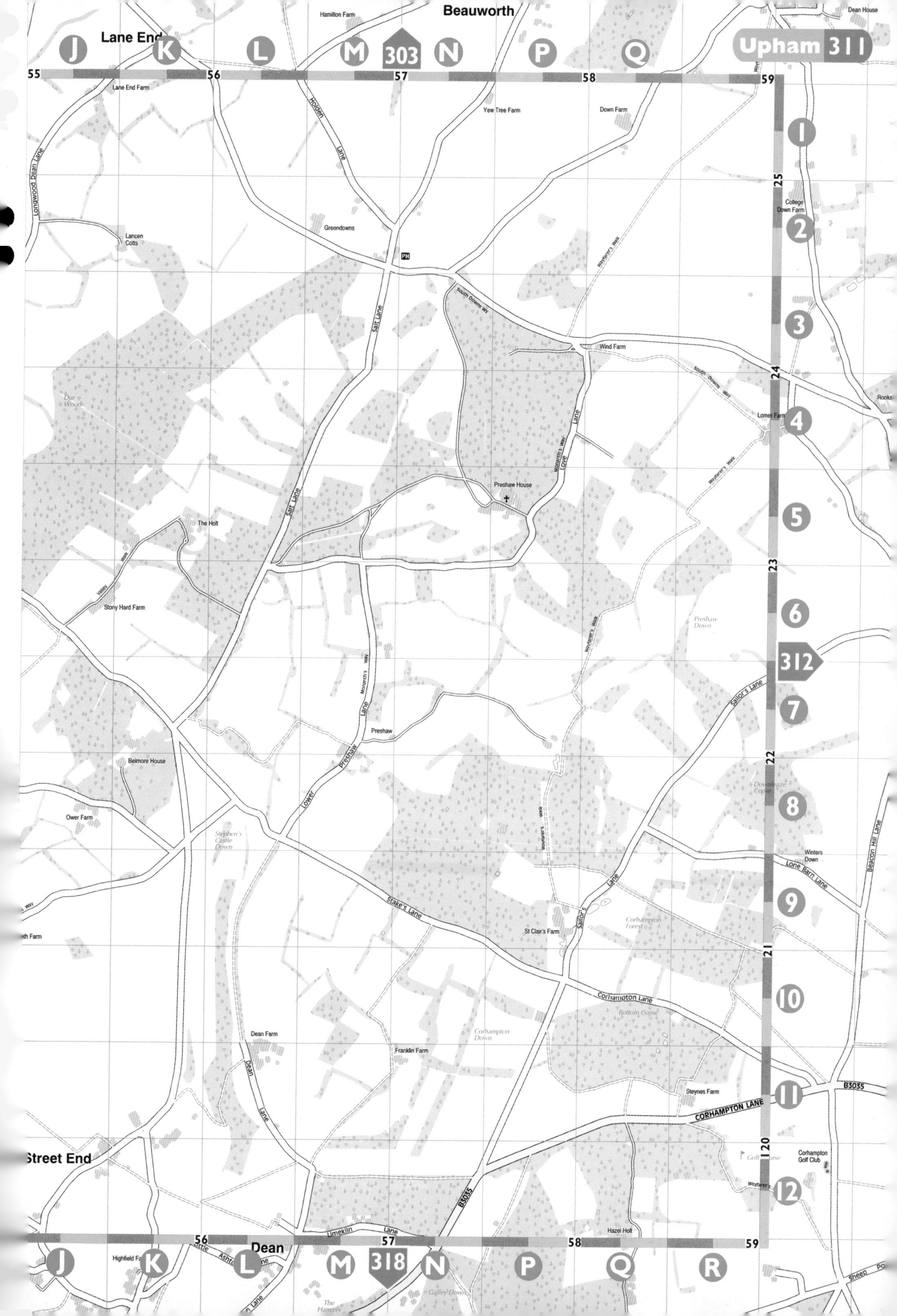

Beauworth
Hamilton Farm
Dean House
Lane End
Upham 311
303
J
K
L
M
N
P
Q
55
56
57
58
59
Lane End Farm
Holden Lane
Yew Tree Farm
Down Farm
Longwood Dean Lane
25
College Down Farm
Lancen Cotts
Greendowns
PH
Wayfarer's Walk
South Downs Way
Salt Lane
Wind Farm
24
South Downs Way
Rooks
Lomer Farm
Love Lane
Monarch's Way
Preshaw House
Wayfarer's Walk
Salt Lane
The Holt
23
Valley Walk
Stony Hard Farm
Preshaw Down
312
Monarch's Way
Sailor's Lane
Preshaw
Preshaw Lane
Lower
22
Belmore House
Downleaze Copse
Ower Farm
Stephen's Castle Down
Winters Down
Lone Barn Lane
Beacon Hill Lane
Stake's Lane
Sailor's Lane
St Clair's Farm
Corhampton Forest
21
Corhampton Lane
Bottom Copse
Dean Farm
Corhampton Down
Franklin Farm
Dean Lane
Steynes Farm
B3035
CORHAMPTON LANE
20
Street End
Golf Course
Corhampton Golf Club
Wayfarer's
B3035
Limekiln Lane
Hazel Holt
Dean
Highfield Fa
Little Ashton Lane
318
R
Sheep
Galley Down
The Hangers
1
2
3
4
5
6
7
8
9
10
11
12

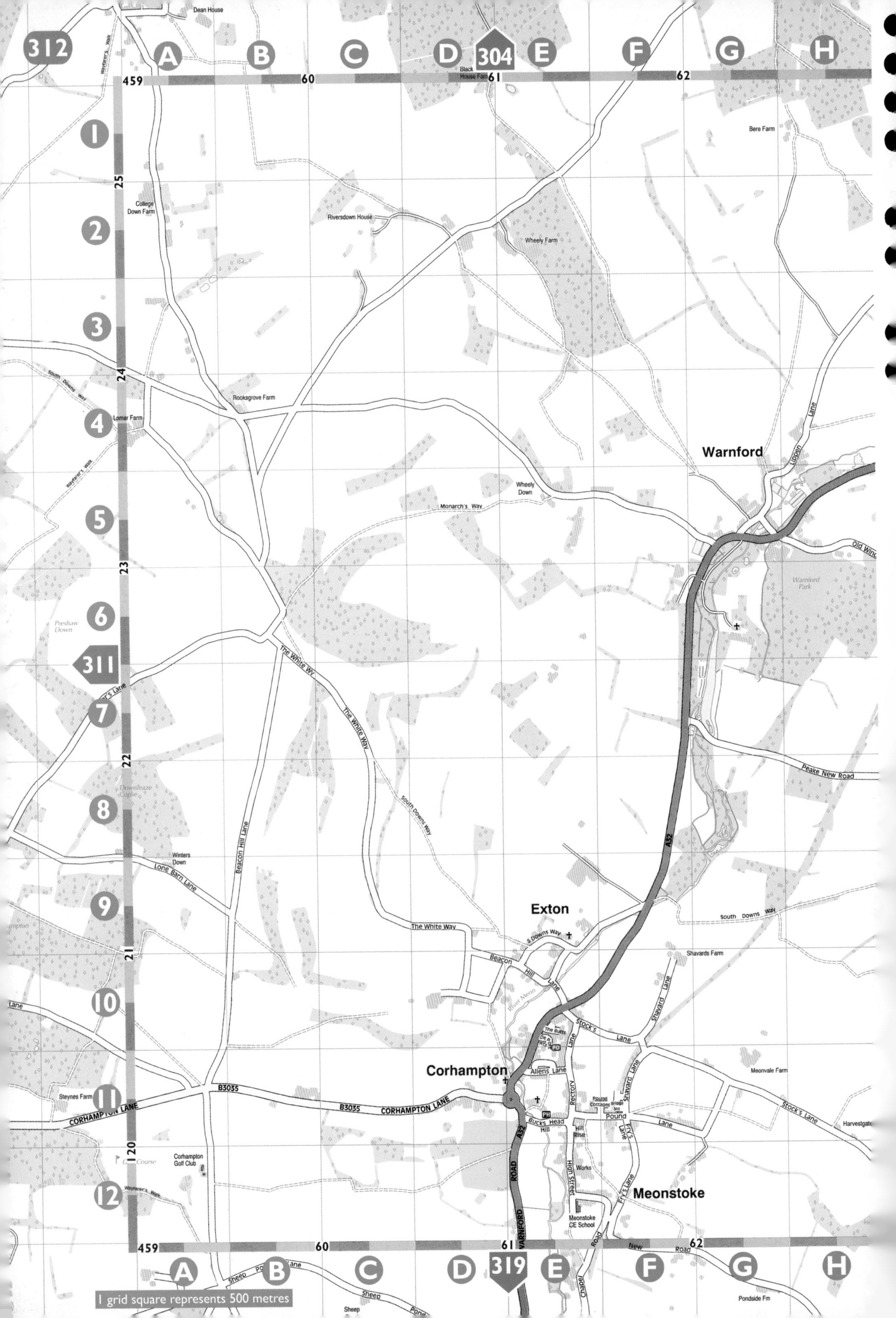

312
304
311
319
Dean House
Black House Farm
Bere Farm
College Down Farm
Riversdown House
Wheely Farm
Rooksgrove Farm
Lomer Farm
South Downs Way
Wayfarer's Walk
Warnford
Wheely Down
Monarch's Way
Old Winchester
Warnford Park
Preshaw Down
The White Way
Peake New Road
Downleaze Copse
Winters Down
Lone Barn Lane
Beacon Hill Lane
South Downs Way
A32
Exton
Shavards Farm
Shavard Lane
Stock's Lane
River Meon
Corhampton
Allens Lane
Meonvale Farm
Steynes Farm
B3035
CORHAMPTON LANE
Bucks Head Hill
Rectory Lane
Pound Cottages
Pound Lane
Fry's Lane
Hill Rise
High Street
Works
Harvestgate
Corhampton Golf Club
Golf Course
Meonstoke
Meonstoke CE School
VARNFORD ROAD
Chapel Road
New Road
Sheep Pond Lane
Pondside Fm
1 grid square represents 500 metres

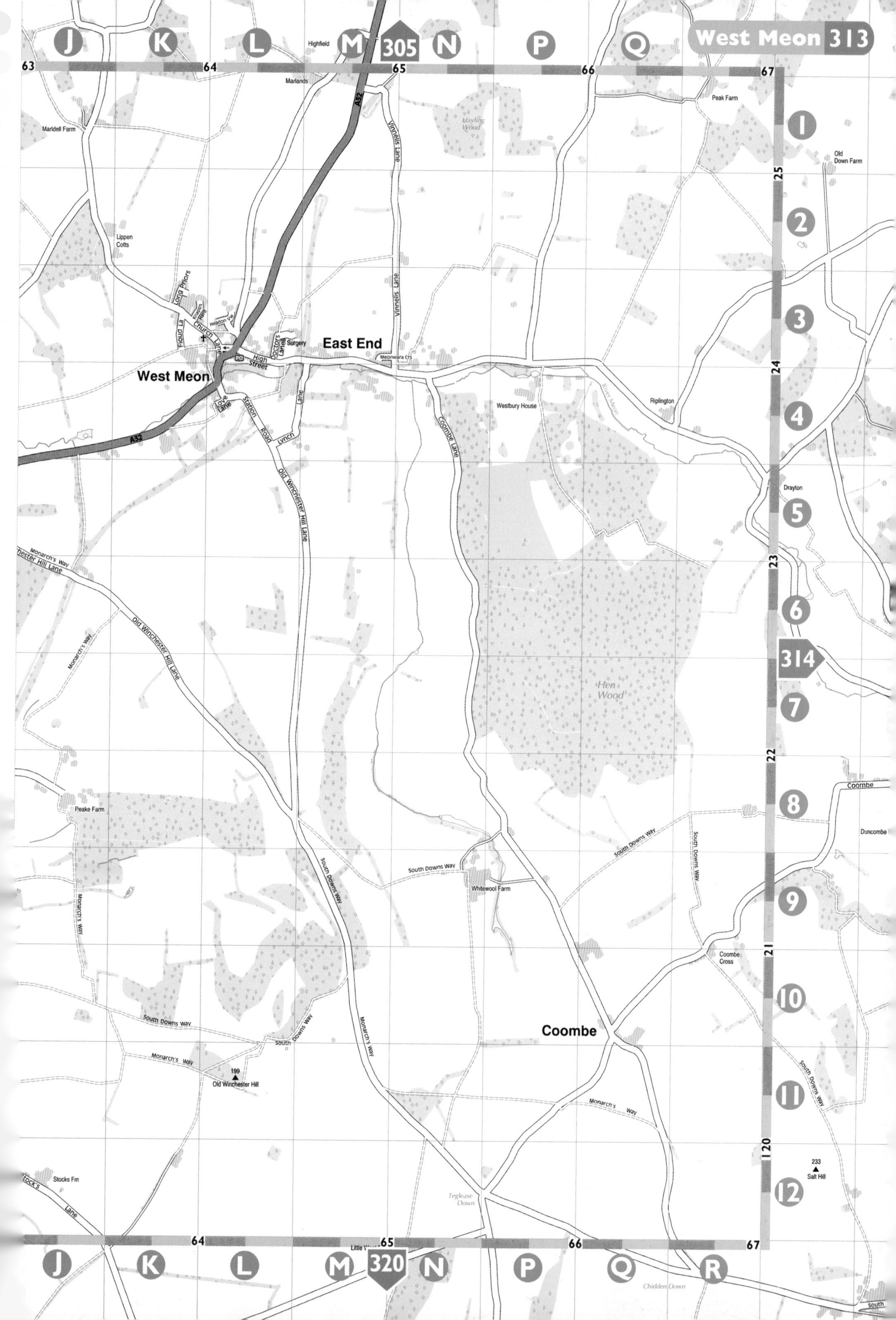

J K L Highfield M 305 N P Q

63 64 65 66 67

Marlands

Mardell Farm

1

Old Down Farm

Lippen Cotts

2

25

Long Priors

3

Doctors Lane Surgery East End Meonwara Ch.

24 4

West Meon High Street Station Road Lynch Vinnells Lane

Westbury House Drayton

5

Riplington

River Meon

23 6

Monarch's Way Chester Hill Lane

314

Hen Wood

7

Old Winchester Hill Lane

22

Peake Farm

Coombe 8

South Downs Way

Duncombe

South Downs Way Whitewool Farm

South Downs Way South Downs Way

9

Monarch's Way

Coombe Cross

South Downs Way 21

South Coombe 10

Monarch's Way South Downs Way

South Monarch's Way

199 Old Winchester Hill

Coombe

Monarch's Way

11

South Downs Way

20

233 Salt Hill

Stocks Fm Stock's Lane

12

Teglease Down

64 65 66 67

J K L M 320 N P Q R

Little Wood

Chidden Down

south

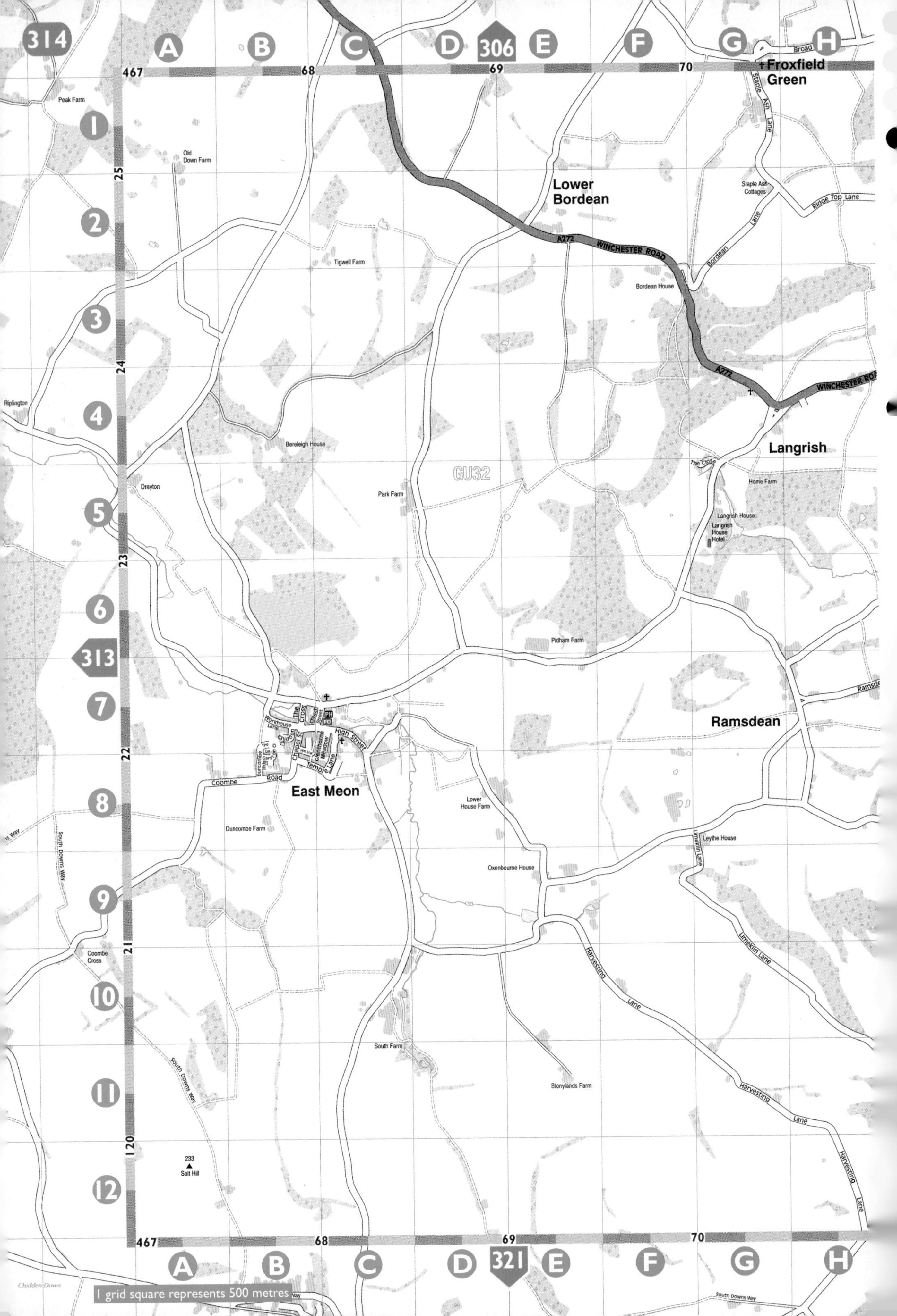

314
306
313
321
A
B
C
D
E
F
G
H
1
2
3
4
5
6
7
8
9
10
11
12
467
68
69
70
25
24
23
22
21
120
Froxfield Green
Broad
Staple Ash Lane
Peak Farm
Old Down Farm
Lower Bordean
Staple Ash Cottages
Ridge Top Lane
Bordean Lane
A272
WINCHESTER ROAD
Bordean House
Tigwell Farm
Riplington
Bereleigh House
Langrish
The Close
Home Farm
Langrish House
Langrish House Hotel
GU32
Drayton
Park Farm
Pidham Farm
Ramsdean
East Meon
Workhouse Lane
The Cross
Church Street
High Street
Chapel St
Hill View
Glenthorne Meadow
Temple Lane
Duncombe Road
Coombe Road
PH
PO
Lower House Farm
Duncombe Farm
South Downs Way
Leythe House
Limekiln Lane
Oxenbourne House
Coombe Cross
Harvesting Lane
South Farm
Stonylands Farm
233
Salt Hill
Chidden Down
1 grid square represents 500 metres

J
K
L
307
M
N
P
Q
71
72
Church Common
73
74
75
Steep
Steep Farm
Steep School
Church Road
Stonerwood Park
Wheeler's Farm
Ridge Top Lane
Ridge
Broadhanger
Bedales School
Ridge Farm
Ridge Common Lane
Dunhurst (Bedales Junior School)
A3
Harrow Lane
Waterworks Road
Lythe Lane
Lythe Farm
Soal Farm
Collyers
Whitehouse Gdns
Bell Hill
Reservoir Lane
Orchard
Monks
Ridge Common
Lythe Lane
Aldersnapp Farm
Tilmore Road
Bell Hill Rdg
Woodbury Av
Long Road
Kingsfernsden Lane
B2070
Buckmore Avenue
Beckham Lane
Stonenam
Stroud End
Stroud Farm
Rothercombe Lane
A272
WINCHESTER ROAD
Winchester Road
Rushes Road
Station Road
Tilmore
North Rd
Highfield Rd
Churchers College
Petersfield Town FC
The Herne Junior School
The Herne Farm Leisure Centre
Willowdale Cl
Stroud
Langrish Primary School
Dukes
Princes Road
Noreuil Rd
Queens Road
Petersfield Station
Osborne Road
Barham Rd
COLLEGE ST
STATION RD
Love Lane
Moggs Mead
PETERSFIELD
Gloucester Close
Council Building
Amey Ind Est
Swan
Chapel St
High St
The Square
Buckingham Road
Bedford Road
Borough Hill
Petersfield Community Hospital
Petersfield Inf Sch
Peter's Rd
DRAGON STREET
TOR WY
Bepton Down
Heath
North Stroud Farm
North Stroud Lane
Ramsdean Road
Petersfield Business Park
Borough Road
Churchers College Junior Department
Superstore
The Avenue
Heath Road West
Heath Pond
Stroudbridge Farm
Grange Road
The Petersfield School
B2070
FORE
Cranford Road
Paddock Way
Larcombe Road
THE CAUSEWAY
Causeway
1
2
3
4
5
6
7
316
SUSSEX ROAD
Petersfield Golf Club (old course)
25
24
23
22
120
Weston Lane
Weston
Wyds Lane
8
Harroway Farm
B2070 THE CAUSEWAY
Nursted House
9
Buriton Business Park
Bolinge Hill Farm
21
Greenway Lane
Ramsdean Down
10
Hangers Way
Cowhouse Farm
Glebe Road
Sumner Rd
Petersfield Rd
Bones Lane
North Lane
Pitcroft Lane
11
271
Butser Hill
Heath
High Street
Buriton Primary School
Kiln Lane
Buriton
Limekiln Lane
South La
Kiln La
Hangers Way
120
12
South Downs Way
Newbarn Road
South Downs Way
Coulters Dean Fm
72
73
74
75
J
K
L
M
322
N
P
Q
R
Was Down

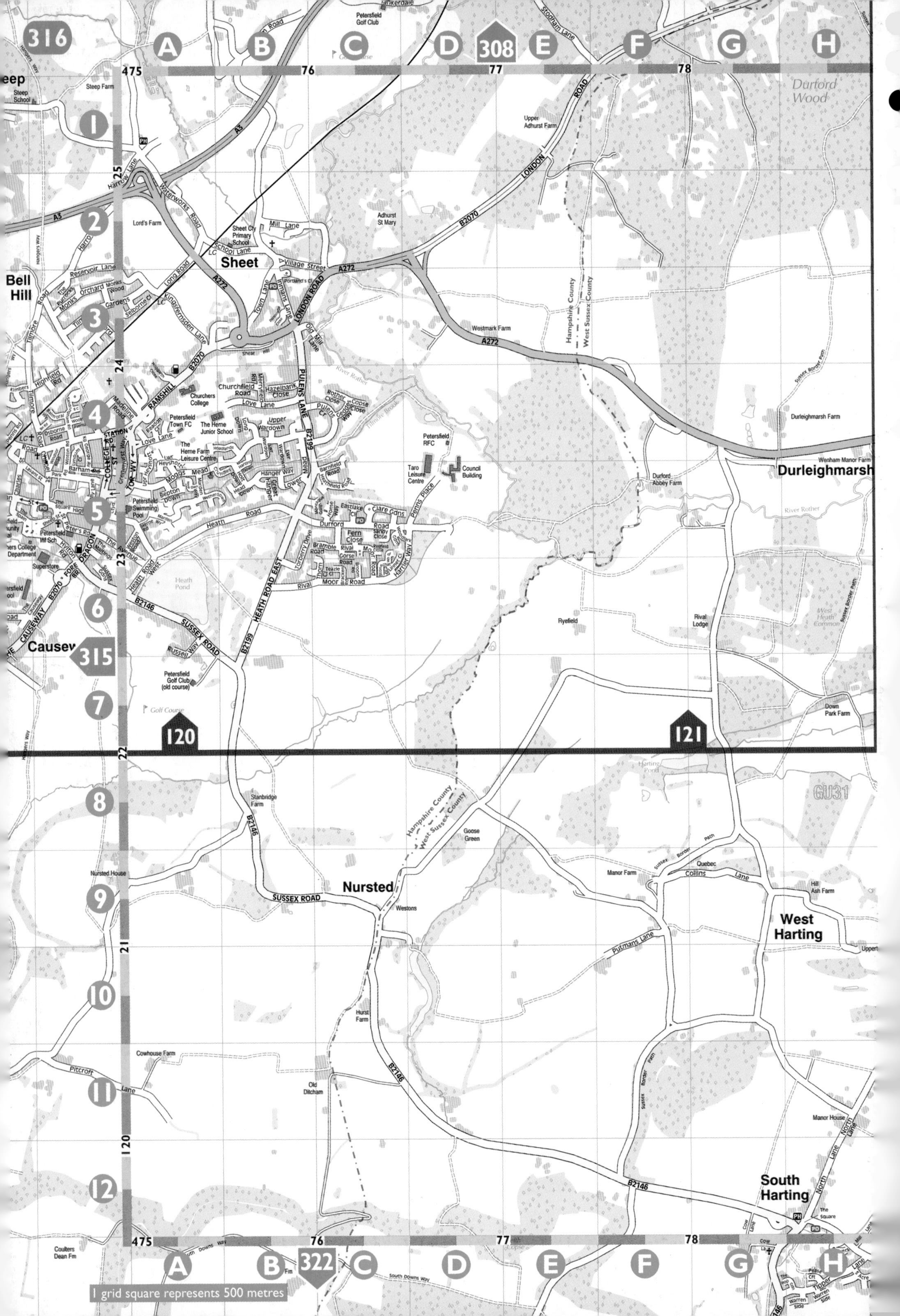
316
308
315
120
121
322
A
B
C
D
E
F
G
H
475
76
77
78
1
2
3
4
5
6
7
8
9
10
11
12
Steep
Steep Farm
Petersfield Golf Club
Durford Wood
Upper Adhurst Farm
Lord's Farm
Sheet
Sheet Cty Primary School
Mill Lane
School Lane
Village Street
Adhurst St Mary
Bell Hill
Reservoir Lane
Monks Orchard
Long Road
Kingsfernsden Lane
London Road
Westmark Farm
Hampshire County
West Sussex County
Churchers College
Churchfield Road
Hazelbank Close
Love Lane
Pulens Lane
Petersfield Town FC
The Herne Junior School
The Herne Farm Leisure Centre
Upper Wardown
Petersfield RFC
Taro Leisure Centre
Council Building
Durleighmarsh Farm
Wenham Manor Farm
Durleighmarsh
Durford Abbey Farm
River Rother
Penns Place
Clare Gdns
Heath Road
Petersfield Swimming Pool
Superstore
Heath Pond
Heath Road East
Sussex Road
Russell Way
Petersfield Golf Club (old course)
Ryefield
Rival Lodge
West Heath Common
Down Park Farm
Causey
Stanbridge Farm
Goose Green
GU31
Nursted House
Nursted
Westons
Manor Farm
Quebec
Collins Lane
Hill Ash Farm
West Harting
Putmans Lane
Hurst Farm
Cowhouse Farm
Pitcroft Lane
Old Ditcham
Manor House
North Lane
South Harting
The Square
Coulters Dean Fm
South Downs Way
A3
A272
B2070
B2146
B2199
1 grid square represents 500 metres

J K L M 309 N P Q
Tullecombe
79 80 81 82 83
Trotten Marsh
Bobbolds Farm
Rogate Common
Borden Wood
Rondle Wood
Borden Lane
Borden
Chithurst Lane
Rogate Lodge
Dangstein
Gatehouse Lane
Halecommon
Terwick Common
Fyning
Slade Lane
Slade Farm
Cumber's Farm
A272
Parsonage Est
Red House Ct
Rogate CE Primary School
Habin Hill
Lane
Gatehouse Farm
Rogate
Carbitts
Haben Farm
Wakeham Farm
Fair Oak
Habin
Sandhill House
Trotton
Rother Lane
River Rother
Mill La
Terwick Lane
Southdowns Country Hotel
Dumpford Lane
Works
Little Barn
Dumpford
Nyewood
Furze Meadow
Greenfields Cl
Dumpford Park Farm
Trotton Road
Goldr Farm
Woodhouse Farm
Elsted Road
Elsted Marsh
Elsted Rough
Elsted Road
Road
Orchard Cl
Hollist Lane
Harting Street
Lane
Elsted
Orchard Cl
PH
Turkey Island
East Harting
323
New House Farm
Redlands
J K L M N P Q R
1 2 3 4 5 6 7 8 9 10 11 12
25 24 23 22 21 120

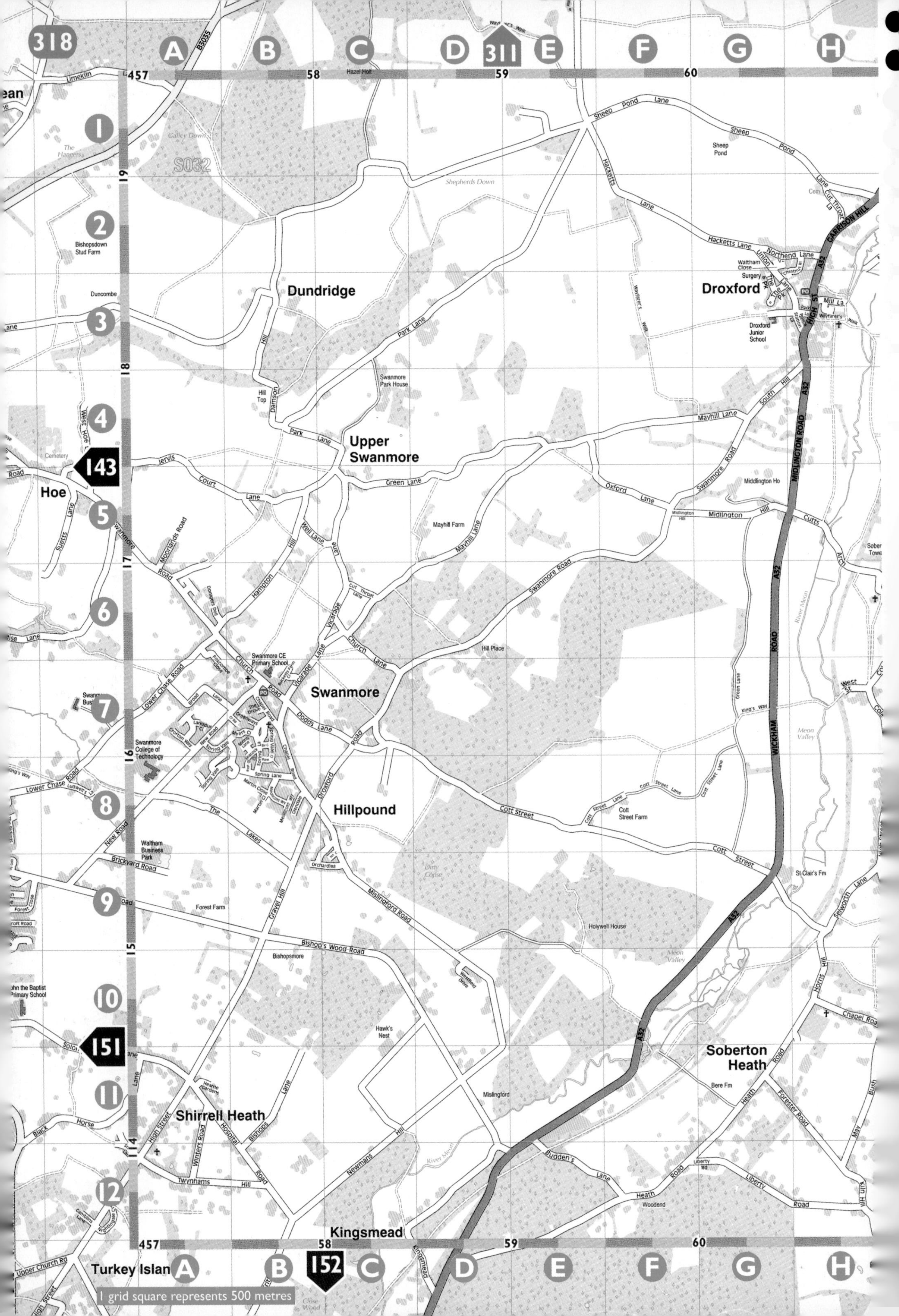
318
311
143
151
152
Dundridge
Droxford
Upper Swanmore
Hoe
Swanmore
Hillpound
Shirrell Heath
Soberton Heath
Kingsmead
Turkey Islan
Sheep Pond Lane
Hacketts Lane
Park Lane
Mayhill Lane
Swanmore Road
Midlington Road
Wickham Road
Cott Street
Bishop's Wood Road
Mislingford Road
Gravel Hill
1 grid square represents 500 metres

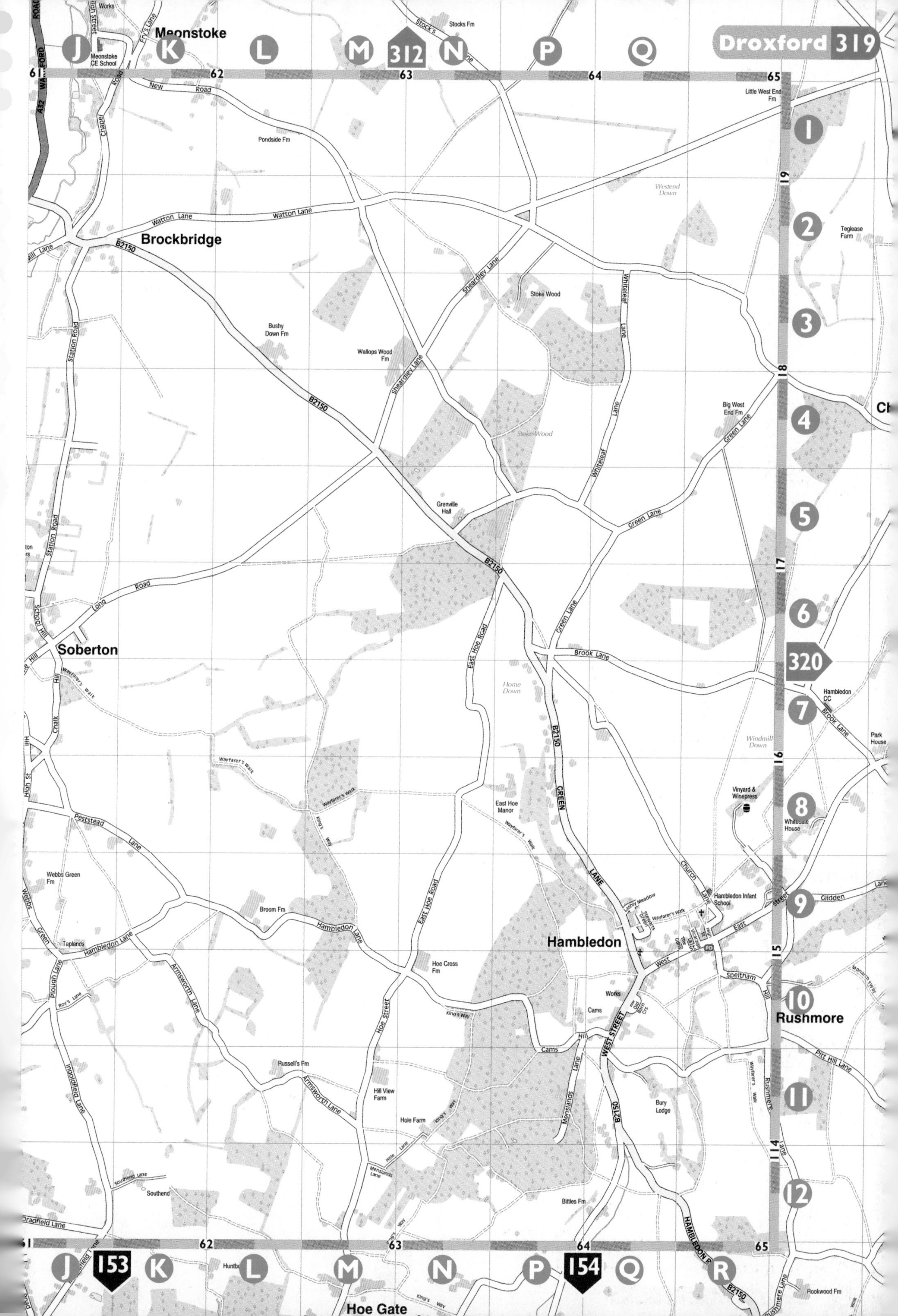
Meonstoke
Meonstoke CE School
Works
Stocks Fm
Little West End Fm
Pondside Fm
Westend Down
Teglease Farm
Watton Lane
Brockbridge
B2150
Stoke Wood
Bushy Down Fm
Wallops Wood Fm
Sheardley Lane
Whiteleaf Lane
Big West End Fm
Green Lane
Station Road
Grenville Hall
Long Road
School Hill
Soberton
East Hoe Road
Brook Lane
Home Down
Hambledon CC
Windmill Down
Park House
Wayfarer's Walk
Vinyard & Winepress
Whitedale House
East Hoe Manor
King's Way
Peststead Lane
Webbs Green Fm
Broom Fm
Hambledon Lane
Church Lane
Hambledon Infant School
Hambledon
East Street
West Street
Speltnam
Rushmore
Clidden
Taplands
Plough Lane
Hoe Cross Fm
Armsworth Lane
Roy's Lane
Hoe Street
Works
Cams
Cams Hill
Pitt Hill Lane
Russell's Fm
Hill View Farm
Hole Farm
Menslands Lane
Hole Lane
Bury Lodge
Rushmere Lane
Southend Lane
Southend
Bittles Fm
Dradfield Lane
Hambledon Road
Hoe Gate
Rookwood Fm
A32 Wickham Road
312
320
153
154
J K L M N P Q R
61 62 63 64 65
19 18 17 16 15 114

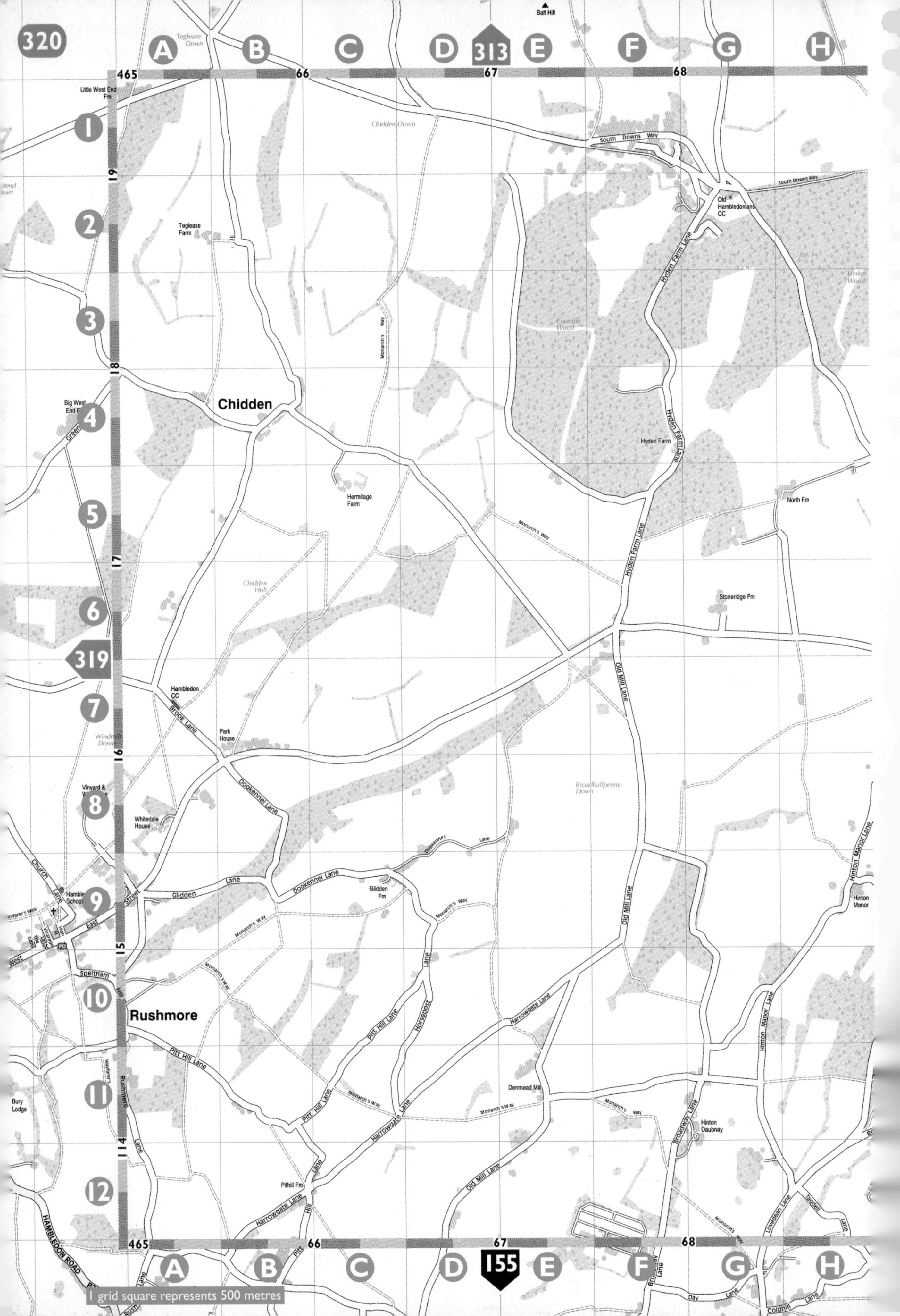
Salt Hill
Teglease Down
313
Little West End Fm
Chidden Down
South Downs Way
Old Hambledonians CC
Teglease Farm
Hyden Farm Lane
Hyden Wood
Coombe Wood
Monarch's Way
Chidden
Big West End Fm
Green
Hyden Farm
Hermitage Farm
North Fm
Chidden Holt
Stoneridge Fm
319
Hambledon CC
Brook Lane
Park House
Old Mill Lane
Windmill Down
Vinyard & Winery
Dookennel Lane
Broadhalfpenny Down
Whitedale House
Church Lane
Hambledon School
Glidden Lane
Glidden Fm
Hinton Manor Lane
Hinton Manor
Wayfarer's Walk
East Street
West Street
Speltnam Hill
Horsepost Lane
Rushmore
Pitt Hill Lane
Harrowgate Lane
Denmead Mill
Bury Lodge
Rushmere Lane
Broadway Lane
Hinton Daubnay
Pithill Fm
HAMBLEDON ROAD
Lovedean Lane
Day Lane
Coldhill Lane
155
1 grid square represents 500 metres

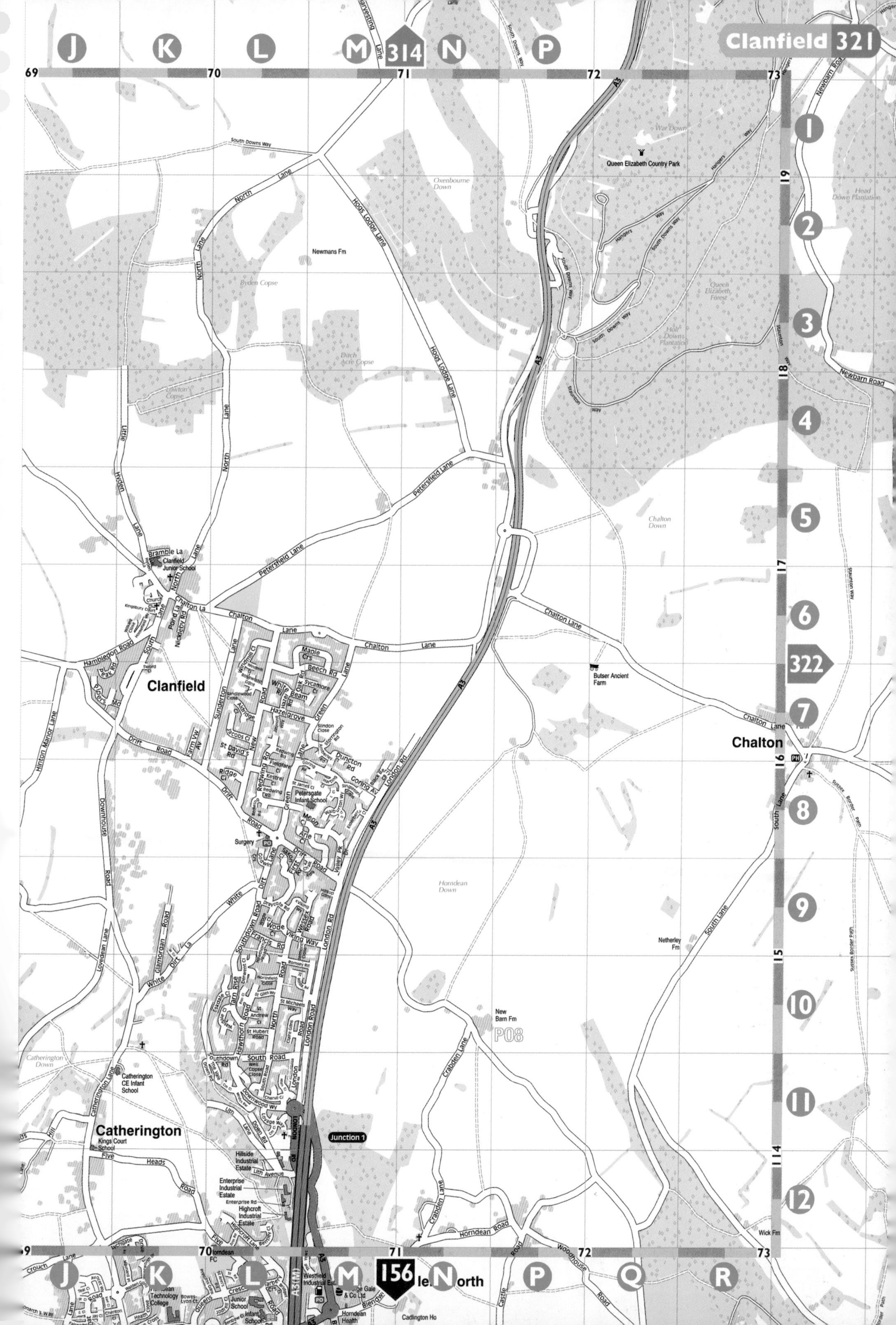

J K L M N P
314
69 70 71 72 73
South Downs Way
North Lane
Hogs Lodge Lane
A3
War Down
Queen Elizabeth Country Park
Oxenbourne Down
Newmans Fm
Byden Copse
Ditch Acre Copse
Chalton Copse
Head Down Plantation
Queen Elizabeth Forest
Holt Downs Plantation
Staunton Way
Newbarn Road
Hangers Way
Little Hyden Lane
Petersfield Lane
Chalton Down
Chalton Lane
Bramble La
Clanfield Junior School
Clanfield
Hambledon Road
Drift Road
Hinton Manor Lane
Downhouse Road
Butser Ancient Farm
322
Chalton
South Lane
Sussex Border Path
Petersgate Infant School
Surgery
London Rd
Horndean Down
Netherley Fm
Southdown Road
Viking Way
White Dirt La
Glamorgan Road
Lovedean Lane
New Barn Fm
PO8
Crabden Lane
Catherington Down
Catherington CE Infant School
Catherington
Kings Court School
Five Heads Road
Hillside Industrial Estate
Enterprise Industrial Estate
Highcroft Industrial Estate
Junction 1
A3(M)
Horndean Road
Woodhouse Road
Wick Fm
Horndean FC
Horndean Technology College
Westfield Industrial Est.
156
Cadlington Ho
Q R
1 2 3 4 5 6 7 8 9 10 11 12
19 18 17 16 15 114

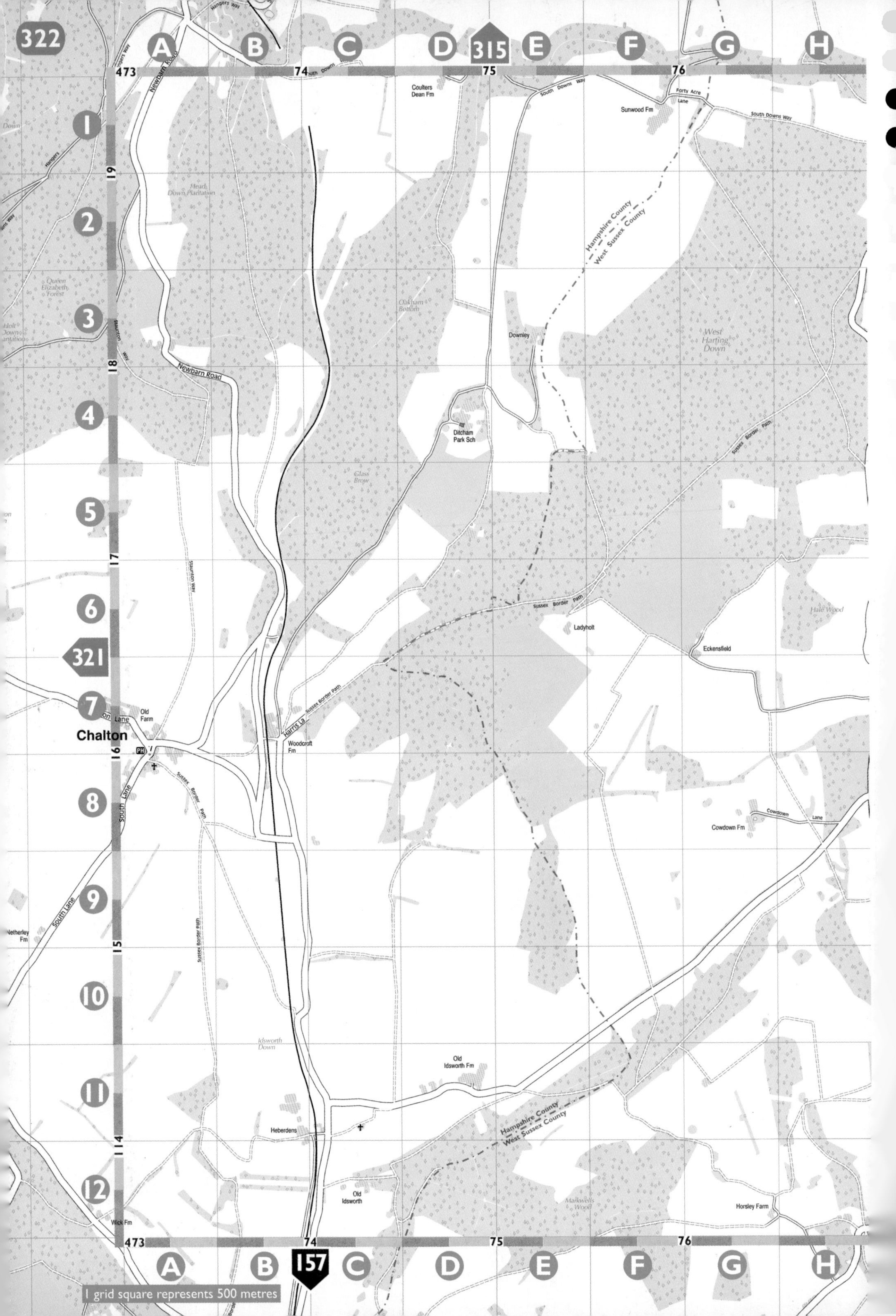
Chalton
Newbarn Road
Old Farm
Woodcroft Fm
Harris La
Sussex Border Path
South Downs Way
Coulters Dean Fm
Sunwood Fm
Forty Acre Lane
Hampshire County
West Sussex County
Downley
Ditcham Park Sch
West Harting Down
Ladyholt
Eckensfield
Hale Wood
Cowdown Fm
Cowdown Lane
Old Idsworth Fm
Heberdens
Old Idsworth
Idsworth Down
Horsley Farm
Wick Fm
Netherley Fm
South Lane
Staunton Way
Queen Elizabeth Forest
Mead Down Plantation
Oakham Bottom
Glass Brow
Markwells Wood
Hangers Way
1 grid square represents 500 metres

315
321
157

South Harting
East Harting
Turkey Island
Foxcombe Fm
Down Place
South Downs Way
Uppark (NT)
Up Park
Round Down
Telegraph House
North Marden Down
Pads Wood
Huckshott Fm
Littlegreen School
Fernbeds Down
Fernbeds Fm
Bevis's Thumb
Long Lane
North Marden
Hill Lands Farm
East Marden
East Marden Down
Compton
School Lane
Compton & Up Marden CE School
Up Marden
Locksash Farm
Locksash Lane
West Marden
Grevitts Copse
B2146
B2141
New Lane
Hill Lane
Telegraph Lane
Eastfield Lane
Orchard Cl
Harting Street
Tipper Lane
Warren Side
Culvers
Leith Copse
317

317

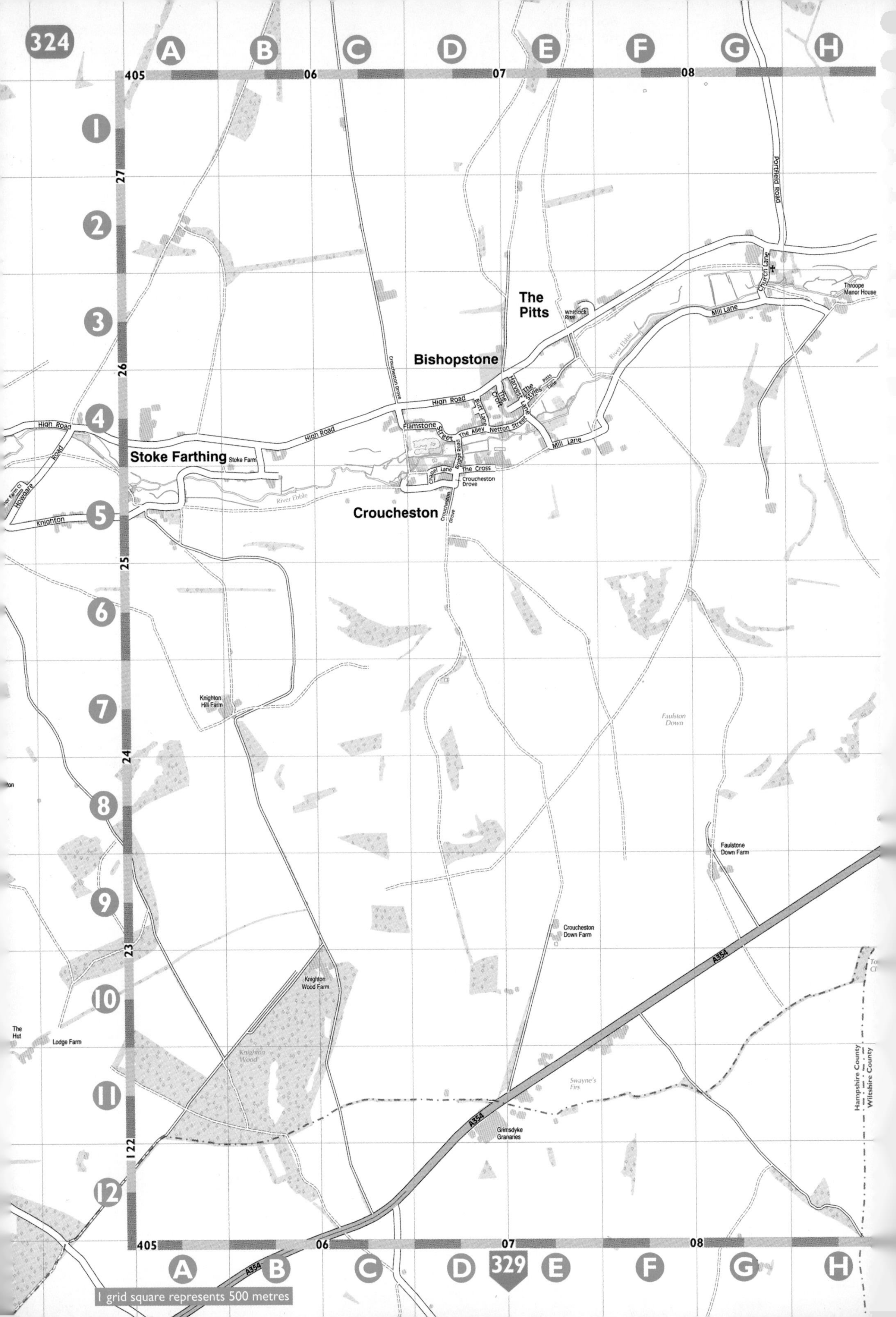

A B C D E F G H

405 06 07 08

1
27
2
3
26
4
5
25
6
7
24
8
9
23
10
11
22
12

405 06 07 08

A B D E F G H

The Pitts

Bishopstone

Whitlock Rise

River Ebble

Mill Lane

Church Lane

Portfield Road

Throope Manor House

Croucheston Drove

High Road

High Road

High Road

Stoke Farthing

Stoke Farm

River Ebble

Knighton

Howgare Road

Flamstone Street

Rectory Lane

Burt Lane

The Alley

Netton Street

The Cross

The Butts

Pitts Lane

Mill Lane

Chapel Lane

Crowcheston Drove

Croucheston

Knighton Hill Farm

Faulston Down

Faulstone Down Farm

Crowcheston Down Farm

A354

Knighton Wood Farm

Knighton Wood

The Hut

Lodge Farm

Swayne's Firs

A354

Grimsdyke Granaries

A354

Hampshire County

Wiltshire County

To CI

1 grid square represents 500 metres

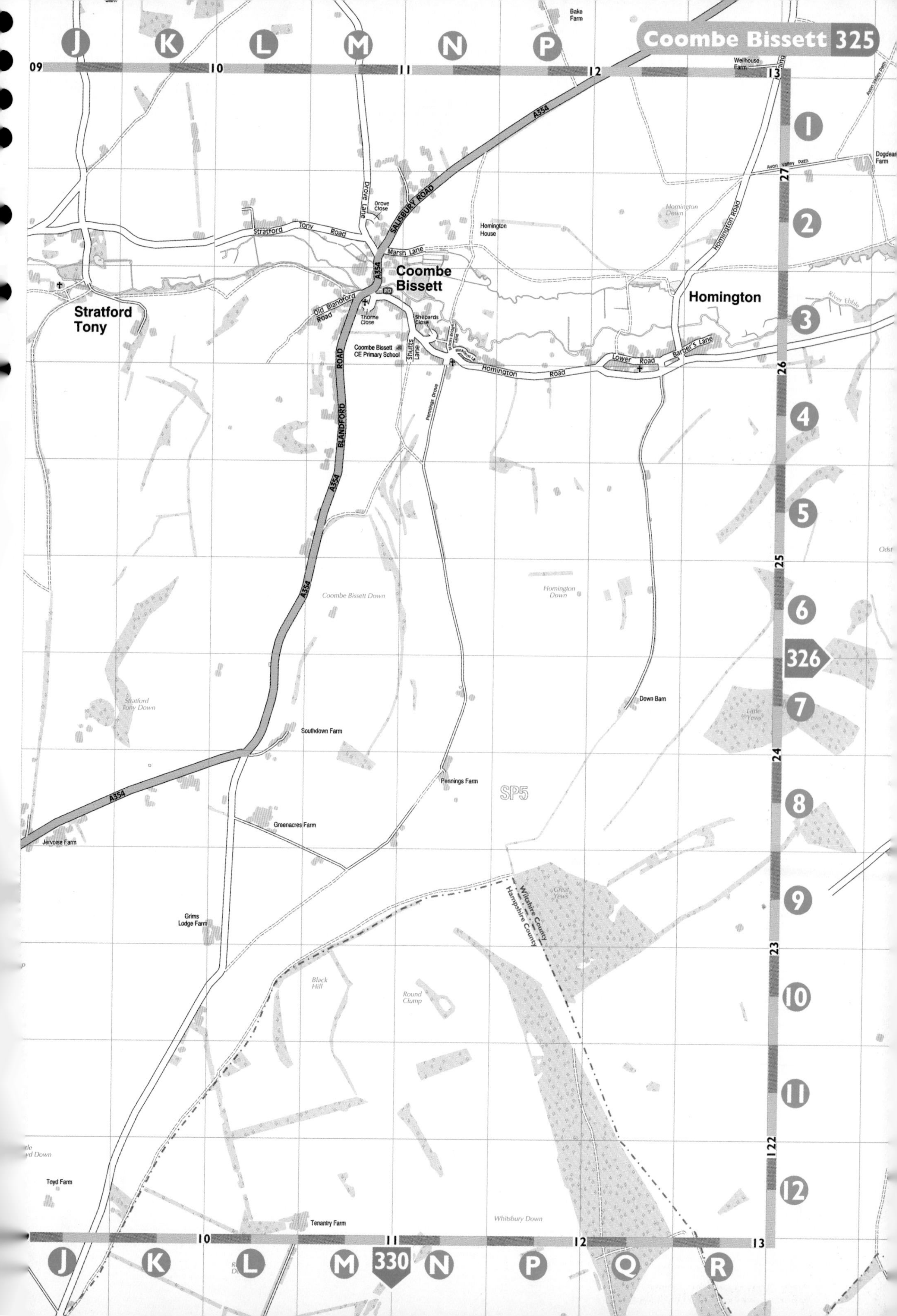
J
K
L
M
N
P
Bake Farm
Wellhouse Farm
A354
SALISBURY ROAD
Avon Valley Path
Dogdean Farm
Drove Lane
Drove Close
Stratford Tony Road
Homington House
Homington Down
Homington Road
Marsh Lane
Coombe Bissett
PO
Homington
River Ebble
Stratford Tony
Old Blandford Road
Thorne Close
Shepards Close
Coombe Bissett CE Primary School
Shutts Lane
Lower Road
Barber's Lane
Homington Road
BLANDFORD ROAD
Pennings Drove
Coombe Bissett Down
Homington Down
326
Down Barn
Stratford Tony Down
Little Yews
Southdown Farm
Pennings Farm
SP5
Greenacres Farm
Jervoise Farm
Wiltshire County
Hampshire County
Great Yews
Grims Lodge Farm
Black Hill
Round Clump
Toyd Farm
Tenantry Farm
Whitsbury Down
330
Q
R
1
2
3
4
5
6
7
8
9
10
11
12

326
A
B
C
D
E
F
G
H
Wellhouse Farm
Homington Road
413
14
15
16
Avon Valley Path
Odstock Road
A&E
Salisbury District Hospital
Dogdean Farm
Road
Manor Farm
Park Lane
Lower Farm
A338
Longford Park
Homington Down
Longford Farm
Homington
River Ebble
Odstock
Nunton
The Old Dairy
PH
PO
Bodenha
Barber's Lane
Odstock Primary Sch
Shepards Close
New Hall Hospital
New Hall
Odstock Road
Nunton Drove
THE HIGHWAY
Odstock Down
Odstock Copse
Matrimony Farm
325
Barn
Clearbury Down
Charlton Manor Farm
Yews Farm
The Giant's Grave
New Court Down Barn
The Giant's Chair
New Court Down
Wick Down
Wick Lane
Wick
Botley's Farm
331
Hampshire County
1
2
3
4
5
6
7
8
9
10
11
12
27
26
25
24
23
122
1 grid square represents 500 metres

J   K   L   M   N   P   Q
17   18   19   20   21

Alderbury

Whaddon

Grimstead
296

Charlton-All-Saints

126

Downton
332

J   K   L   M   N   P   Q   R
17   18   19   20   21

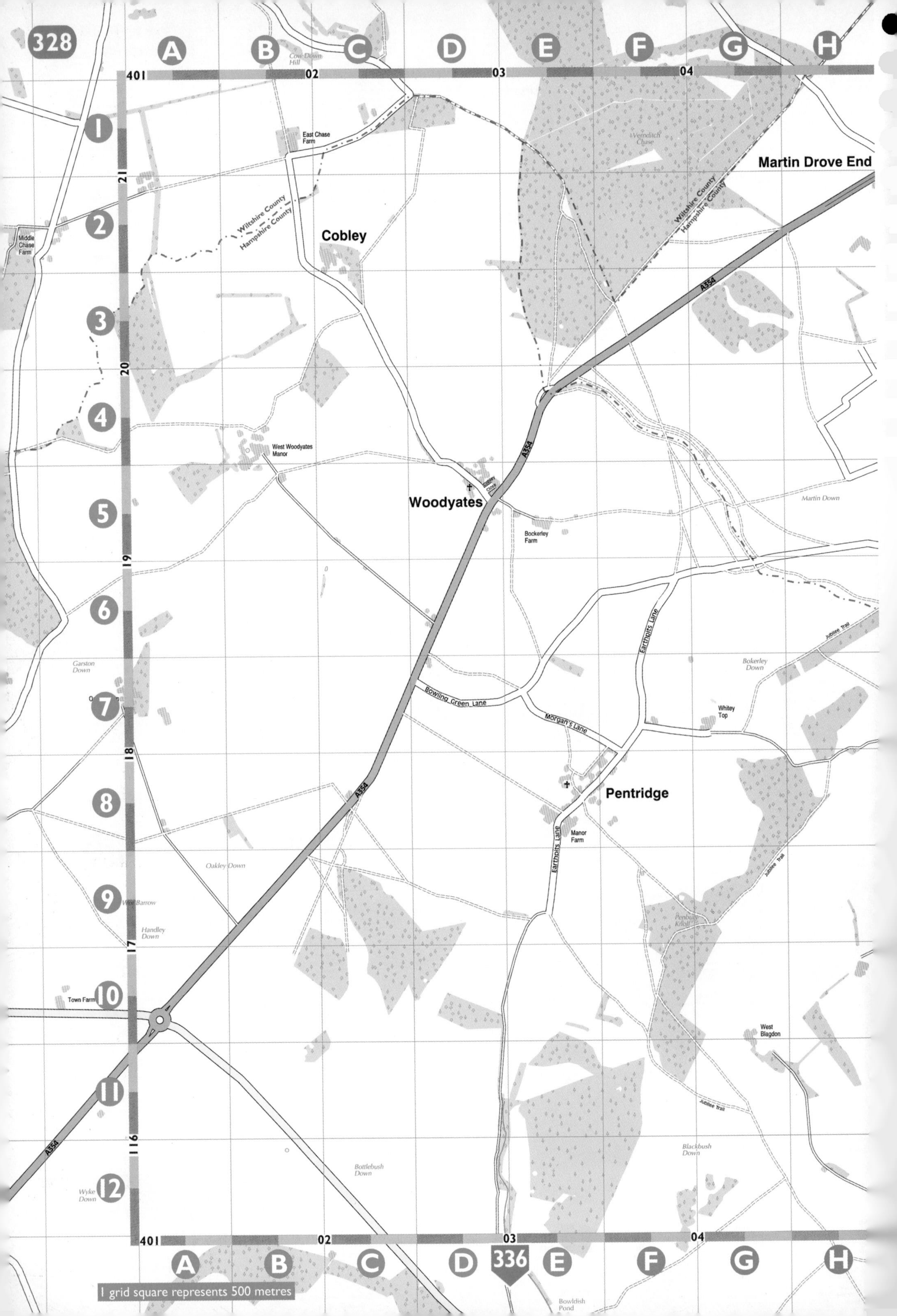

A B C D E F G H

401 02 03 04

1

21

2

3

20

4

5

19

6

7

18

8

9

17

10

11

16

12

401 02 03 04

A B C D E F G H

Cow Down Hill

East Chase Farm

Wiltshire County
Hampshire County

Cobley

Middle Chase Farm

Weirditch Chase

Martin Drove End

Wiltshire County
Hampshire County

A354

West Woodyates Manor

Martin Down

Woodyates

Bockerley Farm

Garston Down

Earthpits Lane

Jubilee Trail

Bokerley Down

Whitey Top

Bowling Green Lane

Morgan's Lane

A354

Pentridge

Oakley Down

Earthpits Lane

Manor Farm

Penbury Knoll

West Barrow

Handley Down

Town Farm

A354

West Blagdon

Jubilee Trail

Blackbush Down

Wyke Down

Bottlebush Down

Bowldish Pond

1 grid square represents 500 metres

J
K
L
M
324
N
P
Q
05
06
07
08
09
A354
Paradise
Martin Drove End
St Brides Farm
Martin Drove End
Downview Rd
Townsend Lane
East Martin
Martin
Sillen Lane
Allen River
Tidpit
Knap Barrow
Grans Barrow
Toyd Down
Knoll Down
330
Hampshire County
Dorset County
National Nature Reserve
North Allenford Farm
Tidpit Common Down
Blackheath Down
Kites Nest Farm
Blagdon Farm
South Allenford Farm
Allen River
Martin Wood
Boulsbury Farm
Stony Lane
Toby's Bottom
Stapleton Farm
Ashley Park Farm
337
R
1
2
3
4
5
6
7
8
9
10
11
12
21
20
19
18
17
116

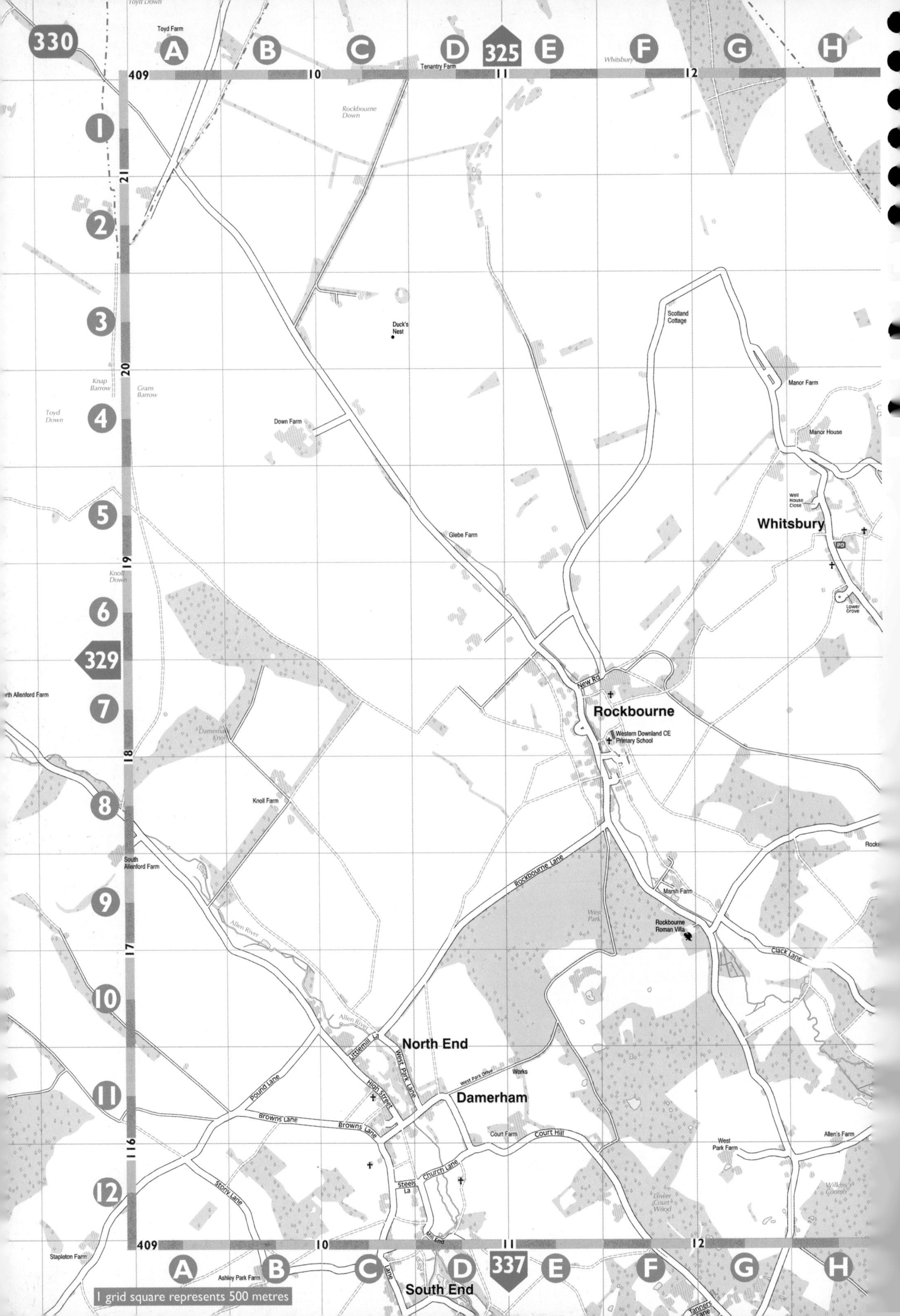

330
325
329
337
A
B
C
D
E
F
G
H
Toyd Farm
Tenantry Farm
Whitsbury
Rockbourne Down
Duck's Nest
Scotland Cottage
Manor Farm
Manor House
Knap Barrow
Grans Barrow
Toyd Down
Down Farm
Well House Close
Whitsbury
Glebe Farm
Knoll Down
Lower Grove
New Rd
Rockbourne
Western Downland CE Primary School
Damerham Knoll
Knoll Farm
South Allenford Farm
Rockbourne Lane
Marsh Farm
Rockbourne Roman Villa
West Park
Allen River
Clack Lane
North End
Littlemill La
West Park Lane
Works
West Park Drive
Damerham
High Street
Pound Lane
Browns Lane
Court Farm
Court Hill
West Park Farm
Allen's Farm
Church Lane
Steels La
Stony Lane
Lower Court Wood
Wilkins Coomb
Mill End
Stapleton Farm
Ashley Park Farm
Lane
South End
Tanners Lane
1 grid square represents 500 metres

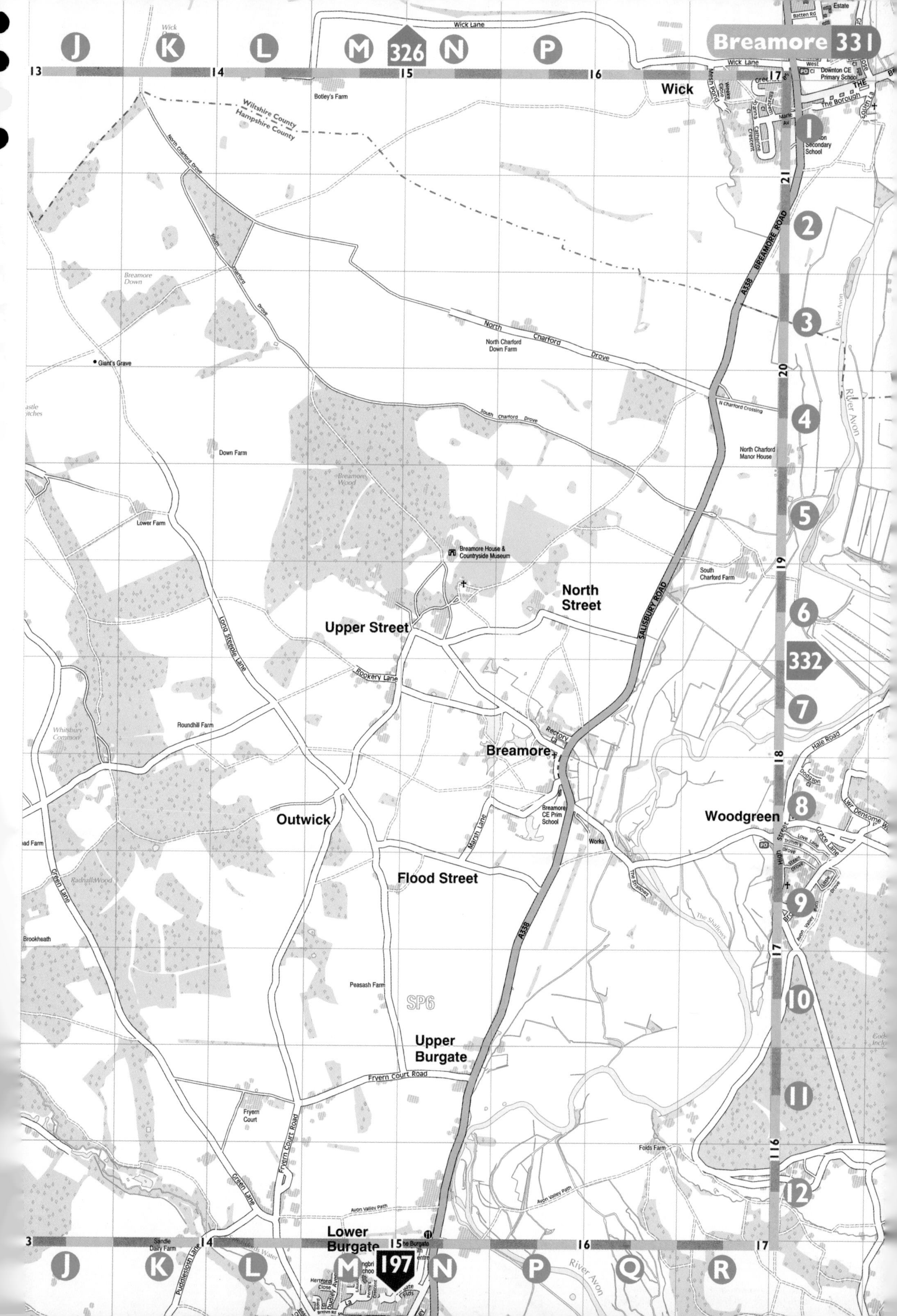

J
K
L
M
326
N
P
13
14
15
16
17
Wick Lane
Wick
Botley's Farm
Wiltshire County
Hampshire County
North Charford Drove
South Charford Drove
Breamore Down
Giant's Grave
North Charford Drove
North Charford Down Farm
N Charford Crossing
North Charford Manor House
A338 BREAMORE ROAD
Down Farm
Breamore Wood
Lower Farm
Breamore House & Countryside Museum
North Street
South Charford Farm
Upper Street
Long Steeple Lane
Rookery Lane
SALISBURY ROAD
Roundhill Farm
Whitsbury Common
Rectory La
Breamore
Breamore CE Prim School
Outwick
Marsh Lane
Works
Woodgreen
Flood Street
The Shallows
Radnall Wood
Green Lane
Brookheath
A338
Peasash Farm
SP6
Upper Burgate
Fryern Court Road
Fryern Court
Folds Farm
Avon Valley Path
Lower Burgate
Sandle Dairy Farm
Puddleslosh Lane
River Avon
Hale Road
Dodgson Cl
High Street
Love Lane
Crace Lane
Lwr Densome Wood
Downton CE Primary School
Secondary School
The Borough
Catherine Crescent
1
2
3
4
5
6
332
7
8
9
10
11
12
21
20
19
18
17
116
197
Q
R

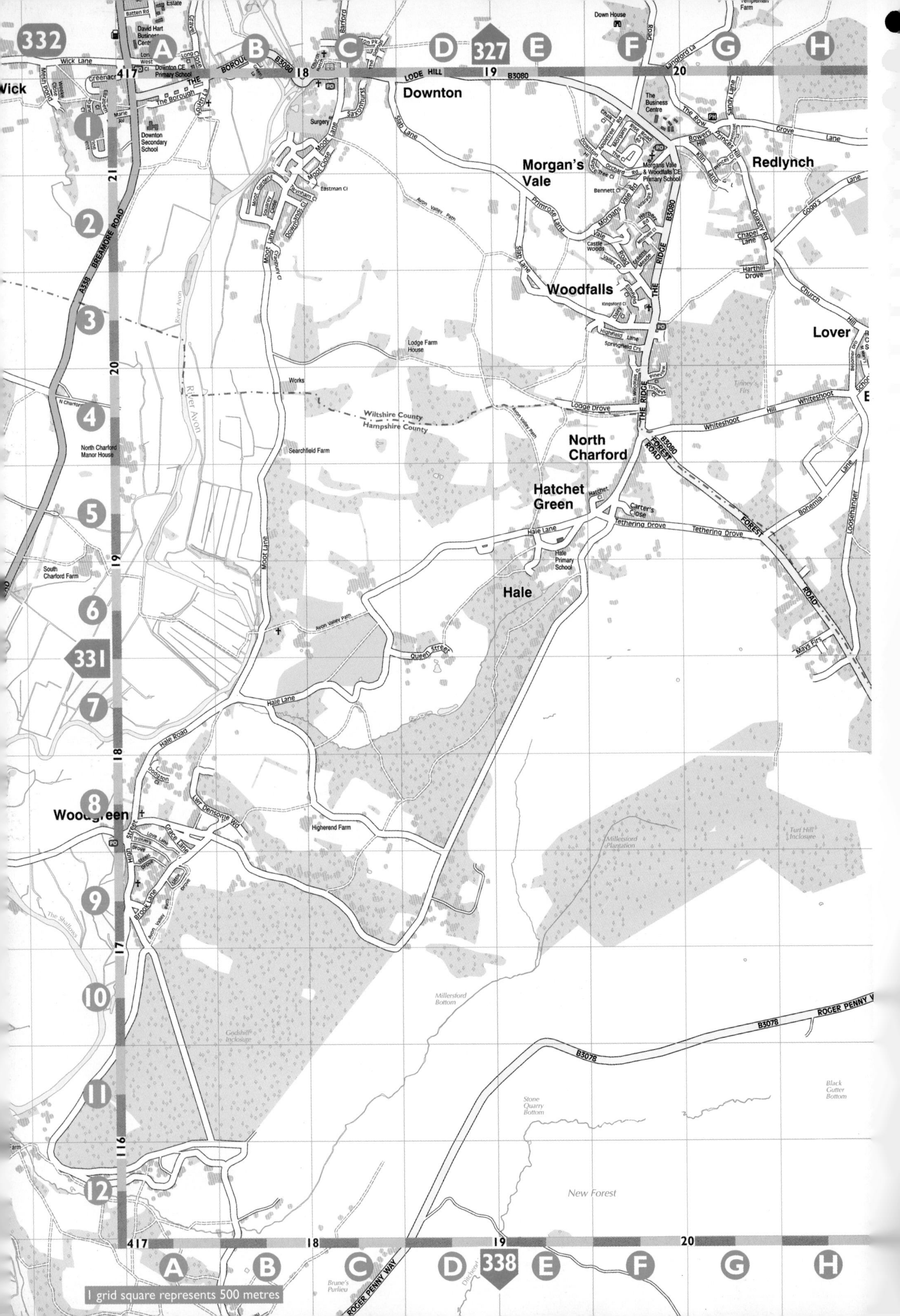
332
327
331
338
A
B
C
D
E
F
G
H
Wick
Downton
Morgan's Vale
Redlynch
Woodfalls
Lover
North Charford
Hatchet Green
Hale
Woodgreen
New Forest
Wick Lane
The Borough
Lode Hill
B3080
B3078
A338
Breamore Road
Moot Lane
Slab Lane
Primrose Lane
The Ridge
Forest Road
Lodge Drove
Whiteshoot Hill
Tethering Drove
Hale Lane
Hale Road
Queen Street
High Street
Brook Lane
Roger Penny Way
River Avon
Avon Valley Path
Wiltshire County
Hampshire County
Lodge Farm House
Works
Searchfield Farm
North Charford Manor House
South Charford Farm
Higherend Farm
Downton Secondary School
Downton CE Primary School
Morgans Vale & Woodfalls CE Primary School
Hale Primary School
The Business Centre
David Hart Business Centre
Down House
Millersford Plantation
Millersford Bottom
Godshill Inclosure
Turf Hill Inclosure
Stone Quarry Bottom
Black Gutter Bottom
Brune's Purlieu
Tinney's Firs
Mays Firs
Bohemia
Loosehanger
Grove Lane
Chapel Lane
Harthill Drove
Church Hill
Sandy Lane
Langford La
The Row
Bowers Hill
Kiln Lane
Quavey Rd
Carter's Close
Highfield Lane
Springfield Crs
Castle Woods
Kingsford Cl
Surgery
Eastman Cl
Downlands Cl
Moot Close
Moot Gardens
Saxonhurst
Barford
Gravel Close
Godson Cl
Grace Lane
Lwr Densome Wd
Love Lane
Trimm's Drove
417
18
19
20
21
116
17
1 grid square represents 500 metres

J K L M **126** N P
21 22 23 24 25

Low Pensworth Farm

Imberley Lane

Vicarage Road

Hamptworth Road

Black Lane

Black Lane

School Rd

Church Ws

Redlynch C E Primary School

Bohemia

Sheawood Copse

Langley Wood

East Copse

Bagfield Copse

Scotland Lane

Glazier's Copse

A36

Stock Lane

I

21

North Common

W. Common Lane

North Common Fm

No. Lane

Barrows Lane

2

3

LYNDHURST ROAD

B3079

Whitterns Hill Farm

Coles's Lane

Landford Lodge

20

Hamptworth Golf & Country Club

4

Landford Primary

Hamptworth Road

Hamptworth Lodge

Hamptworth

Golf Course

LYNDHURST ROAD

B3

5

Loosehanger Copse

Lyburn Road

19

Hamptworth Common

6

334

7

B3080

Golden Cross

Pound Bottom

Cloven Hill Plantation

School Road

York Drove

Pear Drive

18

8

Nomansland Hamptworth Primary School

No

Fore

Lyburn House

North Lane

South Lane

9

Chapel La

17

Franchises Wood

B3080

B3078

Hope Cottage

10

Picket Corner

Pipers Wait

Wiltshire County
Hampshire County

Craws Nest Bottom

11

116

Black Bush Plain

B3078

New Forest

The Butts

12

Islands Thorns Inclosure

Eyeworth Wood

Longcross Plain

78

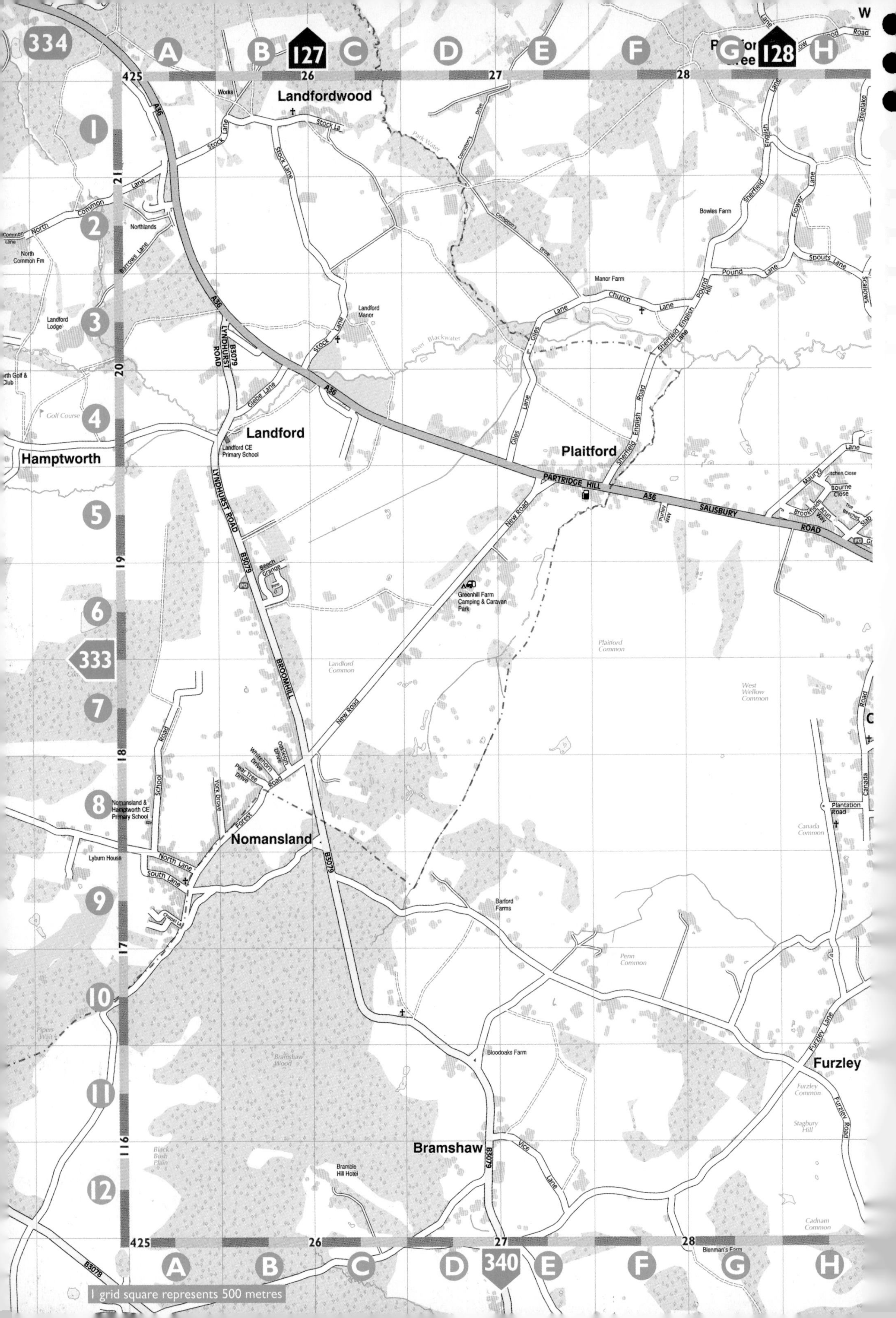
334
127
128
333
340
Landfordwood
Landford
Hamptworth
Plaitford
Nomansland
Bramshaw
Furzley
Landford Common
Plaitford Common
West Wellow Common
Penn Common
Canada Common
Furzley Common
Cadnam Common
Bramshaw Wood
Landford Manor
Landford Lodge
Manor Farm
Bowles Farm
Barford Farms
Bloodoaks Farm
Bramble Hill Hotel
Lyburn House
Northlands
North Common Fm
Greenhill Farm Camping & Caravan Park
Landford CE Primary School
Nomansland & Hamptworth CE Primary School
River Blackwater
Park Water
Golf Course
Stock Lane
Lyndhurst Road
Broomhill
New Road
Partridge Hill
Salisbury Road
Giles Lane
Church Lane
Pound Lane
Spouts Lane
Sherfield English Road
Compton's Drive
Glebe Lane
Forest Road
North Lane
South Lane
Chapel La
School Road
York Drove
Vice Lane
Furzley Lane
Furzley Road
Plantation Road
Canada Road
A36
B3079
B3078
I grid square represents 500 metres

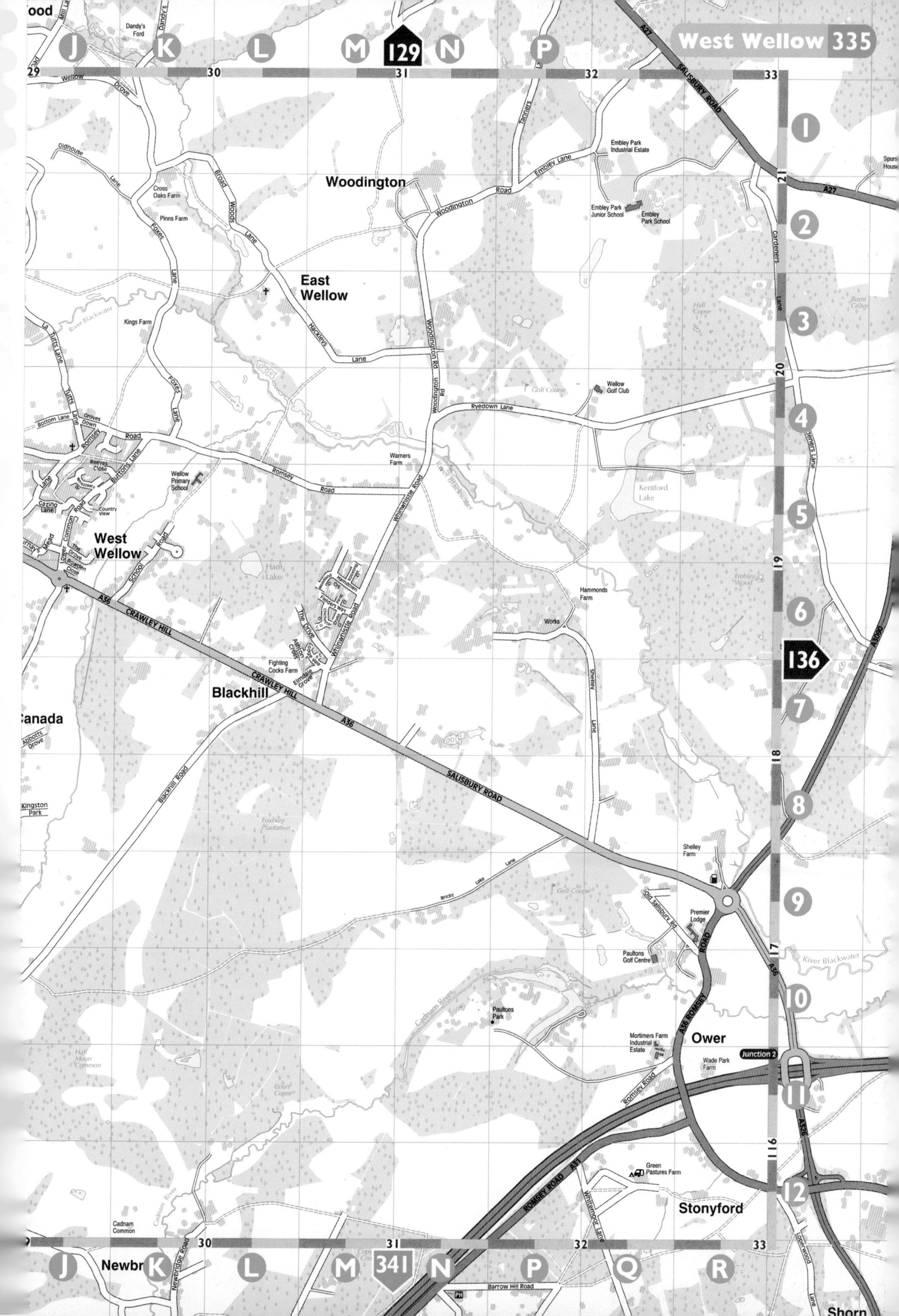
Woodington
East Wellow
West Wellow
Blackhill
Canada
Ower
Stonyford
Embley Park Industrial Estate
Embley Park Junior School
Embley Park School
Cross Oaks Farm
Pinns Farm
Kings Farm
Wellow Golf Club
Kentford Lake
Hammonds Farm
Works
Warners Farm
Wellow Primary School
Fighting Cocks Farm
Ham Lake
Foxbury Plantation
Shelley Farm
Premier Lodge
Paultons Golf Centre
Paultons Park
Mortimers Farm Industrial Estate
Wade Park Farm
Junction 2
Green Pastures Farm
Half Moon Common
Court Copse
Cadnam Common
Kingston Park
Hall Copse
Burnt Grove
Embley Wood
River Blackwater
Cadnam River
SALISBURY ROAD
CRAWLEY HILL
A36
A27
A3090
A31
ROMSEY ROAD
Romsey Road
Woodington Road
Whinwhistle Road
Ryedown Lane
Shelley Lane
Bricky Lake Lane
Blackhill Road
Hackleys Lane
Broad Woods Lane
Foxes Lane
Embley Lane
Gardeners Lane
Newbridge Road
Barrow Hill Road
Whitenbor Lane
Old Salisbury Rd
Abbotts Drove
Tutts Lane
Buttons Lane
Gazing Lane
School Road
Bottom Lane
Groves Down
Reeves Close
Country View
The Drove
Rowden Close
Lower Common Road
Elmdale Grove
Ashton Cross
Fielders Way
The Drive
Hamsdown
Oldhouse Lane
Wellow Drove
Tanners Lane
Dandy's Ford
Newbr
Shorn

129
136
341

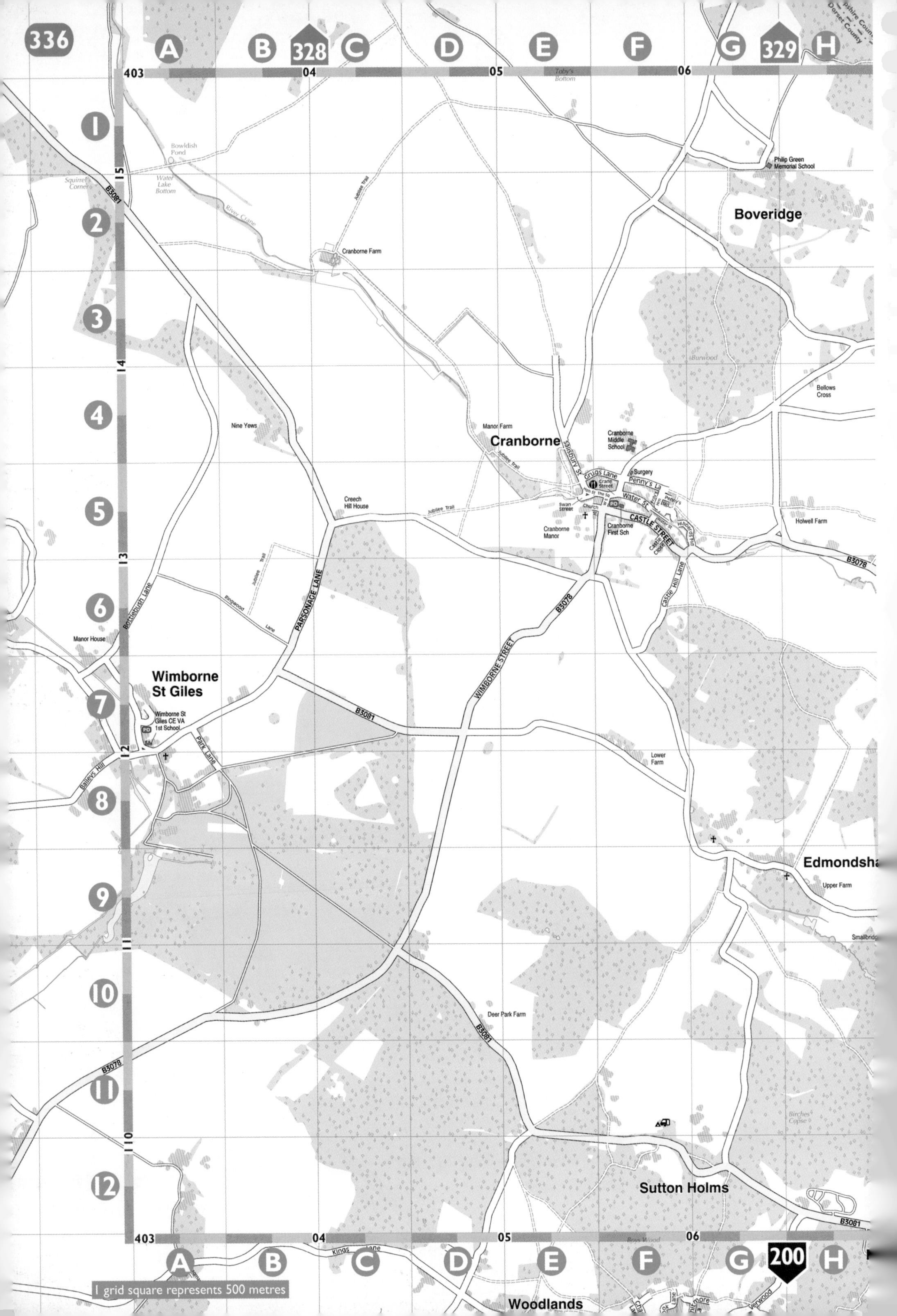

A
B
328
C
D
E
F
G
329
H
403
04
05
06
Toby's Bottom
Bowldish Pond
Squirrel's Corner
Water Lake Bottom
B3081
River Crane
Jubilee Trail
Cranborne Farm
Philip Green Memorial School
Boveridge
Burwood
Bellows Cross
Nine Yews
Manor Farm
Cranborne
Cranborne Middle School
Salisbury St
Grugs Lane
Surgery
Penny's La
Crane Street
Water St
Swan Street
Church
Cranborne Manor
Cranborne First Sch
CASTLE STREET
Holwell Farm
B3078
Creech Hill House
Jubilee Trail
Castle Hill Lane
Ringwood Lane
PARSONAGE LANE
Bennetsbush Lane
Manor House
Wimborne St Giles
Wimborne St Giles CE VA 1st School
B3081
WIMBORNE STREET
Park Lane
Baileys Hill
Lower Farm
Edmondsha
Upper Farm
Smallbridge
Deer Park Farm
B3081
B3078
Birches Copse
Sutton Holms
B3081
Kings Lane
Woodlands
Verwood
200
1
2
3
4
5
6
7
8
9
10
11
12
15
14
13
12
11
10
1 grid square represents 500 metres

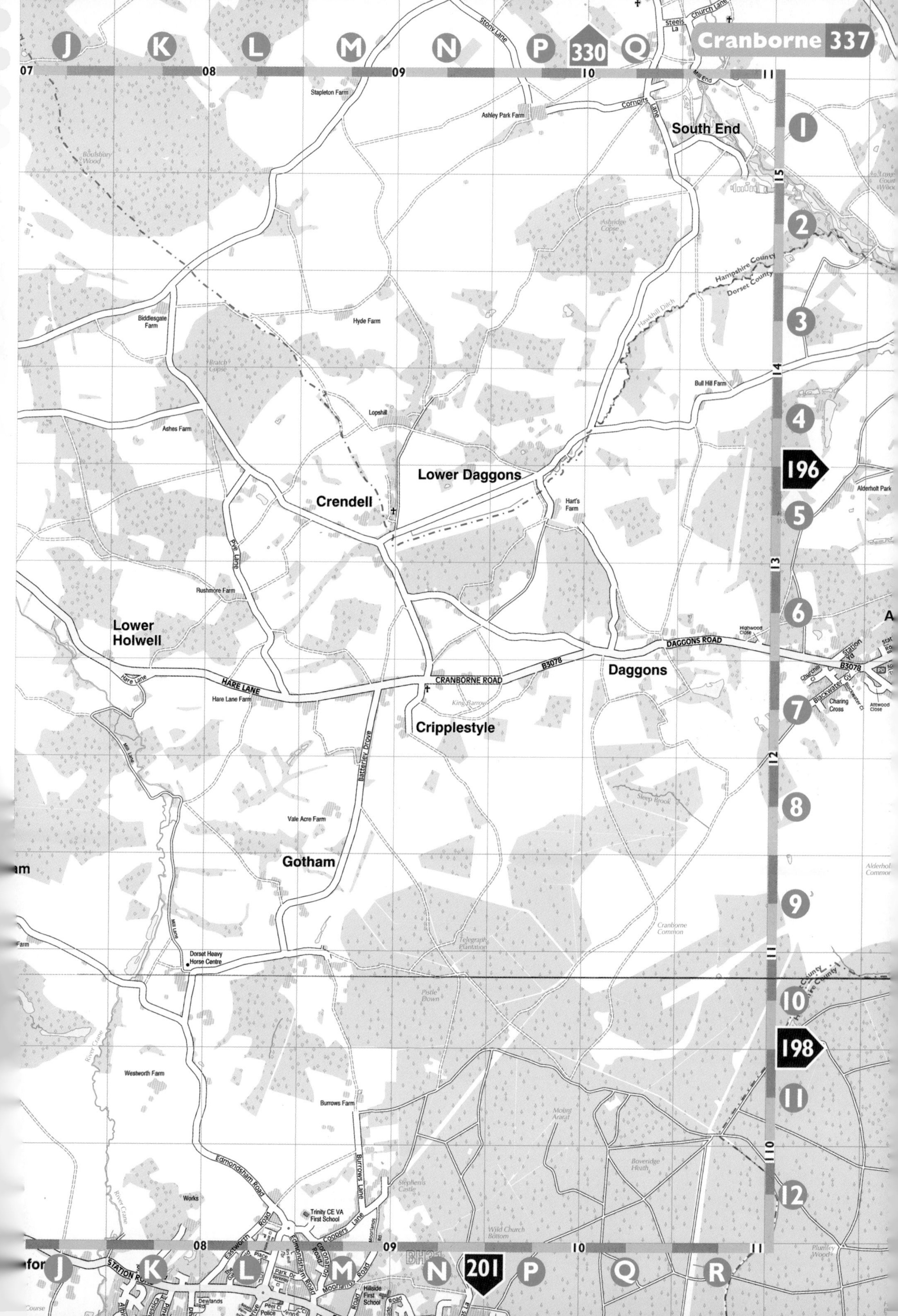

J
K
L
M
N
P
330
Q
Stapleton Farm
Ashley Park Farm
Stony Lane
Church Lane
Steels La
Mill End
Cornpits Lane
South End
Boulsbury Wood
Ashridge Copse
Hampshire County
Dorset County
Hawkhill Ditch
Biddlesgate Farm
Hyde Farm
Bratch Copse
Bull Hill Farm
Lopshill
Ashes Farm
Lower Daggons
196
Alderholt Park
Crendell
Hart's Farm
Pye Lane
Rushmore Farm
Lower Holwell
Highwood Close
DAGGONS ROAD
Station Yd
B3078
Churchill Cl
Blackwater Gv
Charing Cross
Attwood Close
Daggons
Hare Lane
HARE LANE
CRANBORNE ROAD
B3078
Hare Lane Farm
King Barrow
Cripplestyle
Mill Lane
Batterley Drove
Sleep Brook
Vale Acre Farm
Gotham
Alderholt Common
Cranborne Common
Telegraph Plantation
Dorset Heavy Horse Centre
Pistle Down
198
River Crane
Westworth Farm
Burrows Farm
Mount Ararat
Boveridge Heath
Edmondsham Road
Burrows Lane
Stephens Castle
Works
Trinity CE VA First School
Wild Church Bottom
Plumley Wood
Eastworth Road
Edmondsham Road
Coronation Road
Coopers Lane
Moorlands Rd
STATION ROAD
Dewlands Rd
Park Dr
Peel Cl
Police
Hillside First School
1
2
3
4
5
6
7
8
9
10
11
12
07
08
09
10
11
R
201

338
332
342
197
199
New Forest
Godshill
Newgrounds
Blissford
Frogham
Hyde
Hungerford
Ogdens
Furze Hill
Linwood
Mockbeggar
Sandy Balls Holiday Centre
Brune's Purlieu
Roger Penny Way
B3078
Pitts Wood Inclosure
Long Bottom
Hampton Ridge
Alderhill Inclosure
Coopers Hill
Latchmore Bottom
Latchmore Brook
Abbots Well
Ogdens Farm
Hyde Common
Hasley Inclosure
New
Forest
Ogden's Purlieu
Broomy Inclosure
Broomy Plain
Black Barrow
High Corner Inn
Ibsley Common
Whitefield Plantn
Milkham Inclosure
Toms Lane
Linwood Farm
Blissford Road
Broadhill Lane
Abbots Well Road
Abbotswell Road
Blissford Hill
Frogham Hill
Pentons Hill
Gorley Lynch
Hyde Primary School
Ditchend Brook
Dockens Water
Works
Well Lane
Purlieu Lane
1 grid square represents 500 metres

The Butts

Eyeworth Wood

Islands Thorns Inclosure

Longcross Plain

Irons Well

Eyeworth Lodge

Fritham Lodge

Coppice of Linwood

Salisbury Trench

Fritham House

PH

Fritham

Hiscocks Hill

The Butt

King's Garn Gutter Inclosure

Fritham Plain

North Bentley Inclosure

Janesmoor Plain

New

South Bentley Inclosure

Forest

Ames Wood

340

Ocknell Inclosure

Cadman Pool

Holly Hatch Cottage

Holly Hatch Inclosures

Stoney Cross Plain

A31

Broomy Lodge

Ocknell Plain

New

Forest

Slufters Inclosure

Fritham Cross

A31

Puckpits Inclosure

Bratley Arch

A31

King's Garden

Highland Water Inclosure

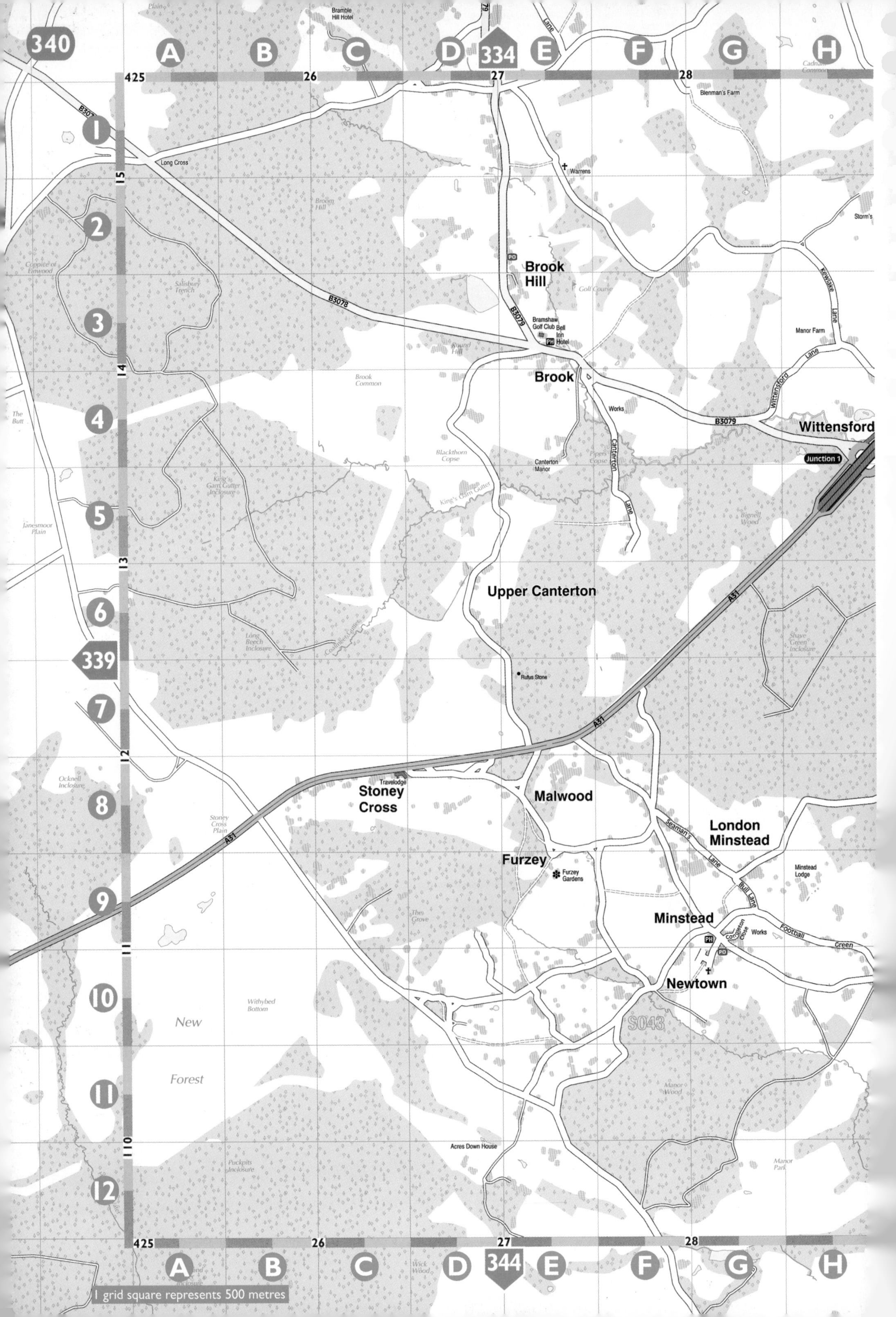

339

A **B** **C** **D** **E** **F** **G** **H**

425   26   27   28

1
2
3
4
5
6
7
8
9
10
11
12

B307

Long Cross

Plain

Bramble Hill Hotel

Blenman's Farm

79

Lane

Warrens

Storm's

Broom Hill

Coppice of Linwood

Salisbury Trench

Golf Course

Kewlake Lane

Manor Farm

Brook Hill

B3078

Bramshaw Golf Club Bell Inn Hotel

PO

B3079

Brook

Round Hill

Brook Common

Works

Canterton Lane

Wittensford Lane

B3079

Wittensford

Junction 1

The Butt

King's Garn Gutter Inclosure

Blackthorn Copse

Pipers Copse

Canterton Manor

Janesmoor Plain

King's Garn Gutter

Bignell Wood

Long Beech Inclosure

Combleywater

Upper Canterton

A31

Shave Green Inclosure

Rufus Stone

Ocknell Inclosure

Travelodge

A31

Stoney Cross

Malwood

Seaman's Lane

London Minstead

Minstead Lodge

Stoney Cross Plain

Furzey

Furzey Gardens

Bull Lane

A31

Minstead

PH

Castle Malwood

Works

Football

Green

The Grove

PO

Newtown

New

Withybed Bottom

S043

Forest

Manor Wood

Acres Down House

Puckpits Inclosure

Manor Park

Wick Wood

A **B** **C** **D** **E** **F** **G** **H**

425   26   27   28

I grid square represents 500 metres

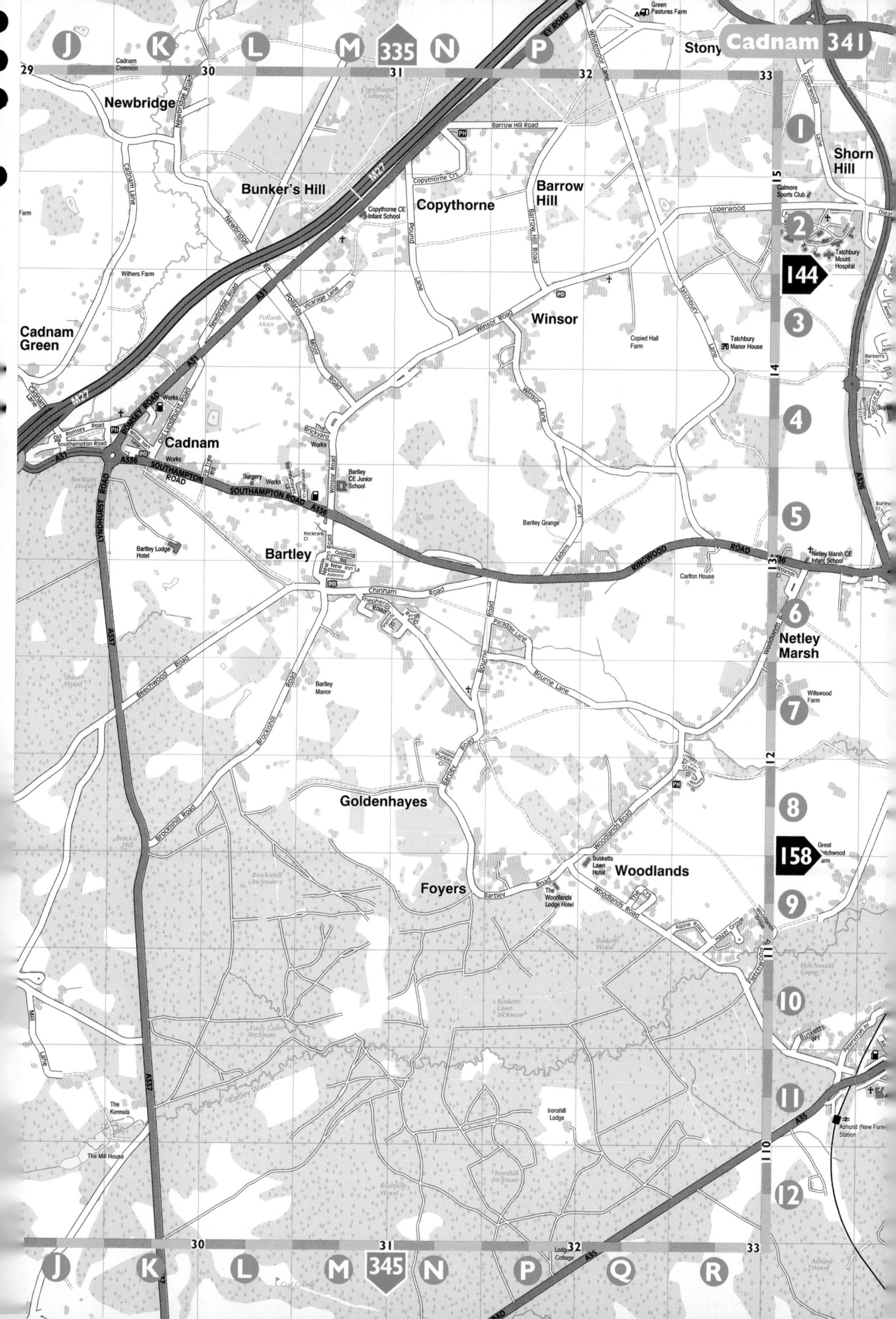
335
Newbridge
Bunker's Hill
Copythorne
Barrow Hill
Winsor
Cadnam Green
Cadnam
Bartley
Shorn Hill
Netley Marsh
Goldenhayes
Woodlands
Foyers
Stony
Green Pastures Farm
Cadnam Common
Copythorne Common
Barrow Hill Road
Copythorne Crs
Copythorne CE Infant School
Pound Lane
Barrow Hill Road
Whitemoor Lane
Tatchbury Lane
Tatchbury Manor House
Tatchbury Mount Hospital
Calmore Sports Club
Copied Hall Farm
Winsor Road
Winsor Lane
Vicarage Lane
Pollards Moor
Pollards Moor Road
Newbridge Road
Cadnam Lane
Withers Farm
Romsey Road
Southampton Road
Old Lyndhurst Road
Lyndhurst Road
Fir Tree Rd
Works
Surgery
Bartley CE Junior School
Rockram Wood
Bartley Lodge Hotel
Bartley Grange
Eadens Lane
Ringwood Road
Carlton House
Netley Marsh CE Infant School
Chinham Road
Shepherds Road
Bourne Road
Paradise Lane
Bourne Lane
Beechwood Road
Shaves Wood
Bartley Manor
Brockishill Road
Brockis Hill
Brockishill Inclosure
Purkiss Cl
Bartley Road
Woodlands Road
Busketts Lawn Hotel
The Woodlands Lodge Hotel
Willswood Farm
Great Fletchwood Farm
Alpine Road
Hazel Grove
Fletchwood Road
Fletchwood Copse
Busketts Wood
Busketts Lawn Inclosure
Furzy Lawn Inclosure
Bartley Water
Ironshill Lodge
Ironshill Inclosure
Rushpole Wood
The Kennels
The Mill House
Mill Lane
Lodge Cottage
Golf Course
Ashurst Wood
Ashurst (New Forest) Station
Busketts Wy
A31
A336
A337
A35
A326
M27
144
158
345

A B C D **338** E F G H

417 18 19 20

1 Mockb ar

2

◄**199**

3

4 Highwood

5

6 North Poulner

Linford

Hangersley

Shobley

BH24

7

8 Poulner

◄**203**

Picket Hill

Foulford

9

Hightown

10

11

Crow

12

Burley Street

417 18 19 20

A B C D **348** E F G H

1 grid square represents 500 metres

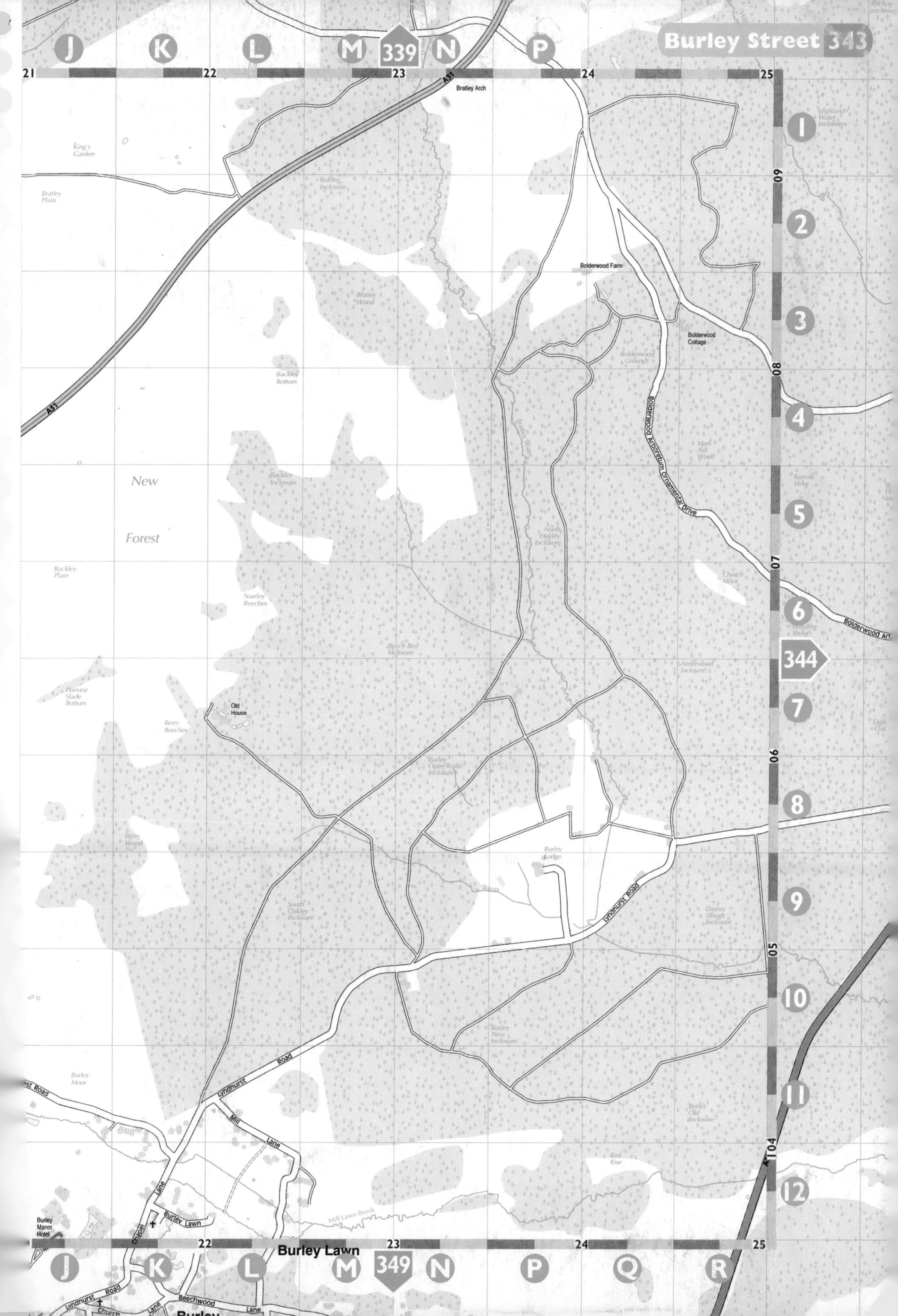

J
K
L
M
339
N
P
21
22
23
24
25
A31
Bratley Arch
King's Garden
Bratley Plain
Bratley Inclosure
Bratley Wood
Backley Bottom
New
Forest
Backley Inclosure
Backley Plain
Soarley Beeches
Beech Bed Inclosure
Harvest Slade Bottom
Old House
Berry Beeches
Berry Wood
Burley Outer Rails Inclosure
Burley Lodge
South Oakley Inclosure
Lyndhurst Road
Burley New Inclosure
Burley Moor
Mill Lane
Burley Lawn
Chapel Lane
Burley Manor Hotel
Mill Lawn Brook
Red Rise
Burley Old Inclosure
Dames Slough Inclosure
Anderwood Inclosure
Church Moor
Winding Shoot
Bolderwood Arboretum Ornamental Drive
Mark Ash Wood
Barrow Moor
North Oakley Inclosure
Bratley Water
Bolderwood Farm
Bolderwood Cottage
Bolderwood Grounds
Highlands Water Inclosure
Bolderwood Arb
A35
1
2
3
4
5
6
7
8
9
10
11
12
09
08
07
06
05
04
344
Burley Lawn
349
J
K
L
M
N
P
Q
R
Lyndhurst Road
Beechwood Lane
Church

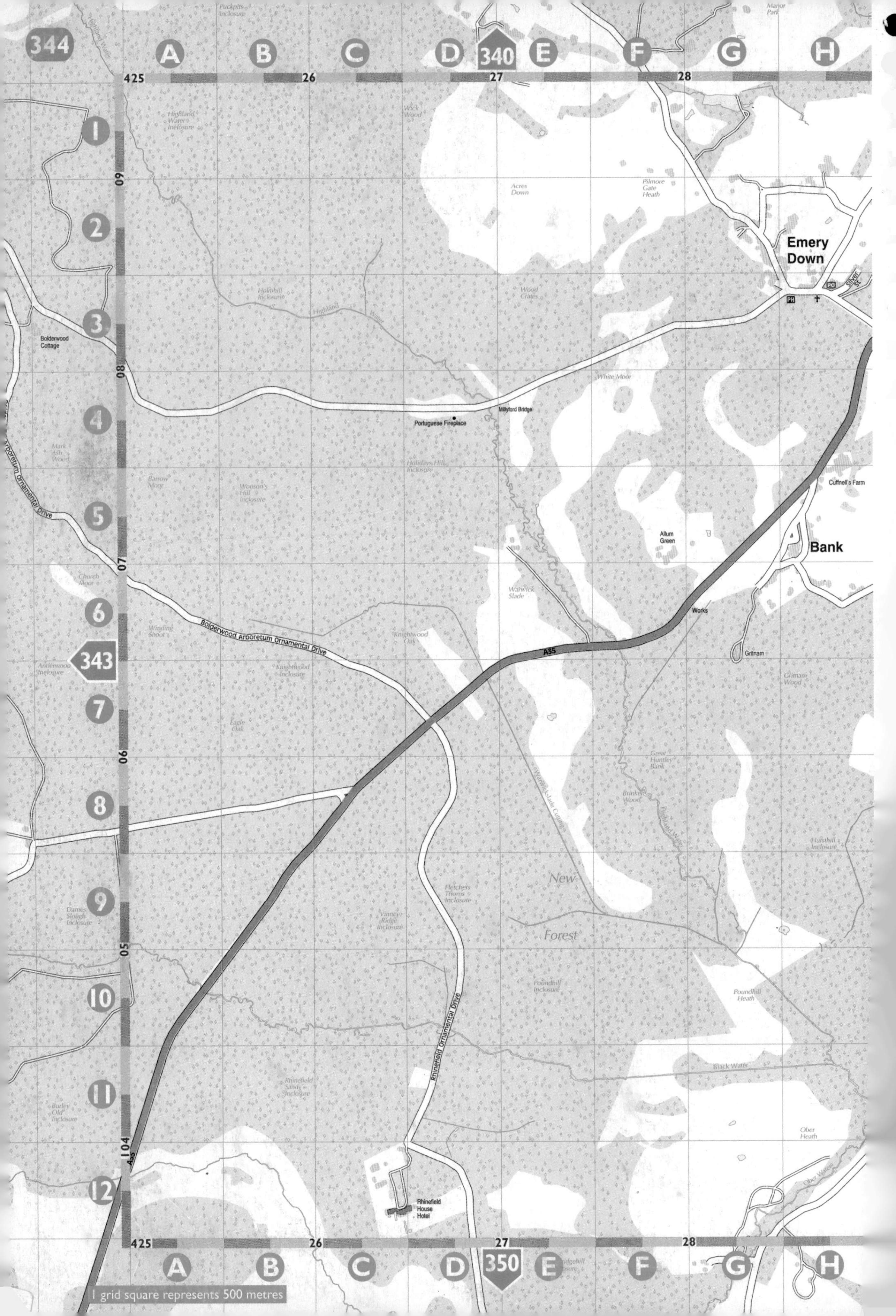

A B C D E F G H

425 26 27 28

1
2
3
4
5
6
343
7
8
9
10
11
12

09
08
07
06
05
04

Highland Water Inclosure

Puckpits Inclosure

Manor Park

Wick Wood

Acres Down

Pilmore Gate Heath

Emery Down

Bolderwood Cottage

Holmhill Inclosure

Highland Water

Wood Crates

PH ✝

White Moor

Cuffnell's Farm

Portuguese Fireplace

Millyford Bridge

Mark Ash Wood

Barrow Moor

Wooson's Hill Inclosure

Holidays Hill Inclosure

Allum Green

Bank

Church Moor

Winding Shoot

Bolderwood Arboretum Ornamental Drive

Knightwood Oak

Warwick Slade

Works

Gritnam

A35

Anderwood Inclosure

Knightwood Inclosure

Gritnam Wood

Eagle Oak

Great Huntley Bank

Brinken Wood

Highland Water

Hursthill Inclosure

Dames Slough Inclosure

Vinney Ridge Inclosure

Fletchers Thorns Inclosure

New

Forest

Poundhill Inclosure

Poundhill Heath

Rhinefield Ornamental Drive

Black Water

Rhinefield Sandy's Inclosure

Bratley Old Inclosure

A35

Ober Heath

Rhinefield House Hotel

Ober Water

Ridgehill Bratley

1 grid square represents 500 metres

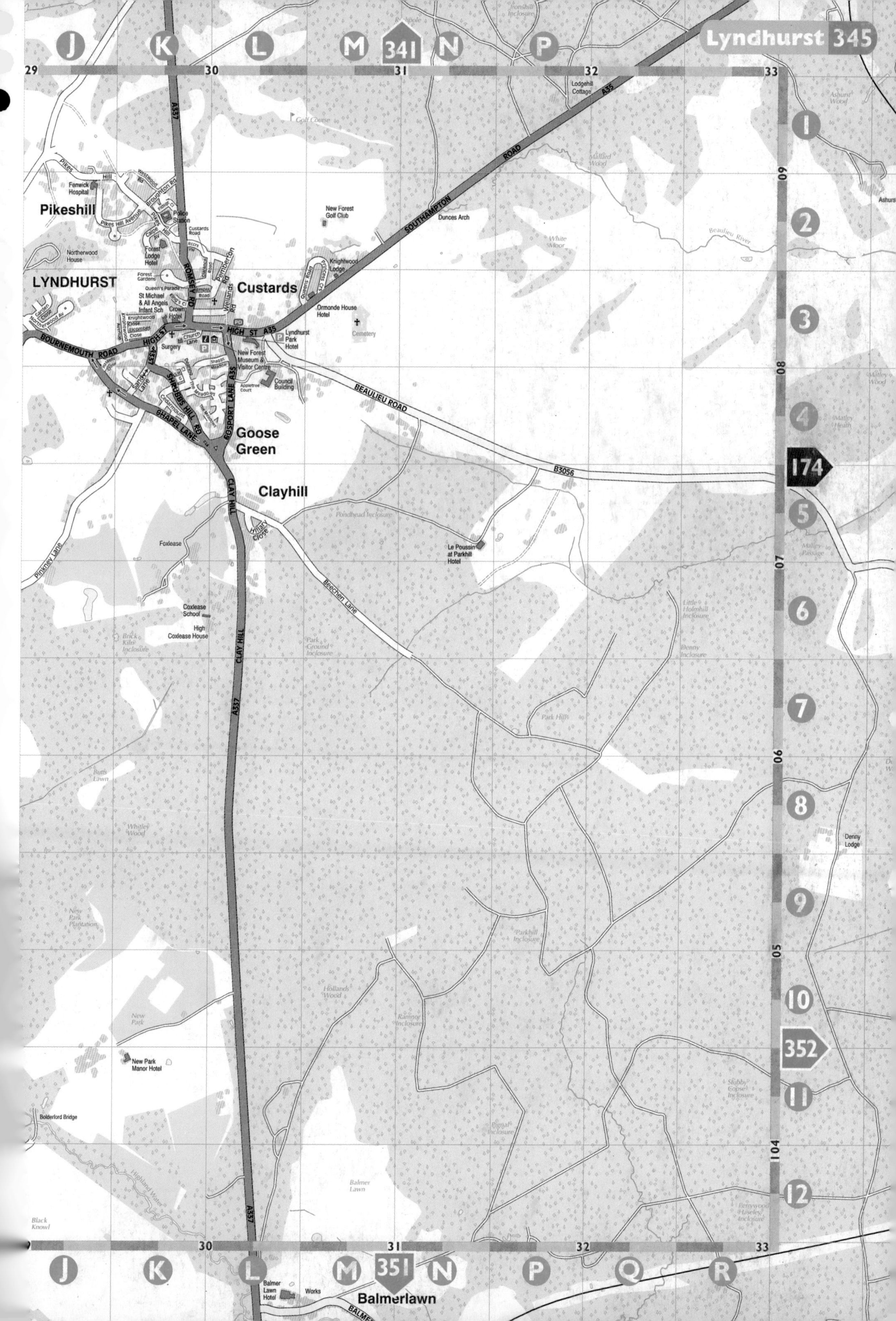

J
K
L
M
341
N
P
29
30
31
32
33
A337
A35
Lodgehill Cottage
Golf Course
SOUTHAMPTON ROAD
Pikes Hill
Fenwick Hospital
Pikeshill
Pikes Hill Avenue
Police Station
Custards Road
Northerwood House
Forest Lodge Hotel
LYNDHURST
Forest Gardens
Queen's Parade
St Michael & All Angels Infant Sch
Crown Hotel
ROMSEY RD
Custards
Wellands Rd
Pemberton
Queens Road
Knightwood Lodge
Ormonde House Hotel
New Forest Golf Club
Dunces Arch
Mallard Wood
White Moor
Beaulieu River
Cemetery
Lyndhurst Park Hotel
HIGH ST
A35
BOURNEMOUTH ROAD
Church Lane
Surgery
New Forest Museum & Visitor Centre
Council Building
Appletree Court
BEAULIEU ROAD
SHRUBBS HILL RD
GOSPORT LANE A35
CHAPEL LANE
Goose Green
B3056
Clayhill
CLAY HILL
Hilltary Close
Pondhead Inclosure
Foxlease
Le Poussin at Parkhill Hotel
Pinkney Lane
Beechen Lane
Coxlease School
High Coxlease House
Brick Kiln Inclosure
Park Ground Inclosure
Little Holmhill Inclosure
Denny Inclosure
Park Hill
Butts Lawn
Whitley Wood
New Park Plantation
Parkhill Inclosure
Hollands Wood
Ramnor Inclosure
New Park
New Park Manor Hotel
Bolderford Bridge
Highland Water
Black Knowl
Balmer Lawn
Denny Lodge
Matley Wood
Matley Heath
Matley Passage
Ashurst Wood
Stubby Copse Inclosure
Perrywood Haseley Inclosure
Balmer Lawn Hotel
Works
Balmerlawn
1
2
3
4
5
6
7
8
9
10
11
12
174
352
351
09
08
07
06
05
104
Q
R

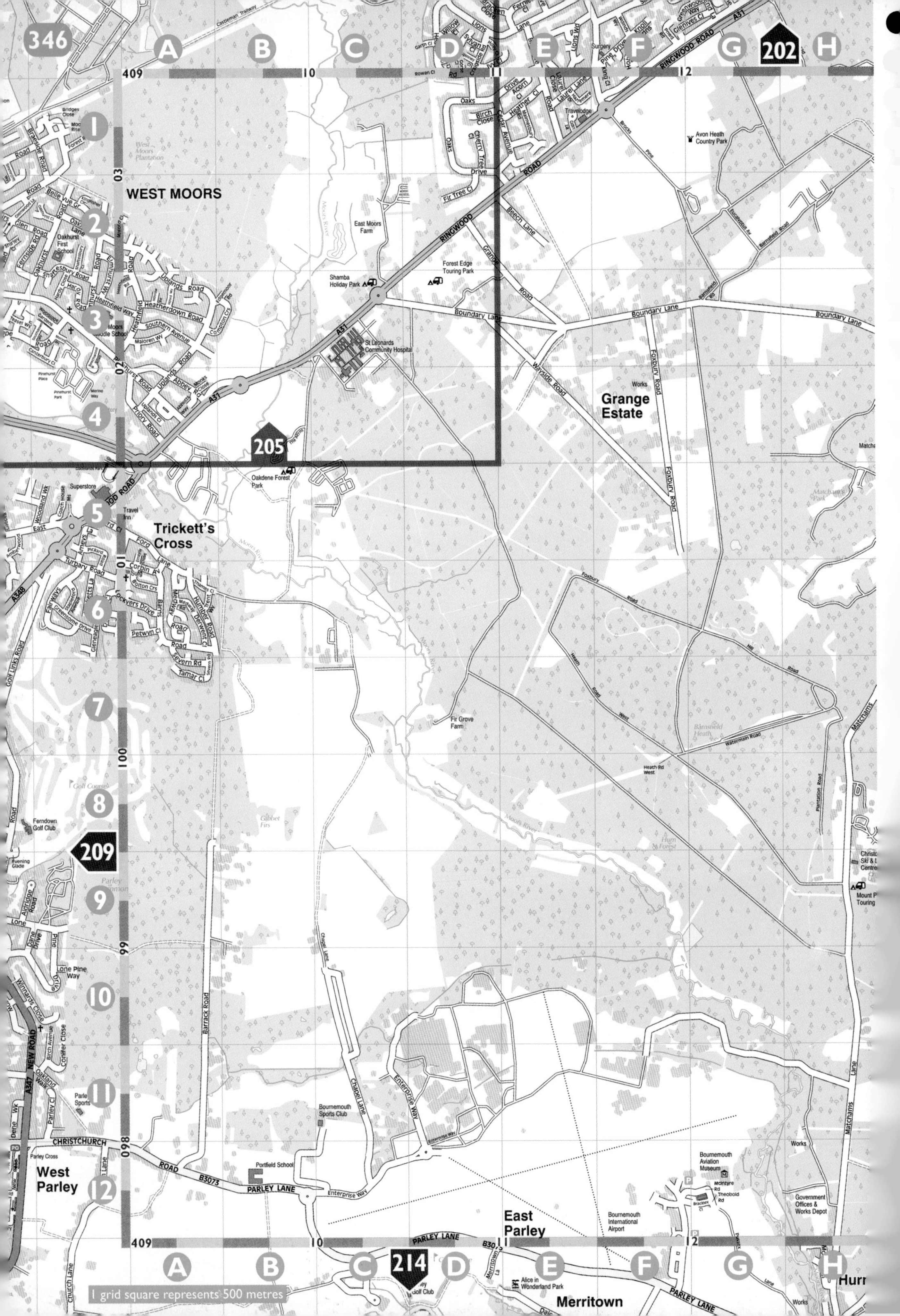
WEST MOORS
Trickett's Cross
Grange Estate
West Parley
East Parley
Merritown
Avon Heath Country Park
East Moors Farm
Forest Edge Touring Park
Shamba Holiday Park
St Leonards Community Hospital
Oakdene Forest Park
Fir Grove Farm
Ferndown Golf Club
Bournemouth Sports Club
Portfield School
Bournemouth Aviation Museum
Bournemouth International Airport
Government Offices & Works Depot
Alice in Wonderland Park
RINGWOOD ROAD
Boundary Lane
Wayside Road
Foxbury Road
Watermain Road
Heath Road West
Plantation Road
Matchams Lane
Barrack Road
Chapel Lane
Enterprise Way
CHRISTCHURCH ROAD
PARLEY LANE
NEW ROAD
Moors River
Gibbet Firs
Barnsfield Heath
Hurn Forest
202
205
209
214
1 grid square represents 500 metres

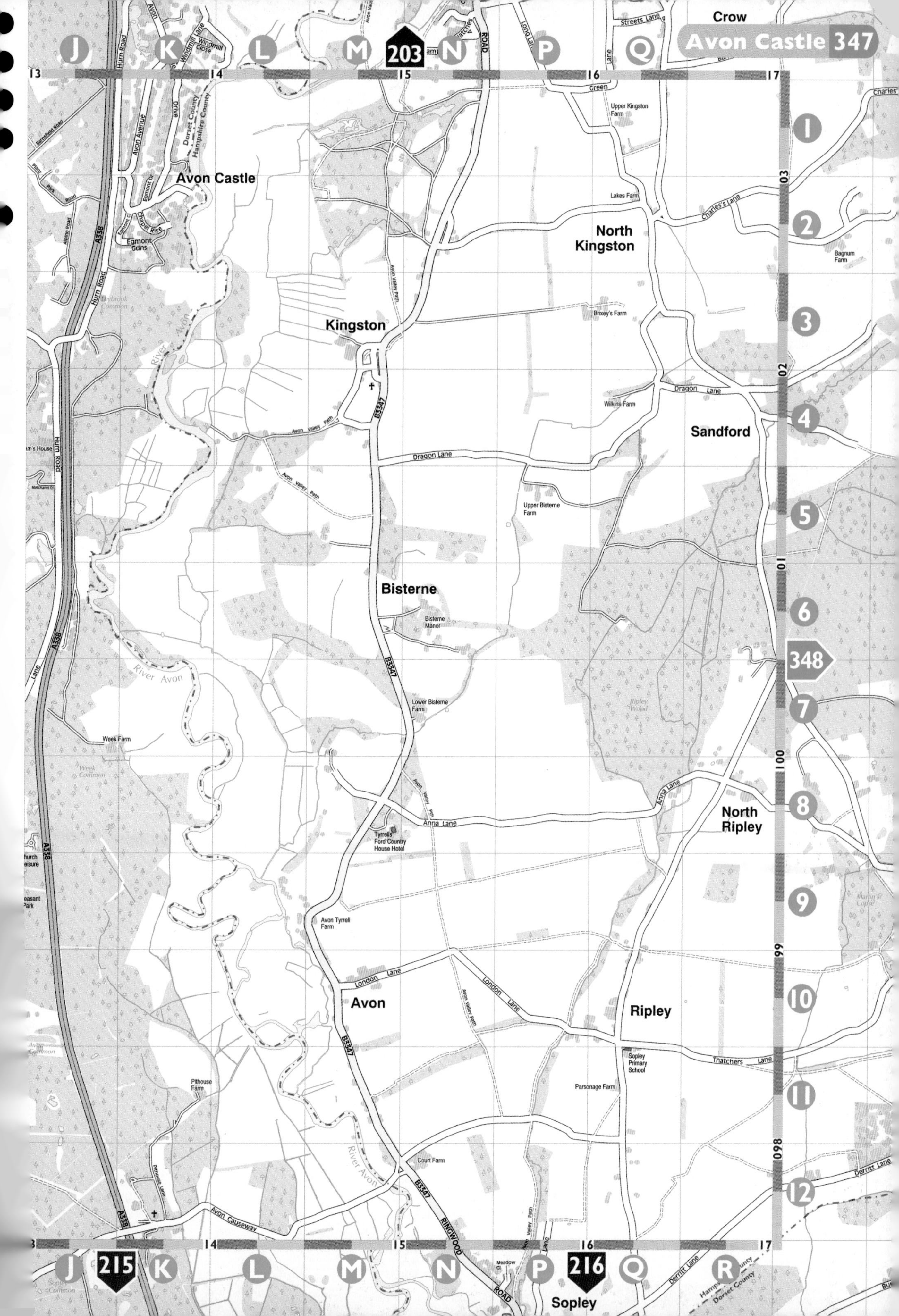
Avon Castle
North Kingston
Kingston
Sandford
Bisterne
North Ripley
Avon
Ripley
Sopley
Crow
Upper Kingston Farm
Lakes Farm
Brixey's Farm
Wilkins Farm
Upper Bisterne Farm
Bisterne Manor
Lower Bisterne Farm
Tyrrells Ford Country House Hotel
Avon Tyrrell Farm
Week Farm
Pithouse Farm
Court Farm
Parsonage Farm
Sopley Primary School
Bagnum Farm
Dragon Lane
Anna Lane
London Lane
Thatchers Lane
Charles's Lane
Derritt Lane
Avon Causeway
Avon Valley Path
Hurn Road
River Avon
Ripley Wood
Week Common
Avon Common
Streets Lane
Egmont Gdns
Chapel Rise
Dorset County
Hampshire County
Ringwood Road
B3347
A338
Meadow
203
348
215
216

Crow
348
342
217
347
A B C D E F G H
1 2 3 4 5 6 7 8 9 10 11 12
Sandford
North Ripley
Burley Beacon
Thorney Hill
Shirley
BRANSGORE
Kingston Great Common National Nature Reserve
Kingston Great Common
Bagnum Farm
Cranes Moor
Burnt Axon
Bisterne Common
Dur Hill Down
Whitten Bottom
Thorney Hill Holms
Avon Tyrrell
Works
Shirley Common
Purlieu
Martin's Copse
Hill Farm
Poors Common
Heathfield
Beech House
Bransgore House
Harrow Wood Farm Caravan Park
Bransgore CE Primary School
The New Medical Cen
Twin Oaks Medical Cen
Harrow Lodge
Charles's Lane
Barrack Lane
Dragon Lane
Anna Lane
Thatchers Lane
Derritt Lane
Pound Lane
Castle Hill Lane
Ringwood Road
Honey Lane
Warnes Lane
Burley Road
Forest Road
School Lane
Brick Lane
Valley Lane
Willow Lane
Dial Cl
Burnt House Lane
Stibbs Way
Bransgore Gdns
Canute Drive
Poplar Lane
Cuckoo Hill Way
Betsy Lane
Pear Tree Cl
Colbourne Close
Brookside Road
Wiltshire Gdns
Wiltshire Rd
West Road
Hill Lane
Lyndhurst Road
Harrow Road
Westbury Cl
Hampshire County
Dorset County
1 grid square represents 500 metres

Burley Lawn
Burley
Bisterne Close
Burley Manor Hotel
Burley Prim School
Burley Golf Club
Lyndhurst Road
Church Lane
Chapel Lane
Beechwood Lane
Bennetts Lane
Southfield
Cott Lane
Bisterne Close
Moorhill Road
Moorhill House Hotel
Golf Course
Shoot Wood
New Forest
Goatspen Plain
Clayhill Bottom
Station Road
Holmsley Passage
Greenberry Bridge
Holmsley Ridge
Holmsley Lodge
Holmsley Inclosure
A35
Wilverley Post
Naked Man
Wilverley Inclosure
Wilverley Plain
Duck Hole
Brownhill Inclosure
Wootton Coppice Inclosure
Avon Water
Broadley Inclosure
Wootton Old Farm
Brownhill Road
Wootton Farm Road
Rhinefield Road
Wilverley Road
HOLMSLEY ROAD
B3058
Manor Farm
Wootton
Eastley Wootton
Plain Heath
Forest Lodge
Ossemsley
North Drive
Ossemsley South Drive
BASHLEY COMMON ROAD B3058
Marlpit Lane
Tiptoe Road
Wootton Road
Daneshurst New Road
North Hinton Farm
Bashley
Hoburne Bashley
343
350
218
J K L M N P Q R
21 22 23 24 25
1 2 3 4 5 6 7 8 9 10 11 12
03 02 01 100 99 098

A   B   C   D   E   F   G   H

Rhinefield House Hotel

344

425   26   27   28

1

2

Crab Tree Earth

Duck Hole

Aldridgehill Inclosure

Ober Water

Beachern Wood

Ober House

Whitemoor

The Coppice

New Forest Drive

North Weirs

3

White Moor

Naked Man

4

Wilverley Plain

Hincheslea Moor

Five Thorns Hill

Burley Road

South Weirs

Burley Road

5

Hincheslea Wood

Blackhamsley House

Ilverley losure

6

349

Long Slade Bottom

Setthorns Cottage

7

Avon Water

Wootton Coppice Inclosure

8

Set Thorns Inclosure

Widden Bottom

Cemetery

9

Broadley Inclosure

Manchester Road

Brighton Road

Durns Town

Eastley Wootton

10

String of Horses Country House Hotel

Mead End Road

Sway Park Ind Est

Station Road

Underwood Dr

St Lukes CE Primary School

Jordans Lane

DURNSTOWN

Back Lane

Pitmore Lane

11

Mead End

Broadley House

Sway

Sway Station

Sway Manor Restaurant & Hotel

Surgery

Church Lane

Birchy Hill

BIRCHY HILL

Chapel Lane

Coombe Lane

South Sway Lane

12

Tiptoe Road

Tiptoe Primary School

Middle Road

Tiptoe

Works

Arnewood Manor

King's Farm

Paul

shley

425   26   27   28

A   B   219   C   D   E   ROAD   F   G   220   H

Northover

ARNEWOOD   BRIDGE

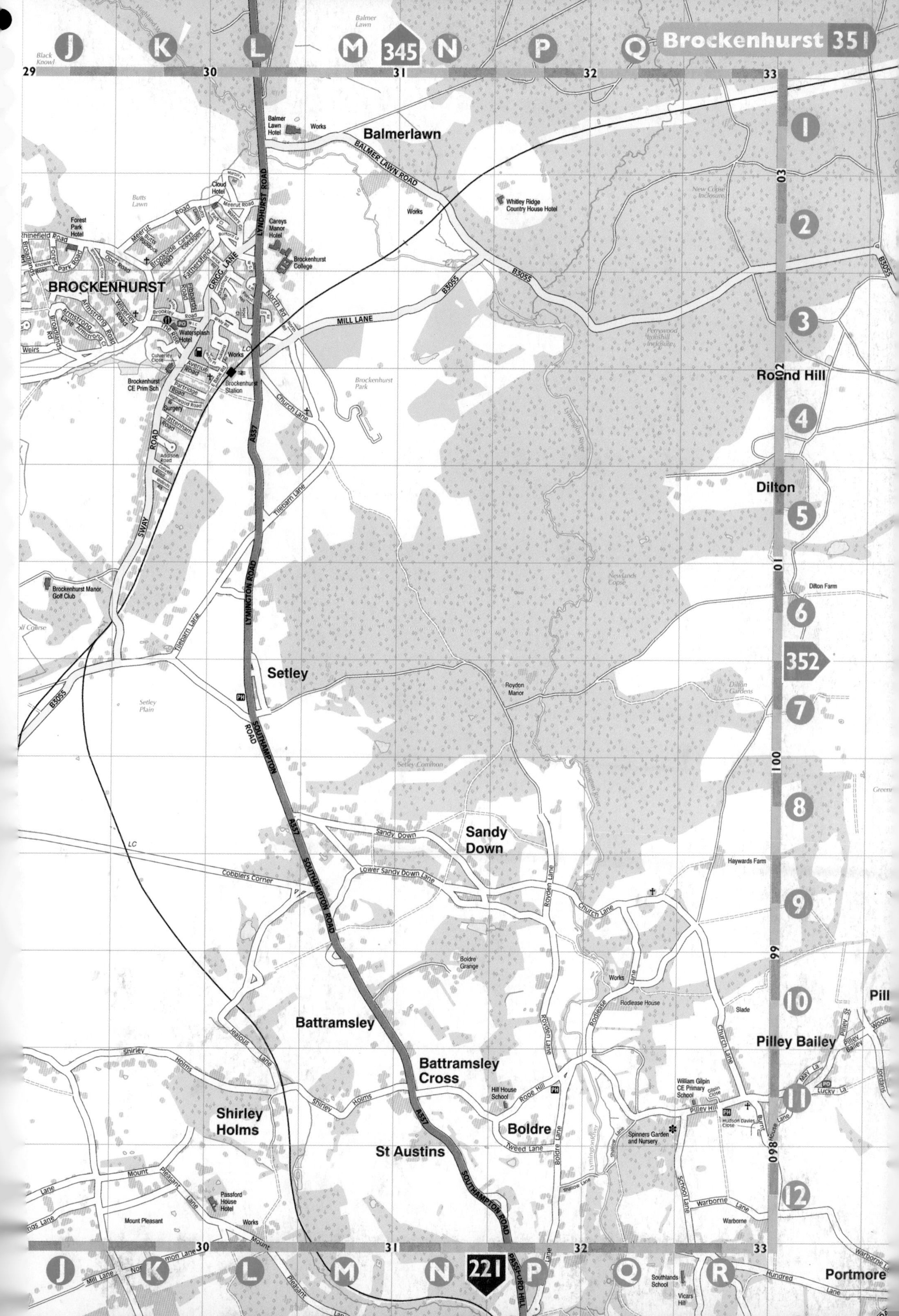
345
221
352
BROCKENHURST
Balmerlawn
Balmer Lawn Hotel
Works
BALMER LAWN ROAD
Cloud Hotel
Careys Manor Hotel
Brockenhurst College
Forest Park Hotel
Whitley Ridge Country House Hotel
B3055
MILL LANE
LYNDHURST ROAD
GRIGG LANE
Watersplash Hotel
Brockenhurst CE Prim Sch
Brockenhurst Station
Church Lane
Brockenhurst Park
Round Hill
Dilton
Dilton Farm
Tilebarn Lane
Brockenhurst Manor Golf Club
LYMINGTON ROAD
A337
Setley
Setley Plain
Roydon Manor
Dilton Gardens
Setley Common
SOUTHAMPTON ROAD
Sandy Down
Lower Sandy Down Lane
Cobblers Corner
Haywards Farm
Church Lane
Roydon Lane
Boldre Grange
Works
Rodlease House
Battramsley
Battramsley Cross
Slade
Pilley Bailey
Pill
Shirley Holms
Hill House School
Rope Hill
Boldre
Tweed Lane
Boldre Lane
William Gilpin CE Primary School
Pilley Hill
Spinners Garden and Nursery
St Austins
Mount Pleasant
Passford House Hotel
Works
School Lane
Warborne Lane
Warborne
PASSFORD HILL
Southlands School
Portmore
Hundred Lane
Vicars Hill
Mill Lane
Jealous Lane

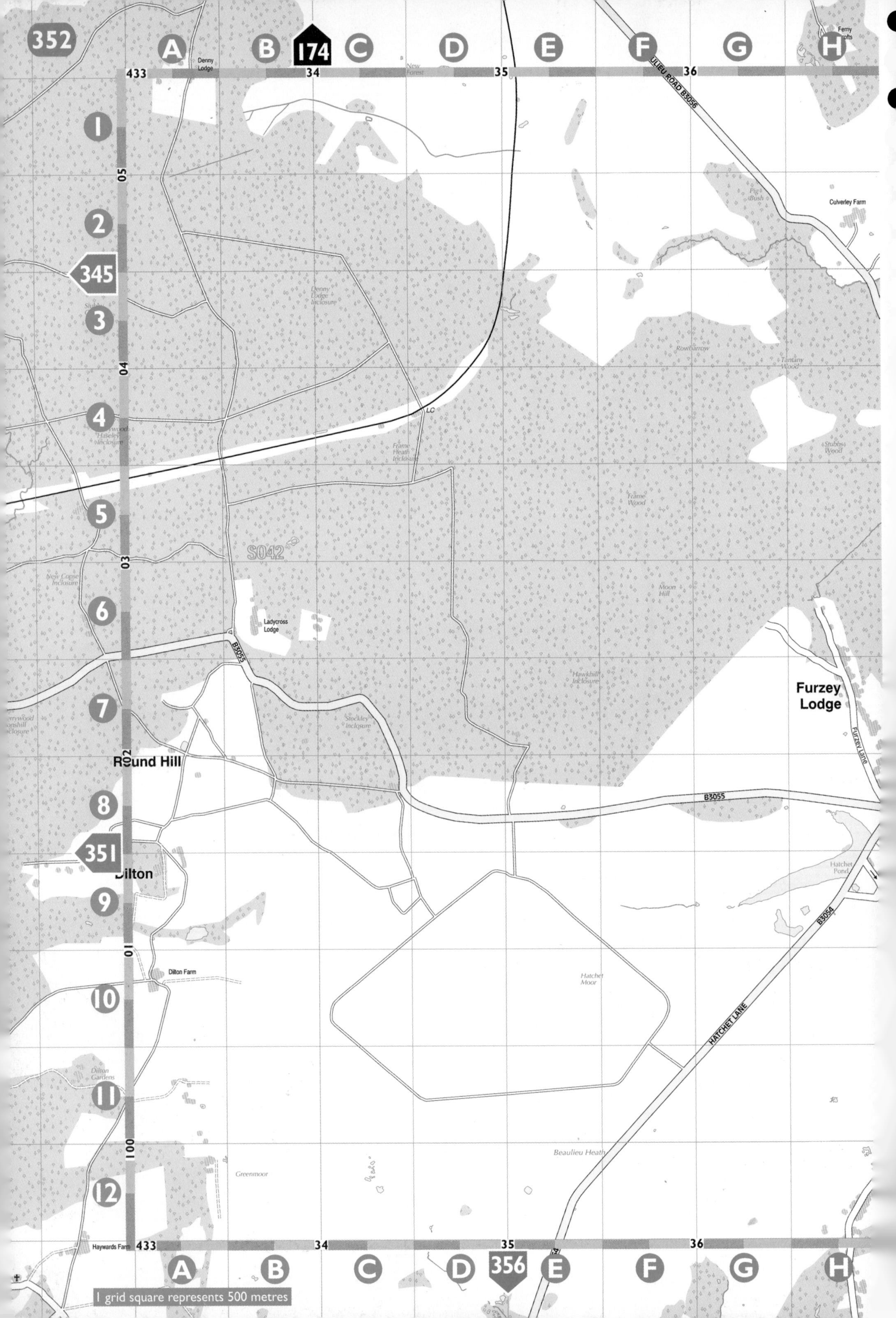

352
174
345
351
356
A
B
C
D
E
F
G
H
433
34
35
36
05
04
03
02
01
100
1
2
3
4
5
6
7
8
9
10
11
12
Denny Lodge
New Forest
LYNDHURST ROAD B3056
Ferny Crofts
Pig Bush
Culverley Farm
Denny Lodge Inclosure
Rowbarrow
Tantany Wood
LC
Frame Heath Inclosure
Stubbs Wood
Frame Wood
SO42
New Copse Inclosure
Moon Hill
Ladycross Lodge
B3055
Hawkhill Inclosure
Stockley Inclosure
Furzey Lodge
Furzey Lane
Round Hill
B3055
Dilton
Hatchet Pond
B3054
Dilton Farm
Hatchet Moor
HATCHET LANE
Dilton Gardens
Beaulieu Heath
Greenmoor
Haywards Farm
1 grid square represents 500 metres

J **175** K L M N P **176** Q

37 38 39 40 41

Ⅰ

Ⅱ

Ⅲ

Ⅳ

Ⅴ

Ⅵ

354

Ⅶ

Ⅷ

Ⅸ

Ⅹ

Ⅺ

Ⅻ

05

04

03

02

01

Fawley Inclosure

King's Hat Inclosure

Crabhat Inclosure

Beaulieu Heath

Stonyford Pond

Foxhunting Inclosure

North Gate

The House in the Wood

Hartford Heath

Shepton Bridge

North Lane

Penerley Lodge

Leygreen Farm

Hides Close

Great Goswell Copse

B3054

Solent Way

BEAULIEU ROAD

Hill Top

Hilltop House

Hatchet Green Lane

Beaulieu : National Motor Museum

Palace House

Beaulieu Abbey

PALACE LANE

PALACE LANE

Moonhills Lane

Moonhills Copse

Otterwood

B3054

Montagu Arms Hotel

Beaulieu Primary School

Beaulieu

HIGH STREET

Carpenters Dock

Dock Lane

Oxley's Copse

The Hummocks

Otterwood

Sunmere Lane

Crossley Lane

Steerl Copse

Hatchet Gate

HATCHET LANE

B3054

The Lodge

Solent Way

Beaulieu River

Dock Lane

Spearbed Copse

Swinesleys Farm

Beufre Farm

Masseys La

East Boldre Road

Heath Lane

Whitmers Lane

Pages Lane

Cara Av

Matthews Lane

PO

Chapel Lane

Wallace Lane

New Inn Lane

Knights Copse

Cripple Gate Lane

East Boldre

Lodge Lane

Solent Way

Keeping Copse

Beaulieu River

Keeping

Ashen Wood

Bucklers Hard

PH

Master Builders House Hotel

Bucklers Hard Village & Maritime Museum

Little Purnel

Newhouse Copse

Lodge Farm

Tilers Copse

Saltershill Copse

Clobb

J K L M **357** N P Q R

38 39 40 41

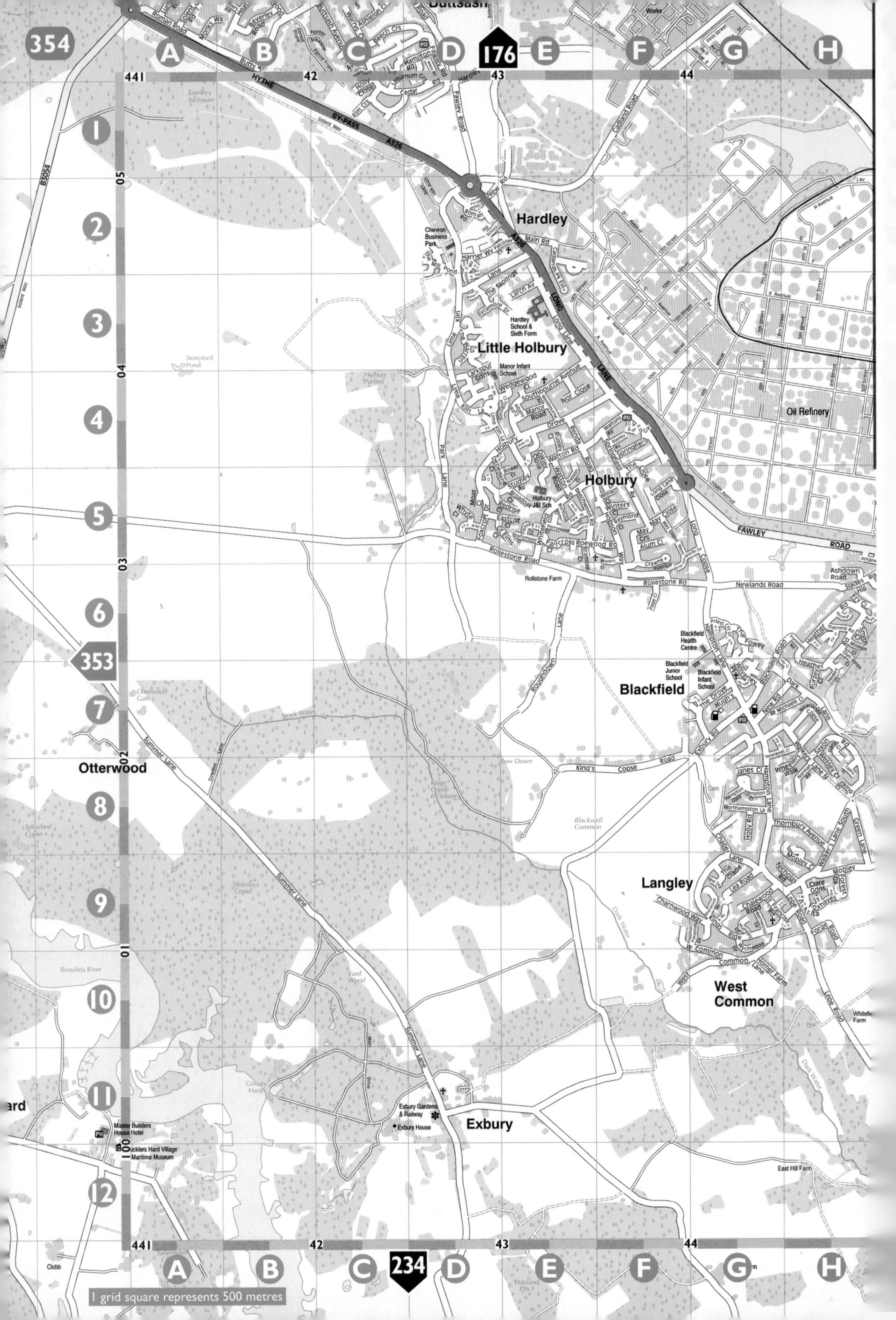

354
176
353
234
Hardley
Little Holbury
Holbury
Blackfield
Langley
West Common
Otterwood
Exbury
Oil Refinery
Hardley School & Sixth Form
Chevron Business Park
Manor Infant School
Holbury J&I Sch
Blackfield Health Centre
Blackfield Junior School
Blackfield Infant School
Rollstone Farm
Exbury Gardens & Railway
Exbury House
Master Builders House Hotel
Bucklers Hard Village Maritime Museum
East Hill Farm
HYTHE BY-PASS
A326
LONG LANE
FAWLEY ROAD
Summer Lane
Rollestone Road
Newlands Road
King's Copse Road
Park Lane
Beaulieu River
Stonyford Pond
Blackwell Common
Row Down
1 grid square represents 500 metres

J
K
L
M
N
P
Q
45
46
47
48
49
Hamble Spit
Cadland Creek
Foreshore
North Trestle Road
South Trestle Road
Burnham Road
Agwi Road
Ashlett Creek
Ashlett
Fawley
Stonehills
FAWLEY BY-PASS
B3053
Northern Access Road
Badminston Farm
Fields Heath
Fields Farm
Badminston Lane
Badminston Drove
Ower
Calshot
Calshot Castle
Calshot Cl
Tristan Close
Castle Lane
Hillhead
Eaglehurst
Mopley Pond
Tom's Down
Badminston Common
Sprat's Down
Stanswood Road
Stanswood Farm
Nelson's Place
Stanswood Bay
Cadland House
Lepe Road
Stone Farm
The Solent
COWES ISLE OF WIGHT
SO45
Fawley Infant School
Fawley Business Centre
School Rd
Church
Copthorne Lane
Clinic
The Pentagon
Chapel La
Gilchrist Gdns
Hook Park Road
New
178
179
235
R
1
2
3
4
5
6
7
8
9
10
11
12
05
04
03
02
01
100

356
352
351
221
A
B
C
D
E
F
G
H
1
2
3
4
5
6
7
8
9
10
11
12
433
34
35
36
99
98
97
96
95
094
Greenmoor
Haywards Farm
Pilley
Pilley Bailey
Pilley St
Wooden House La
William Gilpin CE Primary School
Gilpin Close
May La
Lucky La
Pilley Hill
Hudson Davies Close
Jordans
Holly Lane
Bull Hill
Jordans Lane
School Lane
Warborne La
Warborne
Warborne Lane
Portmore
Hundred Lane
Southlands School
Vicars Hill
B3054
MAIN ROAD
Undershore
Hordle Walhampton School
Lower Buckland
HAMPTON HILL
Monument Lane
SO41
BRIDGE RD
Walhampton
Lymington Town Station
Riverside Bus Park
Community Cen Cinema
Lymington RC Prim S
Stanwell House Hotel
Lymington Pier Station
Ferry Terminal
Elmers Court Hotel
Grove Road
Waterford Lane
Waterford
All Saints Road
Woodside Lane
Viney Road
Maiden Lane
Normandy
Normandy Lane
Saltworks
The Salterns
Solent Way
Crockford Bridge
Crockford Stream
Norley Inclosure
Norleywood Road
Norley Farm
Norleywood
Thatchers Lane
Joys La
Norleywood Road
Main Road
St Leonards Road
Rowes Lane
Broom Hill
East End
Lymington Road
Brook Hill
Newtown Park
Snooks Lane
South Baddesley
South Baddesley Primary School
Snooks Farm
South Baddesley Road
Shotts Lane
Lisle Court
Lisle Court Road
Mill Lane
Sowley Lane
Tanners Lane
The Solent
YARMOUTH
1 grid square represents 500 metres

J
K
L
M
353
N
P
37
38
39
40
41
Newhouse Copse
Tylers Copse
Saltemshill Copse
Clobb
Saltemshill
Newlands
Drokes
Horsemoor Copse
Newlands Plantation
Coopers Wood
Gins
St Leonards Grange
Gins
Gins House
St Leonards Road
Road
Beck Farm
Solent Way
Bergerie
Warren Lane
The Log House
234
Warren Farm
Sowley Lane
Thorns Lane
Thorns Farm
Park Lane
Park Farm
Solent Way
Sowley Pond
Thorns Beach
Thorns Lane
Little Marsh
Park Shore
Sowley Lane
Sandpit Lane
Browns Lane
Pitts Deep Lane
Works
Sandpit Lane
Colgrims
Pitts Deep
99
98
97
96
95
094
1
2
3
4
5
6
7
8
9
10
11
12
Q
R

Abbotstone 290 H6
Abbotswood 131 G5
Abbots Worthy 289 K10
Abbotts Ann 270 G1
Abshot 180 A4
Alderbury 327 M1
Alderholt 196 B6
Aldermaston 37 M5
Aldermaston Soke 44 F1
Aldermaston Wharf 38 C1
Aldermoor 146 A5
Alderney 212 C6
Aldershot 3 H3
Allbrook 134 A6
Alton 106 E5
Alverstoke 14 B8
Alverstoke 190 E6
Ameysford 204 E7
Ampfield 132 C5
Amport 94 B7
Anchorage Park 185 H4
Andover 5 J5
Andover Down 97 J4
Andwell 67 J3
Anmore 155 H4
Anna Valley 95 M7
Ann's Hill 14 A2
Ansteadbrook 119 J7
Anthill Common 154 D2
Applemore 176 A4
Appleshaw 82 D6
Arborfield 238 H4
Arborfield Cross 239 K5
Arborfield Garrison 239 N9
Arford 111 L6
Ash 74 A5
Ashe 90 A4
Ashfield 137 H4
Ashford 196 F3
Ashford Hill 249 J3
Ash Green 74 D8
Ashington 207 G7
Ashlett 355 L5
Ashley 202 E7
Ashley 219 J5
Ashley 300 D1
Ashley Heath 202 C6
Ashmansworth 251 P1
Ashmore Green 28 D4
Ashton 143 H1
Ashurst 158 C6
Ashurst Bridge 158 C3
Ash Vale 74 A2
Avington 290 A11
Avon 347 M10
Avon Castle 347 K2
Awbridge 129 L4
Axford 278 A1
Axmansford 249 N5
Badshot Lea 260 A2
Baffins 193 H1
Bagmore 256 C10
Bagnor 26 D4
Bailey Green 306 A9
Ball Hill 245 Q1
Balmerlawn 351 M1
Bank 344 H5
Bar End 25 K9
Barford 262 E12
Barkham 239 P6
Barrow Hill 341 P2
Bartley 341 L5
Barton-on-Sea 230 F2
Barton Stacey 273 P6
Bashley 219 G1
Bashley Park 219 H2
Basingstoke 6 C3
Bassett 147 G3
Bassett Green 147 G3
Battramsley 351 L10
Battramsley Cross 351 N11
Batt's Corner 109 K5
Baughurst 249 P5
Baybridge 310 C5
Beacon Hill 115 K1
Beacon Hill 210 A6
Bear Cross 212 F2
Bearwood 212 F2
Beaulieu 353 L8
Beauworth 303 N12
Beckley 218 C3
Bedhampton 170 C7
Beech 106 A7
Beech Hill 41 J3
Bell Hill 120 C4
Bentley 259 K11
Bentworth 279 K7
Bickton 197 H6
Bidden 257 M1
Bighton 292 A7
Binley 251 P8
Binsted 108 A5
Birchy Hill 350 G11
Bishop's Green 247 Q1
Bishop's Sutton 291 R12
Bishopstoke 140 C1
Bishopstone 324 D3
Bishop's Waltham 143 J3
Bisterne 347 M6
Bisterne Close 349 M2
Bitterne 161 L1
Bitterne Park 147 K7
Black Dam 7 J8
Blackfield 354 F7
Blackhill 335 L7
Blackmoor 112 B5
Blacknest 108 F5
Blackwater 49 M4
Blackwater 215 H3
Blashford 203 J1
Bleak Hill 198 E1
Blendworth 156 E1
Blissford 338 A4
Boarhunt 167 H3
Bodenham 326 H3
Bohemia 332 H4
Boldre 351 P11
Boorley Green 149 L2
Borden 317 R2
Bordon 113 G2
Boscombe 226 E5
Bossington 299 K1
Botley 150 B6
Boundstone 78 F4
Bournemouth 9 G6
The Bourne 79 G2
Bourne Valley 225 H2
Boveridge 336 G2
Bowling Alley 70 E8
Bowling Green 220 E2
Boyatt Wood 139 M3
Bradley 278 F4
Braishfield 131 J1
Brambridge 134 D4
Bramdean 304 E7
Bramley 46 A4
Bramley Corner 53 K1
Bramley Green 46 D5
Bramshaw 334 D12
Bramshill 240 H5
Bramshott 116 C2
Branksome 224 F3
Branksome Park 224 F6
Bransbury 273 L3
Bransgore 348 D12
Breach 172 D5
Breamore 331 N7
Bridgemary 182 B5
Brighton Hill 93 G4
Brimpton 36 E6
Brimpton Common 249 N2
Broadgate 132 E6
Broad Layings 246 B3
Broadmere 92 F8
Broad Oak 69 J4
Broadoak 149 L5
Broadstone 211 H4
Brockbridge 319 K2
Brockenhurst 351 J3
Brockhampton 16 B6
Brockhurst 190 D2
Brock's Green 247 Q4
Brook 299 L6
Brook 340 E4
Brooke's Hill 144 B4
Brook Hill 340 E2
Broughton 284 E10
Brown Candover 277 K9
Browndown 190 C5
Brown Heath 142 C7
Browninghill Green 249 R9
Bucket Corner 138 C1
Buckland 221 J3
Bucklebury Alley 28 E2
Bucklers Hard 353 Q11
Bucks Horn Oak 109 G4
Buckskin 64 C8
Bull Hill 356 B3
Bunker's Hill 341 L2
Bunstead 133 J2
Burgates 308 E6
Burghclere 246 H5
Burghclere Common 247 J3
Buriton 315 Q11
Burley 349 K1
Burley Beacon 348 G2
Burley Lawn 349 L1
Burley Street 342 G11
Burridge 164 A2
Bursledon 163 G4
Burton 216 C7
Bury's Bank 34 E5
Butlocks Heath 162 D5
Buttermere 243 Q1
Buttsash 177 H8
Butt's Green 298 C11
The Butts 106 E6
Cadley 264 H3
Cadnam 341 K4
Cadnam Green 341 J3
Calmore 144 C7
Calshot 355 P8
Camberley 51 G1
Camel Green 196 D6
Camelsdale 118 A7
Canada 334 H7
Canford Cliffs 237 J1
Canford Heath 211 L7
Canford Magna 208 A7
Carter's Clay 129 G2
Carter's Hill 239 L1
Catherington 321 J11
Catisfield 181 G3
Causeway 120 C7
Causeway 156 B3
Chalton 321 R7
Chandler's Ford 133 K8
Chandlers Green 47 M6
Charleshill 260 E11
Charlton 96 A2
Charlton-All-Saints 327 K8
Charlwood 306 A1
Charminster 214 C7
Charter Alley 52 B4
Chawton 294 D1
Cheriton 303 R7
Chidden 320 B4
Chilbolton 272 E8
Chilbolton Down 287 J2
Chilbridge 206 D1
Chilcomb 123 M7
Chilton Candover 277 N7
Chilworth 138 D7
Chilworth Old Village 138 C6
Chineham 54 B5
Cholderton 268 C3
Christchurch 228 B3
Christmaspie 75 H8
Church Common 307 M12
Church Crookham 71 H3
Church End 54 E2
Church Oakley 91 G2
Churt 262 F11
Chute Cadley 80 F5
Chute Standen 80 D4
Clanfield 321 K7
Clanville 81 F5
Clarken Green 90 F2
Clatford Oakcuts 271 J8
Clayhall 15 G9
Clayhill 345 L5
Cliddesden 93 H5
Cobley 328 D2
Colbury 158 D6
Cold Ash 28 E5
Cold Ash Hill 116 E3
Colden Common 135 G3
Cole Henley 87 M1
Colehill 207 M1
Colemore 306 H2
Collingbourne Ducis 264 G4
Colt Hill 69 H5
Colthrop 36 B1
Combe 244 D6
The Common 282 G10
Compton 77 K7
Compton 124 D5
Compton 219 L5
Compton 323 J10
Compton End 124 C3
Conford 113 M5
Coombe 313 P10
Coombe Bissett 325 M3
Copnor 185 G7
Copythorne 341 N2
Corfe Mullen 210 C2
Corhampton 312 D11
Cosham 169 G8
Cottonworth 272 C8
Couch Green 289 Q9
Court Corner 52 D1
Cove 60 E2
Cowesfield Green 127 J5
Cowgrove 206 D3
Cowplain 155 M5
Coxford 146 A6
Crab Orchard 201 G6
Crampmoor 131 L7
Cranborne 336 D4
Cranbourne 93 H2
Crawley 287 M6
Crawley Hill 51 G3
Creekmoor 211 G8
Crendell 337 M5
Cricket Hill 49 G3
Criddlestyle 197 K3
Cripplestyle 337 N7
Critchell's Green 298 B12
Critchmere 117 L1
Crockerhill 166 A1
Crockham Heath 32 F6
Crondall 259 N1
Crooked Withies 204 B1
Crookham 36 B7
Crookham Village 70 E2
Crosswater 262 E8
Crossways 262 E11
Croucheston 324 C5
Crow 203 M8
Crowdhill 135 J7
Crowthorne 43 G3
Crux Easton 251 Q3
Cuckoo's Corner 281 L4
Cufaude 54 A1
Cupernham 131 G7
Curbridge 150 D8
Curdridge 150 E4
Custards 345 L3
Daggons 337 Q7
Damerham 330 D11
Daneshill 54 A8
Darby Green 49 J2
Deadwater 113 H1
Dean 143 L1
Dean 301 Q1
Deane 90 C3
Deanlane End 157 K3
Deepcut 62 C2
The Dene 250 H8
Denmead 154 F3
Denvilles 17 L2
Dewlands Common 200 F3
Dibden 176 D3
Dibden Purlieu 176 C7
Dilton 351 R5
Dipley 240 G12
Dippenhall 76 B6
Dockenfield 109 M6
Dogmersfield 70 C2
Donnington 26 F6
Dora's Green 76 A3
Downton 231 M1
Downton 332 D1
Drayton 169 J8
Droxford 318 G3
Dry Hill 293 J3
Dudsbury 209 J7
Dummer 103 M3
Dunbridge 298 E11
Dundridge 318 B3
Dunley 252 E8
Durleighmarsh 121 L6
Durley 142 B6
Durley Street 142 C4
Durns Town 350 G10
Durrants 157 H8
Earlstone Common 246 H4
Eashing 261 R11
East Anton 84 E8
East Aston 98 F5
East Boldre 353 K11
East Cholderton 94 B6
East Dean 297 N10
East End 206 E7
East End 245 P5
East End 313 M3
East End 356 H5
East Fields 19 G6
East Green 259 N10
East Grimstead 296 C8
East Harting 323 P1
East Howe 213 J5
Eastland Gate 155 K3
Eastleigh 140 B1
East Liss 308 H9
East Marden 323 R10
East Martin 329 N4
East Meon 314 B8
Eastney 193 J5
East Oakley 91 L2
Eastoke 195 J6
Easton 289 N11
East Parley 346 E12
Eastrop 7 J6
East Stratton 276 C8
East Tisted 294 C11
East Tytherley 298 B5
East Wellow 335 L3
East Winterslow 282 F8
East Woodhay 245 L5
East Worldham 107 L7
Ebblake 201 M4
Ecchinswell 247 P8
Edmondsham 336 H9
Egbury 252 B10
Egypt 274 D7
Eling 159 H3
Ellingham 199 G7
Ellisfield 105 K4
Elson 183 G8
Elstead 263 R1
Elsted 317 N12
Elvetham 58 D3
Elvetham Heath 59 G4
Emery Down 344 H2
Empshott 308 A1
Empshott Green 307 R1
Emsworth 187 L1
Enborne 32 F4
Enborne Row 33 H8
Enham Alamein 84 E5
Ensbury 213 L2
Ensbury Park 213 J6
Eversley 241 P3
Eversley Centre 241 R4
Eversley Cross 42 B8
Everton 220 E7
Ewshot 71 J8
Exbury 354 D11
Exton 312 E9
Faberstown 265 P11
Faccombe 244 H11
Fairmile 215 M7
Fair Oak 141 J2
Fair Oak 249 J5
Fair Oak Green 46 D2
Fareham 10 D5
Farleigh Wallop 105 G2
Farley 296 D4
Farley Hill 239 K11
Farlington 169 K8
Farnborough 61 G4
Farnborough Green 61 J3
Farnborough Park 61 K5
Farnborough Street 61 J3
Farnham 12 F4
Fawley 355 K6
Ferndown 209 H3
Filmore Hill 305 Q8
Finchampstead 241 R1
Finchdean 157 J2
Firsdown 282 B9
Fisher's Pond 135 H6
Fleet 59 J7
Fleet 186 F8
Fleetend 179 M3
Fleetlands 182 C3
Flexford 75 K7
Flexford 132 F8
Flood Street 331 M9
Folly Hill 76 E3
Fordingbridge 197 J3
Forest Gate 154 D1
Forton 14 E1
Forton 98 B8
Fosbury 243 K7
Foulford 342 C9
Four Houses Corner 39 L4
Four Marks 293 N6
Foxdown 89 L2
Foxhills 158 D5
Fox Lane 50 B7
Foyers 341 N9
Fratton 21 M1
Freefolk 88 B6
Freemantle 160 C2
The Frenches 129 H6
Frenchmoor 297 M6
Frensham 262 B5
Friars Cliff 229 J2
Frimley 50 E7
Frimley Green 61 M1
Frimley Ridge 51 J5
Fritham 339 P3
Frithend 109 H8
Frogham 338 A6
Frogmore 49 K2
Frostlane 177 J6
Froxfield Green 306 G12
Fryern Hill 139 K2
Fulflood 24 B4
Fullerton 272 A9
Funtington 173 J1
Funtley 165 L7
Furzedown 299 R5
Furze Hill 338 A9
Furzeley Corner 154 F7
Furzey 340 E9
Furzey Lodge 352 H7
Furzley 334 H11
Fyfield 94 A2
Fyning 317 N3
Gilbert Street 293 K10
Glebe 151 J1
Gobley Hole 104 E4
Godshill 338 A2
Godswinscroft 217 H3
Goldenhayes 341 M8
Golden Hill 219 K5
Golden Pot 280 D1
Goldfinch Bottom 35 J7
Goodworth Clatford 271 P3
Goose Green 345 L4
Goose Hill 248 F1
Gore End 32 B8
Gosport 15 J4
Gosport 132 A6
Gotham 337 L9
Grange Estate 346 F4
Grateley 269 N3
Grayshott 115 H5
Grayswood 119 G3
Greatham 308 E3
Great Lea Common 238 A2
Great Shoddesden 267 N2
Green Cross 262 H11
Greenham 34 C4
The Green 297 P5
Greywell 68 A5
Griggs Green 113 M8
Gundleton 292 B9
Habin 317 M6
Hale 77 H3
Hale 332 E6
Halecommon 317 L3
Halterworth 137 J1
Hambledon 319 P9
Hamble-le-Rice 178 F1
Hambrook 173 G4
Hammer 117 J3
Hammer Bottom 117 H3
Hampreston 208 E6
Hampton Park 147 J5
Hamptworth 333 Q4
Hamstead Marshall 31 M5
Hamworthy 222 E5
Hangersley 342 A6
Hannington 254 F4
Harbridge 199 G3
Harbridge Green 198 F2
Hardley 354 E2
Hardway 191 H1
Harefield 148 C5
Harestock 122 C1
Hartfordbridge 241 P12
Hartley Mauditt 295 L3
Hartley Wespall 47 J7
Hartley Wintney 57 K1
Haslemere 118 D6
Hatch 66 E3
Hatch Bottom 148 D2
Hatchet Gate 353 J8
Hatchet Green 332 E5
Hatch Warren 92 C6
Hatherden 83 L3
Hatt Hill 298 F11
Hattingley 292 G1
Haughurst Hill 249 N3
Havant 16 E1
Hawkley 307 Q5
Hawley 50 A5
Hawley Lane 61 H1
Hawthorn 293 N9
Hayling Island 187 H6
Hazeley 240 G9
Hazeley Bottom 241 J11
Hazeley Lea 240 H9
Headbourne Worthy 288 F11
Headley 111 K7
Headley 248 C3
Headley Down 114 B4
Hearn 114 B1
Heath End 77 H1
Heath End 245 N3
Heath End 249 R3
Heather Row 67 M2
Heatherside 51 L4
Heathfield 181 J3
Heath Green 292 E1
Heckfield 240 C6
Hedge End 149 H5
Hell Corner 31 H7
Henley 243 L5
Hensting 135 K3
Hermitage 172 A5
Herriard 256 B7
Hides Close 353 M4
Highbridge 134 D5
Highbury 184 F2
Highclere 246 B7
Highclere Street 245 R9
Highcliffe 218 A8
High Cross 307 K10
Highfield 147 G6
Hightown 148 E8
Hightown 203 M5
Highwood 342 A4
Hillbourne 211 G6
Hill Brow 309 J10
Hillbutts 206 F1
Hill Head 188 F3
Hill Park 181 K1
Hillpound 318 C8
Hillside 69 J6
Hill Side 308 G8
Hillstreet 144 B3
Hill Top 353 Q4
Hill View 210 D4
Hillyfields 145 J4
Hilsea 184 F4
Hiltingbury 133 K6
Hindhead 115 M4
Hinton 218 A4
Hinton Ampner 304 A8
Hocombe 133 H6
Hoe 143 M5
Hoe Gate 153 M1
Hog Hatch 76 D2
Holbury 354 E5
Holdenhurst 215 G5
Hollington 245 Q8
Hollington Cross 245 R9
Hollywater 113 H3
Holt 56 F7
Holt End 279 L9
Holt Heath 204 C2
Holt Pound 78 B4
Holybourne 107 J1
Homington 325 R3
Hook 56 D7
Hook 179 L5
Hook Park 179 K6
Hopgoods Green 29 L4
Hordle 220 A4
Horndean 156 C2
Horsebridge 299 L3
Horton Common 200 E6
Horton Heath 141 J4
Horton Heath 200 C7
Houghton 285 L11
Hound 162 E6
Hound Green 240 E9
Houndmills 65 G5
Hounsdown 158 E4
Hungerford 197 L7
Hunton 274 G8
Hurn 215 H1
Hursley 133 H1
Hurstbourne Priors 98 E2
Hurstbourne Tarrant 250 G9
Hyde 25 H3
Hyde 197 L6
Hyde End 36 E8
Hythe 177 H4
Ibsley 199 J5
Ibthorpe 250 E8
Ibworth 255 M6
Ifford 227 K1
Inhurst 249 N4
Inkpen 30 C7
Inkpen Common 30 F7
Isington 108 A3
Itchen 161 L5
Itchen Abbas 290 A10
Itchen Stoke 290 F10
Jumpers Common 215 L8
Kempshott 92 C3
Kempshott Park 92 A8
Kent's Oak 129 L3
Keyhaven 233 G5
Kilmeston 303 R11
Kimbridge 298 G12
Kimpton 267 P6
Kingsclere 248 C11
Kingsclere Woodlands 248 E4
Kings Furlong 6 A7
Kingsley 110 C3
Kingsmead 318 C12
King's Somborne 299 P1
Kingston 192 F1
Kingston 347 M3
Kings Worthy 289 J10
Kinson 213 H3
Kintbury 31 G2
Kitwood 293 L9
Knapp 132 D4
Knighton 212 D1
Knights Enham 84 C7
Knowle Village 165 L5
Ladwell 133 H4
Lake 222 D7
Lambs Green 206 E6
Landford 334 B4
Landfordwood 334 B1
Lane End 262 D5
Lane End 303 J12
Lane End 306 B5
Langdown 177 H5
Langley 309 M6
Langley 354 F9
Langley Common 239 M7
Langrish 314 G4
Langstone 186 E2
Lasham 279 P2
Latchmere Green 45 J7
Laverstoke 88 E7
Layland's Green 31 H3
Leagreen 220 A8
Leckford 272 B12
Lee 137 G8
Lee Ground 165 G7
Lee-on-the-Solent 189 K7
Leigh 207 M4
Leigh Park 170 D4
Lepe 235 J2
Lilliput 237 H1
Linchmere 117 G5
Lindford 111 H8
Linford 342 C6
Linkenholt 244 D11
Linwood 338 D12
Liphook 116 A5
Liss 308 G9
Liss Forest 308 F5
Litchfield 252 G8
Little Ann 95 J8
Little Canford 208 C4
Littledown 227 G1
Littledown 243 R8
Little Hoddington 257 L3

Little Holbury 354 D3
Little London 52 F1
Little London 84 F4
Little Posbrook 180 E7
Little Sandhurst 43 J6
Little Shoddesden 267 Q2
Little Somborne 286 B10
Littleton 288 B11
Lockerley 298 A11
Locks Heath 180 A1
London Minstead 340 C8
Long Common 149 M3
Longfleet 223 J4
Longham 209 H7
Longparish 98 D6
Long Park 287 Q8
Longstock 285 N1
Long Sutton 258 C5
Lord's Hill 146 A4
Lordswood 146 D4
Lovedean 155 L2
Lover 332 H3
Lower Bordean 314 E2
Lower Bourne 79 J2
Lower Brook 299 K8
Lower Buckland 221 L3
Lower Bullington 274 A5
Lower Burgate 331 M12
Lower Chute 80 D5
Lower Common 105 K6
Lower Common 241 M3
Lower Daggons 337 N5
Lower Farringdon 294 D5
Lower Froyle 258 G11
Lower Green 30 B7
Lower Hamworthy 223 G7
Lower Holwell 337 K6
Lower Mannington 200 D8
Lower Pennington 221 J8
Lower Ratley 129 M5
Lower Slackstead 131 M1
Lower Swanwick 163 J4
Lower Turmer 198 E5
Lower Upham 310 D12
Lower Wield 278 F6
Lowford 163 G3
Ludgershall 265 N9
Lumley 172 A5
Lychpit 66 B1
Lyde Green 56 A1
Lymington 221 K4
Lymore 232 F2
Lynch 89 G4
Lynch Hill 87 M7
Lyndhurst 345 J3
Malwood 340 E8
Mannington 200 C8
Mapledurwell 67 G5
Marchwood 160 A6
Marley Heights 117 M7
Marsh Benham 32 D1
Marten 242 C3
Martin 329 N5
Martin Drove End 328 G1
Martyr Worthy 289 P10
Mattingley 240 D12
Maybush 145 L6
Mead End 350 C11
Medstead 293 J2
Mengham 195 H5
Meon 188 E1
Meonstoke 312 F12
Merley 207 L7
Merritown 214 E1
Merry Oak 161 L3
Meyrick Park 8 C1
Micheldever 275 P9
Micheldever Station 275 P2
Michelmersh 299 L11
Midanbury 147 M8
Middle Bockhampton 216 F2
Middle Bourne 79 G1
Middleton 98 C7
Middle Wallop 270 A12
Middle Winterslow 282 G9
Midgham 36 E1
Miles's Green 29 L5
Milford on Sea 232 B5
Millbridge 79 H7
Millbrook 159 L1
Mill Green 248 D1
Mill Lane 70 C7
Milton 193 J4
Minstead 340 F9
The Mint 308 G7
Mockbeggar 199 M5
Monk Sherborne 52 D6
Monkwood 305 Q2
Montgomery Lines 73 J4
Monxton 94 D7
Moorcourt 144 C1
Moordown 214 A7
Moorgreen 148 F1
Moor Park 77 M7
Moortown 203 K7
Morestead 125 M4
Morgan's Vale 332 E1
Mortimer 40 A2
Mortimer West End 39 K8
Mottisfont 298 G10
The Mount 246 B5
Mudeford 229 G3
Mullenspond 94 A4
Murrell Green 57 G5
Muscliff 214 B3
Mytchett 61 L5
Mytchett Place 62 B6
Nash's Green 256 E9
Nately Scures 67 L1
Neacroft 217 H2
Neatham 107 L2
Netherton 244 F12
Nether Wallop 284 C2
Netley 162 B6
Netley Hill 148 F8
Netley Marsh 158 A2
New Alresford 291 L10
Newbridge 341 J1
New Brighton 172 A3
Newbury 18 C4
New Cheriton 303 R8
Newfound 91 K1
Newgrounds 338 C2
New Milton 218 E4
Newnham 55 M8
Newton 126 F6
Newton Stacey 273 J7
Newton Tony 268 B7
Newton Valence 294 H10
New Town 162 A3
Newtown 34 B8
Newtown 106 D6
Newtown 116 B6
Newtown 129 H4
Newtown 142 F4
Newtown 153 J1
Newtown 179 K5
Newtown 224 B1
Newtown 340 F10
Nob's Crook 135 G5
No Man's Land 123 M4
Nomansland 334 B8
Norleywood 356 F4
Normandy 75 H4
Norney 261 Q10
Northam 161 J2
North Baddesley 138 A4
North Boarhunt 153 G6
North Bockhampton 216 E1
Northbourne 213 K4
Northbrook 143 J3
Northbrook 275 M8
North Camp 73 H2
North Charford 332 E4
North End 184 F6
North End 245 M2
North End 303 Q5
North End 330 C11
Northfields 125 G5
North Gorley 199 K1
North Hayling 187 J5
North Houghton 285 M8
Northington 276 H12
North Kingston 347 Q2
North Marden 323 R7
Northney 187 J4
North Oakley 254 E7
North Poulner 203 M2
North Ripley 347 R8
North Stoneham 147 K1
North Street 292 G9
North Street 331 P6
North Tidworth 266 G1
North Town 73 L6
North Waltham 103 G2
North Warnborough 68 E4
North Weirs 350 G3
Nunton 326 F3
Nursling 145 J3
Nursted 316 C9
Nutbourne 172 F7
Nutburn 138 B3
Nutcombe 115 K6
Nutley 104 E7
Nyewood 317 L8
Oakdale 223 L2
Oakhanger 295 R4
Oakley 91 J3
Oakley 207 K7
Oakridge 65 K5
Oakshott 307 P8
Ocean Village 23 K7
Odiham 69 G6
Odstock 325 C3
Ogdens 338 B7
Old Alresford 291 L7
Old Basing 66 C2
Old Burghclere 246 G12
Old Milton 218 E7
Old Netley 162 E3
Old Portsmouth 20 C4
Old Shirley 146 A7
Oliver's Battery 124 A1
Ossemsley 349 N11
Otterbourne 124 B8
Otterwood 353 R8
Outwick 331 L8
Overton 89 K5
Over Wallop 269 Q10
Ovington 290 G12
Ower 335 R10
Owlsmoor 43 M6
Owslebury 135 M1
Oxenwood 242 H5
Padworth 38 E3
Padworth Common 38 F6
Palestine 269 L6
Pamber End 52 D3
Pamber Green 44 E8
Pamber Heath 44 D2
Pamphill 206 E2
Pardown 91 K6
Park Gate 164 B7
Parkstone 224 B6
Parley Green 214 C2
Passfield 113 M3
Paulsgrove 168 A8
Peartree Green 161 K4
Peel Common 189 M2
Pennington 221 J6
Penton Corner 95 J3
Penton Grafton 95 G1
Penton Mewsey 83 J8
Pentridge 328 F8
Penwood 246 C4
Peper Harow 261 N11
Perham Down 267 J1
Petersfield 120 B6
Pheonix Green 57 J4
Picket Hill 342 C8
Picket Piece 97 J2
Pikeshill 345 J2
Pilley 356 B2
Pilley Bailey 351 R10
Pirbright 63 M4
Pitch Place 263 N9
Pitt 122 A7
Pitton 282 A12
The Pitts 324 E3
Plaitford 334 E4
Plaitford Green 128 C8
Plastow Green 248 E5
Pokesdown 227 G4
Pondtail 59 M8
Pooksgreen 159 K6
Poole 223 H5
Popham 103 G8
Popley 65 L3
Portchester 167 H8
Portmore 356 A5
Portsea 20 E2
Portsea Island 185 H8
Portsmouth 20 C1
Port Solent 183 M1
Portswood 147 H7
Potbridge 57 J8
Pot Common 263 Q2
Poulner 203 M4
Pound Green 249 P9
Pound Street 246 E5
Powntley Copse 257 M11
Preston Candover 277 Q4
Priddy's Hard 191 J1
Prince's Marsh 308 F10
Prinsted 172 C7
Privett 190 E5
Privett 306 A10
Pucknall 131 M2
Purbrook 169 K3
Purewell 228 C1
Puttenham 261 M3
Pylehill 141 J1
Pyott's Hill 54 C7
Quarley 267 N12
Quidhampton 89 K3
Racedown 267 L10
Rafborough 60 E5
Ragged Appleshaw 82 E6
Rake 309 L8
Ramsdean 314 G7
Ramsdell 52 A5
Ramsnest Common 119 M5
Ratlake 132 E5
Ravenswood Village Settlement 43 G1
Redbridge 145 J8
Redenham 82 B5
Red Hill 157 H7
Red Hill 213 M4
Redlynch 332 G1
Red Rice 271 L4
Ridge 136 C7
Ridge Common 120 A4
The Ridges 42 D4
Ringwood 203 G4
Ripley 347 Q10
Riseley 240 C1
Rockbourne 330 E7
Rockford 199 L7
Rogate 317 L5
Romford 200 D1
Romsey 136 E1
Ropley 292 H12
Ropley Dean 292 E11
Ropley Soke 293 J8
Rossmore 224 E1
Rotherwick 56 A2
Rotten Green 58 F3
Round Hill 351 R4
Row Ash 151 G4
Rowland's Castle 157 K6
Rowledge 109 M1
Rowner 182 C8
Rownhams 145 M1
Runfold 260 A5
Rushcombe Bottom 210 E1
Rushington 158 F2
Rushmoor 263 J5
Rushmore 320 A10
Ryeish Green 238 C4
St Austins 351 M12
St Catherine's Hill 215 L5
St Cross 122 F7
St Denys 147 J8
St Giles's Hill 25 K6
St Ives 202 C7
St Leonards 202 A7
St Mary Bourne 86 C3
Salters Heath 52 F4
Sandbanks 237 H5
Sandford 347 R4
Sandhurst 43 K7
Sandleheath 196 B2
The Sands 260 C6
Sandy Cross 260 D4
Sandy Down 351 N8
Sarisbury 163 L7
Sarson 94 D6
Schoolgreen 238 D4
Seale 260 F4
Selborne 295 L9
Selsmore 195 K6
Setley 351 L7
Shackleford 261 P9
Shalden 280 A4
Shalden Green 257 J12
Shaw 27 K7
Shawford 124 E5
Shedfield 151 K5
Sheet 120 F3
Shepherd's Hill 118 C6
Sherborne St John 52 F8
Sherfield English 128 D7
Sherfield on Loddon 47 G8
Sherfield Park 54 C3
Shinfield 238 D3
Shipton Bellinger 266 D9
Shirley 146 D8
Shirley 348 C10
Shirley Holms 351 L11
Shirley Warren 146 B6
Shirrell Heath 318 A11
Shobley 342 C7
Sholing 148 B8
Sholing Common 148 A7
Shootash 129 K7
Shorley 303 P11
Shorn Hill 144 A5
Shortfield Common 78 F6
Shortheath 78 F2
Shortheath 110 A6
Shottermill 117 L2
Silchester 45 H4
Silkstead 133 L3
Skinners Green 33 H4
Sladen Green 251 P7
The Slade 29 J4
Sleaford 111 G3
Sleight 206 C7
Smannell 85 G6
Soake 155 H5
Soberton 319 J6
Soberton Heath 318 G11
Soldridge 293 J6
Somerford 228 E1
Sopley 216 B1
Southampton 22 C5
South Baddesley 356 E6
South Bockhampton 216 D4
Southbourne 172 E6
Southbourne 227 L5
South Down 124 D7
South End 337 Q1
South Farnborough 61 K7
South Gorley 199 K2
South Ham 92 F1
South Harting 316 G12
South Hayling 194 E6
Southington 89 H5
Southrope 256 E10
Southsea 192 C7
South Tidworth 266 F4
South Town 293 J3
South View 6 E2
South Warnborough 257 Q5
South Weirs 350 H4
Southwick 167 L2
South Wonston 288 C3
Southwood 60 B5
Spanish Green 47 H5
Sparsholt 301 N1
Spearywell 298 F9
Speen 26 E7
Spreakley 78 F8
Springbourne 9 M1
Stamshaw 184 C7
Standford 113 J2
Standon 301 L10
Stanford End 41 L5
Stanley Green 223 H2
Stanmore 122 D7
Stanpit 228 E2
Stapehill 208 E3
Steep 120 C2
Steep Marsh 308 A11
Sterte 223 H5
Steventon 90 D8
Stockbridge 285 P5
Stockcross 26 B7
Stockheath 16 C1
Stoke 187 G6
Stoke 251 L12
Stoke Charity 274 G9
Stoke Common 134 C7
Stoke Farthing 324 A4
Stonehills 355 L6
Stoner Hill 307 M12
Stoney Cross 340 C8
Stony Batter 297 Q4
Stonyford 335 R12
Stony Heath 249 P11
Stonymarsh 299 J11
The Straits 110 C2
Stratfield Mortimer 40 D3
Stratfield Saye 41 H8
Stratfield Turgis 47 J4
Stratford Tony 325 J3
Street End 311 J12
Stroud 315 L4
Strouden 214 D7
Stroud Green 19 G7
Stubbington 189 K1
Stuckton 197 L5
Sunton 264 F2
Sutton Holms 336 F12
Sutton Scotney 274 D8
Swallowfield 238 D10
Swampton 86 B1
Swanmore 318 B7
Swanwick 164 A5
Swarraton 290 H1
Sway 350 E11
Swaythling 147 L5
Sydmonton 247 M12
Tadden 206 D1
Tadley 44 C5
Talbot Heath 225 H1
Talbot Village 213 J8
Talbot Woods 225 K1
Tangley 81 G6
Tapnage 165 J3
Templeton 30 B3
Terwick Common 317 P3
Testwood 144 E7
Thatcham 28 E8
Thorney Hill 348 G8
Thornhill 148 E7
Thornhill Park 148 D5
Thorns Beach 357 P6
Three Ashes 45 K5
Three Legged Cross 201 G8
Three Mile Cross 238 B4
Throop 214 D4
Thruxton 267 R8
Thursley 263 Q8
Tichborne 303 N3
Tidcombe 242 E7
Tidpit 329 P6
Tilford 263 K1
Tilford Common 79 M7
Tilford Reeds 79 M5
Tilly Down 82 D5
Timsbury 130 C1
Tipner 184 B5
Tiptoe 350 B12
Titchfield 180 D3
Titchfield Common 180 A3
Titchfield Park 164 D8
Titcomb 30 F5
Tongham 260 D2
Toothill 137 L7
Totford 277 J12
Tot Hill 246 G3
Totton 145 G8
Townhill Park 147 M6
Towns End 249 L10
Trapshill 30 E8
Trickett's Cross 346 A5
Trotten Marsh 317 Q1
Trotts 159 J5
Tuckton 227 M3
Tufton 99 K2
Tullecombe 309 L12
Tunworth 256 E2
Turbary Common 212 F6
Turgis Green 47 J5
Turkey Island 151 M5
Turlin Moor 222 B4
Turmer 198 F4
Turner's Green 29 K5
Twyford 125 G6
Tye 187 J7
Up Green 48 A2
Upham 310 F10
Up Marden 323 P12
Up Nately 67 K4
Upper Bucklebury 29 L6
Upper Bullington 274 C4
Upper Burgate 331 N10
Upper Canterton 340 D6
Upper Chute 80 B4
Upper Clatford 96 A8
Upper Common 105 H5
Upper Enham 84 D4
Upper Farringdon 294 F5
Upper Froyle 281 N2
Upper Green 244 D1
Upper Hale 76 F2
Upper Pennington 221 G5
Upper Ratley 129 M4
Upper Shirley 146 D6
Upper Slackstead 300 E11
Upper Street 331 M6
Upper Swanmore 318 C4
Upper Wield 278 D10
Upper Wootton 255 Q6
Up Somborne 286 E11
Upton 145 K1
Upton 222 B1
Upton 250 B5
Upton Grey 257 J3
Vernham Bank 243 N10
Vernham Dean 243 P10
Vernham Row 243 M8
Vernham Street 243 R8
Verwood 201 H2
Wadwick 252 A10
Walhampton 356 A8
Walkford 218 B7
Wallington 11 K4
Wallisdown 213 G7
Waltham Chase 143 K8
Walton Heath 167 J1
Wanborough 261 M2
Warblington 17 K6
Warnborough Green 68 D3
Warnford 312 G4
Warren Corner 76 A1
Warren Corner 307 L7
Warsash 179 K3
Wash Common 33 K7
Wash Water 246 D1
Wasing 37 K7
Waterditch 217 G3
Water End 67 K2
Waterford 356 A10
Waterloo 211 G7
Waterlooville 155 J8
Wecock 155 L5
Weeke 24 B1
Well 258 G6
Wellow Wood 128 D8
Westbourne 172 B1
Westbourne 225 H6
West Cliff 8 B8
West Common 354 G10
West Dean 297 K9
West Down 272 D10
West End 10 C8
West End 109 M4
West End 148 E3
West End 292 F4
West End Green 40 D8
Westfield 194 E6
West Fields 18 B5
West Green 57 H3
West Grimstead 296 A11
West Ham 64 E7
West Harting 316 G9
West Heath 52 A3
West Heath 60 E3
West Howe 212 E4
West Hurn 214 F2
West Leigh 171 G3
West Liss 308 F7
West Marden 323 J12
West Meon 313 K4
West Meon Woodlands 305 L10
West Moors 205 J6
Weston 161 L7
Weston 315 M8
Weston Colley 275 L8
Weston Common 148 B8
Weston Corbett 256 H6
Weston Patrick 257 J6
West Parley 209 M8
Westrop Green 28 F1
West Southbourne 227 K3
West Stratton 276 A7
West Tisted 305 N5
West Town 194 E5
West Tytherley 297 P4
West Wellow 335 J5
West Winterslow 282 D11
West Woodhay 245 J1
West Worldham 295 L1
Wexcombe 242 A5
Weybourne 2 C9
Weyhill 94 E2
Whaddon 327 N3
Wheat Hold 249 J6
Wheatley 108 C7
Wherwell 272 C6
Whitchurch 87 L7
Whitehall 69 H2
Whitehill 112 E2
Whiteley 164 D4
Whitenap 137 J1
Whiteparish 127 G4
Whitley Wood 238 C1
Whitmore 200 B2
Whitsbury 330 G5
Whitway 246 F8
Wick 220 B4
Wick 331 Q1
Wickham 152 A4
Wick Hill 42 C2
Widley 169 J6
Wildern 149 J5
Wildhern 84 A2
Wildmoor 55 G3
Willey Green 75 K4
Wilsom 107 G5
Wimble Hill 259 Q6
Wimborne Minster 207 J3
Wimborne St Giles 336 A7
Wimpson 145 L7
Winchester 25 G7
Winchfield 57 L6
Winchfield Hurst 58 A8
Winklebury 64 D6
Winkton 216 C3
Winnall 25 L4
Winslade 256 B3
Winsor 341 P3
Wintershill 142 D3
Winton 225 M1
Wittensford 340 H4
Wivelrod 279 N11
Wolverton 249 K11
Wolverton Common 249 L8
Wonston 274 F9
Woodcot 182 A5
Woodcott 252 B6
Woodfalls 332 E3
Woodgreen 331 R8
Woodhouse 84 E6
Woodington 335 M2
Woodlands 200 A1
Woodlands 341 Q9
Woodlands Common 200 C2
Woodley 131 J7
Woodmancote 172 F2
Woodmancott 276 G3
Woodside 221 L7
Woodspeen 26 C5
Woodyates 328 D5
Woolhampton 37 J2
Woolmer Hill 117 J1
Woolsbridge 205 J1
Woolston 161 L6
Woolton Hill 245 R5
Wootton 349 Q10
Wootton St Lawrence 255 R9
Worlds End 154 A3
Worting 64 C7
Wrecclesham 78 D2
Wyck 281 N8
Wyke 74 F5
Wymering 168 E8
Yateley 48 F2
York Town 50 C4

USING THE STREET INDEX

Street names are listed alphabetically. Each street name is followed by its postal town or area locality, the Postcode District, the page number, and the reference to the square in which the name is found.

Standard index entries are shown as follows:

Aaron Cl *CFDH* BH17 ....**223** M1

Street names and selected addresses not shown on the map due to scale restrictions are shown in the index with an asterisk:

Abbeywood *ASHV* GU12 * **74** B4

GENERAL ABBREVIATIONS

ACC ACCESS
ALY ALLEY
AP APPROACH
AR ARCADE
ASS ASSOCIATION
AV AVENUE
BCH BEACH
BLDS BUILDINGS
BND BEND
BNK BANK
BR BRIDGE
BRK BROOK
BTM BOTTOM
BUS BUSINESS
BVD BOULEVARD
BY BYPASS
CATH CATHEDRAL
CEM CEMETERY
CEN CENTRE
CFT CROFT
CH CHURCH
CHA CHASE
CHYD CHURCHYARD
CIR CIRCLE
CIRC CIRCUS
CL CLOSE
CLFS CLIFFS
CMP CAMP
CNR CORNER
CO COUNTY
COLL COLLEGE
COM COMMON
COMM COMMISSION
CON CONVENT
COT COTTAGE
COTS COTTAGES
CP CAPE
CPS COPSE
CR CREEK
CREM CREMATORIUM
CRS CRESCENT
CSWY CAUSEWAY
CT COURT
CTRL CENTRAL
CTS COURTS
CTYD COURTYARD
CUTT CUTTINGS
CV COVE
CYN CANYON
DEPT DEPARTMENT
DL DALE
DM DAM
DR DRIVE
DRO DROVE
DRY DRIVEWAY
DWGS DWELLINGS
E EAST
EMB EMBANKMENT
EMBY EMBASSY
ESP ESPLANADE
EST ESTATE
EX EXCHANGE
EXPY EXPRESSWAY
EXT EXTENSION
F/O FLYOVER
FC FOOTBALL CLUB
FK FORK
FLD FIELD
FLDS FIELDS
FLS FALLS
FLS FLATS
FM FARM
FT FORT
FWY FREEWAY
FY FERRY
GA GATE
GAL GALLERY
GDN GARDEN
GDNS GARDENS
GLD GLADE
GLN GLEN
GN GREEN
GND GROUND
GRA GRANGE
GRG GARAGE
GT GREAT
GTWY GATEWAY
GV GROVE
HGR HIGHER
HL HILL
HLS HILLS
HO HOUSE
HOL HOLLOW
HOSP HOSPITAL
HRB HARBOUR
HTH HEATH
HTS HEIGHTS
HVN HAVEN
HWY HIGHWAY
IMP IMPERIAL
IN INLET
IND EST INDUSTRIAL ESTATE
INF INFIRMARY
INFO INFORMATION
INT INTERCHANGE
IS ISLAND
JCT JUNCTION
JTY JETTY
KG KING
KNL KNOLL
L LAKE
LA LANE
LDG LODGE
LGT LIGHT
LK LOCK
LKS LAKES
LNDG LANDING
LTL LITTLE
LWR LOWER
MAG MAGISTRATE
MAN MANSIONS
MD MEAD
MDW MEADOWS
MEM MEMORIAL
MKT MARKET
MKTS MARKETS
ML MALL
ML MILL
MNR MANOR
MS MEWS
MSN MISSION
MT MOUNT
MTN MOUNTAIN
MTS MOUNTAINS
MUS MUSEUM
MWY MOTORWAY
N NORTH
NE NORTH EAST
NW NORTH WEST
O/P OVERPASS
OFF OFFICE
ORCH ORCHARD
OV OVAL
PAL PALACE
PAS PASSAGE
PAV PAVILION
PDE PARADE
PH PUBLIC HOUSE
PK PARK
PKWY PARKWAY
PL PLACE
PLN PLAIN
PLNS PLAINS
PLZ PLAZA
POL POLICE STATION
PR PRINCE
PREC PRECINCT
PREP PREPARATORY
PRIM PRIMARY
PROM PROMENADE
PRS PRINCESS
PRT PORT
PT POINT
PTH PATH
PZ PIAZZA
QD QUADRANT
QU QUEEN
QY QUAY
R RIVER
RBT ROUNDABOUT
RD ROAD
RDG RIDGE
REP REPUBLIC
RES RESERVOIR
RFC RUGBY FOOTBALL CLUB
RI RISE
RP RAMP
RW ROW
S SOUTH
SCH SCHOOL
SE SOUTH EAST
SER SERVICE AREA
SH SHORE
SHOP SHOPPING
SKWY SKYWAY
SMT SUMMIT
SOC SOCIETY
SP SPUR
SPR SPRING
SQ SQUARE
ST STREET
STN STATION
STR STREAM
STRD STRAND
SW SOUTH WEST
TDG TRADING
TER TERRACE
THWY THROUGHWAY
TNL TUNNEL
TOLL TOLLWAY
TPK TURNPIKE
TR TRACK
TRL TRAIL
TWR TOWER
U/P UNDERPASS
UNI UNIVERSITY
UPR UPPER
V VALE
VA VALLEY
VIAD VIADUCT
VIL VILLA
VIS VISTA
VLG VILLAGE
VLS VILLAS
VW VIEW
W WEST
WD WOOD
WHF WHARF
WK WALK
WKS WALKS
WLS WELLS
WY WAY
YD YARD
YHA YOUTH HOSTEL

POSTCODE TOWNS AND AREA ABBREVIATIONS

ALDT Aldershot
ALTN Alton
AMSY Amesbury
AND Andover
ASHV Ash Vale
BDST Broadstone
BH/HW/K Brighton Hill/Hatch Warren/Kempshott
BKME/WDN Branksome/Wallisdown
BLKW Blackwater
BMTH Bournemouth
BOR Bordon
BOSC Boscombe
BPWT Bishop's Waltham
BROC Brockenhurst
BSTK Basingstoke
BWD Bearwood
CBLY Camberley
CCLF Canford Cliffs
CFDH Canford Heath
CHAM Cosham
CHAR Charminster
CHCH/BSGR Christchurch/Bransgore
CHFD Chandler's Ford
CHIN Chineham
CHOB/PIR Chobham/Pirbright
CWTH Crowthorne
DEAN Deane/Oakley
EARL Earley
ELGH Eastleigh
EMRTH Emsworth/Southbourne
ENEY Eastney
EPSF Petersfield east
EWKG Wokingham east
FARN Farnborough
FAWY Fawley/Hythe
FBDG Fordingbridge
FERN Ferndown/West Moors
FHAM Fareham
FHAM/PORC Fareham/Porchester
FHAM/STUB Fareham/Stubbington
FLEETN Fleet north
FLEETS Fleet south
FNM Farnham
FRIM Frimley
FUFL Fulflood/Winchester west
GODL Godalming
GPORT Gosport
GSHT Grayshott
HASM Haslemere
HAV Havant
HEND Hedge End
HISD Hayling Island
HLER Hamble-le-Rice
HORN Horndean
HSEA Hilsea
HTWY Hartley Wintney
HUNG Hungerford/Lambourn
ITCH Itchen
KSCL Kingsclere/Rural Newbury
LIPH Liphook
LISS Liss
LSOL/BMARY Lee-on-the-Solent/Bridgemary
LTDN Littledown
LTWR Lightwater
LYMN Lymington
LYND Lyndhurst
MARL Marlborough
MFD/CHID Milford/Chiddingfold
MIDH Midhurst
MOOR/WNTN Moordown/Winton
NARL New Alresford
NBAD North Baddesley
NBNE Northbourne
NEND North End
NMIL/BTOS New Milton/Barton on Sea
NTHA Thatcham north
NTID North Tidworth
NWBY Newbury
ODIM Odiham
OVTN Overton/Rural Basingstoke
PETW Petworth
PLE Poole
PSEA Portsea
PSF Petersfield
PSTN Parkstone
RAND Rural Andover
RCCH Rural Chichester
RFNM Rural Farnham
RGUW Rural Guildford west
RGWD Ringwood
ROMY Romsey
ROWN Rownhams
RSAL Rural Salisbury
RWIN Rural Winchester
SBNE Southbourne
SD/PW St Denys/Portswood
SHAM Southampton
SHST Sandhurst
SSEA Southsea
STHA Thatcham south
STOK Stockbridge
SWGE Swanage
TADY Tadley
THLE Theale/Rural Reading
TOTT Totton
TWDS Talbot Woods
UPTN Upton
VWD Verwood
WBNE Westbourne
WCLF West Cliff
WEND West End
WHAM Wickham
WHCH Whitchurch
WHIT Whitley/Arborfield
WIMB Wimborne Minster
WINC Winchester
WSHM Southampton west
WVILLE Waterlooville/Denmead
WWKG Wokingham west
YTLY Yateley

1

1st St *FAWY* SO45 **355** J5
2nd St *FAWY* SO45 **178** A7
3rd St *FAWY* SO45 **354** H4
4th St *FAWY* SO45 **354** H4
5th St *FAWY* SO45 **354** H3
6th St *FAWY* SO45 **354** G4
7th St *FAWY* SO45 **354** G3
8th St *FAWY* SO45 **354** G4
9th St *FAWY* SO45 **354** F4
10th St *FAWY* SO45 **354** F4
11th St *FAWY* SO45 **354** F3
12th St *FAWY* SO45 **354** F3
13th St *FAWY* SO45 **354** F2
14th St *FAWY* SO45 **354** E3

A

Aaron Cl *CFDH* BH17 **223** M1
Aaron Ct *TOTT* SO40 **159** M6
A Av *FAWY* SO45 **354** F3
Abbatt Cl *RAND* SP11 **265** P10
Abbetts La *CBLY* GU15 **50** D5
Abbey Cl *FAWY* SO45 **177** G5
  NWBY RG14 **18** F9
Abbey Ct *CHIN* RG24 **65** J3
Abbeydore Cl *BOR* GU35 **111** L7
Abbeydore Rd *CHAM* PO6 **168** C7
Abbeyfield Dr *FHAM* PO15 **181** J2
Abbeyfields Cl *HLER* SO31 **162** D6
Abbey Gdns *WIMB* BH21 **208** D3
Abbey Hl *HLER* SO31 **177** M1
Abbey Hill Cl *WINC* SO23 **25** G1
Abbey Hill Rd *WINC* SO23 **24** F1
Abbey Pk *THLE* RG7 **39** M1
Abbey Pas *WINC* SO23 **25** H6
Abbey Rd *ALTN* GU34 **279** N12
  CHIN RG24 **65** K4
  FERN BH22 **205** J8
  FHAM PO15 **181** K2
Abbey Spring La *BROC* SO42 **353** N4
Abbey St *FNM* GU9 **13** G5
Abbey Water *ROMY* SO51 **136** E1
Abbey Wy *FARN* GU14 **61** J4
Abbeywood *ASHV* GU12 * **74** B4
Abbotsbury Rd *BDST* BH18 **210** E3
  ELGH SO50 **140** F2
Abbots Cl *CHCH/BSGR* BH23 **229** M1
  FLEETN GU51 **59** J7
  WVILLE PO7 **169** J4
Abbotsfield *TOTT* SO40 **144** E8
Abbotsfield Cl *ROWN* SO16 **146** C3
Abbotsford *TOTT* SO40 **341** M6
Abbot's Ride *FNM* GU9 **13** M7
Abbots Rd *NWBY* RG14 **18** F7
  THLE RG7 **39** M2
Abbotstone Av *HAV* PO9 **171** G4
Abbots Wy *FHAM* PO15 **181** K3
  HLER SO31 **162** D6
Abbots Well Rd *FBDG* SP6 **338** B5
Abbotswood Cl *ROMY* SO51 **131** J7
Abbott Cl *KBH* RG22 **92** E2
  MOOR/WNTN BH9 **214** A8
Abbott Rd *MOOR/WNTN* BH9 **214** A8
Abbotts Ann Rd *FUFL* SO22 **122** D1
  RAND SP11 **94** E7
Abbotts Cl *NTID* SP9 **266** E1
  RAND SP11 **95** J8
Abbotts Dro *ROMY* SO51 **335** J7
Abbotts Hl *RAND* SP11 **271** J1
Abbotts Rd *ELGH* SO50 **139** L7
  NTID SP9 **266** E1
  WINC SO23 **123** G2
Abbott St *WIMB* BH21 **206** C2
Abbotts Wy *FERN* BH22 **205** J8
  PTSW SO17 **147** H7
Abbottswood Cl *TADY* RG26 **44** B5
A'Becket Ct *PSEA* PO1 **20** D5
Abercrombie Gdns
  ROWN SO16 **146** A4
Aberdare Av *CHAM* PO6 **169** H7
Aberdare Rd *NBNE* BH10 **213** L5
Aberdeen Cl *FHAM* PO15 **10** B2
Aberdeen Rd *PTSW* SO17 **147** J7
Aberdeen Ter *GSHT* GU26 * **115** K5
Aberdour Cl *WEND* SO18 **148** B4
Abex Rd *NWBY* RG14 **19** K4
Abingdon Dr
  CHCH/BSGR BH23 **218** C8
Abingdon Gdns *ROWN* SO16 **146** E5
Abingdon Rd *CFDH* BH17 **211** L8
  SHST GU47 **43** L8
Abinger Rd *LTDN* BH7 **227** G2
Abney Rd *NBNE* BH10 **213** K5
Aborn Pde *THLE* RG7 * **40** A2
Above Bar St *SHAM* SO14 **22** F1
Above Hedges *RSAL* SP5 **296** A1
Above Town *RAND* SP11 **96** A8
Abraham Cl *HEND* SO30 **149** K7
Abshot Cl *FHAM/STUB* PO14 **180** B3
Abshot Rd *FHAM/STUB* PO14 **180** B3
Acacia Av *SHST* GU47 **43** M7
  VWD BH31 **201** L4
Acacia Gdns *HORN* PO8 **156** B3
Acacia Rd *ITCH* SO19 **161** M3
  LYMN SO41 **219** M4
Academy Pl *SHST* GU47 **50** A1
Acanthas Ct *FHAM* PO15 **164** D3
Accentors Cl *ALTN* GU34 **106** F2
Acer Wy *HAV* PO9 **171** H4
Acheulian Cl *FNM* GU9 **13** H9
Achilles Cl *CHIN* RG24 **54** B4
Ackender Rd *ALTN* GU34 **106** E5
Ackrells Md *SHST* GU47 **43** H7
Ackworth Rd *HSEA* PO3 **185** G3
Acland Rd *MOOR/WNTN* BH9 **214** B8
Acorn Cl *BSTK* RG21 **7** L5
  CHAM PO6 **169** L8
  CHCH/BSGR BH23 **215** M8
  FUFL SO22 **24** A1
  LSOL/BMARY PO13 **182** D7
  NMIL/BTOS BH25 **219** J4
  RGWD BH24 **346** E1
  TOTT SO40 **160** A7
Acorn Ct *HLER* SO31 **178** F1
Acorn Dr *NTHA* RG18 **28** F7
  ROWN SO16 **145** L1
Acorn Gv *CHFD* SO53 **138** F4
Acorn Keep *FNM* GU9 **72** D8
Acorn Rd *BLKW* GU17 **49** K3
The Acorns *HLER* SO31 **162** F4
  RGWD BH24 **205** K8
  WIMB BH21 **208** A4
Acorn Wy *VWD* BH31 **201** J2
Acre Ct *AND* SP10 **5** K5
Acre La *HORN* PO8 **156** C7
Acre Pth *AND* SP10 **5** K5
Acres Rd *BWD* BH11 **213** H6
Acton Rd *NBNE* BH10 **213** H7
Adair Rd *ENEY* PO4 **193** G6
Adam Cl *TADY* RG26 **249** Q3
Adames Rd *PSEA* PO1 **192** E2
Adampur Rd *NTID* SP9 **266** C4
Adams Cl *HEND* SO30 **149** H1
Adams Cft *CHOB/PIR* GU24 **63** J1
Adams Dr *FLEETN* GU51 **59** K7
Adamsfield Gdns *NBNE* BH10 **213** J6
Adams Ms *LIPH* GU30 **116** B6
Adamson Cl *CHFD* SO53 **133** K8
Adams Park Rd *FNM* GU9 **77** H4
Adams Rd *FAWY* SO45 **177** G6
Adams Ter *CHAM* PO6 * **185** J2
Adams Wy *ALTN* GU34 **107** G4
Adams Wood Dr *TOTT* SO40 **159** M7
Adastral Rd *CFDH* BH17 **211** L8
Adderbury Av *EMRTH* PO10 **171** M4
Addington Pl
  CHCH/BSGR BH23 * **228** D2
Addiscombe Rd
  CHCH/BSGR BH23 **228** A1
  CWTH RG45 **43** L4
Addison Gdns *ODIM* RG29 **69** G5
Addison Rd *BROC* SO42 **351** K4
  ELGH SO50 **134** B7
  ENEY PO4 **21** L6
  FRIM GU16 **51** G8
  HLER SO31 **163** M6
Addison Sq *RGWD* BH24 **203** K5
Addisson Cl *FUFL* SO22 **122** C7
Addis Sq *PTSW* SO17 * **147** H7
Adelaide Cl *CHCH/BSGR* BH23 **215** M8
Adelaide Pl *FHAM/PORC* PO16 **11** J6
Adelaide Rd *AND* SP10 **5** J5
  PTSW SO17 **147** J8

Adela Verne Cl ITCH SO19 162 E1
Adeline Rd BMTH BH1 226 E4
Adey Cl ITCH SO19 162 B2
Adey's Cl NWBY RG14 19 G7
Adhurst Rd HAV PO9 171 G4
Adlam's La LYMN SO41 350 D9
Adlington Pl FARN GU14 61 L6
Admers Crs LIPH GU30 116 C6
The Admiral Pk HSEA PO3 185 H5
Admirals Cl FAWY SO45 355 K5
Admiral's Keep
LSOL/BMARY PO13 190 A2
Admirals Rd HLER SO31 164 B8
Admirals Wk GPORT PO12 14 A6
PSEA PO1 20 B1
RCCH PO18 173 L1
WCLF BH2 * 8 B8
Admirals Wy AND SP10 96 F4
Admiralty Cl GPORT PO12 191 H2
Admiralty Rd PSEA PO1 20 C2
SBNE BH6 227 M5
Admiralty Wy CBLY GU15 50 B4
TOTT SO40 159 M5
Adrian Cl HTWY RG27 57 M3
Adsdean Cl HAV PO9 170 E4
Adstone La HSEA PO3 185 J4
Adur Cl GPORT PO12 190 F1
WEND SO18 148 B3
Adwood Ct STHA RG19 35 L1
Aerial Rd CHAM PO6 168 B6
Aerodrome Rd
LSOL/BMARY PO13 182 D4
Aerospace Bvd FARN GU14 72 F1
Africa Dr TOTT SO40 159 M7
Agars La LYMN SO41 220 A1
Agarton La LYMN SO41 232 F2
Aggis Farm Rd VWD BH31 201 G2
Aggisters La WWKG RG41 239 Q5
Aghemund Cl CHIN RG24 54 A5
Agincourt Rd NEND PO2 192 D1
Agitor Rd FAWY SO45 178 C7
Agnew Rd LSOL/BMARY PO13 182 C5
Agra Rd NTID SP9 266 C4
Agravaine Cl AND SP10 96 C1
Agricola Wk AND SP10 96 D1
Agricola Wy STHA RG19 35 M2
Aikman La TOTT SO40 158 B1
Ailsa La ITCH SO19 161 K4
Ainger Cl ASHV GU12 3 L1
Ainsdale Rd CHAM PO6 169 K7
Ainsley Gdns ELGH SO50 134 A7
Aintree Cl ELGH SO50 141 K5
NWBY RG14 19 J8
Aintree Dr WVILLE PO7 156 B7
Aintree Rd TOTT SO40 144 C7
Aircraft Esp FARN GU14 61 J7
Aird Cl KSCL RG20 246 A4
Airetons Cl BDST BH18 211 J5
Airfield Rd CHCH/BSGR BH23 228 F1
Airfield Wy CHCH/BSGR BH23 228 F1
Airlie Cnr FUFL SO22 24 D9
Airlie Rd FUFL SO22 24 D8
Airport Service Rd HSEA PO3 185 H3
Airspeed Rd
CHCH/BSGR BH23 229 H1
Ajax Cl CHIN RG24 54 B4
FHAM/STUB PO14 189 K3
Akeshill Cl NMIL/BTOS BH25 219 H3
Alameda Rd WVILLE PO7 169 K4
Alameda Wy WVILLE PO7 169 K4
Alamein Rd ALDT GU11 3 H1
RAND SP11 84 D5
Alanbrooke Cl HTWY RG27 57 L2
Alanbrooke Rd ALDT GU11 73 K2
Alandale Rd ITCH SO19 148 D8
Alan Drayton Wy ELGH SO50 140 E2
Alan Gv FHAM PO15 10 A4
Albacore Av HLER SO31 * 179 L3
Albacore Cl LSOL/BMARY PO13 190 A3
Albany Cl FLEETN GU51 59 K8
NMIL/BTOS BH25 218 F7
Albany Ct BPWT SO32 143 G4
Albany Dr BPWT SO32 143 G4
WIMB BH21 201 G8
Albany Gdns PLE BH15 222 F6
Albany Pk FRIM GU16 50 E7
Albany Rd AND SP10 4 C4
BPWT SO32 143 G4
FAWY SO45 354 E4
FLEETN GU51 59 J8
ROMY SO51 136 E1
SSEA PO5 21 J7
WSHM SO15 160 C2
Albatross Wk
LSOL/BMARY PO13 182 B6
Albemarle Av GPORT PO12 191 H1
Albemarle Rd TWDS BH3 225 M1
Albert Cl HLER SO31 162 C7
Albert Gv SSEA PO5 21 K7
Albert Rd ALDT GU11 3 H3
ALTN GU34 106 E6
BKME/WDN BH12 224 D3
BMTH BH1 8 E5
BPWT SO32 143 H5
CBLY GU15 * 50 E2
CHAM PO6 184 F1
CWTH RG45 43 K3
ELGH SO50 134 B7
FARN GU14 61 J6
FERN BH22 209 K3
FHAM/STUB PO14 189 M2
HEND SO30 149 H7
NMIL/BTOS BH25 218 F6
NWBY RG14 18 D3
SSEA PO5 21 K8
WIMB BH21 210 D3
Albert Rd North SHAM SO14 23 K5
Albert Rd South SHAM SO14 23 K6
Albert St FLEETN GU51 59 H7
GPORT PO12 15 G3
Albion Cl BKME/WDN BH12 224 A1
FHAM/PORC PO16 183 H2
Albion Pl SHAM SO14 22 F4
Albion Rd CHCH/BSGR BH23 215 M7
FBDG SP6 197 H2
SHST GU47 49 K1
Albion Wy VWD BH31 200 F1
Albretia Av HORN PO8 155 K5
Albury Pl CHFD SO53 * 133 H7
Albury Wy STHA RG19 34 F8
Alby Rd BKME/WDN BH12 224 F3
Alcantara Crs SHAM SO14 23 K6
Alcester Rd BKME/WDN BH12 224 D2
Alcot Cl CWTH RG45 43 K4
Alderbrook Cl CWTH RG45 43 G4
Alder Cl ALTN GU34 106 E3
ASHV GU12 74 A1
CHCH/BSGR BH23 216 D7
FAWY SO45 176 C5
NWBY RG14 19 M2
ROMY SO51 137 K2
RWIN SO21 135 G4
TOTT SO40 159 M6
Alder Crs BKME/WDN BH12 224 F1
Alder Dr FBDG SP6 196 B7
Alderfield PSF GU32 120 C6
Alder Gld THLE RG7 39 M1
Alder Gv YTLY GU46 48 E3
Alder Hts BKME/WDN BH12 225 G2
Alder Hill Dr TOTT SO40 144 B8
Alder Hills BKME/WDN BH12 225 G1
Alderholt Rd FBDG SP6 196 C3
Alder La LSOL/BMARY PO13 190 D3
Alderley Rd NBNE BH10 213 K4
Aldermaston Rd TADY RG26 44 A2
TADY RG26 44 D7
Aldermaston Road Rbt
CHIN RG24 65 H4
Aldermaston Rd South
BSTK RG21 6 A1
Aldermoor Av ROWN SO16 146 A4
Aldermoor Cl ROWN SO16 146 C4
Aldermoor Rd
LSOL/BMARY PO13 190 D1
ROWN SO16 146 B4
WVILLE PO7 169 K4
Aldermoor Rd East
WVILLE PO7 169 K3
Alderney Av
BKME/WDN BH12 212 C7
KBH RG22 92 D5
Alderney Cl ROWN SO16 145 L4
Alder Rd BKME/WDN BH12 224 F2
BOR GU35 114 B2
ROWN SO16 145 M5
Alders Cl BSTK RG21 7 K5
Aldershot Rd ASHV GU12 73 M7
CHOB/PIR GU24 63 L7
FLEETN GU51 59 J8
FLEETS GU52 71 H4
RGUW GU3 75 L3
Alders Rd FHAM/PORC PO16 182 B1
The Alders FNM GU9 77 L2
NTHA RG18 28 F8
Alderwood CHIN RG24 54 B5
Alderwood Av CHFD SO53 139 G2
Alderwood Cl HAV PO9 170 A5
Alder Wood Dr HTWY RG27 56 D6
Aldis Gdns PLE BH15 222 E6
Aldrich Rd PSEA PO1 192 A2
Aldridge Cl HORN PO8 321 L7
Aldridge Rd FERN BH22 209 L5
NBNE BH10 213 J3
Aldridge Wy FERN BH22 * 209 M5
Aldrin Cl AND SP10 96 A1
Aldrin Pl FARN GU14 60 D4
Aldroke St CHAM PO6 * 184 F1
Aldsworth Cl CHAM PO6 169 J8
Aldsworth Gdns CHAM PO6 169 J8
Aldwell St SSEA PO5 * 21 J4
Aldwick Cl FARN GU14 61 G2
Aldworth Crs KBH RG22 65 G8
Aldworth Gdns CWTH RG45 43 J3
Alec Rose La PSEA PO1 21 G3
Alecto Rd GPORT PO12 14 E7
Alencon Cl GPORT PO12 183 J8
Alencon Link BSTK RG21 6 F4
Alexander Cl
CHCH/BSGR BH23 228 E2
STOK SO20 285 K11
TOTT SO40 144 D8
WVILLE PO7 * 169 K3
Alexander Gv
FHAM/PORC PO16 10 F8
Alexander Rd OVTN RG25 89 J5
STHA RG19 35 L2
Alexandra Av CBLY GU15 50 C3
HISD PO11 194 F6
Alexandra Cl FAWY SO45 177 G4
Alexandra Ct BOR GU35 112 F1
FARN GU14 61 J7
Alexandra Pk NEND PO2 * 184 D5
Alexandra Rd ALDT GU11 2 B4
ALTN GU34 106 F3
AND SP10 4 F5
ASHV GU12 73 M7
BSTK RG21 6 B5
CHFD SO53 133 M8
FARN GU14 61 J6
FAWY SO45 177 G4
FBDG SP6 197 H2
HEND SO30 149 H7
LYMN SO41 221 J3
PSEA PO1 192 D2
PSTN BH14 224 E4
SBNE BH6 227 H3
WSHM SO15 160 D2
Alexandra St GPORT PO12 14 D1
Alexandra Ter ALDT GU11 * 2 E3
ODIM RG29 * 68 E4
WINC SO23 24 E7
Alexandra Wy HEND SO30 150 A5
Alexandre Ter HTWY RG27 * 46 F7
Alexandria Rd RWIN SO21 274 D7
Alfonso Cl ASHV GU12 3 K6
Alford Rd TWDS BH3 225 K1
Alfred Cl FLEETN GU51 58 F5
TOTT SO40 158 C1
Alfred Gdns AND SP10 96 B2
Alfred Rd FHAM/STUB PO14 189 K1
FNM GU9 13 H5
PSEA PO1 20 F2
Alfred Rose Ct WEND SO18 * 147 L4
Alfred St SHAM SO14 161 H2
Alfrey Cl EMRTH PO10 172 C6
Alfriston Gdns ITCH SO19 162 B1
Alfriston Rd FRIM GU16 62 C1
Algiers Rd HSEA PO3 185 H8
Alhambra Rd ENEY PO4 192 E7
Alice Rd ALDT GU11 3 G3
Alington Cl PSTN BH14 237 H1
Alington Rd PSTN BH14 237 H1
TWDS BH3 226 A2
Alipore Cl PSTN BH14 224 D5
Alison Cl FARN GU14 60 F5
THLE RG7 39 M3
Alison Dr CBLY GU15 51 H3
Alison's Rd ALDT GU11 73 G3
Alison Wy ALDT GU11 2 C3
FUFL SO22 24 E4
Allan Gv ROMY SO51 137 H1
Allaway Av CHAM PO6 167 M8
Allbrook Ct HAV PO9 170 D2
Allbrook Hl ELGH SO50 134 B5
Allbrook Knoll ELGH SO50 134 A5
Allbrook Wy ELGH SO50 134 A4
Allcot Rd HSEA PO3 184 F6
Allden Av ASHV GU12 3 L8
Allden Gdns ASHV GU12 3 L8
Allee Dr LIPH GU30 116 B3
Allenby Cl CFDH BH17 211 H6
Allenby Gv FHAM/PORC PO16 183 J1
Allenby Rd CBLY GU15 50 C2
CFDH BH17 211 H7
GPORT PO12 190 E2
Allen Cl ALTN GU34 107 G3
BSTK RG21 6 A8
Allen Ct WIMB BH21 207 J3
Allendale Av EMRTH PO10 171 L5
Allendale Cl SHST GU47 43 J6
Allen Rd HEND SO30 149 J5
WIMB BH21 207 J4
Allens La BPWT SO32 312 E11
UPTN BH16 222 D3
Allen's Rd SSEA PO5 21 L8
UPTN BH16 222 D3
Allenview Rd WIMB BH21 207 J3
Allen Water Dr FBDG SP6 197 G2
Allerton Cl TOTT SO40 144 D7
The Alley RSAL SP5 324 D4
Alliance Cl LSOL/BMARY PO13 182 D8
Allington La ELGH SO50 141 G5
HEND SO30 148 B1
Allington Rd WSHM SO15 159 K1
Alliston Wy KBH RG22 92 D1
WHCH RG28 87 M8
Allmara Dr WVILLE PO7 169 L3
Allnutt Av BSTK RG21 7 H5
Allotment Rd HLER SO31 163 L7
All Saints Crs FARN GU14 50 A7
All Saints Rd LYMN SO41 221 L6
PSEA PO1 192 D1
Alma Cl ASHV GU12 3 M1
Alma Gdns FRIM GU16 51 M8
Alma La BPWT SO32 142 B2
FNM GU9 77 G1
Alma Rd BOR GU35 113 G1
BOR GU35 114 C3
MOOR/WNTN BH9 226 A1
ROMY SO51 136 F1
SHAM SO14 147 G8
Alma St GPORT PO12 14 D1
Almatade Rd WEND SO18 148 A5
Alma Ter ENEY PO4 193 G5
Alma Wy FNM GU9 77 H1
Almer Rd PLE BH15 222 E5
Almond Av NWBY RG14 27 J7
Almond Cl CHIN RG24 66 C2
CHAM PO6 169 M8
FARN GU14 61 G1
HORN PO8 156 C4
WWKG RG41 239 Q4
Almond Dr NTHA RG18 28 F8
Almond Gv BKME/WDN BH12 224 D1
Almond Rd WSHM SO15 160 C3
Almondsbury Rd CHAM PO6 167 M6
Almondside
LSOL/BMARY PO13 182 E7
Almswood Rd TADY RG26 44 A2
The Aloes FLEETN GU51 59 K8
Alphage Rd
LSOL/BMARY PO13 182 F7
Alpha Rd ASHV GU12 73 L7
Alphington Av FRIM GU16 51 H7
Alphington Gn FRIM GU16 51 G7
Alpine Cl FARN GU14 60 D5
WEND SO18 148 B4
Alpine Ct KBH RG22 92 C1
Alpine Rd BOR GU35 112 F3
RGWD BH24 347 J2
TOTT SO40 341 R9
Alresford Dro RWIN SO21 288 F3
Alresford Rd HAV PO9 170 E4
NARL SO24 291 J12
RWIN SO21 123 M5
WINC SO23 25 L6
Alsford Rd WVILLE PO7 169 K3
Alston Ms STHA RG19 35 J2
Alswitha Ter WINC SO23 * 25 G3
Alten Rd WVILLE PO7 155 J6
Althorpe Dr HSEA PO3 185 J4
Altona Gdns AND SP10 96 B1
Alton Cl ELGH SO50 141 H2
Alton Gv FHAM/PORC PO16 183 J2
Alton La ALTN GU34 293 M8
Alton Ride BLKW GU17 49 L2
Alton Rd FLEETN GU51 59 L7
NBNE BH10 213 H7
ODIM RG29 257 R4
PSTN BH14 224 B5
RFNM GU10 78 B1
Alton Rd East PSTN BH14 224 D6
Alum Chine Rd WBNE BH4 225 H5
Alum Cl FAWY SO45 354 F5
Alumdale Rd WBNE BH4 225 H6
Alumhurst Rd WBNE BH4 225 H6
Alum Wy FHAM/PORC PO16 166 E7
WEND SO18 148 B5
Alvara Rd GPORT PO12 14 D8
Alver Bridge Vw GPORT PO12 14 F7
Alvercliffe Dr GPORT PO12 14 B9
Alver Rd GPORT PO12 14 F6
PSEA PO1 21 L1
Alverstoke Gdns ALDT GU11 2 B5
Alverstone Rd ENEY PO4 193 G4
Alverton Av PLE BH15 223 M5
Alveston Av
FHAM/STUB PO14 181 J4
Alwin Pl FNM GU9 77 G1
Alyth Rd TWDS BH3 225 K2
Amarylis Cl FHAM PO15 164 E8
Amazon Cl BSTK RG21 6 A6
Ambarrow Crs SHST GU47 43 H7
Ambarrow La CWTH RG45 42 F6
Ambassador Cl
CHCH/BSGR BH23 229 G2
Amber Cl BOR GU35 113 G2
Amber Gdns AND SP10 4 B5
Amber Hl CBLY GU15 51 L4
Amberley Cl
CHCH/BSGR BH23 217 L8
HEND SO30 149 M4
NBAD SO52 137 L3
NWBY RG14 18 C1
Amberley Ct TOTT SO40 158 E2
Amberley Gra ALDT GU11 2 C6
Amberley Rd GPORT PO12 183 G8
HORN PO8 321 M7
NEND PO2 184 F5
Amber Rd WIMB BH21 210 C4
Amberslade Wk FAWY SO45 176 F7
Amberwood FERN BH22 209 L1
Amberwood Cl TOTT SO40 144 C6
Amberwood Dr CBLY GU15 51 H1
CHCH/BSGR BH23 218 A6
Amberwood Gdns
CHCH/BSGR BH23 218 A6
Ambledale HLER SO31 163 L8
Ambleside CHCH/BSGR BH23 215 K5
HEND SO30 149 K7
Ambleside Cl FARN GU14 60 E4
FRIM GU16 62 A6
Ambleside Crs FNM GU9 76 E2
Ambleside Gdns ITCH SO19 162 A1
Ambleside Rd LYMN SO41 221 L6
Ambrose Rd TADY RG26 44 B4
Ambury La CHCH/BSGR BH23 216 F8
Amersham Cl GPORT PO12 190 E4
Amery Hl ALTN GU34 106 F4
Amery St ALTN GU34 106 F5
Amesbury Rd AMSY SP4 268 A3
RAND SP11 94 C3
SBNE BH6 227 J2
Amethyst Cl WWKG RG41 239 R1
Amethyst Gv WVILLE PO7 156 B8
Amethyst Rd
CHCH/BSGR BH23 228 F1
Amey Gdns TOTT SO40 144 B7
Ameysford Rd FERN BH22 204 E7
Ameys La FERN BH22 209 M1
Amherst Rd BOR GU35 110 E6
Amoy St WSHM SO15 160 F2
Ampere Rd NWBY RG14 19 G3
Ampfield Cl HAV PO9 170 B4
Ampfield Rd CHAR BH8 214 D5
Amport Cl CHIN RG24 54 C8
FUFL SO22 122 C1
Amport Ct HAV PO9 170 D2
Ampress La LYMN SO41 221 K2
Ampthill Rd WSHM SO15 160 B1
Amsterdam Sq
CHCH/BSGR BH23 228 D1
Amyas Ct ENEY PO4 193 J4
Ancasta Rd SHAM SO14 161 G1
Ancells Rd FLEETN GU51 59 L4
Anchorage Rd HSEA PO3 185 H5
The Anchorage GPORT PO12 15 H5
Anchor Cl BWD BH11 212 F3
CHCH/BSGR BH23 229 G3
RGUW GU3 75 J4
Anchor Ct RCCH PO18 * 172 F7
Anchor Ga PSEA PO1 192 A2
Anchor La PSEA PO1 20 B1
Anchor Meadow FARN GU14 60 F4
Anchor Ms LYMN SO41 221 L4
Anchor Rd BWD BH11 212 F3
KSCL RG20 248 D10
Anchor Yd BSTK RG21 6 F6
KSCL RG20 248 D10
Andalusian Gdns HLER SO31 164 B4
Andeferas Rd AND SP10 96 B1
Anderby Rd ROWN SO16 145 K6
Andersen Cl HLER SO31 164 C4
Anderson Cl HAV PO9 17 G1
ROMY SO51 131 J6
Anderson Crs WHIT RG2 239 L6
Anderson's Rd SHAM SO14 23 K5
Anders Rd RWIN SO21 288 E4
Anderwood Dr LYMN SO41 350 F10
Andes Cl SHAM SO14 23 L6
Andes Rd ROWN SO16 145 H5
Andlers Ash Rd LISS GU33 308 E10
Andover Cl CHCH/BSGR BH23 229 H1
Andover Dro KSCL RG20 33 H8
Andover La RAND SP11 267 N1
Andover Rd BLKW GU17 49 L2
ENEY PO4 192 F6
FUFL SO22 24 F1
KSCL RG20 246 E1
NWBY RG14 33 K8
OVTN RG25 90 C4
RAND SP11 94 D1
RAND SP11 265 R12
RWIN SO21 275 P2
WSHM SO15 160 D2
Andover Rd North FUFL SO22 288 C9
Andover Wy ALDT GU11 3 H9
Andrewartha Rd FARN GU14 61 L7
Andrew Bell St PSEA PO1 192 C2
Andrew Cl FAWY SO45 177 G7
PSEA PO1 192 F2
TOTT SO40 158 D1
Andrew Crs WVILLE PO7 155 K7
Andrewes Cl BPWT SO32 143 J4
Andrew La NMIL/BTOS BH25 219 K6
Andrew Pl FHAM/STUB PO14 189 H2
Andrews Cl BWD BH11 213 G5
FLEETS GU52 71 J2
Andrew's La NARL SO24 293 K11
ODIM RG29 258 D5
Andrews Rd FARN GU14 60 E3
Andromeda Rd ROWN SO16 145 L4
Andwell La HTWY RG27 67 J2
Anfield Cl ELGH SO50 141 J3
Angel Ct NWBY RG14 18 E2
Angel Crs ITCH SO19 148 A5
ITCH SO19 161 M2
Angelica Gdns ELGH SO50 141 J5
Angelica Wy FHAM PO15 164 E4
Angeline Cl CHCH/BSGR BH23 217 M8
Angel La FERN BH22 209 H5
NMIL/BTOS BH25 219 K8
Angel Md THLE RG7 37 J2
Angel Mdw ODIM RG29 69 G5
Angelo Cl WVILLE PO7 156 A8
Angelus Cl FHAM/STUB PO14 189 J2
Angerstein Rd NEND PO2 184 D7
Anglers Pl BSTK RG21 7 K5
Anglers Wy HLER SO31 163 K4
Anglesea Rd
LSOL/BMARY PO13 190 A4
PSEA PO1 20 F3
WSHM SO15 146 B7
Anglesea Ter SHAM SO14 23 K5
Anglesey Arms Rd
GPORT PO12 14 C9
Anglesey Av FARN GU14 60 F1
Anglesey Cl AND SP10 96 C7
CHIN RG24 65 L2
Anglesey Rd ASHV GU12 3 L4
GPORT PO12 14 C9
Anglesey Vw GPORT PO12 * 14 F6
Angora Wy FLEETN GU51 59 K4
Angus Cl FHAM PO15 10 A2
Anjou Cl BWD BH11 212 D3
Anjou Crs FHAM PO15 181 K2
Anker La FHAM/STUB PO14 181 J8
Ankerwyke
LSOL/BMARY PO13 182 B7
Anmore Cl HAV PO9 170 D4
Anmore Dr WVILLE PO7 155 K6
Anmore La WVILLE PO7 155 J4
Anmore Rd WVILLE PO7 155 G4
Annadale NTHA RG18 28 E3
Anna La CHCH/BSGR BH23 347 N8
Annandale Dr RFNM GU10 79 H2
Anne Armstrong Cl ALDT GU11 73 K3
Anne Cl CHCH/BSGR BH23 216 A7
Anne Crs WVILLE PO7 169 L2
Annerley Rd BMTH BH1 9 L4
Annes Wy FLEETS GU52 71 K2
Annet Cl PLE BH15 222 E6
Annettes Cft FLEETS GU52 71 G4
Ann's Hill Rd GPORT PO12 14 C2
Ansell Rd FRIM GU16 51 G8
Anson Cl ALDT GU11 2 C1
CHCH/BSGR BH23 228 F2
LSOL/BMARY PO13 190 D3
RGWD BH24 203 L4
Anson Crs WHIT RG2 238 D1
Anson Dr ITCH SO19 148 C8
Anson Gv FHAM/PORC PO16 167 K7
Anson Rd ELGH SO50 141 J5
ENEY PO4 192 F3
Anstey Cl BSTK RG21 93 J2
BWD BH11 213 G2
Anstey La ALTN GU34 280 F4
Anstey Mill Cl ALTN GU34 107 H3
Anstey Mill La ALTN GU34 107 H3
Anstey Rd ALTN GU34 107 G4
BWD BH11 213 G3
ROMY SO51 131 H7
Antar Cl BSTK RG21 6 A6
Antell's Wy FBDG SP6 196 C6
Anthill Cl WVILLE PO7 154 C3
Anthony Gv GPORT PO12 182 F7
Anthony Pl GSHT GU26 * 115 M7
Anthony's Av PSTN BH14 224 C7
Antler Dr NMIL/BTOS BH25 218 E4
Anton Cl DEAN RG23 91 K3
ROMY SO51 137 J1
Anton La RAND SP11 84 D6
Anton Mill Rd AND SP10 4 F8
Anton Rd AND SP10 5 G8
Antrim Cl KBH RG22 92 D1
Anvil Cl HORN PO8 156 C7
TADY RG26 46 B5
THLE RG7 238 A7
Anvil Crs BDST BH18 210 E3
Anvil Wy TADY RG26 46 B5
Anzac Cl FHAM/STUB PO14 181 J8
Anzio Cl ALDT GU11 2 F2
Apex Dr FRIM GU16 50 F7
Apless La WVILLE PO7 153 M4
Apollo Cl BKME/WDN BH12 224 D1
Apollo Dr BOR GU35 113 G2
WVILLE PO7 169 M5
Apollo Pl WEND SO18 * 148 A5
Apollo Ri FARN GU14 60 D4
Apollo Rd CHFD SO53 139 M1
Appelford Cl STHA RG19 35 K2
Apple Cl BKME/WDN BH12 225 G4
Appledore Ms FARN GU14 61 G1
Appledown Cl NARL SO24 291 M12
Appledown La NARL SO24 304 A1
Applegarth Cl BSTK RG21 7 G8
Applegate Pl HORN PO8 * 156 C3
Apple Gv CHCH/BSGR BH23 215 L6
EMRTH PO10 172 B5
Applelands Cl RFNM GU10 78 E4
Appleshaw Cl FUFL SO22 288 D12
TADY RG26 44 B5
Appleshaw Gn HAV PO9 170 C4
Appleshaw Wy RAND SP11 267 K2
Appleslade Wy
NMIL/BTOS BH25 219 H3
Appleton Cl STOK SO20 269 Q11
Appleton Rd FHAM PO15 181 K3
WEND SO18 147 L7
Appleton Vw ALTN GU34 294 D11
Apple Tree Cl NWBY RG14 33 L5
RSAL SP5 332 F1
Appletree Cl DEAN RG23 91 K4
NMIL/BTOS BH25 219 G7
SBNE BH6 227 J3
TOTT SO40 144 C8
Appletree Ct HEND SO30 150 A5
LYND SO43 345 L4
Apple Tree Gv AND SP10 4 B2
FERN BH22 209 L3
Appletree La THLE RG7 238 B6
Apple Tree Rd FBDG SP6 196 B7
Appletree Rd RSAL SP5 332 F1
Apple Tree Wy SHST GU47 43 M7
Apple Wy CHIN RG24 66 D3
Applewood Gdns ITCH SO19 162 A1
Applewood Gv WVILLE PO7 169 J6
Applewood Pl TOTT SO40 158 C2
Applewood Rd HAV PO9 170 C5
Appley Dr CBLY GU15 50 D3
Approach Rd FNM GU9 13 G5
PSTN BH14 224 B5
The Approach HSEA PO3 * 185 G7
April Cl BWD BH11 213 G4
CBLY GU15 50 E6
WEND SO18 148 B5
April Gv HLER SO31 179 L1
April Sq PSEA PO1 21 J1
Apron Rd STHA RG19 35 G7
Apsley Cl AND SP10 96 B7
Apsley Crs CFDH BH17 211 J7
Apsley Pl CHFD SO53 133 H7
Apsley Rd ENEY PO4 193 G4
Aquila Wy HLER SO31 178 F2
Arabian Gdns FHAM PO15 164 C5
Aragon Rd YTLY GU46 * 48 E4
Aragon Wy MOOR/WNTN BH9 214 B3
The Arboretum OVTN RG25 257 K2
Arborfield Rd WHIT RG2 238 F4
The Arcade ALDT GU11 * 2 F3
BMTH BH1 8 F5
LISS GU33 308 E7
Arcadia Av CHAR BH8 226 B1
Arcadia Cl DEAN RG23 92 C8
ROWN SO16 146 B5
Arcadia Rd CHCH/BSGR BH23 215 M7
Archangel Wy NTHA RG18 29 H8
Archdale Cl NBNE BH10 213 K6
Archers WSHM SO15 * 160 F1
Archers Cl TOTT SO40 144 C6
Archers Rd ELGH SO50 134 A8
WSHM SO15 160 E2
Archery Flds ODIM RG29 69 H5
Archery Gdns ITCH SO19 161 M6
Archery Gv ITCH SO19 161 L6
Archery La FHAM/PORC PO16 11 J4
WINC SO23 24 E6
Archery Ri ALTN GU34 106 E6
Archery Rd ITCH SO19 161 L7
Archway Rd CCLF BH13 224 E4
Arcot Rd NTID SP9 266 D5
Arden Cl WEND SO18 148 B3
Arden Rd MOOR/WNTN BH9 213 M5
Arden Wk NMIL/BTOS BH25 219 H6
Ardglen Rd WHCH RG28 87 K7
Ardingly Crs HEND SO30 149 K2
Ardington Ri WVILLE PO7 169 L5
Ardmore Rd PSTN BH14 224 B4
Ardrossan Av CBLY GU15 51 J4
Ardwell Cl CWTH RG45 43 G3
Arena La ALDT GU11 72 E4
Arenal Dr CWTH RG45 43 K5
Arford Common BOR GU35 111 M6
Arford Rd BOR GU35 111 M6
Argente Cl FLEETN GU51 59 K4
Argosy Cl HLER SO31 179 M3
Argus Rd LSOL/BMARY PO13 189 M5
Argyle Cl BOR GU35 112 F2
Argyle Crs FHAM PO15 10 B3
Argyle Rd CHCH/BSGR BH23 228 E3
NWBY RG14 18 D6
SHAM SO14 23 H1
Argyle St CHOB/PIR GU24 63 G2
Argyll Rd BKME/WDN BH12 224 D2
BOSC BH5 226 E4
Ariel Cl SBNE BH6 228 B4
Ariel Dr SBNE BH6 228 B4
Ariel Rd PSEA PO1 21 L2
Ark Dr FERN BH22 * 209 M5
Arkle Av STHA RG19 34 F1
Ark Royal Crs
LSOL/BMARY PO13 189 L5
Arkwright Cl KSCL RG20 246 B6
Arle Cl HORN PO8 321 L8
NARL SO24 291 L10
Arle Gdns NARL SO24 291 M10
Arley Rd PSTN BH14 224 A6
Arlington Ct NMIL/BTOS BH25 219 H8
Arlington Pl WINC SO23 25 G4
Arlington Ter ALDT GU11 2 D3
Arliss Rd ROWN SO16 146 A7
Arlott Ct WSHM SO15 160 E1
Arlott Dr BSTK RG21 6 F1
Armada Cl ROWN SO16 145 L1
Armada Dr FAWY SO45 176 F6
Arminers Cl GPORT PO12 191 H7
Armitage Av FAWY SO45 176 F7
Armitage Dr FRIM GU16 51 H7
Armory La PSEA PO1 20 D5
The Armoury TOTT SO40 * 160 A5
Armstrong Cl BROC SO42 351 J3
RWIN SO21 288 E4
WVILLE PO7 155 K6
Armstrong Ct ROWN SO16 145 M3
Armstrong La BROC SO42 351 J3

Armstrong Ml FARN GU14 60 D4
Armstrong Ri AND SP10 96 A1
Armstrong Rd BROC SO42 351 J3
CHIN RG24 7 L1
Armstrong Wy FARN GU14 60 B7
Armsworth La BPWT SO32 319 K10
Arnaud Cl NEND PO2 192 D1
Arne Av BKME/WDN BH12 224 E1
Arne Cl KBH RG22 92 F5
Arne Crs BKME/WDN BH12 224 E1
Arnett Av EWKG RG40 42 A1
Arnewood Bridge Rd
LYMN SO41 219 M1
Arnewood Rd SBNE BH6 227 J3
Arnheim Cl ROWN SO16 146 C4
Arnheim Rd ROWN SO16 146 D4
Arnhem Cl ALDT GU11 3 H2
Arnhem Rd NBWY RG14 19 H4
Arnold Cl FERN BH22 205 G5
Arnold Rd ELGH SO50 140 A4
FERN BH22 205 G5
PTSW SO17 147 J6
Arnolds Cl NMIL/BTOS BH25 218 F8
Arnside Rd WVILLE PO7 155 L8
Arnwood Av FAWY SO45 176 F8
Aron Cl PSF GU32 120 C7
Arragon Ct WVILLE PO7 156 A8
Arran Cl CHAM PO6 168 F7
DEAN RG23 91 J2
Arran Wy CHCH/BSGR BH23 218 B7
Arreton HLER SO31 162 C6
Arrow Cl ELGH SO50 134 A8
ITCH SO19 161 K7
Arrow La HTWY RG27 57 K1
Arrow Rd FARN GU14 60 F6
Arrowsmith La WIMB BH21 211 L1
Arrowsmith Rd WIMB BH21 211 K2
Arrow Smith Wy STHA RG19 35 M2
Arters Lawn TOTT SO40 175 H2
Arthur Cl FNM GU9 12 F6
WCLF BH2 8 F2
Arthur La CHCH/BSGR BH23 228 A1
Arthur Rd CHCH/BSGR BH23 228 A1
ELGH SO50 134 A8
FNM GU9 12 F7
NWBY RG14 18 B6
WINC SO23 25 G2
WSHM SO15 160 D1
Arthurs Gdns HEND SO30 149 H1
Arthur St ALDT GU11 3 C4
NEND PO2 192 E1
Artillery Cl CHAM PO6 168 C8
Artillery Dr STHA RG19 35 L3
Artillery Rd ALDT GU11 73 K1
Artillery Ter ENEY PO4 * 193 H4
Artists Wy AND SP10 4 E1
Arun Cl EPSF GU31 120 C7
Arun Ct BSTK RG21 7 J5
Arundel Cl FLEETN GU51 59 K8
LIPH GU30 113 K4
NARL SO24 291 M12
NMIL/BTOS BH25 218 E5
Arundel Dr FHAM/PORC PO16 10 E4
Arundel Gdns DEAN RG23 64 D5
Arundel Pl FNM GU9 12 E3
Arundel Rd CBLY GU15 51 L4
ELGH SO50 134 A6
GPORT PO12 14 B2
TOTT SO40 145 G8
Arundel St PSEA PO1 21 K2
Arundel Wy CHCH/BSGR BH23 229 M1
Arun Rd WEND SO18 148 B2
Arun Wy ROMY SO51 334 H5
Arwood Av TADY RG26 44 D4
Ascension Cl CHIN RG24 65 L3
Ascham Rd CHAR BH8 9 K2
Ascot Cl ALTN GU34 107 G6
FHAM/STUB PO14 180 C2
NWBY RG14 19 J9
Ascot Ct ALDT GU11 2 F4
Ascot Rd BDST BH18 211 G4
ELGH SO50 141 K5
HSEA PO3 193 G1
Ascott Wy NWBY RG14 19 L2
Ascupart St SHAM SO14 23 J3
Asford Gv ELGH SO50 134 D8
Ashbarn Crs FUFL SO22 122 D7
Ashbourne Cl ASHV GU12 74 C5
Ashbourne Rd BOSC BH5 227 H3
Ashbourne Wy STHA RG19 35 H1
Ashbridge Ri CHFD SO53 133 G7
Ashburn Garth RGWD BH24 203 M6
Ashburnham Cl ITCH SO19 161 K3
Ashburton Cl FAWY SO45 176 D5
NARL SO24 291 L11
Ashburton Gdns NBNE BH10 213 K7
Ashburton Rd GPORT PO12 14 B9
NARL SO24 291 L11
SSEA PO5 21 G8
Ashbury Dr FARN GU14 50 C7
Ashbury Rd BOR GU35 112 F2
Ashby Ct WHIT RG2 238 B1
Ashby Pl SSEA PO5 21 H9
Ashby Rd ITCH SO19 162 B1
TOTT SO40 158 D1
Ash Church Rd ASHV GU12 74 B6
Ash Cl ASHV GU12 74 B5
BLKW GU17 49 L3
FAWY SO45 177 G8
FBDG SP6 196 C7
FHAM/STUB PO14 10 A7
GPORT PO12 14 E5
HLER SO31 162 F4
HORN PO8 155 L5
ITCH SO19 148 C6
NBAD SO52 137 M3
NTID SP9 266 G1
ROMY SO51 137 J2
RWIN SO21 134 F4
UPTN BH16 210 B8
Ash Copse HORN PO8 155 M3
Ashcroft La HORN PO8 157 K2
Ashdale Pk EWKG RG40 42 E1
Ashdell Rd ALTN GU34 107 G5
Ashdene WSHM SO15 146 B8
Ashdene Cl WIMB BH21 207 K3
Ashdene Crs ASHV GU12 74 A5
Ashdene Rd ASHV GU12 74 A5
TOTT SO40 158 B6
Ashdown FAWY SO45 354 H5
LSOL/BMARY PO13 182 D7
Ashdown Av FARN GU14 61 L6
Ashdown Cl CFDH BH17 211 L7
CHFD SO53 133 J6
Ashdown Dr CHFD SO53 133 J6
Ashdown Rd CHFD SO53 133 J7
FAWY SO45 354 H6
Ashdown Ter NTID SP9 266 F3
Ashdown Wk
NMIL/BTOS BH25 219 J6
Ashdown Wy ROMY SO51 137 H1
Ashen Cl CHFD SO53 133 J8
Ashe Rd HAV PO9 171 H3
The Ashes THLE RG7 238 B6
Ashfield CHIN RG24 54 B5
Ashfield Gn YTLY GU46 49 H3
Ashfield Rd AND SP10 4 A4
Ashfields RWIN SO21 273 P6
Ashford Cl CHAM PO6 168 E7
FBDG SP6 196 F3
Ashford Crs FAWY SO45 177 H5
Ashford Hill Rd STHA RG19 248 B2
Ashford Rd FBDG SP6 196 E4
SBNE BH6 227 K1
Ash Ga NTHA RG18 29 H8
Ash Green La East ASHV GU12 74 C8
Ash Green La West ASHV GU12 73 M8
Ash Green Rd ASHV GU12 74 C7
Ash Gv CHIN RG24 66 E2
KSCL RG20 248 D10
LIPH GU30 116 D5
LYMN SO41 220 D8
RGWD BH24 203 L5
TOTT SO40 158 C6
Ash Hill Rd ASHV GU12 74 C5
Ashington Cl HORN PO8 156 A5
Ashington Gdns WIMB BH21 206 F8
Ashington La WIMB BH21 207 G7
Ashington Pk
NMIL/BTOS BH25 219 H7
Ash La MFD/CHID GU8 263 Q2
TADY RG26 45 K7
TADY RG26 249 Q3
Ashlawn Gdns AND SP10 5 J8
Ashlea HTWY RG27 56 D6
Ashlea Cl ELGH SO50 141 K2
Ashleigh Cl FAWY SO45 177 G8
Ashleigh Ri NBNE BH10 213 K6
Ashlet Gdns NMIL/BTOS BH25 219 K4
Ashlett Cl FAWY SO45 355 L5
Ashlett Rd FAWY SO45 355 L5
Ashley Cl BMTH BH1 226 E2
FRIM GU16 62 A2
FUFL SO22 122 C1
HAV PO9 170 D4
HLER SO31 164 B5
HORN PO8 155 M3
RFNM GU10 259 P1
RGWD BH24 203 M6
Ashley Common Rd
NMIL/BTOS BH25 219 J4
Ashley Ct HLER SO31 163 G2
Ashley Crs ITCH SO19 162 C2
Ashleycross Cl FAWY SO45 354 F5
Ashley Dr BLKW GU17 49 L4
RGWD BH24 198 E8
Ashley Dr North RGWD BH24 202 B7
Ashley Dr South RGWD BH24 202 B7
Ashley Dr West RGWD BH24 202 B7
Ashley Dro MARL SN8 243 K4
Ashley Gdns BPWT SO32 151 L1
CHFD SO53 139 L3
DEAN RG23 91 K2
Ashley La LYMN SO41 221 L5
NMIL/BTOS BH25 219 K4
Ashley Mdw ROMY SO51 131 G8
Ashley Meads
NMIL/BTOS BH25 219 K4
Ashley Pk RGWD BH24 202 C6
Ashley Rd ALTN GU34 279 K7
BMTH BH1 226 E2
FARN GU14 61 K4
NMIL/BTOS BH25 219 J5
PSTN BH14 224 C3
Ashling Cl CHAR BH8 214 C8
WVILLE PO7 154 F4
Ashling Gdns WVILLE PO7 154 F4
Ashling La NEND PO2 184 D8
Ashling Park Rd WVILLE PO7 154 F4
Ash Lodge Cl ASHV GU12 74 A7
Ash Lodge Dr ASHV GU12 74 A7
Ashlyn Cl FHAM PO15 181 H3
Ashman Rd STHA RG19 35 M1
Ashmead BOR GU35 112 F1
Ashmead Rd ROWN SO16 145 M5
Ashmeads Cl WIMB BH21 208 A2
Ashmeads Wy WIMB BH21 208 A2
Ashmoor La CHIN RG24 67 G2
Ashmore WIMB BH21 207 K4
Ashmore Av NMIL/BTOS BH25 219 H8
PLE BH15 222 F7
Ashmore Cl RSAL SP5 127 H4
Ashmore Crs PLE BH15 222 F7
Ashmore Green Rd NTHA RG18 28 C5
Ashmore Gv CHCH/BSGR BH23 217 L7
Ashmore La RSAL SP5 127 H3
Ashmore Rd FUFL SO22 122 C3
Ashridge FARN GU14 60 F1
Ashridge Av NBNE BH10 213 K3
Ashridge Cl WSHM SO15 146 F8
Ashridge Ct NWBY RG14 18 F6
Ashridge Gdns NBNE BH10 * 213 K3
Ash Rd ASHV GU12 3 L6
KSCL RG20 247 Q1
TOTT SO40 158 B6
Ash St ASHV GU12 73 M7
Ashtead Cl FHAM/PORC PO16 167 G8
Ash Ter NTHA RG18 28 D4
Ashton Cl BPWT SO32 143 G3
Ashton Cross ROMY SO51 335 L6
Ashton La BPWT SO32 143 G2
Ashton Pl CHFD SO53 * 133 H7
HUNG RG17 31 G2
Ashton Rd MOOR/WNTN BH9 213 M6
NWBY RG14 19 G5
Ashton Wy FHAM/STUB PO14 189 K4
Ash Tree Cl DEAN RG23 91 J4
FARN GU14 60 C5
HASM GU27 118 F3
Ashtree Cl NMIL/BTOS BH25 219 K6
Ash Tree Gv KSCL RG20 32 B5
Ash Tree Rd AND SP10 95 L4
WEND SO18 147 L7
Ashurst Bridge Rd TOTT SO40 158 C2
Ashurst Cl FUFL SO22 122 D1
ITCH SO19 162 A3
TADY RG26 44 A4
TOTT SO40 158 B6
Ashurst Rd ASHV GU12 73 M4
CHAM PO6 168 E8
CHAR BH8 214 D5
FERN BH22 204 F5
Ash Wy WWKG RG41 239 R5
Ashwell Av CBLY GU15 51 H2
Ashwood FHAM PO15 164 E7
HLER SO31 180 C2
Ashwood Cl HAV PO9 170 B5
HISD PO11 195 G5
Ashwood Dr BDST BH18 211 J4
NWBY RG14 19 M2
Ashwood Gdns ROWN SO16 146 E5
TOTT SO40 158 C2
Ashwood Wy DEAN RG23 64 F5
Ashworth Dr STHA RG19 35 J2
Askew Dr THLE RG7 238 B5
Aspen Av HLER SO31 179 K4
Aspen Cl BOR GU35 112 F3
HEND SO30 149 K5
RWIN SO21 135 G4
Aspen Dr VWD BH31 201 K2
Aspen Gdns BKME/WDN BH12 224 F1
HTWY RG27 56 D6
Aspen Gv ASHV GU12 73 L8
Aspengrove
LSOL/BMARY PO13 182 E7
Aspen Holt ROWN SO16 147 G3
Aspen Pl NMIL/BTOS BH25 219 H7
Aspen Rd BKME/WDN BH12 224 F1
Aspen Wk TOTT SO40 144 B8
Aspen Wy BKME/WDN BH12 224 F1
HORN PO8 156 A3
Aspin Wy BLKW GU17 49 K3
Asquith Cl CHCH/BSGR BH23 228 D3
Astbury Av BKME/WDN BH12 213 G8
Aster Ct AND SP10 4 B8
Aster Rd KBH RG22 92 C5
ROWN SO16 147 J4
Astley St SSEA PO5 21 G5
Aston Md CHCH/BSGR BH23 215 L4
Aston Rd ENEY PO4 192 F5
WVILLE PO7 155 L8
Astor Crs RAND SP11 265 L10
Astra Ct FAWY SO45 177 G3
Astral Gdns HLER SO31 178 F1
Astra Wk GPORT PO12 15 J5
Astrid Cl HISD PO11 195 J5
Asturias Wy SHAM SO14 23 L6
Asylum Rd WSHM SO15 161 G2
Atalanta Cl ENEY PO4 193 J3
Atbara Rd FLEETS GU52 71 J4
Atheling Rd FAWY SO45 177 G4
Athelstan Rd ITCH SO19 161 L1
SBNE BH6 227 L3
Athena Av WVILLE PO7 169 M5
Athena Cl ELGH SO50 141 G1
Atherfield Rd ROWN SO16 145 L5
Atherley Ct WSHM SO15 146 E8
Atherley Rd HISD PO11 194 E3
WSHM SO15 160 D2
Athlone Ct RAND SP11 84 D4
Atholl Ct AND SP10 96 C1
Atholl Rd BOR GU35 112 F3
Atkinson Cl GPORT PO12 14 D9
Atkins Pl FHAM PO15 181 J1
Atlantic Cl SHAM SO14 23 K8
Atlantic Park Vw WEND SO18 148 A2
Atlantis Av WVILLE PO7 169 M6
Atrebatti Rd SHST GU47 43 L7
Attenborough Cl FLEETN GU51 59 K5
Attfield Cl ASHV GU12 73 M7
Attlee Gdns FLEETS GU52 71 H4
Attwood Cl BSTK RG21 6 A7
FBDG SP6 196 B7
Attwood Dr WHIT RG2 239 L8
Attwoods Dro RWIN SO21 124 D4
Aubrey Cl HISD PO11 194 E4
LYMN SO41 232 F4
Auchinleck Wy ALDT GU11 2 B3
Auckland Cl NTID SP9 266 G2
Auckland Pl BROC SO42 351 K3
Auckland Rd
CHCH/BSGR BH23 229 J1
WSHM SO15 159 M1
Auckland Rd East SSEA PO5 21 H9
Auckland Rd West SSEA PO5 21 G9
Audemer Ct RGWD BH24 203 L4
Audley Cl NWBY RG14 27 M7
Audley Pl ELGH SO50 * 140 F2
Audret Cl FHAM/PORC PO16 183 H2
Augustine Rd CHAM PO6 169 J7
SHAM SO14 161 H2
Augustine Wy AND SP10 95 M1
Augustus Dr DEAN RG23 64 E5
Augustus Gdns CBLY GU15 51 L3
Augustus Wk AND SP10 96 D1
Augustus Wy CHFD SO53 139 L1
Aukland Av BROC SO42 351 L3
Auklet Cl KBH RG22 92 B5
Auriol Dr CHAM PO6 170 A8
Aurora Dr DEAN RG23 92 C8
Austen Av FUFL SO22 124 C1
NBNE BH10 * 213 K2
Austen Cl TOTT SO40 158 D2
WINC SO23 123 G2
Austen Gdns HLER SO31 164 C4
NWBY RG14 19 G9
Austen Gv KBH RG22 93 G2
Austen Rd FARN GU14 61 G2
Austerberry Wy
LSOL/BMARY PO13 182 D8
Auster Cl CHCH/BSGR BH23 229 H1
Austin Av PSTN BH14 224 B6
Austin Cl BMTH BH1 226 D3
Austin Ct CHAM PO6 168 B7
Australia Cl PSEA PO1 21 J2
Aust Rd FHAM/STUB PO14 181 K4
Autumn Cl FERN BH22 209 H1
Autumn Rd BWD BH11 212 D5
TOTT SO40 160 A7
Avalon PSTN BH14 224 C8
Avebury Av NBNE BH10 213 L2
Avebury Gdns CHFD SO53 133 G7
Aveley La FNM GU9 78 F1
Avenger Cl CHFD SO53 139 H3
Avens Cl ELGH SO50 141 J6
Avenue C FAWY SO45 177 L8
Avenue Cl AND SP10 4 D5
LIPH GU30 116 B4
Avenue Ct GPORT PO12 14 C8
Avenue D FAWY SO45 177 L8
Avenue De Cagny
CHOB/PIR GU24 63 M3
Avenue E FAWY SO45 177 L8
Avenue La WCLF BH2 8 D6
Avenue Rd ALTN GU34 256 G12
BROC SO42 351 K3
CHCH/BSGR BH23 218 C7
CHCH/BSGR BH23 227 M1
FARN GU14 61 K4
FHAM/STUB PO14 10 D6
FLEETN GU51 59 H6
FUFL SO22 24 D4
GPORT PO12 15 G3
GSHT GU26 115 K5
HISD PO11 186 F5
LYMN SO41 221 K4
NMIL/BTOS BH25 219 G5
SHAM SO14 147 G8
WCLF BH2 8 C6
WIMB BH21 207 K4
Avenue Sucy CBLY GU15 50 C4
The Avenue ALDT GU11 3 K8
AND SP10 4 D5
BPWT SO32 143 H4
CBLY GU15 50 D4
CCLF BH13 225 G8
CWTH RG45 43 J3
EPSF GU31 120 D6
FERN BH22 204 F5
FHAM PO15 10 B6
FHAM PO15 181 H4
FHAM/STUB PO14 10 D6
FHAM/STUB PO14 181 K3
FLEETN GU51 59 G7
GPORT PO12 14 C8
GSHT GU26 115 K5
HASM GU27 117 M1
LIPH GU30 116 A4
MOOR/WNTN BH9 213 M5
NARL SO24 277 Q9
NARL SO24 291 K11
NTID SP9 266 E4
OVTN RG25 104 F1
PTSW SO17 146 F6
RAND SP11 84 A2
RCCH PO18 173 H5
RFNM GU10 78 D4
RWIN SO21 125 G6
RWIN SO21 273 N1
THLE RG7 40 B3
Avery Cl EWKG RG40 42 B2
Avery La GPORT PO12 190 F1
Aviary Cl RCCH PO18 173 H4
Aviary Ct CHIN RG24 * 54 A8
Aviation Pk West
CHCH/BSGR BH23 * 346 D11
Avington Cl ELGH SO50 134 D7
Avington Ct ROWN SO16 146 F4
Avocet Crs SHST GU47 43 M8
Avocet Quay EMRTH PO10 172 A7
Avocet Wk LSOL/BMARY PO13 182 A6
Avocet Wy HORN PO8 156 A1
Avon Av RGWD BH24 347 K1
Avonborne Wy CHFD SO53 133 H8
Avon Buildings
CHCH/BSGR BH23 228 B1
Avon Castle Dr RGWD BH24 202 F8
Avon Cswy CHCH/BSGR BH23 347 L12
Avoncliffe Rd SBNE BH6 227 L5
Avon Cl ASHV GU12 73 M7
CHAR BH8 226 D2
FARN GU14 60 E1
LSOL/BMARY PO13 189 M7
LYMN SO41 221 J5
PSF GU32 120 C7
Avon Ct AND SP10 96 D2
Avon Crs ROMY SO51 137 J1
Avondale ASHV GU12 73 M1
Avondale Rd ALDT GU11 3 H6
FLEETN GU51 59 J6
PSEA PO1 192 F1
WVILLE PO7 155 M8
Avon Dr RSAL SP5 327 N2
Avon Gdns CHCH/BSGR BH23 348 D11
Avon Gn CHFD SO53 139 K3
Avon Meade FBDG SP6 197 G2
Avon Ms CHAR BH8 226 C2
Avon Pk RGWD BH24 202 F6
Avon Rd CHAR BH8 226 C2
DEAN RG23 91 K3
FERN BH22 205 G7
FNM GU9 13 G6
NTID SP9 266 E3
WEND SO18 147 M7
Avon Rd East
CHCH/BSGR BH23 216 A8
Avon Rd West
CHCH/BSGR BH23 215 M8
Avon Run Cl CHCH/BSGR BH23 229 H3
Avon Run Rd
CHCH/BSGR BH23 229 H3
Avon Valley Pth
CHCH/BSGR BH23 216 C2
FBDG SP6 197 G5
RGWD BH24 203 K1
Avon Vw FBDG SP6 197 M3
Avon View Rd
CHCH/BSGR BH23 216 C5
Avon Wk BSTK RG21 * 7 J5
Avon Wy HEND SO30 148 E2
Avonway NWBY RG14 19 M1
Avon Whf CHCH/BSGR BH23 * 228 C2
Avro Cl WSHM SO15 160 A1
Award Rd FLEETS GU52 71 J3
WIMB BH21 208 F3
Awbridge Rd HAV PO9 170 C4
Axford Cl CHAR BH8 214 D5
Ayesgarth FLEETS GU52 71 K3
Ayjay Cl ALDT GU11 3 G8
Aylen Rd HSEA PO3 185 G6
Aylesbury Rd BMTH BH1 226 D4
NEND PO2 184 F8
Aylesford Wy STHA RG19 36 A2
Aylesham Wy YTLY GU46 48 D2
Ayling Cl LSOL/BMARY PO13 190 C1
Ayling Ct FNM GU9 2 D8
Ayling Hl ALDT GU11 2 C5
Ayling La ALDT GU11 2 D6
Aylings Cl DEAN RG23 64 D8
Aylward's Dr ALTN GU34 294 C5
Aylward St PSEA PO1 20 D2
Aylwards Wy STOK SO20 284 B3
Aylwin Cl BSTK RG21 93 J2
Ayres La KSCL RG20 246 H4
Ayrshire Gdns FLEETN GU51 59 K4
Aysgarth Rd WVILLE PO7 155 L8
Aysha Cl NMIL/BTOS BH25 219 H7
Azalea Av BOR GU35 111 J7
Azalea Cl HAV PO9 171 J4
RGWD BH24 202 C7
Azalea Ct AND SP10 4 B8
Azalea Dr HASM GU27 115 M8
Azalea Gdns FLEETS GU52 71 K3
Azalea Wy CBLY GU15 51 K2
Azura Cl WIMB BH21 205 K2

B

Babbington Rd WHIT RG2 * 238 D2
Babbs Md FNM GU9 12 D5
Babs Flds RFNM GU10 259 L11
Bach Cl KBH RG22 92 F5
Back Down La RGWD BH24 203 M5
Back Dr CWTH RG45 * 43 K5
Back La HUNG RG17 30 F5
LYMN SO41 350 G10
MFD/CHID GU8 260 H12
OVTN RG25 256 F11
RAND SP11 82 E5
RAND SP11 243 P10
RFNM GU10 109 H4
ROMY SO51 298 F7
THLE RG7 37 H6
THLE RG7 39 J8
THLE RG7 238 A8
THLE RG7 249 M1
WHAM PO17 167 L2
Back of the Walls SHAM SO14 23 G5
Back St WINC SO23 122 F8
Bacon Cl ITCH SO19 161 M7
SHST GU47 49 M2
Bacon La HISD PO11 194 D5
RFNM GU10 262 C8
Badajos Rd ALDT GU11 2 C1
Badbury Cl BDST BH18 211 J5
Badbury Vw WIMB BH21 207 K3
Badbury View Rd WIMB BH21 206 D8
Baddesley Cl NBAD SO52 137 M3
Baddesley Rd CHFD SO53 133 G7
Baden Cl NMIL/BTOS BH25 219 H7
Baden Powell Rd LISS GU33 309 J2
Bader Cl HEND SO30 149 J4
Bader Rd CFDH BH17 211 L8
Bader Wy FHAM PO15 164 E7
Badger Brow WVILLE PO7 170 A2
Badger Cl ALTN GU34 293 N5
ELGH SO50 140 F2
FHAM PO15 181 K2
Badger Farm Rd FUFL SO22 122 B7
Badger's Bank CHIN RG24 54 B8
Badgers Cl FLEETS GU52 59 H8
LYMN SO41 350 G10
RGWD BH24 202 B7
Badgers Copse CBLY GU15 51 G5
FHAM PO15 164 B7
NMIL/BTOS BH25 219 J2
Badgers Cft THLE RG7 * 40 A2
Badgers Holt YTLY GU46 48 D3
Badgers Rdg NWBY RG14 33 J8
Badgers Run HLER SO31 163 L6
Badgers Sett CWTH RG45 43 H3
The Badgers HLER SO31 162 C6
Badgers Wk FAWY SO45 176 F6
FERN BH22 209 L1
Badger Wy RFNM GU10 71 K8
VWD BH31 201 H3
Badgerwood Dr FRIM GU16 50 F6
Badminston Dro FAWY SO45 355 L8
Badminston La FAWY SO45 355 L7
Badshear La NARL SO24 304 A5
Badshot Lea Rd FNM GU9 77 M2
Badshot Pk FNM GU9 77 L2
Baffins Rd HSEA PO3 193 G2
Bagber Rd TOTT SO40 158 F1
Bagmore La OVTN RG25 256 A11
Bagnols Wy NWBY RG14 18 A6
Bagshaw Ms ITCH SO19 161 M5
Bagshot Ms ITCH SO19 * 161 M5
Bagwell La ODIM RG29 69 L1
Baigent Cl WINC SO23 25 L5
Bailes La RGUW GU3 75 K6
Bailey Cl FRIM GU16 50 F8
FUFL SO22 24 A9
HEND SO30 149 M6
NMIL/BTOS BH25 219 K4
Bailey Crs PLE BH15 223 J1
Bailey Dr CHCH/BSGR BH23 227 M1
Bailey Gn WEND SO18 148 A2
Baileys Cl BLKW GU17 49 K4
Bailey's Rd SSEA PO5 21 J4
Baily Av NTHA RG18 28 D8
Bain Av CBLY GU15 50 D7
Baird Av KBH RG22 93 G2
Baird Rd FARN GU14 61 J2
WHIT RG2 239 L8
Baiter Gdns PLE BH15 223 J7
Bakehouse Gdns FLEETS GU52 71 K3
Bakehouse Ms ALDT GU11 * 2 F2
Baker Rd BWD BH11 212 F3
Bakers Dro ROWN SO16 145 M2
Bakers Farm Rd VWD BH31 201 G1
Bakers Fld LISS GU33 308 F2
Baker St NEND PO2 192 D1
Balaclava Rd WEND SO18 148 A5
Balcombe Rd CCLF BH13 225 G5
Balderton Cl NEND PO2 184 F4
Baldreys FNM GU9 12 D8
Baldwin Cl CHCH/BSGR BH23 228 D2
Balena Cl CFDH BH17 211 G8
Balfour Cl CHCH/BSGR BH23 217 K8
LSOL/BMARY PO13 190 D2
Balfour Crs NWBY RG14 33 J7
Balfour Dr LISS GU33 308 E8
Balfour Rd ITCH SO19 148 B7
MOOR/WNTN BH9 213 M7
NEND PO2 184 E7
Balintore Ct SHST GU47 49 M1
Balksbury Hl RAND SP11 95 M7
Balksbury Rd RAND SP11 96 A7
Ballam Cl UPTN BH16 222 C1
Ballantyne Rd FARN GU14 61 G2
Ballard Cl KBH RG22 92 E1
NMIL/BTOS BH25 219 H4
PLE BH15 223 J7
ROWN SO16 145 J7
Ballard Rd PLE BH15 223 K7
Balliol Cl FHAM/STUB PO14 180 C3
Balliol Rd NEND PO2 192 E1
Balloon Rd FARN GU14 61 H6
Ball & Wicket La FNM GU9 77 G1
Balmer Lawn Rd BROC SO42 351 M1
Balmoral Av CHAR BH8 214 E7
Balmoral Cl ALTN GU34 106 D5
CHFD SO53 133 H8
LSOL/BMARY PO13 182 D5
ROWN SO16 146 C3
Balmoral Ct KBH RG22 * 92 E1
Balmoral Crs FNM GU9 76 F2
Balmoral Dr FRIM GU16 51 G8
WVILLE PO7 169 J4
Balmoral Rd AND SP10 5 G5
ASHV GU12 74 A4
FHAM PO15 10 B2
PSTN BH14 224 C5
Balmoral Wk NMIL/BTOS BH25 218 F5
Balmoral Wy KBH RG22 92 C5
PSF GU32 120 D5
ROWN SO16 145 K2
Balsan Cl CHIN RG24 64 E4
Balston Rd PSTN BH14 224 A3
Balston Ter PLE BH15 * 223 H6
Baltic Rd HEND SO30 148 E3
Bamber La ALTN GU34 258 F12
Bampton Cl ROWN SO16 145 K8
Banbury Av ITCH SO19 148 C8
Banbury Cl FRIM GU16 61 M1
Banbury Rd CFDH BH17 223 J1
Band Hall Pl HTWY RG27 56 D7
Bangor Rd WSHM SO15 160 B2
Banister Gdns WSHM SO15 160 F1
Banister Ms WSHM SO15 * 160 F1
Banister Rd WSHM SO15 160 F1
Bankhill Dr LYMN SO41 221 K3
Bank Pde BKME/WDN BH12 * 213 G7
Bank Rd ALDT GU11 73 K3
Bank Side EWKG RG40 42 B2
WEND SO18 147 K4
Bankside FNM GU9 2 C9
LYMN SO41 221 K2
Bankside Cl MFD/CHID GU8 263 R1
Bankside Rd
MOOR/WNTN BH9 214 A5
Banks Rd CCLF BH13 237 G5
The Banks ROMY SO51 129 G3
Bank St BPWT SO32 143 K5
Bankview LYMN SO41 221 K2
Bannerman Rd PSF GU32 120 D5
Banning St ROMY SO51 136 E2
Bannister Gdns HTWY RG27 42 A8
YTLY GU46 49 H3
Bannister Pl THLE RG7 36 F6
Bannister Rd THLE RG7 39 M2
Banstead Rd BDST BH18 211 G3
Bapaume Rd HSEA PO3 184 F3
Baptist Hl RAND SP11 86 B2
Barbara Cl FLEETS GU52 71 K2
Barbe Baker Av HEND SO30 148 C2
Barbel Av BSTK RG21 7 L5
Barberry Cl FLEETS GU52 71 J2
Barberry Dr TOTT SO40 144 B7
Barberry Wy BLKW GU17 50 B5
VWD BH31 201 L3
Barber's La RSAL SP5 325 Q3
Barbers Piles PLE BH15 223 H7
Barbon Cl CBLY GU15 51 M5
Barbour Cl ODIM RG29 258 A1
Barcelona Cl AND SP10 5 K3
Barclay Ms FAWY SO45 177 G8
Bardon Wy FHAM/STUB PO14 181 K4
Bardsley Dr FNM GU9 12 C9
Bardwell Cl KBH RG22 64 E8
The Baredown HTWY RG27 67 M1

Bar End Rd WINC SO23 25 J9
Barfield Cl WINC SO23 25 J8
Barfield Rd NTHA RG18 28 C8
Barfields LYMN SO41 221 L4
Barfleur Cl FHAM PO15 181 K2
Barfleur Rd FHAM/STUB PO14 182 A3
Barford Cl CHFD SO53 133 H8
FLEETN GU51 59 M8
Barford La RSAL SP5 327 L12
Bargates CHCH/BSGR BH23 228 B1
Bargate St SHAM SO14 22 F4
Barge Cl ALDT GU11 73 L3
Barge La THLE RG7 41 M4
Barham Cl GPORT PO12 14 F1
Barham Rd PSF GU32 120 D6
Barham Wy NEND PO2 184 D4
Baring Cl RWIN SO21 276 C8
RWIN SO21 290 C9
Baring Rd SBNE BH6 228 A4
WINC SO23 25 K7
Barker Cl WHIT RG2 239 L9
Barker Mill Cl ROWN SO16 145 L2
Barkham Ride EWKG RG40 42 B1
Barkham Rd WHIT RG2 239 L5
Barkham St EWKG RG40 239 Q6
Barlands Cl CHCH/BSGR BH23 216 C6
Barle Cl WEND SO18 148 B3
Barley Down Dr FUFL SO22 122 D8
Barley Mow Cl HTWY RG27 58 B8
Barley Mow Hl BOR GU35 111 M6
Barley Vw OVTN RG25 103 H3
Barley Wy FLEETN GU51 59 K3
Barlow Cl FHAM/STUB PO14 189 H2
Barlows La AND SP10 96 B7
Barlows Rd TADY RG26 44 B5
Barnard Cl FRIM GU16 51 H8
Barnard Wy ALDT GU11 2 D1
Barnbrook Rd HLER SO31 163 L8
Barn Cl CBLY GU15 51 G2
EMRTH PO10 171 K8
HUNG RG17 31 H2
UPTN BH16 222 A1
Barn Close La KSCL RG20 245 P12
Barn Crs NWBY RG14 33 K5
Barncroft FNM GU9 13 G5
RAND SP11 82 C7
Barncroft Wy HAV PO9 16 C1
Barnes Cl FARN GU14 61 K4
HLER SO31 163 K8
ITCH SO19 148 C6
NBNE BH10 213 K5
WINC SO23 122 E7
Barnes Crs NBNE BH10 213 K5
WIMB BH21 207 L4
Barnes La HLER SO31 163 L8
LYMN SO41 220 C8
Barnes Rd FRIM GU16 51 G8
ITCH SO19 148 C6
NBNE BH10 213 K5
PSEA PO1 21 M1
Barnes Wallis Rd FHAM PO15 164 D8
Barnes Wy HAV PO9 170 C5
Barnet Side La PSF GU32 306 H7
Barnetts Wood La NARL SO24 292 E8
Barney Evans Crs HORN PO8 155 K5
Barneyhayes La TOTT SO40 341 L4
Barnfield CHCH/BSGR BH23 217 K8
YTLY GU46 48 F3
Barnfield Cl ALTN GU34 258 G12
EMRTH PO10 172 E4
ITCH SO19 161 L7
Barnfield Ct
FHAM/STUB PO14 10 B8
ITCH SO19 161 M7
Barnfield Ri AND SP10 4 C9
Barnfield Rd EPSF GU31 121 G6
ITCH SO19 161 L7
Barnfield Wy ITCH SO19 161 M7
Barn Fold HORN PO8 * 156 B7
Barn Green Cl WVILLE PO7 154 F4
Barn La ALTN GU34 293 K7
DEAN RG23 91 J4
Barn Meadow Cl FLEETS GU52 71 H5
Barn Piece CHFD SO53 138 F2
Barn Rd BDST BH18 211 H5
Barnsfield Crs TOTT SO40 158 C1
Barnsfield Rd RGWD BH24 346 G3
Barnside Wy LISS GU33 308 F9
Barnsland HEND SO30 148 C2
Barnsley Cl FRIM GU16 62 B7
Barns Rd FERN BH22 346 A6
The Barns OVTN RG25 103 M1
Barnwood Rd FHAM PO15 181 K3
Baroda Rd NTID SP9 266 C4
Baron Rd HLER SO31 178 F1
Barons Md ROWN SO16 145 L5
Barons Rd BWD BH11 212 D2
Barossa Rd CBLY GU15 50 F1
Barracane Dr CWTH RG45 43 K4
Barrack La RGWD BH24 203 M8
Barrack Rd ALDT GU11 2 E3
CHCH/BSGR BH23 215 L8
FERN BH22 346 A10
Barracks La THLE RG7 238 B7
Barra Cl DEAN RG23 91 J2
Barrett's La WHIT RG2 239 K2
Barrie Cl HLER SO31 164 C4
Barrie Rd FNM GU9 76 E1
MOOR/WNTN BH9 213 M5
Barrington Cl ELGH SO50 139 M3
Barron Pl CHIN RG24 64 D4
Barrow Down Gdns ITCH SO19 162 E1
Barrow Dr CHAR BH8 214 F6
Barrowgate Rd CHAR BH8 214 D4
Barrowgate Wy CHAR BH8 214 D5
Barrow Hl RAND SP11 271 N4
Barrow Hill Rd TOTT SO40 341 P1
Barrow Rd CHAR BH8 214 F6
Barrows La LYMN SO41 220 B1
RSAL SP5 333 R2
Barrow Vw WIMB BH21 209 G2
Barrow Wy CHAR BH8 214 F6
Barrs Av NMIL/BTOS BH25 219 G4
Barrs Wood Dr
NMIL/BTOS BH25 219 H4
Barrs Wood Rd
NMIL/BTOS BH25 219 H4
Barry Gdns BDST BH18 210 F3
Barry Rd ITCH SO19 148 C7
Barrys Meadow
FHAM/STUB PO14 * 180 F4
Barry Wy KBH RG22 92 F5
Barters Cl ROWN SO16 145 M7
Barters La BDST BH18 210 F4
Bartholomew Cl HASM GU27 118 C4
NWBY RG14 * 18 D6
WINC SO23 25 G3
Bartholomew St NWBY RG14 18 D6
Bartlemy Cl NWBY RG14 18 A9
Bartlemy Rd NWBY RG14 18 A9
Bartlett Cl FHAM PO15 10 A2
TADY RG26 46 D6
Bartlett Dr LTDN BH7 215 H8
Bartlett Pl FRIM GU16 61 M3
The Bartletts HLER SO31 179 G2
Bartley Av TOTT SO40 158 E2
Bartley Rd TOTT SO40 341 N9
Bartley Wy HTWY RG27 56 E8
Bartok Cl KBH RG22 93 G3
Barton Cha NMIL/BTOS BH25 * 230 F1
Barton Cl ALDT GU11 2 A4
AND SP10 95 M1
ROMY SO51 131 H8
Barton Common La
NMIL/BTOS BH25 219 H8
Barton Common Rd
NMIL/BTOS BH25 231 H1
Barton Court Av
NMIL/BTOS BH25 230 F1
Barton Court Rd
NMIL/BTOS BH25 219 G7
Barton Crs WEND SO18 147 M7
Barton Cft NMIL/BTOS BH25 231 G1
Barton Cross HORN PO8 156 B1
Barton Dr HEND SO30 149 K5
HLER SO31 178 F1
NMIL/BTOS BH25 218 F8
Barton Dro RWIN SO21 274 A8
Barton Gn NMIL/BTOS BH25 231 G2
Barton La NMIL/BTOS BH25 218 D8
Barton Pk ELGH SO50 * 140 C2
Barton Rd ELGH SO50 140 C1
Bartons Ct ODIM RG29 * 68 F5
Barton's Dr YTLY GU46 48 F4
Bartonside Rd
NMIL/BTOS BH25 218 C8
Bartons La CHIN RG24 66 B1
Bartons Rd FBDG SP6 197 H3
HAV PO9 171 G3
The Bartons FBDG SP6 197 H3
Bartons Wy FARN GU14 60 C1
Barton Wy NMIL/BTOS BH25 218 F8
Barton Wood Rd
NMIL/BTOS BH25 230 E1
Bartram Rd TOTT SO40 159 G2
Barwell Cl CWTH RG45 43 H4
Barwell Gv EMRTH PO10 171 L5
Bascott Cl BWD BH11 213 G7
Bascott Rd BWD BH11 212 F7
Bashley Common Rd
NMIL/BTOS BH25 349 Q12
Bashley Cross Rd
NMIL/BTOS BH25 218 E3
Bashley Dr NMIL/BTOS BH25 219 H2
Bashley Rd NMIL/BTOS BH25 219 G1
Basingbourne Cl FLEETS GU52 71 J2
Basingbourne Rd FLEETS GU52 71 H3
Basing Dean ALTN GU34 306 C7
Basing Dr ALDT GU11 3 H9
Basingfield Cl CHIN RG24 66 D4
Basing Ms BPWT SO32 * 143 J5
Basing Rd CHIN RG24 7 M3
HAV PO9 170 E3
Basingstoke Rd ALTN GU34 106 B4
HTWY RG27 47 M2
KSCL RG20 248 E10
RWIN SO21 289 N4
TADY RG26 52 A7
THLE RG7 38 A3
THLE RG7 238 A3
WINC SO23 289 K10
Basing Vw BSTK RG21 7 H4
Basing Wy CHFD SO53 139 G4
Basingwell St BPWT SO32 143 J5
Basin St NEND PO2 184 D8
Bassenthwaite Gdns
BOR GU35 110 F7
Bassett Av ROWN SO16 146 F3
Bassett Cl FRIM GU16 51 G8
ROWN SO16 146 F4
Bassett Crs East ROWN SO16 146 F4
Bassett Crs West ROWN SO16 146 F5
Bassett Dl ROWN SO16 146 F2
Bassett Gdns ROWN SO16 146 E4
Bassett Gn ROWN SO16 147 H3
Bassett Green Cl ROWN SO16 147 H2
Bassett Green Dr ROWN SO16 147 G3
Bassett Green Rd ROWN SO16 147 G2
Bassett Heath Av ROWN SO16 146 F1
Bassett Meadow ROWN SO16 146 F5
Bassett Ms ROWN SO16 146 F3
Bassett Rd BKME/WDN BH12 224 B2
Bassett Rw ROWN SO16 146 F2
Bassett Wood Dr ROWN SO16 146 F2
Bassett Wood Rd ROWN SO16 146 F2
Bat & Ball La FNM GU9 78 E2
Batchelor Crs BWD BH11 212 F5
Batchelor Dr CHIN RG24 66 E3
Batchelor Gn HLER SO31 162 F4
Batchelor Rd BWD BH11 212 F5
Batchelors Barn Rd AND SP10 5 L4
Batcombe Cl BWD BH11 212 E5
Bath Cl ITCH SO19 148 B6
Bath Hill Rbt BMTH BH1 8 F7
Bathing La PSEA PO1 20 A5
Bath La FHAM/PORC PO16 11 K6
Bath La (Lower)
FHAM/PORC PO16 11 K7
Bath Rd BMTH BH1 8 F7
CBLY GU15 50 E2
EMRTH PO10 171 M8
ENEY PO4 192 F5
ITCH SO19 148 B6
LYMN SO41 221 M5
NTHA RG18 28 B8
NTHA RG18 36 B1
NWBY RG14 26 F7
THLE RG7 36 F2
THLE RG7 38 C1
Bath Sq PSEA PO1 20 B5
Bath St SHAM SO14 161 G1
Bathurst Cl HISD PO11 194 E5
Batsford RAND SP11 86 B2
Batstone Wy FERN BH22 209 H2
Battalion Wy STHA RG19 35 L3
Battenburg Av NEND PO2 184 F6
Battenburg Rd GPORT PO12 15 G3
Batten Cl CHCH/BSGR BH23 216 D8
Batten Rd RSAL SP5 327 J12
Battens Av OVTN RG25 89 K5
Battens Wy HAV PO9 170 F4
Batterley Dro WIMB BH21 337 M8
Battery Cl GPORT PO12 182 F8
Battery End NWBY RG14 33 K6
Battery Hl BPWT SO32 143 H4
FUFL SO22 122 C6
Battery Rw PSEA PO1 20 C7
Battle Cl HLER SO31 163 M8
NWBY RG14 26 F8
Battle Rd NWBY RG14 33 J6
Baughurst Rd TADY RG26 249 Q4
THLE RG7 39 G6
B Av FAWY SO45 354 F3
Baverstock Rd
BKME/WDN BH12 213 H8
Baverstocks ALTN GU34 107 G2
The Baxendales NWBY RG14 19 J8
Baxter Rd ITCH SO19 148 E8
Baybridge La BPWT SO32 310 E6
Baybridge Rd HAV PO9 171 H3
Bay Cl ITCH SO19 162 A1
UPTN BH16 222 B2
WIMB BH21 201 G8
Bayfield Av FRIM GU16 51 G6
Bayford Cl FARN GU14 50 C7
Bay Hog La PLE BH15 223 H6
Bayly Av FHAM/PORC PO16 183 K2
Baynard Cl BSTK RG21 7 G1
Bay Rd GPORT PO12 14 A7
ITCH SO19 162 A1
Bays Ct TADY RG26 * 249 R3
Bays Rd LYMN SO41 221 J5
Baythorn Cl NEND PO2 192 D1
Bay Tree Gdns TOTT SO40 159 M7
Bay Trees ITCH SO19 148 E6
Bay Tree Wy CHCH/BSGR BH23 217 K7
Baywood Cl FARN GU14 60 C3
Bazaar Rd NTID SP9 266 D2
Beach Av NMIL/BTOS BH25 230 F1
Beach Dr CHAM PO6 167 M8
Beach Rd CCLF BH13 225 G8
EMRTH PO10 171 L8
HISD PO11 194 E6
LSOL/BMARY PO13 189 L7
SSEA PO5 192 D7
UPTN BH16 222 A2
Beach's Crs TADY RG26 53 G1
Beachway FHAM/PORC PO16 183 K2
Beacon Bottom HLER SO31 164 A6
Beacon Cl HLER SO31 164 A6
LYMN SO41 220 D7
RFNM GU10 78 E3
Beacon Ct FBDG SP6 197 G1
Beacon Dr CHCH/BSGR BH23 229 M1
Beacon Gdns BDST BH18 210 E5
FLEETN GU51 * 59 G7
Beacon Hill Ct GSHT GU26 115 K2
Beacon Hill La BPWT SO32 312 B9
UPTN BH16 210 B5
Beacon Hill Pk GSHT GU26 * 115 H3
Beacon Hill Rd FLEETS GU52 71 K4
GSHT GU26 115 J2
Beacon Mt HLER SO31 164 A6
Beacon Park Crs UPTN BH16 210 A8
Beacon Park Rd UPTN BH16 210 A8
Beacon Rd BDST BH18 210 D5
FARN GU14 61 H8
HEND SO30 148 D4
UPTN BH16 222 B1
WCLF BH2 8 E8
Beaconsfield Av CHAM PO6 185 G1
Beaconsfield Rd
BKME/WDN BH12 224 D3
BSTK RG21 6 F7
CHCH/BSGR BH23 228 B1
FHAM/PORC PO16 11 G8
WVILLE PO7 155 L8
Beacon Sq EMRTH PO10 187 L1
Beacon View Rd
MFD/CHID GU8 263 Q2
Beacon Wy BDST BH18 210 E5
HLER SO31 164 A6
Beale's Cl AND SP10 5 J5
Beales La RFNM GU10 78 D1
Bealeswood La RFNM GU10 109 L6
Bealing Cl ROWN SO16 147 H4
Beal's Pightle TADY RG26 52 B5
Beam Hollow FNM GU9 77 G1
Beamish Rd CFDH BH17 211 M8
Beancroft Rd STHA RG19 35 K2
Bear Cross Av BWD BH11 212 F2
Beard Ct RAND SP11 265 N10
Bear Hl KSCL RG20 248 C11
Bear La FNM GU9 12 F2
NWBY RG14 18 E4
Bearslane Cl TOTT SO40 144 D7
Bearwood Gdns FLEETN GU51 59 J7
Beatrice Rd ENEY PO4 21 M8
WSHM SO15 160 C1
Beattie Ri HEND SO30 149 J2
Beatty Cl HLER SO31 164 B8
RGWD BH24 203 L4
Beatty Ct AND SP10 96 F4
Beatty Dr GPORT PO12 14 B8
Beatty Rd MOOR/WNTN BH9 214 B7
Beauchamp Av
LSOL/BMARY PO13 182 C6
Beauchamp Pl
CHCH/BSGR BH23 228 A1
Beauchamps Gdns LTDN BH7 215 G8
Beauclerk Gn HTWY RG27 57 L7
Beaucroft La WIMB BH21 207 L2
Beaucroft Rd BPWT SO32 151 L1
WIMB BH21 207 K2
Beaufighter Rd FARN GU14 61 G8
Beaufort Av FHAM/PORC PO16 10 C2
Beaufort Cl CHCH/BSGR BH23 229 H1
LSOL/BMARY PO13 190 A2
Beaufort Dr BPWT SO32 143 J4
WIMB BH21 207 J3
Beaufort Rd ASHV GU12 73 M2
BOR GU35 110 F7
FLEETS GU52 71 K1
FNM GU9 13 G2
HAV PO9 16 A3
SBNE BH6 227 J3
SSEA PO5 * 192 D7
WINC SO23 24 E8
Beaufoys Av FERN BH22 209 J1
Beaufoys Cl FERN BH22 209 J1
Beaufront Cl CBLY GU15 51 J1
Beaufront Rd CBLY GU15 51 J1
Beaulieu Av CHCH/BSGR BH23 227 L1
FHAM/PORC PO16 167 G8
HAV PO9 170 D2
Beaulieu Cl FUFL SO22 288 D12
ROWN SO16 146 B3
Beaulieu Ct AND SP10 96 E2
BSTK RG21 7 H5
Beaulieu Gdns BLKW GU17 49 L3
Beaulieu Pl LSOL/BMARY PO13 182 C6
Beaulieu Rd BROC SO42 174 F8
BROC SO42 353 Q4
CHCH/BSGR BH23 227 L1
ELGH SO50 134 A8
FAWY SO45 176 F6
LYND SO43 345 M4
NEND PO2 184 E7
TOTT SO40 175 K3
WBNE BH4 225 H7
Beaumaris Cl AND SP10 4 C8
Beaumaris Gdns FAWY SO45 176 F4
Beaumaris Pde FRIM GU16 51 H8
Beaumond Gn WINC SO23 24 F6
Beaumont Cl FHAM PO15 181 K1
ROWN SO16 146 E5
Beaumont Ct GPORT PO12 * 183 G8
Beaumont Gv ALDT GU11 2 B3
Beaumont Ri FHAM PO15 165 K8
Beaumont Rd CCLF BH13 237 K1
TOTT SO40 159 G1
Beaurepaire Cl TADY RG26 53 M1
Beauworth Av WEND SO18 148 C4
Beaver Dr ELGH SO50 141 G2
Beaver La YTLY GU46 49 G3
Beavers Cl ALTN GU34 106 E4
FNM GU9 12 C4
TADY RG26 249 R3
Beavers Hl FNM GU9 12 B3
Beavers Ms BOR GU35 111 G8
Beavers Rd FNM GU9 12 D4
Beccles Cl PLE BH15 222 F6
Becher Rd PSTN BH14 224 E4
Beck Cl HLER SO31 179 L1
Beckett Cl DEAN RG23 64 C7
Beckett Rd AND SP10 4 D4
Beckford La WHAM PO17 153 L7
Beck Gdns FNM GU9 76 E2
Beckham La PSF GU32 120 B5
Beckhampton Rd PLE BH15 222 E5
Beckley Copse
CHCH/BSGR BH23 218 A6
Beck St PSEA PO1 20 E2
Becton La NMIL/BTOS BH25 231 H1
Becton Md NMIL/BTOS BH25 219 H7
Bedale Wy PLE BH15 223 M3
Beddington Ct CHIN RG24 54 C8
Bede Dr AND SP10 95 M1
Bedenham La
LSOL/BMARY PO13 182 E5
Bedfield La WINC SO23 288 H11
Bedford Av FRIM GU16 61 M3
ITCH SO19 161 L6
Bedford Cl BOR GU35 112 F3
FBDG SP6 197 H1
HAV PO9 17 J6
HEND SO30 149 K6
NWBY RG14 33 J7
Bedford Crs FRIM GU16 61 L2
LTDN BH7 227 J1
Bedford La FRIM GU16 61 M2
Bedford Pl WSHM SO15 160 F2
Bedford Rd PSF GU32 120 B6
Bedford Rd North
BKME/WDN BH12 212 C6
Bedford Rd South
BKME/WDN BH12 212 C6
Bedfordshire Wy WWKG RG41 239 R2
Bedford St GPORT PO12 14 C1
SSEA PO5 21 G4
Bedhampton Hl CHAM PO6 170 A7
Bedhampton Hill Rd HAV PO9 170 B7
Bedhampton Rd HAV PO9 170 C6
NEND PO2 184 F7
Bedhampton Wy HAV PO9 170 F4
Bedser Sq AND SP10 96 D1
Bedwell Cl ROWN SO16 145 M3
Beecham Berry KBH RG22 92 F5
Beecham Rd PSEA PO1 192 E1
Beech Av CBLY GU15 50 F4
CHCH/BSGR BH23 215 K8
RFNM GU10 79 G3
SBNE BH6 227 J4
STOK SO20 270 D8
WEND SO18 161 L1
Beechbank Av CFDH BH17 210 E7
Beechbrook Av YTLY GU46 48 F3
Beech Cl ASHV GU12 73 L8
BDST BH18 210 D4
CHFD SO53 133 K8
FBDG SP6 196 C7
FUFL SO22 124 B1
HLER SO31 178 E2
HORN PO8 * 155 M6
LYMN SO41 220 D8
OVTN RG25 89 K2
RAND SP11 94 A4
RAND SP11 95 J3
ROMY SO51 137 J2
STOK SO20 270 D8
TADY RG26 46 C6
VWD BH31 201 G3
Beech Copse FUFL SO22 122 B3
HEND SO30 * 148 D3
Beech Ct WIMB BH21 207 L4
Beech Crs FAWY SO45 177 C8
Beechcrest Vw HTWY RG27 56 D6
Beechcroft Cl AND SP10 5 G2
CHFD SO53 139 K2
FHAM PO15 181 J3
LIPH GU30 309 P1
Beechcroft Cots
STOK SO20 284 D10
Beechcroft La RGWD BH24 203 K4
Beechcroft Rd GPORT PO12 14 D7
Beechcroft Wy CHFD SO53 139 K2
Beechdale Cl TOTT SO40 144 C6
Beech Dr BLKW GU17 49 M4
Beechen La LYND SO43 345 M6
Beeches Cl RSAL SP5 296 A1
Beeches Hl BPWT SO32 143 K2
The Beeches AND SP10 * 4 C5
ASHV GU12 61 M7
ELGH SO50 141 K3
KBH RG22 92 F6
LTDN BH7 215 G8
ROMY SO51 334 H5
Beechey Rd CHAR BH8 9 J1
Beechfield AMSY SP4 268 B6
Beechfield Ct WSHM SO15 146 A8
Beech Gdns HLER SO31 178 E2
Beech Gra RSAL SP5 334 B6
Beech Gv CHOB/PIR GU24 63 J1
GPORT PO12 14 D6
HISD PO11 195 H4
RAND SP11 272 D6
RWIN SO21 310 A4
Beech Hanger AMSY SP4 268 D3
Beech Hanger End GSHT GU26 115 H5
Beech Hl BOR GU35 114 B4
Beech Hill Rd BOR GU35 111 M6
NTID SP9 266 G1
THLE RG7 41 L2
Beeching Cl ASHV GU12 74 B5
Beechlands Rd ALTN GU34 293 M4
Beech La GSHT GU26 115 H4
RGUW GU3 75 G7
RGWD BH24 346 E2
Beechleigh Pl RGWD BH24 * 203 J4
Beechmount Rd ROWN SO16 146 F3
Beechnut Dr BLKW GU17 49 K2
Beechnut Rd ASHV GU12 3 H4
Beech Ride FLEETS GU52 71 H1
SHST GU47 43 K8
Beech Rd CHFD SO53 133 K8
FARN GU14 61 H1
FHAM PO15 10 B4
FRIM GU16 61 M2
HASM GU27 118 D5
HEND SO30 149 K5
HORN PO8 321 M7
KSCL RG20 247 Q2
NARL SO24 291 M11
TOTT SO40 158 B6
WSHM SO15 160 B2
Beech Tree Cl DEAN RG23 91 J4
Beech Tree Dr FNM GU9 77 L3
Beech Tree Wk ROMY SO51 298 E1
Beech Wk AND SP10 4 A7
STHA RG19 35 L2
Beech Wy DEAN RG23 64 E5
HORN PO8 156 B3
Beechwood CHIN RG24 * 54 A5
FBDG SP6 196 F3
Beechwood Av BOSC BH5 226 F4
NMIL/BTOS BH25 218 E4
WVILLE PO7 169 L2
Beech Wood Cl BDST BH18 211 G5
Beechwood Cl CHFD SO53 133 G7
FLEETN GU51 71 G2
HLER SO31 179 K4
KBH RG22 92 E6
Beechwood Ct LISS GU33 308 G6
Beechwood Crs CHFD SO53 133 G6
Beechwood Gdns BOSC BH5 227 G4
WEND SO18 147 L8
Beechwood La RGWD BH24 349 K1
Beechwood Ri WEND SO18 148 C3
Beechwood Rd ALTN GU34 106 D6
FAWY SO45 354 E5
FERN BH22 205 H7
NEND PO2 184 E4
TOTT SO40 341 K7
Beechwood Wy FAWY SO45 176 C6
Beechworth Rd HAV PO9 17 G4
Beehive Wk PSEA PO1 20 D5
Beethoven Rd KBH RG22 93 G4
Beeton's Av ASHV GU12 74 A4
Beggar's La WINC SO23 25 J5
Beggarwood La DEAN RG23 92 C8
Begonia Cl KBH RG22 92 C5
Begonia Rd ROWN SO16 147 H4
Behrendt Cl GPORT PO12 191 G2
Belaga Cl STOK SO20 270 C7
Belben Cl BKME/WDN BH12 212 D6
Belben Rd BKME/WDN BH12 212 C6
Belbins ROMY SO51 130 F4
Beldham Rd RFNM GU10 12 B9
Belfield Rd SBNE BH6 228 A4
Belfry Ms SHST GU47 43 H8
Belfry Sq DEAN RG23 92 C7
Belfry Wk FHAM/STUB PO14 180 C2
Belgrave Ct BLKW GU17 49 M5
Belgrave Rd CCLF BH13 225 G6
PTSW SO17 147 J6
Belgravia Rd NEND PO2 184 F7
Bellair Rd HAV PO9 17 G5
Belland Dr ALDT GU11 2 B4
Bell Cl FARN GU14 61 J2
Bell Ct RCCH PO18 * 172 F7
Bell Crs WVILLE PO7 169 L2
Bell Davies Rd
FHAM/STUB PO14 189 H3
Bellemoor Rd WSHM SO15 146 D7
Bellever Hl CBLY GU15 51 G3
Bellevue WHCH RG28 87 L7
Belle Vue Cl ASHV GU12 3 M3
SBNE BH6 227 K4
Belle Vue Crs SBNE BH6 227 M4
Belle Vue Gv FERN BH22 205 H6
Bellevue La EMRTH PO10 171 M6
Belle Vue Rd AND SP10 5 J8
ASHV GU12 3 L3
CHIN RG24 66 D2
PSTN BH14 224 C5
SBNE BH6 227 K5
Bellevue Rd ELGH SO50 140 A1
WSHM SO15 161 G2
Bellevue Ter SHAM SO14 161 G2
SSEA PO5 20 E7
Belle Vue Wk FERN BH22 209 L6
Bellew Rd FRIM GU16 62 C1
Bellflower Cl
CHCH/BSGR BH23 217 H8
Bellflower Wy CHFD SO53 138 F1
Bell Heather Cl UPTN BH16 * 210 B8
Bell Hl PSF GU32 120 C4
Bell Hill Rdg PSF GU32 120 C4
Bell Holt NWBY RG14 33 J7
Bellingham Cl CBLY GU15 51 L4
Bell La BLKW GU17 49 L3
HUNG RG17 244 D1
OVTN RG25 105 M6
RFNM GU10 109 L1
Bell Meadow Rd HTWY RG27 56 D7
Bell Rd AND SP10 5 L6
CHIN RG24 7 L2
CHAM PO6 168 D8
Bells La FHAM/STUB PO14 189 J2
Bell St RAND SP11 265 N10
ROMY SO51 136 E1
SHAM SO14 23 H5
WHCH RG28 87 L7
Bell Vale La HASM GU27 118 C8
Belmont Av CHAR BH8 214 C6
Belmont Cl AND SP10 5 K8
FARN GU14 60 F1
FAWY SO45 177 G6
FHAM/STUB PO14 189 K1
HORN PO8 321 L10
VWD BH31 201 J3
Belmont Gv HAV PO9 170 C6
Belmont Hts KBH RG22 92 E7
Belmont Ms CBLY GU15 50 E5
Belmont Pl SSEA PO5 21 H6
Belmont Rd AND SP10 5 J8
CBLY GU15 50 E4
CHFD SO53 139 K5
CWTH RG45 43 K2
NMIL/BTOS BH25 219 J4
PSTN BH14 224 B3
PTSW SO17 147 H8
Belmont St SSEA PO5 21 H6
Belmore Cl PSEA PO1 192 E1
Belmore La LYMN SO41 221 L5
RWIN SO21 310 D3
Belmore Rd LYMN SO41 221 K5
Belney La WHAM PO17 154 E8
Belsize Rd FARN GU14 61 J7
Belstone Ms FARN GU14 61 G1
Belstone Rd TOTT SO40 158 E1
Belton Rd CBLY GU15 51 G3
ITCH SO19 162 B1
Belvedere Cl FLEETN GU51 58 E7
Belvedere Ct BLKW GU17 49 M5
Belvedere Dr NWBY RG14 18 E9
Belvedere Gdns CHIN RG24 54 C4
Belvedere Rd
CHCH/BSGR BH23 228 A1
FARN GU14 61 J6
FAWY SO45 177 G6
TWDS BH3 226 A2
Belverdere Cl PSF GU32 120 D5
Belvidere Rd SHAM SO14 23 L2
Belvidere Ter SHAM SO14 23 L1
Belvoir Cl FHAM/PORC PO16 11 G7
FRIM GU16 51 H7
Bembridge HLER SO31 162 C6
Bembridge Cl ROWN SO16 147 J3
Bembridge Ct CWTH RG45 43 G4
Bembridge Crs ENEY PO4 192 E7
Bembridge Dr HISD PO11 195 J7
Bemister Rd
MOOR/WNTN BH9 214 A8
Bemisters La GPORT PO12 15 L4
Benbow Cl HORN PO8 156 C1
Benbow Ct AND SP10 96 F4
Benbow Crs BKME/WDN BH12 212 E7
Benbow Pl PSEA PO1 20 C2
Benbridge Av BWD BH11 212 F3
Bendeng Cl FLEETN GU51 58 F5
Bendigo Rd CHCH/BSGR BH23 215 L8
Beneden Gn NARL SO24 291 M11
Benedict Cl ROMY SO51 137 J1
Benedict Wy
FHAM/PORC PO16 167 L6
Beneficial St PSEA PO1 20 C3
Benellen Av WBNE BH4 225 J4
Benellen Gdns WBNE BH4 225 J4
Benellen Rd WBNE BH4 225 J3
Benenden Gn NARL SO24 291 M12
Benett Cl NWBY RG14 27 H7
Benett Gdns NWBY RG14 27 H7
Bengal Rd MOOR/WNTN BH9 213 L7
Benger's La ROMY SO51 298 F10

Benham Cha KSCL RG20 26 A7
Benham Dr HSEA PO3 * 184 F4
Benham Dro STOK SO20 283 R2
Benham Gv FHAM/PORC PO16 183 K2
Benham Hl NTHA RG18 28 C8
Benham La THLE RG7 240 D1
Benhams Farm Cl WEND SO18 148 A3
Benhams La LISS GU33 112 B8
Benhams Rd WEND SO18 148 A2
Benin Rd RAND SP11 267 K2
Benjamin Rd PLE BH15 222 E6
Ben La RSAL SP5 296 D5
Benmoor Rd CFDH BH17 211 G8
Benmore Cl NMIL/BTOS BH25 219 J6
Benmore Gdns CHFD SO53 133 H8
Benmore Rd
MOOR/WNTN BH9 214 A7
Bennet Cl ALTN GU34 106 E4
BSTK RG21 7 H1
Bennett Cl RSAL SP5 332 F2
Bennett Ct CBLY GU15 50 E3
Bennett Rd CHAR BH8 226 C2
Bennetts La RGWD BH24 349 L2
Bennetts Ri ALDT GU11 3 J7
Bennion Rd NBNE BH10 213 J5
Benny Hill Cl ELGH SO50 139 M5
Benridge Cl BDST BH18 211 G5
Benson Cl CHCH/BSGR BH23 348 D11
Benson Rd CFDH BH17 223 K1
CWTH RG45 43 H3
WSHM SO15 146 B8
Benta Cl STOK SO20 270 C7
Bentall Pl AND SP10 5 G7
Bentham Rd GPORT PO12 14 E7
Bentham Wy HLER SO31 163 K4
Bentley Cl HORN PO8 321 L12
WINC SO23 288 H10
Bentley Copse CBLY GU15 51 K4
Bentley Ct HAV PO9 171 H3
Bentley Crs FHAM/PORC PO16 10 D3
Bentley Dr WHIT RG2 239 L8
Bentley Gn WEND SO18 148 C4
Bentley Rd MOOR/WNTN BH9 213 M5
Bentley Wy RSAL SP5 282 H11
Bent St STOK SO20 284 A2
Bentworth Cl HAV PO9 170 D4
Benwell Cl ODIM RG29 68 E8
Ben Well Rd CHOB/PIR GU24 63 M1
Bepton Down EPSF GU31 120 E6
Berber Cl FHAM PO15 164 C5
Bercote Cl FUFL SO22 288 B11
Bere Cl CFDH BH17 211 K6
CHFD SO53 133 G8
FUFL SO22 24 A1
Bere Farm La WHAM PO17 152 F8
Bere Hl WHCH RG28 87 L6
Bere Hill Cl WHCH RG28 87 M6
Bere Hill Crs AND SP10 5 L7
Berehurst ALTN GU34 106 F6
Bere Rd WVILLE PO7 154 F4
Beresford Cl AND SP10 96 C7
BKME/WDN BH12 224 D2
FRIM GU16 61 M2
WVILLE PO7 169 L2
Beresford Gdns
CHCH/BSGR BH23 228 E2
CHFD SO53 139 L3
Beresford Ga AND SP10 * 97 G3
Beresford Rd
BKME/WDN BH12 224 D2
CHFD SO53 139 L3
FHAM/STUB PO14 189 K1
LYMN SO41 221 J4
NEND PO2 184 E6
SBNE BH6 227 H4
Bereweeke Av FUFL SO22 24 C1
Bereweeke Cl FUFL SO22 24 B2
Bereweeke Rd FUFL SO22 24 C2
Bereweeke Wy FUFL SO22 24 D1
Berewyk Cl KBH RG22 92 C5
Bergen Crs HEND SO30 149 J7
Berkeley Av BKME/WDN BH12 212 C8
Berkeley Cl FHAM/STUB PO14 189 H2
FLEETN GU51 59 K7
VWD BH31 201 G1
WSHM SO15 160 E1
Berkeley Crs FRIM GU16 51 J8
Berkeley Dr KBH RG22 93 H4
Berkeley Gdns HEND SO30 149 J7
Berkeley Rd NWBY RG14 18 C5
TWDS BH3 225 L1
Berkeley Sq HAV PO9 17 J4
Berkley Av FERN BH22 209 K6
Berkshire Circular Routes
KSCL RG20 33 G4
THLE RG7 40 B2
Berkshire Cl PSEA PO1 21 K3
Berkshire Corpse Rd
ALDT GU11 72 E1
Berkshire Dr STHA RG19 36 A2
Bermuda Cl CHIN RG24 65 L3
Bernard Av ALTN GU34 293 M6
CHAM PO6 169 G8
Bernards Cl CHCH/BSGR BH23 215 L8
Bernard St SHAM SO14 23 H6
Bernersh Cl SHST GU47 43 L7
Berney Rd ENEY PO4 193 J4
Bernina Av WVILLE PO7 155 J6
Bernina Cl WVILLE PO7 155 J6
Bernstein Rd KBH RG22 92 E4
Bernwood Gv FAWY SO45 354 G9
Berrans Av BWD BH11 213 H2
Berrybank SHST GU47 50 A2
Berry Cl HEND SO30 149 K6
Berrydown La OVTN RG25 89 L5
OVTN RG25 105 L8
Berrydown Rd HAV PO9 170 C1
Berryfield Rd LYMN SO41 220 A6
Berry Hl NARL SO24 292 E11
Berrylands LISS GU33 308 G5
Berry La FHAM/STUB PO14 189 G2
RWIN SO21 125 G5
Berry Wy AND SP10 4 A8
Berrywood Gdns HEND SO30 149 H5
Berrywood La NARL SO24 278 F6
Bertie Rd ENEY PO4 193 H4
Bertram Rd NMIL/BTOS BH25 219 J4
Berwick Rd TWDS BH3 225 L2
Berwyn Cl KBH RG22 92 C1
Berwyn Wk FHAM/STUB PO14 10 B7
Beryl Av GPORT PO12 182 F8
Beryton Cl GPORT PO12 * 191 G2
Beryton Rd GPORT PO12 191 G2
Besomer Dro RSAL SP5 332 H4
Bessborough Rd CCLF BH13 237 K1
Bessemer Cl VWD BH31 201 L4
Bessemer Rd BSTK RG21 93 H2
Beswick Av NBNE BH10 213 K7
Beta Rd FARN GU14 60 F3
Bethel Cl FNM GU9 77 H2
Bethel La FNM GU9 77 H2
Bethia Cl CHAR BH8 * 226 D2
Bethia Rd CHAR BH8 226 D2
Betjeman Wk YTLY GU46 48 D4
Betsy Cl CHCH/BSGR BH23 348 D11
Betsy La CHCH/BSGR BH23 348 D11
Betteridge Dr ROWN SO16 145 K2
Betteridge Rd STHA RG19 35 M2
Bettesworth Rd PSEA PO1 192 E1
Bettiscombe Cl CFDH BH17 211 K6
Betty Grove La WWKG RG41 239 M1
Betula Cl WVILLE PO7 170 A2
Beulah Rd ROWN SO16 146 A7
Bevan Cl ITCH SO19 161 L7
Bevan Rd HORN PO8 155 M3
Beveren Cl FLEETN GU51 59 K4
Beverley Cl ASHV GU12 73 M7
BSTK RG21 93 K3
CBLY GU15 51 L2
HLER SO31 164 C8
NTHA RG18 28 E8
Beverley Crs FARN GU14 60 F5
Beverley Gdns BPWT SO32 318 B7
HLER SO31 162 E3
NBNE BH10 213 K5
ROMY SO51 131 H7
Beverley Hts WEND SO18 147 M5
Beverley Rd FAWY SO45 176 F8
FHAM/STUB PO14 189 J3
Beverly Cl LSOL/BMARY PO13 182 D6
The Bevers THLE RG7 40 A2
Beverston Rd CHAM PO6 168 A7
Bevis Cl FAWY SO45 354 H6
HLER SO31 179 K4
Bevis Rd GPORT PO12 14 F3
NEND PO2 184 D7
Bevois Gdns SHAM SO14 161 G1
Bevois Hl PTSW SO17 147 H8
Bevois Valley Rd SHAM SO14 161 H1
Bexington Cl BWD BH11 212 E5
Bexmoor CHIN RG24 66 C2
Bexmoor Wy CHIN RG24 66 C2
Beyne Rd FUFL SO22 124 B1
Bible Flds OVTN RG25 103 L4
Bicester Cl WHCH RG28 87 L7
Bickerley Gdns RGWD BH24 203 H6
Bickerley Rd RGWD BH24 203 H6
Bicknell Rd FRIM GU16 51 G6
Bicton Rd BWD BH11 213 H5
Bidbury La HAV PO9 170 C7
Biddenfield La WHAM PO17 151 K8
Bidden Rd ODIM RG29 68 C6
OVTN RG25 257 L3
Biddesden La RAND SP11 265 P10
Biddlecombe Cl
LSOL/BMARY PO13 182 C8
Bideford Cl FARN GU14 61 G1
ROWN SO16 145 L7
Biggin Wk FHAM/STUB PO14 10 B8
Biggs La EWKG RG40 239 M8
Bighton Dean La NARL SO24 292 B7
Bighton Hl NARL SO24 292 E10
Bighton La NARL SO24 292 A7
Bighton Rd ALTN GU34 292 G3
Bilbao Ct AND SP10 96 F3
Bilberry Cl HLER SO31 179 M2
Bilberry Dr TOTT SO40 159 L6
Billesden Rd CHOB/PIR GU24 63 J2
Billett Av WVILLE PO7 155 M7
Billing Av EWKG RG40 42 A2
Billing Cl ENEY PO4 193 H5
Billington Gdns HEND SO30 149 K3
Billington Wy NTHA RG18 28 E6
Billy Lawn Av HAV PO9 170 F4
Bilton Rd CHIN RG24 54 A7
Bilton Wy HSEA PO3 185 J6
Bindon Cl BKME/WDN BH12 224 E1
ROWN SO16 146 A6
Bindon Rd ROWN SO16 146 A6
Binfields Cl CHIN RG24 54 B7
Bingham Av PSTN BH14 237 J1
Bingham Dr LYMN SO41 221 L5
Bingham Rd CHCH/BSGR BH23 228 E1
MOOR/WNTN BH9 214 A8
VWD BH31 201 J4
Bingley Cl ALTN GU34 106 E4
BSTK RG21 7 H1
Binley Bottom RAND SP11 251 M12
Binnacle Wy CHAM PO6 168 B8
Binness Wy CHAM PO6 185 L1
Binnie Rd BKME/WDN BH12 224 E3
Binsey Cl ROWN SO16 145 L8
Binstead Cl ROWN SO16 147 J3
Binstead Rd ALTN GU34 108 F4
Binsted Dr BLKW GU17 49 M3
Binsteed Rd NEND PO2 184 E8
Binton La RFNM GU10 260 C6
Birch Av CHCH/BSGR BH23 216 C5
FERN BH22 209 M7
FLEETN GU51 59 H7
NMIL/BTOS BH25 218 D2
Birch Cl BOR GU35 113 G2
HORN PO8 155 L5
LISS GU33 308 G8
PSTN BH14 224 E5
RFNM GU10 78 E4
RGWD BH24 205 M5
ROMY SO51 137 J2
ROWN SO16 146 A6
RWIN SO21 134 F4
WIMB BH21 210 D2
Birch Dl FAWY SO45 177 H6
Birchdale Cl HLER SO31 179 K4
Birchdale Rd WIMB BH21 207 K3
Birch Dr BLKW GU17 49 M5
CHAR BH8 215 G6
LSOL/BMARY PO13 182 C4
Birchen Cl HLER SO31 164 C8
The Birches Cl NBAD SO52 137 M3
Birches Crest KBH RG22 92 F6
The Birches BLKW GU17 49 K3
FARN GU14 60 D4
WEND SO18 148 B4
Birchett Rd ALDT GU11 2 E3
FARN GU14 60 E3
Birchfields CBLY GU15 50 E4
Birch Gv BOR GU35 112 F3
ELGH SO50 139 M2
FERN BH22 204 F6
HTWY RG27 56 D6
STOK SO20 272 F10
Birchland Cl THLE RG7 39 L6
Birchlands TOTT SO40 158 D3
Birch La THLE RG7 39 M7
Birchmore Cl
LSOL/BMARY PO13 182 C6
Bircholt Rd LIPH GU30 113 K8
Birch Rd BOR GU35 114 B2
EWKG RG40 42 C1
HEND SO30 149 K5
RGWD BH24 202 D8
ROWN SO16 139 G8
ROWN SO16 146 A6
TADY RG26 249 Q2
THLE RG7 39 M1
Birch Side CWTH RG45 43 H2
Birch Tree Cl EMRTH PO10 171 M4
Birch Tree Dr EMRTH PO10 171 M4
Birchview Cl YTLY GU46 48 E4
Birch Wk FERN BH22 * 209 M5
Birch Wy ASHV GU12 74 A1
Birchwood CHIN RG24 54 B5
Birch Wd ITCH SO19 148 E7
Birchwood Cl
CHCH/BSGR BH23 217 L8
Birchwood Dr FBDG SP6 196 C7
Birchwood Gdns HEND SO30 149 J4
Birchwood Rd NWBY RG14 19 M1
PSTN BH14 224 D5
UPTN BH16 222 B2
Birchy Hl LYMN SO41 350 G11
Bird Fld CHFD SO53 138 E2
Birdham Rd HISD PO11 195 L6
Birdhaven RFNM GU10 78 E3
Birdlip Cl HORN PO8 156 A2
Birdlip Rd CHAM PO6 168 B7
Bird's Hill Rd PLE BH15 223 L4
Birds La THLE RG7 36 E1
Birdwood Gv
FHAM/PORC PO16 166 F8
Birdwood Rd CBLY GU15 50 B2
Birinus Rd WINC SO23 25 H3
Birkdale Av CHAM PO6 169 J7
Birkdale Ct BDST BH18 211 G3
Birkdale Rd BDST BH18 211 G3
Birkenholme Cl BOR GU35 114 C4
Birmingham Ct
LSOL/BMARY PO13 * 190 D3
Biscay Cl FHAM/STUB PO14 189 H1
Bishearne Gdns LISS GU33 308 E7
Bishop Cl BKME/WDN BH12 225 J1
Bishop Ct RGWD BH24 203 J5
Bishop Rd MOOR/WNTN BH9 214 A8
Bishops Cl FLEETS GU52 71 J1
LTDN BH7 226 F2
NTID SP9 266 F4
TADY RG26 44 A3
TOTT SO40 144 E8
Bishops Ct ELGH SO50 134 D7
Bishops Crs ITCH SO19 161 M4
Bishopsfield Rd
FHAM/STUB PO14 10 B8
Bishops Ga FHAM/STUB PO14 180 C1
Bishop's La BPWT SO32 143 J5
BPWT SO32 318 B11
Bishop's Md FNM GU9 12 E4
Bishops Rd FNM GU9 76 F2
ITCH SO19 161 L5
Bishopstoke La ELGH SO50 134 E6
Bishopstoke Mnr ELGH SO50 * 140 D1
Bishopstoke Rd ELGH SO50 140 C1
HAV PO9 170 E3
Bishop St PSEA PO1 20 D2
Bishop Sumner Dr FNM GU9 77 G2
Bishop's Vw ALTN GU34 293 K6
Bishop's Wy AND SP10 4 E4
Bishopswood La TADY RG26 249 Q3
Bishop's Wood Rd BPWT SO32 318 B9
Bishopswood Rd TADY RG26 249 R3
Bisterne Cl RGWD BH24 349 M2
Bitham La HUNG RG17 30 B8
Bittern Cl ALDT GU11 2 E8
GPORT PO12 191 H1
KBH RG22 92 B4
SHST GU47 43 M8
Bitterne Cl HAV PO9 170 F2
Bitterne Crs ITCH SO19 148 A6
Bitterne Rd ITCH SO19 161 M2
Bitterne Rd East WEND SO18 148 B6
Bitterne Rd West WEND SO18 161 L1
Bitterne Village ITCH SO19 148 A6
Bitterne Wy ITCH SO19 161 L2
LYMN SO41 221 K6
VWD BH31 201 J3
Blackberry Cl ALTN GU34 293 N5
Black Berry Cl HORN PO8 321 M8
Blackberry Dr ELGH SO50 141 H3
Blackberry La ALTN GU34 293 N6
CHCH/BSGR BH23 228 F2
Blackberry Ter SHAM SO14 161 H1
Blackberry Wk CHIN RG24 7 M1
Blackbird Cl CFDH BH17 210 E8
HORN PO8 155 M4
KBH RG22 92 B4
SHST GU47 43 M8
Blackbird Ct AND SP10 96 D2
Blackbird Rd ELGH SO50 139 K6
Blackbird Wy
CHCH/BSGR BH23 348 E12
LSOL/BMARY PO13 189 M5
Blackbrook House Dr
FHAM PO15 10 B5
Blackbrook Park Av
FHAM PO15 10 C5
Blackbrook Rd FHAM PO15 10 B5
Blackburn Ct
LSOL/BMARY PO13 * 190 D3
Blackburn Rd
BKME/WDN BH12 224 B2
Blackbushe Cl ROWN SO16 145 M3
Blackbushe Pk YTLY GU46 * 48 E3
Blackbushes Rd FLEETN GU51 59 G2
HTWY RG27 48 A7
Blackbush Rd LYMN SO41 232 B2
Blackcap Cl HAV PO9 157 G7
Black Dam Rbt CHIN RG24 7 L5
Black Dam Wy BSTK RG21 7 J9
Blackdown Cl FAWY SO45 176 D6
KBH RG22 92 C1
Blackdown Crs HAV PO9 170 E4
Blackdown Rd FRIM GU16 62 C1
Blackdown Wy STHA RG19 35 J2
Blackfield La FERN BH22 205 G5
Blackfield Rd CHAR BH8 214 D5
FAWY SO45 354 H6
Blackfriars Cl SSEA PO5 21 J4
Blackfriars Rd SSEA PO5 21 J3
Blackheath Rd FNM GU9 76 E1
Black Hl VWD BH31 201 J2
Blackhill Rd ROMY SO51 335 K8
Black Horse La BPWT SO32 151 J3
Blackhouse La WHAM PO17 153 G8
Blacklands Rd THLE RG7 29 L7
Black La RSAL SP5 282 A12
RSAL SP5 333 K4
Blackman Gdns ALDT GU11 3 H7
Blackmoor Rd LISS GU33 112 C6
Black Moor Rd VWD BH31 201 L4
Blackmore La MARL SN8 265 M7
PSF GU32 307 J8
Blacknest Rd ALTN GU34 108 E2
Black Pond La RFNM GU10 79 G2
Blacksmith Cl WIMB BH21 210 D3
Blackstocks La HTWY RG27 67 K3
Blackstone Cl FARN GU14 60 D2
Black Swan Yd AND SP10 5 J5
Blackthorn Cl ITCH SO19 161 M3
LYMN SO41 221 H6
RWIN SO21 288 C4
Blackthorn Crs FARN GU14 50 B8
Blackthorn Dr GPORT PO12 183 G7
HISD PO11 195 J5
NTHA RG18 28 F7
Blackthorne Cl BOR GU35 113 G1
Blackthorn Gn RWIN SO21 135 G4
Blackthorn Rd HISD PO11 195 J5
ITCH SO19 161 M3
Blackthorn Wy DEAN RG23 64 E6
VWD BH31 201 K5
Blackwater Cl ASHV GU12 74 A7
BSTK RG21 7 H5
CHAM PO6 168 D8
DEAN RG23 91 K3
FBDG SP6 196 A7
THLE RG7 238 B7
Blackwater Dr TOTT SO40 144 D7
WIMB BH21 211 K1
Blackwater Gv FBDG SP6 196 A7
Blackwater Ms TOTT SO40 144 D7
Blackwater Pk ASHV GU12 73 L7
Blackwater Vw EWKG RG40 42 C6
Blackwater Wy ASHV GU12 3 M7
Blackwell Rd RWIN SO21 288 C6
Bladon Cl HAV PO9 17 L1
Bladon Rd ROWN SO16 146 C6
Blagdon Cl STHA RG19 34 D5
Blair Av PSTN BH14 224 C4
Blair Cl NMIL/BTOS BH25 218 E5
Blaire Pk YTLY GU46 42 D8
Blair Rd BSTK RG21 6 D8
Blaise Cl FARN GU14 61 K5
Blake Cl CWTH RG45 43 L4
ODIM RG29 68 E8
ROWN SO16 145 J3
Blake Ct AND SP10 5 H2
Blakedene Rd PSTN BH14 224 B7
Blake Hill Av PSTN BH14 224 C7
Blake Hill Crs PSTN BH14 224 C7
Blakemere Crs CHAM PO6 168 C7
Blakeney Rd ROWN SO16 145 K6
Blake Rd CHAM PO6 169 K7
GPORT PO12 15 G3
Blake's La TADY RG26 44 C3
Blakesley La HSEA PO3 185 J4
Blakes Ride YTLY GU46 48 D2
Blanchard Rd BPWT SO32 143 H4
Blandford Cl PLE BH15 222 F6
Blandford Rd PLE BH15 222 F7
RSAL SP5 325 L6
UPTN BH16 222 C2
WIMB BH21 206 C7
Blandford Rd North
UPTN BH16 210 B8
Bland's Cl THLE RG7 39 M2
Blaney Wy WIMB BH21 210 C2
Blanket St ALTN GU34 107 M8
Blankney Cl FHAM/STUB PO14 189 H2
Blann Cl ROWN SO16 145 J3
Blaven Wk FHAM/STUB PO14 10 B7
Bleaklow Cl ROWN SO16 145 M8
Blechynden Ter WSHM SO15 22 D2
Bledlow Cl NWBY RG14 33 K7
Blencowe Dr CHFD SO53 138 E3
Blendon Dr AND SP10 4 A3
Blendworth Crs HAV PO9 170 E5
Blendworth La HORN PO8 156 D1
WEND SO18 148 C5
Blendworth Rd ENEY PO4 * 193 G4
Blenheim Av PTSW SO17 147 G7
Blenheim Cl ALTN GU34 107 G5
ALTN GU34 293 M5
CHFD SO53 138 F4
RFNM GU10 260 C1
TOTT SO40 158 D2
Blenheim Ct ENEY PO4 193 G5
FARN GU14 61 K6
Blenheim Crs FNM GU9 76 E2
LYMN SO41 219 L4
Blenheim Dr CHCH/BSGR BH23 229 H1
Blenheim Gdns FAWY SO45 176 D6
GPORT PO12 183 H8
HAV PO9 17 L2
PTSW SO17 147 H6
Blenheim Pk ALDT GU11 73 J1
Blenheim Rd ALDT GU11 73 J1
CHIN RG24 66 E3
ELGH SO50 140 A2
HORN PO8 156 A3
NWBY RG14 18 C4
Bleriot Crs FHAM PO15 164 E7
Blighmont Crs WSHM SO15 160 B2
Blighton La RFNM GU10 260 B6
Blind La BPWT SO32 141 J7
BPWT SO32 150 E2
FBDG SP6 199 L3
WHAM PO17 151 M7
WIMB BH21 207 H2
Bliss Cl KBH RG22 93 G3
WVILLE PO7 169 L3
Blissford Cl HAV PO9 171 H2
Blissford Cross FBDG SP6 338 A4
Blissford Hl FBDG SP6 338 A6
Blissford Rd FBDG SP6 338 A4
Bloomfield Av
MOOR/WNTN BH9 213 M6
Bloomsbury Wk ITCH SO19 161 L6
Bloomsbury Wy BLKW GU17 49 L5
Blossom Cl AND SP10 95 L5
HEND SO30 149 L6
Blossom Sq PSEA PO1 20 D1
Bloswood Dr WHCH RG28 87 K7
Bloswood La WHCH RG28 87 H6
Blount Rd PSEA PO1 20 E6
Bloxworth Rd
BKME/WDN BH12 212 F8
Blue Ball Cnr WINC SO23 * 25 J5
Blue Ball Hl WINC SO23 25 J5
Bluebell Cl AND SP10 95 L5
CHCH/BSGR BH23 217 H8
WVILLE PO7 169 M2
Bluebell Copse HLER SO31 179 M2
Bluebell Dr THLE RG7 39 M1
Bluebell La CFDH BH17 210 E7
Bluebell Rd BOR GU35 111 J7
ROWN SO16 147 H4
Bluebell Wy FHAM PO15 164 D4
NTHA RG18 28 F7
Blueberry Gdns AND SP10 95 L5
Bluecoats NTHA RG18 28 F8
Bluehaven Wk HTWY RG27 56 B7
Blueprint Portfield Rd
HSEA PO3 185 G6
Blue Prior Ct FLEETS GU52 71 G5
Bluestar Gdns HEND SO30 149 J2
Bluff Cove ALDT GU11 3 K1
Blundell La HLER SO31 163 J2
Blunden Cl BSTK RG21 93 H3
Blunden Rd FARN GU14 60 F3
Blunt Rd DEAN RG23 92 B8
Blyth Av STHA RG19 35 L2
Blyth Cl CHCH/BSGR BH23 215 K4
ROWN SO16 145 K6
Blythe Rd WIMB BH21 210 D2
Blythswood Ct
NMIL/BTOS BH25 230 F1
Blythwood Dr FRIM GU16 50 F6
Boakes Pl TOTT SO40 158 C6
Boames La KSCL RG20 32 F7
Boardwalk Wy TOTT SO40 160 A4
Boarhunt Cl PSEA PO1 21 J2
Boarhunt Rd WHAM PO17 11 M1
Boar's Br TADY RG26 53 G2
Bobgreen Ct WHIT RG2 238 C2
Bob Hann Cl BKME/WDN BH12 224 E3
Bockhampton Rd
CHCH/BSGR BH23 216 E3
Bodin Gdns NWBY RG14 34 A4
Bodley Rd CCLF BH13 237 K1
Bodmin Cl KBH RG22 92 D1
STHA RG19 35 J2
Bodmin Rd CHAM PO6 168 A8
ELGH SO50 140 E1
Bodorgan Rd WCLF BH2 8 E4
Bodowen Cl CHCH/BSGR BH23 216 D6
Bodowen Rd
CHCH/BSGR BH23 216 D6
Bodycoats Rd CHFD SO53 139 K2
Bofors Rd FARN GU14 61 G8
Bogmoor Cl ALTN GU34 293 M6
Bognor Rd BDST BH18 210 F4
Bohemia La RSAL SP5 332 H5
Boiler Rd PSEA PO1 191 M2
Bolde Cl HSEA PO3 185 H5
Boldens Rd GPORT PO12 191 H7
Bolderford Br BROC SO42 345 J11
Bolderwood Arboretum
Ornamental Dr LYND SO43 343 Q4
Bolderwood Cl ELGH SO50 140 F1
Boldre Cl BKME/WDN BH12 224 E1
HAV PO9 170 C4
NMIL/BTOS BH25 218 D8
Boldre La LYMN SO41 221 K1
Boldrewood THLE RG7 39 M1
Boldrewood Rd ROWN SO16 146 E4
Boleyn Crs MOOR/WNTN BH9 214 C4
Bolhinton Av TOTT SO40 159 K7
Bolingbroke Wy STHA RG19 35 M1
Bolle Rd ALTN GU34 106 D6
Bolley Av BOR GU35 110 D7
Bolton Crs FERN BH22 346 A6
KBH RG22 93 G1
Bolton Dr GPORT PO12 191 J1
Bolton Rd SBNE BH6 227 L5
The Boltons WVILLE PO7 169 L5
Bonchurch Cl ROWN SO16 147 J3
Bonchurch Rd ENEY PO4 193 G3
Bond Av FERN BH22 204 F4
Bond Cl CHIN RG24 54 A8
LYMN SO41 350 F9
TADY RG26 44 A3
Bondfields Crs HAV PO9 170 F2
Bond Rd PLE BH15 223 M3
WEND SO18 147 L7
Bond St SHAM SO14 161 J2
Bone La NWBY RG14 19 H4
Bonemill La KSCL RG20 33 K2
Bones La EPSF GU31 315 P11
Bonfire Cnr PSEA PO1 20 C1
Bonham Rd TWDS BH3 225 M1
Bonhams Cl ALTN GU34 107 L1
Boniface Cl TOTT SO40 144 D8
Boniface Crs ROWN SO16 145 L5
Bonington Cl
CHCH/BSGR BH23 216 E8
Bonners Fld RFNM GU10 259 L11
Boon Wy DEAN RG23 91 J2
Boothby Cl TOTT SO40 159 G2
Bordean La PSF GU32 314 G3
Borden Gates AND SP10 5 H7
Borden La LIPH GU30 317 R2
Border Dr UPTN BH16 222 C3
Border End HASM GU27 * 117 K2
Border Rd HASM GU27 117 K2
UPTN BH16 222 C3
Borderside YTLY GU46 48 C2
Bordon Cl TADY RG26 44 A4
Bordon Rd HAV PO9 170 F4
The Boreen BOR GU35 114 B3
Boreham Rd SBNE BH6 227 K5
Borelli Ms FNM GU9 13 G3
Borkum Cl AND SP10 96 B1
Borley Rd CFDH BH17 211 G8
Borman Wy RWIN SO21 288 E4
Borodin Cl KBH RG22 93 H4
Borough Court Rd HTWY RG27 57 G2
Borough Gv PSF GU32 120 C7
Borough Hl PSF GU32 120 C6
Borough Rd PSF GU32 120 B7
The Borough FNM GU9 12 F3
RFNM GU10 259 N2
RSAL SP5 332 A1
Borovere Cl ALTN GU34 106 E6
Borovere Gdns ALTN GU34 106 E6
Borovere La ALTN GU34 106 E6
Borrowdale Rd ROWN SO16 145 L7
Borsberry Cl AND SP10 5 K4
Borthwick Rd BMTH BH1 226 E3
Boscawen Wy STHA RG19 36 A2
Boscobel Rd FUFL SO22 24 E2
Boscombe Cliff Rd BOSC BH5 226 E5
Boscombe Grove Rd
BMTH BH1 226 E3
Boscombe Overcliff Dr
BOSC BH5 226 F5
Boscombe Spa Rd BOSC BH5 226 D4
Boscowen Cl AND SP10 96 F4
Bosham Rd NEND PO2 184 F8
Bosham Wk
LSOL/BMARY PO13 182 B6
Bosley Cl CHCH/BSGR BH23 215 L6
Bosley Wy CHCH/BSGR BH23 215 L6
Bosmere Gdns EMRTH PO10 171 L7
Bosmere Rd HISD PO11 195 L6
Bossington Cl ROWN SO16 145 L3
Bostock Cl RWIN SO21 301 P1
Boston Rd CHAM PO6 168 E7
Bosuns Cl FHAM/PORC PO16 182 B2
Bosville ELGH SO50 134 A6
Boswell Cl HEND SO30 149 M5
ITCH SO19 148 C6
Bosworth Ms
MOOR/WNTN BH9 214 B4
Botany Bay Rd ITCH SO19 162 B1
Botany Cl STHA RG19 35 M1
Botany Hl RFNM GU10 260 B7
Botisdone Cl RAND SP11 243 P10
Botley Dr HAV PO9 170 D3
Botley Gdns ITCH SO19 162 E1
Botley Rd BPWT SO32 150 D4
ELGH SO50 141 K4
HEND SO30 148 F3
HLER SO31 164 A5
ITCH SO19 162 C2
NBAD SO52 137 M3
ROMY SO51 137 G1
Bottle La HTWY RG27 47 M6
Bottom La ROMY SO51 335 J4
Boulevards ALDT GU11 * 2 F3
Boulnois Av PSTN BH14 224 E5
Boulter La WHAM PO17 168 A1
Boulters Rd ASHV GU12 3 H4
Boulton Rd SSEA PO5 21 L7
Boundary Acre HLER SO31 149 H8
Boundary Cl WSHM SO15 159 M2
Boundary Dr WIMB BH21 207 K2
Boundary La RGWD BH24 205 M7
Boundary Rd FARN GU14 60 C7
GSHT GU26 115 K5
HLER SO31 162 F4
MOOR/WNTN BH9 213 K8
NWBY RG14 19 H5
RFNM GU10 109 L5
Boundary Wk WHAM PO17 165 L5
Boundary Wy CHAM PO6 169 H6
HAV PO9 16 D4
Bound La HISD PO11 195 G6
Boundstone FAWY SO45 176 F5
Boundstone Cl RFNM GU10 78 F3
Boundstone Rd RFNM GU10 78 D4
Boundway LYMN SO41 350 B11
Bounty Ri BSTK RG21 6 D7
Bounty Rd BSTK RG21 6 D7
Bourley La RFNM GU10 71 M6
Bourley Rd FLEETS GU52 71 L4
Bourne Arch NTHA RG18 28 D8

Bourne Av WCLF BH2 8 C5
WSHM SO15 146 C7
Bourne Cl HORN PO8 156 B2
ROMY SO51 334 H5
RWIN SO21 124 B8
WBNE BH4 8 A5
Bourne Ct ALDT GU11 2 E6
AND SP10 5 L1
BSTK RG21 * 7 J4
WIMB BH21 207 K3
Bourne Dene RFNM GU10 78 E3
Bourne Fld CHIN RG24 53 G8
Bournefields RWIN SO21 125 H5
Bourne Firs RFNM GU10 79 H3
Bourne Gv FNM GU9 13 L9
Bourne Grove Cl FNM GU9 13 M9
Bourne Grove Dr RFNM GU10 79 J1
Bourne Hts FNM GU9 * 13 H8
Bourne La NTID SP9 266 E9
RWIN SO21 125 G5
TOTT SO40 341 P7
Bourne Meadow RAND SP11 86 C3
Bournemouth Ar BMTH BH1 * 8 E6
Bournemouth Av
GPORT PO12 191 G1
Bournemouth International
Centre Rbt WCLF BH2 8 E7
Bournemouth Rd LYND SO43 345 J3
PSTN BH14 224 C4
RAND SP11 269 L7
ROWN SO16 139 G8
Bournemouth Rd Castle Hl
PSTN BH14 224 B4
Bournemouth Station Rbt
BMTH BH1 9 J4
Bourne Ri MARL SN8 264 G3
Bourne Rd CHAM PO6 168 B8
NTID SP9 266 F2
STHA RG19 28 D8
TOTT SO40 341 N7
WSHM SO15 22 B1
The Bourne FLEETS GU52 71 J2
Bourne Valley Rd
BKME/WDN BH12 225 G3
Bourne Vw NTID SP9 * 266 F1
RAND SP11 * 86 D4
Bourne View Cl EMRTH PO10 172 D4
Bournewood Dr WBNE BH4 225 J4
Bourton Gdns LTDN BH7 215 H8
Bouverie Cl NMIL/BTOS BH25 218 F7
Boveridge Gdns
MOOR/WNTN BH9 214 B4
Bovington Cl CFDH BH17 211 M7
Bowater Cl TOTT SO40 144 C7
Bowater Wy TOTT SO40 144 C8
Bowcombe HLER SO31 162 C5
Bowcott Hl BOR GU35 111 M7
Bowden La PTSW SO17 147 J6
Bowden Rd BKME/WDN BH12 212 C6
Bow Dr HTWY RG27 46 F8
Bowenhurst Gdns
FLEETS GU52 71 J4
Bowenhurst La RFNM GU10 70 D7
Bowenhurst Rd FLEETS GU52 71 J3
Bower Cl FAWY SO45 354 E5
ITCH SO19 161 M7
Bower Rd CHAR BH8 214 D8
RFNM GU10 78 E3
Bowers Cl HORN PO8 156 A4
Bowers Grove La ALTN GU34 292 G9
Bowers Hl RSAL SP5 332 G1
Bowers La RAND SP11 243 N9
Bowerwood Rd FBDG SP6 196 E4
Bowes Hl HAV PO9 157 J5
Bowes-Lyon Ct HORN PO8 156 B1
Bowes Rd STHA RG19 35 K2
Bow Fld HTWY RG27 56 E7
Bow Gdns HTWY RG27 46 F8
Bow Gv HTWY RG27 46 F7
Bowland Ri CHFD SO53 139 G1
NMIL/BTOS BH25 219 J6
Bowland Wy FAWY SO45 354 G9
Bowler Av HSEA PO3 192 F2
Bowler Ct HSEA PO3 192 F2
Bowling Court Gn FRIM GU16 61 L1
Bowling Green Dr HTWY RG27 56 B7
Bowling Green La RSAL SP5 328 D7
Bowling Green Rd NTHA RG18 28 C7
Bowman Ct CWTH RG45 43 G4
ITCH SO19 162 B1
Bowman Rd CHIN RG24 54 B4
Bowmonts Rd TADY RG26 44 D4
Bow St ALTN GU34 106 E6
Bowyer Cl BSTK RG21 6 C7
Boxall's Gv ALDT GU11 2 E8
Boxall's La FNM GU9 2 D7
Box Cl CFDH BH17 223 H1
Boxhalls La ALDT GU11 2 D7
Boxwood Cl WVILLE PO7 169 L2
Boyatt Crs ELGH SO50 134 A4
Boyatt La ELGH SO50 134 A5
Boyce Cl KBH RG22 92 E4
Boyd Cl FHAM/STUB PO14 189 H3
Boyd Rd BKME/WDN BH12 224 F2
LSOL/BMARY PO13 182 B5
Boyes La RWIN SO21 135 G3
Boyle Crs WVILLE PO7 169 K3
Boyne Mead Rd WINC SO23 288 H9
Boyne Ri WINC SO23 288 H8
Boyneswood Cl ALTN GU34 293 N4
Boyneswood La ALTN GU34 293 M4
Boyneswood Rd ALTN GU34 293 N4
Boynton Cl CHFD SO53 133 H8
Brabant Cl HLER SO31 164 B5
Brabazon Dr
CHCH/BSGR BH23 229 H1
Brabazon Rd FHAM PO15 164 D7
WIMB BH21 207 M7
Brabon Rd FARN GU14 60 F3
Brabourne Av FERN BH22 209 J4
Bracebridge CBLY GU15 50 C3
Bracher Cl AND SP10 5 J4
Bracken Bank CHIN RG24 54 B8
Brackenbury AND SP10 4 A3
Bracken Cl LSOL/BMARY PO13 190 A2
NBAD SO52 138 A5
RGWD BH24 205 M4
RSAL SP5 327 M1
Bracken Crs ELGH SO50 140 F2
Brackendale Cl FRIM GU16 51 G5
Brackendale Ct WIMB BH21 200 F8
Brackendale Rd CBLY GU15 50 F4
CHAR BH8 214 C8
Brackendene ASHV GU12 74 C5
Bracken Gln PLE BH15 223 L4
Bracken Heath HORN PO8 156 B7
Brackenhill CCLF BH13 225 G7
Brackenhill Rd WIMB BH21 208 A1
Bracken La BOR GU35 112 C4
ROWN SO16 146 A7
YTLY GU46 48 C2
Bracken Pl ELGH SO50 147 G1
Bracken Rd EPSF GU31 121 G7
FERN BH22 209 H1
NBAD SO52 138 A5
SBNE BH6 227 J4
The Brackens CWTH RG45 43 J1
FAWY SO45 176 D5
HLER SO31 180 B2
KBH RG22 92 E6
Brackens Wy LYMN SO41 221 M6
Bracken Wy CHCH/BSGR BH23 218 B7
Brackenway Rd CHFD SO53 133 J8
Brackenwood CBLY GU15 51 M3
Bracklesham Cl FARN GU14 61 G1
ITCH SO19 161 M5
Bracklesham Pl
NMIL/BTOS BH25 230 F1
Bracklesham Rd HISD PO11 195 M7
LSOL/BMARY PO13 182 D8
Brackley Av ELGH SO50 141 H2
HTWY RG27 57 K2
Brackley Cl CHCH/BSGR BH23 346 G12
Brackley Wy KBH RG22 92 E3
TOTT SO40 144 D8
Bracknell La HTWY RG27 57 L1
Bracknell Rd CWTH RG45 43 M2
Bradburne Rd WCLF BH2 8 C5
Bradbury Cl WHCH RG28 87 K7
Bradford Ct
LSOL/BMARY PO13 * 190 C2
Bradford Rd
MOOR/WNTN BH9 214 C4
SSEA PO5 21 K4
Brading Av ENEY PO4 193 G6
LSOL/BMARY PO13 182 C6
Brading Cl ROWN SO16 147 J3
Bradley Cl HUNG RG17 31 H3
Bradley Ct HAV PO9 171 H3
Bradley Gn ROWN SO16 146 B4
Bradley-Moore Sq NTHA RG18 29 G7
Bradley Peak FUFL SO22 122 C3
Bradley Rd FUFL SO22 122 C1
Bradly Rd FHAM PO15 181 J3
Bradman Sq AND SP10 * 96 D1
Bradpole Rd CHAR BH8 214 E7
Bradshaw Cl ELGH SO50 141 L2
Bradstock Cl
BKME/WDN BH12 212 F8
Bradwell Cl AND SP10 95 M1
Braehead FAWY SO45 176 F6
Braemar Av CHAM PO6 185 H1
SBNE BH6 228 A4
Braemar Cl FHAM PO15 10 B1
FRIM GU16 51 H8
LSOL/BMARY PO13 182 D6
SBNE BH6 228 A4
Braemar Dr CHCH/BSGR BH23 217 M7
DEAN RG23 91 J2
Braemar Rd
LSOL/BMARY PO13 182 D5
Braemore Cl STHA RG19 35 K3
Braeside Cl FUFL SO22 122 B8
HASM GU27 115 M8
Braeside Crs ITCH SO19 161 L3
Braeside Rd FERN BH22 205 G5
ITCH SO19 161 L3
RGWD BH24 202 A8
Brahms Rd KBH RG22 93 G4
Braidley Rd WCLF BH2 8 E4
Brailswood Rd PLE BH15 223 K4
Braintree Rd CHAM PO6 168 D7
Brairwood Gdns HISD PO11 194 F5
Braishfield Cl ROWN SO16 145 M7
Braishfield Gdns CHAR BH8 214 D6
Braishfield Rd HAV PO9 171 G4
ROMY SO51 131 J7
Brake Rd FARN GU14 60 E7
Bramber Rd GPORT PO12 191 G1
Bramble Bank FRIM GU16 62 A2
Bramble Cl ELGH SO50 134 B7
FAWY SO45 354 E5
FBDG SP6 196 C7
FHAM/STUB PO14 189 G3
HAV PO9 171 J5
Bramble Ct FERN BH22 204 F6
Bramble Dr ROMY SO51 131 J7
Bramblegate CWTH RG45 43 J2
ELGH SO50 * 141 K3
Bramble Hl CHFD SO53 139 H2
NARL SO24 291 M11
Bramble La CHCH/BSGR BH23 218 B7
HLER SO31 163 L7
HORN PO8 321 K5
Bramble Ms WEND SO18 148 A4
Bramble Rd ENEY PO4 21 L5
EPSF GU31 121 G6
Brambles Cl ALTN GU34 293 M6
ASHV GU12 74 B7
RWIN SO21 135 G4
Brambles Rd
LSOL/BMARY PO13 189 K5
The Brambles CWTH RG45 42 F2
NWBY RG14 33 L4
RFNM GU10 * 259 N2
Brambleton Av FNM GU9 12 E8
Bramble Wk LYMN SO41 221 J4
Bramble Wy CHIN RG24 66 E2
CHCH/BSGR BH23 348 D11
LSOL/BMARY PO13 182 A6
Bramblewood Pl FLEETN GU51 59 G7
Brambling Cl KBH RG22 92 B5
ROWN SO16 146 B2
Brambling Rd HAV PO9 157 H7
The Bramblings TOTT SO40 158 C1
Bramblys Cl BSTK RG21 6 D6
Bramblys Dr BSTK RG21 6 C6
Bramcote CBLY GU15 51 L3
Bramdean Cl TADY RG26 44 B5
Bramdean Dr HAV PO9 170 D3
Bramdean Rd WEND SO18 148 D5
Bramdown Hts KBH RG22 92 D6
Bramham Moor
FHAM/STUB PO14 189 H2
Bramley Cl ALTN GU34 107 G5
LYMN SO41 221 L6
WVILLE PO7 155 M8
Bramley Crs ITCH SO19 162 B2
Bramley Gdns EMRTH PO10 172 B6
GPORT PO12 191 G7
Bramley Green Rd TADY RG26 46 C6
Bramley Gv CWTH RG45 42 F3
Bramley La BLKW GU17 49 K3
TADY RG26 46 B4
Bramley Rd CBLY GU15 50 D6
FERN BH22 209 J2
HTWY RG27 46 F7
NBNE BH10 213 J3
TADY RG26 52 F3
THLE RG7 45 H3
The Bramleys RSAL SP5 127 H5
Bramley Wk BOR GU35 112 D2
Bramling Av YTLY GU46 48 D2
Brampton Gdns KBH RG22 92 D7
Brampton La HSEA PO3 185 J4
Brampton Rd PLE BH15 223 K2
Bramshaw Cl FUFL SO22 122 C1
Bramshaw Ct HAV PO9 171 H3
Bramshaw Gdns CHAR BH8 214 D5
Bramshaw Wy
NMIL/BTOS BH25 218 D8
Bramshill Cl WHIT RG2 239 L8
Bramshot Dr FLEETN GU51 59 J6
Bramshot La FLEETN GU51 60 A3
Bramshott Ct LIPH GU30 * 114 A8
Bramshott Dr HTWY RG27 56 D7
Bramshott Rd ENEY PO4 192 F4
FARN GU14 60 A6
ITCH SO19 161 M8
Bramston Rd WSHM SO15 146 C8
Bramwell Cl STHA RG19 35 M2
Brancaster Av AND SP10 95 M1
Branches La ROMY SO51 128 F6
Branders Cl SBNE BH6 228 A4
Branders La SBNE BH6 228 A3
Brandon Cl ALTN GU34 106 D4
CBLY GU15 51 M4
Brandon Rd FLEETS GU52 71 G4
SSEA PO5 21 J9
Brandy Bottom BLKW GU17 * 49 G5
Brandy Mt NARL SO24 291 M10
Branewick Cl FHAM PO15 180 D1
Branksea Av PLE BH15 222 D7
Branksea Cl PLE BH15 222 E7
Branksome Av STOK SO20 272 E9
WSHM SO15 146 C7
Branksome Cl CBLY GU15 51 G2
FUFL SO22 122 B6
NMIL/BTOS BH25 219 H6
STOK SO20 272 D9
Branksome Dene Rd
WBNE BH4 225 H6
Branksome Hill Rd SHST GU47 50 A1
WBNE BH4 225 H3
Branksome Park Rd CBLY GU15 51 G2
Branksome Towers
CCLF BH13 225 H8
Branksome Wood Gdns
WCLF BH2 8 B3
Branksomewood Rd
FLEETN GU51 59 G7
Branksome Wood Rd
WBNE BH4 225 J3
Bransbury Cl ROWN SO16 146 C4
Bransbury Rd ENEY PO4 193 H5
Bransgore Av HAV PO9 170 C4
Bransgore Gdns
CHCH/BSGR BH23 348 D11
Bransley Cl ROMY SO51 131 H7
Branson Rd BOR GU35 113 G1
Branton Cl KBH RG22 92 E1
Brants Cl WHIT RG2 239 L6
Branwell Cl CHCH/BSGR BH23 216 A7
Branwood Cl LYMN SO41 220 E7
Brasenose Cl
FHAM/STUB PO14 180 B3
Brasher Cl ELGH SO50 141 G2
Brassey Cl MOOR/WNTN BH9 214 A7
Brassey Rd FUFL SO22 24 E2
MOOR/WNTN BH9 213 M7
Brassey Ter
MOOR/WNTN BH9 * 213 M7
Brasted Ct ENEY PO4 193 H3
Braunfels Wk KSCL RG20 18 A6
Braybourne Cl STOK SO20 299 Q2
Braye Cl SHST GU47 43 L7
Breach Av EMRTH PO10 172 D4
Breachfield KSCL RG20 246 H5
Breach La HTWY RG27 47 G8
RAND SP11 80 D4
Breadels Fld DEAN RG23 92 C8
Breamore Cl ELGH SO50 134 A6
NMIL/BTOS BH25 218 E5
Breamore Rd RSAL SP5 331 R2
WEND SO18 148 D5
Brean Cl ROWN SO16 145 L5
Brecon Av CHAM PO6 169 H7
Brecon Cl CHFD SO53 139 H5
FARN GU14 60 D1
FAWY SO45 176 E5
FHAM/STUB PO14 10 A7
NBNE BH10 213 L2
NMIL/BTOS BH25 219 J6
Brecon Rd ITCH SO19 148 C7
Bredenbury Crs CHAM PO6 168 C7
Bredon Wk FHAM/STUB PO14 10 B8
Bredy Cl CFDH BH17 211 K7
Breech Cl HSEA PO3 * 184 F4
The Breech CBLY GU15 50 A1
Bremble Cl BKME/WDN BH12 212 C6
Bremen Gdns AND SP10 96 B2
Brenchley Cl
FHAM/PORC PO16 183 G1
Brendon Cl CHAR BH8 * 214 E6
FAWY SO45 176 D6
Brendon Gn ROWN SO16 145 M8
Brendon Rd FARN GU14 60 D1
FHAM/STUB PO14 181 K4
Brent Cl STHA RG19 35 K2
Brent Ct EMRTH PO10 171 L8
Brentwood Crs WEND SO18 148 A3
Bret Harte Rd FRIM GU16 51 G7
Breton Cl FHAM PO15 164 B5
Brewells La LISS GU33 309 L6
Brewer Cl HLER SO31 164 B8
KBH RG22 92 E1
Brewers Cl FARN GU14 61 G3
Brewers La LSOL/BMARY PO13 182 C6
NARL SO24 305 R5
RWIN SO21 124 F7
Brewer St PSEA PO1 21 G1
Brewery Common THLE RG7 40 B2
Brewhouse La HTWY RG27 57 M1
Brewhouse Sq GPORT PO12 15 J2
Brewster Cl HORN PO8 156 A5
Briar Cl CHCH/BSGR BH23 228 F2
GPORT PO12 190 E5
HORN PO8 156 B3
PLE BH15 223 L3
Briardene Ct TOTT SO40 158 E1
Briarfield Gdns HORN PO8 156 B2
Briar La ALTN GU34 293 N5
Briarlea Rd THLE RG7 39 M6
Briars Cl FARN GU14 60 D5
The Briars ASHV GU12 74 B7
FLEETS GU52 71 J2
WVILLE PO7 * 155 J7
Briarswood ROWN SO16 146 B7
Briarswood Ri FAWY SO45 176 D6
Briarswood Rd UPTN BH16 222 C1
Briar Wy ROMY SO51 131 J7
TADY RG26 44 C4
WIMB BH21 208 B3
Briar Wd LISS GU33 308 G5
Briarwood Cl
FHAM/PORC PO16 11 G7
Briarwood Dr EWKG RG40 42 A2
Briarwood Rd TOTT SO40 158 C2
Brickfield La CHFD SO53 139 H3
LYMN SO41 221 M3
Brickfield Rd PTSW SO17 147 J6
Brickfields Cl CHIN RG24 54 B8
Brickiln La ALTN GU34 293 R2
Brick Kiln La ALTN GU34 106 C4
NARL SO24 305 P5
Brick La CHCH/BSGR BH23 348 G8
FLEETN GU51 59 J6
Brickmakers Rd RWIN SO21 134 F4
Bricksbury Hl FNM GU9 77 G1
Brickwoods ROMY SO51 131 H8
Brickworth La RSAL SP5 126 C4
Brickworth Rd RSAL SP5 126 E4
Brickyard La WIMB BH21 206 A8
WIMB BH21 209 G2
Brickyard Rd BPWT SO32 151 M1
The Brickyard TOTT SO40 341 M4
Bricky Lake La ROMY SO51 335 N9
Bridefield Cl HORN PO8 155 K5
Bridefield Crs HORN PO8 155 K5
Bridge Ap PLE BH15 223 H7
Bridge Cl HLER SO31 163 H3
Bridge End CBLY GU15 50 D4
Bridgefield FNM GU9 13 J3
Bridgefoot Dr
FHAM/PORC PO16 11 K6
Bridgefoot Pth EMRTH PO10 171 M8
Bridge Industries
FHAM/PORC PO16 11 K2
Bridge La RWIN SO21 124 E5
Bridgemary Av
LSOL/BMARY PO13 182 D5
Bridgemary Gv
LSOL/BMARY PO13 182 C3
Bridgemary Rd
LSOL/BMARY PO13 182 C3
Bridgemary Wy
LSOL/BMARY PO13 * 182 C3
Bridge Md BPWT SO32 312 F11
Bridgemead FRIM GU16 50 F8
Bridge Mdw LISS GU33 308 F8
Bridge Pl NBNE BH10 213 K1
Bridge Rd ALDT GU11 2 F6
CBLY GU15 50 D5
EMRTH PO10 171 M7
FARN GU14 60 F4
HASM GU27 118 C5
HLER SO31 163 H4
HLER SO31 163 M6
ITCH SO19 161 K5
LYMN SO41 221 M4
NARL SO24 291 K11
ODIM RG29 68 E4
ROMY SO51 136 F1
RSAL SP5 324 D5
Bridgers Cl ROWN SO16 145 L3
Bridges Av CHAM PO6 167 M7
Bridges Cl ELGH SO50 139 M5
FERN BH22 205 H5
Bridgeside Cl PSEA PO1 21 K2
Bridge Sq FNM GU9 13 G4
The Bridges RGWD BH24 203 G5
THLE RG7 39 J7
Bridge St AND SP10 5 H6
CHCH/BSGR BH23 228 C2
FBDG SP6 197 H3
FHAM/STUB PO14 181 G4
NWBY RG14 18 E4
OVTN RG25 89 J4
WHAM PO17 152 A4
WHAM PO17 167 K2
WINC SO23 25 J6
Bridget Cl HORN PO8 156 C1
Bridge Ter SHAM SO14 * 23 K6
Bridgetts La RWIN SO21 289 P6
Bridge Wk YTLY GU46 48 F1
Bridgewater Rd
BKME/WDN BH12 224 D2
The Bridgeway ITCH SO19 * 161 L5
Bridgwater Ct WSHM SO15 22 A1
Bridle Cl ALTN GU34 294 D11
GSHT GU26 115 G5
UPTN BH16 222 D1
Bridle Ct ALDT GU11 2 B3
Bridle Crs LTDN BH7 215 J8
Bridle Wy WIMB BH21 208 B2
Bridleways VWD BH31 201 G2
Bridlington Av WSHM SO15 146 D8
Bridport Rd BKME/WDN BH12 212 F8
VWD BH31 201 H2
Bridport St PSEA PO1 21 H2
Brierley Av FERN BH22 209 L7
Brierley Cl NBNE BH10 213 L5
Brierley Rd NBNE BH10 213 L4
Briff La THLE RG7 29 K6
Brigantine Rd HLER SO31 179 L3
Brighstone Cl ROWN SO16 147 J3
Brightlands Av SBNE BH6 227 M4
Brighton Av GPORT PO12 182 F8
Brighton Rd ALDT GU11 3 K7
LYMN SO41 350 E9
WSHM SO15 160 F1
Brighton Wy KBH RG22 92 F4
Bright Rd PLE BH15 223 K2
Brightside WVILLE PO7 169 K2
Brightside Rd ROWN SO16 145 M6
Brights La HISD PO11 194 F3
Brightstone La ALTN GU34 294 A6
Brightstone Rd CHAM PO6 184 E1
Brightwells Rd FNM GU9 13 G3
Brimley Hill Ct KSCL RG20 248 D10
Brimpton La THLE RG7 249 M1
Brimpton Rd THLE RG7 36 E3
Brindle Cl ALDT GU11 3 G8
ROWN SO16 147 G3
Brinksway FLEETN GU51 59 J8
Brinn's La BLKW GU17 49 L3
Brinsons Cl CHCH/BSGR BH23 216 C5
Brinton La FAWY SO45 177 G3
Brinton's Rd SHAM SO14 23 H1
Brinton's Ter SHAM SO14 161 G2
Brisbane Rd
CHCH/BSGR BH23 215 L7
Brislands La ALTN GU34 292 H9
Bristol Ct LSOL/BMARY PO13 * 190 C2
Bristol Rd ENEY PO4 192 F6
Bristow Rd CBLY GU15 50 D5
Britain St PSEA PO1 20 D3
Britannia Cl BOR GU35 113 G1
Britannia Dr DEAN RG23 92 C8
Britannia Gdns HEND SO30 149 H1
Britannia Rd PSTN BH14 224 A5
SHAM SO14 23 K1
SSEA PO5 21 K5
Britannia Rd North SSEA PO5 21 K5
Britannia Wy
CHCH/BSGR BH23 229 H1
GPORT PO12 191 J1
Briton St SHAM SO14 22 F6
Britten Cl ASHV GU12 74 B6
Britten Rd KBH RG22 93 G4
LSOL/BMARY PO13 189 L6
Britten Wy WVILLE PO7 169 L4
Brixey Cl BKME/WDN BH12 224 C1
Brixey Rd BKME/WDN BH12 224 C1
Broadacres FLEETN GU51 58 F8
Broad Av CHAR BH8 214 D8
Broadbent Cl ROWN SO16 145 K2
Broad Chalke Down
FUFL SO22 122 C8
Broad Cft HAV PO9 157 J6
Broadcut FHAM/PORC PO16 11 K3
Broadfields Cl LYMN SO41 232 D3
Broad Gdns CHAM PO6 169 L8
Broad Gn SHAM SO14 23 H2
Broadhalfpenny La TADY RG26 44 C3
Broad Ha'Penny RFNM GU10 78 E3
Broadhill La FBDG SP6 197 M4
Broadhurst FARN GU14 60 C4
Broadhurst Av NBNE BH10 213 L4
Broadhurst Gv CHIN RG24 66 B1
Broadlands FARN GU14 61 L6
FRIM GU16 51 H8
Broadlands Av ELGH SO50 134 A7
SBNE BH6 227 M4
WVILLE PO7 169 L2
Broadlands Cl CHAR BH8 214 D5
CHCH/BSGR BH23 218 B6
Broadlands Rd BROC SO42 351 J3
PTSW SO17 147 H5
Broad La BPWT SO32 318 A7
LYMN SO41 221 M5
NBAD SO52 137 L3
NTHA RG18 29 H4
WVILLE PO7 154 B2
Broadlaw Wk
FHAM/STUB PO14 10 B9
Broad Leaze HTWY RG27 56 C6
Broadley Cl FAWY SO45 354 E4
Broadly Cl LYMN SO41 221 H6
Broadmayne Rd
BKME/WDN BH12 224 F1
Broadmead FARN GU14 60 D5
Broadmeadow Cl TOTT SO40 158 E1
Broadmeadow End NTHA RG18 35 M1
Broadmeadows La
WVILLE PO7 170 A1
Broadmead Rd ROWN SO16 145 K2
Broad Mead Rd WIMB BH21 201 G7
Broadmere Av HAV PO9 170 F3
Broadmere Rd DEAN RG23 92 C7
Broadmoor Rd WIMB BH21 210 C2
Broad Oak HEND SO30 149 L5
Broadoak TADY RG26 44 D4
Broadoak Cl FAWY SO45 354 E5
Broad Oak La ODIM RG29 69 J5
Broad Rd RAND SP11 270 D1
RCCH PO18 173 H6
Broadsands Dr GPORT PO12 190 D5
Broadshard La RGWD BH24 203 J3
The Broads WIMB BH21 207 F2
Broadstone Wy BDST BH18 210 F7
Broad St NARL SO24 291 M10
PSEA PO1 20 B6
Broadview Cl ALTN GU34 108 A5
Broad View La FUFL SO22 124 A1
Broad Wk FRIM GU16 51 G6
Broadwater Av PSTN BH14 224 B6
Broadwater Rd ROMY SO51 136 E2
WEND SO18 147 M5
Broad Wy FARN GU14 61 G8
HLER SO31 162 E7
PSF GU32 306 H12
THLE RG7 41 K5
Broadway SBNE BH6 228 A4
STHA RG19 35 K1
WHCH RG28 87 M8
Broadway La CHAR BH8 214 C5
HORN PO8 155 K2
Broadway Pk EPSF GU31 120 D8
The Broadway AND SP10 5 G6
NBNE BH10 213 K2
PTSW SO17 * 147 H7
SHST GU47 49 K1
WINC SO23 25 H6
Broadwell Rd RFNM GU10 78 D2
Broad Woods La ROMY SO51 335 L1
Brocas Dr BSTK RG21 7 H1
Brocas Rd THLE RG7 39 M3
Brock Cl FRIM GU16 51 M8
Brockenhurst Av HAV PO9 170 D2
Brockenhurst Dr YTLY GU46 48 F3
Brockenhurst Rd ALDT GU11 3 G6
MOOR/WNTN BH9 214 B6
Brockham Hill La ALTN GU34 280 G1
Brockhampton La HAV PO9 16 D5
Brockhampton Rd HAV PO9 16 B6
Brockhills La NMIL/BTOS BH25 219 J3
Brockhurst Ldg FNM GU9 78 F1
Brockhurst Rd GPORT PO12 190 F1
Brockishill Rd LYND SO43 341 K8
Brocklands HAV PO9 16 B4
YTLY GU46 48 D4
Brockley Rd NBNE BH10 213 K4
Brocks Cl FAWY SO45 176 D6
Brocks Pine RGWD BH24 346 F1
Brockwood Bottom
NARL SO24 304 G11
Brodrick Av GPORT PO12 14 D7
Brog St WIMB BH21 206 C7
Brokenford Av TOTT SO40 159 G1
Brokenford La TOTT SO40 158 F1
Broken Wy KSCL RG20 247 K2
Brokle Cl FLEETS GU52 71 G4
Bromelia Cl TADY RG26 46 B4
Bromley Rd WEND SO18 147 M7
Brompton Rd ENEY PO4 192 F6
Bromyard Crs CHAM PO6 168 C8
Bronte Av CHCH/BSGR BH23 216 A7
Bronte Cl TOTT SO40 158 D2
Bronte Gdns FHAM PO15 164 C4
Bronte Ri NWBY RG14 34 B4
Bronte Wy ITCH SO19 161 L2
Bronze Cl DEAN RG23 92 C8
Brook Av FNM GU9 2 D8
HLER SO31 179 J1
NMIL/BTOS BH25 219 H4
Brook Cl FLEETN GU51 59 J8
HLER SO31 179 K1
NBAD SO52 138 A5
NBNE BH10 213 J4
Brookdale Cl BDST BH18 211 G4
WVILLE PO7 155 L8
Brook Dr VWD BH31 201 K4
Brooke Cl WINC SO23 288 H8
Brookers Cnr CWTH RG45 43 L3
Brooker's Hl WHIT RG2 238 D2
Brookers La
LSOL/BMARY PO13 182 A5
Brookers Rw CWTH RG45 43 L2
Brook Farm Av FHAM PO15 10 C5
Brookfield Cl CHIN RG24 54 C5
HAV PO9 16 D2
Brookfield Gdns HLER SO31 163 M8
Brookfield Pl PTSW SO17 * 147 H6
Brookfield Rd ASHV GU12 73 L6
ELGH SO50 141 H2
PSEA PO1 21 M1
Brookfields ROMY SO51 334 H5
Brook Gdns EMRTH PO10 171 K8
FARN GU14 60 F6
Brook Gn TADY RG26 44 D4
Brook Hl LYMN SO41 356 E5
Brookhouse Rd FARN GU14 60 F5
Brookland Cl LYMN SO41 221 J5
Brooklands ALDT GU11 2 B4
Brooklands Cl FNM GU9 77 H1
RFNM GU10 259 M11
Brooklands Rd BPWT SO32 143 J4
FNM GU9 2 A9
HAV PO9 170 B6
Brooklands Wy FNM GU9 2 A9
Brook La CHCH/BSGR BH23 217 G1
FBDG SP6 332 A9
HEND SO30 149 M6
HLER SO31 179 J3
WIMB BH21 200 B1
WIMB BH21 210 C2
WVILLE PO7 319 P6
Brookley Cl RFNM GU10 77 M5
Brookley Rd BROC SO42 351 L3
Brookly Gdns FLEETN GU51 59 K7
Brooklyn Cl RWIN SO21 134 C1
Brooklyn Ct NMIL/BTOS BH25 218 F5
Brooklyn Dr WVILLE PO7 155 M8
Brooklynn Cl BPWT SO32 151 L2

Brookmead Ct FNM GU9 12 D5
Brookmeadow FHAM PO15 10 C5
Brookmead Wy HAV PO9 16 E8
Brook Rd BKME/WDN BH12 224 C3
CBLY GU15 50 D4
ELGH SO50 141 J2
LYMN SO41 221 M6
NBNE BH10 213 J4
WEND SO18 148 A5
WIMB BH21 207 L5
Brook Rw FAWY SO45 * 177 H6
Brooksby Cl BLKW GU17 49 K3
Brooks Cl RGWD BH24 203 K6
WHCH RG28 87 M8
Brookside FBDG SP6 199 L2
FNM GU9 77 G2
LSOL/BMARY PO13 182 B3
SHST GU47 49 L1
TOTT SO40 158 F3
Brookside Av WSHM SO15 159 M1
Brookside Cl
CHCH/BSGR BH23 348 C11
WVILLE PO7 154 F4
Brookside Pk FARN GU14 * 50 C7
Brookside Rd BROC SO42 351 K2
CHCH/BSGR BH23 348 C12
HAV PO9 16 B6
WIMB BH21 207 M4
Brookside Wk TADY RG26 44 C4
Brookside Wy
CHCH/BSGR BH23 217 L7
HEND SO30 148 E2
WEND SO18 147 L4
Brooks Rd NTHA RG18 29 G8
The Brooks WINC SO23 * 25 H5
Brook St BPWT SO32 143 J5
Brook Ter FBDG SP6 197 H4
The Brook NARL SO24 291 M8
Brookvale Cl BSTK RG21 6 C5
Brookvale Rd PTSW SO17 147 G7
Brook Va ROWN SO16 146 A6
Brook Wy CHCH/BSGR BH23 229 J1
ROMY SO51 131 H6
Brookway NWBY RG14 34 E1
RAND SP11 95 L8
Brookwood Av ELGH SO50 139 M5
Brookwood Rd FARN GU14 61 K4
ROWN SO16 145 K8
Broom Acres FLEETS GU52 71 H2
SHST GU47 43 K8
Broom Cl ENEY PO4 193 K4
WVILLE PO7 170 A3
Broome Cl YTLY GU46 48 E1
Broomfield MFD/CHID GU8 261 J12
Broomfield Crs
LSOL/BMARY PO13 190 B1
Broomfield Dr FBDG SP6 196 C7
Broomfield La LYMN SO41 221 L4
RFNM GU10 78 E7
Broomfield Rd BOR GU35 112 D2
Broom Gv WWKG RG41 239 R4
Broom Hl LYMN SO41 356 H5
Broomhill RFNM GU10 71 K8
RSAL SP5 334 B7
THLE RG7 * 38 A1
Broomhill Rd FARN GU14 60 D3
Broomhill Ter RSAL SP5 * 334 B6
Broom Hill Wy ELGH SO50 139 M1
Broomleaf Cnr FNM GU9 13 K4
Broomleaf Rd FNM GU9 13 K3
Broomrigg Rd FLEETN GU51 58 F6
Broom Rd BKME/WDN BH12 212 C7
EPSF GU31 121 G7
Brooms Gv ITCH SO19 162 D1
Broom Sq ENEY PO4 193 K4
Broom Wy BLKW GU17 49 M4
LSOL/BMARY PO13 189 M5
Broomwood Wy RFNM GU10 79 G2
Broomy Cl FAWY SO45 176 C4
Brougham La GPORT PO12 14 C1
Brougham Pl FNM GU9 76 F1
Brougham Rd SSEA PO5 21 G5
Brougham St GPORT PO12 14 C1
Broughton Av NBNE BH10 213 L4
Broughton Cl NBNE BH10 213 L5
ROWN SO16 146 A7
Broughton Ct HSEA PO3 185 J4
Broughton Ms FRIM GU16 51 H7
Broughton Rd LYND SO43 345 K2
STOK SO20 284 G6
Brown Cft HTWY RG27 56 B7
Browndown Rd
LSOL/BMARY PO13 190 C5
Brownen Rd
MOOR/WNTN BH9 214 B8
Brownhill Cl CHFD SO53 139 J1
Brownhill Ct ROWN SO16 145 L5
Brownhill Rd CHFD SO53 139 J1
NBAD SO52 138 B4
NMIL/BTOS BH25 349 M9
Brownhill Wy ROWN SO16 145 J5
Browning Av BOSC BH5 226 F4
CHAM PO6 167 L7
ITCH SO19 148 D6
Browning Cl CBLY GU15 51 L4
CHIN RG24 65 L4
ELGH SO50 139 M5
HLER SO31 164 C3
NTHA RG18 28 E8
TOTT SO40 158 D1
Browning Dr FUFL SO22 24 B4
Browning Rd
BKME/WDN BH12 224 D2
FLEETS GU52 71 G5
Brownings Cl LYMN SO41 221 G4
Brownlow Av ITCH SO19 148 A6
Brownlow Cl PSEA PO1 192 D1
Brownlow Gdns ITCH SO19 148 A6
Browns Cl TADY RG26 46 A4
Brownsea Av WIMB BH21 210 D2
Brownsea Cl NMIL/BTOS BH25 218 E5
Brownsea Rd CCLF BH13 237 G5
Brownsea View Av PSTN BH14 224 B7
Brownsfield Rd NTHA RG18 35 J1
Browns La FBDG SP6 330 C11
LYMN SO41 357 J7
Brownsover Rd FARN GU14 60 C4
Browns Wk RFNM GU10 78 D3
Brownwich La
FHAM/STUB PO14 180 D7
The Brow WVILLE PO7 169 J6
Broxburn Cl CHFD SO53 133 L7
Broxhead Farm Rd BOR GU35 111 G4
Broxhead Rd HAV PO9 171 G2
Bruan Rd NWBY RG14 33 M4
Bruce Cl FHAM/PORC PO16 10 F2
Bruce Rd ENEY PO4 192 F6
Brudenell Av CCLF BH13 237 J1
Brudenell Rd CCLF BH13 237 J1
Brue Cl CHFD SO53 139 H1
Brummell Rd NWBY RG14 18 A1
Brune La LSOL/BMARY PO13 182 A7
Brunel Cl HEND SO30 149 K3
RWIN SO21 275 P2
VWD BH31 201 L4
Brunel Rd BSTK RG21 65 G6
NEND PO2 184 E5
TOTT SO40 144 D5
WSHM SO15 159 J1
Brunel Wy FHAM PO15 164 D7
Brune Wy FERN BH22 209 K5
Brunstead Pl
BKME/WDN BH12 225 H4
Brunstead Rd
BKME/WDN BH12 225 G4
Brunswick Cl ELGH SO50 141 H2
Brunswick Gdns CHOB/PIR GU24 63 K1
Brunswick Gdns HAV PO9 16 A3
Brunswick Pl BSTK RG21 93 H3
LYMN SO41 221 L4
WSHM SO15 160 F2
Brunswick Rd CHOB/PIR GU24 63 K2
ELGH SO50 141 H1
FRIM GU16 62 D2
Brunswick Sq SHAM SO14 23 G6
Brunswick St SSEA PO5 21 G5
Bruntile Cl FARN GU14 61 K7
Bruyn Rd FBDG SP6 197 J3
Bryanstone Cl FLEETS GU52 71 J2
Bryanstone Rd TWDS BH3 225 L1
Bryanston Rd ITCH SO19 161 K4
Bryant Rd BKME/WDN BH12 213 G8
Bryce Gdns ALDT GU11 3 K9
Bryces La NARL SO24 277 J9
Brydes Rd RAND SP11 265 M10
Bryher Island CHAM PO6 184 B1
Brympton Cl FBDG SP6 196 E2
Bryn Rd RFNM GU10 78 D1
Bryon Rd WIMB BH21 207 J2
Bryony Cl BDST BH18 210 F5
HLER SO31 * 179 M2
Bryony Gdns ELGH SO50 141 J6
Bryony Wy WVILLE PO7 170 A2
Bryson Rd CHAM PO6 168 D8
Bubb La HEND SO30 149 H1
Bub La CHCH/BSGR BH23 228 E2
Buccaneers Cl
CHCH/BSGR BH23 228 D2
Buccleuch Rd CCLF BH13 225 G8
Bucehayes Cl
CHCH/BSGR BH23 218 A8
Buchanan Av LTDN BH7 226 E2
Buchanan Dr EWKG RG40 42 A1
Buchanan Rd ROWN SO16 145 M3
Buchan Av FHAM PO15 164 C4
Buchan Ct FAWY SO45 176 C6
Buckby La BSTK RG21 7 K4
HSEA PO3 185 J4
Bucketts Farm Cl BPWT SO32 318 B7
Buckfast Cl CHIN RG24 65 J3
Buckholt Rd STOK SO20 284 C10
Buckhurst Rd FRIM GU16 61 M2
Buckingham Cl ALTN GU34 106 D5
Buckingham Ct KBH RG22 92 C4
Buckingham Ga WSHM SO15 146 E8
Buckingham Gn PSEA PO1 192 D1
Buckingham Pde KBH RG22 92 C4
Buckingham Rd
BKME/WDN BH12 224 D1
NWBY RG14 18 B7
PSF GU32 120 B6
Buckingham St PSEA PO1 21 H1
Buckland Av KBH RG22 92 F3
Buckland Cl ELGH SO50 134 A7
FARN GU14 61 J1
WVILLE PO7 155 K6
Buckland Dene LYMN SO41 221 K3
Buckland Gdns TOTT SO40 144 C6
Buckland Gv
CHCH/BSGR BH23 217 L6
Buckland Pth NEND PO2 192 D1
Buckland Rd
BKME/WDN BH12 224 C3
Buckland St NEND PO2 192 E1
Buckland Ter
BKME/WDN BH12 224 C3
Bucklers Ct HAV PO9 170 D1
Bucklers Rd GPORT PO12 183 J8
The Bucklers LYMN SO41 232 A3
Bucklers Wy CHAR BH8 214 D5
Buckmore Av PSF GU32 120 B5
Bucksey Rd
LSOL/BMARY PO13 182 C8
Bucks Head Hl BPWT SO32 312 E11
Buckskin La KBH RG22 92 C2
Buckstone Cl LYMN SO41 220 E7
Buckthorn Cl BDST BH18 210 F6
TOTT SO40 144 A8
Budden's La WHAM PO17 318 E12
Buddens Meadow
WIMB BH21 210 C4
Buddens Rd WHAM PO17 152 A4
Buddle Hl FBDG SP6 197 L8
Buddlesgate RWIN SO21 274 D9
Budd's Cl BSTK RG21 6 C6
Budds La BOR GU35 110 E8
ROMY SO51 130 E7
Bude Cl CHAM PO6 167 M7
Buffbeards La HASM GU27 117 L1
Buffins Cnr ODIM RG29 68 E6
Buffins Rd ODIM RG29 68 E6
Bugdens La VWD BH31 201 H2
Bugkingham Wy FRIM GU16 51 H8
Bugle St SHAM SO14 22 F6
Bulbeck Rd HAV PO9 16 E5
Bulbery RAND SP11 270 H1
Buldowne Wk LYMN SO41 350 F9
Bulford Rd NTID SP9 266 B7
Bullar Rd WEND SO18 161 L1
Bullar St SHAM SO14 161 H2
Bull Dro WINC SO23 123 H7
Buller Ct FARN GU14 61 J7
Buller Rd ALDT GU11 73 H4
Bullers Rd FNM GU9 77 J2
Bullfinch Cl CFDH BH17 210 F7
TOTT SO40 158 C1
Bull Hl LISS GU33 309 L8
LYMN SO41 356 B3
Bullington La RWIN SO21 273 Q5
Bull La BPWT SO32 151 K1
LYND SO43 340 G9
THLE RG7 240 B1
Bullrush Cl FAWY SO45 176 F7
Bulls Copse La HORN PO8 156 A2
Bulls Copse Rd TOTT SO40 158 F4
Bulls Down Cl HTWY RG27 46 E7
Bulls Dro RSAL SP5 297 N6
Bulpits Hl RAND SP11 243 Q10
Bunch La HASM GU27 118 A5
Bunch Wy HASM GU27 118 A6
Bungalow Rd FARN GU14 61 H6
Bungler's Hl THLE RG7 238 H10
Bunkers Hl NWBY RG14 33 J7
WVILLE PO7 154 D5
Bunnian Pl BSTK RG21 6 F2
Bunns La WVILLE PO7 153 L3
Bunny La ROMY SO51 130 F2
RSAL SP5 128 A4
Bunstead La RWIN SO21 133 K2
Bunting Gdns HORN PO8 155 M4
Bunting Ms KBH RG22 92 D5
Bunting Rd FERN BH22 204 D8
Buntings ALTN GU34 106 F2
The Buntings FNM GU9 12 B9
Burbidge Gv ENEY PO4 193 G6
Burbridge Cl CFDH BH17 211 L8
Burbury Woods CBLY GU15 51 G2
Burbush Cl FAWY SO45 354 E5
Burchell Rd NWBY RG14 27 G7
Burcombe Rd NBNE BH10 213 J3
Burcote Dr HSEA PO3 185 H4
Burdale Dr HISD PO11 195 K5
Burdens Heath NTHA RG18 29 J5
Burdock Cl CHCH/BSGR BH23 217 H7
RAND SP11 271 P4
Bure Cl CHCH/BSGR BH23 229 H2
Bure Haven Dr
CHCH/BSGR BH23 229 G2
Bure Homage Gdns
CHCH/BSGR BH23 229 H2
Bure Homage La
CHCH/BSGR BH23 229 G2
Bure La CHCH/BSGR BH23 229 H3
Bure Pk CHCH/BSGR BH23 229 H2
Bure Rd CHCH/BSGR BH23 229 H2
Burfield KSCL RG20 246 A7
Burford Cl CHCH/BSGR BH23 215 K7
Burford Cl La BROC SO42 351 L2
Burford Lea MFD/CHID GU8 261 J12
Burford Rd CBLY GU15 50 D4
Burgage Fld WHCH RG28 87 M6
Burgate Cl HAV PO9 170 D5
Burgate Flds FBDG SP6 197 J1
Burgess Cl BWD BH11 212 F4
HISD PO11 195 K7
ODIM RG29 68 E6
Burgess Fld WIMB BH21 200 C2
Burgess Gdns ROWN SO16 146 E5
Burgess La KSCL RG20 31 J7
Burgess Rd BSTK RG21 6 D2
PTSW SO17 147 H4
WSHM SO15 146 D6
Burghclere Rd HAV PO9 171 H2
ITCH SO19 161 M8
Burghead Cl SHST GU47 49 M1
Burgh Hill Rd LIPH GU30 113 M5
Burgoyne Rd CBLY GU15 51 J2
ITCH SO19 148 E8
SSEA PO5 192 D7
Burgundy Cl HLER SO31 179 M2
Buriton Cl FHAM/PORC PO16 167 K7
Buriton Rd FUFL SO22 288 D12
Buriton St PSEA PO1 21 J1
Burkal Dr AND SP10 84 C8
Burke Dr ITCH SO19 148 C6
Burleigh Rd FRIM GU16 50 F8
NEND PO2 184 F8
SBNE BH6 227 K2
Burley Cl CHFD SO53 139 H4
HAV PO9 171 H2
NMIL/BTOS BH25 218 D8
TOTT SO40 158 B1
VWD BH31 201 G3
Burley Down CHFD SO53 139 H4
Burley La OVTN RG25 101 M3
Burley Lawn RGWD BH24 343 K12
Burley Rd BKME/WDN BH12 224 C2
BROC SO42 350 E5
CHCH/BSGR BH23 216 C3
CHCH/BSGR BH23 348 E11
FUFL SO22 288 D12
Burley Wy BLKW GU17 49 L2
Burlingham Cl WHIT RG2 238 C2
Burlington Ar BMTH BH1 * 8 F5
Burlington Ct ALDT GU11 2 D5
BLKW GU17 49 L5
Burlington Rd NEND PO2 184 E7
WSHM SO15 160 E2
Burmah Rd North FAWY SO45 178 C6
Burmah Rd South FAWY SO45 178 D6
Burma Wy TOTT SO40 159 M8
Burmese Cl FHAM PO15 164 C5
Burnaby Cl KBH RG22 92 E1
Burnaby Rd PSEA PO1 20 E3
WBNE BH4 225 J7
Burnbake Rd VWD BH31 201 H3
Burnbank Gdns TOTT SO40 158 E1
Burnbrae Rd FERN BH22 209 K7
Burn Cl VWD BH31 201 K4
Burne Cl RWIN SO21 288 D6
Burne-Jones Dr SHST GU47 49 M2
Burnett Av CHCH/BSGR BH23 227 L1
Burnett Cl FAWY SO45 177 H6
FUFL SO22 122 C2
WEND SO18 147 L7
Burnett Rd CHCH/BSGR BH23 227 M1
GPORT PO12 14 B1
Burnetts Flds ELGH SO50 141 J5
Burnetts Gdns ELGH SO50 141 K5
Burnetts La HEND SO30 141 H8
Burney Bit TADY RG26 44 E4
Burney Rd GPORT PO12 190 E5
Burngate Rd PLE BH15 222 E6
Burnham Beeches CHFD SO53 139 H2
Burnham Cha WEND SO18 148 B5
Burnham Dr CHAR BH8 226 C1
Burnham Rd CHAM PO6 169 K7
CHCH/BSGR BH23 216 C6
FBDG SP6 197 H1
TADY RG26 249 R2
Burnhams Cl AND SP10 96 C1
Burnhams Wk GPORT PO12 15 K3
Burnham Wd
FHAM/PORC PO16 10 E1
Burnleigh Gdns
NMIL/BTOS BH25 219 J4
Burnley Cl TADY RG26 44 B5
Burnmoor Meadow
EWKG RG40 42 A6
Burnsall Cl FARN GU14 61 H2
Burns Av FLEETS GU52 71 K2
Burns Cl CHIN RG24 65 L4
ELGH SO50 139 L7
FARN GU14 60 F2
RWIN SO21 288 E4
Burnside CHCH/BSGR BH23 217 K8
FLEETN GU51 59 J7
LSOL/BMARY PO13 182 B3
WVILLE PO7 156 A7
Burns Pl ROWN SO16 146 A6
Burns Rd ELGH SO50 139 M7
ITCH SO19 148 D7
SBNE BH6 227 K1
Burnt Hill Rd RFNM GU10 78 E2
Burnt Hill Wy RFNM GU10 78 F3
Burnt House La
CHCH/BSGR BH23 348 D11
FHAM/STUB PO14 189 K1
LYMN SO41 351 R11
Burrard Gv LYMN SO41 221 M6
Burr Cl RWIN SO21 134 F4
Burrell Rd FRIM GU16 50 E8
Burrfields Rd HSEA PO3 185 H7
Burridge Rd HLER SO31 164 A2
Burrill Av CHAM PO6 169 G8
Burrowfields KBH RG22 92 D6
Burrow Rd RWIN SO21 301 N3
Burrows Cl HAV PO9 17 H1
Burrows La VWD BH31 337 M12
The Burrows TADY RG26 44 A3
Burrwood Gdns ASHV GU12 74 A4
Bursledon Hts HLER SO31 163 H3
Bursledon Pl WVILLE PO7 169 K3
Bursledon Rd HEND SO30 149 H7
ITCH SO19 148 B6
WVILLE PO7 169 K3
Bursledon Ter NTID SP9 * 266 E8
Burtley Rd SBNE BH6 227 L5
Burton Cl CHCH/BSGR BH23 216 C7
RGWD BH24 205 M3
Burtoncroft CHCH/BSGR BH23 216 C5
Burton Hall Pl
CHCH/BSGR BH23 216 C5
Burton Rd CCLF BH13 225 G5
CHCH/BSGR BH23 228 E1
WSHM SO15 160 E1
Burton's Gdns CHIN RG24 66 D2
Burtons Hl HUNG RG17 31 H2
Burt's Hl WIMB BH21 207 J2
Burt's La WIMB BH21 200 C8
Burwood Gv HISD PO11 195 G4
Bury Brickfield Pk
TOTT SO40 * 159 J4
Bury Cl GPORT PO12 14 F5
Bury Crs GPORT PO12 14 E5
Burydown Md OVTN RG25 103 H3
Buryfields ODIM RG29 69 G6
Bury Hall La GPORT PO12 14 A6
Bury Hill Cl RAND SP11 95 M8
Bury La TOTT SO40 159 H3
Bury Rd CCLF BH13 224 F7
DEAN RG23 64 F6
GPORT PO12 14 C5
TOTT SO40 159 L6
Bury's Bank Rd STHA RG19 34 D5
Bushell Rd PLE BH15 223 J1
Bushells Farm FBDG SP6 197 G4
Bushey La ALTN GU34 * 280 E4
Bushey Rd CHAR BH8 214 C7
Bushmead Dr RGWD BH24 202 A7
Bushnells Dr KSCL RG20 248 C9
Bush St West SSEA PO5 * 21 G6
Bush St East SSEA PO5 21 G6
Bushy Md WVILLE PO7 169 J5
Bushywarren La OVTN RG25 256 B7
Busk Crs FARN GU14 60 F5
Busket La WINC SO23 25 H6
Busketts Wy TOTT SO40 158 A6
Butcher St PSEA PO1 20 C3
Bute Dr CHCH/BSGR BH23 230 B1
Butler Cl KBH RG22 64 E8
Butler Rd CWTH RG45 43 K2
Butlers Cl ROMY SO51 298 C11
Butlers La RGWD BH24 203 L3
Butser Wk FHAM/STUB PO14 10 B8
Butson Cl NWBY RG14 18 A4
Butt Cl RAND SP11 265 L9
Buttenshaw Av WHIT RG2 239 M8
Buttenshaw Cl WHIT RG2 239 N8
Buttercup Cl BOR GU35 111 J7
FAWY SO45 177 G7
HEND SO30 149 G6
Buttercup Dr
CHCH/BSGR BH23 217 H7
Buttercup Pl NTHA RG18 28 F8
Buttercup Wy HLER SO31 179 L1
Butterfield CBLY GU15 50 D4
Butterfield Rd ROWN SO16 146 E4
Butterfly Dr CHAM PO6 168 A6
Butter Furlong Rd RSAL SP5 327 R1
Butteridge Rl ROMY SO51 129 L2
Buttermer Cl RFNM GU10 78 C1
Buttermere Cl BOR GU35 110 F7
FARN GU14 60 E4
ROWN SO16 145 L6
Buttermere Ct ASHV GU12 * 73 M4
Buttermere Dr CBLY GU15 51 M4
KBH RG22 92 C3
Buttermere Gdns NARL SO24 291 M12
The Buttery CHCH/BSGR BH23 228 D1
Butt La RSAL SP5 324 D4
Button's La ALTN GU34 307 M2
ROMY SO51 335 J5
Buttsash Av FAWY SO45 177 G8
Butts Ash Gdns FAWY SO45 177 G7
Butts Ash La FAWY SO45 176 F8
Butts Bridge Hl FAWY SO45 177 G6
Buttsbridge Rd FAWY SO45 177 G7
Butts Cl FUFL SO22 24 B2
ITCH SO19 148 D8
Butt's Crs ITCH SO19 148 C8
Butts Lake THLE RG7 * 38 B2
Butts La BPWT SO32 143 K4
Butts Lawn BROC SO42 351 K2
Butts Meadow HTWY RG27 56 C7
Butts Ms ALTN GU34 106 E6
Butts Paddock BROC SO42 351 K2
Butts Rd ALTN GU34 106 E7
ITCH SO19 162 B2
Butt's Sq ITCH SO19 148 C8
The Butts BPWT SO32 312 E10
THLE RG7 45 H4
Butt St RAND SP11 265 L10
The Butty BSTK RG21 7 K4
Byerley Cl EMRTH PO10 172 B1
Byerley Rd PSEA PO1 192 F2
Byes La THLE RG7 45 H5
Byeways FAWY SO45 176 F6
KSCL RG20 246 B6
Byfields Rd KSCL RG20 248 C10
Byfleet Av CHIN RG24 66 D3
Byng Wk AND SP10 96 F4
By-Pass Rd ROMY SO51 136 E2
RWIN SO21 274 B8
Byrd Cl WVILLE PO7 169 L3
Byrd Gdns KBH RG22 92 E5
Byron Av FRIM GU16 51 K5
FUFL SO22 24 A5
Byron Cl BPWT SO32 143 L4
CHIN RG24 65 L3
FHAM/PORC PO16 10 E3
FLEETN GU51 59 J8
NWBY RG14 33 M5
RAND SP11 265 M10
YTLY GU46 48 D4
Byron Dr CWTH RG45 43 K5
Byron Rd BOSC BH5 226 F4
ELGH SO50 134 B8
ITCH SO19 148 D6
NEND PO2 184 F8
NMIL/BTOS BH25 218 E8
Byways YTLY GU46 48 D3
Byworth Cl FNM GU9 12 B3
Byworth Rd FNM GU9 12 B4

C

Cable St SHAM SO14 23 L1
ELGH SO50 140 A2
Cabot Dr FAWY SO45 176 C5
Cabot La CFDH BH17 211 H8
Cabot Wy NMIL/BTOS BH25 218 F5
Cabrol Rd FARN GU14 61 G3
Cabul Rd NTID SP9 266 D3
Cadet Wy FLEETS GU52 71 K4
Cadgwith Pl CHAM PO6 184 B1
Cadhay Cl NMIL/BTOS BH25 218 E5
Cadland Rd FAWY SO45 354 F1
Cadlands Park Est FAWY SO45 354 E2
Cadley Rd MARL SN8 264 H3
Cadnam Cl ALDT GU11 3 J9
DEAN RG23 91 K2
Cadnam La TOTT SO40 341 J4
Cadnam Rd ENEY PO4 193 H5
Cadnam Wy CHAR BH8 214 D5
Cadogan Rd ALDT GU11 73 K1
RGWD BH24 203 K5
Cador Dr FHAM/PORC PO16 183 H2
Caerleon Av ITCH SO19 148 C6
Caerleon Cl GSHT GU26 115 J2
Caerleon Dr AND SP10 84 C8
ITCH SO19 148 B6
Caernarvon FRIM GU16 51 H8
Caernarvon Cl DEAN RG23 64 E7
Caernarvon Gdns CHFD SO53 139 G4
Caer Peris Vw
FHAM/PORC PO16 167 J6
Caesar Cl AND SP10 96 D1
Caesar Ct ALDT GU11 2 B3
Caesar's Wy BDST BH18 210 E4
WHCH RG28 87 K6
Cains Cl FHAM/STUB PO14 189 J1
Caird Av NMIL/BTOS BH25 219 H5
Cairn Cl FRIM GU16 51 K5
Cairngorm Cl KBH RG22 64 D8
Cairngorm Pl FARN GU14 60 E1
Cairngorm Rd STHA RG19 35 K2
Cairns Cl CHCH/BSGR BH23 215 M8
Cairo Ter NEND PO2 192 D1
Caister Cl FERN BH22 209 J2
Caistor Cl ROWN SO16 146 A4
Caithness Cl DEAN RG23 91 J2
Caker's La ALTN GU34 107 K6
Caker Stream Rd ALTN GU34 107 H4
Calabrese HLER SO31 164 B5
Calard Dr NTHA RG18 28 C7
Calbourne HLER SO31 162 C5
Calcot Hl BPWT SO32 150 E1
Calcot La BPWT SO32 150 E2
Calcott Pk YTLY GU46 48 E2
Calder Cl ROWN SO16 145 L8
Calder Ct AND SP10 96 E2
Calder Rd CFDH BH17 211 M8
Calderwood Dr ITCH SO19 148 A8
Caledonia Dr FAWY SO45 176 D5
Caledonian Cl
CHCH/BSGR BH23 229 H1
Caledon Rd PSTN BH14 224 D5
Calender Cl ALTN GU34 106 F6
California Cl TOTT SO40 144 B7
Calkin Cl CHCH/BSGR BH23 216 A7
Calleva Cl KBH RG22 92 D5
Callowing Cl RWIN SO21 134 F4
Calluna Rd BKME/WDN BH12 212 B7
Calmore Cl CHAR BH8 214 D5
Calmore Crs TOTT SO40 144 B7
Calmore Dr TOTT SO40 144 C7
Calmore Gdns TOTT SO40 158 C1
Calmore Rd TOTT SO40 144 C8
Calpe Av LYND SO43 345 K2
Calshot Cl FAWY SO45 355 P8
Calshot Dr CHFD SO53 139 G4
Calshot Rd FAWY SO45 355 K5
HAV PO9 170 C1
Calshot Wy FRIM GU16 62 A1
LSOL/BMARY PO13 182 B7
Calthorpe Rd FLEETN GU51 59 G6
Calton Gdns ALDT GU11 3 J9
Calvecroft LIPH GU30 116 C4
Calvert Cl ASHV GU12 3 M5
Calvin Cl CBLY GU15 51 K4
Calvin Rd MOOR/WNTN BH9 213 M8
Camargue Cl HLER SO31 164 B4
Camber Pl PSEA PO1 20 B6
Camberry Cl BSTK RG21 7 G9
Cambria Dr FAWY SO45 176 D5
Cambrian Cl CBLY GU15 50 D3
HLER SO31 163 G2
Cambrian Rd FARN GU14 60 D1
Cambrian Ter SSEA PO5 * 21 J6
Cambrian Wk
FHAM/STUB PO14 181 M5
Cambrian Wy KBH RG22 92 D1
Cambridge Dr CHFD SO53 139 J5
Cambridge Gdns
CHCH/BSGR BH23 215 M6
Cambridge Gn
FHAM/STUB PO14 180 C2
Cambridge Rd ALDT GU11 2 C3
CWTH RG45 43 L4
GPORT PO12 190 E2
LSOL/BMARY PO13 189 M8
PSEA PO1 20 E5
SHAM SO14 147 G8
WCLF BH2 8 B5
Cambridge Rd East FARN GU14 61 K7
Cambridge Rd West
FARN GU14 61 J7
Camcross Cl CHAM PO6 * 168 B7
Camden Cl MOOR/WNTN BH9 214 B7
Camden St GPORT PO12 14 D1
Camden Wk FLEETN GU51 59 L7
Camel Green Rd FBDG SP6 196 D6
Camelia Cl HAV PO9 171 H5
NBAD SO52 138 A3
Camelia Gdns WEND SO18 148 A2
Camelia Gv ELGH SO50 141 L2
Camellia Cl WIMB BH21 201 G7
Camellia Gdns
NMIL/BTOS BH25 219 H6
Camellia Wy WWKG RG41 239 R1
Camelot Cl AND SP10 96 C2
Camelot Crs
FHAM/PORC PO16 167 H7
Camelsdale Rd HASM GU27 117 M3
Camel Wy FARN GU14 61 G8
Cameron Cl
LSOL/BMARY PO13 182 C5
Cameron Rd ALDT GU11 73 K1
CHCH/BSGR BH23 228 D1
Camfield Cl BSTK RG21 7 G9
Camford Cl DEAN RG23 92 C8
Camilla Cl TOTT SO40 144 B7
Camlea Cl BSTK RG21 7 G9
Camley Cl ITCH SO19 161 L7
Cammel Rd FERN BH22 209 K6
Camomile Dr RAND SP11 265 M10
Campbell Cl ALDT GU11 3 J9
FLEETN GU51 59 G7
RAND SP11 269 L5
YTLY GU46 49 H2
Campbell Pl FRIM GU16 51 H5
Campbell Rd ALDT GU11 2 E1
BMTH BH1 226 E3
CHCH/BSGR BH23 216 C5
ELGH SO50 140 B3
RWIN SO21 273 N2
SSEA PO5 21 K6
TADY RG26 46 D6
Campbell St SHAM SO14 * 161 J2
Campbell Wy ELGH SO50 141 J2
Camp Farm Rd ALDT GU11 73 K3
Camp Fld STOK SO20 299 Q1
Camp Hl RFNM GU10 260 A8
Campion Cl BLKW GU17 50 B5
BOR GU35 111 J8
ELGH SO50 141 J6
HLER SO31 179 L3
LYMN SO41 221 L3
WVILLE PO7 170 A2
Campion Dr ROMY SO51 131 J7
Campion Gv CHCH/BSGR BH23 228 F2

Campion Rd ITCH SO19 148 D7
Campion Wy HTWY RG27 57 M1
LYMN SO41 221 L3
WINC SO23 289 J10
Camp Rd BOR GU35 110 F7
FARN GU14 61 J8
LSOL/BMARY PO13 182 D5
THLE RG7 39 J1
Campsie Cl KBH RG22 64 D8
Camrose Wy BSTK RG21 7 G9
Cams Bay Cl
FHAM/PORC PO16 166 F7
Cams Hall Est
FHAM/PORC PO16 11 M8
Cams Hl FHAM/PORC PO16 11 M6
WVILLE PO7 319 P11
Camus Cl FLEETS GU52 70 F3
Cam Wk BSTK RG21 7 J5
Camwood Cl BSTK RG21 7 G9
Canada Rd FRIM GU16 51 M8
ITCH SO19 161 L6
ROMY SO51 334 H8
Canada Wy BOR GU35 110 F8
LIPH GU30 116 C5
Canal Cl ALDT GU11 73 K3
ODIM RG29 68 E4
ROMY SO51 131 G7
Canal La RSAL SP5 327 N2
Canalside RSAL SP5 327 N2
Canal View Rd NWBY RG14 19 M4
Canal Wk NWBY RG14 18 E4
ROMY SO51 130 F8
SHAM SO14 23 G5
SSEA PO5 21 J3
Canberra Cl GPORT PO12 14 B5
HTWY RG27 48 C1
Canberra Rd
CHCH/BSGR BH23 215 L7
ROWN SO16 145 H4
Canberra Wy DEAN RG23 92 C8
FARN GU14 60 F8
Candleford Ga LIPH GU30 * 116 B4
Candlemas Pl PTSW SO17 * 147 G8
Candover Cl TADY RG26 44 B5
Candy La WEND SO18 148 E5
Candys Cl WIMB BH21 206 E6
Candys La WIMB BH21 206 E6
Canes La BOR GU35 111 H7
Canford Av BWD BH11 212 F7
Canford Bottom WIMB BH21 208 C2
Canford Cliffs Av PSTN BH14 224 D6
Canford Cliffs Rd CCLF BH13 224 E6
Canford Cl BPWT SO32 151 L5
ROWN SO16 145 K6
Canford Crs CCLF BH13 237 K1
Canford Heath Rd CFDH BH17 211 K7
Canford Magna WIMB BH21 207 M6
Canford Rd BWD BH11 213 G7
PLE BH15 223 K4
Canford View Dr WIMB BH21 208 B2
Canford Wy BKME/WDN BH12 212 C6
Canhouse La LISS GU33 309 M9
Canning Rd ASHV GU12 3 L3
Cannock Wk FHAM/STUB PO14 10 B9
Cannon Cl BDST BH18 210 F7
Cannon Hill Gdns WIMB BH21 208 B1
Cannon Hill Rd WIMB BH21 208 A1
Cannon St LYMN SO41 221 M4
WSHM SO15 146 C8
Canoe Cl HLER SO31 179 M3
Canon's Barn Cl
FHAM/PORC PO16 167 J7
Canons Cl NTID SP9 266 F4
Canon's Ct KSCL RG20 248 C10
Canon St WINC SO23 24 F7
Cansfield End NWBY RG14 18 D3
Canterbury Av ITCH SO19 162 C1
Canterbury Cl FERN BH22 205 G7
KBH RG22 92 D4
LSOL/BMARY PO13 190 B4
Canterbury Dr FAWY SO45 176 C5
Canterbury Rd ASHV GU12 74 A5
ENEY PO4 192 F5
FARN GU14 61 K6
FHAM/STUB PO14 189 J1
Canterton La LYND SO43 340 F4
Canton St WSHM SO15 160 F2
Canute Dr CHCH/BSGR BH23 348 D11
Canute Rd SHAM SO14 23 K6
WINC SO23 25 K8
Capella Gdns FAWY SO45 176 D5
Capel Ley WVILLE PO7 169 L4
Capers End La BPWT SO32 150 E3
Capesthorne
CHCH/BSGR BH23 229 H3
Capper Rd CBLY GU15 50 C1
Capstone Pl CHAR BH8 226 D2
Capstone Rd CHAR BH8 226 C2
Captains Cl GPORT PO12 182 F8
Captains Pl SHAM SO14 23 J6
Captain's Rw LYMN SO41 221 M4
PSEA PO1 20 C6
Carberry Dr FHAM/PORC PO16 183 H1
Carbery Av SBNE BH6 227 K4
Carbery Ct HAV PO9 170 D1
Carbery Gdns SBNE BH6 227 L3
Carbery Rw SBNE BH6 * 227 J4
Carbis Cl CHAM PO6 184 A1
Carbonel Cl DEAN RG23 64 C7
Cardew Rd LISS GU33 308 G9
Cardiff Rd NEND PO2 184 D6
Cardigan Rd BKME/WDN BH12 224 F4
MOOR/WNTN BH9 213 M8
Cardinal Dr WVILLE PO7 156 B7
Cardinal Ms AND SP10 * 4 F5
The Cardinals RFNM GU10 260 D1
Cardinal Wy HLER SO31 180 B2
Carey Rd ITCH SO19 148 C7
MOOR/WNTN BH9 213 M6
Careys Cots BROC SO42 351 K2
Careys Rd CHAR BH8 214 D4
Carfax Av RFNM GU10 73 M8
Cargate Av ALDT GU11 2 E4
Cargate Gv ALDT GU11 2 D5
Cargate Hl ALDT GU11 2 D4
Cargate Ter ALDT GU11 2 D5
Carisbrooke FRIM GU16 51 H8
HLER SO31 162 C5
Carisbrooke Av
FHAM/STUB PO14 189 G2
Carisbrooke Cl DEAN RG23 64 E6
HAV PO9 17 J3
NARL SO24 291 M12
Carisbrooke Ct
NMIL/BTOS BH25 218 F5
ROMY SO51 131 G7
Carisbrooke Crs CHFD SO53 139 L3
PLE BH15 222 D5
Carisbrooke Dr ITCH SO19 161 M2
Carisbrooke Rd ENEY PO4 192 F4
LSOL/BMARY PO13 182 B5
Carisbrooke Wy
CHCH/BSGR BH23 217 L7
Carless Cl LSOL/BMARY PO13 190 D1
Carleton Cl HTWY RG27 56 B8
Carlin Pl CBLY GU15 50 E4
Carlinwark Dr CBLY GU15 51 H1
Carlisle Cl DEAN RG23 64 E6
Carlisle Rd RFNM GU10 262 H5
ROWN SO16 146 B8
SSEA PO5 21 K3
Carlton Av NMIL/BTOS BH25 230 D1
Carlton Cl FRIM GU16 51 K5
Carlton Crs FLEETS GU52 71 K2
WSHM SO15 160 F2
Carlton Gv PSTN BH14 224 D3
Carlton Pl WSHM SO15 160 F2
Carlton Rd BMTH BH1 9 M3
BOR GU35 114 C4
FHAM/PORC PO16 167 K7
GPORT PO12 15 H4
WSHM SO15 160 F1
Carlton Wy GPORT PO12 15 H3
Carlyle Rd GPORT PO12 14 E2
SBNE BH6 227 K2
Carlyn Dr CHFD SO53 139 K1
Carlyon Cl FARN GU14 61 J4
FRIM GU16 61 M4
Carmans La RWIN SO21 124 D5
Carmarthen Av CHAM PO6 169 H7
Carmarthen Cl FARN GU14 60 F1
Carmichael Wy KBH RG22 92 E4
Carmine Ct
LSOL/BMARY PO13 * 190 C2
Carmino Ter LIPH GU30 * 116 B4
Carnac Ct FHAM/PORC PO16 * 11 L8
Carnarvon Rd BMTH BH1 226 E4
GPORT PO12 14 C4
NEND PO2 184 F8
Carnation Rd ROWN SO16 147 J4
Carne Cl CHFD SO53 133 J8
Carnegie Cl PSTN BH14 224 D3
Carnegie Rd NWBY RG14 18 F5
Carolina Pl EWKG RG40 42 A1
Caroline Av CHCH/BSGR BH23 228 E3
Caroline Gdns FHAM PO15 181 J2
Caroline Pl GPORT PO12 14 F1
Caroline Rd BWD BH11 213 H5
Caroline Wy FRIM GU16 51 H7
Carolyn Cl ITCH SO19 161 L6
Carpathia Cl WEND SO18 148 A2
Carpenter Cl ENEY PO4 * 193 G5
FAWY SO45 177 G4
LYMN SO41 221 K3
Carpenter Rd RWIN SO21 273 N2
Carpenters NARL SO24 291 M11
Carpenters Cl HTWY RG27 46 F7
Carpenter's Ct KBH RG22 92 F2
Carpenter's Down CHIN RG24 65 K2
Carran Wk FHAM/STUB PO14 10 B9
Carraway FHAM PO15 164 D5
Carrbridge Cl TWDS BH3 225 K1
Carrbridge Rd TWDS BH3 225 K1
Carrick La YTLY GU46 49 G2
Carrick Wy NMIL/BTOS BH25 219 J6
Carrington Cl LYMN SO41 232 E4
Carrington Crs TADY RG26 44 B4
Carrington La ASHV GU12 61 M8
LYMN SO41 232 E3
Carroll Av FERN BH22 209 K3
Carroll Cl BKME/WDN BH12 225 G2
ELGH SO50 141 K3
Carronade Wk HSEA PO3 184 F3
Carshalton Av CHAM PO6 169 H8
Carsworth Wy CFDH BH17 212 A6
Carters Av PLE BH15 222 D4
Carter's Clay Rd ROMY SO51 129 H3
Carter's Cl FBDG SP6 332 F5
Carter's La PLE BH15 223 J6
TOTT SO40 175 L3
Carter's Meadow AND SP10 95 M2
Carters Wk FNM GU9 72 D8
Carthage Cl CHFD SO53 139 M1
Carthagena RWIN SO21 274 D8
Carthona Dr FLEETS GU52 71 H1
Cartref Cl VWD BH31 201 H2
Cartwright Cl NBNE BH10 213 J4
Cartwright Dr FHAM PO15 180 F2
Carvers La RGWD BH24 203 J5
Cary Cl NWBY RG14 33 K6
Carysfort Rd BMTH BH1 226 D4
Cascades Ap PSEA PO1 21 G1
Cashmoor Cl
BKME/WDN BH12 224 F1
Cask St PSEA PO1 * 192 C2
Caslake Cl NMIL/BTOS BH25 218 F7
Caspar John Cl
FHAM/STUB PO14 189 H3
Caspian Cl HLER SO31 164 B5
Cassel Av WBNE BH4 225 H7
Cassino Cl ALDT GU11 3 G2
Casterbridge La RAND SP11 94 F2
Casterbridge Rd FERN BH22 209 H5
Castle Av CHCH/BSGR BH23 217 L8
HAV PO9 17 K5
Castle Cl CBLY GU15 51 H4
LYMN SO41 232 E5
SSEA PO5 21 G6
WIMB BH21 336 F5
Castle Ct RAND SP11 265 L9
WSHM SO15 160 A2
Castlecraig Ct SHST GU47 * 49 M1
Castledene Crs PSTN BH14 224 A6
Castle Farm La WHAM PO17 152 B6
Castle Fld FNM GU9 12 E2
Castle Gate Cl CHAR BH8 214 C6
Castle Gv FHAM/PORC PO16 183 K1
NWBY RG14 27 H7
Castle Hl FNM GU9 12 D2
THLE RG7 239 J9
Castle Hill La RGWD BH24 342 F12
WIMB BH21 336 F6
Castle La CHFD SO53 139 G4
FAWY SO45 355 P9
NBAD SO52 138 B4
NWBY RG14 27 G8
RSAL SP5 327 N3
SHAM SO14 22 F5
Castle La East LTDN BH7 215 H8
Castle La West
MOOR/WNTN BH9 214 B5
Castlemain Av SBNE BH6 227 J3
Castlemans La HISD PO11 187 G7
Castleman Trailway
CFDH BH17 210 E8
FERN BH22 204 E5
RGWD BH24 205 M3
WIMB BH21 207 J8
WIMB BH21 208 D1
Castleman Wy RGWD BH24 203 J6
Castlemews RGWD BH24 202 E7
Castle Point CHAR BH8 * 214 E6
Castle Ri ODIM RG29 68 E4
WINC SO23 289 J7
Castle Rd ALDT GU11 2 A1
BSTK RG21 6 F8
CBLY GU15 51 H3
HAV PO9 157 G6
HLER SO31 162 B6
MOOR/WNTN BH9 213 M7
SSEA PO5 20 F7
WEND SO18 147 L6
WHAM PO17 167 M2
Castle Rw GPORT PO12 * 15 L4
Castleshaw Cl ROWN SO16 159 M1
Castle Sq SHAM SO14 22 F5
Castle St ALTN GU34 293 J1
CHCH/BSGR BH23 228 B2
FHAM/PORC PO16 183 K1
FHAM/STUB PO14 180 F4
FLEETS GU52 71 H1
FNM GU9 12 F2
PLE BH15 223 J7
RAND SP11 265 L9
SHAM SO14 161 G1
WIMB BH21 336 F5
Castleton Av NBNE BH10 213 K2
Castle Vw GPORT PO12 183 H8
Castle View Rd
FHAM/PORC PO16 183 K2
Castleway HAV PO9 17 K5
Castle Wy SHAM SO14 22 F4
Castlewood CHFD SO53 * 139 J4
RGWD BH24 202 F7
Castle Woods RSAL SP5 332 F2
Castor Ct FLEETS GU52 71 K3
YTLY GU46 48 D1
Caswall Ride YTLY GU46 49 G3
Caswell Cl FARN GU14 60 F2
Catalina Cl CHCH/BSGR BH23 229 G2
Catalina Dr PLE BH15 223 L7
Catamaran Cl HLER SO31 179 M3
Catchmoor RSAL SP5 * 327 K8
Cateran Cl ROWN SO16 145 M8
Caterham Cl CHOB/PIR GU24 63 L2
Catesby Gdns YTLY GU46 48 C3
Cathay Gdns FAWY SO45 176 C5
Cathedral Vw WINC SO23 25 J8
Catherine Cl HEND SO30 148 E2
Catherine Crs RSAL SP5 331 R1
Catherine Gdns HEND SO30 148 E2
Catherine Rd NWBY RG14 18 E6
Catherines Wk RAND SP11 270 H1
Catherington La HORN PO8 321 J11
Catherington Wy HAV PO9 170 F4
Catisfield La FHAM PO15 181 H3
Catisfield Rd ENEY PO4 193 H4
FHAM PO15 181 J3
Catkin Cl CHIN RG24 54 B5
Catmint Cl CHFD SO53 138 F1
Caton Cl BKME/WDN BH12 213 H8
Cattistock Rd CHAR BH8 214 E7
Cattle La RAND SP11 95 J8
Caunter Rd NWBY RG14 26 F8
Causeway Crs TOTT SO40 145 G8
Causeway Farm HORN PO8 156 B2
The Causeway EPSF GU31 120 D7
FHAM/PORC PO16 166 E7
HTWY RG27 240 C5
RSAL SP5 282 G10
STOK SO20 284 B2
Causton Rd DEAN RG23 92 D8
Cavalier Cl CHIN RG24 66 E2
FAWY SO45 176 C5
NWBY RG14 27 L7
Cavalier Rd CHIN RG24 66 E2
Cavalier Wy ALTN GU34 106 D6
Cavalry Ct ALDT GU11 2 B3
Cavan Crs CFDH BH17 211 H7
Cavanna Cl LSOL/BMARY PO13 182 B5
Cavan's Rd ALDT GU11 73 J2
Cavel Ct CHIN RG24 54 C8
Cavell Dr CHAM PO6 168 E7
Cavendish Cl ROMY SO51 131 H7
WVILLE PO7 * 155 M8
Cavendish Ct BLKW GU17 49 M5
NWBY RG14 28 A7
Cavendish Dr WVILLE PO7 169 M1
Cavendish Gdns FLEETS GU52 71 G3
Cavendish Gv WINC SO23 123 H1
WSHM SO15 146 F8
Cavendish Ms ALDT GU11 2 E5
WSHM SO15 146 F8
Cavendish Pl BMTH BH1 9 G2
Cavendish Rd ALDT GU11 2 F4
BMTH BH1 9 G2
FLEETS GU52 71 H4
SSEA PO5 21 J7
WCLF BH2 8 F2
C Av FAWY SO45 354 F3
Caversham Cl HEND SO30 148 D4
ITCH SO19 148 A8
PLE BH15 222 E5
Caves Farm Cl SHST GU47 43 J8
Cawdor Rd TWDS BH3 225 K1
Cawte Rd WSHM SO15 160 C2
Caxton Av ITCH SO19 148 B6
Caxton Cl AND SP10 95 L3
CHCH/BSGR BH23 228 F1
Cayman Cl CHIN RG24 65 L3
Cecil Av CHAR BH8 214 C8
ROWN SO16 146 B7
TOTT SO40 158 C6
Cecil Cl WIMB BH21 210 E2
Cecil Gv SSEA PO5 20 F7
Cecil Hl CHAR BH8 214 B8
Cecil Pl SSEA PO5 20 F7
Cecil Rd BKME/WDN BH12 224 D2
BOSC BH5 226 E4
ITCH SO19 161 M5
Cedar Av BLKW GU17 49 M3
CHCH/BSGR BH23 215 K8
NBNE BH10 213 K2
RGWD BH24 205 M5
RGWD BH24 * 346 E1
WSHM SO15 146 D8
Cedar Cl ASHV GU12 73 L8
GPORT PO12 183 G7
HEND SO30 149 J5
HLER SO31 162 F4
TADY RG26 44 D6
UPTN BH16 210 B8
WINC SO23 288 H8
WVILLE PO7 169 L2
Cedar Ct HASM GU27 118 C6
Cedar Crs HORN PO8 156 C3
NBAD SO52 137 M3
Cedar Dr FLEETN GU51 59 L7
KSCL RG20 248 C10
LYMN SO41 220 D8
WIMB BH21 208 B3
Cedar Gdns HAV PO9 17 G2
SHAM SO14 147 G8
Cedar Gv HSEA PO3 193 H1
STHA RG19 35 J1
Cedar Lawn ROMY SO51 131 J7
Cedar Ldg HASM GU27 * 118 E7
Cedarmount LYND SO43 345 K4
Cedar Mt NWBY RG14 33 M4
Cedar Pl CHCH/BSGR BH23 348 D11
Cedar Rd ELGH SO50 139 L7
FARN GU14 61 J5
FAWY SO45 354 C1
SHAM SO14 147 G8
Cedars Cl SHST GU47 43 H8
The Cedars FHAM/PORC PO16 10 C1
FLEETN GU51 59 K8
Cedars Vw RSAL SP5 298 A5
Cedar Ter HTWY RG27 * 57 K3
Cedar Tree Cl DEAN RG23 91 J4
Cedar Vw FLEETS GU52 71 K2
Cedar Wk AND SP10 4 A8
FUFL SO22 * 24 D6
Cedar Wy DEAN RG23 64 F5
FERN BH22 204 E8
FHAM/STUB PO14 10 A7
Cedarways FNM GU9 78 F1
Cedarwood CHIN RG24 * 54 A5
WINC SO23 289 J9
Cedar Wood Cl ELGH SO50 141 L2
TOTT SO40 144 C8
Cedric Cl FAWY SO45 354 H8
Celandine Av HLER SO31 179 M2
HORN PO8 156 B5
Celandine Cl CHCH/BSGR BH23 217 H8
CHFD SO53 138 F3
CWTH RG45 43 L2
Celandine Ct YTLY GU46 48 C1
Celandine Gv NTHA RG18 35 M1
Celia Cl WVILLE PO7 156 B8
Cellars Farm Rd SBNE BH6 228 A5
Celtic Dr AND SP10 4 C8
Cement Ter SHAM SO14 22 F5
Cemetery Av PLE BH15 223 M2
Cemetery Hl ODIM RG29 69 G6
Cemetery La EMRTH PO10 172 C3
OVTN RG25 257 K3
WVILLE PO7 154 F3
Cemetery Rd FLEETN GU51 71 G1
WIMB BH21 207 H3
WSHM SO15 146 E8
Centaur St NEND PO2 184 D8
Centaury Gdns ELGH SO50 141 J5
Centenary Cl LYMN SO41 350 G10
Centenary Gdns HAV PO9 16 F3
Centenary Wy BMTH BH1 226 E3
Central Av BKME/WDN BH12 224 E2
WIMB BH21 210 D1
Central Br SHAM SO14 23 J5
Central Dr FERN BH22 * 205 K8
WCLF BH2 8 D2
Central Rd BOR GU35 110 F6
CHAM PO6 185 J1
FHAM/PORC PO16 183 H1
SHAM SO14 23 H7
Central Sq WHAM PO17 165 L5
Central Station Br WSHM SO15 22 C2
Central St PSEA PO1 21 J1
RAND SP11 265 M10
Central Wy AND SP10 97 G3
Centre Dr CHIN RG24 54 B7
Centre La LYMN SO41 220 E7
Centre Pl RGWD BH24 203 H5
Centre Terrace Rd FARN GU14 61 G8
Centre Wy HLER SO31 180 A1
Centurion Cl SHST GU47 43 M8
Centurion Ga ENEY PO4 193 K5
Centurion Wy KBH RG22 92 D6
Century Cl OVTN RG25 93 J5
Century Dr THLE RG7 238 C7
Cerdic Ms HLER SO31 163 G8
Cerne Cl MOOR/WNTN BH9 214 B4
NBAD SO52 137 L4
WEND SO18 148 B3
Chadderton Gdns PSEA PO1 20 E6
Chaddesley Gln CCLF BH13 237 J2
Chaddesley Pines CCLF BH13 237 K2
Chaddesley Wood Rd
CCLF BH13 237 K3
Chadswell Meadow HAV PO9 16 A4
Chadwell Av ITCH SO19 148 B8
Chadwick Rd ELGH SO50 139 M6
Chafen Rd WEND SO18 147 K8
Chaffers Cl ODIM RG29 258 B6
Chaffey Cl RGWD BH24 203 L4
Chaffinch Cl CFDH BH17 210 F7
KBH RG22 92 C4
NMIL/BTOS BH25 218 F6
TOTT SO40 144 C8
Chaffinch Gn HORN PO8 155 L4
Chaffinch Wy
FHAM/PORC PO16 166 F8
LSOL/BMARY PO13 189 M5
Chalbury Ct CFDH BH17 212 A6
Chalcraft Cl LIPH GU30 116 A4
Chalcrafts ALTN GU34 107 G3
Chaldecott Gdns NBNE BH10 213 J4
Chaldon Rd CFDH BH17 211 M6
Chale Cl LSOL/BMARY PO13 182 C6
Chalet Hl BOR GU35 113 G1
Chalewood Rd FAWY SO45 354 G9
Chalfont Av CHCH/BSGR BH23 215 K5
Chalfont Dr FARN GU14 61 J6
Chalford Rd NWBY RG14 18 A5
Chalice Ct HEND SO30 149 G6
Chalk Cl ALTN GU34 293 M6
Chalkcroft La RAND SP11 83 H8
Chalk Hl BPWT SO32 319 J7
STOK SO20 286 D11
WEND SO18 148 C3
Chalk La MFD/CHID GU8 261 P8
WHAM PO17 166 B1
Chalkpit La RAND SP11 94 F7
Chalk Pit La RSAL SP5 297 P3
Chalkpit Rd CHAM PO6 168 B6
Chalk Rdg HORN PO8 321 M9
WINC SO23 25 M7
Chalkridge Rd CHAM PO6 169 G7
Chalk's Cl RSAL SP5 332 F1
Chalk V CHIN RG24 66 E3
STOK SO20 286 D12
Chalky Copse HTWY RG27 56 C6
Chalky Hl ALTN GU34 292 E2
Chalky La HTWY RG27 70 B5
Challenger Wy FAWY SO45 176 D4
Challenor Cl EWKG RG40 42 B1
Challis Cl KBH RG22 92 E2
Challis Ct RAND SP11 265 N10
SHAM SO14 23 H5
Challoner Cl KBH RG22 92 E1
Chalmers Wy HLER SO31 178 E1
Chaloner Crs FAWY SO45 177 G7
Chalton Crs HAV PO9 170 D3
Chalton La HORN PO8 321 K6
Chalvington Rd CHFD SO53 139 J4
Chalybeate Cl ROWN SO16 146 B6
Chamberhouse Mill Rd
STHA RG19 35 M3
Chamberlain Gv
FHAM/STUB PO14 10 E8
Chamberlain Rd PTSW SO17 147 G5
Chamberlain's Gdns WHIT RG2 239 L6
Chamber La RFNM GU10 76 A8
Chamberlayne Rd ELGH SO50 140 A3
HLER SO31 162 A6
HLER SO31 162 F4
Chambers Av ROMY SO51 137 H1
Chambers Cl ROWN SO16 145 J3
Chambers Rd ASHV GU12 74 B2
Chamomile Gdns FARN GU14 60 C3
Champion Cl LYMN SO41 232 E4
Champion Wy FLEETS GU52 71 J3
Champney Cl BOR GU35 112 E3
Chancellors La BPWT SO32 149 L1
Chancel Rd HLER SO31 180 B1
Chander Cl FERN BH22 209 L4
Chandler Rd BSTK RG21 93 J2
Chandlers Cl HISD PO11 195 J5
LTDN BH7 215 H8
Chandlers La YTLY GU46 48 E1
Chandlers Rd ASHV GU12 74 B4
Chandlers Wy HLER SO31 164 B6
Chandos Av BKME/WDN BH12 213 G8
Chandos Ri PSEA PO1 * 21 H2
Chandos Rd NWBY RG14 33 M4
Chandos St SHAM SO14 23 H5
Channels Farm Rd
ROWN SO16 147 K3
Channel Wy SHAM SO14 23 L7
Chant Cl CHCH/BSGR BH23 228 D1
RAND SP11 272 D6
Chantrell Wk FHAM PO15 181 K1
Chantreys FLEETN GU51 58 F8
Chantry Cl CHCH/BSGR BH23 217 M7
FNM GU9 12 B4
HTWY RG27 56 C8
Chantry La RAND SP11 80 A3
Chantry Ms KBH RG22 92 D5
Chantry Rd GPORT PO12 190 F1
HORN PO8 321 K12
SHAM SO14 23 K5
The Chantrys FNM GU9 12 B5
Chantry St AND SP10 5 H5
The Chantry
FHAM/STUB PO14 180 C1
Chantry Wy AND SP10 5 H5
Chapel Cl CHIN RG24 66 D1
OVTN RG25 103 M3
RAND SP11 94 D6
ROMY SO51 * 131 K2
STOK SO20 285 L11
WIMB BH21 210 C2
Chapel Ct NTHA RG18 29 G8
Chapel Crs ITCH SO19 148 A8
Chapel Dro ELGH SO50 141 J5
HEND SO30 149 H6
Chapel Gdns BOR GU35 111 H7
Chapel Hl BSTK RG21 6 D3
RSAL SP5 327 R2
Chapel La BPWT SO32 150 E4
BROC SO42 353 J10
CHCH/BSGR BH23 346 C9
ELGH SO50 134 B3
FARN GU14 50 B8
FAWY SO45 354 G8
LYMN SO41 350 H11
LYND SO43 345 K4
PLE BH15 223 J6
RAND SP11 84 D6
RAND SP11 251 L12
RAND SP11 265 L10
RAND SP11 269 P4
RGWD BH24 349 K1
ROMY SO51 128 E2
ROMY SO51 299 M12
RSAL SP5 324 D5
RSAL SP5 327 K7
RSAL SP5 332 G2
RSAL SP5 334 A9
RWIN SO21 302 A2
STHA RG19 249 K3
STOK SO20 284 D9
TADY RG26 249 K8
THLE RG7 38 F7
THLE RG7 238 B6
THLE RG7 240 C1
TOTT SO40 158 E3
WIMB BH21 200 B1
WIMB BH21 207 H3
WIMB BH21 210 C3
Chapel Md HTWY RG27 42 A8
Chapel Pond Dr ODIM RG29 68 E5
Chapel Ri RGWD BH24 347 K2
Chapel River Cl AND SP10 4 B6
Chapel Rd BPWT SO32 318 B7
BPWT SO32 318 H10
BPWT SO32 319 J1
CBLY GU15 50 D3
HEND SO30 148 E2
HLER SO31 163 L6
KSCL RG20 26 A6
PSTN BH14 224 A4
RFNM GU10 109 L1
SHAM SO14 23 J4
Chapel Rw HTWY RG27 57 M2
Chapelside FHAM/STUB PO14 181 G4
Chapel Sq CBLY GU15 50 B2
Chapel St FARN GU14 61 K2
GPORT PO12 183 H8
NEND PO2 * 184 E8
NTHA RG18 35 L1
OVTN RG25 103 G3
PSF GU32 120 D5
PSF GU32 314 B8
SSEA PO5 * 20 F6
Chaplains Av HORN PO8 155 K5
Chaplains Cl HORN PO8 155 K4
Chaplain's Hl CWTH RG45 43 M4
Chaplins Ter NTID SP9 * 266 F1
Chappell Cl LIPH GU30 116 C4
Chapter Ter HTWY RG27 57 M2
Charborough Rd BDST BH18 211 H5
Charden Rd ELGH SO50 141 G3
LSOL/BMARY PO13 182 D8
Charfield Cl FHAM/STUB PO14 181 K4
FUFL SO22 122 E7
Charing Cl RGWD BH24 203 J6
Charity Vw WHAM PO17 165 L5
Chark La LSOL/BMARY PO13 189 M4
Charlcot Cl WHCH RG28 99 L1
Charlcot Farm WHCH RG28 99 L1
Charldon Gn CHIN RG24 54 C8
Charlecote Cl FARN GU14 61 K5
Charlecote Dr CHFD SO53 133 G8
Charledown Cl OVTN RG25 89 J5
Charledown Rd OVTN RG25 89 J5
Charlemont Dr
FHAM/PORC PO16 11 M5
Charlesbury Av GPORT PO12 14 A5
Charles Cl HTWY RG27 56 C7
WINC SO23 123 G2
WVILLE PO7 169 K2
Charles Crs NMIL/BTOS BH25 219 H3
Charles Dalton Ct AND SP10 * 5 G6
Charles Dickens St PSEA PO1 21 G3
Charles Gdns NBNE BH10 213 J6
Charles Hl RFNM GU10 260 C10
Charles Keightley Ct
WIMB BH21 207 K5
Charles Knott Gdns
WSHM SO15 160 F1
Charles Richards Cl
BSTK RG21 6 D8
Charles Rd CHCH/BSGR BH23 216 F8
PLE BH15 223 K5
Charles's La RGWD BH24 347 R2
Charles St CBLY GU15 50 E3
KBH RG22 64 F8
NWBY RG14 33 K6
PSEA PO1 21 J1
PSF GU32 120 C6
SHAM SO14 23 H5
Charleston Cl HISD PO11 194 E4
Charleston Rd FAWY SO45 177 K8
Charles Watts Wy HEND SO30 148 E5
Charles Wy WVILLE PO7 155 K7
Charlesworth Dr WVILLE PO7 155 K7
Charlesworth Gdns
WVILLE PO7 155 K7
Charliejoy Gdns SHAM SO14 161 J2
Charlie Soar Ct ELGH SO50 140 A2
Charlock Cl NTHA RG18 29 G7
Charlotte Cl AND SP10 96 F4
BKME/WDN BH12 225 J1
CHCH/BSGR BH23 229 G2
FNM GU9 72 D8

Charlotte Dr GPORT PO12 191 J1
Charlotte Pl SHAM SO14 161 G2
WSHM SO15 23 G1
Charlotte St PSEA PO1 21 G1
Charlton Cl LYMN SO41 219 M5
MOOR/WNTN BH9 214 C4
Charlton Ct SHST GU47 43 M7
Charlton La THLE RG7 238 C11
Charlton Pl NWBY RG14 18 F2
Charlton Rd AND SP10 4 E3
WSHM SO15 160 D1
Charlwood La ALTN GU34 293 N12
Charminster Av
MOOR/WNTN BH9 214 B7
Charminster Cl
MOOR/WNTN BH9 214 B6
WVILLE PO7 155 L8
Charminster Pl
MOOR/WNTN BH9 * 214 C6
Charminster Rd CHAR BH8 214 B7
Charmouth Gv PSTN BH14 224 A4
Charmouth Ter ROWN SO16 * 146 A7
Charmus Rd TOTT SO40 144 B6
Charmwen Crs HEND SO30 148 C2
Charmwood Cl NWBY RG14 27 H7
Charnock Cl LYMN SO41 219 M5
Charnwood
LSOL/BMARY PO13 182 D6
Charnwood Av
MOOR/WNTN BH9 214 B5
Charnwood Cl AND SP10 5 K8
CHFD SO53 133 J6
FERN BH22 205 G6
KBH RG22 92 D1
TOTT SO40 144 D7
Charnwood Crs CHFD SO53 133 J6
Charnwood Dr FBDG SP6 197 G2
Charnwood Gdns CHFD SO53 133 J6
Charnwood Wy FAWY SO45 354 F9
Charterhouse Wy HEND SO30 149 H3
Charter Rd BWD BH11 212 D2
NWBY RG14 33 M4
Charter Wk HASM GU27 * 118 C6
Chart House Rd ASHV GU12 74 A1
Chartwell FNM GU9 78 D2
FRIM GU16 61 L3
Chartwell Cl ELGH SO50 134 B6
FHAM/STUB PO14 180 C3
Chartwell Dr HAV PO9 17 L1
Chartwell Gdns ALDT GU11 73 J1
Chase Cl LISS GU33 308 G8
Chase Farm Cl BPWT SO32 151 L1
Chase Fld ALTN GU34 294 D6
Chase Gv BPWT SO32 151 L1
Chase La HASM GU27 118 E8
Chase Pln GSHT GU26 * 115 J7
Chase Rd BOR GU35 111 H7
LISS GU33 308 G8
Chaseside LTDN BH7 215 G8
The Chase CWTH RG45 43 J2
FARN GU14 61 K2
FHAM/STUB PO14 180 D2
GPORT PO12 14 A5
NWBY RG14 27 H5
RGWD BH24 202 F7
VWD BH31 201 L2
Chasewater Av HSEA PO3 193 G1
Chatburn Av HORN PO8 155 M5
Chatfield Av NEND PO2 184 A7
Chatfield Cl FARN GU14 61 J6
Chatfield Rd
LSOL/BMARY PO13 182 B4
Chatham Cl GPORT PO12 191 J1
Chatham Dr PSEA PO1 20 E7
Chatham Rd FUFL SO22 122 C7
Chatsworth Av CHAM PO6 185 G2
HASM GU27 118 C4
Chatsworth Cl FHAM PO15 181 J3
Chatsworth Dr AND SP10 4 B7
Chatsworth Gn KBH RG22 92 E6
Chatsworth Gv FNM GU9 76 F2
Chatsworth Hts CBLY GU15 51 J1
Chatsworth Rd CHAR BH8 226 B2
ELGH SO50 134 B6
FARN GU14 61 L5
ITCH SO19 148 A7
PSTN BH14 224 B3
Chatsworth Wy
NMIL/BTOS BH25 218 E5
The Chatters THLE RG7 239 J9
Chaucer Av AND SP10 4 A2
CHAM PO6 167 L7
Chaucer Cl CHIN RG24 65 L3
FHAM/PORC PO16 10 D4
RWIN SO21 288 E3
WIMB BH21 207 J2
WVILLE PO7 155 L6
Chaucer Crs NWBY RG14 27 G7
Chaucer Dr LYMN SO41 232 D3
Chaucer Gv CBLY GU15 50 F3
Chaucer Rd CCLF BH13 224 E8
CWTH RG45 43 K4
FARN GU14 60 F2
ITCH SO19 148 D6
Chaucombe Pl
NMIL/BTOS BH25 218 F7
Chaundler Rd WINC SO23 25 H1
Chaundlers Cft RFNM GU10 259 P3
Chauntsingers Rd ALTN GU34 106 F4
Chaveney Cl FAWY SO45 176 F7
Chawton Cl FLEETN GU51 58 E5
FUFL SO22 288 D12
WEND SO18 148 D4
Chawton Park Rd ALTN GU34 106 B8
Cheam Rd BDST BH18 210 F4
Cheam Wy TOTT SO40 144 D7
Cheap St NWBY RG14 18 E4
Cheavley Cl AND SP10 95 L4
Cheddar Cl ITCH SO19 161 L5
Cheddington Rd
MOOR/WNTN BH9 214 A4
Chedington Cl CFDH BH17 211 L6
Chedworth Crs CHAM PO6 168 A7
Cheesecombe Farm La
LISS GU33 307 R6
Cheesemans La RCCH PO18 173 J2
Cheetah Rd FARN GU14 61 H6
Chelmer Ct BSTK RG21 7 J5
Chelmsford Rd NEND PO2 184 F6
UPTN BH16 222 B1
Chelsea Rd SSEA PO5 21 K7
Cheltenham Crs
LSOL/BMARY PO13 189 M6
Cheltenham Gdns HEND SO30 149 J2
Cheltenham Rd
BKME/WDN BH12 224 C3
CHAM PO6 168 C8
Chelveston Crs ROWN SO16 145 M4
Chelwood Dr SHST GU47 43 H7
Chene Rd WIMB BH21 207 K4
Cheping Gdns HEND SO30 150 A6
Chepstow Cl CHFD SO53 139 H2
TOTT SO40 144 C8
Chepstow Ct WVILLE PO7 156 B7
Chequer La THLE RG7 41 L6
Chequers La HTWY RG27 48 A1
Chequers Rd BSTK RG21 6 F5
Cherberry Cl FLEETN GU51 59 K4
Cherbourg Rd ELGH SO50 139 M7
Cherford Rd BWD BH11 213 H6
Cherita Ct PLE BH15 223 M2
Cheriton Av LTDN BH7 215 J8
WEND SO18 148 C5
Cheriton Cl FUFL SO22 24 B3
HAV PO9 170 D3
HORN PO8 156 A1
NWBY RG14 19 G8
TADY RG26 44 B5
Cheriton La NARL SO24 304 C3
Cheriton Rd ELGH SO50 139 M8
FUFL SO22 24 C3
GPORT PO12 14 B4
Cheriton Wy BLKW GU17 49 M3
WIMB BH21 207 J2
Cherque La LSOL/BMARY PO13 182 A8
Cherrett Cl BWD BH11 212 F4
Cherries Dr MOOR/WNTN BH9 213 L6
Cherrimans Orch HASM GU27 117 M2
Cherry Cl HTWY RG27 56 D6
LSOL/BMARY PO13 189 M7
NWBY RG14 18 D1
PSTN BH14 224 B4
RWIN SO21 288 D4
Cherrydale Rd CBLY GU15 51 M3
Cherry Dro ELGH SO50 141 J6
Cherry Gdns BPWT SO32 143 K5
Cherrygarth Rd FHAM PO15 181 J3
Cherry Gv FERN BH22 209 J2
Cherryhill Gv ALDT GU11 2 C5
Cherry Hill Gv UPTN BH16 222 B2
Cherry Ldg ASHV GU12 * 3 H4
Cherryton Gdns FAWY SO45 354 D5
Cherry Tree Av
FHAM/STUB PO14 181 K4
HASM GU27 117 M1
HORN PO8 156 B6
NTID SP9 266 G1
Cherry Tree Cl FARN GU14 * 60 C3
LYMN SO41 220 D8
RGWD BH24 205 M5
SHST GU47 43 M7
Cherry Tree Dr
NMIL/BTOS BH25 218 E3
Cherry Tree Gv WWKG RG41 239 R4
Cherry Tree Rd AND SP10 4 C2
RFNM GU10 109 L1
Cherry Wk WSHM SO15 146 C8
Cherryway ALTN GU34 106 E3
Cherrywood CHIN RG24 * 54 A5
HEND SO30 149 H6
Cherrywood Gdns TOTT SO40 158 C1
HISD PO11 194 F4
Cherrywood Rd FARN GU14 61 G1
Chervil Cl CHFD SO53 138 F2
HORN PO8 321 L11
Cherville St ROMY SO51 130 E8
Cherwell Crs ROWN SO16 145 L8
Cherwell Gdns CHFD SO53 139 K3
Cheshire Cl FHAM PO15 164 F7
Cheshire Dr CHAR BH8 215 G6
Cheshire Wy EMRTH PO10 172 E4
Chesildene Av CHAR BH8 214 D6
Chesildene Dr CHAR BH8 214 D5
Chesil St WINC SO23 25 J7
Chesil Ter WINC SO23 25 J7
Chesilton Crs FLEETS GU52 71 J4
Chesil Wd WINC SO23 * 25 M7
Cheslyn Rd HSEA PO3 193 H2
Chessel Av BOSC BH5 226 F4
ITCH SO19 161 L1
Chessel Crs ITCH SO19 161 M2
Chester Cl ASHV GU12 74 B6
NWBY RG14 19 K9
Chester Crs
LSOL/BMARY PO13 190 B4
Chesterfield Cl CCLF BH13 224 F8
Chesterfield Rd BSTK RG21 7 H8
HSEA PO3 193 G1
NWBY RG14 18 E7
Chester Pl BSTK RG21 6 C7
SSEA PO5 21 J8
Chester Rd ASHV GU12 74 B5
CCLF BH13 225 G6
WEND SO18 148 A3
WINC SO23 25 J6
Chesters Rd CBLY GU15 51 K3
Chesterton Gdns HORN PO8 155 L5
Chesterton Pl FHAM PO15 164 C4
Chesterton Rd NTHA RG18 28 E7
Chester Wy RFNM GU10 260 D2
Chestnut Av AND SP10 4 F9
ASHV GU12 260 C1
CBLY GU15 51 J2
CHCH/BSGR BH23 215 K8
CHFD SO53 139 J5
ENEY PO4 192 F4
FNM GU9 12 C8
FUFL SO22 288 C11
HASM GU27 118 C5
HAV PO9 170 B5
HORN PO8 156 C3
NMIL/BTOS BH25 219 G8
NTID SP9 266 F1
RGWD BH24 198 D6
RWIN SO21 134 F3
SBNE BH6 227 J4
TOTT SO40 158 C5
WWKG RG41 239 Q2
Chestnut Bank CHIN RG24 66 D1
Chestnut Cl ALTN GU34 106 E3
BLKW GU17 * 50 A3
CHFD SO53 139 J6
FLEETN GU51 59 L4
GSHT GU26 115 H5
LIPH GU30 116 D5
ROMY SO51 137 K2
WVILLE PO7 154 F4
Chestnut Ct ASHV GU12 3 M3
BOR GU35 113 G2
Chestnut Crs NWBY RG14 18 F1
STOK SO20 270 D8
WHIT RG2 238 E4
Chestnut End BOR GU35 111 M8
Chestnut Gv FLEETN GU51 59 K6
WIMB BH21 208 E2
Chestnut Pl STOK SO20 270 D8
Chestnut Ri BPWT SO32 318 G3
ELGH SO50 139 K7
Chestnut Rd BROC SO42 351 L3
FARN GU14 61 G3
ROWN SO16 146 A6
Chestnut Sq STOK SO20 270 D8
The Chestnuts HLER SO31 180 A2
Chestnut Wk GPORT PO12 183 G8
Chestnut Wy
CHCH/BSGR BH23 216 C5
FHAM/STUB PO14 180 C3
Cheswell Gdns FLEETN GU51 71 G2
Chetnole Cl CFDH BH17 211 M7
Chettle Rd ITCH SO19 148 E7
Chetwode Pl ALDT GU11 3 K8
Chetwode Ter ALDT GU11 2 A4
Chetwode Wy CFDH BH17 211 H6
Chetwynd Dr ROWN SO16 146 F4
Chetwynd Rd ENEY PO4 21 L6
ROWN SO16 146 F4
Chevening Ct ENEY PO4 * 193 H3
Cheviot Cl CBLY GU15 51 L4
FARN GU14 60 E1
KBH RG22 92 D1
NWBY RG14 33 J7
Cheviot Dr FAWY SO45 176 D5
FLEETN GU51 59 K4
Cheviot Gn HLER SO31 179 K4
Cheviot Rd ROWN SO16 145 L8
SHST GU47 43 H7
Cheviot Wk
FHAM/STUB PO14 181 M5
Cheviot Wy VWD BH31 201 H3
Chewter Cl ENEY PO4 192 E7
Chewton Common Rd
CHCH/BSGR BH23 218 A7
Chewton Farm Rd
CHCH/BSGR BH23 218 C7
Chewton Ldg
CHCH/BSGR BH23 218 B8
Chewton Wy
CHCH/BSGR BH23 218 B7
Cheylesmore Dr FRIM GU16 51 M5
Cheyne Gdns WBNE BH4 225 J6
Cheyne Wy FARN GU14 60 F1
LSOL/BMARY PO13 189 M7
Chichester Av HISD PO11 194 F6
Chichester Cl AND SP10 4 A4
HEND SO30 149 J3
HLER SO31 179 L1
LSOL/BMARY PO13 182 B6
ROMY SO51 335 M6
Chichester Pl KBH RG22 93 G2
Chichester Rd ASHV GU12 74 A5
HISD PO11 187 J7
NEND PO2 184 E8
RGWD BH24 203 L4
WEND SO18 148 A5
Chichester Wk WIMB BH21 207 L7
Chickenhall La ELGH SO50 140 C2
Chickerell Cl
MOOR/WNTN BH9 214 B5
Chick's La MARL SN8 264 F4
Chidden Cl PSF GU32 314 B7
Chidden Holt CHFD SO53 139 G3
Chideock Cl BKME/WDN BH12 224 E2
Chidham Cl HAV PO9 16 D2
Chidham Dr HAV PO9 16 C2
Chidham La RCCH PO18 173 J7
Chidham Rd CHAM PO6 169 G7
Chidham Sq HAV PO9 16 C3
Chidham Wk HAV PO9 16 D2
Chigwell Rd CHAR BH8 214 C7
Chilbolton Av FUFL SO22 24 A4
Chilbolton Ct HAV PO9 171 H2
Chilcomb Cl
LSOL/BMARY PO13 189 M6
Chilcombe Cl HAV PO9 170 E5
Chilcombe Rd SBNE BH6 * 227 H3
Chilcomb La WINC SO23 123 H7
Chilcomb Rd WEND SO18 148 C4
Chilcote Rd HSEA PO3 193 G1
Chilcroft Rd HASM GU27 117 M1
Childerstone Cl LIPH GU30 116 B4
Childe Sq NEND PO2 184 C6
Chilfrome Cl CFDH BH17 211 J7
Chilgrove Rd CHAM PO6 169 J8
Chilham Cl ELGH SO50 134 A5
FRIM GU16 51 H8
Chillandham La RWIN SO21 289 Q3
Chilland La RWIN SO21 289 Q10
Chillenden Ct TOTT SO40 158 C2
Chillerton HLER SO31 162 C6
Chillingham Wy CBLY GU15 50 E4
Chilling La HLER SO31 179 L7
Chillington Gdns CHFD SO53 133 H7
Chilmark Ct LISS GU33 308 F8
Chilsdown Wy WVILLE PO7 169 L3
Chiltern Av FARN GU14 60 D4
Chiltern Cl FARN GU14 60 C4
FLEETS GU52 71 K3
HASM GU27 118 B7
NMIL/BTOS BH25 218 F7
NWBY RG14 33 J7
TOTT SO40 158 D3
WBNE BH4 225 H3
Chiltern Dr NMIL/BTOS BH25 218 E8
VWD BH31 201 H2
Chiltern Gn ROWN SO16 145 L8
Chiltern Rd SHST GU47 43 H7
Chiltern Wk FHAM/STUB PO14 10 C9
Chiltern Wy KBH RG22 92 C1
Chiltlee Cl LIPH GU30 116 C4
Chiltlee Mnr LIPH GU30 116 C4
Chiltley La LIPH GU30 116 D6
Chiltley Wy LIPH GU30 116 C6
Chilton Farm Pk FARN GU14 * 60 C4
Chilton Rdg KBH RG22 92 D7
Chilworth Cl ROWN SO16 138 D7
Chilworth Dro ROWN SO16 138 D7
Chilworth Gdns HORN PO8 * 321 L8
Chilworth Gv GPORT PO12 14 D2
Chilworth Rd ROWN SO16 138 E7
Chine Av ITCH SO19 161 L2
Chine Cl HLER SO31 164 A8
Chine Crs WCLF BH2 8 B7
Chine Crescent Rd WCLF BH2 8 B7
Chineham Cl FLEETN GU51 58 E5
Chineham Farm Cots
CHIN RG24 65 M3
Chineham La CHIN RG24 65 J2
Chineham Park Ct CHIN RG24 65 M4
The Chine LSOL/BMARY PO13 182 E7
RFNM GU10 78 D3
Chine Wk FERN BH22 209 L7
Chingford Av FARN GU14 61 J3
Chinham Rd TOTT SO40 341 M6
Chinnock Cl FLEETS GU52 71 H1
Chippendale Cl TADY RG26 249 Q3
Chipstead Rd CHAM PO6 168 F8
Chirk Pl ROMY SO51 137 G1
Chisels La CHCH/BSGR BH23 217 H2
Chisholm Cl ROWN SO16 145 M3
Chiswell Rd CFDH BH17 211 K7
Chitty Rd ENEY PO4 193 G6
Chivers Cl KBH RG22 92 D1
SSEA PO5 21 H6
Chivers Dr EWKG RG40 42 A1
Chloe Gdns BKME/WDN BH12 224 D1
Chobham Rd FRIM GU16 51 G6
Cholderton Rd AMSY SP4 268 A5
RAND SP11 269 K1
Cholseley Dr FLEETN GU51 59 G5
Cholsey Cl STHA RG19 35 M1
Chopin Rd KBH RG22 92 F4
Chorley Cl PLE BH15 223 J2
Chris Crs UPTN BH16 * 222 C1
Chrismas Av ASHV GU12 3 K5
Chrismas Pl ASHV GU12 3 K5
Christchurch Bay Rd
NMIL/BTOS BH25 230 F1
Christchurch By-Pass
CHCH/BSGR BH23 228 B1
Christchurch Cl FLEETS GU52 71 H4
Christchurch Dr BLKW GU17 49 L2
Christchurch Gdns CHAM PO6 169 H6
WINC SO23 122 E7
Christchurch Rd BMTH BH1 9 K5
CHCH/BSGR BH23 215 H2
FERN BH22 209 H6
LTDN BH7 226 F3
LYMN SO41 231 M1
NMIL/BTOS BH25 218 E8
RGWD BH24 203 H5
WINC SO23 24 E8
Christie Av HLER SO31 164 C4
Christie Hts NWBY RG14 34 B4
Christie Wk YTLY GU46 48 E4
Christine Cl ASHV GU12 73 M7
Christmas Hl RWIN SO21 274 C10
Christmaspie Av RGUW GU3 75 H7
Christopher Ct NWBY RG14 19 H6
Christopher Crs PLE BH15 223 J2
Christopher Wy EMRTH PO10 171 M6
Christy Ct TADY RG26 44 C5
Christy Est ASHV GU12 * 73 L6
Church Av FARN GU14 61 J6
Church Bank Rd RWIN SO21 276 B7
Church Brook TADY RG26 44 A6
Church Cir FARN GU14 61 J7
Church Cl AND SP10 5 J5
CHOB/PIR GU24 63 M1
ELGH SO50 134 C8
HASM GU27 118 F2
HLER SO31 180 B1
HORN PO8 321 K6
KSCL RG20 32 E6
NBAD SO52 138 A4
Church Ct FLEETN GU51 59 H7
Church End WSHM SO15 160 C1
Churcher Cl GPORT PO12 190 D5
Churcher Rd EMRTH PO10 172 B2
Church Farm FBDG SP6 197 H4
Church Farm Barns THLE RG7 40 D3
Church Farm Cl FAWY SO45 176 B2
OVTN RG25 103 G2
Churchfield VWD BH31 201 G2
Churchfield Crs PLE BH15 223 L4
Churchfield La RGWD BH24 199 G3
Churchfield Rd EPSF GU31 120 F5
PLE BH15 223 L5
Church Flds BOR GU35 111 L7
Churchfields BOR GU35 110 D3
FAWY SO45 355 K5
Churchfields Rd RWIN SO21 124 F6
Church Ga STHA RG19 35 K1
Church Gv FLEETN GU51 59 G7
Church Hams EWKG RG40 239 R10
Church Hatch RSAL SP5 327 L12
Church Hl ALDT GU11 3 J6
CBLY GU15 51 G3
HEND SO30 148 C3
LYMN SO41 232 E3
RSAL SP5 332 H3
STOK SO20 284 C3
VWD BH31 201 G2
WIMB BH21 200 B2
Church Hill Ter RFNM GU10 * 259 P2
Churchill Av ASHV GU12 3 J6
BPWT SO32 143 G3
ODIM RG29 68 F8
Churchill Cl ALTN GU34 106 F6
ALTN GU34 293 M5
FBDG SP6 196 A7
FHAM/STUB PO14 180 C3
HTWY RG27 57 K1
NTID SP9 264 D12
ODIM RG29 68 F8
TADY RG26 44 D5
WINC SO23 288 H7
Churchill Ct HORN PO8 * 156 A2
Churchill Crs
BKME/WDN BH12 224 C2
BOR GU35 111 M8
FARN GU14 50 D8
Churchill Dr EMRTH PO10 171 M4
Churchill Gdns
BKME/WDN BH12 224 C3
Churchill Ms GPORT PO12 * 14 C1
Churchill Plaza BSTK RG21 * 6 F4
Churchill Rd BKME/WDN BH12 224 C3
BMTH BH1 226 D3
WIMB BH21 207 K5
Churchill Sq ENEY PO4 193 H6
Churchill Wy AND SP10 5 L2
BSTK RG21 6 E4
Churchill Wy East BSTK RG21 7 H4
Churchill Wy West AND SP10 4 A1
BSTK RG21 6 A5
KBH RG22 64 F7
Church Lands TADY RG26 53 M1
Church La ALTN GU34 107 J1
ALTN GU34 279 K10
ALTN GU34 306 A9
ASHV GU12 74 B6
BOR GU35 111 K6
BPWT SO32 141 M6
BPWT SO32 150 D4
BPWT SO32 318 C6
BROC SO42 351 L4
BROC SO42 353 K11
CHIN RG24 66 D2
CHCH/BSGR BH23 228 B2
CHOB/PIR GU24 63 K3
DEAN RG23 64 C8
ELGH SO50 134 E4
EWKG RG40 42 A4
EWKG RG40 239 Q7
FARN GU14 60 E4
FAWY SO45 355 J5
FBDG SP6 330 D12
FERN BH22 213 M1
FUFL SO22 288 A10
GSHT GU26 115 J5
HASM GU27 118 C5
HAV PO9 17 K7
HEND SO30 149 H7
HEND SO30 150 A7
HISD PO11 187 J5
HLER SO31 163 H4
HTWY RG27 57 M4
HTWY RG27 240 C6
HUNG RG17 244 D6
KSCL RG20 32 E6
KSCL RG20 245 R4
KSCL RG20 247 J5
LIPH GU30 116 B2
LISS GU33 308 B1
LYMN SO41 221 L5
LYMN SO41 350 F11
LYMN SO41 351 P9
LYND SO43 345 K3
MARL SN8 243 Q2
NARL SO24 291 R12
NARL SO24 292 G12
NARL SO24 304 E8
NMIL/BTOS BH25 218 F7
NTID SP9 266 F4
NWBY RG14 26 F8
OVTN RG25 93 J5
OVTN RG25 105 K3
PSF GU32 313 K3
PTSW SO17 147 H6
RAND SP11 243 N8
RAND SP11 265 L10
RAND SP11 271 Q3
RCCH PO18 173 L1
RFNM GU10 76 B1
RFNM GU10 78 D1
RFNM GU10 109 L1
RFNM GU10 259 L10
RGWD BH24 349 J1
ROMY SO51 128 D5
ROMY SO51 129 L4
ROMY SO51 131 J1
ROMY SO51 136 E1
ROMY SO51 298 H11
ROMY SO51 334 F3
ROWN SO16 144 F3
RSAL SP5 282 A12
RSAL SP5 324 G3
RSAL SP5 327 J7
RWIN SO21 125 G4
RWIN SO21 134 F4
RWIN SO21 289 M11
RWIN SO21 301 N1
STHA RG19 35 K1
STOK SO20 284 C3
STOK SO20 285 L10
TADY RG26 248 H10
THLE RG7 36 F6
THLE RG7 45 L3
THLE RG7 238 B4
THLE RG7 239 K10
WHIT RG2 238 D3
WHIT RG2 239 J4
WINC SO23 289 J10
WVILLE PO7 319 R9
Church Lane Cnr LYMN SO41 * 351 R11
Church La East ALDT GU11 2 F5
Church La West ALDT GU11 2 D5
Church Md LYMN SO41 221 L6
Church Mdw NTID SP9 266 E8
Church Ms RAND SP11 * 95 L8
Churchmoor Rd WIMB BH21 208 A3
Church Pth ASHV GU12 74 A5
EMRTH PO10 171 M8
FHAM/PORC PO16 11 J5
GPORT PO12 15 K5
HORN PO8 156 D2
HTWY RG27 56 B8
Church Pth North PSEA PO1 * 21 H1
Church Rd ALDT GU11 3 J7
ALTN GU34 294 E5
BPWT SO32 151 K5
BPWT SO32 318 B6
CBLY GU15 50 B1
ELGH SO50 134 D7
EMRTH PO10 172 B3
EMRTH PO10 172 D7
FERN BH22 209 J3
FHAM/PORC PO16 183 L2
FLEETN GU51 59 G6
FRIM GU16 50 F8
GPORT PO12 14 C8
HASM GU27 118 C5
HISD PO11 195 G4
HLER SO31 179 K4
HLER SO31 180 B1
ITCH SO19 161 K7
KSCL RG20 26 A7
LIPH GU30 116 C2
NWBY RG14 27 J7
OVTN RG25 89 J4
OVTN RG25 103 G3
PSEA PO1 21 J1
PSF GU32 120 C2
PSTN BH14 224 A4
ROMY SO51 136 E1
ROMY SO51 299 M10
RSAL SP5 296 C5
SBNE BH6 227 M5
SHST GU47 43 H7
SHST GU47 43 M7
STOK SO20 285 M1
STOK SO20 299 Q1
TADY RG26 44 B6
TADY RG26 44 E3
THLE RG7 38 A5
THLE RG7 39 J7
WHAM PO17 153 H1
WIMB BH21 201 G7
Church Rd East CWTH RG45 43 K3
FARN GU14 61 K7
Church Rd West CWTH RG45 43 K4
FARN GU14 61 J7
Church Sq BSTK RG21 6 E5
Church St ALDT GU11 2 D3
ALTN GU34 106 F4
ALTN GU34 279 L7
BPWT SO32 310 F10
BSTK RG21 6 E5
CHCH/BSGR BH23 228 B2
CWTH RG45 43 K4
FBDG SP6 197 G4
FHAM/STUB PO14 180 F4
HUNG RG17 31 G2
KSCL RG20 245 R5
LISS GU33 308 D6
MARL SN8 264 G5
NARL SO24 292 G12
ODIM RG29 68 F6
PLE BH15 223 H7
PSEA PO1 192 C1
PSF GU32 314 B7
RAND SP11 250 G9
RAND SP11 272 E6
RFNM GU10 259 N2
ROMY SO51 136 E1
RSAL SP5 296 A10
RWIN SO21 275 N9
WHCH RG28 87 L8
WIMB BH21 207 H3
WIMB BH21 336 E5
WSHM SO15 146 C8
Church Street Rbt PSEA PO1 192 C1
Church Vw ASHV GU12 74 A6
EMRTH PO10 * 172 B3
ENEY PO4 193 G4
HTWY RG27 56 D7
HTWY RG27 57 L4
ODIM RG29 257 P5
YTLY GU46 48 F1
Church View Cl ITCH SO19 162 A1
Church Wk RSAL SP5 333 J3
Churchward Gdns HEND SO30 149 J2
Churn Cl CHIN RG24 66 D1
Churt Rd BOR GU35 114 A1
Churt Wynde GSHT GU26 115 K1
Chute Cswy MARL SN8 242 F8
RAND SP11 80 D1
Chute Cl TADY RG26 46 B4
Cibbons Rd CHIN RG24 54 B5
Cinderford Cl CHAM PO6 168 B7
Cinnamon La PLE BH15 223 H7
Circle Hill Rd CWTH RG45 43 L3
The Circle MOOR/WNTN BH9 * 214 A4
SSEA PO5 21 J9
WHAM PO17 151 M8
Circular Rd PSEA PO1 20 E1
The Circus WVILLE PO7 168 A6
Cirrus Gdns HLER SO31 178 F2
City Rd WINC SO23 24 F4
Civic Centre Rd HAV PO9 16 E2
SHAM SO14 22 F2
Civic Wy FHAM/PORC PO16 11 J5
Clack La FBDG SP6 330 G10
Clacton Rd CHAM PO6 168 D8
Claire Gdns HORN PO8 321 L10

Clandon Ct FARN GU14 61 K5
Clandon Dr ELGH SO50 139 M2
Clanfield Cl CHFD SO53 139 K2
Clanfield Dr CHFD SO53 139 K2
Clanfield Ride BLKW GU17 49 M3
Clanfield Rd WEND SO18 148 C5
Clanfield Wy CHFD SO53 139 K2
Clanwilliam Rd
LSOL/BMARY PO13 189 L6
Clappers Farm Rd THLE RG7 40 A8
Clapps Gate Rd TADY RG26 44 E3
Clare Cl FHAM/STUB PO14 180 C3
Clare Gdns EPSF GU31 121 G6
FAWY SO45 354 H9
Clare Lodge Cl
CHCH/BSGR BH23 348 C11
Clare Md RFNM GU10 109 M1
Claremont Av CBLY GU15 51 H3
MOOR/WNTN BH9 214 B6
Claremont Cl ELGH SO50 134 A6
Claremont Crs NWBY RG14 19 L2
WSHM SO15 160 A1
Claremont Gdns WVILLE PO7 169 L4
Claremont Rd
MOOR/WNTN BH9 214 B6
PSEA PO1 21 L3
WSHM SO15 160 A1
Clarence Cl ASHV GU12 3 K3
RAND SP11 265 L10
Clarence Dr CBLY GU15 51 K1
Clarence Esp SSEA PO5 20 E9
Clarence Pde SSEA PO5 20 F8
Clarence Park Rd LTDN BH7 227 G2
Clarence Rd FLEETN GU51 59 H8
GPORT PO12 15 K3
LYND SO43 345 L3
PSTN BH14 * 224 A5
SSEA PO5 192 D7
Clarence St PSEA PO1 192 C2
Clarence Whf GPORT PO12 * 15 K3
Clarendon Av AND SP10 4 D8
Clarendon Cl BDST BH18 211 G4
ROMY SO51 131 H7
Clarendon Ct BLKW GU17 49 M5
Clarendon Crs
FHAM/STUB PO14 180 B3
Clarendon Gdns NWBY RG14 18 F2
Clarendon Ms SSEA PO5 * 192 D7
Clarendon Pk LYMN SO41 221 K6
Clarendon Pl PSEA PO1 192 D2
Clarendon Rd BDST BH18 210 E5
CHCH/BSGR BH23 228 A1
HAV PO9 16 D5
ROWN SO16 146 A8
RSAL SP5 327 M1
SSEA PO5 21 J9
WBNE BH4 8 A7
Clarendon St PSEA PO1 192 D2
Clarendon Wy RSAL SP5 283 L10
STOK SO20 284 B10
STOK SO20 285 L12
STOK SO20 300 B4
WINC SO23 122 F8
Clares Green Rd THLE RG7 238 B5
Clarewood Dr CBLY GU15 51 G2
Clarke Crs CBLY GU15 50 A1
Clarke's La RAND SP11 81 H6
Clarkes Rd PSEA PO1 192 F2
Clark Ms WHCH RG28 87 L7
Clark's Cl RGWD BH24 203 J5
Clarks Hl RFNM GU10 76 A6
Clatford Ldg RAND SP11 * 95 L7
Claude Ashby Cl WEND SO18 147 L4
Claudeen Cl WEND SO18 147 L3
Claudia Ct GPORT PO12 14 B1
Claudius Cl AND SP10 84 D8
CHFD SO53 139 M1
Claudius Dr DEAN RG23 64 E5
Claudius Gdns CHFD SO53 139 M2
Clausentum Cl CHFD SO53 139 L1
Clausentum Rd SHAM SO14 161 G1
WINC SO23 122 F7
Clausen Wy LYMN SO41 221 J7
Claxton St PSEA PO1 21 J2
Claybank Sp HSEA PO3 185 G7
Claycart Rd ALDT GU11 2 A1
Claydon Av ENEY PO4 193 G4
Claydon Gdns FARN GU14 50 C7
Clayford Av FERN BH22 209 H1
Clayford Cl CFDH BH17 211 K6
Clayhall Rd GPORT PO12 14 E9
Clay Hl BROC SO42 345 L7
Clayhill Cl BPWT SO32 143 K8
Clay Hill Crs NWBY RG14 27 M7
Clayhill Rd THLE RG7 39 M1
Claylake Dr VWD BH31 201 J3
Claylands Ct BPWT SO32 143 H4
Claylands Rd BPWT SO32 143 H4
Clay La LYND SO43 345 K4
Claypit Rd ROMY SO51 132 C2
Claypits La FAWY SO45 176 C5
Claypitt La ALTN GU34 306 G6
Clay's La ALTN GU34 107 L7
Clay St RSAL SP5 127 G5
Claythorpe Rd KBH RG22 92 D1
Clayton Barracks ALDT GU11 73 K4
Clayton Cl HTWY RG27 57 L3
Clayton Ct FNM GU9 * 12 F4
Clayton Rd FARN GU14 50 B7
Cleasby Cl ROWN SO16 159 L1
Clease Wy RWIN SO21 124 C5
Cleaver Wy KBH RG22 92 E1
Clee Av FHAM/STUB PO14 181 K4
Cleethorpes Rd ITCH SO19 148 B8
Cleeve Cl CHAM PO6 168 B7
Cleeves Cl BKME/WDN BH12 212 D6
The Cleeves TOTT SO40 158 C2
Clegg Rd ENEY PO4 193 G5
Clematis Cl CHCH/BSGR BH23 217 J8
Clemence Gdns WHCH RG28 87 L7
Clement Attlee Wy CHAM PO6 168 B8
Clements Cl ALTN GU34 108 A5
THLE RG7 238 A7
Clem's Wy ROMY SO51 298 C11
Clere Gdns CHIN RG24 54 B6
Clerewater Pl STHA RG19 34 F1
Cleric Ct FHAM/STUB PO14 180 D1
Clevedge Wy ODIM RG29 68 E4
Clevedon Ct FARN GU14 61 K5
FRIM GU16 51 J8
Cleveland Cl KBH RG22 92 D2
NMIL/BTOS BH25 230 D1
Cleveland Ct WEND SO18 148 A3
Cleveland Dr FAWY SO45 176 D6
FHAM/STUB PO14 181 K4
Cleveland Gdns BMTH BH1 9 M1
Cleveland Gv NWBY RG14 18 D3
Cleveland Rd BMTH BH1 226 D3
GPORT PO12 14 F6
SSEA PO5 21 L5
WEND SO18 147 M6
Clevelands Cl CHFD SO53 133 H7
Cleves La OVTN RG25 257 K2
Clewborough Dr CBLY GU15 51 K2
Clewers Hl BPWT SO32 143 K8
Clewers La BPWT SO32 143 K8
Cliddesden Ct BSTK RG21 93 K2
Cliddesden La KBH RG22 92 F6
Cliddesden Rd BSTK RG21 6 F8
Cliff Crs NMIL/BTOS BH25 230 F1
Cliff Dr CCLF BH13 237 L2
CHCH/BSGR BH23 229 J2
Cliffe Av HLER SO31 178 E1
Cliffe Rd NMIL/BTOS BH25 230 E1
Clifford Dibben Ms
SHAM SO14 146 F8
Clifford Pl ELGH SO50 141 J2
Clifford Rd MOOR/WNTN BH9 214 A7
Clifford St SHAM SO14 23 J2
Cliff Rd FHAM/STUB PO14 188 F3
LYMN SO41 232 A4
WSHM SO15 22 A1
The Cliffs HUNG RG17 * 31 H1
Cliff Ter NMIL/BTOS BH25 * 230 F2
Cliff Wy RWIN SO21 124 D6
Clifton Cl RFNM GU10 78 E4
Clifton Crs WVILLE PO7 155 H4
Clifton Gdns FERN BH22 209 J4
FRIM GU16 61 M2
WEND SO18 148 C3
Clifton Hl FUFL SO22 24 E5
Clifton Rd FUFL SO22 24 D4
LSOL/BMARY PO13 190 A4
NWBY RG14 18 A5
PSTN BH14 224 D6
SBNE BH6 227 K5
SSEA PO5 21 G9
WSHM SO15 146 A8
Clifton St GPORT PO12 14 B1
PSEA PO1 21 L1
Clifton Ter BSTK RG21 6 F3
FUFL SO22 24 E5
SSEA PO5 * 21 G9
Clingan Rd SBNE BH6 227 K2
Clinkley Rd NARL SO24 305 M5
Clinton Cl CHCH/BSGR BH23 218 B6
Clinton Rd LYMN SO41 221 L3
WVILLE PO7 155 J5
Clipper Cl HLER SO31 179 L3
Clitheroe Rd FARN GU14 49 H7
Cliveden Cl FERN BH22 209 J1
Clive Gv FHAM/PORC PO16 183 J1
Clive Rd ASHV GU12 3 L5
CHCH/BSGR BH23 217 L6
MOOR/WNTN BH9 213 M7
PSEA PO1 21 M1
Clock House Ct HASM GU27 * 118 C6
Clockhouse Rd FARN GU14 61 H4
Clock St PSEA PO1 20 C3
Clocktower Dr ENEY PO4 193 H6
The Cloisters ALTN GU34 * 106 F4
FHAM PO15 181 J2
FRIM GU16 50 F7
LYMN SO41 * 221 L5
RGWD BH24 203 L6
ROMY SO51 130 E8
ROWN SO16 147 G4
The Close Bellfield
FHAM/STUB PO14 180 F5
The Close BDST BH18 210 E5
CHAM PO6 185 G1
DEAN RG23 * 64 F5
FAWY SO45 354 F5
FHAM/PORC PO16 167 J8
FNM GU9 13 K6
FRIM GU16 50 E8
HEND SO30 149 H6
LYMN SO41 350 E10
NMIL/BTOS BH25 219 G8
NTHA RG18 28 D8
PSF GU32 314 F5
RAND SP11 83 L2
RGWD BH24 202 C8
RGWD BH24 202 F8
RGWD BH24 203 H5
RSAL SP5 332 F1
RWIN SO21 * 134 D3
TADY RG26 52 D6
WEND SO18 148 D5
WINC SO23 25 G7
Closewood Rd WVILLE PO7 155 G7
Closeworth Rd FARN GU14 61 L8
Clough La RGWD BH24 348 H1
RSAL SP5 282 F9
Clough's Rd RGWD BH24 203 K5
Clouston Rd FARN GU14 60 F3
Clovelly Dr GSHT GU26 115 J1
Clovelly Rd EMRTH PO10 171 L8
EMRTH PO10 172 D5
ENEY PO4 193 G4
GSHT GU26 115 J2
HISD PO11 187 J4
SHAM SO14 161 G2
Cloverbank WINC SO23 288 H6
Clover Cl BOR GU35 111 J7
CHCH/BSGR BH23 217 H8
HLER SO31 179 L2
LSOL/BMARY PO13 182 C6
Clover Ct NMIL/BTOS BH25 219 K4
Clover Dr CFDH BH17 210 F7
Clover Fld CHIN RG24 54 B8
Clover Gdns RAND SP11 265 M10
Clover La YTLY GU46 48 C2
Cloverleaf Wy CHIN RG24 66 D4
Clover Ms AND SP10 5 K6
The Clovers BKME/WDN BH12 213 G8
Clover Wy HEND SO30 149 G6
ROMY SO51 131 J8
Clowes Av SBNE BH6 228 B5
Club House La BPWT SO32 151 L1
Clubhouse Rd ALDT GU11 72 F3
Club La CWTH RG45 43 M3
NTID SP9 266 E4
Clump Hl WIMB BH21 200 C7
Clumps Rd RFNM GU10 79 J4
Clydebank Rd NEND PO2 184 D8
Clyde Ct AND SP10 5 L1
GPORT PO12 14 B1
Clyde Rd CFDH BH17 211 H6
GPORT PO12 14 B1
Clydesdale Dr TOTT SO40 * 144 B8
Clydesdale Rd HLER SO31 164 B5
Clydesdale Wy TOTT SO40 144 B8
Coach Hl FHAM/STUB PO14 180 F4
RAND SP11 80 D8
Coach Hill Cl CHFD SO53 139 H1
Coach Hill La RGWD BH24 342 G11
Coach House Cl FRIM GU16 51 G5
Coach House Gdns
FLEETN GU51 59 J5
Coach House Ms ENEY PO4 * 193 J4
FERN BH22 209 M1
Coach House Pl BMTH BH1 9 H2
Coachmans Copse
WEND SO18 148 A2
Coachman's Ct NWBY RG14 27 K7
Coachmans Halt WVILLE PO7 * 319 Q10
Coach Rd HLER SO31 178 E2
The Coach Rd RSAL SP5 297 P4
Coachways AND SP10 5 G8
Coal Park La HLER SO31 163 L3
Coalville Rd ITCH SO19 148 B8
Coastguard Cl GPORT PO12 14 A9
Coastguard Wy
CHCH/BSGR BH23 228 E4
Coate Dr RWIN SO21 288 D6
Coates Cl KBH RG22 93 H3
Coates Rd ITCH SO19 148 D8
Coates Wy WVILLE PO7 169 L3
Coat Gdns FAWY SO45 177 G5
Cobalt Ct LSOL/BMARY PO13 * 190 C2
Cobbets Rdg RFNM GU10 260 A7
Cobbett Cl FUFL SO22 122 C7
Cobbett Gn KBH RG22 93 G2
Cobbett Hill Rd RGUW GU3 75 L1
Cobbett Rd WEND SO18 161 L1
Cobbett's La BLKW GU17 49 H4
Cobbetts Ms FNM GU9 * 12 E3
Cobbetts Wy FNM GU9 78 D2
Cobbett Wy HEND SO30 149 L5
Cobblers Cnr LYMN SO41 351 L9
Cobblewood EMRTH PO10 171 M5
Cobbs La PLE BH15 223 L2
Cobb's Rd WIMB BH21 207 L2
Cobden Av HSEA PO3 185 G8
WEND SO18 147 L8
Cobden Crs WEND SO18 147 M8
Cobden Gdns WEND SO18 147 L7
Cobden La HASM GU27 118 D5
Cobden Ri WEND SO18 * 147 L7
Cobden St GPORT PO12 14 E2
Cobham Rd MOOR/WNTN BH9 214 A5
WIMB BH21 208 F1
Cobham Wy WIMB BH21 207 L7
Coblands Av TOTT SO40 158 D1
Cobley Cl RSAL SP5 328 D5
Coburg St PSEA PO1 21 K2
SHAM SO14 161 J2
Cochcrane Cl
LSOL/BMARY PO13 190 D2
Cochrane Cl STHA RG19 35 L1
Cock-a-Dobby SHST GU47 43 J8
Cockerell Cl FHAM PO15 164 C7
WIMB BH21 207 M7
Cockleshell Gdns ENEY PO4 193 J5
Cockleshell Sq GPORT PO12 15 J3
Cocklydown La TOTT SO40 158 E3
Cockshott La PSF GU32 307 N10
Cody Cl ASHV GU12 73 M3
Cody Rd FARN GU14 60 F5
Coe Cl ALDT GU11 2 E4
Cogdean Cl WIMB BH21 206 E8
Cogdeane Rd CFDH BH17 211 K6
Cogdean Wk WIMB BH21 206 E8
Cogdean Wy WIMB BH21 206 E8
Coghlan Cl FHAM/PORC PO16 11 G3
Cokenor Wd RFNM GU10 78 D2
Coker Cl FUFL SO22 24 D4
Colbeck FLEETS GU52 71 K4
Colborne Av WIMB BH21 207 M3
Colborne Cl LYMN SO41 221 L3
PLE BH15 223 K7
Colbourne Cl
CHCH/BSGR BH23 348 C12
Colbred Cnr FLEETN GU51 59 L4
Colburn Cl ROWN SO16 145 K6
Colbury Gv HAV PO9 170 C4
Colchester Av ELGH SO50 134 E8
Colchester Rd CHAM PO6 168 D7
Cold Ash Hl NTHA RG18 28 E4
Cold East Cl HLER SO31 163 L7
Coldeast Wy HLER SO31 163 M7
Colden La NARL SO24 291 N7
Coldharbour OVTN RG25 103 G3
Cold Harbour Cl WHAM PO17 151 M8
Coldharbour Farm Rd
EMRTH PO10 171 M7
Cold Harbour La FARN GU14 50 B8
Coldharbour La ROWN SO16 137 H8
Coldhill La HORN PO8 155 L1
Cole Av ALDT GU11 2 C1
Colebrook Av HSEA PO3 193 H1
WSHM SO15 146 C7
Colebrook Pl WINC SO23 25 J7
Colebrook St WINC SO23 25 H7
Colebrook Wy AND SP10 4 B6
Cole Cl AND SP10 84 C8
Coleford Bridge Rd FRIM GU16 61 L4
Coleford Cl FRIM GU16 61 M5
Coleford Paddocks FRIM GU16 61 M4
Cole Hl BPWT SO32 318 H7
Colehill Crs MOOR/WNTN BH9 214 B5
Colehill Gdns BPWT SO32 143 G4
Colehill La WIMB BH21 207 L2
Coleman Cl BSTK RG21 65 L5
Coleman Rd ASHV GU12 3 L5
BWD BH11 213 G5
Coleman St SHAM SO14 23 J3
Colemere Gdns
CHCH/BSGR BH23 217 M7
Colemore Rd LTDN BH7 227 J1
Colemore Sq HAV PO9 * 170 F4
Colenso Rd FHAM/PORC PO16 10 F4
Colenzo Dr AND SP10 5 K2
Coleridge Av YTLY GU46 49 G3
Coleridge Cl CWTH RG45 43 L4
HLER SO31 179 K3
Coleridge Gdns HORN PO8 155 M4
Coleridge Gn
CHCH/BSGR BH23 216 F8
Coleridge Rd CHAM PO6 167 M7
Coles Av PLE BH15 222 E6
Colesbourne Rd CHAM PO6 168 B7
Coles Cl RWIN SO21 125 G5
Coles Gdns PLE BH15 222 E6
Coles Mede RWIN SO21 134 B1
Coleson Hill Rd RFNM GU10 78 D3
Coleson Rd WEND SO18 147 L8
Coles's La RSAL SP5 333 N3
Coleville Av FAWY SO45 355 K5
Coleville Rd FARN GU14 60 F3
Coley La STOK SO20 272 D8
Colin Cl WIMB BH21 210 D3
Colinton Av FHAM/PORC PO16 167 K7
Collards Ga HASM GU27 * 118 D6
Collards La HASM GU27 118 D6
Collard Wy LISS GU33 308 F8
Collaroy Rd NTHA RG18 28 E5
College Cl HAV PO9 157 J7
HLER SO31 178 F2
College Gdns FNM GU9 12 E3
College Hl HASM GU27 118 C6
College Hill Ter HASM GU27 118 C6
College La OVTN RG25 105 K6
PSEA PO1 20 C3
College Piece THLE RG7 39 M6
College Pl WSHM SO15 161 G2
College Ride CBLY GU15 50 F1
College Rd ASHV GU12 74 A5
BOSC BH5 227 G4
BSTK RG21 6 B4
ITCH SO19 161 L6
PSEA PO1 20 C2
RGWD BH24 203 J5
SHST GU47 50 A1
WVILLE PO7 169 L6
College St EPSF GU31 120 D6
PSEA PO1 20 C3
SHAM SO14 23 H5
WINC SO23 25 G7
College Wk WINC SO23 25 H8
Collens Fld CHOB/PIR GU24 63 L5
Collett Cl HEND SO30 149 H2
Colley Cl WINC SO23 123 G1
Collier Cl FARN GU14 60 D3
PTSW SO17 147 J8
Collingbourne Av SBNE BH6 227 K2
Collingbourne Dr CHFD SO53 139 G2
Collington Crs CHAM PO6 168 B7
Collingwood FARN GU14 61 L6
Collingwood Ri CBLY GU15 51 J1
Collingwood Rd SSEA PO5 21 K8
WIMB BH21 205 G2
Collingwood Wk AND SP10 96 F4
Collingworth Cl HLER SO31 164 B6
Collingworth Ri FHAM PO15 164 B7
Collins Cl AND SP10 96 A1
CHFD SO53 138 F2
NWBY RG14 19 J1
Collins Ct NTID SP9 264 E12
Collins Gdns ASHV GU12 74 B6
Collins La EPSF GU31 316 F9
RGWD BH24 203 J5
RWIN SO21 133 J1
Collins Rd ENEY PO4 193 G6
Collis Rd HSEA PO3 185 G8
Collwood Cl PLE BH15 223 J1
Collyers Crs LIPH GU30 116 E4
Collyers Rd BROC SO42 351 K5
Colne Av ROWN SO16 145 K5
Colne Valley Wy RWIN SO21 274 B5
WHCH RG28 88 D7
Colne Wy ASHV GU12 74 A7
BSTK RG21 7 J5
Colonnade Rd BOSC BH5 227 G3
The Colonnade ITCH SO19 * 161 K5
Colpoy St SSEA PO5 20 F5
Colson Cl WINC SO23 25 K4
Colson Rd WINC SO23 25 K4
Colt Cl ROWN SO16 145 M3
WIMB BH21 208 B2
Colthrop La STHA RG19 36 B3
Colthrop Wy STHA RG19 36 B2
Colton Copse CHFD SO53 138 F2
Coltsfoot Cl HEND SO30 149 H5
Coltsfoot Dr HLER SO31 179 L2
WVILLE PO7 169 M3
Coltsfoot Pl HTWY RG27 56 E6
Colts Foot Rd BOR GU35 111 J7
Coltsfoot Wk ROMY SO51 131 J7
Coltsmead CHAM PO6 167 M8
Colts Rd ROWN SO16 145 L1
Columbia Ct EWKG RG40 42 A1
Columbian Wy NBNE BH10 213 J6
Columbia Rd NBNE BH10 213 K6
Columbia Trees La NBNE BH10 213 J7
Columbine Cl
CHCH/BSGR BH23 217 H7
Columbine Rd KBH RG22 92 C4
Columbus Dr FARN GU14 60 C5
Columbus Wy AND SP10 97 G4
Colville Cl BOSC BH5 227 G3
Colville Dr BPWT SO32 143 K4
Colville Rd BOSC BH5 227 G3
CHAM PO6 169 G8
Colvin Gdns CHFD SO53 133 H8
Colwell Cl ROWN SO16 145 K8
Colwell Rd CHAM PO6 184 F1
Colwyn Cl YTLY GU46 48 D2
Colyer Cl KBH RG22 92 E1
Combe La FARN GU14 61 G2
Combe Ri RFNM GU10 79 H3
Combe Rd LISS GU33 308 H11
Comber Rd MOOR/WNTN BH9 213 M5
Comet Cl ASHV GU12 73 M3
Comet Wy CHCH/BSGR BH23 229 G2
Comfrey Cl FARN GU14 60 C3
HORN PO8 321 L11
ROMY SO51 131 J7
Comines Wy HEND SO30 148 E6
Comley Hl HAV PO9 171 J1
Comley Rd MOOR/WNTN BH9 213 M6
Commercial Pl PSEA PO1 21 H1
Commercial Rd ASHV GU12 3 K6
PLE BH15 223 M4
PSEA PO1 21 G2
TOTT SO40 159 G1
WCLF BH2 8 D6
WSHM SO15 22 F1
Commercial St WEND SO18 148 B5
Common Barn La
LSOL/BMARY PO13 * 189 M5
Common Cl CHFD SO53 133 J8
Commonfield La EWKG RG40 239 P8
Common Gdns CHFD SO53 133 J8
Common Hl ALTN GU34 292 H2
Common Hill Rd ROMY SO51 131 K2
Common La FHAM/STUB PO14 180 D4
WHAM PO17 153 L7
Common Rd CHFD SO53 133 J8
EMRTH PO10 172 F1
RSAL SP5 127 H5
STHA RG19 248 C4
Commonside EMRTH PO10 172 B1
Common St PSEA PO1 * 21 K1
The Common RSAL SP5 282 H10
Compass Cl
LSOL/BMARY PO13 190 D2
Compass Fld HTWY RG27 56 D7
Compass Point HLER SO31 * 178 E2
Compass Rd CHAM PO6 168 B8
Complins ALTN GU34 107 H2
Compound Rd FARN GU14 61 G6
Compton Av PSTN BH14 224 D6
Compton Beeches
RGWD BH24 202 C7
Compton Cl ELGH SO50 139 M2
FLEETS GU52 71 K3
FUFL SO22 124 B1
HAV PO9 16 E1
HTWY RG27 56 D8
LSOL/BMARY PO13 190 A2
SHST GU47 43 L7
VWD BH31 201 H2
Compton Crs FERN BH22 205 J7
Compton Dr PSTN BH14 224 C6
Compton Gdns PSTN BH14 224 C6
Compton Rd FLEETS GU52 71 K3
NEND PO2 184 F5
NMIL/BTOS BH25 219 G6
TOTT SO40 145 G8
WINC SO23 24 E7
Compton's Dr ROMY SO51 334 D2
Compton Sq AND SP10 96 E1
Compton St RWIN SO21 124 C4
Compton Wk SHAM SO14 23 G1
Compton Wy FUFL SO22 124 B1
RFNM GU10 77 L6
Conan Rd NEND PO2 184 E4
Concorde Wy FHAM PO15 164 E7
Conde Wy BOR GU35 112 F2
Condor Av FHAM/PORC PO16 182 F1
Condor Cl ITCH SO19 161 K5
WIMB BH21 205 K3
Condor Rd FARN GU14 61 H6
Coneygar La FERN BH22 209 G5
Coney Gn WINC SO23 25 G1
Conference Dr HLER SO31 180 B1
Conference Pl LYMN SO41 221 L6
Conford Ct HAV PO9 170 D2
Congleton Cl LYND SO43 340 G9
Congreve Cl THLE RG7 37 M5
Conholt Hl RAND SP11 81 H1
Conholt La RAND SP11 81 K1
Conholt Rd AND SP10 96 C7
Conifer Av PSTN BH14 224 B6
Conifer Cl BOR GU35 112 E3
CHCH/BSGR BH23 215 K5
FAWY SO45 176 E5
FERN BH22 209 M7
FLEETS GU52 71 H3
FUFL SO22 24 D3
HORN PO8 * 156 A6
RGWD BH24 205 M4
TADY RG26 249 Q2
Conifer Crs LYMN SO41 221 H5
Conifer Crest NWBY RG14 33 J8
Conifer Dr CBLY GU15 51 J2
RCCH PO18 173 J4
Conifer Gv LSOL/BMARY PO13 182 C4
Conifer Ms FHAM/PORC PO16 167 K7
Conifer Rd ROWN SO16 146 A4
The Conifers CWTH RG45 43 J1
Conigar Rd EMRTH PO10 171 M5
Coningham Rd WHIT RG2 238 C2
Coniston Av BWD BH11 212 E3
HSEA PO3 185 G8
Coniston Cl CBLY GU15 51 L5
FARN GU14 60 E5
STHA RG19 35 G1
VWD BH31 201 G3
Coniston Ct ASHV GU12 * 73 M4
Coniston Dr FNM GU9 76 E2
Coniston Gdns HEND SO30 149 J7
Coniston Gv NARL SO24 291 M12
Coniston Rd BOR GU35 110 E7
ELGH SO50 139 M6
KBH RG22 92 D4
RGWD BH24 * 203 K6
ROWN SO16 145 J8
Coniston Wk
FHAM/STUB PO14 10 B9
Coniston Wy FLEETS GU52 71 G3
Connaught Barracks
ALDT GU11 73 K2
Connaught Cl BOR GU35 112 F2
CWTH RG45 43 H5
NMIL/BTOS BH25 218 E8
YTLY GU46 48 D2
Connaught Crs
BKME/WDN BH12 224 E2
CHOB/PIR GU24 63 M1
Connaught Rd ASHV GU12 3 K3
BOSC BH5 227 H3
CBLY GU15 51 H3
CHOB/PIR GU24 63 M1
FLEETN GU51 59 J8
HAV PO9 17 H4
NEND PO2 184 D6
NWBY RG14 19 G4
RWIN SO21 288 C6
Connell Rd PLE BH15 223 J3
Connemara Crs HLER SO31 164 B5
Connigar Cl
LSOL/BMARY PO13 190 C1
Connop Wy FRIM GU16 51 H5
Conqueror Wy
FHAM/STUB PO14 189 K2
Conrad Gdns FHAM PO15 164 C4
The Conservatory WINC SO23 * 25 J6
Consort Cl ELGH SO50 134 B7
PSTN BH14 224 C3
Consort Ct FHAM/PORC PO16 * 11 J6
Consort Dr CBLY GU15 51 L1
Consort Rd ELGH SO50 134 B7
Constable Cl BSTK RG21 7 K9
FERN BH22 209 J4
GPORT PO12 191 J7
ITCH SO19 162 C2
Constable Ct AND SP10 5 G3
Constable's Ga WINC SO23 24 E6
Constable Wy SHST GU47 50 A2
Constantine Av CHFD SO53 139 L2
Constantine Cl CHFD SO53 139 M2
Constantine Sq AND SP10 * 96 D2
Constantine Wy KBH RG22 92 C6
Constant Rd FARN GU14 60 A6
Constitution Hill Rd
PSTN BH14 223 M4
Convent La EMRTH PO10 171 M8
Conway Cl CHFD SO53 139 H5
NMIL/BTOS BH25 219 H5
Conway Dr FARN GU14 60 D3
NTHA RG18 28 D7
Conways Dr PSTN BH14 224 A4
Cook Cl RGWD BH24 203 L4
Cooke Rd BKME/WDN BH12 224 F2
Cookham Cl SHST GU47 43 L7
Cook Rw WIMB BH21 207 H4
Cooks La EMRTH PO10 172 E5
ROMY SO51 128 D1
ROMY SO51 130 A4
TOTT SO40 144 C6
Cook St SHAM SO14 23 H4
Coolarne Ri CBLY GU15 51 J2
Coolers Farm STOK SO20 284 E10
Coombe Av NBNE BH10 213 L6
Coombe Cl FRIM GU16 50 F8
Coombe Ct STHA RG19 35 L1
Coombedale HLER SO31 180 B2
Coombe Dr FLEETN GU51 59 L7
Coombe Farm Av
FHAM/PORC PO16 10 F7
Coombe Gdns NBNE BH10 213 K6
Coombehurst Dr BSTK RG21 93 K2
Coombe La LYMN SO41 350 H11
PSF GU32 313 N4
ROMY SO51 129 M5
Coombe Rd GPORT PO12 191 H1
PSF GU32 314 A8
YTLY GU46 48 D1
Coombes La WWKG RG41 239 Q4
Coombe Sq STHA RG19 35 L1
Coombs Cl HORN PO8 321 L11
The Cooperage ALTN GU34 106 E5
Cooper Cl WHIT RG2 238 C1
Cooper Dean Dr CHAR BH8 214 F7
Cooper Gv FHAM/PORC PO16 183 K2
Cooper Rd HSEA PO3 193 H1
TOTT SO40 158 C5
Cooper's Cl ROMY SO51 335 M6
RWIN SO21 288 D6
WEND SO18 148 C3
Coopers Ct TADY RG26 46 B5
Coopers Crs NTHA RG18 28 E8
Cooper's Hl HTWY RG27 241 R9
Coopers Hill Dr CHOB/PIR GU24 63 J1
Cooper's La ITCH SO19 161 K5
TADY RG26 46 A5
VWD BH31 201 H1
Cope Hall La NWBY RG14 33 H5
Copeland Dr PSTN BH14 224 B6
Copeland Rd ROWN SO16 145 K7
Copelands Cl CBLY GU15 51 M4
Copenhagen Cl WHIT RG2 238 C1
Copes La HTWY RG27 240 G5
Copinger Cl TOTT SO40 158 C2
Copland Cl KBH RG22 92 E4
Copnor Cl KSCL RG20 245 Q4
Copnor Rd NEND PO2 184 F4
Copped Hall Dr CBLY GU15 51 L2
Copped Hall Wy CBLY GU15 51 L2
Copper Beech Cl
BKME/WDN BH12 225 G4
Copper Beech Dr CHAM PO6 169 L8

Copper Beech Gdns
NBNE BH10 213 K6
Copperfield Rd ROWN SO16 147 G3
Copperfields TOTT SO40 158 B1
Coppers Cl FBDG SP6 196 C6
Copper St SSEA PO5 20 F6
Coppice Av FERN BH22 209 H1
Coppice Cl FNM GU9 77 J2
FUFL SO22 122 C3
NMIL/BTOS BH25 219 K4
NWBY RG14 19 G9
RGWD BH24 202 B8
TADY RG26 249 P4
Coppice Gdns CWTH RG45 43 H3
YTLY GU46 48 E3
Coppice Hl BPWT SO32 143 J5
Coppice Ms DEAN RG23 64 E6
Coppice Rd KSCL RG20 248 E10
TOTT SO40 144 C6
The Coppice BROC SO42 350 H2
CHCH/BSGR BH23 229 H2
HORN PO8 156 A2
LSOL/BMARY PO13 182 D6
Coppice Vw NBNE BH10 213 L5
Coppice Wy FHAM PO15 181 K1
Coppid Hl WWKG RG41 * 239 Q5
Coppins Gv FHAM/PORC PO16 183 J2
Copse Av FNM GU9 2 A8
NMIL/BTOS BH25 219 H6
Copse Cl CBLY GU15 51 J3
EPSF GU31 121 G5
LISS GU33 308 G8
NBAD SO52 137 M4
PLE BH15 223 M5
RWIN SO21 124 C8
TOTT SO40 158 F2
WVILLE PO7 169 K6
Copse Edge MFD/CHID GU8 263 Q1
Copse End CBLY GU15 51 H2
Copse Fld CHIN RG24 54 C8
Copse La HISD PO11 187 G8
HLER SO31 178 F2
LSOL/BMARY PO13 182 D7
NARL SO24 276 G9
ODIM RG29 258 B5
ROWN SO16 138 F7
Copse Rd HASM GU27 117 K3
NMIL/BTOS BH25 219 H6
OVTN RG25 89 K2
RGWD BH24 348 H2
VWD BH31 201 H2
WEND SO18 147 M6
The Copse CHFD SO53 139 L3
DEAN RG23 103 M1
FARN GU14 60 D5
FHAM PO15 165 K8
RFNM GU10 78 D4
RSAL SP5 327 M2
TADY RG26 44 A4
TOTT SO40 * 341 P7
Copse Vw ITCH SO19 148 E7
Copse View Cl CHIN RG24 54 B5
Copse Wy CHCH/BSGR BH23 217 L8
EWKG RG40 42 A1
RFNM GU10 78 D2
Copsewood Av CHAR BH8 214 E7
Copsewood Rd FAWY SO45 176 F5
TOTT SO40 158 C5
WEND SO18 147 L6
Copsey Cl CHAM PO6 169 K8
Copsey Gv CHAM PO6 169 K8
Copthorne La FAWY SO45 355 L5
Copythorne Cl CHAR BH8 214 D6
Copythorne Crs TOTT SO40 341 N2
Copythorn Rd NEND PO2 184 F7
Coracle Cl HLER SO31 179 M3
Coral Cl FHAM/PORC PO16 183 J2
Coral Ct LSOL/BMARY PO13 * 190 C2
Coralin Gv WVILLE PO7 156 B7
Coram Cl WINC SO23 123 G2
Coranation Rd WVILLE PO7 155 L8
Corbar Rd CHCH/BSGR BH23 215 L8
Corbett Rd WVILLE PO7 169 K2
Corbiere Av BKME/WDN BH12 212 D7
Corbiere Cl ROWN SO16 145 L5
Corbin Av FERN BH22 346 A6
Corbin Rd LYMN SO41 221 H6
Corbould Rd FAWY SO45 176 F7
Corby Crs HSEA PO3 185 H4
Cordale Rd BSTK RG21 6 D8
Cordelia Cl FAWY SO45 176 D5
Cordelia Gdns ASHV GU12 61 M8
Corderoy Cl STHA RG19 35 M2
Corfe Cl FHAM/STUB PO14 189 G2
NARL SO24 291 L12
Corfe Gdns FRIM GU16 51 H7
Corfe Halt Cl WIMB BH21 206 E7
Corfe Lodge Rd BDST BH18 210 D5
Corfe View Rd PSTN BH14 224 B5
WIMB BH21 210 C3
Corfe Wk DEAN RG23 64 E6
Corfe Wy BDST BH18 210 E5
FARN GU14 61 L7
Corfield Cl EWKG RG40 42 A5
Corhampton Crs HAV PO9 170 D4
Corhampton La BPWT SO32 311 R11
Corhampton Rd SBNE BH6 227 J2
Coriander Cl FARN GU14 60 C4
Coriander Dr TOTT SO40 158 B1
Coriander Wy FHAM PO15 164 D4
Corinna Gdns FAWY SO45 176 D5
Corinthian Cl AND SP10 84 D8
KBH RG22 92 E5
Corinthian Rd CHFD SO53 139 L1
Cork La TOTT SO40 159 M6
Cormorant Cl
FHAM/PORC PO16 166 F8
KBH RG22 92 B4
Cormorant Dr FAWY SO45 177 H6
Cornaway La
FHAM/PORC PO16 183 H1
Cornbrook Gv HORN PO8 156 C7
Cornbunting Cl SHST GU47 49 M1
Cornelia Cl FARN GU14 * 60 D5
Cornelia Crs BKME/WDN BH12 225 G2
Cornelius Dr WVILLE PO7 156 B7
Cornel Rd ITCH SO19 161 M3
Corner Md WVILLE PO7 154 F4
Cornes Cl FUFL SO22 24 A5
Cornfield FHAM/PORC PO16 166 B4
Cornfield Cl CHFD SO53 138 F2
Cornfield Rd
LSOL/BMARY PO13 189 M6
Cornfields AND SP10 5 K9
YTLY GU46 48 D4
The Cornfields KBH RG22 92 E5
Cornflower Cl HLER SO31 179 L2
WWKG RG41 239 R1
Cornflower Dr
CHCH/BSGR BH23 217 J7
Cornflower Wy RAND SP11 265 M11
Cornford Wy
CHCH/BSGR BH23 217 K8
Cornforth Rd TOTT SO40 144 C7
Cornish Cl KBH RG22 92 E1
Cornish Gdns NBNE BH10 213 K7
Corn Market ROMY SO51 136 E1
Cornpits La FBDG SP6 337 Q1
Cornwall Cl CBLY GU15 51 H1
WWKG RG41 239 R2
Cornwall Crs WEND SO18 147 M6
Cornwallis Crs PSEA PO1 192 C2
Cornwallis Rd LYMN SO41 232 B4
Cornwall Rd BOR GU35 112 F3
CHFD SO53 139 J5
PSEA PO1 21 L3
WEND SO18 147 M6
Cornwell Cl LSOL/BMARY PO13 190 D1
NEND PO2 184 B6
Coronado Rd GPORT PO12 191 H2
Coronation Av
MOOR/WNTN BH9 213 M6
UPTN BH16 222 B1
Coronation Cl KSCL RG20 246 H5
ODIM RG29 69 H5
Coronation Pde HLER SO31 178 E1
Coronation Rd ALDT GU11 3 H8
BPWT SO32 318 B7
BSTK RG21 7 H2
HISD PO11 195 L7
NTID SP9 264 E12
RAND SP11 265 N10
VWD BH31 201 H1
YTLY GU46 48 F1
Corporation Rd BMTH BH1 9 K3
Correlli Rd KBH RG22 93 H4
Corringway FLEETS GU52 71 K2
Corry Rd GSHT GU26 115 J2
Corsair Cl LSOL/BMARY PO13 190 A3
Corsair Dr FAWY SO45 176 D4
Corscombe Cl CFDH BH17 211 L6
Corsham Wy CWTH RG45 43 K2
Cortina Wy HEND SO30 149 J7
Cortry Cl BKME/WDN BH12 225 G1
Cort Wy FHAM PO15 165 J8
Corunna Main AND SP10 5 K3
Corvette Av HLER SO31 179 M3
Cosford Cl ELGH SO50 141 G2
Cosham Park Av CHAM PO6 184 F1
Cossack Gn SHAM SO14 23 H3
Cossack La WINC SO23 25 H5
Coster Cl NWBY RG14 26 F7
Cosworth Dr FAWY SO45 176 D5
Cotes Av PSTN BH14 224 A3
Cotlands Rd BMTH BH1 9 K4
Cotsalls ELGH SO50 141 J3
Cotswold Cl FARN GU14 60 E1
FAWY SO45 176 D5
HAV PO9 170 E2
KBH RG22 64 D8
VWD BH31 201 H3
Cotswold Rd ROWN SO16 145 M8
SHST GU47 43 H7
Cotswold Wk
FHAM/STUB PO14 181 M5
Cottage Cl WVILLE PO7 154 F5
Cottage Gdns
BKME/WDN BH12 224 C3
FARN GU14 60 F4
Cottage Gn HTWY RG27 57 M3
RAND SP11 271 P4
Cottage Gv GPORT PO12 14 E3
SSEA PO5 21 H5
Cottage La LISS GU33 307 R8
Cottage Ms FBDG SP6 197 G2
RGWD BH24 203 H5
Cottage Rd STOK SO20 269 Q12
Cottagers La LYMN SO41 220 A5
Cottage Vw PSEA PO1 21 J2
Cottes Wy FHAM/STUB PO14 189 G3
Cottesway East
FHAM/STUB PO14 189 G3
Cottington Cl KSCL RG20 248 E10
Cott La RGWD BH24 349 K2
Cottle Cl BSTK RG21 93 J2
Cotton Cl ALDT GU11 2 C1
BDST BH18 210 F3
ELGH SO50 140 E1
Cotton Dr EMRTH PO10 171 L5
Cott St BPWT SO32 318 D8
Cott Street La BPWT SO32 318 E8
Cotwell Av HORN PO8 156 B4
Coulmere Rd GPORT PO12 14 C1
Coulsdon Rd HEND SO30 149 J6
Coultas Rd CHFD SO53 133 L6
Council Rd BSTK RG21 6 E7
Countess Cl WIMB BH21 207 L8
Countess Gdns LTDN BH7 214 F8
Country Vw FHAM/STUB PO14 181 H8
ROMY SO51 335 J5
County Gdns
FHAM/STUB PO14 181 J4
County Gates La WBNE BH4 225 H4
Course Park Crs
FHAM/STUB PO14 180 D2
Court Barn La
LSOL/BMARY PO13 189 M5
Court Cl CHAM PO6 185 H1
CHCH/BSGR BH23 228 E1
LIPH GU30 116 B5
LYMN SO41 221 K6
TOTT SO40 144 C6
Court Dro OVTN RG25 89 H1
Courtenay Dr WIMB BH21 207 J2
Courtenay Pl LYMN SO41 221 L6
Courtenay Rd FNM GU9 77 J2
PSTN BH14 224 B4
WINC SO23 123 G2
Court Gdns CBLY GU15 50 F3
Court Hl FBDG SP6 330 E11
Courthill Rd PSTN BH14 224 C4
Court House Cl FAWY SO45 177 G4
Courtland Gdns ROWN SO16 147 H3
Courtlands Rd NWBY RG14 19 G8
Courtlands Ter HORN PO8 * 156 A4
Court La ALTN GU34 292 H10
CHAM PO6 185 H1
STOK SO20 286 F10
Court Ldg LYMN SO41 * 221 K6
Court Md CHAM PO6 185 H1
Courtmoor Av FLEETS GU52 71 H1
Courtmount Gv CHAM PO6 169 G8
Court Rd ALDT GU11 2 F2
LSOL/BMARY PO13 189 L5
MOOR/WNTN BH9 214 B7
WINC SO23 289 J11
WSHM SO15 160 F1
Court Royal Ms WSHM SO15 * 146 F8
Courts Hill Rd HASM GU27 118 B6
Courts Mount Rd HASM GU27 118 B6
The Courtyard EPSF GU31 120 D6
The Court Yd STHA RG19 * 35 K1
Cousins Gv ENEY PO4 193 G6
Covena Rd SBNE BH6 227 K2
Coventry Cl KBH RG22 92 D4
WIMB BH21 210 C4
Coventry Ct
LSOL/BMARY PO13 * 190 D2
Coventry Crs CFDH BH17 211 G7
Coventry Rd WSHM SO15 160 F2
Coverack Wy CHAM PO6 184 B1
Cove Rd FARN GU14 60 F4
FLEETN GU51 59 L5
NBNE BH10 213 J6
Covert Gv WVILLE PO7 170 A3
Coverts Cl FNM GU9 77 J4
The Covert FARN GU14 50 A8
ROMY SO51 137 H2
Covey Cl FARN GU14 50 C8
Covey Wy NARL SO24 291 K12
Covington Rd EMRTH PO10 172 B1
Cowan Rd WVILLE PO7 169 K3
Coward Rd GPORT PO12 14 B9
Cowdown La RAND SP11 271 R1
RCCH PO18 322 G8
Cowdray Cl ELGH SO50 140 F2
ROWN SO16 146 B4
Cowdray Pk ALTN GU34 106 F6
FHAM/STUB PO14 189 G2
Cowdrey Gdns CHAR BH8 214 F6
Cowdrey Hts CHIN RG24 7 L2
Cowdrey Sq AND SP10 * 96 D1
Cow Drove Hl STOK SO20 285 P12
Cowdrys Fld WIMB BH21 207 H2
Cowell Dr LTDN BH7 215 H8
Cowes La HLER SO31 179 K6
Cowfold La HTWY RG27 56 C2
Cowgrove Rd WIMB BH21 206 C4
WIMB BH21 207 G3
Cow La CHAM PO6 184 D1
EPSF GU31 323 L1
FHAM/PORC PO16 183 L1
RAND SP11 267 P5
Cowley Cl ROWN SO16 145 L6
Cowley Dr RWIN SO21 288 D6
Cowley Rd CFDH BH17 211 K8
LYMN SO41 221 J4
Cowleys La BROC SO42 354 A8
Cowleys Rd CHCH/BSGR BH23 216 C6
Cowper Av NMIL/BTOS BH25 219 G7
Cowper Rd ITCH SO19 148 D6
MOOR/WNTN BH9 213 M6
PSEA PO1 * 192 E1
Cowpitts La RGWD BH24 203 M2
Cowshot Crs CHOB/PIR GU24 63 K1
Cowslade NWBY RG14 26 F7
Cowslease Cl ROMY SO51 129 L3
Cowslease Cots
ROMY SO51 129 L3
Cowslip Bank CHIN RG24 54 B8
Cowslip Cl BOR GU35 111 J8
HLER SO31 179 L3
LSOL/BMARY PO13 182 C6
Cowslip Crs NTHA RG18 28 F7
Cowslip Rd BDST BH18 210 E6
Cox Av MOOR/WNTN BH9 214 B5
Coxbridge Mdw FNM GU9 12 B5
Cox Cl MOOR/WNTN BH9 214 B4
Cox Dl FHAM/STUB PO14 180 C3
Coxes Meadow PSF GU32 120 C4
Coxeter Rd NWBY RG14 18 A1
Coxford Cl ROWN SO16 146 A6
Coxford Dro ROWN SO16 146 A5
Coxford Rd ROWN SO16 146 C5
Coxgreen SHST GU47 49 M2
Coxheath Rd FLEETS GU52 71 G2
Coxmoor Cl FLEETS GU52 71 L3
Cox Rw CHFD SO53 139 K5
Cox's Dr ITCH SO19 162 B2
Coxs Hl RWIN SO21 125 G4
Cox's La THLE RG7 36 D1
Coxstone La RGWD BH24 203 J6
Coy Pond Rd
BKME/WDN BH12 225 G3
Cozens Cl ITCH SO19 161 K7
Crabapple Cl TOTT SO40 158 C1
Crabbe Ct SSEA PO5 21 H5
Crabbs Wy TOTT SO40 158 B1
Crabbswood La LYMN SO41 350 C12
Crabden La HORN PO8 321 N12
Crableck La HLER SO31 163 J7
Crab Orchard Wy WIMB BH21 201 G6
Crabs Hl TADY RG26 248 H11
Crabthorne Farm La
FHAM/STUB PO14 189 H1
Crabton Close Rd BOSC BH5 226 F3
Crabtree ROWN SO16 145 M7
Crabtree Cl CHCH/BSGR BH23 216 C6
Crabtree Gdns BOR GU35 111 L7
Crabtree La BOR GU35 111 L7
RFNM GU10 262 G10
Crabtree Rd CBLY GU15 50 D6
Crabtree Wy CHIN RG24 66 D4
Crabwood Cl ROWN SO16 145 M6
Crabwood Ct HAV PO9 170 D1
Crabwood Dr HEND SO30 148 E3
Crabwood Rd ROWN SO16 145 L6
Cracknore Hard TOTT SO40 160 C6
Cracknore Hard La TOTT SO40 160 C6
Cracknore Rd WSHM SO15 22 A2
Cradle La BOR GU35 109 J8
Craigmoor Av CHAR BH8 214 E7
Craigmoor Cl CHAR BH8 214 F7
Craigmoor Wy CHAR BH8 214 E6
Craigside Rd RGWD BH24 205 M4
Craigwell Rd WVILLE PO7 169 K4
Craigwood Dr FERN BH22 209 L4
Crake Pl SHST GU47 43 M8
Crampmoor La ROMY SO51 131 L8
Cramptons ALTN GU34 106 A6
Cranberry Cl TOTT SO40 159 M7
Cranborne Crs
BKME/WDN BH12 212 E8
Cranborne Gdns CHFD SO53 133 H7
Cranborne Rd CHAM PO6 169 G7
FBDG SP6 337 N7
WCLF BH2 8 D7
Cranborne Wk
FHAM/STUB PO14 181 L5
Cranbourne Cl WSHM SO15 146 D7
Cranbourne Ct BSTK RG21 93 H2
Cranbourne Dr RWIN SO21 134 B1
Cranbourne La BSTK RG21 93 H2
Cranbourne Rd GPORT PO12 15 G6
Cranbrook Ct FLEETN GU51 59 J5
Cranbrook Rd
BKME/WDN BH12 224 B2
Cranbury Av SHAM SO14 161 H2
Cranbury Cl RSAL SP5 332 B2
RWIN SO21 134 B1
Cranbury Ct ITCH SO19 161 M5
Cranbury Gdns HLER SO31 162 F3
Cranbury Pl SHAM SO14 161 G2
Cranbury Rd ELGH SO50 140 A3
ITCH SO19 161 M5
Crane Cl LSOL/BMARY PO13 182 B6
VWD BH31 201 G1
Crane Ct SHST GU47 43 M8
Crane Dr VWD BH31 201 G2
Cranemoor Av
CHCH/BSGR BH23 217 L6
Cranemoor Cl
CHCH/BSGR BH23 217 L6
Cranemoor Gdns
CHCH/BSGR BH23 217 M6
Cranesfield CHIN RG24 53 G8
Cranes Ms PLE BH15 223 K5
Cranes Rd CHIN RG24 52 F8
Crane St WIMB BH21 336 F5
Craneswater Av ENEY PO4 21 M9
Craneswater Ga ENEY PO4 192 E7
Craneswater Pk ENEY PO4 21 M9
Crane Wy WIMB BH21 205 K2
Cranfield Av WIMB BH21 207 K3
Cranford Av FLEETS GU52 71 G3
Cranford Dr ALTN GU34 107 J2
Cranford Gdns CHFD SO53 133 H8
Cranford Park Dr YTLY GU46 48 F2
Cranford Rd PSF GU32 120 C7
Cranford Wy PTSW SO17 147 G6
Cranleigh Av PSEA PO1 192 E2
Cranleigh Cl SBNE BH6 227 L3
Cranleigh Ct FARN GU14 60 F4
Cranleigh Gdns SBNE BH6 227 L3
Cranleigh Rd
FHAM/PORC PO16 183 G1
HEND SO30 149 J6
PSEA PO1 192 E2
SBNE BH6 227 K2
Cranmer Dr ROWN SO16 145 J3
Cranmer Rd MOOR/WNTN BH9 213 M8
Cranmore HLER SO31 162 C5
Cranmore Cl ALDT GU11 2 A5
Cranmore Gdns ALDT GU11 2 B5
Cranmore La ALDT GU11 2 A6
Cranmore Rd FRIM GU16 61 M4
Crantock Gv CHAR BH8 214 F6
Cranwell Cl BWD BH11 212 E4
CHCH/BSGR BH23 348 D11
Cranworth Rd FUFL SO22 24 E3
Crasswell St PSEA PO1 21 H1
Craven Cl HUNG RG17 31 H3
RFNM GU10 79 G2
Craven Ct FHAM PO15 10 A2
Craven Dene NWBY RG14 19 H2
Craven Rd CHFD SO53 139 K2
HUNG RG17 30 B6
NWBY RG14 18 A5
Craven St SHAM SO14 23 H2
Craven Wk SHAM SO14 23 H2
Craven Wy HUNG RG17 31 H2
Crawford Cl ROWN SO16 145 K3
Crawford Dr FHAM/PORC PO16 10 C1
Crawford Gdns CBLY GU15 50 D3
Crawford Pl NWBY RG14 18 D3
Crawlboys La RAND SP11 265 M9
Crawley Av HAV PO9 171 G2
Crawley Dr CBLY GU15 51 H2
Crawley Hl CBLY GU15 51 H3
ROMY SO51 335 L7
Crawley Rdg CBLY GU15 51 H2
Crawley Wood Cl CBLY GU15 51 H3
Crawshaw Rd PSTN BH14 224 B6
Crawte Av FAWY SO45 354 F6
Crawts Rd OVTN RG25 89 J5
Craydown La STOK SO20 270 A10
Creasey Rd BWD BH11 213 G3
Credenhill Rd CHAM PO6 168 C7
Credon Cl FARN GU14 60 E3
Creech Rd BKME/WDN BH12 224 C3
Creech Vw WVILLE PO7 154 E4
Creedy Dr CHCH/BSGR BH23 228 A3
Creedy Gdns WEND SO18 148 A1
Creek End EMRTH PO10 187 M1
Creekmoor La CFDH BH17 210 F7
Creek Rd GPORT PO12 15 J4
HISD PO11 195 K6
Creighton Rd WSHM SO15 159 M2
Cremorne Pl EPSF GU31 120 D5
Cremyll Cl FHAM/STUB PO14 189 J2
Crerar Cl FARN GU14 60 D5
Crescent Cl FUFL SO22 122 B8
Crescent Dr NMIL/BTOS BH25 230 F1
Crescent Gdns
FHAM/PORC PO16 * 10 F6
Crescent La ASHV GU12 74 B3
Crescent Rd FHAM/PORC PO16 10 F6
GPORT PO12 191 G7
HLER SO31 179 M1
NBAD SO52 137 M3
PSTN BH14 224 E4
VWD BH31 201 J2
WCLF BH2 8 C5
WIMB BH21 207 J4
The Crescent ALTN GU34 293 M4
AND SP10 95 L4
BMTH BH1 226 E4
ELGH SO50 134 A8
EMRTH PO10 172 D6
FARN GU14 61 J5
FERN BH22 * 205 K8
FLEETN GU51 70 E2
FNM GU9 72 D8
HLER SO31 162 C6
HTWY RG27 54 D3
HUNG RG17 * 31 G2
ITCH SO19 162 A2
NMIL/BTOS BH25 218 C8
RAND SP11 96 A8
RAND SP11 250 G9
RAND SP11 271 P3
ROMY SO51 131 H8
RWIN SO21 125 G6
THLE RG7 40 A2
TOTT SO40 159 L7
TOTT SO40 341 Q9
WVILLE PO7 169 J4
YTLY GU46 48 F1
Crescent Wk FERN BH22 209 L6
Cressey Rd ROMY SO51 136 F1
Cress Gdns AND SP10 4 E8
Cresswell Rd NWBY RG14 19 M1
Cressy Rd NEND PO2 192 D1
Cresta Gdns FERN BH22 209 L6
Crest Cl FHAM/PORC PO16 11 M5
Crestland Cl HORN PO8 156 A5
Crest Rd BKME/WDN BH12 224 C2
The Crest WVILLE PO7 169 J6
Crest Wy ITCH SO19 148 C8
Creswell Cl WHIT RG2 238 B2
Crete La FAWY SO45 176 F7
Crete Rd FAWY SO45 176 F8
Cribb Cl CFDH BH17 223 L1
Crichel Mount Rd PSTN BH14 224 C8
Crichel Rd MOOR/WNTN BH9 214 A8
Cricket Cl CHCH/BSGR BH23 228 F3
RWIN SO21 287 M6
Cricket Dr HORN PO8 156 A3
Cricketers KSCL RG20 26 A6
Cricketers Wy AND SP10 96 E1
Cricket Field Gv CWTH RG45 43 M4
Cricket Gn HTWY RG27 57 M2
Cricket Green La HTWY RG27 57 M2
Cricket Hl EWKG RG40 42 B6
Cricket Hill La BLKW GU17 48 F5
YTLY GU46 49 G3
Cricket La RFNM GU10 79 H2
Cricket Lea BOR GU35 111 H7
Cricklade Pl AND SP10 4 D3
Cricklemede BPWT SO32 143 K5
Cricklewood Cl BPWT SO32 143 K5
Crigdon Cl ROWN SO16 145 L8
Crimea Rd ALDT GU11 3 H3
MOOR/WNTN BH9 225 M1
Cringle Av SBNE BH6 228 A4
Crinoline Gdns ENEY PO4 193 G6
Cripley Rd FARN GU14 60 E3
Cripplecrutch Hl
MFD/CHID GU8 119 M6
Cripple Gate La BROC SO42 353 K11
Crispin Cl CHCH/BSGR BH23 217 M8
ELGH SO50 141 J6
HLER SO31 164 B8
Crispstead La WINC SO23 122 F7
Crisspyn Cl HORN PO8 * 156 B2
Critchmere Hl HASM GU27 117 L1
Critchmere La HASM GU27 117 L2
Critchmere V HASM GU27 117 K2
Criterion Ar BMTH BH1 * 8 E6
Crittall Cl LYMN SO41 350 G10
Cricket Cl GSHT GU26 115 K2
Crockford Br LYMN SO41 356 D2
Crockford Cl NMIL/BTOS BH25 219 H3
Crockford La CHIN RG24 65 M2
Crockford Rd EMRTH PO10 172 B2
RSAL SP5 327 Q2
Crocus Md NTHA RG18 29 G8
Crocus Wy WWKG RG41 239 R1
Croft Av AND SP10 5 H8
Croft Cl WIMB BH21 210 D1
Crofters Cl FRIM GU16 51 M7
SHST GU47 43 J8
Crofters Meadow CHIN RG24 54 B8
Croft Gdns ALTN GU34 106 E4
AND SP10 5 H9
Croft Hts RSAL SP5 127 H5
Croftlands Av
FHAM/STUB PO14 189 J1
Croft La HISD PO11 187 G7
NWBY RG14 18 B2
RFNM GU10 259 N3
YTLY GU46 48 E1
Crofton Av LSOL/BMARY PO13 189 J4
Crofton Cl CHCH/BSGR BH23 215 L8
PTSW SO17 147 G7
WVILLE PO7 169 J3
Crofton La FHAM/STUB PO14 189 H3
Crofton Rd ENEY PO4 193 H4
NEND PO2 184 E6
Crofton Wy BPWT SO32 318 A7
HLER SO31 179 J3
Croft Rd ALDT GU11 3 H7
BKME/WDN BH12 224 B2
CHCH/BSGR BH23 217 H2
CHCH/BSGR BH23 228 F1
DEAN RG23 91 J2
MOOR/WNTN BH9 213 M6
NEND PO2 * 184 D7
NWBY RG14 18 D9
RGWD BH24 203 L3
THLE RG7 39 M6
THLE RG7 238 C6
The Crofts KBH RG22 92 E6
The Croft AMSY SP4 268 B6
CHFD SO53 139 J5
FHAM/STUB PO14 181 J8
HUNG RG17 31 G2
RSAL SP5 324 D4
TOTT SO40 144 C6
Croft Wy FRIM GU16 51 H7
Cromarty Av ENEY PO4 193 H4
Cromarty Cl FHAM/STUB PO14 189 H1
Cromarty Rd ROWN SO16 145 L3
Crombie Cl HORN PO8 155 M4
Cromer Gdns
BKME/WDN BH12 224 F3
Cromer Rd BKME/WDN BH12 224 F3
CHAM PO6 168 D7
CHAR BH8 226 D1
ROWN SO16 145 K7
Cromhall Cl FHAM/STUB PO14 181 J4
Crompton Wy FHAM PO15 164 C7
Cromwell Cl CHIN RG24 66 D2
Cromwell Pl BOSC BH5 227 H3
NWBY RG14 18 E3
Cromwell Rd
BKME/WDN BH12 224 D3
BOSC BH5 227 H3
BSTK RG21 6 D2
CBLY GU15 50 F1
ENEY PO4 193 H6
FUFL SO22 24 B9
NWBY RG14 27 L7
WIMB BH21 207 K4
WSHM SO15 160 F1
Cromwell Ter NWBY RG14 * 26 F7
Cromwell Wy FARN GU14 61 H1
Crondall Av HAV PO9 170 E2
Crondall Ct CBLY GU15 50 D4
Crondall End YTLY GU46 48 E1
Crondall La RFNM GU10 76 A6
Crondall Rd FLEETN GU51 70 E5
RFNM GU10 259 Q9
Crooked Hays Cl TOTT SO40 159 M7
Crooked Walk La WHAM PO17 167 L5
Crookham Cl HAV PO9 170 C4
TADY RG26 44 B6
Crookham Reach FLEETS GU52 71 G3
Crookham Rd FLEETN GU51 71 G2
ITCH SO19 161 M8
Crookhorn La WVILLE PO7 169 L7
Crooksbury Rd RFNM GU10 77 M5
Cropmark Wy KBH RG22 92 D5
Cropper Cl STHA RG19 36 A1
Crosby Gdns YTLY GU46 48 C1
Crosby Hill Dr CBLY GU15 51 H1
Crosby Rd WBNE BH4 225 J7
Crosby Wy FNM GU9 12 D5
Crosfield Cl ROMY SO51 335 M6
Crossbill Cl HORN PO8 * 156 A1
Crossborough Gdns
BSTK RG21 * 7 H6
Crossborough Hl BSTK RG21 7 H7
Crossfell Wk FHAM/STUB PO14 10 B9
Cross Gdns FRIM GU16 61 M2
Crosshouse Rd SHAM SO14 23 L6
Cross Keys Pas WINC SO23 * 25 H6
Crossland Cl GPORT PO12 15 G7
Crossland Dr HAV PO9 17 G1
Cross La AND SP10 4 E4
BPWT SO32 143 G1
FRIM GU16 61 M2
HORN PO8 156 A3
KSCL RG20 245 Q12
THLE RG7 41 K1
Crossmead Av
NMIL/BTOS BH25 219 G6
Cross & Pillory La ALTN GU34 * 106 F5
Cross Rd ASHV GU12 74 B5
FARN GU14 60 E7
ITCH SO19 161 L1
LSOL/BMARY PO13 190 A4
Cross St ALDT GU11 2 E3
BPWT SO32 143 J4
BSTK RG21 6 E6
FARN GU14 61 J8
PSEA PO1 20 D2
SSEA PO5 * 21 J4
WINC SO23 24 F5
The Cross PSF GU32 314 B7
RGWD BH24 349 J1
RSAL SP5 324 D5
STOK SO20 299 Q1
Crosstrees HLER SO31 * 163 M6
Crosswater La RFNM GU10 262 E8
Cross Wy CHCH/BSGR BH23 215 K7
HAV PO9 16 C3
RWIN SO21 124 D7
Crossways ASHV GU12 3 K5
LYMN SO41 220 D7
RFNM GU10 262 E11
Crossways Rd GSHT GU26 115 K5
The Crossways AND SP10 4 F4
GPORT PO12 14 E1
UPTN BH16 222 C1

The Crossway
FHAM/PORC PO16 167 J8
Crosswell Cl ITCH SO19 148 C7
Croucher's Cft FUFL SO22 122 B3
Croucheston Dro RSAL SP5 324 C3
Crouch La HORN PO8 156 A1
Crow Arch La RGWD BH24 203 K6
Crowder Ter FUFL SO22 24 E6
Crowfield Dr STHA RG19 35 H1
Crow La RGWD BH24 203 L7
Crowley Dr ALTN GU34 107 G5
Crown Acre Cl STHA RG19 35 J1
Crown Cl BKME/WDN BH12 224 C3
WVILLE PO7 169 L5
Crown Dr FNM GU9 77 L3
Crownfields ODIM RG29 68 F6
Crown Gdns FLEETN GU51 59 K8
Crown La CHIN RG24 66 C2
FNM GU9 77 L3
HTWY RG27 67 K1
RAND SP11 265 L10
Crown Md STHA RG19 * 35 J1
WIMB BH21 207 J4
Crown Pl SHST GU47 * 43 M7
Crown St PSEA PO1 21 K1
WSHM SO15 146 B8
Crown Wk WINC SO23 * 25 G4
Crown Yd STHA RG19 * 35 M3
Crowsbury Cl EMRTH PO10 171 L5
Crows La ALTN GU34 294 E5
Crows Nest La BPWT SO32 149 M3
Crowsport HLER SO31 179 G1
Crowther Cl ITCH SO19 148 C8
Crowthorne Rd SHST GU47 43 K8
Croyde Cl FARN GU14 61 G2
Croydon Cl ROWN SO16 146 A4
Croye Cl AND SP10 4 E5
Cruikshank Lea SHST GU47 50 A2
Crummock Rd CHFD SO53 139 G1
Crundles EPSF GU31 120 E6
Crusader Ct GPORT PO12 191 J1
Crusader Rd BWD BH11 212 D4
HEND SO30 149 K7
Crusaders Wy CHFD SO53 138 F2
Cruse Cl LYMN SO41 350 F10
Crystal Wy WVILLE PO7 156 B8
Cucklington Gdns
MOOR/WNTN BH9 214 B5
Cuckmere La ROWN SO16 145 K8
Cuckoo Bushes La CHFD SO53 133 H8
Cuckoo Cl OVTN RG25 103 G3
Cuckoo Hill Wy
CHCH/BSGR BH23 348 E11
Cuckoo La FHAM/STUB PO14 181 H8
Cuckoo Rd BKME/WDN BH12 212 A8
Cudnell Av BWD BH11 212 F2
Cudworth Md HEND SO30 149 K3
Cufaude La TADY RG26 54 B2
Cuffelle Cl CHIN RG24 54 C5
Cuffnells Cl RGWD BH24 199 K4
The Cul-de-Sac
NMIL/BTOS BH25 * 218 C8
Culford Av TOTT SO40 158 F2
Culford Cl CHAR BH8 214 F6
Culford Wy TOTT SO40 158 F2
Cull Cl BKME/WDN BH12 213 J8
Cullen Cl YTLY GU46 48 E3
Cullens Ms ALDT GU11 * 2 E4
Culley Vw NARL SO24 291 M12
Culliford Crs CFDH BH17 211 L6
Cull La NMIL/BTOS BH25 219 H3
Culloden Cl FHAM PO15 10 B3
Culloden Rd FHAM/STUB PO14 181 M6
Cull's Rd RGUW GU3 75 H7
Cullwood La NMIL/BTOS BH25 219 J3
Culver HLER SO31 162 C5
Culver Cl ROWN SO16 145 K6
Culver Dr HISD PO11 195 J7
Culverhayes Pl WIMB BH21 207 H2
Culverhayes Rd WIMB BH21 207 H2
Culverin Sq HSEA PO3 * 185 G4
Culverlands Crs ASHV GU12 73 M5
Culverley Cl BROC SO42 351 K3
Culver Ms WINC SO23 * 25 G7
Culver Rd BSTK RG21 6 C9
ENEY PO4 193 G6
NMIL/BTOS BH25 218 F6
NWBY RG14 33 M4
SHST GU47 43 M7
WINC SO23 24 F8
Culvers EPSF GU31 323 M1
Culverwell Gdns WINC SO23 24 F7
Culvery Gdns WEND SO18 148 A2
Cumberland Av CHFD SO53 139 L3
EMRTH PO10 171 L4
KBH RG22 93 G3
Cumberland Cl CHFD SO53 139 L2
Cumberland Pl WSHM SO15 22 E1
Cumberland Rd CBLY GU15 51 L4
SSEA PO5 * 21 L3
Cumberland St PSEA PO1 20 D1
SHAM SO14 23 J3
Cumberland Wy FAWY SO45 176 D5
WWKG RG41 239 R2
Cumber Rd HLER SO31 179 L1
Cumbria Ct FARN GU14 61 L7
Cumbrian Wy ROWN SO16 145 L8
Cummins Cl AND SP10 5 K6
Cummins Gn HLER SO31 163 G3
Cumnor Rd BMTH BH1 9 G5
Cunard Av WSHM SO15 146 C8
Cunard Rd SHAM SO14 23 H8
Cundell Wy WINC SO23 288 H7
Cunningham Av BPWT SO32 143 G4
Cunningham Cl BWD BH11 213 G5
CHCH/BSGR BH23 229 G2
RGWD BH24 203 L4
Cunningham Crs BWD BH11 213 G5
ITCH SO19 148 B8
Cunningham Dr HLER SO31 164 B8
LSOL/BMARY PO13 182 D5
Cunningham Gdns HLER SO31 162 E4
Cunningham Pl BWD BH11 213 G5
Cunningham Rd HORN PO8 156 C1
WVILLE PO7 169 L3
Cunnington Rd FARN GU14 61 L7
Cupernham Cl ROMY SO51 131 G8
Cupernham La ROMY SO51 131 G5
Curdridge Cl HAV PO9 171 G3
Curdridge La BPWT SO32 151 G2
Curlew Cl EMRTH PO10 171 L8
FERN BH22 209 H1
KBH RG22 92 C3
ROWN SO16 146 B3
STHA RG19 35 J1
Curlew Dr FAWY SO45 177 H6
FHAM/PORC PO16 166 F8
Curlew Gdns HORN PO8 155 M4
Curlew Pth ENEY PO4 * 193 H3
Curlew Rd CHAR BH8 214 D6
CHCH/BSGR BH23 229 G2
Curlews ALTN GU34 106 F2
The Curlews VWD BH31 201 J3
Curlew Sq ELGH SO50 139 L6
Curlieu Rd PLE BH15 223 L2
Curling Wy NWBY RG14 19 K1
Curly Bridge Cl FARN GU14 50 B8
Curly's Wy THLE RG7 238 D10
Curnock Ct NWBY RG14 * 18 B7
Curridge Rd NWBY RG14 27 L1
Curtis Cl BOR GU35 111 L6
CBLY GU15 51 L1
Curtis La BOR GU35 111 L6
Curtis Md NEND PO2 184 F4
Curtis Rd ALTN GU34 107 G6
BKME/WDN BH12 224 C3
Curtiss Gdns GPORT PO12 14 A4
The Curve HORN PO8 155 M2
LSOL/BMARY PO13 182 B6
Curzon Br CHOB/PIR GU24 63 G3
Curzon Dr FLEETS GU52 71 J3
Curzon Howe Rd PSEA PO1 20 D2
Curzon Pl LYMN SO41 221 K6
Curzon Rd BMTH BH1 226 D2
PSTN BH14 224 A5
WVILLE PO7 169 L1
Curzon Wy CHCH/BSGR BH23 217 K8
Cusden Dr AND SP10 5 G2
Custards Rd LYND SO43 345 K2
Cutbush La WEND SO18 148 A1
WHIT RG2 238 E2
Cuthbert Rd ASHV GU12 74 A2
PSEA PO1 192 F2
Cuthburga Rd WIMB BH21 207 J3
Cuthbury Cl WIMB BH21 207 G4
Cuthbury Gdns WIMB BH21 207 G3
Cutler Cl BKME/WDN BH12 225 J1
NMIL/BTOS BH25 219 J5
Cutlers La FHAM/STUB PO14 189 J1
Cutlers Pl WIMB BH21 208 A3
Cut Pound ALTN GU34 106 E5
Cutter Av HLER SO31 179 L3
Cut Throat La BPWT SO32 318 C6
BPWT SO32 318 H2
Cutts Arch BPWT SO32 318 H5
Cutts Rd ALDT GU11 73 K1
Cuxhaven Wy AND SP10 96 B1
Cygnet Cl STHA RG19 35 H1
Cygnet Ct FHAM/PORC PO16 166 F8
Cygnet Rd CHAM PO6 185 M1
Cygnus Gdns FAWY SO45 176 C5
Cynthia Cl BKME/WDN BH12 224 B1
Cynthia Rd BKME/WDN BH12 224 B1
Cypress FARN GU14 50 B7
Cypress Av ITCH SO19 161 M3
Cypress Crs HORN PO8 156 A3
Cypress Dr FLEETN GU51 59 L7
Cypress Gdns HEND SO30 150 A5
TOTT SO40 158 C1
Cypress Gv ASHV GU12 73 M1
RAND SP11 95 L5
Cypress Rd BOR GU35 112 C1
Cypress Wy GSHT GU26 115 K6
Cyprus Rd FHAM/STUB PO14 180 C3
FRIM GU16 51 M8
KBH RG22 92 E7
NEND PO2 184 E8
Cyril Rd CHAR BH8 226 C2
Cyril Vokins Rd NWBY RG14 34 E2

D

Dacombe Cl UPTN BH16 222 C1
Dacombe Dr UPTN BH16 222 C1
Dacre Cl AND SP10 95 M1
Daffodil Cl KBH RG22 92 C4
Daffodil Rd ROWN SO16 147 J4
Daggons Rd FBDG SP6 337 Q6
Dahlia Cl KBH RG22 92 C4
Dahlia Ct AND SP10 4 B8
Dahlia Rd ROWN SO16 147 G4
Daintree Cl ITCH SO19 162 D1
Dairy Cl CHCH/BSGR BH23 228 D1
RSAL SP5 332 F3
WIMB BH21 210 B4
Dairy Gate Rd FARN GU14 61 H8
Dairy La ROWN SO16 145 G4
Dairymoor WHAM PO17 152 A4
Daisy La GPORT PO12 14 D4
HLER SO31 180 B1
Daisy Md WVILLE PO7 170 A2
Daisy Rd ROWN SO16 147 J4
Dalby Crs NWBY RG14 19 J9
Dale Cl FUFL SO22 288 A11
PLE BH15 223 M2
RFNM GU10 78 D1
Dale Dr LSOL/BMARY PO13 182 B3
Dale Gdns SHST GU47 43 J8
Dale Rd FAWY SO45 176 F5
FHAM/STUB PO14 189 K1
PLE BH15 223 M2
ROWN SO16 146 C6
Dales Cl WIMB BH21 208 C2
Dales Dr WIMB BH21 208 B3
Dales La CHCH/BSGR BH23 214 E1
Dales Wy TOTT SO40 144 B8
The Dale WVILLE PO7 169 J6
Dale Valley Cl ROWN SO16 146 C6
Dale Valley Gdns ROWN SO16 146 C6
Dale Valley Rd PLE BH15 223 L1
ROWN SO16 146 C5
Dale Vw HASM GU27 117 M3
Dalewood KBH RG22 92 C2
Dalewood Av BWD BH11 212 E3
Dalewood Rd FHAM PO15 181 K3
Dalkeith Arcade BMTH BH1 8 F5
Dalkeith Rd CCLF BH13 225 G7
WIMB BH21 210 D4
Dalkeith Steps BMTH BH1 * 8 F5
Dalley Ct SHST GU47 49 M1
Dalling Rd BKME/WDN BH12 225 G3
Dallington Cl
FHAM/STUB PO14 189 J3
Dalmally Gdns WEND SO18 147 L8
Dalmeny Rd SBNE BH6 228 A5
Dalston Cl CBLY GU15 51 M5
Damask Gdns WVILLE PO7 156 B7
Damen Cl HEND SO30 149 H7
Damerham Rd CHAR BH8 214 D5
Dampier Cl LSOL/BMARY PO13 190 C1
Damsel La OVTN RG25 278 B1
Damsel Pth BSTK RG21 7 K5
Damson Crs ELGH SO50 141 G3
Damson Hl BPWT SO32 318 B4
Danbury Ct EMRTH PO10 172 A4
Dancers Meadow CHIN RG24 65 H1
Dances Cl AND SP10 5 J3
Dances La WHCH RG28 87 L6
Dances Wy HISD PO11 194 E4
Dandelion Cl
LSOL/BMARY PO13 182 B5
Dando Rd WVILLE PO7 155 G4
Dandy's Ford La ROMY SO51 128 F8
Danebury Cl HAV PO9 170 E2
Danebury Gdns CHFD SO53 139 G4
Danebury Rd KBH RG22 92 D6
Danebury Wy ROWN SO16 145 K5
Dane Cl FAWY SO45 354 H7
Danecourt Cl PSTN BH14 223 M4
Danecourt Rd PSTN BH14 223 M4
Danecrest Rd LYMN SO41 219 M5
Dane Dr FERN BH22 209 L5
Danegeld Cl AND SP10 84 D8
Danehurst New Rd
LYMN SO41 350 A12
Danehurst Pl AND SP10 95 L4
HLER SO31 180 A2
Dane Rd LYMN SO41 232 A2
Danesbrook La WVILLE PO7 170 A1
Danesbury Av SBNE BH6 227 M4
Danesbury Mdw
NMIL/BTOS BH25 219 J3
Danes Cl NMIL/BTOS BH25 231 G1
Daneshill Ct CHIN RG24 54 B8
Daneshill Dr CHIN RG24 54 C8
Danes Rd FHAM/PORC PO16 167 H7
ROMY SO51 129 K4
WINC SO23 25 G2
The Danes BSTK RG21 7 G5
Danestream Cl LYMN SO41 232 D4
Daneswood Rd
NMIL/BTOS BH25 219 J5
Daniell's Cl LYMN SO41 221 L5
Daniell's Wk LYMN SO41 221 L6
Daniel Rd WHCH RG28 87 M8
Dankworth Rd KBH RG22 92 E4
Danley La HASM GU27 117 G5
Dansie Cl PSTN BH14 224 B4
Danvers Cl STHA RG19 35 K2
Danvers Dr FLEETS GU52 70 F4
Daphne Dr FLEETS GU52 71 G5
Dapple Pl TOTT SO40 160 A7
Darby Green La BLKW GU17 49 K3
Darby Green Rd BLKW GU17 49 J3
Darby's Cl PLE BH15 223 K2
Darby's Cnr CFDH BH17 211 J6
Darby's La PLE BH15 223 K2
Darby's La North CFDH BH17 223 K1
Darent Ct BSTK RG21 7 J5
Dare's La RFNM GU10 71 G7
Dark La CHIN RG24 65 G1
CHCH/BSGR BH23 218 A4
FAWY SO45 354 H7
NARL SO24 303 R7
NARL SO24 304 B2
RGUW GU3 261 M4
Darlee Ga HLER SO31 * 162 F3
Darleydale Cl SHST GU47 43 M6
Darley Rd FERN BH22 209 J5
Darlington Gdns WSHM SO15 146 D8
Darlington Rd BSTK RG21 6 D1
ENEY PO4 21 L6
Darracott Cl CBLY GU15 51 K1
Darracott Rd BOSC BH5 227 G4
Darren Cl FHAM/STUB PO14 181 K8
Darset Av FLEETN GU51 59 J6
Dart Cl EWKG RG40 42 B1
NTHA RG18 28 D7
Dart Ct AND SP10 96 E2
Dartington Rd ELGH SO50 134 D7
Dartmouth Rd HSEA PO3 185 G6
Dartmouth Wk KBH RG22 92 E1
Dartmouth Wy KBH RG22 92 E1
Dart Rd FARN GU14 60 D2
WEND SO18 148 B1
Darvill Hts FNM GU9 * 13 H4
Darvill Rd NARL SO24 292 E11
Darvills La FNM GU9 13 H3
Darwin Av CHCH/BSGR BH23 215 L7
Darwin Cl LSOL/BMARY PO13 189 M5
Darwin Gv ALDT GU11 3 K1
Darwin Rd ELGH SO50 134 B8
WSHM SO15 160 D1
Darwin Wy LSOL/BMARY PO13 190 D2
Dashwood Cl ALTN GU34 106 D6
Dasna Rd NTID SP9 266 D3
Daulston Rd PSEA PO1 192 E1
Daunch Cl NTID SP9 266 D1
Dauntsey Dro RAND SP11 94 C2
Dauntsey La RAND SP11 94 C3
Davenport Cl
LSOL/BMARY PO13 190 C2
UPTN BH16 222 C1
Davenport Ga AND SP10 95 L3
Daventry La HSEA PO3 185 J4
D Av FAWY SO45 354 F2
David Newberry Dr
LSOL/BMARY PO13 190 A2
David's Gdn RSAL SP5 296 A1
David's La RGWD BH24 202 E7
Davidson Cl FAWY SO45 177 H4
David Wy PLE BH15 222 D6
Davis Cl LSOL/BMARY PO13 182 C8
Davis Fld NMIL/BTOS BH25 218 F6
Davis Gdns SHST GU47 50 A1
Davis Rd PSTN BH14 224 E3
Davy Cl KBH RG22 65 G7
Dawkins Rd PLE BH15 222 D5
Dawkins Wy NMIL/BTOS BH25 219 G6
Daw La HISD PO11 186 F8
Dawlish Av WSHM SO15 146 D8
Dawnay Cl ROWN SO16 147 K3
Dawn Cl NBNE BH10 213 J6
Dawney Hl CHOB/PIR GU24 63 L2
Dawneys Rd CHOB/PIR GU24 63 L3
Dawn Gdns FUFL SO22 122 C6
Daws Av BWD BH11 213 H6
Dawsmere Cl CBLY GU15 51 L3
Dawson Rd ITCH SO19 162 C2
RWIN SO21 273 N1
Day La HORN PO8 155 K1
Daylesford Cl PSTN BH14 224 A6
Dayrell Cl TOTT SO40 144 B7
Day's Ct WIMB BH21 207 K4
Dayshes Cl LSOL/BMARY PO13 182 B5
Dayslondon Rd WVILLE PO7 169 K3
Daytona Dr STHA RG19 36 B2
Deacon Cl ITCH SO19 148 A7
Deacon Crs ITCH SO19 148 A6
Deacon Gdns BWD BH11 213 G3
Deacon Rd BWD BH11 213 G3
HLER SO31 180 B2
ITCH SO19 148 A7
RAND SP11 267 P4
Deadbrook La ASHV GU12 3 M1
Deadman's La BSTK RG21 7 K5
STHA RG19 34 B6
Deadmoor La KSCL RG20 246 G2
Deal Cl FHAM/STUB PO14 181 J8
Deal Rd CHAM PO6 168 E7
Dean Cl FUFL SO22 122 C2
PLE BH15 222 E5
Dean Ct HEND SO30 149 H5
Deane Ct HAV PO9 * 171 H3
Deane Down Dro FUFL SO22 288 B12
The Deanery CHFD SO53 133 H8
Deanes Cl BSTK RG21 7 G2
Deane's Park Rd
FHAM/PORC PO16 11 L6
Deanfield Cl HLER SO31 178 F2
Dean La BPWT SO32 311 L11
HORN PO8 157 K3
RSAL SP5 127 H4
RWIN SO21 301 Q1
Dean Park Crs BMTH BH1 8 F4
Dean Park Rd BMTH BH1 8 F4
Dean Ri RAND SP11 250 H9
Dean Rd CHAM PO6 184 F1
ELGH SO50 141 H3
RSAL SP5 296 D9
RSAL SP5 297 L7
WEND SO18 148 A5
Deans Cl NTID SP9 266 F4
Deans Ct LYMN SO41 232 D3
Deans Court La WIMB BH21 207 H4
Deanscroft Rd NBNE BH10 213 L4
Deans Dell PSF GU32 307 J11
Deans Ga FHAM/STUB PO14 189 J3
Deans Gv WIMB BH21 207 K1
Deansleigh Rd LTDN BH7 215 H7
Dean's Rd BOSC BH5 227 H3
The Deans BMTH BH1 8 F3
Dean St PSEA PO1 20 D3
Dean Swift Crs PSTN BH14 224 C8
Deanswood Rd TADY RG26 44 A4
The Dean NARL SO24 291 L10
Dear Hay La PLE BH15 223 J6
Dearing Cl LYND SO43 345 K4
Decies Rd PSTN BH14 224 B3
De Courtenai Cl BWD BH11 212 E3
Decouttere Cl FLEETS GU52 71 G3
Dee Cl CHFD SO53 139 G3
Deedman Cl ASHV GU12 74 A6
Deepcut Bridge Rd FRIM GU16 51 M7
Deep Dene HASM GU27 117 L2
Deepdene RFNM GU10 79 H2
Deeping Cl ITCH SO19 161 M7
Deeping Ga WVILLE PO7 170 A1
Deep La BSTK RG21 6 A5
Deep Well Dr CBLY GU15 51 G3
Deerfield Cl TADY RG26 46 D6
Deerhurst Cl TOTT SO40 158 C2
Deerhurst Crs CHAM PO6 168 A7
Deerleap BOR GU35 * 114 C4
Deer Leap FHAM PO15 165 K7
Deerleap La TOTT SO40 158 E8
Deerleap Wy FAWY SO45 177 G5
NMIL/BTOS BH25 219 H2
Deer Park Cl NMIL/BTOS BH25 218 F4
Deer Park Vw ODIM RG29 69 G5
Deer Rock Rd CBLY GU15 51 H1
Deeside KBH RG22 * 92 E1
Dee Wy PLE BH15 223 H6
Defender Rd ITCH SO19 161 K5
Defender Wk ITCH SO19 161 K5
De Grouchy La PTSW SO17 147 G7
De Haviland Cl WIMB BH21 207 M6
De Havilland Wy
CHCH/BSGR BH23 229 G3
Delamere Gdns NBNE BH10 213 L5
Delamere Rd ENEY PO4 21 M6
De La Warr Rd LYMN SO41 232 C4
Delft Cl HLER SO31 179 M1
Delft Gdns WVILLE PO7 155 K6
Delft Ms CHCH/BSGR BH23 228 D1
Delhi Cl PSTN BH14 224 D5
Delhi Rd NBNE BH10 213 L6
Delibes Rd KBH RG22 93 H4
Delilah Rd PLE BH15 222 D6
De Lisle Cl NEND PO2 184 F4
De Lisle Rd TWDS BH3 225 M1
Delius Av ITCH SO19 162 D1
Delius Cl KBH RG22 93 G3
Delius Wk WVILLE PO7 169 L3
Dellands OVTN RG25 89 J5
Dellands La OVTN RG25 89 H4
Dell Cl BDST BH18 210 E4
CHAM PO6 169 H6
ELGH SO50 141 J3
HASM GU27 118 A5
Dellcrest Pth CHAM PO6 169 H7
Dellfield DEAN RG23 91 K1
PSF GU32 307 J10
Dellfield Cl CHAM PO6 168 A7
Dell Gv FRIM GU16 51 H6
Delling Cl RCCH PO18 173 M8
Dell Piece East HORN PO8 156 D3
Dell Piece West HORN PO8 156 C3
Dell Quay Cl FHAM/STUB PO14 182 A6
Dell Rd AND SP10 4 E2
EWKG RG40 42 C5
WEND SO18 147 M6
WINC SO23 25 L8
The Dell CHIN RG24 66 E3
FHAM/PORC PO16 11 M6
FNM GU9 77 G1
HAV PO9 170 B6
KSCL RG20 248 D10
NMIL/BTOS BH25 218 C8
RAND SP11 243 Q10
RAND SP11 269 P3
YTLY GU46 48 E3
Delme Dr FHAM/PORC PO16 11 L4
Delphi Wy WVILLE PO7 169 M6
Delph Rd WIMB BH21 207 K8
Delta Cl CHCH/BSGR BH23 229 G1
De-lucy Av NARL SO24 291 K11
Delville Cl FARN GU14 60 D5
De Mauley Rd CCLF BH13 224 E8
De Montfort Rd NWBY RG14 26 F7
WIMB BH21 207 K7
De Mowbray Wy LYMN SO41 221 K6
Dempsey Cl ITCH SO19 148 B8
Denbigh Cl ELGH SO50 139 M3
TOTT SO40 158 D3
Denbigh Dr FHAM/PORC PO16 10 D3
Denbigh Gdns ROWN SO16 146 F4
Denbigh Rd HASM GU27 118 D7
Denby Rd PLE BH15 223 K4
Dene Cl ASHV GU12 74 C6
BOR GU35 112 F2
HASM GU27 118 C6
HLER SO31 163 L8
NARL SO24 292 D11
RFNM GU10 79 H2
RGWD BH24 203 L3
ROWN SO16 146 F1
Dene Ct AND SP10 5 J7
Dene Hollow CHAM PO6 169 K8
Dene La RFNM GU10 79 H2
Dene La West RFNM GU10 79 H3
Dene Pth AND SP10 5 K7
Dene Rd AND SP10 5 J7
FARN GU14 60 F5
TOTT SO40 158 C6
Deneside Copse LYMN SO41 221 H7
Deneside Gdns LYMN SO41 221 H6
The Dene NARL SO24 292 D12
Deneve Av CFDH BH17 211 J7
Dene Wk FERN BH22 209 L7
RFNM GU10 79 J2
Dene Wy NWBY RG14 27 H7
TOTT SO40 158 C5
Denewood Copse FERN BH22 204 F5
Denewood Rd FERN BH22 204 F4
WBNE BH4 225 H6
Denewulf Cl BPWT SO32 143 J4
Denham Cl CFDH BH17 211 L5
FHAM/STUB PO14 189 H2
WINC SO23 24 F1
Denham Dr CHCH/BSGR BH23 217 M7
KBH RG22 92 E2
YTLY GU46 48 F3
Denham Gdns HLER SO31 162 B7
Denhill Cl HISD PO11 194 E3
Denholm Cl RGWD BH24 203 M3
Denison Rd CFDH BH17 211 J7
Denman Cl FLEETN GU51 59 L7
Denmark La PLE BH15 223 K5
Denmark Rd
MOOR/WNTN BH9 213 M7
NWBY RG14 19 G4
PLE BH15 223 K5
Denmark Sq ASHV GU12 3 M2
Denmark St ASHV GU12 3 M2
Denmead NMIL/BTOS BH25 219 K4
Denmead Rd SBNE BH6 227 K1
TADY RG26 44 B4
WEND SO18 148 C4
Denning Cl FLEETS GU52 71 G1
Denning Md AND SP10 4 E6
Dennis Rd WIMB BH21 210 D3
Dennistoun Av
CHCH/BSGR BH23 228 F1
Dennistoun Cl CBLY GU15 50 F3
Dennis Wy LISS GU33 308 G9
Denny Cl FAWY SO45 355 K5
Denton Cl STHA RG19 35 J2
Denton Wy FRIM GU16 50 F6
Denville Av FHAM/PORC PO16 183 K2
Denville Cl CHAM PO6 169 M8
Denvilles Cl HAV PO9 17 J2
Denzil Av HLER SO31 162 C6
Depedene Cl FAWY SO45 354 D4
De Port Hts BPWT SO32 312 E10
Deptford La ODIM RG29 68 C5
Derby Ct LSOL/BMARY PO13 * 190 C2
Derby Flds ODIM RG29 68 E2
Derby Rd BMTH BH1 9 M4
ELGH SO50 139 M6
HASM GU27 118 B5
NEND PO2 184 D7
NWBY RG14 18 D7
SHAM SO14 23 J1
De Redvers Rd PSTN BH14 224 C6
Dereham Wy
BKME/WDN BH12 224 F2
Deridene Ct TOTT SO40 158 D2
Derlyn Rd FHAM/PORC PO16 10 F5
Derritt La CHCH/BSGR BH23 216 C1
Derrybrian Gdns
NMIL/BTOS BH25 219 G6
Derry Cl ASHV GU12 73 M3
Derry Rd FARN GU14 50 B7
Derwent Av ASHV GU12 73 M4
Derwent Cl BOR GU35 110 F7
FARN GU14 60 D4
FERN BH22 346 A6
FHAM/STUB PO14 181 K8
FNM GU9 76 E2
HORN PO8 321 L10
MOOR/WNTN BH9 214 A6
WEND SO18 148 B3
Derwent Ct AND SP10 96 E2
Derwent Dr TOTT SO40 144 B8
Derwent Gdns NARL SO24 291 M12
Derwent Rd KBH RG22 92 C3
LSOL/BMARY PO13 189 M7
NMIL/BTOS BH25 219 H3
ROWN SO16 145 L7
STHA RG19 35 G1
Derwentwater Rd WIMB BH21 207 K6
Desborough Cl CHAM PO6 168 A7
Desborough Rd ELGH SO50 140 A3
Dettingen Crs FRIM GU16 51 M8
Devenish Rd FUFL SO22 122 D1
Dever Cl RWIN SO21 275 N9
Deverel Cl CHCH/BSGR BH23 216 A8
Deverell Pl WVILLE PO7 169 J5
Dever Wy DEAN RG23 91 K3
The Devil's Hwy CWTH RG45 43 G3
Devils La LIPH GU30 116 E5
Devine Gdns ELGH SO50 140 D2
Devon Cl FLEETN GU51 59 K4
SHST GU47 49 M1
Devon Dr CHFD SO53 139 J5
Devon Rd ALDT GU11 72 E1
BOR GU35 112 F1
CHCH/BSGR BH23 215 L8
HSEA PO3 185 G5
PLE BH15 223 L3
Devonshire Av ENEY PO4 193 G5
Devonshire Dr CBLY GU15 51 H1
Devonshire Gdns FAWY SO45 177 G8
HLER SO31 162 F2
Devonshire Pl ALDT GU11 2 C5
BSTK RG21 6 C7
Devonshire Rd WSHM SO15 160 F2
Devonshire Sq ENEY PO4 192 F4
Devonshire Wy
FHAM/STUB PO14 181 J4
Dewar Cl FHAM PO15 164 C7
Dewberry Down NTHA RG18 29 H8
Deweys La RAND SP11 265 M10
Dewlands Rd VWD BH31 200 F2
Dewlands Wy VWD BH31 200 F2
Dew La ELGH SO50 139 M5
Dewlish Cl CFDH BH17 212 A6
Dewpond Wk CHIN RG24 54 B8
Dexter Sq AND SP10 * 96 E1
Dexter Wy FLEETN GU51 59 K4
Dial Cl CHCH/BSGR BH23 348 E10
Diamond Cl FBDG SP6 197 G4
Diamond Hl CBLY GU15 51 G1
Diamond Rdg CBLY GU15 50 F1
Diamond St SSEA PO5 * 20 F6
Diamond Wy FARN GU14 60 E8
Diana Cl EMRTH PO10 171 L4
GPORT PO12 190 E4
KBH RG22 93 G1
THLE RG7 238 A7
Diana Wy WIMB BH21 210 E1
Dibble Dr NBAD SO52 137 M5
Dibden Cl CHAR BH8 214 D5
HAV PO9 170 C4
Dibden Lodge Cl FAWY SO45 176 F3
Dibles Pk HLER SO31 * 179 L3
Dibles Rd HLER SO31 179 L3
Dibley Cl KBH RG22 92 E1
Dickens Cl NEND PO2 192 D1
Dickens Dell TOTT SO40 158 B1
Dickens Dr HLER SO31 164 C3
Dickens La OVTN RG25 66 B6
Dickenson Wk NARL SO24 291 M12
Dickens Rd SBNE BH6 227 K1
Dickens Wk NWBY RG14 34 A4
Dickens Wy YTLY GU46 48 E4
Dicker's La ALTN GU34 107 G4
Dickson Pl WHAM PO17 152 A4
Didcot Rd CFDH BH17 211 K8
WSHM SO15 146 C7
Dieppe Crs NEND PO2 184 E4
Dieppe Gdns GPORT PO12 14 B4
Digby Rd NWBY RG14 18 B1
Diligence Cl HLER SO31 163 G3
Dilly La HTWY RG27 57 L4
NMIL/BTOS BH25 231 G1
Dimond Cl WEND SO18 147 L7
Dimond Hl WEND SO18 147 L7
Dimond Rd WEND SO18 147 L6
Dines Cl RAND SP11 250 F9
Dingle Rd BOSC BH5 227 H4
Dingle Wy HLER SO31 164 A8
Dingley Rd PLE BH15 223 K2
Dingley Wy FARN GU14 61 G8
Dinham Rd NMIL/BTOS BH25 219 K4
Dinorben Av FLEETS GU52 71 G1
Dinorben Beeches
FLEETS GU52 71 G1
Dinorben Cl FLEETS GU52 71 H1
Dippenhall Rd RFNM GU10 259 R6
Dippenhall St RFNM GU10 259 Q3

Diprose Rd WIMB BH21 ....210 E1
Discovery Cl
FHAM/STUB PO14 * 181 J7
Disraeli Rd CHCH/BSGR BH23 ....228 D2
Ditcham Crs HAV PO9 ....170 E4
Ditchbury LYMN SO41 ....221 K2
Dittany Gdns NTHA RG18 ....28 F7
Ditton Cl FHAM/STUB PO14 ....189 J1
The Dittons EWKG RG40 ....42 A2
Divers Cl ALTN GU34 ....106 F2
Dixon Rd HTWY RG27 ....46 D8
Dixons La STOK SO20 ....284 D9
Dockenfield Cl HAV PO9 * 170 C4
Dockenfield St RFNM GU10 ....109 H5
Dock La BROC SO42 ....353 Q8
Dock Rd GPORT PO12 ....15 H5
Doctors Dro RAND SP11 ....250 F9
Doctor's Hl ROMY SO51 ....128 F4
Doctors La PSF GU32 ....313 L3
Dodds La BPWT SO32 ....318 B7
Dodgson Cl FBDG SP6 ....332 A8
Dodwell La HLER SO31 ....163 H1
Doe Copse Wy
NMIL/BTOS BH25 ....218 E4
Dogflud Wy FNM GU9 ....13 H2
Dogkennel La WVILLE PO7 ....320 B8
Dogwood Dell WVILLE PO7 ....169 M3
Dogwood Rd BDST BH18 ....210 E6
Doiley Bottom RAND SP11 ....251 M8
Dolbery Rd North
BKME/WDN BH12 ....212 D6
Dolbery Rd South
BKME/WDN BH12 ....212 C7
Doles Hl WWKG RG41 ....239 R5
Dollis Dr FNM GU9 ....13 J1
Dollis Gn TADY RG26 ....46 B5
Dolman Rd GPORT PO12 ....15 H6
NWBY RG14 ....18 E1
Dolomans La RAND SP11 ....250 F9
Dolphin Av NBNE BH10 ....213 L3
Dolphin Cl ELGH SO50 ....140 F2
HASM GU27 ....117 L2
Dolphin Ct FHAM/STUB PO14 ....181 H8
Dolphin Crs GPORT PO12 ....14 F6
Dolphin Hl RWIN SO21 ....125 G6
Dolphin Pl NMIL/BTOS BH25 ....230 F1
Dolphin Wy GPORT PO12 ....15 K9
Dolton Rd ROWN SO16 ....145 M5
Doman Rd CBLY GU15 ....50 C4
Dome Aly WINC SO23 ....25 G7
Dominica Cl CHIN RG24 ....65 L2
Dominion Rd BWD BH11 ....212 E5
Domitian Gdns CHIN RG24 ....64 E4
Domoney Cl STHA RG19 ....35 L1
Domum Rd NEND PO2 ....184 F6
WINC SO23 ....25 J8
Domvilles Ap NEND PO2 ....184 B7
Donaldson Rd CHAM PO6 ....184 F2
Doncaster Rd ELGH SO50 ....140 A4
Donigers Dell BPWT SO32 ....318 A6
Donlan Dr FARN GU14 ....60 C7
Donnelly Rd SBNE BH6 ....227 M3
Donnelly St GPORT PO12 ....14 C1
Donnington Cl CBLY GU15 ....50 D4
Donnington Dr
CHCH/BSGR BH23 ....229 H1
CHFD SO53 ....139 G5
Donnington Gv PTSW SO17 ....147 H6
Donnington Pk NWBY RG14 ....27 H6
Donnington Sq NWBY RG14 ....27 H7
Donoughmore Rd BMTH BH1 ....226 D4
Dora's Green La RFNM GU10 ....259 R6
Dorcas Cl WVILLE PO7 ....156 A7
Dorcas Ct CBLY GU15 ....50 D5
Dorchester Cl DEAN RG23 ....64 D7
Dorchester Gdns PLE BH15 ....223 L3
Dorchester Rd HTWY RG27 ....56 C7
PLE BH15 ....223 L2
UPTN BH16 ....222 A1
Dorchester Wy ODIM RG29 ....68 B4
Dore Av FHAM/PORC PO16 ....167 H8
Doreen Cl FARN GU14 ....49 M8
Dores La ROMY SO51 ....131 M1
Dorian Gv NARL SO24 ....291 K12
Doric Cl CHFD SO53 ....139 M1
Dorking Crs CHAM PO6 ....184 F1
Dorland Gdns TOTT SO40 ....158 D2
Dormer Cl CWTH RG45 ....43 J3
NWBY RG14 ....33 L6
Dormington Rd CHAM PO6 ....168 C7
Dormy Cl HLER SO31 ....179 K1
Dormy Wy LSOL/BMARY PO13 ....182 B7
Dorneywood Wy NWBY RG14 ....19 L2
Dornie Rd CCLF BH13 ....237 J1
Dornmere La WVILLE PO7 ....170 A1
Dorothy Dymond St
PSEA PO1 * 21 G3
Dorrel Cl KBH RG22 ....92 D6
Dorrien Rd GPORT PO12 ....191 H1
Dorrita Av HORN PO8 ....156 A4
Dorrita Cl ENEY PO4 ....192 F6
The Dorrits TOTT SO40 ....158 B1
Dorset Av FERN BH22 ....209 K5
Dorset Cl HORN PO8 ....156 B2
Dorset Lake Av PSTN BH14 ....224 B8
Dorset Rd ASHV GU12 ....74 A3
CHCH/BSGR BH23 ....216 F8
CHFD SO53 ....139 J5
WBNE BH4 ....225 J3
Dorset St PTSW SO17 ....161 G2
Dorset Wy PLE BH15 ....223 K1
Dorstone Rd CHAM PO6 ....168 C7
Doswell Wy BSTK RG21 ....7 G2
Douai Cl FARN GU14 ....61 J4
Doublet Cl STHA RG19 ....35 G1
Doughty Wy AND SP10 ....97 G3
Douglas Av CHCH/BSGR BH23 ....227 M2
Douglas Cl UPTN BH16 ....222 C1
Douglas Crs ITCH SO19 ....148 D6
Douglas Gdns
BKME/WDN BH12 ....224 E3
HAV PO9 ....171 G4
Douglas Gv RFNM GU10 ....79 G3
Douglas Ms SBNE BH6 ....227 J3
Douglas Ride KSCL RG20 ....246 A4
Douglas Rd BKME/WDN BH12 ....224 E3
HSEA PO3 ....192 F1
RAND SP11 ....95 K5
SBNE BH6 ....227 L5
Douglas Wy FAWY SO45 ....176 F4
Doulton Gdns PSTN BH14 ....224 B6
Doussie Cl UPTN BH16 ....210 A8
Dove Cl AND SP10 ....96 D2
HORN PO8 ....155 M4
KBH RG22 ....92 B3
Dovecote Rd WHIT RG2 ....238 B1
Dove Dl ELGH SO50 ....139 K6
Dovedale Cl SHST GU47 ....43 M6
Dove Gdns HLER SO31 ....164 B7
Dover Cl CCLF BH13 ....225 G5
DEAN RG23 ....64 F6
FHAM/STUB PO14 ....189 H1
NARL SO24 ....291 M12
Dover Ct HISD PO11 ....194 E3
Dovercourt Rd CHAM PO6 ....185 G2
Dover Rd CCLF BH13 ....225 G5
HSEA PO3 ....185 G8
Dover St SHAM SO14 ....161 G1
Doves Ct ALTN GU34 ....107 G2
Doveshill Crs NBNE BH10 ....213 K5
Doveshill Gdns NBNE BH10 ....213 K5
Doves La RSAL SP5 ....127 G5
Doveton Wy NWBY RG14 ....19 H1
Doveys Cl RGWD BH24 ....348 H1
Dowden Gv ALTN GU34 ....106 F3
Dowding Ct CWTH RG45 * 43 L2
Dowds Cl HEND SO30 ....149 H4
Dowlands Cl NBNE BH10 ....213 K4
Dowlands Rd NBNE BH10 ....213 J4
Dowley Ct FHAM/STUB PO14 * 180 F4
Down End CHAM PO6 ....169 J7
Down End Rd CHAM PO6 ....169 J7
Downend Rd
FHAM/PORC PO16 ....166 F7
Downey Cl BWD BH11 ....212 F6
Down Farm La FUFL SO22 ....288 C8
Down Farm Pl HORN PO8 * 321 L11
Down Ga NARL SO24 ....291 L12
Downham Cl HORN PO8 ....155 M5
Downhouse Rd HORN PO8 ....321 J8
Downing St FNM GU9 ....12 F3
Downland Cl HEND SO30 ....149 M5
HLER SO31 ....164 A8
Downland Pl CFDH BH17 * 211 L8
HEND SO30 ....149 H8
Downlands Cl RSAL SP5 ....332 B2
Downlands Rd FUFL SO22 ....122 B8
Downlands Wy RWIN SO21 ....288 D4
Down La OVTN RG25 ....67 J6
Downley Point HAV PO9 * 171 H4
Downley Rd HAV PO9 ....171 H4
Down Lodge Cl FBDG SP6 ....196 C6
Down Rd HORN PO8 ....321 L11
RAND SP11 ....267 M5
Downs Cl FARN GU14 ....60 E1
WVILLE PO7 ....169 M5
Downscroft Gdns HEND SO30 ....149 H5
Downside GSHT GU26 ....115 K1
LSOL/BMARY PO13 ....182 D6
Downside Av ITCH SO19 ....148 A6
Downside Rd FUFL SO22 ....122 B2
WVILLE PO7 ....169 J5
Downsland Rd BSTK RG21 ....6 B6
Downs La MARL SN8 ....243 P1
Down's Park Av TOTT SO40 ....159 G2
Down's Park Crs TOTT SO40 ....159 G2
Down's Park Rd TOTT SO40 ....159 G2
Downs Rd RWIN SO21 ....288 D4
STOK SO20 ....269 Q9
Down St OVTN RG25 ....103 M3
RCCH PO18 ....173 M3
Downs Vw ALTN GU34 ....107 L1
Downsview Rd BOR GU35 ....114 C3
Downsview Wy RAND SP11 ....267 K2
Downs Wy ALTN GU34 ....106 D6
The Downsway
FHAM/PORC PO16 ....167 J8
Downton Cl CHAR BH8 ....214 C5
Downton Hl RSAL SP5 ....332 E1
Downton La LYMN SO41 ....231 M2
Downton Rd WEND SO18 ....147 M6
Downview Cl GSHT GU26 ....115 K2
Downview Rd FBDG SP6 ....329 L4
Downwood Cl FAWY SO45 ....176 C6
FBDG SP6 ....196 F2
Downwood Wy HORN PO8 ....321 L11
Down Yhonda MFD/CHID GU8 ....263 Q1
Doyle Av NEND PO2 ....184 E4
Doyle Cl NEND PO2 ....184 E4
Doyle Ct ITCH SO19 ....161 M7
Doyle Gdns YTLY GU46 * 48 E3
Doyne Rd PSTN BH14 ....224 E4
Dpdn La BWD BH11 ....212 E3
Dradfield La BPWT SO32 ....319 J12
Dragon Est CHAM PO6 * 185 L1
Dragonfly Dr CHIN RG24 ....54 B8
Dragon La RGWD BH24 ....347 N4
Dragon St EPSF GU31 ....120 D7
Dragoon Cl ITCH SO19 ....148 C8
Dragoon Ct ALDT GU11 ....2 B3
Dragoon Wy
CHCH/BSGR BH23 ....227 M1
Drake Av FRIM GU16 ....62 A7
Drake Cl CHCH/BSGR BH23 ....228 F2
EWKG RG40 ....42 A1
HLER SO31 ....164 B7
NMIL/BTOS BH25 ....218 F5
RGWD BH24 ....203 L3
TOTT SO40 ....159 M6
Drake Ct AND SP10 ....96 F4
Drake Rd ELGH SO50 ....134 E8
LSOL/BMARY PO13 ....189 K5
PLE BH15 ....223 J7
Drakes Cl FAWY SO45 ....176 F6
Drakes Rd FERN BH22 * 209 M5
Draper Cl STHA RG19 ....35 K2
Draper Rd BWD BH11 ....213 G4
CHCH/BSGR BH23 ....228 E1
Drapers Copse FAWY SO45 ....176 D4
Draycote Rd HORN PO8 ....321 L9
Draycott Rd NBNE BH10 ....213 K6
Draymans Wy ALTN GU34 ....106 F5
Drayton Cl ITCH SO19 ....161 M8
Drayton La CHAM PO6 ....169 H7
Drayton Pl TOTT SO40 ....158 D1
Drayton Rd NEND PO2 ....184 E7
Drayton St FUFL SO22 ....122 C6
Draytons Vw STHA RG19 ....34 C5
Dreadnought Rd
FHAM/STUB PO14 ....181 L7
Dresden Dr HORN PO8 ....155 K6
Dreswick Cl CHCH/BSGR BH23 ....215 K4
Drew Cl BKME/WDN BH12 ....225 J1
Drewett Cl WHIT RG2 ....238 C2
Drifters Dr FRIM GU16 ....51 M7
Drift La RCCH PO18 ....173 J7
Drift Rd BOR GU35 ....112 D4
FHAM/PORC PO16 ....11 L3
HORN PO8 ....321 L8
STOK SO20 ....273 K10
The Drift HAV PO9 ....157 H7
Driftway Rd HTWY RG27 ....56 E7
Driftwood Gdns ENEY PO4 ....193 J6
TOTT SO40 ....158 C2
Drill Shed Rd NEND PO2 ....184 B7
Drinkwater Cl ELGH SO50 ....139 M5
The Drive BKME/WDN BH12 ....224 D3
DEAN RG23 ....91 K3
EMRTH PO10 ....172 D6
FHAM/PORC PO16 ....10 E5
FNM GU9 ....12 F9
GODL GU7 ....261 Q12
HAV PO9 ....16 E1
HEND SO30 ....148 C1
LSOL/BMARY PO13 ....182 A6
NWBY RG14 ....18 B9
ROMY SO51 ....127 M7
ROMY SO51 ....335 L6
TOTT SO40 ....158 F3
Drove Cl RSAL SP5 ....325 M2
RWIN SO21 ....124 F7
Drove Hl STOK SO20 ....272 E9
Drove La NARL SO24 ....291 J10
NTHA RG18 ....28 D2
Drove Rd ITCH SO19 ....148 B8
STOK SO20 ....272 E9
WHAM PO17 ....168 A4
Drovers End FLEETN GU51 ....59 L4
Drovers Wy ASHV GU12 ....74 C7
FNM GU9 ....76 E2
The Drove AND SP10 ....4 B5
BPWT SO32 ....142 D4
BPWT SO32 ....318 B7
ELGH SO50 ....141 K6
FAWY SO45 ....354 G7
HEND SO30 ....148 F1
ROMY SO51 ....335 J5
RWIN SO21 ....124 F7
TOTT SO40 ....144 B7
WEND SO18 ....148 A5
Droxford Cl GPORT PO12 * 14 B4
Droxford Crs TADY RG26 ....44 A5
Droxford Rd BPWT SO32 ....318 C8
LTDN BH7 ....227 H2
Druce Wy STHA RG19 ....35 K1
Druids Cl FERN BH22 ....209 K6
Druitt Rd CHCH/BSGR BH23 ....216 F8
Drum Md PSF GU32 ....120 C6
Drummond Cl ALTN GU34 ....293 K6
FUFL SO22 ....122 E7
Drummond Rd BMTH BH1 ....226 D4
FAWY SO45 ....177 G4
HEND SO30 ....149 J3
PSEA PO1 ....192 D2
Drummond Wy CHFD SO53 ....133 H8
Drury Cl WHCH RG28 ....98 F4
Drury La ALTN GU34 ....279 L7
THLE RG7 ....40 B4
Drury Rd WBNE BH4 ....225 H6
Dryden Av CHAM PO6 ....167 L7
Dryden Cl CHIN RG24 ....65 L4
FHAM/PORC PO16 ....10 D4
NTHA RG18 ....28 E7
RGWD BH24 ....202 A7
WVILLE PO7 ....155 K6
Dryden Pl LYMN SO41 ....232 D3
Dryden Rd FARN GU14 ....60 F2
ITCH SO19 ....148 F7
Dryden Wy LIPH GU30 ....116 A3
Drysdale Ms ENEY PO4 * 193 H6
Duchess Cl ALTN GU34 ....106 E5
CWTH RG45 ....43 K1
Duchess of Kent Barracks
ALDT GU11 ....73 H5
Ducking Stool La
CHCH/BSGR BH23 ....228 B2
Duck Island La RGWD BH24 ....203 H6
Ducklands BOR GU35 ....113 G2
Duck La BWD BH11 ....212 F4
Duckmead La LISS GU33 ....308 H6
Ducks La STOK SO20 ....284 B2
Duddon Cl WEND SO18 ....148 B3
Duddon Wy BSTK RG21 ....7 K5
Dudleston Heath Dr
HORN PO8 ....156 B6
Dudley Av FBDG SP6 ....197 H1
LYMN SO41 ....219 M6
Dudley Cl BOR GU35 ....112 E3
DEAN RG23 ....64 D7
Dudley Gdns NBNE BH10 ....213 K3
Dudley Rd HSEA PO3 ....193 G1
NBNE BH10 ....213 K3
Dudmoor Farm Rd
CHCH/BSGR BH23 ....215 M5
Dudmoor La CHCH/BSGR BH23 ....215 M4
Dudsbury Av FERN BH22 ....209 K4
Dudsbury Crs FERN BH22 ....209 K4
Dudsbury Gdns FERN BH22 ....209 L8
Dudsbury Rd FERN BH22 ....209 K7
Duffield La EMRTH PO10 ....172 D3
Dugald Drummond St
PSEA PO1 ....21 G3
Dugdell Cl FERN BH22 ....209 M2
Duisburg Wy SSEA PO5 ....20 E7
Duke Cl AND SP10 * 96 F3
Duke Crs PSEA PO1 ....192 D1
Duke Rd HEND SO30 ....149 K7
Dukes Cl ALTN GU34 ....106 D6
FNM GU9 * 76 E2
PSF GU32 ....120 B5
Dukes Dr BWD BH11 ....212 E3
Dukesfield CHCH/BSGR BH23 ....215 K6
Dukes Md FLEETN GU51 ....58 F8
Dukes Meadow RCCH PO18 ....173 L1
Dukes Pk ALDT GU11 ....73 K2
Duke's Ride CWTH RG45 ....43 H4
THLE RG7 ....45 H4
Dukes Rd GPORT PO12 ....191 G2
SHAM SO14 ....147 H8
Duke St RWIN SO21 ....275 P9
SHAM SO14 ....23 J5
Dukes Walk Service Rd
WVILLE PO7 ....169 L1
Dukes Wd CWTH RG45 ....43 K3
Dukeswood Dr FAWY SO45 ....176 F7
Duke Ter HAV PO9 * 170 D4
Dulsie Rd TWDS BH3 ....225 J1
Dumas Cl YTLY GU46 ....48 E3
Du Maurier Cl FLEETS GU52 ....71 G5
Dumbarton Cl NEND PO2 ....184 D8
Dumbleton Cl ITCH SO19 ....148 F7
Dummer Ct HAV PO9 ....170 D2
Dummer Down La
OVTN RG25 ....103 K5
Dummer La RAND SP11 ....80 C2
Dummer Ms WINC SO23 ....24 F7
Dummers Rd ROMY SO51 ....131 K1
Dumpers Dro ELGH SO50 ....141 K6
Dumpford La EPSF GU31 ....317 M8
Dump Rd FARN GU14 ....60 E7
Dunbar Cl ROWN SO16 ....145 M3
Dunbar Crs CHCH/BSGR BH23 ....217 M6
Dunbar Rd ENEY PO4 ....193 H4
FRIM GU16 ....61 M1
TWDS BH3 ....225 L2
Dunbridge La ROMY SO51 ....298 G12
Duncan Cl ITCH SO19 ....161 L8
Duncan Ct AND SP10 ....96 F4
Duncan Rd HLER SO31 ....164 B7
NMIL/BTOS BH25 ....219 K4
SSEA PO5 ....21 K8
Duncan's Cl RAND SP11 ....94 A2
Duncans Dr FHAM/STUB PO14 ....181 H4
Duncliff Rd SBNE BH6 ....228 A4
Duncombe Dr RGWD BH24 ....202 D2
Duncombe Rd PSF GU32 ....314 B8
Duncton Rd HORN PO8 ....321 M7
Dundaff Cl CBLY GU15 ....51 J3
Dundas Cl HSEA PO3 ....185 H6
Dundas La HSEA PO3 ....185 H7
Dundas Rd CFDH BH17 ....211 L8
Dundas Sp HSEA PO3 ....185 H6
Dundee Cl FHAM PO15 ....10 B2
Dundee Rd PTSW SO17 ....147 J7
Dundonald Cl HISD PO11 ....195 G3
ITCH SO19 ....161 K7
Dundridge La BPWT SO32 ....143 L3
Dundry Wy HEND SO30 ....149 J5
Dunedin Cl FERN BH22 ....209 H5
NTID SP9 ....266 G2
Dunedin Dr FERN BH22 ....209 H5
Dunedin Gdns FERN BH22 ....209 H5
Dunedin Gv CHCH/BSGR BH23 ....229 J1
Dunford Cl NMIL/BTOS BH25 ....218 E8
Dunford Rd BKME/WDN BH12 ....224 D3
Dungells Farm Cl YTLY GU46 ....48 F4
Dungells La YTLY GU46 ....48 E4
Dunhills La RAND SP11 ....84 E4
Dunhurst Cl HAV PO9 ....171 G5
Dunkeld Rd GPORT PO12 ....190 F1
TWDS BH3 ....225 K2
Dunkirk Cl ROWN SO16 ....146 D4
Dunkirk Rd ROWN SO16 ....146 D4
Dunkirt La RAND SP11 ....270 G1
Dunley's Hl ODIM RG29 ....68 E5
Dunlin Cl CHCH/BSGR BH23 ....229 H3
ENEY PO4 ....193 K3
Dunmow Hl FLEETN GU51 ....59 J6
Dunmow Rd AND SP10 ....5 K8
Dunn Cl ENEY PO4 ....193 H5
Dunn Crs HUNG RG17 ....31 H3
Dunnings La NBAD SO52 ....137 L3
Dunnock Cl HAV PO9 ....157 H7
FERN BH22 ....204 D8
Dunsbury Wy HAV PO9 ....170 E3
Dunsell's La NARL SO24 ....292 H11
Dunsford Crs DEAN RG23 ....64 E5
Dunsmore Cl SSEA PO5 ....21 G5
Dunsmore Gdns YTLY GU46 ....48 C3
Dunstable Wk
FHAM/STUB PO14 ....181 K5
Dunstall Pk FARN GU14 ....61 G1
Dunstan Rd NTHA RG18 ....29 G8
Dunstan's Dro RAND SP11 ....250 E7
Dunstans La PSTN BH14 ....223 M2
Dunster Cl ROWN SO16 ....146 C3
Dunvegan Dr ROWN SO16 ....146 C3
Dunyeats Rd BDST BH18 ....211 H4
Dunyeats Rbt WIMB BH21 ....211 K3
Duouro Cl TADY RG26 ....249 P4
Dupree Dr ENEY PO4 ....193 G5
Durban Cl ROMY SO51 ....131 G7
Durban Rd PSEA PO1 ....192 F1
Durbidges STHA RG19 ....248 C4
Durdells Av BWD BH11 ....213 G3
Durdells Gdns BWD BH11 ....213 G3
Durford Ct HAV PO9 ....170 D2
Durford Rd EPSF GU31 ....121 G6
Durham Dr FRIM GU16 ....51 M7
Durham Gdns WVILLE PO7 ....169 M3
Durham St GPORT PO12 ....14 C1
PSEA PO1 ....21 H2
Durham Wy KBH RG22 ....92 D4
Durland Cl NMIL/BTOS BH25 ....219 G7
Durlands Rd HORN PO8 ....321 L12
Durley Av HORN PO8 ....155 M5
Durley Brook Rd BPWT SO32 ....141 M6
Durley Chine Rd WCLF BH2 ....8 B6
Durley Chine Rd South
WCLF BH2 ....8 B8
Durley Cl AND SP10 ....4 C7
Durley Crs TOTT SO40 ....158 D3
Durley Gdns WCLF BH2 ....8 B8
Durley Hall La BPWT SO32 ....142 B3
Durley Rd ELGH SO50 ....141 L5
GPORT PO12 ....190 F2
WCLF BH2 ....8 C7
Durley Rd South WCLF BH2 ....8 C7
Durley Rbt WCLF BH2 ....8 C7
Durley St BPWT SO32 ....142 D5
Durlston Crs CHCH/BSGR BH23 ....215 K4
Durlston Rd PSTN BH14 ....224 C6
ROWN SO16 ....145 J7
Durnford Cl STOK SO20 ....272 E8
Durnford Rd SHAM SO14 ....161 H2
Durngate Pl WINC SO23 ....25 J5
Durngate Ter WINC SO23 ....25 J5
Durnsford Av FLEETS GU52 ....71 J1
Durnstown LYMN SO41 ....350 G10
Durrant Rd PSTN BH14 ....224 C5
WCLF BH2 ....8 D4
Durrants Gdns HAV PO9 ....157 H8
Durrants Rd HAV PO9 ....171 H1
Durrant Wy LYMN SO41 ....350 F10
Durrington Pl LTDN BH7 ....227 H2
Durrington Rd LTDN BH7 ....227 H1
Dursley Crs CHAM PO6 ....168 C8
Durweston Cl
MOOR/WNTN BH9 ....214 B5
Dutton La ELGH SO50 ....140 B1
Duttons Rd ROMY SO51 ....130 E8
Dyehouse Rd MFD/CHID GU8 ....263 N8
Dyer Rd WSHM SO15 ....160 C1
Dymewood Rd WIMB BH21 ....205 G1
Dymoke St EMRTH PO10 ....171 L4
Dymott Cl WSHM SO15 ....22 A1
Dyneley Gn WEND SO18 ....148 A3
Dyram Cl ELGH SO50 ....139 M3
Dysart Av CHAM PO6 ....185 H1
Dyserth Cl ITCH SO19 ....162 B3
Dyson Dr WINC SO23 ....123 G2
Dysons Cl NWBY RG14 ....18 B4

E

Eadens La TOTT SO40 ....341 P5
Eagle Av HORN PO8 ....155 K4
Eagle Cl ALTN GU34 ....106 F2
CHFD SO53 ....139 H4
CWTH RG45 ....43 J1
FHAM/PORC PO16 ....166 F8
KBH RG22 ....92 B4
Eagle Rd BKME/WDN BH12 ....225 G4
KSCL RG20 ....247 Q2
LSOL/BMARY PO13 ....189 K5
Eagles Nest SHST GU47 ....43 J7
Eames La LISS GU33 ....307 R4
Eardley Av AND SP10 ....4 A4
Earle Rd WBNE BH4 ....225 J7
Earlham Dr PSTN BH14 ....224 C4
Earl of Chester Dr FRIM GU16 ....51 M8
Earlsbourne FLEETS GU52 ....71 K4
Earls Cl ELGH SO50 ....141 G2
Earlsdon St SSEA PO5 ....21 G4
Earlsdon Wy
CHCH/BSGR BH23 ....217 M8
Earls Gv CBLY GU15 ....51 G2
Earls Rd FHAM/PORC PO16 ....11 G9
SHAM SO14 ....147 G8
Earlswood Dr FBDG SP6 ....196 B7
Earlswood Pk
NMIL/BTOS BH25 ....219 K3
Earnley Rd HISD PO11 ....195 M6
Earthpits La RSAL SP5 ....328 E9
Eashing La GODL GU7 ....261 R12
Eastacre FUFL SO22 ....24 D1
East Av FNM GU9 ....77 H2
NMIL/BTOS BH25 ....230 C1
TWDS BH3 ....225 J2
East Bank Rd BROC SO42 ....351 L4
East Bargate SHAM SO14 ....23 G4
East Beach BMTH BH1 * 8 F7
East Boldre Rd BROC SO42 ....353 J9
East Borough WIMB BH21 ....207 J3
Eastbourne Av GPORT PO12 ....182 F8
WSHM SO15 ....146 D8
Eastbourne Rd HSEA PO3 ....185 G8
Eastbrook Cl GPORT PO12 ....182 F8
HLER SO31 ....164 A7
Eastbrooke Rd ALTN GU34 ....107 G4
Eastbrook Rw WIMB BH21 * 207 J3
East Cams Cl
FHAM/PORC PO16 ....166 F7
Eastchurch Cl ROWN SO16 ....145 M4
Eastcliff Cl LSOL/BMARY PO13 ....189 L5
East Cliffe WINC SO23 ....25 J7
East Cliff Wy
CHCH/BSGR BH23 ....229 J1
East Cl NMIL/BTOS BH25 ....218 D8
East Cosham Rd CHAM PO6 ....169 H8
Eastcot Cl FAWY SO45 ....354 D5
Eastcott Cl LTDN BH7 ....215 G8
East Ct CHAM PO6 ....169 H8
Eastcroft Rd GPORT PO12 ....14 C2
East Dean Rd ROMY SO51 ....297 R10
East Dr ELGH SO50 ....134 D8
RGWD BH24 * 205 K8
Eastern Av AND SP10 ....5 J7
HSEA PO3 ....193 H2
Eastern Pde ENEY PO4 ....192 F7
FHAM/PORC PO16 ....11 H9
Eastern Rd ASHV GU12 ....3 M3
ASHV GU12 ....73 L6
BOR GU35 ....110 F6
CHAM PO6 ....185 K2
ENEY PO4 ....193 H3
HAV PO9 ....16 F3
HEND SO30 ....148 D3
HSEA PO3 ....185 J4
LYMN SO41 ....221 K4
NEND PO2 ....184 B6
Eastern Ter ENEY PO4 * 193 G6
Eastern Villas Rd ENEY PO4 * 192 D7
Eastern Wy FHAM/PORC PO16 ....11 J6
LYMN SO41 ....232 F4
Easter Rd MOOR/WNTN BH9 ....214 A6
Eastfield Av BSTK RG21 ....7 H5
FHAM/STUB PO14 ....181 M6
East Field Cl EMRTH PO10 ....172 E4
Eastfield Cl AND SP10 ....5 L5
RGWD BH24 ....203 L5
Eastfield La EPSF GU31 ....323 Q1
RGWD BH24 ....203 L5
Eastfield Rd AND SP10 ....5 K5
CHAM PO6 ....168 B6
ENEY PO4 ....193 G5
East Flexford La RGUW GU3 ....261 R2
Eastgate St SHAM SO14 ....23 G5
WINC SO23 ....25 J6
East Gn BLKW GU17 ....49 L4
East Harting St EPSF GU31 ....323 P1
East Hl LYMN SO41 ....221 L4
WINC SO23 ....25 J8
East Hill Cl FHAM/PORC PO16 ....11 L4
East Hill Dr LISS GU33 ....308 G9
East Hoe Rd WVILLE PO7 ....319 N9
East House Av
FHAM/STUB PO14 ....189 K2
East Howe La NBNE BH10 ....213 J4
Eastlake Av
BKME/WDN BH12 ....224 B2
Eastlake Cl EPSF GU31 ....121 G6
Eastlands NMIL/BTOS BH25 ....219 H7
East La LYMN SO41 ....220 E7
NARL SO24 ....290 H12
Eastleigh Rd ELGH SO50 ....141 J3
East Leigh Rd HAV PO9 ....171 J5
East Ldg FHAM PO15 ....181 J3
East Lodge Pk CHAM PO6 ....169 M8
Eastlyn Rd TADY RG26 ....44 E3
Eastman Cl RSAL SP5 ....332 C2
Eastmans Fld STOK SO20 ....272 E9
Eastmead FARN GU14 ....61 H5
Eastmeare Ct TOTT SO40 ....158 C2
Eastney Farm Rd ENEY PO4 ....193 J5
Eastney Rd ENEY PO4 ....193 H5
Eastney St ENEY PO4 ....193 G6
Eastoke Av HISD PO11 ....195 K7
Easton Common Hl RSAL SP5 ....283 J10
Easton La RWIN SO21 ....123 K2
WINC SO23 ....25 L4
East Overcliff Dr BMTH BH1 ....9 H7
Eastover Ct HAV PO9 ....170 D2
East Park Ter SHAM SO14 ....23 G1
East Portway AND SP10 ....95 L4
East Quay Rd PLE BH15 ....223 J7
East Ring RFNM GU10 ....260 E1
East Rd FAWY SO45 ....177 K8
RWIN SO21 ....273 Q5
WHAM PO17 ....168 A2
Eastrop La BSTK RG21 ....7 G5
Eastrop Rbt BSTK RG21 ....7 G4
Eastrop Wy BSTK RG21 ....7 G4
East Station Rd ASHV GU12 ....3 G4
East St AND SP10 ....5 J6
EMRTH PO10 ....172 B3
FHAM/PORC PO16 ....11 K6
FHAM/STUB PO14 ....180 F4
FNM GU9 ....13 G2
HAV PO9 ....16 F5
NARL SO24 ....291 M10
PLE BH15 ....223 J6
PSEA PO1 ....20 B5
SHAM SO14 ....23 G4
WIMB BH21 ....207 H4
WVILLE PO7 ....319 R9
East Surrey St PSEA PO1 ....21 H2
East View Rd RGWD BH24 ....203 K5
Eastville Rd ELGH SO50 ....141 J3
East Wy CHAR BH8 ....214 B7
WIMB BH21 ....210 D3
Eastways BPWT SO32 ....143 J5
Eastwood ROMY SO51 ....128 C7
Eastwood Av FERN BH22 ....209 L2
Eastwood Cl HISD PO11 ....195 H4
Eastwood Ct ROMY SO51 * 136 E1
East Woodhay Rd FUFL SO22 ....288 D12
Eastwood Rd NEND PO2 ....184 E4
Eastworth Rd VWD BH31 ....201 G1
Eaton Rd CBLY GU15 ....50 D4
CCLF BH13 ....225 G6
E Av FAWY SO45 ....354 G3
Ebblake Cl VWD BH31 ....201 L5
Ebble Cl NTID SP9 ....266 F1
Ebden Rd WINC SO23 ....25 K4
Ebery Gv HSEA PO3 ....193 H2
Ebor Cl FERN BH22 ....209 L6
Ebor Rd BKME/WDN BH12 ....224 D2
Ecchinswell Rd KSCL RG20 ....248 B10
Eccles Rd PLE BH15 ....223 G6
Echo Barn La RFNM GU10 ....78 C3
Ecton La HSEA PO3 ....185 J5
Eddeys Cl BOR GU35 ....114 B2
Eddeys La BOR GU35 ....114 B3
Eddy Rd ASHV GU12 ....3 J4
Eddystone Rd TOTT SO40 ....144 D5
Edelvale Rd WEND SO18 ....148 B3
Edelweiss Cl RAND SP11 ....265 M11
Edenbridge Rd ENEY PO4 ....193 H3
Edenbridge Wy HLER SO31 ....163 M6
Eden Gv WIMB BH21 ....207 K5
Eden Ri FHAM/PORC PO16 ....11 G8
Eden Rd WEND SO18 ....148 B2
Eden St PSEA PO1 * 21 H1
Eden Wk CHFD SO53 ....139 G3
Edgar Cl AND SP10 ....84 D8
Edgar Crs FHAM/PORC PO16 ....183 K2
Edgar Rd WINC SO23 ....24 E9
Edgarton Rd CFDH BH17 ....211 K5
Edgbarrow Ct CWTH RG45 * 43 J5
Edgbarrowhill Star CWTH RG45 ....43 J5
Edgbarrow Ri SHST GU47 ....43 J6

Edgcumbe Park Dr CWTH RG45 43 J3
Edgecombe Crs
LSOL/BMARY PO13 182 C8
Edgecombe La NWBY RG14 27 L7
Edgedale Cl CWTH RG45 43 K4
Edgefield Gv HORN PO8 156 C7
Edgehill Cl KBH RG22 92 D1
Edgehill Rd MOOR/WNTN BH9 213 L8
WEND SO18 147 M7
Edgell Rd EMRTH PO10 172 B2
Edgemoor Rd FERN BH22 205 K7
FRIM GU16 51 L5
Edgerly Gdns CHAM PO6 184 F2
Edgeware Rd ENEY PO4 193 G3
Edgewood Cl CWTH RG45 43 J1
Edifred Rd MOOR/WNTN BH9 214 A4
Edinburgh Rd PSEA PO1 20 F2
WINC SO23 288 H7
Edington Cl BPWT SO32 143 H3
Edington Rd WINC SO23 25 G1
Edison Rd BSTK RG21 65 G5
Edith Haisman Cl WSHM SO15 22 B1
Edmondsham Rd VWD BH31 337 L12
Edmund Rd ENEY PO4 21 M6
Edmunds Cl HEND SO30 149 K7
NMIL/BTOS BH25 218 F7
Edney Cl FLEETS GU52 71 K2
Edneys La WVILLE PO7 155 G3
Edrich Sq AND SP10 * 96 D2
Edric's Gn AMSY SP4 268 D3
Edward Av CBLY GU15 50 C3
ELGH SO50 134 D8
Edward Cl FAWY SO45 354 G7
Edward Gdns HAV PO9 170 C7
Edward Gv FHAM/PORC PO16 167 L7
Edward Rd ALTN GU34 107 G3
BWD BH11 213 H5
CHCH/BSGR BH23 216 F8
FAWY SO45 177 G4
FNM GU9 13 G9
PSTN BH14 224 C3
WINC SO23 122 E8
WSHM SO15 160 C1
Edwards Cl CHAM PO6 168 B7
WVILLE PO7 155 M6
Edward St ALDT GU11 2 D3
Edward Ter NARL SO24 * 291 N11
Edwina Cl ITCH SO19 161 M2
NBAD SO52 138 A4
RGWD BH24 203 L3
Edwina Dr CFDH BH17 211 H6
Edwin Cl STHA RG19 35 M1
Eeklo Pl NWBY RG14 18 F8
Eelmoor Br ALDT GU11 72 C2
Eelmoor Plain Rd ALDT GU11 72 D4
Eelmoor Rd ALDT GU11 72 D3
FARN GU14 60 F6
Effingham Gdns ITCH SO19 148 C8
Efford Wy LYMN SO41 221 H6
Egan Cl NEND PO2 184 F5
Egbert Rd WINC SO23 25 G2
Egbury Rd RAND SP11 86 C2
Egdon Cl FERN BH22 209 H6
Egdon Ct UPTN BH16 222 B1
Egdon Dr WIMB BH21 207 L8
Egerton Gdns CHAR BH8 * 226 D2
Egerton Rd CHAR BH8 226 D2
SHST GU47 50 A2
Eggars Cl ALTN GU34 107 H4
Eggars Fld RFNM GU10 259 M11
Eggar's Hl ALDT GU11 2 E7
Eggleton Cl FLEETS GU52 71 G3
Eglantine Cl HORN PO8 156 B4
Eglantine Wk HORN PO8 156 B4
Eglinton Rd RFNM GU10 262 H6
Egmont Cl RGWD BH24 347 J2
Egmont Dr RGWD BH24 347 K2
Egmont Gdns RGWD BH24 347 K2
Egmont Rd UPTN BH16 222 B4
Egret Gdns ALDT GU11 2 E8
Eight Acres GSHT GU26 115 J1
ROMY SO51 137 H1
Elaine Gdns HORN PO8 155 M3
Elan Cl WEND SO18 148 B3
Eland Rd ASHV GU12 3 L5
Elbe Wy AND SP10 96 B1
Elbow Cnr BSTK RG21 6 E5
Elcombes Cl LYND SO43 345 K3
Elden Rd NTID SP9 264 G11
Elderberry Bank CHIN RG24 54 B8
Elderberry Cl ELGH SO50 141 G2
HORN PO8 321 M8
Elderberry La
CHCH/BSGR BH23 228 F2
Elderberry Rd BOR GU35 111 J7
Elderberry Wy HORN PO8 156 B4
Elder Cl FUFL SO22 122 C8
HLER SO31 179 M2
TOTT SO40 160 A7
Elder Crs AND SP10 4 A8
Elderfield Cl EMRTH PO10 172 A3
Elderfield Rd HAV PO9 170 D1
Elder Gn RWIN SO21 135 G4
Eldergrove FARN GU14 61 L6
Elder Rd HAV PO9 17 K1
Eldon Av NMIL/BTOS BH25 218 E8
Eldon Cl NMIL/BTOS BH25 218 E8
STOK SO20 299 Q2
Eldon Dr RFNM GU10 79 H3
Eldon Pl WBNE BH4 * 225 H5
Eldon Rd MOOR/WNTN BH9 213 L7
ROMY SO51 299 R12
STOK SO20 299 Q3
Eldon St SSEA PO5 21 G5
Eldridge Gdns ROMY SO51 130 F8
Eleanor Cl LIPH GU30 113 K4
Eleanor Ct RAND SP11 265 L10
Eleanor Dr BWD BH11 212 D3
Eleanor Gdns
CHCH/BSGR BH23 215 L8
Eleanors Wd
FHAM/PORC PO16 * 167 H7
Electron Wy CHFD SO53 139 J2
Elettra Av WVILLE PO7 155 K7
Elfin Dr FERN BH22 209 J1
Elgar Av CWTH RG45 43 K2
Elgar Cl CHAM PO6 * 167 L8
GPORT PO12 14 B9
KBH RG22 93 G4
Elgar Rd ITCH SO19 162 C1
NBNE BH10 213 K4
Elgars Ct LYMN SO41 * 221 M4
Elgar Wk WVILLE PO7 169 M4
Elgin Cl FAWY SO45 177 G5
FHAM PO15 10 C3
Elgin Rd BLKW GU17 49 G7
CHAM PO6 184 F2
PSTN BH14 224 C6
WBNE BH4 8 B1
WSHM SO15 22 A1
Elgin Wy FRIM GU16 61 M1
Elijah Cl PLE BH15 222 E6
Eling Cl FUFL SO22 122 D1
Eling Ct HAV PO9 170 D2
Eling Hl TOTT SO40 159 H3
Eling La TOTT SO40 159 G2
Eliot Cl CBLY GU15 51 K1
NTHA RG18 28 E7
Eliot Dr HASM GU27 117 L2
Elise Cl LTDN BH7 215 H8
Elizabethan Ri OVTN RG25 103 G2
Elizabeth Av CHCH/BSGR BH23 215 M8
NWBY RG14 33 K5
Elizabeth Cl HEND SO30 148 D3
RSAL SP5 331 R1
WHAM PO17 151 M8
WINC SO23 288 H7
Elizabeth Ct
FHAM/STUB PO14 * 181 M5
Elizabeth Crs LYMN SO41 220 A6
Elizabeth Dr FLEETS GU52 71 J3
Elizabeth Gdns ENEY PO4 192 F6
FAWY SO45 177 G7
Elizabeth Rd
FHAM/STUB PO14 189 K2
KBH RG22 65 G8
PLE BH15 223 K5
UPTN BH16 * 222 C1
WHAM PO17 152 A4
WIMB BH21 207 J3
WVILLE PO7 169 M2
Elizabeth Rout Cl THLE RG7 238 C6
Elizabeth Wy BPWT SO32 143 H5
ELGH SO50 134 B7
Eliza Pl GPORT PO12 15 G3
Elkhams Cl LYMN SO41 220 D7
Elkins Gv RFNM GU10 * 12 A4
Elkstone Rd CHAM PO6 168 B7
Ellachie Ms GPORT PO12 191 H7
Ellachie Rd GPORT PO12 191 H7
Elland Cl ELGH SO50 141 J3
Ellidene Ct TOTT SO40 158 E3
Ellen Dr FLEETN GU51 59 K4
Ellen Gdns CHFD SO53 139 G3
TADY RG26 46 A5
Elleray Ct ASHV GU12 74 A3
Ellerslie Cl FHAM/STUB PO14 189 G3
Ellery Gv LYMN SO41 221 L3
Elles Cl FARN GU14 61 H5
Ellesfield Dr FERN BH22 209 K5
Ellesmere Orch EMRTH PO10 172 B2
Elles Rd FARN GU14 61 G6
Ellingham Cl NARL SO24 291 M11
Ellingham Dr RGWD BH24 198 F7
Ellingham Dro RGWD BH24 199 L7
Ellingham Rd
NMIL/BTOS BH25 218 D8
Ellington Cl RAND SP11 95 K5
Ellington Dr KBH RG22 92 E5
Elliot Cl TOTT SO40 158 D2
Elliot Ri HEND SO30 149 J2
Elliott Rd BWD BH11 212 E5
Ellisfield Rd HAV PO9 170 E4
Ellison Wy RFNM GU10 260 D1
Ellis Rd CWTH RG45 43 K2
ITCH SO19 148 E7
Ellis's Hl WHIT RG2 239 M4
Ellwood Av ITCH SO19 148 E7
Ellwood Cl ITCH SO19 148 E6
Elm Av CHCH/BSGR BH23 215 L7
LYMN SO41 221 J7
NMIL/BTOS BH25 219 G6
Elm Bank YTLY GU46 48 E1
Elm Bank Rd AND SP10 5 H7
Elm Cl BOR GU35 113 G1
HISD PO11 195 G5
RAND SP11 265 P10
RAND SP11 267 R8
ROWN SO16 * 146 F4
RSAL SP5 282 A12
STOK SO20 270 D8
Elm Crs BPWT SO32 310 E10
FAWY SO45 354 C1
FNM GU9 77 H1
Elmcroft Cl FRIM GU16 61 M1
Elmdale Cl HLER SO31 179 K4
Elmdale Gv ROMY SO51 335 L7
Elmers Wy CHCH/BSGR BH23 348 D11
Elmes Dr WSHM SO15 159 M1
Elmes Rd MOOR/WNTN BH9 213 L6
Elmeswelle Rd HORN PO8 156 A2
Elm Farm Gv KSCL RG20 * 248 D10
Elmfield Cl RSAL SP5 332 F3
Elmfield West Block
WSHM SO15 * 22 B2
Elm Gdns HEND SO30 148 D2
WBNE BH4 225 J3
Elmgate Dr LTDN BH7 226 F1
Elm Gv ELGH SO50 139 M6
FNM GU9 77 G1
GPORT PO12 14 F2
HISD PO11 195 G5
KSCL RG20 248 D10
NTHA RG18 28 D7
SSEA PO5 21 H6
Elm Grove Rd FARN GU14 61 H4
Elmhurst TADY RG26 44 B5
Elmhurst Rd BWD BH11 213 G3
FERN BH22 205 H7
FHAM/PORC PO16 11 G7
GPORT PO12 15 G4
NTHA RG18 28 C7
Elmhurst Wy FERN BH22 205 H6
Elm La HAV PO9 16 E4
RFNM GU10 73 M8
Elmleigh Rd HAV PO9 16 E2
Elmore Av LSOL/BMARY PO13 189 M7
Elmore Cl LSOL/BMARY PO13 189 M7
Elmore Dr RGWD BH24 202 A6
Elmore Rd LSOL/BMARY PO13 189 M8
Elm Park Rd HAV PO9 16 F3
Elm Pl ALDT GU11 3 J7
Elm Rd BPWT SO32 143 L4
CHIN RG24 64 F2
FNM GU9 77 H1
FUFL SO22 24 D4
HAV PO9 17 H6
NARL SO24 291 M11
OVTN RG25 89 K2
Elms Av PSTN BH14 224 A7
STHA RG19 35 L1
Elms Cl FBDG SP6 196 C2
PSTN BH14 224 A7
Elmside HTWY RG27 * 46 F7
Elmsleigh Gdns ROWN SO16 147 G4
Elmsleigh Rd FARN GU14 61 G4
Elmslie Gdns HLER SO31 162 F3
Elms Rd ALDT GU11 2 F4
FHAM/PORC PO16 11 G9
FLEETN GU51 59 L7
HTWY RG27 56 C7
Elmstead Rd CCLF BH13 224 F8
The Elms AND SP10 4 F6
BLKW GU17 * 49 M4
RFNM GU10 260 D1
Elm St SHAM SO14 23 K4
SSEA PO5 * 20 F6
Elms Wy SBNE BH6 227 L4
Elm Ter LISS GU33 308 E7
SHAM SO14 23 K5
Elm Tree Cl TOTT SO40 158 B6
Elmtree Gdns ROMY SO51 137 J2
Elmtree Rd CHAM PO6 169 L8
Elm Tree Wk FERN BH22 209 L8
Elm Vw ASHV GU12 74 B5
Elmwood CHIN RG24 * 54 A5
Elmwood Av FBDG SP6 196 F2
WVILLE PO7 169 L2
Elmwood Cl ALTN GU34 106 D6
Elmwood Rd NEND PO2 184 E4
Elmwood Wy
CHCH/BSGR BH23 229 M1
DEAN RG23 64 E5
Elphinstone Rd
CHCH/BSGR BH23 218 B8
SSEA PO5 21 G8
Elsenwood Crs CBLY GU15 51 J2
Elsenwood Dr CBLY GU15 51 J1
Elsfred Rd FHAM/STUB PO14 189 G3
Elsley Cl FRIM GU16 61 M2
Elson La GPORT PO12 183 G8
Elson Rd GPORT PO12 182 F8
Elstead Gdns WVILLE PO7 169 J4
Elstead Rd MFD/CHID GU8 261 Q10
RFNM GU10 260 E3
Elsted Rd MIDH GU29 317 P12
Elston Pl ASHV GU12 3 J6
Elston Rd ASHV GU12 3 J6
Elstree Rd ITCH SO19 161 L3
Eltham Cl LTDN BH7 215 H8
Elvetham Cl FLEETN GU51 59 H5
Elvetham Crs FLEETN GU51 58 F5
Elvetham Heath FLEETN GU51 58 B7
Elvetham Heath Wy
FLEETN GU51 58 F5
Elvetham La HTWY RG27 241 P12
Elvetham Pl FLEETN GU51 59 G5
Elvetham Rd FLEETN GU51 58 F6
Elvin Cl LYMN SO41 219 M4
Elwell Gn HISD PO11 194 F5
Elwyn Rd BMTH BH1 9 L2
Ely Cl FRIM GU16 62 A1
Ely Ct LSOL/BMARY PO13 * 190 D3
Emanuel St NEND PO2 192 D1
Embankment Wy RGWD BH24 203 K6
Emberley Cl FERN BH22 346 A6
Emblen Crs WHIT RG2 239 L6
Embleton Rd BOR GU35 114 B2
Embley Cl TOTT SO40 144 D6
Embley La ROMY SO51 335 P2
Embsay Rd HLER SO31 163 K4
Emden Rd AND SP10 96 B1
Emerald Cl ITCH SO19 148 A6
RGWD BH24 202 A6
WVILLE PO7 170 A1
Emer Cl NBAD SO52 138 A3
Emerson Cl PLE BH15 223 J6
Emerson Rd PLE BH15 223 J6
Emery Down Dr FLEETN GU51 58 E5
Emily Cl CHCH/BSGR BH23 216 A7
Emmanuel Cl
FHAM/STUB PO14 180 C2
Emmett Rd ROWN SO16 145 M3
Emmons Cl HLER SO31 178 F3
Empress Av FARN GU14 61 H3
Empress Pk SHAM SO14 * 161 H1
Empress Rd LYND SO43 345 K3
SHAM SO14 23 J9
Empress Wy RAND SP11 265 M10
Empshott Rd ENEY PO4 192 F4
Empson Wk
LSOL/BMARY PO13 189 M6
Emsbrook Dr EMRTH PO10 171 M6
Emsworth Common Rd
EMRTH PO10 171 K3
Emsworth House Cl
EMRTH PO10 171 L7
Emsworth Rd HAV PO9 17 G5
LYMN SO41 221 L4
NEND PO2 184 E7
WSHM SO15 146 B8
Enborne Ct NWBY RG14 * 33 K3
Enborne Ga NWBY RG14 33 K3
Enborne Gv NWBY RG14 18 B6
Enborne Lodge La NWBY RG14 33 J6
Enborne Pl NWBY RG14 18 B6
Enborne Rd KSCL RG20 33 J3
NWBY RG14 18 B6
Enborne St KSCL RG20 33 G8
Enborne Wy THLE RG7 36 F6
Encombe Cl BKME/WDN BH12 212 F8
Endeavour Cl GPORT PO12 15 J5
WSHM SO15 160 B1
Endeavour Wy FAWY SO45 176 F3
Enderwood Cl TOTT SO40 * 144 B8
Endfield Cl CHCH/BSGR BH23 215 M7
Endfield Rd CHCH/BSGR BH23 215 M8
MOOR/WNTN BH9 214 A6
Endle St SHAM SO14 23 K5
Endofield Cl FHAM/STUB PO14 181 M6
Enfield Av PLE BH15 223 L2
Enfield Crs PLE BH15 223 L2
Enfield Gv ITCH SO19 161 L6
Enfield Rd ASHV GU12 74 B3
PLE BH15 223 L2
Englands Wy BWD BH11 212 D4
Englefield Rd WEND SO18 161 K1
Englesfield CBLY GU15 51 L3
English Rd WSHM SO15 160 B1
English Wd CHIN RG24 64 E5
Enham Arch Rbt AND SP10 5 H2
Enham La AND SP10 96 A1
Enmill La FUFL SO22 301 R7
Ennel Copse NBAD SO52 138 A4
Ennerdale Cl HORN PO8 321 L10
KBH RG22 92 D2
Ennerdale Gdns NARL SO24 291 M12
WEND SO18 148 B3
Ennerdale Gv FNM GU9 76 E2
Ennerdale Rd BOR GU35 110 F7
FHAM/STUB PO14 181 K8
ROWN SO16 145 L6
Ennerdale Wy STHA RG19 35 G1
Ensbury Av NBNE BH10 213 K7
Ensbury Br FERN BH22 213 L1
Ensbury Cl NBNE BH10 213 K7
Ensbury Park Rd
MOOR/WNTN BH9 213 L6
Ensign Dr LSOL/BMARY PO13 190 D2
Ensign Wy HLER SO31 178 E2
Enterprise Cl HLER SO31 179 L3
Enterprise Ct CHIN RG24 65 M5
Enterprise Rd HORN PO8 321 L12
ROWN SO16 138 C7
Enterprise Wy
CHCH/BSGR BH23 346 D12
SHAM SO14 23 J7
STHA RG19 36 A2
Epping Cl WEND SO18 148 B3
Epsom Cl ELGH SO50 141 K5
Epsom Crs NWBY RG14 19 H8
Epsom Down ALTN GU34 106 F6
Epts Rd FARN GU14 61 G8
Epworth Rd NEND PO2 184 F7
Equine Wy NWBY RG14 34 B5
Erica Cl HLER SO31 179 M1
HORN PO8 156 B5
Erica Dr WIMB BH21 210 D2
Erica Wy HORN PO8 156 B4
Ericksen Rd BWD BH11 213 J5
Eric Rd FHAM/STUB PO14 189 J2
Erleigh Dene NWBY RG14 18 C8
Erles Rd LIPH GU30 116 C4
Ernest Cl EMRTH PO10 171 M7
RFNM GU10 78 F2
Ernest Rd HAV PO9 170 C4
PSEA PO1 192 E1
Erpingham Rd
BKME/WDN BH12 225 G3
Erskine Cl TADY RG26 44 F3
Erskine Rd FUFL SO22 24 D7
Escombe Rd ELGH SO50 140 D1
Escur Cl NEND PO2 184 F4
Esdaile La RGWD BH24 348 H1
Esher Cl KBH RG22 92 F3
Esher Gv WVILLE PO7 155 J6
Eskdale Cl HORN PO8 321 L10
Eskdale Ct ASHV GU12 * 73 M4
Eskdale Wy CBLY GU15 51 L4
Esmond Cl EMRTH PO10 171 M8
Esmonde Cl
LSOL/BMARY PO13 * 189 M6
Esmonde Wy CFDH BH17 211 M8
Esplanade CCLF BH13 237 L1
ENEY PO4 192 E7
PLE BH15 223 J5
Esplanade Gdns ENEY PO4 193 J6
The Esplanade GPORT PO12 15 L4
Essex Av CHCH/BSGR BH23 215 M6
Essex Cl FRIM GU16 62 A1
Essex Pl NWBY RG14 * 26 F7
Essex Rd BOR GU35 110 F8
BSTK RG21 6 D5
ENEY PO4 193 G4
Essex St NWBY RG14 33 K5
Esslemont Rd ENEY PO4 21 M6
Estancia Cl
LSOL/BMARY PO13 192 F5
Estella Rd NEND PO2 184 D8
Estridge Cl HLER SO31 162 F3
Ethelbert Dr AND SP10 95 M1
Ethelbert Rd WIMB BH21 207 K4
Ethelburt Av ROWN SO16 147 J3
Ethelred Gdns TOTT SO40 158 C2
Ethel Rd PSEA PO1 21 L1
Eton Cl KBH RG22 92 C6
Eton Gdns WBNE BH4 225 H4
Eton Pl FNM GU9 76 F1
Eton Rd SSEA PO5 21 L4
Ettrick Rd CCLF BH13 225 G7
Etwall RAND SP11 267 N12
Eucalyptus Av RGWD BH24 346 G2
Europa Cl TADY RG26 46 B5
European Wy SHAM SO14 23 J8
Euryalus Rd
FHAM/STUB PO14 181 M6
Euskirchen Wy KBH RG22 64 F7
Euston Gv RGWD BH24 203 K6
Euston Rd ENEY PO4 193 H3
Evans Cl BWD BH11 212 F7
NEND PO2 184 B6
RGWD BH24 202 A6
STOK SO20 269 Q10
Evans Rd ENEY PO4 193 G4
Evans St SHAM SO14 23 H4
Evelegh Rd CHAM PO6 169 K8
Eveley Cl BOR GU35 112 D4
Evelyn Av ALDT GU11 3 H7
Evelyn Cl BPWT SO32 143 L8
Evelyn Crs WSHM SO15 146 D8
Evelyn Rd MOOR/WNTN BH9 214 A7
Evelyn Woods Rd ALDT GU11 73 J1
Evendon's La WWKG RG41 239 R5
Evening Gld FERN BH22 209 L5
Evenlode Rd ROWN SO16 145 L7
Evenlode Wy SHST GU47 43 L8
Everdene Cl FERN BH22 209 J6
Everdon La HSEA PO3 185 J4
Everest Rd CHCH/BSGR BH23 216 E8
CWTH RG45 43 K2
Everglades Av HORN PO8 155 M5
Everglades Cl FERN BH22 209 K1
Evergreen Cl TOTT SO40 159 M7
WIMB BH21 201 G8
WVILLE PO7 169 K1
Evergreen Rd FRIM GU16 51 H6
Evergreens RGWD BH24 202 A7
TOTT SO40 * 159 G2
Evering Av BKME/WDN BH12 212 D7
Evering Gdns
BKME/WDN BH12 212 C7
Everlea Cl LYMN SO41 220 D7
Everleigh Rd MARL SN8 264 F4
Everon Gdns NMIL/BTOS BH25 219 H7
Eversfield Cl AND SP10 4 E5
Evershot Rd CHAR BH8 214 E7
Eversley Crs HAV PO9 170 D4
Eversley Dr FLEETN GU51 58 E5
Eversley Pl FUFL SO22 122 D7
Eversley Rd WHIT RG2 239 L6
Eversley St HTWY RG27 241 N3
Everton Rd LYMN SO41 219 M4
Evesham Cl LTDN BH7 215 G8
ROWN SO16 147 H3
Evesham Wk CHIN RG24 65 K3
SHST GU47 43 L7
Evingar Gdns WHCH RG28 87 L6
Evingar Rd WHCH RG28 87 L6
Evreux Cl STHA RG19 * 35 M2
Ewart Ct FAWY SO45 177 G3
Ewart Rd PSEA PO1 192 E1
Ewell Wy TOTT SO40 144 D7
Ewer Common GPORT PO12 14 F8
Ewhurst Cl HAV PO9 170 D4
Ewhurst Rd TADY RG26 255 Q1
Ewing Wy NWBY RG14 18 F9
Ewins Cl ASHV GU12 74 A6
Ewshot La FLEETS GU52 71 H5
Exbury Cl ELGH SO50 140 F2
Exbury Dr BWD BH11 212 F3
Exbury Rd FAWY SO45 354 G8
HAV PO9 171 G3
Exbury Wy AND SP10 4 C7
Excellent Rd
FHAM/STUB PO14 181 M7
Excelsior Rd PSTN BH14 224 C6
Exchange Rd PSEA PO1 20 F3
Exeter Cl ELGH SO50 139 M3
EMRTH PO10 171 M5
HLER SO31 179 M1
KBH RG22 92 D5
WEND SO18 148 A3
Exeter Ct LSOL/BMARY PO13 * 190 C2
Exeter Crs WCLF BH2 8 E7
Exeter Gdns YTLY GU46 48 D1
Exeter Park Rd WCLF BH2 8 E7
Exeter Rd ASHV GU12 74 A5
ENEY PO4 192 F6
WCLF BH2 8 E7
WEND SO18 148 A4
Exford Av WEND SO18 148 C4
Exford Dr WEND SO18 148 C5
Exhibition Rd FARN GU14 61 G8
Exleigh Cl ITCH SO19 148 B6
Exmoor Cl KBH RG22 92 D1
Exmoor Rd STHA RG19 35 J1
Exmouth Gdns ELGH SO50 141 J5
Exmouth Rd GPORT PO12 183 G8
SSEA PO5 21 K8
Express Wy NWBY RG14 34 E2
Exton Gdns FHAM/PORC PO16 167 J7
Exton Rd HAV PO9 171 H3
SBNE BH6 227 K1
Eyebright Cl ELGH SO50 141 J6
Eyeworth Wk FAWY SO45 176 C4
Eynham Av ITCH SO19 148 C6
Eynham Cl ITCH SO19 148 B6
Eyre Cl TOTT SO40 158 D2
Eyres Dr RSAL SP5 327 N2

F

Faber Cl HAV PO9 171 G4
Fabian Cl BSTK RG21 6 C6
WVILLE PO7 156 A8
Factory Rd ELGH SO50 140 A2
UPTN BH16 222 D2
Fairacre KSCL RG20 246 B4
Fairacre Ri FHAM/STUB PO14 181 H4
Fairacres RFNM GU10 * 78 D4
Fairbairn Wk CHFD SO53 138 F2
Fairbourne Cl HORN PO8 * 155 L6
Fair Cl NWBY RG14 * 18 E6
WHCH RG28 87 L8
Fairclose WHCH RG28 87 K8
Fairclose Dr FUFL SO22 288 B11
Faircross Cl FAWY SO45 354 E5
Fairdown Cl WINC SO23 25 M6
Fairfax Cl FUFL SO22 122 B7
Fairfax Ct ITCH SO19 148 E6
Fairfax Ms FARN GU14 61 K6
ITCH SO19 148 E6
Fairfax Pl NWBY RG14 28 A7
Fairfax Rd FARN GU14 61 H1
Fair Fld ROMY SO51 131 G7
Fairfield CHCH/BSGR BH23 228 B1
WHCH RG28 87 L6
WVILLE PO7 154 F4
Fairfield Av FHAM/STUB PO14 10 B9
Fairfield Cl CHCH/BSGR BH23 228 B1
EMRTH PO10 171 M6
FAWY SO45 176 F4
LYMN SO41 221 L5
WIMB BH21 207 L3
Fairfield Dr FRIM GU16 51 G5
Fairfield Gn ALTN GU34 293 N5
Fairfield Pk THLE RG7 * 39 M7
Fairfield Rd FUFL SO22 24 D3
HAV PO9 16 F4
NMIL/BTOS BH25 230 E1
RWIN SO21 124 D7
WIMB BH21 207 K4
Fairfield Sq CHAM PO6 168 E8
Fairfields Rd BSTK RG21 6 E8
Fairfield Ter HAV PO9 * 16 F4
The Fairfield FNM GU9 13 H4
Fair Gn ITCH SO19 148 B7
The Fairground RAND SP11 94 F2
Fairholme Gdns FNM GU9 13 H6
Fairhome Cl GPORT PO12 191 G1
Fairies Dr FERN BH22 * 209 M5
Fair Isle Cl FHAM/STUB PO14 189 H1
Fairisle Rd ROWN SO16 145 L4
Fairland Cl FLEETS GU52 59 K8
Fair La RWIN SO21 123 M4
Fairlawn Cl ROWN SO16 145 M2
Fairlawn Rd TADY RG26 44 D5
Fairlead Dr LSOL/BMARY PO13 190 D2
Fairlea Rd EMRTH PO10 171 M5
LYMN SO41 221 L4
Fairlie RGWD BH24 203 L3
Fairlie Cl HEND SO30 149 H1
Fairlie Pk RGWD BH24 203 K3
Fairlight Gdns ALTN GU34 293 N5
Fairlight La LYMN SO41 350 B11
Fairmead Cl SHST GU47 50 A1
Fairmead Ct CBLY GU15 50 E4
Fairmead Rd WHIT RG2 238 E3
Fairmead Wk HORN PO8 156 A5
Fairmead Wy TOTT SO40 158 E3
Fairmile FLEETS GU52 71 J2
Fairmile Rd CHCH/BSGR BH23 215 M7
Fair Oak HAV PO9 16 E1
Fair Oak La THLE RG7 46 E1
Fairoak Rd ELGH SO50 140 D2
Fairoak Wy TADY RG26 249 P3
Fairthorne Gdns GPORT PO12 14 D5
Fairthorne Ri CHIN RG24 66 E3
Fair Vw NARL SO24 291 L12
Fairview Cl FAWY SO45 177 G5
ROMY SO51 131 H7
Fairview Crs BDST BH18 211 G3
Fairview Dr BDST BH18 211 G3
FAWY SO45 176 F6
ROMY SO51 131 H8
Fairview Gdns FNM GU9 77 H2
Fairview Meadow DEAN RG23 91 K4
Fairview Pde FAWY SO45 177 G6
Fairview Rd ASHV GU12 74 B5
BDST BH18 211 G3
BOR GU35 114 B3
RAND SP11 94 E2
Fairview Ter BOR GU35 * 114 A2
Fairwater Cl LSOL/BMARY PO13 182 B7
Fairway Cl LIPH GU30 309 P1
Fairway Dr CHCH/BSGR BH23 227 M2
Fairway Gdns ROWN SO16 145 L3
Fairway Hts CBLY GU15 51 K2
Fairway Rd FAWY SO45 176 F4
PSTN BH14 224 C8
Fairways FERN BH22 209 M2
GSHT GU26 115 H2
RAND SP11 94 D2
The Fairway BOR GU35 112 D3
FARN GU14 60 B8
FHAM/PORC PO16 167 J8
FNM GU9 77 H1
FRIM GU16 51 J5
HAV PO9 157 J6
LSOL/BMARY PO13 182 C7
NMIL/BTOS BH25 231 H1
Fairwood Rd VWD BH31 201 L3
Fairy Crossway HORN PO8 156 B6
Faithfulls Dro STOK SO20 285 J12
Fakenham Wy SHST GU47 43 M7
Falaise Cl ALDT GU11 3 G2
ROWN SO16 146 C4
Falaise Rd STOK SO20 270 C8
Falcon Cl FHAM/PORC PO16 166 F8
GPORT PO12 191 J1
KBH RG22 92 B3
NTID SP9 266 F1
Falcon Coppice KSCL RG20 246 B4
Falcon Dr CHCH/BSGR BH23 229 H3
Falconer Ct FAWY SO45 354 D2
Falconer Dr PLE BH15 222 E4
Falcon Flds FAWY SO45 355 K5
TADY RG26 44 B2
Falcon House Gdns KSCL RG20 246 A4
Falcon Rd HORN PO8 156 A1
Falcon Sq ELGH SO50 139 L7
Falcon Vw FUFL SO22 122 C8
Falcon Wy BPWT SO32 149 M3
YTLY GU46 * 48 D2
Falconwood Cl FBDG SP6 196 F3
Falkland Dr NWBY RG14 18 C9
Falkland Garth NWBY RG14 33 K5
Falkland Rd CHIN RG24 65 L3
CHFD SO53 139 J5
NEND PO2 184 D4
NWBY RG14 33 K6
WSHM SO15 160 A1

Falklands Cl
LSOL/BMARY PO13 189 M5
Falklands Rd NEND PO2 * 184 E4
Falkner Rd FNM GU9 12 D3
Falkners Cl FLEETN GU51 59 L4
Fallow Fld FUFL SO22 122 C8
Fallowfield FLEETN GU51 59 L4
YTLY GU46 48 D1
Falmouth Cl CBLY GU15 51 J4
Falmouth Rd CHAM PO6 167 M7
WHIT RG2 238 C1
Falmouth Wy STHA RG19 35 M1
Falstaff Wy TOTT SO40 158 E3
Fancy Rd BKME/WDN BH12 212 B8
Fannys La THLE RG7 29 K3
Fanshawe St SHAM SO14 161 G2
Fantails ALTN GU34 106 F2
Faraday Cl WHIT RG2 239 L9
Faraday Ct CHIN RG24 * 65 M4
Faraday Rd CHIN RG24 65 M4
FARN GU14 61 J2
NWBY RG14 19 G3
Faraday Wy EWKG RG40 239 N8
Farcroft Rd PSTN BH14 224 B3
Farcrosse Cl SHST GU47 43 L8
Fareham Dr YTLY GU46 48 D1
Fareham Hts
FHAM/PORC PO16 * 11 M3
Fareham Park Rd FHAM PO15 165 J8
Fareham Rd
LSOL/BMARY PO13 182 C3
WHAM PO17 152 A5
WHAM PO17 167 L3
Faringdon Cl SHST GU47 43 L7
Faringdon Rd WEND SO18 148 D5
Farleigh Cl HAV PO9 170 D3
Farleigh La OVTN RG25 104 C3
Farleigh Ri BSTK RG21 93 L2
Farleigh Rd OVTN RG25 93 K3
Farley Castle THLE RG7 * 239 J9
Farley Cl ELGH SO50 141 K3
FUFL SO22 122 B8
Farley Ct FARN GU14 * 61 K6
Farley La ROMY SO51 300 B11
Farley Mount Rd RWIN SO21 301 L6
Farley St STOK SO20 284 B2
Farlington Av CHAM PO6 169 J7
Farlington Rd NEND PO2 184 E7
Farm Cl CWTH RG45 43 L1
RGWD BH24 203 J4
YTLY GU46 48 F3
Farm Ct FRIM GU16 * 51 H6
Farmdene Cl
CHCH/BSGR BH23 * 217 K8
Farm Dr FLEETN GU51 59 K4
Far Meadow Wy EMRTH PO10 171 K8
Farm Edge Rd
FHAM/STUB PO14 189 J3
Farmers Cl WHIT RG2 238 B2
Farmers Wk LYMN SO41 220 D8
WIMB BH21 207 H2
Farmery Cl ELGH SO50 147 K4
Farm Gdns HSEA PO3 184 F4
Farm Ground Cl HTWY RG27 56 E7
Farm House Cl
FHAM/STUB PO14 181 J7
Farmhouse Wy HORN PO8 156 A3
Farm La CHCH/BSGR BH23 229 G3
RCCH PO18 172 F7
RFNM GU10 259 N3
Farm Lane Cl WVILLE PO7 169 K2
Farm La North
NMIL/BTOS BH25 219 G8
Farm La South
NMIL/BTOS BH25 231 G1
Farmlea Rd CHAM PO6 167 M8
Farm Rd ASHV GU12 73 L5
FERN BH22 204 F6
FHAM/STUB PO14 180 E2
FRIM GU16 51 G6
RAND SP11 95 J6
Farmside Gdns HSEA PO3 184 F4
Farm Vw EMRTH PO10 171 M5
YTLY GU46 48 F3
Farm View Av HORN PO8 321 K7
Farm View Dr CHIN RG24 54 C5
Farm Wk ASHV GU12 74 C8
Farnborough Ga FARN GU14 * 61 J1
Farnborough Rd ALDT GU11 2 C1
FARN GU14 61 J1
Farnborough St FARN GU14 61 K3
Farnham By-Pass FNM GU9 12 B7
Farnham La HASM GU27 118 A3
Farnham Park Cl FNM GU9 76 F2
Farnham Rd BKME/WDN BH12 225 G1
BOR GU35 110 F6
FLEETN GU51 59 M7
LISS GU33 308 E8
ODIM RG29 69 H5
PSF GU32 120 F1
RFNM GU10 260 F11
Farnleys Md LYMN SO41 221 L6
Faroe Cl CHIN RG24 65 M3
Faroes Cl FHAM/STUB PO14 * 189 H1
Farrell Cl CBLY GU15 50 E5
Farriers Cl TADY RG26 46 B5
WIMB BH21 208 B2
Farrier's Fld OVTN RG25 105 J4
Farriers Wk GPORT PO12 15 K3
Farriers Wy HORN PO8 156 C7
Farrier Wy FHAM/PORC PO16 182 B2
Farringdon Rd HAV PO9 171 G4
Farringdon Wy TADY RG26 44 B5
Farringford Rd ITCH SO19 148 D6
Farrs Av AND SP10 5 K8
Farthingale Ter PSEA PO1 * 20 D6
Farthing Flds BOR GU35 111 L7
Farthings Ga WVILLE PO7 169 L5
Farwell Cl CHCH/BSGR BH23 216 C5
Farwell Rd BKME/WDN BH12 212 C6
Fastnet Cl ROWN SO16 145 L3
Fastnet Wy FHAM/STUB PO14 189 H1
Fathersfield BROC SO42 351 K3
Fathoms Reach HISD PO11 194 E4
F Av FAWY SO45 354 H2
Faversham Rd SHST GU47 43 M7
Fawcett Rd ENEY PO4 21 L4
NMIL/BTOS BH25 218 F6
Fawconer Rd KSCL RG20 248 D10
Fawley By-pass FAWY SO45 355 K5
Fawley Ct HAV PO9 171 H3
Fawley Gn CHAR BH8 214 D5
Fawley La ALTN GU34 305 R8
RWIN SO21 125 M4
Fawley Rd FAWY SO45 177 H8
NEND PO2 184 E3
WSHM SO15 160 A2
Fawn Gdns NMIL/BTOS BH25 218 F4
Fay Cl FHAM/STUB PO14 189 J2
Fayre Rd FHAM/PORC PO16 10 F9
Fayrewood Cha KBH RG22 92 D5
Fearon Rd NEND PO2 184 E6
Feathers La BSTK RG21 6 F6
Feildon Ct KSCL RG20 248 C11
Felbridge Cl FRIM GU16 51 H6
Feld Wy CHIN RG24 66 C1
Felix Rd GPORT PO12 191 H1
Fell Cl HLER SO31 164 A8
Fell Dr LSOL/BMARY PO13 189 M5
Fellows Rd FARN GU14 61 K7
Felmer Dr WINC SO23 289 J9
Feltham Cl ROMY SO51 131 J8
Felton Crs CHCH/BSGR BH23 217 M8
Felton Rd PSTN BH14 223 M3
Feltons Pl HSEA PO3 184 F3
Fen Av FHAM/PORC PO16 182 B1
Fencott Pl BSTK RG21 6 E2
Fenleigh Cl NMIL/BTOS BH25 219 H8
Fennel Cl CHIN RG24 54 C4
FARN GU14 60 B4
NWBY RG14 27 M7
Fennel Gdns LYMN SO41 221 K3
Fennell Cl WVILLE PO7 155 K7
Fenton Rd SBNE BH6 227 J2
Ferbies FLEETS GU52 71 J2
Ferguson Cl BSTK RG21 93 J2
Fermor Dr ALDT GU11 2 C1
Fernbank EWKG RG40 239 R10
Fern Bank WIMB BH21 205 G1
Fern Barrow
BKME/WDN BH12 213 H8
Fernbrae Cl RFNM GU10 78 F6
Fern Cl CHCH/BSGR BH23 216 C6
CWTH RG45 43 K1
EPSF GU31 121 G6
FBDG SP6 196 C7
FRIM GU16 51 L5
Ferncote Rd BOR GU35 113 G1
Ferncroft Cl FHAM/STUB PO14 189 J3
Ferncroft Gdns NBNE BH10 213 K3
Ferncroft Rd NBNE BH10 213 K3
Ferndale HEND SO30 149 K7
WVILLE PO7 169 M1
Ferndale Ct STHA RG19 35 K1
Ferndale Gdns HTWY RG27 56 C6
Ferndale Ms
LSOL/BMARY PO13 182 B4
Ferndale Rd AND SP10 4 C3
FLEETS GU52 71 H3
NMIL/BTOS BH25 219 H4
TOTT SO40 159 M7
Ferndene Wy WEND SO18 147 M8
Ferndown Cl DEAN RG23 92 C8
Ferndown Gdns FARN GU14 60 E4
Ferndown, Stour &
Forest Trail FERN BH22 209 G7
Fern Dr FLEETN GU51 71 G2
HAV PO9 17 G2
Ferneham Rd FHAM PO15 181 J2
Ferney Cl ALTN GU34 294 D1
Ferney La ALTN GU34 278 D12
Fernglade NMIL/BTOS BH25 219 G5
Fernheath Cl BWD BH11 213 G6
Fernheath Rd BWD BH11 213 G5
Fernhill Cl CFDH BH17 212 A6
FARN GU14 50 A7
FNM GU9 76 F2
Fernhill Dr FNM GU9 76 F2
Fernhill La FARN GU14 50 B7
FNM GU9 76 F1
NMIL/BTOS BH25 219 G2
Fern Hill La ROMY SO51 300 B12
Fernhill Rd BLKW GU17 50 A6
FARN GU14 60 E3
NMIL/BTOS BH25 219 G4
Fernhills Rd FAWY SO45 177 H7
Fernhill Wk FARN GU14 50 B7
Fernhurst Cl HISD PO11 194 E5
Fernhurst Rd ENEY PO4 192 F4
Fernie Cl FHAM/STUB PO14 189 H2
Ferniehurst CBLY GU15 51 H4
Fernlea BOR GU35 112 D3
Fernlea Av FERN BH22 209 K4
Fernlea Cl FERN BH22 209 K4
RGWD BH24 202 A8
Fernlea Gdns FERN BH22 209 K4
ROWN SO16 146 E5
Fernlea Wy FAWY SO45 176 D5
Fernleigh Ri FRIM GU16 62 C1
Fern Rd FAWY SO45 176 F5
ITCH SO19 161 M6
Fernside Av PSTN BH14 223 M4
Fernside Rd FERN BH22 205 G6
MOOR/WNTN BH9 213 K8
PLE BH15 223 L4
Ferns Md FNM GU9 12 D5
The Ferns FNM GU9 * 77 G1
Fern Wy FHAM PO15 180 D1
Fernway Cl WIMB BH21 208 B4
Fernwood Cl RGWD BH24 202 D7
Fernyhurst Av ROWN SO16 145 M2
Ferrell Fld HTWY RG27 56 B7
Ferrier Gv NWBY RG14 19 G9
Ferris Av CHAR BH8 214 C6
Ferris Cl CHAR BH8 214 D6
Ferris Pl CHAR BH8 214 D6
Ferrol Rd GPORT PO12 15 G1
Ferry Point LYMN SO41 * 356 A8
Ferry Rd ENEY PO4 193 K5
FAWY SO45 176 F5
HISD PO11 194 A4
PLE BH15 223 H7
SBNE BH6 227 M5
SWCE BH19 236 E8
Ferry Wy CCLF BH13 237 G5
Festing Gv ENEY PO4 192 F6
Festing Rd ENEY PO4 192 F6
Festival Wy BSTK RG21 6 F5
Feversham Av CHAR BH8 214 E7
Fey Rd GPORT PO12 15 G3
Fibbards Rd BROC SO42 351 K3
Fiddlers Fld ALTN GU34 280 B4
Field Cl HLER SO31 180 B2
LSOL/BMARY PO13 182 B3
ROMY SO51 137 G1
ROWN SO16 147 J3
RWIN SO21 124 C6
Fielden Cl NBAD SO52 137 M4
Field End FNM GU9 77 K4
WINC SO23 289 J9
Fielders Ct ALTN GU34 106 F5
The Fielders HTWY RG27 42 A8
Fielders Wy ROMY SO51 335 M6
Fieldfare Av YTLY GU46 48 C2
Fieldfare Cl HORN PO8 321 L8
Fieldfare Ct TOTT SO40 144 C8
Field Gate Dr KSCL RG20 248 C10
Fieldhouse Dr
LSOL/BMARY PO13 189 M4
Fielding Gdns CWTH RG45 43 K4
Fielding Rd SHST GU47 50 A2
Field La FRIM GU16 51 G7
Fieldmore Rd GPORT PO12 191 H1
Field Pl LIPH GU30 116 B5
NMIL/BTOS BH25 218 D8
VWD BH31 201 G1
Fieldridge NWBY RG14 27 L7
Field Rd FARN GU14 50 B7
Fields Cl FAWY SO45 354 G7
Field Stores Ap ALDT GU11 3 J1
Field Vw CHFD SO53 138 F2
Field Wk LYMN SO41 221 K3
Field Wy ASHV GU12 73 L6
CHCH/BSGR BH23 217 K7
FBDG SP6 338 A2
RFNM GU10 260 D1
RWIN SO21 124 C6
WIMB BH21 206 E8
WVILLE PO7 154 F4
Fieldway FLEETN GU51 58 F8
HASM GU27 118 C5
RGWD BH24 203 K4
Fifield La RFNM GU10 79 G6
Fifth Av CHAM PO6 168 E8
HAV PO9 17 K2
Fifth Rd NWBY RG14 18 A8
Fifth St PSEA PO1 192 F1
STHA RG19 34 F7
Filmer Cl LSOL/BMARY PO13 182 D8
Filmorehill La ALTN GU34 305 P9
Filton Cl TOTT SO40 144 C8
Filton Rd LYMN SO41 221 K4
Fincham End Dr CWTH RG45 43 H4
Finchampstead Rd EWKG RG40 42 A3
Finch Cl TADY RG26 44 C5
Finchdean Rd HAV PO9 157 J6
HAV PO9 170 D4
Finches Gn ALTN GU34 106 F2
The Finches PTSW SO17 147 H6
Finchfield Av BWD BH11 212 F2
Finchleigh Pl ODIM RG29 * 68 F6
Finchmead La PSF GU32 315 M4
Finch Rd ENEY PO4 193 K5
Finch's La RWIN SO21 124 F6
Findhorn Cl SHST GU47 49 M1
The Findings FARN GU14 50 A8
Findon Rd GPORT PO12 183 H8
Fingle Dr AND SP10 4 D5
Finisterre St FHAM/STUB PO14 181 H8
Finkley Rd RAND SP11 85 H7
Fintry Pl FARN GU14 60 E1
Finzi Cl ITCH SO19 162 C1
Fiona Cl WINC SO23 25 L4
Fir Acre Rd ASHV GU12 74 A2
Fir Av NMIL/BTOS BH25 219 H6
Firbank Rd MOOR/WNTN BH9 214 B8
Fir Cl FERN BH22 205 G5
FLEETN GU51 59 H8
Fir Copse Rd WVILLE PO7 169 K5
Fir Croft Dr CHFD SO53 139 K3
Fir Dr BLKW GU17 49 M5
Firecrest Cl ROWN SO16 146 B3
Firecrest Rd KBH RG22 92 B6
Fire Station Rd ALDT GU11 3 G1
Fire Thorn Cl FLEETS GU52 71 H2
Firfield Rd FNM GU9 78 E1
Firglen Dr YTLY GU46 48 F1
Fir Gv BOR GU35 112 D3
Firgrove Cl NBAD SO52 137 M4
Firgrove Ct FNM GU9 13 G5
Firgrove Crs HSEA PO3 184 F3
Firgrove Hl FNM GU9 13 G6
Firgrove La WHAM PO17 152 F6
Firgrove Pde FARN GU14 * 61 H4
Firgrove Rd BOR GU35 112 D3
FARN GU14 61 H4
HTWY RG27 48 C2
NBAD SO52 137 M4
WSHM SO15 160 C1
Firlands Av CBLY GU15 50 F3
Firlands Ri CHAM PO6 170 A7
Firmain Rd BKME/WDN BH12 212 D7
Firmount Cl LYMN SO41 220 E7
Firmstone Rd WINC SO23 25 L5
Fir Rd TOTT SO40 158 B6
Firs Av WVILLE PO7 155 M6
Firs Cl EWKG RG40 42 B1
FARN GU14 61 J6
Firs Crs WINC SO23 288 G8
Firs Dr HEND SO30 149 G7
Firs Glen Rd FERN BH22 205 G6
MOOR/WNTN BH9 213 K8
VWD BH31 201 H3
Firshill CHCH/BSGR BH23 217 L7
Firside Rd WIMB BH21 210 C4
Firs La ODIM RG29 68 E6
PSTN BH14 224 B8
Firs Rd RSAL SP5 285 A8
RSAL SP5 327 N2
First Av CHAM PO6 168 F8
CHAM PO6 169 L8
EMRTH PO10 172 D6
HAV PO9 17 J3
HORN PO8 321 L9
THLE RG7 44 C2
WSHM SO15 159 K1
The Firs AND SP10 * 4 D5
BMTH BH1 9 H4
HUNG RG17 30 E7
LIPH GU30 116 B5
LSOL/BMARY PO13 182 D7
NTHA RG18 28 D8
ROWN SO16 146 F4
First Marine Av
NMIL/BTOS BH25 230 F1
First St FAWY SO45 177 L8
First St East STHA RG19 35 G7
Firs Wy DEAN RG23 64 D5
WHCH RG28 87 L7
Firsway WHCH RG28 87 L7
Firth Cl THLE RG7 45 H4
Fir Tree Av HASM GU27 117 K2
Fir Tree Cl ELGH SO50 141 J5
RGWD BH24 205 M6
Firtree Cl SHST GU47 43 H8
Firtree Cnr TADY RG26 249 Q2
Firtree Crs LYMN SO41 219 M5
Firtree Gdns HORN PO8 156 C3
Firtree Gv FAWY SO45 * 177 G8
Fir Tree Hl FBDG SP6 196 C6
Fir Tree La CHCH/BSGR BH23 217 K7
ELGH SO50 141 H5
NWBY RG14 28 A8
Fir Tree Rd HISD PO11 195 G5
TOTT SO40 341 L5
Firtree Wy FLEETN GU51 59 K8
ITCH SO19 148 B7
Fir Vale Rd BMTH BH1 8 F5
Firway GSHT GU26 114 E3
Firwood Cl CHFD SO53 133 J8
Firwood Dr CBLY GU15 50 E3
Fisgard Rd GPORT PO12 191 H1
Fisher Cl AND SP10 96 F4
FHAM/STUB PO14 189 H1
Fisherman's Av SBNE BH6 227 H4
Fisherman's La THLE RG7 38 A5
Fishermans Quay
LYMN SO41 * 221 M4
Fishermans Rd PLE BH15 223 J7
The Fishermans EMRTH PO10 172 A6
Fishermans Wk HISD PO11 195 L6
Fishermen's Cl ALDT GU11 73 L3
Fisher Rd LSOL/BMARY PO13 182 C5
Fishers Gv CHAM PO6 185 L1
Fishers Hl FHAM PO15 181 G2
Fisher's La NTHA RG18 28 C3
Fisher's Rd TOTT SO40 159 G2
Fishery La HISD PO11 195 J6
Fishlake Mdw ROMY SO51 130 F7
Fiske Cl BSTK RG21 64 E8
Fitzgerald Cl HLER SO31 164 C4
Fitzharris Av
MOOR/WNTN BH9 226 A1
Fitzherbert Rd CHAM PO6 185 K1
Fitzherbert Sp CHAM PO6 185 L1
Fitzherbert St PSEA PO1 192 C2
Fitzhugh Pl WSHM SO15 160 F1
Fitzhugh St SHAM SO14 22 E2
Fitzmaurice Rd
CHCH/BSGR BH23 215 L8
Fitzpain Cl FERN BH22 209 K6
Fitzpain Rd FERN BH22 209 K6
Fitzpatrick Ct CHAM PO6 * 168 D7
Fitzroy Cl ROWN SO16 146 F1
Fitzroy Dr LSOL/BMARY PO13 189 M5
LSOL/BMARY PO13 190 A1
Fitzroy Rd FLEETN GU51 58 F7
Fitzwilliam Av
FHAM/STUB PO14 189 G2
Fitzwilliam Cl BWD BH11 212 E3
Fitzworth Av UPTN BH16 222 C4
Fitzwygram Crs HAV PO9 16 E1
Five Acres RCCH PO18 173 L1
Five Acres Cl BOR GU35 111 H7
Five Ash Rd ALTN GU34 293 L4
Five Bells La STOK SO20 284 A3
Five Bridges Rd WINC SO23 124 E1
Five Elms Dr ROMY SO51 137 H2
Fivefields Cl WINC SO23 25 L7
Fivefields Rd WINC SO23 25 M7
Five Heads Rd HORN PO8 321 J12
Five Post La GPORT PO12 191 H2
Flaghead Chine Rd CCLF BH13 237 K2
Flaghead Rd CCLF BH13 237 K1
Flag Staff Gn GPORT PO12 15 J1
Flagstaff Sq STHA RG19 35 L2
Flag Wk HORN PO8 155 M3
Flambard Av
CHCH/BSGR BH23 215 M7
Flambard Rd PSTN BH14 224 C6
Flamborough Cl ROWN SO16 145 K6
Flamingo Ct
FHAM/PORC PO16 166 F8
Flamstone St RSAL SP5 324 C4
Flanders Rd HEND SO30 149 H4
The Flashett RSAL SP5 282 H10
Flathouse Rd PSEA PO1 192 C1
The Flats BLKW GU17 49 K4
Flatt Rd RCCH PO18 173 H6
Flaxfield Ct BSTK RG21 6 D5
Flaxfield Rd BSTK RG21 6 D5
Flaxfields End FBDG SP6 197 G3
Flazen Cl BWD BH11 212 D5
Flecker Cl NTHA RG18 28 E7
Fleet Cl LSOL/BMARY PO13 182 D7
Fleet End Bottom HLER SO31 179 M4
Fleetend Cl HAV PO9 170 E2
Fleet End Rd HLER SO31 179 M4
Fleet Hl EWKG RG40 241 Q2
Fleet La EWKG RG40 241 P2
Fleet Rd FARN GU14 60 C4
FLEETN GU51 59 H7
FLEETS GU52 72 A1
HTWY RG27 57 M2
Fleet's Cnr CFDH BH17 223 H1
Fleets La PLE BH15 223 J2
Fleet Ter ELGH SO50 * 134 B3
Fleetwood Cl NWBY RG14 27 M7
Fleming Av NBAD SO52 138 A4
Fleming Cl FARN GU14 61 K2
RAND SP11 265 M10
WHIT RG2 239 L9
Fleming Ct NBAD SO52 * 138 B4
Fleming Pl ROMY SO51 130 F8
RWIN SO21 134 F3
Fleming Rd FUFL SO22 122 C1
NWBY RG14 19 G3
ROWN SO16 147 K4
Flensburg Cl AND SP10 96 B1
Fletcher Cl BSTK RG21 6 B7
FAWY SO45 176 D5
NBNE BH10 * 213 K5
Fletcher Rd NBNE BH10 213 K5
Fletchers Fld LIPH GU30 116 B5
Fletchwood La TOTT SO40 158 B2
Fletchwood Rd TOTT SO40 341 R10
Fleur-de-Lys Pk LYMN SO41 * 351 R11
Fleuret Cl FAWY SO45 177 G8
Flexford Cl CHFD SO53 133 G7
KSCL RG20 246 B7
Flexford La LYMN SO41 220 C2
Flexford Rd NBAD SO52 138 F1
RGUW GU3 75 H8
Flinders Cl AND SP10 97 H3
Flinders Ct ENEY PO4 193 H6
Flint Cl AND SP10 4 B9
ITCH SO19 148 E8
Flint La RAND SP11 82 F4
Flint St SSEA PO5 20 F6
Floating Bridge Rd SHAM SO14 23 L6
The Flood RSAL SP5 282 F9
Floral Farm WIMB BH21 207 M6
Floral Wy NTHA RG18 28 F7
RAND SP11 4 A9
Floreat Gdns NWBY RG14 18 A7
Florence Cl ROMY SO51 335 M6
YTLY GU46 48 E2
Florence Ct AND SP10 96 D1
Florence Portal Cl WHCH RG28 88 D7
Florence Rd BOSC BH5 226 E4
FLEETS GU52 71 K2
ITCH SO19 161 L6
PSTN BH14 224 C4
SHST GU47 50 A1
SSEA PO5 192 D7
Florence Wy CHIN RG24 64 E4
Florentine Wy WVILLE PO7 156 A8
The Florins HLER SO31 180 A3
WVILLE PO7 169 L5
Floriston Gdns
NMIL/BTOS BH25 219 K5
Florrie Pl ALTN GU34 * 294 D5
Floud La PSF GU32 313 K3
Flowerdown Cl TOTT SO40 144 C8
Flower La ROMY SO51 334 H2
Flowers Cl HLER SO31 178 E1
Flume Rd FAWY SO45 178 C8
Flushards LYMN SO41 221 M5
Focus Wy AND SP10 96 F3
Foden Rd ALDT GU11 2 F4
Fokerham Rd STHA RG19 35 M2
Foldsgate Cl LYND SO43 345 K2
Folkestone Rd HSEA PO3 193 G1
Folly Cl FLEETS GU52 71 J1
Folly Farm La RGWD BH24 202 E6
Folly Fld BPWT SO32 143 K5
Folly Hl FNM GU9 76 E3
Folly La EPSF GU31 120 D6
RSAL SP5 327 L1
TADY RG26 46 D4
Folly La North FNM GU9 76 F1
Folly La South FNM GU9 76 E2
Folly Rd HUNG RG17 30 C6
Folly Rbt AND SP10 5 G3
The Folly NWBY RG14 19 G8
Font Cl FHAM/STUB PO14 180 C1
Fontley Rd FHAM PO15 181 G1
Fontmell Rd BDST BH18 211 J6
Fontwell Cl ASHV GU12 3 L2
TOTT SO40 144 C7
Fontwell Dr ALTN GU34 106 F6
Fontwell Gdns ELGH SO50 141 K5
Fontwell Ms HORN PO8 156 B7
Fontwell Rd NWBY RG14 19 H8
SSEA PO5 21 J8
Foord Rd HEND SO30 149 H8
Football Gn LYND SO43 340 G9
Footner Cl ROMY SO51 131 J6
Footners La CHCH/BSGR BH23 216 C6
Forbes Cha SHST GU47 49 M1
Forbes Cl ROWN SO16 145 M2
Forbes Rd WINC SO23 288 H8
Forbury La HUNG RG17 31 H5
Forbury Rd SSEA PO5 21 J4
Ford Av CHFD SO53 139 K4
Ford Cl FERN BH22 209 M1
Fordingbridge Rd ENEY PO4 193 H5
FBDG SP6 196 D5
Fordington Av FUFL SO22 24 B4
Fordington Rd FUFL SO22 24 C4
Ford La FERN BH22 346 A5
ODIM RG29 68 B8
RFNM GU10 78 F2
THLE RG7 238 G12
Ford Rd GPORT PO12 190 F2
Fore Br EPSF GU31 120 D7
The Forehead THLE RG7 40 F4
Foreland Cl CHCH/BSGR BH23 215 K4
Foreland Ct HISD PO11 195 J6
Foreland Rd UPTN BH16 222 B4
Foreman Pk ASHV GU12 74 B6
Foreman Rd ASHV GU12 74 B7
Foreshore North FAWY SO45 178 B6
Foreshore South FAWY SO45 178 B6
Forest Av HORN PO8 155 M5
Forest Cl BPWT SO32 151 L1
CHCH/BSGR BH23 217 K7
CHFD SO53 133 J8
HORN PO8 155 M5
NBAD SO52 137 L3
TADY RG26 249 Q2
VWD BH31 201 M4
Forest Cnr LISS GU33 308 C5
Forest Court Hills RGWD BH24 203 M6
Forestdale GSHT GU26 115 K5
Forest Dean FLEETN GU51 59 L4
WHIT RG2 238 C1
Forest Dr CHIN RG24 54 B4
NTID SP9 266 G2
RFNM GU10 79 G4
Forest Edge FAWY SO45 355 J5
Forest Edge Cl RGWD BH24 205 M3
Forest Edge Rd RGWD BH24 342 A11
Forest End FLEETS GU52 71 H2
WVILLE PO7 169 K1
Forest End Rd SHST GU47 43 H7
Forester Rd BPWT SO32 318 G11
Foresters Ga FAWY SO45 354 G9
Foresters Rd FAWY SO45 354 H6
Forest Front FAWY SO45 176 F8
Forest Gdns BPWT SO32 151 L1
LYND SO43 345 K3
Forest Ga FAWY SO45 354 H9
Forest Gate Gdns LYMN SO41 221 K7
Forest Gld RFNM GU10 109 K1
Forest Glade Cl BROC SO42 350 H3
Forest Hall BROC SO42 351 L3
Forest Hills CBLY GU15 50 D4
Forest Hills Dr WEND SO18 147 L5
Forest Hill Wy FAWY SO45 176 F6
Forestlake Av RGWD BH24 203 M6
Forest La BOR GU35 111 J6
FAWY SO45 354 D2
RAND SP11 80 B4
RAND SP11 97 H6
RGWD BH24 342 B10
TADY RG26 44 D6
VWD BH31 201 G1
WHAM PO17 152 C7
Forest Lane Cl LIPH GU30 116 A4
Forest Links Rd WIMB BH21 204 D7
Forest Md WVILLE PO7 154 F5
Forest Meadow FAWY SO45 177 G8
Forest Oak Dr
NMIL/BTOS BH25 219 G3
Forest Park Rd BROC SO42 351 J2
Forest Pines NMIL/BTOS BH25 219 G3
Forest Ri CHCH/BSGR BH23 217 K6
LISS GU33 308 G6
Forest Rd BOR GU35 112 F3
BPWT SO32 151 M1
CCLF BH13 225 G6
CHCH/BSGR BH23 348 G8
CHFD SO53 133 K8
CWTH RG45 43 L3
FBDG SP6 332 G5
FERN BH22 205 H5
LISS GU33 308 E3
RGWD BH24 342 H11
RSAL SP5 334 B8
WVILLE PO7 154 A4
Forestside Av HAV PO9 171 G3
Forestside Gdns RGWD BH24 203 L3
The Forestside VWD BH31 201 M3
Forest Vw BROC SO42 350 H3
NMIL/BTOS BH25 218 D3
SHAM SO14 22 F5
Forest View Cl
MOOR/WNTN BH9 214 A6
Forest View Dr WIMB BH21 209 G2
Forest View Rd
MOOR/WNTN BH9 214 A5
Forest Wy CHCH/BSGR BH23 217 L7
LSOL/BMARY PO13 182 D6
LYMN SO41 220 D7
TOTT SO40 144 A6
WIMB BH21 209 G3
Forfield Dr DEAN RG23 92 C7
Forge Cl FNM GU9 13 K1
HLER SO31 163 G3
HUNG RG17 31 G2
TADY RG26 46 C6
Forge Fld AND SP10 5 J3
Forge La ALDT GU11 72 F2
Forge Rd BOR GU35 110 D3
FAWY SO45 354 H9
Forneth Gdns FHAM PO15 181 H4
Forster Rd SHAM SO14 161 G1
The Forsters THLE RG7 * 37 M5
Forsyth Gdns NBNE BH10 213 J7
Forsythia Cl HAV PO9 171 H4
HEND SO30 149 H4
Forsythia Pl ITCH SO19 161 M3
Fort Cumberland Cl PLE BH15 222 D6
Fort Cumberland Rd
ENEY PO4 193 K5
Fortescue Rd
BKME/WDN BH12 224 D1
TWDS BH3 226 A2
Fort Fareham Rd
FHAM/STUB PO14 181 M6
Forth Cl CHFD SO53 139 H3
FARN GU14 60 D2
FHAM/STUB PO14 189 H1
Forth Ct AND SP10 5 L1
Fort Hill Dr DEAN RG23 64 E6
Forties Cl FHAM/STUB PO14 * 181 H8
Forton Rd GPORT PO12 14 C1
PSEA PO1 192 E2
Fort Rd GPORT PO12 191 G7
ITCH SO19 161 L5
Fortrose Cl SHST GU47 49 M1
Fortunes Wy CHAM PO6 169 M7
Forty Acre La EPSF GU31 322 F1
Forum Cl DEAN RG23 64 D7

The Forum FHAM PO15 * 164 E6
Forward Dr LYMN SO41 221 J6
Fosseway CWTH RG45 43 H3
Foster Cl FHAM/STUB PO14 181 J8
Foster Rd GPORT PO12 14 E6
PSEA PO1 192 D2
Foul La ALTN GU34 293 K1
Founders Wy
LSOL/BMARY PO13 182 D6
Foundry Crs HLER SO31 163 G4
Foundry La HASM GU27 118 A6
WSHM SO15 160 C2
Foundry Rd RAND SP11 95 L8
RSAL SP5 332 F1
Fountains Cl CHIN RG24 65 J3
Fountain St PSEA PO1 21 G2
Four Acre HEND SO30 150 A6
Four Acre Coppice HTWY RG27 56 E7
Four Lanes Cl CHIN RG24 54 C5
Four Oaks KSCL RG20 246 B6
Four Posts Hl WSHM SO15 22 C1
Fourshells Cl FAWY SO45 354 H6
Fourth Av CHAM PO6 168 E8
HAV PO9 17 J3
Fourth St PSEA PO1 192 F2
STHA RG19 34 F7
Fourways RAND SP11 * 271 R1
Four Wells Rd WIMB BH21 208 A1
Fowey Cl CHFD SO53 139 H1
Fowey Ct GPORT PO12 * 183 J8
The Fowey FAWY SO45 354 G6
Fowler Av FARN GU14 61 H6
Fowler Rd FARN GU14 60 F6
Fowler's Rd ALDT GU11 73 J3
HEND SO30 149 H4
Fowler's Wk NBAD SO52 138 D6
Foxborough THLE RG7 238 D10
Foxbury Cl FAWY SO45 177 G6
Foxbury Gv FHAM/PORC PO16 183 H1
Foxbury La EMRTH PO10 172 C2
LSOL/BMARY PO13 182 D4
Foxbury Rd RGWD BH24 346 E6
Fox Cl ELGH SO50 140 F2
Foxcombe Cl BPWT SO32 318 A6
Foxcote EWKG RG40 42 C1
Foxcote Gdns
NMIL/BTOS BH25 * 218 F5
Foxcott Cl ITCH SO19 161 M8
Foxcotte Cl AND SP10 95 M2
Foxcotte La RAND SP11 95 K2
Foxcotte Rd AND SP10 95 M1
Foxcott Gv HAV PO9 170 F3
Fox Cft FLEETS GU52 71 J3
Foxcroft Dr FAWY SO45 354 D5
WIMB BH21 208 B3
Foxdown OVTN RG25 89 J2
Foxdown Cl CBLY GU15 50 E3
Fox Dr YTLY GU46 48 F1
Foxes Cl VWD BH31 201 H3
WVILLE PO7 169 L2
Foxes La ROMY SO51 335 K2
Fox Farm RAND SP11 270 A1
Fox Fld LYMN SO41 220 D7
Foxglade FAWY SO45 354 H9
Foxglove Cl CHCH/BSGR BH23 217 J8
KBH RG22 92 C5
WWKG RG41 239 R1
Foxglove Dr BOR GU35 113 G2
Foxglove Pl NMIL/BTOS BH25 219 K4
Foxgloves FHAM/PORC PO16 11 J1
UPTN BH16 222 B1
The Foxgloves HEND SO30 149 K7
Foxglove Wy NTHA RG18 28 F7
Foxhayes La FAWY SO45 354 H9
Fox Heath FARN GU14 60 C5
Foxhills TOTT SO40 158 C4
VWD BH31 201 K2
Foxhills Cl TOTT SO40 158 C5
Fox Hills La ASHV GU12 74 C5
Foxholes Rd PLE BH15 223 M2
SBNE BH6 227 M4
Foxhunter Wy STHA RG19 34 F1
Foxhurst Rd ASHV GU12 74 A3
Foxlands FAWY SO45 354 H9
Fox La DEAN RG23 91 L1
FUFL SO22 122 C7
HTWY RG27 42 B8
WIMB BH21 208 C3
Foxlea Gdns GPORT PO12 191 H1
Foxley Cl BLKW GU17 49 L3
Foxley Dr HSEA PO3 185 H4
Foxmoor Cl DEAN RG23 91 K1
Fox Pond La LYMN SO41 221 J6
Fox Rd HASM GU27 117 L2
RFNM GU10 79 G2
Fox's Furlong CHIN RG24 54 D4
Fox's La KSCL RG20 248 C11
Fox's Wk FAWY SO45 354 H9
Foxtail Dr FAWY SO45 176 F7
Foxtail Gdns RAND SP11 265 M10
Fox Wy RFNM GU10 71 K8
Foxwood FLEETN GU51 59 L5
Foxwood Av
CHCH/BSGR BH23 228 F3
Fox Yd FNM GU9 12 E3
Foxy Paddock FAWY SO45 354 H9
Foye La FLEETS GU52 71 K3
Foy Gdns HLER SO31 179 J3
Foyle Pk BSTK RG21 93 K2
Foyle Rd CHFD SO53 139 H2
Frampton Cl NMIL/BTOS BH25 219 J3
RWIN SO21 134 F3
Frampton Pl RGWD BH24 203 J5
Frampton Rd
MOOR/WNTN BH9 214 A8
Frampton Wy TOTT SO40 158 F2
WINC SO23 289 J9
France Hill Dr CBLY GU15 50 E3
Frances Rd BMTH BH1 9 L4
BSTK RG21 6 D7
WVILLE PO7 169 K5
The Frances NTHA RG18 28 F8
Francis Av BWD BH11 212 D5
ENEY PO4 192 F5
Francis Cl LSOL/BMARY PO13 190 A3
Francis Gdns WINC SO23 123 H2
Francis Pl FHAM/STUB PO14 189 K2
Francis Rd BKME/WDN BH12 224 E3
HORN PO8 321 L9
Frankland Crs PSTN BH14 224 E5
Frankland Ter EMRTH PO10 172 A6
Franklin Av HTWY RG27 57 L1
TADY RG26 44 A3
Franklin Rd
LSOL/BMARY PO13 190 C1
MOOR/WNTN BH9 214 A5
NMIL/BTOS BH25 219 J4
RWIN SO21 125 G5
Franklyn Av ITCH SO19 148 A8
Franklyn Cl UPTN BH16 222 B1
Frankston Rd SBNE BH6 227 J4
Franks Wy PLE BH15 224 B1
Frankton Wy GPORT PO12 15 K3
Fraryden EMRTH PO10 172 D6
Fraser Cl CHIN RG24 66 D2
ROWN SO16 145 M2
Fraser Gdns EMRTH PO10 172 E4
Fraser Md SHST GU47 50 A2
Fraser Rd BKME/WDN BH12 212 F7
HAV PO9 16 B2
LSOL/BMARY PO13 182 C4
NEND PO2 184 B6
SSEA PO5 21 J4
WINC SO23 288 H8
Frater La GPORT PO12 183 G7
Fratton Rd PSEA PO1 21 L1
Fratton Wy ELGH SO50 141 J3
ENEY PO4 192 F3
Frayslea FAWY SO45 177 G7
Freda Rd CHCH/BSGR BH23 227 M2
Freda Routh Gdns ELGH SO50 141 K2
Frederica Rd
MOOR/WNTN BH9 213 L8
Frederick St ALDT GU11 2 E3
SHAM SO14 161 H2
Freedom Ct FAWY SO45 177 G4
Freegrounds Av HEND SO30 149 J6
Freegrounds Cl HEND SO30 149 J6
Freegrounds Rd HEND SO30 149 J6
Freelands Dr FLEETS GU52 71 G3
Freemans Cl WIMB BH21 208 B2
Freemans La WIMB BH21 208 B3
Freemantle Cl BSTK RG21 65 M5
ITCH SO19 161 M3
Freemantle Common Rd
ITCH SO19 161 M3
Freemantle Rd GPORT PO12 191 H1
Freesia Cl WWKG RG41 239 R1
Freestone Rd SSEA PO5 21 J9
Free St BPWT SO32 143 K4
Fremantle Rd RAND SP11 267 K1
Frenches La ROMY SO51 129 H7
French Gdns BLKW GU17 49 M4
Frenchies Vw WVILLE PO7 154 E4
Frenchmans Creek
FLEETS GU52 71 G4
Frenchmans Rd PSF GU32 120 C5
Frenchmoor La RSAL SP5 297 M9
French Rd CFDH BH17 211 H7
LISS GU33 309 K1
French's Farm Rd UPTN BH16 222 A1
French St PSEA PO1 * 20 C6
SHAM SO14 2 F6
Frendstaple Rd WVILLE PO7 170 A3
Frensham Av FLEETN GU51 59 L7
Frensham Cl HEND SO30 149 J6
NBNE BH10 213 L5
YTLY GU46 48 D2
Frensham Ct RFNM GU10 78 F4
Frensham Heights Rd
RFNM GU10 78 E6
Frensham La BOR GU35 111 J6
Frensham Rd CWTH RG45 43 K1
ENEY PO4 192 F4
FNM GU9 13 H9
Frensham V RFNM GU10 79 G4
Frere Av FLEETN GU51 71 G1
Frescade Crs BSTK RG21 6 C8
Freshfield Gdns WVILLE PO7 155 L8
Freshfield Rd WSHM SO15 160 B1
Freshfield Sq WSHM SO15 160 B1
Freshwater Dr PLE BH15 222 D4
Freshwater Rd CHAM PO6 184 E1
CHCH/BSGR BH23 229 J2
Freshwood Dr YTLY GU46 48 E4
Friarscroft HLER SO31 162 B5
Friars Cft TOTT SO40 144 B6
Friars Fld FNM GU9 12 E2
Friarsgate WINC SO23 25 H5
Friars Pond Rd FHAM PO15 181 J3
Friars Rd CHCH/BSGR BH23 229 H2
ELGH SO50 139 M7
NWBY RG14 18 E9
Friars Wk NMIL/BTOS BH25 219 G8
Friars Wy WEND SO18 147 K4
Friary Cl SSEA PO5 21 H8
Friday's Heron WIMB BH21 336 F5
Friend Av ASHV GU12 3 M5
Friesian Cl FLEETN GU51 59 K4
Frimley Green Rd FRIM GU16 61 L1
Frimley Grove Gdns FRIM GU16 50 F7
Frimley Hall Dr CBLY GU15 51 H2
Frimley High St FRIM GU16 50 F8
Frimley Rd ASHV GU12 62 A8
CBLY GU15 50 D4
Fritham Cl TOTT SO40 158 C1
Fritham Gdns CHAR BH8 214 D5
Fritham Rd WEND SO18 148 C4
Frith End Rd ALTN GU34 108 F4
Frith Hill Rd FRIM GU16 51 J7
Frith La WHAM PO17 152 A2
Frithmead Cl BSTK RG21 93 J2
Frobisher Av
BKME/WDN BH12 212 F7
Frobisher Cl
CHCH/BSGR BH23 228 F2
LSOL/BMARY PO13 190 C2
RGWD BH24 203 L4
Frobisher Gdns EMRTH PO10 171 M8
ITCH SO19 148 C8
Frobisher Gv
FHAM/PORC PO16 183 J1
Froddington Rd SSEA PO5 21 K4
Frog Grove La RGUW GU3 75 M4
Froghall FAWY SO45 176 F7
Frogham Hl FBDG SP6 197 L5
Frog La FBDG SP6 197 G5
HTWY RG27 55 M1
OVTN RG25 67 H3
TADY RG26 45 H7
Frogmore FHAM/STUB PO14 181 J4
Frogmore Gv BLKW GU17 49 J4
Frogmore La HORN PO8 156 A2
ROWN SO16 145 K5
Frogmore Park Dr BLKW GU17 49 M4
Frogmore Rd BLKW GU17 49 L4
ENEY PO4 192 F4
Frogs Hole KSCL RG20 248 C10
Frome Cl BSTK RG21 7 J4
DEAN RG23 91 L3
FARN GU14 60 D2
TOTT SO40 160 A6
Frome Rd WEND SO18 148 A1
Fromond Cl LYMN SO41 221 L3
Fromond Rd FUFL SO22 122 C1
Fromont Dr STHA RG19 35 K1
Frosthole Cl FHAM PO15 10 B1
Frosthole Crs FHAM PO15 10 A2
Frost La FAWY SO45 177 J6
Frost Rd BWD BH11 212 F5
Froud Cl HTWY RG27 56 B8
Frouds La THLE RG7 37 M2
Froud Wy WIMB BH21 210 C4
Froxfield Cl FUFL SO22 288 D12
Froxfield Gdns
FHAM/PORC PO16 167 J7
Froxfield Rd HAV PO9 171 H3
Froyle Ct HAV PO9 171 H3
Froyle La ODIM RG29 257 Q5
Fry Cl FAWY SO45 354 H6
HLER SO31 163 G8
Fryer Cl BWD BH11 213 H3
Fryern Ar CHFD SO53 * 139 L1
Fryern Cl CHFD SO53 139 L2
Fryern Court Rd FBDG SP6 331 L12
Fryers Cl WINC SO23 289 J8
Fryer's Copse WIMB BH21 208 C2
Fryers Rd WIMB BH21 201 G8
Fry's La BPWT SO32 312 F12
LYMN SO41 220 D7
YTLY GU46 49 G1
Fry Sq AND SP10 * 96 D2
Fugelmere Rd FLEETN GU51 59 L6
Fulbrook La MFD/CHID GU8 260 H10
Fulbrook Wy ODIM RG29 68 F8
Fulflood Rd HAV PO9 170 E3
Fuller Cl STHA RG19 35 M2
Fullers La KSCL RG20 245 P5
Fullers Rd RFNM GU10 78 B4
Fullers V BOR GU35 111 M7
Fullerton Cl HAV PO9 171 H3
ITCH SO19 161 M8
Fullerton Rd LYMN SO41 221 J4
RAND SP11 271 J2
RAND SP11 271 R8
Fullerton Wy TADY RG26 44 C5
Fulmar Cl KBH RG22 92 B5
ROWN SO16 146 B3
Fulmar Dr FAWY SO45 177 H6
Fulmar Rd CHCH/BSGR BH23 229 G3
Fulmer Wk HORN PO8 155 L4
Fulwood Av BWD BH11 212 E3
Funtington Rd NEND PO2 184 F8
Funtley Hl FHAM/PORC PO16 165 L8
Funtley Rd FHAM PO15 165 K7
Furdies WVILLE PO7 154 E4
Furley Cl WINC SO23 25 K5
The Furlong RGWD BH24 203 H5
Furneaux Gdns
FHAM/PORC PO16 11 G1
Furnell Rd PLE BH15 223 K7
Furness Rd SSEA PO5 192 D7
Furniss Wy HISD PO11 194 D4
Furnston Gv EMRTH PO10 172 E5
Furse Cl CBLY GU15 51 K4
Furse Hill Rd NTID SP9 266 F3
Further Vell-Mead FLEETS GU52 71 G4
Fury Wy FHAM/STUB PO14 189 H1
Furzebrook Cl CFDH BH17 211 L6
Furze Cl ASHV GU12 74 A1
ITCH SO19 148 A7
Furze Cft NMIL/BTOS BH25 219 G7
Furzedale Gdns FAWY SO45 177 H7
Furzedale Pk FAWY SO45 177 H7
Furzedown Crs HAV PO9 171 G3
Furzedown La RAND SP11 94 A7
Furzedown Ms FAWY SO45 177 H7
Furzedown Rd PTSW SO17 147 G6
STOK SO20 299 R4
Furze Dr RAND SP11 267 K2
Furzehall Av FHAM/PORC PO16 11 J1
Furze Hill Crs CWTH RG45 43 L4
Furze Hill Dr PSTN BH14 224 C7
Furze Hill Rd BOR GU35 114 C4
Furzelands Rd WIMB BH21 201 G8
Furze La ENEY PO4 193 K3
Furzeley Rd WVILLE PO7 154 F6
Furze Meadow EPSF GU31 317 L8
Furzen La OVTN RG25 105 K5
Furze Rd ITCH SO19 148 A7
TADY RG26 249 R2
Furze Vale Rd BOR GU35 114 B4
Furze Wy HORN PO8 156 B4
Furzey Cl FAWY SO45 354 H7
Furzey La BROC SO42 352 H7
Furzey Rd UPTN BH16 222 B2
Furzley Ct HAV PO9 170 C2
Furzley La ROMY SO51 334 H11
Furzley Rd ROMY SO51 334 H11
Fushia Cl HAV PO9 171 J4
Fushsia Gdns ROWN SO16 146 D6
Fuzzy Dro KBH RG22 92 B4
Fyeford Cl ROWN SO16 145 M2
Fyfield Cl BLKW GU17 49 M3
FHAM PO15 164 C4
Fyfield La RAND SP11 94 C2
Fyfield Rd RAND SP11 94 D2
STHA RG19 35 K2
Fyfield Wy FUFL SO22 288 B11
RAND SP11 267 K2
Fylingdales STHA RG19 35 J2
Fylingdales Cl KBH RG22 92 C1
Fyning St PSEA PO1 21 J1

G

Gable End FARN GU14 * 61 H4
Gables Cl ASHV GU12 74 A3
FARN GU14 61 G4
Gables Ct ROWN SO16 146 F3
Gables Rd FLEETS GU52 71 H4
Gables Wy STHA RG19 36 B2
Gabriel Dr CBLY GU15 51 K4
The Gabriels NWBY RG14 33 K6
Gaffney Cl ALDT GU11 73 K1
Gage Cl CHIN RG24 66 B1
TOTT SO40 160 A6
Gaiger Av HTWY RG27 54 D3
Gainsborough Av HUNG RG17 31 H2
NMIL/BTOS BH25 219 H3
Gainsborough Cl CBLY GU15 51 H1
FARN GU14 61 K6
Gainsborough Ct AND SP10 4 F2
Gainsborough Ms
FHAM/STUB PO14 180 F4
Gainsborough Rd BSTK RG21 93 L2
LTDN BH7 226 F1
RGWD BH24 202 A7
Gainsford Rd ITCH SO19 161 L3
Gain's Rd ENEY PO4 193 L8
Galahad Cl AND SP10 96 C2
Galaxie Rd HORN PO8 156 B4
Gale Barracks ALDT GU11 * 73 H4
Gale Moor Av GPORT PO12 190 D5
Galileo Pk AND SP10 * 95 L3
Gallaghers Md AND SP10 95 K4
Galleon Cl HLER SO31 179 M3
Galleon Pl GPORT PO12 15 J1
The Galleries ALDT GU11 * 2 F2
Galley La STHA RG19 248 B3
The Gallops FHAM/STUB PO14 180 D2
The Gallop YTLY GU46 48 F1
Gallop Wy BKME/WDN BH12 225 J1
Galloway Cl FLEETN GU51 59 L4
KBH RG22 92 D1
Galloway Rd PLE BH15 222 D4
Gallows Dr FERN BH22 209 K7
Gallwey Rd ALDT GU11 73 J5
Gally Hill Rd FLEETS GU52 71 H4
Galsworthy Rd TOTT SO40 158 D1
Galton Av CHCH/BSGR BH23 227 M2
Galt Av CHAM PO6 169 K8
Galway Rd YTLY GU46 * 48 E4
Gamble Cl ITCH SO19 161 M4
Gambledown La ROMY SO51 128 E3
Gamblins La BPWT SO32 151 M4
Gander Dr CHIN RG24 64 E4
Gangbridge La RAND SP11 85 M1
Ganger Rd ROMY SO51 131 J6
Gannet Cl FAWY SO45 177 H6
KBH RG22 92 B5
ROWN SO16 146 B3
The Gannets
FHAM/STUB PO14 189 H2
Gapemouth Rd FRIM GU16 62 E3
Garbett Rd WINC SO23 25 L5
Garbetts Wy RFNM GU10 260 C2
Garbitts La EPSF GU31 317 M5
Garden City FAWY SO45 176 A2
Garden Cl AND SP10 5 K6
FARN GU14 60 E6
HISD PO11 194 F5
HTWY RG27 56 B7
KSCL RG20 248 D10
LYND SO43 345 J3
NMIL/BTOS BH25 219 G7
OVTN RG25 277 R3
Garden Close La NWBY RG14 33 K8
Gardeners Gn NTID SP9 266 D9
Gardener's Hill Rd RFNM GU10 78 F4
Gardeners La ROMY SO51 335 R2
Gardenia Dr FHAM PO15 180 E1
Garden La RGWD BH24 346 E1
SSEA PO5 21 G7
WINC SO23 25 H5
Garden Ms HLER SO31 179 J3
Garden Rd RGWD BH24 348 H2
Gardens Crs PSTN BH14 224 B8
Gardens Rd PSTN BH14 224 B8
The Gardens CHOB/PIR GU24 63 M3
FHAM/PORC PO16 11 J2
HAV PO9 17 K6
RCCH PO18 173 M3
RFNM GU10 260 D1
WVILLE PO7 319 R9
Gardens Vw BMTH BH1 9 L3
Garden Ter SSEA PO5 21 K9
Garden Wk FERN BH22 209 L1
Gardiner Cl TOTT SO40 160 A6
Gardner Rd CHCH/BSGR BH23 215 L8
FHAM/STUB PO14 180 F5
RGWD BH24 203 K6
Garendon Ct FBDG SP6 197 G2
Garfield Av BMTH BH1 226 D3
Garfield Cl BPWT SO32 143 J4
Garfield Rd BPWT SO32 143 J4
CBLY GU15 50 E3
HLER SO31 162 A6
ITCH SO19 161 L1
NEND PO2 184 D8
Garford Crs NWBY RG14 33 K4
Garland Av EMRTH PO10 171 M5
Garland Rd PLE BH15 223 K4
Garland Wy TOTT SO40 144 B8
Garnet Fld YTLY GU46 48 C3
Garnet Rd BOR GU35 113 G2
Garnett Cl FHAM/STUB PO14 181 J8
Garnier Pk WHAM PO17 152 A4
Garnier Rd WINC SO23 123 G7
Garnier St PSEA PO1 21 K2
Garnock Rd ITCH SO19 161 K6
Garratt Cl HEND SO30 149 J2
Garrett Cl ITCH SO19 162 A3
KSCL RG20 248 C9
Garrick Gdns ITCH SO19 162 A2
Garrick Wy FRIM GU16 61 L2
Garrison Hl BPWT SO32 318 H2
Garrow Dr LYMN SO41 221 L3
Garsdale Cl BWD BH11 213 G2
Garsons Rd EMRTH PO10 172 D6
Garston Cl PSF GU32 314 B8
Garston Mede STOK SO20 272 E8
Garstons Cl FHAM/STUB PO14 180 F4
Garstons Rd FHAM/STUB PO14 180 F4
Gar St WINC SO23 24 F6
Garth Cl FNM GU9 12 D9
RGWD BH24 205 M4
Garth Rd MOOR/WNTN BH9 214 A7
THLE RG7 40 A3
The Garth ALTN GU34 107 G4
ASHV GU12 73 M7
FARN GU14 61 K4
FAWY SO45 176 E6
Garton Rd ITCH SO19 161 K5
Gascoigne La NARL SO24 292 F11
Gashouse Hl HLER SO31 162 C7
Gaskell Cl ALTN GU34 107 J2
Gaskell Ms NWBY RG14 19 G9
Gason Hill Rd NTID SP9 264 E12
Gaston La ALTN GU34 294 E5
ODIM RG29 257 P2
Gatcombe HLER SO31 162 C5
Gatcombe Av HSEA PO3 184 F6
Gatcombe Dr NEND PO2 184 F5
Gatcombe Gdns
FHAM/STUB PO14 181 H4
WEND SO18 148 A2
Gatehouse La EPSF GU31 317 R2
Gate House Rd
FHAM/PORC PO16 183 G1
Gatekeeper Cl WINC SO23 25 M5
Gaters Hl WEND SO18 * 148 A1
The Gates FLEETN GU51 59 L4
Gatwick Cl ROWN SO16 146 A4
Gaulter Cl HAV PO9 17 G1
Gauvain Cl ALTN GU34 107 G6
Gavan St ITCH SO19 148 D7
G Av FAWY SO45 354 H4
Gawaine Cl AND SP10 84 C8
Gaydon Ri BWD BH11 212 E4
Gaylyn Wy FHAM/STUB PO14 181 H4
Gaywood Dr NWBY RG14 19 L1
Gaza Av BROC SO42 353 J10
Gazing La ROMY SO51 335 J5
Geale's Crs ALTN GU34 107 G3
Geddes Wy EPSF GU31 121 G5
Gemini Cl ROWN SO16 145 M4
Geneva Av SBNE BH6 227 K3
Genoa Cl LYMN SO41 221 J7
Genoa Ct AND SP10 96 D1
Gentles La LIPH GU30 114 A7
Gento Cl HEND SO30 149 L6
Geoffrey Av WVILLE PO7 169 H6
Geoffrey Crs
FHAM/PORC PO16 182 B2
George Byng Wy NEND PO2 184 C8
George Curl Wy ELGH SO50 147 M2
George Denyer Cl HASM GU27 118 C5
George Eyston Dr FUFL SO22 24 A8
George Gdns ALDT GU11 3 K8
Georgeham Rd SHST GU47 43 M6
George Rd FLEETN GU51 59 K7
LYMN SO41 232 C3
George St BSTK RG21 6 B5
CHOB/PIR GU24 63 G2
ELGH SO50 140 A1
GPORT PO12 15 H2
KSCL RG20 248 D10
PSEA PO1 192 E1
George Vi Rd NTID SP9 264 E12
George Yd AND SP10 5 J6
The George Yd NARL SO24 291 M10
Georgia Cl AND SP10 4 B9
Georgia Gdns TADY RG26 44 E4
Georgia La RAND SP11 270 A1
Georgian Cl CBLY GU15 51 G1
RGWD BH24 203 J4
Georgian Wy NBNE BH10 213 M4
Georgina Cl BKME/WDN BH12 213 J8
Gerald Rd TWDS BH3 226 A2
Gerald Sq ALTN GU34 107 G2
Gerard Crs ITCH SO19 148 D6
Germaine Cl CHCH/BSGR BH23 217 M8
German Rd TADY RG26 46 C6
Gerring Rd WHIT RG2 239 L9
Gershwin Rd KBH RG22 92 E4
Gervis Crs PSTN BH14 224 A4
Gervis Pl BMTH BH1 8 E6
Gervis Rd BMTH BH1 9 K6
Gibbet La CBLY GU15 51 J1
Gibbons Cl SHST GU47 49 L1
Gibb's Acre CHOB/PIR GU24 63 M4
Gibbs Cl EWKG RG40 42 A2
Gibbs' La BOR GU35 110 C6
Gibbs Rd SHAM SO14 22 F2
Gibbs Wy YTLY GU46 48 D4
Gibraltar Cl FHAM PO15 181 K2
Gibraltar Rd ENEY PO4 193 K5
FHAM/STUB PO14 181 M6
Gibson Cl FHAM PO15 164 E7
LSOL/BMARY PO13 189 M6
Gibson Rd CFDH BH17 223 L1
Giddylake WIMB BH21 207 J2
Gid La ALTN GU34 281 P1
Giffard Dr FARN GU14 60 F2
Giffards Meadow FNM GU9 13 L5
Gifford Cl FHAM PO15 10 A2
Gilbard Ct CHIN RG24 54 C5
Gilbert Cl CHIN RG24 65 L3
FBDG SP6 196 D6
LSOL/BMARY PO13 182 D8
LYMN SO41 221 K6
Gilbert Md HISD PO11 194 E4
Gilbert Rd CHAR BH8 226 D2
FRIM GU16 50 E7
Gilbert's Gn NTID SP9 266 E9
Gilberts Mead Cl RAND SP11 95 K8
Gilberts Piece MARL SN8 264 G3
Gilbert St NARL SO24 292 H11
Gilbert Wy WVILLE PO7 169 L3
Gilbert White Wy ALTN GU34 106 F3
Gilbury Cl WEND SO18 147 L4
Gilchrist Gdns HLER SO31 179 J5
Giles Cl FHAM/PORC PO16 11 H1
GPORT PO12 191 G2
HEND SO30 149 K3
NWBY RG14 * 18 B5
Giles Ct TADY RG26 44 C4
Giles La ROMY SO51 334 E3
Giles Rd TADY RG26 44 C4
Gilkicker Rd GPORT PO12 191 J7
Gillam Rd NBNE BH10 213 K4
Gillcrest FHAM PO15 164 C8
Gillett Rd BKME/WDN BH12 225 J1
Gillham's La HASM GU27 117 G4
Gillian Av ASHV GU12 3 K6
Gillian Cl ASHV GU12 3 L6
Gillies Dr CHIN RG24 64 E4
The Gillies FHAM/PORC PO16 10 F6
Gillingham Cl
MOOR/WNTN BH9 214 C5
WINC SO23 289 J9
Gillingham Rd LYMN SO41 232 D4
Gillman Rd CHAM PO6 169 L8
Gilpin Cl ITCH SO19 148 D7
LYMN SO41 351 R11
Gilpin Hl LYMN SO41 350 F10
Gilroy Cl NWBY RG14 33 J6
Gins La BROC SO42 357 R3
Gipsy La WWKG RG41 239 M1
Girton Cl FHAM/STUB PO14 180 C3
Gisbourne Cl NTID SP9 266 G2
Gitsham Gdns WVILLE PO7 169 J5
Gladdis Rd BWD BH11 212 F4
Glade Cl CHIN RG24 54 B6
Gladeland Rd FERN BH22 205 H8
Gladelands Cl BDST BH18 210 E4
Gladelands Pk FERN BH22 209 M1
Gladelands Wy BDST BH18 210 E4
The Glades HLER SO31 164 A8
The Glade CHFD SO53 133 M7
FAWY SO45 354 G9
FHAM PO15 165 K8
FNM GU9 77 H1
FRIM GU16 61 M6
HISD PO11 195 J6
NWBY RG14 33 M5
RFNM GU10 109 H3
RGWD BH24 202 A7
WVILLE PO7 156 A8
Gladiator Wy FARN GU14 61 G8
Gladstone Cl
CHCH/BSGR BH23 228 D2
HUNG RG17 31 H2
Gladstone Gdns
FHAM/PORC PO16 183 J1
Gladstone La NTHA RG18 28 E4
Gladstone Rd
BKME/WDN BH12 224 C3
GPORT PO12 191 G1
ITCH SO19 148 B8
LTDN BH7 226 F3
Gladstone Rd East LTDN BH7 226 F3
Gladstone Rd West BMTH BH1 226 E3
Gladstone St WINC SO23 24 F4
Gladys Av HORN PO8 156 A4
NEND PO2 184 D6
Glaisdale STHA RG19 35 J2
Glamis Av NBNE BH10 213 L3
Glamis Cl DEAN RG23 91 K2
FRIM GU16 61 M1
WVILLE PO7 156 A8
Glamorgan Rd HORN PO8 321 K10
Glasgow Rd ENEY PO4 193 H5
Glasslaw Rd WEND SO18 148 A4
Glasspool WVILLE PO7 154 E3
Glastonbury Cl CHIN RG24 65 J4
Glaston Hill Rd HTWY RG27 241 P4
Glayshers Hl BOR GU35 114 A2
Glaziers La RGUW GU3 75 J6
Gleadowe Av
CHCH/BSGR BH23 227 M2
Glebe Cl ALDT GU11 2 F8
ALTN GU34 279 M6
HISD PO11 194 E3
OVTN RG25 103 M3
RSAL SP5 296 A1
TADY RG26 44 C5
Glebe Cnr WHAM PO17 152 B5
Glebe Ct ELGH SO50 141 K2
FLEETN GU51 59 H7
HEND SO30 150 A4
PTSW SO17 147 G6
Glebe Dr LSOL/BMARY PO13 182 C7
Glebefield Gdns CHAM PO6 168 E8
Glebe Flds ALTN GU34 279 M6
Glebefields LYMN SO41 232 D3
NWBY RG14 27 K7
Glebeland Rd CBLY GU15 50 B4
Glebelands RAND SP11 271 R2
STHA RG19 35 J1
Glebe La DEAN RG23 64 C8
HTWY RG27 57 M3
KSCL RG20 26 A7
RFNM GU10 263 J7
RSAL SP5 334 B4
Glebe Meadow OVTN RG25 89 J4
RSAL SP5 297 N10
Glebe Park Av CHAM PO6 170 A7
Glebe Rd BOR GU35 111 L7
EPSF GU31 315 P11
FARN GU14 60 F3

RFNM GU10 259 P2
The Glebe BLKW GU17 50 A4
FHAM/STUB PO14 189 J3
Glenair Av PSTN BH14 224 A5
Glenair Rd PSTN BH14 224 A5
Glenavon NMIL/BTOS BH25 219 H6
Glenavon Gdns YTLY GU46 48 F4
Glenavon Rd
CHCH/BSGR BH23 217 M7
Glenbrook Wk
FHAM/STUB PO14 181 J4
Glencarron Wy ROWN SO16 146 E5
Glen Cl AND SP10 4 C5
GSHT GU26 115 J2
NMIL/BTOS BH25 218 D8
Glencoe Cl FRIM GU16 51 H8
Glencoe Rd BKME/WDN BH12 224 D3
LTDN BH7 226 F1
PSEA PO1 192 F1
Glencoyne Gdns ROWN SO16 145 M6
Glenda Cl HLER SO31 179 K4
Glen Dl HAV PO9 157 K7
Glendale BPWT SO32 318 B8
HLER SO31 180 B2
Glendale Av FERN BH22 209 K2
NWBY RG14 33 J7
Glendale Cl CHCH/BSGR BH23 215 K5
WIMB BH21 207 J3
Glendale Pk FLEETN GU51 58 E6
Glendale Rd SBNE BH6 228 A4
TADY RG26 44 A3
Glendene Pk
NMIL/BTOS BH25 * 218 E3
Glendon Av NBNE BH10 213 J2
Glendowan Rd CHFD SO53 139 G1
Glendrive NMIL/BTOS BH25 218 C8
Gleneagles Av PSTN BH14 224 D6
Gleneagles Cl DEAN RG23 92 C7
FERN BH22 209 M2
Gleneagles Dr FARN GU14 60 C5
HORN PO8 156 B6
Glenelg FHAM PO15 10 C3
Glenesha Gdns FHAM PO15 181 K2
Glen Eyre Dr ROWN SO16 147 G3
Glen Eyre Rd ROWN SO16 146 F3
Glen Eyre Wy ROWN SO16 147 G4
Glenferness Av TWDS BH3 225 K2
Glen Fern Rd BMTH BH1 9 G5
Glenfield Av WEND SO18 161 M1
Glenfield Cl RSAL SP5 282 H10
Glenfield Crs WEND SO18 161 M1
Glenfield Wy WEND SO18 161 M1
Glengariff Rd PSTN BH14 224 C6
Glengarry NMIL/BTOS BH25 219 J6
Glengarry Wy
CHCH/BSGR BH23 229 J2
Glenhurst Cl BLKW GU17 50 A4
Glenives Cl RGWD BH24 202 B8
Glenlea GSHT GU26 115 L7
Glenlea Cl HEND SO30 148 D3
Glenlea Dr HEND SO30 148 D3
Glenlea Hollow GSHT GU26 115 L8
Glenleigh Av CHAM PO6 184 F1
Glenleigh Pk HAV PO9 17 K3
Glenme Adows Dr BWD BH11 213 H3
Glenmoor Cl NBNE BH10 213 K7
Glenmoor Rd FERN BH22 209 J5
MOOR/WNTN BH9 213 K8
Glenmore Cl STHA RG19 * 35 K2
Glenmount Dr PSTN BH14 224 B3
Glenmount Rd FRIM GU16 62 A6
Glenney Cl LSOL/BMARY PO13 190 A2
Glenn Rd HEND SO30 148 D2
HLER SO31 163 L6
Glen Rd BOSC BH5 226 E4
FLEETN GU51 59 H8
GSHT GU26 115 J2
HLER SO31 163 M5
ITCH SO19 161 K7
PSTN BH14 224 B4
Glenroyd Gdns SBNE BH6 227 K4
Glenside FAWY SO45 176 F5
HEND SO30 * 148 D3
NMIL/BTOS BH25 230 B1
Glenside Av ITCH SO19 148 D8
Glen Spey NMIL/BTOS BH25 219 K6
The Glen CCLF BH13 224 E8
FNM GU9 77 G2
LSOL/BMARY PO13 182 E7
TADY RG26 44 E3
Glenthorne Cl
FHAM/STUB PO14 189 K3
Glenthorne Meadow
PSF GU32 314 C8
Glenthorne Rd HSEA PO3 185 G7
Glenville Cl CHCH/BSGR BH23 218 B6
Glenville Gdns GSHT GU26 115 M4
NBNE BH10 213 J6
Glenville Rd CHCH/BSGR BH23 218 B6
NBNE BH10 213 J6
Glenwood Av ROWN SO16 147 G3
Glenwood Ct ELGH SO50 141 L2
Glenwood Gdns HORN PO8 155 M6
Glenwood La FERN BH22 205 G6
Glenwood Rd EMRTH PO10 172 D5
FERN BH22 205 G6
VWD BH31 201 H3
Glenwood Wy FERN BH22 205 G6
Glidden Cl PSEA PO1 21 J2
Glidden La WVILLE PO7 320 A9
Glissons FERN BH22 209 G6
Globe Farm La BLKW GU17 49 K3
Globe Yd AND SP10 5 H6
Glorney Md FNM GU9 77 L2
Gloster Ct FHAM PO15 164 C7
Gloucester Cl ALTN GU34 293 L6
FRIM GU16 61 L2
PSF GU32 120 B6
Gloucester Dr KBH RG22 92 D5
Gloucester Rd ALDT GU11 3 J9
BKME/WDN BH12 224 E3
LTDN BH7 226 F3
NWBY RG14 18 B5
PSEA PO1 192 A2
WVILLE PO7 169 M2
Gloucester Sq SHAM SO14 23 G6
Gloucester Ter SSEA PO5 21 G6
Gloucester Vw SSEA PO5 21 G6
Glyn Dr FHAM/STUB PO14 189 J2
Glyn Jones Cl FAWY SO45 354 H6
Glynswood CBLY GU15 51 H5
RFNM GU10 78 E4
Glynville Cl WIMB BH21 208 A1
Glynville Rd WIMB BH21 208 A1
Glyn Wy FHAM/STUB PO14 189 J2
Goatacre Rd ALTN GU34 292 G3
Goathorn Cl UPTN BH16 222 D4
Goat La BSTK RG21 7 C5
Goch Wy AND SP10 96 B2
Goddard Cl WHIT RG2 238 E3
Goddard Dr THLE RG7 36 F1
Goddards Cl HTWY RG27 46 F8
Goddards Firs DEAN RG23 91 L4
Goddards La CBLY GU15 50 D5
Goddards Md AND SP10 4 D7
Goddard Sq AND SP10 96 D2
Godfrey Cl SHST GU47 49 M1
Godfrey Pink Wy BPWT SO32 143 K5
Godmanston Cl CFDH BH17 212 A7
Godshill Cl CHAR BH8 214 D5
Godwin Cl EMRTH PO10 171 L5
FUFL SO22 122 C1
Godwin Crs HORN PO8 321 L8
Godwit Cl GPORT PO12 183 H8
Godwit Rd ENEY PO4 193 J3
Gofton Av CHAM PO6 185 H1
Gogg's La RSAL SP5 332 H2
Goldcrest Cl
FHAM/PORC PO16 * 166 E8
HORN PO8 156 A1
YTLY GU46 48 D2
Goldcrest Gdns ROWN SO16 146 A3
Goldcrest La TOTT SO40 144 C8
Golden Ct HEND SO30 148 F2
Golden Crs LYMN SO41 220 D7
Goldenfield Cl LIPH GU30 116 D5
Golden Flds LIPH GU30 116 D5
Golden Gv SHAM SO14 23 J2
Golden Hind Pk FAWY SO45 176 F6
Goldenleas Dr BWD BH11 212 D5
Golden Lion Rbt BSTK RG21 93 K3
Goldfinch Cl ALDT GU11 2 D7
NMIL/BTOS BH25 218 F6
Goldfinch Gdns KBH RG22 92 B6
Goldfinch La
LSOL/BMARY PO13 189 M5
Goldfinch Rd CFDH BH17 210 E8
Goldfinch Wy RWIN SO21 288 E3
Gold Hl BOR GU35 * 110 E3
Goldhill RFNM GU10 79 G2
Golding Cl STHA RG19 35 M2
Gold La ALDT GU11 73 L4
Gold Mead Cl LYMN SO41 221 L6
Goldney Rd CBLY GU15 51 K4
Goldring Cl HISD PO11 195 G5
Goldsmith Av ENEY PO4 21 M3
Goldsmith Cl NTHA RG18 28 E7
TOTT SO40 158 D1
Goldsmith Rd ELGH SO50 139 M7
Goldsmith Wy CWTH RG45 43 K4
Gold St SSEA PO5 20 F6
Goldwell Dr NWBY RG14 18 C2
Goldwire Dr CHFD SO53 138 F3
Gole Rd CHOB/PIR GU24 63 K2
Golf Course Rd ROWN SO16 146 E2
Golf Dr CBLY GU15 51 H4
Golf La BOR GU35 112 D3
Golf Links Av GSHT GU26 115 H2
Golf Links Rd BDST BH18 211 H3
FERN BH22 209 L3
Goliath Rd PLE BH15 222 D6
Gomer La GPORT PO12 190 E4
Gondreville Gdns FLEETS GU52 71 G4
Gong Hl RFNM GU10 79 H5
Gong Hill Dr RFNM GU10 79 H4
Goodden Crs FARN GU14 60 F6
The Goodens NARL SO24 303 Q7
Goodison Cl ELGH SO50 141 H3
Goodlands V HEND SO30 149 G6
Goodman Cl BSTK RG21 6 A7
Goodwood Rd BKME/WDN BH12 224 D1
Goodsell Cl FHAM/STUB PO14 189 H2
Goodwin Cl ROWN SO16 145 K6
Goodwood Cl ALTN GU34 106 F6
FHAM/STUB PO14 180 C2
GPORT PO12 183 H8
THLE RG7 39 M2
WVILLE PO7 156 B7
Goodwood Ct EMRTH PO10 172 E6
Goodwood Gdns TOTT SO40 144 C8
Goodwood Pl FARN GU14 61 L5
Goodwood Rd ELGH SO50 139 L4
SSEA PO5 21 L7
Goodwood Wy NWBY RG14 19 K8
Goodwyns Cl NTID SP9 266 D9
Goodwyns Gn ALTN GU34 107 G2
Goodyers ALTN GU34 107 G5
Goose Gn HTWY RG27 56 B6
Goose Green Wy STHA RG19 35 L2
Goose La HTWY RG27 56 C6
Gordon Av CBLY GU15 50 D4
FLEETS GU52 71 K2
SHAM SO14 147 G8
WINC SO23 25 M8
Gordon Cl BSTK RG21 7 H2
Gordon Crs CBLY GU15 50 E4
Gordon Mt CHCH/BSGR BH23 218 B7
Gordon Palmer Cl THLE RG7 40 D3
Gordon Rd ALDT GU11 2 F4
BKME/WDN BH12 225 G3
BMTH BH1 226 D4
BPWT SO32 150 F3
CBLY GU15 50 E4
CHCH/BSGR BH23 218 A8
CHFD SO53 133 K7
CWTH RG45 43 M5
EMRTH PO10 172 B7
FARN GU14 61 K8
FHAM/PORC PO16 10 E5
GPORT PO12 14 D5
LYMN SO41 221 J5
NTHA RG18 28 C7
NWBY RG14 19 G5
PSEA PO1 20 E7
WIMB BH21 207 L4
WINC SO23 25 H3
WVILLE PO7 169 K2
Gordon Rd South
BKME/WDN BH12 225 G4
Gordon Ter ITCH SO19 162 A2
Gordon Wk YTLY GU46 49 G3
Gordon Wy CHCH/BSGR BH23 216 C7
Gore End Rd KSCL RG20 245 P1
Gore Rd NMIL/BTOS BH25 218 E6
Gorey Rd BKME/WDN BH12 212 D7
Goring Av HORN PO8 321 M8
Goring Fld FUFL SO22 122 C3
Goring La THLE RG7 39 M3
Gorleston Rd
BKME/WDN BH12 224 F3
Gorley Ct HAV PO9 170 C2
Gorley Lynch FBDG SP6 197 M7
Gorley Rd RGWD BH24 203 L4
Gorran Av LSOL/BMARY PO13 182 C7
The Gorrings STOK SO20 299 Q2
Gorsecliff Rd NBNE BH10 213 K7
Gorse Cl FNM GU9 78 E2
HLER SO31 179 M2
NMIL/BTOS BH25 219 K4
RGWD BH24 205 M4
Gorse Cottage Dr NTHA RG18 28 D3
Gorsedown Cl BOR GU35 112 D3
Gorsefield Rd
NMIL/BTOS BH25 219 H3
Gorse Hill Cl PLE BH15 223 L3
Gorse Hill Crs PLE BH15 223 L3
Gorse Hill Rd PLE BH15 223 L3
Gorse Knoll Dr VWD BH31 201 G1
Gorseland Ct FERN BH22 209 L5
Gorselands NWBY RG14 33 K7
TADY RG26 44 B3
YTLY GU46 48 E4
Gorselands Cl ASHV GU12 74 A3
BOR GU35 114 C4
Gorselands Rd WEND SO18 148 B3
Gorselands Wy
LSOL/BMARY PO13 182 D8
Gorse La RFNM GU10 78 E2
UPTN BH16 222 C1
Gorse Ride North EWKG RG40 42 A1
Gorse Ride South EWKG RG40 42 A1
Gorse Rd EPSF GU31 121 G6
FRIM GU16 51 G6
WIMB BH21 210 C3
Gorseway FLEETS GU52 71 J1
The Gorseway HISD PO11 194 D5
Gort Cl ALDT GU11 73 L1
Gort Crs ITCH SO19 148 B8
Gort Rd BWD BH11 213 H5
CFDH BH17 211 G7
Goscombs La NARL SO24 292 B9
Gosling Cl CFDH BH17 223 M1
Goslings Cft ALTN GU34 295 L7
Gosnell Cl FRIM GU16 51 M5
Gosport La LYND SO43 345 L4
Gosport Rd FHAM/PORC PO16 11 G9
FHAM/STUB PO14 189 K2
LSOL/BMARY PO13 189 M7
Gosport St LYMN SO41 221 M4
Gostrode La MFD/CHID GU8 119 M5
Gough Crs CFDH BH17 211 H6
Gough Rd FLEETN GU51 59 G6
Gough's Meadow SHST GU47 49 K1
Gould Cl NWBY RG14 19 H4
RAND SP11 265 L10
Government House Rd
ALDT GU11 73 G1
Government Rd ALDT GU11 73 L4
Governor's Rd CBLY GU15 50 B2
Gover Rd ROWN SO16 145 J7
Gower Cl BSTK RG21 6 F2
Gower Crs HTWY RG27 56 D7
Gower Pk SHST GU47 49 M1
Grace Bennett Cl FARN GU14 * 61 G1
Grace Dieu Gdns HLER SO31 * 162 F3
Grace La FBDG SP6 332 A8
Gracemere Crs KBH RG22 92 B5
Grace Sq AND SP10 96 E2
Gracious St ALTN GU34 295 K8
Graddidge Wy TOTT SO40 158 D1
Gradwell La ALTN GU34 293 L8
Graemar La ROMY SO51 128 C7
Grafton Cl BOR GU35 113 G2
CHCH/BSGR BH23 228 D2
GPORT PO12 191 J1
TWDS BH3 226 A1
Grafton Gdns LYMN SO41 221 J7
ROWN SO16 146 C3
Grafton Rd TWDS BH3 226 A2
WINC SO23 24 E8
Grafton St NEND PO2 192 C1
Grafton Wy KBH RG22 64 F8
Graham Rd ENEY PO4 21 M7
GPORT PO12 191 G2
SHAM SO14 161 H2
Graham St SHAM SO14 161 J2
Grainger Cl KBH RG22 93 G3
Grainger Gdns ITCH SO19 162 C1
Grammar School La
WIMB BH21 207 H4
Grammarsham La
OVTN RG25 105 H2
Grampian Rd SHST GU47 43 H6
Grampian Wy KBH RG22 92 D1
Granada Cl HORN PO8 156 A5
Granada Pl AND SP10 5 H3
Granada Rd ENEY PO4 192 E7
HEND SO30 149 G7
The Granary NWBY RG14 * 18 D4
Granby Gv PTSW SO17 147 H5
Granby Rd MOOR/WNTN BH9 214 A4
Grand Av CBLY GU15 50 E2
SBNE BH6 227 J4
Grand Pde FUFL SO22 288 C11
HISD PO11 195 G6
PLE BH15 * 223 H7
PSEA PO1 20 C7
Grand Trunk Rd NTID SP9 266 C4
Grange Av CWTH RG45 43 K2
Grange Cl GPORT PO12 14 B1
HAV PO9 17 J3
LYMN SO41 220 E8
RAND SP11 94 A2
WEND SO18 147 L4
Grange Ct HLER SO31 162 B6
RFNM GU10 * 260 C2
Grange Crs GPORT PO12 190 F2
Grange Dr HEND SO30 149 K4
Grange Farm Rd ASHV GU12 74 A5
Grange Gdns
BKME/WDN BH12 224 E1
Grange La HTWY RG27 57 K3
LSOL/BMARY PO13 182 C8
Grange Ms ROMY SO51 131 J7
Grange Rd ASHV GU12 74 B7
BDST BH18 211 G4
CBLY GU15 51 G3
CHCH/BSGR BH23 229 H1
CHOB/PIR GU24 63 K3
FARN GU14 61 H1
FLEETS GU52 71 H3
HEND SO30 149 K5
HLER SO31 162 B6
LSOL/BMARY PO13 190 D4
NARL SO24 291 L11
NEND PO2 184 D7
PSF GU32 120 C7
RFNM GU10 79 M8
RFNM GU10 260 C2
RGWD BH24 205 M6
ROWN SO16 146 B7
SBNE BH6 227 K5
WINC SO23 122 E8
The Grange LYMN SO41 220 B8
NWBY RG14 33 J7
Grangewood Gdns ELGH SO50 141 H2
Grantham Av HLER SO31 178 E1
Grantham Rd BMTH BH1 226 E3
ELGH SO50 139 M6
ITCH SO19 161 M2
Grantley Ct FNM GU9 78 D2
Grantley Dr FLEETS GU52 71 H1
Grantley Rd BOSC BH5 226 F4
Grant Rd CHAM PO6 169 K8
CWTH RG45 43 L5
Grant's Av BMTH BH1 226 D2
Grants Cl BMTH BH1 226 D2
Granville Cl HAV PO9 17 H5
Granville Pl WINC SO23 25 J8
Granville Rd BOSC BH5 227 G3
PSTN BH14 224 B3
Granville St SHAM SO14 23 K4
Grasdean Cl WEND SO18 148 A3
Grasmere ELGH SO50 139 M6
Grasmere Cl BOR GU35 110 F7
CHCH/BSGR BH23 215 K5
WEND SO18 148 B3
Grasmere Gdns
NMIL/BTOS BH25 219 H3
Grasmere Rd BOSC BH5 227 G4
CCLF BH13 237 G5
FARN GU14 60 E5
FNM GU9 76 E2
Grasmere Wy
FHAM/STUB PO14 181 K8
Graspan Rd RAND SP11 265 P11
Grassington Pl STHA RG19 35 K2
Grassmead STHA RG19 35 M2
Grassmere Wy HORN PO8 156 B7
Grassymead FHAM PO15 164 C8
Grateley Cl ITCH SO19 161 M8
Grateley Crs HAV PO9 170 C4
Grateley Dro RAND SP11 269 M3
Grateley Rd AMSY SP4 268 D3
Gratton Cl RWIN SO21 274 D8
Gravel Cl NARL SO24 277 L8
RSAL SP5 327 J12
Gravel Hl BPWT SO32 318 B9
CFDH BH17 211 J5
KSCL RG20 26 A7
WIMB BH21 207 K7
Gravel Hill Rd RFNM GU10 259 Q11
Gravel La ALTN GU34 293 J7
RGWD BH24 203 H5
RWIN SO21 273 P6
Gravelly Cl KSCL RG20 245 N1
TADY RG26 44 C6
Gravel Rd FARN GU14 61 K8
FLEETS GU52 71 K2
FNM GU9 76 F1
Graveney Sq AND SP10 96 D2
Gray Cl CFDH BH17 211 M8
HLER SO31 179 M3
Graycot Cl NBNE BH10 213 J3
Grayland Cl HISD PO11 194 E5
Grayling Md ROMY SO51 130 F7
Graylings WSHM SO15 * 146 A8
Grays Av FAWY SO45 177 H5
Grays Cl ELGH SO50 134 F4
GPORT PO12 190 E5
HASM GU27 118 E4
ROMY SO51 137 G1
Grays Ct PSEA PO1 20 D5
Grayshot Dr BLKW GU17 49 L3
Grayshott Cl FUFL SO22 288 D12
Grayshott Laurels BOR GU35 111 J6
Grayshott Rd BOR GU35 114 C3
ENEY PO4 192 F4
GPORT PO12 14 B5
Grayson Cl LSOL/BMARY PO13 190 A2
Grayswood Dr FRIM GU16 62 A7
Grayswood Ms HASM GU27 * 118 F2
Grayswood Rd HASM GU27 118 D4
Gray's Yd PLE BH15 * 223 J7
Grazeley Rd THLE RG7 40 E3
THLE RG7 238 A4
Great Austins FNM GU9 13 J7
Great Binfields Crs CHIN RG24 54 B8
Great Binfields Rd CHIN RG24 54 B8
Great Br ROMY SO51 130 E6
Greatbridge Rd ROMY SO51 130 E5
Great Copse Dr HAV PO9 170 F3
Great Cft RSAL SP5 282 A9
Great Elms Cl FAWY SO45 354 D5
Greater Horseshoe Wy
WHAM PO17 165 L4
Greatfield Cl FARN GU14 50 D8
Greatfield Rd FARN GU14 50 C8
Great Field Rd FUFL SO22 122 D1
Greatfield Wy HAV PO9 157 H6
Great Gays FHAM/STUB PO14 189 G3
Great Hanger EPSF GU31 120 F6
Great La WHCH RG28 87 L7
Great Lea THLE RG7 238 A3
Great Md LYND SO43 * 345 K4
WVILLE PO7 155 G5
Great Minster St WINC SO23 25 G6
Great Oaks Cha CHIN RG24 54 A6
Great Severals HUNG RG17 31 G2
Great Sheldons Coppice
HTWY RG27 56 C6
Great Southsea St SSEA PO5 21 G6
Great Well Dr ROMY SO51 130 F8
Greatwood Cl FAWY SO45 177 G6
Greaves Cl NBNE BH10 * 213 J5
Grebe Cl ALTN GU34 106 F2
CFDH BH17 210 E8
CHCH/BSGR BH23 229 G2
EMRTH PO10 172 B2
FHAM/PORC PO16 166 F8
HORN PO8 155 L4
KBH RG22 92 B5
LYMN SO41 232 E4
Green Acre ALDT GU11 2 D5
Greenacre KSCL RG20 248 D10
NMIL/BTOS BH25 219 G8
Greenacre Cl UPTN BH16 222 C2
Greenacre Gdns WVILLE PO7 169 K4
Greenacres BOR GU35 111 H8
KSCL RG20 246 A4
RFNM GU10 260 A6
RSAL SP5 331 R1
RWIN SO21 273 N6
Greenacres Cl NBNE BH10 213 L1
Green Acres Cl RGWD BH24 202 F7
Greenacres Dr RWIN SO21 134 C1
Greenaway La HLER SO31 179 L2
Greenbank Crs ROWN SO16 146 F3
Greenbanks Cl LYMN SO41 232 D3
Greenbanks Gdns
FHAM/PORC PO16 11 L4
Greenberry Br RGWD BH24 349 L5
Greenbirch Cl KBH RG22 92 B5
Green Bottom WIMB BH21 208 A1
Greenbury Cl DEAN RG23 64 E7
Green Cl FAWY SO45 177 G4
NARL SO24 291 M7
PLE BH15 223 K7
RSAL SP5 127 H4
RWIN SO21 288 E4
TOTT SO40 341 R8
Greenclose La WIMB BH21 207 K4
Green Crs LSOL/BMARY PO13 182 C7
Greencroft FARN GU14 61 H4
Green Cross La RFNM GU10 262 G11
Greendale Cl FHAM PO15 165 K8
The Greendale FHAM PO15 165 K8
Green Dro RAND SP11 84 D2
Green End YTLY GU46 48 F1
Green End Cl THLE RG7 * 238 B6
Greenfield Cl LIPH GU30 116 C3
Greenfield Crs HORN PO8 156 C4
Greenfield Gdns
NMIL/BTOS BH25 219 H8
Greenfield Ri HORN PO8 156 B5
Greenfield Rd FNM GU9 78 D1
PLE BH15 223 L2
Greenfields EPSF GU31 317 L9
LISS GU33 308 G8
RAND SP11 84 E4
RSAL SP5 296 A10
Greenfields Av ALTN GU34 106 E4
TOTT SO40 144 E7
Greenfields Cl EPSF GU31 317 L8
Greenfield Wy CWTH RG45 43 J1
Green Finch Cl CWTH RG45 * 43 H2
Greenfinch Cl CFDH BH17 * 210 F7
ELGH SO50 139 K7
Greenfinch Wk RGWD BH24 203 L6
Green Glades FLEETS GU52 71 H3
Greenham Cl STHA RG19 34 D4
Greenham Rd NWBY RG14 18 F6
Greenhanger RFNM GU10 262 F12
Greenhaven YTLY GU46 48 D3
Greenhaven Cl AND SP10 5 L6
Greenhayes BDST BH18 211 J6
Greenhays Ri WIMB BH21 207 J3
Greenhill Av FUFL SO22 24 C5
Green Hill Cl CBLY GU15 51 L2
Greenhill Cl FNM GU9 78 E1
FUFL SO22 24 C5
WIMB BH21 207 K2
Greenhill La ROWN SO16 137 L8
WIMB BH21 207 K2
Green Hill Rd CBLY GU15 51 L2
Greenhill Rd FNM GU9 13 K8
FUFL SO22 24 B5
WIMB BH21 207 K2
Greenhill Ter FUFL SO22 24 C5
Greenhill Wy FNM GU9 78 E2
Green Hollow Cl
FHAM/PORC PO16 10 C1
Greenholme CBLY GU15 51 M3
Greening Wd GSHT GU26 * 115 M3
Green Jacket Cl FUFL SO22 122 E7
Greenlands KSCL RG20 246 A3
Greenlands Rd CBLY GU15 50 D7
KSCL RG20 248 D10
NWBY RG14 19 G9
Green La ALTN GU34 293 K8
ALTN GU34 293 N12
BLKW GU17 49 L3
BPWT SO32 318 C5
FAWY SO45 354 H8
FBDG SP6 197 H2
FBDG SP6 331 J9
FERN BH22 209 G7
FNM GU9 12 D8
FNM GU9 77 K2
GPORT PO12 14 C8
GPORT PO12 183 J8
HASM GU27 118 B8
HISD PO11 194 E6
HLER SO31 162 E3
HLER SO31 163 K4
HLER SO31 164 A3
HLER SO31 179 G2
HLER SO31 179 M3
HORN PO8 321 M7
HSEA PO3 185 G5
HTWY RG27 57 L3
NARL SO24 292 A11
NARL SO24 305 M6
NBNE BH10 213 J5
NMIL/BTOS BH25 219 H8
NWBY RG14 18 B5
OVTN RG25 105 J4
PSF GU32 307 K7
RAND SP11 94 E7
RCCH PO18 173 L6
RFNM GU10 109 L6
RFNM GU10 260 B10
RFNM GU10 262 F12
RGWD BH24 203 J5
RGWD BH24 347 P1
ROMY SO51 131 L8
ROWN SO16 138 F7
ROWN SO16 145 L6
RSAL SP5 327 K12
SHST GU47 43 L8
STHA RG19 35 J1
TADY RG26 44 E8
THLE RG7 39 J2
THLE RG7 40 F8
TOTT SO40 144 C4
WVILLE PO7 153 M5
WVILLE PO7 154 E3
WVILLE PO7 319 P6
YTLY GU46 48 D1
Green Lane Cl CBLY GU15 50 E1
Green La East RGUW GU3 75 G8
Green La West ASHV GU12 74 E8
Greenlea Cl CHAM PO6 169 H6
Greenlea Crs ROWN SO16 147 K3
Greenlea Rd GPORT PO12 190 F1
Greenleas FRIM GU16 51 G6
Greenleas Cl YTLY GU46 48 E1
Green Leys FLEETS GU52 71 H4
Greenmead Av LYMN SO41 220 D7
Green Meadows La
RAND SP11 271 Q2
Green Park Cl WINC SO23 123 H2
Green Park Rd ROWN SO16 159 L1
Green Pond Cnr HAV PO9 17 J5
Green Pond La ROMY SO51 132 C5
Green Ride Cl HTWY RG27 * 241 K8
Green Rd FHAM/STUB PO14 181 J8
GPORT PO12 14 C8
MOOR/WNTN BH9 214 B8
PLE BH15 223 J6
SSEA PO5 21 G6
Greensand Wy FNM GU9 13 H4
GSHT GU26 118 A2
MFD/CHID GU8 263 Q9
RFNM GU10 263 K2
Greens Cl BPWT SO32 143 H4
ELGH SO50 141 G3
Greenside CWTH RG45 43 H3
Greensleeves Av BDST BH18 211 H2
Greens Meade RSAL SP5 332 F2
Greensome Dr FERN BH22 209 M2
Green Springs RFNM GU10 259 P1
Green Stile ALTN GU34 293 J2
Green St BOR GU35 281 R12
Greensward La WHIT RG2 239 J5
The Green AND SP10 96 A2
FNM GU9 77 G2
FNM GU9 77 M2
FRIM GU16 61 M2
HLER SO31 163 L6
HTWY RG27 58 A2
HUNG RG17 31 H3
LISS GU33 308 E7
OVTN RG25 89 K4
PSF GU32 314 B7
RFNM GU10 260 C7
ROMY SO51 131 J6
RSAL SP5 127 H4
RSAL SP5 296 A1
RSAL SP5 327 L1
RWIN SO21 273 Q5
STOK SO20 270 D8
TADY RG26 44 C6
WBNE BH4 * 225 J3
WHCH RG28 87 M7
Green Wk FHAM PO15 10 A1
Green Wy ASHV GU12 73 L5
KBH RG22 64 E8
Greenway HTWY RG27 46 F8
Greenway Cl LYMN SO41 221 J4
Greenway Crs UPTN BH16 222 A1
Greenway La EPSF GU31 315 N10
Greenway Rd GPORT PO12 14 E1
Greenways BPWT SO32 318 B7
CHCH/BSGR BH23 217 M8
CHFD SO53 139 K2
FLEETS GU52 71 H2
KSCL RG20 246 A3
LYMN SO41 232 C3
ROWN SO16 147 K3
SHST GU47 43 K7
Greenways Av CHAR BH8 214 C5
Greenways Rd BROC SO42 351 L3
The Greenwich FAWY SO45 354 G6
Greenwich Wy AND SP10 96 C2

Greenwood Av *CHAM* PO6 168 D8
FERN BH22 209 K2
PSTN BH14 224 C8
ROWN SO16 145 K2
Greenwood Cl
FHAM/PORC PO16 166 A4
ROMY SO51 131 G8
Greenwood Copse
RGWD BH24 202 B8
Greenwood Dr *CHIN* RG24 54 B4
Greenwood La *BPWT* SO32 142 A4
Greenwood Rd
CHOB/PIR GU24 63 H2
CWTH RG45 43 J2
MOOR/WNTN BH9 213 L7
Greenwoods *NMIL/BTOS* BH25 219 H7
WHCH RG28 87 L6
Greenwood Wy *RGWD* BH24 202 B8
Greetham St *SSEA* PO5 21 H3
Gregory Cl *BSTK* RG21 65 L5
Gregory Gdns *TOTT* SO40 144 C7
Gregory La *BPWT* SO32 142 B7
Gregson Av
LSOL/BMARY PO13 182 C5
Gregson Cl *LSOL/BMARY* PO13 182 C5
Greig Rd *KBH* RG22 93 G3
Grenadier Cl *HLER* SO31 180 B2
Grenadier Rd *ASHV* GU12 74 B4
Grenadiers Wy *FARN* GU14 60 C5
Grendon Cl *ROWN* SO16 147 H3
Grenehurst Wy *EPSF* GU31 120 D6
Grenfell Rd *MOOR/WNTN* BH9 213 M5
Grensell Cl *HTWY* RG27 42 A8
Grenville Cl *LIPH* GU30 116 C4
RGWD BH24 203 L3
Grenville Dr *FLEETN* GU51 71 G1
Grenville Gdns *FAWY* SO45 177 G7
FRIM GU16 61 L2
Grenville Rd *ENEY* PO4 21 L6
MFD/CHID GU8 261 P9
WIMB BH21 207 K4
Gresham Rd
MOOR/WNTN BH9 214 A7
Gresham Wy *FRIM* GU16 61 L2
Gresley Gdns *HEND* SO30 149 J2
Gresley Rd *BSTK* RG21 7 H3
Grevillea Av *FHAM* PO15 180 E1
Greville Cl *ALDT* GU11 2 E2
Greville Gn *EMRTH* PO10 171 L5
Greville Rd *WSHM* SO15 160 D1
Greyberry Copse Rd *STHA* RG19 34 D4
Greyfriars Rd *FHAM* PO15 181 J2
Greyhound Cl *ASHV* GU12 73 M7
HEND SO30 149 H1
Greyhound La *OVTN* RG25 89 J5
Greys Ct *ALDT* GU11 2 A3
Greys Farm Cl *NARL* SO24 303 R8
Greyshott Av
FHAM/STUB PO14 181 J4
Greystead Pk *RFNM* GU10 78 C2
Greystoke Av *BWD* BH11 212 F2
Greystoke Ct *CWTH* RG45 43 J4
Greywell Av *ROWN* SO16 146 C4
Greywell Cl *TADY* RG26 44 A4
Greywell Rd *CHIN* RG24 66 F3
HAV PO9 170 E3
HTWY RG27 67 L4
Grieve Cl *RFNM* GU10 260 C1
Griffen Cl *ELGH* SO50 140 E2
Griffin Ct *PTSW* SO17 147 J8
Griffin Wk *LSOL/BMARY* PO13 190 C2
Griffin Wy North *HTWY* RG27 56 D5
Griffin Wy South *HTWY* RG27 56 D5
Griffiths Cl *STHA* RG19 35 M2
Griffiths Gdns *BWD* BH11 213 H3
Griffon Cl *FARN* GU14 60 D5
HLER SO31 163 G3
Grigg La *BROC* SO42 351 L3
Grimstead Rd *RSAL* SP5 296 C6
RSAL SP5 327 Q2
Grindle Cl *NTHA* RG18 28 E7
Gritanwood Rd *ENEY* PO4 193 H5
Grosvenor Cl *KBH* RG22 92 D7
PTSW SO17 147 J6
RGWD BH24 205 M3
Grosvenor Ct *BLKW* GU17 49 M5
Grosvenor Dr *WINC* SO23 123 H2
Grosvenor Gdns *BMTH* BH1 226 E4
HEND SO30 148 D3
PTSW SO17 147 J6
Grosvenor House
WSHM SO15 * 160 F2
Grosvenor Lawn *NWBY* RG14 * 18 A5
Grosvenor Ms *LYMN* SO41 * 221 K3
PTSW SO17 * 147 J6
Grosvenor Rd *ALDT* GU11 2 E3
ALTN GU34 293 J6
CHFD SO53 133 L7
PTSW SO17 147 J6
WBNE BH4 225 J5
Grosvenor Sq *WSHM* SO15 160 F2
Grosvenor St *SSEA* PO5 21 H4
Grove Av *FHAM/PORC* PO16 183 J2
GPORT PO12 15 G3
Grovebury *HLER* SO31 180 A2
Grove Cl *BSTK* RG21 7 G9
EWKG RG40 43 G1
Grove Cross Rd *FRIM* GU16 50 F7
Grove End Rd *FNM* GU9 12 E9
Grove Farm Pk *FRIM* GU16 * 61 M7
Grovefields Av *FRIM* GU16 50 F7
Grove Gdns *ITCH* SO19 162 B3
Groveland Rd *NWBY* RG14 26 F7
Grovelands *RFNM* GU10 79 J1
Grovelands Rd *FUFL* SO22 122 B3
THLE RG7 238 C6
Grove La *RSAL* SP5 332 H1
Groveley Rd *CHCH/BSGR* BH23 228 E2
WBNE BH4 225 H6
Grovely Av *BOSC* BH5 226 F4
Grovely Wy *ROMY* SO51 131 L7
Grove Pastures *LYMN* SO41 221 L5
Grove Pl *ITCH* SO19 162 B2
LYMN SO41 221 L5
Grove Rd *ALTN* GU34 106 F6
ASHV GU12 74 A4
BKME/WDN BH12 224 B2
BMTH BH1 * 9 H6
BSTK RG21 7 H9
CBLY GU15 51 G3
CHAM PO6 185 J1
FHAM/PORC PO16 10 E6
FLEETS GU52 71 K3
GPORT PO12 191 H2
GSHT GU26 115 J2
HAV PO9 16 F5
LSOL/BMARY PO13 189 L6
LYMN SO41 221 M5
NMIL/BTOS BH25 231 G1
NWBY RG14 26 F7
RWIN SO21 124 D7
WIMB BH21 207 J4
WSHM SO15 160 C1
Grove Rd East
CHCH/BSGR BH23 216 A8
Grove Rd North *SSEA* PO5 21 H6
Grove Rd South *SSEA* PO5 21 H7
Grove Rd West
CHCH/BSGR BH23 215 M8
Groves Cl *RWIN* SO21 288 C4
Groves Down *ROMY* SO51 335 J4
Groves Lea *THLE* RG7 39 M6
The Grove *ALDT* GU11 2 F4
CHCH/BSGR BH23 215 L7
EMRTH PO10 172 B3
FARN GU14 61 K7
FERN BH22 209 J4
FHAM/STUB PO14 189 H2
FRIM GU16 50 F7
HLER SO31 162 D5
HLER SO31 163 G3
ITCH SO19 162 B3
LIPH GU30 116 B4
MOOR/WNTN BH9 213 M5
NTHA RG18 28 F8
RAND SP11 83 H8
VWD BH31 201 J3
Grower Gdns *BWD* BH11 213 G4
Grugs La *WIMB* BH21 336 E5
Gruneisen Rd *NEND* PO2 184 C6
Guardhouse Rd *PSEA* PO1 192 B1
Guardian Ct *MFD/CHID* GU8 263 Q1
Guardroom Rd *NEND* PO2 184 B7
Guernsey Cl *CHIN* RG24 65 L2
ROWN SO16 145 L5
Guernsey Dr *FLEETN* GU51 59 K4
Guernsey Rd
BKME/WDN BH12 212 D7
Guessens La
FHAM/STUB PO14 180 F4
Guest Av *BKME/WDN* BH12 224 F2
Guest Cl *BKME/WDN* BH12 225 G2
Guest Rd *ELGH* SO50 140 D1
UPTN BH16 222 B1
Guildford Cl *EMRTH* PO10 172 D5
Guildford Ct
LSOL/BMARY PO13 * 190 D3
Guildford Dr *CHFD* SO53 139 H5
Guildford Rd *ALDT* GU11 3 L8
ASHV GU12 74 D5
CHOB/PIR GU24 63 M4
FLEETN GU51 59 L7
FNM GU9 13 K1
FRIM GU16 62 A3
PSEA PO1 21 M2
Guildford Rd East *FARN* GU14 61 J7
Guildford Rd West *FARN* GU14 61 J7
Guildford St *SHAM* SO14 * 23 K1
Guildhall Sq *PSEA* PO1 21 G3
Guildhall Wk *PSEA* PO1 20 F4
Guildhill Rd *SBNE* BH6 227 L4
Guillemont Flds *FARN* GU14 60 D3
Guillemot Cl *FAWY* SO45 177 H5
Guillemot Gdns
LSOL/BMARY PO13 182 B5
Guinea Ct *CHIN* RG24 54 C5
Gull Cl *LSOL/BMARY* PO13 182 B6
Gulley Rd *FARN* GU14 61 G8
Gulliver Cl *PSTN* BH14 224 C8
The Gulls *TOTT* SO40 159 M6
Gullycroft Md *HEND* SO30 149 H5
Gun Hl *ALDT* GU11 3 G1
Gunners La *RWIN* SO21 277 J6
Gunners Ms *BPWT* SO32 143 K4
Gunners Pk *BPWT* SO32 143 L4
Gunners Rw *ENEY* PO4 193 H6
Gunners Wy *GPORT* PO12 182 F8
LSOL/BMARY PO13 183 G7
Gunns Farm *LIPH* GU30 116 C6
Gunstore Rd *HSEA* PO3 185 G4
Gunville Crs *MOOR/WNTN* BH9 214 B5
Gunville Hl *RSAL* SP5 283 J10
Gunville Rd *RSAL* SP5 282 H10
Gunwharf Quays *PSEA* PO1 20 C4
Gunwharf Rd *PSEA* PO1 20 C5
Gurdons *ALTN* GU34 106 D7
Gurjun Cl *UPTN* BH16 210 A8
Gurnard Rd *CHAM* PO6 184 E1
Gurnays Md *ROMY* SO51 334 H5
Gurney Rd *ENEY* PO4 193 H4
WIMB BH21 210 E2
WSHM SO15 146 C8
Gussage Rd *BKME/WDN* BH12 212 E8
Gutner La *HISD* PO11 187 J7
Guttridge La *TADY* RG26 44 A4
Gwatkin Cl *HAV* PO9 170 C5
Gwenlyn Rd *UPTN* BH16 222 C2
Gwyn Cl *NWBY* RG14 33 M4
Gwynne Rd *BKME/WDN* BH12 224 E3
Gypsy La *HORN* PO8 155 M3
RGWD BH24 203 K4

H

Haarlem Ms *CHCH/BSGR* BH23 228 D1
Habershon Dr *FRIM* GU16 51 M6
Habin Hl *EPSF* GU31 317 M4
Hack Dr *RWIN* SO21 134 F4
Hacketts La *BPWT* SO32 318 G2
Hackett Wy *FHAM/STUB* PO14 182 A2
Hackleys La *ROMY* SO51 335 M3
Hacks La *RWIN* SO21 287 M5
Hackupps La *ROMY* SO51 299 L11
Hackwood Cl *AND* SP10 4 B7
Hackwood Cots
BSTK RG21 93 L2
Hackwood La *OVTN* RG25 93 K6
Hackwood Rd *BSTK* RG21 6 F7
Hackwood Road Rbt *BSTK* RG21 7 G8
Hackworth Gdns *HEND* SO30 149 J2
Hadden Rd *CHAR* BH8 214 D8
Haddon Cl *FHAM* PO15 10 B6
Haddon Dr *ELGH* SO50 134 A7
Haddons Dr *WIMB* BH21 204 F2
Hadleigh Gdns *ELGH* SO50 134 A7
Hadleigh Pl *BSTK* RG21 6 D5
Hadleigh Rd *CHAM* PO6 * 168 D8
Hadley Fld *FAWY* SO45 354 D3
Hadleys *RFNM* GU10 109 L1
Hadley Wy *BDST* BH18 210 E5
Hadow Rd *BWD* BH11 213 J5
Hadrian Cl *FERN* BH22 209 K6
Hadrian Rd *AND* SP10 96 D1
Hadrians *FNM* GU9 77 J4
Hadrians Cl *CHFD* SO53 139 L1
Hadrians Wy *DEAN* RG23 64 E5
Hadrian Wy *ROWN* SO16 146 E1
WIMB BH21 206 E8
Haflinger Dr *HLER* SO31 164 B4
Haglane Copse *LYMN* SO41 221 H6
Hagley Rd *FLEETN* GU51 59 G6
Hahnemann Rd *WCLF* BH2 8 C7
Haig Av *PSTN* BH14 224 E7
Haig La *FLEETS* GU52 71 K3
Haig Rd *AND* SP10 4 C4
ASHV GU12 3 K4
CBLY GU15 50 B2
ELGH SO50 141 G3
NARL SO24 291 M10
Haileybury Gdns *HEND* SO30 149 H3
Hailsham Cl *SHST* GU47 43 M7
Hailstone Rd *BSTK* RG21 65 K4
Hainault Dr *VWD* BH31 201 J2
Haining Gdns *FRIM* GU16 62 A5
Haking Rd *CHCH/BSGR* BH23 228 D1
Halcyon Dr *RAND* SP11 94 A4
Halden Cl *ROMY* SO51 131 H7
Hale Av *NMIL/BTOS* BH25 219 H6
Hale Cl *NARL* SO24 292 G11
Hale Gdns *NMIL/BTOS* BH25 219 H6
Hale House La *RFNM* GU10 262 G11
Hale La *FBDG* SP6 332 B7
Hale Pl *FNM* GU9 77 J3
Hale Reeds *FNM* GU9 77 H2
Hale Rd *FBDG* SP6 332 A7
FNM GU9 13 K1
Hales Dr *HEND* SO30 149 G7
Hales Fld *HASM* GU27 118 C6
Hale St North *PSEA* PO1 192 D2
Hale St South *PSEA* PO1 192 D2
Hale Wy *FRIM* GU16 50 F7
Halewood Wy
CHCH/BSGR BH23 215 M8
Halfacre Cl *THLE* RG7 238 B5
Half Moon Hl *HASM* GU27 118 C6
Halfpenny La *PSEA* PO1 * 20 D6
Halifax Cl *AND* SP10 4 E3
FARN GU14 60 F5
Halifax Ct *HEND* SO30 * 148 C2
Halifax Pl *NTHA* RG18 28 E8
Halifax Ri *WVILLE* PO7 169 M1
Halifax Wy *CHCH/BSGR* BH23 229 H1
FARN GU14 72 F1
Halimote Rd *ALDT* GU11 2 F4
Hall Cl *BPWT* SO32 143 K4
CBLY GU15 51 G2
Hall Dr *FLEETS* GU52 71 K2
Hallet Cl *WEND* SO18 148 A2
Hallett Cl *WEND* SO18 148 A2
Hallett Rd *HAV* PO9 17 K3
Halletts Cl *FHAM/STUB* PO14 189 J1
Hall Farm Crs *YTLY* GU46 48 E3
The Halliards
FHAM/PORC PO16 182 B1
Halliday Cl *BSTK* RG21 93 J2
GPORT PO12 14 F3
Halliday Crs *ENEY* PO4 193 J5
Hall Lands La *ELGH* SO50 141 K2
Hall La *ALTN* GU34 295 J6
YTLY GU46 48 E3
Hall Rd *ALTN* GU34 107 G2
BWD BH11 212 F5
FARN GU14 61 H7
Halls Farm Cl *FUFL* SO22 122 E1
The Hall Wy *FUFL* SO22 288 B11
Halsey Cl *GPORT* PO12 14 B6
Halstead Rd *CHAM* PO6 168 D8
WEND SO18 147 M6
Halstock Crs *CFDH* BH17 211 K6
Halter Pth *PLE* BH15 222 E5
Halter Ri *WIMB* BH21 208 C2
Halters End *GSHT* GU26 115 G5
The Halters *NWBY* RG14 34 B5
Halterworth Cl *ROMY* SO51 137 H1
Halterworth La *ROMY* SO51 131 J8
Halton Cl *CHCH/BSGR* BH23 348 D12
Halton Rd *RAND* SP11 267 K1
Haltons Cl *TOTT* SO40 144 D7
Halyard Cl *LSOL/BMARY* PO13 190 D1
Hambert Wy *TOTT* SO40 158 E3
Hamble Av *BLKW* GU17 49 M3
Hamble Cl *DEAN* RG23 91 K3
HLER SO31 179 J3
Hamble Ct *AND* SP10 5 L1
BSTK RG21 7 K5
CHFD SO53 139 K3
Hambledon Cl *FUFL* SO22 288 D12
Hambledon Gdns *SBNE* BH6 227 J2
Hambledon La *BPWT* SO32 319 J10
Hambledon Pde
WVILLE PO7 * 155 J6
Hambledon Rd *HORN* PO8 321 J7
LTDN BH7 227 H1
WVILLE PO7 155 H6
Hambledon Wy *HTWY* RG27 54 D3
Hamble Dr *TADY* RG26 44 D4
Hamble House Gdns
HLER SO31 179 G2
Hamble La *HLER* SO31 162 E8
WVILLE PO7 169 L3
Hamble Pk *HLER* SO31 * 179 M3
Hamble Rd *GPORT* PO12 14 B4
PLE BH15 223 M1
Hamble Springs *BPWT* SO32 143 K5
Hambleton Cl *CBLY* GU15 51 K5
Hamblewood *HEND* SO30 150 A6
Ham Br *STHA* RG19 34 E1
Hambridge *NWBY* RG14 19 M4
Hambridge La *NWBY* RG14 34 E2
Hambridge Rd *NWBY* RG14 19 J5
Hambrook Hl (North)
RCCH PO18 173 H3
Hambrook Hl (South)
RCCH PO18 173 H4
Hambrook Rd *GPORT* PO12 14 C1
Hambrook St *SSEA* PO5 20 F7
Hamburg Cl *AND* SP10 96 B1
Hamdown Crs *ROMY* SO51 335 M6
Hameldon Cl *ROWN* SO16 159 L1
Hamelyn Cl *BSTK* RG21 6 C7
Hamelyn Rd *BSTK* RG21 6 C7
Hamesmoor Rd *FRIM* GU16 61 L4
Hamesmoor Wy *FRIM* GU16 61 M4
Hamfield Dr *HISD* PO11 194 E4
Hamilton Cl *BMTH* BH1 226 D3
BOR GU35 111 H8
BSTK RG21 65 G5
CHCH/BSGR BH23 228 F4
HAV PO9 16 F7
NWBY RG14 18 F9
PLE BH15 222 E6
Hamilton Ct *LYMN* SO41 232 C4
NWBY RG14 18 F9
Hamilton Crs *PLE* BH15 222 E6
Hamilton Gv
LSOL/BMARY PO13 182 B7
Hamilton Ms *FAWY* SO45 177 H7
Hamilton Pk *RSAL* SP5 327 L12
Hamilton Pl *ALDT* GU11 2 D5
LYMN SO41 * 221 K5
Hamilton Rd *BMTH* BH1 226 D4
CHAM PO6 167 L8
ELGH SO50 140 D1
FAWY SO45 177 H8
FLEETS GU52 71 K2
LISS GU33 309 K2
PLE BH15 222 E6
SSEA PO5 21 J8
WIMB BH21 210 E3
Ham La *EMRTH* PO10 172 D7
FERN BH22 209 H6
GPORT PO12 183 G7
HORN PO8 320 H12
MFD/CHID GU8 261 J12
TADY RG26 249 M6
WIMB BH21 208 C3
Hamlash La *RFNM* GU10 79 G7
Hamlet Gdns *RAND* SP11 84 D6
Hamlet Wy *GPORT* PO12 182 F7
Hammer Hl *HASM* GU27 117 J4
Hammer La *GSHT* GU26 114 E1
GSHT GU26 115 J8
LIPH GU30 117 G2
Hammersley Rd *ALDT* GU11 73 H1
Hammerwood Copse
HASM GU27 117 K3
Ham Ml *NWBY* RG14 * 19 L3
Hammond Cl *FHAM* PO15 181 K2
STHA RG19 35 L2
Hammond Rd *BSTK* RG21 6 D8
FHAM PO15 10 A3
Hammonds Cl *TOTT* SO40 144 E8
Hammond's Gn *TOTT* SO40 144 D8
Hammonds Heath *THLE* RG7 40 B2
Hammond's La *NARL* SO24 292 G12
TOTT SO40 144 E8
Hammond Sq *AND* SP10 * 96 D2
Hammonds Wy *TOTT* SO40 144 E8
Hampden La *SBNE* BH6 227 H3
Hampdens *NWBY* RG14 33 J6
The Hampdens *NWBY* RG14 * 33 J6
Hampshire Cl *ASHV* GU12 3 M8
CHCH/BSGR BH23 215 M6
KBH RG22 92 C1
Hampshire Hatches La
RGWD BH24 203 J8
Hampshire Rd *BOR* GU35 110 F8
Hampshire St *PSEA* PO1 192 E1
Hampshire Ter *PSEA* PO1 20 F5
Hampshire Wy *WWKG* RG41 239 R2
Hampton Cl *FAWY* SO45 354 G8
FLEETS GU52 71 J4
WVILLE PO7 170 A1
Hampton Dr *RGWD* BH24 203 K3
Hampton Gdns *FAWY* SO45 354 G8
Hampton Gv *FHAM* PO15 181 H3
Hampton Hl *BPWT* SO32 318 B6
Hampton La *FAWY* SO45 354 G6
FUFL SO22 122 C3
Hampton Rd *FNM* GU9 76 E2
NWBY RG14 18 D7
Hamptworth Rd *RSAL* SP5 333 K3
Hamstead Meadow
RCCH PO18 173 J7
Hamtun Crs *TOTT* SO40 144 E7
Hamtun Gdns *TOTT* SO40 144 E7
Hamtun Rd *ITCH* SO19 162 C2
Hamtun St *SHAM* SO14 22 F5
Hanbidge Crs
LSOL/BMARY PO13 182 D4
Hanbury Wy *CBLY* GU15 50 E5
Hancombe Rd *SHST* GU47 43 J6
Handcroft Cl *RFNM* GU10 70 F8
Handel Cl *KBH* RG22 92 F3
Handel Rd *WSHM* SO15 160 F2
Handel Ter *WSHM* SO15 22 D1
Handford La *YTLY* GU46 48 F4
Handford Pl *WSHM* SO15 160 F2
Handley Rd *GPORT* PO12 190 F2
Hangerfield Cl *YTLY* GU46 48 E3
Hanger Rd *TADY* RG26 249 R3
The Hangers *BPWT* SO32 143 K2
BPWT SO32 311 N12
Hangers Wy *ALTN* GU34 107 G4
EPSF GU31 315 N12
HORN PO8 321 Q2
The Hanger *BOR* GU35 111 L5
Hanger Wy *EPSF* GU31 120 F6
Hanham Rd *WIMB* BH21 207 J3
WIMB BH21 210 D3
Hankinson Rd
MOOR/WNTN BH9 214 A8
Hanley Rd *WSHM* SO15 146 D8
Hanlon Cl *BWD* BH11 213 G4
Hanmore Rd *CHIN* RG24 54 A6
Hannah Gdns *WVILLE* PO7 155 M8
Hannah Wy *LYMN* SO41 220 F2
Hannam's Farm *RFNM* GU10 259 N2
Hannay Ri *ITCH* SO19 148 D7
Hannington Rd *HAV* PO9 170 D1
LTDN BH7 227 G3
Hann Rd *ROWN* SO16 145 L2
Hanns Wy *ELGH* SO50 140 A2
Hanover Buildings *SHAM* SO14 23 G4
Hanover Cl *AND* SP10 4 B8
FRIM GU16 51 G7
YTLY GU46 48 F1
Hanover Ct *PSEA* PO1 * 20 D5
Hanover Dr *FLEETN* GU51 59 L4
Hanover Gdns *BSTK* RG21 93 J2
FARN GU14 60 E2
FHAM/PORC PO16 11 G1
Hanover Gn *CFDH* BH17 * 211 M8
Hanoverian Wy *FHAM* PO15 164 C5
Hanover Md *NWBY* RG14 * 33 K6
Hanover St *PSEA* PO1 20 C2
Hanson Cl *CBLY* GU15 51 K1
Hanson Rd *AND* SP10 4 D3
Hanway Rd *NEND* PO2 184 D8
Ha'Penny Dell *WVILLE* PO7 * 169 L5
Harbeck Rd *CHAR* BH8 214 C5
Harborough Rd *WSHM* SO15 160 F2
Harbour Cl *FARN* GU14 50 C8
TOTT SO40 * 160 C6
Harbour Crs *CHCH/BSGR* BH23 228 E3
Harbour Hill Crs *PLE* BH15 223 L3
Harbour Hill Rd *PLE* BH15 223 L3
Harbourne Gdns *WEND* SO18 148 B2
Harbour Pde *SHAM* SO14 22 E3
Harbour Rd *GPORT* PO12 15 K3
HISD PO11 194 C4
SBNE BH6 228 A5
Harbourside *HAV* PO9 186 F2
Harbour Vw
FHAM/PORC PO16 183 J2
Harbour View Cl *PSTN* BH14 224 A3
Harbour View Rd *PSTN* BH14 224 A3
Harbour Wy *EMRTH* PO10 172 A6
NEND PO2 184 C6
Harbridge Ct *HAV* PO9 170 D1
Harbridge Dro *FBDG* SP6 196 E8
Harbury Ct *NWBY* RG14 18 F6
Harcombe Cl *CFDH* BH17 211 L5
Harcourt Cl *HORN* PO8 156 A4
Harcourt Rd *BOSC* BH5 227 G3
CBLY GU15 50 D3
FHAM/STUB PO14 181 H5
GPORT PO12 14 D3
PSEA PO1 192 E1
WEND SO18 147 K8
Harding La *ELGH* SO50 141 H1
Harding Rd *GPORT* PO12 190 F2
Hardings La *HTWY* RG27 57 M2
Hardley La *FAWY* SO45 354 D1
The Hard *PSEA* PO1 20 C2
Hardwicke Cl *ROWN* SO16 145 M6
Hardwicke Wy *HLER* SO31 178 D2
Hardwick Rd *CHFD* SO53 139 K2
Hardy Av *YTLY* GU46 48 E4
Hardy Cl *FERN* BH22 205 H7
HLER SO31 164 B8
NMIL/BTOS BH25 218 F5
NTHA RG18 28 E7
WSHM SO15 160 B2
Hardy Crs *WIMB* BH21 207 K5
Hardy Dr *FAWY* SO45 177 H7
Hardyfair Cl *RAND* SP11 94 F2
Hardy Gn *CWTH* RG45 43 K4
Hardy La *BSTK* RG21 6 C7
Hardy Rd *CHAM* PO6 185 L1
ELGH SO50 139 M7
FERN BH22 205 H7
PSTN BH14 224 D4
Hardys Fld *KSCL* RG20 248 C9
Harebell Cl *FHAM/PORC* PO16 11 J1
HTWY RG27 57 M1
Harebell Dr *NTHA* RG18 29 G8
Harebell Gdns *HTWY* RG27 57 M1
Harefield Ct *ROMY* SO51 131 H8
Harefield Rd *PTSW* SO17 147 J5
Hare La *NMIL/BTOS* BH25 219 K5
RWIN SO21 125 G8
WIMB BH21 337 L7
Haresfoot Cl *RCCH* PO18 173 K1
Hares Gn *LTDN* BH7 215 G8
Hare's La *HTWY* RG27 58 A1
Harestock Cl *FUFL* SO22 288 D11
Harestock Rd *FUFL* SO22 288 D12
HAV PO9 16 B1
Harewood Av *LTDN* BH7 226 F1
Harewood Cl *ELGH* SO50 134 A7
Harewood Crs *LTDN* BH7 226 F1
Harewood Dr *NTHA* RG18 28 E4
Harewood Gdns *LTDN* BH7 226 F1
Harewood Gn *LYMN* SO41 233 H4
Harewood Pl *LTDN* BH7 227 H2
Harfield Cl *HTWY* RG27 56 C7
Harford Cl *LYMN* SO41 221 H7
Harford Rd *BKME/WDN* BH12 212 C8
Harkness Dr *WVILLE* PO7 156 B8
Harkwood Dr *PLE* BH15 222 F4
Harland Crs *WSHM* SO15 146 D7
Harland Rd *SBNE* BH6 228 A4
Harlaxton Cl *ELGH* SO50 139 M3
Harlech Cl *DEAN* RG23 64 E7
Harlech Dr *CHFD* SO53 139 G4
Harlech Rd *BLKW* GU17 49 M4
Harlequin Gv *FHAM* PO15 10 B5
Harleston Rd *CHAM* PO6 168 D7
Harleston Vls *WIMB* BH21 207 K4
Harlington Wy *FLEETN* GU51 59 G8
Harlyn Rd *ROWN* SO16 145 M7
Harman Rd *LSOL/BMARY* PO13 182 C5
Harmsworth Rd *TADY* RG26 44 B4
Harness Cl *WHIT* RG2 238 B2
WIMB BH21 208 B2
Harold Cl *TOTT* SO40 158 D2
Harold Gdns *ALTN* GU34 107 G3
Harold Jackson Ter *BSTK* RG21 7 G7
Harold Rd *EMRTH* PO10 172 B2
ENEY PO4 21 M7
FHAM/STUB PO14 189 K1
HISD PO11 195 H6
HUNG RG17 31 J2
WSHM SO15 160 C1
Harpdon Pde *YTLY* GU46 48 F1
Harper's Rd *ASHV* GU12 74 C6
Harpton Cl *YTLY* GU46 48 F1
Harpway La *CHCH/BSGR* BH23 216 C2
The Harrage *ROMY* SO51 136 F1
Harrier Cl *HORN* PO8 156 A2
LSOL/BMARY PO13 189 M6
ROWN SO16 146 B2
Harrier Dr *WIMB* BH21 207 K6
Harriers Cl *CHCH/BSGR* BH23 217 K8
Harrier Wy *EPSF* GU31 121 G7
FAWY SO45 354 D2
Harriet Cl *FHAM/STUB* PO14 189 H2
Harrington Cl *NWBY* RG14 27 M7
Harris Av *HEND* SO30 149 J4
Harris Hl *KBH* RG22 92 D5
Harris La *HORN* PO8 322 B7
Harrison Av *BMTH* BH1 226 D2
Harrison Cl *CHCH/BSGR* BH23 216 C5
Harrison Rd *FHAM/PORC* PO16 11 G3
PTSW SO17 147 J5
Harrison Wy *FERN* BH22 205 G5
Harris Rd *LSOL/BMARY* PO13 182 C5
Harroway *WHCH* RG28 87 K3
Harroway La *RAND* SP11 95 J2
Harrow Cl *CHCH/BSGR* BH23 217 H1
Harrow Down *FUFL* SO22 122 D8
Harrowgate La *WVILLE* PO7 320 B12
Harrow La *PSF* GU32 120 D3
Harrow Rd *CHCH/BSGR* BH23 217 G1
SSEA PO5 21 L4
Harrow Wy *AND* SP10 4 A2
OVTN RG25 90 D1
RAND SP11 95 J2
The Harrow Wy *KBH* RG22 93 G3
Harry Barrow Cl *RGWD* BH24 203 J5
Hart Cl *FARN* GU14 50 A8
NMIL/BTOS BH25 218 F4
Hartford Bridge Flats
HTWY RG27 241 Q11
Hartford Ct *HTWY* RG27 57 L2
Hartford Ri *CBLY* GU15 50 F2
Hartford Rd *HTWY* RG27 57 L2
Hart Hl *FAWY* SO45 177 J7
Harthill Dro *RSAL* SP5 332 G3
Harting Cl *HORN* PO8 321 M8
Harting Down *EPSF* GU31 120 F6
Harting Gdns
FHAM/PORC PO16 167 J7
Harting Rd *SBNE* BH6 227 K1
Hartington Rd *GPORT* PO12 190 F2
SHAM SO14 23 K1
Hartland Ct *EMRTH* PO10 172 D5
Hartland Pl *FARN* GU14 61 G1
Hartland's Rd
FHAM/PORC PO16 11 H6
Hartley Av *PTSW* SO17 147 H6
Hartley Cl *BLKW* GU17 49 K3
ELGH SO50 141 G3
FAWY SO45 177 G7
Hartley Ct *ROWN* SO16 147 G4
Hartley Gdns *TADY* RG26 44 B5
Hartley La *HTWY* RG27 47 H6
Hartley Meadow *WHCH* RG28 87 K7
Hartley Rd *ELGH* SO50 141 G2
NEND PO2 184 D5
Hartleys *THLE* RG7 45 H4
Hartley Wk *FAWY* SO45 176 F7
Hartmead Rd *STHA* RG19 35 L1
Hart Plain Av *HORN* PO8 155 L6
Hartsbourne Dr *LTDN* BH7 215 H8
Harts Cl *WHIT* RG2 239 L6
Harts Farm Wy *HAV* PO9 16 A7
Harts Hill Rd *NTHA* RG18 29 G8
Hartshill Rd *TADY* RG26 249 R4
Harts La *KSCL* RG20 246 G6
Hartsleaf Cl *FLEETN* GU51 59 H8
Harts Leap Cl *SHST* GU47 43 J7
Harts Leap Rd *SHST* GU47 43 J8
Harts Wy *LYMN* SO41 220 D7
Hartswood *CHIN* RG24 54 A6
The Hart *FNM* GU9 12 E3
Hartwell Rd *HSEA* PO3 185 H4
Hartwood Gdns *HORN* PO8 155 L6
Harvest Cl *FUFL* SO22 122 D8
YTLY GU46 48 D4
Harvest Crs *FLEETN* GU51 59 K3
Harvest Dr *WWKG* RG41 239 P1
Harvester Dr *FHAM* PO15 181 H3
Harvester Wy *LYMN* SO41 221 K2
Harvest Gn *NWBY* RG14 18 A8
Harvesting La *PSF* GU32 314 E10
Harvest La *RSAL* SP5 324 E4
Harvest Rd *CHFD* SO53 138 F2
WVILLE PO7 154 E4
Harvest Wy *CHIN* RG24 54 B8
Harvey Ct *FAWY* SO45 354 G6

Harvey Crs HLER SO31 179 M2
Harvey Gdns FAWY SO45 177 H5
Harvey Pl AND SP10 96 F4
Harvey Rd BOSC BH5 227 G3
ELGH SO50 140 E1
FARN GU14 60 C3
WIMB BH21 207 M7
Harveys Fld OVTN RG25 89 J4
Harwell Rd CFDH BH17 223 K1
Harwich Rd CHAM PO6 168 D7
Harwood Cl
LSOL/BMARY PO13 182 C4
TOTT SO40 144 D8
Harwood Pl WINC SO23 289 J8
Harwood Ri KSCL RG20 246 B3
Harwood Rd
LSOL/BMARY PO13 182 C5
Haselbury Rd TOTT SO40 158 F1
Haselfoot Gdns WEND SO18 148 E5
Haselworth Dr GPORT PO12 191 H7
Haskells Cl LYND SO43 345 J4
Haskells Rd BKME/WDN BH12 224 B1
Haslar Br GPORT PO12 15 L6
Haslar Crs WVILLE PO7 155 J6
Haslar Rd GPORT PO12 15 J8
Hasle Dr HASM GU27 118 B7
Haslemere Av
CHCH/BSGR BH23 217 M8
Haslemere Cl FRIM GU16 51 L5
Haslemere Gdns HISD PO11 195 M6
Haslemere Pl
CHCH/BSGR BH23 218 A8
Haslemere Rd EMRTH PO10 172 D4
ENEY PO4 192 F6
LIPH GU30 116 D4
Hasler Rd CFDH BH17 211 J6
Haslop Rd WIMB BH21 207 M1
The Hassocks WVILLE PO7 170 A1
Hastards La ALTN GU34 295 L8
Hasted Dr NARL SO24 291 L12
Haste Hl HASM GU27 118 D7
Haste Hill Top HASM GU27 * 118 D7
Hastings Av GPORT PO12 182 F8
Hastings Cl FRIM GU16 62 A1
KBH RG22 64 D7
Hastings Rd CFDH BH17 211 H6
CHAR BH8 214 F6
Hatchbury La RAND SP11 243 Q10
Hatch Ct HAV PO9 170 C1
Hatchers La RWIN SO21 125 M7
The Hatches FNM GU9 12 B8
FRIM GU16 61 M2
Hatchet Cl FBDG SP6 332 F5
Hatchet La BROC SO42 352 G11
RAND SP11 83 J3
Hatchetts Dr HASM GU27 117 J2
Hatchgate Cl NTHA RG18 28 E6
Hatch La CHIN RG24 66 D3
LISS GU33 309 J8
Hatchley La RWIN SO21 310 B10
Hatch Md HEND SO30 148 C2
Hatch Pond La CFDH BH17 211 J8
Hatch Pond Rd CFDH BH17 211 J8
Hatch Ride CWTH RG45 43 K1
Hatch Rw KBH RG22 92 E6
Hatchwarren Gdns KBH RG22 93 G5
Hatchwarren La KBH RG22 92 E5
Hatch Warren La KBH RG22 93 G5
Hatfield Ct CBLY GU15 50 D3
NMIL/BTOS BH25 218 E5
Hatfield Gdns FARN GU14 61 L5
LTDN BH7 215 H8
Hatfield Rd ENEY PO4 193 G5
Hathaway Cl ELGH SO50 134 B8
Hathaway Gdns CHIN RG24 65 L4
WVILLE PO7 156 B7
Hathaway Rd SBNE BH6 227 K4
Hatherden Av PSTN BH14 223 M3
Hatherden Ct AND SP10 * 5 J5
Hatherell Cl HEND SO30 148 D3
Hatherley Crs
FHAM/PORC PO16 183 H1
Hatherley Dr
FHAM/PORC PO16 167 H8
Hatherley Rd CHAM PO6 168 A7
FUFL SO22 24 D3
Hatherwood YTLY GU46 * 49 H3
Hatley Rd WEND SO18 148 B4
Hattem Pl AND SP10 96 B2
Hattingley Rd ALTN GU34 292 G1
Hatt La ROMY SO51 298 G10
Haughurst Hl STHA RG19 249 M4
Havant Farm Cl HAV PO9 16 F1
Havant Rd CHAM PO6 168 F8
HAV PO9 17 J6
HISD PO11 187 G8
HORN PO8 156 D3
NEND PO2 184 D7
Havant St PSEA PO1 20 C3
Havelock Rd
BKME/WDN BH12 225 G3
HLER SO31 179 J3
SHAM SO14 22 E2
SSEA PO5 21 K5
Havelock Wy
CHCH/BSGR BH23 217 K6
Haven Crs FHAM/STUB PO14 188 F3
Havendale HEND SO30 149 K7
Haven Gdns NMIL/BTOS BH25 219 H6
Haven Rd CCLF BH13 237 K2
HISD PO11 195 L7
WIMB BH21 210 C2
Havenstone Wy WEND SO18 147 K4
The Haven ELGH SO50 134 B7
ENEY PO4 193 H3
GPORT PO12 14 E9
HEND SO30 * 149 H8
HUNG RG17 31 G2
H Av FAWY SO45 354 H2
Haven Wy FNM GU9 77 H4
Haverstock Rd
MOOR/WNTN BH9 214 B6
Haviland Rd BMTH BH1 226 F3
WIMB BH21 209 G1
Haviland Rd East LTDN BH7 226 F3
Haviland Rd West BMTH BH1 226 E4
Havisham Rd NEND PO2 * 192 D1
Hawden Rd BWD BH11 213 G7
Haweswater Cl BOR GU35 110 F7
Haweswater Ct ASHV GU12 * 73 M4
Hawfinch Cl ROWN SO16 146 B2
Hawkchurch Gdns CFDH BH17 211 L6
Hawk Cl FHAM/STUB PO14 189 H2
KBH RG22 92 B4
WIMB BH21 208 A1
Hawke Cl AND SP10 96 F3
Hawker Cl WIMB BH21 207 M7
Hawker Rd ASHV GU12 73 M3
Hawkers Cl TOTT SO40 144 E7
Hawkes Cl HTWY RG27 57 L1
Hawke St PSEA PO1 20 C2
Hawkeswood Rd WEND SO18 161 J1
Hawkewood Av WVILLE PO7 155 K6
Hawkfield La BSTK RG21 6 D7
Hawkhill FAWY SO45 176 C4
Hawkhurst Cl ITCH SO19 162 A3
Hawkins Cl RGWD BH24 203 L3
Hawkins Gv FLEETN GU51 70 F2
Hawkins Rd BKME/WDN BH12 212 F7
LSOL/BMARY PO13 182 D6
Hawkins Wy FLEETS GU52 59 L8
Hawkley Cl HAV PO9 170 E2
Hawkley Dr TADY RG26 44 C5
Hawkley Gn ITCH SO19 161 M8
Hawkley Rd LISS GU33 307 R5
Hawkshaw Cl LIPH GU30 116 D4
Hawkswood Av FRIM GU16 51 H6
Hawkwell FHAM/PORC PO16 166 F8
FLEETS GU52 71 K4
Hawkwood Rd BOSC BH5 226 E4
Hawley Gn BLKW GU17 50 A5
Hawley Gv BLKW GU17 50 A6
Hawley La FARN GU14 50 D8
Hawley Rd BLKW GU17 50 B5
Haworth Cl CHCH/BSGR BH23 216 A7
Hawswater Cl ROWN SO16 145 M7
Hawthorn Cl ASHV GU12 73 L8
ELGH SO50 141 J2
FHAM/PORC PO16 167 H7
HEND SO30 149 K6
NARL SO24 291 M11
NMIL/BTOS BH25 219 J4
RWIN SO21 135 G4
RWIN SO21 275 P10
Hawthorn Ct EPSF GU31 121 G6
FARN GU14 61 J8
Hawthorn Crs CHAM PO6 185 G2
Hawthorn Dr CFDH BH17 210 F7
LYMN SO41 350 F10
Hawthorne Cl NTHA RG18 28 F7
RAND SP11 269 P4
Hawthorne Crs BLKW GU17 50 A4
Hawthorne Gv HISD PO11 195 G4
Hawthorne Rd TOTT SO40 144 D8
Hawthorn La ALTN GU34 293 P8
HLER SO31 163 L7
RFNM GU10 109 M1
Hawthorn Ri HTWY RG27 56 D6
Hawthorn Rd ALTN GU34 293 M8
CHCH/BSGR BH23 216 E6
FAWY SO45 176 F5
FRIM GU16 51 H6
HORN PO8 321 L11
MOOR/WNTN BH9 213 M8
NTID SP9 266 F1
NWBY RG14 18 E1
PTSW SO17 147 G6
WVILLE PO7 154 D4
Hawthorns ALTN GU34 106 E3
The Hawthorns BPWT SO32 * 143 G3
CHCH/BSGR BH23 228 F2
ELGH SO50 139 L7
TADY RG26 249 Q4
TOTT SO40 160 A7
Hawthorn Wy DEAN RG23 64 E6
Hayburn Rd ROWN SO16 145 K6
Haydn Cl WINC SO23 288 H8
Haydn Rd KBH RG22 92 F4
Haydock Cl ALTN GU34 106 F6
TOTT SO40 144 C8
Haydock Ms WVILLE PO7 156 B7
Haydon Rd CCLF BH13 225 H7
Hay Down La RAND SP11 94 A7
Hayes Av LTDN BH7 226 E2
Hayes Cl FHAM PO15 181 K1
STOK SO20 299 P2
WIMB BH21 208 A4
Hayes La WIMB BH21 208 B4
WWKG RG41 239 Q4
Hayes Md FAWY SO45 354 D3
Hayeswood Rd WIMB BH21 208 A2
Hayle Rd WEND SO18 148 B2
Hayley Cl FAWY SO45 176 F8
Hayley La ODIM RG29 257 R3
Hayling Av HSEA PO3 193 H1
Hayling Billy Coastal Pth
HISD PO11 194 E1
Hayling Cl FHAM/STUB PO14 181 K4
GPORT PO12 183 J8
Haymoor Rd PLE BH15 224 A1
Haynes Av PLE BH15 223 K4
Haynes Wy FAWY SO45 176 E7
Haysoms Cl NMIL/BTOS BH25 219 H7
Haysoms Dr NWBY RG14 34 B5
Hay St PSEA PO1 20 E2
Hayter Gdns ROMY SO51 131 G8
Hayters Wy FBDG SP6 196 C6
Hayward Cl TOTT SO40 158 D1
Hayward Ct FAWY SO45 354 D3
Haywards Crs VWD BH31 201 G3
Haywarden Pl HTWY RG27 57 M1
Haywards Farm Cl VWD BH31 201 G3
Haywards La WIMB BH21 206 C8
The Haywards NTHA RG18 28 F8
Hayward Wy VWD BH31 200 F3
Haywood Dr FLEETS GU52 71 J1
Hazel Av FARN GU14 60 F6
Hazelbank EWKG RG40 239 R10
Hazelbank Cl EPSF GU31 120 F5
LIPH GU30 116 D4
Hazel Cl AND SP10 4 B9
CHCH/BSGR BH23 217 J7
CHFD SO53 133 J6
DEAN RG23 91 K3
FBDG SP6 196 C7
RWIN SO21 135 G3
Hazelcombe OVTN RG25 89 K5
Hazel Coppice HTWY RG27 56 D6
Hazeldean Dr HAV PO9 157 H7
Hazeldene CHIN RG24 54 B6
Hazeldene Rd LIPH GU30 113 K8
Hazeldown Cl ROWN SO16 145 L3
Hazel Dr FERN BH22 204 F8
Hazeleigh Av ITCH SO19 161 L6
Hazeley Cl HTWY RG27 57 L1
Hazeley Rd RWIN SO21 125 G6
Hazel Farm Rd TOTT SO40 158 C1
Hazel Gn TADY RG26 249 P3
Hazel Gv FUFL SO22 122 D7
GSHT GU26 115 L7
HLER SO31 180 B2
NTHA RG18 28 F7
TOTT SO40 341 R9
Hazelgrove HORN PO8 321 L7
Hazelholt Dr HAV PO9 16 A1
Hazell Av NBNE BH10 213 H6
Hazell Rd FNM GU9 12 A4
Hazel Rd ALTN GU34 293 N5
ASHV GU12 260 G1
FRIM GU16 62 A6
HORN PO8 321 L7
ITCH SO19 161 K5
LYMN SO41 221 G4
Hazelton Cl LTDN BH7 215 G8
Hazelwood CHIN RG24 * 54 A4
FHAM/STUB PO14 181 H7
Hazelwood Av HAV PO9 170 B5
NMIL/BTOS BH25 218 E4
Hazelwood Cl DEAN RG23 64 F5
Hazelwood Dr DEAN RG23 64 F5
VWD BH31 201 K4
Hazelwood Rd WEND SO18 148 A3
Hazely Cl HTWY RG27 57 L1
Hazlebury Rd CFDH BH17 223 G1
Hazlemere Dr RGWD BH24 346 E1
Hazleton Int HORN PO8 * 156 C2
Hazleton Wy HORN PO8 156 B3
Hazlewood MFD/CHID GU8 261 J12
Head Down EPSF GU31 120 F6
Headington Cl KBH RG22 92 F4
Headland Dr HLER SO31 164 A8
Headley Cl
LSOL/BMARY PO13 * 189 M6
NARL SO24 291 M12
Headley Flds BOR GU35 111 L8
Headley Hill Rd BOR GU35 111 M7
Headley La LIPH GU30 113 L2
Headley Rd BOR GU35 111 J7
GSHT GU26 114 F4
LIPH GU30 116 A2
Headmore La ALTN GU34 293 Q7
Headon Vw PSF GU32 313 L3
Heads Farm Cl NBNE BH10 213 L3
Heads La HUNG RG17 31 G7
NBNE BH10 213 L3
Headswell Av NBNE BH10 213 L4
Headswell Crs NBNE BH10 213 L4
Headswell Gdns NBNE BH10 213 L4
Heanor Cl NBNE BH10 213 J6
Heardman Cl STHA RG19 35 M2
Hearmon Cl YTLY GU46 48 F2
Hearne Gdns BPWT SO32 318 A11
Hearn V BOR GU35 114 A1
Hearsey Gdns BLKW GU17 49 L2
Heath Av PLE BH15 223 K1
Heath Cl ELGH SO50 141 K3
FNM GU9 77 G1
GSHT GU26 115 J1
HORN PO8 156 B1
WIMB BH21 208 B1
Heathcote Cl ASHV GU12 * 74 A5
Heathcote Pl RWIN SO21 133 H1
Heathcote Rd ASHV GU12 74 B5
BMTH BH1 226 F4
BOR GU35 113 G1
CBLY GU15 50 F3
CHFD SO53 139 K2
NEND PO2 184 F7
Heath Cots GSHT GU26 * 115 J2
Heath End Farm TADY RG26 249 Q3
Heath End Rd TADY RG26 249 Q3
Heathen St BPWT SO32 142 B8
Heatherbank Rd WBNE BH4 225 J5
Heatherbrae Gdns NBAD SO52 137 M4
Heatherbrae La UPTN BH16 222 B2
Heather Cha ELGH SO50 141 G2
Heather Cl ALDT GU11 2 A4
ASHV GU12 74 B3
BOR GU35 112 D3
CHAR BH8 214 D4
CHCH/BSGR BH23 218 A7
EWKG RG40 42 A1
FNM GU9 78 D2
LSOL/BMARY PO13 182 B6
LYMN SO41 220 A5
RCCH PO18 173 M3
RGWD BH24 346 E1
TOTT SO40 158 E1
WIMB BH21 210 E2
WVILLE PO7 169 M2
Heather Ct WEND SO18 148 C5
Heatherdale Rd CBLY GU15 50 E4
Heatherdeane Rd PTSW SO17 147 G6
Heatherdell UPTN BH16 222 B2
Heatherden Cl WHIT RG2 238 C1
Heatherdene Av CWTH RG45 43 G4
Heatherdene Rd CHFD SO53 133 L7
Heatherdown Rd FERN BH22 205 J7
Heatherdown Wy FERN BH22 205 J7
Heather Dr AND SP10 4 F3
BOR GU35 111 H7
FERN BH22 209 K1
FLEETS GU52 71 H3
NTHA RG18 28 F7
TADY RG26 249 R2
Heatherfield EPSF GU31 315 P11
Heather Gdns FHAM PO15 181 K1
NWBY RG14 33 L5
Heather Gv HTWY RG27 57 L1
Heatherlands Ri
BKME/WDN BH12 224 D3
Heatherlands Rd ROWN SO16 138 F8
Heather La HTWY RG27 67 L3
Heatherlea Rd SBNE BH6 227 K4
Heatherley Cl CBLY GU15 50 D3
Heatherley Rd CBLY GU15 50 D3
Heather Md FRIM GU16 51 H6
Heathermount Dr CWTH RG45 43 H2
Heather Rd EPSF GU31 121 G6
FAWY SO45 354 H6
NBNE BH10 213 K5
Heather Row La HTWY RG27 67 M3
Heatherstone Av FAWY SO45 176 F8
Heatherton Ms EMRTH PO10 171 M5
Heatherview Cl NBAD SO52 137 M3
Heather View Rd
BKME/WDN BH12 224 F1
Heather Wk CHOB/PIR GU24 63 K2
Heatherway CWTH RG45 43 J3
Heather Wy FERN BH22 209 K1
GSHT GU26 115 M4
KBH RG22 92 C5
Heath Farm Cl FERN BH22 209 J5
Heath Farm Rd FERN BH22 209 J5
Heath Farm Wy FERN BH22 209 J5
Heathfield FAWY SO45 176 F6
Heathfield Av
BKME/WDN BH12 213 G8
FHAM/STUB PO14 181 K3
Heathfield Cl ITCH SO19 162 B1
Heathfield Ct FLEETN GU51 71 G1
Heathfield Rd CHFD SO53 133 J6
EPSF GU31 121 G6
FERN BH22 205 J7
ITCH SO19 162 B1
KBH RG22 92 A5
NEND PO2 184 D8
Heathfields TADY RG26 249 Q3
Heathfield Wy FERN BH22 205 H7
Heath Gdns HLER SO31 162 D5
Heath Green La ALTN GU34 292 E1
Heath Hl RFNM GU10 111 L1
Heath Hill Rd North
CWTH RG45 43 K3
Heath Hill Rd South
CWTH RG45 43 K3
Heath House Cl HEND SO30 149 H8
Heath House Gdns
HEND SO30 149 H8
Heathhouse La HEND SO30 149 H8
Heathlands KSCL RG20 246 C4
Heathlands Av FERN BH22 209 K6
Heathlands Cl
CHCH/BSGR BH23 216 C5
CHFD SO53 133 J8
VWD BH31 201 J2
Heathlands Rd CHFD SO53 133 J8
Heathland St ALDT GU11 2 F3
Heath La BROC SO42 353 J9
FNM GU9 77 G1
MARL SN8 243 P1
NTHA RG18 28 E7
RFNM GU10 259 Q2
Heath Lawns FHAM PO15 181 K3
Heathman St STOK SO20 284 C2
Heath Ride CWTH RG45 42 F4
EWKG RG40 42 D2
Heath Ri CBLY GU15 50 F3
Heath Rd CHCH/BSGR BH23 218 B7
EPSF GU31 120 E6
HASM GU27 117 K3
HLER SO31 179 M1
ITCH SO19 148 A7
LYMN SO41 219 M5
NBAD SO52 138 A5
RGWD BH24 205 M4
TADY RG26 44 E3
WHAM PO17 318 F12
Heath Rd East EPSF GU31 120 F7
Heath Rd North HLER SO31 179 M1
Heath Rd South HLER SO31 179 M1
Heath Rd West
CHCH/BSGR BH23 346 E6
EPSF GU31 120 E7
Heathrow Copse TADY RG26 249 P4
Heathside La GSHT GU26 115 K2
Heathside Pk CBLY GU15 51 L1
Heathside Wy HTWY RG27 57 L1
The Heath WVILLE PO7 155 G4
Heath V AND SP10 5 J7
Heathvale Bridge Rd
ASHV GU12 74 A2
Heathview HTWY RG27 56 E6
Heathway CBLY GU15 50 F3
Heathway Cl CBLY GU15 50 F3
Heathwood Av
NMIL/BTOS BH25 218 E8
Heathwood Cl YTLY GU46 48 F1
Heathwood Rd
MOOR/WNTN BH9 213 L8
Heathy Cl NMIL/BTOS BH25 218 F8
Heathyfields Rd FNM GU9 76 D2
Heaton Rd GPORT PO12 190 F1
NBNE BH10 213 H6
Heavytree Rd PSTN BH14 224 B4
Hebden Cl STHA RG19 35 J3
Hebrides Cl FHAM/STUB PO14 189 H1
Heckfield Cl HAV PO9 171 H3
Heckford La PLE BH15 223 K4
Heckford Rd PLE BH15 223 K4
WIMB BH21 210 C3
Hector Cl WVILLE PO7 169 L6
Hector Rd FHAM/STUB PO14 182 A3
Heddon Wk FARN GU14 61 G1
Hedera Rd HLER SO31 179 M1
Hedgecroft YTLY GU46 * 48 D2
Hedge End Rd AND SP10 5 L8
Hedgehog La HASM GU27 118 B7
Hedgerley NMIL/BTOS BH25 219 H8
Hedgerow Cl ROWN SO16 145 L2
Hedgerow Dr WEND SO18 148 B3
Hedgerow Gdns EMRTH PO10 171 M5
The Hedgerows CHIN RG24 54 C8
Hedges Cl NTID SP9 266 D9
The Hedges ELGH SO50 * 141 K6
Hedgeway NWBY RG14 19 K1
Hedley Cl FAWY SO45 354 H7
Hedley Gdns HEND SO30 149 H1
Heenan Cl FRIM GU16 61 L1
Heidelberg Rd ENEY PO4 192 F4
Heights Ap UPTN BH16 222 C1
Heights Rd UPTN BH16 210 C8
The Heights FHAM/PORC PO16 11 L3
HEND SO30 149 G6
Hei-lin Wy RAND SP11 265 L10
Heinz Burt Cl ELGH SO50 139 M5
Hele Cl BSTK RG21 93 J2
Helena Rd ENEY PO4 192 F6
Helen Ct FARN GU14 61 H4
Helford Ct AND SP10 96 E2
Helford Gdns WEND SO18 148 B2
Helksham Cl SHST GU47 43 M7
Hellyer Rd ENEY PO4 193 G5
Helm Cl LSOL/BMARY PO13 190 D2
Helsby Cl FHAM/STUB PO14 10 A8
Helsted Cl GPORT PO12 190 E4
Helston Dr EMRTH PO10 171 L5
Helston Rd CHAM PO6 167 M7
Helvellyn Rd ROWN SO16 145 M8
Helyar Rd CHAR BH8 214 F6
Hemdean Gdns HEND SO30 148 D3
Hemlock Rd HORN PO8 155 K4
Hemlock Wy CHFD SO53 138 F3
Hemming Cl TOTT SO40 158 E2
Hemmingway Gdns
FHAM PO15 164 C4
Hempland La ALTN GU34 306 A8
Hempsted Rd CHAM PO6 168 B7
Hemsley Wk HORN PO8 155 M4
Henbury Cl CFDH BH17 212 A6
WIMB BH21 210 D2
Henbury Ri WIMB BH21 210 D2
Henbury View Rd WIMB BH21 210 D2
Henderson Rd ENEY PO4 193 H5
Hendford Rd NBNE BH10 213 K6
Hendon Rd BOR GU35 112 F2
Hendren Sq AND SP10 96 D2
Hendy Cl SSEA PO5 21 J7
Henery St GPORT PO12 * 15 H4
Hengest Cl AND SP10 95 M1
Hengistbury Rd
NMIL/BTOS BH25 218 E8
SBNE BH6 227 M5
Hengist Pk SBNE BH6 * 228 B4
Hengist Rd BMTH BH1 226 D4
Henley Cl FARN GU14 50 A8
Henley Dr FRIM GU16 61 L1
Henley Gdns FHAM PO15 165 K8
LTDN BH7 227 G1
YTLY GU46 48 F3
Henley Ga CHOB/PIR GU24 63 J8
Henley Pk RGUW GU3 * 75 K2
Henley Rd ENEY PO4 192 F5
Henning's Park Rd PLE BH15 223 K3
Henry Cl FAWY SO45 354 D2
Henry Rd ELGH SO50 134 D8
WSHM SO15 160 C1
The Henrys NTHA RG18 28 F8
Henry St WSHM SO15 * 160 F2
Henshaw Crs NWBY RG14 33 K4
Henstead Rd WSHM SO15 160 F2
Hensting La RWIN SO21 135 J5
Henty Rd ROWN SO16 146 A8
Henville Cl LSOL/BMARY PO13 182 D8
Henville Rd CHAR BH8 9 L1
Henwick Cl NTHA RG18 28 C6
Henwick La NTHA RG18 28 C8
Henwood Down EPSF GU31 120 E6
Hepplewhite Cl TADY RG26 249 Q3
Hepplewhite Dr KBH RG22 92 C5
Hepworth Cl AND SP10 5 H2
ITCH SO19 162 C2
Hepworth Cft SHST GU47 50 A2
Herald Rd HEND SO30 149 H3
Herbert Av BKME/WDN BH12 212 C8
Herberton Rd SBNE BH6 227 J3
Herbert Rd ENEY PO4 21 L9
FLEETN GU51 59 G7
GPORT PO12 14 B3
NMIL/BTOS BH25 219 H5
RSAL SP5 332 F2
WBNE BH4 225 H6
Herbert St PSEA PO1 192 C1
Herbert Walker Av WSHM SO15 22 E5
Herbs End FARN GU14 60 C3
Hercules Rd PLE BH15 222 D5
Hercules St NEND PO2 184 D8
Hereford Cl ODIM RG29 68 E6
Hereford Ct
LSOL/BMARY PO13 * 190 C2
Hereford La FNM GU9 76 F2
Hereford Md FLEETN GU51 59 K4
Hereford Rd DEAN RG23 64 E7
SSEA PO5 21 J7
Hereward Cl ROMY SO51 137 H1
Herewood Cl NWBY RG14 18 C1
Heriard Pl DEAN RG23 92 C7
Heritage Gdns
FHAM/PORC PO16 183 G1
Heritage Pk DEAN RG23 92 D7
Heritage Vw DEAN RG23 92 D7
Heritage Wy GPORT PO12 183 J8
Hermes Cl FLEETN GU51 59 L7
Hermes Ct GPORT PO12 * 183 J8
Hermes Rd LSOL/BMARY PO13 189 K5
Hermitage Cl ALTN GU34 106 E6
BPWT SO32 * 143 G4
FARN GU14 61 K7
FRIM GU16 51 H7
HAV PO9 170 E4
WIMB BH21 * 201 G8
Hermitage Rd NTHA RG18 28 D2
PSTN BH14 224 A2
Herm Rd BKME/WDN BH12 212 C7
Herne Rd CHAM PO6 168 E8
EPSF GU31 120 E6
Heroes Wk WHIT RG2 238 B1
Heron Cl ALTN GU34 106 F2
ENEY PO4 193 H3
FLEETS GU52 71 L3
FRIM GU16 61 M4
LYMN SO41 350 F10
Heron Court Rd
MOOR/WNTN BH9 226 A1
Herondale HASM GU27 117 L2
Heron Dr WIMB BH21 208 A1
Heron La ROMY SO51 130 D2
Heron Pk CHIN RG24 54 B7
Heron Quay EMRTH PO10 172 A7
Herons Cl FHAM/STUB PO14 181 J8
Heron Sq ELGH SO50 139 L7
Herons Ri AND SP10 5 K9
Herons Wy CHOB/PIR GU24 63 K2
Heron Wy KBH RG22 92 C4
LSOL/BMARY PO13 182 A5
STHA RG19 35 H1
THLE RG7 38 B1
Heron Wood Rd ASHV GU12 3 M7
Herretts Gdns ASHV GU12 3 M5
Herrett St ASHV GU12 3 L6
Herriard Wy TADY RG26 44 C5
Herrick Cl FRIM GU16 51 L5
ITCH SO19 148 D8
Herridge Cl TADY RG26 46 D6
Herriot Ct YTLY GU46 48 E4
Herriott Cl HORN PO8 156 A3
Herstone Cl CFDH BH17 211 M7
Hertford Cl FBDG SP6 197 H1
Hertford Pl PSEA PO1 192 D1
Hertsfield FHAM/STUB PO14 164 C8
Hesketh Cl RGWD BH24 202 C7
Hester Rd ENEY PO4 193 H4
Hesters Vw ODIM RG29 258 B6
Hestia Cl ROMY SO51 131 J8
Heston Cl CHCH/BSGR BH23 215 K4
Heston Wy FERN BH22 204 F5
Hewett Cl FHAM/STUB PO14 180 F5
Hewett Rd FHAM/STUB PO14 180 F5
NEND PO2 184 E6
Hewetts Ri HLER SO31 179 J4
Hewitt Cl GPORT PO12 191 G1
Hewitt Rd PLE BH15 222 E4
Hewitt's Rd WSHM SO15 22 B2
Hewshott Gv LIPH GU30 116 E3
Hewshott La LIPH GU30 116 D3
The Hexagon AND SP10 4 B8
Hexham Cl SHST GU47 43 M6
Heyes Dr ITCH SO19 162 C1
Heysham Rd BDST BH18 211 G5
WSHM SO15 146 B8
Heyshott Rd ENEY PO4 192 F4
Heytesbury Rd SBNE BH6 227 K3
Heyward Rd ENEY PO4 21 L5
Heywood Gn ITCH SO19 148 E7
Hibberds Fld WIMB BH21 336 F5
Hibberd Wy NBNE BH10 213 K7
Hibbs Cl UPTN BH16 222 C1
Hibiscus Crs AND SP10 95 L5
Hibiscus Gv BOR GU35 113 G2
Hickes Cl BWD BH11 212 F4
Hickory Cl UPTN BH16 210 A8
Hickory Dr FUFL SO22 288 C12
Hickory Gdns HEND SO30 148 D1
Hicks Cl TADY RG26 44 C4
Hicks La BLKW GU17 49 K3
Hides Cl WHCH RG28 87 L8
Highams Cl KSCL RG20 248 E10
Highbank Av WVILLE PO7 169 H5
Highbank Gdns FBDG SP6 197 H3
High Beeches FRIM GU16 50 F6
High Beech Gdns AND SP10 5 L7
Highbridge Rd ELGH SO50 134 D5
PSTN BH14 224 C5
Highbury Cl ELGH SO50 141 J3
NMIL/BTOS BH25 219 H5
Highbury Crs CBLY GU15 51 J1
Highbury Gv CHAM PO6 185 G2
HASM GU27 118 C4
Highbury Rd RAND SP11 95 M8
Highbury St PSEA PO1 20 D5
Highbury Wy CHAM PO6 184 F2
Highclere Av HAV PO9 170 D4
Highclere Dr CBLY GU15 51 J1
Highclere Rd ASHV GU12 3 L6
ROWN SO16 146 D5
Highclere Wy CHFD SO53 139 G5
Highcliff Av SHAM SO14 147 G8
Highcliffe Dr ELGH SO50 134 A5
Highcliffe Rd
CHCH/BSGR BH23 217 G8
GPORT PO12 14 B5
WINC SO23 25 J8
Highcroft La HORN PO8 321 L12
High Cross PSF GU32 307 J10
High Cross La PSF GU32 306 G11
Highcrown St PTSW SO17 147 G6
Highdown FLEETN GU51 59 J6
Highdowns KBH RG22 92 E6
High Dr KBH RG22 92 E2
LSOL/BMARY PO13 182 C7
Higher Blandford Rd
BDST BH18 211 G3
WIMB BH21 210 F2
Highercombe Rd HASM GU27 118 E4
Higher Md CHIN RG24 66 B1
Higher Merley La WIMB BH21 206 E8
Highfield LYMN SO41 221 K5
RWIN SO21 125 G7
Highfield Av ALDT GU11 2 F7
FHAM/STUB PO14 10 C8
LYMN SO41 221 J5
NWBY RG14 18 E5
PTSW SO17 146 F5
RGWD BH24 203 J4
RWIN SO21 125 G7

WVILLE PO7 155 M7
Highfield Cha BSTK RG21 6 B5
Highfield Cl ALDT GU11 3 G7
CHFD SO53 139 K2
FARN GU14 60 F4
FNM GU9 78 F1
LYMN SO41 350 F10
PTSW SO17 147 G6
WIMB BH21 210 E3
WVILLE PO7 155 M7
Highfield Crs GSHT GU26 115 L4
PTSW SO17 147 H6
RSAL SP5 282 F10
Highfield Dr RGWD BH24 203 J3
Highfield Gdns ALDT GU11 2 F7
LISS GU33 308 H8
LYMN SO41 350 F10
Highfield La LIPH GU30 116 D6
MFD/CHID GU8 263 P11
PTSW SO17 147 G6
RGUW GU3 261 L5
RSAL SP5 332 F3
Highfield Pth FARN GU14 60 F4
Highfield Rd CHFD SO53 139 L2
FARN GU14 60 F4
FERN BH22 204 F4
GPORT PO12 190 F2
LYMN SO41 221 J4
MOOR/WNTN BH9 213 L6
NWBY RG14 18 D9
PSEA PO1 21 K2
PSF GU32 120 D5
PTSW SO17 146 F7
RGWD BH24 203 J4
WIMB BH21 210 E3
Highfields OVTN RG25 89 K5
Highfield Ter FUFL SO22 24 D6
High Firs Gdns ROMY SO51 137 J1
High Firs Rd ITCH SO19 148 B7
ROMY SO51 131 J8
Highgate La FARN GU14 61 J3
Highgate Rd HSEA PO3 185 G7
Highgrove FARN GU14 61 H1
Highgrove Cl TOTT SO40 158 D3
Highgrove Rd HSEA PO3 185 H8
High Howe Cl BWD BH11 212 E4
High Howe Gdns BWD BH11 212 E4
High Howe La BWD BH11 212 E5
Highland Av CHCH/BSGR BH23 218 B7
Highland Cl EMRTH PO10 171 L8
Highland Dr DEAN RG23 91 J2
FLEETN GU51 59 K5
Highland Rd ASHV GU12 3 L3
EMRTH PO10 171 L7
ENEY PO4 192 F5
PSTN BH14 224 B3
WIMB BH21 207 K3
Highlands Av WWKG RG41 239 Q3
Highlands Cl FAWY SO45 177 G6
FNM GU9 78 F1
NBAD SO52 137 L3
Highlands Crs NBNE BH10 213 J4
Highlands Rd AND SP10 5 M6
CHAM PO6 169 K8
FHAM PO15 181 H4
FNM GU9 77 G1
KBH RG22 92 C1
NMIL/BTOS BH25 219 H8
Highland St ENEY PO4 193 G6
Highlands Wy FAWY SO45 176 F6
RSAL SP5 127 H4
Highland Ter ENEY PO4 192 F5
Highland View Cl WIMB BH21 207 K3
High La HASM GU27 118 C4
High Lawn Wy HAV PO9 170 E3
High Md FERN BH22 209 G6
FHAM PO15 10 A1
High Mead La FERN BH22 209 G7
High Meadow ITCH SO19 148 C6
Highmoor Cl WIMB BH21 * 210 D3
Highmoor Rd BWD BH11 213 G7
PSTN BH14 224 C5
WIMB BH21 210 D3
Highmoors CHIN RG24 54 A5
Highmount Cl WINC SO23 25 K7
Highnam Gdns HLER SO31 163 M8
High Oaks Cl HLER SO31 180 A1
High Oaks Gdns BWD BH11 212 E4
High Park Rd BDST BH18 210 E4
FNM GU9 12 F2
Highpath Wy CHIN RG24 64 E5
High Pitfold GSHT GU26 115 K7
Highridge ALTN GU34 106 D6
High Ridge Crs
NMIL/BTOS BH25 219 J6
High Rd ELGH SO50 147 K3
RSAL SP5 324 B4
High St ALDT GU11 2 E2
ALTN GU34 106 F5
ALTN GU34 293 K1
AND SP10 5 J5
ASHV GU12 3 H4
BOR GU35 111 L7
BOR GU35 112 F1
BPWT SO32 143 J5
BPWT SO32 151 L5
BPWT SO32 312 E12
BPWT SO32 318 H3
BPWT SO32 318 H9
BROC SO42 353 M8
CBLY GU15 50 F2
CHAM PO6 184 F1
CHCH/BSGR BH23 228 B2
CWTH RG45 43 L4
ELGH SO50 140 A3
EMRTH PO10 171 M8
EPSF GU31 120 D6
EPSF GU31 315 P11
FARN GU14 61 J8
FAWY SO45 177 G3
FBDG SP6 197 H3
FBDG SP6 330 C11
FBDG SP6 332 A9
FHAM/PORC PO16 11 J4
FHAM/STUB PO14 180 F4
GPORT PO12 15 K4
HASM GU27 118 D5
HEND SO30 148 D3
HEND SO30 150 A5
HLER SO31 163 H5
HTWY RG27 57 M2
HUNG RG17 31 H1
LSOL/BMARY PO13 189 L6
LYMN SO41 221 L5
LYMN SO41 232 E4
LYND SO43 345 K3
MARL SN8 264 G3
NTID SP9 266 E8
ODIM RG29 68 F6
OVTN RG25 89 J4
PLE BH15 223 H7
PSEA PO1 20 C6
PSF GU32 313 L3
PSF GU32 314 C7
RAND SP11 265 L10
RAND SP11 269 P3
RFNM GU10 109 L1
RGWD BH24 202 A6
RGWD BH24 203 H5
RSAL SP5 296 A1
RSAL SP5 327 L1
RWIN SO21 125 G7
SHAM SO14 23 G6
SHST GU47 43 H8
STHA RG19 35 K1
STOK SO20 284 C3
STOK SO20 284 D9
STOK SO20 285 N5
TOTT SO40 159 G1
WHAM PO17 167 M3
WIMB BH21 207 H3
WIMB BH21 336 E5
WINC SO23 24 F5
WVILLE PO7 319 R9
High St North PLE BH15 223 K5
High Thicket Rd RFNM GU10 109 K8
Hightown Gdns RGWD BH24 203 K6
Hightown Hl RGWD BH24 203 M6
Hightown Rd RGWD BH24 203 K6
High Trees ELGH SO50 141 L2
WVILLE PO7 155 M8
Hightrees Av CHAR BH8 214 E7
High Trees Dr FUFL SO22 24 C1
High Trees Wk FERN BH22 209 K1
High Vw FHAM/PORC PO16 167 J7
PSF GU32 120 D5
Highview Cl CHCH/BSGR BH23 215 L5
High View Cl FARN GU14 61 G4
Highview Gdns
BKME/WDN BH12 224 C1
High View Rd FARN GU14 61 G4
High View Wy WEND SO18 147 M8
High Wk FHAM PO15 10 A1
High Wy BDST BH18 210 F5
Highway CWTH RG45 43 J3
Highways Rd RWIN SO21 124 C7
The Highway RSAL SP5 326 H6
Highwood Cl FBDG SP6 337 R6
NWBY RG14 27 K6
YTLY GU46 48 E4
Highwood La RGWD BH24 199 L8
ROMY SO51 131 K8
Highwood Rdg KBH RG22 92 D6
Highwood Rd BROC SO42 351 K4
LSOL/BMARY PO13 190 C1
PSTN BH14 224 E4
Higworth La HISD PO11 194 F3
Hilary Av CHAM PO6 185 G1
Hilary Cl WHIT RG2 238 C1
Hilary Dr CWTH RG45 43 K2
Hilary Rd CFDH BH17 211 J7
Hilborn Wy EWKG RG40 239 N7
Hilda Gdns WVILLE PO7 155 G5
Hilda Rd BKME/WDN BH12 224 E2
Hilden Wy FUFL SO22 288 A11
Hilder Gdns FARN GU14 61 K5
Hiley Rd PLE BH15 223 J2
Hilfield BLKW GU17 49 H3
Hilland Ri BOR GU35 111 M8
Hillary Cl FHAM/PORC PO16 10 C3
FNM GU9 12 F9
LYND SO43 345 L5
Hillary Rd BSTK RG21 6 B1
CHCH/BSGR BH23 216 E8
FNM GU9 12 E9
Hill Barn La RWIN SO21 274 A6
Hillborough Crs SSEA PO5 21 J7
Hillbourne Rd CFDH BH17 211 G6
Hillbrook Ri FNM GU9 76 E2
Hillbrow Cl FHAM PO15 181 K1
Hill Brow Cl HAV PO9 157 H7
Hill Brow Rd LISS GU33 308 F9
Hillbrow Rd SBNE BH6 227 H2
Hillbury Av AND SP10 4 D8
Hillbury Pk FBDG SP6 * 196 D7
Hillbury Rd FBDG SP6 196 D7
Hill Cl CHCH/BSGR BH23 217 G1
ELGH SO50 135 J7
NWBY RG14 33 K5
Hill Ct FARN GU14 50 B7
Hill Crs THLE RG7 * 37 J2
Hillcrest FLEETN GU51 59 J5
FNM GU9 * 72 D8
Hill Crest MFD/CHID GU8 263 R1
Hillcrest Av CHFD SO53 139 K2
FERN BH22 209 J1
Hillcrest Cl MOOR/WNTN BH9 214 A5
NBAD SO52 137 M3
Hillcrest Ct DEAN RG23 64 D6
Hillcrest Dr CHFD SO53 139 K2
Hill Crest Dr RFNM GU10 78 D2
Hill Crest Gdns BPWT SO32 143 K8
Hillcrest Rd BKME/WDN BH12 224 A3
CBLY GU15 51 K1
MOOR/WNTN BH9 214 A5
WIMB BH21 210 C3
Hill Cft FHAM PO15 180 D1
Hillcroft RSAL SP5 * 332 F2
Hilldene Wy HEND SO30 148 E3
Hillditch LYMN SO41 221 K2
Hilldown Rd PTSW SO17 147 G5
Hilldowns Av NEND PO2 184 C6
Hill Dr FHAM PO15 181 K1
Hill Farm Cl HASM GU27 * 117 M3
Hill Farm Rd NARL SO24 305 R3
WSHM SO15 160 E2
Hillgarth GSHT GU26 115 K3
Hillgrove Rd WEND SO18 147 M5
Hill Head Rd FHAM/STUB PO14 189 G3
Hill House Hl LIPH GU30 113 M5
Hillhouse La STHA RG19 248 E4
Hill Houses La NARL SO24 303 P7
Hillier Wy WINC SO23 25 H1
Hill La CHCH/BSGR BH23 348 C12
EPSF GU31 323 N2
ROWN SO16 146 D5
RWIN SO21 134 F3
Hillman Rd PSTN BH14 224 D3
Hillmead Gdns HAV PO9 170 B6
Hill Meadow OVTN RG25 89 J2
Hillmeadow VWD BH31 201 J4
Hill Park Rd FHAM PO15 165 K8
GPORT PO12 14 A1
Hill Pl HLER SO31 163 H4
Hill Ri BPWT SO32 312 E11
RWIN SO21 125 G6
Hill Rd DEAN RG23 91 K4
FHAM/PORC PO16 167 K7
FNM GU9 77 H1
GSHT GU26 115 J2
HASM GU27 118 C6
NWBY RG14 18 A2
RGWD BH24 346 G6
RWIN SO21 273 M2
WHIT RG2 239 M7
Hillsborough Ct FARN GU14 50 A8
Hillsborough Pk CBLY GU15 51 L3
Hill School RFNM GU10 78 D1
Hillside CBLY GU15 50 B1
FUFL SO22 288 B11
RAND SP11 95 H8
TADY RG26 249 P8
WHCH RG28 88 A7
Hillside Av ROMY SO51 137 G1
WEND SO18 147 L7
WVILLE PO7 169 H6
Hillside Cl ALTN GU34 106 F3
BOR GU35 114 A2
CHFD SO53 139 K2
FLEETN GU51 70 E2
FUFL SO22 122 C2
RSAL SP5 297 K10
Hillside Ct AND SP10 4 E6
Hillside Crs CHAM PO6 167 M7
FRIM GU16 61 M1
Hillside Dr CHCH/BSGR BH23 215 K4
Hillside Gdns WIMB BH21 210 C4
Hillside La FNM GU9 77 H1
Hillside Rd ALDT GU11 2 D7
ASHV GU12 74 B5
BKME/WDN BH12 212 F7
FNM GU9 2 B9
FUFL SO22 122 C3
HASM GU27 117 M3
LYMN SO41 221 J5
ODIM RG29 69 H7
RFNM GU10 78 F5
RWIN SO21 287 L12
VWD BH31 201 J1
WIMB BH21 200 C1
WIMB BH21 210 C3
Hillside Vls AND SP10 4 C1
Hillsley Rd CHAM PO6 167 M6
Hillson Dr FHAM PO15 181 J1
Hillsons Rd HEND SO30 150 B5
Hillstead Ct BSTK RG21 6 F7
Hill St PLE BH15 223 J6
ROMY SO51 144 C2
Hilltop FUFL SO22 288 C11
Hill Top Av NTID SP9 264 E12
Hilltop Cl FERN BH22 209 H1
Hilltop Crs CHAM PO6 169 H6
Hilltop Dr ITCH SO19 148 C8
Hilltop Gdns HORN PO8 321 M9
Hilltop Rd FERN BH22 209 H1
OVTN RG25 89 J2
WIMB BH21 210 E3
WVILLE PO7 168 A6
Hilltop Vw YTLY GU46 48 D3
Hillview HORN PO8 156 C3
Hill Vw PSF GU32 314 B7
THLE RG7 238 A7
Hill View Pk ELGH SO50 * 135 H7
Hill View Rd FERN BH22 209 J2
FHAM/PORC PO16 167 J7
FNM GU9 12 B3
KBH RG22 93 G1
ROMY SO51 131 J2
Hillview Rd FAWY SO45 176 F5
NBNE BH10 213 K4
Hill Wk FHAM PO15 181 K1
Hill Wy RGWD BH24 202 A7
The Hillway CHFD SO53 139 K1
FHAM/PORC PO16 167 J8
Hilly Cl RWIN SO21 310 B4
Hillyfields ROWN SO16 145 J4
Hilsea Crs NEND PO2 184 E3
Hiltingbury Cl CHFD SO53 133 K7
Hiltingbury Rd CHFD SO53 133 H7
HAV PO9 171 G3
Hiltom Rd RGWD BH24 203 K5
Hilton Cl PLE BH15 224 A2
Hilton Rd GPORT PO12 15 H7
NMIL/BTOS BH25 219 H4
Hinaidi Wy FARN GU14 60 F8
Hinchliffe Cl PLE BH15 222 F6
Hinchliffe Rd PLE BH15 222 F6
Hindell Cl FARN GU14 50 C8
Hindhead Rd HASM GU27 115 L8
Hinkler Rd ITCH SO19 148 D7
Hinstock Cl FARN GU14 61 G5
Hinton Cl CWTH RG45 43 K1
HAV PO9 170 C4
TADY RG26 44 B5
Hinton Crs ITCH SO19 148 E7
Hinton Dr CWTH RG45 43 K1
Hinton Flds WINC SO23 289 J10
Hinton Hl NARL SO24 304 B8
Hinton Manor La HORN PO8 320 G11
Hinton Rd BMTH BH1 8 F6
Hinton Wood Av
CHCH/BSGR BH23 217 L6
Hintonwood La
CHCH/BSGR BH23 217 L6
Hinwood Cl STOK SO20 284 D9
Hipley Rd HAV PO9 171 G5
Hirst Copse RAND SP11 86 C2
Hirst Rd FAWY SO45 177 H5
Hirtes Av WHIT RG2 238 E3
Hispano Av FHAM PO15 164 C5
Hitches La FLEETN GU51 70 E1
Hither Gn EMRTH PO10 172 E4
Hitherwood Cl HORN PO8 156 B7
Hives Wy LYMN SO41 221 K2
H Jones Crs ALDT GU11 3 K1
Hoadlands EPSF GU31 120 E5
Hoad's Hl WHAM PO17 152 B6
Hobart Dr FAWY SO45 177 H5
Hobart Rd NMIL/BTOS BH25 218 F6
Hobb La HEND SO30 149 K6
Hobbs Cl NARL SO24 292 A12
Hobbs Pk RGWD BH24 202 B8
Hobbs Rd BKME/WDN BH12 212 C8
Hobbs Sq AND SP10 96 E2
Hobby Cl HSEA PO3 185 G4
Hobson Wy FAWY SO45 354 F5
Hoburne Gdns
CHCH/BSGR BH23 217 J7
Hoburne La CHCH/BSGR BH23 217 J7
Hockford La THLE RG7 249 L1
Hockham Ct HAV PO9 170 C1
Hockley Cl CHAM PO6 168 D8
Hockley Link RWIN SO21 124 E3
Hocombe Dr CHFD SO53 133 H6
Hocombe Park Cl CHFD SO53 133 H6
Hocombe Rd CHFD SO53 133 H6
Hocombe Wood Rd
CHFD SO53 133 G6
Hodder Cl CHFD SO53 139 H3
Hodges Cl CFDH BH17 223 L1
HAV PO9 17 G1
Hoeford Cl FHAM/PORC PO16 182 B2
Hoe La ROMY SO51 137 J6
Hoe Rd BPWT SO32 143 L5
Hoe St WVILLE PO7 153 M2
The Hoe LSOL/BMARY PO13 182 E7
Hogarth Cl BSTK RG21 7 L7
ITCH SO19 162 B2
ROMY SO51 131 H7
SHST GU47 50 A2
Hogarth Ct AND SP10 4 E2
Hogarth Wy CHAR BH8 214 F6
Hoggarth Cl EPSF GU31 120 E4
Hoghatch La FNM GU9 76 E2
Hogmoor Rd BOR GU35 110 D8
Hogs Lodge La HORN PO8 321 M2
Hogue Av NBNE BH10 213 K3
Hogwood La EWKG RG40 239 N10
HEND SO30 140 E6
Holbeche Cl YTLY GU46 48 C3
Holbein Cl BSTK RG21 7 J9
Holborne Cl NWBY RG14 33 J7
Holbrook Cl FNM GU9 2 D7
Holbrook Rd FHAM/PORC PO16 11 G7
PSEA PO1 21 K2
Holbrook Wy ALDT GU11 3 G8
Holbury Cl CHAR BH8 214 E5
Holbury Ct HAV PO9 171 H3
Holbury Dro FAWY SO45 354 D4
Holbury La RSAL SP5 297 Q9
Holcombe Rd UPTN BH16 222 B2
Holcot La HSEA PO3 185 J4
Holcroft Rd ITCH SO19 148 E7
Holdaway Cl WINC SO23 289 J9
Holdenbury Ct HSEA PO3 185 J3
Holdenhurst Av LTDN BH7 227 J1
Holdenhurst Cl HORN PO8 321 L11
Holdenhurst Rd BMTH BH1 9 J5
CHAR BH8 215 G5
Holden La RWIN SO21 311 M1
Holder Rd ASHV GU12 73 L7
Holdfast La HASM GU27 118 F4
Holding La NARL SO24 303 L10
Hole La BPWT SO32 151 G3
RFNM GU10 259 L7
WVILLE PO7 319 M12
Holes Bay Rd PLE BH15 223 H4
Holes Cl LYMN SO41 219 M4
Holkham Cl ROWN SO16 145 L5
Hollam Cl FHAM/STUB PO14 181 H4
Hollam Crs FHAM/STUB PO14 181 H4
Hollam Dr FHAM/STUB PO14 181 H4
Hollam Rd ENEY PO4 193 H4
Holland Cl FNM GU9 13 L6
Holland Dr AND SP10 96 B1
Holland Gdns FLEETN GU51 59 J8
Holland Pk HLER SO31 179 M1
Holland Pl LSOL/BMARY PO13 182 D6
ROWN SO16 146 B7
Holland Rd ENEY PO4 21 L5
ITCH SO19 161 K6
TOTT SO40 158 C1
The Hollands STHA RG19 35 L1
Hollands Wood Dr
NMIL/BTOS BH25 219 H3
Holland Wy BDST BH18 210 F3
Hollies Cl LYMN SO41 350 F11
The Hollies FARN GU14 * 50 B7
NWBY RG14 33 K7
Hollingbourne Cl WEND SO18 147 K8
Hollington La KSCL RG20 245 Q8
Hollington Pl STHA RG19 * 35 J1
Hollist La EPSF GU31 317 L12
Hollis Wood Dr RFNM GU10 78 C3
Hollman Dr ROMY SO51 130 D8
Holloway Av BWD BH11 212 F3
Hollow La BOR GU35 111 L6
HISD PO11 194 F5
WHIT RG2 238 E3
Hollowshot La KSCL RG20 248 C11
TADY RG26 248 G12
The Hollow GODL GU7 261 R12
KSCL RG20 248 C10
STOK SO20 284 E12
Holly Av FRIM GU16 51 K5
Hollybank LSOL/BMARY PO13 189 M7
Holly Bank Cl HORN PO8 156 C3
Hollybank Crs FAWY SO45 176 F4
Hollybank La EMRTH PO10 171 M4
Hollybank Rd FAWY SO45 176 F5
Hollybrook Av ROWN SO16 146 C5
Hollybrook Cl ROWN SO16 146 B7
Hollybrook Gdns HLER SO31 164 A7
Hollybrook Pk BOR GU35 113 G1
Hollybrook Rd ROWN SO16 146 C6
Hollybush La ALDT GU11 73 L2
HTWY RG27 42 A8
TADY RG26 249 R10
THLE RG7 39 M2
Hollybush Ride EWKG RG40 42 E3
Holly Cl ASHV GU12 3 K3
BOR GU35 114 C3
FARN GU14 61 G4
FAWY SO45 354 C1
HLER SO31 179 L1
RGWD BH24 205 M4
TADY RG26 46 C6
UPTN BH16 222 A1
Hollycombe Cl LIPH GU30 116 C6
Holly Ct CWTH RG45 * 43 H3
Hollycroft STHA RG19 249 J3
Holly Dell ROWN SO16 146 E3
Holly Dr CHIN RG24 66 E2
WVILLE PO7 170 A2
Hollyfields Cl CBLY GU15 50 D3
Holly Gdns CHCH/BSGR BH23 216 D7
HEND SO30 148 D1
LYMN SO41 232 C3
Holly Green Ri BWD BH11 212 E4
Holly Gv FHAM/PORC PO16 165 L8
VWD BH31 200 F3
Holly Hatch Rd TOTT SO40 158 E2
Holly Hedge Cl FRIM GU16 51 G6
Holly Hedge La CFDH BH17 211 J8
Holly Hedge Rd FRIM GU16 51 G6
Holly Hl ROWN SO16 146 F3
Holly Hill Cl ROWN SO16 146 E3
Holly Hill La HLER SO31 163 K7
Hollyhock Cl KBH RG22 92 C4
Holly La CHCH/BSGR BH23 218 C6
LYMN SO41 356 B3
NMIL/BTOS BH25 219 J4
NTHA RG18 29 K1
THLE RG7 45 H4
Holly Ldg CHFD SO53 * 139 J5
Holly Ms ROWN SO16 * 146 F4
Holly Oak Rd ROWN SO16 146 A5
Hollyridge HASM GU27 118 C6
Holly Rd ASHV GU12 3 K3
FARN GU14 60 F4
FAWY SO45 354 G8
TOTT SO40 158 B6
Holly St GPORT PO12 15 H4
Hollytree Gdns FRIM GU16 50 F8
Holly Tree Pk RWIN SO21 274 C8
Hollytrees FLEETN GU51 71 G2
Holly Wk AND SP10 4 A8
Hollywater Rd LIPH GU30 113 H4
Holly Wy BLKW GU17 49 M4
Hollywell Dr CHAM PO6 184 B1
Hollywood Cl NBAD SO52 137 M4
Hollywood La LYMN SO41 221 K3
Holman Cl HORN PO8 156 A6
TADY RG26 46 D6
Holmbrook Cl FARN GU14 60 C4
Holmbury Av CWTH RG45 43 J1
Holm Cl RGWD BH24 203 L3
Holmdale Rd GPORT PO12 190 F1
Holme Cl CWTH RG45 43 J1
Holmefield Av
FHAM/STUB PO14 181 M6
Holme Rd CHCH/BSGR BH23 218 B8
Holmes Cl HLER SO31 162 B6
KBH RG22 92 E6
Holmes Ct AND SP10 4 C6
Holmesland Dr HEND SO30 149 M5
Holmesland La HEND SO30 149 M5
Holmfield Av LTDN BH7 227 J1
Holmgrove FHAM/STUB PO14 180 C1
Holm Hill La CHCH/BSGR BH23 218 B1
Holmhurst Av
CHCH/BSGR BH23 217 M7
Holm Oak Cl FUFL SO22 288 A11
VWD BH31 201 G1
Holmsley Cl LYMN SO41 221 H6
WEND SO18 148 C5
Holmsley Ct TOTT SO40 * 144 B8
Holmsley Pas RGWD BH24 349 L5
Holmsley Rd NMIL/BTOS BH25 349 M10
Holmwood Garth RGWD BH24 203 M6
Holne Ct ENEY PO4 193 J5
Holnest Rd CFDH BH17 211 K7
Holst Cl KBH RG22 93 G5
Holst Wy WVILLE PO7 169 M3
Holt Cl FARN GU14 61 J1
WHAM PO17 151 M8
Holt Cots STHA RG19 249 K4
Holt Ct ITCH SO19 161 L8
Holt Down EPSF GU31 120 F6
Holt End La ALTN GU34 279 J10
Holt Gdns HAV PO9 157 H5
Holt La HTWY RG27 68 E1
RAND SP11 81 K4
TADY RG26 249 K8
Holt Pound La RFNM GU10 78 A3
Holt Rd BKME/WDN BH12 224 F2
HUNG RG17 31 H2
WIMB BH21 200 F8
WSHM SO15 160 F1
Holt Wy HTWY RG27 56 E6
Holtwood Rd KSCL RG20 32 B6
Holworth Cl BWD BH11 212 E5
Holy Barn Cl KBH RG22 92 C3
Holyborne Rd ROMY SO51 137 H1
Holybourne Rd HAV PO9 16 E1
Holyhook Cl CWTH RG45 43 J2
Holyrood Av PTSW SO17 147 H6
Holyrood Cl WVILLE PO7 170 A1
Holywell Cl CFDH BH17 211 K5
FARN GU14 61 G1
Holywell Ct STHA RG19 35 K1
Home Cl NARL SO24 278 E10
NARL SO24 292 A11
Home Farm Cl FARN GU14 61 K2
FAWY SO45 177 H6
Home Farm Gdns AND SP10 95 M1
Home Farm Rd HTWY RG27 58 D1
Home Farm Wy VWD BH31 201 G2
Homefield MFD/CHID GU8 * 263 Q9
ROMY SO51 131 G7
Home Field Dr ROWN SO16 145 J3
Homefield Rd CHAM PO6 185 J1
EMRTH PO10 172 B2
Homefield Wy HORN PO8 321 K6
Home La RWIN SO21 301 N1
Homelea Cl FARN GU14 50 D8
Homeleigh Crs ASHV GU12 62 A8
Home Md OVTN RG25 103 H3
WVILLE PO7 154 F5
Home Mead Cl NWBY RG14 33 L4
Home Park Rd YTLY GU46 48 E2
Homer Cl HORN PO8 155 L6
LSOL/BMARY PO13 182 B8
Homer Farm La FAWY SO45 354 G10
Home Rd BWD BH11 213 H2
Homer Pk FAWY SO45 * 354 G10
Home Rule Rd HLER SO31 164 A8
Homeside Rd
MOOR/WNTN BH9 214 A6
Homestead Rd ALTN GU34 292 H3
Homesteads Rd KBH RG22 92 C4
Home Wy EPSF GU31 121 G6
Homewell HAV PO9 16 E5
Homewood Cl
NMIL/BTOS BH25 219 J5
Homington Rd RSAL SP5 325 N4
Hone Hl SHST GU47 49 K1
Honeybottom Rd TADY RG26 44 B3
Honeybourne Crs SBNE BH6 228 A4
Honeycritch La PSF GU32 307 M9
Honey La ALTN GU34 295 M9
FHAM PO15 165 K7
RGWD BH24 348 G2
Honeyleaze DEAN RG23 92 C7
Honeysuckle Cl CWTH RG45 43 J1
FUFL SO22 122 D8
HLER SO31 164 A7
KBH RG22 92 C4
LSOL/BMARY PO13 * 182 B5
YTLY GU46 48 C2
Honeysuckle Ct WVILLE PO7 169 M3
Honeysuckle Gdns LYMN SO41 220 C7
Honeysuckle La BOR GU35 114 B3
CFDH BH17 210 F7
Honeysuckle Rd ROWN SO16 147 H4
Honeysuckle Wy
CHCH/BSGR BH23 217 H8
CHFD SO53 139 G2
Honeywood Cl HSEA PO3 184 F4
TOTT SO40 144 D7
Honister Gdns FLEETN GU51 59 L6
Hood Cl AND SP10 96 F4
HLER SO31 164 B8
NBNE BH10 213 H7
Hood Crs NBNE BH10 213 H7
Hood Rd WEND SO18 148 A4
Hook Cl CHFD SO53 133 G6
NWBY RG14 34 C5
Hook Common HTWY RG27 68 B1
Hook Crs CHFD SO53 133 G6
Hooke Cl CFDH BH17 212 A6
Hook La HLER SO31 179 M6
NARL SO24 292 E12
RGUW GU3 261 P6
TADY RG26 249 M6
TADY RG26 255 N8
Hook Park Est HLER SO31 * 179 K6
Hook Park Rd HLER SO31 179 J5
Hookpit Farm La WINC SO23 288 H8
Hook Rd HTWY RG27 56 C3
HTWY RG27 68 C1
KSCL RG20 248 E10
ODIM RG29 68 B4
ROMY SO51 132 E5
Hook's Farm Wy HAV PO9 16 B1
Hook's La HAV PO9 16 B2
Hookstile La FNM GU9 13 G6
Hook Water Rd CHFD SO53 133 G6
Hookwood La RAND SP11 80 C5
ROMY SO51 132 F6
Hoopersmead OVTN RG25 93 J5
Hoopers Wy DEAN RG23 91 K3
Hope Fountain CBLY GU15 51 H4
Hope Grant's Rd ALDT GU11 73 G4
Hope La FNM GU9 76 F2
Hopeman Cl SHST GU47 49 M1
Hope Rd HEND SO30 148 E2
Hope St MFD/CHID GU8 260 H12
PSEA PO1 192 C2
Hopeswood LISS GU33 308 F1
Hope Wy ALDT GU11 2 D1
Hopfield Cl WVILLE PO7 169 L2
Hopfield Ms WVILLE PO7 169 L2
Hopfield Rd HTWY RG27 57 L3
Hop Gdn FLEETS GU52 71 G4
Hop Garden Rd HTWY RG27 56 B7
Hop Gdns NWBY RG14 * 27 K7
The Hop Gdn EPSF GU31 323 M1
Hopkins Cl CHAM PO6 * 167 L8
CHAR BH8 215 G6
Hopkins Ct ENEY PO4 193 H6
Hopkinson Wy AND SP10 95 K3
Hopton Garth CHIN RG24 54 C7
Hopwood Cl NWBY RG14 19 L1
Horace Rd BOSC BH5 226 E4

Hordle La *LYMN* SO41 219 M8
Hordle Rd *HAV* PO9 170 C4
Horlock Rd *BROC* SO42 351 L2
Hormer Cl *SHST* GU47 43 M7
Hornbeam Cl *FARN* GU14 60 C3
HEND SO30 149 K6
RWIN SO21 288 E4
SHST GU47 43 M7
WWKG RG41 239 R5
Hornbeam Gdns *HEND* SO30 148 D2
Hornbeam Pl *HTWY* RG27 56 D6
Hornbeam Rd *CHFD* SO53 138 E3
HAV PO9 17 K1
Hornbeams *THLE* RG7 238 C9
Hornbeam Wy *WIMB* BH21 207 K3
Hornby Cl *HLER* SO31 179 K4
Hornchurch Rd *ROWN* SO16 145 M3
Horndean Prec *HORN* PO8 * 156 D1
Horndean Rd *EMRTH* PO10 171 K4
HORN PO8 321 N12
Horne Rd *STHA* RG19 35 L2
Hornet Cl *FHAM* PO15 181 K2
GPORT PO12 15 H7
Hornet Rd *FHAM/STUB* PO14 181 M7
Horning Rd *BKME/WDN* BH12 224 F3
Horn Rd *FARN* GU14 60 E3
Horns Dro *ROWN* SO16 145 L2
Horns Hl *BPWT* SO32 318 H10
Horns Hill Cl *ROWN* SO16 145 K2
Horsa Cl *SBNE* BH6 227 L4
Horsa Ct *SBNE* BH6 227 L4
Horsa Rd *SBNE* BH6 227 L4
Horsea La *NEND* PO2 184 D4
Horsea Rd *NEND* PO2 184 E3
Horsebridge Rd *HAV* PO9 171 G4
STOK SO20 284 G12
STOK SO20 299 M3
Horsebridge Wy *ROWN* SO16 145 L3
Horsecroft *ROMY* SO51 130 F8
Horsefair Ct *ROMY* SO51 136 E1
Horse La *ALTN* GU34 292 H9
Horsepost La *WVILLE* PO7 320 D10
Horse Sands Cl *ENEY* PO4 193 K5
Horseshoe Bend *GSHT* GU26 115 G5
Horseshoe Cl
FHAM/STUB PO14 180 D2
WIMB BH21 208 B2
Horseshoe Crs *BOR* GU35 113 G1
Horseshoe Dr *ROMY* SO51 131 H6
TOTT SO40 144 A6
Horseshoe End *NWBY* RG14 34 B5
Horseshoe La *ASHV* GU12 74 A2
RAND SP11 250 F8
Horseshoe Ldg *HLER* SO31 179 L3
Horsham Av *NBNE* BH10 213 J2
Horsham Rd *SHST* GU47 43 M7
Horton Cl *MOOR/WNTN* BH9 214 C5
Horton Rd *LSOL/BMARY* PO13 182 C4
RGWD BH24 205 L2
WIMB BH21 200 E8
Horton Wy *ELGH* SO50 140 F3
VWD BH31 200 F3
Horwood Gdns *BSTK* RG21 93 H2
Hosker Rd *BOSC* BH5 227 H3
Hosketts La *STOK* SO20 284 A3
Hospital Hl *ALDT* GU11 2 E2
Hospital La *FHAM/PORC* PO16 183 L2
Hospital Rd *ALDT* GU11 73 G5
BPWT SO32 318 A11
Hostel Rd *FARN* GU14 61 H8
Hotspur Cl *FAWY* SO45 176 F3
Houchin St *BPWT* SO32 143 J5
Houghton Cl *HAV* PO9 * 171 H2
Houlton Rd *PLE* BH15 223 L4
Hound Cl *HLER* SO31 162 D7
Hound Green Cl *HTWY* RG27 240 D9
Houndmills Rd *BSTK* RG21 65 G6
Houndown La *MFD/CHID* GU8 263 N7
Hound Rd *HLER* SO31 162 D6
Hound Road Gdns *HLER* SO31 162 D7
Hounds Wy *WIMB* BH21 208 B3
Hound Wy *HLER* SO31 162 D6
Houndwell Pl *SHAM* SO14 23 H4
Hounsdown Av *TOTT* SO40 158 F3
Hounsdown Cl *TOTT* SO40 158 F3
Hounslow Cl *PLE* BH15 222 E6
Hoursome Ct *DEAN* RG23 92 D8
House Cl *RWIN* SO21 135 G3
House Farm Rd *GPORT* PO12 190 E4
Houseman Rd *FARN* GU14 60 F2
Hoveton Gv *CHFD* SO53 133 H8
Howard Cl *CHCH/BSGR* BH23 228 F2
CHFD SO53 139 K4
ELGH SO50 141 J2
FLEETN GU51 59 L7
LSOL/BMARY PO13 190 A1
RGWD BH24 348 H2
WEND SO18 147 L4
Howard Cole Wy *ALDT* GU11 2 B3
Howard Dr *FARN* GU14 60 B4
Howard Rd *BSTK* RG21 7 G9
CHAR BH8 226 C1
NEND PO2 184 E4
NWBY RG14 18 E7
VWD BH31 201 H2
WSHM SO15 160 D2
Howard's Gv *WSHM* SO15 146 C8
Howard's La *ALTN* GU34 107 J1
Howards Md *LYMN* SO41 221 H6
Howe Cl *CHCH/BSGR* BH23 228 F3
NMIL/BTOS BH25 218 F5
Howe La *VWD* BH31 201 H3
Howell Cl *WHIT* RG2 239 L8
Howe Rd *LSOL/BMARY* PO13 190 C2
Howerts Cl *HLER* SO31 179 K5
Howes Gdns *FLEETN* GU51 71 G2
Howeth Cl *NBNE* BH10 213 K5
The Howe *FARN* GU14 60 B7
Howeth Rd *NBNE* BH10 213 J4
Howlett Cl *LYMN* SO41 221 J4
Howton Cl *NBNE* BH10 * 213 J3
Howton Rd *NBNE* BH10 213 J3
Hoxley Rd *NBNE* BH10 213 K4
Hoyal Rd *PLE* BH15 222 D5
Hoylake Cl *LSOL/BMARY* PO13 182 C7
Hoylake Rd *CHAM* PO6 169 J7
Hoylecroft Cl *FHAM* PO15 10 A1
Hubbard Rd *BSTK* RG21 6 A1
Hubert Rd *WINC* SO23 122 E8
Huddington Gld *HTWY* RG27 48 C3
Hudson Cl *BKME/WDN* BH12 212 C6
LIPH GU30 116 C5
LSOL/BMARY PO13 190 C2
RGWD BH24 203 L4
Hudson Ct *TOTT* SO40 158 D2
Hudson Davies Cl *LYMN* SO41 351 R11
Hudson Rd *SSEA* PO5 21 J5
Hudsons Meadow *HTWY* RG27 240 D9
Hugh's Cl *FAWY* SO45 354 G7
Huish La *OVTN* RG25 66 D6
Hulbert Rd *WVILLE* PO7 169 M1
Hulbert Wy *KBH* RG22 92 E2
Hulfords La *HTWY* RG27 241 N11
Hullam La *ALTN* GU34 294 H11
Hull Crs *BWD* BH11 212 D4
Hulles Wy *NBAD* SO52 137 M4
Hull Rd *BWD* BH11 212 D4
Hull Wy *BWD* BH11 212 E4
Hulse Rd *WSHM* SO15 146 F8
Hulton Cl *ITCH* SO19 161 K7
Humber Cl *FHAM/STUB* PO14 189 H1
NTHA RG18 28 D7
Humber Ct *AND* SP10 5 M1
Humber Gdns *HLER* SO31 163 G3
Humber La *NTID* SP9 266 D4
Humber Rd *FERN* BH22 346 A6
Humberstone Rd *AND* SP10 5 H8
Humbers Vw *STOK* SO20 299 Q3
Humber Wy *SHST* GU47 43 M8
The Hummicks *BROC* SO42 353 Q8
Humming Bird Ct *KBH* RG22 92 B4
Hundred Acres Rd
WHAM PO17 152 E5
Hundred La *LYMN* SO41 221 M1
The Hundred *ROMY* SO51 136 E1
WVILLE PO7 155 K7
Hungerfield Cl
CHCH/BSGR BH23 348 C11
Hungerford *HLER* SO31 162 F5
Hungerford Cl *SHST* GU47 43 L8
Hungerford Hl *FBDG* SP6 197 K7
Hungerford La *RAND* SP11 81 G2
RAND SP11 83 K1
Hungerford Rd *CHAR* BH8 214 D5
MARL SN8 243 N2
Hunnels Cl *FLEETS* GU52 71 G5
Hunt Av *HLER* SO31 162 C6
Hunt Cl *RWIN* SO21 288 E4
Hunter Cl *CHCH/BSGR* BH23 229 G1
FAWY SO45 354 D2
LSOL/BMARY PO13 190 D1
WIMB BH21 208 C2
Hunter Rd *ENEY* PO4 192 F5
FARN GU14 60 F5
Hunters Cha *BPWT* SO32 318 C9
LIPH GU30 116 B3
Hunters Cl *DEAN* RG23 91 K1
VWD BH31 201 L3
Hunters Ct *HLER* SO31 * 163 H1
Hunters Crs *ROMY* SO51 131 J7
TOTT SO40 158 B2
Hunter's Hl *THLE* RG7 39 M1
TOTT SO40 158 D5
Hunters Ldg *FHAM* PO15 181 H4
Hunters Ride *WVILLE* PO7 169 L1
Hunters Rd *LISS* GU33 309 K2
Hunters Wy *ELGH* SO50 141 G2
THLE RG7 238 A7
Huntfield Rd
MOOR/WNTN BH9 214 B5
Huntingdon Cl
FHAM/STUB PO14 180 C3
Huntingdon Dr *WIMB* BH21 207 L7
Huntingdon Gdns
CHCH/BSGR BH23 215 M6
ELGH SO50 141 K5
Huntingdon House Dr
GSHT GU26 115 L4
Huntingford Cl *GSHT* GU26 * 115 J1
Hunting Ga *AND* SP10 95 L4
Huntley Cl *CHAM* PO6 * 168 B7
Huntly Rd *TWDS* BH3 225 K2
Huntly Wy *WEND* SO18 161 M1
Hunton Cl *ROWN* SO16 146 D5
Hunton Down La *RWIN* SO21 274 G8
Hunton La *RWIN* SO21 274 F8
Hunt Rd *CHCH/BSGR* BH23 216 F8
PLE BH15 223 L4
Huntsbottom La *LISS* GU33 308 H9
Hunts Cl *HTWY* RG27 56 E7
Hunts Common *HTWY* RG27 57 M1
Hunts Hill Rd *RGUW* GU3 75 G3
Huntsman's Ms *FRIM* GU16 61 M4
Huntsmead *ALTN* GU34 107 G5
Huntsmoor Rd *TADY* RG26 44 A3
Hunts Pond Rd *HLER* SO31 164 B8
Huntvale Rd
MOOR/WNTN BH9 214 B5
The Hurdles *CHCH/BSGR* BH23 215 L8
FHAM/STUB PO14 180 D2
Hurdle Wy *RWIN* SO21 124 C4
Hurland La *BOR* GU35 111 M8
Hurlands Cl *FNM* GU9 77 K4
Hurlands Pl *FNM* GU9 77 K4
Hurlingham Gdns *ROWN* SO16 147 G3
Hurn Br *CHCH/BSGR* BH23 215 H2
Hurn Cl *RGWD* BH24 202 F6
Hurn Ct *HAV* PO9 171 H2
Hurn Court La
CHCH/BSGR BH23 214 F2
Hurne Ct *BSTK* RG21 * 7 J5
Hurn La *RGWD* BH24 202 F6
Hurn Rd *CHCH/BSGR* BH23 215 L5
RGWD BH24 347 J4
Hurn Wy *CHCH/BSGR* BH23 215 K7
Huron Dr *LIPH* GU30 116 D5
Hurricane Dr *ROWN* SO16 145 L2
Hurricane Wy *FARN* GU14 72 F1
Hursley Cl *LTDN* BH7 227 J1
Hursley Dr *FAWY* SO45 354 G9
Hursley Park Rd *RWIN* SO21 133 H2
Hursley Rd *HAV* PO9 170 D3
RWIN SO21 133 H4
Hurstbourne Av
CHCH/BSGR BH23 217 L7
Hurstbourne Cl *HAV* PO9 * 170 D2
Hurstbourne Pl *ITCH* SO19 * 161 M8
Hurst Cl *CHCH/BSGR* BH23 218 C6
CHFD SO53 139 G4
FHAM/STUB PO14 189 G3
LIPH GU30 116 A3
NMIL/BTOS BH25 218 D8
TOTT SO40 144 F8
Hurstdene Rd *CHAR* BH8 214 C6
Hurst Gn *LSOL/BMARY* PO13 182 B6
Hurst Green Cl *HORN* PO8 156 B6
ITCH SO19 162 A3
Hurst Hl *PSTN* BH14 224 C8
Hurst La *ALTN* GU34 306 F9
RWIN SO21 310 A10
Hurst Lea *LYMN* SO41 * 221 K7
Hurstly La *LYMN* SO41 * 351 M9
Hurstmere Cl *GSHT* GU26 115 K5
Hurst Rd *ALDT* GU11 73 J5
FARN GU14 50 D8
LYMN SO41 232 E5
RGWD BH24 203 J3
The Hurst *HTWY* RG27 58 B7
Hurstville Dr *WVILLE* PO7 169 M2
Hurstwood Av *EMRTH* PO10 172 E5
Hurtmore Rd *MFD/CHID* GU8 261 P10
Hussar Cl *CHCH/BSGR* BH23 227 M1
Hussar Ct *ALDT* GU11 2 A3
WVILLE PO7 * 155 J7
Hussell La *ALTN* GU34 293 K1
Hussey Cl *WINC* SO23 123 G2
Hussey's La *ALTN* GU34 258 G11
Hutton Cl *NWBY* RG14 19 G1
Hutton Rd *ASHV* GU12 74 A2
Hutton Sq *AND* SP10 96 E2
Hutwood Rd *ROWN* SO16 139 G8
Huxley Cl *HLER* SO31 180 B2
Huxley Ct *FAWY* SO45 176 C6
Hyacinth Cl *CFDH* BH17 210 F7
KBH RG22 92 C4
Hyde Abbey Rd *WINC* SO23 25 G4
Hyde Church La *WINC* SO23 25 G3
Hyde Church Pth *WINC* SO23 25 G2
Hyde Cl *LYMN* SO41 350 F10
TOTT SO40 158 B1
WINC SO23 24 F3
WSHM SO15 146 C7
Hyde End La *STHA* RG19 36 D7
THLE RG7 238 C4
Hyde End Rd *THLE* RG7 238 C6
Hyde Ga *WINC* SO23 25 G3
Hyde House Gdns *WINC* SO23 * 25 G3
Hyde La *FBDG* SP6 197 L6
KSCL RG20 247 Q6
RFNM GU10 259 M1
RFNM GU10 263 K11
Hyden Farm La *HORN* PO8 320 F6
Hyde Park Rd *SSEA* PO5 21 H4
Hyde Rd *NBNE* BH10 213 J3
Hydes Platt *THLE* RG7 45 H4
Hyde St *SSEA* PO5 * 21 G6
WINC SO23 25 G4
The Hyde *NMIL/BTOS* BH25 218 E4
Hylton Ct *TADY* RG26 44 C4
Hylton Rd *EPSF* GU31 120 D6
Hymans Wy *TOTT* SO40 158 E1
Hynesbury Rd
CHCH/BSGR BH23 229 J2
Hyson Crs *RAND* SP11 265 P10
Hyssop Cl *FHAM* PO15 164 D5
Hythe By-Pass *FAWY* SO45 176 B4
Hythe Cl *TADY* RG26 44 B5
Hythe Rd *CHAM* PO6 168 E8
PLE BH15 224 A1
TOTT SO40 159 M8

I

Ibbertson Cl *CHAR* BH8 214 F6
Ibbertson Rd *CHAR* BH8 214 F6
Ibbertson Wy *CHAR* BH8 214 F6
Ibbett Rd *NBNE* BH10 213 J6
Ibbotson Wy *TOTT* SO40 158 D3
Iberian Wy *CBLY* GU15 51 J2
Ibsen Cl *HLER* SO31 164 C4
Ibsley Cl *CHAR* BH8 226 C2
Ibsley Dro *RGWD* BH24 199 J3
Ibsley Gv *HAV* PO9 16 A1
Ibworth La *TADY* RG26 254 H5
Icarus Pl *WVILLE* PO7 169 M6
Icknield Wy *AND* SP10 84 D8
Iddesleigh Rd *TWDS* BH3 225 M2
Iden Ct *NWBY* RG14 19 H2
Idsworth Cl *HORN* PO8 156 E2
Idsworth Rd *HORN* PO8 156 B6
HSEA PO3 185 G8
Iford Br *CHCH/BSGR* BH23 215 K8
Iford Ct *HAV* PO9 171 H2
Iford Gdns *LTDN* BH7 227 J1
Iford La *SBNE* BH6 227 L1
Ilbury Cl *WHIT* RG2 238 E3
Ilex Cl *TADY* RG26 44 E3
WINC SO23 288 H8
YTLY GU46 48 D2
Ilex Crs *HLER* SO31 179 M1
Ilex Wk *HISD* PO11 195 J5
Iley La *LYMN* SO41 233 J1
Ilford Cl *SBNE* BH6 227 M2
Ilkley Wy *STHA* RG19 35 J2
Illingworth Cl *TADY* RG26 46 D6
Ilynton Av *RSAL* SP5 282 A9
Imadene Crs *BOR* GU35 111 H8
Imber Cl *ITCH* SO19 148 C8
Imber Dr *CHCH/BSGR* BH23 217 M8
Imber Rd *WINC* SO23 25 L4
Imber Wy *ITCH* SO19 148 C8
Imbrecourt *CCLF* BH13 237 K1
Imjin Cl *ALDT* GU11 3 H1
Imperial Av *WSHM* SO15 160 B1
Imperial Rd *SHAM* SO14 161 H1
Imperial Wy *WHIT* RG2 238 A1
WSHM SO15 160 C3
Implacable Rd
LSOL/BMARY PO13 189 K5
Impstone Rd *TADY* RG26 44 F3
Imran Ct *ASHV* GU12 3 J6
Ingersley Ri *HEND* SO30 148 D3
Ingle Dell *CBLY* GU15 50 F4
Ingledene Cl *GPORT* PO12 14 E5
HAV PO9 16 A3
Ingle Gln *EWKG* RG40 * 42 C1
FAWY SO45 177 G7
Ingle Gn *TOTT* SO40 144 B7
Ingles Edge *HUNG* RG17 30 D8
Inglesham Wy *PLE* BH15 222 E5
Ingleside *HLER* SO31 162 C5
Ingleside Cl *FHAM/STUB* PO14 181 H4
Ingleton Rd *ROWN* SO16 145 K7
Inglewood Av *CBLY* GU15 51 M3
CHAR BH8 214 F7
Inglewood Dr *KBH* RG22 92 D6
NMIL/BTOS BH25 219 H6
Inglewood Rd *HUNG* RG17 30 A3
Inglis Rd *SSEA* PO5 21 L6
Ingoldfield La *WHAM* PO17 153 J1
Ingram Wk *WIMB* BH21 207 K4
Ings Cl *ALTN* GU34 106 F6
Ingworth Rd
BKME/WDN BH12 225 G3
Inhams La *WVILLE* PO7 154 D4
Inhams Rd *ALTN* GU34 107 K2
Inhams Wy *THLE* RG7 45 G4
Inhurst Av *WVILLE* PO7 156 A8
Inhurst La *STHA* RG19 249 N3
Inhurst Rd *NEND* PO2 184 E6
Inhurst Wy *TADY* RG26 249 R3
Inkerman Rd *ITCH* SO19 161 K5
Inkpen Gdns *CHIN* RG24 54 C8
Inkpen Rd *HUNG* RG17 30 A4
HUNG RG17 31 G2
Inlands Rd *RCCH* PO18 172 F5
Inmans La *PSF* GU32 120 F4
Innisfail Gdns *ALDT* GU11 2 C6
Insley Crs *BDST* BH18 210 E3
Institute Rd *ASHV* GU12 3 L6
Instow Gdns *FARN* GU14 61 G1
Interchange Pk *HSEA* PO3 * 185 J5
International Wy *ITCH* SO19 161 L8
Inval Hl *HASM* GU27 118 C4
Inveravon *CHCH/BSGR* BH23 228 F3
Inverclyde Rd *PSTN* BH14 224 C4
Invergordon Av *CHAM* PO6 185 H1
Inverkip Cl
LSOL/BMARY PO13 * 189 L5
Inverleigh Rd *SBNE* BH6 227 K2
Inverness Av *FHAM* PO15 10 A2
Inverness Rd *GPORT* PO12 14 D1
NEND PO2 192 E1
Inverness Wy *SHST* GU47 49 M1
Invincible Rd *FARN* GU14 61 C5
FHAM/STUB PO14 189 H3
Inwood Rd *LISS* GU33 308 G9
Ionic Cl *CHFD* SO53 139 M1
Iping Av *HAV* PO9 170 D3
Ipley Wy *FAWY* SO45 177 G6
Ipoh Cl *STOK* SO20 270 C7
Ipswich Rd *WBNE* BH4 225 H4
Ireland Wy *WVILLE* PO7 169 L3
Iris Cl *KBH* RG22 92 C5
Irish Hill Rd *HUNG* RG17 31 H2
Iris Rd *MOOR/WNTN* BH9 213 M7
ROWN SO16 147 H4
Ironbridge Crs *HLER* SO31 164 A6
Ironbridge La *ENEY* PO4 193 J4
Iron Mill Cl *FHAM* PO15 181 K1
Ironmill La *FHAM* PO15 165 H7
Irvine Cl *FHAM/PORC* PO16 10 E2
Irvine Dr *FARN* GU14 50 A8
Irvine Wy *CHCH/BSGR* BH23 216 E8
Irving Rd *ROWN* SO16 145 M7
SBNE BH6 227 K3
Irwell Cl *BSTK* RG21 7 J5
CHFD SO53 139 G3
Isaac Newton Rd *WHIT* RG2 239 M8
Isaacs Cl *BKME/WDN* BH12 225 H1
Isambard Brunel Rd *PSEA* PO1 21 G3
Isington La *ALTN* GU34 108 A1
Isington Rd *ALTN* GU34 281 R4
Isis Cl *ROWN* SO16 145 L8
Isis Wy *SHST* GU47 43 M8
Island Cl *HISD* PO11 187 G5
Island Farm Rd *THLE* RG7 39 L3
Island View Av
CHCH/BSGR BH23 229 H2
Island View Cl *LYMN* SO41 232 E5
Island View Rd
NMIL/BTOS BH25 230 D1
Island View Ter *NEND* PO2 184 C7
Islay Gdns *CHAM* PO6 168 F7
Itchel La *RFNM* GU10 259 M1
Itchen Av *ELGH* SO50 140 F2
Itchen Cl *DEAN* RG23 91 K3
PSF GU32 120 C7
ROMY SO51 334 H5
Itchen Ct *AND* SP10 5 M1
Itchenor Rd *HISD* PO11 195 M6
Itchen Rd *HAV* PO9 171 H2
Itchenside Cl *WEND* SO18 147 M4
Itchen Vw *NARL* SO24 290 F11
Itchen Wy *ELGH* SO50 134 B6
ITCH SO19 161 K5
NARL SO24 303 P4
RWIN SO21 289 K11
RWIN SO21 290 C11
WINC SO23 25 J8
Itchin Cl *TOTT* SO40 158 D2
Ithica Cl *HISD* PO11 195 G4
Ivamy Pl *BWD* BH11 212 F6
Ivanhoe Rd *EWKG* RG40 239 N10
WSHM SO15 146 D7
Ivar Gdns *CHIN* RG24 54 C8
Ively Rd *FARN* GU14 60 C7
Ives Cl *YTLY* GU46 48 D1
Ivor Cl *FAWY* SO45 354 E4
Ivor Rd *PLE* BH15 223 G7
WIMB BH21 210 D4
Ivy Cl *FUFL* SO22 122 E7
RGWD BH24 205 M4
TOTT SO40 144 E6
Ivy Ct *WVILLE* PO7 169 K4
Ivy Dene *ITCH* SO19 148 D8
Ivydene Crs *RCCH* PO18 173 H7
Ivydene Gdns *HORN* PO8 156 A4
Ivy Down La *DEAN* RG23 91 G1
Ivyhole Hl *HTWY* RG27 241 R12
Ivyhouse La *PSF* GU32 307 J9
Ivy La *FNM* GU9 12 F3
HEND SO30 148 B2
RGWD BH24 203 J1
Ivy Rd *ASHV* GU12 73 L6
PTSW SO17 147 J8
WIMB BH21 207 K8
Iwerne Cl *MOOR/WNTN* BH9 214 B4

J

Jacaranda Cl *FHAM* PO15 180 E1
Jacaranda Rd *BOR* GU35 112 F2
Jack Cl *CHFD* SO53 138 E2
Jack Cockerill Wy *SSEA* PO5 * 192 D7
Jackdaw Cl *HORN* PO8 155 L4
KBH RG22 92 B4
Jackdaw Ri *ELGH* SO50 139 K7
Jackie Wigg Gdns *TOTT* SO40 158 F1
Jacklyns Cl *NARL* SO24 291 L12
Jacklyns La *NARL* SO24 291 L12
Jackmans Cl *ITCH* SO19 161 K5
Jackman's Hl *RWIN* SO21 310 A1
Jackson Cl *CHAM* PO6 185 J2
Jackson Rd *BKME/WDN* BH12 224 C2
Jacobean Cl *CHCH/BSGR* BH23 218 B7
Jacob Rd *CBLY* GU15 50 C1
Jacobs Cl *HORN* PO8 321 L7
ROMY SO51 137 G1
Jacob's Gutter La *TOTT* SO40 158 F3
Jacobs Rd *PLE* BH15 222 E6
Jacob's St *PSEA* PO1 21 H1
Jacobs Wk *TOTT* SO40 158 E4
Jacomb Pl
LSOL/BMARY PO13 * 182 D6
Jacqueline Av *WVILLE* PO7 169 K4
Jacqueline Rd
BKME/WDN BH12 224 B1
Jade Ct *LSOL/BMARY* PO13 * 190 C2
Jagdalik Rd *NTID* SP9 266 E4
Jago Rd *PSEA* PO1 20 B1
Jaguar Rd *FARN* GU14 61 H6
Jamacia Pl *GPORT* PO12 15 G5
Jamaica Pl *GPORT* PO12 15 G5
Jamaica Rd *GPORT* PO12 15 K2
James Callaghan Dr
CHAM PO6 168 A6
James Cl *BSTK* RG21 65 L5
HISD PO11 194 E5
LSOL/BMARY PO13 182 C4
James Copse Rd *HORN* PO8 155 M3
James Grieve Av *HLER* SO31 180 A2
Jameson Rd
MOOR/WNTN BH9 213 L7
James Rd *ALDT* GU11 73 K1
BKME/WDN BH12 225 G3
CBLY GU15 50 D6
HAV PO9 16 B2
LSOL/BMARY PO13 182 C4
James St *SHAM* SO14 23 J3
James Watt Rd *EWKG* RG40 239 N8
James Wy *CBLY* GU15 50 D6
Jamrud Rd *NTID* SP9 266 D3
Janaway Gdns *PTSW* SO17 147 J8
Janes Cl *FAWY* SO45 354 G8
Jan Smuts Cl *LISS* GU33 309 K3
Janson Rd *WSHM* SO15 160 C1
Japonica Cl *WWKG* RG41 239 R4
Japonica Wy *HAV* PO9 171 J4
Jardine Sq *AND* SP10 96 E2
Jarndyce Wk *NEND* PO2 * 192 C1
Jarvis Cl *HTWY* RG27 42 A8
Jarvis Flds *HLER* SO31 163 H4
Jasmine Cl *WWKG* RG41 239 R1
Jasmine Ct *AND* SP10 4 C8
FHAM PO15 164 D3
LSOL/BMARY PO13 * 190 C2
LYMN SO41 221 K4
Jasmine Gv *WVILLE* PO7 170 A2
Jasmine Rd *HEND* SO30 149 H4
KBH RG22 92 D4
Jasmine Wk *FHAM/STUB* PO14 10 A8
Jasmine Wy *BOR* GU35 113 G2
HORN PO8 321 L7
Jasmond Rd *CHAM* PO6 184 F2
Jason Pl *WVILLE* PO7 169 L6
Jason Wy *GPORT* PO12 * 182 F8
Jaundrells Cl *NMIL/BTOS* BH25 219 J5
Java Dr *FHAM* PO15 164 C5
Java Rd *SHAM* SO14 23 K9
J Av *FAWY* SO45 354 H2
Jay Cl *FHAM/STUB* PO14 181 H8
HORN PO8 156 A1
Jays Cl *BSTK* RG21 93 K3
KBH RG22 93 H4
Jay's Ct *CHCH/BSGR* BH23 218 B8
Jays Nest Cl *BLKW* GU17 49 M4
Jealous La *LYMN* SO41 351 L10
Jedburgh Cl *STHA* RG19 35 M1
Jefferson Av *CHAR* BH8 226 D2
Jefferson Rd *BSTK* RG21 65 K5
Jeffries Cl *ROWN* SO16 145 L3
Jellicoe Av *GPORT* PO12 14 B8
Jellicoe Cl *PSTN* BH14 223 M3
Jellicoe Ct *AND* SP10 * 96 F4
Jellicoe Dr *CHCH/BSGR* BH23 228 F2
Jenkins Cl *HEND* SO30 150 A5
Jenkins Gv *HSEA* PO3 193 H1
Jenner Cl *VWD* BH31 201 G1
Jenner Wy *ALTN* GU34 107 G2
ROMY SO51 131 J8
Jennie Green La *ALTN* GU34 279 J10
Jennings Rd *PSTN* BH14 224 C6
TOTT SO40 145 G8
Jenny's Wk *YTLY* GU46 49 G2
Jenson Gdns *AND* SP10 4 C6
Jephcote Rd *BWD* BH11 212 F4
Jermyns La *ROMY* SO51 131 J5
Jerome Cnr *CWTH* RG45 43 L5
Jerome Ct *ITCH* SO19 148 D6
Jerram Cl *GPORT* PO12 14 A7
Jerrett's La *ROWN* SO16 145 K5
Jersey Brow Rd *FARN* GU14 61 G6
Jersey Cl *BKME/WDN* BH12 212 C7
CHIN RG24 65 L2
FHAM/STUB PO14 189 K3
FLEETN GU51 59 K4
ROWN SO16 145 L5
Jersey Rd *BKME/WDN* BH12 212 D7
NEND PO2 184 E8
Jervis Ct *AND* SP10 96 F3
Jervis Court La *BPWT* SO32 318 A4
Jervis Dr *GPORT* PO12 14 E1
Jervis Rd *NEND* PO2 184 C6
Jesmond Av *CHCH/BSGR* BH23 217 M8
Jesmond Dene *NWBY* RG14 18 C2
Jesmond Gv *HLER* SO31 180 A3
Jessamine Rd *ROWN* SO16 146 B6
Jesse Cl *BLKW* GU17 49 H3
Jessett Dr *FLEETS* GU52 71 G4
Jessica Av *VWD* BH31 200 F1
Jessica Cl *WVILLE* PO7 156 B7
Jessica Crs *TOTT* SO40 144 B7
Jessie Rd *ENEY* PO4 21 M5
GPORT PO12 14 D5
HAV PO9 170 C5
Jessie Ter *SHAM* SO14 23 H6
Jessop Cl *FAWY* SO45 176 F3
Jessopp Cl *NBNE* BH10 213 M4
Jessopp Rd *WIMB* BH21 208 B2
Jesty Rd *NARL* SO24 291 K12
Jetty Rd *FAWY* SO45 178 B7
Jewell Rd *CHAR* BH8 214 F7
Jewry St *WINC* SO23 25 G5
Jex Blake Cl *ROWN* SO16 146 B4
Jibbs Meadow *TADY* RG26 46 B5
Jimmy Brown Av *WIMB* BH21 205 G3
Jinny La *ROMY* SO51 130 E3
Joanna Cl *RSAL* SP5 331 R1
Jobson Cl *WHCH* RG28 87 L7
Jockey La *ELGH* SO50 134 E7
Jodrell Cl *HORN* PO8 156 C1
Joe Bigwood Cl *ROWN* SO16 145 K3
John Bunyan Cl *FHAM* PO15 164 C4
John Cl *ALDT* GU11 2 A6
John Darling Ml *ELGH* SO50 * 134 A8
John Eggars Sq *ALTN* GU34 107 G3
John Hunt Cl *STHA* RG19 35 L2
John Morgan Cl *HTWY* RG27 56 D5
Johnson Dr *EWKG* RG40 42 D1
Johnson Rd *WIMB* BH21 209 G1
Johnson St *SHAM* SO14 23 H3
Johnson Vw *FHAM* PO15 164 E6
Johnson Wy *FLEETS* GU52 71 H2
RAND SP11 265 L11
Johns Rd *FHAM/PORC* PO16 11 G9
ITCH SO19 161 K5
Johnstone Rd
CHCH/BSGR BH23 228 E2
Johnston Rd *PLE* BH15 223 K1
John St *SHAM* SO14 23 H6
Jolliffe Av *PLE* BH15 223 K4
Jolliffe Rd *PLE* BH15 223 K4
Jonas Nichols Sq *SHAM* SO14 23 J3
Jonathan Cl *LYMN* SO41 221 L3
Jonathan Hl *KSCL* RG20 247 K1
Jones La *FAWY* SO45 176 F4
Jopps Cnr *CHCH/BSGR* BH23 216 C4
Jordan Cl *THLE* RG7 238 D7
Jordans La *LYMN* SO41 350 G9
LYMN SO41 356 B3
THLE RG7 39 M2
Joseph St *GPORT* PO12 * 15 H4
Joshua Cl *PLE* BH15 222 E6
Josian Wk *SHAM* SO14 23 J2
Jouldings La *HTWY* RG27 239 K12
Joule Rd *AND* SP10 95 K3
BSTK RG21 6 B1
Jowitt Dr *NMIL/BTOS* BH25 218 F6
Joys La *LYMN* SO41 356 E4
STOK SO20 272 E8
Joys Rd *WIMB* BH21 201 G8
Jubilee Av *CHAM* PO6 167 L8
Jubilee Cl *ELGH* SO50 139 M7
FARN GU14 60 C4
RGWD BH24 203 L4
TADY RG26 44 E3
WIMB BH21 210 E1
Jubilee Ct *FHAM/STUB* PO14 182 A1
LYMN SO41 350 F11
Jubilee Crs *BKME/WDN* BH12 224 D3
Jubilee Dr *ASHV* GU12 74 A2
Jubilee Gdns *NBNE* BH10 213 K6
WEND SO18 148 A5
Jubilee Hall Rd *FARN* GU14 61 J4
Jubilee La *GSHT* GU26 115 J5
RFNM GU10 78 E3
Jubilee Rd *ALDT* GU11 3 H8
BSTK RG21 6 E7
ENEY PO4 192 F5
EWKG RG40 42 B3
FBDG SP6 196 E3
FHAM/PORC PO16 167 K8
FRIM GU16 62 A6
GPORT PO12 14 F2
NWBY RG14 19 G6
PSTN BH14 224 D3
ROMY SO51 130 E8
WIMB BH21 210 E2

WVILLE PO7 155 L8
Jubilee Ter SSEA PO5 20 F6
Jubilee Trail WIMB BH21 336 C2
Jukes Wk HEND SO30 148 F2
Julia Cl CHCH/BSGR BH23 217 M8
Julian Cl ROWN SO16 146 F2
Julian Rd ITCH SO19 162 B1
Julian Ter BOSC BH5 * 227 H3
Julie Av FHAM PO15 10 A5
Juliet Ct WVILLE PO7 * 156 A8
Julius Cl CHIN RG24 64 E4
CHFD SO53 139 L2
Julkes La WHIT RG2 239 L1
Julyan Av BKME/WDN BH12 213 G8
Jumar Cl HLER SO31 179 K5
Jumpers Av CHCH/BSGR BH23 215 L8
Jumpers Rd CHCH/BSGR BH23 215 M8
Jumps Rd RFNM GU10 262 F9
Junction Rd AND SP10 4 F4
MOOR/WNTN BH9 213 M8
RSAL SP5 327 N1
TOTT SO40 159 G1
UPTN BH16 222 D4
Junction Ter NWBY RG14 19 J5
June Dr DEAN RG23 64 D7
Juniper Cl AND SP10 4 A7
BOR GU35 112 C2
CHIN RG24 54 C4
FERN BH22 204 E8
FUFL SO22 122 D7
LYMN SO41 221 H6
NBAD SO52 137 M3
WIMB BH21 201 G8
Juniper Rd FARN GU14 60 C3
HORN PO8 * 321 L11
RSAL SP5 282 A9
WEND SO18 161 M1
Juniper Sq HAV PO9 16 F6
The Junipers WWKG RG41 239 R4
Jupiter Cl ROWN SO16 145 L4
Jupiter Wy WIMB BH21 206 E8
Jura Cl CHAM PO6 168 F7
Jurds Lake Wy ITCH SO19 161 K7
Jurd Wy HLER SO31 162 F3
Justice Cl STHA RG19 35 M2
Justin Cl FHAM/STUB PO14 10 A6
Justin Gdns NBNE BH10 213 L4
Justinian Cl CHFD SO53 139 M1
Jute Cl FHAM/PORC PO16 167 H7
Jutland Cl FHAM PO15 164 B5
Jutland Crs AND SP10 84 B8
Juventu Cl HAV PO9 171 G5

K

Kamptee Copse
NMIL/BTOS BH25 219 H2
Kanes Hl ITCH SO19 148 F6
Kangaw Pl PLE BH15 222 D6
Karachi Cl NTID SP9 266 E1
Karen Av CHAM PO6 185 J2
Kassassin St ENEY PO4 193 G6
Kassel Cl WVILLE PO7 156 B7
Katherine Chance Cl
CHCH/BSGR BH23 216 C5
Kathleen Cl BSTK RG21 93 J2
Kathleen Rd ITCH SO19 162 B1
Kathryn Cl TOTT SO40 144 B7
Katrina Gdns HISD PO11 195 G3
Katrine Crs CHFD SO53 139 G1
Katterns Cl CHCH/BSGR BH23 215 L6
Kayak Cl HLER SO31 179 L3
Kay Cl CHCH/BSGR BH23 228 E2
Kay Crs BOR GU35 114 B2
Kayleigh Cl TOTT SO40 158 D2
Keable Rd RFNM GU10 78 D1
Kealy Rd GPORT PO12 191 G2
Kearsney Av NEND PO2 184 E6
Keats Av CHAM PO6 167 L7
LYMN SO41 232 D3
Keats Cl CHIN RG24 65 L3
FUFL SO22 122 C8
HLER SO31 164 B3
HORN PO8 155 M4
RWIN SO21 288 D4
Keats Rd WEND SO18 148 C6
Keats Wy CWTH RG45 43 K1
YTLY GU46 48 D4
Keble Cl CHFD SO53 139 J4
Keble Rd CHFD SO53 139 J4
Keble St FUFL SO22 122 C6
Keeble Cl NBNE BH10 213 K2
Keeble Crs NBNE BH10 213 K2
Keeble Rd NBNE BH10 213 K2
Keel Cl HSEA PO3 185 J5
LSOL/BMARY PO13 190 D1
Keepers Cl CHFD SO53 139 H2
Keeper's Hl RAND SP11 94 C7
Keepers La ROMY SO51 298 E10
WIMB BH21 208 E3
Keeps Md KSCL RG20 248 C9
The Keep FHAM/PORC PO16 183 K1
Kefford Cl HORN PO8 * 156 B2
Keighley Av BDST BH18 210 F6
Keighley Cl STHA RG19 35 J2
Keith Cl GPORT PO12 191 H2
Keith Lucas Rd FARN GU14 60 F6
Keith Rd TWDS BH3 225 J2
Kelburn Cl CHFD SO53 139 H1
Kellaway Rd CFDH BH17 211 M8
Kellett Rd WSHM SO15 146 D8
Kelly Cl CFDH BH17 211 M8
Kellynch Cl ALTN GU34 106 E4
Kelly Rd WVILLE PO7 169 L3
Kellys Wk AND SP10 4 C6
Kelmscott Gdns CHFD SO53 133 G7
Kelsall Gdns NMIL/BTOS BH25 219 G5
Kelsey Av EMRTH PO10 172 E5
EWKG RG40 42 A2
Kelsey Cl FHAM/STUB PO14 180 B3
LISS GU33 308 G7
Kelsey Gv YTLY GU46 49 G3
Kelvin Cl FAWY SO45 177 G5
WHIT RG2 239 L9
Kelvin Gv FHAM/PORC PO16 167 K8
HLER SO31 162 C6
Kelvin Hl KBH RG22 93 G2
Kelvin Rd ELGH SO50 139 M6
NWBY RG14 19 G2
Kembers La OVTN RG25 67 G4
Kemmel Rd RAND SP11 267 J1
Kemmitt Wy AND SP10 4 C9
Kemnal Pk HASM GU27 118 D4
Kemp Rd MOOR/WNTN BH9 213 M8
Kempshott Gdns KBH RG22 92 C4
Kempshott Gv KBH RG22 64 C8
Kempshott La KBH RG22 92 C3
Kempton Cl ALTN GU34 106 F6
NWBY RG14 19 K8
Kempton Ct FARN GU14 60 F6
Kempton Pk WVILLE PO7 156 B7
Kemshott Ct HAV PO9 170 D2
Ken Berry Ct HAV PO9 171 H2
The Kench HISD PO11 * 194 A4
Kendal Av HSEA PO3 185 G7
ROWN SO16 145 L8
WHIT RG2 238 E2
Kendal Cl CHFD SO53 139 L1
FARN GU14 * 60 E4
HORN PO8 156 A4
NTHA RG18 28 E8
Kendal Gdns KBH RG22 92 D3
Kendal Gv CBLY GU15 51 M4
Kendrick Rd NWBY RG14 33 K7
Kenilworth Cl
LSOL/BMARY PO13 189 M5
NMIL/BTOS BH25 219 H5
Kenilworth Crs FLEETN GU51 59 L6
Kenilworth Dr ELGH SO50 134 A6
Kenilworth Gdns HEND SO30 148 E3
Kenilworth Rd DEAN RG23 64 E6
FARN GU14 60 C3
FLEETN GU51 59 K7
SSEA PO5 * 192 D7
WSHM SO15 160 F2
Kenley Rd BOR GU35 114 B3
Kenmore Cl FLEETS GU52 71 K3
FRIM GU16 50 F8
TOTT SO40 158 D3
Kennard Ct NMIL/BTOS BH25 218 F5
Kennard Rd NMIL/BTOS BH25 218 F4
Kennart Rd CFDH BH17 223 G1
Kennedy Av FHAM PO15 165 L8
Kennedy Cl NWBY RG14 33 K6
WVILLE PO7 169 L4
Kennedy Crs GPORT PO12 190 E6
Kennedy Rd ROWN SO16 145 M5
Kennel La RFNM GU10 79 G6
Kennel Rd FUFL SO22 288 B12
Kennels La FARN GU14 60 C6
Kennet Cl ASHV GU12 74 A7
BSTK RG21 7 J5
FARN GU14 60 D2
GPORT PO12 191 H7
STHA RG19 35 L1
WEND SO18 148 B1
Kennet Ct AND SP10 * 96 E2
Kennet Rd NTID SP9 266 G2
NWBY RG14 18 D5
PSF GU32 120 C7
Kennet Side NWBY RG14 19 J4
Kennett Pl NWBY RG14 19 G2
Kennett Rd ROMY SO51 131 J8
Kennet Wy DEAN RG23 91 K3
Kennington La TOTT SO40 341 M5
Kennington Rd CFDH BH17 211 K8
Ken Rd SBNE BH6 227 L4
Kensington Cl ELGH SO50 134 D7
Kensington Dr WCLF BH2 8 B3
Kensington Flds FAWY SO45 176 D6
Kensington Gdns
FHAM/STUB PO14 180 C2
Kensington Pk LYMN SO41 232 C4
Kensington Rd GPORT PO12 15 G6
NEND PO2 184 F6
Kenson Gdns ITCH SO19 148 A8
Kent Cl WWKG RG41 239 R3
Kent Gv FHAM/PORC PO16 183 J2
Kentidge Rd WVILLE PO7 169 K3
Kentish Rd WSHM SO15 160 C1
Kent La RGWD BH24 199 G3
Kenton Cl FRIM GU16 51 H6
Kent Rd BKME/WDN BH12 224 E2
BOR GU35 112 F2
CHFD SO53 139 J5
FLEETN GU51 59 K7
LSOL/BMARY PO13 182 B4
PTSW SO17 147 J7
SSEA PO5 21 G7
Kent St PSEA PO1 20 D3
SHAM SO14 23 L1
Kenwith Av FLEETN GU51 59 L7
Kenwood Rd
FHAM/PORC PO16 183 K3
Kenwyn Cl WEND SO18 148 B2
Kenya Rd FHAM/PORC PO16 183 H1
Kenyon Cl PLE BH15 223 L1
Kenyon Rd NEND PO2 184 F6
PLE BH15 223 L1
Kenyons Yd AND SP10 4 C5
Keogh Barracks FRIM GU16 62 A8
Keogh Cl FRIM GU16 62 B7
Keppel Cl RGWD BH24 203 K5
Kerchers Fld OVTN RG25 89 J5
Kerfield Wy HTWY RG27 56 D7
Kerley Rd WCLF BH2 * 8 D8
Kern Cl ROWN SO16 145 M5
Kerrfield FUFL SO22 24 A7
Kerrfield Ms FUFL SO22 24 B6
Kerry Cl CHFD SO53 139 J2
FLEETN GU51 59 K3
LYMN SO41 221 J5
Kersey Crs NWBY RG14 27 G7
Kersley Crs ODIM RG29 68 E8
Kersley Gdns ITCH SO19 148 A8
Kesteven Wy WEND SO18 148 A4
Kestrel Cl BPWT SO32 143 G4
BPWT SO32 149 M3
FERN BH22 209 H1
FHAM/STUB PO14 181 H8
FUFL SO22 122 D8
HORN PO8 321 L8
NTID SP9 266 G1
RFNM GU10 76 B1
ROWN SO16 146 B3
STHA RG19 35 H1
TOTT SO40 159 L7
UPTN BH16 210 B8
Kestrel Ct RGWD BH24 203 J4
TADY RG26 * 53 H8
Kestrel Dr CHCH/BSGR BH23 229 G2
Kestrel Pl CHAM PO6 185 M1
Kestrel Rd ELGH SO50 139 L6
FARN GU14 61 H6
KBH RG22 92 C3
Kestrel Wy FBDG SP6 196 D7
Keswick Av HSEA PO3 185 G8
Keswick Cl CBLY GU15 51 L4
Keswick Rd BOSC BH5 226 F4
ITCH SO19 161 K5
NMIL/BTOS BH25 219 H3
Keswick Wy VWD BH31 201 G3
Ketchers Fld ALTN GU34 295 M10
Ketelbey Ri KBH RG22 93 H5
Kettering Ter NEND PO2 184 C8
Kevin Cl KSCL RG20 248 F10
Kevins Dr YTLY GU46 49 G1
Kevins Gv FLEETN GU51 59 K7
Kevlyn Crs HLER SO31 162 F3
Kewlake La ROMY SO51 340 H2
Kew La HLER SO31 163 G5
Kew Wk AND SP10 4 C7
Keydell Av HORN PO8 156 A3
Keydell Cl HORN PO8 156 A3
Keyes Cl BKME/WDN BH12 212 F7
CHCH/BSGR BH23 228 F2
LSOL/BMARY PO13 182 C4
Keyes Rd LSOL/BMARY PO13 182 C5
Keyhaven Cl
LSOL/BMARY PO13 182 A6
Keyhaven Dr HAV PO9 170 C3
Keyhaven Rd LYMN SO41 232 E4
Keynes Cl FLEETS GU52 71 K4
Keynsham Rd ITCH SO19 148 B6
Keynsham Wy SHST GU47 43 M6
Keysworth Av
NMIL/BTOS BH25 230 F1
Keysworth Rd UPTN BH16 222 C4
The Key FLEETN GU51 58 F5
Khandala Gdns WVILLE PO7 169 M4
Khartoum Rd PTSW SO17 147 G6
Khyber Rd BKME/WDN BH12 224 D3
Kidmore La WVILLE PO7 154 F2
Kielder Cl CHFD SO53 139 G1
Kielder Gv LSOL/BMARY PO13 182 D6
Kiel Dr AND SP10 84 B8
Kildare Rd BOR GU35 110 F8
Kilford Ct HEND SO30 150 A6
Kilham La FUFL SO22 122 B6
Killarney Cl ITCH SO19 162 E1
Killinghurst La HASM GU27 119 J6
Kilmarnock Rd
MOOR/WNTN BH9 213 M7
Kilmartin Gdns FRIM GU16 51 H7
Kilmeston Rd NARL SO24 303 R8
Kilmington Wy
CHCH/BSGR BH23 217 M8
Kilmiston Cl PSEA PO1 192 E1
Kilmiston Dr
FHAM/PORC PO16 167 J7
Kilmore Dr CBLY GU15 51 K4
Kilmuir Cl SHST GU47 49 M1
Kiln Acre FHAM/PORC PO16 * 11 H2
Kiln Cl FAWY SO45 176 E5
RSAL SP5 327 P3
WIMB BH21 210 C4
Kiln Fld LISS GU33 308 E7
Kiln Flds HASM GU27 118 C4
Kiln Gdns HTWY RG27 57 L2
Kiln Hl BPWT SO32 318 H12
THLE RG7 238 H9
Kiln La EPSF GU31 315 N12
NARL SO24 291 M7
RFNM GU10 79 G2
ROMY SO51 131 H2
RSAL SP5 332 G1
RWIN SO21 134 B2
TADY RG26 52 C7
THLE RG7 40 C3
WVILLE PO7 153 K4
Kiln Ride EWKG RG40 42 C1
Kiln Ride Extension EWKG RG40 42 C2
Kiln Rd CHIN RG24 65 G1
FHAM/PORC PO16 165 M8
HSEA PO3 185 G7
NWBY RG14 27 L7
Kilnside WVILLE PO7 154 F5
The Kilns ALTN GU34 * 107 H5
FNM GU9 * 77 H3
Kiln Wy ALDT GU11 3 G8
GSHT GU26 114 E3
VWD BH31 201 L4
Kilnyard Cl TOTT SO40 144 D7
Kilpatrick Cl NEND PO2 * 184 D8
Kilwich Wy FHAM/PORC PO16 183 H2
Kimbell Rd KBH RG22 93 H2
Kimber Cl CHIN RG24 54 B6
Kimberley FLEETS GU52 71 K4
Kimberley Cl AND SP10 95 M2
CHCH/BSGR BH23 215 M8
ELGH SO50 141 K2
Kimberley Rd ENEY PO4 193 G6
KBH RG22 93 G1
LISS GU33 309 J2
PSTN BH14 224 B5
SBNE BH6 227 J2
Kimber Rd BWD BH11 * 212 F5
Kimbers PSF GU32 120 C5
Kimbers Cl NWBY RG14 * 18 D4
Kimbers Dr NWBY RG14 26 E7
Kimbers La FNM GU9 13 K1
TADY RG26 44 D7
Kimbolton Rd HSEA PO3 193 G2
Kimbridge Crs HAV PO9 171 G2
Kimbridge La ROMY SO51 129 M1
Kimmeridge Av
BKME/WDN BH12 212 C8
Kimpton Cl LSOL/BMARY PO13 189 M6
Kimpton Ct HAV PO9 * 171 H2
Kimpton Dr FLEETN GU51 58 E5
Kineton Rd WSHM SO15 146 E7
King Alfred Pl WINC SO23 25 G3
King Alfred Ter WINC SO23 25 G3
King Arthur's Ct CHAM PO6 * 169 K8
King Arthur's Wy AND SP10 96 C1
King Charles St PSEA PO1 20 C5
King Cl RGWD BH24 202 B8
King Cup Av HLER SO31 179 M2
Kingcup Cl BDST BH18 210 E6
Kingdom Cl FHAM PO15 164 D7
King Edward Av
MOOR/WNTN BH9 213 M6
ROWN SO16 146 A8
King Edward's Crs NEND PO2 184 D6
Kingfisher Cl BOR GU35 113 G2
FARN GU14 60 C2
FERN BH22 205 H6
FLEETS GU52 71 J3
HAV PO9 157 H7
HISD PO11 195 J6
HLER SO31 163 G8
HORN PO8 155 L4
KBH RG22 92 B3
SBNE BH6 227 L2
THLE RG7 38 C1
WHCH RG28 * 87 L7
Kingfisher Copse HLER SO31 180 B1
Kingfisher Ct NWBY RG14 19 L4
Kingfisher Dr EMRTH PO10 172 B2
YTLY GU46 48 D2
Kingfisher Pk WIMB BH21 * 205 G2
Kingfisher Rd ELGH SO50 139 K6
Kingfishers FHAM/PORC PO16 166 F8
NTID SP9 266 E9
The Kingfishers VWD BH31 201 J3
Kingfisher Wk ASHV GU12 73 M5
Kingfisher Wy
CHCH/BSGR BH23 229 G3
RGWD BH24 203 K3
ROMY SO51 130 F8
TOTT SO40 159 L7
King George Av EPSF GU31 120 D5
MOOR/WNTN BH9 213 M6
King George Cl FARN GU14 61 K6
King George Ms EPSF GU31 120 D5
King George Rd AND SP10 4 B4
FHAM/PORC PO16 183 J1
King George's Av WSHM SO15 159 M2
King Henry I St PSEA PO1 20 F3
King John Av BWD BH11 212 D3
FHAM/PORC PO16 183 H1
King John Rd KSCL RG20 248 D10
King Johns Rd ODIM RG29 68 E4
Kingland Rd PLE BH15 223 K6
King La PSF GU32 307 K12
STOK SO20 269 P6
King Richard I Rd PSEA PO1 20 F4
King Richard Dr BWD BH11 212 D3
Kings Acre STOK SO20 299 Q1
Kings Apartments CBLY GU15 50 E4
Kings Arms La RGWD BH24 203 H5
Kings Arms Rw RGWD BH24 203 H5
King's Av CHCH/BSGR BH23 227 M2
FUFL SO22 122 E7
HLER SO31 178 E1
PSTN BH14 224 D6
RFNM GU10 73 L8
Kingsbere Av NBNE BH10 213 H6
Kingsbere Rd PLE BH15 223 L3
Kingsbridge Copse HTWY RG27 56 A8
Kingsbridge Hl THLE RG7 238 A10
Kingsbridge Rd NWBY RG14 18 A7
PSTN BH14 224 C5
Kingsbury Ct HORN PO8 321 K6
Kingsbury Rd SHAM SO14 161 H1
Kingsbury's La RGWD BH24 203 H5
Kingsclear Pk CBLY GU15 50 F4
Kingsclere Av HAV PO9 170 D3
ITCH SO19 161 M8
Kingsclere Cl ITCH SO19 161 M7
Kingsclere Rd BSTK RG21 6 B2
DEAN RG23 64 A2
OVTN RG25 89 J2
King's Cl CHFD SO53 139 K1
FERN BH22 204 F7
HAV PO9 157 G6
LYND SO43 345 K3
RWIN SO21 125 G5
WINC SO23 288 H7
Kings Copse Av HEND SO30 149 K6
King's Copse Rd FAWY SO45 354 E8
HEND SO30 149 J7
Kingscote Rd CHAM PO6 167 M6
HORN PO8 155 K5
King's Ct RFNM GU10 73 L8
Kings Crs LYMN SO41 221 J4
PSTN BH14 224 E6
Kingscroft FLEETN GU51 59 J8
Kingscroft Ct HAV PO9 16 B5
King's Croft La HAV PO9 170 C7
Kingsdown Pl PSEA PO1 * 21 L3
Kingsdown Rd WVILLE PO7 155 J6
Kingsdown Wy WEND SO18 147 M6
King's Elms RWIN SO21 273 P5
Kingsey Av EMRTH PO10 171 L8
Kingsfernsden La PSF GU32 120 E4
Kings Fld HLER SO31 163 G3
Kingsfield LYMN SO41 356 A10
RGWD BH24 203 J6
Kings Field Gdns HLER SO31 163 G3
Kingsfold Av WEND SO18 147 M5
Kingsford Cl RSAL SP5 332 F3
Kings Furlong Centre BSTK RG21 6 C8
Kings Furlong Dr BSTK RG21 6 B8
Kingsgate Rd WINC SO23 122 F7
Kingsgate St WINC SO23 25 G8
Kings Head Ms EPSF GU31 * 317 P1
King's Hl ALTN GU34 279 P12
Kings Keep FLEETS GU52 71 J2
SHST GU47 43 K7
Kingsland Cl CHAM PO6 168 C7
Kingsland Gra NWBY RG14 33 L4
Kingsland Rd ALTN GU34 106 E5
Kings La LYMN SO41 351 J12
PSF GU32 306 G10
RFNM GU10 78 D2
RWIN SO21 123 M6
Kingsley Av CBLY GU15 50 E4
SBNE BH6 228 A4
Kingsley Bungalows
NARL SO24 * 291 K12
Kingsley Cl CWTH RG45 43 K5
NWBY RG14 27 K7
SBNE BH6 228 A4
WHIT RG2 238 B1
Kingsley Gdns TOTT SO40 158 B1
Kingsley Pk WHCH RG28 87 L6
Kingsley Pl FUFL SO22 122 E7
Kingsley Rd ENEY PO4 193 H5
FARN GU14 60 F2
GPORT PO12 190 F1
HTWY RG27 241 Q4
WSHM SO15 160 B1
Kingsley Sq FLEETN GU51 58 E4
Kingsmead ALTN GU34 106 F5
FARN GU14 61 H4
FRIM GU16 61 L1
RAND SP11 95 L8
ROMY SO51 * 335 J5
WHAM PO17 152 C1
Kingsmead Av
FHAM/STUB PO14 189 K3
Kings Meadow AND SP10 5 J6
OVTN RG25 89 J4
Kings Mede HORN PO8 156 B2
Kingsmill Cl GPORT PO12 14 B5
Kingsmill Rd BSTK RG21 93 J2
CFDH BH17 223 L1
Kings Orch DEAN RG23 91 K4
Kings Paddock RSAL SP5 282 E11
Kings Pde FLEETN GU51 * 59 J6
King's Park Dr LTDN BH7 226 E2
King's Park Rd BMTH BH1 226 E2
WSHM SO15 161 G2
The Kings Peace GSHT GU26 * 115 J5
Kings Pightle CHIN RG24 54 B5
King's Ride CBLY GU15 50 F1
FAWY SO45 354 G9
King's Rd ALDT GU11 2 B4
ALTN GU34 106 D6
CHFD SO53 139 J2
CWTH RG45 43 K4
EMRTH PO10 171 L8
FHAM/PORC PO16 11 G6
FLEETN GU51 59 K7
FUFL SO22 122 C6
GPORT PO12 14 F4
HASM GU27 118 A6
HISD PO11 195 G3
HORN PO8 155 M5
KBH RG22 93 G1
LSOL/BMARY PO13 189 L5
LYMN SO41 221 K4
NMIL/BTOS BH25 219 J4
NWBY RG14 18 F5
PSEA PO1 20 B1
PSF GU32 120 B5
RAND SP11 84 D5
SSEA PO5 20 F6
THLE RG7 45 G3
TWDS BH3 226 A1
Kingsroad Rbt PSEA PO1 20 E6
Kings Rd West NWBY RG14 18 F5
King's Saltern Rd LYMN SO41 356 A10
Kings Somborne Rd
ROMY SO51 300 B11
King's Ter EMRTH PO10 171 M8
PSEA PO1 20 F6
Kingston HLER SO31 162 C5
Kingston Cl AND SP10 4 D9
Kingston Crs NEND PO2 184 D8
Kingston Gdns FHAM PO15 165 K8
Kingston Pk LYMN SO41 221 J6
ROMY SO51 335 J8
Kingston Rd GPORT PO12 14 B2
NEND PO2 184 E8
PLE BH15 223 K4
WSHM SO15 160 D2
King St EMRTH PO10 172 A6
EMRTH PO10 172 B3
GPORT PO12 15 K3
ODIM RG29 69 G5
SHAM SO14 23 H5
SSEA PO5 21 G5
THLE RG7 40 A2
WIMB BH21 207 H4
Kingsvale Ct BSTK RG21 6 B8
King's Wk CBLY GU15 50 B2
WHCH RG28 87 L7
WINC SO23 25 H6
King's Wy BPWT SO32 142 E1
BPWT SO32 318 G7
BPWT SO32 319 M8
FHAM/PORC PO16 166 F8
FHAM/PORC PO16 182 F1
NARL SO24 303 M2
RWIN SO21 290 A10
RWIN SO21 302 D8
WHAM PO17 153 M7
WINC SO23 123 H1
WVILLE PO7 153 M3
Kingsway ALDT GU11 2 C5
AND SP10 97 G2
BLKW GU17 49 M3
CHFD SO53 139 K2
FERN BH22 204 D8
HISD PO11 187 G5
SHAM SO14 23 H2
Kingsway Cl CHCH/BSGR BH23 215 M7
Kingsway Gdns AND SP10 96 C1
CHFD SO53 133 L8
The Kingsway
FHAM/PORC PO16 167 J8
Kingswell Cl NBNE BH10 213 K6
Kingswell Gdns NBNE BH10 213 H6
Kingswell Gv NBNE BH10 213 H6
Kingswell Rd NBNE BH10 213 J6
Kingswell St PSEA PO1 * 21 G2
Kingswood TOTT SO40 160 A7
Kingswood Firs GSHT GU26 115 J6
Kingswood La GSHT GU26 115 J6
Kingswood Ri ALTN GU34 293 K6
Kings Worthy Rd FLEETN GU51 58 E4
Kingsworthy Rd HAV PO9 170 F5
King's Yd AND SP10 5 J5
King William St PSEA PO1 20 D1
Kinnell Cl EMRTH PO10 171 M8
Kinross Crs CHAM PO6 185 H1
Kinross Rd TOTT SO40 158 F1
TWDS BH3 225 L2
Kinsbourne Av NBNE BH10 213 K6
Kinsbourne Cl ITCH SO19 148 F6
Kinsbourne Ri ITCH SO19 148 F7
Kinsbourne Wy ITCH SO19 148 E7
Kinson Av PLE BH15 224 A2
Kinson Gv NBNE BH10 213 J2
Kinson Park Rd NBNE BH10 213 K2
Kinson Rd NBNE BH10 213 H6
Kintbury Cross Ways
HUNG RG17 31 H5
Kintbury Rd HUNG RG17 30 F6
Kintbury Sq HUNG RG17 31 G2
Kintyre Cl DEAN RG23 91 J2
Kintyre Rd CHAM PO6 168 F7
Kinver Cl ROMY SO51 131 H7
Kipling Cl HLER SO31 164 B3
NTHA RG18 28 E7
YTLY GU46 48 E4
Kipling Ct ITCH SO19 161 M7
Kipling Rd ELGH SO50 139 M5
NEND PO2 184 E5
PSTN BH14 224 B3
Kipling Wk KBH RG22 93 G1
Kirby Cl PLE BH15 223 M2
Kirby Rd NEND PO2 184 E6
Kirby Wy SBNE BH6 227 K4
Kirkee Rd NTID SP9 266 E3
Kirk Gdns TOTT SO40 158 F3
Kirkham Av CHCH/BSGR BH23 216 C5
Kirkham Cl SHST GU47 43 M6
Kirk Knoll BOR GU35 111 M7
Kirkstall Rd ENEY PO4 192 D7
Kirkstone Cl CBLY GU15 51 M4
Kirkway BDST BH18 211 H4
Kirkwood Crs THLE RG7 39 M1
Kirriemuir Gdns ASHV GU12 74 D5
Kirtley Cl CHAM PO6 185 J2
Kirton Rd CHAM PO6 185 J1
Kitchener Crs CFDH BH17 211 H6
Kitchener Rd ALDT GU11 73 K2
LISS GU33 309 J2
PTSW SO17 147 J5
Kitchers Cl LYMN SO41 350 F9
Kitcombe La ALTN GU34 294 C7
Kite Cl HORN PO8 155 L4
Kites Croft Cl
FHAM/STUB PO14 180 C3
Kitnocks Hl BPWT SO32 150 E4
Kitscroft Rd NBNE BH10 213 J3
Kittiwake Cl
LSOL/BMARY PO13 182 B6
SBNE BH6 227 K2
Kitt's La NARL SO24 305 L10
RFNM GU10 262 F12
Kitwalls La LYMN SO41 232 D3
Kitwood Gn HAV PO9 * 171 H3
Kitwood La ALTN GU34 293 N9
Kitwood Rd ALTN GU34 293 M9
Kivernell Rd LYMN SO41 232 C4
Kiwi Cl PLE BH15 223 L5
Knapp Cl CHCH/BSGR BH23 216 A8
The Knapp Cl MARL SN8 264 F5
Knapp La ROMY SO51 132 D4
TADY RG26 44 D6
Knapp Mill Av
CHCH/BSGR BH23 216 A8
Knapps Hard PSF GU32 313 K3
Knatchbull Cl ROMY SO51 136 F1
Knellers La TOTT SO40 158 D4
Knight Cl FLEETN GU51 70 E2
WINC SO23 25 G1
Knightcrest Pk LYMN SO41 * 220 E7
Knight Gdns CHAM PO6 185 K1
Knighton Heath Cl BWD BH11 212 E4
Knighton Heath Rd
BWD BH11 212 E4
Knighton La BWD BH11 212 D1
Knighton Pk NMIL/BTOS BH25 218 E8
Knighton Rd ITCH SO19 161 M5
Knights Bank Rd
FHAM/STUB PO14 188 F3
Knightsbridge Dr STHA RG19 247 R1
Knightsbridge Rd CBLY GU15 51 G1
RAND SP11 84 E5
Knights Cl HLER SO31 179 L3
Knights La KSCL RG20 245 Q1
Knights Lea KSCL RG20 245 P1
Knights Rd BWD BH11 212 D3
Knightstone Gra FAWY SO45 177 G6
Knight St BSTK RG21 6 B6
Knights Wy ALTN GU34 106 D5
CBLY GU15 51 L4
Knightswood Vw
CHFD SO53 * 139 J2
Knightwood Av HAV PO9 171 G3
LYND SO43 345 K3
Knightwood Cl
CHCH/BSGR BH23 217 L8
LYND SO43 345 K3
TOTT SO40 158 B6
Knightwood Rd CHFD SO53 138 F4
FAWY SO45 177 H6

Knobcrook Rd WIMB BH21 207 H2
Knockhundred La GSHT GU26 115 H8
Knockwood La STOK SO20 284 A1
Knole Gdns BMTH BH1 226 D4
Knole Rd BMTH BH1 226 D3
Knoll Cl FLEETN GU51 59 J6
Knoll Ct FLEETN GU51 59 J5
Knoll Gdns RGWD BH24 202 B8
Knoll La WIMB BH21 206 B7
Knoll Rd CBLY GU15 50 F2
FLEETN GU51 59 J6
Knollys Rd ALDT GU11 72 F5
THLE RG7 44 F3
The Knook SHST GU47 * 49 M1
Knottgrass Rd HLER SO31 179 L2
Knowland Dr LYMN SO41 232 D3
Knowle Av WHAM PO17 165 L5
Knowle Crs KSCL RG20 248 D10
Knowle Ga WHAM PO17 165 L5
Knowle Hl ELGH SO50 134 B5
Knowle La ELGH SO50 141 L4
Knowle Rd BROC SO42 351 J2
WHAM PO17 165 M5
Knowles Av CWTH RG45 43 H4
Knowles Cl CHCH/BSGR BH23 228 E1
Knowles Meadow LISS GU33 308 H11
The Knowle BOR GU35 114 B2
The Knowlings WHCH RG28 87 M8
Knowlton Gdns
MOOR/WNTN BH9 214 B4
Knowlton Rd CFDH BH17 211 M6
Knowsley Crs CHAM PO6 185 G1
Knowsley Rd CHAM PO6 184 F1
Knox Cl FLEETS GU52 71 G3
Knox Rd HAV PO9 16 B4
NEND PO2 184 C7
Knox Ter ALTN GU34 * 107 G4
Knyght Cl ROMY SO51 137 G4
Knyveton Rd BMTH BH1 9 M4
Kohat Cl NTID SP9 266 D1
Kohat Ct ALDT GU11 2 C3
Kohima Cl ALDT GU11 3 H1
Komat Rd NTID SP9 266 E3
Kootenay Av WEND SO18 148 E5
Kooyong Cl ROMY SO51 335 M6
Krooner Rd CBLY GU15 50 D5
Kynegils Rd FUFL SO22 24 B1
Kynon Cl GPORT PO12 183 J8
Kyrchil La WIMB BH21 207 L2
Kyrchil Wy WIMB BH21 207 M1
Kytes La BPWT SO32 142 B7

L

Labrador Dr PLE BH15 223 K7
Laburnum Av CHAM PO6 185 J1
Laburnum Cl ALDT GU11 2 E4
FERN BH22 209 H2
NBAD SO52 138 A3
VWD BH31 201 L3
Laburnum Crs FAWY SO45 354 C1
Laburnum Dr LYMN SO41 220 D8
Laburnum Gv ELGH SO50 140 A1
HISD PO11 195 H4
NEND PO2 184 E7
NWBY RG14 18 E1
Laburnum Pas ALDT GU11 2 E3
Laburnum Rd ALDT GU11 2 E4
FHAM/PORC PO16 182 B2
FNM GU9 2 A9
HEND SO30 149 K6
ROWN SO16 147 J4
WVILLE PO7 169 L2
Laburnums HTWY RG27 * 46 F7
The Laburnums BLKW GU17 49 K3
Laburnum Wy DEAN RG23 64 F6
Lacey Crs PSTN BH14 224 A2
Lackford Av TOTT SO40 158 E2
Lacon Cl WEND SO18 147 L8
Lacy Cl WIMB BH21 207 K2
Lacy Dr WIMB BH21 207 J2
Ladram Rd GPORT PO12 190 E4
Ladwell Cl NWBY RG14 33 K7
Lady Betty's Dr FHAM PO15 164 E6
Ladybridge Rd WVILLE PO7 169 J4
Ladycross Rd FAWY SO45 177 G6
Lady Diana Ct RAND SP11 265 M10
Ladygate Dr GSHT GU26 115 G5
Lady Godley Cl NTID SP9 266 E3
Lady Jane Wk RAND SP11 265 M10
Ladysmith Cl
CHCH/BSGR BH23 228 E1
Ladysmith Pl BOR GU35 110 E7
Ladywell La NARL SO24 291 M9
Ladywood ELGH SO50 139 M2
Ladywood Av FARN GU14 60 C4
Laffan's Rd ALDT GU11 72 F3
ODIM RG29 68 F8
Laffan Tr ALDT GU11 72 C2
Lagado Cl PSTN BH14 224 C8
Lagland St PLE BH15 223 J6
Lagoon Rd PSTN BH14 224 B8
Lahore Cl NTID SP9 266 E1
Lahore Rd NTID SP9 266 E3
Laidlaw Cl BKME/WDN BH12 213 H8
Lainston Cl FUFL SO22 22 C2
Lake Av PLE BH15 222 D7
Lake Ct TADY RG26 44 D4
Lake Crs PLE BH15 222 E5
Lake Dr BOR GU35 113 G1
PLE BH15 222 D6
Lake End Wy CWTH RG45 43 J4
Lake Farm Cl HEND SO30 149 J4
Lake Grove Rd
NMIL/BTOS BH25 218 F4
Lakeland Dr FRIM GU16 51 G7
Lakeland Gdns TOTT SO40 159 L7
Lakelands Dr WSHM SO15 160 C2
Lake La RFNM GU10 109 L6
Lake Rd BPWT SO32 150 F4
BWD BH11 213 H2
CHFD SO53 133 L8
FRIM GU16 62 A2
ITCH SO19 161 K6
PLE BH15 222 E6
PSEA PO1 21 H1
VWD BH31 201 K3
Laker Sq AND SP10 96 E2
Lakeside ELGH SO50 139 M8
LSOL/BMARY PO13 189 M8
RGWD BH24 203 L6
WHAM PO17 165 L7
Lakeside Av HSEA PO3 193 H2
ROWN SO16 145 L3
Lakeside Cl AND SP10 95 M2
ASHV GU12 73 M4
Lakeside Ct FLEETN GU51 59 K5
Lakeside Dr HTWY RG27 241 K8
Lakeside Gdns FARN GU14 60 D1
HAV PO9 17 G2
Lakeside Rd ALDT GU11 73 G1
ASHV GU12 73 M4
CCLF BH13 225 G7
The Lake Side BLKW GU17 49 M4
Lakesmere Rd HORN PO8 156 C2
The Lakes BPWT SO32 318 A8
Lake Vw HTWY RG27 * 57 M1
Lakeview Dr RGWD BH24 203 L6
Lakewood Cl CHFD SO53 133 K8
Lakewood Rd
CHCH/BSGR BH23 217 M7
CHFD SO53 133 K8
TOTT SO40 158 C5
Lamb Cl AND SP10 5 L6
NTHA RG18 28 E7
Lambdens Wk TADY RG26 44 B4
Lambdown Ap RAND SP11 267 J2
Lambdown Ter RAND SP11 266 H2
Lamberhurst Cl ITCH SO19 162 A4
Lambert Cl WVILLE PO7 169 L3
Lambert Crs BLKW GU17 49 L4
Lamborne Cl SHST GU47 43 J7
Lambourn Cl
FHAM/STUB PO14 181 K4
Lambourne Cl FAWY SO45 176 F7
FHAM/STUB PO14 181 K4
RAND SP11 94 A4
RWIN SO21 301 N1
Lambourne Dr HLER SO31 180 A1
Lambourne Rd WEND SO18 148 B2
Lambourne Wy RAND SP11 94 A4
RFNM GU10 260 C1
Lambourn Rd KSCL RG20 26 E6
Lambourn Sq CHFD SO53 139 G2
Lambourn Valley Wy
KSCL RG20 26 D4
NWBY RG14 18 B4
Lambs Cl CFDH BH17 211 J7
Lambsgreen La WIMB BH21 206 F6
Lambs La THLE RG7 238 A8
Lambs Rw CHIN RG24 66 B1
Lamerton Rd BOR GU35 110 E8
Lammas Rd FAWY SO45 177 G6
Lamp Acres NWBY RG14 27 K7
Lampard La RFNM GU10 262 D10
Lampards Cl HTWY RG27 56 B2
Lampeter Av CHAM PO6 169 H8
Lampton Gdns
MOOR/WNTN BH9 213 M7
Lanark Cl FRIM GU16 51 G6
Lancaster Av FNM GU9 13 H7
Lancaster Cl AND SP10 4 E2
ASHV GU12 73 M3
BDST BH18 210 F3
CHCH/BSGR BH23 229 J1
FHAM/PORC PO16 167 H7
HLER SO31 163 G3
LSOL/BMARY PO13 190 B4
NTHA RG18 28 E8
Lancaster Ct HEND SO30 * 148 C2
Lancaster Dr BDST BH18 210 F3
CBLY GU15 50 F2
VWD BH31 201 G2
Lancaster Rd BSTK RG21 6 C2
FARN GU14 61 H7
ROWN SO16 145 M5
WIMB BH21 204 C8
Lancaster Wy FARN GU14 61 J1
WVILLE PO7 169 M2
Lancer Cl CHCH/BSGR BH23 227 M1
Lancer Ct ALDT GU11 2 A3
Lance's Hl ITCH SO19 161 M1
Landale Cl RAND SP11 84 D5
Lander Cl PLE BH15 223 K7
Landford Gdns CHAR BH8 214 D6
Landford Wy CHAR BH8 214 D6
Landguard Rd ENEY PO4 193 G5
WSHM SO15 160 D2
Landon Ct GPORT PO12 14 C9
Landon Rd LSOL/BMARY PO13 182 D8
Landport St PSEA PO1 20 F5
PSEA PO1 21 J1
Landport Ter PSEA PO1 20 F5
Landport Vw PSEA PO1 21 H1
Landsdowne St SSEA PO5 20 F5
Landseer Cl BSTK RG21 7 J9
SHST GU47 50 A2
Landseer Ct AND SP10 4 F2
Landseer Rd ITCH SO19 162 C1
WBNE BH4 225 J5
Lands End La BOR GU35 111 G7
Lands End Rd HLER SO31 163 H5
Lane End TADY RG26 46 B6
Lane End Cl WHIT RG2 238 E2
Lane End Dr EMRTH PO10 171 M8
Lane End Vls WHIT RG2 * 238 E2
Lanehays Rd FAWY SO45 176 F5
Lanesbridge Cl TOTT SO40 341 R7
Lanes End FHAM/STUB PO14 189 J2
The Lanes NMIL/BTOS BH25 219 G3
Laneswood FHAM/STUB PO14 39 L7
The Lane BMTH BH1 * 9 M1
ENEY PO4 192 F6
FAWY SO45 355 K5
GPORT PO12 191 G7
MFD/CHID GU8 263 P8
TADY RG26 44 B4
Langbar Cl ITCH SO19 161 L2
Langbrook Cl HAV PO9 16 E7
Langdale Av CHAM PO6 185 H1
Langdale Cl FARN GU14 60 E4
ROWN SO16 145 M8
Langdale Ct ASHV GU12 * 73 M3
Langdon Cl CBLY GU15 51 L4
Langdon Rd PSTN BH14 224 C4
Langdown Firs FAWY SO45 * 177 G5
Langdown Lawn FAWY SO45 177 G6
Langdown Lawn Cl
FAWY SO45 177 G6
Langdown Rd FAWY SO45 177 G5
Langford La RSAL SP5 327 P12
Langford Rd NEND PO2 192 F1
Langham Cl NBAD SO52 137 M4
Langham Rd ALTN GU34 106 E5
Langhorn Rd ROWN SO16 147 J4
Langley Cha RGWD BH24 202 C7
Langley Cl FLEETS GU52 71 H4
Langley Common Rd
EWKG RG40 239 M7
Langley Dr ALDT GU11 2 F6
CBLY GU15 50 F2
Langley Gdn FBDG SP6 197 J1
Langley Lodge Gdns
FAWY SO45 354 G9
Langley Rd CHCH/BSGR BH23 217 L7
NEND PO2 184 E8
PSTN BH14 224 F4
WSHM SO15 160 A2
Langrish Cl HAV PO9 171 G2
Langrish Rd ROWN SO16 146 B4
Langside Av BKME/WDN BH12 213 G8
Langstone Av HAV PO9 16 E8
Langstone Br HISD PO11 187 G3
Langstone High St HAV PO9 186 F2
Langstone Rd HAV PO9 16 E9
HSEA PO3 193 G2
Langstone Wk
FHAM/STUB PO14 181 J4
LSOL/BMARY PO13 182 B6
Langton Cl FUFL SO22 24 A1
NMIL/BTOS BH25 219 H8
Langton Dr BOR GU35 114 A1
Langton Farm Gdns PSEA PO1 192 E1
Langton Rd BPWT SO32 143 H4
LTDN BH7 226 F3
Langtons NARL SO24 291 N11
Lanham La FUFL SO22 301 Q5
Lankhills Rd WINC SO23 24 F1
Lansdown Av
FHAM/PORC PO16 183 K2
Lansdowne Av AND SP10 4 D8
WINC SO23 122 F7
WVILLE PO7 169 H5
Lansdowne Cl ROMY SO51 130 E8
Lansdowne Gdns BMTH BH1 9 H3
THLE RG7 238 C7
Lansdowne Hl SHAM SO14 22 F5
Lansdowne Rd ALDT GU11 2 E4
ALTN GU34 107 G3
BMTH BH1 9 G1
FRIM GU16 51 J8
WSHM SO15 160 A1
The Lansdowne Rbt BMTH BH1 9 H5
Lansley Rd BSTK RG21 65 K4
Lantana Cl WVILLE PO7 169 M2
Lanyard Dr LSOL/BMARY PO13 190 D2
Lapin La KBH RG22 92 D7
Lapthorn Cl
LSOL/BMARY PO13 182 B4
Lapwing Cl ENEY PO4 193 J3
GPORT PO12 191 H1
HORN PO8 156 A1
KBH RG22 92 B5
Lapwing Dr TOTT SO40 144 C8
Lapwing Gv FHAM/PORC PO16 166 F8
Lapwing Ri WHCH RG28 87 K6
Lapwing Rd WIMB BH21 208 A1
Lara Cl CHAR BH8 214 D5
Larch Av FAWY SO45 354 E3
Larch Cl CFDH BH17 210 F7
HEND SO30 148 D1
LIPH GU30 116 B5
LSOL/BMARY PO13 190 A3
LYMN SO41 219 M5
NWBY RG14 26 F7
RGWD BH24 202 C8
STOK SO20 270 D8
WINC SO23 288 H8
Larchdale Cl HLER SO31 179 K4
Larch Dr AND SP10 95 L5
KSCL RG20 248 D10
Larches Gdns FHAM PO15 181 J3
Larchfield Rd FLEETS GU52 71 J1
Larchfield Wy HORN PO8 156 C3
Larch Rd BOR GU35 114 B2
ROWN SO16 146 A5
Larch Rw FBDG SP6 197 M2
Larchside Cl THLE RG7 238 B6
Larch Wy FARN GU14 60 C5
FERN BH22 204 E8
HLER SO31 162 F4
Larchwood CHIN RG24 54 A4
Larchwood Av HAV PO9 170 B4
Larchwood Gld CBLY GU15 51 J1
Larchwood Rd TOTT SO40 158 C2
Larcombe Rd PSF GU32 120 B8
Larg Dr FUFL SO22 288 C12
Lark Cl AND SP10 96 D2
KBH RG22 92 B4
Larkfield CHIN RG24 54 B5
Larkfield Cl FNM GU9 12 A2
Larkfield Rd FNM GU9 12 A3
Lark Hill Ri FUFL SO22 122 D8
Larkhill Rd HSEA PO3 184 F4
Larkin Cl RAND SP11 * 265 N10
Lark Ri LIPH GU30 116 A3
Lark Rd CHCH/BSGR BH23 229 G2
Larks Barrow Hl WHCH RG28 87 L2
Larks Cl FERN BH22 209 H1
Larksfield Av
MOOR/WNTN BH9 214 B5
Larkshill Cl NMIL/BTOS BH25 219 H4
Larkspur Cha ITCH SO19 148 E7
Larkspur Cl ALDT GU11 2 F8
BPWT SO32 318 A7
HLER SO31 179 L2
WWKG RG41 239 R1
Larkspur Dr CHFD SO53 138 F1
TOTT SO40 159 L8
Larkspur Gdns FAWY SO45 354 D4
HEND SO30 149 J6
NTHA RG18 29 H8
Larks Ri FERN BH22 209 H1
Larkswood Cl SHST GU47 43 J7
Larkswood Dr CWTH RG45 43 K3
Larkwhistle Farm Rd
RWIN SO21 275 R3
Larmer Cl FLEETN GU51 70 F1
Larwood Sq AND SP10 96 E1
Lascelles Rd LTDN BH7 227 H2
Lascombe La RGUW GU3 261 L4
Laser Cl HLER SO31 179 L3
Lasham Gn HAV PO9 * 171 H3
Lasham Rd FLEETN GU51 58 E4
Lasham Wk FHAM/STUB PO14 181 K5
Lashly Meadow WVILLE PO7 319 Q9
Latch Farm Av
CHCH/BSGR BH23 216 A8
Latchmore Dr FAWY SO45 176 C4
Latchmore Forest Gv
HORN PO8 155 M5
Latchmore Gdns HORN PO8 155 L5
Latchwood La RFNM GU10 79 H3
Latelie Cl HLER SO31 162 B7
Latham Av FRIM GU16 51 G6
Latham Cl ELGH SO50 141 H2
Latham Ct WSHM SO15 160 B1
Latham Rd ELGH SO50 141 H2
ROMY SO51 130 F8
Latimer Ct HSEA PO3 * 185 H5
Latimer Rd MOOR/WNTN BH9 213 M8
Latimers Cl CHCH/BSGR BH23 217 M7
Latimer St ROMY SO51 136 E1
SHAM SO14 23 H6
Laud Cl NWBY RG14 27 M7
Lauder Cl EMRTH PO10 172 D4
FRIM GU16 51 G6
Lauderdale FARN GU14 60 D6
Launcelot Cl AND SP10 96 C1
Launcelyn Cl NBAD SO52 137 M5
Launceston Dr ELGH SO50 139 M3
Laundry La CBLY GU15 50 A3
HTWY RG27 240 D7
LYMN SO41 232 E4
Laundry Rd ROWN SO16 146 B6
Laurel Cl CBLY GU15 50 F4
CHCH/BSGR BH23 217 K7
DEAN RG23 91 K3
FARN GU14 60 C5
FAWY SO45 176 E5
GPORT PO12 191 J1
HLER SO31 164 B8
ITCH SO19 161 K5
LYMN SO41 219 L4
ODIM RG29 68 E5
RGWD BH24 202 A8
WIMB BH21 210 D2
Laureldene RGUW GU3 24 H7
Laurel Dr BDST BH18 211 H4
Laurel Gdns ALDT GU11 2 F8
BDST BH18 211 J4
HLER SO31 164 B8
Laurel Gv RFNM GU10 78 D3
Laurel La RGWD BH24 346 E1
Laurel Rd HLER SO31 164 B8
HORN PO8 156 C4
The Laurels AND SP10 4 D3
BROC SO42 * 351 K4
BSTK RG21 7 H2
FERN BH22 209 J1
FLEETN GU51 59 J7
FNM GU9 2 C8
NTHA RG18 * 28 E7
Laurence Ct RAND SP11 265 M10
Lauren Wy TOTT SO40 144 B7
Lauriston Dr CHFD SO53 133 H7
Laurus Cl WVILLE PO7 170 A3
Lavant Cl HORN PO8 156 B7
Lavant Dr HAV PO9 17 G1
Lavant St PSF GU32 120 C6
Lavell's La THLE RG7 40 C8
Lavender Cl ITCH SO19 161 M3
VWD BH31 201 L3
Lavender Ct AND SP10 4 C8
FHAM PO15 164 D3
Lavender Gdns BOR GU35 112 F2
Lavender La RFNM GU10 78 D4
Lavender Rd CHAR BH8 214 D4
KBH RG22 92 C5
LYMN SO41 219 L5
WVILLE PO7 170 A2
Lavender Wy BDST BH18 210 D5
Laverock Lea
FHAM/PORC PO16 167 J7
Laverstoke Cl ROWN SO16 145 L3
Laverstoke La OVTN RG25 100 E4
WHCH RG28 88 E7
Lavey's La FHAM PO15 165 H6
Lavington Gdns NBAD SO52 137 M5
Lavinia Rd BKME/WDN BH12 224 C1
GPORT PO12 14 D3
Lawday Link FNM GU9 76 E1
Lawday Pl FNM GU9 76 E1
Lawday Place La FNM GU9 76 E1
Lawford Crs YTLY GU46 48 F2
Lawford Ri
MOOR/WNTN BH9 * 214 A5
Lawford Rd MOOR/WNTN BH9 214 A5
Lawford Wy TOTT SO40 144 E8
Lawn Cl LSOL/BMARY PO13 182 D8
LYMN SO41 232 E4
Lawn Dr HLER SO31 180 A2
Lawn Rd ELGH SO50 134 B8
FUFL SO22 288 C11
LYMN SO41 221 H5
LYMN SO41 232 E4
PTSW SO17 147 H8
Lawns Cl WIMB BH21 208 C2
Lawnside Rd WSHM SO15 146 A8
Lawns Rd WIMB BH21 208 B2
The Lawns CHCH/BSGR BH23 218 B8
FARN GU14 60 E5
Lawn St WINC SO23 25 H5
Lawnswood ELGH SO50 * 141 K3
Lawnswood Cl FAWY SO45 176 E7
HORN PO8 155 M6
Lawn Vw NMIL/BTOS BH25 218 D3
Lawrence Av HORN PO8 155 L6
Lawrence Cl AND SP10 4 E1
CHIN RG24 65 L3
Lawrence Ct CHAR BH8 226 C2
Lawrencedale Ct BSTK RG21 6 B6
Lawrence Dr PSTN BH14 224 E7
Lawrence Gv ITCH SO19 161 M6
Lawrence Houses RAND SP11 269 P3
Lawrence La FBDG SP6 197 K8
Lawrence Md HUNG RG17 31 G2
Lawrence Pl NWBY RG14 27 L7
Lawrence Rd FHAM PO15 10 C4
FLEETS GU52 59 H8
RGWD BH24 203 L2
SSEA PO5 21 L7
Lawrences La NTHA RG18 28 F6
Lawrence Wk
LSOL/BMARY PO13 * 190 D2
Lawrence Wy CBLY GU15 50 B4
Lawson Cl HLER SO31 163 K4
Lawson Rd BKME/WDN BH12 224 B2
SSEA PO5 21 L5
Laws Ter ALDT GU11 3 J2
Laxton Cl HLER SO31 180 B1
ITCH SO19 162 A2
Layard Dr WIMB BH21 207 K7
Lay Fld HTWY RG27 56 B7
Layland's Gn HUNG RG17 31 H3
Layton Rd BKME/WDN BH12 224 D3
LSOL/BMARY PO13 182 C5
Lazy Acre EMRTH PO10 172 D6
Lea Cl ASHV GU12 74 A7
BSTK RG21 7 K4
FNM GU9 77 L2
Leacock Cl BPWT SO32 318 B8
Lea Ct FNM GU9 2 D8
Lea Cft CWTH RG45 43 K2
Leaden Vere ODIM RG29 258 B4
Leafy La FHAM PO15 164 E6
Lealand Gv CHAM PO6 169 K8
Lealand Rd CHAM PO6 185 K1
Leamington Crs
LSOL/BMARY PO13 189 M6
Leamington Rd
MOOR/WNTN BH9 226 A1
Leander Cl ELGH SO50 134 A7
Leander Dr GPORT PO12 191 J1
Lea-Oak Gdns FHAM PO15 181 K1
Leaphill Rd LTDN BH7 227 G2
Lea Rd CBLY GU15 50 D6
FAWY SO45 354 G9
Learoyd Rd CFDH BH17 223 K1
Lear Rd GPORT PO12 14 F3
Leaside Wy ROWN SO16 147 K3
Lea Springs FLEETN GU51 70 F1
The Lea FLEETN GU51 70 F1
VWD BH31 201 J3
Leatherhead Gdns HEND SO30 149 K2
Lea Wy ASHV GU12 73 M5
BWD BH11 212 E2
Leaway FNM GU9 * 77 L3
The Leaway
FHAM/PORC PO16 167 K8
Leawood Rd FLEETN GU51 70 F1
Lea Wood Rd FLEETN GU51 71 G1
Lebanon Rd WSHM SO15 159 K1
Le Borowe FLEETS GU52 71 G4
Lechlade Gdns FHAM PO15 165 K8
LTDN BH7 215 G8
Leckford Cl FHAM/PORC PO16 167 J7
WEND SO18 148 D4
Leckford La STOK SO20 285 Q4
Leckford Rd HAV PO9 171 H2
Lecole Wk HEND SO30 * 150 A5
Ledbury Rd CHAM PO6 168 C7
CHCH/BSGR BH23 228 F3
Lederle La LSOL/BMARY PO13 182 C3
Ledgard Cl PSTN BH14 224 B4
Ledwell Ct GPORT PO12 15 J1
Lee Church La ROMY SO51 136 F8
Lee Ct ALDT GU11 3 J6
Leedam Rd NBNE BH10 213 K4
Lee Dro ROMY SO51 137 G7
Lee Lands LYMN SO41 221 K7
Lee La ROMY SO51 137 G8
Leep La GPORT PO12 14 F9
Lee Rd ALDT GU11 2 A3
GPORT PO12 191 G2
Lees Cl CHCH/BSGR BH23 215 K4
Leesland Rd GPORT PO12 14 C2
Lees La GPORT PO12 14 E2
Leeson Dr FERN BH22 204 D8
Leeson Rd LTDN BH7 226 E1
Lefroy Av BSTK RG21 7 H1
Lefroy's Fld RFNM GU10 70 F8
Leger Cl FLEETS GU52 71 G3
Legge Crs ALDT GU11 2 A4
Legg La WIMB BH21 207 K4
Legion Cl PLE BH15 222 E6
Legion La WINC SO23 289 J9
Legion Rd HISD PO11 195 G4
PLE BH15 222 E6
Lehar Cl KBH RG22 92 F4
Leicester Ct
LSOL/BMARY PO13 * 190 D3
Leicester Pl AND SP10 5 G6
Leicester Rd CCLF BH13 224 F5
WSHM SO15 146 D6
Leicester Wy WINC SO23 25 M2
Leigham Vale Rd SBNE BH6 227 K4
Leigh Cl AND SP10 5 L7
Leigh Common WIMB BH21 207 L3
Leigh Fld THLE RG7 39 M6
Leigh Gdns AND SP10 5 L7
WIMB BH21 207 K4
Leigh La FNM GU9 13 L8
WIMB BH21 207 M3
Leigh Pk LYMN SO41 221 J4
Leigh Rd AND SP10 5 L7
CHFD SO53 139 J4
FHAM/PORC PO16 10 E4
HAV PO9 16 F2
NMIL/BTOS BH25 219 G4
PTSW SO17 147 G7
WIMB BH21 207 J4
Leighton Av WSHM SO15 146 B8
Leighton Rd ITCH SO19 161 L5
Leipzig Barracks FLEETS GU52 71 K6
Leipzig Rd FLEETS GU52 71 K5
Leith Av FHAM/PORC PO16 167 K7
Leith Cl CWTH RG45 43 J1
Leith Dr ALDT GU11 2 D2
Le Marchant Rd FRIM GU16 51 H5
Lemon Gv BOR GU35 112 E3
Lemon Rd WSHM SO15 160 B1
Lena Cl RAND SP11 265 L10
Lendorber Av CHAM PO6 185 G1
Lendore Rd FRIM GU16 50 F8
Lennel Gdns FLEETS GU52 71 L2
Lennon Wy KBH RG22 92 E5
Lennox Cl CHFD SO53 133 L8
GPORT PO12 191 H7
ROWN SO16 145 M3
Lennox Rd KBH RG22 93 G2
Lennox Rd North SSEA PO5 21 J8
Lennox Rd South SSEA PO5 21 J9
Len Smart Ct BSTK RG21 65 L5
Lensyd Gdns HORN PO8 155 M2
Lenten St ALTN GU34 106 E5
Lentham Cl CFDH BH17 211 K7
Lent Hill Ct FUFL SO22 * 24 B9
Lentune Wy LYMN SO41 221 K6
Leofric Ct ENEY PO4 193 J5
Leominster Rd CHAM PO6 168 B7
Leonard Cl FRIM GU16 50 F8
Leonard Rd GPORT PO12 15 H3
Leonardslee Crs NWBY RG14 19 L2
Leopald Av FARN GU14 61 H3
Leopold Dr BPWT SO32 143 H5
Leopold St ENEY PO4 21 M8
Le Patourel Cl
CHCH/BSGR BH23 228 D1
Lepe Rd FAWY SO45 354 H9
Leroux Cl WSHM SO15 22 E1
Lerryn Rd LSOL/BMARY PO13 182 D6
Leslie Rd MOOR/WNTN BH9 213 L8
PSTN BH14 224 A5
Leslie Southern Ct NWBY RG14 19 G2
Lesser Horseshoe Cl
WHAM PO17 165 L4
Lester Av HAV PO9 170 C6
Lester Rd GPORT PO12 14 A3
Lestock Wy FLEETN GU51 59 L7
Levell Ct RAND SP11 265 M10
Leven Av WBNE BH4 8 A2
Leven Cl CHFD SO53 133 G8
WBNE BH4 8 A3
Leventhorpe Ct GPORT PO12 15 C5
Levern Dr FNM GU9 77 C2
Leveson Cl GPORT PO12 14 A7
Levet's La PLE BH15 223 H6
Leviathan Cl
FHAM/STUB PO14 189 K2
Levignen Cl FLEETS GU52 70 F3
Lewendon Rd NWBY RG14 27 G7
Lewens Cl WIMB BH21 207 J4
Lewes Cl ELGH SO50 134 A6
Lewesdon Dr BDST BH18 210 F4
Lewin Cl RWIN SO21 135 G4
Lewins Wk HLER SO31 162 F3
Lewis Cl BSTK RG21 7 H1
FAWY SO45 176 C6
Lewisham Wy SHST GU47 43 M7
Lewis Rd EMRTH PO10 172 A3
Lewis Silkin Wy ROWN SO16 146 A4
Lewry Cl HEND SO30 149 J5
Lexby Rd TOTT SO40 159 G2
Lexden Gdns HISD PO11 194 E4
Lexington Gv WHIT RG2 238 C2
Leybourne Av NBNE BH10 213 K3
WEND SO18 147 M8
Leybourne Cl NBNE BH10 213 J3
Leydene Av CHAR BH8 214 F7
Leydene Cl CHAR BH8 214 F7
Leydene Pk PSF GU32 * 320 G2
Leyland Cl GPORT PO12 14 F7
Leyland Gdns WHIT RG2 238 E3
Leyland Rd BKME/WDN BH12 212 E6
Ley Rd FARN GU14 50 C8
Leys Gdns NWBY RG14 18 D2
Leyside CHCH/BSGR BH23 228 F2
CWTH RG45 43 J3
Leyton Rd SHAM SO14 161 J2
Leyton Wy AND SP10 4 D9
Liam Cl HAV PO9 171 G4
The Liberties BPWT SO32 * 318 H10
Liberty Cl WIMB BH21 205 K2
Liberty Rd BPWT SO32 318 G12
The Liberty WVILLE PO7 154 E5
Library Gdns HAV PO9 16 D1
Library La RWIN SO21 287 M12
Library Rd BKME/WDN BH12 224 E3
FARN GU14 61 H6
FERN BH22 209 K3
MOOR/WNTN BH9 213 M7
TOTT SO40 159 G1
Lichen Wy TOTT SO40 159 M6
Lichfield Ct
LSOL/BMARY PO13 * 190 D3
Lichfield Rd FHAM/STUB PO14 180 C1
HSEA PO3 193 G2
Lickfolds Rd RFNM GU10 109 L2
Liddell Cl EWKG RG40 42 A5
Liddel Wy CHFD SO53 139 G3
Liddiards Wy WVILLE PO7 169 L5

Lidiard Gdns ENEY PO4 193 H6
Liederbach Dr VWD BH31 201 L4
Lightfoot Gv BSTK RG21 93 K2
Lightsfield DEAN RG23 91 K2
Light's La RSAL SP5 327 M1
Lilac Cl AND SP10 4 A7
BOR GU35 112 F2
HAV PO9 171 J5
RGWD BH24 203 K4
Lilac Rd ROWN SO16 147 H4
The Lilacs WWKG RG41 239 Q5
Lilac Wy DEAN RG23 64 F6
Lille Barracks ALDT GU11 61 K8
The Lillies ELGH SO50 141 K5
Lilliput Rd PSTN BH14 224 C8
Lillywhite Crs AND SP10 84 D8
Lily Av WVILLE PO7 169 H6
Lily Cl KBH RG22 92 C5
Limberline Rd HSEA PO3 185 G4
Limberline Sp HSEA PO3 185 G3
Limbrey Hl OVTN RG25 257 K3
Lime Av ALTN GU34 106 E3
CBLY GU15 51 J2
ITCH SO19 148 A7
Lime Cl FAWY SO45 176 E6
ITCH SO19 148 A7
NWBY RG14 19 M2
PLE BH15 223 M2
RWIN SO21 135 G4
Limecroft YTLY GU46 48 E3
Lime Dr FLEETN GU51 59 K4
Lime Gdns BSTK RG21 7 L5
HEND SO30 148 D1
Lime Gv ALTN GU34 106 E3
CHAM PO6 168 B7
HISD PO11 194 C5
LYMN SO41 220 D8
Lime Kiln La FAWY SO45 354 D2
Limekiln La BPWT SO32 143 M1
PSF GU32 314 G9
PSF GU32 315 J12
Limekiln Lane Est
FAWY SO45 * 354 D3
Limekiln Rd RAND SP11 80 D7
Lime Rd NARL SO24 291 M11
Limes Av KSCL RG20 247 J5
Limes Cl LIPH GU30 116 C1
LISS GU33 308 F8
Limes Rd FARN GU14 60 C3
The Limes LSOL/BMARY PO13 182 D7
TADY RG26 46 D6
TOTT SO40 160 A7
Lime St ALDT GU11 2 D3
SHAM SO14 23 H5
Limetree Av KSCL RG20 246 D10
Lime Tree Cl FBDG SP6 196 B7
Limetree Wk WINC SO23 25 M5
Lime Tree Wy CHIN RG24 54 A5
Lime Wk AND SP10 4 A8
FAWY SO45 176 E6
Limited Rd MOOR/WNTN BH9 214 A7
Limmer Cl WWKG RG41 239 Q4
Linacre Rd ITCH SO19 148 D8
Lin Brook Dr RGWD BH24 203 L2
Linchmere Rd HASM GU27 117 J5
Lincoln Av BMTH BH1 226 D2
CHCH/BSGR BH23 215 M6
Lincoln Cl ASHV GU12 74 A3
CBLY GU15 51 K4
FHAM/STUB PO14 180 C1
KBH RG22 92 D5
Lincoln Ct LSOL/BMARY PO13 * 190 D3
NWBY RG14 18 C5
WSHM SO15 146 E6
Lincoln Gn ALTN GU34 106 E6
Lincoln Ri HORN PO8 156 A4
Lincoln Rd BKME/WDN BH12 224 D1
FARN GU14 61 G7
PSEA PO1 21 M2
Lincolns Ri ELGH SO50 134 B4
Linda Gv HORN PO8 155 M5
Linda Rd FAWY SO45 355 K5
Lindbergh Rd WIMB BH21 204 C8
Lindberg Ri FHAM PO15 164 E7
Lind Cl WVILLE PO7 169 M5
Linden Av CHIN RG24 66 D3
ODIM RG29 69 H4
Linden Cl BPWT SO32 151 L1
FERN BH22 209 K7
NWBY RG14 18 C1
RAND SP11 265 N10
Linden Ct CBLY GU15 51 H1
Linden Dr LISS GU33 308 F8
Linden Gdns HEND SO30 149 K7
Linden Gv CHFD SO53 133 J8
GPORT PO12 14 E6
HISD PO11 195 G5
Linden Lea FHAM/PORC PO16 167 J7
Lindenmuth Wy STHA RG19 34 F7
Linden Rd BKME/WDN BH12 224 C2
BOR GU35 114 B3
FERN BH22 209 K7
MOOR/WNTN BH9 214 A5
ROMY SO51 136 F1
ROWN SO16 146 A4
Lindens Cl EMRTH PO10 171 M5
The Lindens CHCH/BSGR BH23 216 D5
FNM GU9 13 K6
Linden Wk NBAD SO52 137 M3
Linden Wy HAV PO9 * 170 F5
HORN PO8 156 B3
LYMN SO41 221 J4
Lindford Cha BOR GU35 111 H7
Lindford Rd BOR GU35 111 G6
Lindford Wey BOR GU35 111 H7
Lindisfarne Cl CHAM PO6 185 G1
Lindley Av ENEY PO4 193 G6
Lindley Gdns NARL SO24 291 M12
Lind Rd GPORT PO12 191 J7
Lindsay Rd CCLF BH13 225 G4
ITCH SO19 148 E6
Lindum Dene ALDT GU11 2 E5
Lindway HLER SO31 164 A7
Lineside CHCH/BSGR BH23 216 C8
The Lines KSCL RG20 248 D9
Linford Cl NMIL/BTOS BH25 219 G4
Linford Ct HAV PO9 170 D1
Linford Crs ROWN SO16 146 D5
Linford Rd RGWD BH24 203 M3
Ling Crs BOR GU35 114 B2
Ling Dl ROWN SO16 146 F1
Lingdale Rd SBNE BH6 227 K2
Lingen Cl AND SP10 96 B1
Lingfield Cl ALTN GU34 106 F6
CHIN RG24 66 E3
Lingfield Gdns WEND SO18 147 M5
Lingfield Rd NWBY RG14 19 J9
Lingmala Gv FLEETS GU52 71 K3
Ling Rd BKME/WDN BH12 212 B7
Lingwood Av
CHCH/BSGR BH23 228 F2
Lingwood Cl ROWN SO16 146 F1
Lingwood Wk ROWN SO16 146 F1
Linhorns La NMIL/BTOS BH25 219 G2
Linkenholt Wy HAV PO9 170 C3
Linklater Pth PSEA PO1 192 D1
Link Ri WIMB BH21 210 E2
Link Rd ALTN GU34 107 G2
CHAM PO6 168 B6
FARN GU14 60 D8
KSCL RG20 248 E10
NWBY RG14 18 E6
RGWD BH24 203 L3
ROWN SO16 145 M5
Links Dr CHCH/BSGR BH23 215 K7
Linkside Av CHAR BH8 214 E8
Linkside East GSHT GU26 115 H1
Linkside North GSHT GU26 115 H1
Linkside South GSHT GU26 115 J2
Linkside West GSHT GU26 115 H1
Links La HAV PO9 157 H5
HISD PO11 194 C5
Links Rd FUFL SO22 24 A3
PSTN BH14 224 D6
The Links BOR GU35 112 D3
LSOL/BMARY PO13 182 C7
Links View Av PSTN BH14 224 E7
Links View Wy ROWN SO16 146 F2
Links Wy FARN GU14 60 C5
The Link AND SP10 95 L4
WVILLE PO7 156 A7
YTLY GU46 48 E1
Link Vw NWBY RG14 * 27 H5
Link Wy DEAN RG23 91 K3
NTHA RG18 28 D8
WHIT RG2 239 L6
Linkway CBLY GU15 50 E4
CWTH RG45 43 H3
FHAM/STUB PO14 189 J3
FLEETS GU52 71 H2
Linmead Dr BWD BH11 213 G2
Linnet Cl EPSF GU31 121 G7
HORN PO8 155 L4
KBH RG22 92 C2
RGWD BH24 203 L6
Linnet Ct NMIL/BTOS BH25 218 F5
Linnet Rd CFDH BH17 210 E8
Linnet Sq ELGH SO50 139 K7
Linnets Rd NARL SO24 291 L12
The Linnets FHAM/PORC PO16 182 F1
TOTT SO40 144 C8
Linnets Wy ALTN GU34 106 F3
Linnies La LYMN SO41 220 A1
Linsford La FRIM GU16 61 M5
Linstead Rd FARN GU14 50 A8
Linsted La BOR GU35 111 K5
Linthorpe Rd PLE BH15 223 L4
Linton Cl TADY RG26 44 C5
Linton Dr AND SP10 85 J7
Linwood Cl FAWY SO45 177 G6
Linwood Rd MOOR/WNTN BH9 226 B1
Lion Cl OVTN RG25 89 J5
Lionheart Cl BWD BH11 212 D3
Lionheart Wy HLER SO31 162 F3
Lion & Lamb Wy FNM GU9 12 E3
Lion & Lamb Yd FNM GU9 * 12 E3
Lion La GSHT GU26 115 M7
Lion Md HASM GU27 117 M2
Lion Rd FARN GU14 61 H6
Lions Fld BOR GU35 295 R4
Lions Ga FBDG SP6 * 197 H3
Lions Hill Wy RGWD BH24 205 L3
Lions La RGWD BH24 205 M4
Lion St PSEA PO1 20 E2
Lions Wd RGWD BH24 202 A8
Lion Ter PSEA PO1 20 E2
Lion Wy FLEETS GU52 71 K3
Liphook Rd BOR GU35 111 H7
BOR GU35 112 E4
HASM GU27 117 G4
Lipizzaner Flds HLER SO31 164 B4
Lippen La BPWT SO32 312 H5
Lipscombe Cl NWBY RG14 18 A5
Lipscombe Ri ALTN GU34 106 F3
Lisbon Rd WSHM SO15 160 D2
Liskeard Dr FARN GU14 61 G2
Lisle Cl FUFL SO22 124 A1
LYMN SO41 221 K5
NWBY RG14 27 H7
Lisle Ct FUFL SO22 24 D9
Lisle Court Rd LYMN SO41 356 B8
Lisle Wy EMRTH PO10 171 L5
Lismoyne Cl FLEETN GU51 59 H6
Liss Rd ENEY PO4 192 F4
Lister Rd KBH RG22 93 M3
Litchfield Cl AND SP10 95 H1
Litchfield Crs WEND SO18 147 M7
Litchfield Rd FUFL SO22 288 D12
WEND SO18 147 M7
Litchford Rd NMIL/BTOS BH25 219 J4
Lith Av HORN PO8 321 L12
Lith La HORN PO8 321 L11
The Litter KSCL RG20 248 D10
Little Abshot Rd
FHAM/STUB PO14 180 B4
Little Aldershot La STHA RG19 249 R1
Little Anglesey Rd GPORT PO12 14 C8
Little Arthur St NEND PO2 * 192 E1
Little Ashton La BPWT SO32 143 K1
Little Austins Rd FNM GU9 13 K7
Little Barn Pl LISS GU33 308 H8
Little Barrs Dr
NMIL/BTOS BH25 219 H4
Little Basing CHIN RG24 66 B1
Little Binfield CHIN RG24 54 C7
Little Bull La BPWT SO32 151 K2
Little Copse AND SP10 4 C9
FLEETS GU52 71 H1
YTLY GU46 48 E1
Little Copse Cha CHIN RG24 54 A6
Little Cnr WVILLE PO7 154 F5
Littlecroft Av
MOOR/WNTN BH9 214 B5
Little Croft Rd
BKME/WDN BH12 224 B2
Little Dean La OVTN RG25 257 N3
Little Dene Copse LYMN SO41 221 H6
Little Dewlands VWD BH31 200 F2
Littledown Av LTDN BH7 226 E1
Littledown Dr LTDN BH7 226 E1
Little Dro FBDG SP6 332 A9
Little Drove Rd STOK SO20 272 E9
Little Fallow CHIN RG24 54 B8
Littlefield Cl ASHV GU12 74 A7
Littlefield Crs CHFD SO53 138 E2
Littlefield Gdns ASHV GU12 74 A7
Littlefield Rd ALTN GU34 107 G4
Little Forest Rd WBNE BH4 8 B1
Little Fox Dr FHAM PO15 164 B7
Little Foxes EWKG RG40 42 C1
Little Frith EWKG RG40 42 F2
Little Gays FHAM/STUB PO14 188 F2
Little George St PSEA PO1 192 E1
Little Gn GPORT PO12 14 C8
Littlegreen Av HAV PO9 171 G5
Little Green La FNM GU9 78 E1
Little Green Orch GPORT PO12 * 14 C8
Little Hambrook St SSEA PO5 * 20 F6
Little Hayes La RWIN SO21 290 B9
Little Hoddington Cl
OVTN RG25 257 L3
Little Hyden La HORN PO8 321 K5
Little Knowle Hl KSCL RG20 248 F8
Little Lance's Hl ITCH SO19 161 M1
Little La GPORT PO12 14 C8
THLE RG7 29 L6
Little London Rd THLE RG7 45 G6
Little Md WVILLE PO7 155 G5
Littlemead Cl CFDH BH17 223 G1
Littlemeads ROMY SO51 136 D1
Littlemill La FBDG SP6 330 C11
Little Minster St WINC SO23 25 G6
Little Moor SHST GU47 43 L7
Littlemoor Av BWD BH11 212 D4
Little Oak Rd ROWN SO16 146 F4
Littlepark Av HAV PO9 170 B5
Little Park Cl HEND SO30 149 H6
Little Park Farm Rd
FHAM PO15 164 C7
Little Quob La HEND SO30 148 E2
Little Shore La BPWT SO32 143 J5
Little Southsea St SSEA PO5 20 F6
Little Thurbans Cl FNM GU9 78 E2
Littleton Gv HAV PO9 170 F4
Littleton La RWIN SO21 301 P2
Little Vigo YTLY GU46 48 D4
Little Wellington St ALDT GU11 2 F3
Little Woodfalls Dr RSAL SP5 332 F4
Littlewood Gdns HEND SO30 148 D3
HLER SO31 179 L1
Little Woodham La
LSOL/BMARY PO13 190 C3
Littleworth Rd MFD/CHID GU8 261 J9
RFNM GU10 260 D7
Litton Gdns DEAN RG23 91 K3
Liverpool Ct
LSOL/BMARY PO13 * 190 D3
Liverpool Rd
FHAM/STUB PO14 181 M6
PSEA PO1 21 M2
Liverpool St SHAM SO14 161 G1
Livery Rd RSAL SP5 282 E11
RSAL SP5 296 F6
Livesay Gdns HSEA PO3 192 F2
Livia Cl AND SP10 84 D8
Livingstone Rd AND SP10 97 G3
BKME/WDN BH12 224 C2
BOSC BH5 227 H4
CHCH/BSGR BH23 228 D2
NWBY RG14 19 G5
SHAM SO14 147 G8
SSEA PO5 21 K6
WIMB BH21 207 L4
Llangar Gv CWTH RG45 43 J3
Llewellin Cl UPTN BH16 222 C1
Lloyd Av TOTT SO40 159 L7
Lloyd's La TADY RG26 255 N3
Loader Cl WINC SO23 289 J9
Loaders Cl MOOR/WNTN BH9 214 A8
Loane Rd ITCH SO19 161 M5
Lobelia Rd ROWN SO16 147 J4
Locarno Rd HSEA PO3 184 F6
Loch Rd PSTN BH14 224 E3
Lock Appoach CHAM PO6 184 A1
Locke Cl RAND SP11 269 L5
Lockerley Cl LYMN SO41 221 L6
Lockerley Crs ROWN SO16 145 M6
Lockerley Rd HAV PO9 171 G5
ROMY SO51 129 K3
Locke Rd HEND SO30 149 J4
LIPH GU30 116 D4
Locke's Dro RAND SP11 250 A8
Lockhams Rd BPWT SO32 150 F4
Lock Rd ALDT GU11 73 K3
Locksash La RCCH PO18 323 J12
Locksbridge La TADY RG26 53 M2
Locksheath Cl HAV PO9 170 D2
Locksheath Park Rd
HLER SO31 180 B3
Lockside Ct THLE RG7 38 C1
Lock's La RWIN SO21 301 N1
Locksley Dr FERN BH22 209 J5
Locksley Rd ELGH SO50 139 L7
Locksmead BSTK RG21 7 K4
Lock Sq AND SP10 96 E2
Locks Rd HLER SO31 164 A8
Locksway Rd ENEY PO4 193 J4
Lockswood Keep HLER SO31 * 164 A8
Lockswood Rd HLER SO31 179 M1
Lock Vw CHAM PO6 184 A1
Lockwood Cl FARN GU14 50 A8
Lockyers Dr FERN BH22 209 M2
Lockyers Rd WIMB BH21 206 E8
Loddon Cl CBLY GU15 51 J2
Loddon Ct BSTK RG21 93 K2
Loddon Dr BSTK RG21 7 J5
Loddon Rd FARN GU14 60 D2
Loddon Wy ASHV GU12 74 A7
Lode Hl RSAL SP5 332 D1
Loders Cl CFDH BH17 211 J5
Lodge Av CHAM PO6 169 G8
Lodgebury Cl EMRTH PO10 172 E6
Lodge Cl AND SP10 4 C5
PSTN BH14 224 E4
Lodge Ct PSTN BH14 224 E4
Lodge Dr FAWY SO45 176 F7
RAND SP11 94 F2
Lodge Dro RSAL SP5 332 E4
Lodge Gdns GPORT PO12 14 C6
Lodge Gv YTLY GU46 49 H2
Lodge Hill Cl RFNM GU10 79 H2
Lodge Hill Rd RFNM GU10 79 H2
Lodge La BROC SO42 353 L10
RAND SP11 82 D1
Lodge Rd CHCH/BSGR BH23 215 L8
HAV PO9 170 B7
HLER SO31 180 B1
LYMN SO41 221 H5
SHAM SO14 161 G1
The Lodge WSHM SO15 * 160 F1
Lodge V ROMY SO51 335 M6
Lodsworth FARN GU14 60 D5
Lodsworth Cl HORN PO8 321 M8
Loewy Crs BKME/WDN BH12 212 D6
Lofting Cl ELGH SO50 140 E2
Logan Cl ROWN SO16 145 M3
Loggon Rd BSTK RG21 93 J3
Loman Rd FRIM GU16 62 A5
Lomax Cl HEND SO30 149 J3
Lombard Av SBNE BH6 227 K3
Lombard St MFD/CHID GU8 261 K10
PSEA PO1 20 C5
Lombardy Cl
LSOL/BMARY PO13 182 E6
VWD BH31 201 K3
Lombardy Ri WVILLE PO7 169 M3
Lomer La RGWD BH24 196 E8
Lomond Cl DEAN RG23 91 J3
NEND PO2 184 D8
Londesborough Rd ENEY PO4 21 M6
Londlandes FLEETS GU52 71 G4
London Av NEND PO2 184 D6
London La CHCH/BSGR BH23 347 N10
London Ml NEND PO2 * 184 D7
London Rd ALTN GU34 107 J2
AND SP10 5 L5
BLKW GU17 50 A4
BSTK RG21 7 G6
CBLY GU15 50 F1
CHIN RG24 66 D4
CHAM PO6 168 F8
EPSF GU31 120 F4
HORN PO8 321 M9
HTWY RG27 57 L3
HTWY RG27 67 J1
LIPH GU30 116 C4
NEND PO2 184 D8
NWBY RG14 18 F2
ODIM RG29 69 H4
OVTN RG25 89 H5
RAND SP11 97 L3
STHA RG19 35 L1
STOK SO20 285 Q4
WHCH RG28 88 B7
WINC SO23 288 H12
WSHM SO15 160 F2
WVILLE PO7 155 M6
WVILLE PO7 169 H6
London St AND SP10 5 J6
BSTK RG21 6 F6
WHCH RG28 87 L7
Lone Barn La BPWT SO32 312 A9
Lone Pine Dr FERN BH22 209 L5
Lone Pine Wy FERN BH22 209 M6
Lone Va WVILLE PO7 169 J5
Longacre ASHV GU12 73 M6
NWBY RG14 33 K4
Longacre Cl LISS GU33 308 G8
Long Acre Ct PSEA PO1 192 E1
Longacre Ri CHIN RG24 54 A6
Longacres FHAM/STUB PO14 164 C8
Longbarrow Cl CHAR BH8 * 214 F7
Long Barrow Cl RWIN SO21 288 E3
Long Beech Dr FARN GU14 60 C5
TOTT SO40 158 D2
Long Bottom RAND SP11 82 C1
Long Br FNM GU9 13 G4
Longbridge Cl HTWY RG27 47 G7
TOTT SO40 144 D6
Longbridge Rd TADY RG26 46 B5
Long Cl HUNG RG17 31 H2
RSAL SP5 327 J12
Longclose Rd HEND SO30 149 K5
Long Cl West RSAL SP5 327 J12
Long Copse FAWY SO45 354 G5
Long Copse Cha CHIN RG24 54 A6
Long Copse La EMRTH PO10 171 M4
Longcroft RFNM GU10 259 L11
Longcroft Cl BSTK RG21 6 C6
Longcroft Rd KSCL RG20 248 C9
STHA RG19 35 L2
Long Cross Hl BOR GU35 111 L7
Long Cross La KBH RG22 92 C6
Long Curtain Rd PSEA PO1 20 D7
Longdean Cl CHAM PO6 168 A7
Longdene Rd HASM GU27 118 B6
Longdon Dr
LSOL/BMARY PO13 189 M5
Long Down EPSF GU31 120 F5
Longdown FLEETS GU52 71 H2
Longdown Cl RFNM GU10 79 G2
Longdown Rd RFNM GU10 78 F3
SHST GU47 43 J7
Long Dr HEND SO30 148 E2
LSOL/BMARY PO13 182 C7
Long Dro RSAL SP5 296 D7
Longespee Rd WIMB BH21 207 K8
Longfellow Pde CHIN RG24 * 65 L4
Longfield DEAN RG23 91 J1
Longfield Cl ENEY PO4 193 J3
FARN GU14 50 C8
OVTN RG25 103 G3
Longfield Dr BWD BH11 213 G2
FERN BH22 209 L8
Longfield Rd ASHV GU12 74 A6
EMRTH PO10 171 L5
LYMN SO41 220 B6
WINC SO23 123 K4
Longfleet Dr WIMB BH21 212 A1
Longfleet Rd PLE BH15 223 L4
Longford Cl CBLY GU15 50 F4
Long Garden Pl FNM GU9 12 F2
Long Garden Wk FNM GU9 12 F3
Long Garden Wk East FNM GU9 12 F3
Long Garden Wk West
FNM GU9 12 F2
Long Garden Wy FNM GU9 12 E3
Long Gv TADY RG26 249 P2
THLE RG7 29 K7
Longham Br NBNE BH10 213 G1
Long Hl RFNM GU10 260 C7
Longhope Dr RFNM GU10 78 E2
Longhouse Gn WINC SO23 25 M5
Longlands Rd EMRTH PO10 172 D6
Long La CHIN RG24 54 C6
FAWY SO45 354 E3
HLER SO31 163 G4
NTHA RG18 28 B2
NWBY RG14 27 L5
ODIM RG29 69 H8
RCCH PO18 323 Q9
RGWD BH24 203 K8
TOTT SO40 159 K7
WIMB BH21 207 K1
Long Lane Cl FAWY SO45 354 F5
Longleat Gdns
NMIL/BTOS BH25 218 E5
ROWN SO16 146 B3
Longleat Sq FARN GU14 61 L5
Long Leaze RAND SP11 251 L12
Longley Rd FNM GU9 13 J5
Longmead FLEETS GU52 71 J2
KSCL RG20 246 B3
LISS GU33 308 F9
Longmead Av ELGH SO50 134 D8
Longmead Gdns HAV PO9 16 F8
Longmeadow FRIM GU16 51 H5
Longmeadow Gdns
FAWY SO45 177 G4
Longmeadow La CFDH BH17 210 E8
Longmead Rd RGWD BH24 342 H12
WEND SO18 147 M6
Long Mickle SHST GU47 43 J7
Longmoor Cl EWKG RG40 42 A2
Longmoor Dr LIPH GU30 113 K8
Longmoor La THLE RG7 40 A1
Longmoor Rd BSTK RG21 6 C7
LIPH GU30 113 J8
LISS GU33 308 G2
Longmore Av ITCH SO19 161 K6
Longmore Crs ITCH SO19 161 K6
Longmore Rd WHIT RG2 238 D2
Longmynd Dr
FHAM/STUB PO14 181 K4
Longparish Rd RAND SP11 272 E5
WHCH RG28 98 F3
Long Priors PSF GU32 313 K3
Longridge Rd HEND SO30 149 J6
Long Rd BPWT SO32 319 J6
NBNE BH10 213 J4
PSF GU32 120 E4
The Long Rd RFNM GU10 109 M1
Longrogden La OVTN RG25 256 D1
Longs Ct WHCH RG28 87 L7
Longshore Wy ENEY PO4 193 K4
Longs La FHAM/STUB PO14 189 J1
Longstaff Gdns
FHAM/PORC PO16 10 D2
Long Steeple La FBDG SP6 331 L6
Longstock Cl AND SP10 4 C7
CHIN RG24 54 D4
ITCH SO19 162 A4
Longstock Crs TOTT SO40 158 D1
Longstock Rd HAV PO9 171 H2
RAND SP11 271 P8
Longs Wk PSEA PO1 192 D1
Long Wk RWIN SO21 289 L12
Long Water Dr GPORT PO12 191 J7
Longwater La EWKG RG40 42 A6
Longwater Rd HTWY RG27 42 B8
Longwood Av HORN PO8 155 M5
Longwood Copse La DEAN RG23 92 B8
Longwood Dean La
RWIN SO21 311 J2
Longwood Rd RWIN SO21 310 C4
Lonnen Rd WIMB BH21 207 M1
Lonsdale Av CHAM PO6 185 G1
FHAM/PORC PO16 183 K2
Lonsdale Rd TWDS BH3 225 M1
Loosehanger RSAL SP5 332 H5
Loperwood TOTT SO40 341 R2
Loperwood La TOTT SO40 144 A4
Loraine Av CHCH/BSGR BH23 218 C8
Lord Cl CFDH BH17 223 M1
Lordington Cl CHAM PO6 169 H8
Lord Mountbatten Cl
WEND SO18 147 L4
Lordsfield Gdns OVTN RG25 89 H4
Lord's Hill Centre East
ROWN SO16 145 M3
Lord's Hill Centre West
ROWN SO16 145 M4
Lord's Hill Wy ROWN SO16 145 M4
Lordswood ELGH SO50 134 E5
THLE RG7 45 G4
Lordswood Cl ROWN SO16 146 D5
Lordswood Gdns ROWN SO16 146 D4
Lordswood Rd ROWN SO16 146 C4
Loreille Cl ROWN SO16 145 L1
Lorne Park Rd BMTH BH1 9 G5
Lorne Pl WEND SO18 * 148 A5
Lorne Rd SSEA PO5 21 L5
Lothian Rd CHOB/PIR GU24 63 G2
Loughwood Cl ELGH SO50 134 A6
Louisburg Rd BOR GU35 110 F6
Louise Margaret Rd ALDT GU11 3 H1
Loundyes Cl NTHA RG18 28 D8
Lovage Gdns TOTT SO40 158 C1
Lovage Rd FHAM PO15 164 D5
Lovage Wy HORN PO8 321 L11
Lovatt Gv FHAM PO15 181 K1
Lovedean La HORN PO8 155 M2
Lovedon La WINC SO23 289 J8
Lovegroves CHIN RG24 54 C5
Love La AND SP10 5 J7
BPWT SO32 311 P5
EPSF GU31 120 F5
FBDG SP6 332 A8
KSCL RG20 248 D10
NWBY RG14 27 H6
ODIM RG29 68 F8
PSF GU32 313 L4
ROMY SO51 136 E1
RWIN SO21 125 H7
Lovell Cl RAND SP11 267 R9
RWIN SO21 288 E4
Lovells Wk NARL SO24 291 L11
Loveridge Cl AND SP10 84 D8
BSTK RG21 93 J2
Lovers La RFNM GU10 262 C5
Love's Cl THLE RG7 39 M1
Loves Wd THLE RG7 39 M7
Lovett Rd HSEA PO3 184 F5
Lovington La RWIN SO21 290 E12
Lowa Cl NTID SP9 266 E3
Lowa Rd NTID SP9 266 E2
Lowcay Rd SSEA PO5 21 K9
Lowden Cl FUFL SO22 122 D8
Lowe Cl ALDT GU11 2 C1
Lower Alfred St SHAM SO14 161 H2
Lower Ashley Rd
NMIL/BTOS BH25 219 K5
Lower Banister St
WSHM SO15 160 F2
Lower Bartons FBDG SP6 197 H3
Lower Baybridge La
RWIN SO21 310 B7
Lower Bellfield
FHAM/STUB PO14 180 F5
Lower Bere Wd WVILLE PO7 169 M1
Lower Blandford Rd
BDST BH18 211 H5
Lower Broadmoor Rd
CWTH RG45 43 M4
Lower Brookfield Rd
PSEA PO1 * 21 M1
Lower Brook St BSTK RG21 6 A5
WINC SO23 25 H5
Lower Brownhill Rd
ROWN SO16 145 K5
Lower Buckland Rd
LYMN SO41 221 K3
Lower Canal Wk SHAM SO14 23 G6
Lower Canes YTLY GU46 48 C2
Lower Chase Rd BPWT SO32 318 A7
Lower Chestnut Dr BSTK RG21 6 A9
Lower Church La FNM GU9 12 F4
Lower Church Pth PSEA PO1 21 H2
Lower Church Rd
FHAM/STUB PO14 180 C1
SHST GU47 43 G7
Lower Common HTWY RG27 241 L3
Lower Common La
WIMB BH21 205 J1
Lower Common Rd
ROMY SO51 335 J6
Lower Crabbick La
WVILLE PO7 154 B4
Lower Densome Wd
FBDG SP6 332 A8
Lower Derby Rd NEND PO2 184 C7
Lower Drayton La CHAM PO6 185 J1
Lower Duncan Rd HLER SO31 164 B7
Lower Earley Wy (West)
WHIT RG2 238 E1
Lower Eashing GODL GU7 261 Q12
Lower Evingar Rd WHCH RG28 87 L7
Lower Farlington Rd
CHAM PO6 169 L8
Lower Farm Ct STHA RG19 34 F3
Lower Farm La ROMY SO51 132 B5
Lower Farnham Rd ALDT GU11 3 J8
Lower Forbury Rd SSEA PO5 * 21 J4
Lower Golf Links Rd
BDST BH18 211 H3
Lower Gv FBDG SP6 330 H6
Lower Grove Rd HAV PO9 17 G6
Lower Ham La MFD/CHID GU8 261 J12
Lower Hanger HASM GU27 117 J2
Lower Heyshott EPSF GU31 120 E5
Lower Lamborough La
NARL SO24 303 R7
Lower La BPWT SO32 143 K4
Lower Md EPSF GU31 120 F6
LISS GU33 308 F8
STOK SO20 270 D8
Lower Mead End Rd
LYMN SO41 350 D12
Lower Moor YTLY GU46 48 F3
Lower Moors Rd RWIN SO21 134 F3
Lower Mortimer Rd ITCH SO19 161 K5
Lower Mount St FLEETN GU51 58 E5
Lower Mullin's La FAWY SO45 176 F4
Lower Neatham Mill La
ALTN GU34 107 L2

Lower Nelson St ALDT GU11 2 E2
Lower Newport Rd ASHV GU12 3 M6
Lower New Rd HEND SO30 148 D3
Lower Northam Rd
HEND SO30 149 J6
Lower Paice La ALTN GU34 292 G4
Lower Pennington La
LYMN SO41 221 K7
Lower Pool Rd HTWY RG27 241 K8
Lower Preshaw La
BPWT SO32 311 M8
Lower Quay Cl
FHAM/PORC PO16 11 H8
Lower Quay Rd
FHAM/PORC PO16 11 H8
Lower Rd HASM GU27 118 F2
HAV PO9 170 C7
RSAL SP5 325 Q3
RSAL SP5 327 K8
RWIN SO21 288 C4
Lower St Helens Rd
HEND SO30 149 J7
Lower Sandhurst Rd
EWKG RG40 42 C6
Lower Sandy Down La
LYMN SO41 351 M9
Lower South Vw FNM GU9 13 G2
Lower Spinney HLER SO31 179 J5
Lower St HASM GU27 118 C6
ROMY SO51 131 H1
Lower Swanwick Rd
HLER SO31 163 K4
Lower Terrace Rd FARN GU14 61 G8
Lower Turk St ALTN GU34 106 F5
Lower Vicarage Rd ITCH SO19 161 K5
Lower Wardown EPSF GU31 120 F5
Lower Wy STHA RG19 34 F1
Lower Weybourne La FNM GU9 77 K2
Lower William St SHAM SO14 161 K2
Lower Wokingham Rd
EWKG RG40 42 F2
Lower Woodside LYMN SO41 221 L8
Lower York St SHAM SO14 161 K2
Lowestoft Rd CHAM PO6 168 D7
Loweswater Gdns BOR GU35 110 F7
Lowford Hl HLER SO31 162 F3
Lowicks Rd RFNM GU10 262 H6
Lowland Rd WVILLE PO7 154 E4
Lowlands Rd BLKW GU17 49 L4
KBH RG22 92 C1
Low La FNM GU9 77 M2
Lowndes Buildings FNM GU9 12 F2
Lowry Cl SHST GU47 49 M2
Lowry Ct AND SP10 4 F2
Lowry Gdns ITCH SO19 162 C2
Lowther Gdns CHAR BH8 9 L1
Lowther Rd CHAR BH8 226 A2
Loxwood Av FLEETN GU51 71 G1
Loxwood Cl THLE RG7 238 A4
Loxwood Rd HORN PO8 155 M2
Loyalty La CHIN RG24 66 D2
Luard Ct HAV PO9 17 J5
Lubeck Dr AND SP10 96 B1
Lucas Cl ROWN SO16 145 M3
YTLY GU46 48 F3
Lucas Fld HASM GU27 117 L2
Lucas Rd BKME/WDN BH12 224 C2
Luccombe Pl WSHM SO15 146 D6
Luccombe Rd WSHM SO15 146 D6
Lucerne Av SBNE BH6 227 K3
WVILLE PO7 155 J7
Lucerne Gdns HEND SO30 149 H6
Lucerne Rd LYMN SO41 232 D4
Lucewood La RSAL SP5 296 A6
Luckham Cl MOOR/WNTN BH9 214 B6
Luckham Pl MOOR/WNTN BH9 214 B6
Luckham Rd
MOOR/WNTN BH9 214 B6
Luckham Rd East
MOOR/WNTN BH9 214 B6
Lucknow St PSEA PO1 21 L3
Lucky La LYMN SO41 356 A3
Ludcombe WVILLE PO7 154 F3
Ludgershall Rd MARL SN8 264 G5
NTID SP9 266 F1
Ludlow Cl DEAN RG23 64 F7
FRIM GU16 62 A1
NWBY RG14 28 A8
Ludlow Gdns DEAN RG23 64 F7
Ludlow Rd CHAM PO6 168 C7
ITCH SO19 161 L4
Ludshott Gv BOR GU35 114 B3
Ludwell's La BPWT SO32 143 M8
Lugano Cl WVILLE PO7 155 K7
Luke Rd ALDT GU11 2 A6
Luke Rd East ALDT GU11 2 B6
Lukin Dr ROWN SO16 145 J3
Lulworth Av PLE BH15 222 E7
Lulworth Cl CHFD SO53 139 H5
FARN GU14 61 G1
HISD PO11 195 G3
PLE BH15 222 E6
ROWN SO16 145 L6
Lulworth Crs PLE BH15 222 E7
Lulworth Gn ROWN SO16 145 L6
Lulworth Rd
LSOL/BMARY PO13 189 L6
Lumby Dr RGWD BH24 203 K4
Lumby Drive Pk RGWD BH24 203 K4
Lumley Rd EMRTH PO10 172 A5
Lumsden Av WSHM SO15 160 C1
Lumsden Rd ENEY PO4 193 K5
Lundy Cl CHIN RG24 65 M3
ROWN SO16 145 L3
Lune Cl BSTK RG21 7 J5
Lune Ct AND SP10 5 M1
Lunedale Rd FAWY SO45 176 E8
Lupin Cl KBH RG22 92 C4
Lupin Gdns FUFL SO22 122 B2
Lupin Rd ROWN SO16 147 J3
Luscombe Rd PSTN BH14 224 C6
Luther Rd MOOR/WNTN BH9 213 M8
Lutman St EMRTH PO10 171 L4
Luton Rd ITCH SO19 148 B8
Lutyens Cl CHIN RG24 54 B8
Luxton Cl HEND SO30 149 M4
Luzborough La ROMY SO51 137 J3
Lyall Pl FNM GU9 76 F1
Lyburn Cl ROWN SO16 146 C4
Lyburn Rd RSAL SP5 333 Q6
Lych Gate Cl SHST GU47 43 H8
Lych Gate Ct RGWD BH24 203 L6
Lychgate Dr HORN PO8 156 B1
Lychgate Gn
FHAM/STUB PO14 181 J7
Lyde Cl DEAN RG23 91 K3
Lydford Cl FARN GU14 * 61 G1
FRIM GU16 62 A1
Lydford Gdns BWD BH11 213 G6
Lydford Rd BWD BH11 213 G6
Lydgate LYMN SO41 232 A3
TOTT SO40 158 D1
Lydgate Cl ITCH SO19 148 D8
Lydgate Gn ITCH SO19 148 D8
Lydgate Rd ITCH SO19 148 D8
Lydiard Cl ELGH SO50 134 A7
Lydlinch Cl FERN BH22 209 K7
Lydlynch Rd TOTT SO40 158 E1
Lydney Cl CHAM PO6 168 C8
Lydney Rd HLER SO31 179 M2
Lydwell Cl BWD BH11 212 F3
Lye Copse Av FARN GU14 50 D8
Lyell Rd BKME/WDN BH12 224 C2
Lyeway La NARL SO24 292 H12
Lyeway Rd ALTN GU34 293 L11
Lyford Rd BSTK RG21 6 F2
Lymbourn Rd HAV PO9 17 G5
Lyme Cl ELGH SO50 139 M3
Lyme Crs CHCH/BSGR BH23 217 M8
Lymefields LYMN SO41 232 E2
Lymer La ROWN SO16 145 J2
Lymer Vls ROWN SO16 * 145 J2
Lymington Av YTLY GU46 48 E3
Lymington Bottom
ALTN GU34 293 M7
Lymington Bottom Rd
ALTN GU34 293 L4
Lymington Cl ALTN GU34 293 L6
KBH RG22 92 D6
Lymington Ri ALTN GU34 293 M6
Lymington Rd BROC SO42 351 L6
CHCH/BSGR BH23 229 K1
LYMN SO41 232 E2
LYMN SO41 356 G7
NMIL/BTOS BH25 218 F7
Lymington Road Shelley Hl
CHCH/BSGR BH23 229 J1
Lymore La LYMN SO41 220 E8
Lymore Va LYMN SO41 232 E1
Lynams FLEETS GU52 71 G5
Lynchborough Rd LIPH GU30 113 K4
Lynch Cl FUFL SO22 24 C1
Lynchford La FARN GU14 61 L7
Lynchford Rd ALDT GU11 61 K8
Lynch Hl WHCH RG28 87 L7
Lynch Hill Pk WHCH RG28 87 M7
Lynch La PSF GU32 313 L4
Lynch Rd FNM GU9 13 L4
The Lynch OVTN RG25 89 G4
WHCH RG28 87 L7
Lyn Ct BSTK RG21 7 J4
Lyndale Cl LYMN SO41 232 E3
Lyndale Dr FLEETN GU51 59 M7
Lyndale Rd HLER SO31 164 B8
Lynden Cl FHAM/STUB PO14 181 H4
Lynden Ga ITCH SO19 162 A1
Lyndford Ter FLEETS GU52 71 H1
Lyndhurst Av BLKW GU17 49 L2
FNM GU9 260 A2
Lyndhurst Cl FUFL SO22 288 D12
HISD PO11 195 G6
Lyndhurst Dr KBH RG22 92 E6
Lyndhurst Rd BROC SO42 351 L2
CHCH/BSGR BH23 216 F4
CHCH/BSGR BH23 217 H7
FLEETN GU51 58 E4
GPORT PO12 14 C3
NEND PO2 184 F6
RGWD BH24 349 J1
RSAL SP5 334 A5
TOTT SO40 341 J5
Lyndock Cl ITCH SO19 * 161 L6
Lyndock Pl ITCH SO19 161 L6
Lyndsey Cl FARN GU14 60 B4
Lyndum Cl EPSF GU31 120 D6
Lyndum Pl BOR GU35 * 111 H7
Lyneham Rd CWTH RG45 43 K3
Lyne Pl HORN PO8 156 B2
Lynes La RGWD BH24 203 H5
Lynford Av FUFL SO22 122 E2
Lynford Wy FUFL SO22 122 E2
Lynn Rd CFDH BH17 211 M8
NEND PO2 184 F8
Lynn Wy FARN GU14 60 F1
WINC SO23 289 J10
Lynric Cl NMIL/BTOS BH25 230 F1
Lynton Cl FNM GU9 12 C9
Lynton Ct TOTT SO40 158 E2
Lynton Crs CHCH/BSGR BH23 215 K5
Lynton Gdns FHAM/PORC PO16 10 C1
Lynton Gv HSEA PO3 185 G8
Lynton Meadow STOK SO20 272 E7
Lynton Rd BOR GU35 112 F1
HEND SO30 149 J5
PSF GU32 120 C5
Lynwood Av WVILLE PO7 155 K5
Lynwood Cl BOR GU35 111 J7
FERN BH22 209 K1
Lynwood Dr AND SP10 4 D6
FRIM GU16 62 A5
WIMB BH21 207 L8
Lynwood Gdns HTWY RG27 56 C7
Lynx Cl ELGH SO50 140 F2
Lyon Av NMIL/BTOS BH25 219 H5
Lyon Cl STHA RG19 35 M2
Lyon Rd BKME/WDN BH12 212 E6
CWTH RG45 43 L2
Lyon St SHAM SO14 161 G2
Lyon Wy FRIM GU16 50 E7
Lysander Cl CHCH/BSGR BH23 229 H1
Lysander Wy FARN GU14 61 H7
WVILLE PO7 156 A8
Lysons Av ASHV GU12 61 M8
Lysons Rd ALDT GU11 2 F4
Lyss Ct LISS GU33 308 F8
Lysses Ct FHAM/PORC PO16 11 K5
Lysses Pth FHAM/PORC PO16 11 K5
Lyster Rd FBDG SP6 197 J2
Lystra Rd MOOR/WNTN BH9 214 A5
Lytchett Dr BDST BH18 210 F6
Lytchett Wy UPTN BH16 222 B2
Lyteltane Rd LYMN SO41 221 K6
Lytham Rd BDST BH18 211 G5
WEND SO18 148 A4
Lythe La PSF GU32 315 L3
Lytton Rd BMTH BH1 9 L2
BSTK RG21 7 H5
FAWY SO45 177 H6

M

Mabbs La HTWY RG27 57 L4
Mabett Cl WHIT RG2 239 L8
Mabey Av NBNE BH10 213 K6
Mabey Cl GPORT PO12 15 G9
Mablethorpe Rd CHAM PO6 168 E7
Macadam Av CWTH RG45 * 43 M1
Macadam Wy AND SP10 95 K3
Macandrew Rd CCLF BH13 237 K1
Macarthur Crs WEND SO18 148 A4
Macaulay Av CHAM PO6 167 M7
Macaulay Rd BDST BH18 211 G4
Maccullum Rd RAND SP11 84 D4
Macdonald Rd FNM GU9 76 F1
Maclaren Rd
MOOR/WNTN BH9 213 M5
Maclean Rd BWD BH11 212 F5
Macnaghten Rd WEND SO18 161 K1
Macnaghten Woods CBLY GU15 51 G2
Macrae Rd YTLY GU46 48 E2
Madden Cl GPORT PO12 14 A7
Maddison St SHAM SO14 22 F4
Maddocks Hl NARL SO24 292 F12
Maddoxford Wy BPWT SO32 149 M3
Madeira Cl CHIN RG24 65 M3
Madeira Pl NWBY RG14 18 E6
Madeira Rd BMTH BH1 9 G4
NEND PO2 184 E5
PSTN BH14 224 D3
Madeley Rd FLEETS GU52 71 K2
Madeline Crs
BKME/WDN BH12 224 B1
Madeline Rd EPSF GU31 120 D5
Madison Av BMTH BH1 226 D2
Madison Cl LSOL/BMARY PO13 182 E8
Madison Ct FHAM/PORC PO16 11 K6
Madox Brown End SHST GU47 50 A2
Madrid Rd AND SP10 5 M3
Mafeking Rd ENEY PO4 192 F5
Magazine La TOTT SO40 160 A5
Magazine Rd FARN GU14 60 D8
Magdala Rd CHAM PO6 184 F1
HISD PO11 194 E5
Magdalene Wy
FHAM/STUB PO14 180 C3
Magdalen Hl WINC SO23 25 J6
Magdalen La
CHCH/BSGR BH23 228 A2
Magdalen Ms WINC SO23 * 25 J6
Magdalen Rd NEND PO2 184 E5
Magdalen Rw PSF GU32 120 C6
Magellan Cl AND SP10 97 G3
Magennis Cl
LSOL/BMARY PO13 190 D1
Magenta Ct
LSOL/BMARY PO13 * 190 C2
Magill Cl THLE RG7 238 B6
Magister Dr
LSOL/BMARY PO13 190 A3
Magna Cl BWD BH11 212 F2
Magna Gdns BWD BH11 212 F2
Magna Rd WIMB BH21 208 B8
Magnolia Cl AND SP10 4 C7
FAWY SO45 176 C4
FHAM/STUB PO14 10 A7
SBNE BH6 228 A3
SHST GU47 43 M7
VWD BH31 201 L4
Magnolia Ct CHIN RG24 65 J3
Magnolia Gv ELGH SO50 141 L2
Magnolia Rd ITCH SO19 161 M3
Magnolia Wy FLEETS GU52 71 J1
HORN PO8 156 C4
Magnus Dr KBH RG22 92 D5
Magpie Cl BOR GU35 113 G2
CHAR BH8 214 C5
FHAM/PORC PO16 166 E8
KBH RG22 92 B4
RFNM GU10 71 K8
STHA RG19 35 H1
Magpie Dr TOTT SO40 158 C1
Magpie Gdns ITCH SO19 148 B8
Magpie Gv NMIL/BTOS BH25 218 F6
Magpie La ELGH SO50 139 L6
Magpie Rd HORN PO8 157 J3
Magpie Wk HORN PO8 155 K4
Mag's Barrow FERN BH22 209 L6
Maguire Dr FRIM GU16 51 L5
Mahler Cl KBH RG22 93 H4
Maida Rd ALDT GU11 73 H4
Maiden La LYMN SO41 221 M7
Maidenthorn La OVTN RG25 103 H3
Maidford Gv HSEA PO3 * 185 J4
Maidment Cl BWD BH11 212 E4
Maidstone Crs CHAM PO6 168 E7
Main Dr FAWY SO45 354 C10
WHAM PO17 168 A2
Main Gate Rd FARN GU14 61 H6
Main Rd ELGH SO50 135 H6
EMRTH PO10 172 D6
FAWY SO45 176 A1
FAWY SO45 354 E2
FUFL SO22 288 A10
LSOL/BMARY PO13 182 D4
LYMN SO41 356 A6
LYMN SO41 356 H3
PSEA PO1 20 B2
RCCH PO18 173 J7
RWIN SO21 134 B2
RWIN SO21 134 F2
RWIN SO21 135 H5
RWIN SO21 310 B4
TADY RG26 44 D6
TOTT SO40 158 E4
TOTT SO40 159 M7
Mainsail Dr FHAM/PORC PO16 11 G8
Mainstone ROMY SO51 136 D3
Mainstone Cl FRIM GU16 62 C1
Mainstone Crs CHOB/PIR GU24 63 K2
Mainstream Ct ELGH SO50 140 D1
Main St STHA RG19 35 G8
Maisemore Gdns EMRTH PO10 171 K8
Maison Belle Vue ITCH SO19 * 161 M7
Maitland Rd FARN GU14 61 H8
Maitlands Cl RFNM GU10 260 C2
Maitland St PSEA PO1 192 D1
Majendie Cl NWBY RG14 26 F8
Majestic Rd KBH RG22 92 C7
ROWN SO16 145 H4
Majorca Av AND SP10 5 M3
Malan Cl CFDH BH17 211 L8
Malcolm Cl CHFD SO53 133 L7
HLER SO31 180 B1
Malcolm Rd CHFD SO53 133 L7
Malcomb Cl SBNE BH6 228 A5
Malcroft Ms TOTT SO40 160 A7
Maldive Rd CHIN RG24 65 M3
Maldon Cl ELGH SO50 140 D1
Maldon Rd CHAM PO6 * 168 D8
ITCH SO19 161 L4
Malham Gdns KBH RG22 92 D7
Malham Rd STHA RG19 35 L3
Malibres Rd CHFD SO53 133 M8
Malin Cl FHAM/STUB PO14 189 H1
ROWN SO16 145 L4
Malins Rd NEND PO2 192 D1
Mallard Cl AND SP10 96 D2
ASHV GU12 73 M6
BPWT SO32 143 G4
CHAR BH8 214 C7
CHCH/BSGR BH23 229 G2
HASM GU27 117 L2
KBH RG22 92 B5
LYMN SO41 220 A5
NARL SO24 291 M10
ROMY SO51 130 F8
Mallard Ct NWBY RG14 18 C4
Mallard Gdns HEND SO30 149 J2
LSOL/BMARY PO13 182 B6
Mallard Rd CHAR BH8 214 D7
ENEY PO4 193 H3
HAV PO9 157 H7
WIMB BH21 208 A1
Mallards ALTN GU34 106 F3
Mallards Rd HLER SO31 162 F5
The Mallards FHAM/PORC PO16 10 F1
FRIM GU16 51 H6
HAV PO9 16 D8
Mallard Wy EMRTH PO10 172 C2
THLE RG7 38 B1
YTLY GU46 * 48 D2
Mallett Cl HEND SO30 149 L3
Mallory Cl CHCH/BSGR BH23 216 F8
Mallory Crs FHAM/PORC PO16 10 E2
Mallow Cl BDST BH18 210 E5
BOR GU35 111 J7
CHAM PO6 * 168 F8
CHCH/BSGR BH23 217 J8
WVILLE PO7 169 M2
Mallow Gdns NTHA RG18 28 F7
Mallow Rd HEND SO30 149 G6
The Mallows NMIL/BTOS BH25 219 K4
The Mall CHFD SO53 * 139 L1
NEND PO2 * 184 D7
NTID SP9 266 C4
RGWD BH24 349 J1
Malmesbury Cl ELGH SO50 141 J2
Malmesbury Ct CHAR BH8 226 C2
Malmesbury Fld KBH RG22 92 F4
Malmesbury Flds KBH RG22 * 92 F4
Malmesbury Gdns FUFL SO22 24 A1
Malmesbury Park Pl CHAR BH8 9 M1
Malmesbury Park Rd
CHAR BH8 226 C2
Malmesbury Pl WSHM SO15 160 D1
Malmesbury Rd RGWD BH24 346 E1
ROMY SO51 130 E8
WSHM SO15 160 D1
Malmsbury Cl
CHCH/BSGR BH23 228 B3
Malmsbury Rd BOR GU35 112 F2
Maloren Wy FERN BH22 205 J7
Malory Cl ITCH SO19 148 D6
Malpass Rd RWIN SO21 288 C6
Malshanger La DEAN RG23 91 J1
Malta Cl CHIN RG24 65 L3
Malta Rd FRIM GU16 51 M8
NEND PO2 184 E8
Maltby's ALTN GU34 295 L8
Malthouse PLE BH15 223 J6
Malthouse Cl FLEETS GU52 71 G3
ROMY SO51 130 E8
RWIN SO21 289 M11
Malthouse Gdns TOTT SO40 159 M7
Malt House La RAND SP11 84 E5
Malthouse La
FHAM/PORC PO16 11 G5
NARL SO24 292 A7
RAND SP11 80 B4
RCCH PO18 173 M3
TADY RG26 44 D6
Malthouse Mdw LIPH GU30 116 C4
Malthouse Ms ALTN GU34 107 J2
Malthouse Rd NEND PO2 184 D8
Maltings Cl ALTN GU34 106 F6
The Maltings EPSF GU31 120 D6
FHAM/PORC PO16 11 L3
LIPH GU30 116 D4
NWBY RG14 18 D5
TADY RG26 46 B6
Malt La BPWT SO32 143 J4
Malus Cl FHAM/STUB PO14 181 M5
Malvern Av FHAM/STUB PO14 10 A8
Malvern Cl BPWT SO32 143 K5
KBH RG22 92 C1
MOOR/WNTN BH9 214 A5
Malvern Ct NWBY RG14 18 D7
Malvern Dr FAWY SO45 176 D5
Malvern Gdns HEND SO30 149 K2
Malvern Ms EMRTH PO10 171 M7
Malvern Rd BLKW GU17 49 H7
FARN GU14 60 D1
GPORT PO12 14 B2
LISS GU33 308 H10
MOOR/WNTN BH9 214 A6
ROWN SO16 146 C6
SSEA PO5 192 D7
Malvern Ter ROWN SO16 * 146 D6
Malwood Av ROWN SO16 146 D5
Malwood Cl HAV PO9 171 G2
Malwood Gdns TOTT SO40 144 C8
Malwood Rd FAWY SO45 176 F4
Malwood Rd West FAWY SO45 176 F4
Manaton Wy HEND SO30 149 H3
Manchester Ct
LSOL/BMARY PO13 * 190 D3
Manchester Rd HLER SO31 162 A7
LYMN SO41 350 F9
PSEA PO1 21 M2
Mancroft Av
FHAM/STUB PO14 189 J3
Mandale Cl BWD BH11 213 G5
Mandale Rd BWD BH11 212 F5
Mandarin Ct NWBY RG14 * 19 J5
Mandarin Wy
LSOL/BMARY PO13 * 190 C2
Mandela Wy WSHM SO15 22 C1
Manderley LYMN SO41 232 E5
Mandora Rd ALDT GU11 73 H4
Manfield Rd ASHV GU12 74 A6
Manica Cl BOR GU35 112 F1
Manley Bridge Rd RFNM GU10 78 C4
Manley James Cl ODIM RG29 69 G5
Manley Rd HLER SO31 162 F3
Mann Cl WHCH RG28 87 M8
Manners La ENEY PO4 21 L4
Manners Rd ENEY PO4 21 M4
Manning Av CHCH/BSGR BH23 217 J7
Manningford Cl WINC SO23 123 G1
Mannings Heath Rd
BKME/WDN BH12 212 B6
Mannington Pl WCLF BH2 8 C6
Mannington Wy FERN BH22 204 F6
Manns Cl WEND SO18 148 C2
Mannyngham Wy ROMY SO51 130 D1
Manor Av BKME/WDN BH12 212 C7
Manor Bridge Ct NTID SP9 266 F1
Manor Cl ALTN GU34 107 G2
FBDG SP6 197 H3
FERN BH22 209 L3
HASM GU27 117 L2
HAV PO9 16 F4
HLER SO31 162 F3
KBH RG22 92 C6
LYMN SO41 232 D3
NTID SP9 266 E9
RAND SP11 271 J1
RFNM GU10 260 D1
TOTT SO40 158 E2
WHAM PO17 152 A6
WINC SO23 25 K4
Manor Copse AND SP10 84 D7
Manor Ct FLEETS GU52 71 J4
RGWD BH24 203 J4
VWD BH31 201 H2
Manor Crs CHAM PO6 185 H1
CHOB/PIR GU24 63 K1
HLER SO31 162 F3
Manor Farm Cl ASHV GU12 * 73 M7
NMIL/BTOS BH25 218 F7
Manor Farm Gn RWIN SO21 124 F7
Manor Farm Gv ELGH SO50 * 140 E2
Manor Farm La ROMY SO51 299 M11
Manor Farm Rd FBDG SP6 196 E3
NBNE BH10 213 J2
WEND SO18 147 K7
Manor Flds LIPH GU30 116 D4
Manor Gdns EMRTH PO10 172 D5
RFNM GU10 79 H3
RGWD BH24 203 J4
VWD BH31 201 H2
Manor House Av WSHM SO15 159 L2
Manor La CHIN RG24 66 D2
NTHA RG18 28 A8
STHA RG19 36 D5
VWD BH31 201 H3
Manor Lodge Rd HAV PO9 157 H8
Manor Ms CHAM PO6 169 J8
Manor Park Av HSEA PO3 185 G8
Manor Park Dr EWKG RG40 42 A2
YTLY GU46 48 F3
Manor Park Est ASHV GU12 * 3 J4
Manor Pl NWBY RG14 26 F7
Manor Ri RAND SP11 96 A8
Manor Rd ALDT GU11 2 D6
ALTN GU34 107 G2
AND SP10 4 E3
ASHV GU12 73 M7
BMTH BH1 9 L6
BPWT SO32 142 D5
CHIN RG24 65 G1
CHCH/BSGR BH23 228 A2
ELGH SO50 140 E2
EMRTH PO10 172 D5
FARN GU14 61 K5
FAWY SO45 354 E4
FNM GU9 77 J4
HISD PO11 195 G2
LYMN SO41 232 D2
NMIL/BTOS BH25 219 H5
PSEA PO1 192 E1
RGWD BH24 203 J5
ROWN SO16 138 D7
RSAL SP5 298 A5
RWIN SO21 124 F7
TOTT SO40 176 A3
VWD BH31 201 H2
Manor Rd North ITCH SO19 161 L4
Manor Rd South ITCH SO19 161 L5
Manorside Cl RFNM GU10 73 M8
The Manor WHIT RG2 238 E3
Manor Vw THLE RG7 * 36 F5
Manor Wk ASHV GU12 3 G5
Manor Wy EMRTH PO10 172 D5
HISD PO11 195 G6
LSOL/BMARY PO13 189 L6
VWD BH31 201 H1
Mans Br WEND SO18 147 M4
Mansbridge Rd ELGH SO50 140 A3
WEND SO18 147 M4
Manse La TADY RG26 44 D6
Mansel Cl BKME/WDN BH12 225 J1
Mansel Ct ROWN SO16 145 L6
Mansell Cl FAWY SO45 176 E8
Mansell Dr NWBY RG14 33 J7
Mansel Rd East ROWN SO16 145 L7
Mansel Rd West ROWN SO16 145 K6
Mansfield Cl FERN BH22 209 K6
PSTN BH14 224 C4
Mansfield La WHAM PO17 151 H8
Mansfield Rd KBH RG22 93 G2
LSOL/BMARY PO13 182 C8
MOOR/WNTN BH9 213 L7
PSTN BH14 224 C4
RGWD BH24 203 H5
Mansion Dr HTWY RG27 241 K8
Mansion House St
NWBY RG14 * 18 D4
Mansion Rd ENEY PO4 192 E7
WSHM SO15 160 D2
Mansvid Av CHAM PO6 185 H1
Mantle Cl LSOL/BMARY PO13 190 D1
Mantle Sq NEND PO2 184 B6
Manton Rd PLE BH15 222 E5
Maple Cl ALTN GU34 106 F3
ASHV GU12 73 M1
BLKW GU17 49 L3
CHCH/BSGR BH23 229 M1
EMRTH PO10 171 M6
FHAM PO15 181 J3
LSOL/BMARY PO13 189 M7
NARL SO24 291 L12
NMIL/BTOS BH25 231 H1
ROMY SO51 137 J2
SHST GU47 43 H7
STOK SO20 270 D8
Maple Crs BSTK RG21 65 K5
HORN PO8 321 L6
NWBY RG14 18 E1
RAND SP11 265 P10
Maple Dr CWTH RG45 43 L1
FERN BH22 204 E8
RSAL SP5 282 A9
WINC SO23 288 H8
WVILLE PO7 155 G5
Maple Gdns TOTT SO40 158 C2
YTLY GU46 48 F3
Maple Gv TADY RG26 44 C4
Maplehurst Cha KBH RG22 92 D7
Maple Leaf Cl FARN GU14 60 F5
Maple Leaf Dr BOR GU35 110 F8
Maple Ldg HASM GU27 * 118 E8
Maple Rd FAWY SO45 177 H8
MOOR/WNTN BH9 213 M8
PLE BH15 223 K5
SSEA PO5 21 J9
WEND SO18 161 L1
Maple Sq ELGH SO50 139 L7
The Maples CHFD SO53 133 J8
Maple Ter NTID SP9 * 266 C1
Mapleton Rd HEND SO30 149 K6
Mapletree Av HORN PO8 156 C3
Maple Wk ASHV GU12 3 M7
RAND SP11 4 A8
Maple Wy BOR GU35 114 B2
Maple Wd HAV PO9 170 B7
Maplewood Cl TOTT SO40 158 C2
Maplin Rd ROWN SO16 145 K6
Mapperton Cl CFDH BH17 212 A6
Marabout Cl CHCH/BSGR BH23 228 D1
Maralyn Av WVILLE PO7 169 L2
Marathon Pl ELGH SO50 141 H2
Marazan Rd HSEA PO3 185 H6
Marbrean Cl FBDG SP6 196 E2
Marchant Cl STHA RG19 34 D5
Marchant Rd AND SP10 4 D7
March Cl AND SP10 5 K3
Marchwood By-Pass
TOTT SO40 158 F3
Marchwood Rd HAV PO9 170 E2
NBNE BH10 213 J5
TOTT SO40 159 J4
WSHM SO15 160 B2
Marchwood Ter TOTT SO40 * 159 M6
Marconi Rd NWBY RG14 19 G2
Marcus Cl ELGH SO50 141 H2
Marcuse Flds RCCH PO18 173 L8
Mardale CBLY GU15 51 L4
Mardale Rd ROWN SO16 145 K8
Marden Wy EPSF GU31 120 E6
Mardon Cl ELGH SO50 147 L3
Mare La RWIN SO21 125 L5
Mareth Cl ALDT GU11 3 H2
Margam Av ITCH SO19 161 M3
Margards La VWD BH31 200 F3
Margaret Cl WHIT RG2 238 C1
WVILLE PO7 155 K7
Margaret Rd KBH RG22 64 F8
Margarita Rd FHAM PO15 10 A4
Margate Rd SSEA PO5 21 J5
Margery's Ct PSEA PO1 * 20 D3
Margha Rd NTID SP9 266 E2

Marguerite Cl TADY RG26 46 B5
Marian Cl WIMB BH21 210 C4
Marianne Cl WSHM SO15 159 M2
Marianne Rd
BKME/WDN BH12 213 J8
WIMB BH21 208 A1
Marian Rd WIMB BH21 210 C4
Marie Av RSAL SP5 331 R1
Marie Cl BKME/WDN BH12 224 D1
Marie Rd ITCH SO19 162 C1
Marigold Cl CWTH RG45 43 H1
FHAM PO15 10 A4
KBH RG22 92 C4
Marina Cl EMRTH PO10 172 A6
Marina Dr HLER SO31 179 G2
PSTN BH14 224 B7
Marina Gv FHAM/PORC PO16 183 J2
HSEA PO3 193 H2
Marina Keep CHAM PO6 184 A1
The Marina BOSC BH5 226 E5
Marine Ct ENEY PO4 193 G6
Marine Dr NMIL/BTOS BH25 230 E1
Marine Dr East
NMIL/BTOS BH25 231 G2
Marine Dr West
NMIL/BTOS BH25 230 D1
Marine Pde SHAM SO14 23 K4
Marine Pde East
LSOL/BMARY PO13 189 M8
Marine Pde West
LSOL/BMARY PO13 189 K5
Marine Prospect
NMIL/BTOS BH25 230 F1
Marine Rd SBNE BH6 227 K5
Mariner's Cl HLER SO31 163 G8
TADY RG26 44 D6
Mariners Dr RGUW GU3 75 H5
Mariners Ms FAWY SO45 177 G4
Mariners Wk ENEY PO4 193 H3
Mariners Wy GPORT PO12 15 J6
HLER SO31 179 J3
Marine Wk HISD PO11 195 K5
Marino Wy EWKG RG40 239 N10
Marion Rd ENEY PO4 21 M9
Maritime Av TOTT SO40 159 M5
Maritime Wk SHAM SO14 23 J8
Maritime Wy SHAM SO14 23 H7
Marjoram Cl FARN GU14 60 B4
Marjoram Crs HORN PO8 156 B5
Marjoram Wy FHAM PO15 164 D5
Markall Cl NARL SO24 303 R7
Mark Cl HSEA PO3 184 F4
WSHM SO15 160 A1
Marken Cl HLER SO31 179 L1
Market Cl PLE BH15 223 J6
Market La WINC SO23 25 G6
Market Pde HAV PO9 16 E4
Market Pl BSTK RG21 6 F6
NWBY RG14 18 E4
RGWD BH24 203 H5
SHAM SO14 23 G6
Market Sq ALTN GU34 106 F5
Market St ALTN GU34 106 F5
ELGH SO50 140 B3
NWBY RG14 18 E5
PLE BH15 223 H7
WINC SO23 25 G6
Marketway PSEA PO1 192 C2
Market Wy WIMB BH21 207 K4
Markham Av NBNE BH10 213 K2
Markham Cl NBNE BH10 213 K1
Markham Ct CBLY GU15 50 F2
Markham Rd
MOOR/WNTN BH9 214 A8
Mark's La NMIL/BTOS BH25 219 G2
Markson Rd RWIN SO21 288 C4
Mark's Rd FHAM/STUB PO14 189 L2
MOOR/WNTN BH9 213 M5
Marks Tey Rd
FHAM/STUB PO14 181 J7
Mark Wy RSAL SP5 * 297 R9
Markway Cl EMRTH PO10 171 K7
Marlborough Cl FLEETN GU51 59 M8
WVILLE PO7 169 K3
Marlborough Ct FAWY SO45 176 E6
Marlborough Gdns DEAN RG23 91 K2
HEND SO30 149 J1
Marlborough Gv
FHAM/PORC PO16 183 J1
Marlborough Pk HAV PO9 17 K2
Marlborough Pl LYMN SO41 221 K3
WIMB BH21 207 K3
Marlborough Ri CBLY GU15 51 G2
Marlborough Rd CHFD SO53 133 L7
GPORT PO12 190 F2
MARL SN8 264 G2
PSTN BH14 224 C4
WBNE BH4 225 J5
WSHM SO15 146 B8
Marlborough Rw PSEA PO1 20 D1
Marlborough St AND SP10 5 H4
Marlborough Vw FARN GU14 60 C3
Marldell Cl HAV PO9 171 G3
Marles Cl LSOL/BMARY PO13 190 D1
Marley Av NMIL/BTOS BH25 218 E4
Marley Cl NMIL/BTOS BH25 218 F5
Marley Combe Rd HASM GU27 117 M3
Marley La HASM GU27 117 L3
Marley Mt LYMN SO41 350 C11
Marlhill Cl WEND SO18 147 M6
Marlin Cl LSOL/BMARY PO13 190 D2
Marline Rd BKME/WDN BH12 224 D2
Marl La FBDG SP6 196 F2
Marlott Rd PLE BH15 223 J3
Marlow Cl FHAM PO15 165 L8
Marlow Dr CHCH/BSGR BH23 215 L5
Marlowe Cl CHIN RG24 65 L4
Marlowe Ct WVILLE PO7 155 K7
The Marlowes NWBY RG14 33 M4
Marlow Rd BPWT SO32 143 G3
Marlpit Dr CHCH/BSGR BH23 218 A6
Marlpit La EMRTH PO10 173 G2
NMIL/BTOS BH25 349 Q12
Marl's La TADY RG26 53 K8
Marls Rd HEND SO30 149 L6
Marmion Av SSEA PO5 21 J8
Marmion Gn CHCH/BSGR BH23 228 F1
Marmion Rd SSEA PO5 21 H8
Marne Rd WEND SO18 148 A5
Marnhull Rd PLE BH15 223 K4
Marpet Cl BWD BH11 212 F2
Marples Wy HAV PO9 16 B5
Marquis Wy BWD BH11 212 D3
Marram Cl LYMN SO41 221 L2
Marrels Wd WVILLE PO7 169 J4
Marrowbrook Cl FARN GU14 61 G5
Marrowbrook La FARN GU14 60 F6
Marryat Rd NMIL/BTOS BH25 218 F5
Marsden Ct WHCH RG28 88 E6
Marsden Rd CHAM PO6 168 B8
Marshal Cl ALTN GU34 106 E6
Marshall Cl FARN GU14 60 F1
FRIM GU16 51 M6
Marshall Gdns BSTK RG21 6 F1
Marshall Rd HISD PO11 195 J6
SHST GU47 49 M1
Marshalls Ct NWBY RG14 26 F7
Marshall Sq AND SP10 * 96 E2
WSHM SO15 146 F8
Marshall Wy HEND SO30 148 F3
Marshal Rd CFDH BH17 211 H7
Marsh Cl BOR GU35 113 H1
CHAM PO6 185 J2
Marshcourt CHIN RG24 54 B8
Marshfield WIMB BH21 207 M1
Marshfield Cl TOTT SO40 159 K7
Marsh Gdns HEND SO30 149 J2
Marshlands Cl
CHCH/BSGR BH23 228 D2
Marshlands Rd CHAM PO6 185 K1
Marshlands Sp CHAM PO6 185 L1
Marsh La CHCH/BSGR BH23 215 M6
FAWY SO45 178 B8
FBDG SP6 331 N8
HTWY RG27 48 A3
LYMN SO41 221 L2
NWBY RG14 18 E3
RSAL SP5 325 M2
SHAM SO14 23 H5
UPTN BH16 222 A1
Marsh Rd NTHA RG18 29 G8
The Marsh FAWY SO45 177 G3
Marshwood Av CFDH BH17 211 M6
WVILLE PO7 170 A1
Marston Cl NMIL/BTOS BH25 219 H3
Marston Dr FARN GU14 61 H1
NWBY RG14 27 M7
Marston Ga WINC SO23 25 G4
Marston Gv CHCH/BSGR BH23 217 L7
Marston La HSEA PO3 185 H4
Marston Rd FNM GU9 12 B5
ITCH SO19 148 D7
NMIL/BTOS BH25 219 H3
PLE BH15 223 H6
Marsum Cl AND SP10 84 B8
Martel Cl CBLY GU15 51 L1
Martello Cl GPORT PO12 190 D5
Martello Pk CCLF BH13 237 L1
Martello Rd CCLF BH13 224 F7
The Martells NMIL/BTOS BH25 231 H1
Martin Av FHAM/STUB PO14 189 K2
WVILLE PO7 155 G4
Martin Cl BPWT SO32 318 B8
BSTK RG21 65 L5
CFDH BH17 222 F1
LSOL/BMARY PO13 189 M5
NTID SP9 266 G2
Martindale Av CBLY GU15 51 L5
WIMB BH21 208 B3
Martin Drove End FBDG SP6 329 J2
Martingale Cl UPTN BH16 222 D1
Martingale Ct ALDT GU11 2 B3
Martin Rd FHAM/STUB PO14 189 K2
HAV PO9 171 G4
HSEA PO3 185 G8
Martins Cl ALTN GU34 107 G3
BLKW GU17 49 M4
FERN BH22 209 L1
Martins Dr FERN BH22 209 L1
Martins Flds RWIN SO21 124 C3
Martins Hill Cl
CHCH/BSGR BH23 216 C7
Martins Hill La
CHCH/BSGR BH23 216 C7
Martins La STOK SO20 272 G9
Martins Pk FARN GU14 * 60 D1
Martins Ri RSAL SP5 126 F4
Martin's Rd BROC SO42 351 L2
The Martins ELGH SO50 141 K3
STHA RG19 35 M2
Martin St BPWT SO32 143 H5
Martins Wy FERN BH22 209 L1
Martins Wd CHIN RG24 54 B5
Martin Wy AND SP10 96 D2
FRIM GU16 51 G7
Martley Gdns HEND SO30 149 K2
Marvic Ct HAV PO9 170 E2
Marvin Wy HEND SO30 149 L5
WEND SO18 148 C6
Marwell Cl LTDN BH7 227 G1
Marwell Rd FLEETN GU51 58 E4
Marybridge Cl TOTT SO40 158 E2
Maryfield SHAM SO14 23 J4
Maryland EWKG RG40 239 R9
Maryland Cl WEND SO18 147 M5
Maryland Gdns LYMN SO41 232 B4
Maryland Rd UPTN BH16 222 C4
Mary La ALTN GU34 293 R8
FERN BH22 204 F6
OVTN RG25 103 G2
Mary Rose Cl FHAM PO15 10 A1
The Mary Rose St PSEA PO1 * 21 G3
Masdar Gdns EWKG RG40 42 A2
Masefield Av CHAM PO6 167 M7
Masefield Cl ELGH SO50 139 M5
Masefield Crs HORN PO8 155 M5
Masefield Gn ITCH SO19 148 D6
Masefield Rd NTHA RG18 28 E8
Maskell Wy FARN GU14 60 C5
Maslen Mws DEAN RG23 92 D8
Mason Cl YTLY GU46 * 49 G3
Mason Pl SHST GU47 43 H8
Mason Rd FARN GU14 60 E2
Masons Yd WINC SO23 * 24 F6
Mason Wy ALDT GU11 3 G8
Masseys La BROC SO42 353 J9
Masten Crs LSOL/BMARY PO13 182 C8
Matapan Rd NEND PO2 184 D4
Matchams Cl RGWD BH24 347 J5
Matchams La RGWD BH24 346 H7
Matchlock Ms NWBY RG14 * 27 L7
Matheson Rd ROWN SO16 145 M2
Mathews Ter ALDT GU11 * 3 J2
Mathias Wk KBH RG22 92 F6
Matilda Dr KBH RG22 92 D5
Matilda Pl WINC SO23 * 25 H4
Matley Gdns TOTT SO40 158 B1
Matlock Rd FERN BH22 209 J5
Matrons Cots RSAL SP5 327 P3
Matthew Rd FNM GU9 2 A6
Matthews Cl HAV PO9 170 C5
STHA RG19 35 H1
Matthews La BROC SO42 353 J10
Matthews Wy DEAN RG23 91 L3
Mattock Wy CHIN RG24 54 B5
Maturin Cl LYMN SO41 221 K5
The Maultway CBLY GU15 51 M4
Maundeville Crs
CHCH/BSGR BH23 215 L8
Maundeville Rd
CHCH/BSGR BH23 215 L8
Maunsell Wy HEND SO30 149 J1
Maureen Cl BKME/WDN BH12 212 B8
Maurepas Wy WVILLE PO7 169 K1
Mauretania Rd ROWN SO16 145 H4
Maurice Rd ENEY PO4 193 J4
Maurys La ROMY SO51 334 H5
Mavins Rd FNM GU9 13 J7
Mavis Crs HAV PO9 16 E3
Mavis Rd MOOR/WNTN BH9 214 B7
Maw Cl KBH RG22 93 H4
Maxine Cl SHST GU47 43 K7
Maxstoke Cl SSEA PO5 21 J3
Maxwell Rd BDST BH18 210 D5
CCLF BH13 237 L1
ENEY PO4 193 G5
ITCH SO19 162 A1
MOOR/WNTN BH9 226 A1
May Av LYMN SO41 221 K3
Maybray King Wy ITCH SO19 148 A5
Maybrick Cl SHST GU47 43 H7
Maybrook CHIN RG24 54 B4
Maybury Cl FRIM GU16 50 F8
Maybush Dr RCCH PO18 173 H7
May Bush La BPWT SO32 318 H11
Maybush Rd ROWN SO16 145 L6
May Cl BOR GU35 111 L8
CHIN RG24 66 E2
FAWY SO45 354 F5
SHST GU47 43 M8
May Copse FAWY SO45 354 F5
May Crs ASHV GU12 73 L7
FAWY SO45 354 F5
Maydman Sq HSEA PO3 193 G2
Mayfair Ct HEND SO30 150 A5
Mayfair Dr NWBY RG14 18 A7
Mayfair Gdns BWD BH11 213 G4
WSHM SO15 160 F1
Mayfield RFNM GU10 109 M1
Mayfield Av PSTN BH14 224 E5
TOTT SO40 144 E8
Mayfield Cl FERN BH22 209 J2
FHAM/STUB PO14 189 K1
FNM GU9 77 M2
NTID SP9 266 D9
Mayfield Ct HTWY RG27 241 R4
Mayfield Dr FERN BH22 209 K2
Mayfield Rdg KBH RG22 92 D7
Mayfield Rd CBLY GU15 * 50 D7
FARN GU14 60 F1
FBDG SP6 196 E2
GPORT PO12 14 F6
MOOR/WNTN BH9 214 A6
NEND PO2 184 E6
PTSW SO17 147 H5
Mayfield Wy FERN BH22 209 J2
Mayflower Cl CHIN RG24 54 A6
CHFD SO53 139 H3
FHAM/STUB PO14 189 J3
LYMN SO41 356 A9
Mayflower Dr YTLY GU46 48 C1
Mayflower Rd BOR GU35 112 E4
WSHM SO15 146 C8
Mayflower Rbt WSHM SO15 22 E6
The Mayflowers ROWN SO16 147 G4
Mayfly Cl FBDG SP6 197 H2
Mayford Rd BKME/WDN BH12 225 H2
May Gdns BWD BH11 212 E5
CHCH/BSGR BH23 218 B6
Mayhall Rd HSEA PO3 185 G7
Mayhill La BPWT SO32 318 D5
The Maying WHIT RG2 238 B2
Maylands Av ENEY PO4 193 G4
Maylands Rd HAV PO9 170 B6
May La LYMN SO41 356 A3
Mayles Cl WHAM PO17 152 A5
Mayles Cnr WHAM PO17 165 K4
Mayles La WHAM PO17 165 L4
Mayles Rd ENEY PO4 193 H4
Maylings Farm Rd
FHAM/PORC PO16 10 D2
Maynard Cl LSOL/BMARY PO13 182 C4
NTHA RG18 28 E7
Maynard Pl HORN PO8 156 B1
Maynard Rd TOTT SO40 158 F1
Maynard's Wd CHIN RG24 54 A6
Mayo Cl PSEA PO1 192 D1
Mayors La NWBY RG14 18 E5
Mayow Cl STHA RG19 35 M2
May Pl BSTK RG21 6 F6
Mayridge FHAM/STUB PO14 180 C1
May Rd WSHM SO15 160 C1
Mays Firs FBDG SP6 332 H6
May's La FHAM/STUB PO14 181 K8
May Tree Cl FUFL SO22 122 C8
Maytree Cl HLER SO31 180 A1
Maytree Gdns HORN PO8 155 L5
May Tree Rd AND SP10 4 B3
Maytree Rd CHFD SO53 133 K6
FHAM/PORC PO16 10 E6
HORN PO8 155 L5
Mayvale Cl TOTT SO40 159 M7
Maywood Dr CBLY GU15 51 K1
McCartney Wk KBH RG22 92 E5
McFauld Wy WHCH RG28 87 L8
McGrigor Barracks ALDT GU11 73 H5
McIntyre Rd CHCH/BSGR BH23 346 G12
McKay Cl ALDT GU11 3 K1
McKinley Rd WBNE BH4 225 J6
McNaughton Cl FARN GU14 60 C5
McWilliam Cl
BKME/WDN BH12 213 J8
McWilliam Rd
MOOR/WNTN BH9 214 A6
Meacher Cl TOTT SO40 144 E8
Meadbrook Gdns CHFD SO53 139 J2
Mead Cl FBDG SP6 197 G2
AND SP10 4 E7
CFDH BH17 211 G7
ROMY SO51 137 H1
Mead Crs WEND SO18 147 K5
Meadcroft Cl HLER SO31 179 K4
Meadend Cl HAV PO9 171 H3
Mead End Rd LYMN SO41 350 D11
WVILLE PO7 155 G5
Meadens La RSAL SP5 325 N3
Meade Rd RAND SP11 265 N10
Mead Gdns HTWY RG27 57 K1
Meadham La OVTN RG25 254 B5
Mead Hatchgate HTWY RG27 56 C6
Mead Hawks LISS GU33 308 E7
Mead Hedges AND SP10 4 D8
Mead La FNM GU9 12 E4
Meadow Av HLER SO31 164 A8
Meadow Bank FNM GU9 12 E5
Meadowbank RWIN SO21 287 L11
Meadowbank Rd FHAM PO15 181 K3
Meadow Cl ASHV GU12 61 M7
BLKW GU17 49 M4
BPWT SO32 143 K8
CHCH/BSGR BH23 216 B1
CHCH/BSGR BH23 217 G1
FBDG SP6 197 G2
FERN BH22 209 K7
HEND SO30 148 E2
HISD PO11 186 F5
LIPH GU30 116 C4
NARL SO24 291 M11
NBAD SO52 138 A5
RGWD BH24 203 K3
RGWD BH24 348 H2
STHA RG19 35 J1
TOTT SO40 158 F3
Meadow Ct FBDG SP6 197 H2
RSAL SP5 127 J4
Meadow Court Cl
MOOR/WNTN BH9 214 A5
Meadowcroft Cl RWIN SO21 134 C1
Meadow Dr RAND SP11 271 P4
Meadow Edge WVILLE PO7 169 H6
Meadow Farm La WIMB BH21 206 D8
Meadow Gdns BPWT SO32 143 L8
Meadow Gate Av FARN GU14 60 F6
Meadow Gv VWD BH31 201 K3
Meadowhead Rd ROWN SO16 146 F5
Meadowland CHIN RG24 54 A5
CHCH/BSGR BH23 228 E2
WINC SO23 288 H9
Meadowlands HAV PO9 17 H5
LYMN SO41 221 J4
Meadow La CHCH/BSGR BH23 216 C6
HLER SO31 179 G2
HTWY RG27 57 L2
Meadowmead Av WSHM SO15 160 A1
Meadow Pound WHCH RG28 87 M7
Meadowridge KBH RG22 92 E7
Meadow Ri BDST BH18 210 F3
HORN PO8 156 B5
OVTN RG25 103 H3
Meadow Rd BSTK RG21 93 J3
FARN GU14 61 H1
LYMN SO41 221 J6
NMIL/BTOS BH25 219 H4
NWBY RG14 18 D9
RGWD BH24 203 K4
Meadows Cl CFDH BH17 210 C8
Meadows Dr UPTN BH16 222 C1
Meadowside Cl WEND SO18 147 L4
The Meadows
FHAM/PORC PO16 11 K1
HTWY RG27 46 F7
LYND SO43 345 K4
RFNM GU10 262 F11
Meadow St SSEA PO5 * 20 F6
Meadowsweet WVILLE PO7 156 B7
Meadowsweet Cl NTHA RG18 29 G8
Meadowsweet Rd CFDH BH17 210 E8
Meadowsweet Wy CHAM PO6 168 D7
ELGH SO50 141 J6
Meadow Ter
FHAM/PORC PO16 * 10 F5
The Meadow ROMY SO51 130 F7
WVILLE PO7 154 F4
Meadow V HASM GU27 118 A6
Meadow Vw BOR GU35 113 G1
FLEETS GU52 71 G3
RAND SP11 * 94 D2
WHCH RG28 87 K7
Meadow View Rd BWD BH11 212 E4
Meadow Wk LISS GU33 308 F8
LSOL/BMARY PO13 182 B3
Meadow Wy AND SP10 4 A5
ASHV GU12 73 M5
BLKW GU17 49 L3
FAWY SO45 355 J5
FUFL SO22 122 C8
LIPH GU30 116 C3
NMIL/BTOS BH25 231 G1
RFNM GU10 109 M1
RGWD BH24 203 K4
VWD BH31 201 K4
Mead Park Sq STOK SO20 270 D8
Mead Rd AND SP10 4 E7
CHFD SO53 139 J2
GSHT GU26 115 M4
LYMN SO41 221 H6
WINC SO23 122 E8
The Meads CHFD SO53 139 C3
HASM GU27 117 M2
ROMY SO51 136 D1
The Mead CHIN RG24 66 D2
FARN GU14 * 61 H5
FAWY SO45 176 E5
LIPH GU30 116 B3
LISS GU33 308 F8
LSOL/BMARY PO13 182 B5
PSF GU32 120 B7
Mead Wy FHAM/PORC PO16 11 G2
Meadway FRIM GU16 51 H6
HASM GU27 117 M2
WVILLE PO7 156 A7
The Meadway
CHCH/BSGR BH23 217 K6
Mears Rd ELGH SO50 141 K2
Meath Cl HISD PO11 195 J7
Mede Cl OVTN RG25 89 K5
Medina Cl CHFD SO53 139 L3
Medina Gdns DEAN RG23 91 K3
Medina Rd CHAM PO6 168 D8
WSHM SO15 146 B7
Medina Wy CHCH/BSGR BH23 229 J2
Medlar Cl CHCH/BSGR BH23 216 D7
HEND SO30 149 K6
Medlar Dr BLKW GU17 50 B5
Medlicott Wy BPWT SO32 318 B8
Medonte Cl FLEETN GU51 59 K8
Medstead Rd ALTN GU34 279 Q11
HAV PO9 170 F5
Medwall Gn ITCH SO19 148 D7
Medway Av DEAN RG23 91 K2
Medway Cl NTHA RG18 28 D7
Medway Ct AND SP10 96 E2
BSTK RG21 7 K5
Medway Dr CHFD SO53 133 G8
FARN GU14 60 E1
Medway Rd FERN BH22 346 A6
Meerut Rd BROC SO42 351 L2
NTID SP9 266 E2
Meeting House La
RGWD BH24 203 H5
Megana Wy ROMY SO51 131 J3
Megan Rd HEND SO30 148 D2
Meggeson Av WEND SO18 148 A2
Megson Dr LSOL/BMARY PO13 190 A2
Meitner Cl TADY RG26 46 B4
Melbourne Pl SSEA PO5 20 F4
Melbourne Rd CHAR BH8 226 C2
CHCH/BSGR BH23 215 L7
HEND SO30 149 J6
Melbourne St SHAM SO14 23 K4
Melbury Av BKME/WDN BH12 224 E1
Melbury Cl FERN BH22 209 K4
LYMN SO41 221 K5
Melchet Cl ROMY SO51 128 B7
Melchet Rd WEND SO18 148 C4
Meldrum Cl NWBY RG14 33 J6
Melford Gdns KBH RG22 92 C2
Melick Cl TOTT SO40 159 M6
Meliot Ri AND SP10 84 C8
Mellersh Cl FLEETS GU52 71 G4
Mellor Cl CHAM PO6 168 D8
Mellstock Rd PLE BH15 223 J3
Melrose Av FARN GU14 60 C3
Melrose Cl BOR GU35 112 F2
ENEY PO4 193 H4
Melrose Ct NMIL/BTOS BH25 * 219 J5
TOTT SO40 144 C7
Melrose Gdns GPORT PO12 190 F1
WHIT RG2 239 L6
Melrose Rd WSHM SO15 146 D6
Melrose Wk CHIN RG24 65 J4
Melverley Gdns WIMB BH21 207 K3
Melville Av FRIM GU16 51 H7
Melville Cl ROWN SO16 146 C3
Melville Rd ENEY PO4 193 J6
GPORT PO12 191 G1
MOOR/WNTN BH9 213 L8
Melville Ter FNM GU9 * 12 E4
Membury Cl FRIM GU16 62 A1
Memorial Rd HTWY RG27 56 C8
Mendip Cl KBH RG22 92 C1
NMIL/BTOS BH25 219 H6
VWD BH31 201 H3
Mendip Gdns FAWY SO45 176 D6
Mendip Rd FARN GU14 60 E1
ROWN SO16 145 M8
VWD BH31 201 H2
Mendips Rd FHAM/STUB PO14 181 K4
Mendips Wk
FHAM/STUB PO14 181 K4
Mengham Av HISD PO11 195 G6
Mengham La HISD PO11 195 H5
Mengham Rd HISD PO11 195 G5
Menin Wy FNM GU9 13 K6
Menslands La WVILLE PO7 319 M12
Mentone Rd PSTN BH14 224 A5
Menzies Cl ROWN SO16 145 M3
Meon Cl FARN GU14 60 D2
HORN PO8 321 L8
LSOL/BMARY PO13 182 B6
PSF GU32 120 C5
ROMY SO51 137 J1
TADY RG26 44 A3
Meon Ct WEND SO18 148 D4
Meon Crs CHFD SO53 139 K2
Meon Rd DEAN RG23 91 K3
ENEY PO4 193 H4
LTDN BH7 227 H1
ROMY SO51 137 J1
Meon Wk BSTK RG21 * 7 H5
Meonwara Crs PSF GU32 313 M3
Mercer Cl KBH RG22 64 E8
Mercer Wy ROMY SO51 130 F8
Merchants Pl WINC SO23 25 H5
Merchants Wk SHAM SO14 22 E6
Merchistoun Rd HORN PO8 156 C1
Mercia Av AND SP10 95 M1
Mercury Cl BOR GU35 113 G1
ROWN SO16 145 M4
Mercury Gdns HLER SO31 163 G8
Mercury Pl WVILLE PO7 169 L6
Merdon Av CHFD SO53 133 K8
Merdon Cl CHFD SO53 133 K8
Mere Cft FHAM PO15 180 D1
Meredith Cl CHCH/BSGR BH23 228 D1
Meredith Gdns TOTT SO40 158 D2
Meredith Rd NEND PO2 184 E5
Meredun Cl RWIN SO21 133 H1
Mereoak La THLE RG7 238 A3
Merepond La ALTN GU34 306 C9
Merganser Cl GPORT PO12 191 H1
Meriden Cl CCLF BH13 237 L1
Meriden Rd SSEA PO5 20 F4
Meridian Pk AND SP10 5 HI
The Meridians
CHCH/BSGR BH23 227 M3
Merino Wy FERN BH22 205 H8
Merivale FLEETN GU51 58 F8
Merlewood Cl WCLF BH2 8 E2
Merley Dr CHCH/BSGR BH23 218 A8
Merley Gdns WIMB BH21 207 K7
Merley La WIMB BH21 207 K7
Merley Park Rd WIMB BH21 206 E8
Merley Ways WIMB BH21 207 K5
Merlin Cl AND SP10 96 C1
BPWT SO32 143 H4
HORN PO8 155 L4
RGWD BH24 203 L6
Merlin Dr HSEA PO3 185 G4
Merlin Gdns FHAM/PORC PO16 167 H7
HEND SO30 149 H5
Merlin Md KBH RG22 92 B6
Merlin Rd ALTN GU34 293 M6
FARN GU14 61 H6
Merlins Cl FNM GU9 13 G6
Merlin Wy CHCH/BSGR BH23 229 G3
CHFD SO53 138 F1
FARN GU14 60 D5
Mermaid Rd FHAM/STUB PO14 181 M7
Mermaid Wy SHAM SO14 * 23 J7
Merriatt Cl BSTK RG21 93 K2
Merrick Wy CHFD SO53 132 F8
Merridale Rd ITCH SO19 161 L4
Merriefield Av BDST BH18 211 J2
Merriefield Dr BDST BH18 211 H2
Merrieleas Cl CHFD SO53 139 J1
Merrieleas Dr CHFD SO53 139 J1
Merriemeade Cl FAWY SO45 176 E7
Merrifield WIMB BH21 207 L1
Merrifield Cl BDST BH18 211 H2
Merrileas Gdns KBH RG22 92 C4
Merritown La
CHCH/BSGR BH23 214 D1
Merrivale Av SBNE BH6 227 L3
Merrivale Cl FAWY SO45 176 E5
Merrivale Rd NEND PO2 184 E5
Merron Cl YTLY GU46 48 E3
Merrow Av BKME/WDN BH12 225 H2
Merrydown La CHIN RG24 54 B5
Merryfield CHIN RG24 54 A5
FHAM/STUB PO14 164 C8
Merryfield Av HAV PO9 170 D3
Merryfield Cl
CHCH/BSGR BH23 348 C12
VWD BH31 201 H2
Merryfield La NBNE BH10 213 J4
Merryfield Rd EPSF GU31 120 F5
Merry Gdns NBAD SO52 138 A3
Merryman Dr CWTH RG45 43 H2
Merryoak Gn ITCH SO19 161 M3
Merryoak Rd ITCH SO19 161 M4
Merrywood Pk CBLY GU15 51 H4
Mersea Gdns ITCH SO19 148 A8
Mersey Ct AND SP10 5 M1
Mersey Wy NTHA RG18 28 D7
Mersham Gdns WEND SO18 161 M1
Merstone Rd
LSOL/BMARY PO13 182 C6
Merthyr Av CHAM PO6 169 H7
Merton Av FHAM/PORC PO16 183 K2
Merton Cl FBDG SP6 197 H1
Merton Crs FHAM/PORC PO16 183 K2
Merton Rd BSTK RG21 6 B2
PTSW SO17 147 H6
SSEA PO5 21 H7
Meryl Rd ENEY PO4 193 J4
Meryon Rd NARL SO24 291 L12
Mesh Pond RSAL SP5 326 H12
Mesh Rd ROMY SO51 299 L10
Metcalfe Av FHAM/STUB PO14 189 K1
Meteor Wy FARN GU14 61 G7
Methuen Cl CHAR BH8 9 L1
Methuen Rd CFDH BH17 211 H6
CHAR BH8 9 J1
ENEY PO4 193 G5
LISS GU33 309 J1
Methuen St SHAM SO14 161 G1
Metuchen Wy HEND SO30 149 J8
Meudon Av FARN GU14 61 H5
Mewsey Ct HAV PO9 170 D1
Mews La FUFL SO22 24 D6
The Mews AND SP10 5 K8
CHFD SO53 * 139 J5
EPSF GU31 120 E5
FAWY SO45 354 H9
HAV PO9 170 E4
ROWN SO16 145 M2
TADY RG26 46 D6
Mey Cl WVILLE PO7 169 M1
Meynell Cl ELGH SO50 139 M5
Meyrick Cl CHCH/BSGR BH23 217 G1
Meyrick Dr NWBY RG14 33 J7
Meyrick Park Crs TWDS BH3 225 M2
Meyrick Rd BMTH BH1 9 J6
HAV PO9 16 B4

NEND PO2 184 C7
Michael Crook Cl HAV PO9 170 C5
Michaelmas Cl YTLY GU46 48 F4
Michaelmas Dro RAND SP11 94 D3
Michaels Wy ELGH SO50 141 K2
FAWY SO45 176 F4
Micheldever Cl WHCH RG28 99 M1
Micheldever Gdns WHCH RG28 99 M1
Micheldever Rd AND SP10 5 K6
WHCH RG28 87 M8
Michelgrove Rd BOSC BH5 226 E5
Michelmersh Cl ROWN SO16 145 L3
Michelmersh Gn CHAR BH8 214 D6
Michigan Wy TOTT SO40 144 B8
Mickleham Cl
BKME/WDN BH12 213 H8
Mickle Hl SHST GU47 43 J7
Midanbury Broadway
WEND SO18 * 147 M7
Midanbury Crs WEND SO18 147 M7
Midanbury La WEND SO18 147 L8
Midanbury Wk WEND SO18 147 M8
Midas Cl WVILLE PO7 169 M5
Middle Av FNM GU9 13 J8
Middlebere Crs UPTN BH16 222 C4
Middle Bourne La RFNM GU10 78 F2
Middlebridge St ROMY SO51 136 E2
Middlebrook BPWT SO32 143 J4
Middle Brook St WINC SO23 25 H6
Middle Church La FNM GU9 12 F4
Middle Cl CBLY GU15 51 L2
NWBY RG14 33 K5
Middle Common Rd
LYMN SO41 221 G5
Middlecroft La GPORT PO12 14 B1
Middlefield FNM GU9 12 D9
Middle Gordon Rd CBLY GU15 50 E3
Middle Hl ALDT GU11 2 F2
Middlehill Dr WIMB BH21 208 B2
Middlehill Rd WIMB BH21 208 A1
Middle La RGWD BH24 203 J5
Middle Md FHAM/STUB PO14 181 H4
HTWY RG27 56 C7
Middle Meadow LISS GU33 308 G8
Middlemoor Rd FRIM GU16 51 G8
Middle Old Pk FNM GU9 76 D4
Middle Park Wy HAV PO9 170 D2
Middle Rd FUFL SO22 24 D4
HLER SO31 164 B7
ITCH SO19 162 A1
LYMN SO41 221 K5
LYMN SO41 350 B12
NBAD SO52 138 A3
NBNE BH10 213 J3
PLE BH15 223 L2
Middlesex Rd ENEY PO4 193 G5
Middle St CCLF BH13 236 C3
SHAM SO14 161 G1
SSEA PO5 21 G4
Middleton Cl FHAM/STUB PO14 10 A9
WEND SO18 148 A2
Middleton Ct NWBY RG14 28 A7
Middleton Gdns BSTK RG21 6 F1
FARN GU14 60 E2
Middleton Ms
NMIL/BTOS BH25 218 F7
Middleton Park Farm
RAND SP11 * 98 B6
Middleton Ri HORN PO8 * 321 M8
Middleton Rd CBLY GU15 51 G2
NBNE BH10 213 L6
RGWD BH24 203 J4
RSAL SP5 282 F9
The Middleway RAND SP11 97 K4
Midfield Cl FHAM/STUB PO14 181 M5
Midhurst Rd HASM GU27 118 B7
LIPH GU30 116 C5
Midland Rd MOOR/WNTN BH9 213 M7
Midlands Est HEND SO30 148 C3
Midlane Cl BSTK RG21 93 J2
Midlington Hl BPWT SO32 318 G5
Midlington Rd BPWT SO32 318 H5
Midway FAWY SO45 176 F5
Midway Rd NEND PO2 184 E3
Midways FHAM/STUB PO14 189 J3
Midwood Av CHAR BH8 214 F7
Mike Hawthorn Dr FNM GU9 13 H2
Milbeck Cl HORN PO8 156 A5
Milborne Crs
BKME/WDN BH12 224 E1
Milbourne Rd FERN BH22 209 J2
Milburn Cl WBNE BH4 225 J4
Milburn Rd WBNE BH4 225 H4
The Milburns ROMY SO51 130 D1
Milbury Crs ITCH SO19 148 A6
Milden Cl FRIM GU16 62 A2
Milden Gdns FRIM GU16 62 A2
Mildmay Ct ODIM RG29 69 G6
Mildmay St FUFL SO22 122 D7
Milebush Rd ENEY PO4 193 J3
Mile End Rd PSEA PO1 192 C1
Miles Rd ASHV GU12 74 B5
Miles's La RSAL SP5 127 J1
Milestone Rd PLE BH15 223 K2
Milford Cl FERN BH22 205 H6
HAV PO9 170 D5
Milford Ct LYMN SO41 232 E4
Milford Crs LYMN SO41 232 E4
Milford Dr BWD BH11 212 F3
Milford Gdns CHFD SO53 139 L2
Milford Rd LYMN SO41 220 F7
MFD/CHID GU8 261 J12
NMIL/BTOS BH25 231 J1
PSEA PO1 21 J2
Military Rd FHAM/PORC PO16 11 M3
FHAM/PORC PO16 166 E6
GPORT PO12 190 E1
HSEA PO3 184 F3
PSEA PO1 192 B2
Milkingpen La CHIN RG24 66 D1
Milkwood Ct TOTT SO40 158 B1
Millais Rd ITCH SO19 161 L5
Milland Rd WINC SO23 25 K9
Millard Cl BSTK RG21 65 H5
Mill Bank HUNG RG17 31 G1
Millbank St SHAM SO14 23 M1
Millbridge Gdns ITCH SO19 148 B8
Millbridge Rd YTLY GU46 42 D8
Millbrook Cl CHFD SO53 139 H3
LISS GU33 308 G8
Millbrook Dr HAV PO9 171 G2
Millbrook Point Rd
WSHM SO15 160 A2
Millbrook Rd East WSHM SO15 160 C3
Millbrook Rd West
WSHM SO15 159 M2
Mill Chase Rd BOR GU35 113 G1
Mill Cl HASM GU27 117 L2
HISD PO11 186 F6
ROWN SO16 145 K3
WVILLE PO7 155 H4
Mill Copse Rd HASM GU27 118 B8
Mill Cnr FLEETN GU51 59 L3
Mill Ct FBDG SP6 * 197 G3
Mill Dro MARL SN8 264 D1
Mill End EMRTH PO10 172 B6
FBDG SP6 330 D12
Millennium Ct BSTK RG21 6 A5
Miller Cl NMIL/BTOS BH25 219 J4
Miller Dr FHAM/PORC PO16 10 D2
Miller Rd CHCH/BSGR BH23 228 D1
Millers La FUFL SO22 301 R9
Miller's Pond Gdns ITCH SO19 161 M5
Millers Rd TADY RG26 44 B4
Millers Yd RWIN SO21 * 274 C8
Millfield CFDH BH17 223 G1
Millgreen La STHA RG19 248 D2
Millhams Rd BWD BH11 213 G1
Millhams St CHCH/BSGR BH23 228 B2
Millhams St North
CHCH/BSGR BH23 228 B2
Mill Hl HEND SO30 150 A5
NARL SO24 291 M9
Mill Hill Av NTID SP9 264 E12
Mill Hill Cl PSTN BH14 224 B5
Milliken Cl FAWY SO45 354 H6
Millins Cl SHST GU47 43 M7
Mill La ALTN GU34 107 J3
BOR GU35 111 K7
BPWT SO32 150 D1
BPWT SO32 318 H3
BROC SO42 351 M3
BROC SO42 352 B6
CHCH/BSGR BH23 215 H2
CHCH/BSGR BH23 218 B8
CHOB/PIR GU24 63 K5
EMRTH PO10 172 B4
EPSF GU31 317 R8
EPSF GU31 323 M1
FHAM PO15 181 G3
GPORT PO12 14 F1
HAV PO9 170 C7
HTWY RG27 55 L2
KSCL RG20 247 Q8
LISS GU33 307 R2
LYMN SO41 220 E1
LYMN SO41 221 M4
LYMN SO41 356 F8
LYND SO43 341 J10
NARL SO24 291 Q11
NWBY RG14 18 F4
ODIM RG29 68 E3
PSF GU32 120 C1
PSTN BH14 224 B6
RAND SP11 98 E7
RFNM GU10 262 B5
RGWD BH24 343 L11
ROMY SO51 128 E8
ROMY SO51 136 D1
ROWN SO16 144 E4
RSAL SP5 282 H8
RSAL SP5 324 E4
STHA RG19 36 B2
THLE RG7 38 C1
THLE RG7 46 E3
WHAM PO17 152 A3
WIMB BH21 207 H3
WIMB BH21 337 K7
WVILLE PO7 168 E4
YTLY GU46 42 F8
Mill Meadow LYMN SO41 232 C3
Millmere YTLY GU46 48 F1
Mill Pond La RCCH PO18 173 M3
Mill Pond Rd GPORT PO12 14 E1
The Mill Pond FAWY SO45 354 D2
Mill Quay EMRTH PO10 172 A7
Mill Reef Cl STHA RG19 34 F1
Mill Ri ROMY SO51 298 F12
Mill Rd CHIN RG24 64 E4
CHCH/BSGR BH23 216 A8
EMRTH PO10 172 B2
FHAM/PORC PO16 10 F8
GPORT PO12 191 G2
LISS GU33 308 G7
RCCH PO18 173 L3
TOTT SO40 159 G1
WSHM SO15 160 A1
WVILLE PO7 155 G4
WVILLE PO7 169 K2
Mill Rd (North) CHAR BH8 214 D5
Mill Rd (South) CHAR BH8 214 D6
Mill Rythe La HISD PO11 195 G1
Mills Rd NEND PO2 184 D8
Mill Stream FNM GU9 77 J2
Millstream Cl AND SP10 4 F9
CFDH BH17 223 G1
WIMB BH21 207 J4
Millstream Ri ROMY SO51 136 D1
The Millstream HASM GU27 117 L3
Mill St FHAM/STUB PO14 181 G4
Millvina Cl TOTT SO40 341 R8
Mill Wy TOTT SO40 158 E3
Millway Cl AND SP10 4 C7
Millway Rd AND SP10 4 C6
Millworth La WHIT RG2 238 E4
Millyford Br LYND SO43 344 E4
Millyford Cl NMIL/BTOS BH25 218 D8
Milne Cl FAWY SO45 176 C6
Milner Ct WSHM SO15 146 C8
Milne Rd CFDH BH17 211 H7
Milner Pl FUFL SO22 24 D9
Milner Rd WBNE BH4 225 J6
Milnthorpe La FUFL SO22 24 C7
Milsom Cl WHIT RG2 238 E3
The Milsons STOK SO20 285 P6
Milton Av AND SP10 4 B3
Milton Cl CHIN RG24 65 L4
PSTN BH14 224 D5
Milton Gn NMIL/BTOS BH25 * 218 F7
Milton Gv HLER SO31 180 B3
NMIL/BTOS BH25 219 H6
Milton Md NMIL/BTOS BH25 218 F6
Milton Pde WVILLE PO7 155 L6
Milton Park Av ENEY PO4 193 G4
Milton Rd CHAR BH8 9 H1
ELGH SO50 134 B7
HSEA PO3 193 G2
PSTN BH14 224 D5
WIMB BH21 207 J2
WSHM SO15 160 E2
WVILLE PO7 155 K7
Milverton Cl CHCH/BSGR BH23 217 L7
Milverton Rd FUFL SO22 24 C4
TOTT SO40 159 G2
Milvil Rd LSOL/BMARY PO13 189 L7
Mimosa Av WIMB BH21 207 L8
Mimosa Cl BOR GU35 111 J7
FHAM PO15 164 E8
Mimosa Ct AND SP10 4 B7
Mimosa Dr ELGH SO50 141 L2
Minchens La TADY RG26 46 A3
Mincingfield La BPWT SO32 142 D8
Minden Cl AND SP10 96 B1
CHIN RG24 54 A7
The Mindens NTID SP9 * 266 E9
Minden Wy FUFL SO22 122 C7
Minehurst Rd FRIM GU16 61 M4
Minerva Cl WVILLE PO7 169 L6
Minerva Crs PSEA PO1 * 20 C5
Minerva Rd FARN GU14 61 H7
Ministry Rd STHA RG19 35 G7
Minley Cl FARN GU14 60 E4
Minley Ct HAV PO9 171 H3
Minley Gv FLEETN GU51 59 K5
Minley Rd FARN GU14 49 G7
FLEETN GU51 59 K5
Minnitt Rd GPORT PO12 15 L4
Minstead Av WEND SO18 148 C4
Minstead Cl FUFL SO22 288 D12
TADY RG26 44 B6
Minstead Dr YTLY GU46 48 E3
Minstead Rd ENEY PO4 193 H5
NBNE BH10 213 J5
Minster Cl FHAM PO15 181 J3
Minster Ct CBLY GU15 * 50 B4
Minster La WINC SO23 25 G6
Minster Pk WIMB BH21 * 205 G2
Minster Vw WIMB BH21 207 J3
Minster Wy UPTN BH16 210 B8
Mintern Cl ELGH SO50 134 D7
Minterne Rd CHCH/BSGR BH23 228 E3
MOOR/WNTN BH9 214 A6
PSTN BH14 237 H1
Minters Lepe WVILLE PO7 169 L5
Mint Rd LISS GU33 308 H6
Mirabella Cl ITCH SO19 161 K6
Mirror Cl HLER SO31 179 M3
Mislingford Rd BPWT SO32 318 C9
Missenden Acres HEND SO30 149 K4
Mission Rd BDST BH18 211 G6
Misslebrook La NBAD SO52 138 D4
Mistletoe Rd YTLY GU46 48 F4
Mitchell Av HTWY RG27 57 L3
Mitchell Cl AND SP10 95 K3
FHAM PO15 164 D7
ITCH SO19 161 K5
NMIL/BTOS BH25 231 G1
Mitchell Dr ELGH SO50 141 J1
Mitchell Gdns KBH RG22 92 E5
Mitchell Rd CFDH BH17 211 M8
ELGH SO50 140 B2
HAV PO9 170 B5
WIMB BH21 209 G1
Mitchells Cl ROMY SO51 136 F1
RSAL SP5 332 F2
Mitchell Wy ELGH SO50 140 A5
ELGH SO50 147 M2
HSEA PO3 185 H5
Mitford Rd NARL SO24 291 K11
Mitre Copse ELGH SO50 140 F2
Mizen Wy LSOL/BMARY PO13 190 D2
Moat Cl FAWY SO45 354 D5
TADY RG26 46 A4
Moat Dr GPORT PO12 190 D5
Moat Hl WEND SO18 147 M5
Moat La NMIL/BTOS BH25 218 F7
Mockbeggar La RGWD BH24 199 J5
Moffat Rd CHCH/BSGR BH23 228 D1
Moffatts Cl SHST GU47 43 J8
Moggs Md EPSF GU31 120 E6
Mole Cl FARN GU14 60 D2
Mole Hl WVILLE PO7 169 M3
Mole Rd WHIT RG2 239 M3
Molesworth Rd GPORT PO12 14 F5
Mollison Ri FHAM PO15 164 D6
Molyneux Rd
NMIL/BTOS BH25 219 K5
Momford Rd FUFL SO22 124 B1
Monachus La HTWY RG27 57 M1
Monarch Cl HLER SO31 180 B2
KBH RG22 92 C7
WVILLE PO7 170 A1
Monarch's Wy BPWT SO32 310 C9
BPWT SO32 313 K11
HAV PO9 157 M7
HORN PO8 156 D3
ROMY SO51 132 C4
ROMY SO51 298 H12
RSAL SP5 283 Q11
STOK SO20 284 F10
WVILLE PO7 320 C3
Monarch Wy FUFL SO22 122 C6
HEND SO30 148 F2
Monastery Rd WEND SO18 161 L1
Monckton Rd GPORT PO12 191 H7
HSEA PO3 184 F6
Mon Crs WEND SO18 148 C5
Moneyer Rd AND SP10 96 B1
Moneyfield Av HSEA PO3 185 G8
Moneyfield La HSEA PO3 * 185 G8
Moneyfly Rd VWD BH31 201 K3
Mongers Piece CHIN RG24 54 C4
Monier Williams Rd
RWIN SO21 273 M1
Moniton Est KBH RG22 * 64 D8
Monks Brook Cl ELGH SO50 139 L7
Monks Cl FARN GU14 61 J4
FERN BH22 205 J8
NTID SP9 266 E1
Monkshanger FNM GU9 13 M3
Monk Sherborne Rd
TADY RG26 255 R1
Monkshood Cl
CHCH/BSGR BH23 217 H7
Monks La NWBY RG14 33 M5
Monks Orch PSF GU32 120 D4
Monks Pl TOTT SO40 158 D2
Monks Ri FLEETN GU51 58 F7
Monks Rd HLER SO31 162 B6
WINC SO23 25 G3
Monks Wk FAWY SO45 176 E8
RFNM GU10 79 K1
Monks Wy ELGH SO50 139 M7
FHAM/STUB PO14 189 H4
WEND SO18 147 L4
WIMB BH21 212 C3
Monks' Well RFNM GU10 260 A8
Monkswell Gn
CHCH/BSGR BH23 228 D2
Monks Wd PSF GU32 120 D4
Monks Wood Cl ELGH SO50 147 H2
Monkswood Cl NWBY RG14 33 K5
Monks Wood Crs TADY RG26 44 B5
Monkton Cl FERN BH22 209 K2
Monkton Crs
BKME/WDN BH12 212 E8
Monkton La FNM GU9 77 J3
TOTT SO40 158 D2
Monktons La THLE RG7 40 C3
Monkwood Cl HAV PO9 170 D3
Monkworthy Dr RGWD BH24 202 B7
Monmouth Cl CHFD SO53 139 H2
VWD BH31 201 K4
Monmouth Dr VWD BH31 201 K4
Monmouth Rd NEND PO2 184 D6
Monmouth Sq FUFL SO22 * 122 B6
Monnow Gdns WEND SO18 148 B3
Monroe Cl GPORT PO12 190 E5
Monsal Av FERN BH22 209 J5
Mons Barracks ALDT GU11 73 J3
Mons Cl ALDT GU11 73 L1
Mons Ct WINC SO23 24 E5
Montacute Cl FARN GU14 61 K4
Montacute Dr STHA RG19 35 M2
Montacute Wy WIMB BH21 207 L8
Montagu Cl GPORT PO12 183 J8
Montague Av ITCH SO19 162 D1
Montague Cl CBLY GU15 50 D3
ITCH SO19 162 D1
Montague Gdns EPSF GU31 121 G6
Montague Pl BSTK RG21 6 F8
Montague Rd BOSC BH5 227 H4
NEND PO2 184 E7
Montague Ter NWBY RG14 18 E9
Montagu Rd CHCH/BSGR BH23 230 B1
Monteagle La YTLY GU46 48 D3
Monteray Dr LYMN SO41 219 M4
Monterey Dr HAV PO9 171 G4
HLER SO31 180 A2
Montfort Cl ROMY SO51 137 J1
Montfort Hts ROMY SO51 137 J1
Montfort Rd ROMY SO51 137 J2
Montgomerie Rd SSEA PO5 21 J4
Montgomery Av BWD BH11 213 H5
TOTT SO40 144 D8
Montgomery Cl FUFL SO22 122 C7
SHST GU47 43 K8
Montgomery Dr THLE RG7 238 B6
Montgomery Rd FARN GU14 60 F5
HAV PO9 17 G4
LSOL/BMARY PO13 182 C4
NWBY RG14 18 A9
RAND SP11 84 D5
WEND SO18 148 A4
Montgomery Wk WVILLE PO7 169 J3
Montgomery Wy CHFD SO53 139 H5
Montpelier Cl HLER SO31 180 C1
Montrose Av
FHAM/PORC PO16 167 L7
Montrose Cl BOR GU35 112 F3
FLEETN GU51 59 K8
FRIM GU16 51 G6
HEND SO30 149 L6
VWD BH31 201 H2
Montrose Dr NBNE BH10 213 H6
Montserrat Pl CHIN RG24 65 L2
Montserrat Rd CHIN RG24 65 L2
LSOL/BMARY PO13 189 L6
Monument Cha BOR GU35 113 G3
Monument Cl NWBY RG14 33 K5
Monument La LYMN SO41 356 A8
WHAM PO17 167 H4
Monxton Rd RAND SP11 95 H5
RAND SP11 269 Q3
Moody Rd FHAM/STUB PO14 189 H3
Moody's Hl RSAL SP5 297 J10
Moon Cl TOTT SO40 159 L7
Moonhills La BROC SO42 353 P6
Moonrakers Wy
CHCH/BSGR BH23 217 L7
Moonscross Av TOTT SO40 158 F4
Moons Hl RFNM GU10 78 F6
Moor Cl BOR GU35 112 D1
EWKG RG40 42 A1
Moor Court La RWIN SO21 301 M1
Moorcroft Av
CHCH/BSGR BH23 216 C6
Moorcroft Cl RWIN SO21 274 D9
Moordown Cl
MOOR/WNTN BH9 214 A5
Moore Av BWD BH11 213 G5
Moore Cl AND SP10 5 H2
FLEETS GU52 71 J3
NMIL/BTOS BH25 218 F7
RFNM GU10 73 M8
Moore Crs HLER SO31 162 B6
Moore Gdns GPORT PO12 14 A4
Moore Rd CHOB/PIR GU24 63 H2
FLEETS GU52 71 J3
Moorfield HASM GU27 117 M3
Moorfield Gv
MOOR/WNTN BH9 213 M6
Moorfields Rd CCLF BH13 224 F8
Moorfoot Gdns KBH RG22 92 D1
Moorgreen Pk HEND SO30 * 148 F2
Moorgreen Rd HAV PO9 171 G3
HEND SO30 148 F2
Moorhams Av KBH RG22 92 C6
Moorhill Gdns WEND SO18 148 E5
Moorhill Rd HEND SO30 148 D4
RGWD BH24 349 J2
Moorings Cl PLE BH15 222 F7
The Moorings BSTK RG21 7 K4
FHAM/PORC PO16 182 B1
Moorings Wy ENEY PO4 193 J2
Moorland Av NMIL/BTOS BH25 218 F8
Moorland Cl FAWY SO45 176 D5
HLER SO31 164 A8
Moorland Crs UPTN BH16 222 B1
Moorland Ga RGWD BH24 203 J7
Moorland Pde UPTN BH16 * 222 B1
Moorland Rd BMTH BH1 226 D4
PSEA PO1 21 M1
Moorlands Cl BROC SO42 350 H3
FLEETN GU51 59 K8
GSHT GU26 115 L4
Moorlands Crs WEND SO18 148 A4
Moorlands Ri FERN BH22 205 H5
Moorlands Rd BPWT SO32 318 A6
CBLY GU15 50 C4
FERN BH22 205 G6
VWD BH31 201 H1
Moorland Wy UPTN BH16 222 B1
Moor La RSAL SP5 126 E7
Moor Pk HORN PO8 156 B6
Moor Park La FNM GU9 13 M1
RFNM GU10 77 K5
Moor Park Wy FNM GU9 77 K6
Moor Rd BDST BH18 211 H3
FARN GU14 50 C8
FRIM GU16 51 H8
HASM GU27 117 J3
LISS GU33 308 H3
Moors Cl CHCH/BSGR BH23 215 H1
RWIN SO21 134 F3
Moorside FERN BH22 * 205 K8
Moorside Cl BWD BH11 213 H5
FARN GU14 50 C7
Moorside Rd BWD BH11 213 G5
FERN BH22 205 G6
WIMB BH21 210 D3
WINC SO23 25 M1
Moors La MFD/CHID GU8 263 Q1
The Moors RFNM GU10 260 D1
STHA RG19 35 K2
Moortown Av CHAM PO6 169 J7
Moortown Dr WIMB BH21 208 B8
Moortown La RGWD BH24 203 K8
Moorvale Rd
MOOR/WNTN BH9 214 A6
Moor Vw CHIN RG24 66 C1
Moor View Rd PLE BH15 223 L2
Moot Cl AND SP10 84 D8
RSAL SP5 332 C2
Moot Gdns RSAL SP5 332 B2
Moot La RSAL SP5 332 B2
Mopley FAWY SO45 354 H9
Mopley Cl FAWY SO45 354 H9
Morant Rd RGWD BH24 203 K3
Moraunt Cl GPORT PO12 183 H8
Moraunt Dr FHAM/PORC PO16 183 H2
Moray Av SHST GU47 49 M1
Mordaunt Dr CWTH RG45 43 K5
Mordaunt Rd SHAM SO14 161 G1
Morden Av FERN BH22 209 J4
Morden Rd MOOR/WNTN BH9 213 M7
Moreland Cl ALTN GU34 106 F6
Moreland Rd GPORT PO12 14 E3
Morelands Rd WVILLE PO7 169 L4
Morestead Rd RWIN SO21 123 J8
Moreton Cl FLEETS GU52 71 H4
RFNM GU10 262 E11
Moreton Rd MOOR/WNTN BH9 214 B4
Morgan Le Fay Dr CHFD SO53 138 F1
Morgan Rd ENEY PO4 193 J4
HEND SO30 149 J7
Morgans Dr FHAM/STUB PO14 181 J7
Morgan's La RSAL SP5 328 E7
Morgans Rise Rd RSAL SP5 332 F1
Morgans Vale Rd RSAL SP5 332 F2
Morgaston Rd TADY RG26 53 H5
Morland Rd ALDT GU11 3 H9
WSHM SO15 146 C7
Morland's Rd ALDT GU11 73 K3
Morley Cl BOSC BH5 227 G3
CHCH/BSGR BH23 216 C5
ITCH SO19 161 M2
YTLY GU46 48 D3
Morley College WINC SO23 * 25 G6
Morley Crs HORN PO8 156 A5
Morley Dr BPWT SO32 143 J4
Morley Rd BOSC BH5 227 G3
BSTK RG21 93 J3
ENEY PO4 193 G6
FNM GU9 13 H6
Morningside Av
FHAM/PORC PO16 167 K7
Mornington Cl AND SP10 96 C7
TADY RG26 249 P3
Mornington Dr FUFL SO22 122 C2
Mornington Rd BOR GU35 112 C2
Mornish Rd CCLF BH13 224 F6
Morpeth Av TOTT SO40 144 F8
Morris Cl FAWY SO45 176 D4
LSOL/BMARY PO13 182 C4
Morrison Av BKME/WDN BH12 224 F2
Morris Ri CHIN RG24 54 A6
Morris Rd CFDH BH17 211 K8
FARN GU14 61 K8
WSHM SO15 22 D1
Morris St HTWY RG27 56 A8
Morse Rd KBH RG22 65 G8
Morshead Crs
FHAM/PORC PO16 10 D2
Mortimer Cl CHCH/BSGR BH23 229 G2
HLER SO31 162 B6
HTWY RG27 57 K4
TOTT SO40 144 D7
WHIT RG2 238 C1
WINC SO23 288 H10
Mortimer Gdns TADY RG26 44 C5
Mortimer La BSTK RG21 6 D5
THLE RG7 40 D1
Mortimer Rd CHAM PO6 168 C7
CHAR BH8 214 B7
HEND SO30 150 A6
ITCH SO19 161 L4
Mortimers Dr ELGH SO50 141 K2
Mortimers La ELGH SO50 141 K2
Mortimer Wy NBAD SO52 137 M5
Mortimore Rd GPORT PO12 190 F2
Morton Cl FRIM GU16 61 M1
Morval Cl FARN GU14 60 E4
Mosaic Cl ITCH SO19 148 F8
Mosdell Rd EMRTH PO10 172 D6
Moselle Cl FARN GU14 60 D3
Moss Cl LISS GU33 308 G8
Mosscrop Ct BSTK RG21 6 D7
Moss Dr TOTT SO40 159 M6
Mossleigh Av ROWN SO16 145 M3
Mossley Av BKME/WDN BH12 212 F7
Moss Rd WINC SO23 25 K5
Motcombe Rd CCLF BH13 225 G7
Mothes House TADY RG26 44 C5
Mottisfont Cl WSHM SO15 160 A2
Mottisfont Rd ELGH SO50 134 A8
Moulsham Copse La YTLY GU46 48 D1
Moulsham La YTLY GU46 48 D1
Moulshay La HTWY RG27 54 E3
Mound Cl GPORT PO12 14 C6
Mountain Ash Cl WEND SO18 148 C5
Mountbatten Av ROMY SO51 136 F1
Mountbatten Cl
CHCH/BSGR BH23 229 G3
LSOL/BMARY PO13 182 C4
NWBY RG14 27 L7
Mountbatten Ct AND SP10 96 F3
FUFL SO22 122 E1
Mountbatten Dr FERN BH22 209 J3
WVILLE PO7 169 J2
Mountbatten Pl WINC SO23 289 J8
Mountbatten Ri SHST GU47 43 H7
Mountbatten Rd CCLF BH13 225 H7
CHAR BH8 214 F6
ELGH SO50 134 A7
TOTT SO40 144 D8
Mountbatten Sq ENEY PO4 193 H6
Mount Carmel Rd RAND SP11 269 K7
Mount Cl FUFL SO22 122 E1
KSCL RG20 246 B6
NMIL/BTOS BH25 219 G7
NWBY RG14 18 E8
Mount Dr CHFD SO53 139 L4
FHAM PO15 181 H4
Mounters La ALTN GU34 106 D7
Mountfield FAWY SO45 176 E4
Mount Grace Dr PSTN BH14 237 H1
Mount Hermon Rd RAND SP11 269 L6
Mount House Cl FAWY SO45 177 G3
Mountjoy Cl WIMB BH21 207 M6
Mount La ROMY SO51 128 F1
Mount Pleasant FNM GU9 12 C4
HTWY RG27 57 M2
RGWD BH24 203 J4
ROMY SO51 * 136 E2
SHST GU47 43 J7
TADY RG26 44 A4
WINC SO23 288 H10
Mount Pleasant Dr CHAR BH8 214 F7
CHCH/BSGR BH23 348 E11
Mount Pleasant La
LYMN SO41 351 L12
Mount Pleasant Rd ALTN GU34 106 F6
ASHV GU12 3 J3
BOR GU35 111 H7
GPORT PO12 14 E8
PLE BH15 223 K6
SHAM SO14 161 H1
Mount Rd BWD BH11 213 G4
KSCL RG20 246 B5
NTHA RG18 28 F8
PSTN BH14 224 B3
Mountsom's La ALTN GU34 294 F4
Mounts Wy FLEETN GU51 58 E5
Mount Temple ROMY SO51 137 G1
The Mount BOR GU35 114 A2
FLEETN GU51 59 J6
HASM GU27 118 F2
LSOL/BMARY PO13 182 E7
NWBY RG14 * 18 E9
RGWD BH24 203 M4
ROWN SO16 146 A7
ROWN SO16 146 F4
Mount Vw ALDT GU11 2 E5
ELGH SO50 134 B8
Mountview Av
FHAM/PORC PO16 167 L7
Mountwood Rd EMRTH PO10 172 D5
Mourne Cl KBH RG22 64 D8
Mousehole La FAWY SO45 177 G5
WEND SO18 147 M8
Mousehole Rd CHAM PO6 167 M7
Mowbray Rd ITCH SO19 148 B8
Moxhams FBDG SP6 * 197 H3
Mozart Cl KBH RG22 93 G4

Muccleshell Cl HAV PO9 171 G4
Mudberry La RCCH PO18 173 L6
Muddyford Rd RSAL SP5 327 P11
Mudeford CHCH/BSGR BH23 228 F3
Mudeford Green Cl
CHCH/BSGR BH23 228 F3
Mudeford La
CHCH/BSGR BH23 228 F2
Mude Gdns CHCH/BSGR BH23 229 G3
Mud La HTWY RG27 241 M3
Mulberry Av CHAM PO6 185 G1
FHAM/STUB PO14 189 J3
Mulberry Cl ASHV GU12 74 A4
CWTH RG45 43 L4
GPORT PO12 14 E5
SHST GU47 43 M8
Mulberry Cnr CHFD SO53 * 139 G4
Mulberry Ct ALTN GU34 293 N5
Mulberry Gdns FBDG SP6 197 G4
Mulberry La CHAM PO6 185 G1
Mulberry Rd TOTT SO40 159 M7
Mulberry Wk WSHM SO15 146 C8
Mulberry Wy CHIN RG24 54 B5
Mulfords Hl TADY RG26 44 C4
Mulgrave Rd FRIM GU16 51 H6
Mull Cl DEAN RG23 91 J2
Mullen Cl ITCH SO19 161 L4
Mullins Cl BKME/WDN BH12 213 J8
BSTK RG21 65 L5
Mullin's La FAWY SO45 176 F6
Mullion Cl CHAM PO6 184 B1
Mulroy Dr CBLY GU15 51 J2
Mumby Rd GPORT PO12 15 K3
Munday's Boro RGUW GU3 261 L4
Munday's Boro Rd RGUW GU3 261 M4
Mundays Rw HORN PO8 321 L11
Munkle Marsh STHA RG19 * 36 A1
Munnings Cl BSTK RG21 7 J9
Munnings Ct AND SP10 4 E2
Munnings Dr SHST GU47 49 M2
Munro Crs WSHM SO15 159 M1
Munster Rd NEND PO2 184 D6
PSTN BH14 224 D5
Murefield Rd PSEA PO1 21 K2
Muriel Rd WVILLE PO7 155 L8
Murley Rd MOOR/WNTN BH9 214 A8
Murray Cl AND SP10 96 B7
FHAM PO15 10 B4
ITCH SO19 148 E6
Murray Rd FARN GU14 60 F5
HORN PO8 156 C2
Murray's La PSEA PO1 191 M2
Murray's Rd ALDT GU11 73 K3
Murrell Rd ASHV GU12 74 A5
Murrells La CBLY GU15 50 D5
Muscliffe Ct HAV PO9 171 H3
Muscliffe La MOOR/WNTN BH9 214 A4
Muscliffe Pk
MOOR/WNTN BH9 214 C4
Muscliffe Rd
MOOR/WNTN BH9 213 M8
Muscott Cl NTID SP9 266 D9
Museum Hl HASM GU27 118 D6
Museum Rd PSEA PO1 20 E5
Musgrave Cl KBH RG22 92 F4
Musgrove Gdns ALTN GU34 106 E4
Musket Copse CHIN RG24 66 C2
Mussett Cl TOTT SO40 158 E1
Muss La STOK SO20 299 Q1
Mustang Av FHAM PO15 164 B5
Myers Cl BPWT SO32 318 B7
Myers Wy FRIM GU16 51 M6
Myland Cl BSTK RG21 65 L5
Mylen Rd AND SP10 4 D4
My Lords La HISD PO11 195 H5
Mylum Cl WHIT RG2 238 C2
Myrtle Av FHAM/PORC PO16 183 K1
TOTT SO40 158 D2
Myrtle Cl LSOL/BMARY PO13 182 B5
LYMN SO41 219 M4
Myrtle Dr BLKW GU17 49 M4
Myrtle Gv HSEA PO3 193 H2
Myrtle Rd CHAR BH8 226 C2
ROWN SO16 146 B4
Mytchett Farm Pk FRIM GU16 * 61 M6
Mytchett Heath FRIM GU16 62 A5
Mytchett Lake Rd FRIM GU16 62 A7
Mytchett Place Rd FRIM GU16 62 A5
Mytchett Rd FRIM GU16 61 M4
Myvern Cl FAWY SO45 354 F5

N

Nada Rd CHCH/BSGR BH23 217 K7
Nadder Rd NTID SP9 266 F2
Nailsworth Rd CHAM PO6 168 B7
Naini Tal Rd NTID SP9 266 E1
Nairn Cl FRIM GU16 51 G6
Nairn Rd CCLF BH13 237 K1
TWDS BH3 225 L2
Naish Ct HAV PO9 170 C1
Naish Dr GPORT PO12 183 G7
Naish Est NMIL/BTOS BH25 * 218 D8
Naish Rd NMIL/BTOS BH25 230 D1
Namu Rd MOOR/WNTN BH9 213 L7
Nansen Av PLE BH15 223 K3
Napier Cl ALDT GU11 73 L1
CWTH RG45 43 L4
NTID SP9 266 G2
Napier Crs FHAM PO15 181 J3
Napier Dr CBLY GU15 51 J1
Napier Rd CWTH RG45 43 L4
HORN PO8 156 C2
ITCH SO19 148 E7
PLE BH15 222 C5
SSEA PO5 21 K9
Napier Wk AND SP10 96 F3
Napoleon Av FARN GU14 61 H2
Napoleon Dr DEAN RG23 64 E5
Narrow La RGWD BH24 203 M4
ROMY SO51 136 E1
Narvik Rd NEND PO2 184 D4
Naseby Ri NWBY RG14 27 M7
Naseby Rd MOOR/WNTN BH9 214 A7
Nash Cl BSTK RG21 7 G1
FARN GU14 60 F4
FAWY SO45 176 D6
Nashe Cl FHAM PO15 181 K1
Nashe Wy FHAM PO15 181 J2
Nash Mdw ODIM RG29 257 Q4
Nash Rd FAWY SO45 176 D7
Nasmith Cl LSOL/BMARY PO13 190 D4
Nately Rd OVTN RG25 67 M5
Nathen Gdns PLE BH15 222 D5
Nations Hl WINC SO23 288 H9
Navarino Ct LYMN SO41 * 221 M5
Navigator's Wy HEND SO30 149 J4
Navy Rd PSEA PO1 192 A2
The Naylors THLE RG7 238 D10
Nea Cl CHCH/BSGR BH23 217 K8
Neacroft Cl NMIL/BTOS BH25 218 D8
Nea Dr RGWD BH24 198 C7
Nea Rd CHCH/BSGR BH23 217 L8
Neath Rd BSTK RG21 7 J4
Neath Wy CHFD SO53 139 G3
Needles Point LYMN SO41 232 D4
Neelands Gv CHAM PO6 167 L8
Neilson Cl CHFD SO53 139 J1
Nelson Av FHAM/PORC PO16 183 H1
NEND PO2 184 D6
Nelson Cl ASHV GU12 3 K4
FAWY SO45 354 E5
FNM GU9 72 D8
NMIL/BTOS BH25 218 F5
ROMY SO51 130 F8
STOK SO20 285 P5
Nelson Ct FHAM/STUB PO14 181 M6
Nelson Crs HORN PO8 * 156 C1
Nelson Dr CHCH/BSGR BH23 228 F2
Nelson Ga WSHM SO15 22 D1
Nelson La WHAM PO17 167 J5
Nelson Pl LYMN SO41 221 M5
Nelson Rd BKME/WDN BH12 225 H4
ELGH SO50 134 D8
FNM GU9 72 D8
GPORT PO12 14 F5
PSEA PO1 192 D1
SSEA PO5 21 H7
WINC SO23 25 L7
WSHM SO15 160 C2
Nelsons Gdns HEND SO30 149 J1
Nelson St ALDT GU11 2 E2
Nelson Wk AND SP10 96 E2
Nelson Wy CBLY GU15 50 B4
Nene Ct AND SP10 * 96 E2
Nepaul Rd NTID SP9 266 E1
Nepean Cl GPORT PO12 191 H7
Neptune Rd BOR GU35 113 G2
FHAM PO15 181 J2
FHAM/STUB PO14 181 M7
Neptune Wy SHAM SO14 23 J7
Nerissa Cl WVILLE PO7 156 B8
Nerquis Cl ROMY SO51 131 H8
Nesbitt Cl LSOL/BMARY PO13 182 B5
Nessus St NEND PO2 184 D8
Nestor Cl AND SP10 4 E2
Netherfield Cl ALTN GU34 106 E4
HAV PO9 17 H6
Netherhall Gdns WBNE BH4 225 J5
Nether Hill La BPWT SO32 150 B2
Netherhouse Moor
FLEETN GU51 70 F2
Netherton Rd GPORT PO12 190 F1
Nether Vell-Mead FLEETS GU52 71 G4
Netherwood Pl WIMB BH21 207 G3
Netley Cliff HLER SO31 * 162 B7
Netley Cl CHFD SO53 139 H5
PLE BH15 224 A1
Netley Firs Rd ITCH SO19 148 F8
Netley Hill Est ITCH SO19 * 148 F8
Netley Lodge Cl HLER SO31 162 C7
Netley Rd FHAM/STUB PO14 180 C3
SSEA PO5 21 G8
Netley St FARN GU14 61 J8
Netley Ter SSEA PO5 21 G9
Nettlebeds La NARL SO24 291 R6
Nettlestone HLER SO31 162 C5
Nettlestone Rd ENEY PO4 * 193 G6
Nettleton Cl CFDH BH17 223 L1
Netton St RSAL SP5 324 D4
Neuvic Wy WHCH RG28 87 M8
Nevada Cl FARN GU14 60 D5
Neva Rd WEND SO18 147 M8
Neville Av FHAM/PORC PO16 183 K2
Neville Cl AND SP10 5 K9
BSTK RG21 93 K2
Neville Dr ROMY SO51 130 F7
STHA RG19 35 L1
Neville Duke Rd FARN GU14 50 B8
Neville Gdns EMRTH PO10 171 L5
Neville Rd HSEA PO3 193 G1
Neville Shute Rd HSEA PO3 185 G5
New Acres EWKG RG40 * 43 G1
Newall Rd RAND SP11 95 J5
Newark Rd BLKW GU17 49 G7
New Barn Cl FLEETN GU51 70 F1
New Barn La ALTN GU34 106 F6
RAND SP11 272 D4
Newbarn Rd EPSF GU31 322 A1
HAV PO9 170 C5
Newbold Rd NWBY RG14 26 F7
Newbolt Cl HORN PO8 155 L5
NTHA RG18 28 E7
Newbolt Rd CHAM PO6 167 M7
New Borough Rd WIMB BH21 207 J5
New Br CHCH/BSGR BH23 215 G5
Newbridge HLER SO31 162 C6
New Bridge La BSTK RG21 7 K4
Newbridge Rd TOTT SO40 341 K1
Newbridge Wy LYMN SO41 221 J7
New Brighton Rd
EMRTH PO10 171 M6
Newbroke Rd
LSOL/BMARY PO13 182 E8
Newburgh St WINC SO23 24 E4
Newbury Cl ELGH SO50 141 H2
Newbury Dr NBNE BH10 213 K7
Newbury Pl HLER SO31 179 M2
Newbury Rd AND SP10 96 D2
KSCL RG20 248 B9
RAND SP11 84 D2
WHCH RG28 87 L7
WSHM SO15 146 C7
Newbury St AND SP10 5 J5
HUNG RG17 31 H2
WHCH RG28 87 L7
Newchurch Rd TADY RG26 44 A3
New Cliffe Gdns HEND SO30 149 H7
Newcomb Cl AND SP10 96 B7
Newcombe Rd FERN BH22 204 F5
SBNE BH6 227 L2
WSHM SO15 160 E2
Newcomen Rd NEND PO2 184 C6
Newcome Pl ASHV GU12 3 L8
Newcome Rd FNM GU9 2 A9
PSEA PO1 21 L1
New Cottages La End
RWIN SO21 * 303 J12
New Crs RAND SP11 265 L11
Newcroft Gdns
CHCH/BSGR BH23 216 A8
New Cut HISD PO11 186 F5
New Dawn Cl FARN GU14 60 D5
New Down La WVILLE PO7 169 G6
New Dro RAND SP11 265 L11
Newells La RCCH PO18 173 L4
Newenham Rd LYMN SO41 221 L6
New Farm Rd NARL SO24 291 K11
RWIN SO21 276 B9
Newfield Av FARN GU14 60 E2
Newfield Rd ASHV GU12 74 A2
LISS GU33 308 G6
New Forest Dr BROC SO42 350 H3
Newfoundland Dr PLE BH15 223 K7
Newfoundland Rd FRIM GU16 51 M8
Newgate La FHAM/STUB PO14 182 A2
New Harbour Rd PLE BH15 223 H7
New Harbour Rd South
PLE BH15 223 H8
New House La RAND SP11 82 C5
New Inn La BROC SO42 353 J11
TOTT SO40 341 M6
New Inn Rd TOTT SO40 341 M6
Newland Av GPORT PO12 14 C4
Newlands FHAM PO15 181 J3
FLEETS GU52 71 J2
Newlands Av WSHM SO15 160 D1
Newlands Cl CHFD SO53 138 E3
FAWY SO45 354 G8
YTLY GU46 48 F3
Newlands Copse FAWY SO45 354 H7
Newlands Dr ASHV GU12 74 B4
Newlands La WVILLE PO7 154 F7
Newlands Rd
CHCH/BSGR BH23 228 F1
FAWY SO45 354 G6
FRIM GU16 50 D7
LTDN BH7 227 G2
NMIL/BTOS BH25 219 H7
WVILLE PO7 169 K3
Newlands Wy BDST BH18 210 D5
New La EPSF GU31 323 M2
HAV PO9 17 G3
LYMN SO41 232 F5
NMIL/BTOS BH25 218 F2
STOK SO20 285 Q12
Newlease Rd WVILLE PO7 169 M3
Newlyn Wk ROMY SO51 131 G7
Newlyn Wy BKME/WDN BH12 224 E1
CHAM PO6 184 A1
Newman La ALTN GU34 107 H3
Newmans Cl FERN BH22 205 G3
Newmans Copse Rd
TOTT SO40 159 G4
Newmans Ct FNM GU9 76 E2
Newmans Hl WHAM PO17 318 C12
Newman's La FERN BH22 204 E3
Newman St ROWN SO16 146 B8
Newmarket Cl ELGH SO50 141 K5
Newmer Ct HAV PO9 170 C2
New Merrifield WIMB BH21 207 L1
New Mill La HTWY RG27 241 L2
New Mill Rd HTWY RG27 241 L2
Newmorton Rd
MOOR/WNTN BH9 214 A4
Newney Cl NEND PO2 184 F4
Newnham Ct HAV PO9 * 171 H3
Newnham La CHIN RG24 54 F8
HTWY RG27 55 L7
Newnham Pk HTWY RG27 56 B8
Newnham Rd HTWY RG27 55 M8
New Odiham Rd ALTN GU34 106 D2
New Orch PLE BH15 223 H6
New Paddock Cl ALTN GU34 107 J2
New Pde NBNE BH10 * 213 L5
New Park Rd SBNE BH6 227 J4
New Pines RSAL SP5 * 327 P3
Newport Cl CHFD SO53 139 G4
NWBY RG14 19 H2
Newport La ROMY SO51 131 H2
Newport Rd ASHV GU12 3 K5
GPORT PO12 14 A2
NWBY RG14 19 H2
New Quay Rd PLE BH15 223 G7
New Rd BKME/WDN BH12 224 D2
BLKW GU17 50 A4
BOR GU35 112 E3
BPWT SO32 143 K2
BPWT SO32 143 M8
BPWT SO32 319 K1
BSTK RG21 6 F6
CWTH RG45 43 L3
ELGH SO50 141 H2
EMRTH PO10 172 B3
EMRTH PO10 172 E6
FAWY SO45 177 H8
FAWY SO45 354 G7
FBDG SP6 330 E7
FERN BH22 209 K3
FERN BH22 209 L8
FHAM/PORC PO16 10 F5
FLEETS GU52 71 K2
FUFL SO22 288 A10
HASM GU27 117 M3
HAV PO9 16 B3
HLER SO31 162 B6
HLER SO31 163 M4
HLER SO31 179 K4
HORN PO8 155 L2
HORN PO8 321 L7
HTWY RG27 48 A1
HTWY RG27 56 C7
HTWY RG27 57 L2
LYMN SO41 233 G4
NBNE BH10 213 L3
NEND PO2 192 E1
NWBY RG14 19 G7
ODIM RG29 68 E4
RFNM GU10 260 D2
RGWD BH24 199 K4
ROMY SO51 130 D1
ROMY SO51 131 G8
RSAL SP5 334 C7
RWIN SO21 134 F3
RWIN SO21 275 P2
SHAM SO14 23 G2
SHST GU47 43 J8
STHA RG19 34 D5
STOK SO20 269 Q12
TADY RG26 44 A5
TADY RG26 52 E1
TOTT SO40 158 C6
WIMB BH21 200 C1
New Rd East NEND PO2 184 F8
New Road Hl THLE RG7 37 H1
Newstead Rd SBNE BH6 227 K4
New St AND SP10 5 J2
BSTK RG21 6 E6
LYMN SO41 221 L4
PLE BH15 223 H6
RGWD BH24 203 J6
STOK SO20 285 P6
THLE RG7 41 G8
Newton Cl FHAM/STUB PO14 181 J8
RSAL SP5 127 G5
Newton La ALTN GU34 294 E8
ROMY SO51 136 E1
RSAL SP5 126 D8
Newton Morrell PSTN BH14 224 D5
Newton Pl
LSOL/BMARY PO13 189 L5
Newton Rd CCLF BH13 224 E8
FARN GU14 61 K2
NMIL/BTOS BH25 219 H8
RWIN SO21 125 G5
WEND SO18 147 L7
Newton Vls RAND SP11 * 265 P11
Newton Wy RFNM GU10 260 C1
New Town FHAM/PORC PO16 167 K8
Newtown TADY RG26 44 A4
Newtown Cl AND SP10 4 D6
Newtown La HISD PO11 194 E4
RGWD BH24 199 L3
WIMB BH21 206 D8
Newtown Rd ELGH SO50 134 A8
HLER SO31 179 J4
ITCH SO19 162 A2
LIPH GU30 116 C5
NWBY RG14 18 E8
ROMY SO51 129 H5
SHST GU47 43 K8
VWD BH31 201 J2
New Valley Rd LYMN SO41 232 C4
New Vls KSCL RG20 * 245 P1
New Wokingham Rd
CWTH RG45 43 J2
Nexus Pk ASHV GU12 61 M8
Nicholas Cl CHCH/BSGR BH23 218 B6
Nicholas Crs FHAM PO15 10 C4
Nicholas Gdns NBNE BH10 213 J6
Nicholas Rd FAWY SO45 354 G9
Nicholl Pl LSOL/BMARY PO13 182 C6
Nichol Rd CHFD SO53 133 K7
Nicholson Cl CFDH BH17 211 L8
Nicholson Wk ROWN SO16 145 K2
Nicholson Wy HAV PO9 16 D1
Nichols Rd SHAM SO14 23 J1
Nickel Cl WINC SO23 25 K4
Nickel St SSEA PO5 20 F7
Nickleby Gdns TOTT SO40 158 B1
Nickleby Rd HORN PO8 321 K6
Nickson Cl CHFD SO53 133 H8
Nideggan Cl STHA RG19 35 K1
Nightingale Av ELGH SO50 139 K6
Nightingale Cl FARN GU14 60 C2
FUFL SO22 122 B6
GPORT PO12 190 F2
HAV PO9 157 G7
ROMY SO51 137 G1
VWD BH31 201 J3
Nightingale Ct EMRTH PO10 172 B2
Nightingale Crs BPWT SO32 151 M4
Nightingale Dr FRIM GU16 62 A5
TOTT SO40 144 C8
Nightingale Gdns CHIN RG24 64 E4
HTWY RG27 56 C7
SHST GU47 43 K8
Nightingale Gv WSHM SO15 160 C1
Nightingale La RCCH PO18 173 G3
THLE RG7 40 D2
Nightingale Pk HAV PO9 17 J5
Nightingale Ri OVTN RG25 89 K5
Nightingale Rd ASHV GU12 74 C5
BOR GU35 113 G2
HLER SO31 162 F4
PSF GU32 120 B7
SSEA PO5 20 F8
The Nightingales NWBY RG14 18 F9
Nightingale Wk HLER SO31 162 C8
Nightjar Cl CFDH BH17 210 E8
HORN PO8 156 A2
RFNM GU10 71 K8
Nile Rd PTSW SO17 147 G6
Nile St EMRTH PO10 171 M8
Nimrod Dr LSOL/BMARY PO13 190 D2
Nimrod Wy WIMB BH21 208 F2
Nine Elms La WHAM PO17 166 E4
Nine Mile Ride EWKG RG40 42 F1
Ninian Cl ELGH SO50 141 J3
Ninian Park Rd HSEA PO3 185 G6
Niton Cl LSOL/BMARY PO13 182 C6
Noads Cl FAWY SO45 176 F6
Noads Wy FAWY SO45 176 F6
Nobbs La PSEA PO1 20 D5
Nobes Av LSOL/BMARY PO13 182 C5
Nobes Cl LSOL/BMARY PO13 182 D6
Noble Cl BWD BH11 212 F7
Noble Rd HEND SO30 149 K6
Nob's Crook RWIN SO21 135 G5
Noctule Ct WHAM PO17 165 K4
Noel Cl BROC SO42 351 L3
Noel Rd NBNE BH10 213 H7
Nogarth Cl ROMY SO51 131 H7
Nomad Cl WEND SO18 148 B3
The Nook ELGH SO50 134 B7
LSOL/BMARY PO13 182 E7
Noon Gdns VWD BH31 201 K2
Noon Hill Dr VWD BH31 201 K2
Noon Hill Rd VWD BH31 201 K2
Norbury Cl CHFD SO53 139 H1
Norbury Gdns HLER SO31 178 E2
Norcliffe Cl BWD BH11 213 H5
Norcliffe Rd PTSW SO17 147 G8
Norden Cl BSTK RG21 6 F2
Nordik Gdns HEND SO30 149 J7
Nore Crs EMRTH PO10 171 K7
Nore Down Wy RCCH PO18 323 J12
Nore Farm Av EMRTH PO10 171 K7
Nores Rd WHIT RG2 238 D1
Noreuil Rd PSF GU32 120 B6
Norfolk Av CHCH/BSGR BH23 215 M7
Norfolk Rd GPORT PO12 190 F1
WSHM SO15 146 D8
Norfolk St SSEA PO5 21 G6
Norgett Wy FHAM/PORC PO16 183 H2
Norham Av ROWN SO16 146 C6
Norham Cl ROWN SO16 146 C6
Norland Rd ENEY PO4 21 L6
Norlands NTHA RG18 28 E7
Norlands Dr RWIN SO21 124 C8
Norley Cl HAV PO9 170 E3
Norleywood
CHCH/BSGR BH23 217 M8
Norleywood Rd LYMN SO41 356 D3
Norman Av BKME/WDN BH12 224 F2
Norman Cl BOR GU35 113 G1
FHAM/PORC PO16 183 K2
Norman Court La RAND SP11 96 B8
Normandy Cl LYMN SO41 350 E10
ROWN SO16 145 K2
Normandy Common La
RGUW GU3 75 H4
Normandy Dr
CHCH/BSGR BH23 228 D1
Normandy Gdns GPORT PO12 14 B4
Normandy La LYMN SO41 221 M6
Normandy Rd NEND PO2 184 D4
Normandy St ALTN GU34 107 G4
Normandy Wy FBDG SP6 197 G2
PLE BH15 222 D6
TOTT SO40 159 M5
Norman Gdns
BKME/WDN BH12 224 F2
HEND SO30 149 G7
Normanhurst Av CHAR BH8 214 D7
Norman Rd ENEY PO4 21 L7
FAWY SO45 354 H8
GPORT PO12 14 C2
HISD PO11 195 H6
WINC SO23 24 E9
WSHM SO15 22 A1
Normanton Cl
CHCH/BSGR BH23 215 M7
Normanton Rd BSTK RG21 65 K5
Norman Wy HAV PO9 170 C6
Normay Ri NWBY RG14 33 J7
Normoor Rd THLE RG7 39 M3
Norn Hl BSTK RG21 7 H2
Norn Hill Cl BSTK RG21 7 H2
Norris Br FARN GU14 60 A8
Norris Cl BOR GU35 112 D3
RGWD BH24 202 A8
ROMY SO51 131 J6
Norris Gdns HAV PO9 17 H6
NMIL/BTOS BH25 219 G7
RWIN SO21 288 D4
Norris Hl WEND SO18 147 L7
Norris Hill Rd FLEETS GU52 71 M1
Norrish Rd BKME/WDN BH12 224 C3
Norset Rd FHAM PO15 181 J2
Northam Br SHAM SO14 161 J2
Northam Ms PSEA PO1 * 21 J2
Northampton La FAWY SO45 354 G8
Northam Rd SHAM SO14 23 K1
Northam St PSEA PO1 21 K2
Northanger Cl ALTN GU34 106 E4
Northarbour Rd CHAM PO6 184 D1
North Av FNM GU9 77 H1
NBNE BH10 213 K2
NEND PO2 184 E3
North Battery Rd NEND PO2 184 B6
Northbourne Av NBNE BH10 213 K4
Northbourne Cl FAWY SO45 177 G7
Northbourne Gdns
NBNE BH10 213 L3
Northbourne Pl NBNE BH10 213 K3
Northbrook Av WINC SO23 25 K6
Northbrook Cl PSEA PO1 192 D1
WINC SO23 25 L6
Northbrook Rd ALDT GU11 3 G6
BDST BH18 211 G6
SHAM SO14 23 J1
Northbrook St NWBY RG14 18 E3
North Charford Crossing
FBDG SP6 331 R4
North Charford Dro FBDG SP6 331 K1
North Cl ASHV GU12 3 M5
FARN GU14 50 C8
GPORT PO12 14 A5
HAV PO9 17 G6
LYMN SO41 221 M4
ROMY SO51 131 J7
North Common La LYMN SO41 220 F1
RSAL SP5 333 R2
Northcote Av NEND PO2 184 F8
Northcote Rd ASHV GU12 74 A1
BMTH BH1 9 K3
ENEY PO4 21 M7
FARN GU14 60 E2
PTSW SO17 147 J6
North Crs HISD PO11 195 H5
Northcroft La NWBY RG14 18 C3
Northcroft Rd GPORT PO12 14 B1
Northcroft Ter NWBY RG14 18 D4
North Cross St GPORT PO12 15 K4
Northdene Rd CHFD SO53 139 J3
North Downs Wy RFNM GU10 77 L6
RGUW GU3 261 K5
North Dr CHOB/PIR GU24 63 J2
FERN BH22 * 205 K8
FUFL SO22 288 B11
NMIL/BTOS BH25 349 N11
North East Cl ITCH SO19 148 B7
North East Rd ITCH SO19 148 A8
North End Av NEND PO2 184 D6
North End Cl CHFD SO53 139 J4
North End Gv NEND PO2 184 D6
Northend La BPWT SO32 318 G2
North End La FBDG SP6 196 F8
NARL SO24 303 R5
Northern Access Rd
FAWY SO45 355 M6
Northern Anchorage
ITCH SO19 23 M5
ITCH SO19 161 K5
Northern Av AND SP10 5 H3
NWBY RG14 27 J6
Northern Pde NEND PO2 184 D5
Northern Rd CHAM PO6 168 F8
Northerwood Av LYND SO43 345 J3
Northerwood Cl NBAD SO52 137 M4
Northey Rd SBNE BH6 227 L2
North Farm Rd FARN GU14 50 A8
North Fld OVTN RG25 89 J3
Northfield Av
FHAM/STUB PO14 181 M5
Northfield Cl ASHV GU12 3 M4
BPWT SO32 143 G3
FLEETS GU52 * 71 K2
HORN PO8 321 L10
Northfield La ALTN GU34 106 C8
Northfield Pk
FHAM/PORC PO16 * 167 H7
Northfield Rd FLEETS GU52 71 K2
HTWY RG27 46 F7
LYMN SO41 232 E3
NTHA RG18 28 D8
RGWD BH24 203 J3
WEND SO18 147 M5
Northfields Farm La
WHAM PO17 152 A3
North Front SHAM SO14 23 H2
North Fryerne YTLY GU46 42 F8
Northgate Av NEND PO2 192 F1
Northgate Dr CBLY GU15 51 J1
Northgate La OVTN RG25 105 K3
North Gate Rd FARN GU14 61 H6
Northgate Wy KBH RG22 92 C6
North Greenlands LYMN SO41 221 J6
North Head LYMN SO41 232 A3
North Hl CHAM PO6 168 B6
FHAM/PORC PO16 11 G1
North Hill Cl FUFL SO22 24 F1
Northington Rd NARL SO24 290 E2
RWIN SO21 290 D7
Northlands Cl TOTT SO40 144 D8
Northlands Dr WINC SO23 25 G1
Northlands Gdns WSHM SO15 160 E1
Northlands Rd ELGH SO50 140 A1
ROMY SO51 137 J2
TOTT SO40 144 D8
WSHM SO15 160 E1
North La ALDT GU11 3 L1
BROC SO42 353 L3
EPSF GU31 315 Q11
EPSF GU31 316 H12
HORN PO8 321 K3
HORN PO8 321 K6
RSAL SP5 297 N2
RSAL SP5 334 A9
Northleigh Cnr WEND SO18 * 147 L3
Northleigh La WIMB BH21 207 L3
North Ldg FBDG SP6 * 196 B4
THLE RG7 * 41 G1
North Lodge Rd PSTN BH14 224 E4
Northmead FARN GU14 61 H4
Northmead Dr CFDH BH17 210 F8
Northmere Dr
BKME/WDN BH12 224 F1
Northmere Rd
BKME/WDN BH12 224 E2
North Millers Dl CHFD SO53 133 G7
Northmore Cl HLER SO31 164 B7
Northmore Rd HLER SO31 164 B7
Northney La HISD PO11 187 J4
Northney Rd HISD PO11 187 H4
Northolt Gdns ROWN SO16 146 A4
Northover La LYMN SO41 219 L1
Northover Rd HSEA PO3 185 H8
LYMN SO41 221 G4
North Pde BOR GU35 110 E6
North Poulner Rd RGWD BH24 203 K2
North Rd ALDT GU11 73 K1
BROC SO42 351 L3
FAWY SO45 176 E6
HORN PO8 321 L10
LTDN BH7 226 E3
PLE BH15 223 G6
PSF GU32 120 D5
PSTN BH14 224 A4
PTSW SO17 147 J8
WINC SO23 288 H8

WVILLE PO7 168 A6
North Rd East WHAM PO17 168 A2
North Rd West WHAM PO17 167 M2
North Shore Rd HISD PO11 194 D4
North Side RFNM GU10 260 E1
Northside La NARL SO24 292 B9
North Sq WHAM PO17 165 L5
North St EMRTH PO10 171 M7
HAV PO9 16 A3
HAV PO9 16 F4
KSCL RG20 248 D10
LYMN SO41 221 J6
NARL SO24 291 R11
PLE BH15 223 J6
PSEA PO1 20 D2
North Street Ar HAV PO9 16 F3
North Stroud La PSF GU32 315 J6
North Town RWIN SO21 125 G5
North Trestle Rd FAWY SO45 178 B6
Northumberland Rd
BOR GU35 112 F3
SHAM SO14 23 K1
SSEA PO5 * 21 L3
North Vw FUFL SO22 24 D4
North View Rd TADY RG26 44 D5
North Wallington
FHAM/PORC PO16 11 K3
North Walls WINC SO23 25 J5
North Warnborough St
ODIM RG29 68 D5
North Wy AND SP10 96 F2
HAV PO9 16 D4
RAND SP11 97 G2
Northway FHAM PO15 180 E1
NTHA RG18 28 E7
NWBY RG14 19 G6
WWKG RG41 239 R1
Northways
FHAM/STUB PO14 189 K2
North Weirs BROC SO42 350 H3
Northwick HTWY RG27 48 A1
Northwood Cl ROWN SO16 147 G2
Northwood Dr NWBY RG14 19 J1
Northwood La HISD PO11 187 G7
Northwood Rd NEND PO2 184 E4
Northwood Sq
FHAM/PORC PO16 11 G4
Nortoft Rd CHAR BH8 226 B2
Norton Cl CHCH/BSGR BH23 228 D1
ITCH SO19 161 L5
NWBY RG14 33 J6
WHAM PO17 167 M2
WVILLE PO7 169 K1
Norton Dr FHAM/PORC PO16 10 F3
Norton Ride CHIN RG24 66 B1
Norton Rd CBLY GU15 51 L4
MOOR/WNTN BH9 213 L7
THLE RG7 240 C2
WHAM PO17 167 M2
Norton Wy PLE BH15 223 G7
Norton Welch Cl NBAD SO52 138 B4
Norway Rd HSEA PO3 184 F4
Norwich Av CBLY GU15 51 G5
WCLF BH2 8 B5
Norwich Av West WBNE BH4 8 A5
Norwich Cl HLER SO31 163 L8
KBH RG22 92 D5
Norwich Pl
LSOL/BMARY PO13 189 L5
Norwich Rd CHAM PO6 168 D7
WCLF BH2 8 C6
WEND SO18 147 M6
Norwood Pl BOSC BH5 227 H3
Nottingham Pl
LSOL/BMARY PO13 189 L5
Nouale La RGWD BH24 203 M5
Novello Cl KBH RG22 92 F5
Novello Gdns WVILLE PO7 169 L3
Noyce Dr ELGH SO50 141 K3
Noyce Gdns CHAR BH8 215 H6
Nuffield Rd CFDH BH17 211 K8
WHIT RG2 239 M9
Nugee Ct CWTH RG45 43 K3
Nugent Rd SBNE BH6 227 M4
Nunns Pk RSAL SP5 127 H4
Nuns Rd WINC SO23 25 H2
Nuns Wk WINC SO23 25 H2
Nunton Dro RSAL SP5 326 B8
Nursery Cl CHIN RG24 54 C5
EMRTH PO10 171 M5
FLEETN GU51 59 M8
FRIM GU16 61 M1
HTWY RG27 56 C6
LSOL/BMARY PO13 182 B5
Nursery Fld LISS GU33 308 E9
Nursery Gdns CHFD SO53 139 J5
FUFL SO22 24 B5
HORN PO8 156 A3
ITCH SO19 148 B6
ROMY SO51 137 G1
Nursery Gv HEND SO30 149 J7
Nursery La FHAM/STUB PO14 189 J3
Nursery Rd ALTN GU34 107 G4
HAV PO9 170 C6
MOOR/WNTN BH9 214 A5
NARL SO24 291 M11
RGWD BH24 203 J6
WEND SO18 147 K7
Nursery Ter ODIM RG29 * 68 E4
Nursling Crs HAV PO9 171 G3
Nursling Gn CHAR BH8 214 D6
Nursling St ROWN SO16 145 J3
Nutash FHAM PO15 164 C8
Nutbane Cl AND SP10 4 B6
Nutbane La RAND SP11 83 H5
Nutbean La THLE RG7 238 F11
Nutbeem Rd ELGH SO50 140 A2
Nutbourne FNM GU9 2 B8
Nutbourne Rd CHAM PO6 185 K1
HISD PO11 195 L7
Nutburn Rd NBAD SO52 138 B4
Nutchers Dro STOK SO20 299 Q1
Nutcombe La GSHT GU26 115 L7
Nutfield Ct ROWN SO16 145 L5
Nutfield Pl PSEA PO1 192 D2
Nutfield Rd ROWN SO16 145 K2
Nuthatch Cl CFDH BH17 222 F1
FERN BH22 204 D8
HAV PO9 157 H7
KBH RG22 92 B5
RFNM GU10 76 B1
Nutley Cl BOR GU35 112 F2
BWD BH11 212 F4
YTLY GU46 48 F3
Nutley La OVTN RG25 104 B3
Nutley Rd HAV PO9 170 D3
Nutley Wy BWD BH11 212 F5
Nutmeg Ct FARN GU14 60 C3
Nutsey Av TOTT SO40 144 D6
Nutsey La TOTT SO40 144 E6
Nutshalling Av ROWN SO16 145 L3
Nutshalling Cl TOTT SO40 144 C6
Nutshell La FNM GU9 77 G2
Nutter's La WHIT RG2 238 C7
Nutwick Rd HAV PO9 17 K1
Nutwood Wy TOTT SO40 144 E6
Nyewood Av
FHAM/PORC PO16 167 K7
Nyria Wy GPORT PO12 15 J5

O

Oakapple Gdns CHAM PO6 169 L8
Oak Av CHCH/BSGR BH23 215 K8
SHST GU47 43 M7
Oak Bank AND SP10 5 H8
Oakbank Rd ELGH SO50 140 C1
ITCH SO19 161 K5
Oak Cl BPWT SO32 310 F11
BSTK RG21 7 K5
DEAN RG23 91 K3
FAWY SO45 176 E7
FERN BH22 209 L7
HORN PO8 155 L6
KSCL RG20 248 E10
LYND SO43 * 345 K4
NTID SP9 266 G1
OVTN RG25 89 J5
RSAL SP5 296 C5
STOK SO20 270 D8
TADY RG26 249 P4
WIMB BH21 210 C3
WSHM SO15 159 J1
Oak Coppice Cl ELGH SO50 141 G2
Oak Ct FNM GU9 12 F6
LYMN SO41 * 221 J6
Oakcroft La FHAM/STUB PO14 181 J7
Oakdale Rd PLE BH15 223 L2
Oakdene ALTN GU34 106 E3
LSOL/BMARY PO13 182 D7
TOTT SO40 158 B1
Oakdene Cl WIMB BH21 207 K3
Oakdown Rd
FHAM/STUB PO14 189 K1
Oak Dr ELGH SO50 141 J2
NWBY RG14 18 C6
RSAL SP5 327 M1
THLE RG7 39 M2
Oakenbrow FAWY SO45 176 D6
LYMN SO41 350 E9
Oaken Copse CBLY GU15 51 L1
FLEETS GU52 71 K4
Oaken Copse Crs FARN GU14 61 H1
Oaken Gv NWBY RG14 33 K4
The Oakes FHAM/STUB PO14 181 H8
Oak Farm Cl BLKW GU17 49 L3
Oakfield Ct HAV PO9 * 171 H3
Oakfield Pl FARN GU14 60 C4
Oakfield Rd BLKW GU17 50 A4
PLE BH15 223 J2
TADY RG26 44 E3
TOTT SO40 158 F1
TOTT SO40 341 M5
Oakfields CBLY GU15 * 50 D3
ELGH SO50 134 A5
Oakfields Cl KSCL RG20 247 P8
Oak Gdns LYMN SO41 220 D8
Oak Gn ALTN GU34 * 293 N5
Oak Green Wy WEND SO18 148 A4
Oak Grove Crs CBLY GU15 50 B2
Oakgrove Rd ELGH SO50 140 E2
Oak Hanger Cl HTWY RG27 56 D7
Oakhanger Rd BOR GU35 110 C7
Oakhill HLER SO31 163 H3
Oak Hl NARL SO24 291 M12
Oakhill Cl CHFD SO53 139 L3
HLER SO31 163 H3
Oakhill Ct CHFD SO53 139 L3
Oakhill Rd BOR GU35 114 B3
Oakhurst GSHT GU26 115 K5
Oakhurst Cl FERN BH22 205 H6
HLER SO31 162 C6
Oakhurst Dr WVILLE PO7 156 A8
Oakhurst Gdns CHAM PO6 169 H6
Oakhurst La FERN BH22 205 H6
Oakhurst Rd FERN BH22 205 H7
PTSW SO17 147 G5
Oakhurst Wy HLER SO31 162 C6
Oakland Av FNM GU9 2 A8
Oakland Dr TOTT SO40 159 M7
Oakland Rd WHCH RG28 87 L7
Oaklands HASM GU27 118 C5
HTWY RG27 57 L3
LYMN SO41 221 M6
NTHA RG18 27 L1
RWIN SO21 288 D4
YTLY GU46 48 F2
Oaklands Av TOTT SO40 158 F1
Oaklands Cl FBDG SP6 197 G2
FUFL SO22 122 B6
VWD BH31 201 G2
Oaklands Gdns
FHAM/STUB PO14 180 C3
Oaklands Gv HORN PO8 155 L5
Oaklands La CWTH RG45 43 J2
Oaklands Rd HAV PO9 17 H4
PSF GU32 120 C5
The Oaklands CHFD SO53 139 H5
Oaklands Wy DEAN RG23 64 E6
FAWY SO45 176 C6
FHAM/STUB PO14 180 C3
ROWN SO16 146 F4
Oakland Wk FERN BH22 209 L7
Oak La RGWD BH24 203 K4
Oaklea ASHV GU12 74 A3
Oaklea Dr HTWY RG27 241 L2
Oaklea Gdns TADY RG26 46 D6
Oaklea La RSAL SP5 327 N2
Oakleigh Crs TOTT SO40 158 E2
Oakleigh Dr RSAL SP5 334 B7
Oakleigh Gdns ROMY SO51 137 G1
Oakleigh Wy
CHCH/BSGR BH23 229 M1
Oakley Cl FAWY SO45 354 E4
Oakley Dr FLEETN GU51 59 J8
Oakley Gdns UPTN BH16 222 A1
Oakley Hl WIMB BH21 207 K5
Oakley La DEAN RG23 91 K2
WIMB BH21 207 M6
Oakley Rd BOR GU35 110 F7
CBLY GU15 50 D4
HAV PO9 170 D3
NWBY RG14 19 L1
ROMY SO51 298 G10
ROWN SO16 145 M8
TADY RG26 254 F5
WIMB BH21 207 K6
Oakley Straight WIMB BH21 207 L7
Oak Ldg HASM GU27 * 118 E8
Oakmead TADY RG26 46 A4
Oakmead Gdns BWD BH11 212 F4
Oakmeadow Cl EMRTH PO10 172 A3
Oakmead Rd CFDH BH17 210 F8
Oakmont Dr WVILLE PO7 155 M6
Oakmount Av CHFD SO53 139 K4
PTSW SO17 147 G7
TOTT SO40 144 F8
Oakmount Rd CHFD SO53 139 K4
Oak Park Dr HAV PO9 17 G1
Oakridge Centre BSTK RG21 65 L5
Oak Ridge Cl NWBY RG14 33 L4
Oakridge Rd BSTK RG21 65 K4
WSHM SO15 145 K8
Oak Rd BPWT SO32 143 K4
CHAR BH8 226 C2
FARN GU14 61 J5
FAWY SO45 176 E7
FBDG SP6 196 B7
FHAM PO15 181 K2
HLER SO31 162 F4
HORN PO8 321 L7
ITCH SO19 161 K6
NMIL/BTOS BH25 219 J5
UPTN BH16 222 C2
Oaks Coppice HORN PO8 156 A2
Oaks Dr RGWD BH24 205 M5
Oakshott Dr HAV PO9 171 G3
Oaks Md VWD BH31 * 201 H2
The Oaks ALTN GU34 293 L1
AND SP10 * 4 D5
FLEETN GU51 58 F7
HLER SO31 162 F4
ITCH SO19 161 M3
TADY RG26 44 A4
VWD BH31 201 G1
YTLY GU46 48 F3
Oak St GPORT PO12 15 H4
Oakthorn Cl
LSOL/BMARY PO13 190 C2
Oak Tree Cl ASHV GU12 3 M7
BOR GU35 111 M8
RWIN SO21 134 F4
TADY RG26 44 B3
Oaktree Ct LYMN SO41 232 C4
Oak Tree Dr EMRTH PO10 171 L4
HTWY RG27 56 D6
LISS GU33 308 G8
Oak Tree Farm RCCH PO18 173 H5
Oak Tree Gdns HEND SO30 149 H6
Oak Tree La HASM GU27 117 K2
Oak Tree Rd BOR GU35 112 E3
STHA RG19 35 L2
WEND SO18 147 K7
Oaktrees ASHV GU12 73 M7
FNM GU9 76 F2
Oak Tree Ter AND SP10 * 5 J5
Oak Tree Vw FNM GU9 77 H2
Oak Tree Wy ELGH SO50 134 A7
Oaktree Wy SHST GU47 43 J7
Oak V HEND SO30 148 B1
Oakway ASHV GU12 73 K8
RFNM GU10 259 L12
Oakway Dr FRIM GU16 51 G7
Oakwood CHIN RG24 54 B5
FLEETS GU52 71 J4
Oakwood Av HAV PO9 170 B5
NMIL/BTOS BH25 219 J4
RWIN SO21 134 C1
Oakwood Cl CHFD SO53 133 K7
HLER SO31 179 L4
MOOR/WNTN BH9 214 B6
ROMY SO51 131 J7
RWIN SO21 129 C8
Oakwood Ct HEND SO30 148 E2
Oakwood Dr ALTN GU34 * 106 E5
ROWN SO16 146 D3
Oakwood Gv RSAL SP5 327 M1
Oakwood Rd
CHCH/BSGR BH23 217 M7
CHFD SO53 133 K8
HISD PO11 194 F5
MOOR/WNTN BH9 214 A6
NEND PO2 184 E4
Oakwood Wy HLER SO31 179 G1
Oasthouse Dr FLEETN GU51 59 L4
Oast House La FNM GU9 77 H3
Oast La ALDT GU11 3 G8
Oates Rd MOOR/WNTN BH9 213 L7
Oatfield Gdns TOTT SO40 144 C7
Oatlands ROMY SO51 130 F8
Oatlands Cl BPWT SO32 149 M3
Oatlands Rd BPWT SO32 149 M3
WHIT RG2 238 F4
Oatsheaf Pde FLEETN GU51 * 59 H8
Oban Cl DEAN RG23 91 J2
Oban Rd TWDS BH3 225 L1
O'Bee Gdns TADY RG26 249 R3
Obelisk Rd ITCH SO19 161 K6
Obelisk Wy CBLY GU15 50 E2
Oberfield Rd BROC SO42 350 H2
Oberon Cl WVILLE PO7 156 A8
Ober Rd BROC SO42 351 J2
Oberursel Wy ALDT GU11 2 D2
Occupation La
FHAM/STUB PO14 180 E5
Ocean Cl FHAM PO15 181 K2
Oceania Crs DEAN RG23 92 B8
Ocean Pk HSEA PO3 * 185 H7
Ocean Rd FHAM/STUB PO14 181 M7
SHAM SO14 23 H9
Ocean Wy SHAM SO14 23 K8
Ochil Cl KBH RG22 92 D1
Ockendon Cl SSEA PO5 21 G5
Ocknell Gv FAWY SO45 176 C5
Octavia Cl WIMB BH21 207 M3
Octavia Gdns CHFD SO53 139 M1
Octavia Hl FUFL SO22 24 B9
Octavian Cl KBH RG22 92 D5
Octavia Rd WEND SO18 147 L4
Octavius Ct WVILLE PO7 156 B7
Oddfellows Rd NWBY RG14 18 D5
Odell Cl FHAM/PORC PO16 10 C1
Odette Gdns TADY RG26 44 B3
Odiham Cl ROWN SO16 145 M4
Odiham Rd HTWY RG27 57 K4
HTWY RG27 69 J1
RFNM GU10 71 H8
THLE RG7 240 C1
Odstock Rd RSAL SP5 326 C5
Officers Rw TADY RG26 46 D6
Oglander Rd WINC SO23 25 H1
Ogle Rd SHAM SO14 22 F3
O'Gorman Av FARN GU14 61 H6
Okeford Rd BDST BH18 211 H6
Okement Cl WEND SO18 148 B2
Okingham Cl SHST GU47 43 M7
Olaf Cl AND SP10 84 D8
Olave Cl LSOL/BMARY PO13 * 189 L6
Old Acre Rd ALTN GU34 106 E6
Old Agwi Rd FAWY SO45 178 C7
Old Barn Cl CHCH/BSGR BH23 215 K6
OVTN RG25 103 G3
RGWD BH24 203 L5
Oldbarn Cl TOTT SO40 144 C6
Old Barn Crs WVILLE PO7 319 Q10
Old Barn Farm Rd WIMB BH21 205 J3
Old Barn La RFNM GU10 262 H10
Old Barn Rd CHCH/BSGR BH23 215 K6
Old Basing Ml BSTK RG21 6 F4
Old Bath Rd NWBY RG14 18 B1
Old Beggarwood La DEAN RG23 92 C7
Oldberg Gdns KBH RG22 93 H4
Old Bisley Rd FRIM GU16 51 J6
Old Blandford Rd RSAL SP5 325 M3
Old Bound Rd UPTN BH16 222 C3
Old Brickfield Rd ALDT GU11 3 G8
Old Brickyard Rd FBDG SP6 196 D2
Old Bridge House Rd
HLER SO31 163 H4
Old Bridge Rd ENEY PO4 21 M9
LTDN BH7 215 K8
Oldbury Cl FRIM GU16 51 H8
Oldbury Ct ROWN SO16 145 K6
Oldbury Wy FHAM/STUB PO14 181 J4
Old Canal ENEY PO4 * 193 H4
Old Canal Pl BSTK RG21 7 K4
Old Chapel Cl RSAL SP5 327 M1
Old Chapel La ASHV GU12 74 A6
Old Christchurch Rd BMTH BH1 8 F5
LYMN SO41 220 D7
Old Church La FNM GU9 13 J9
Old Coach Rd NTID SP9 266 H8
Old Coastguard Rd CCLF BH13 237 G4
Old Commercial Rd
NEND PO2 192 C1
Old Common HLER SO31 164 A8
Old Common Gdns HLER SO31 180 A1
Old Common Rd BSTK RG21 7 J7
Old Common Wy RAND SP11 265 M10
Old Compton La FNM GU9 13 M4
Old Copse Rd HAV PO9 17 G2
Oldcorne Hollow HTWY RG27 48 C3
Old Cove Rd FLEETN GU51 59 K5
Old Cracknore Cl TOTT SO40 159 M6
Old Cricket Ms WSHM SO15 146 F8
Old Cross Tree Wy ASHV GU12 74 C8
The Old Dairy RSAL SP5 326 F3
Old Dean Rd CBLY GU15 50 F1
Old Down RWIN SO21 310 B1
Old Down Cl KBH RG22 92 C3
Old Down Rd AND SP10 4 E2
Olde Farm Dr BLKW GU17 49 K3
Oldenburg HLER SO31 164 B4
Old English Dr AND SP10 84 B8
Old Farm Cl RGWD BH24 203 L2
Old Farm Dr WEND SO18 147 M6
Old Farm La EMRTH PO10 172 B3
FHAM/STUB PO14 189 J3
Old Farm Pl ASHV GU12 73 M4
Old Farm Rd PLE BH15 223 L2
Old Farm Wk LYMN SO41 221 K5
Old Farm Wy CHAM PO6 185 L1
Old Farnham La FNM GU9 13 H7
RFNM GU10 259 Q7
Oldfield Vw HTWY RG27 57 L3
The Old Flour Ml
EMRTH PO10 * 172 A6
Old Forge End SHST GU47 49 K1
Old Forge Gdns STOK SO20 * 284 D9
Old Forge Rd WIMB BH21 208 F2
Old Foundry Ms HTWY RG27 56 C7
Old Frensham Rd RFNM GU10 79 H2
Old Garden Cl
FHAM/STUB PO14 180 C2
Old Gdns FUFL SO22 122 F2
Oldgate Gdns NEND PO2 * 184 F4
Old Gosport Rd
FHAM/PORC PO16 11 H8
Old Green La CBLY GU15 50 E1
Old Guildford Rd FRIM GU16 62 C3
Old Ham La WIMB BH21 208 D4
Old Haslemere Rd HASM GU27 118 C7
Old Heath Wy FNM GU9 * 77 G1
Old Hillside Rd FUFL SO22 122 C3
The Old Hl RAND SP11 272 D6
Oldhouse La ROMY SO51 335 J1
The Old Iron Foundry
STOK SO20 299 P1
Old Ivy La WEND SO18 148 B2
Old Kempshott La KBH RG22 92 C1
Old Kennels Cl FUFL SO22 124 A1
Old Kennels La RWIN SO21 301 Q11
Old Kiln Cl RFNM GU10 262 F10
Old Kiln La RFNM GU10 262 F10
Old Kiln Rd UPTN BH16 222 C1
Old La ALDT GU11 2 E8
ASHV GU12 73 L5
KSCL RG20 31 L3
RFNM GU10 109 L8
STHA RG19 249 J3
Old Litten La PSF GU32 307 N9
Old London Rd STOK SO20 285 Q5
Old Lyndhurst Rd TOTT SO40 341 K4
Old Magazine Cl TOTT SO40 159 M6
Old Manor Cl WIMB BH21 207 L4
Old Manor Farm HAV PO9 * 170 B7
Old Manor Wy CHAM PO6 185 H1
Old Market Sq BSTK RG21 6 F6
Old Micheldever Rd RAND SP11 97 J7
Old Mill La EPSF GU31 120 F4
HORN PO8 320 D12
Old Mill Pl HASM GU27 117 M1
Old Mill Wy ROWN SO16 146 A7
Old Milton Gn
NMIL/BTOS BH25 218 F7
Old Milton Rd
NMIL/BTOS BH25 218 F7
Old Mulberry Cl NBNE BH10 213 G7
Old Newtown Rd NWBY RG14 18 D8
Old Odiham Rd ALTN GU34 280 D1
Old Orch PLE BH15 223 J7
Old Orchards LYMN SO41 221 M6
The Old Orch FNM GU9 12 B9
ODIM RG29 257 P4
Old Palace Farm STOK SO20 299 Q2
Old Park Cl FNM GU9 76 E2
Old Park La FNM GU9 76 D1
Old Park Rd NARL SO24 304 G1
Old Parsonage Ct RWIN SO21 134 C1
Old Pasture Rd FRIM GU16 51 H5
Old Pharmacy Ct CWTH RG45 * 43 L4
Old Pines Cl FERN BH22 209 L4
Old Pond Cl FRIM GU16 50 D7
Old Portsmouth Rd CBLY GU15 51 J4
MFD/CHID GU8 263 R8
Old Potbridge Rd HTWY RG27 57 J7
Old Priory Cl HLER SO31 179 G2
Old Priory Rd SBNE BH6 227 M4
Old Pumphouse Cl
FLEETN GU51 59 K6
The Old Quarry HASM GU27 117 M4
Old Reading Rd BSTK RG21 7 G4
Old Rectory Cl EMRTH PO10 172 B3
WIMB BH21 206 D8
Old Rectory Dr ASHV GU12 74 B6
Old Rectory Gdns FARN GU14 61 K4
WINC SO23 289 K10
Old Rectory La RWIN SO21 125 G5
Old Rectory Rd CHAM PO6 169 L8
Old Redbridge Rd WSHM SO15 145 J8
Old Reservoir Rd CHAM PO6 185 K1
Old River WVILLE PO7 154 F5
Old Rd GPORT PO12 15 H6
ROMY SO51 131 G8
SHAM SO14 23 J7
WIMB BH21 207 H4
The Old Rd CHAM PO6 184 F2
Old Romsey Rd TOTT SO40 341 J4
The Old Rope Wk PLE BH15 * 222 F7
Old St John's Ms
MOOR/WNTN BH9 213 M5
Old Salisbury La ROMY SO51 129 L7
Old Salisbury Rd RAND SP11 271 K1
ROMY SO51 335 Q9
Old Sandpit La UPTN BH16 210 A6
Old Sawmill Cl VWD BH31 200 F1
Old Sawmill La CWTH RG45 43 L2
The Old Sawmills HUNG RG17 30 E6
Old School Cl ASHV GU12 74 A5
FAWY SO45 354 D2
FERN BH22 209 J3
FLEETN GU51 * 59 J7
HLER SO31 162 C5
HTWY RG27 57 M2
Old School Dr HISD PO11 195 H6
Old School Gdns HEND SO30 148 E2
Old School La YTLY GU46 48 E2
Old School Pl STOK SO20 * 284 D9
Old School Rd HTWY RG27 56 A8
LISS GU33 308 F8
Old Shamblehurst La
HEND SO30 149 J2
Old Stacks Gdns RGWD BH24 203 L6
Old Star PSEA PO1 20 C2
Old Station Ap WINC SO23 25 K6
Old Station Rd RWIN SO21 290 A9
Old Station Wy BOR GU35 110 C7
Old Stockbridge Rd
RAND SP11 269 P6
STOK SO20 270 C7
Old Stoke Rd RWIN SO21 288 G2
Old St FHAM/STUB PO14 181 H8
Old Timbers HISD PO11 194 F5
Old Town Ms FNM GU9 * 12 D4
Old Turnpike FHAM/PORC PO16 11 H3
Old Vicarage Cl NBNE BH10 213 L2
Old Vicarage La STOK SO20 299 Q1
The Old Vineries FBDG SP6 196 F3
Old Vyne La TADY RG26 249 R11
Old Wareham Rd
BKME/WDN BH12 224 A1
UPTN BH16 210 A6
The Old Well Cl ITCH SO19 162 C1
Old Welmore YTLY GU46 49 G3
Old Whitley Wood La
WHIT RG2 238 C2
Old Winchester Hill La
BPWT SO32 312 H5
Old Winton Garages AND SP10 5 J8
Old Winton Rd AND SP10 5 J7
Old Wokingham Rd CWTH RG45 43 L1
Oldwood Cha FARN GU14 60 B5
Old Worting Rd KBH RG22 64 E8
Old Wymering La CHAM PO6 168 E8
Oleander Cl CWTH RG45 43 H1
HLER SO31 164 A7
Oleander Dr TOTT SO40 144 B6
Olinda St PSEA PO1 21 M1
Olive Crs FHAM/PORC PO16 183 K2
Olive Gv RAND SP11 269 L7
Olive Rd ROWN SO16 146 A4
Oliver Ri ALTN GU34 106 F4
Oliver Rd ENEY PO4 192 F5
LYMN SO41 221 J5
WEND SO18 147 K5
Oliver's Battery Crs FUFL SO22 122 B8
Oliver's Battery Gdns
FUFL SO22 124 B1
Oliver's Battery Rd North
FUFL SO22 122 B7
Oliver's Battery Rd South
FUFL SO22 124 B1
Olivers Cl TADY RG26 46 C6
TOTT SO40 158 B1
Oliver's La TADY RG26 46 C4
Olivers Rd WIMB BH21 208 A2
Oliver's Wk CHIN RG24 66 B1
Olivers Wy WIMB BH21 208 A2
Olivia Cl WVILLE PO7 156 A7
Olympic Wy ELGH SO50 141 H1
Omdurman Rd PTSW SO17 147 G6
Omega ALTN GU34 107 H5
Omega Pk ALTN GU34 107 H5
Omega St SSEA PO5 21 J3
Omer's Ri THLE RG7 39 M1
Onibury Cl WEND SO18 148 A3
Onibury Rd WEND SO18 148 A3
Onslow Cl CHIN RG24 54 A7
Onslow Gdns WIMB BH21 207 K2
Onslow Rd SHAM SO14 161 G2
SSEA PO5 192 D7
Ontario Wy LIPH GU30 116 C5
Openfields BOR GU35 111 L6
Ophir Gdns BMTH BH1 9 K2
Ophir Rd CHAR BH8 9 J1
NEND PO2 184 D6
Oracle Dr WVILLE PO7 169 L5
Orange Gv LSOL/BMARY PO13 182 D7
RAND SP11 269 L7
Orange La STOK SO20 269 Q10
Orange Rw EMRTH PO10 171 M8
Oratory Gdns CCLF BH13 224 F8
Orbit Cl EWKG RG40 42 B2
Orchard Av ELGH SO50 140 F3
PSTN BH14 223 M6
Orchard Cl ASHV GU12 74 A3
CHCH/BSGR BH23 228 A2
EPSF GU31 317 L12
FARN GU14 50 B7
FAWY SO45 355 K5
FBDG SP6 197 H2
FERN BH22 209 L3
FNM GU9 77 L2
GPORT PO12 183 G7
HISD PO11 194 F6
HORN PO8 156 C2
MFD/CHID GU8 260 H12
NARL SO24 291 M12
NBAD SO52 137 M3
NWBY RG14 27 L7
RGUW GU3 75 H7
RGWD BH24 203 J4
RWIN SO21 134 F3
RWIN SO21 288 C4
THLE RG7 37 J2
THLE RG7 238 B6
TOTT SO40 158 F3
WIMB BH21 210 D1
Orchard Ct HEND SO30 149 L5
VWD BH31 201 J3
Orchard Dene Dr THLE RG7 38 C2
Orchard Dro ELGH SO50 * 141 K6
Orchard End RFNM GU10 109 M1
Orchardene NWBY RG14 19 H2
Orchard Gdns ALDT GU11 3 K7
FBDG SP6 197 H3
Orchard Ga SHST GU47 43 K8
Orchard Gv FHAM/PORC PO16 183 G1
HORN PO8 155 M5
NMIL/BTOS BH25 219 G7
Orchard La ALTN GU34 107 G4
EMRTH PO10 172 A6
ROMY SO51 136 E1
SHAM SO14 23 H5
WIMB BH21 210 D1
Orchardlea BPWT SO32 318 B9
Orchard Mt RGWD BH24 * 203 J4
Orchard Pl SHAM SO14 23 H6
Orchard Rd AND SP10 4 C3
ELGH SO50 141 J2
ENEY PO4 21 M4
FARN GU14 61 G4
FNM GU9 77 L2
GPORT PO12 15 K1
HAV PO9 16 F6
HISD PO11 195 G6
HLER SO31 179 M2
KBH RG22 64 E8
RSAL SP5 332 F1
RWIN SO21 288 C4
THLE RG7 40 B3
Orchard St WCLF BH2 8 D6
Orchards Wy HEND SO30 148 D3

PTSW SO17 147 G6
Orchard Ter ALTN GU34 107 G4
The Orchard BWD BH11 212 D2
CHAM PO6 184 F1
CHCH/BSGR BH23 348 E12
HASM GU27 117 M3
HTWY RG27 56 C6
LYMN SO41 232 D4
OVTN RG25 89 J4
ROWN SO16 138 E7
STHA RG19 * 34 F1
TADY RG26 44 D4
TOTT SO40 * 341 P7
WVILLE PO7 154 F4
Orchard Wk FUFL SO22 122 D2
Orchard Wy ALDT GU11 3 K7
CBLY GU15 50 D6
FAWY SO45 176 E6
RGUW GU3 75 H7
Orcheston Rd CHAR BH8 226 C2
Orchid Ct AND SP10 4 B8
Orchid Dr RAND SP11 265 M11
Orchid Wy CHCH/BSGR BH23 228 C1
Ordnance Ct HSEA PO3 * 185 G3
Ordnance Rd ALDT GU11 3 H2
GPORT PO12 15 J4
NTID SP9 266 F2
WSHM SO15 161 G2
Ordnance Rw PSEA PO1 20 C3
Ordnance Wy TOTT SO40 160 A5
Oregon Cl ITCH SO19 148 A8
Oregon Wk EWKG RG40 239 R9
Orford Cl CHCH/BSGR BH23 215 K4
Oriana Wy ROWN SO16 145 H4
Oriel Dr FHAM/STUB PO14 180 C3
Oriel Hl CBLY GU15 50 F4
Oriel Rd NEND PO2 184 D6
Orient Dr FUFL SO22 122 C1
Orion Av GPORT PO12 191 J1
Orion Cl FHAM/STUB PO14 189 K2
ROWN SO16 145 M4
Orkney Cl CHIN RG24 65 M3
ROWN SO16 145 L4
Orkney Rd CHAM PO6 168 F7
Ormesby Dr CHFD SO53 133 H8
Ormond Cl ELGH SO50 141 H1
Ormonde Rd CCLF BH13 225 G6
Ormsby Rd SSEA PO5 21 H7
Orpen Rd ITCH SO19 162 C1
Orpine Cl FHAM PO15 180 F1
Orsmond Cl WVILLE PO7 169 L2
Orwell Cl FARN GU14 60 E1
ROWN SO16 145 L7
Orwell Crs FHAM/STUB PO14 180 C2
Orwell Rd PSF GU32 120 C7
Osborn Crs LSOL/BMARY PO13 182 B4
Osborne Cl ALTN GU34 106 D5
BSTK RG21 6 C1
WVILLE PO7 170 A1
Osborne Dr CHFD SO53 139 L3
FLEETS GU52 71 K1
Osborne Gdns ELGH SO50 141 L2
Osborne Pl WHAM PO17 165 L5
Osborne Rd AND SP10 4 F6
FARN GU14 61 J8
GPORT PO12 15 J2
HLER SO31 179 K4
LSOL/BMARY PO13 189 L6
MOOR/WNTN BH9 213 L8
NMIL/BTOS BH25 219 H5
PSF GU32 120 D5
PSTN BH14 224 B5
SSEA PO5 20 F8
TOTT SO40 159 G1
WIMB BH21 207 K4
Osborne Rd North PTSW SO17 147 J7
Osborne Rd South PTSW SO17 147 J8
Osborne View Rd
FHAM/STUB PO14 189 G3
Osborn Rd FHAM/PORC PO16 11 H5
FNM GU9 77 H4
Osborn Rd South
FHAM/PORC PO16 11 G5
Osborn Sq FHAM/PORC PO16 11 J6
Osborn Wy HTWY RG27 56 D8
Osier Cl NEND PO2 184 C6
Oslands Dr HLER SO31 163 K5
Osler Cl TADY RG26 46 B5
Osnaburgh Hl CBLY GU15 50 D3
Osprey Cl CHCH/BSGR BH23 229 G3
ROWN SO16 146 B3
TOTT SO40 159 L7
Osprey Dr HISD PO11 195 H5
Osprey Gdns ALDT GU11 2 F8
LSOL/BMARY PO13 189 M6
Osprey Quay EMRTH PO10 172 B7
Osprey Rd DEAN RG23 92 B3
Ossemsley South Dr
NMIL/BTOS BH25 349 N12
Osterley Cl HEND SO30 149 L5
Osterly Rd ITCH SO19 161 L3
Oswald Cl MOOR/WNTN BH9 213 L6
Oswald Rd MOOR/WNTN BH9 213 L6
Othello Dr WVILLE PO7 156 A8
Ottawa Dr LIPH GU30 116 C5
Otterbourne Crs HAV PO9 170 D3
TADY RG26 44 B6
Otterbourne Hl CHFD SO53 134 A3
Otterbourne Rd RWIN SO21 124 C8
Otter Cl CWTH RG45 43 J1
ELGH SO50 141 G2
UPTN BH16 222 B2
VWD BH31 201 J3
Otter Rd PLE BH15 223 M2
Otters Wk NMIL/BTOS BH25 219 J2
Ouse Cl CHFD SO53 133 G8
Ouse Ct AND SP10 96 E2
Outer Cir ROWN SO16 146 A4
Outlands La HEND SO30 150 D6
Outram Rd SSEA PO5 21 K6
Oval Gdns GPORT PO12 14 A6
Oval Rd ROMY SO51 298 B12
The Oval AND SP10 * 96 E1
LISS GU33 308 F8
NTID SP9 * 266 E3
Overbecks NWBY RG14 19 L2
Overbridge Sq NWBY RG14 34 E1
Overbrook FAWY SO45 176 F6
Overbrook Wy NBAD SO52 137 L3
Overbury Rd PSTN BH14 224 C5
Overcliff Ri ROWN SO16 146 E4
Overcombe Cl CFDH BH17 211 L6
Overdale Pl BOR GU35 * 112 F3
Overdale Ri FRIM GU16 51 G5
Overdale Wk BOR GU35 112 F3
Over Links Dr PSTN BH14 224 D6
Overstand Crs LYMN SO41 232 D5
Overton Cl ALDT GU11 260 A2
Overton Crs HAV PO9 170 D3
Overton Rd RWIN SO21 275 P2
Oviat Cl TOTT SO40 158 B1
Ovington Av LTDN BH7 227 J1
Ovington Gdns LTDN BH7 227 J1
Owen Cl LSOL/BMARY PO13 190 C1
Owen Rd ELGH SO50 139 M6
NWBY RG14 27 K6
Owen's Rd FUFL SO22 24 E2
Owen St ENEY PO4 193 G6
Owletts Gv NWBY RG14 19 L2
Owlsmoor Rd SHST GU47 43 M8
Owls Rd BOSC BH5 226 E5
VWD BH31 201 J3
Owslebury Bottom
RWIN SO21 310 A3
Owslebury Gv HAV PO9 170 F3
Oxburgh Cl ELGH SO50 139 M3
Ox Dro RAND SP11 97 J2
RAND SP11 267 M6
RWIN SO21 288 F4
Ox Drove Ri RAND SP11 97 K1
Oxdrove Wy NARL SO24 277 M10
NARL SO24 291 R4
OVTN RG25 278 B6
RWIN SO21 289 Q4
Oxenden Ct RFNM GU10 73 L8
Oxenden Rd RFNM GU10 73 L8
Oxford Av SBNE BH6 227 H3
SHAM SO14 23 H1
Oxford Cl FHAM/PORC PO16 10 D3
Oxford La BPWT SO32 318 F5
BWD BH11 213 H2
Oxford Ms SHAM SO14 * 23 H6
Oxford Rd BMTH BH1 9 J4
FARN GU14 61 J7
GPORT PO12 14 A2
NWBY RG14 18 D1
RWIN SO21 274 C9
SHAM SO14 161 G1
SSEA PO5 21 L7
Oxford St NWBY RG14 18 D2
SHAM SO14 23 H6
Oxford Ter LYMN SO41 * 350 G10
Oxlease Cl ROMY SO51 131 G7
Oxlease La OVTN RG25 256 A9
Oxleys Cl FHAM/STUB PO14 181 H4
Oxted Ct ENEY PO4 193 H3
Oyster Cl KBH RG22 92 C5
Oyster Est CHAM PO6 * 185 K2
Oyster Ms PSEA PO1 20 C6
Oyster Quay CHAM PO6 184 B2
Oyster St PSEA PO1 20 C6
Ozier Rd WEND SO18 148 A2

P

Pacific Cl SHAM SO14 23 L8
Packenham Rd BSTK RG21 6 B7
Pack La DEAN RG23 91 K1
KBH RG22 92 D2
Packridge La ROMY SO51 137 M7
Packway FNM GU9 13 K9
Padbury Cl NEND PO2 * 184 F4
Paddington Gv BWD BH11 212 D5
Paddington Rd NEND PO2 184 F7
Paddock Cl BKME/WDN BH12 224 B2
CBLY GU15 51 J2
RGWD BH24 202 B8
RWIN SO21 288 E4
WIMB BH21 209 G2
Paddock Ct HTWY RG27 57 L3
Paddock End WVILLE PO7 154 F5
Paddock Fld STOK SO20 272 F7
Paddockfields CHIN RG24 66 D1
Paddock Gdns LYMN SO41 221 K3
Paddock Gv VWD BH31 201 J3
Paddock Rd KBH RG22 92 F1
NWBY RG14 18 D8
The Paddocks FAWY SO45 355 K5
RGUW GU3 75 J7
The Paddock BOR GU35 111 L7
BROC SO42 351 K3
CWTH RG45 43 J2
ELGH SO50 134 B6
FBDG SP6 338 A6
FHAM/STUB PO14 181 J8
GPORT PO12 14 C6
GSHT GU26 115 G4
HASM GU27 118 A4
HTWY RG27 57 M1
KSCL RG20 248 C10
NWBY RG14 19 K5
RFNM GU10 * 78 D4
RGWD BH24 * 205 K8
TOTT SO40 144 C6
WINC SO23 289 J10
Paddock Wy HASM GU27 119 G2
LIPH GU30 116 B3
NARL SO24 291 L12
PSF GU32 120 B7
Padfield Cl SBNE BH6 227 L2
Padget Rd RGWD BH24 203 L3
Padnell Av HORN PO8 156 B6
Padnell Rd HORN PO8 156 B5
Padstow Pl FBDG SP6 197 G4
Padwell Rd SHAM SO14 161 G1
Padwick Av CHAM PO6 169 G8
Padwick Cl BSTK RG21 6 C7
Padworth La THLE RG7 38 E1
Padworth Rd THLE RG7 39 L4
Paffard Cl LSOL/BMARY PO13 190 C1
Page Cl FAWY SO45 354 F6
Pages La BROC SO42 353 J10
Paget Cl CBLY GU15 51 K1
NTID SP9 264 D12
WIMB BH21 208 A1
Paget Rd BWD BH11 213 G4
GPORT PO12 14 C9
Paget St SHAM SO14 23 K5
Pagham Cl EMRTH PO10 172 A6
Pagham Gdns HISD PO11 195 M6
Paice La ALTN GU34 293 J4
Paices Hl THLE RG7 38 A8
Paignton Av HSEA PO3 185 G8
Paignton Rd ROWN SO16 145 M8
Paimpol Pl ROMY SO51 * 136 E2
Pain's Rd SSEA PO5 21 J5
Painswick Cl CHAM PO6 168 C8
HLER SO31 163 M6
Painter Cl HSEA PO3 185 H5
Painters Pightle HTWY RG27 56 B7
Paisley Rd SBNE BH6 227 J3
Pakenham Dr ALDT GU11 2 E1
Palace Cl STOK SO20 299 P2
Palace Ga ODIM RG29 68 F5
Palace La BROC SO42 353 N7
Palace Ms BPWT SO32 * 143 J5
Pale La HTWY RG27 58 C6
Palestine Rd RAND SP11 269 K6
Palfrey Rd NBNE BH10 213 K4
Palk Rd HAV PO9 16 B4
Pallant Gdns
FHAM/PORC PO16 11 M4
The Pallant HAV PO9 16 F4
Pallet Cl RWIN SO21 134 F4
Pallot Cl HLER SO31 162 F4
Palmer Dr AND SP10 96 F4
Palmer Pl NMIL/BTOS BH25 219 G4
Palmer Rd PLE BH15 223 J3
Palmers Cl ELGH SO50 141 K2
Palmer's Rd EMRTH PO10 171 M7
Palmerston Av
CHCH/BSGR BH23 228 D2
FHAM/PORC PO16 11 H5
Palmerston Cl FARN GU14 60 D5
UPTN BH16 222 D1
Palmerston Dr
FHAM/STUB PO14 182 A1
Palmerstone Ms BMTH BH1 226 E3
Palmerston Rd BMTH BH1 226 E4
HISD PO11 195 G4
PSTN BH14 224 D4
SHAM SO14 23 G2
SSEA PO5 21 H9
UPTN BH16 222 C1
Palmerston St ROMY SO51 136 F1
Palmerston Wy GPORT PO12 190 E6
Palmers Yd KSCL RG20 247 Q6
Palm Hall Cl WINC SO23 25 L6
Palm Rd ROWN SO16 145 M5
Palmyra Rd GPORT PO12 191 G1
Pamber Heath Rd TADY RG26 44 D4
Pamber Rd THLE RG7 45 C3
Pamela Av CHAM PO6 167 M8
Pamplyn Cl LYMN SO41 221 J4
Pangbourne Av CHAM PO6 185 H1
Pangbourne Cl ITCH SO19 148 A8
Pankridge St RFNM GU10 259 P1
Pannall Rd GPORT PO12 191 G1
Pannells RFNM GU10 79 H3
Panorama Rd CCLF BH13 237 C5
Pans Cnr FERN BH22 * 209 M5
Pan's Gdns CBLY GU15 51 H4
Pan St PSEA PO1 * 21 H1
Pansy Rd ROWN SO16 147 G4
Pantheon Rd CHFD SO53 139 M1
Pantile Dr HTWY RG27 56 E7
Pantiles BOR GU35 * 114 B3
The Pantiles FBDG SP6 196 F3
Pantings La KSCL RG20 246 B6
Panton Cl EMRTH PO10 * 171 L5
Panwell Rd WEND SO18 148 A5
Papermakers OVTN RG25 89 K5
Paper Mill La ALTN GU34 107 G4
The Parade ASHV GU12 * 74 A4
BSTK RG21 * 7 H3
FRIM GU16 * 50 F8
LSOL/BMARY PO13 * 182 B5
NMIL/BTOS BH25 * 219 K5
PSEA PO1 20 C1
TADY RG26 * 44 B3
Paradise La BPWT SO32 143 L6
EMRTH PO10 172 B2
FHAM/PORC PO16 11 M6
TOTT SO40 341 P6
Paradise St PLE BH15 223 H7
PSEA PO1 21 H2
Parchment St WINC SO23 25 G5
The Parchment HAV PO9 16 E5
Pardoe Cl HEND SO30 149 J7
Pardown DEAN RG23 91 K5
Pardys Hl WIMB BH21 206 C8
Parfitts Cl FNM GU9 12 C4
Parham Dr ELGH SO50 139 M4
Parham Rd GPORT PO12 15 G1
NBNE BH10 213 J6
Parish Cl ASHV GU12 74 B7
FNM GU9 76 E2
Parish Rd FARN GU14 61 H8
PLE BH15 223 L5
Park Ap WHAM PO17 165 L5
Park Av CBLY GU15 50 E4
CHIN RG24 66 D3
LYMN SO41 221 K4
MFD/CHID GU8 261 N11
NBNE BH10 213 J2
NTHA RG18 28 F8
WINC SO23 25 H4
WVILLE PO7 169 K4
Park Cl BOR GU35 110 E3
BROC SO42 351 L2
CHCH/BSGR BH23 216 C5
DEAN RG23 91 J2
FAWY SO45 177 H4
GPORT PO12 14 A1
HASM GU27 118 F3
LYMN SO41 232 E3
NMIL/BTOS BH25 219 J3
RFNM GU10 109 G2
TOTT SO40 159 K7
WINC SO23 123 G2
Park Close Rd ALTN GU34 107 G3
Parkcorner La WHIT RG2 239 M2
Park Corner Rd HTWY RG27 57 M1
Park Crs EMRTH PO10 171 K7
Park Dr VWD BH31 201 G1
Park Dro STOK SO20 270 A8
Park End NWBY RG14 18 F2
Parker Cl GPORT PO12 183 G7
Parker Gdns WVILLE PO7 169 J6
Parker Rd MOOR/WNTN BH9 225 M1
Parkers Cl RGWD BH24 203 L3
Park Farm Av FHAM PO15 165 J8
Park Farm Cl FHAM PO15 181 K1
Park Farm Rd WVILLE PO7 169 K4
Parkfields YTLY GU46 48 F3
Park Gdns BSTK RG21 7 J8
Park Gln FHAM PO15 164 C8
Park Gv CHAM PO6 184 F1
Park Hl FLEETS GU52 71 H4
Parkhill Cl BLKW GU17 49 M4
Park Hill Cl FAWY SO45 354 E5
Parkhill Rd BLKW GU17 49 M4
Park Homer Dr WIMB BH21 207 M2
Park Homer Rd WIMB BH21 207 M1
Park House Farm Wy
HAV PO9 170 C3
Parkhurst Flds RFNM GU10 262 F11
Park Lake Rd PLE BH15 223 L6
Parkland Cl VWD BH31 201 M4
Parkland Dr NMIL/BTOS BH25 218 F8
Parkland Gv FNM GU9 2 C7
Parklands HLER SO31 164 A8
WEND SO18 147 L7
Parklands Av HORN PO8 156 A3
Parklands Cl CHFD SO53 139 J1
GPORT PO12 14 E1
Park La ALTN GU34 258 G12
BPWT SO32 318 C3
BPWT SO32 318 H3
CBLY GU15 * 50 E3
CHIN RG24 66 D3
CHAM PO6 185 G1
ELGH SO50 134 B4
EWKG RG40 241 N1
FAWY SO45 354 D4
FBDG SP6 196 B6
FHAM/PORC PO16 10 F3
FHAM/STUB PO14 189 J1
HAV PO9 156 C8
HAV PO9 170 C5
HORN PO8 156 A6
KSCL RG20 32 B3
LYMN SO41 232 D4
LYMN SO41 357 P6
NARL SO24 305 K1
NBNE BH10 213 M4
NTHA RG18 28 F7
NWBY RG14 * 19 G2
RAND SP11 267 N12
RSAL SP5 296 G4
RWIN SO21 125 G7
RWIN SO21 289 K10
THLE RG7 40 C6
TOTT SO40 159 J6
WIMB BH21 200 B2
WIMB BH21 207 J4
WIMB BH21 336 A7
Park Pde HAV PO9 170 E4
Park Pl FLEETS GU52 71 H3
Park Prewett CHIN RG24 * 65 G3
Park Rd ALDT GU11 3 H7
BMTH BH1 9 H3
BPWT SO32 143 G4
CBLY GU15 50 E3
CHFD SO53 133 J8
EMRTH PO10 172 D5
FARN GU14 61 L7
FBDG SP6 197 H2
FNM GU9 77 H4
FUFL SO22 122 F2
GPORT PO12 14 F8
HASM GU27 118 C6
HISD PO11 194 C4
LYMN SO41 221 K4
LYMN SO41 232 E4
NMIL/BTOS BH25 218 F7
NMIL/BTOS BH25 219 J3
NTID SP9 266 F2
PLE BH15 223 M5
PSEA PO1 20 C4
PSF GU32 120 D6
SHST GU47 49 L1
WSHM SO15 160 C2
WVILLE PO7 154 F3
WVILLE PO7 169 J4
Park Rd North HAV PO9 16 E4
Park Rd South HAV PO9 16 E5
Park Rw FNM GU9 12 F2
Parkside CHCH/BSGR BH23 217 K7
FNM GU9 77 G2
HAV PO9 170 C6
RGWD BH24 203 H6
TOTT SO40 158 F3
Parkside Av ROWN SO16 145 K8
Parkside Gdns FUFL SO22 122 C2
NBNE BH10 213 L6
Parkside La NARL SO24 305 J2
Parkside Rd BSTK RG21 7 G8
NTHA RG18 28 F7
PSTN BH14 224 C4
Parkstone Av ENEY PO4 192 E7
PSTN BH14 224 D4
Parkstone Dr CBLY GU15 50 E4
Parkstone Hts PSTN BH14 223 M3
Parkstone Rd NARL SO24 305 M2
PLE BH15 223 M5
Park St BOR GU35 112 F1
CBLY GU15 50 E2
GPORT PO12 14 F3
NWBY RG14 18 E2
ROWN SO16 146 B8
SSEA PO5 20 F5
Park Ter NWBY RG14 18 E2
Park Terraces GPORT PO12 * 15 H4
The Park BPWT SO32 318 G3
NMIL/BTOS BH25 230 C1
Park Vw ELGH SO50 * 134 B3
HEND SO30 149 H5
HEND SO30 150 A5
Parkview Cl AND SP10 4 C1
Parkville Rd ROWN SO16 147 K4
Park Wk FHAM PO15 181 J1
SHAM SO14 23 G2
Parkwater Rd RSAL SP5 127 J7
Park Wy FERN BH22 205 G6
HAV PO9 16 D4
NWBY RG14 18 E2
Parkway CBLY GU15 50 E5
CWTH RG45 43 J3
FHAM PO15 164 F5
Parkway Dr CHAR BH8 214 E8
Parkway Gdns CHFD SO53 139 J1
The Parkway
LSOL/BMARY PO13 182 B6
ROWN SO16 147 G3
Parkwood Cl CHIN RG24 54 B4
Parkwood Rd BOSC BH5 227 H4
WIMB BH21 207 J4
Parley Cl FERN BH22 209 M7
Parley Cross FERN BH22 209 L8
Parley La CHCH/BSGR BH23 346 B12
Parley Rd MOOR/WNTN BH9 214 A6
Parliamentary Rd
CHOB/PIR GU24 63 G2
Parliament Pl FUFL SO22 122 C8
Parmiter Dr WIMB BH21 207 L4
Parmiter Rd WIMB BH21 207 L4
Parmiter Wy WIMB BH21 207 L4
Parnell Ct AND SP10 95 L3
Parnell La ROMY SO51 299 Q10
Parnell Rd ELGH SO50 139 M6
Parr Rd CHAM PO6 168 D8
Parr St PSTN BH14 224 A4
Parry Cl CHAM PO6 167 L8
Parry Rd ITCH SO19 148 D8
Parsonage Barn La
RGWD BH24 203 J4
Parsonage Cl ALTN GU34 294 E5
EPSF GU31 120 F4
Parsonage Est EPSF GU31 317 L4
Parsonage Hl RSAL SP5 296 B5
Parsonage La BPWT SO32 142 B6
WIMB BH21 336 B6
Parsonage Park Dr FBDG SP6 197 G2
Parsonage Rd BMTH BH1 9 G6
SHAM SO14 161 H2
Parsonage Wy FRIM GU16 51 G7
Parsons Cl FLEETS GU52 71 H3
HASM GU27 118 C4
HSEA PO3 184 F4
NWBY RG14 18 A5
WHIT RG2 239 N9
Parsons Fld SHST GU47 43 K8
Parsons Gn HASM GU27 118 C4
Parsons La GSHT GU26 115 J2
Part La THLE RG7 240 C1
Partridge Av YTLY GU46 48 D2
Partridge Cl CHCH/BSGR BH23 229 G3
FHAM/PORC PO16 * 166 E8
FRIM GU16 51 G7
KBH RG22 92 B5
RFNM GU10 71 K8
RWIN SO21 273 P5
Partridge Down FUFL SO22 124 B1
Partridge Dr PSTN BH14 224 B7
Partridge Gdns HORN PO8 155 K4
Partridge Gn ALTN GU34 106 F3
NMIL/BTOS BH25 219 H2
Partridge Hl RSAL SP5 334 E5
Partridge Rd BROC SO42 351 K4
FAWY SO45 176 F7
Partridge Wk PSTN BH14 224 C7
Partry Cl CHFD SO53 133 G8
Pascoe Cl PSTN BH14 224 A4
Passage La HLER SO31 179 H3
Passfield Av ELGH SO50 139 L6
Passfield Cl ELGH SO50 139 L6
Passfield Rd LIPH GU30 113 L4
Passfield Wk HAV PO9 * 171 H3
Passford Hl LYMN SO41 221 K1
Passingham Wk HORN PO8 156 A4
The Pastures
FHAM/STUB PO14 164 C8
NARL SO24 303 Q6
WINC SO23 288 H7
WVILLE PO7 154 E5
Pat Bear Cl WSHM SO15 145 J8
Patchins Rd UPTN BH16 222 B4
Patchway Dr
FHAM/STUB PO14 181 J4
Paternoster Rw WINC SO23 25 H6
Paterson Cl FRIM GU16 51 L5
KBH RG22 92 E5
Paterson Rd LISS GU33 309 J2
Pathfields Cl HASM GU27 118 D5
The Pathfinders FARN GU14 60 C5
Patricia Cl HEND SO30 148 D2
Patricia Dr HEND SO30 149 K5
Patrick's Cl LISS GU33 308 G8
Patten Av YTLY GU46 48 E3
Pattinson Crs RAND SP11 95 J5
Pattinson Rd WHIT RG2 * 238 D2
Paul Cl ALDT GU11 2 B6
Paulet Cl WEND SO18 148 A3
Paulet Lacave Av ROWN SO16 145 K2
Paulet Pl CHIN RG24 66 D2
FUFL SO22 122 E7
Pauletts La TOTT SO40 144 B5
Paul's Fld HTWY RG27 42 A8
Paulsgrove Rd NEND PO2 184 F8
Pauls La LYMN SO41 350 H12
Paulson Cl CHFD SO53 133 J8
Pauncefoot Hl ROMY SO51 136 C3
Pauncefote Rd BOSC BH5 227 G3
Pauntley Rd CHCH/BSGR BH23 228 E3
Pavan Gdns NBNE BH10 213 J5
Pavilion Cl ELGH SO50 141 J4
Pavilion Rd ALDT GU11 2 A4
HEND SO30 149 K4
The Pavilions End CBLY GU15 50 F5
Pavilions Wy GPORT PO12 15 J3
Pavy Cl STHA RG19 35 M2
Pawley Cl RFNM GU10 260 D1
Pawmers Md FLEETS GU52 71 G5
Pax Hl RFNM GU10 259 K12
Paxton Cl HEND SO30 149 K7
KBH RG22 92 D5
Paxton Rd FHAM/STUB PO14 10 D6
Payne Cl WIMB BH21 205 G3
Paynes Cl STHA RG19 248 C4
STOK SO20 284 D9
Paynesdown Rd STHA RG19 35 H1
Paynes Hay Rd ROMY SO51 299 R12
Paynes La STOK SO20 284 D9
Payne's Meadow CHIN RG24 54 C8
Payne's Rd WSHM SO15 160 C2
Peabody Rd FARN GU14 61 K7
Peace Cl CHCH/BSGR BH23 348 C12
Peachey Dr STHA RG19 35 M2
Peach Gv RAND SP11 269 L7
Peach Rd ROWN SO16 146 A4
Peach Tree Cl FARN GU14 61 G1
Peacock Cl FHAM/PORC PO16 166 E8
Peacock La PSEA PO1 20 D6
Peacock Pl WINC SO23 25 M5
Peak Cl ROWN SO16 145 M8
Peak Dr FHAM/STUB PO14 181 K4
Peake New Rd BPWT SO32 312 H8
Peakfield RFNM GU10 262 C5
WVILLE PO7 154 E4
Peak La BPWT SO32 310 H12
FHAM/STUB PO14 181 K5
Peak Rd HORN PO8 321 J7
The Peak HAV PO9 157 J6
Pealsham Gdns FBDG SP6 197 G2
Pearce Av PSTN BH14 224 A7
Pearce Ct GPORT PO12 15 H3
Pearce Rd UPTN BH16 222 B2
Pearces Pl KSCL RG20 * 248 D10
Pear Cl BKME/WDN BH12 225 H4
Pearl Gdns NBNE BH10 213 J4
Pearl Rd NBNE BH10 213 J4
Pearman Dr AND SP10 96 F4
Pearson Av PSTN BH14 224 B3
Pearson Gdns NBNE BH10 213 K2
Peartree LYMN SO41 * 221 L6
Pear Tree Av FLEETN GU51 59 H6
Peartree Av ITCH SO19 161 L4
Pear Tree Cl BOR GU35 111 H8
BPWT SO32 149 M2
CHCH/BSGR BH23 348 C12
FBDG SP6 196 B6
Peartree Cl FHAM/STUB PO14 189 K1
ITCH SO19 161 K4
Peartree Ct LYMN SO41 221 L6
Pear Tree Dr RSAL SP5 334 B8
Pear Tree La NWBY RG14 27 L7
RFNM GU10 109 M1
Pear Tree Rd BOR GU35 111 H7
Peartree Rd FAWY SO45 176 E6
ITCH SO19 161 K4
Pease Cft EPSF GU31 323 M1
Peat Common MFD/CHID GU8 263 Q2
Peat Moor Cl FLEETN GU51 59 G6
Peatmoor Cl FLEETN GU51 59 G6
Peatmore Dr CHOB/PIR GU24 63 J2
Pebble Cl HISD PO11 195 H6
Pebble Ct TOTT SO40 159 M6
Pebble Hl HUNG RG17 31 H5
Pebmarsh Rd CHAM PO6 168 D8
Pecche Pl CHIN RG24 54 C7
Peckham Av NMIL/BTOS BH25 219 G6
Peckham Cl HLER SO31 180 C2
Peckmoor Dr STHA RG19 34 C5
Pedam Cl ENEY PO4 193 G5
Peddlars Gv YTLY GU46 49 G2
Peel Av FRIM GU16 62 A1
Peel Cl BKME/WDN BH12 224 C3
ROMY SO51 131 J7
VWD BH31 201 G1
Peel Ct HTWY RG27 57 L2
Peel Gdns KSCL RG20 248 C9
Peel Pl SSEA PO5 21 G5
Peel Rd GPORT PO12 15 H3
Peel St SHAM SO14 23 L1
Peewit Hl HLER SO31 163 G1
Peewit Hill Cl HLER SO31 163 G1
Pegasus Av ASHV GU12 73 L5
LYMN SO41 220 A6
Pegasus Cl HASM GU27 117 K3
HLER SO31 178 F2
ROWN SO16 145 M4
STHA RG19 28 C8
Pegasus Ct WHCH RG28 * 87 L6
Pegasus Rd FARN GU14 * 60 F1
FARN GU14 61 H6
Pelham Cl BOR GU35 112 F3
CHIN RG24 66 D3
CHCH/BSGR BH23 228 D2
Pelham Pl RFNM GU10 78 E4
Pelham Rd GPORT PO12 14 E3
SSEA PO5 21 H7
Pelhams Pk NBNE BH10 * 213 J2
Pelham Ter EMRTH PO10 172 A6
Pelican Cl FHAM PO15 181 K2
Pelican Ct AND SP10 5 J3
Pelican La NWBY RG14 18 E2
Pelican Md RGWD BH24 203 L6
Pelican Rd FHAM/STUB PO14 181 M7
TADY RG26 44 E2
Pelton Rd BSTK RG21 6 B3
Pembers Cl ELGH SO50 141 K2

Pemberton Rd LYND SO43 345 L3
Pembrey Cl ROWN SO16 145 M3
Pembridge Rd FBDG SP6 197 J1
Pembroke Broadway
CBLY GU15 50 E3
Pembroke Cl ELGH SO50 139 M3
PSEA PO1 20 D6
ROMY SO51 136 F1
TOTT SO40 145 G8
Pembroke Crs
FHAM/STUB PO14 189 G2
Pembroke Rd
BKME/WDN BH12 224 D1
DEAN RG23 64 D7
FUFL SO22 288 C11
ITCH SO19 148 B8
NWBY RG14 18 D3
PSEA PO1 20 E7
WBNE BH4 225 H6
Pembury Pl ASHV GU12 3 J5
Pembury Rd
FHAM/STUB PO14 181 K8
HAV PO9 17 H6
Pemerton Rd BSTK RG21 7 H1
FUFL SO22 122 D1
Penarth Av CHAM PO6 169 H8
Penarth Cl ITCH SO19 148 B6
Penarth Pl WINC SO23 * 25 G6
Pen Cl AND SP10 5 M6
Pendennis Cl DEAN RG23 64 D6
Pendennis Rd CHAM PO6 167 M8
Pendle Cl ROWN SO16 145 M8
Pendle Gn ROMY SO51 298 B11
Pendleton Gdns FAWY SO45 354 G7
Pendragon Wy CBLY GU15 51 M4
Pendred Rd WHIT RG2 238 C2
Pendula Wy ELGH SO50 134 E7
Penelope Gdns HLER SO31 162 F2
Penfold Cft FNM GU9 77 K4
Penfords Paddock
BPWT SO32 143 K5
Pengelly Av NBNE BH10 213 L3
Pengilly Rd FNM GU9 12 E4
Penhale Gdns
FHAM/STUB PO14 180 B3
Penhale Rd PSEA PO1 21 M2
Penhale Wy TOTT SO40 158 E3
Penhurst Rd HAV PO9 170 B6
Peninsular Cl CBLY GU15 51 K1
Peninsula Rd FUFL SO22 24 D7
Peninsula Sq WINC SO23 24 E6
Penistone Cl ITCH SO19 162 B3
Penjar Av WVILLE PO7 169 J4
Penk Rdg CHAM PO6 169 M8
Pennant Hills HAV PO9 170 B6
Pennant Pk
FHAM/PORC PO16 * 11 J1
Pennant Wy CHCH/BSGR BH23 228 F1
Pennard Wy CHFD SO53 139 G4
Penn Cl NMIL/BTOS BH25 218 E7
Pennefather's Rd ALDT GU11 72 F5
Pennerly Ct HAV PO9 170 D1
Penner Rd HAV PO9 16 C8
Penn Hill Av PSTN BH14 224 D5
Pennine Gdns FAWY SO45 176 D6
Pennine Rd ROWN SO16 159 M1
Pennine Wk FHAM/STUB PO14 10 A9
Pennine Wy CHFD SO53 139 K4
FARN GU14 60 E1
KBH RG22 92 D1
LSOL/BMARY PO13 190 A4
VWD BH31 201 H3
Pennings Dro RSAL SP5 325 N4
Pennings Rd NTID SP9 264 E10
Pennington Cl ELGH SO50 134 F4
FERN BH22 204 F7
LYMN SO41 221 J6
Pennington Crs FERN BH22 204 F6
Pennington Ov LYMN SO41 221 H6
Pennington Rd FERN BH22 204 F7
Pennington Wy FHAM PO15 181 K1
Penn Rd NWBY RG14 26 F7
Penns Pl EPSF GU31 121 H6
Penns Rd PSF GU32 120 C5
Penns Wd FARN GU14 61 K7
Penns Yd FNM GU9 12 E3
Penn Wy GPORT PO12 190 E5
Pennycress HLER SO31 179 L2
Penny Hedge
NMIL/BTOS BH25 219 H8
Penny Hl MARL SN8 264 G4
Penny La EMRTH PO10 172 B6
STOK SO20 285 Q7
Penny Pl WVILLE PO7 * 169 L5
Penny's Cl FBDG SP6 197 H1
Penny's Crs FBDG SP6 197 H1
Penny's Hatch KSCL RG20 248 E10
Pennys La FBDG SP6 197 H2
RSAL SP5 296 C5
WIMB BH21 336 F5
Penny's Md WIMB BH21 336 F5
Penny St PSEA PO1 20 C7
Pennywell Gdns
NMIL/BTOS BH25 219 K4
Penrhyn Av CHAM PO6 169 H8
Penrhyn Cl ALDT GU11 3 G5
ELGH SO50 139 M3
Penrith Cl VWD BH31 201 G3
Penrith Rd BOSC BH5 227 G4
BSTK RG21 6 C6
Penrose Cl NEND PO2 184 D6
NWBY RG14 27 H7
Penrose Rd FERN BH22 209 K2
Penryn Dr BOR GU35 114 C3
Pensford Cl CWTH RG45 43 K1
Penshurst Ri FRIM GU16 51 H8
Penshurst Wy ELGH SO50 134 A6
The Pentagon FAWY SO45 355 J6
Pentere Rd HORN PO8 156 A2
Pentire Av WSHM SO15 146 D6
Pentire Wy WSHM SO15 146 D6
Pentland Cl FAWY SO45 176 D6
KBH RG22 92 D1
Pentland Ri FHAM/PORC PO16 167 K7
The Pentlands HUNG RG17 31 J2
Penton Ct HAV PO9 171 H2
Penton La RAND SP11 83 H6
Penton Pl WINC SO23 * 25 K8
Penton Rd RWIN SO21 125 G5
Pentons Hl FBDG SP6 197 M6
Pentridge Wy TOTT SO40 158 D3
Penwith Dr HASM GU27 117 K4
Penwood Gn HAV PO9 * 171 H3
Penwood Hts KSCL RG20 246 C4
Penwood Rd KSCL RG20 246 E1
Peperham Rd HASM GU27 118 C4
Peper Harow HORN PO8 156 B2
Peper Harow La
MFD/CHID GU8 261 N10
Peppard Cl WEND SO18 148 A5
Pepperbox Ri RSAL SP5 327 P2
Peppercorn Wy HEND SO30 149 H1
Pepys Av ITCH SO19 148 D7
Pepys Cl ENEY PO4 192 F5
GPORT PO12 191 H7
Percivale Rd CHFD SO53 138 F4
Percival Rd NEND PO2 184 F8
Percy Chandler St PSEA PO1 21 J1
Percy Cl FAWY SO45 176 F3
Percy Rd BOSC BH5 226 E5
ENEY PO4 21 L5
GPORT PO12 15 G4
ROWN SO16 146 A8
Peregrine Cl TOTT SO40 158 C2
Peregrine Rd
CHCH/BSGR BH23 229 G2
The Peregrines
FHAM/PORC PO16 166 F8
Pergin Crs CFDH BH17 223 H1
Pergin Wy CFDH BH17 223 H1
Perham Crs RAND SP11 265 N10
Perins Cl NARL SO24 291 K12
Periwinkle Cl BOR GU35 111 J7
Pern Dr HEND SO30 150 A5
Peronne Cl HSEA PO3 184 F3
Peronne Rd HSEA PO3 184 F3
Perowne St ALDT GU11 2 D3
Perran Rd ROWN SO16 145 K7
Perring Av FARN GU14 50 A8
Perring Rd FARN GU14 61 G7
Perry Dr FLEETN GU51 58 F7
Perryfield Gdns LTDN BH7 215 H8
Perry Gdns PLE BH15 223 J7
Perryhill Dr SHST GU47 43 H7
Perry Wy BOR GU35 111 M8
FNM GU9 76 F1
Perrywood Cl FAWY SO45 354 E5
Perrywood Gdns TOTT SO40 144 B8
Perseus Pl WVILLE PO7 169 M5
Perseus Ter PSEA PO1 * 20 C5
Pershore Cl HLER SO31 180 A1
Pershore Rd CHIN RG24 65 K3
Persian Dr HLER SO31 164 B5
Persley Rd NBNE BH10 213 K4
Perth Cl CHCH/BSGR BH23 215 L7
Perth Rd ENEY PO4 193 H4
LSOL/BMARY PO13 182 D5
RAND SP11 267 K1
Pervin Rd CHAM PO6 184 F1
Peststead La BPWT SO32 319 J8
Peter Ashley Rd CHAM PO6 169 K7
Peterborough Ct
LSOL/BMARY PO13 * 190 D3
Peterborough Rd CHAM PO6 168 E7
Peter Grant Wy FERN BH22 209 J3
Peters Cl HLER SO31 179 L1
UPTN BH16 222 C2
Peterscroft Av TOTT SO40 158 A7
Petersfield DEAN RG23 91 K4
Petersfield Cl CHIN RG24 54 C4
Petersfield La HORN PO8 321 L6
Petersfield Pl LTDN BH7 227 H1
Petersfield Rd BOR GU35 112 E3
EPSF GU31 315 P11
HAV PO9 16 F1
LISS GU33 308 E3
LTDN BH7 227 G2
NARL SO24 292 D12
NARL SO24 303 R8
RWIN SO21 302 A6
WINC SO23 25 L7
Petersham Cl WVILLE PO7 155 K7
Petersham Rd CFDH BH17 210 F8
Peters Rd FERN BH22 * 209 M5
HLER SO31 179 M1
Petit Rd MOOR/WNTN BH9 214 A5
Petrel Cft KBH RG22 92 C4
Petrel Wk LSOL/BMARY PO13 182 B6
Petrie Rd LSOL/BMARY PO13 189 M6
Petticoat La RSAL SP5 332 G1
Pettinger Gdns PTSW SO17 147 K8
Petty Cl ROMY SO51 137 G1
Pettycot Crs
LSOL/BMARY PO13 182 B5
Petty's Brook Rd CHIN RG24 54 B4
Petunia Cl KBH RG22 92 C4
Petworth Cl FRIM GU16 51 H8
KBH RG22 92 D6
Petworth Gdns ELGH SO50 134 A7
ROWN SO16 146 C3
Petworth Rd HASM GU27 118 D7
HSEA PO3 193 H2
Petwyn Cl FERN BH22 346 A6
Pevensey Cl ROWN SO16 145 K7
Pevensey Wy FRIM GU16 51 J8
Peveral Wk KBH RG22 92 F1
Peverell Rd UPTN BH16 222 B4
Peverells Rd CHFD SO53 139 L2
Peverells Wood Av CHFD SO53 139 L1
Peverells Wood Cl CHFD SO53 139 M1
Peveril Cl RGWD BH24 202 B6
Peveril Rd ITCH SO19 161 L4
Pewsey Pl WSHM SO15 146 D6
Pheaben's Fld TADY RG26 46 A5
Pheasant Cl KBH RG22 92 B4
NTID SP9 266 F2
RWIN SO21 273 P5
Pheasant Copse FLEETN GU51 58 F6
Pheby Rd KBH RG22 92 F2
Phelipps Rd WIMB BH21 210 E2
Pheonix Wy
LSOL/BMARY PO13 182 C7
Philip Rd WVILLE PO7 169 M3
Philips Crs BOR GU35 111 M7
Phillimore Rd ROWN SO16 147 K4
Phillips Cl BOR GU35 111 M7
RFNM GU10 73 L8
ROWN SO16 145 L2
Philpott Dr TOTT SO40 159 M7
Phoenix Cl HLER SO31 163 G3
Phoenix Ct HTWY RG27 57 K4
KSCL RG20 248 D10
Phoenix Park Ter BSTK RG21 6 E3
Phoenix Sq NEND PO2 184 E4
Phoenix Ter HTWY RG27 57 K4
Phyldon Cl BKME/WDN BH12 224 B3
Phyldon Rd BKME/WDN BH12 224 B2
Pickard Rd FERN BH22 209 M1
Pickaxe La ODIM RG29 257 P8
Pickering Cl BDST BH18 211 G6
Picket Cl FBDG SP6 197 H2
Picketts Hl BOR GU35 111 J3
Picket Twenty RAND SP11 97 G4
Pickford Rd MOOR/WNTN BH9 213 L7
Pickford St ALDT GU11 3 G3
Pickwick Cl TOTT SO40 158 B1
Pickwick Gdns CBLY GU15 51 K4
Picton Cl CBLY GU15 51 L1
Picton Rd AND SP10 96 B7
Pier Ap BMTH BH1 8 F8
Pier Head Rd NEND PO2 184 B8
Pierrefondes Av FARN GU14 61 H3
Pier Rd PSEA PO1 20 E8
Pier St LSOL/BMARY PO13 189 L6
Pigeon Cl TADY RG26 46 C6
Pigeonhouse Fld RWIN SO21 274 C8
Pigeon House La WVILLE PO7 168 D5
Pigeonhouse Yd RWIN SO21 274 C8
Pigeons Farm Rd STHA RG19 34 D5
Pike Cl ALDT GU11 3 K2
Pikes Hl LYND SO43 345 K2
Pikes Hill Av LYND SO43 345 J2
Pike St NWBY RG14 19 H1
Pilands Wood Rd HLER SO31 162 F4
Pilchards Av ELGH SO50 141 H1
Pilcot Rd HTWY RG27 70 D2
Pilford Heath Rd WIMB BH21 208 A1
Pilgrim Cl NMIL/BTOS BH25 219 J4
Pilgrim Pk RGWD BH24 203 L4
Pilgrim Pl WEND SO18 147 L4
Pilgrims Cl CHFD SO53 138 F3
FNM GU9 12 D7
Pilgrims Ga FUFL SO22 24 C3
Pilgrims Pk RGWD BH24 * 203 L4
Pilgrims Vw ASHV GU12 74 C8
Pilgrims Wy AND SP10 5 M2
BOR GU35 111 L7
CFDH BH17 223 G1
FHAM/STUB PO14 189 H3
Pilley Bailey LYMN SO41 356 A2
Pilley Hl LYMN SO41 351 R11
Pilley St LYMN SO41 356 A2
Pill Hl RSAL SP5 127 G4
Pilning Cl FHAM/STUB PO14 181 J4
Pilot Hight Rd BWD BH11 213 G5
Pilsdon Dr CFDH BH17 211 L6
Pimpern Cl CFDH BH17 211 L6
Pimpernel Cl HLER SO31 179 L2
Pimpernel Pl NTHA RG18 29 H8
Pimpernel Wy CHIN RG24 66 B1
Pinchington La NWBY RG14 34 B5
Pindar Pl NWBY RG14 28 A7
Pine Av BKME/WDN BH12 224 F1
CBLY GU15 50 F4
CHOB/PIR GU24 63 M2
SBNE BH6 227 J4
Pine Bank GSHT GU26 115 L4
Pinecliffe Av SBNE BH6 227 J4
Pinecliffe Rd NMIL/BTOS BH25 230 C1
Pinecliff Rd CCLF BH13 225 G8
Pine Cl ASHV GU12 74 A2
CBLY GU15 50 A1
FAWY SO45 176 F6
FERN BH22 209 J1
FUFL SO22 124 B1
NBAD SO52 137 M3
NMIL/BTOS BH25 218 E8
RSAL SP5 334 B6
RWIN SO21 288 E4
STOK SO20 270 D8
TOTT SO40 158 C5
Pine Ct FRIM GU16 * 62 A5
Pine Crs CHCH/BSGR BH23 229 L1
CHFD SO53 133 J8
Pine Dr BLKW GU17 50 A5
CCLF BH13 224 F5
EWKG RG40 42 C1
RGWD BH24 202 B8
THLE RG7 39 M6
WEND SO18 148 D5
Pine Dr East WEND SO18 148 E5
Pine End FERN BH22 * 209 M5
Pinefield Rd WEND SO18 147 M6
Pinefields Cl CWTH RG45 43 K3
Pine Glen Av FERN BH22 204 D8
Pine Gv FLEETS GU52 71 K3
HAV PO9 17 H5
RFNM GU10 79 J2
Pinegrove Rd ITCH SO19 161 M5
Pinehill Ri SHST GU47 43 K8
Pinehill Rd BOR GU35 113 G2
CWTH RG45 43 K4
Pineholt Cl RGWD BH24 202 C7
Pinehurst TADY RG26 44 B5
Pinehurst Av
CHCH/BSGR BH23 228 F3
FARN GU14 61 H6
Pinehurst Cl HORN PO8 156 C6
Pinehurst Pk FERN BH22 205 H8
Pinehurst Pl FERN BH22 205 H8
Pinehurst Rd FARN GU14 61 G6
FERN BH22 205 H7
ROWN SO16 146 F2
Pinelands Rd ROWN SO16 138 F8
Pine Manor Rd RGWD BH24 205 M3
Pine Mount Rd CBLY GU15 50 F4
Pine Rdg NWBY RG14 27 L7
Pine Ridge Dr RFNM GU10 78 F3
Pine Rd ALTN GU34 293 N5
BPWT SO32 143 K4
CHFD SO53 133 J7
FBDG SP6 196 B7
MOOR/WNTN BH9 213 M7
ROMY SO51 137 J2
WIMB BH21 206 E7
Pinesprings Dr BDST BH18 210 E6
Pines Rd FLEETN GU51 59 H6
LIPH GU30 113 L8
The Pines AND SP10 4 E4
CBLY GU15 51 H1
FBDG SP6 197 M2
FHAM/PORC PO16 167 G7
Pinetops Cl LYMN SO41 221 G5
Pine Tree Cl WIMB BH21 207 K3
Pine Tree Gdns HORN PO8 156 A6
Pine Tree Gln WBNE BH4 225 J5
Pinetree Houses NTID SP9 * 266 G1
Pine Trees Cl
FHAM/STUB PO14 181 K4
Pinetree Wk CFDH BH17 210 F8
Pine Vale Crs NBNE BH10 213 M5
Pine Vw BOR GU35 114 B2
Pine View Cl FNM GU9 77 L3
HASM GU27 118 C4
UPTN BH16 222 C2
Pineview Cl HLER SO31 163 G3
RSAL SP5 332 F4
Pine View Rd VWD BH31 200 F1
Pine Wk AND SP10 4 A8
FERN BH22 205 G5
HLER SO31 164 A7
LISS GU33 308 G6
ROWN SO16 146 F1
VWD BH31 201 K3
Pine Wy ROWN SO16 146 F1
Pinewood CHIN RG24 * 54 A5
LSOL/BMARY PO13 182 E7
Pinewood Av CWTH RG45 43 L2
HAV PO9 170 B5
NBNE BH10 213 K3
Pinewood Cl
CHCH/BSGR BH23 218 A7
FHAM/STUB PO14 181 K8
NBNE BH10 213 K3
ROMY SO51 131 J7
SHST GU47 43 H8
TADY RG26 249 P3
UPTN BH16 222 A1
Pinewood Crs FARN GU14 60 C3
FAWY SO45 177 H6
Pinewood Dr FAWY SO45 177 H6
KSCL RG20 247 J2
Pinewood Gdns FERN BH22 209 K1
Pinewood Hl FLEETN GU51 59 J6
Pinewood Pk FARN GU14 60 D1
ITCH SO19 148 F7
Pinewood Rd ASHV GU12 74 D5
CCLF BH13 225 H7
CHCH/BSGR BH23 217 M7
FERN BH22 209 J1
LYMN SO41 219 M5
RGWD BH24 202 B8
Pinewood Rd West
UPTN BH16 222 A1
Pinkerton Rd KBH RG22 92 E2
Pinkney La LYND SO43 345 J6
Pink Rd NEND PO2 184 E8
Pinks Hl FHAM/PORC PO16 11 M4
Pinks La TADY RG26 249 Q3
Pinnell Cl KBH RG22 92 C6
Pinsley Dr WHAM PO17 168 A2
Pintail Cl KBH RG22 92 B5
Pinto Cl FHAM PO15 164 B5
Pipers Ash RGWD BH24 203 L4
Pipers Cl TOTT SO40 158 D2
Pipers Ct STHA RG19 * 36 A2
Pipers Cft FLEETS GU52 71 H4
Pipers Dr CHCH/BSGR BH23 229 G1
Pipers La STHA RG19 35 M3
Pipers Md HORN PO8 321 J7
Pipers Patch FARN GU14 61 H4
Pipers Wy STHA RG19 35 M3
Piping Cl RWIN SO21 134 F4
Piping Rd RWIN SO21 134 F4
Pipistrelle Wk WHAM PO17 165 L4
Pipit Cl GPORT PO12 191 H1
STHA RG19 35 H1
Pippin Cl CHCH/BSGR BH23 215 L6
LYMN SO41 221 L6
Pipsons Cl YTLY GU46 48 F2
Pirbright Rd FARN GU14 61 J5
RGUW GU3 74 F4
Pirbright Ter CHOB/PIR GU24 * 63 M4
Pirelli St SHAM SO14 22 E3
Pirelli Wy ELGH SO50 140 A2
Pirrie Cl WSHM SO15 146 D7
Pitcairn Cl CHIN RG24 65 L2
Pitcairn Ms ENEY PO4 * 193 H6
Pitchponds Rd HLER SO31 179 J4
Pitcot La RWIN SO21 310 B5
Pitcroft La EPSF GU31 315 R11
Pitcroft Rd NEND PO2 184 D7
Pitfield La THLE RG7 40 C4
Pitfold Av HASM GU27 117 K2
Pitfold Cl HASM GU27 117 L2
Pither Rd ODIM RG29 68 E8
Pithouse La CHCH/BSGR BH23 347 K12
Pitman Cl KBH RG22 92 D2
Pitmore Cl ELGH SO50 134 B4
Pitmore La LYMN SO41 350 H10
Pitmore Rd ELGH SO50 134 B4
Pitreavie Rd CHAM PO6 185 G2
Pittard Rd BSTK RG21 6 B8
Pitter Cl FUFL SO22 288 B11
Pitthall TADY RG26 * 255 M3
Pitt Hill La WVILLE PO7 320 A11
Pitt La RFNM GU10 262 A6
Pittmore Rd CHCH/BSGR BH23 216 C6
Pitton Rd RSAL SP5 296 B4
Pitt Rd WSHM SO15 160 C2
Pitts Deep La LYMN SO41 357 J7
Pitts La AND SP10 5 G8
RSAL SP5 324 E4
Pitts Pl NMIL/BTOS BH25 219 K6
Pitt Wy FARN GU14 60 F3
Pit Wk AMSY SP4 268 D5
Pitwines Cl PLE BH15 223 K6
Pitymoor La WHAM PO17 168 B4
Place Crs WVILLE PO7 169 M3
Place House Cl FHAM PO15 181 J3
Place La RWIN SO21 124 D4
Plaitford Gv HAV PO9 170 C4
Plantaganet Crs BWD BH11 212 D3
Plantation Dr
CHCH/BSGR BH23 218 A6
TOTT SO40 159 L7
Plantation Rd AND SP10 4 C6
CFDH BH17 211 J7
CHCH/BSGR BH23 346 H8
LISS GU33 308 H10
NTID SP9 266 F3
ROMY SO51 334 H8
TADY RG26 249 R2
The Plantation BPWT SO32 150 E2
RSAL SP5 282 E11
Plantation Wy BOR GU35 112 C4
Plant Park Rd RGWD BH24 347 J1
Plants Cl ROMY SO51 335 M7
Plassey Crs BWD BH11 213 H3
Plassey Rd NTID SP9 266 E1
Platform Rd SHAM SO14 23 G7
Platoff Rd LYMN SO41 221 L8
Player Ct FBDG SP6 197 H1
Players Crs TOTT SO40 158 E3
Playfair Rd SSEA PO5 21 J5
Playfields Dr
BKME/WDN BH12 224 E2
Pleasance Wy
NMIL/BTOS BH25 218 F5
Pleasant Hl TADY RG26 44 B4
Pleasant Rd ENEY PO4 193 H4
Plecy Cl FERN BH22 209 K5
Plemont Cl BKME/WDN BH12 212 E7
Pless Rd LYMN SO41 232 A3
Plough Gdns STOK SO20 284 D10
Plough La BPWT SO32 319 J10
HTWY RG27 240 H9
Plough Rd YTLY GU46 49 G1
Plough Wy FUFL SO22 122 D8
Plover Cl AND SP10 96 D2
FHAM/STUB PO14 189 H2
KBH RG22 92 C3
ROWN SO16 146 B3
Plover Dr LYMN SO41 232 F4
Plover Reach ENEY PO4 193 H3
Plover Rd TOTT SO40 158 C1
Plovers Down FUFL SO22 124 B1
Plovers Ri CHOB/PIR GU24 63 L1
Plovers Rd HORN PO8 156 A2
Plovers Wy ALTN GU34 107 G3
P.L.P.H. Rd FAWY SO45 178 B7
Plumer Rd CFDH BH17 211 G7
LISS GU33 309 J1
Plumpton Gdns HSEA PO3 185 H5
Plumpton Gv WVILLE PO7 156 B7
Plumpton Rd NWBY RG14 19 J8
Plumpton Wy ALTN GU34 106 F6
Pluto Rd ELGH SO50 139 M5
Plymouth Dr
FHAM/STUB PO14 189 H2
Plymouth St SSEA PO5 21 H4
Poachers Fld ODIM RG29 257 Q5
Pococks La LISS GU33 307 R5
Poets Wy FUFL SO22 24 B4
Poffley Pl STHA RG19 36 A1
Poinsettia Cl FHAM PO15 180 E1
Pointout Cl ROWN SO16 146 E5
Pointout Rd ROWN SO16 146 E5
Poland La ODIM RG29 69 G2
Polden Cl FARN GU14 60 E1
Polesden Cl CHFD SO53 133 H8
Poles La LYMN SO41 221 L7
RWIN SO21 133 H2
Police Station La BPWT SO32 318 H3
Polkerris Wy FLEETS GU52 71 K4
Pollard Gv CBLY GU15 51 L4
Pollards Moor Rd TOTT SO40 341 L3
Polmear Cl FLEETS GU52 71 K4
The Polygon WSHM SO15 22 E1
Pomona Cl FERN BH22 209 K2
Pompeys La FERN BH22 209 G4
Pond Cl NMIL/BTOS BH25 219 G5
NWBY RG14 33 K5
OVTN RG25 89 J6
TOTT SO40 159 M6
Pond Cft YTLY GU46 49 G2
Pondhead Cl FAWY SO45 354 E5
Pond La HORN PO8 321 K6
RFNM GU10 262 C8
Pond Piece WVILLE PO7 154 F5
Pond Rd BOR GU35 114 A4
FARN GU14 61 H6
HLER SO31 163 M6
TADY RG26 46 C6
Pondside La BPWT SO32 143 J3
Pondtail Cl FLEETN GU51 59 L8
Pondtail Gdns FLEETN GU51 59 L8
Pondtail Rd FLEETN GU51 59 L8
Pondview Cl FLEETN GU51 59 L6
Ponsonby Rd PSTN BH14 224 D4
Pony Dr UPTN BH16 222 D1
Pook Hl MFD/CHID GU8 119 L1
Pook La HAV PO9 17 J7
WHAM PO17 166 B4
Pookles La ALTN GU34 281 P11
Pooksgreen TOTT SO40 159 K6
Poole Br PLE BH15 223 H7
Poole Hl WCLF BH2 8 C6
Poole La BWD BH11 212 F4
Poole Rd CCLF BH13 224 F4
ITCH SO19 161 L4
UPTN BH16 222 C1
WBNE BH4 225 H4
WCLF BH2 8 B6
WIMB BH21 207 J4
Pool Rd ALDT GU11 3 K9
HTWY RG27 57 L1
Poors Farm Rd CHIN RG24 55 G8
Popes Hl KSCL RG20 248 C10
Popes La BPWT SO32 310 C12
TOTT SO40 158 F1
Popes Md HASM GU27 118 C5
Popes Rd PLE BH15 223 K2
Popham Ct HAV PO9 170 C2
Popham La OVTN RG25 103 G4
Poplar Cl CHCH/BSGR BH23 218 B8
CHCH/BSGR BH23 348 E12
FRIM GU16 62 A5
HTWY RG27 46 F7
TADY RG26 249 P4
WIMB BH21 207 K3
Poplar Crs RGWD BH24 203 K5
Poplar Dr FHAM/STUB PO14 10 A8
TOTT SO40 159 K7
Poplar Gv HISD PO11 195 G4
Poplar La CHCH/BSGR BH23 348 E11
Poplar Pl NWBY RG14 27 J7
Poplar Rd ITCH SO19 161 M2
NMIL/BTOS BH25 219 K4
Poplars Cl FARN GU14 60 C3
The Poplars BPWT SO32 151 L1
Poplar Wk FNM GU9 77 H1
Poplar Wy HEND SO30 149 K5
NBAD SO52 137 M3
RGWD BH24 203 K5
Popley Wy CHIN RG24 65 H4
Poppy Cl CHCH/BSGR BH23 217 H8
HLER SO31 179 M2
RAND SP11 95 L5
Poppy Dr NTHA RG18 29 H8
Poppy Flds CHIN RG24 54 C8
Poppyfields CHFD SO53 139 G2
Poppy Rd ROWN SO16 147 J3
Porchester Cl AND SP10 95 M1
Porchester Rd ITCH SO19 161 L5
NWBY RG14 18 E8
Porlock Cl STHA RG19 * 35 K2
Porlock Rd ROWN SO16 145 J7
Portacre Ri BSTK RG21 6 A8
Portal Cl RAND SP11 95 K5
Portal Rd ELGH SO50 140 D1
ITCH SO19 148 B8
LSOL/BMARY PO13 182 C5
TOTT SO40 158 D1
WINC SO23 25 K8
Portarlington Cl WBNE BH4 8 A7
Portarlington Rd WBNE BH4 225 J5
Portchester Ct BMTH BH1 9 K2
Portchester Hts
FHAM/PORC PO16 167 K7
Portchester La WHAM PO17 167 J2
Portchester Pl BMTH BH1 9 K2
Portchester Ri ELGH SO50 134 A5
Portchester Rd CHAR BH8 9 H1
FHAM/PORC PO16 167 G8
NEND PO2 184 E8
Portelet Cl BKME/WDN BH12 212 D7
Portelet Pl HEND SO30 149 J7
Porteous Crs CHFD SO53 139 M2
Porter Cl ODIM RG29 * 68 E8
Porter End NWBY RG14 19 H9
Porter Rd CFDH BH17 223 H1
KBH RG22 93 H3
Portersbridge St ROMY SO51 136 E1
Porters Cl AND SP10 4 B3
OVTN RG25 103 M3
Porter's La SHAM SO14 22 F6
WIMB BH21 208 C2
Portesberry Rd CBLY GU15 50 F2
Portesbery Hill Dr CBLY GU15 50 F1
Portesham Gdns
MOOR/WNTN BH9 214 B4
Portesham Wy CFDH BH17 211 L5
Portfield Cl CHCH/BSGR BH23 216 A8
Portfield Rd CHCH/BSGR BH23 228 A1
Port Hamble HLER SO31 * 179 G1
Portiswood Cl TADY RG26 44 D4
Portland Dr FLEETS GU52 71 H4
GPORT PO12 190 D5
Portland Gv AND SP10 5 H5
Portland Rd
MOOR/WNTN BH9 214 A8
SSEA PO5 21 H8
WVILLE PO7 169 L1
Portland's Cl PSF GU32 120 F4
Portland Sq LISS GU33 308 F8
Portland St FHAM/PORC PO16 11 H6
PSEA PO1 20 E3
SHAM SO14 22 F3
Portland Ter FNM GU9 * 77 H4
SHAM SO14 22 F4
SSEA PO5 * 21 H8
Port La RWIN SO21 133 H1
Portman Crs SBNE BH6 227 H4
Portman Rd LTDN BH7 226 F3
Portman Ter SBNE BH6 * 227 H4
Portmore Cl BDST BH18 211 H2
Portobello Gv
FHAM/PORC PO16 167 K7
Port Royal St SSEA PO5 * 21 K3
Portsdown Av CHAM PO6 169 J8
Portsdown Hill Rd CHAM PO6 168 F7
WHAM PO17 167 G6
Portsdown Rd CHAM PO6 167 L8
Portside Cl TOTT SO40 160 A5
Portsmouth Crs KBH RG22 92 F1
Portsmouth Rd BPWT SO32 310 B12
CBLY GU15 51 J2
CHAM PO6 184 F2
ELGH SO50 135 J6
FRIM GU16 51 G5
GSHT GU26 115 J7
HLER SO31 162 F3
HORN PO8 156 C2
ITCH SO19 161 L6

ITCH SO19 162 B2
LIPH GU30 116 B7
LIPH GU30 117 G1
LSOL/BMARY PO13 189 M8
MFD/CHID GU8 263 R10
Portsmouth Wk KBH RG22 92 F2
Portsmouth Wy KBH RG22 92 F2
Portsview Av
FHAM/PORC PO16 167 K8
Portsview Gdns
FHAM/PORC PO16 167 K7
Portswood Av PTSW SO17 147 H8
Portswood Dr
MOOR/WNTN BH9 214 A4
Portswood Pk PTSW SO17 147 H8
Portswood Rd HAV PO9 170 D2
NEND PO2 184 E3
PTSW SO17 147 H8
Portview Rd WEND SO18 147 M6
Port Wy CHAM PO6 168 A8
Portway TADY RG26 249 P3
THLE RG7 240 C2
Portway Cl AND SP10 4 A5
WEND SO18 148 B5
Portway Pl DEAN RG23 64 D7
Posbrooke Rd ENEY PO4 193 G4
Posbrook La
FHAM/STUB PO14 180 E7
Postern Cl FHAM/PORC PO16 167 K8
Post Horn La HTWY RG27 56 A3
Posting House Ms NWBY RG14 18 B1
Post Office La OVTN RG25 103 M3
RGWD BH24 202 C7
Post Office Rd BMTH BH1 8 E6
HUNG RG17 30 E7
WVILLE PO7 169 J3
Potbridge Rd ODIM RG29 57 H8
Pot La CHIN RG24 55 H8
Potley Hill Rd YTLY GU46 49 H3
Potteries La FRIM GU16 61 M5
The Potteries FARN GU14 60 D2
FHAM/PORC PO16 11 H2
Potterne Wy WIMB BH21 201 J4
Potterne Wood Cl VWD BH31 201 L4
Potters Crs ASHV GU12 74 B5
Potters Fld LISS GU33 308 G8
Potters Ga FNM GU9 12 D3
Potters Heron Cl ROMY SO51 132 E5
Potters Heron La ROMY SO51 132 E5
Potters La HTWY RG27 47 H5
Potters Wy PSTN BH14 224 C6
Pottery Dro STOK SO20 269 N10
Pottery La HUNG RG17 30 D7
RCCH PO18 173 H7
RFNM GU10 78 D2
Pottery Rd PSTN BH14 224 A6
Poulner Cl ITCH SO19 162 A3
Poulner Ct HAV PO9 170 C2
Poulner Hl RGWD BH24 203 M4
Poulner Pk RGWD BH24 203 L3
Poultons Cl OVTN RG25 89 J6
Poultons Rd OVTN RG25 89 J5
Pound Cl BOR GU35 111 M7
LSOL/BMARY PO13 182 D8
NARL SO24 278 D10
PLE BH15 223 M3
RGWD BH24 203 J4
TADY RG26 46 A5
Pound Cots BPWT SO32 312 E11
Pound Farm La ASHV GU12 74 D7
Pound Ga ALTN GU34 107 G3
Pound Gate Dr
FHAM/STUB PO14 180 C3
Pound Hl NARL SO24 291 L10
ROMY SO51 334 G3
Pound La BPWT SO32 312 F11
FBDG SP6 330 B11
KSCL RG20 246 G6
NWBY RG14 26 F8
PLE BH15 223 L3
RGWD BH24 348 G3
ROMY SO51 132 B6
ROMY SO51 334 G3
STHA RG19 35 G1
TOTT SO40 158 F6
TOTT SO40 341 N2
Pound Lea HISD PO11 195 G3
Pound Meadow HTWY RG27 47 G8
Pound Rd ASHV GU12 3 H4
CHAM PO6 168 B6
HLER SO31 162 F4
LYMN SO41 221 H5
OVTN RG25 89 K5
STOK SO20 269 Q10
WINC SO23 289 J8
Pound St NWBY RG14 18 D6
WEND SO18 148 A5
Pound Tree Rd SHAM SO14 23 G3
Poveys Md KSCL RG20 248 E10
Powell Crs TOTT SO40 158 F3
Powell Rd PSTN BH14 224 B5
Power Rd PSEA PO1 192 E2
Powerscourt Rd NEND PO2 184 E8
NMIL/BTOS BH25 230 D1
Powis Cl NMIL/BTOS BH25 219 H5
Poyle Rd RFNM GU10 260 E1
Poyner Cl FHAM/PORC PO16 11 G4
Poynings Crs BSTK RG21 93 L2
Poynings Pl PSEA PO1 20 D6
Poynters Cl AND SP10 4 F1
Poyntz Rd OVTN RG25 89 J4
Prancing Horse Cl STHA RG19 35 L1
The Precinct GPORT PO12 * 15 K4
HISD PO11 * 195 G5
WVILLE PO7 169 L1
Precosa Rd HEND SO30 149 L7
Prelate Wy FHAM/STUB PO14 180 C2
Premier Pde WEND SO18 * 147 M5
Premier Wy ROMY SO51 137 K3
Prentice Cl FARN GU14 50 D8
Prescelly Cl KBH RG22 64 D8
Preshaw Cl ROWN SO16 146 C4
Preston Cl UPTN BH16 222 C1
Preston La CHCH/BSGR BH23 216 D5
Preston Pl NWBY RG14 27 M7
Preston Rd NEND PO2 184 F7
PLE BH15 223 J2
Preston Wy CHCH/BSGR BH23 217 K8
Prestwick La HASM GU27 119 G2
Prestwood Cl
NMIL/BTOS BH25 218 F7
Prestwood Rd HEND SO30 149 J6
Pretoria Cl LISS GU33 309 J2
Pretoria Rd ENEY PO4 192 F5
HEND SO30 149 H7
RAND SP11 265 P11
Pricketts Hl BPWT SO32 151 M5
Prideaux-Brune Av
LSOL/BMARY PO13 182 C4
Priest Croft Dr FAWY SO45 354 G6
Priest Down DEAN RG23 92 D7
Priestfields FHAM/STUB PO14 180 C2
Priestlands ROMY SO51 130 E8
Priestlands Cl TOTT SO40 158 A2
Priestlands La LYMN SO41 221 J5
Priestlands Rd LYMN SO41 221 J5
Priest La CHCH/BSGR BH23 216 B1
Priestley Cl TOTT SO40 158 D1
Priestley Rd CHIN RG24 65 G3
NBNE BH10 213 H7
Priestwood Cl WEND SO18 148 D5
Primate Rd FHAM/STUB PO14 180 D2
Prime One AND SP10 * 97 G3
Primrose Cl CHFD SO53 138 F4
HEND SO30 149 J7
LSOL/BMARY PO13 182 C3
Primrose Dr HTWY RG27 57 L1
Primrose Gdns CFDH BH17 210 F7
FARN GU14 60 E5
KBH RG22 92 D7
Primrose La LISS GU33 309 L8
RSAL SP5 332 E2
Primrose Rd RAND SP11 265 M10
ROWN SO16 147 G4
Primrose Wy
CHCH/BSGR BH23 217 J8
HLER SO31 179 M2
ROMY SO51 131 J8
SHST GU47 43 K7
WIMB BH21 210 E1
Primula Rd BOR GU35 113 G1
Prince Albert Gdns AND SP10 4 F6
Prince Albert Rd ENEY PO4 193 G5
Prince Alfred St GPORT PO12 14 E6
Prince Charles Cl RAND SP11 265 M9
Prince Charles Crs FARN GU14 50 D8
Prince Cl AND SP10 96 F2
Prince Dr SHST GU47 43 J7
Prince George's St HAV PO9 16 F4
Prince George St PSEA PO1 20 D2
Prince Hold Rd STHA RG19 35 G1
Prince of Wales Av
WSHM SO15 160 A1
Prince of Wales Cl
WVILLE PO7 * 170 A1
Prince of Wales Rd
GPORT PO12 15 H4
WBNE BH4 225 J4
Prince Rd FHAM/STUB PO14 181 M6
ROWN SO16 145 L1
Prince's Av ALDT GU11 73 J3
Princes Buildings WINC SO23 * 25 H5
Princes Cl BOR GU35 112 E3
BPWT SO32 143 H4
RSAL SP5 332 G1
Princes Ct SHAM SO14 161 J2
Princes' Crs KBH RG22 93 G1
Princes Dr WVILLE PO7 156 A7
Princes Hl RSAL SP5 332 G1
Princes Pl FUFL SO22 122 E7
NEND PO2 * 192 D1
NMIL/BTOS BH25 219 J5
Princes Rd FERN BH22 209 K3
PSF GU32 120 B5
ROMY SO51 130 E8
WSHM SO15 160 D2
Princess Av CHCH/BSGR BH23 228 B2
Princess Cl HEND SO30 148 E2
Princess Crs LYND SO43 345 M2
Princess Dr ALTN GU34 106 D5
Princess Gdns HORN PO8 156 B1
Princess Marina Dr WHIT RG2 239 M9
Princess Mary Gdns
RAND SP11 265 M10
Princess Rd BKME/WDN BH12 225 G4
TOTT SO40 158 B6
Prince's St PSEA PO1 192 D1
SHAM SO14 161 J2
Princess Wy CBLY GU15 50 E3
Princes Wy ALDT GU11 2 E2
Pringles Cl FERN BH22 209 L3
Pringles Dr FERN BH22 209 L3
Prinstead Cl WINC SO23 25 J9
Prinsted Cl CHAM PO6 185 K1
Prinsted La EMRTH PO10 172 D7
Prinsted Wk
FHAM/STUB PO14 181 K4
Prior Croft Cl CBLY GU15 51 J4
Prior End CBLY GU15 51 J3
Prior Rd CBLY GU15 51 K4
Priors Barton WINC SO23 122 F7
Priors Cl CHCH/BSGR BH23 229 J1
EMRTH PO10 172 E5
FARN GU14 50 D8
KSCL RG20 248 D10
Priorsdean Av HSEA PO3 193 G2
Priorsdean Crs HAV PO9 170 D4
Priors Dean Rd FUFL SO22 288 D12
Priors Hatch La GODL GU7 261 R7
Priors Keep FLEETS GU52 59 L8
Prior's La BLKW GU17 49 J3
Priors Leaze La RCCH PO18 172 F5
Priors Rd CFDH BH17 211 G8
TADY RG26 44 A3
Priors Wk WIMB BH21 207 H3
Priors Wy FUFL SO22 124 B1
The Priors Wy NARL SO24 * 305 R2
Priors Wd CWTH RG45 42 F4
HASM GU27 117 M2
Priorswood RGUW GU3 261 R6
Priory Av PTSW SO17 147 K7
Priory Cl BPWT SO32 143 H4
FLEETN GU51 58 F8
PTSW SO17 147 K7
RSAL SP5 327 P2
Priory Ct CBLY GU15 * 50 B3
Priory Crs ENEY PO4 193 G4
Priory Gdns CHIN RG24 66 D1
FHAM/PORC PO16 167 J8
WVILLE PO7 155 L7
Priory La HTWY RG27 57 L4
RFNM GU10 79 H8
WHCH RG28 88 C5
Priory Pl NWBY RG14 34 B6
Priory Quay
CHCH/BSGR BH23 * 228 C3
Priory Rd ELGH SO50 139 M7
ENEY PO4 193 G6
FERN BH22 205 J8
FHAM PO15 181 K2
GPORT PO12 183 H8
HLER SO31 162 B6
NWBY RG14 18 E8
PTSW SO17 147 J8
WCLF BH2 8 D7
WHAM PO17 168 A2
Priory St FARN GU14 61 K4
The Priory BPWT SO32 143 H5
Priory View Pl
MOOR/WNTN BH9 214 A5
Priory View Rd
CHCH/BSGR BH23 216 C6
MOOR/WNTN BH9 214 A5
Pritchard Cl STHA RG19 34 D5
Private Rd LYMN SO41 * 221 L3
Privet La RAND SP11 82 B8
Privet Rd BOR GU35 111 J7
MOOR/WNTN BH9 213 L8
Privett Cl CHIN RG24 54 C8
Privett Pl GPORT PO12 190 E4
Privett Rd FHAM PO15 181 J2
LSOL/BMARY PO13 190 C5
PSF GU32 306 H10
WVILLE PO7 169 K5
Prochurch Rd HORN PO8 156 B4
Proctor Cl ITCH SO19 148 D7
Proctor Dr NBAD SO52 137 M5
Proctor La PSEA PO1 192 F3
Promenade CCLF BH13 237 L1
The Promenade EMRTH PO10 187 M1
FAWY SO45 177 G3
NEND PO2 * 184 D7
Propeller Rd FARN GU14 61 H6
Propsperous St PLE BH15 223 J7
Prospect Av FARN GU14 61 H2
Prospect La HAV PO9 171 H3
Prospect Pl CHFD SO53 139 J2
FAWY SO45 177 G3
HAV PO9 16 D3
NWBY RG14 18 E7
Prospect Rd ASHV GU12 74 A3
FARN GU14 61 G4
NARL SO24 291 K12
NEND PO2 192 C1
RFNM GU10 109 L1
Protea Gdns
FHAM/STUB PO14 180 F4
Provene Cl BPWT SO32 143 L8
Provene Gdns BPWT SO32 143 K8
Providence Hl HLER SO31 163 G2
Providence Pk ROWN SO16 146 F3
Provident Wy BSTK RG21 6 E4
Provost St FBDG SP6 197 H4
Pruetts La LISS GU33 308 F11
Prunus Cl FERN BH22 209 H1
ROWN SO16 146 C3
Prunus Dr FERN BH22 209 H1
Puckridge Gate Rd ALDT GU11 72 D2
Puckridge Hill Rd ALDT GU11 72 E3
Puckshott Wy HASM GU27 118 D4
Pudbrooke Gdns HEND SO30 149 H4
Pudding La WINC SO23 288 H12
Puddleslosh La FBDG SP6 196 F1
Puddletown Crs CFDH BH17 211 M6
Puffers Wy NWBY RG14 18 A6
Puffin Cl KBH RG22 92 B6
ROWN SO16 146 B3
Puffin Crs FHAM/STUB PO14 181 H8
Puffin Gdns
LSOL/BMARY PO13 182 B5
Puffin Wk HORN PO8 155 K4
Pug's Hole RSAL SP5 297 N5
Pulens Crs EPSF GU31 121 G5
Pulens La EPSF GU31 120 F5
Pullman Ct FERN BH22 204 F6
Pullman Wy RGWD BH24 203 J6
Pump La HORN PO8 156 A3
LSOL/BMARY PO13 182 C7
Punsholt La NARL SO24 305 N9
Purbeck Av PLE BH15 222 E7
Purbeck Cl UPTN BH16 * 222 B1
Purbeck Dr FHAM/STUB PO14 181 K4
VWD BH31 201 H3
Purbeck Rd NMIL/BTOS BH25 230 D1
WCLF BH2 8 C6
Purbrook Cl ROWN SO16 146 C4
Purbrook Gdns WVILLE PO7 169 J3
Purbrook Heath Rd
WVILLE PO7 168 F3
Purbrook Rd PSEA PO1 21 M3
TADY RG26 44 A4
Purbrook Wy HAV PO9 170 B4
WVILLE PO7 169 M4
Purcell Cl KBH RG22 93 H3
WVILLE PO7 169 L3
Purcell Rd CWTH RG45 43 K1
ITCH SO19 162 D1
Purchase Rd
BKME/WDN BH12 225 J1
Purewell CHCH/BSGR BH23 228 D2
Purewell Cl CHCH/BSGR BH23 228 E2
Purewell Cross Rd
CHCH/BSGR BH23 228 D1
Purkess Cl CHFD SO53 139 K1
Purkiss Cl TOTT SO40 341 N7
Purley Wy FRIM GU16 51 G8
ROMY SO51 334 F5
Purlieu La FBDG SP6 338 B1
Purmerend Cl FARN GU14 60 C3
The Purrocks PSF GU32 120 D4
Pursers Farm THLE RG7 238 B5
Purslane Gdns FHAM PO15 180 F1
Purvis Gdns ITCH SO19 162 B2
Pussex La CHCH/BSGR BH23 346 G12
Putmans La EPSF GU31 316 F10
Puttenham Heath Rd
RGUW GU3 261 P4
Puttenham Hl RGUW GU3 261 N3
Puttenham La MFD/CHID GU8 261 N7
Puttenham Rd CHIN RG24 54 C5
RFNM GU10 260 G4
Puttock Cl HASM GU27 117 K3
Pycroft Cl HISD PO11 187 J5
ITCH SO19 161 M3
Pye Cl WIMB BH21 210 D1
Pye La WIMB BH21 207 H4
WIMB BH21 337 L5
Pyestock Crs FARN GU14 60 B4
Pye St PSEA PO1 192 C2
Pyland's La HLER SO31 163 H1
Pyle Cl HORN PO8 156 A4
Pyle Hl NWBY RG14 19 H8
Pylewell Rd FAWY SO45 177 G3
Pyotts Copse CHIN RG24 54 C7
Pyotts Ct CHIN RG24 54 C7
Pyotts Hl CHIN RG24 54 C7
Pyrford Cl GPORT PO12 190 E5
WVILLE PO7 155 K6
Pyrford Ms LYMN SO41 221 L6
Pytchley Cl FHAM/STUB PO14 189 G2

Q

The Quadrangle ELGH SO50 134 A8
FARN GU14 * 50 E8
The Quadrant ASHV GU12 74 A4
Quail Wy HORN PO8 156 A2
Quantock Cl KBH RG22 92 D1
Quantock Rd ROWN SO16 145 L8
The Quantocks FAWY SO45 176 D6
STHA RG19 35 K2
Quarely Rd HAV PO9 170 C2
Quarrington Cl STHA RG19 35 L2
Quarry La YTLY GU46 49 G3
Quarry Rd WIMB BH21 208 A1
WINC SO23 25 K7
Quarterdeck Av NEND PO2 184 B7
Quarters Rd FARN GU14 61 J6
Quartremaine Rd HSEA PO3 185 H5
Quartz Cl WWKG RG41 239 R1
Quavey Rd RSAL SP5 332 G2
Quay Hvn HLER SO31 163 K4
Quay La GPORT PO12 15 L4
Quayle Dr BWD BH11 212 F2
Quay Point CHAM PO6 * 168 C8
Quay Rd CHCH/BSGR BH23 228 B3
Quayside HEND SO30 * 150 A6
Quayside Rd WEND SO18 161 K1
Quayside Wk TOTT SO40 159 M5
Quay St FHAM/PORC PO16 11 J7
LYMN SO41 221 M4
The Quay PLE BH15 223 J7
Quebec Cl LIPH GU30 116 C5
Quebec Gdns BLKW GU17 49 M4
HLER SO31 162 F3
Queen Anne Dr WIMB BH21 211 L1
Queen Anne's Dr HAV PO9 170 C6
Queen Anne's Ga FNM GU9 77 H1
Queen Elizabeth Av
LYMN SO41 221 K4
Queen Elizabeth Cl ASHV GU12 74 A6
Queen Elizabeth Dr ALDT GU11 2 D3
Queen Katherine Rd
LYMN SO41 221 M5
Queen Mary Av BSTK RG21 6 F2
CBLY GU15 50 C3
MOOR/WNTN BH9 213 M6
Queen Mary Cl FLEETN GU51 59 H6
Queen Mary Rd
FHAM/PORC PO16 183 K1
Queen Rd FHAM/STUB PO14 181 M6
Queen's Av ALDT GU11 73 H3
AND SP10 4 F5
CHCH/BSGR BH23 228 B3
Queensbury Pl BLKW GU17 49 L5
Queen's Cl FARN GU14 61 H8
FAWY SO45 177 G5
FERN BH22 204 F7
LSOL/BMARY PO13 * 189 L6
RAND SP11 265 M10
Queens Ct FNM GU9 76 F1
Queens Crs FHAM/STUB PO14 189 K1
HORN PO8 156 B1
SSEA PO5 21 H7
Queensfield OVTN RG25 103 M3
Queens Gdns FBDG SP6 197 H2
WBNE BH4 8 A4
Queen's Gate Rd FARN GU14 73 H1
Queens Gv NMIL/BTOS BH25 219 J4
SSEA PO5 21 H8
WVILLE PO7 169 K3
Queensland Rd BOSC BH5 227 G3
Queens La FNM GU9 76 F1
Queensmead
CHCH/BSGR BH23 216 A7
FARN GU14 61 H5
Queens Md FUFL SO22 122 C6
Queen's Pde LYND SO43 345 K3
WVILLE PO7 169 L1
Queen's Park Av CHAR BH8 214 C8
Queen's Park Gdns CHAR BH8 226 C1
Queen's Park Rd CHAR BH8 226 D1
Queen's Park South Dr
CHAR BH8 226 D1
Queen's Park West Dr
CHAR BH8 226 C1
Queen's Pl SSEA PO5 21 H7
Queens Ride CWTH RG45 43 J1
NBAD SO52 137 L4
Queens Rd ALDT GU11 2 D3
ALTN GU34 106 E5
BSTK RG21 6 B4
CBLY GU15 50 D4
CHCH/BSGR BH23 228 E2
CHFD SO53 133 K7
CHOB/PIR GU24 63 L1
FARN GU14 61 K8
FERN BH22 209 K1
FHAM/PORC PO16 11 G6
FLEETS GU52 71 J1
FNM GU9 77 G2
FUFL SO22 24 B6
GPORT PO12 15 G3
HLER SO31 179 J4
KSCL RG20 248 E10
LIPH GU30 309 N1
LSOL/BMARY PO13 189 M8
LYND SO43 345 L3
NEND PO2 184 E8
NWBY RG14 19 G6
ODIM RG29 68 E5
PSEA PO1 191 M2
PSF GU32 120 B5
PSTN BH14 224 D4
WBNE BH4 8 A5
WHCH RG28 99 M1
WIMB BH21 210 D3
WSHM SO15 146 C6
WVILLE PO7 155 L7
Queen's Ter SHAM SO14 23 H6
Queenstown Rd WSHM SO15 160 D2
Queen St ASHV GU12 3 M2
EMRTH PO10 172 A6
FBDG SP6 332 D7
PSEA PO1 20 C2
RWIN SO21 124 F7
Queens Vw HLER SO31 162 B6
Queens Wy HUNG RG17 31 H2
SHAM SO14 23 G6
SSEA PO5 21 H7
Queensway FRIM GU16 62 A1
HISD PO11 187 G5
NMIL/BTOS BH25 218 E5
RGWD BH24 203 K5
The Queensway
FHAM/PORC PO16 167 H8
Queenswood Av CHAR BH8 214 E7
Queenswood Dr FERN BH22 209 K1
Queenwood Ri STOK SO20 284 D10
Queenwood Rd STOK SO20 284 D10
Quennells Hl RFNM GU10 78 C2
Querida Cl HLER SO31 163 K4
Quilter Cl ITCH SO19 148 D8
Quilter Rd KBH RG22 92 F3
Quince La WIMB BH21 207 K2
Quince Tree Wy HTWY RG27 56 D7
Quintin Cl CHCH/BSGR BH23 217 M8
Quinton Cl SSEA PO5 21 J4
Quintrell Av FHAM/PORC PO16 167 G8
Quob Farm Cl HEND SO30 148 E1
Quob La HEND SO30 148 E1
The Quomp RGWD BH24 203 J5

R

Racecourse Vw LYND SO43 345 K2
Rachel Cl ELGH SO50 141 H2
Rack Cl AND SP10 5 J5
Rackclose Rd ALTN GU34 106 E5
Rackfield HASM GU27 117 K1
Rackstraw Rd SHST GU47 43 M7
Racton Av CHAM PO6 185 H1
Racton Rd EMRTH PO10 171 M5
Radar Rd FARN GU14 60 D7
Radcliffe Cl FRIM GU16 61 M1
Radcliffe Rd SHAM SO14 161 H3
Radclyffe Rd FHAM/PORC PO16 11 K3
Radford Cl FNM GU9 77 J3
Radford Gdns BSTK RG21 93 H2
Radical Ride EWKG RG40 42 B1
Radipole Rd CFDH BH17 211 M6
Radleigh Gdns TOTT SO40 144 B8
Radley Cl HEND SO30 149 J3
Radnor St SSEA PO5 21 H4
Radstock Rd ITCH SO19 161 L5
Radway Crs WSHM SO15 146 D8
Radway Rd WSHM SO15 146 D8
Raebarn Cl NARL SO24 303 R7
Raeburn Dr HEND SO30 149 J5
Raeburn Wy SHST GU47 49 M2
Rae Rd FARN GU14 61 H7
RAF Gate Rd FARN GU14 61 H7
Raghill THLE RG7 38 D6
Raglan Cl ASHV GU12 3 J5
CHFD SO53 138 F4
FRIM GU16 51 H8
Raglan Gdns BWD BH11 213 G6
Raglan St SSEA PO5 21 J3
Ragmore La PSF GU32 307 J7
Railside THLE RG7 37 M2
Rails La HISD PO11 195 H6
Railton Cl WHIT RG2 238 D1
Railway Rd LISS GU33 309 K1
NWBY RG14 19 G5
Railway Triangle CHAM PO6 * 185 H2
Railway Vw PSEA PO1 21 J2
Rainbow Cl CHIN RG24 66 E3
Rainham Cl KBH RG22 92 B5
Rakemakers ALTN GU34 107 K1
Rake Rd LIPH GU30 309 R10
LISS GU33 308 H8
Raleigh Cl CHCH/BSGR BH23 228 F3
NMIL/BTOS BH25 218 F5
RGWD BH24 203 L4
Raleigh Wy CBLY GU15 51 H5
Raley Rd HLER SO31 180 A2
Ralph Rd WIMB BH21 210 E1
Ram Aly STHA RG19 248 G4
Ramalley La CHFD SO53 139 H1
Rambler Dr
LSOL/BMARY PO13 190 C2
Ramblers Md RAND SP11 95 H1
Ramblers Wy HORN PO8 156 B7
Ramillies Cl ALDT GU11 73 L1
Ramley Rd LYMN SO41 220 F3
Rampart Gdns HSEA PO3 184 F3
Rampart Rd WEND SO18 161 K1
Rampart Rw GPORT PO12 15 L6
The Ramparts AND SP10 4 C9
The Rampart LYMN SO41 221 K3
Rampton Rd WHCH RG28 87 M8
Ramptons La THLE RG7 39 H6
Rampton's Meadow
TADY RG26 44 D5
Ramsay Pl LSOL/BMARY PO13 182 C6
Ramsay Rd WINC SO23 289 J9
Ramsdale Av HAV PO9 170 C3
Ramsdean Rd PSF GU32 314 H7
Ramsdell Cl TADY RG26 44 B5
Ramsdell Rd FLEETN GU51 58 F5
TADY RG26 52 D3
TADY RG26 249 J11
Ramsey Rd HISD PO11 195 G5
Ramshill EPSF GU31 120 E5
Ramsholt Cl OVTN RG25 103 G3
Rances Wy FUFL SO22 122 E7
Randall Cl TOTT SO40 144 C6
Randall Rd CHFD SO53 133 K6
Randalls La RGWD BH24 342 G11
Randolph Dr FARN GU14 60 C5
Randolph Rd BMTH BH1 226 E4
NEND PO2 184 E5
PSTN BH14 224 C3
Randolph St WSHM SO15 160 C1
Ranelagh Gdns WSHM SO15 160 E1
Ranelagh Rd
CHCH/BSGR BH23 229 M1
HAV PO9 16 B4
NEND PO2 184 C7
WINC SO23 24 E9
Ranfurly Gdns FAWY SO45 176 E6
Range Gdns ITCH SO19 162 B1
Range Gn NEND PO2 184 C5
Range Ride CBLY GU15 50 B1
Range Rd EWKG RG40 42 D1
FARN GU14 60 D6
Rankine Cl FNM GU9 77 L2
Rankine Rd CHIN RG24 65 M5
Rannoch Cl FHAM PO15 10 A2
Ransome Cl FHAM/STUB PO14 180 F5
Ranvilles La FHAM/STUB PO14 181 H5
Rapallo Cl FARN GU14 61 J4
Raphael Cl BSTK RG21 7 K8
Rapley's Fld CHOB/PIR GU24 63 L4
Rapson Cl CHAM PO6 168 C7
Rareridge La BPWT SO32 143 L4
Rashleigh Ct FLEETS GU52 71 K4
Rasset Md FLEETS GU52 71 G5
Ratcliffe Rd FARN GU14 50 B8
FAWY SO45 176 F7
HEND SO30 149 J5
Ratlake La ROMY SO51 132 F4
Rattigan Gdns HLER SO31 164 C4
Ravel Cl KBH RG22 93 G3
Ravelin Cl RFNM GU10 259 P3
Raven Cl LSOL/BMARY PO13 190 C2
NTID SP9 266 F2
YTLY GU46 48 D2
Raven Rd HTWY RG27 56 C7
SHAM SO14 161 H2
Ravens Cl FHAM/STUB PO14 189 K1
Ravenscourt Rd LYMN SO41 221 K5
SBNE BH6 227 J3
Ravenscroft HTWY RG27 56 D6
Ravens Cft HTWY RG27 * 56 E7
Ravenscroft Cl ASHV GU12 74 C5
HLER SO31 162 F3
Ravenscroft Wy BPWT SO32 149 M3
Ravensdale Cl
BKME/WDN BH12 224 C2
Raven Sq ALTN GU34 106 F2
ELGH SO50 139 K6
Ravenstone Rd CBLY GU15 51 M3
Ravens Wy LYMN SO41 232 D4
Ravenswood
FHAM/STUB PO14 * 180 C1
Ravenswood Av CWTH RG45 43 G3
Ravenswood Dr CBLY GU15 51 J3
Ravensworth Rd THLE RG7 39 L6
Raven Wy CHCH/BSGR BH23 229 G3
Ravine Rd BOSC BH5 227 H4
CCLF BH13 224 F8
Rawlings Ct RAND SP11 265 M10
Rawlings Rd HTWY RG27 56 D8
Rawlinson Rd ALDT GU11 73 J2
CBLY GU15 50 B2
Raygnoldes FLEETS GU52 71 G5
Rayleigh Rd BSTK RG21 6 D5
Raymond Cl FAWY SO45 354 F5
HEND SO30 148 F1
VWD BH31 201 K2
Raymond Rd CHAM PO6 167 L7
WSHM SO15 160 D1
Rayner Dr WHIT RG2 239 L8
Rayners Gdns ROWN SO16 147 K4
Raynes Rd LSOL/BMARY PO13 189 M8
Reading Dr North HTWY RG27 241 K8
Reading Rd BLKW GU17 49 K4
CHIN RG24 54 C5
CHIN RG24 65 M4
EWKG RG40 239 M12
FARN GU14 61 J7
HTWY RG27 46 F8
HTWY RG27 48 B1
HTWY RG27 56 D6
HTWY RG27 240 E12
HTWY RG27 241 R4
THLE RG7 38 F7
THLE RG7 39 M4

WHIT RG2 239 J4
Reading Rd North
FLEETN GU51 58 F6
Reading Road Rbt CHIN RG24 65 M4
Reading Rd South FLEETS GU52 59 H8
Reading Room La BPWT SO32 150 D4
Readon Cl EPSF GU31 120 E5
Read's Fld ALTN GU34 293 M6
Rebbeck Rd LTDN BH7 227 G3
Rebecca Cl FLEETS GU52 71 G5
The Recess ELGH SO50 134 B7
Record Rd EMRTH PO10 171 L7
Recreation Cl FARN GU14 50 B7
Recreation La THLE RG7 238 B6
Recreation Rd AND SP10 5 H4
BKME/WDN BH12 224 E2
ODIM RG29 68 E6
RAND SP11 265 M10
RFNM GU10 109 L1
Rectory Av CHAM PO6 169 M7
WIMB BH21 206 D7
Rectory Cl FHAM/STUB PO14 189 J1
GPORT PO12 14 D8
NWBY RG14 18 C7
SHST GU47 43 H8
TADY RG26 44 C6
Rectory Ct HEND SO30 149 M5
Rectory Hl RSAL SP5 297 K9
RSAL SP5 297 N3
Rectory La BPWT SO32 312 E11
FBDG SP6 331 P7
LIPH GU30 116 D1
RFNM GU10 259 M12
RSAL SP5 327 N2
RWIN SO21 290 C8
STOK SO20 284 D10
TADY RG26 254 G1
Rectory Pl RAND SP11 94 F2
Rectory Rd DEAN RG23 91 G3
FARN GU14 61 J4
HAV PO9 16 E6
HTWY RG27 56 C8
PLE BH15 223 J2
RSAL SP5 327 N2
THLE RG7 38 F5
Reculver Wy AND SP10 95 M1
Redan Cl CHCH/BSGR BH23 229 M1
Redan Gdns ASHV GU12 3 H3
Redan Hill Est ASHV GU12 * 3 K3
Redan Rd ASHV GU12 3 J3
The Redan GPORT PO12 191 J7
Red Barn Av
FHAM/PORC PO16 167 J7
Red Barn La FHAM PO15 165 L8
Redbreast Rd
MOOR/WNTN BH9 214 A5
Redbreast Rd North
MOOR/WNTN BH9 214 A5
Redbridge Cswy WSHM SO15 145 H8
Redbridge Dr AND SP10 4 E8
Redbridge Gv HAV PO9 170 D5
Redbridge Hl ROWN SO16 145 M7
Redbridge La CHIN RG24 7 M5
ROWN SO16 145 J6
Redbridge Rd WSHM SO15 145 K8
Redbrook Ter FBDG SP6 * 197 J5
Redcar Av HSEA PO3 185 G7
Redcliffe Cl CHCH/BSGR BH23 216 C6
Redcote Cl WEND SO18 148 B5
Redcotts La WIMB BH21 207 H3
Redcotts Rd WIMB BH21 207 H3
Redcrest Gdns CBLY GU15 51 H3
Redcroft La HLER SO31 163 G3
Redenham Dro RAND SP11 82 C4
Redfield Ct NWBY RG14 19 M2
Redfields La FLEETS GU52 71 G7
The Redfords TOTT SO40 144 E7
Redgauntlet EWKG RG40 42 A2
Redhearne Flds RFNM GU10 262 E10
Red Hl ALTN GU34 293 M3
HTWY RG27 240 G11
KSCL RG20 251 Q2
RAND SP11 251 L6
Redhill ROWN SO16 146 E4
Redhill Av NBNE BH10 213 L6
Redhill Cl NBNE BH10 213 L6
ROWN SO16 146 E4
Redhill Ct NBNE BH10 * 214 A4
Redhill Crs MOOR/WNTN BH9 213 M5
Red Hill Crs ROWN SO16 146 E4
Redhill Dr NBNE BH10 213 L6
Redhill Rd HAV PO9 157 H7
Red Hill Wy ROWN SO16 146 E5
Redhoave Rd CFDH BH17 211 L7
Redhorn Cl UPTN BH16 222 C4
Red House Ct EPSF GU31 317 M4
Red House La MFD/CHID GU8 263 Q1
Redhouse Park Gdns
GPORT PO12 190 E2
Redlands BKME/WDN BH12 224 F3
Redlands Dr ITCH SO19 161 M2
Redlands Gv ENEY PO4 193 J4
Redlands La EMRTH PO10 171 M4
FHAM/STUB PO14 10 D6
RFNM GU10 259 Q1
Red La BOR GU35 114 B1
OVTN RG25 105 L8
RSAL SP5 297 N5
THLE RG7 38 D7
WIMB BH21 206 A8
Red Leaves BPWT SO32 151 L2
Red Lion La BSTK RG21 6 F6
FNM GU9 12 F6
OVTN RG25 89 J4
Red Ldg CHFD SO53 139 H5
Redlynch Cl HAV PO9 * 171 H4
Redmans Vw VWD BH31 200 F2
Redmayne CBLY GU15 51 L4
Redmoor Cl ITCH SO19 161 L2
Red Oaks RFNM GU10 * 109 L1
Red Oaks Cl FERN BH22 209 H1
Red Oaks Dr FHAM PO15 164 C7
Redon Wy AND SP10 4 E2
Red Post La RAND SP11 95 G4
Red Rice Rd RAND SP11 271 L3
Redrise Cl FAWY SO45 354 D5
Redshank Cl CFDH BH17 210 F7
Redshank Ct STHA RG19 35 G1
Redshank Rd HORN PO8 156 A1
Redvers Buller Rd ALDT GU11 73 J1
Redvers Rd CHCH/BSGR BH23 228 E1
Redward Rd ROWN SO16 145 M3
Redwing Ct ENEY PO4 193 J3
Redwing Gdns TOTT SO40 144 C8
Redwing Rd HORN PO8 321 L8
KBH RG22 92 B5
Redwood Cl FAWY SO45 176 D5
HEND SO30 148 C2
LYMN SO41 221 J3
RGWD BH24 203 K5
Redwood Dr CBLY GU15 51 M4
FERN BH22 204 E8
FHAM/PORC PO16 167 H8
Redwood Gdns TOTT SO40 158 C1
Redwood Gv HAV PO9 171 G4
Redwood La ALTN GU34 279 L12
Redwood Rd UPTN BH16 210 A8
Redwoods Wy FLEETS GU52 71 K4
Redwood Wy ROWN SO16 147 G2
Reed Cl ALDT GU11 73 K2
Reed Dr TOTT SO40 159 M6
Reeder Cl FBDG SP6 197 G3
Reedmace Cl WVILLE PO7 * 170 A2
Reeds La LISS GU33 309 L6
Reed's Pl GPORT PO12 14 D2
Reeds Rd GPORT PO12 191 H1
The Reeds Rd RFNM GU10 79 H7
Reed Wk NWBY RG14 19 J1
Rees Rd RWIN SO21 288 C6
Reeves Cl ROMY SO51 335 J5
Reeves Rd ASHV GU12 3 J4
Reeves Wy HLER SO31 162 F4
Regal Cl CHAM PO6 168 F8
Regency Crs CHCH/BSGR BH23 215 M8
Regency Gdns WVILLE PO7 169 K2
Regency Pl FHAM PO15 10 A5
Regent Cl FLEETN GU51 59 J8
RWIN SO21 124 C8
Regent Ct BSTK RG21 7 G2
Regent Dr LTDN BH7 214 F8
Regent Pl SSEA PO5 20 F7
Regent Rd CHFD SO53 139 K2
Regents Ct HAV PO9 16 E7
NWBY RG14 18 D3
Regents Ga HLER SO31 163 L7
Regent's Gv WSHM SO15 * 146 B8
Regent's Park Gdns
WSHM SO15 160 B1
Regent's Park Rd
WSHM SO15 160 A1
Regents Pl SHST GU47 43 L8
Regent St FLEETN GU51 59 J8
PSEA PO1 192 C1
SHAM SO14 22 F3
Regent Wy CHCH/BSGR BH23 228 B2
FRIM GU16 51 H7
Regiment Cl FARN GU14 * 60 C5
Reginald Rd ENEY PO4 193 G5
Regis Cl WHIT RG2 238 D1
Regnum Dr NWBY RG14 27 K7
Reid St CHCH/BSGR BH23 228 A1
Reith Wy AND SP10 95 K3
Relay Rd WVILLE PO7 155 K8
Reliant Cl CHFD SO53 139 H3
CHFD SO53 139 H4
Rembrandt Cl BSTK RG21 7 K8
WWKG RG41 239 R2
Remembrance Gdns CHIN RG24 54 A6
Remembrance Rd NWBY RG14 18 A6
Rempstone Rd WIMB BH21 207 K7
Renault Dr BDST BH18 211 G7
Renda Rd FAWY SO45 354 E4
Renny Rd PSEA PO1 21 M3
Renoir Cl BSTK RG21 7 J9
Renouf Cl LYMN SO41 221 J5
Renown Cl CHFD SO53 139 H3
Renown Gdns HORN PO8 155 M3
Renown Wy CHIN RG24 54 B4
Repton Cl GPORT PO12 190 E4
Repton Gdns HEND SO30 149 K2
Reservoir La HEND SO30 149 G6
PSF GU32 120 D4
Reservoir Rd FARN GU14 60 D7
Rest-a-Wyle Av HISD PO11 195 G3
Restormel Cl DEAN RG23 64 D6
Retreat Rd WIMB BH21 207 K4
The Retreat ELGH SO50 134 B8
SSEA PO5 21 H7
TOTT SO40 159 G3
Reuben Dr PLE BH15 222 D6
Reuben's Crs TADY RG26 44 B5
Revelstoke Av FARN GU14 61 H2
Revenge Cl ENEY PO4 193 J2
Rewlands Dr FUFL SO22 288 C12
Reynards Cl TADY RG26 44 B4
Reynolds Cl BSTK RG21 7 K7
Reynolds Ct AND SP10 4 F2
Reynolds Dl TOTT SO40 158 D3
Reynolds Gn SHST GU47 49 M2
Reynolds Rd ELGH SO50 141 K3
WSHM SO15 146 C8
Reyntiens Vw ODIM RG29 69 G6
Rhine Banks FARN GU14 60 D3
Rhinefield Cl BROC SO42 351 J2
ELGH SO50 140 F2
HAV PO9 * 170 C4
Rhinefield Ornamental Dr
BROC SO42 344 D11
Rhinefield Rd BROC SO42 350 H2
NMIL/BTOS BH25 349 N10
Rhiners Cl LYMN SO41 350 F9
Rhodes Sq AND SP10 96 E1
Rhododendron Rd FRIM GU16 51 K8
Rhyme Hall Ms FAWY SO45 355 K5
Ribble Cl BDST BH18 211 G6
CHFD SO53 139 K3
Ribble Ct ROWN SO16 145 L7
Ribble Pl FARN GU14 60 E2
Ribble Wy BSTK RG21 7 J5
Ricardo Crs CHCH/BSGR BH23 229 G2
Rice Gdns UPTN BH16 222 D4
Richard Cl FLEETN GU51 71 G1
UPTN BH16 210 B8
Richard Gv GPORT PO12 183 G7
Richards Cl ASHV GU12 * 74 A3
HLER SO31 180 B1
Richborough Dr AND SP10 95 L1
Richlans Rd HEND SO30 149 J6
Richmond Av STHA RG19 35 G1
Richmond Cl BOR GU35 112 F3
CHFD SO53 133 H7
FARN GU14 60 D5
FLEETS GU52 71 H2
FRIM GU16 51 H7
HISD PO11 194 E4
TOTT SO40 144 B7
Richmond Dr HISD PO11 194 D4
Richmond Gdns BMTH BH1 8 F5
PTSW SO17 147 H7
WVILLE PO7 * 169 J3
Richmond Hl WCLF BH2 8 E5
Richmond Hill Dr WCLF BH2 8 E5
Richmond Hill Rbt WCLF BH2 8 E4
Richmond La ROMY SO51 131 G7
Richmond Pk RWIN SO21 124 D8
Richmond Park Av CHAR BH8 226 C1
Richmond Park Cl CHAR BH8 * 226 D2
Richmond Park Crs CHAR BH8 226 C1
Richmond Park Rd CHAR BH8 226 B2
Richmond Pl PSEA PO1 20 E3
SSEA PO5 21 H8
Richmond Ri
FHAM/PORC PO16 167 J7
Richmond Rd BSTK RG21 6 D2
GPORT PO12 14 C5
LSOL/BMARY PO13 189 K6
PSTN BH14 224 C4
SHST GU47 50 A1
SSEA PO5 21 J9
WIMB BH21 207 K4
WSHM SO15 160 C2
Richmond St SHAM SO14 23 H5
Richmond Ter SSEA PO5 * 21 G9
Richmond Wood Rd
CHAR BH8 226 C1
Richville Rd ROWN SO16 146 A8
Rickman Cl WHIT RG2 239 L7
Ridding Cl WSHM SO15 146 C7
Riddings La STHA RG19 248 G2
Riders La HAV PO9 170 E4
Rideway Cl CBLY GU15 50 D4
Ridge Cl HORN PO8 321 L8
KBH RG22 92 E7
Ridge Common La PSF GU32 120 A3
Ridgefield Gdns
CHCH/BSGR BH23 217 K8
Ridge La HEND SO30 164 D1
HTWY RG27 55 M7
ROMY SO51 136 B7
Ridge Moor Cl GSHT GU26 115 L3
Ridgemount Av ROWN SO16 146 F3
Ridgemount Gdns PLE BH15 222 E5
Ridges Cl RAND SP11 84 F4
The Ridge NTHA RG18 28 F4
RSAL SP5 332 F4
Ridge Top La PSF GU32 314 H2
Ridgeway BDST BH18 211 H4
FERN BH22 209 L8
FUFL SO22 122 C7
WIMB BH21 206 D8
Ridgeway Cl CHAM PO6 167 M7
CHFD SO53 139 L3
ELGH SO50 141 J1
Ridgeway La LYMN SO41 221 K6
Ridgeway Rd FNM GU9 13 H8
The Ridgeway ALTN GU34 106 F6
CHOB/PIR GU24 63 M1
FHAM/PORC PO16 166 E7
Ridgewood Cl FAWY SO45 176 C5
Ridgewood Dr FRIM GU16 51 M5
Ridgway HAV PO9 16 A5
Ridgway Hill Rd FNM GU9 13 G8
Ridgway Pde FNM GU9 * 13 H8
Ridgway Rd FNM GU9 13 G9
The Ridings BPWT SO32 143 L8
ELGH SO50 141 G2
FRIM GU16 51 K5
LISS GU33 308 H8
NEND PO2 184 F5
Riding Wy WWKG RG41 239 R2
Ridley Cl FAWY SO45 354 E4
FLEETS GU52 71 H1
Ridley Rd MOOR/WNTN BH9 213 M8
Ridleys Piece ODIM RG29 257 Q4
Ridout Cl NBNE BH10 213 H7
Rifle Wy FARN GU14 60 C5
Rigby Rd SHAM SO14 147 H8
Riggs Gdns BWD BH11 212 F6
Rigler Rd PLE BH15 223 G7
Riley La CHIN RG24 66 D1
Riley Rd RWIN SO21 288 E6
Rimbault Cl ALDT GU11 73 K1
Rimbury Wy
CHCH/BSGR BH23 216 A8
Rimes's La TADY RG26 249 R6
Rimmington Rd HORN PO8 155 L5
Ringbury LYMN SO41 221 K2
Ringlet Wy WINC SO23 25 M5
Ringsgreen La PSF GU32 307 L9
Ringshall Gdns TADY RG26 46 A5
The Ring ROWN SO16 146 E1
Ringway North CHIN RG24 65 G5
Ringway South BSTK RG21 6 D9
Ringway West KBH RG22 65 G8
Ringwood Dr NBAD SO52 137 M4
Ringwood La WIMB BH21 336 B6
Ringwood Rd
BKME/WDN BH12 212 D6
BLKW GU17 49 L2
CHCH/BSGR BH23 347 N12
ENEY PO4 193 H5
FARN GU14 61 J1
FBDG SP6 196 C8
FBDG SP6 197 J4
FERN BH22 209 H8
PSTN BH14 223 M2
TOTT SO40 158 A1
VWD BH31 201 H1
WIMB BH21 200 F8
WIMB BH21 205 J1
Ripley Gv HSEA PO3 185 G8
Ripon Cl CBLY GU15 51 M5
Ripon Ct LSOL/BMARY PO13 * 190 D3
Ripon Gdns WVILLE PO7 156 B7
Ripon Rd BLKW GU17 49 H7
MOOR/WNTN BH9 214 A8
Ripplesmore Cl SHST GU47 43 K8
Ripplewood TOTT SO40 160 A7
Ripstone Gdns PTSW SO17 147 H5
The Rise BROC SO42 351 K3
CWTH RG45 43 H3
EWKG RG40 241 N2
NTHA RG18 28 E4
THLE RG7 * 40 C3
WVILLE PO7 169 K6
Ritchie Ct ITCH SO19 148 B8
Ritchie Pl FERN BH22 204 F4
Ritchie Rd BWD BH11 213 H4
Rival Moor Rd EPSF GU31 120 F7
River Cl ALTN GU34 293 M6
WIMB BH21 207 J2
Riverdale RFNM GU10 78 C1
Riverdale Av WVILLE PO7 170 A1
Riverdale Cl FBDG SP6 197 H2
Riverdale La CHCH/BSGR BH23 228 A2
Riverdene Pl WEND SO18 147 K8
River Gdns LYMN SO41 232 E4
River Gn HLER SO31 179 G2
Riverhead NARL SO24 292 A12
Riverhead Cl ENEY PO4 193 H3
River La FHAM PO15 165 J6
FNM GU9 78 C1
Riverlea Rd CHCH/BSGR BH23 228 A2
Rivermead Cl ROMY SO51 136 D1
Rivermead Gdns
CHCH/BSGR BH23 215 L6
Rivermead Rd CBLY GU15 50 D6
Rivermede BOR GU35 111 G8
River Pde AND SP10 * 5 L1
River Pk NWBY RG14 19 H3
River Rd YTLY GU46 48 D1
River Rw FNM GU9 12 A8
Rivers Cl FARN GU14 61 L7
Riversdale Cl ITCH SO19 161 L8
Riversdale Rd SBNE BH6 228 A4
Riverside ELGH SO50 140 D1
NBNE BH10 * 213 M4
RGWD BH24 203 H6
WHCH RG28 * 87 L7
Riverside Av FHAM/PORC PO16 11 L2
LTDN BH7 215 J7
Riverside Cl CHIN RG24 66 D1
CHOB/PIR GU24 63 M1
FARN GU14 60 F3
LISS GU33 308 F8
OVTN RG25 89 K4
TOTT SO40 341 N6
Riverside Gdns ROMY SO51 136 E2
Riverside Gn STOK SO20 299 Q1
Riverside La SBNE BH6 227 M3
Riverside Ms WHAM PO17 * 152 A5
Riverside Pl FBDG SP6 197 H3
Riverside Rd FERN BH22 204 F6
SBNE BH6 227 M3
Riverside Wy CBLY GU15 50 C5
Riversmeet RFNM GU10 260 A12
Rivers Reach LYMN SO41 * 221 M5
River's St SSEA PO5 21 J4
River St EMRTH PO10 172 B2
Riverview TOTT SO40 158 F3
River View Cl STOK SO20 272 D8
River View Rd WEND SO18 147 K6
River Wk NWBY RG14 19 J1
WEND SO18 147 L5
River Wy AND SP10 5 L1
CHCH/BSGR BH23 215 K6
HAV PO9 17 G1
RL Stevenson Av WBNE BH4 225 H5
Roads Hl HORN PO8 320 H11
Road Vw NEND PO2 184 C8
Robert Cecil Av WEND SO18 147 L4
Robert Mays Rd ODIM RG29 68 E6
Roberts Cl LYMN SO41 220 E7
WHAM PO17 152 A4
WINC SO23 288 H7
Robertsfield STHA RG19 34 F1
Roberts La CFDH BH17 223 G1
Robertson Cl NWBY RG14 34 B4
Robertson Rd NARL SO24 291 L12
Robertson Wy ASHV GU12 73 M7
Roberts Rd ASHV GU12 3 L4
CBLY GU15 50 C2
CFDH BH17 211 H7
FAWY SO45 176 F4
GPORT PO12 190 F2
LISS GU33 309 J2
LTDN BH7 227 G2
RAND SP11 265 L11
RWIN SO21 273 P4
TOTT SO40 158 F3
WSHM SO15 22 B1
Robert Wy FRIM GU16 61 M5
Robert Whitworth Dr
ROMY SO51 130 F7
Robina Cl WVILLE PO7 170 A1
Robin Cl ALTN GU34 107 G2
ASHV GU12 73 M2
KBH RG22 92 C4
Robin Crs NMIL/BTOS BH25 218 D3
Robin Gdns CHCH/BSGR BH23 216 A8
HORN PO8 155 K4
TOTT SO40 144 C8
Robin Gv NMIL/BTOS BH25 218 F6
Robin Hill Dr CBLY GU15 51 J5
Robin Hood Cl FARN GU14 61 G1
Robinia Gn ROWN SO16 146 C3
Robin La SHST GU47 43 L8
Robins Cl FHAM/STUB PO14 189 J1
NWBY RG14 33 M5
Robins Grove Crs YTLY GU46 48 D2
Robins Hl HUNG RG17 30 E6
Robins Meadow
FHAM/STUB PO14 180 C3
Robinson Rd
FHAM/STUB PO14 189 H3
Robinson Wy BOR GU35 113 G2
HSEA PO3 185 J5
Robin Sq ELGH SO50 139 J7
Robins Wy CHCH/BSGR BH23 229 H3
Robinswood Dr FERN BH22 204 F8
Robin Wy AND SP10 96 D2
Rochester Cl KBH RG22 92 D4
Rochester Ct
LSOL/BMARY PO13 * 190 D3
Rochester Gv FLEETN GU51 59 H8
Rochester Rd BWD BH11 213 H4
ENEY PO4 192 F5
Rochester St SHAM SO14 23 L2
Rochford Rd BSTK RG21 6 C5
CHAM PO6 168 D8
Rockall Cl ROWN SO16 145 L3
Rockbourne Cl HAV PO9 170 C4
Rockbourne Gdns
NMIL/BTOS BH25 218 D8
Rockbourne La FBDG SP6 330 E9
Rockbourne Rd FUFL SO22 288 D12
Rockdale Dr GSHT GU26 115 K5
Rockery Cl FAWY SO45 176 C4
The Rockery FARN GU14 60 D5
Rocket Rd FARN GU14 60 D7
Rockfield Wy SHST GU47 * 43 M8
Rockford Cl SBNE BH6 227 M5
Rock Gdns ALDT GU11 2 C4
Rockingham Rd NWBY RG14 18 C5
Rockingham Wy
FHAM/PORC PO16 167 H8
Rock La RFNM GU10 78 E3
Rockleigh Dr TOTT SO40 158 D4
Rockleigh Rd ROWN SO16 146 D5
Rockley Rd PLE BH15 222 E6
Rockmoor La RAND SP11 243 R6
Rockram Cl TOTT SO40 341 M5
Rockram Gdns FAWY SO45 176 C5
Rockrose Wy CHAM PO6 168 A6
Rockstone La SHAM SO14 161 G2
Rockstone Pl WSHM SO15 160 F2
Rockville Dr WVILLE PO7 169 L1
Rodbourne Cl LYMN SO41 220 D8
Rodfield La RWIN SO21 302 H9
Rodgate La MFD/CHID GU8 119 L7
Roding Cl BSTK RG21 7 J5
Rodlease La LYMN SO41 351 Q10
Rodmel Ct FARN GU14 61 L7
Rodney Cl BKME/WDN BH12 213 G8
LSOL/BMARY PO13 190 C2
Rodney Ct AND SP10 96 F3
Rodney Dr CHCH/BSGR BH23 228 F2
Rodney Rd ENEY PO4 192 F3
Rodney Wy HORN PO8 156 B2
Rodway WIMB BH21 207 J4
Rodwell Cl NBNE BH10 213 J2
Roebuck Av FHAM PO15 165 K7
Roebuck Cl CHAM PO6 184 F1
NMIL/BTOS BH25 219 H5
Roebuts Cl NWBY RG14 18 C9
Roedeer Copse HASM GU27 117 L2
Roe Downs Rd ALTN GU34 293 K2
Roentgen Rd CHIN RG24 7 M1
Roeshot Crs CHCH/BSGR BH23 217 L7
Roewood Cl FAWY SO45 354 E5
Roewood Rd FAWY SO45 354 E5
Rogate Gdns
FHAM/PORC PO16 167 J7
Roger Penny Wy FBDG SP6 338 C1
Rogers Cl ELGH SO50 134 E8
GPORT PO12 191 H2
Rogers Ct ALTN GU34 106 F4
Rogers Md HISD PO11 186 F5
Rogers Rd ELGH SO50 134 E8
Rokeby Cl NWBY RG14 34 A5
Roke La ODIM RG29 69 J8
Rokers La MFD/CHID GU8 261 P9
Roker Wy ELGH SO50 141 H3
Rokes Pl YTLY GU46 48 C2
Roland Cl HORN PO8 156 B2
Rollesbrook Gdns WSHM SO15 160 E2
Rollestone Rd FAWY SO45 354 D5
Rolls Dr SBNE BH6 228 B4
Roman Cl CHFD SO53 139 L1
Roman Dr ROWN SO16 146 E1
Roman Gdns FAWY SO45 176 D7
Roman Gn WVILLE PO7 154 E4
Roman Gv FHAM/PORC PO16 183 K2
Roman Hts WIMB BH21 206 E8
Roman Ride CWTH RG45 42 F3
Roman Rd BDST BH18 210 E4
DEAN RG23 64 D8
FAWY SO45 176 C6
ROWN SO16 138 E7
RWIN SO21 125 G7
STOK SO20 285 M5
WHCH RG28 253 K9
Romans Fld THLE RG7 45 H4
Romans Ga THLE RG7 44 F3
Romans' Rd WINC SO23 24 F8
Roman Wy AND SP10 84 D8
DEAN RG23 64 C7
FAWY SO45 176 D7
FNM GU9 77 J4
HAV PO9 170 C6
NTHA RG18 28 C8
RWIN SO21 273 Q5
WIMB BH21 206 C4
The Romany FARN GU14 60 A7
Romayne Cl FARN GU14 61 G3
Romford Rd HLER SO31 179 K4
Romill Cl WEND SO18 148 B1
Romney Cl NBNE BH10 * 213 L5
Romney Rd FARN GU14 60 E7
NBNE BH10 213 L4
Romsey Av FHAM/PORC PO16 167 G8
HSEA PO3 193 H2
Romsey Cl ALDT GU11 260 A2
BLKW GU17 49 L2
CHIN RG24 65 J3
ELGH SO50 140 A1
Romsey Rd ELGH SO50 140 A1
FUFL SO22 24 C6
HORN PO8 321 L10
LYND SO43 345 K2
RAND SP11 272 A4
ROMY SO51 335 J4
ROWN SO16 145 K3
RSAL SP5 127 H4
STOK SO20 283 R1
STOK SO20 284 D11
STOK SO20 299 N3
TOTT SO40 335 P12
TOTT SO40 341 K4
Romyns Ct FHAM/STUB PO14 10 C6
Rookcliff Wy LYMN SO41 232 C4
Rookery Av FHAM PO15 164 C5
Rookery Gra HLER SO31 164 B5
Rookery La FBDG SP6 331 M7
STOK SO20 284 E10
The Rookery EMRTH PO10 172 A5
WHCH RG28 87 L7
Rookes Cl HORN PO8 156 B2
Rookes La LYMN SO41 221 K6
Rook Hill Rd CHCH/BSGR BH23 229 H2
Rook La RWIN SO21 275 N9
Rookley HLER SO31 162 C5
Rooksbridge FAWY SO45 176 C5
Rooksbury Cft HAV PO9 171 G3
Rooksbury Rd AND SP10 4 D8
Rooksdown Av CHIN RG24 64 E4
Rooksdown La CHIN RG24 64 E3
Rooks Down Rd FUFL SO22 122 D7
Rooksfield KSCL RG20 247 Q2
Rooksnest La HUNG RG17 31 G7
Rooksway Gv
FHAM/PORC PO16 166 F8
Rookswood ALTN GU34 106 F3
KSCL RG20 26 B6
Rookswood Cl HTWY RG27 56 D7
Rookwood Cl ELGH SO50 134 B6
Rookwood Gdns FBDG SP6 196 F3
Rookwood La ALTN GU34 292 G5
Rookwood Vw WVILLE PO7 154 F3
Roosevelt Crs BWD BH11 213 H2
Rope Hl LYMN SO41 351 P11
Ropers La UPTN BH16 222 D1
Rope Wk STHA RG19 35 J1
The Rope Wk
FHAM/PORC PO16 * 11 H8
Ropley Cl ITCH SO19 162 A4
TADY RG26 44 A5
Ropley Rd ALTN GU34 293 R11
HAV PO9 171 H3
LTDN BH7 227 J1
Rorkes Drift FRIM GU16 61 M4
Rosamund Av WIMB BH21 207 L7
Rosary Gdns YTLY GU46 * 48 F2
Roscrea Cl SBNE BH6 228 B4
Roscrea Dr SBNE BH6 228 B4
Rosebank Cl ROWN SO16 145 L3
TADY RG26 44 B4
Rosebank Ldg ROWN SO16 * 145 L3
Rosebay Cl ELGH SO50 141 J6
Rosebay Ct WVILLE PO7 169 M3
Rosebay Gdns HTWY RG27 56 E6
Roseberry Cl KBH RG22 92 D7
Rosebery Av BOSC BH5 185 G1
Rosebery Cl VWD BH31 201 L3
Rosebery Crs ELGH SO50 134 B6
Rosebery Rd BOSC BH5 227 G3
NARL SO24 291 L11
Rosebud Av MOOR/WNTN BH9 214 A6
Rosebury Av FAWY SO45 177 G7
Rose Cl FAWY SO45 177 G6
HEND SO30 149 J4
KBH RG22 92 D4
Rosecrae Cl NMIL/BTOS BH25 218 F4
Rose Crs PLE BH15 223 M2
Rosecroft Wy WHIT RG2 238 E3
Rosedale ASHV GU12 3 J3
Rosedale Av ROMY SO51 137 G1
Rosedale Cl CHCH/BSGR BH23 228 E2
FHAM/STUB PO14 180 F4
Rosedale Gdns STHA RG19 35 J2
Rosedene Gdns FLEETN GU51 59 H6
Rosedene La SHST GU47 49 M1
The Rose Est HTWY RG27 * 56 D8
Rose Gdns FARN GU14 60 D5
MOOR/WNTN BH9 214 A6
Rose Hl HORN PO8 156 A2
Rosehill Cl CHCH/BSGR BH23 * 348 D11
Rosehill Dr CHCH/BSGR BH23 348 D11
Rosehip Cl ELGH SO50 141 G3
Rosehip Wy CHIN RG24 66 B1
Rose Hodson Pl DEAN RG23 64 E5
Roselands HEND SO30 148 D4
HORN PO8 156 A3
Roselands Cl ELGH SO50 141 H1
Roselands Gdns PTSW SO17 147 G6
Roseleigh Dr TOTT SO40 158 E2
Rosemary Av ASHV GU12 62 A8
Rosemary Cl FARN GU14 60 D3
Rosemary Dr TADY RG26 44 B6
Rosemary Gdns
BKME/WDN BH12 224 B1
BLKW GU17 49 L3
FHAM PO15 164 D4
HEND SO30 149 J7
Rosemary La BLKW GU17 49 L2
PSEA PO1 20 C3
RFNM GU10 78 C4
Rosemary Price Ct
HEND SO30 * 149 J4
Rosemary Rd
BKME/WDN BH12 224 C1
Rosemary Wy HORN PO8 156 B4
Rosemoor Gdns NWBY RG14 19 K1
Rosemoor Gv CHFD SO53 133 H7
Rosemount Rd WBNE BH4 225 H6

Rosendale Rd CHFD SO53 139 K4
Rose Rd SHAM SO14 147 G8
TOTT SO40 159 G2
The Rosery GPORT PO12 191 H7
Rosetta Rd ENEY PO4 193 H4
Rose Wk FLEETN GU51 59 H6
Rosewall Rd ROWN SO16 145 M5
Rosewarne Ct WINC SO23 24 F3
Rosewood CHIN RG24 * 54 A5
LSOL/BMARY PO13 182 E7
Rosewood Gdns HORN PO8 321 L7
NMIL/BTOS BH25 218 F4
TOTT SO40 160 A7
Rosewood Rd BOR GU35 111 J7
Rosewood Ter NTID SP9 * 266 G1
Rosier Cl STHA RG19 35 M2
Rosina Cl WVILLE PO7 156 B8
Roslin Rd TWDS BH3 225 L1
Roslin Rd South TWDS BH3 225 K1
Rosoman Rd ITCH SO19 161 M4
Rossan Av HLER SO31 179 K5
Ross Cl BSTK RG21 93 J2
Ross Gdns BWD BH11 212 C5
ROWN SO16 146 A6
Rossington Av WEND SO18 161 M1
Rossington Wy WEND SO18 161 M1
Rossini Cl KBH RG22 93 G4
Rossiters Quay
CHCH/BSGR BH23 * 228 C2
Rossley Cl CHCH/BSGR BH23 217 L6
Rosslyn Cl NBAD SO52 138 A4
Ross Ms HLER SO31 * 162 A6
Rossmore Gdns ALDT GU11 2 C5
Rossmore Rd
BKME/WDN BH12 212 C8
Ross Rd RGWD BH24 203 L3
Ross Wy LSOL/BMARY PO13 189 M5
Rostron Cl WEND SO18 148 A1
Rosyth Rd WEND SO18 161 M1
Rotary Cl WIMB BH21 207 M1
Rotary Ct HLER SO31 162 B6
Rothay Ct BSTK RG21 7 J5
Rothbury Cl ITCH SO19 * 148 A8
TOTT SO40 144 D7
Rothbury Pk NMIL/BTOS BH25 219 H6
Rotherbank Farm La
LISS GU33 308 F6
Rother Cl EPSF GU31 121 G5
SHST GU47 43 L8
WEND SO18 148 B3
Rothercombe La PSF GU32 315 L4
Rother Dl ITCH SO19 162 E1
Rotherfield Rd BOSC BH5 227 H5
CHCH/BSGR BH23 218 A7
Rother Rd FARN GU14 60 E2
Rotherwick Cl HAV PO9 171 H3
Rotherwick La HTWY RG27 47 L8
Rotherwick Rd TADY RG26 44 B5
Rothesay Dr
CHCH/BSGR BH23 229 L1
Rothesay Rd GPORT PO12 191 G1
TWDS BH3 225 J2
Rothsbury Dr CHFD SO53 139 H2
Rothschild Cl ITCH SO19 161 L7
Rothville Pl CHFD SO53 133 H6
Rothwell Cl CHAM PO6 168 A7
Rotten Green Rd FLEETN GU51 59 G2
Rotten Hl OVTN RG25 88 F6
Rotterdam Dr
CHCH/BSGR BH23 228 D1
Rotunda Est ALDT GU11 3 H3
Roughdown La FAWY SO45 354 E7
Roumelia La BOSC BH5 226 E4
The Roundabouts LISS GU33 308 G7
Roundaway La RAND SP11 83 G2
Round Cl YTLY GU46 49 H3
Round End NWBY RG14 33 K7
Roundfield THLE RG7 29 K6
Roundhaye Rd BWD BH11 212 F3
Round Hl FBDG SP6 197 H3
Roundhill Cl WEND SO18 148 A3
Roundhouse Dr TOTT SO40 158 B2
Roundhouse Meadow
EMRTH PO10 172 A7
Roundhuts Ri WINC SO23 25 M5
Roundmead Rd BSTK RG21 6 C6
Roundway CBLY GU15 51 L2
WVILLE PO7 155 M8
Roundway Cl CBLY GU15 51 L2
Roundway Ct AND SP10 4 C5
Roundways BWD BH11 * 212 F5
Rounton Rd FLEETS GU52 71 J3
Routs Wy ROWN SO16 145 L1
Rowallan Av
LSOL/BMARY PO13 182 B7
Rowan Av HORN PO8 156 B6
Rowan Cha RFNM GU10 78 E3
Rowan Cl BPWT SO32 318 B8
CHCH/BSGR BH23 217 K8
FLEETN GU51 59 L7
HLER SO31 162 F4
LSOL/BMARY PO13 189 M7
LYMN SO41 350 F11
RGWD BH24 205 M4
ROMY SO51 137 J2
ROWN SO16 145 M5
RWIN SO21 288 E4
TOTT SO40 158 D2
Rowan Ct ENEY PO4 192 F4
NTID SP9 * 266 F1
Rowan Dl FLEETS GU52 71 H3
Rowan Dr CFDH BH17 210 E7
CHCH/BSGR BH23 217 K8
CWTH RG45 43 L1
NWBY RG14 27 J7
VWD BH31 201 K4
Rowan Gdns HEND SO30 149 K6
Rowan Rd HAV PO9 171 H5
TADY RG26 44 C5
Rowans Cl FARN GU14 50 A7
Rowanside Cl BOR GU35 114 C4
Rowans Pk LYMN SO41 221 K5
The Rowans GSHT GU26 115 K6
TOTT SO40 159 M7
Rowan Wy FHAM/STUB PO14 181 J4
Rowbarrow Cl CFDH BH17 211 L6
Rowborough Rd WEND SO18 147 M8
Rowbury Rd HAV PO9 170 D2
Rowcroft Cl ASHV GU12 74 A2
Rowcroft Rd WHIT RG2 239 M9
Rowdell Cots NARL SO24 292 G11
Rowden Cl ROMY SO51 335 J6
Rowe Ashe Wy HLER SO31 179 M1
Rowena Rd SBNE BH6 227 M3
Rowes La LYMN SO41 356 H5
Rowhay La BPWT SO32 310 C11
Rowhill Av ALDT GU11 2 C6
Rowhill Crs ALDT GU11 2 C7
Rowhill Dr FAWY SO45 176 C5
Rowhills FNM GU9 2 A7
Rowhills Cl FNM GU9 2 C7
Rowin Cl HISD PO11 195 K6
Rowland Av PLE BH15 223 L3
Rowland Rd CHAM PO6 167 L7
FHAM PO15 10 C4
Rowlands Av WVILLE PO7 155 L7
Rowlands Castle Rd
HORN PO8 156 F2
Rowlands Cl CHFD SO53 139 G4
THLE RG7 39 J7
Rowlands Hl WIMB BH21 207 J3
Rowlands Wk WEND SO18 148 A2
Rowlett Rd LYMN SO41 221 L5
Rowley Cl HEND SO30 149 M4
Rowley Dr HEND SO30 149 M4
Rowlings Rd FUFL SO22 122 D1
Rowner Cl LSOL/BMARY PO13 182 C7
Rowner La LSOL/BMARY PO13 182 C8
Rowner Rd LSOL/BMARY PO13 182 B7
Rownhams Cl ROWN SO16 145 L2
Rownhams La NBAD SO52 137 M3
ROWN SO16 145 M1
Rownhams Pk ROWN SO16 * 137 L8
Rownhams Rd CHAR BH8 214 C5
HAV PO9 170 D3
NBAD SO52 138 A5
ROWN SO16 145 M6
Rownhams Rd North
ROWN SO16 145 M3
Rownhams Wy ROWN SO16 145 L2
Rowse Cl ROMY SO51 130 F7
The Row RSAL SP5 332 G1
Row Wood La
LSOL/BMARY PO13 182 B7
Roxbee Cox Rd FARN GU14 60 A7
Roxburgh Cl CBLY GU15 51 L4
Roxburghe Cl BOR GU35 112 F2
Royal Albert Wk ENEY PO4 * 21 M8
Royal Clarence Yd
GPORT PO12 * 15 J1
Royal Cl DEAN RG23 92 C7
Royal Crescent Rd SHAM SO14 23 K5
The Royal Crs NTID SP9 266 G1
Royale Cl ALDT GU11 3 K7
Royal Gdns HAV PO9 157 G7
Royal Ga ENEY PO4 193 H6
Royal Oak Cl YTLY GU46 49 G2
Royal Oak Rd NBNE BH10 213 J3
Royal Sovereign Av
FHAM/STUB PO14 181 M7
Royal Wy WVILLE PO7 170 A1
Royce Cl AND SP10 95 K3
Royden La LYMN SO41 351 P9
Roydon Cl FUFL SO22 122 D7
Roy's La BPWT SO32 319 J10
Royster Cl CFDH BH17 211 J7
Royston Av ELGH SO50 134 A7
Royston Cl PTSW SO17 147 H6
Royston Dr WIMB BH21 207 K3
Royston Pl NMIL/BTOS BH25 219 H8
Rozelle Cl FUFL SO22 288 A11
Rozelle Rd PSTN BH14 224 C4
Rubens Cl BSTK RG21 93 M2
NMIL/BTOS BH25 219 G4
Ruby Rd ITCH SO19 148 A6
Rudd Hall Ri CBLY GU15 50 F5
Rudd La ROMY SO51 130 E1
Rudgwick Cl
FHAM/PORC PO16 167 H8
Rudland Cl STHA RG19 35 K2
Rudmore Sq NEND PO2 184 C8
Ruffield Cl FUFL SO22 122 C2
Rufford Cl ELGH SO50 134 A6
FLEETS GU52 71 J2
Rufford Gdns SBNE BH6 227 L3
Rufus Cl CHFD SO53 133 L8
ROWN SO16 145 K2
Rufus Gdns TOTT SO40 158 C1
Rugby Rd CFDH BH17 211 G7
SSEA PO5 21 L4
Rumbridge Gdns TOTT SO40 159 G1
Rumbridge St TOTT SO40 158 F2
Rune Dr AND SP10 84 B8
Runnymede FHAM PO15 165 K8
HEND SO30 148 D3
Runnymede Av BWD BH11 212 D2
Runnymede Ct HEND SO30 148 C3
Runton Rd BKME/WDN BH12 224 F3
The Runway
CHCH/BSGR BH23 229 H1
Runwick La RFNM GU10 76 B7
Rupert Rd NWBY RG14 33 M4
Rushall Cl EARL RG6 238 E1
Rushall La WIMB BH21 210 A4
Rushcombe Wy WIMB BH21 210 E2
Rushden Wy FNM GU9 77 H1
Rushes Farm PSF GU32 120 C5
Rushes Rd PSF GU32 120 C5
The Rushes BSTK RG21 7 K5
TOTT SO40 159 M6
Rushfield Rd LISS GU33 308 F9
Rushford Warren
CHCH/BSGR BH23 228 F4
Rushington Av TOTT SO40 158 F2
Rushington La TOTT SO40 158 E3
Rushmere La WVILLE PO7 154 D1
Rushmere Rd SBNE BH6 227 J1
Rushmoor Cl FLEETS GU52 71 J1
Rushmoor Rd ALDT GU11 72 E5
Rushton Crs TWDS BH3 225 M2
Ruskin Av MOOR/WNTN BH9 214 B5
Ruskin Cl BSTK RG21 7 L8
Ruskin Ct CWTH RG45 * 43 H4
Ruskin Rd ELGH SO50 134 A8
ENEY PO4 193 G4
Ruskin Wy HORN PO8 155 M4
WWKG RG41 239 R2
Rusland Cl CHFD SO53 139 H1
Russell Cl LSOL/BMARY PO13 189 M6
Russell Cotes Rd BMTH BH1 9 G7
Russell Ct BLKW GU17 49 M3
Russell Dr CHCH/BSGR BH23 228 D2
ROMY SO51 298 F12
Russell Gdns RGWD BH24 202 D7
UPTN BH16 222 C4
Russell Pl FHAM/PORC PO16 10 F5
PTSW SO17 147 H7
Russell Rd BSTK RG21 7 G9
HAV PO9 16 F1
LSOL/BMARY PO13 189 M7
NWBY RG14 18 B5
WINC SO23 25 H1
Russell St GPORT PO12 14 D1
SHAM SO14 23 H5
Russell Wy EPSF GU31 120 E7
Russel Rd NBNE BH10 213 J2
Russet Cl FERN BH22 209 K2
LYMN SO41 * 221 M5
NARL SO24 291 L12
RFNM GU10 260 C1
Russet Gdns CBLY GU15 50 F5
EMRTH PO10 172 B6
Russet Gld ALDT GU11 2 A5
FNM GU9 72 D8
Russett Cl BPWT SO32 318 B8
Russett Rd ALTN GU34 107 G5
Russetts Dr FLEETN GU51 59 J8
Rustan Cl ELGH SO50 141 K2
HEND SO30 * 149 H6
Rustic Gln FLEETS GU52 71 H3
Ruth Cl FARN GU14 60 C3
Rutherford Rd CHIN RG24 65 M4
Rutland Cl ALDT GU11 2 F1
Rutland Gdns HLER SO31 163 G3
Rutland Rd CHCH/BSGR BH23 215 M7
MOOR/WNTN BH9 214 B8
Rutland Wy WEND SO18 148 A3
Ruxley Cl FAWY SO45 354 E4
Ryall Dr CFDH BH17 211 K7
Ryan Cl FERN BH22 209 J1
Ryan Gdns FERN BH22 209 J1
Ryan Mt SHST GU47 43 J8
Rycroft Meadow DEAN RG23 92 C8
Rydal Cl BOR GU35 110 F7
CBLY GU15 51 M3
CHAM PO6 168 B7
CHCH/BSGR BH23 215 K4
FARN GU14 60 D5
KBH RG22 92 C2
Rydal Dr FLEETS GU52 71 G3
STHA RG19 28 C8
Rydal Rd GPORT PO12 183 G8
Ryde Pl LSOL/BMARY PO13 190 A4
Ryde Ter SHAM SO14 23 K5
Ryebeck Rd FLEETS GU52 71 J3
Rye Cl CHFD SO53 138 F2
FARN GU14 60 E2
FLEETN GU51 59 L3
Rye Cft FLEETS GU52 71 G4
Ryecroft FHAM/STUB PO14 180 C2
HAV PO9 17 K4
Ryecroft Av BWD BH11 212 E3
Ryecroft Gdns BLKW GU17 50 A4
Rye Dl TOTT SO40 158 C5
Ryedown La ROMY SO51 335 N4
Ryefield Cl EPSF GU31 121 G6
Ryeish La THLE RG7 238 C5
Ryeland Cl FLEETN GU51 * 59 L3
Ryelaw Rd FLEETS GU52 71 J3
Rye Paddock La FAWY SO45 178 B8
Rylandes Ct ROWN SO16 145 M5
Ryle Rd FNM GU9 12 F7
Ryon Cl AND SP10 84 C8
Ryves Av YTLY GU46 48 C3

S

Sabre Ct ALDT GU11 2 B3
Sackville St SSEA PO5 21 G5
Saddleback Wy FLEETN GU51 59 K4
Saddle Cl WIMB BH21 208 C2
Saddler Cnr SHST GU47 49 K1
Saddlers Cl ELGH SO50 134 A6
RWIN SO21 274 C8
Saddlers Scarp GSHT GU26 115 G4
Saddlewood CBLY GU15 50 E4
Sadlers End WWKG RG41 239 P1
Sadlers La FAWY SO45 177 G7
Sadlers Wk EMRTH PO10 172 A6
Saffron Cl CHIN RG24 54 B4
NWBY RG14 18 D3
Saffron Dr CHCH/BSGR BH23 217 H8
Saffron Wy BWD BH11 212 D5
FHAM PO15 164 D4
Sage Cl WVILLE PO7 170 A2
Sagecroft Rd NTHA RG18 28 E7
Sages La ALTN GU34 306 A7
Sailor's La BPWT SO32 311 Q9
MFD/CHID GU8 263 M10
Sainfoin La DEAN RG23 91 K4
Sainsbury Cl AND SP10 4 E8
St Agatha's Rd HLER SO31 163 G8
St Alban's Av CHAR BH8 226 C1
St Albans Ct
LSOL/BMARY PO13 * 190 D3
St Alban's Crs CHAR BH8 226 B1
St Alban's Rd CHAR BH8 226 B1
ENEY PO4 192 F5
HAV PO9 171 G4
SHAM SO14 23 K1
St Aldhelm's Cl CCLF BH13 224 F5
St Aldhelm's Rd CCLF BH13 224 F4
St Alphege Gdns AND SP10 96 B2
St Andrew Cl HORN PO8 321 L10
St Andrews Cl CWTH RG45 43 H2
NBAD SO52 137 L3
ROMY SO51 130 D2
St Andrews Pk ELGH SO50 141 J6
St Andrews Rd BDST BH18 211 G3
BOR GU35 112 D2
CHAM PO6 169 M8
GPORT PO12 14 F5
HISD PO11 195 H6
KBH RG22 92 F1
NTID SP9 266 E2
SHAM SO14 23 H1
SSEA PO5 21 J6
St Andrew's Wy FRIM GU16 61 M1
St Anne's Av SBNE BH6 227 L3
St Annes Cl FUFL SO22 122 C7
RAND SP11 271 P4
St Anne's Gdns ITCH SO19 161 L6
LYMN SO41 221 K5
St Anne's Gv
FHAM/STUB PO14 181 M5
St Annes La BPWT SO32 151 K5
St Anne's Rd ITCH SO19 161 L6
UPTN BH16 222 B1
St Ann's Cl AND SP10 4 F7
St Ann's Crs GPORT PO12 14 C1
St Ann's Rd HORN PO8 156 C1
St Anthony's Rd WCLF BH2 8 E2
St Aubin's Av ITCH SO19 148 A7
St Aubins Cl ALTN GU34 293 M6
St Aubin's Pk HISD PO11 194 D5
St Aubyns Ct PLE BH15 * 223 H6
St Aubyns La RGWD BH24 342 A7
St Augustine Gdns PTSW SO17 147 K7
St Augustine Rd ENEY PO4 192 F5
St Augustine's Cl ASHV GU12 3 M4
St Augustin's Rd WCLF BH2 8 E1
St Austell Cl ELGH SO50 140 E1
St Austins GSHT GU26 * 115 K5
St Barbara's Cl TADY RG26 46 D6
St Barbara Wy NEND PO2 184 F4
St Barbe Cl ROMY SO51 137 G2
St Bartholomew Gdns
SSEA PO5 21 K6
St Benedict's Cl ALDT GU11 2 E5
St Birinus Gdns AND SP10 96 B1
St Birstan Gdns AND SP10 96 B2
St Blaize Rd ROMY SO51 131 J8
St Bonnet Dr BPWT SO32 143 J4
St Brelades Av
BKME/WDN BH12 212 D7
St Catherines WIMB BH21 207 J4
St Catherine's Hl THLE RG7 39 L7
St Catherine's Rd ELGH SO50 134 A7
FRIM GU16 51 J7
HISD PO11 194 C5
SBNE BH6 227 L5
WEND SO18 147 L7
WINC SO23 25 K8
St Catherines's Wy
CHCH/BSGR BH23 215 K5
St Catherine St SSEA PO5 192 D7
St Catherines Vw
HEND SO30 * 149 G6
St Catherines Wy
FHAM/PORC PO16 166 E7
St Chad's Av NEND PO2 184 E6
St Christopher Av
FHAM/PORC PO16 11 H2
St Christophers Cl ASHV GU12 3 L2
HASM GU27 * 118 A6
KBH RG22 92 E1
NBAD SO52 137 M4
St Christophers Pl FARN GU14 60 F5
St Christopher's Rd FARN GU14 61 G5
HASM GU27 118 A6
HAV PO9 170 C5
St Clair Rd CCLF BH13 237 K2
St Clares Av HAV PO9 170 D1
St Cleeve Wy FERN BH22 209 J5
St Clements Cl ROMY SO51 130 E8
St Clements Gdns BMTH BH1 226 D3
St Clement's Rd BMTH BH1 226 D3
PLE BH15 224 B1
St Clement St WINC SO23 24 F6
St Colman's Av CHAM PO6 169 G8
St Cross Rd FNM GU9 13 G2
FRIM GU16 62 A1
RFNM GU10 259 P3
WINC SO23 124 E1
St Cuthberts Cl HLER SO31 164 B8
St Cuthberts La HLER SO31 164 B8
St David's Cl FARN GU14 50 B8
FNM GU9 2 B9
ODIM RG29 68 E6
TOTT SO40 144 C7
St Davids Ct
LSOL/BMARY PO13 * 190 C2
St Davids Rd HLER SO31 179 M1
HORN PO8 321 L7
KBH RG22 93 G1
NWBY RG14 18 D5
SSEA PO5 21 K5
UPTN BH16 222 B1
St Denys' Rd PTSW SO17 147 J7
St Donats Pl NWBY RG14 18 F6
St Edmondsbury Ct
LSOL/BMARY PO13 * 190 D3
St Edmund Cl
FHAM/STUB PO14 180 B3
St Edmund's Rd ROWN SO16 146 B8
St Edward's Rd GPORT PO12 14 F5
HLER SO31 162 B5
SSEA PO5 21 G7
St Elizabeth Cl WHIT RG2 238 B1
St Elizabeth's Av WEND SO18 148 B5
St Evox Cl ROWN SO16 145 M3
St Faith's Cl GPORT PO12 14 C3
St Faiths Rd PSEA PO1 21 H1
WINC SO23 122 F7
St Francis Av WEND SO18 148 B4
St Francis Cl FAWY SO45 354 G9
St Francis Ct NEND PO2 * 184 E4
St Francis Pl HAV PO9 170 E5
St Francis Rd FAWY SO45 354 G9
GPORT PO12 191 J7
St Gabriels Lea CHIN RG24 54 C5
St Gabriel's Rd WEND SO18 148 B5
St George Cl HLER SO31 162 F3
St Georges PLE BH15 * 223 H7
St George's Av
BKME/WDN BH12 212 B8
CHAR BH8 214 C8
HAV PO9 17 K4
NWBY RG14 18 C6
St George's Cl CHAR BH8 214 C8
CHCH/BSGR BH23 217 K8
FNM GU9 * 77 M2
St Georges Ct
FHAM/PORC PO16 11 G8
St Georges Crs FBDG SP6 197 H2
St Georges Dr BWD BH11 212 D5
CHCH/BSGR BH23 348 E12
FERN BH22 209 J4
St Georges Ms FNM GU9 12 F2
St George's Rd ASHV GU12 3 G5
CBLY GU15 50 F2
CHAM PO6 168 F8
ENEY PO4 193 G6
FBDG SP6 197 H2
FNM GU9 13 J5
HISD PO11 194 D5
HLER SO31 179 M1
NTID SP9 266 E2
PSEA PO1 20 D4
RFNM GU10 77 M4
St George's Rd East ASHV GU12 3 H4
St Georges Sq PSEA PO1 * 20 D3
St Georges St SHAM SO14 23 H4
WINC SO23 25 H6
St Georges Wk GPORT PO12 15 J3
St George's Wk WVILLE PO7 169 L1
St George's Wy PSEA PO1 20 D3
St Georges Yd FNM GU9 12 F3
St Giles Cl WINC SO23 25 K7
St Giles Hl WINC SO23 25 K6
St Giles Wy HORN PO8 321 L10
St Helena Gdns WEND SO18 147 M5
St Helena Wy
FHAM/PORC PO16 167 K8
St Helen's Cl ENEY PO4 192 F6
St Helens Crs SHST GU47 43 K8
St Helens Pde ENEY PO4 192 E7
St Helens Rd GPORT PO12 190 E5
HISD PO11 194 D5
St Helier Rd BKME/WDN BH12 212 D7
St Hellen's Rd CHAM PO6 169 K8
St Hermans Rd HISD PO11 195 J6
St Hilda Av HORN PO8 321 L10
St Hubert Rd AND SP10 4 D6
HORN PO8 321 L10
St Ives End La RGWD BH24 202 C7
St Ives Gdns WCLF BH2 8 F2
St Ives Pk RGWD BH24 202 C7
St Ives Wd RGWD BH24 202 D7
St James' Av FNM GU9 77 H4
St James Cl HORN PO8 321 L8
PLE BH15 223 H7
TADY RG26 46 D7
St James' La FUFL SO22 24 D6
St James Pk CHFD SO53 * 133 G8
St James' Rd EMRTH PO10 171 M7
FLEETN GU51 59 H8
HEND SO30 148 D2
LYMN SO41 350 G10
WIMB BH21 209 G2
St James's Cl WSHM SO15 146 C7
St James's Park Rd
ROWN SO16 146 C6
St James's Rd SSEA PO5 21 G5
WSHM SO15 146 C7
St James's Sq BOSC BH5 227 G3
St James's St PSEA PO1 20 E2
St James St RAND SP11 265 L10
St James' Ter FNM GU9 13 H1
FUFL SO22 24 E6
St James' Vls WINC SO23 24 E7
St James Wy
FHAM/PORC PO16 167 K8
St John Cl TADY RG26 46 C6
St John's Av WVILLE PO7 169 L5
St John's Cl GPORT PO12 14 E2
HISD PO11 194 E5
HTWY RG27 56 D7
ROWN SO16 145 L1
WIMB BH21 207 K4
St Johns Ct FARN GU14 * 60 D3
TOTT SO40 159 M7
St Johns Dr TOTT SO40 159 L7
St John's Gdns
MOOR/WNTN BH9 213 M7
ROMY SO51 130 F8
St Johns Glebe ROWN SO16 145 M2
St Johns Gv FNM GU9 12 F8
St John's Hl WIMB BH21 207 K3
St Johns North WINC SO23 25 J6
St John's Piece DEAN RG23 91 K4
St John's Rd AND SP10 5 J4
BOSC BH5 226 E5
CHAM PO6 169 G8
CHCH/BSGR BH23 228 A2
DEAN RG23 91 K2
ELGH SO50 134 B8
EMRTH PO10 172 C5
FARN GU14 60 E4
FNM GU9 12 F8
HAV PO9 170 C4
HEND SO30 149 G8
HLER SO31 180 B2
HTWY RG27 57 M3
NMIL/BTOS BH25 219 G1
NWBY RG14 18 E7
PLE BH15 223 K4
SHST GU47 49 K1
STHA RG19 35 J1
THLE RG7 40 A3
WINC SO23 25 K5
St Johns South WINC SO23 25 J6
St Johns Sq GPORT PO12 14 F2
St John's St FAWY SO45 177 G4
WINC SO23 25 J6
St Joseph's Crs CHIN RG24 54 B6
St Josephs Ms SSEA PO5 * 21 H6
St Joseph's Rd ALDT GU11 2 F5
ASHV GU12 3 G5
St Just Cl AMSY SP4 268 B7
FERN BH22 209 H5
St Lawrence Rd ALTN GU34 106 F4
ELGH SO50 134 A8
SHAM SO14 23 J6
St Ledger's Pl CHAR BH8 * 226 D2
St Ledger's Rd CHAR BH8 226 D1
St Leger Ct NWBY RG14 18 B1
St Leonards RAND SP11 269 P3
St Leonard's Av CHIN RG24 54 C5
HISD PO11 195 G5
St Leonards Cl FHAM PO15 180 E1
St Leonard's Rd CHAR BH8 226 B2
LYMN SO41 356 H5
WINC SO23 25 L8
St Leonards Wy RGWD BH24 205 M3
St Lukes Cl HEND SO30 149 J3
KBH RG22 92 E2
St Luke's Rd GPORT PO12 191 G2
TWDS BH3 225 M1
St Margaret's Av
CHCH/BSGR BH23 228 A2
St Margaret's Cl WEND SO18 148 B5
WIMB BH21 207 G3
St Margaret's Hl WIMB BH21 207 G2
St Margarets La
FHAM/STUB PO14 180 E3
St Magarets Rd ELGH SO50 134 D8
HISD PO11 195 G5
NBNE BH10 213 H6
PLE BH15 223 J4
St Marks Cl CHFD SO53 * 133 M7
FARN GU14 61 J7
GPORT PO12 191 G7
STHA RG19 35 J1
TADY RG26 46 C6
St Marks Pl FNM GU9 * 76 F1
St Mark's Rd BWD BH11 213 H5
GPORT PO12 191 G7
LYMN SO41 221 H5
NEND PO2 184 D7
St Martin's Cl ROWN SO16 145 L5
WINC SO23 25 K5
St Martins Rd UPTN BH16 222 A1
St Mary Gv LYMN SO41 220 A6
St Marys ROMY SO51 * 136 E2
St Mary's Av GPORT PO12 14 D8
TADY RG26 46 D6
St Marys Cl ALTN GU34 106 F6
CHCH/BSGR BH23 348 D12
RSAL SP5 332 H3
SHST GU47 43 L8
WINC SO23 289 J11
St Mary's Ct BSTK RG21 7 G5
TADY RG26 46 D6
St Mary's Meadow RAND SP11 95 J8
St Marys Paddock
NTHA RG18 * 28 E3
St Mary's Pl NWBY RG14 18 F2
SHAM SO14 23 H4
St Mary's Rd ASHV GU12 74 A3
BMTH BH1 226 D2
CBLY GU15 50 E2
ELGH SO50 134 D8
FERN BH22 209 J3
FHAM/STUB PO14 181 J8
HISD PO11 194 F5
HLER SO31 162 C6
HTWY RG27 57 L3
KSCL RG20 248 D10
LISS GU33 308 F8
NWBY RG14 18 F2
PLE BH15 223 L4
PSEA PO1 192 F2
SHAM SO14 23 H1
THLE RG7 40 A2
St Mary's Ter RWIN SO21 125 G6
St Mary St FUFL SO22 122 D7
SHAM SO14 23 J4
St Matthews Cl SHAM SO14 23 H1
St Matthews Ct GPORT PO12 15 K3
St Matthew's Rd CHAM PO6 168 F8
FUFL SO22 122 D2
St Merrin's Cl NBNE BH10 213 J4
St Michaels Av NTID SP9 266 E3
St Michaels Cl FAWY SO45 354 G7
FLEETN GU51 59 L8
OVTN RG25 103 G3
PLE BH15 222 E5
VWD BH31 201 H3
St Michaels Ct CHAM PO6 168 B7
St Michael's Gdns WINC SO23 24 F7
St Michael's Gv
FHAM/STUB PO14 10 D9
St Michael's Rd ASHV GU12 3 G5
CBLY GU15 * 50 D3
FARN GU14 61 H2
HAV PO9 170 C5
HLER SO31 179 M2
KBH RG22 92 E1
NWBY RG14 18 C6
PSEA PO1 20 F4
SHST GU47 43 H8
TOTT SO40 144 F7
VWD BH31 201 H4
WCLF BH2 8 C6
WINC SO23 24 F8
St Michaels Sq SHAM SO14 22 F5
St Michael's St SHAM SO14 22 F5
St Michaels Wy HORN PO8 321 L10
St Monica Rd ITCH SO19 162 A1
St Neot's Rd HTWY RG27 241 M5
St Nicholas WINC SO23 288 H10

St Nicholas Av
LSOL/BMARY PO13 190 C1
St Nicholas Cl FLEETN GU51 59 H7
RAND SP11 265 P10
St Nicholas Ct KBH RG22 64 F8
St Nicholas' Rd HAV PO9 170 C5
NWBY RG14 18 D5
St Nicholas St PSEA PO1 20 D6
St Omer Barracks ALDT GU11 73 K3
St Osmund's Rd PSTN BH14 224 C5
St Patricks Av NTID SP9 266 D3
St Patrick's La LISS GU33 309 J7
St Patrick's Rd KBH RG22 93 G1
St Pauls Cl RFNM GU10 260 D1
St Paul's Hl FUFL SO22 24 E4
St Paul's La BMTH BH1 9 J4
St Paul's Pl BMTH BH1 9 J4
St Pauls Rd BMTH BH1 9 J3
HLER SO31 163 L6
KBH RG22 93 G1
SSEA PO5 20 F4
St Pauls Rbt BMTH BH1 9 H3
St Paul's Sq SSEA PO5 * 20 F5
St Peter's Av HISD PO11 187 J6
St Peters Cl NTID SP9 266 E9
RAND SP11 271 R2
St Peter's Gdns RFNM GU10 78 D2
YTLY GU46 48 F2
St Peters Gv SSEA PO5 21 J6
St Peters Md ASHV GU12 74 B6
St Peters Pk ALDT GU11 2 A5
St Peter's Rd BMTH BH1 8 F5
HISD PO11 187 J6
KBH RG22 92 E1
PSF GU32 120 D6
PSTN BH14 224 A4
St Peters Rbt BMTH BH1 9 G6
St Peter's Sq EMRTH PO10 171 M8
St Peter's St BPWT SO32 143 J4
St Peter St WINC SO23 25 G5
St Peter's Wy FRIM GU16 61 M1
St Philip's Wy WEND SO18 148 B5
St Pirans Av HSEA PO3 193 G1
St Richards Gdns
WVILLE PO7 * 169 J3
St Richards Rd NWBY RG14 27 K7
St Ronans Av ENEY PO4 21 M8
St Ronan's Rd ENEY PO4 21 M8
St Sebastian Crs
FHAM/PORC PO16 11 H1
St Simon Cl HLER SO31 180 B1
St Simons Rd SSEA PO5 21 K9
St Stephens Cl HASM GU27 118 C5
St Stephens La VWD BH31 201 J2
St Stephen's Rd FUFL SO22 24 B1
NEND PO2 184 E8
WCLF BH2 8 C4
St Stephen's Wy WCLF BH2 8 E5
St Swithin Wy AND SP10 96 B2
St Swithun Cl BPWT SO32 143 H4
St Swithun's Cl ROMY SO51 131 K7
St Swithun's Rd BMTH BH1 9 K3
NEND PO2 184 F6
St Swithun's Rd South
BMTH BH1 9 K4
St Swithuns Ter WINC SO23 * 25 G7
St Swithun St WINC SO23 24 F7
St Theresas Cl HAV PO9 170 C5
St Thomas Av HISD PO11 194 D5
St Thomas Cl AND SP10 96 A1
BSTK RG21 6 D1
FHAM/PORC PO16 11 J2
St Thomas Pk LYMN SO41 221 K4
St Thomas's Cl NBNE BH10 213 K6
St Thomas's Ct PSEA PO1 20 D5
St Thomas's Rd GPORT PO12 183 H8
St Thomas's St LYMN SO41 221 K5
PSEA PO1 20 C6
St Thomas St WINC SO23 24 F7
St Tristan Cl HLER SO31 180 B1
St Ursula Gv SSEA PO5 21 J6
St Valerie Rd GPORT PO12 14 F7
WCLF BH2 8 E2
St Vigor Wy RWIN SO21 134 F3
St Vincent Crs HORN PO8 156 B2
St Vincent Rd GPORT PO12 191 H2
SSEA PO5 21 J8
St Vincent St SSEA PO5 * 20 F4
St Winifred's Rd ROWN SO16 146 C6
WCLF BH2 8 E2
Salamanca CWTH RG45 43 G3
Salcombe Av HSEA PO3 185 G7
Salcombe Cl CHFD SO53 139 H4
Salcombe Crs TOTT SO40 158 E2
Salcombe Rd NWBY RG14 18 A7
TOTT SO40 158 E2
WSHM SO15 160 C1
Salcot Rd WINC SO23 25 G1
Salem St WSHM SO15 146 C7
Salerno Cl ALDT GU11 2 F2
Salerno Dr GPORT PO12 14 B4
Salerno Pl PLE BH15 222 D6
Salerno Rd NEND PO2 184 D4
ROWN SO16 146 C4
Salesian Vw FARN GU14 61 L8
Salet Wy WVILLE PO7 156 B7
Salford Cl WHIT RG2 238 C1
Salisbury Cl ALTN GU34 107 G6
ELGH SO50 134 B8
ODIM RG29 68 E6
Salisbury Gdns KBH RG22 64 E8
Salisbury Gv FRIM GU16 62 A5
Salisbury La STOK SO20 269 Q12
Salisbury Rd AND SP10 4 C8
ASHV GU12 74 A6
BLKW GU17 49 L3
BMTH BH1 226 E4
CHAM PO6 185 G1
CHCH/BSGR BH23 216 B2
ENEY PO4 192 F6
FARN GU14 61 J4
FBDG SP6 197 J2
FBDG SP6 331 Q6
NARL SO24 291 L11
NTID SP9 266 E11
PSTN BH14 224 C3
PTSW SO17 147 G5
RAND SP11 95 L7
RAND SP11 269 L6
RAND SP11 270 F6
RAND SP11 271 J3
RGWD BH24 199 J3
RGWD BH24 203 H4
ROMY SO51 129 H6
ROMY SO51 334 G5
ROMY SO51 335 N8
RSAL SP5 325 M2
RSAL SP5 327 J11
STOK SO20 284 B6
TOTT SO40 144 E6
Salisbury Road Ar TOTT SO40 * 158 F1
Salisbury St FBDG SP6 197 H3
WIMB BH21 336 E4
Salisbury Ter FRIM GU16 62 A5
LSOL/BMARY PO13 189 M7
Salmon Cl THLE RG7 238 B6
Salmon Dr ELGH SO50 140 F2
Salmond Rd RAND SP11 95 K4
WHIT RG2 238 C2
Salmons Rd ODIM RG29 68 E6
Salterns Av ENEY PO4 193 H3
Salterns Cl HISD PO11 195 J5
Salterns Est FHAM/PORC PO16 11 H9
Salterns La FAWY SO45 178 B8
FHAM/PORC PO16 182 B1
HISD PO11 195 H5
HLER SO31 163 G6
Salterns Rd FHAM/STUB PO14 189 H4
PSTN BH14 224 A5
Salterns Wy PSTN BH14 224 B8
Salter Rd CCLF BH13 237 G5
Salters Acres FUFL SO22 122 C2
Salters Heath Rd TADY RG26 52 D6
Salters La FUFL SO22 122 B2
Saltgrass La LYMN SO41 233 G5
Saltings Rd UPTN BH16 222 B2
The Saltings CHAM PO6 185 L1
HAV PO9 186 F2
Salt La BPWT SO32 311 L5
Saltmarsh La HISD PO11 194 E3
Saltmarsh Rd SHAM SO14 23 K6
Saltmead PTSW SO17 147 K7
Salt Meat La GPORT PO12 15 J1
Saltram Rd FARN GU14 61 L6
Salvia Cl WVILLE PO7 170 A2
Salwey Rd HEND SO30 149 K7
Samarkand Cl CBLY GU15 51 K4
Samber Cl LYMN SO41 221 J4
Sampage Cl WHIT RG2 238 C2
Sampan Cl HLER SO31 179 L3
Samples Wy CFDH BH17 211 M8
Sampson Rd
FHAM/STUB PO14 181 M6
PSEA PO1 20 B1
Samson Cl LSOL/BMARY PO13 190 D1
Samson Rd PLE BH15 222 D5
Samuel Rd PSEA PO1 192 F2
Sam Whites Hl RAND SP11 96 A8
San Carlos Ap ALDT GU11 3 K2
Sancreed Rd
BKME/WDN BH12 224 E1
Sanctuary Pl HTWY RG27 57 M1
Sandbanks Dr KBH RG22 92 D5
Sandbanks Rd PLE BH15 223 M5
PSTN BH14 224 A5
Sandbourne Rd CCLF BH13 225 H7
PLE BH15 223 K4
Sandcroft Cl GPORT PO12 190 E5
Sandecotes Rd PSTN BH14 224 C5
Sanderling Rd ENEY PO4 193 J3
Sanderlings RGWD BH24 203 L6
The Sanderlings HISD PO11 195 G6
Sandford Av GPORT PO12 190 D4
Sandford Cl KSCL RG20 248 F10
MOOR/WNTN BH9 214 C5
Sandford Ct ALDT GU11 2 B4
Sandford Rd ALDT GU11 2 D3
FNM GU9 76 F1
TADY RG26 44 A4
Sandford Wy BDST BH18 210 F5
Sandheath Rd GSHT GU26 115 J1
Sand Hl FARN GU14 61 H1
Sandhill La LSOL/BMARY PO13 190 A1
Sandhills Cl CFDH BH17 211 K6
Sandhurst Dr WIMB BH21 205 J1
Sandhurst La BLKW GU17 49 K2
Sandhurst Rd CWTH RG45 43 K5
WSHM SO15 160 E2
YTLY GU46 49 G2
San Diego Rd GPORT PO12 191 H2
Sandisplatt FHAM/STUB PO14 181 J4
Sandle Copse FBDG SP6 196 D3
Sandleford Cl WHIT RG2 238 C2
Sandleford Pde NWBY RG14 * 34 A5
Sandleford Ri NWBY RG14 34 A5
Sandleford Rd HAV PO9 170 D1
Sandleheath Rd FBDG SP6 196 B4
Sandlewood Cl HORN PO8 321 L7
TOTT SO40 144 C8
Sandmartin Cl
NMIL/BTOS BH25 230 F1
Sandown Cl ALTN GU34 107 G6
BLKW GU17 49 M3
GPORT PO12 190 E5
Sandown Crs ALDT GU11 3 G9
Sandown Dr FRIM GU16 50 F6
Sandown Rd CHAM PO6 184 E1
CHCH/BSGR BH23 228 E2
WSHM SO15 146 B7
Sandown Wy NWBY RG14 19 J8
Sandpiper Cl CFDH BH17 210 F7
HORN PO8 156 A1
TOTT SO40 159 L7
Sandpiper Rd ROWN SO16 146 A3
Sandpiper Wy KBH RG22 92 B5
Sandpit Hl KSCL RG20 246 E1
Sandpit La LYMN SO41 357 L8
THLE RG7 238 H11
Sandport Gv
FHAM/PORC PO16 183 H1
Sandringham Cl ALTN GU34 106 D5
CHFD SO53 138 F4
MOOR/WNTN BH9 214 B4
Sandringham Gdns
MOOR/WNTN BH9 214 B4
Sandringham La PSEA PO1 * 21 L2
Sandringham Rd
FHAM/STUB PO14 181 H4
PSEA PO1 21 L2
PSF GU32 120 D5
PSTN BH14 224 B5
WEND SO18 147 L7
The Sandringhams RSAL SP5 327 P3
Sandringham Wy FRIM GU16 51 H8
Sandrock HASM GU27 118 C6
Sandrock Hill Rd RFNM GU10 78 D2
Sandsbury La PSF GU32 315 M3
Sands Cl RFNM GU10 260 B6
Sands Rd RFNM GU10 260 A6
The Sands BOR GU35 112 C2
Sandy Brow WVILLE PO7 169 K4
Sandy Cl EPSF GU31 121 G6
Sandycroft HLER SO31 179 K4
Sandy Down LYMN SO41 351 M8
Sandy Field Crs HORN PO8 155 L5
Sandy Hill Rd FNM GU9 76 E1
Sandyhurst Cl CFDH BH17 211 J7
Sandy La BPWT SO32 151 J3
CBLY GU15 51 G2
CHCH/BSGR BH23 215 L6
ELGH SO50 141 H2
FARN GU14 60 C2
FHAM/STUB PO14 180 F4
FLEETS GU52 71 J4
GSHT GU26 115 M6
HASM GU27 117 J1
HASM GU27 118 E3
HTWY RG27 57 M3
LISS GU33 309 L9
LYND SO43 345 K4
NBAD SO52 138 B4
RFNM GU10 79 G7
RFNM GU10 262 G6
RCUW GU3 75 K4
RGWD BH24 202 B8
ROMY SO51 131 G5
RSAL SP5 332 G1
SBNE BH6 227 H3
SHST GU47 43 H7
TADY RG26 44 D4
UPTN BH16 222 A2
VWD BH31 201 J2
WIMB BH21 201 G6
WIMB BH21 206 B3
WWKG RG41 239 R4
Sandy Mead Rd CHAR BH8 214 F7
Sandy Plot CHCH/BSGR BH23 216 C7
Sandy Point Rd HISD PO11 195 L7
Sandys Cl KBH RG22 93 G1
Sandys Rd KBH RG22 65 G8
Sandy Wy NBNE BH10 213 L5
Sankey La FLEETN GU51 59 M4
Sanross Cl FHAM/STUB PO14 189 G3
Santina Cl FNM GU9 72 D8
Saor Ms AND SP10 4 F4
Sapley La OVTN RG25 89 J5
The Saplings FAWY SO45 354 D3
Sapphire Cl GPORT PO12 191 H1
WVILLE PO7 * 170 A1
Sapphire Rdg WVILLE PO7 170 A1
Saracen Cl LYMN SO41 221 J7
Saracens Rd CHFD SO53 139 M1
Sarah Cl LTDN BH7 215 H8
Sarah Sands Cl
CHCH/BSGR BH23 216 D8
Sarah Wy FARN GU14 61 H4
Sargood Cl STHA RG19 35 L2
Sarisbury Cl TADY RG26 44 A4
Sark Rd BKME/WDN BH12 212 D8
Sarnia Ct ROWN SO16 145 L5
Sarson Cl RAND SP11 94 D6
Sarson La RAND SP11 94 D5
Sarum Av FERN BH22 205 G4
Sarum Cl FUFL SO22 122 C5
NTID SP9 266 D9
STOK SO20 269 R12
Sarum Hl BSTK RG21 6 D6
Sarum Rd CHFD SO53 139 L2
FUFL SO22 24 A6
TADY RG26 44 A3
Sarum St PLE BH15 223 H7
Sarum Vw FUFL SO22 122 B6
Sarum Wk LYMN SO41 221 K2
Satchell La HLER SO31 163 G8
Saturn Cl ROWN SO16 145 M4
Saulfland Dr CHCH/BSGR BH23 217 K8
Saulfland Pl CHCH/BSGR BH23 217 K8
Saunders Cl
LSOL/BMARY PO13 190 A1
Saunders Gdn TADY RG26 44 B4
Saunders La ROMY SO51 129 L3
Saunders Ms ENEY PO4 193 H6
Saunton Gdns FARN GU14 61 G2
Savernake Cl
LSOL/BMARY PO13 182 D6
ROMY SO51 131 H7
Savile Crs BOR GU35 112 F1
Saville Cl ELGH SO50 134 D7
GPORT PO12 14 A6
Saville Gdns CBLY GU15 51 K3
FHAM/PORC PO16 10 D1
Savoy Cl AND SP10 5 J6
Savoy Gv BLKW GU17 49 M5
The Sawmills BPWT SO32 142 B7
Sawyer Cl FUFL SO22 122 C3
Saxholm Cl ROWN SO16 146 F2
Saxholm Dl ROWN SO16 146 F2
Saxholm Wy ROWN SO16 146 F2
Saxley Ct HAV PO9 170 C2
Saxonbury Rd SBNE BH6 227 L2
Saxon Cl FHAM/PORC PO16 167 H7
HLER SO31 179 L3
HORN PO8 321 L8
Saxon Ct AND SP10 96 C1
STHA RG19 35 G1
Saxon Cft FNM GU9 13 G5
Saxonford Rd
CHCH/BSGR BH23 229 J1
Saxon Gdns HEND SO30 149 G7
Saxonhurst RSAL SP5 332 C1
Saxonhurst Cl NBNE BH10 213 L3
Saxonhurst Gdns NBNE BH10 213 L4
Saxonhurst Rd NBNE BH10 213 K4
Saxon King Gdns SBNE BH6 228 B4
Saxon Leas RSAL SP5 282 G10
Saxon Pl LYMN SO41 221 K2
Saxon Ri MARL SN8 264 H3
Saxon Rd FAWY SO45 354 H7
WINC SO23 25 G3
WSHM SO15 22 A2
Saxon Wk CHFD SO53 139 L3
Saxon Wy AND SP10 84 B8
CHIN RG24 66 B1
FBDG SP6 196 C7
ROMY SO51 137 H1
Saxony Wy YTLY GU46 * 48 E4
Sayers Cl FRIM GU16 61 L1
NWBY RG14 34 B4
Sayers Rd ELGH SO50 140 D2
SBAC Tr ALDT GU11 72 D5
Scafell Av FHAM/STUB PO14 181 K4
Scallows La ROMY SO51 334 H3
Scantabout Av CHFD SO53 139 L1
Scant Rd RCCH PO18 173 K3
Scant Rd (East) RCCH PO18 173 J4
Scant Rd (West) RCCH PO18 173 H4
Scarf Rd CFDH BH17 223 M1
Scarlatti Rd KBH RG22 93 H4
Scarlet Oaks CBLY GU15 51 G5
Scarlett's Rd ALDT GU11 73 G5
Scholars' Wk CHAM PO6 185 J1
School Cl CHFD SO53 139 H3
LYMN SO41 221 J6
RAND SP11 243 Q11
VWD BH31 201 J1
School Dell RCCH PO18 173 L3
School Flds BOR GU35 110 D3
School Hl BPWT SO32 319 J6
CWTH RG45 43 M4
RFNM GU10 78 D2
RFNM GU10 260 F4
RSAL SP5 327 L2
SHST GU47 43 J7
School La BWD BH11 213 H3
CHCH/BSGR BH23 348 G8
CHFD SO53 139 H3
CHOB/PIR GU24 63 L5
EMRTH PO10 171 M8
EMRTH PO10 172 B1
HLER SO31 179 G3
LISS GU33 308 F8
LYMN SO41 221 L4
LYMN SO41 232 E2
LYMN SO41 351 R12
MFD/CHID GU8 261 Q10
NARL SO24 291 R11
NARL SO24 292 G12
PLE BH15 223 J3
PSF GU32 120 E3
RCCH PO18 172 F7
RCCH PO18 323 K10
RFNM GU10 79 H2
RFNM GU10 259 M11
RCUW GU3 74 F4
RCUW GU3 261 N4
RGWD BH24 202 C7
RGWD BH24 203 J5
RWIN SO21 290 B9
STOK SO20 270 B12
STOK SO20 284 C9
THLE RG7 39 M2
THLE RG7 45 H3
THLE RG7 240 E1
WIMB BH21 205 H1
WIMB BH21 207 H3
WINC SO23 288 H11
WVILLE PO7 154 D3
YTLY GU46 48 D2
School Rd BOR GU35 110 F8
BPWT SO32 318 F10
CHCH/BSGR BH23 348 G8
FAWY SO45 177 G4
FAWY SO45 355 K5
GPORT PO12 182 F7
GSHT GU26 115 H5
HASM GU27 117 M3
HAV PO9 16 D5
HLER SO31 165 G4
RFNM GU10 109 L1
ROMY SO51 131 J7
ROMY SO51 335 K6
RSAL SP5 332 H4
RSAL SP5 333 J3
RSAL SP5 334 A8
RWIN SO21 124 F6
THLE RG7 29 F3
THLE RG7 238 E12
TOTT SO40 159 G2
WHAM PO17 152 A5
WWKG RG41 239 M6
Schooner Wy HLER SO31 179 L3
HSEA PO3 193 J2
Schroeder Cl BSTK RG21 93 J2
Schubert Rd KBH RG22 93 G4
The Scimitars
FHAM/STUB PO14 189 H1
Scivier's La BPWT SO32 142 C2
Scotland Cl ASHV GU12 74 A3
ELGH SO50 141 L2
Scotland Farm Rd ASHV GU12 74 A3
Scotland Hl SHST GU47 43 J8
Scotland La HASM GU27 118 C7
RSAL SP5 333 Q1
Scotlands Cl HASM GU27 118 B7
Scotlands Dr HASM GU27 118 B7
Scotney Ct HAV PO9 171 H2
Scotney Rd BSTK RG21 65 K5
Scots Ct HTWY RG27 56 E6
Scott Cl AND SP10 97 G3
BKME/WDN BH12 212 F7
FHAM/STUB PO14 181 J8
RWIN SO21 135 G4
STOK SO20 299 Q2
Scotter Rd ELGH SO50 140 D1
LTDN BH7 227 H3
Scott-Paine Dr FAWY SO45 177 H4
Scott Rd BKME/WDN BH12 212 F8
ELGH SO50 139 M6
HSEA PO3 184 F3
ITCH SO19 161 M7
PSEA PO1 20 B1
Scott's Ct FARN GU14 61 H1
Scott's Gn CHCH/BSGR BH23 216 F8
Scotts Hills La
CHCH/BSGR BH23 228 D2
Scratchface La HAV PO9 170 C6
WVILLE PO7 169 M4
Scrivens Md STHA RG19 35 M1
Scrubbs La NARL SO24 304 C1
Scullards La SHAM SO14 22 F3
Scures Rd HTWY RG27 56 B7
Seabank Cl UPTN BH16 222 A1
Seabird Wy FHAM/PORC PO16 11 H9
Seabourne Pl BOSC BH5 227 H3
Seabourne Rd BOSC BH5 227 H4
Sea Breeze Gdns ENEY PO4 193 J5
Seabreeze Wy LYMN SO41 232 A2
Seacombe Gn ROWN SO16 145 K7
Seacombe Rd CCLF BH13 237 G5
Sea Crest Rd
LSOL/BMARY PO13 189 M7
Seacroft Av NMIL/BTOS BH25 218 E8
Seafield Cl NMIL/BTOS BH25 230 F1
Seafield Dr SBNE BH6 227 L2
Seafield Park Rd
FHAM/STUB PO14 189 H3
Seafield Rd CHCH/BSGR BH23 229 J2
FHAM/PORC PO16 183 H1
HSEA PO3 185 G7
NMIL/BTOS BH25 218 E8
ROWN SO16 145 K6
SBNE BH6 227 K4
Seafields EMRTH PO10 171 L8
Seafire Wy FARN GU14 72 E1
Seaford Cl HLER SO31 162 F3
Sea Front HISD PO11 194 F6
Seagarth La ROWN SO16 146 D5
Seager's Ct PSEA PO1 20 B6
Seagrim Rd CHAR BH8 214 C5
Sea Grove Av HISD PO11 195 G6
Seagrove Rd NEND PO2 184 D7
Seagull Cl ENEY PO4 * 193 J2
KBH RG22 92 B4
Seagull La EMRTH PO10 171 M7
Seagull Rd CHAR BH8 214 C7
The Seagulls
LSOL/BMARY PO13 190 A4
Seahorse Wk GPORT PO12 15 K3
Sea Kings FHAM/STUB PO14 189 H2
Sea La LSOL/BMARY PO13 189 J4
Sealark Rd GPORT PO12 191 J1
Seale La RFNM GU10 260 B4
RCUW GU3 261 K4
Seale Rd MFD/CHID GU8 260 F8
Seal Rd BSTK RG21 6 F5
Seaman's La LYND SO43 340 F8
Seamead FHAM/STUB PO14 189 J4
Sea Mill Gdns PSEA PO1 20 D3
Seamoor La WBNE BH4 225 H5
Seamoor Rd CCLF BH13 225 H5
Searing Wy TADY RG26 44 A3
Searle Rd FNM GU9 13 G7
Searles Cl NARL SO24 291 M11
Searles Hl RWIN SO21 125 G6
Searl's La HTWY RG27 56 D4
Sea Rd BOSC BH5 226 E5
ITCH SO19 161 K4
LYMN SO41 232 E4
NMIL/BTOS BH25 218 E8
SBNE BH6 227 M5
Seaton Av HSEA PO3 185 G8
Seaton Cl CHCH/BSGR BH23 218 B8
FHAM/STUB PO14 189 J2
LYMN SO41 221 L3
WEND SO18 148 C3
Seaton Rd CBLY GU15 50 D3
CHCH/BSGR BH23 218 B8
Seatown Cl CFDH BH17 212 A7
Sea Vw LYMN SO41 * 350 F12
Seaview Av FHAM/PORC PO16 167 L7
Seaview Cl HLER SO31 162 B7
Sea View Rd BKME/WDN BH12 224 A3
CHAM PO6 169 J8
UPTN BH16 222 A1
Seaview Rd CHCH/BSGR BH23 218 C7
HISD PO11 195 K5
NMIL/BTOS BH25 230 D1
Seaward Av NMIL/BTOS BH25 230 E1
SBNE BH6 227 H4
Seaward Rd FAWY SO45 177 H5
ITCH SO19 161 L4
Seaway NMIL/BTOS BH25 219 H8
Seaway Av CHCH/BSGR BH23 229 J2
Seaway Crs ENEY PO4 193 J4
Seaway Gv FHAM/PORC PO16 183 J2
Seawinds LYMN SO41 232 A3
Sebastian Gv WVILLE PO7 156 A8
Sebastopol Rd ALDT GU11 3 G3
Second Av CHAM PO6 168 E8
CHAM PO6 185 L1
EMRTH PO10 172 D6
HAV PO9 17 J3
THLE RG7 44 C2
WSHM SO15 159 K1
Second Marine Av
NMIL/BTOS BH25 231 G2
Second St FAWY SO45 177 L8
STHA RG19 35 G8
Second St East STHA RG19 35 G7
Sedbergh Rd ROWN SO16 145 K7
Seddon Cl NMIL/BTOS BH25 219 H8
Sedgefield Cl CHAM PO6 167 M8
TOTT SO40 144 C8
Sedgefield Rd NWBY RG14 19 J9
Sedge Gv NTHA RG18 29 G8
Sedgeley Gv GPORT PO12 183 G8
Sedgemead HLER SO31 162 B7
Sedgemoor FARN GU14 61 H1
Sedgewick Cl
LSOL/BMARY PO13 182 C8
Sedgewick Rd ELGH SO50 140 D1
ITCH SO19 148 C7
Sedgley Cl SSEA PO5 21 J5
Sedgley Rd MOOR/WNTN BH9 213 L8
Seebys Oak SHST GU47 49 M2
Seeviours Ct WHCH RG28 87 L7
Segars La RWIN SO21 124 F7
Segensworth Rd FHAM PO15 164 D8
Sek Kong Cl STOK SO20 270 C8
Selangor Av EMRTH PO10 171 K7
Selborne Av ALDT GU11 3 J9
HAV PO9 170 D3
WEND SO18 148 C4
Selborne Cl BLKW GU17 49 L2
HTWY RG27 56 D7
PSF GU32 120 E4
Selborne Gdns FNM GU9 12 C9
GPORT PO12 14 B4
Selborne Pl FUFL SO22 122 D7
Selborne Rd ALTN GU34 106 F8
LISS GU33 308 C2
Selborne Wk WEND SO18 148 C4
Selborne Wy BOR GU35 112 C2
Selbourne Dr ELGH SO50 134 A8
Selbourne Rd HAV PO9 16 D5
TOTT SO40 144 D8
Selbourne Ter PSEA PO1 21 L3
Selby Cl BDST BH18 211 G5
Selby Wk CHIN RG24 65 K4
Seldon Cl FUFL SO22 122 B8
Seldown PLE BH15 223 K5
Seldown Br PLE BH15 223 K6
Seldown La PLE BH15 223 K5
Seldown Rd PLE BH15 223 K5
Selfridge Av SBNE BH6 228 B5
Selfridge Cl SBNE BH6 228 B5
Selhurst Wy ELGH SO50 141 J3
Seliot Cl PLE BH15 223 K3
Selkirk Cl WIMB BH21 207 L7
Sellwood Rd HLER SO31 162 C6
Sellwood Wy
NMIL/BTOS BH25 218 D8
Selman Cl FAWY SO45 177 H4
Selsdon Av ROMY SO51 131 H8
Selsey Av ENEY PO4 193 G6
GPORT PO12 182 F8
Selsey Cl HISD PO11 195 M6
ROWN SO16 145 L6
Selsmore Av HISD PO11 195 J6
Selsmore Rd HISD PO11 195 G5
Selwood Pk NBNE BH10 * 213 J1
Selworth La BPWT SO32 318 H9
Selworthy Cl PSTN BH14 224 A6
Selwyn Dr YTLY GU46 48 D2
Selwyn Gdns ELGH SO50 134 A7
Sengana Cl HEND SO30 149 K6
Senlac Rd ROMY SO51 137 H1
Sennen Pl CHAM PO6 184 A1
Sentinel Cl WVILLE PO7 156 B7
Sepen Meade FLEETS GU52 71 G4
Seps 4 Rd FAWY SO45 178 B8
September Cl HEND SO30 148 D3
Seremban Cl STOK SO20 270 C7
Serle Cl TOTT SO40 158 B1
Serle Gdns TOTT SO40 158 D2
Sermon Rd FUFL SO22 122 B3
Serpentine Rd
FHAM/PORC PO16 11 G2
PLE BH15 223 J5
SSEA PO5 20 F9
WVILLE PO7 169 J5
Setley Gdns CHAR BH8 214 E5
Seton Dr HTWY RG27 56 B8
Setters Cl RWIN SO21 134 F4
Set Thorns Rd LYMN SO41 350 G10
Settle Cl ROWN SO16 146 B8
Settlers Cl PSEA PO1 21 J1
The Sett YTLY GU46 48 D3
Sevenoaks Dr LTDN BH7 215 G8
THLE RG7 238 A5
Sevenoaks Rd CHAM PO6 168 E8
Seventh St STHA RG19 34 F7
The Severals CHIN RG24 65 G1
Severn Cl CHAM PO6 168 B7
FHAM/PORC PO16 167 G8
NTHA RG18 28 D7
SHST GU47 43 L8
Severn Ct AND SP10 96 E2
Severn Gdns DEAN RG23 91 K3
Severn Rd FARN GU14 60 E2
FERN BH22 346 A7
ROWN SO16 145 L8
Severn Wy BSTK RG21 7 K5
HEND SO30 148 D2
Seville Crs AND SP10 5 L3
Seward Ri ROMY SO51 131 J8
Sewell Cl NTHA RG18 27 L3
Seymour Av WHIT RG2 238 E3
Seymour Cl CHFD SO53 139 L3
NEND PO2 192 D1
TOTT SO40 144 C7
Seymour La NBAD SO52 137 M4
Seymour Rd BOR GU35 114 C4
KBH RG22 92 E2
LSOL/BMARY PO13 189 M8
RGWD BH24 203 K3
ROWN SO16 146 C5
Shackleford Rd
MFD/CHID GU8 261 P9
Shackleton Cl ASHV GU12 73 M2
Shackleton Rd
LSOL/BMARY PO13 182 D8
Shackleton Sq AND SP10 * 96 E1
CHCH/BSGR BH23 348 D11
Shadwell Rd NEND PO2 184 E6

Shady Nook FNM GU9 76 F2
Shaftesbury Av CHFD SO53 139 J4
PTSW SO17 147 H7
WVILLE PO7 169 K4
Shaftesbury Cl FERN BH22 205 H6
Shaftesbury Mt BLKW GU17 49 L5
Shaftesbury Rd CHAR BH8 226 C2
FERN BH22 205 H7
PLE BH15 223 K5
SSEA PO5 21 G8
Shaftesbury St FBDG SP6 197 G3
Shaftsbury Rd GPORT PO12 15 G5
Shaggs Meadow LYND SO43 345 L3
Shakespeare Av AND SP10 4 A3
PTSW SO17 147 H8
Shakespeare Dr TOTT SO40 144 D6
Shakespeare Gdns FARN GU14 60 D3
HORN PO8 155 L5
Shakespeare Rd CHIN RG24 65 L4
ELGH SO50 134 A8
ELGH SO50 139 M3
NTHA RG18 28 E8
PSEA PO1 192 E2
SBNE BH6 227 K1
WIMB BH21 207 J2
Shalbourne Ri CBLY GU15 50 F3
Shalbourne Rd GPORT PO12 191 G1
Shalcombe HLER SO31 162 C5
Shalden Rd ASHV GU12 3 L6
Shaldon Cl ROWN SO16 146 C4
Shaldon Rd HAV PO9 171 H2
Shaldon Wy FLEETN GU51 58 F8
Shales Rd WEND SO18 148 B5
Shallow La LYMN SO41 351 P12
The Shallows FBDG SP6 331 Q9
Shamblehurst La HEND SO30 149 J3
Shamblehurst La North
BPWT SO32 149 K1
Shamblehurst La South
HEND SO30 149 J4
Shamrock Cl FRIM GU16 50 F8
GPORT PO12 15 J5
Shamrock Quay SHAM SO14 * 161 K2
Shamrock Rd ITCH SO19 161 K5
Shamrock Wy FAWY SO45 177 G3
Shanklin Ct ASHV GU12 3 K5
Shanklin Crs WSHM SO15 146 D7
Shanklin Rd ENEY PO4 21 M5
WSHM SO15 146 D6
Shannon Cl FHAM PO15 181 K2
Shannon Ct AND SP10 96 E2
Shannon Rd FHAM/STUB PO14 181 H8
FHAM/STUB PO14 181 M7
FHAM/STUB PO14 182 A3
Shannon Wy CHFD SO53 139 H2
Shapland Av BWD BH11 212 E3
Shappen Hill La RGWD BH24 348 H2
Shapton Cl FAWY SO45 354 D4
Shapwick Rd PLE BH15 223 G7
Shard Cl VWD BH31 201 J2
Sharf Rd BKME/WDN BH12 225 G1
Sharlands Cl BDST BH18 211 H5
Sharon Rd HEND SO30 148 C2
Sharpley Cl FBDG SP6 197 G1
Sharpness Cl
FHAM/STUB PO14 * 181 J4
Sharps Cl HSEA PO3 185 H5
Sharps Rd HAV PO9 171 H3
Sharvells Rd LYMN SO41 232 C3
Shavard La BPWT SO32 312 F11
Shaves La NMIL/BTOS BH25 219 G3
Shaw Br NWBY RG14 * 27 K7
Shaw Cl AND SP10 95 L4
TOTT SO40 158 D1
WEND SO18 148 A2
Shaw Farm Rd NWBY RG14 27 K7
Shawfield La ASHV GU12 73 M6
Shawfield Rd ASHV GU12 73 M7
HAV PO9 17 H6
Shawford Cl ROWN SO16 146 E4
TOTT SO40 158 B1
Shawford Gdns CHAR BH8 214 D6
Shawford Gv HAV PO9 170 C3
Shawford Rd CHAR BH8 214 D5
RWIN SO21 124 F6
Shaw Hl MARL SN8 264 H8
NWBY RG14 27 K7
Shaw La TADY RG26 249 R6
Shaw Pk CWTH RG45 43 K5
Shaw Pightle HTWY RG27 56 B7
Shaw Rd NWBY RG14 19 G1
RGWD BH24 203 L2
Shaws Wk AND SP10 5 H6
Sheardley La BPWT SO32 319 M4
Shearer Rd PSEA PO1 192 E1
Shear Hl EPSF GU31 120 F4
Shears Brook Cl
CHCH/BSGR BH23 348 D11
Shears Rd ELGH SO50 140 E1
Shearwater Av
FHAM/PORC PO16 166 E8
Shearwater Cl
LSOL/BMARY PO13 182 B6
Shearwater Dr CHAM PO6 185 M1
Sheep Dro STOK SO20 283 R4
Sheep Fair AND SP10 5 L5
Sheep Fair Cl AND SP10 5 L5
Sheephatch La RFNM GU10 79 M3
Sheephouse FNM GU9 13 G7
Sheep Pond La BPWT SO32 318 E1
Sheep St PSF GU32 120 D6
Sheepwash La KSCL RG20 247 J2
TADY RG26 255 R2
WVILLE PO7 154 F8
Sheerlands Rd EWKG RG40 239 L10
Sheffield Cl ELGH SO50 134 D7
FARN GU14 60 F4
Sheffield Ct
LSOL/BMARY PO13 * 190 C2
Sheffield Rd PSEA PO1 21 L2
Shelbourne Cl CHAR BH8 226 D2
Shelbourne Rd CHAR BH8 226 C2
Sheldon's La HTWY RG27 56 C7
Sheldon's Rd HTWY RG27 56 F7
Sheldrake Gdns LYMN SO41 220 B4
ROWN SO16 146 B3
Sheldrake Rd
CHCH/BSGR BH23 229 G3
Shelford Rd ENEY PO4 193 H4
Shellcroft HLER SO31 179 K4
Shelley Av CHAM PO6 167 L7
Shelley Cl BMTH BH1 226 E3
CHIN RG24 65 L4
CHCH/BSGR BH23 229 J1
FLEETN GU51 59 J8
FUFL SO22 24 A4
RGWD BH24 202 A7
RWIN SO21 290 A10
Shelley Ct CBLY GU15 50 E3
Shelley Gdns BMTH BH1 226 E3
HORN PO8 155 L5
Shelley La ROMY SO51 335 Q7
Shelley Rd BMTH BH1 226 E3
ELGH SO50 139 M7
ITCH SO19 148 D6
NTHA RG18 28 E8
PSTN BH14 224 D3
TOTT SO40 144 D6
Shelley Rd East BMTH BH1 226 E3
Shelleys La ALTN GU34 107 L7
Shelley Wk YTLY GU46 48 D3
Shell La ALTN GU34 306 G2
Shelly Ri FARN GU14 60 F2
Shelton Rd SBNE BH6 227 J2
Shenley Cl FHAM PO15 181 J2
Shenstone Ct
NMIL/BTOS BH25 * 219 G7
Shepards Cl FHAM/STUB PO14 181 J4
Shepherd Cl CHCH/BSGR BH23 217 M7
Shepherd & Flock Roundabout
FNM GU9 13 M1
Shepherds Cl FUFL SO22 122 B8
RSAL SP5 325 N3
RSAL SP5 326 C4
TOTT SO40 341 M6
Shepherds Down NARL SO24 291 L12
Shepherds Hey Rd TOTT SO40 144 B7
Shepherd's Hl HASM GU27 118 C6
RGWD BH24 198 E6
Shepherds La RGWD BH24 198 C6
RWIN SO21 133 M2
Shepherds Purse Cl
HLER SO31 179 M2
Shepherds Ri RAND SP11 243 Q11
Shepherds Rd TOTT SO40 341 M6
WINC SO23 25 M5
Shepherds Rw AND SP10 5 L6
Shepherds Spring La AND SP10 5 H4
Shepherds Wk FARN GU14 60 E1
Shepherds Wy CWTH RG45 43 G4
LIPH GU30 116 D5
LTDN BH7 227 G1
LYMN SO41 220 C7
RFNM GU10 260 A12
ROWN SO16 145 J3
Sheppard Cl HORN PO8 156 A2
WHCH RG28 87 L8
Sheppard Rd BSTK RG21 93 J2
Sheppards Fld WIMB BH21 207 H2
Sheppard Sq AND SP10 * 96 E2
Shepton Br BROC SO42 352 H3
Sheraton Av KBH RG22 92 D5
Sheraton Cl BLKW GU17 50 A4
Sherborn Crs CFDH BH17 211 M7
Sherborne Ct ELGH SO50 139 M2
Sherborne Dr FERN BH22 209 K4
Sherborne Rd BSTK RG21 6 C1
CHIN RG24 65 H2
FARN GU14 61 K8
PTSW SO17 147 H6
Sherborne Wy HEND SO30 149 J6
Sherbrooke Cl WINC SO23 289 J8
Sherfield Av HAV PO9 171 G3
Sherfield Cl CHAR BH8 214 D6
Sherfield English La
ROMY SO51 334 G2
Sherfield English Rd RSAL SP5 334 F5
Sherfield Rd TADY RG26 46 B5
Sheridan Cl ALDT GU11 2 F6
FUFL SO22 122 C7
ITCH SO19 148 C7
Sheridan Crs TADY RG26 249 Q3
Sheridan Gdns HLER SO31 164 C4
TOTT SO40 158 D1
Sheridan Rd FRIM GU16 50 F8
Sheringham Rd
BKME/WDN BH12 224 F3
CHAM PO6 * 168 D7
Sherington Cl FARN GU14 61 H2
Sherley Gn HLER SO31 162 F3
Sherlock Lea HTWY RG27 48 A1
Shermin's Bank
CHCH/BSGR BH23 228 E3
Sherrardmead NWBY RG14 27 K7
Sherrin Cl PLE BH15 223 K3
Sherringham Cl FAWY SO45 355 K5
Sherrington Wy KBH RG22 93 H3
Sherwin Crs FARN GU14 50 D8
Sherwin Wk GPORT PO12 14 C7
Sherwood Av FERN BH22 209 J5
HEND SO30 149 J8
PSTN BH14 223 M6
Sherwood Cl
CHCH/BSGR BH23 227 M1
KBH RG22 92 E6
LISS GU33 308 G5
ROWN SO16 146 B2
Sherwood Dr VWD BH31 201 K2
Sherwood Gdns HLER SO31 163 L8
Sherwood Rd CHFD SO53 133 L7
GPORT PO12 14 D4
Sherwood Ter ALTN GU34 * 107 G5
Sherwood Wy FAWY SO45 354 G9
Shetland Cl CHAM PO6 168 F7
TOTT SO40 144 B8
Shetland Ri HLER SO31 164 B6
Shetland Rd CHIN RG24 65 L3
Shetland Vw VWD BH31 201 L2
Shetland Wy FLEETN GU51 59 K4
Shildon Cl CBLY GU15 51 M5
Shillinglee WVILLE PO7 169 L5
Shillingstone Dr
MOOR/WNTN BH9 214 C4
Shillingstone Gdns
BKME/WDN BH12 224 F1
Shillito Rd BKME/WDN BH12 224 D3
Shinewill Gdns ROWN SO16 145 L8
Shinfield Pk WHIT RG2 * 238 E1
Shinfield Rd WHIT RG2 238 E2
Shingle Bank Dr LYMN SO41 232 D4
Ship Aly FARN GU14 61 J2
Shipbuilding Rd PSEA PO1 191 M2
Shipcote La BPWT SO32 143 J2
Ship La FARN GU14 61 J2
Ship Leopard St PSEA PO1 20 C3
Shipley Cl ALTN GU34 107 G3
Shipley Ct LIPH GU30 116 B5
Shipley Rd RWIN SO21 125 G5
Shipstal Cl UPTN BH16 222 C4
Shipton Wy KBH RG22 92 E2
Shire Av FLEETN GU51 59 L5
Shire Cl HLER SO31 164 B5
HORN PO8 156 B7
Shire Ct ALDT GU11 2 A3
Shires Cl RGWD BH24 203 J8
Shires Cps SBNE BH6 227 M5
Shires Md VWD BH31 201 J2
The Shires HEND SO30 149 G6
WWKG RG41 239 R4
Shires Wy YTLY GU46 42 F8
Shirley Av ENEY PO4 193 J4
WHIT RG2 238 C1
WIMB BH21 207 K6
WSHM SO15 146 C8
Shirley Cl CHCH/BSGR BH23 348 D11
FERN BH22 205 G6
Shirley High St ROWN SO16 146 B8
Shirley Holms LYMN SO41 351 K11
Shirley Park Rd ROWN SO16 146 B8
Shirley Rd BKME/WDN BH12 224 B2
MOOR/WNTN BH9 214 A7
SSEA PO5 21 L9
UPTN BH16 * 221 J3
WSHM SO15 146 C8
Shirley Towers WSHM SO15 * 146 C8
Shoddesden La RAND SP11 265 N12
Shoe La ALDT GU11 73 G2
BPWT SO32 310 F10
Sholing Ct HAV PO9 170 D2
Sholing Rd ITCH SO19 161 L4
Shooters Hill Cl ITCH SO19 162 B1
Shooters Wy BSTK RG21 7 G1
Shoot Hl WHAM PO17 153 K5
Shoot La LSOL/BMARY PO13 182 A8
Shop La HLER SO31 162 E1
NWBY RG14 27 H6
Shore Av HSEA PO3 193 H2
UPTN BH16 222 C2
Shore Cl LYMN SO41 * 232 D4
UPTN BH16 222 C2
Shore Crs BPWT SO32 143 K5
Shorefield Crs LYMN SO41 232 C3
Shorefield Rd LYMN SO41 231 M2
TOTT SO40 159 M6
Shorefield Wy LYMN SO41 232 C3
Shore Gdns UPTN BH16 222 B3
Shorehaven CHAM PO6 167 M8
Shore La BPWT SO32 143 K5
UPTN BH16 222 B3
Shore Rd FAWY SO45 177 H4
HLER SO31 179 J3
PSTN BH14 237 H1
Shorewell HLER SO31 162 C5
Shorewood Cl HLER SO31 180 A3
Short Cl BKME/WDN BH12 213 G8
Short Dale Rd ALDT GU11 260 A2
Shortfield Rd RFNM GU10 79 G7
Shortheath Crest FNM GU9 78 B7
Shortheath La THLE RG7 39 K1
Shortheath Rd FNM GU9 78 E2
Short Hl ROMY SO51 131 J7
Short La RAND SP11 95 J3
Short Rd FHAM/STUB PO14 189 G2
Short Rw PSEA PO1 20 D1
Shorts Cl CHCH/BSGR BH23 216 C7
Shorts Rd ELGH SO50 141 H2
Short St ALDT GU11 2 E2
RAND SP11 265 M10
Shortwood Copse DEAN RG23 92 B7
Shorwell HLER SO31 162 C5
Shotterfield Ter LISS GU33 308 F8
Shottermill Pk HASM GU27 * 117 L1
Shotters Hill Cl HEND SO30 148 D3
Shotters La ALTN GU34 294 F10
Shottsford Rd PLE BH15 223 J3
Shotts La LYMN SO41 356 C8
Shraveshill Cl TOTT SO40 144 D7
The Shrave ALTN GU34 293 Q4
Shrewsbury Ter NWBY RG14 * 18 B7
Shrivenham Cl SHST GU47 43 M8
Shrubbery Cl
FHAM/PORC PO16 183 J1
The Shrubbery FARN GU14 60 D5
GPORT PO12 190 F1
Shrubb's Av LYMN SO41 221 L4
Shrubbs Hill Gdns LYND SO43 345 K4
Shrubbs Hill Rd LYND SO43 345 K4
Shrubbs La RFNM GU10 78 D4
Shrubland Cl WEND SO18 148 B4
Shute End Rd RSAL SP5 327 L3
Shutts La RSAL SP5 325 N3
Shyshack La TADY RG26 249 Q3
Sian Cl FLEETS GU52 71 K3
Sibelius Cl KBH RG22 93 G5
Sibland Cl FHAM/STUB PO14 181 K4
Sickle Rd HASM GU27 117 M3
Sickles Rd BOR GU35 110 D2
Sidbury Circular Rd NTID SP9 266 D1
Sidbury Hts NTID SP9 * 264 E12
Sidbury Hill Av NTID SP9 264 E12
Siddal Cl ITCH SO19 162 C1
Sidestrand Rd ALDT GU11 72 E1
NWBY RG14 33 K4
The Sidings ALDT GU11 3 J1
HLER SO31 162 D7
RSAL SP5 327 L12
Sidlaw Cl KBH RG22 92 C1
Sidlaws Rd FARN GU14 60 D1
Sidlesham Cl HISD PO11 195 M6
Sidmouth Av HSEA PO3 185 G8
Sidmouth Rd AND SP10 5 M5
Silchester Cl AND SP10 4 C1
WCLF BH2 8 E3
Silchester Rd HSEA PO3 193 H1
TADY RG26 44 C3
TADY RG26 53 G2
TADY RG26 53 K1
Silkin Gdns TOTT SO40 158 B2
Silk Mill La OVTN RG25 89 H4
Silkstead Av HAV PO9 170 F2
Silkstead La RWIN SO21 133 M3
Silkweavers Rd AND SP10 5 J4
Sillen La FBDG SP6 329 K5
Silver Birch Av
FHAM/STUB PO14 10 A7
Silver Birch Cl
BKME/WDN BH12 225 G4
FLEETS GU52 71 H3
LISS GU33 308 G8
Silver Birches HLER SO31 162 F4
WWKG RG41 239 Q5
Silver Birch Rd AND SP10 4 C3
Silverdale FLEETS GU52 71 J2
NMIL/BTOS BH25 219 H8
Silverdale Cl BDST BH18 210 E4
Silverdale Crs FBDG SP6 196 C6
Silverdale Dr WVILLE PO7 155 J6
Silverdale Rd TADY RG26 44 B3
WSHM SO15 160 E1
Silver Dr FRIM GU16 51 L5
Silverglades YTLY GU46 48 E4
Silver Hl WINC SO23 25 H6
Silver La THLE RG7 39 G4
Silverlock Cl NEND PO2 * 184 D8
Silverlock Pl EMRTH PO10 * 172 B1
Silver Park Cl FLEETS GU52 71 K2
Silversands Gdns HISD PO11 195 H6
Silvers End FAWY SO45 177 G7
Silver St CHCH/BSGR BH23 228 B2
LYMN SO41 219 M4
LYND SO43 344 H3
RSAL SP5 327 K1
SSEA PO5 20 F6
Silvers Wd TOTT SO40 144 C7
Silverthorne Wy WVILLE PO7 155 K8
Silvertrees EMRTH PO10 171 M6
HLER SO31 163 L6
Silver Wy CHCH/BSGR BH23 217 L8
Silverweed Cl CHFD SO53 138 F1
Silver Wd RSAL SP5 327 L1
Silverwood Cl FUFL SO22 122 D7
WIMB BH21 207 K6
Silverwood Dr CBLY GU15 51 J1
Silvester Cl BSTK RG21 7 H1
Silvester Rd HORN PO8 155 L6
Silvester Wy FLEETS GU52 71 G4
Silwood Cl FUFL SO22 24 B2
Simmonds Cl PLE BH15 223 K3
Simmondstone La
RFNM GU10 262 D10
Simmons Cl HEND SO30 149 J4
Simmons Fld NTHA RG18 29 H8
Simmons Gn HISD PO11 195 J5
Simms Farm La THLE RG7 39 M8
Simnel St SHAM SO14 * 22 F5
Simonds Ct WINC SO23 25 H1
Simonds Rd RAND SP11 285 L10
Simons Cl CHIN RG24 54 B6
Simons Rd CHIN RG24 54 A6
Simon Wy WEND SO18 148 E5
Simpson Cl FHAM/PORC PO16 167 J8
Simpson Rd NEND PO2 184 C7
Sims Ct TADY RG26 46 D6
Sinah La HISD PO11 194 C5
Sinclair Rd ROWN SO16 146 A3
Sindlesham Rd WHIT RG2 239 L5
Sine Cl FARN GU14 50 D8
Singleton Dr NBNE BH10 213 J6
Singleton Gdns HORN PO8 321 M8
Singleton Wy TOTT SO40 144 B8
Sinhurst Rd CBLY GU15 50 D4
Sir Christopher Cl FAWY SO45 177 H4
Sirdar Rd PTSW SO17 147 J5
Sir Galahad Rd CHFD SO53 138 F2
Sir George's Rd WSHM SO15 160 D2
Sir Lancelot Cl CHFD SO53 138 F2
Siskin Cl BPWT SO32 143 G4
FERN BH22 209 H1
ROWN SO16 146 A3
Siskin Gv WVILLE PO7 170 A2
Siskin Rd ENEY PO4 193 J3
Sissinghurst Cl ITCH SO19 162 A3
Sissinghurst Rd
FHAM/PORC PO16 183 H1
Six Oaks Rd NBAD SO52 138 A3
Sixpenny Cl BKME/WDN BH12 224 F1
HLER SO31 180 A3
Sixth Av CHAM PO6 168 E8
Sixth St STHA RG19 34 F7
Sizer Wy FAWY SO45 176 C4
Skates La TADY RG26 44 D7
Skew Rd RAND SP11 269 P1
WHAM PO17 167 J6
Skilman Dr STHA RG19 35 M1
Skinner's Green La KSCL RG20 32 D6
NWBY RG14 33 H4
Skinner St PLE BH15 223 J7
Skipper Cl TOTT SO40 160 A5
Skipper Wy
LSOL/BMARY PO13 189 M7
Skippetts La East BSTK RG21 93 L2
Skippetts La West BSTK RG21 93 L2
Skippons Cl NWBY RG14 33 J6
Skipton Cl BDST BH18 211 G6
Skipton Rd CHFD SO53 139 K4
Skye Cl CHAM PO6 168 F7
Sky End La LYMN SO41 220 A6
Skylark Cl DEAN RG23 92 B5
Skylark Mdw FHAM PO15 164 F7
Skylark Ri WHCH RG28 87 K6
Skylings NWBY RG14 19 J2
Skys Wood Rd CHFD SO53 138 F2
Slab La ROMY SO51 334 H5
RSAL SP5 332 C1
Slade Cl LYMN SO41 220 A5
Slade La EPSF GU31 317 J4
Slade Rd CHOB/PIR GU24 63 K1
Slades Farm Rd NBNE BH10 213 J7
Slades Hl FAWY SO45 354 H6
Slade's La NBNE BH10 213 J8
Slater Cl TOTT SO40 144 B8
Sleepbrook Cl VWD BH31 201 G2
Sleepers Delle Gdns FUFL SO22 24 C8
Sleepers Hill Gdns FUFL SO22 24 A8
Sleepers' Hl FUFL SO22 24 A8
Sleight La WIMB BH21 206 C8
Slepe Crs BKME/WDN BH12 212 F8
Slessor Cl RAND SP11 95 K5
Slim Cl ALDT GU11 73 L1
Slim Rd CBLY GU15 50 E2
Slindon Cl HORN PO8 321 M7
Slindon St PSEA PO1 21 H2
Slingsby Cl PSEA PO1 20 E6
Slinn Rd CHCH/BSGR BH23 228 E1
Slipper Ml EMRTH PO10 * 172 A7
Slipper Rd EMRTH PO10 172 A7
Slip Wy PLE BH15 223 H6
The Slipway CHAM PO6 * 184 A1
Sloane Av FAWY SO45 354 F4
Sloane Ct FAWY SO45 354 F4
Sloane Pk BPWT SO32 151 K5
Sloe Tree Cl HLER SO31 180 C2
Slough La WIMB BH21 200 A6
Smallcutts Av EMRTH PO10 172 D5
Smallfield Dr HTWY RG27 56 E7
Smallridge KSCL RG20 33 J8
Smannell Rd AND SP10 96 D1
RAND SP11 84 F6
Smay Down La MARL SN8 242 H5
Smeaton Rd AND SP10 95 K2
Smeeton Rd
LSOL/BMARY PO13 189 M6
Smith Cl FAWY SO45 354 H6
Smithe Cl ELGH SO50 140 A1
Smithfield La BOR GU35 262 A11
Smithfield Pl
MOOR/WNTN BH9 213 M7
Smith Gv HEND SO30 149 J7
Smith's Fld ROMY SO51 131 G7
Smiths La BPWT SO32 151 M4
Smith's Md OVTN RG25 103 H3
Smithson Cl BKME/WDN BH12 213 H8
Smith St GPORT PO12 14 D4
Smithy Cl ALTN GU34 107 K1
Smithy La BOR GU35 111 L2
NMIL/BTOS BH25 218 F2
The Smithy TADY RG26 46 B5
WVILLE PO7 154 E4
Smugglers La NARL SO24 305 Q2
Smugglers La North
CHCH/BSGR BH23 217 J8
Smugglers La South
CHCH/BSGR BH23 217 L8
Smugglers' Wy RFNM GU10 260 C8
Smugglers Wood Rd
CHCH/BSGR BH23 217 J7
Smythe Rd ITCH SO19 162 D1
Snailing La LISS GU33 308 B6
Snail's La RGWD BH24 203 J1
Snailslynch FNM GU9 13 J3
Snake La KSCL RG20 26 C6
Snakemoor La BPWT SO32 141 L7
Snapdragon Cl HLER SO31 179 M2
Snape Cl LSOL/BMARY PO13 182 C8
Snellgrove Cl TOTT SO40 144 C6
Snellgrove Pl TOTT SO40 144 C6
Snoddington Rd RAND SP11 267 K9
Snode Hl ALTN GU34 106 A5
Snooks La LYMN SO41 356 B6
Snowberry Crs HAV PO9 171 H5
Snowdon Cl STHA RG19 35 K2
Snowdon Dr FHAM/STUB PO14 10 A8
Snowdon Rd FARN GU14 60 E1
WBNE BH4 225 J4
Snowdrop Cl HLER SO31 179 M2
KBH RG22 92 C4
Snowdrop Copse NTHA RG18 29 H8
Snowdrop Gdns
CHCH/BSGR BH23 217 H7
Snowhill WHAM PO17 * 167 K2
Soake Rd WVILLE PO7 155 H5
Soalwood La PSF GU32 307 K11
Soame's La NARL SO24 305 N1
Sobers Sq AND SP10 96 E1
Soberton Rd CHAR BH8 226 D1
HAV PO9 170 E5
Soke Hl ALTN GU34 293 J8
Soke Rd THLE RG7 38 E8
The Soke NARL SO24 291 M9
Solartron Rd FARN GU14 61 G5
Solby's Rd BSTK RG21 6 C5
Soldiers Ri EWKG RG40 42 F1
Soldridge Cl HAV PO9 171 H2
Soldridge Rd ALTN GU34 293 J5
Solent Av ITCH SO19 148 E6
LYMN SO41 221 M5
Solent Cl CHFD SO53 139 L2
LYMN SO41 221 M5
Solent Dr FAWY SO45 176 F4
HISD PO11 194 F6
HLER SO31 179 K6
KBH RG22 92 D5
NMIL/BTOS BH25 231 G1
Solent Mdw HLER SO31 179 G3
Solent Rd CHAM PO6 169 J8
CHCH/BSGR BH23 218 B6
FAWY SO45 176 E8
FHAM/STUB PO14 189 G3
HAV PO9 16 D5
SBNE BH6 228 A5
WSHM SO15 22 C4
Solent Twentyseven
CHAM PO6 * 185 J2
Solent Vw FHAM/PORC PO16 167 H7
Solent Wy BROC SO42 353 P9
FHAM/STUB PO14 189 G3
GPORT PO12 15 L6
GPORT PO12 190 E5
HAV PO9 16 A7
HAV PO9 17 L8
HSEA PO3 193 K2
LSOL/BMARY PO13 190 A5
LYMN SO41 232 F4
SHAM SO14 23 G7
Solly Cl BKME/WDN BH12 224 E1
Solomons La BPWT SO32 151 M2
Solomon Wy PLE BH15 222 D6
Solona Cl CHFD SO53 139 M1
Somborne Dr HAV PO9 170 F3
Somborne Park Rd STOK SO20 286 A7
Somerby Rd PLE BH15 223 K2
Somerford Av
CHCH/BSGR BH23 217 H8
Somerford Cl ITCH SO19 148 A6
Somerford Rd
CHCH/BSGR BH23 228 F1
Somerford Wy
CHCH/BSGR BH23 228 E1
Somerley Rd
MOOR/WNTN BH9 226 A1
Somerley Vw RGWD BH24 203 J4
Somers Cl FUFL SO22 122 D7
Somerset Av BOR GU35 112 F1
WEND SO18 148 C5
Somerset Cl WWKG RG41 239 R2
Somerset Crs CHFD SO53 139 J5
Somerset Rd
CHCH/BSGR BH23 227 L1
FARN GU14 61 J7
LTDN BH7 226 F3
PTSW SO17 147 J6
SSEA PO5 192 D7
Somerset Ter WSHM SO15 160 B2
Somers Rd SSEA PO5 21 H5
Somers Rd North PSEA PO1 21 K3
Somerton Av WEND SO18 148 B5
Somerton Cl NMIL/BTOS BH25 219 K5
Somerton Gv STHA RG19 35 J2
Somervell Cl GPORT PO12 14 C9
Somervell Dr FHAM/PORC PO16 10 E2
Somerville Cl WWKG RG41 239 R4
Somerville Ct AND SP10 96 F3
Somerville Crs YTLY GU46 49 G2
Somerville Rd RGWD BH24 203 L4
WCLF BH2 8 B6
WINC SO23 289 J7
Somme Rd RAND SP11 265 K12
Sonnet Wy WVILLE PO7 156 B8
Sonning Cl KBH RG22 92 B5
Sonninge Cl SHST GU47 43 M8
Soper Gv BSTK RG21 6 E2
Sopers La CFDH BH17 211 G7
CHCH/BSGR BH23 228 A3
Sopers Rw CHIN RG24 * 66 C2
Sopley Cl NMIL/BTOS BH25 218 D8
Sopley Ct HAV PO9 171 H2
Sopwith Cl CHCH/BSGR BH23 229 H2
STOK SO20 299 Q2
Sopwith Crs WIMB BH21 207 M7
Sopwith Pk AND SP10 95 K3
Sopwith Rd ELGH SO50 139 M5
Sopwith Wy HLER SO31 163 L4
Sorrel Cl NWBY RG14 27 M7
ROMY SO51 131 J7
WVILLE PO7 170 A2
Sorrel Dr FHAM PO15 164 D5
Sorrel Gdns BDST BH18 210 F6
Sorrell Cl HLER SO31 179 M2
Sorrell's Cl CHIN RG24 54 B5
Sorrell Wy CHCH/BSGR BH23 217 H8
Sotherington La ALTN GU34 295 M10
South Acre EPSF GU31 323 M1
Southampton Cl BLKW GU17 49 L2
Southampton Hl
FHAM/STUB PO14 180 F3
Southampton Rd BROC SO42 351 L7
CHAM PO6 167 M8
ELGH SO50 140 A4
FAWY SO45 176 E4
FBDG SP6 197 K3
FHAM PO15 164 C8
FHAM/PORC PO16 11 G4
FHAM/STUB PO14 180 D2
LYMN SO41 221 K3
LYND SO43 345 N2
RGWD BH24 203 J4
ROMY SO51 137 G2
RSAL SP5 327 L1
TOTT SO40 341 K5
Southampton St FARN GU14 61 H8
WSHM SO15 160 F2
South Atlantic Dr ALDT GU11 3 J1
South Av FAWY SO45 354 G5
FNM GU9 77 H2
NEND PO2 184 E4
NMIL/BTOS BH25 219 H6
South Baddesey Rd
LYMN SO41 356 B8
South Beta Rd FARN GU14 61 H6
Southbourne Av CHAM PO6 185 H1
EMRTH PO10 172 B6
FAWY SO45 354 E4
Southbourne Coast Rd
SBNE BH6 227 L5
Southbourne Gv SBNE BH6 227 H4
Southbourne Overcliff Dr
SBNE BH6 227 J5
Southbourne Rd LYMN SO41 221 J5
SBNE BH6 227 J4
Southbrook Cl CFDH BH17 212 A6
HAV PO9 16 E7
Southbrook Pl RWIN SO21 275 N9
Southbrook Rd HAV PO9 16 E8
RCCH PO18 173 L3
WSHM SO15 22 C2
Southby Dr FLEETN GU51 59 K7

South Charford Dro FBDG SP6 331 K2
Southcliff LSOL/BMARY PO13 189 L5
Southcliffe Rd
CHCH/BSGR BH23 229 H2
NMIL/BTOS BH25 218 D8
Southcliff Rd SHAM SO14 161 G1
South Cliff Rd WCLF BH2 8 E7
South Cl GPORT PO12 14 B8
HAV PO9 17 G6
NARL SO24 291 K11
ROMY SO51 131 J7
Southcote Dr CBLY GU15 51 J3
Southcote Rd BMTH BH1 9 L3
South Ct HLER SO31 178 E2
Southcroft Rd GPORT PO12 14 A2
South Cross St GPORT PO12 15 K4
Southdene Rd CHFD SO53 139 J3
Southdown Rd CHAM PO6 169 G8
HORN PO8 321 L9
RWIN SO21 124 D6
STHA RG19 34 F1
TADY RG26 44 A3
Southdowns NARL SO24 291 M7
South Downs Wy BPWT SO32 311 R3
BPWT SO32 312 C8
EPSF GU31 323 Q3
NARL SO24 303 K8
PSF GU32 313 N9
PSF GU32 320 F1
WINC SO23 25 K8
Southdown Vw WVILLE PO7 155 J6
Southdown Wy FERN BH22 205 H7
South Dr CHOB/PIR GU24 63 J2
FERN BH22 * 346 B5
FUFL SO22 288 A12
NTID SP9 266 E4
ROMY SO51 130 B5
South East Crs ITCH SO19 148 A8
South East Rd ITCH SO19 148 A8
Southend NTHA RG18 28 E6
South End Cl RWIN SO21 133 H2
Southend La BPWT SO32 319 K12
South End Rd AND SP10 5 K9
Southend Rd BSTK RG21 6 C5
Southern Av FERN BH22 205 J7
Southern Gdns TOTT SO40 158 E1
Southern Haye HTWY RG27 57 L3
Southernhay Rd VWD BH31 201 K2
Southern La NMIL/BTOS BH25 218 F8
Southern Oaks
NMIL/BTOS BH25 218 F7
Southern Rd BOR GU35 110 F7
BSTK RG21 6 E7
CBLY GU15 50 E2
HEND SO30 148 D4
LYMN SO41 221 K4
SBNE BH6 227 J4
WSHM SO15 22 C3
Southern Wy FARN GU14 60 D5
FNM GU9 13 H5
Southey Rd CHCH/BSGR BH23 216 F8
Southfield RGWD BH24 203 J6
Southfield La RGWD BH24 349 L2
Southfield Ms RGWD BH24 203 J6
Southfields Cl BPWT SO32 143 J4
South Front SHAM SO14 23 H3
Southgate St WINC SO23 24 F6
Southgate Vls WINC SO23 * 24 F7
South Gv FLEETN GU51 59 L4
LYMN SO41 221 M5
South Ham Rd KBH RG22 65 G8
South Haven Cl UPTN BH16 222 B4
South Hl BPWT SO32 318 G4
FBDG SP6 196 C6
South Hurst BOR GU35 112 F3
Southill Av BKME/WDN BH12 224 C2
Southill Gdns
MOOR/WNTN BH9 214 A7
Southill Rd BKME/WDN BH12 224 C2
MOOR/WNTN BH9 214 A7
Southington Cl OVTN RG25 89 G4
Southington La OVTN RG25 89 H4
South Kinson Dr BWD BH11 213 G4
Southlands CHIN RG24 54 A5
LYMN SO41 221 J6
Southlands Av SBNE BH6 227 M4
WIMB BH21 210 D2
Southlands Cl ASHV GU12 74 A7
Southlands Rd ASHV GU12 74 A7
South La ASHV GU12 74 B7
EMRTH PO10 172 E3
EPSF GU31 315 P12
HORN PO8 321 K6
HORN PO8 321 R9
RSAL SP5 332 A1
RSAL SP5 334 A9
Southlawns Wk
NMIL/BTOS BH25 218 F7
Southlea Av SBNE BH6 227 M3
Southleigh Gv HISD PO11 194 F4
Southleigh Rd EMRTH PO10 171 M5
HAV PO9 17 J5
South Loading Rd
GPORT PO12 * 15 K4
South Ldg FHAM PO15 181 H3
South Meadow CWTH RG45 43 M5
Southmead Rd ALDT GU11 3 G6
FHAM PO15 181 K3
South Millers Dl CHFD SO53 139 H1
South Mill Rd WSHM SO15 159 M1
Southmoor La HAV PO9 16 B8
South Normandy PSEA PO1 20 D5
South Pde ENEY PO4 192 D7
South Park Rd
BKME/WDN BH12 213 G8
South Pl LSOL/BMARY PO13 190 A4
South Rdg ODIM RG29 69 G6
South Rd ASHV GU12 73 M4
BMTH BH1 226 E3
CHAM PO6 185 K1
HISD PO11 194 F5
HORN PO8 321 L11
KSCL RG20 248 E10
LIPH GU30 116 C7
NARL SO24 291 K11
PSEA PO1 192 E1
PTSW SO17 147 J8
STOK SO20 284 E11
WHAM PO17 168 A2
WIMB BH21 210 E2
Southrope Gn OVTN RG25 256 E9
Southsea Ter SSEA PO5 20 F7
South Side RFNM GU10 260 D1
Southside Rd RAND SP11 98 D7
South Sp CHAM PO6 168 B6
South St AND SP10 5 H6
ELGH SO50 140 A4
EMRTH PO10 171 M8
FARN GU14 61 L7
FAWY SO45 177 G5
FHAM/STUB PO14 180 F4
FNM GU9 13 G3
GPORT PO12 15 G5
HAV PO9 16 F6
LYMN SO41 221 J6
NARL SO24 292 G12
SSEA PO5 20 F6
South Sway La LYMN SO41 350 G12
South Ter PSEA PO1 20 C2
South Town Rd ALTN GU34 293 K2
South Trestle Rd FAWY SO45 178 C7
South Vw FUFL SO22 24 D5
South View Cl RWIN SO21 274 D9
South View Cots
WHCH RG28 88 C5
Southview Gdns AND SP10 5 J7
South View Gdns NWBY RG14 19 G2
South View Pl WCLF BH2 8 C7
Southview Ri ALTN GU34 106 E4
Southview Rd BOR GU35 114 B3
South View Rd
CHCH/BSGR BH23 228 A2
FUFL SO22 124 B1
WSHM SO15 146 D8
South View Ter RAND SP11 86 C4
Southville Rd BOSC BH5 227 H3
South Wk ASHV GU12 3 M3
Southwark Cl YTLY GU46 48 E2
South Wy AND SP10 97 G3
RSAL SP5 327 N2
Southway CBLY GU15 50 D4
FHAM PO15 180 E1
Southways FHAM/STUB PO14 189 K2
South Weirs BROC SO42 350 H5
Southwell Park Rd CBLY GU15 50 D3
South West Coast Pth
SWGE BH19 237 G8
South Western Crs PSTN BH14 224 B6
Southwick Av
FHAM/PORC PO16 167 L7
Southwick Cl FUFL SO22 288 D12
Southwick Ct
FHAM/STUB PO14 182 A2
Southwick Hill Rd CHAM PO6 168 E7
Southwick Pl SBNE BH6 227 J1
Southwick Rd CHAM PO6 168 C6
SBNE BH6 227 J2
WHAM PO17 152 C5
WVILLE PO7 154 E4
Southwood Av
CHCH/BSGR BH23 218 A7
SBNE BH6 227 J4
Southwood Cl
CHCH/BSGR BH23 218 A7
FERN BH22 209 J3
South Wood Gdns HLER SO31 179 M1
Southwood La FLEETN GU51 60 A5
Southwood Rd ALTN GU34 280 B4
FARN GU14 49 G7
FARN GU14 60 E4
FARN GU14 61 F2
HISD PO11 195 J6
NEND PO2 184 E4
Sovereign Av GPORT PO12 191 J1
Sovereign Cl LTDN BH7 214 F8
TOTT SO40 144 B8
Sovereign Crs
FHAM/STUB PO14 180 A3
Sovereign Dr CBLY GU15 51 L1
ENEY PO4 193 J3
HEND SO30 149 L6
Sovereign La WVILLE PO7 169 L5
Sovereign Wy ELGH SO50 139 M2
Sowcroft La ODIM RG29 257 Q11
Sowden Cl HEND SO30 149 H5
Sowley La LYMN SO41 356 G7
Spackman Cl STHA RG19 35 K2
Spain La ALTN GU34 279 J1
The Spain PSF GU32 120 C6
Spalding Rd ITCH SO19 148 D7
Spa Meadow Cl STHA RG19 34 C4
Spaniard's La ROMY SO51 136 F5
Sparkford Cl FUFL SO22 24 D8
LTDN BH7 215 H8
Sparkford Rd FUFL SO22 24 D8
Spa Rd SHAM SO14 22 F4
Sparrow Cl HORN PO8 155 M4
Sparrow Ct LSOL/BMARY PO13 189 M5
Sparrowgrove RWIN SO21 124 C8
Sparrowhawk Cl RFNM GU10 71 K8
Sparrow Sq ELGH SO50 139 K6
Sparsholt Cl HAV PO9 170 C3
Sparsholt Rd ITCH SO19 161 M8
RWIN SO21 301 M9
Spartan Cl FHAM/STUB PO14 181 J7
Spartina Dr LYMN SO41 221 L2
Sparvells HTWY RG27 42 A8
Spats La BOR GU35 111 M4
Speakers Corner Rbt
SHAM SO14 23 G4
Spear Rd SHAM SO14 147 G8
Speckled Wood Rd CHIN RG24 65 K3
Specks La ENEY PO4 193 G4
Speedwell Cl HLER SO31 179 M2
Speedwell Dr
CHCH/BSGR BH23 217 H8
Speedwell Wy NTHA RG18 29 H8
Speen Hill Cl NWBY RG14 18 A2
Speen La NWBY RG14 18 B2
Speen Lodge Ct NWBY RG14 18 A1
Speen Pl NWBY RG14 18 A1
Speggs Wk HEND SO30 149 J6
Speltham Hl WVILLE PO7 319 R10
Spencer Cl ALTN GU34 293 M5
FLEETS GU52 71 L3
FRIM GU16 61 L2
HISD PO11 * 195 G5
TADY RG26 44 E3
WWKG RG41 239 R2
Spencer Ct FHAM/STUB PO14 189 L2
Spencer Dr LSOL/BMARY PO13 189 M7
Spencer Gdns HORN PO8 155 L5
Spencer Rd BMTH BH1 9 M3
CCLF BH13 224 E8
ELGH SO50 139 L6
EMRTH PO10 171 L4
ENEY PO4 192 F6
ITCH SO19 148 D6
NMIL/BTOS BH25 219 G5
NWBY RG14 33 K6
WHIT RG2 238 B1
Spenlow Cl NEND PO2 184 D8
Spenser Cl ALTN GU34 107 G3
HLER SO31 179 K4
Sperrin Cl KBH RG22 92 D1
Spetisbury Cl
MOOR/WNTN BH9 214 B5
Spey Ct AND SP10 96 E2
Spicer La BWD BH11 212 E3
Spicers ALTN GU34 107 G5
Spicer's Hl TOTT SO40 158 F3
Spicer St PSEA PO1 * 21 H1
Spicer's Wy TOTT SO40 158 E2
Spicewood FHAM PO15 10 A4
Spiders Island RSAL SP5 327 P2
Spiers Cl TADY RG26 44 D4
Spiers La NARL SO24 277 N9
Spinacre NMIL/BTOS BH25 219 H8
Spindle Cl BDST BH18 210 F6
HAV PO9 17 L1
Spindle Warren HAV PO9 17 L1
Spindlewood Cl
NMIL/BTOS BH25 219 G7
ROWN SO16 147 G2
Spindlewood Wy TOTT SO40 159 M8
Spinnaker Cl HISD PO11 194 E4
LSOL/BMARY PO13 190 D1
Spinnaker Dr NEND PO2 184 D4
Spinnaker Gra HISD PO11 187 J4
Spinnaker Vw CHAM PO6 170 A7
Spinners Cl FERN BH22 205 G7
Spinney Cl HORN PO8 155 L5
RGWD BH24 205 M4
Spinney Dl FAWY SO45 177 H6
Spinney Gdns FAWY SO45 177 H6
Spinneys La FERN BH22 209 K3
The Spinney CBLY GU15 51 L2
ELGH SO50 141 G2
FHAM/PORC PO16 166 F7
FLEETN GU51 58 F8
GSHT GU26 115 G4
HASM GU27 * 117 K3
HASM GU27 118 C4
HORN PO8 156 A2
HTWY RG27 56 C6
LSOL/BMARY PO13 182 D7
NARL SO24 304 E7
RGWD BH24 202 B6
ROWN SO16 146 F2
RWIN SO21 124 C5
TOTT SO40 144 C7
WVILLE PO7 154 F5
YTLY GU46 48 E1
Spinney Wk WEND SO18 147 M5
Spinney Wy NMIL/BTOS BH25 219 G2
Spitalfields Rd ALTN GU34 106 F4
Spitalhatch ALTN GU34 107 H5
Spitfire End WINC SO23 123 K4
Spitfire La STOK SO20 284 H4
Spitfire Loop ELGH SO50 147 M1
Spitfire Wy FARN GU14 60 E8
HLER SO31 178 F2
Spithead Av GPORT PO12 191 J7
Spittlefields RGWD BH24 203 K5
Spoil La RFNM GU10 260 D1
Spokane Cl ALDT GU11 2 D6
Spouts La ROMY SO51 334 H2
Sprat's Hatch La ODIM RG29 69 M3
Spray Leaze RAND SP11 265 P10
Spriggs Cl STHA RG19 35 K2
Springbank Rd LTDN BH7 214 F8
Spring Cl CHIN RG24 64 F1
ELGH SO50 141 J2
ITCH SO19 161 M4
VWD BH31 201 H3
Spring Crs PTSW SO17 147 H8
Springcroft
LSOL/BMARY PO13 182 B3
Springcross Av BLKW GU17 49 M5
Springdale Av BDST BH18 210 F3
Springdale Gv WIMB BH21 210 E4
Springdale Rd WIMB BH21 210 D4
Springfarm Rd HASM GU27 117 L3
Springfield DEAN RG23 91 K2
Springfield Av
CHCH/BSGR BH23 215 K6
FAWY SO45 354 F4
HTWY RG27 57 L1
SBNE BH6 228 A4
Springfield Cl AND SP10 96 F4
HAV PO9 170 B6
LYMN SO41 356 A9
VWD BH31 201 H3
WHAM PO17 152 A4
Springfield Crs PSTN BH14 224 B4
RSAL SP5 332 F3
Springfield Dr TOTT SO40 158 E2
Springfield Gdns
NMIL/BTOS BH25 219 K6
Springfield Gv FAWY SO45 354 F4
Springfield La FLEETN GU51 59 G7
NWBY RG14 34 A4
Springfield Pl CHIN RG24 * 66 D1
Springfield Rd ASHV GU12 74 A3
CBLY GU15 51 J3
PSTN BH14 224 A3
TADY RG26 44 E3
VWD BH31 201 H3
Springfields Cl RWIN SO21 134 F3
Springfield Wy
FHAM/STUB PO14 189 J3
Springford Cl ROWN SO16 146 B4
Springford Crs ROWN SO16 146 C5
Springford Gdns ROWN SO16 146 B4
Springford Rd ROWN SO16 146 B5
Spring Garden La GPORT PO12 15 H3
Spring Gdns BKME/WDN BH12 224 D3
CBLY GU15 51 J3
EMRTH PO10 171 M8
EWKG RG40 * 42 B3
FARN GU14 61 G1
NARL SO24 291 K12
NBAD SO52 137 M3
PSEA PO1 20 F3
THLE RG7 238 B7
Spring Gv HLER SO31 163 G3
Spring Hill La RAND SP11 86 B2
Springhill Rd CHFD SO53 139 J2
Spring Hills ITCH SO19 148 C8
Springhurst NWBY RG14 * 34 B4
Springlakes Est ASHV GU12 * 73 L5
Spring La BPWT SO32 318 B8
ELGH SO50 140 D1
FNM GU9 76 E1
KSCL RG20 246 H6
NMIL/BTOS BH25 219 K6
NTHA RG18 28 E4
RWIN SO21 134 F3
THLE RG7 38 C6
THLE RG7 40 A1
THLE RG7 240 A1
Spring La West FNM GU9 76 E2
Springles La FHAM PO15 165 G7
Spring Meadow MARL SN8 264 G4
Spring Ms AND SP10 5 J3
Spring Pl ROMY SO51 136 E1
Spring Rd BMTH BH1 9 M2
FAWY SO45 177 G4
HLER SO31 163 M6
ITCH SO19 161 M2
LYMN SO41 356 A9
The Springs THLE RG7 40 D8
Spring St PSEA PO1 21 G2
The Spring WVILLE PO7 154 F5
Spring V BPWT SO32 318 B7
HORN PO8 156 B4
Springvale Av LTDN BH7 214 F8
WINC SO23 288 H10
Springvale Rd WINC SO23 288 H11
Springwater Cl BWD BH11 213 G5
Springwater Dr
CHCH/BSGR BH23 228 D2
Springwater Rd BWD BH11 213 G5
Spring Wy NARL SO24 291 L12
Springwell La HTWY RG27 241 M12
Springwood Av WVILLE PO7 169 M2
Spring Woods FLEETS GU52 71 H1
SHST GU47 43 L7
Spruce Av BOR GU35 112 D1
WVILLE PO7 170 A1
Spruce Cl AND SP10 95 L5
CFDH BH17 210 E7
HLER SO31 179 K4
RWIN SO21 288 E3
Spruce Dr ITCH SO19 148 E7
TOTT SO40 144 B8
Spruce Wy FLEETN GU51 59 M7
Spur Cl WIMB BH21 208 C2
Spurcroft Rd STHA RG19 35 K2
Spurgeon Rd LTDN BH7 227 H2
Spur Hill Av PSTN BH14 224 D5
Spurlings Rd WHAM PO17 166 D4
Spur Rd CHAM PO6 168 F8
PSTN BH14 224 D4
WVILLE PO7 169 L1
Spurs Ct ALDT GU11 2 B3
The Spur GPORT PO12 14 A9
WHAM PO17 152 A4
Spybush La NARL SO24 277 K9
Square Cl WIMB BH21 * 208 F5
Squarefield Gdns HTWY RG27 56 E6
The Square BSTK RG21 * 7 H3
EMRTH PO10 172 B3
EPSF GU31 316 H12
FAWY SO45 355 K5
FERN BH22 * 205 K8
GPORT PO12 183 H8
HTWY RG27 54 D3
LYMN SO41 221 J5
PSF GU32 120 D6
ROMY SO51 129 H4
SHAM SO14 22 F2
STHA RG19 35 G8
STOK SO20 284 C2
THLE RG7 238 B6
WHAM PO17 152 A5
WIMB BH21 336 F5
WINC SO23 25 G6
Squarey Cl RSAL SP5 332 B2
Squires Hill La RFNM GU10 260 A11
Squires Wk ITCH SO19 161 L7
Squirrel Cl ELGH SO50 140 F2
FHAM PO15 164 C7
SHST GU47 43 K8
Squirrel Dr DEAN RG23 104 B1
ITCH SO19 162 A1
Squirrel La FARN GU14 61 G3
Squirrels Cl CHCH/BSGR BH23 215 K6
Squirrels Drey CWTH RG45 43 H3
Squirrels Wk FAWY SO45 176 F6
Stable Cl FHAM/STUB PO14 180 D2
HTWY RG27 56 B7
Stable Ct NWBY RG14 27 K7
Stable Rd BOR GU35 110 E6
Stables Rd NTID SP9 266 E4
Stable Vw YTLY GU46 48 F1
Stacey Cl BKME/WDN BH12 224 C1
Stacey Ct HAV PO9 170 D1
Stacey Gdns CHAR BH8 214 F6
Stacey's Farm Rd
MFD/CHID GU8 263 R1
Staff College Rd CBLY GU15 50 D2
Stafford Rd BMTH BH1 9 H5
PSF GU32 120 D4
SSEA PO5 21 J7
WSHM SO15 160 D1
Staff Rd ASHV GU12 3 K3
ROMY SO51 299 K12
Stagbrake Cl FAWY SO45 354 D5
Stag Cl ELGH SO50 140 F2
NMIL/BTOS BH25 218 E4
Stag Hl KBH RG22 92 F2
Stag Oak La CHIN RG24 54 A4
Stagshorn Rd HORN PO8 156 C1
Stags La RWIN SO21 310 A3
Stagswood VWD BH31 200 F2
Stag Wy FHAM PO15 165 K7
Stainer Cl ITCH SO19 162 D1
Stainers La RWIN SO21 288 C4
Staith Cl ITCH SO19 162 C7
Stake La FARN GU14 61 G4
Stakes Hill Rd WVILLE PO7 169 L1
Stakes La BPWT SO32 142 E2
BPWT SO32 311 M9
Stakes Rd WVILLE PO7 169 K4
Stalbridge Dr FERN BH22 209 K4
Stalbridge Rd CFDH BH17 223 G1
Stalham Rd BKME/WDN BH12 224 F2
Stallard Cl EMRTH PO10 171 L7
Stallards La RGWD BH24 203 H5
Stalybridge Cl HLER SO31 164 A6
Stamford Av FRIM GU16 51 H7
HISD PO11 194 E5
Stamford Rd SBNE BH6 227 K3
Stamford St PSEA PO1 21 K1
Stamford Wy ELGH SO50 141 J3
Stamshaw Rd NEND PO2 184 D7
Stanbridge La ROMY SO51 130 B5
Stanbridge Rd HAV PO9 171 H4
Stanbury Cl RAND SP11 94 A4
RCCH PO18 173 M7
Stanbury Rd RAND SP11 94 A4
Stancomb Broad La
ALTN GU34 292 G6
Stancombe La ALTN GU34 280 C3
ALTN GU34 292 H5
Standard Wy
FHAM/PORC PO16 11 K1
Standen Rd ROWN SO16 145 J3
Standford Hl BOR GU35 113 J3
Standford La BOR GU35 113 J1
Standford St SHAM SO14 23 K4
Standing Hl RSAL SP5 297 L4
Stanfield TADY RG26 44 B4
Stanfield Rd BKME/WDN BH12 224 D1
FERN BH22 209 J2
MOOR/WNTN BH9 213 L8
Stanford Cl CHAM PO6 168 D8
Stanford Ct HAV PO9 171 H3
Stanford Ri LYMN SO41 350 F10
Stanford Rd KBH RG22 92 F5
Stanham Cl RWIN SO21 288 D6
Stanhope Rd CBLY GU15 50 C3
PSEA PO1 21 G2
Stanier Wy HEND SO30 149 J2
Stanley Av HSEA PO3 185 H8
Stanley Cl FHAM PO15 10 A5
GPORT PO12 183 G7
VWD BH31 201 J3
Stanley Dr FARN GU14 * 60 C5
Stanley Green Rd PLE BH15 223 J3
Stanley Hl CHOB/PIR GU24 63 J3
Stanley La SSEA PO5 21 H8
Stanley Rd BMTH BH1 9 L2
CHCH/BSGR BH23 218 A8
EMRTH PO10 172 A6
FAWY SO45 354 F4
LYMN SO41 221 M6
NEND PO2 184 C7
NWBY RG14 19 G6
PLE BH15 223 J7
PTSW SO17 147 J7
TOTT SO40 144 D7
Stanley St SSEA PO5 21 H8
Stanmore Gdns THLE RG7 39 M7
Stanmore La FUFL SO22 122 C6
Stannington Cl
NMIL/BTOS BH25 219 G6
Stannington Crs TOTT SO40 144 F8
Stannington Wy TOTT SO40 144 F8
Stanpit CHCH/BSGR BH23 228 E3
Stanstead Cl HAV PO9 157 J6
Stanstead Rd ELGH SO50 139 M4
Stansted Crs HAV PO9 171 H2
Stansted Rd SSEA PO5 21 K5
Stanswood Rd FAWY SO45 355 L11
HAV PO9 170 D2
Stanton Dr FLEETN GU51 59 G8
Stanton Rd NBNE BH10 213 J6
PSF GU32 120 C5
WSHM SO15 159 M1
Stapehill Crs WIMB BH21 208 C3
Stapehill Rd WIMB BH21 208 E6
Staple Ash La PSF GU32 314 G1
Staple Cl WVILLE PO7 155 K7
Staple Close La PLE BH15 223 J2
Staple Cross WHAM PO17 153 H8
Staplecross La
CHCH/BSGR BH23 216 D8
Stapleford Av FERN BH22 209 M2
Stapleford Cl ROMY SO51 131 H6
Stapleford La BPWT SO32 141 M7
Staple Gdns WINC SO23 24 F5
Staplehurst Cl ITCH SO19 162 A3
Staplers Reach
LSOL/BMARY PO13 182 B7
Stapleton Cl NWBY RG14 33 J6
Stapleton Rd HSEA PO3 185 G8
Staplewood La TOTT SO40 159 K7
Stapley La NARL SO24 305 M2
Stares Cl LSOL/BMARY PO13 190 C1
Star Hl HTWY RG27 241 P11
RFNM GU10 262 D10
Star Hill Dr RFNM GU10 262 D9
Starina Gdns WVILLE PO7 156 B8
Star La ASHV GU12 73 M6
KSCL RG20 246 B6
Starlight Farm Cl VWD BH31 201 K1
Starling Cl KBH RG22 92 B4
Starling Sq ELGH SO50 139 K6
Starting Gates NWBY RG14 19 J8
The Starting Ga NWBY RG14 19 J7
Statham Sq AND SP10 96 E1
Station Ap ALTN GU34 293 M5
AND SP10 4 E4
ASHV GU12 74 A1
BDST BH18 211 G4
BLKW GU17 50 A4
EMRTH PO10 * 171 M7
NARL SO24 291 M11
NWBY RG14 18 E5
PSEA PO1 20 C3
RAND SP11 265 M9
RAND SP11 269 M5
Station Cl RWIN SO21 290 A10
WHAM PO17 152 A4
Station Hl ELGH SO50 140 B1
FNM GU9 13 H4
HEND SO30 150 C5
HLER SO31 163 H5
NARL SO24 292 D11
OVTN RG25 89 K2
RWIN SO21 290 A10
WINC SO23 24 F4
Station La CHFD SO53 139 J2
Station Rd ALDT GU11 3 G3
ALTN GU34 107 G4
BOR GU35 110 F7
BPWT SO32 143 J5
BPWT SO32 319 J3
CHAM PO6 185 J2
CHCH/BSGR BH23 217 L5
CHCH/BSGR BH23 228 A1
DEAN RG23 91 H2
EPSF GU31 120 D5
FARN GU14 61 H4
FBDG SP6 196 B6
FBDG SP6 196 D2
FERN BH22 204 F6
FHAM/PORC PO16 167 K8
FRIM GU16 50 E7
GPORT PO12 190 F1
HISD PO11 194 E4
HLER SO31 162 C6
HLER SO31 163 H4
HLER SO31 164 A7
HSEA PO3 185 G8
HTWY RG27 56 C7
HTWY RG27 57 M7
ITCH SO19 161 M5
ITCH SO19 162 A1
KSCL RG20 246 C1
LIPH GU30 116 B6
LISS GU33 308 F8
LYMN SO41 350 F10
NARL SO24 291 M10
NMIL/BTOS BH25 219 H7
NTID SP9 266 F3
NWBY RG14 18 E6
OVTN RG25 89 K4
OVTN RG25 93 K5
PSF GU32 120 C5
PSF GU32 313 L4
PSTN BH14 224 B5
RAND SP11 269 N4
RFNM GU10 259 L12
RGWD BH24 349 M4
ROMY SO51 130 F8
ROMY SO51 136 E1
ROWN SO16 145 G4
STHA RG19 35 L1
STOK SO20 272 D9
THLE RG7 37 J2
THLE RG7 40 E3
VWD BH31 200 F1
WHAM PO17 152 A4
WHCH RG28 87 L6
WIMB BH21 207 K5
WINC SO23 24 E4
WSHM SO15 145 J8
Station Rd East ASHV GU12 73 M1
Station Rd North TOTT SO40 * 159 G1
Station Rd South TOTT SO40 * 159 G1
Station St LYMN SO41 221 M4
PSEA PO1 21 G2
Station Ter WIMB BH21 207 K5
Station Vw ASHV GU12 62 A8
Station Yd FBDG SP6 196 A6
Staunton Av HISD PO11 194 D5
Staunton Rd HAV PO9 16 C4
Staunton St PSEA PO1 192 C2
Staunton Wy HAV PO9 16 C2
HORN PO8 321 P4
Stavedown Rd RWIN SO21 288 C4
Stead Cl HISD PO11 195 H5
Stedman Rd BOSC BH5 227 H3
Steele Cl CHFD SO53 139 K4
Steeles Rd ALDT GU11 73 H4
Steels Dro FBDG SP6 332 A9
Steels La FBDG SP6 330 C12
Steel St SSEA PO5 20 F6
Steep Cl FHAM/PORC PO16 * 167 J7
Steepdene PSTN BH14 224 B5
Steeple Cl CFDH BH17 211 K5
Steeple Dr ALTN GU34 106 F4
Steepleton Rd BDST BH18 211 J5
Steeple Wy FHAM/STUB PO14 180 D1
Steepways GSHT GU26 115 H2
Steerforth Cl NEND PO2 192 D1
Steinbeck Cl FHAM PO15 164 C4
Stein Rd EMRTH PO10 172 D4
Stem La NMIL/BTOS BH25 218 E3
Stenbury Dr OVTN RG25 277 R4
Stenbury Wy HLER SO31 162 C5
Stenhurst Rd PLE BH15 223 L2
Stephen Cl HORN PO8 156 B6

Stephendale Rd FNM GU9 77 H4
Stephen Langton Dr
BWD BH11 212 D3
Stephen Martin Gdns
FBDG SP6 197 G2
Stephen Rd FHAM PO15 10 D5
Stephen's Cl THLE RG7 39 M6
Stephens Firs THLE RG7 39 M6
Stephenson Cl AND SP10 95 L3
GPORT PO12 14 C9
NTHA RG18 28 F8
Stephenson Rd BSTK RG21 65 G6
FHAM PO15 180 E2
TOTT SO40 144 D6
WHIT RG2 239 N9
Stephenson Wy HEND SO30 149 H1
Stephens Rd TADY RG26 44 C4
THLE RG7 39 M6
Steplake Rd ROMY SO51 334 H1
Step Ter FUFL SO22 24 D5
Sterling Pk AND SP10 95 L3
Sterte Av PLE BH15 223 H4
Sterte Av West PLE BH15 223 H4
Sterte Cl PLE BH15 223 J4
Sterte Rd PLE BH15 223 J4
Steuart Rd WEND SO18 161 K1
Stevens Dro STOK SO20 285 K11
Stevens Gn RAND SP11 86 C3
Stevens Hl YTLY GU46 49 G3
Stevenson Crs PSTN BH14 224 D5
Stevenson Rd RWIN SO21 273 N2
SBNE BH6 228 A5
Stevensons Cl WIMB BH21 207 J4
Steventon Rd OVTN RG25 103 G3
WEND SO18 148 C5
Stewards Ri RFNM GU10 78 D1
Stewart Cl CHAR BH8 9 M1
Stewart Rd CHIN RG24 54 A7
CHAR BH8 226 B2
Stewarts Gn WVILLE PO7 319 Q9
Stewarts Wy FERN BH22 209 L1
Steyning Ter HAV PO9 * 16 F3
Stibbs Wy CHCH/BSGR BH23 348 E11
Stickle Down FRIM GU16 51 M8
Stile Gdns HASM GU27 117 M2
Stiles Dr AND SP10 96 F4
Stillions Cl ALTN GU34 107 G5
Stillmore Rd BWD BH11 212 D5
Stillwater Pk RGWD BH24 * 203 L2
Stilwell Cl YTLY GU46 49 G2
Stinchar Dr CHFD SO53 139 G3
Stinsford Cl MOOR/WNTN BH9 214 B4
Stinsford Rd CFDH BH17 211 K7
Stirling Av WVILLE PO7 169 M1
Stirling Cl ASHV GU12 73 M3
FARN GU14 61 G5
FRIM GU16 51 G6
NMIL/BTOS BH25 219 H5
TOTT SO40 145 G7
Stirling Crs HEND SO30 149 J3
TOTT SO40 145 G8
Stirling Rd MOOR/WNTN BH9 225 L1
Stirling St NEND PO2 184 D8
Stirling Wy CHCH/BSGR BH23 229 H2
FARN GU14 72 D1
NTHA RG18 28 E8
Stirrup Cl UPTN BH16 222 D1
WIMB BH21 208 C2
Stirrup Pightle NWBY RG14 34 B5
Stoatley Hollow HASM GU27 118 A4
Stoatley Ri HASM GU27 118 A4
Stoatley River HASM GU27 118 A4
Stoborough Dr BDST BH18 211 G6
Stockbridge Cl CFDH BH17 212 B6
CHIN RG24 54 D4
HAV PO9 171 H3
Stockbridge Dr ALDT GU11 260 A2
Stockbridge Rd FUFL SO22 24 A1
RAND SP11 271 J9
ROMY SO51 130 C1
RWIN SO21 274 C8
RWIN SO21 287 L8
STOK SO20 299 Q1
Stockbridge Wy YTLY GU46 48 F4
Stocker Cl BSTK RG21 93 J2
Stocker Pl LSOL/BMARY PO13 182 D6
Stockers Av FUFL SO22 24 A1
Stockheath La HAV PO9 16 C2
Stockheath Rd HAV PO9 170 F4
Stockheath Wy HAV PO9 170 F5
Stockholm Dr HEND SO30 149 J8
Stock La RSAL SP5 334 A1
Stockley Cl FAWY SO45 354 E5
Stocks Bridge La RSAL SP5 325 N3
Stocks La ALTN GU34 305 Q11
BPWT SO32 312 E10
Stockton Av FLEETN GU51 59 H6
Stockton Cl HEND SO30 149 K5
Stockton Pk FLEETN GU51 59 H6
Stockwood Ri CBLY GU15 51 H3
Stockwood Wy FNM GU9 2 D8
Stoddart Av ITCH SO19 161 M2
Stodham La EPSF GU31 121 J1
Stoke Charity Rd RWIN SO21 288 G5
Stoke Common Rd ELGH SO50 134 E7
Stoke Gdns GPORT PO12 15 G5
Stoke Hts ELGH SO50 141 H1
Stoke Hl RAND SP11 85 K1
Stoke Hills FNM GU9 13 J1
Stoke La RAND SP11 251 J11
Stoken La HTWY RG27 57 H1
Stoke Pde GPORT PO12 * 15 G5
Stoke Park Rd ELGH SO50 134 E8
Stoke Rd GPORT PO12 14 F5
RAND SP11 85 G5
RAND SP11 250 H10
ROWN SO16 146 A7
WINC SO23 123 G1
Stokes Av PLE BH15 223 J4
Stokesay Cl FAWY SO45 177 G8
Stokes Bay Rd GPORT PO12 190 D6
Stokes La STHA RG19 249 N3
Stokesway GPORT PO12 * 15 G5
Stoke Wood Cl ELGH SO50 141 H2
Stoke Wood Rd TWDS BH3 225 M1
Stonechat Cl EPSF GU31 121 G7
FERN BH22 204 D8
Stonechat Dr TOTT SO40 144 B8
Stonechat Rd HORN PO8 156 A2
Stone Cl AND SP10 4 C9
RSAL SP5 282 G10
Stone Copse NTHA RG18 28 A5
Stonecrop Cl BDST BH18 210 E6
Stone Crop Cl HLER SO31 179 L3
Stonedene Cl BOR GU35 114 B4
Stone Gdns CHAR BH8 215 G6
Stonegate CBLY GU15 51 L2
Stoneham Cemetery Rd
WEND SO18 147 M4
Stoneham Cl PSF GU32 120 B5
ROWN SO16 147 K3
Stoneham La ELGH SO50 139 L8
ROWN SO16 147 K3
Stoneham Pk PSF GU32 120 B5
Stoneham Wy ELGH SO50 147 L3
Stonehill Pk BOR GU35 114 B4
Stonehill Rd BOR GU35 114 C4
Stonehills FAWY SO45 355 L6
Stonehouse Ri FRIM GU16 51 G7
Stonehouse Rd LIPH GU30 116 D4
Stone La GPORT PO12 14 F6
WIMB BH21 207 G2
Stoneleigh Av LYMN SO41 219 M4
Stoneleigh Cl
FHAM/PORC PO16 167 H8
Stoneleigh Ct FRIM GU16 51 H7
Stoners Cl LSOL/BMARY PO13 182 B5
Stone Sq HAV PO9 170 F4
Stone St ASHV GU12 3 M6
SSEA PO5 20 F6
Stone Ter ELGH SO50 * 134 B3
Stoney Bottom GSHT GU26 115 J5
Stoney Cl YTLY GU46 48 F4
Stoney Ct FUFL SO22 122 E2
Stoney Cross RAND SP11 265 M10
Stoneyfields FNM GU9 13 L6
Stoney La ALTN GU34 293 M4
FUFL SO22 122 E2
NWBY RG14 27 M6
STHA RG19 35 L1
Stony La CHCH/BSGR BH23 216 B6
FBDG SP6 330 A12
PSEA PO1 20 C1
Stony La South
CHCH/BSGR BH23 228 C2
Stonymoor Cl FAWY SO45 354 E5
Stookes Wy YTLY GU46 48 D4
Stopples La LYMN SO41 219 M5
Storrington Rd HORN PO8 321 M7
Story La BDST BH18 211 H4
Stourbank Rd
CHCH/BSGR BH23 228 A2
Stourcliffe Av SBNE BH6 227 J4
Stour Cl PSF GU32 120 C7
WEND SO18 148 A1
WIMB BH21 208 D4
Stourcroft Dr
CHCH/BSGR BH23 215 K6
Stourfield Rd BOSC BH5 227 H4
Stourhead Cl AND SP10 4 B7
FARN GU14 61 K4
Stourpaine Rd CFDH BH17 211 K6
Stour Pk NBNE BH10 * 213 L2
Stour Rd CHAR BH8 226 D2
CHCH/BSGR BH23 228 A2
DEAN RG23 91 K3
Stourvale Av
CHCH/BSGR BH23 215 K8
Stourvale Gdns CHFD SO53 139 K3
Stourvale Pl BOSC BH5 227 H3
Stourvale Rd SBNE BH6 227 H3
Stour Valley Wy
MOOR/WNTN BH9 214 C2
SBNE BH6 227 L1
SBNE BH6 228 E6
WIMB BH21 206 E4
WIMB BH21 208 A7
Stour View Gdns WIMB BH21 206 E7
Stour Wk CHAR BH8 214 D4
Stour Wy CHCH/BSGR BH23 215 K6
Stourwood Av SBNE BH6 227 J4
Stourwood Rd SBNE BH6 227 K4
Stouts La CHCH/BSGR BH23 348 D11
Stovold's Wy ALDT GU11 2 C6
Stowe Cl HEND SO30 149 K3
Stowe Rd ENEY PO4 193 H4
Stradbrook
LSOL/BMARY PO13 182 B7
Stragwyne Cl NBAD SO52 137 L3
The Straight Mile ROMY SO51 131 L7
Strand SHAM SO14 23 G4
Strand St PLE BH15 223 H7
The Strand HISD PO11 195 J7
Stranding St ELGH SO50 139 M5
Strategic Pk HEND SO30 * 148 F5
Stratfield Av TADY RG26 44 B5
Stratfield Dr CHFD SO53 133 H7
Stratfield Pk WVILLE PO7 * 155 J8
Stratfield Pl NMIL/BTOS BH25 218 E5
Stratfield Rd BSTK RG21 65 K4
Stratfield Saye Rd TADY RG26 46 C3
Stratford Pl ELGH SO50 134 B8
LYMN SO41 221 K3
Stratford Rd ASHV GU12 61 M8
WVILLE PO7 156 A8
Stratford Tony Rd RSAL SP5 325 L2
Strathfield Rd AND SP10 96 B7
Strathmore Dr VWD BH31 201 J2
Strathmore Rd GPORT PO12 15 H4
NBNE BH10 214 A4
Stratton Cl CHAM PO6 168 C8
RWIN SO21 276 C8
Stratton La RWIN SO21 276 E11
Stratton Pk KBH RG22 92 D2
Stratton Rd BSTK RG21 93 H2
MOOR/WNTN BH9 214 C4
WINC SO23 25 K7
WSHM SO15 146 C7
Stratton Wk FARN GU14 61 G1
Strauss Rd KBH RG22 92 E4
Stravinsky Rd KBH RG22 93 H4
Strawberry Cl CHOB/PIR GU24 63 K2
Strawberry Ct FRIM GU16 51 M8
Strawberry Flds BROC SO42 353 K10
HEND SO30 149 G6
TADY RG26 46 B5
Strawberry Hl HLER SO31 179 M1
NWBY RG14 18 D2
Strawberry Md ELGH SO50 141 H3
Stream Farm Cl RFNM GU10 79 H1
Streamleaze
FHAM/STUB PO14 180 C3
Streamside FLEETN GU51 59 J8
Stream Valley Rd RFNM GU10 79 G2
Street End HTWY RG27 58 D4
NBAD SO52 138 B3
Streets La RGWD BH24 203 L8
The Street ALTN GU34 108 A5
CHIN RG24 66 C2
FLEETN GU51 70 F3
HTWY RG27 56 A3
MFD/CHID GU8 261 P9
MFD/CHID GU8 263 Q8
ODIM RG29 68 B6
ODIM RG29 258 B5
RFNM GU10 78 C2
RFNM GU10 109 L6
RFNM GU10 260 D3
RFNM GU10 262 C5
RGUW GU3 261 M4
RSAL SP5 127 G4
RSAL SP5 127 M5
RSAL SP5 282 D10
RSAL SP5 296 C5
TADY RG26 53 M2
THLE RG7 38 A5
THLE RG7 40 B3
THLE RG7 238 C10
Streetway Rd RAND SP11 269 M5
Strete Mt CHCH/BSGR BH23 * 228 E1
Stride Av HSEA PO3 193 H2
Strides La RGWD BH24 203 H5
Strides Wy TOTT SO40 158 B1
Strode Gdns RGWD BH24 202 D7
Strode Rd NEND PO2 184 C6
Strokins Rd KSCL RG20 248 D9
Strongs Cl ROMY SO51 131 H8
Stroud Cl CHIN RG24 54 A6
WIMB BH21 208 A2
Strouden Av CHAR BH8 214 C8
Strouden Ct HAV PO9 170 D1
Stroud End PSF GU32 315 M4
Strouden Rd
MOOR/WNTN BH9 214 A7
Stroud Gdns CHCH/BSGR BH23 228 E2
Stroud Gn NWBY RG14 19 G7
Stroud Green La
FHAM/STUB PO14 181 L7
Stroud La CHCH/BSGR BH23 228 E2
FLEETN GU51 70 E3
Stroudley Av CHAM PO6 185 J2
Stroudley Rd CHIN RG24 66 A1
Stroudley Wy HEND SO30 149 K2
Stroud Park Av
CHCH/BSGR BH23 228 E2
Strouds Meadow NTHA RG18 28 E5
Stroudwood La BPWT SO32 142 A1
RWIN SO21 310 A11
Stroudwood Rd HAV PO9 171 G5
Struan Cl RGWD BH24 202 B6
Struan Ct RGWD BH24 202 C6
Struan Dr RGWD BH24 202 B6
Struan Gdns RGWD BH24 202 B6
Stuart Cl FARN GU14 61 G3
FHAM/STUB PO14 189 J2
UPTN BH16 222 B1
Stuart Crs FUFL SO22 122 E7
Stuart Rd CHCH/BSGR BH23 218 B8
NWBY RG14 33 J6
Stubbington Av BOR GU35 112 E3
NEND PO2 184 E7
Stubbington Gn
FHAM/STUB PO14 189 J1
Stubbington La
FHAM/STUB PO14 189 J2
Stubbington Wy ELGH SO50 141 K3
Stubbs Ct AND SP10 4 F2
Stubbs Dro HEND SO30 149 K5
Stubbs Folly SHST GU47 49 M1
Stubbs Moor Rd FARN GU14 60 F3
Stubbs Rd BSTK RG21 93 L2
ITCH SO19 162 C2
Stuckton Rd FBDG SP6 197 J4
Studland Cl ROWN SO16 145 K7
WHIT RG2 238 C1
Studland Dr LYMN SO41 232 B3
Studland Rd
LSOL/BMARY PO13 189 L6
ROWN SO16 145 K7
WBNE BH4 225 J7
Studley Av FAWY SO45 354 E5
Studley Cl CHCH/BSGR BH23 218 C8
Studley Ct NMIL/BTOS BH25 218 D8
Stukeley Rd BSTK RG21 6 B7
Sturdee Cl FRIM GU16 51 G7
Sturminster Rd
MOOR/WNTN BH9 214 B4
Sturt Av HASM GU27 117 M3
Sturt Rd FNM GU9 76 F1
FRIM GU16 61 M3
HASM GU27 118 A8
The Styles RSAL SP5 324 E4
Sudbury Rd CHAM PO6 168 D8
Suetts La BPWT SO32 143 M5
Suffield La RGUW GU3 261 K8
Suffolk Av CHCH/BSGR BH23 215 M6
WSHM SO15 160 D1
Suffolk Cl CHFD SO53 139 J6
WIMB BH21 208 C2
WWKG RG41 239 R2
Suffolk Ct FRIM GU16 51 M8
Suffolk Dr CHFD SO53 139 J6
FHAM PO15 164 B5
Suffolk Rd AND SP10 4 F7
ENEY PO4 193 G5
WCLF BH2 8 B5
Suffolk Rd South WBNE BH4 8 A4
Sullivan Cl CHAM PO6 167 L8
FARN GU14 61 G4
Sullivan Rd CBLY GU15 50 C3
ITCH SO19 162 D1
KBH RG22 93 H4
Sullivan Wy WVILLE PO7 169 L3
Sultan Rd EMRTH PO10 171 M7
NEND PO2 192 D1
Sumar Cl FHAM/STUB PO14 181 K7
Summercroft Wy FERN BH22 205 G5
Summer Down La TADY RG26 255 L11
Summer Fld WIMB BH21 208 B4
Summerfield Cl
CHCH/BSGR BH23 216 C6
Summerfield Gdns
ROWN SO16 147 K3
Summerfield La RFNM GU10 78 E6
Summerfields CHIN RG24 54 C4
FHAM/STUB PO14 180 B3
LTDN BH7 226 F1
Summer Flds VWD BH31 201 H4
Summer Gdns CBLY GU15 51 L3
Summerhill Rd HORN PO8 155 M5
Summerlands Rd ELGH SO50 141 J2
Summerlands Wk HAV PO9 * 171 H3
Summer La BROC SO42 354 A7
Summerleigh Wk
FHAM/STUB PO14 181 K7
Summerlug THLE RG7 40 A3
Summers Av BWD BH11 213 H2
Summers La CHCH/BSGR BH23 216 D7
Summers St SHAM SO14 161 H2
Summertrees Ct
NMIL/BTOS BH25 219 K4
Summit Av FARN GU14 60 C5
Summit Cl EWKG RG40 42 B2
Summit Wy WEND SO18 147 M7
Sumner Rd EPSF GU31 315 P11
FNM GU9 13 H1
Sunbeam Wy GPORT PO12 14 F7
Sun Brow HASM GU27 117 M3
Sunbury Cl BOR GU35 113 G1
Sunbury Ct FHAM PO15 165 L8
Sunderland Dr
CHCH/BSGR BH23 229 H1
Sunderland Pl NTHA RG18 28 E8
Sunderton La HORN PO8 321 L7
Sundew Cl CHCH/BSGR BH23 217 J7
NMIL/BTOS BH25 219 K4
Sundew Rd BDST BH18 210 E6
Sundridge Cl CHAM PO6 168 E8
Sunflower Cl KBH RG22 92 C5
Sun Hill Crs NARL SO24 291 M12
Sun La NARL SO24 291 M12
THLE RG7 240 B2
Sunley Cl NWBY RG14 33 K6
Sunningdale FAWY SO45 176 F6
Sunningdale Cl ELGH SO50 140 F2
LSOL/BMARY PO13 182 C7
Sunningdale Crs NBNE BH10 213 J4
Sunningdale Gdns
WEND SO18 148 B5
Sunningdale Rd
FHAM/PORC PO16 183 K1
HSEA PO3 193 G2
Sunnybank RAND SP11 95 G6
Sunnybank Ms ASHV GU12 * 74 B5
Sunnybank Rd FARN GU14 60 D2
WIMB BH21 208 B2
Sunnydell La FNM GU9 78 E2
Sunnydown Rd FUFL SO22 124 A1
Sunnyfield Ri HLER SO31 163 G3
Sunnyfield Rd
NMIL/BTOS BH25 219 G8
Sunnyheath HAV PO9 170 E4
Sunnyhill MARL SN8 264 G4
Sunny Hill Rd ALDT GU11 72 D6
BKME/WDN BH12 224 D3
Sunnyhill Rd SBNE BH6 227 H3
Sunnylands Av SBNE BH6 227 M4
Sunny Md DEAN RG23 91 K4
Sunnymead Dr WVILLE PO7 155 J6
Sunnymoor Rd BWD BH11 213 G7
Sunnyside FLEETN GU51 59 G6
KSCL RG20 * 248 C11
Sunnyside Cl AND SP10 95 M2
Sunnyside Rd
BKME/WDN BH12 224 D2
BOR GU35 114 C4
Sunnyview Cl ASHV GU12 3 K4
Sunny Wk PSEA PO1 20 B2
Sunny Wy TOTT SO40 158 F1
Sun Ray Est SHST GU47 43 H8
Sunridge Cl BKME/WDN BH12 225 G2
Sunset Av TOTT SO40 144 E8
Sunset Rd TOTT SO40 144 E8
Sunshine Av HISD PO11 195 H6
Sun St PSEA PO1 20 D3
Suntrap Gdns HISD PO11 * 195 H6
Sunvale Av HASM GU27 117 K2
Sunvale Cl HASM GU27 117 K2
ITCH SO19 162 B1
Sunwood Rd HAV PO9 170 D3
Surbiton Rd ELGH SO50 134 B7
Surrey Av CBLY GU15 50 C4
Surrey Cl CHCH/BSGR BH23 215 M6
TOTT SO40 158 D3
Surrey Gdns WBNE BH4 225 J4
Surrey Rd BKME/WDN BH12 225 G3
CHFD SO53 139 J5
ITCH SO19 161 K6
Surrey Rd South WBNE BH4 225 J4
Surrey St PSEA PO1 21 G2
Sussex Border Pth
EMRTH PO10 187 M5
EPSF GU31 316 F11
HAV PO9 157 K4
HORN PO8 322 A8
LIPH GU30 116 C7
LISS GU33 309 M6
MFD/CHID GU8 119 M7
Sussex Cl MOOR/WNTN BH9 214 B4
Sussex Gdns EPSF GU31 120 D7
FLEETN GU51 59 K4
Sussex La THLE RG7 238 C7
Sussex Pl SSEA PO5 * 21 G7
Sussex Rd CHFD SO53 139 K5
EPSF GU31 120 E7
SHAM SO14 23 G3
SSEA PO5 21 G7
Sussex St WINC SO23 24 F5
Sussex Ter SSEA PO5 21 G7
Sutcliffe Sq AND SP10 * 96 E1
Sutherland Av BDST BH18 210 E3
Sutherland Cl BOR GU35 112 F3
ROMY SO51 131 H7
Sutherland Ct AND SP10 4 F2
Sutherland Rd ENEY PO4 21 M6
ROWN SO16 145 M3
Sutherlands NWBY RG14 33 L5
Sutherlands Ct CHFD SO53 139 J2
Sutherlands Wy CHFD SO53 139 H1
Sutton Cl CFDH BH17 212 A6
HORN PO8 155 K5
HSEA PO3 185 H4
Sutton Fld BOR GU35 112 E3
Sutton Gdns WINC SO23 25 G5
Sutton Pl BROC SO42 351 L3
Sutton Rd BSTK RG21 6 E1
HORN PO8 155 K5
MOOR/WNTN BH9 214 B7
NWBY RG14 26 F7
TOTT SO40 144 D7
Sutton Wood La NARL SO24 292 C8
Swains Cl TADY RG26 44 B4
Swains Rd TADY RG26 44 B4
Swaledale Gdns FLEETN GU51 59 K4
Swale Dr CHFD SO53 139 G1
Swale Rd FARN GU14 60 D2
Swallow Cl ALTN GU34 107 G2
CFDH BH17 210 F8
HAV PO9 17 J1
KBH RG22 92 B4
NTID SP9 266 F2
TOTT SO40 158 B2
YTLY GU46 48 D2
Swallow Ct LSOL/BMARY PO13 189 M5
Swallow Dr LYMN SO41 232 F4
Swallowfield Dr WHIT RG2 238 B2
Swallowfield Rd THLE RG7 238 G10
Swallowfields AND SP10 96 D2
Swallow Sq ELGH SO50 139 K6
Swallow Wd FHAM/PORC PO16 11 G1
Swanage Cl ITCH SO19 161 L5
Swanage Rd
LSOL/BMARY PO13 189 L6
Swan Barn Rd HASM GU27 118 D6
Swan Cl EMRTH PO10 172 A7
HLER SO31 163 K5
Swancote FHAM/PORC PO16 166 F8
Swan Ct AND SP10 5 J5
HTWY RG27 57 M2
NWBY RG14 * 18 D4
Swan Dr THLE RG7 38 C1
Swan La SHST GU47 49 K2
WINC SO23 24 F4
Swanley Cl ELGH SO50 134 A7
Swan Md RGWD BH24 203 L6
Swan Ms ODIM RG29 68 E4
Swanmore Av ITCH SO19 162 B1
Swanmore Cl FUFL SO22 288 C12
LTDN BH7 227 H1
Swanmore Rd BPWT SO32 143 M5
BPWT SO32 318 E6
HAV PO9 170 D1
LTDN BH7 227 H2
Swansbury Dr CHAR BH8 215 G6
Swan St KSCL RG20 248 C11
PSF GU32 120 C6
WIMB BH21 336 E5
Swans Wk HISD PO11 * 195 H5
Swanton Cl FHAM/STUB PO14 189 K1
Swanton Gdns CHFD SO53 * 139 H1
Swan Wy FLEETN GU51 70 F1
Swanwick La HLER SO31 163 L4
Swanwick Shore Rd
HLER SO31 163 K5
Swanwick Wk TADY RG26 44 B4
Swarraton Rd HAV PO9 171 G4
Sway Ct HAV PO9 * 171 H3
Sway Gdns CHAR BH8 214 D6
Sway Rd BROC SO42 351 K5
LYMN SO41 220 E3
NMIL/BTOS BH25 219 H2
Swaythling Rd HAV PO9 170 D2
HEND SO30 148 B2
Swedish Houses TADY RG26 44 C5
The Sweep RGWD BH24 203 H5
Sweetbriar CWTH RG45 * 43 J1
Sweetbriar Gdns WVILLE PO7 169 M3
Sweethills Crs HLER SO31 164 B4
Sweetzer's Piece THLE RG7 39 L6
Swelling Hl ALTN GU34 293 L10
Sweyns Lease BROC SO42 353 J10
Swift Cl AND SP10 96 D2
CFDH BH17 210 F8
ELGH SO50 139 K6
FUFL SO22 122 D7
HORN PO8 156 A1
LSOL/BMARY PO13 189 M5
Swift Gdns ITCH SO19 161 K7
Swift Hollow ITCH SO19 161 K7
Swift Rd FNM GU9 76 F1
ITCH SO19 161 L7
Swift's Cl RFNM GU10 77 M7
Swinburn Gdns HORN PO8 155 M4
Swincombe Ri WEND SO18 148 B3
Swingate Rd FNM GU9 13 J8
Swing Swang La CHIN RG24 66 B1
Swiss Cl RFNM GU10 78 D4
Swiss Rd WVILLE PO7 169 L1
Switchback La RFNM GU10 78 E5
Swivelton La WHAM PO17 167 G5
Sword Cl GPORT PO12 190 E6
HORN PO8 321 K7
Swordfish Dr
CHCH/BSGR BH23 229 H1
Swordfish Wy FARN GU14 72 E1
Sword Sands Rd HSEA PO3 193 J1
Swordsman's Rd FRIM GU16 51 M8
Sycamore Av CHFD SO53 133 J7
Sycamore Cl CFDH BH17 210 F7
CHCH/BSGR BH23 215 K8
FHAM/STUB PO14 180 C4
FRIM GU16 51 G7
HLER SO31 162 F4
HORN PO8 155 L5
HORN PO8 321 L7
LSOL/BMARY PO13 182 E7
LYMN SO41 232 C3
NBAD SO52 137 M3
NTID SP9 266 G2
ROMY SO51 137 J2
SHST GU47 49 K1
Sycamore Crs FLEETN GU51 71 G2
Sycamore Dr ASHV GU12 73 M1
FAWY SO45 354 D3
FRIM GU16 51 G6
HISD PO11 194 E4
RFNM GU10 78 E2
WINC SO23 288 H8
Sycamore Pl WIMB BH21 208 D3
Sycamore Ri NWBY RG14 27 L6
Sycamore Rd BPWT SO32 143 L4
FARN GU14 61 K6
FAWY SO45 176 F5
LYMN SO41 219 M4
ROWN SO16 146 A6
The Sycamores BLKW GU17 49 K3
FARN GU14 61 K5
Sycamore Wk AND SP10 4 B7
Sycamore Wy DEAN RG23 64 F6
Sydenham Ter PSEA PO1 21 K3
The Sydings NWBY RG14 26 F7
Sydling Cl CFDH BH17 212 B6
Sydmanton Cl ROMY SO51 137 G2
Sydmonton Ct HAV PO9 171 H2
Sydney Av HLER SO31 178 E1
Sydney Cl CWTH RG45 43 L1
STHA RG19 * 35 L1
Sydney Loader Pl BLKW GU17 49 J2
Sydney Rd BDST BH18 211 G5
BOR GU35 112 F1
CHCH/BSGR BH23 215 L7
ELGH SO50 134 D8
GPORT PO12 14 F4
WSHM SO15 146 B7
Sydney Smith Av FARN GU14 61 H7
Syers Rd LISS GU33 308 F8
Sylmor Gdns
MOOR/WNTN BH9 214 A6
Sylvan Av ITCH SO19 148 C6
Sylvan Cl LYMN SO41 220 B6
RGWD BH24 205 M4
Sylvan Dr NBAD SO52 137 M4
Sylvan La HLER SO31 179 G2
Sylvan Rdg SHST GU47 43 J7
Sylvan Rd BKME/WDN BH12 224 B2
The Sylvans FAWY SO45 176 D5
Sylvan Vw WVILLE PO7 169 M2
Sylvan Wy FLEETS GU52 71 H3
Sylvester Cl NWBY RG14 27 G7
Sylvia Cl BSTK RG21 6 D8
Sylvia Crs TOTT SO40 144 E7
Symes Rd PLE BH15 222 E4
ROMY SO51 137 H1
Symonds Cl CHFD SO53 139 K4
Symonds St WINC SO23 25 G7
Sympson Rd TADY RG26 44 D3
Syon Pl FARN GU14 61 K4
Sywell Crs HSEA PO3 185 H4
Szabo Crs RGUW GU3 75 H7

T

Tadburn Cl CHFD SO53 139 K3
ROMY SO51 137 G1
Tadburn Gn ROMY SO51 * 136 E2
Tadburn Rd ROMY SO51 137 G2
Tadden Wk BDST BH18 210 F6
Tadfield Rd ROMY SO51 137 G1
Tadham Pl STHA RG19 35 J2
Tadley Cl FLEETN GU51 58 F4
Tadley Common Rd TADY RG26 44 C3
Tadley Hl TADY RG26 44 C5
Tadpole La RFNM GU10 71 K7
Tagdell La HORN PO8 320 H12
Taiping Rd STOK SO20 270 C7
Tait Cl CFDH BH17 223 L1
Tait Pl LSOL/BMARY PO13 182 D7
Talbot Av TWDS BH3 225 L1
Talbot Cl FRIM GU16 62 A4
HAV PO9 170 C5
NWBY RG14 27 G7
ROWN SO16 146 F4
Talbot Dr BKME/WDN BH12 213 H8
CHCH/BSGR BH23 217 M6
Talbot Hill Rd
MOOR/WNTN BH9 213 K8
Talbot Mdw BKME/WDN BH12 213 H8
Talbot Ms NBNE BH10 213 H7
Talbot Ri NBNE BH10 213 J7
Talbot Rd ENEY PO4 21 M5
FAWY SO45 176 D7
FHAM PO15 180 E2
FNM GU9 12 E7
HAV PO9 16 A1
MOOR/WNTN BH9 213 L8
Talgarth Dr FARN GU14 61 K6
Talisman Cl CWTH RG45 42 F3
Talland Rd FHAM/STUB PO14 180 B3
Tallis Gdns KBH RG22 93 G3
Talmey Cl CHIN RG24 54 A5
Tamar Cl FERN BH22 346 A7
FHAM/PORC PO16 167 G7

Tamar Down WVILLE PO7 170 A1
Tamar Dr DEAN RG23 91 K3
Tamar Gv FAWY SO45 176 E5
Tamarisk Cl ENEY PO4 193 J5
FHAM/STUB PO14 189 J4
KBH RG22 92 E7
WVILLE PO7 170 A3
Tamarisk Cl NTHA RG18 29 H8
Tamarisk Gdns WEND SO18 147 L8
Tamarisk Rd HEND SO30 149 H5
Tamella Rd HEND SO30 149 L6
Tammys Turn
FHAM/STUB PO14 181 H4
Tamorisk Dr TOTT SO40 158 C2
Tamworth Dr FLEETN GU51 59 K4
Tamworth Pl GPORT PO12 14 F6
Tamworth Rd HSEA PO3 193 G2
LTDN BH7 226 F3
Tanfield La WHAM PO17 165 M1
Tanfield Pk WHAM PO17 165 M1
Tangier Cl ALDT GU11 2 C3
Tangier La BPWT SO32 142 F5
Tangier Rd HSEA PO3 193 G1
Tanglewood EWKG RG40 42 C1
FHAM/PORC PO16 10 E1
TOTT SO40 160 A7
Tanglewood Cl WVILLE PO7 169 J4
Tangley Wk HAV PO9 * 171 H3
Tangmere Cl
CHCH/BSGR BH23 229 H2
Tangmere Dr ROWN SO16 145 M4
Tangway CHIN RG24 54 B4
Tangyes Cl FHAM/STUB PO14 189 K1
Tanhouse Cl HEND SO30 149 J7
Tanhouse La ALTN GU34 106 E4
HEND SO30 149 K8
Tan Howse Cl LTDN BH7 215 H8
Tankerdale La PSF GU32 121 G1
Tanker Rd FARN GU14 61 H7
Tankerton Cl CHAM PO6 168 E8
Tankerville Rd ITCH SO19 161 K5
Tank Rd CBLY GU15 50 B3
The Tanneries
FHAM/STUB PO14 * 181 G4
HAV PO9 * 16 D5
Tanner's Brook Wy
WSHM SO15 159 M2
Tanners Cl THLE RG7 39 M3
Tanners La FBDG SP6 196 B1
FHAM/STUB PO14 181 L6
HASM GU27 118 C5
LYMN SO41 356 G8
ROMY SO51 335 P1
WVILLE PO7 154 F3
Tanner's Rdg WVILLE PO7 169 L5
Tanners Rd NBAD SO52 138 A4
The Tanners FHAM/STUB PO14 180 C4
Tanner St WINC SO23 25 H6
Tanners Wy DEAN RG23 91 K2
Tansy Cl WVILLE PO7 170 A2
Tansy Meadow CHFD SO53 138 F4
The Tanyards CHFD SO53 133 H7
Taplin Dr HEND SO30 149 J4
Taplings Cl FUFL SO22 122 D1
Taplings Rd FUFL SO22 122 D1
Taplin's Farm La HTWY RG27 58 A5
Taranto Rd ROWN SO16 146 C4
Tarbat Ct SHST GU47 43 M8
Tarbery Crs HORN PO8 156 C1
Target Rd NEND PO2 184 C5
Tarius Cl LSOL/BMARY PO13 182 D6
Tarleton Rd CHAM PO6 168 B7
Tarn Cl FARN GU14 60 E6
Tarn Dr CFDH BH17 210 F7
Tarn Howes Cl STHA RG19 35 G1
Tarn La NWBY RG14 18 C9
Tarn Ri HORN PO8 321 L10
Tarn Rd GSHT GU26 115 K5
Tarragon Cl FARN GU14 60 C4
Tarrant Cl CFDH BH17 211 L6
Tarrant Gdns HAV PO9 16 D1
Tarrant Rd MOOR/WNTN BH9 214 B5
Taskers Dr RAND SP11 95 L7
Tasman Cl CHCH/BSGR BH23 215 M8
SHAM SO14 23 K8
Tasman Ct SHAM SO14 23 K8
Tasmania Cl CHIN RG24 65 L2
Taswell Rd SSEA PO5 21 K9
Tatchbury La TOTT SO40 341 R3
Tate Rd WSHM SO15 145 J8
Tate Sq AND SP10 * 96 E1
Tates Rd FAWY SO45 177 H6
Tatnam Rd PLE BH15 223 J4
Tattenham Rd BROC SO42 351 K4
Tattershall Crs
FHAM/PORC PO16 183 H1
Tatwin Cl ITCH SO19 148 D7
Tatwin Crs ITCH SO19 148 D7
Taunton Dr WEND SO18 148 B5
Tavells Cl TOTT SO40 159 L7
Tavell's La TOTT SO40 159 L7
Taverner Cl BSTK RG21 7 J1
PLE BH15 223 K7
Taverners Cl ITCH SO19 162 D1
Tavistock Cl ROMY SO51 131 H7
Tavistock Gdns FARN GU14 61 H1
HAV PO9 17 J5
Tavistock Rd FLEETN GU51 58 F8
Tavy Cl CHFD SO53 139 H2
Taw Dr CHFD SO53 139 H1
Tawny Gv ALTN GU34 293 L6
Tawny Owl Cl
FHAM/STUB PO14 181 H8
Tawny Rw SHST GU47 * 43 M8
Tay Cl FARN GU14 60 E2
Taylor Dr CHAR BH8 214 D4
TADY RG26 46 D6
Taylor's Buildings PLE BH15 223 J7
Taylors Cl BOR GU35 111 H7
Taylors La BOR GU35 111 H7
Taylor Wy VWD BH31 201 J2
Teachers Wy FAWY SO45 354 D4
Teal Cl FHAM/PORC PO16 166 F8
HISD PO11 195 H5
HORN PO8 156 A1
TOTT SO40 158 C1
Teal Crs KBH RG22 92 B5
Teasel Cl RAND SP11 265 M11
Teasel Wy FERN BH22 205 G7
Teazle Cl EPSF GU31 121 G7
Tebourba Dr GPORT PO12 14 C7
Tebourba Wy WSHM SO15 159 M1
Technology Rd CFDH BH17 211 G7
Tedder Cl BWD BH11 213 H5
RAND SP11 95 K5
Tedder Rd BWD BH11 213 H5
LSOL/BMARY PO13 182 D5
WEND SO18 148 A4
Tedder Wy TOTT SO40 158 D1
Teddington Rd ENEY PO4 193 G4
Tees Cl CHFD SO53 139 G1
FARN GU14 60 E2
Teg Down Meads FUFL SO22 122 B3
Tegg Down Rd NARL SO24 304 D1
Teignmouth Rd GPORT PO12 190 F1
HSEA PO3 185 G8
Tekels Av CBLY GU15 50 F4
Tekels Wy CBLY GU15 51 H5
Telconia Cl BOR GU35 114 C4
Telegraph La ALTN GU34 293 P5
EPSF GU31 323 Q2
Telegraph Rd HEND SO30 148 E4
Telegraph Wy RWIN SO21 302 B5
Telephone Rd ENEY PO4 21 M4
Telford Gdns HEND SO30 149 L2
Telford Rd BSTK RG21 65 G5
NEND PO2 184 E5
WIMB BH21 204 C8
Telford Wy FHAM PO15 164 C7
Teme Crs ROWN SO16 145 L8
Teme Rd ROWN SO16 145 L8
Tempest Av WVILLE PO7 156 B7
Templar Cl SHST GU47 43 J8
Templars Mede CHFD SO53 139 H5
Templars Wy CHFD SO53 138 F4
Templecombe Rd ELGH SO50 140 F3
Temple Gdns ITCH SO19 161 M6
Temple La PSF GU32 314 B8
Templemere
FHAM/STUB PO14 181 J5
Temple Ms BMTH BH1 * 226 D2
Templer Av FARN GU14 61 G7
Templer Cl BKME/WDN BH12 212 F7
Temple Rd ITCH SO19 161 M6
LISS GU33 308 G6
Temple's Cl RFNM GU10 260 A7
Temple St PSEA PO1 21 H1
Templeton Cl NEND PO2 * 184 E5
Tenby Cl WEND SO18 148 A4
Tenby Dr CHFD SO53 139 G4
Tenby Rd FRIM GU16 51 J8
Tench Wy ROMY SO51 130 F8
Tennyson Cl BPWT SO32 143 L4
FAWY SO45 354 D3
Tennyson Crs WVILLE PO7 155 K7
Tennyson Gdns
FHAM/PORC PO16 10 E4
Tennyson Rd ELGH SO50 139 M6
MOOR/WNTN BH9 213 M6
NEND PO2 184 F8
NTHA RG18 28 E8
PSTN BH14 224 A5
PTSW SO17 147 H8
TOTT SO40 144 D6
WIMB BH21 207 J2
Tennyson's La HASM GU27 118 E8
Tennyson Wy KBH RG22 93 G1
Tensing Cl FHAM/PORC PO16 10 E1
Tensing Rd CHCH/BSGR BH23 228 E1
Tenterton Av ITCH SO19 162 B3
Terence Av CFDH BH17 211 J7
Terence Rd WIMB BH21 210 C3
Terminus Ter SHAM SO14 23 J6
Tern Cl FAWY SO45 177 H6
KBH RG22 92 B5
Tern Ct SBNE BH6 227 K2
Tern Wk ENEY PO4 193 H3
Terrace Rd WCLF BH2 8 D6
The Terrace CBLY GU15 50 B3
CWTH RG45 43 M3
FARN GU14 * 61 K5
Terrier Cl HEND SO30 149 J1
Terrington Av
CHCH/BSGR BH23 217 L7
Terriote Cl CHFD SO53 139 J1
Terry Cl DEAN RG23 92 B8
Tesimond Dr YTLY GU46 48 C3
Tess Farm Rd RWIN SO21 134 F4
Testbourne Av TOTT SO40 158 D1
Testbourne Cl TOTT SO40 158 D1
Testbourne Rd TOTT SO40 158 D1
Test Cl PSF GU32 120 C8
Testcombe Rd GPORT PO12 14 D7
Testlands Av ROWN SO16 145 K2
Test La ROWN SO16 145 H5
Test Ms WHCH RG28 87 L7
Test Mills ROMY SO51 * 130 D8
Test Ri STOK SO20 272 E9
Test Rd SHAM SO14 161 H8
WHCH RG28 87 L8
Test Wy BSTK RG21 7 J5
MARL SN8 244 B6
RAND SP11 86 A2
RAND SP11 98 D7
RAND SP11 244 C10
RAND SP11 272 D4
RAND SP11 272 H2
ROMY SO51 130 A6
ROMY SO51 298 G9
RWIN SO21 273 K2
STOK SO20 285 R2
TOTT SO40 145 G7
Testwood Av TOTT SO40 144 E7
Testwood Crs TOTT SO40 144 D6
Testwood La TOTT SO40 144 F7
Testwood Pl TOTT SO40 145 G8
Testwood Rd HAV PO9 170 D3
WSHM SO15 160 B2
Tethering Dro FBDG SP6 332 G5
Tetney Cl ROWN SO16 145 L5
Teviot Rd CHFD SO53 139 G3
Tewkesbury Av FHAM PO15 181 J1
GPORT PO12 191 G1
Tewkesbury Cl CHIN RG24 65 K3
CHAM PO6 168 D8
Texas Dr FUFL SO22 124 B2
Thackeray Ml
FHAM/PORC PO16 11 J5
Thackeray Rd PTSW SO17 147 H8
Thackham's La HTWY RG27 57 H3
The Thakerays STHA RG19 35 K2
Thames Cl FARN GU14 60 E2
FERN BH22 346 A6
WEND SO18 148 B2
Thames Ct AND SP10 5 M1
BSTK RG21 7 K5
Thames Dr FHAM PO15 165 K8
Thamesmead Cl GPORT PO12 190 F1
Thames Ms PLE BH15 * 223 H7
Thames St PLE BH15 223 H7
Thatched Cottage Pk
LYND SO43 * 345 M2
Thatchers La
CHCH/BSGR BH23 347 R11
LYMN SO41 356 F4
Theal Cl SHST GU47 43 M8
Theatre Ms SSEA PO5 * 21 K8
Theatre Rd FARN GU14 61 H8
The Itchen Br ITCH SO19 23 M6
Theobalds Wy FRIM GU16 51 L5
Theobold Rd
CHCH/BSGR BH23 346 G12
Theseus Rd
LSOL/BMARY PO13 189 K5
Thetchers Cl NMIL/BTOS BH25 219 H3
Thetford Gdns CHFD SO53 139 G1
Thetford Rd BKME/WDN BH12 224 F2
Thibet Rd SHST GU47 43 L8
The Thicket FHAM/PORC PO16 166 F7
LSOL/BMARY PO13 182 E7
ROMY SO51 137 J2
SSEA PO5 * 21 J7
WVILLE PO7 169 K6
Third Av CHAM PO6 168 E8
HAV PO9 17 H3
WSHM SO15 159 M2
Third St East STHA RG19 35 G7
Thirlmere ELGH SO50 139 M6
Thirlmere Cl BOR GU35 110 F7
FARN GU14 60 E4
FHAM/STUB PO14 181 K8
Thirlmere Crs FLEETS GU52 71 G3
Thirlmere Rd ROWN SO16 145 L6
Thirlstane Firs CHFD SO53 139 H4
Thirsk Ct ASHV GU12 3 L2
Thirtover NTHA RG18 28 D3
Thirt Wy STOK SO20 272 G11
Thistlebarrow Rd LTDN BH7 226 E2
Thistledown HORN PO8 156 B3
Thistledown Cl AND SP10 4 D3
Thistledowne Gdns
EMRTH PO10 172 B6
Thistle Rd CHFD SO53 138 F3
HEND SO30 149 H6
Thomas Cl TOTT SO40 158 D2
Thomas Lewis Wy PTSW SO17 147 J7
Thomas Merriman Ct
NWBY RG14 * 18 E5
Thomas Rd NBAD SO52 138 A4
Thompson Dr STHA RG19 35 L2
Thompsons Cl CHOB/PIR GU24 63 K4
Thompson's La RWIN SO21 135 M5
WVILLE PO7 154 C3
Thorburn Cha SHST GU47 50 A2
Thoresby Ct NMIL/BTOS BH25 218 E5
Thornbrake Rd GPORT PO12 15 H6
Thornbury Av FAWY SO45 354 G8
WSHM SO15 160 E1
Thornbury Cl CWTH RG45 43 K3
FHAM/STUB PO14 181 J4
Thornbury Hts CHFD SO53 133 M7
Thornbury Rd SBNE BH6 228 A4
Thornbury Wd CHFD SO53 133 M7
Thorncliffe Cl NEND PO2 184 F4
Thorn Cl ELGH SO50 134 A7
EPSF GU31 121 G7
RFNM GU10 78 D4
Thorncombe Cl CFDH BH17 211 L7
Thorn Ct ALTN GU34 293 M6
Thorn Crs ALTN GU34 293 M6
Thorncroft Rd PSEA PO1 21 M3
Thorndike Cl ROWN SO16 146 A6
Thorn Dr ALTN GU34 293 M6
Thorne Cl CWTH RG45 43 J1
RSAL SP5 325 M3
VWD BH31 201 G1
WWKG RG41 239 R5
Thorneley Rd KSCL RG20 248 D10
Thorness Cl ROWN SO16 145 J7
Thorney Cl FHAM/STUB PO14 181 K4
Thorney Vw HISD PO11 * 187 J6
Thornfield STHA RG19 248 B1
Thornfield Dr
CHCH/BSGR BH23 217 M7
Thornfield Gn BLKW GU17 50 B5
Thornford Rd STHA RG19 35 H8
Thorngate RSAL SP5 * 297 N4
Thorngate Wy GPORT PO12 15 K4
Thornham La EMRTH PO10 172 B8
Thornham Rd
NMIL/BTOS BH25 219 K5
Thornhill Av ITCH SO19 148 D6
Thornhill Cl FAWY SO45 354 H6
Thornhill Park Rd WEND SO18 148 D5
Thornhill Rd ALDT GU11 73 K4
FAWY SO45 354 H6
ROWN SO16 146 D4
Thornhill Vw GSHT GU26 * 115 K5
Thornhill Wy CHIN RG24 54 C5
Thorni Av FHAM PO15 181 J1
Thorn La ALTN GU34 293 N6
Thornleigh Rd ITCH SO19 161 L6
Thornley Rd NBNE BH10 213 K4
Thorn Rd CFDH BH17 211 J5
RFNM GU10 78 D4
Thorns La LYMN SO41 357 M5
Thornton Av HLER SO31 179 J3
Thornton Cl CHAM PO6 169 H6
TADY RG26 46 D6
WIMB BH21 210 C3
Thornton End ALTN GU34 107 J2
Thornton Rd GPORT PO12 183 H8
Thornycroft Av ITCH SO19 161 L6
Thornycroft Rbt KBH RG22 65 G7
Thornyhurst Rd FRIM GU16 62 A4
Thorold Rd CHFD SO53 133 L7
FNM GU9 13 G2
WEND SO18 147 L7
Thorpe Gdns ALTN GU34 106 D4
Threadgill Wy NTID SP9 266 C9
Three Acre Dr
NMIL/BTOS BH25 218 F8
Three Acre Rd NWBY RG14 33 M4
Three Acres WVILLE PO7 155 G5
Three Castles Pth HTWY RG27 48 C1
NARL SO24 278 D6
NARL SO24 291 M1
ODIM RG29 68 B6
OVTN RG25 67 J7
RWIN SO21 289 J12
RWIN SO21 290 E8
Three Cross Rd WIMB BH21 205 G2
Threefield La SHAM SO14 23 H5
Three Firs Wy THLE RG7 39 M3
Three Gates La HASM GU27 118 D5
Three Horse Shoes La
ALTN GU34 305 N10
Three Oaks ITCH SO19 148 E7
Three Stiles Rd FNM GU9 12 B2
Three Tun Cl PSEA PO1 20 D3
Thresher Cl HORN PO8 156 C7
Threshers Cnr FLEETN GU51 59 L4
Throgmorton Rd YTLY GU46 48 C3
Throop Cl CHAR BH8 215 G6
Throop Rd CHAR BH8 214 E4
Throopside Av
MOOR/WNTN BH9 214 D4
Thrush Cl KBH RG22 92 B4
Thrush Rd BKME/WDN BH12 212 C7
Thrush Wk HORN PO8 155 L5
Thruxton Ct ITCH SO19 161 L3
Thruxton Rd HAV PO9 170 C3
Thuillier Rd RWIN SO21 273 N2
Thumwood CHIN RG24 54 B5
Thundery Hl RFNM GU10 260 D4
Thurbans Rd FNM GU9 78 E1
Thurbern Rd NEND PO2 184 E6
Thurmell Cl HEND SO30 149 J8
Thurmond Crs FUFL SO22 122 C6
Thurmond Rd FUFL SO22 122 C6
Thursby Rd CHCH/BSGR BH23 217 M6
Thursley Rd MFD/CHID GU8 263 P7
MFD/CHID GU8 263 Q2
RFNM GU10 263 J9
Thurston Cl CHFD SO53 139 K1
Thurstons ALTN GU34 108 A6
Thwaite Rd BKME/WDN BH12 225 H3
Thyme Av FHAM PO15 164 D4
Thyme Cl CHIN RG24 54 C4
Thyme Ct FARN GU14 60 C3
Tibb's Meadow RAND SP11 80 B4
Tiberius Cl DEAN RG23 64 E5
Tiberius Rd AND SP10 96 D1
Tichborne Cl BLKW GU17 49 M3
Tichborne Down NARL SO24 303 Q1
Tichborne Gv HAV PO9 170 D3
Tichborne Pl ASHV GU12 3 L7
Tichborne Rd ELGH SO50 139 M8
WEND SO18 148 D4
Tichborne Wy
LSOL/BMARY PO13 182 D7
Tichbourne Cl FRIM GU16 51 H5
Tickenor Dr EWKG RG40 42 B1
Tickhill Cl EARL RG6 238 F1
Tickleford Dr ITCH SO19 162 A4
Tickner Cl HEND SO30 149 L7
Ticonderoga Gdns ITCH SO19 161 L7
Tidemill Cl CHCH/BSGR BH23 216 A8
Tides Reach WEND SO18 147 K8
Tides Wy TOTT SO40 159 M6
Tideway Gdns ENEY PO4 193 J4
Tidworth Rd HAV PO9 170 F4
MARL SN8 264 F5
RAND SP11 265 K11
Tiffany Cl LYMN SO41 219 M4
WWKG RG41 239 R2
Tiffield Cl HSEA PO3 185 J4
Tiger Moth Cl
LSOL/BMARY PO13 190 A2
Tigerseye Cl WWKG RG41 239 R1
Tigwells Fld ODIM RG29 257 Q4
Tilbrook Rd WSHM SO15 146 A8
Tilburg Rd CHCH/BSGR BH23 228 D1
Tilbury's Cl BOR GU35 112 F1
Tilden Rd RWIN SO21 124 C7
Tile Barn Cl FARN GU14 61 G2
Tilebarn La BROC SO42 351 L5
Tilford Rd FNM GU9 13 J5
GSHT GU26 115 M3
HORN PO8 155 M2
RFNM GU10 263 J1
Tilford St RFNM GU10 263 J1
Tillington Gdns HORN PO8 321 M8
Tilmore Gdns PSF GU32 120 D4
Tilmore Rd PSF GU32 120 D4
Tilney Cl ALTN GU34 106 E4
Timber Bank FRIM GU16 62 A3
Timber Cl FNM GU9 * 12 E3
Timbercroft Cl ALTN GU34 293 L7
Timberlake Rd BSTK RG21 6 E5
Timberlane WVILLE PO7 169 K4
Timberley La RSAL SP5 333 J2
Timberley Pl CWTH RG45 43 G4
Timberly Cl FAWY SO45 354 E4
Timbermill Ct HASM GU27 117 M2
The Timbers FHAM PO15 181 J3
Timor Cl CHIN RG24 65 L3
HLER SO31 164 B4
Timothy Cl NBNE BH10 213 K3
Timpson Rd PSEA PO1 192 E2
Timsbury Crs HAV PO9 16 C1
Timsbury Dr ROWN SO16 145 M6
Timson Cl TOTT SO40 158 C2
Tincleton Gdns
MOOR/WNTN BH9 214 B4
Tindal Cl YTLY GU46 48 F2
Tindale Rd ROWN SO16 145 L6
Tinker Aly ELGH SO50 140 A5
Tinley Gdns ODIM RG29 69 H5
Tinneys Cl RSAL SP5 332 F4
Tintagel Cl AND SP10 96 C1
DEAN RG23 64 E6
Tintagel Dr FRIM GU16 51 H7
Tintagel Wy CHAM PO6 184 B1
Tintern Cl CHIN RG24 65 H4
CHAM PO6 167 M7
Tintern Gv WSHM SO15 22 C1
Tintern Rd GPORT PO12 14 D4
Tipner Gn NEND PO2 184 C5
Tipner La NEND PO2 184 C5
Tipner Rd NEND PO2 184 C6
Tipper La EPSF GU31 323 M1
Tippet Gdns KBH RG22 93 H4
Tiptoe Rd NMIL/BTOS BH25 350 A11
Tiptree Cl ELGH SO50 134 A7
Tisbury Cl FLEETN GU51 59 G5
Tisted Ct HAV PO9 * 171 H3
Titchfield Cl TADY RG26 44 C5
Titchfield Hl FHAM/STUB PO14 181 G4
Titchfield La FHAM PO15 165 J4
Titchfield Park Rd FHAM PO15 180 D1
Titchfield Rd
FHAM/STUB PO14 181 G5
Titcombe Wy HUNG RG17 31 G2
Tithe Barn LYMN SO41 221 L3
Tithelands La NARL SO24 304 H8
Tithe Md ROMY SO51 130 F7
Tithe Meadow KBH RG22 92 E7
The Tithe WVILLE PO7 154 F5
Tithewood Cl CHFD SO53 133 H6
Tittymouse La RAND SP11 94 E2
Titus Gdns WVILLE PO7 156 A8
Tiverton Rd DEAN RG23 64 E7
Tivoli Cl CHFD SO53 139 M1
Toad La BLKW GU17 50 A4
Tobago Cl CHIN RG24 65 K3
Tobruk Cl RAND SP11 84 D5
Tobruk Rd RAND SP11 267 K2
Toby St PSEA PO1 21 G1
Todber Cl BWD BH11 212 D5
Todmore LISS GU33 308 F1
Tokar St ENEY PO4 193 G6
Tokio Rd HSEA PO3 185 G7
Toledo Gv AND SP10 5 L2
Tolefrey Gdns CHFD SO53 138 F2
Tollard Cl BKME/WDN BH12 212 E8
Tollbar Wy HEND SO30 149 G4
Tollerford Rd CFDH BH17 211 K6
Tollgate CHFD SO53 139 J6
Tollgate Cl DEAN RG23 91 K1
Tollgate Rd AND SP10 4 B2
HLER SO31 163 K4
Tollway CHIN RG24 54 C5
Tolpuddle Gdns
MOOR/WNTN BH9 214 B4
Tolpuddle Wy YTLY GU46 49 H3
Tolstoi Rd PSTN BH14 224 A2
Tomkyns Cl CHFD SO53 138 F2
Tomlin Cl STHA RG19 35 K3
Tomlins Av FRIM GU16 51 H6
Tomlins Cl TADY RG26 44 B5
Tomlinscote Wy FRIM GU16 51 J6
Tomlinson Dr EWKG RG40 42 C2
Tommy Green Wk ELGH SO50 139 M5
Toms La RGWD BH24 338 C12
Tonbridge St SSEA PO5 21 H8
Tonge Rd BWD BH11 213 H2
Tongham Mdw RFNM GU10 260 C1
Tongham Rd ASHV GU12 3 L7
RFNM GU10 260 B3
Tonnant Cl FHAM/STUB PO14 189 K3
Toogoods Wy ROWN SO16 145 K3
Toomer Cl FAWY SO45 354 H6
Toomers Whf NWBY RG14 * 18 E4
Toothill Rd ROMY SO51 137 J7
Topaz Gv WVILLE PO7 156 B8
Tope Rd WHIT RG2 239 M8
Topiary Gdns HLER SO31 164 B8
The Topiary CHIN RG24 54 C8
FARN GU14 60 E5
PSTN BH14 223 M3
Toplady Pl FNM GU9 77 G1
Top La RGWD BH24 203 J5
Top Terrace Rd FARN GU14 61 G8
Torbay Rd PSTN BH14 224 C5
Torberry Dr EPSF GU31 120 F7
Torch Cl ELGH SO50 141 H2
Tor Cl FHAM/PORC PO16 166 E7
WVILLE PO7 169 M5
Torcross Cl ITCH SO19 161 L6
Torfrida Ct ENEY PO4 193 J5
Tormead FAWY SO45 176 F5
Tornay Gv NBAD SO52 137 M4
Toronto Pl GPORT PO12 14 F3
Toronto Rd NEND PO2 192 E1
Torquay Av GPORT PO12 183 G8
WSHM SO15 146 C8
Torque Cl ITCH SO19 148 E8
Torre Cl ELGH SO50 134 A6
Torridge Gdns WEND SO18 148 B1
Torrington Cl BOR GU35 * 111 J7
ITCH SO19 148 A8
Torrington Rd NEND PO2 184 E5
Tor Rd FNM GU9 12 B4
Tortworth Cl
FHAM/STUB PO14 181 K4
Tor Wy EPSF GU31 120 E6
Torwood Gdns ELGH SO50 140 F2
Tosson Cl ROWN SO16 * 145 L8
Totford La RFNM GU10 261 J5
Totland Cl FARN GU14 61 G2
ROWN SO16 145 L8
Totland Rd CHAM PO6 184 E1
LSOL/BMARY PO13 182 C6
Totmel Rd CFDH BH17 212 A6
Totnes Cl ELGH SO50 139 M3
Tottehale Cl NBAD SO52 137 M5
Tottenham Cl TADY RG26 46 B4
Tottenham Rd PSEA PO1 192 E2
Tottenham Wk SHST GU47 43 M7
Totterdown THLE RG7 39 M3
Totters La HTWY RG27 57 H7
Totton By-Pass TOTT SO40 159 G2
Tournai Cl ALDT GU11 73 L1
Tournerbury La HISD PO11 195 G4
Tourney Rd BWD BH11 212 D2
Tovey Ct AND SP10 96 F3
Tovey Pl WINC SO23 289 J8
Tower Cl AND SP10 95 M1
GPORT PO12 190 D5
Tower Gdns HAV PO9 186 F2
Tower Hl FARN GU14 61 G5
Tower La ELGH SO50 140 C2
WIMB BH21 207 K2
Tower Pl HEND SO30 148 D3
Tower Rd BMTH BH1 226 E3
CCLF BH13 225 H7
GSHT GU26 115 L4
LIPH GU30 116 B4
WINC SO23 24 F4
Tower Rd West CCLF BH13 225 G7
Towers Dr CWTH RG45 43 K4
Towers Farm WIMB BH21 210 D1
Tower St ALTN GU34 106 E6
EMRTH PO10 172 A6
PSEA PO1 20 B6
WINC SO23 24 F5
Towers Wy WIMB BH21 210 D1
Town Centre East Jct
CHIN RG24 7 M3
Town Cl NARL SO24 292 H12
Towngate Br PLE BH15 223 J6
Towngate Ms RGWD BH24 * 203 J6
Town Hall Rd HAV PO9 16 F5
Townhill Wy WEND SO18 148 A4
Town La EPSF GU31 120 F4
Town Mill La WHCH RG28 87 M7
Town Mills NWBY RG14 * 18 E4
Town Quay SHAM SO14 22 F7
Townsend RSAL SP5 282 A12
Townsend Cl BSTK RG21 6 B6
BWD BH11 213 H2
Townsend La FBDG SP6 329 J4
Townside Pl CBLY GU15 50 F2
Townsville Rd
MOOR/WNTN BH9 214 B6
Towpath Md ENEY PO4 193 J4
Toynbee Cl ELGH SO50 140 A1
Toynbee Rd ELGH SO50 140 A1
Tozer Cl BWD BH11 212 F6
Trade St KSCL RG20 245 R4
Trafalgar Cl CHFD SO53 139 H3
Trafalgar Ct FHAM/STUB PO14 181 M5
FNM GU9 12 F5
Trafalgar Pl PSEA PO1 21 L1
Trafalgar Rd
MOOR/WNTN BH9 225 M1
WSHM SO15 160 C2
Trafalgar Sq GPORT PO12 14 E2
Trafalgar St WINC SO23 24 F6
Trafalgar Wy CBLY GU15 50 B4
FAWY SO45 177 H7
STOK SO20 285 P6
Trafford Rd FRIM GU16 50 F8
Trafford Wy ELGH SO50 141 H3
Trajan Wk AND SP10 96 D1
Trampers La WHAM PO17 153 G7
Tranby Rd ITCH SO19 161 L4
Tranmere Cl LYMN SO41 221 M6
Tranmere Rd ENEY PO4 193 H4
Transport Rd FARN GU14 61 H7
Travellers Cnr THLE RG7 * 39 L7
Travellers End FUFL SO22 24 B2
Travis La SHST GU47 49 M1
Treadwheel Rd HORN PO8 157 G2
Treagore Rd TOTT SO40 144 C7
Trearnan Cl ROWN SO16 145 M8
Treble Cl FUFL SO22 122 B8
Trebor Av FNM GU9 13 J6
Tredegar Rd ENEY PO4 192 F5
Tredenham Cl FARN GU14 61 J8
Tree Av HASM GU27 115 M8
Treebys Cl CHCH/BSGR BH23 216 D7
Treeside CHCH/BSGR BH23 217 J6
Treeside Av TOTT SO40 159 G1
Treeside Dr FNM GU9 2 A9
Treeside Rd WSHM SO15 146 C8
Tree Side Wy WVILLE PO7 155 L7
Trefoil Cl HTWY RG27 57 L1
WVILLE PO7 169 M1
Trefoil Dro NTHA RG18 29 H8
Trefoil Wy CHCH/BSGR BH23 217 J8
Tregaron Av CHAM PO6 185 H1
Tregolls Dr FARN GU14 61 J5
Tregonwell Rd WCLF BH2 8 D6
Trellis Dr CHIN RG24 54 C8
Treloar Rd HISD PO11 195 M7
Treloyhan Cl CHFD SO53 139 K4
Tremayne Wk CBLY GU15 51 L4
Tremona Rd ROWN SO16 146 C6
Trenchard Rd RAND SP11 95 K5
Trenchmead Gdns CHIN RG24 64 F4
Trenley Cl FAWY SO45 354 E5
Trent Cl FARN GU14 60 E2
WEND SO18 147 M7
Trent Ct AND SP10 5 M1
Trent Crs NTHA RG18 28 D7
Trentham Av LTDN BH7 215 H8
Trentham Cl LTDN BH7 215 H8
Trenton Cl FRIM GU16 51 J6
Trent Rd WEND SO18 147 M7
Trent Wy BSTK RG21 7 K5
FERN BH22 346 A6
HEND SO30 148 D2

LSOL/BMARY PO13 189 M7
Tresham Crs YTLY GU46 48 C2
Tresillian Gdns WEND SO18 148 B2
Tresillian Wy
CHCH/BSGR BH23 218 B6
Trevis Rd ENEY PO4 193 J4
Trevone Cl TOTT SO40 158 E3
Trevor Rd ENEY PO4 21 M7
Trevose Cl CHFD SO53 139 K4
LSOL/BMARY PO13 182 C7
Trevose Crs CHFD SO53 139 K4
Trevose Wy FHAM/STUB PO14 180 B8
Triangle La FHAM/STUB PO14 180 E8
The Triangle
NMIL/BTOS BH25 * 230 C1
NWBY RG14 34 B5
RSAL SP5 127 H4
WCLF BH2 8 C6
WEND SO18 * 147 L7
Tribe Rd GPORT PO12 14 D3
Tricketts La FERN BH22 209 M2
Trigon Rd PLE BH15 223 K1
Trimaran Cl HLER SO31 179 L3
Trimaran Rd HLER SO31 179 L3
Trimmers Cl FNM GU9 76 F1
Trimmers Fld FNM GU9 13 L5
Trimmers Wd GSHT GU26 115 K2
Trimm's Dro FBDG SP6 332 A8
Trims Ct OVTN RG25 89 J4
Trinidad Cl CHIN RG24 65 K3
Trinidad Crs BKME/WDN BH12 212 C8
Trinity Cl GPORT PO12 15 K5
Trinity Flds FNM GU9 76 E2
Trinity Gdns FHAM/PORC PO16 10 F5
Trinity Gn GPORT PO12 15 L5
Trinity Hl ALTN GU34 279 J12
FNM GU9 76 E2
Trinity Ri RAND SP11 83 H8
Trinity Rd ALTN GU34 279 J11
BMTH BH1 9 H5
SHAM SO14 23 H1
Trinity St FHAM/PORC PO16 11 G5
Tristan Cl FAWY SO45 355 N9
Tristram Cl CHFD SO53 138 F4
Triumph Cl FHAM PO15 181 K2
Triumph Rd FHAM/STUB PO14 181 M7
Troak Cl CHCH/BSGR BH23 216 E8
Trojan Wy WVILLE PO7 169 M5
Troon Crs CHAM PO6 169 J7
Troon Rd BDST BH18 211 G3
Trosnant Rd HAV PO9 16 C2
Trotsford Meadow BLKW GU17 49 L4
Trotton Rd EPSF GU31 317 R8
Trotts La TOTT SO40 159 J4
Trout Rd HASM GU27 117 L2
Trout Wk NWBY RG14 27 K7
Trowbridge Cl ROWN SO16 145 L2
Trowe's La THLE RG7 41 K4
THLE RG7 238 D11
Trueman Sq AND SP10 * 96 E1
Truman Rd BWD BH11 213 H2
Trunk Rd FARN GU14 60 C4
Truro Ct LSOL/BMARY PO13 * 190 C2
Truro Ri ELGH SO50 140 E1
Truro Rd CHAM PO6 167 M8
Truscott Av MOOR/WNTN BH9 226 A1
Trussell Cl FUFL SO22 122 D1
Trussell Crs FUFL SO22 122 D1
Trust Cl HTWY RG27 56 B7
Tryplets FLEETS GU52 70 F5
Tubb's La KSCL RG20 246 B6
TADY RG26 52 C4
Tuckers La PLE BH15 222 F7
Tucks Cl CHCH/BSGR BH23 348 C11
Tuckton Cl SBNE BH6 227 K4
Tuckton Rd SBNE BH6 227 K4
Tudor Av EMRTH PO10 171 L4
Tudor Cl FBDG SP6 196 C7
FHAM/PORC PO16 167 H7
GSHT GU26 115 K6
HISD PO11 194 F6
LSOL/BMARY PO13 182 E8
TADY RG26 53 L2
TOTT SO40 144 C8
Tudor Ct FHAM/STUB PO14 * 181 M5
PLE BH15 223 L2
TADY RG26 44 B3
Tudor Crs CHAM PO6 184 F2
Tudor Dr YTLY GU46 48 F4
Tudor Gdns HEND SO30 149 G7
Tudor Rd BDST BH18 211 H4
NWBY RG14 18 F7
Tudor Wy FLEETS GU52 71 J4
WINC SO23 288 H8
Tudor Wood Cl ROWN SO16 146 F4
Tuffin Cl ROWN SO16 145 J3
Tukes Av LSOL/BMARY PO13 182 B4
Tulip Cl KBH RG22 92 C5
Tulip Gdns HAV PO9 170 C6
HLER SO31 179 M1
Tulip Rd ROWN SO16 147 J4
Tulls La BOR GU35 113 K2
Tull Wy NTHA RG18 28 B8
Tumulus Cl ITCH SO19 148 F8
Tunball La MARL SN8 243 J9
Tunbridge Crs LIPH GU30 116 B3
Tunbridge La LIPH GU30 116 B2
Tunnel Hl RSAL SP5 327 L2
Tunnel Rd FARN GU14 60 E7
Tunstall Rd CHAM PO6 168 D7
ITCH SO19 148 E8
Tunworth Cl FLEETN GU51 59 G4
Tunworth Ct HAV PO9 171 H3
TADY RG26 44 C5
Tunworth Ms TADY RG26 44 C4
Tunworth Rd OVTN RG25 67 G4
Tuppenny La EMRTH PO10 172 C6
Turbary Cl BKME/WDN BH12 212 E8
Turbary Ct UPTN BH16 * 210 C8
Turbary Gdns TADY RG26 44 B3
Turbary Rd BKME/WDN BH12 224 D1
FERN BH22 209 M1
Turgis Rd FLEETN GU51 59 G4
Turin Ct AND SP10 84 D8
Turks La PSTN BH14 224 A7
THLE RG7 39 M8
Turk St ALTN GU34 106 F5
Turlin Rd UPTN BH16 222 C4
Turnberry Cl CHCH/BSGR BH23 227 M2
Turnberry Dr DEAN RG23 92 C7
Turner Av LSOL/BMARY PO13 182 E8
Turner Cl BSTK RG21 7 L7
Turner Ct AND SP10 4 F2
Turner Pl SHST GU47 49 M2
Turner Rd PSEA PO1 192 D1
Turners Av FLEETN GU51 59 G4
Turners Dr STHA RG19 35 L1
Turners Farm Crs LYMN SO41 220 A6
Turner's Green La HTWY RG27 58 F3
Turners Wy FLEETN GU51 58 F5
The Turnery STHA RG19 35 J1
Turnfields STHA RG19 35 K1
Turnill Ct RAND SP11 * 84 D5
Turnpike Cots OVTN RG25 89 K4
Turnpike Down WINC SO23 25 M5
Turnpike Rd NTHA RG18 28 A8
NWBY RG14 19 M1
Turnpike Wy DEAN RG23 91 J2
HEND SO30 149 G6
Turnstone End YTLY GU46 48 D2
Turnstone Gdns ROWN SO16 146 B3
Turnworth Cl BDST BH18 211 J5
Turtle Cl FHAM/STUB PO14 181 H8
Tuscan Wk CHFD SO53 139 L2
Tuscany Wy WVILLE PO7 156 B8
YTLY GU46 * 48 E4
The Tussocks TOTT SO40 159 M6
Tutland Rd NBAD SO52 137 M4
Tutor Cl HLER SO31 178 F1
Tutts La ROMY SO51 335 J4
Tweedale Rd
MOOR/WNTN BH9 214 C5
Tweed Cl CHFD SO53 139 G1
FARN GU14 60 E2
Tweed La LYMN SO41 351 P12
Tweedsmuir Cl FARN GU14 60 D5
KBH RG22 64 D8
Twelve Acre Crs FARN GU14 60 D3
Twemlow Av PSTN BH14 223 M6
Tweseldown Rd FLEETS GU52 71 K4
Twiggs End Cl HLER SO31 163 M8
Twiggs La TOTT SO40 175 K2
Twiggs Lane End TOTT SO40 175 J3
Twineham Gdns RSAL SP5 327 N2
Twinley La WHCH RG28 253 L12
Twin Oaks Cl BDST BH18 211 G5
Twisell Thorne FLEETS GU52 71 G4
Twittens Wy HAV PO9 16 F5
Two Gate La OVTN RG25 89 K5
Two Gate Meadow OVTN RG25 89 K4
Two Rivers Wy NWBY RG14 19 M3
Twyford Av NEND PO2 184 D5
WSHM SO15 146 C7
Twyford Cl CHAR BH8 214 D6
Twyford Dr
LSOL/BMARY PO13 189 M6
Twyford La RFNM GU10 78 F2
Twyford Rd ELGH SO50 134 B6
Twyford Wy CFDH BH17 212 A6
Twynham Av
CHCH/BSGR BH23 228 A2
Twynham Cl RSAL SP5 332 B2
Twynham Rd SBNE BH6 227 M4
Twynhams Hl BPWT SO32 318 A12
Tydehams NWBY RG14 33 L5
Tyfield CHIN RG24 65 G1
Tyler Dr WHIT RG2 239 L9
Tylers Cl LYMN SO41 221 K3
Tyler's La THLE RG7 29 K2
The Tyleshades ROMY SO51 137 G2
Tylney La HTWY RG27 55 M7
Tylney Vw HTWY RG27 * 56 C8
Tylston Meadow LIPH GU30 116 B3
Tyndalls GSHT GU26 115 M4
Tyne Cl CHFD SO53 139 G3
FARN GU14 60 E2
Tyne Ct AND SP10 5 M1
Tynedale Cl GPORT PO12 182 F8
MOOR/WNTN BH9 214 C4
Tyneham Av BKME/WDN BH12 212 B8
Tyne Wy HEND SO30 148 E2
NTHA RG18 28 D7
Tyrell Rd CHFD SO53 139 J1
Tyrells Cft AND SP10 5 L5
Tyrells La RGWD BH24 342 G12
Tyrrell Gdns CHAR BH8 215 G6
Tyrrells Ct CHCH/BSGR BH23 348 D11
Tyseley Rd SSEA PO5 21 H4
Tytherley Gn CHAR BH8 214 D6
Tytherley Rd RSAL SP5 283 J10
WEND SO18 148 C4

U

Ubsdell Cl NMIL/BTOS BH25 219 G5
Uddens Dr WIMB BH21 208 E2
Ullswater Av FARN GU14 60 E5
WEND SO18 148 B3
Ullswater Cl BOR GU35 110 F7
FNM GU9 76 E2
STHA RG19 35 G1
Ullswater Ct ASHV GU12 * 73 M3
Ullswater Gv NARL SO24 291 M12
Ullswater Rd ROWN SO16 145 L7
WIMB BH21 207 J6
Undercliff Dr BMTH BH1 9 H7
Undercliff Rd BOSC BH5 226 E5
Underdown Av WVILLE PO7 169 K6
Underhill La FNM GU9 78 F1
Undershore LYMN SO41 221 L2
Underwood Av ASHV GU12 73 L7
Underwood Cl CFDH BH17 211 H7
ROWN SO16 * 146 E4
Underwood Rd ELGH SO50 134 D8
HASM GU27 117 M1
ROWN SO16 146 E4
Unicorn Rd LSOL/BMARY PO13 189 K5
PSEA PO1 21 G1
Union La BPWT SO32 318 C2
KSCL RG20 248 D7
Union Pl PSEA PO1 21 K1
Union Ri LISS GU33 309 K2
Union Rd FNM GU9 13 G4
FRIM GU16 51 M8
HAV PO9 16 D4
SHAM SO14 161 H2
Union St ALDT GU11 2 E3
AND SP10 5 J5
CHOB/PIR GU24 63 G2
FARN GU14 61 G4
FHAM/PORC PO16 11 K6
PSEA PO1 20 D2
WINC SO23 25 J5
University Crs PTSW SO17 147 H5
University Pkwy ROWN SO16 138 C7
University Rd PTSW SO17 147 G5
Unwin Cl ITCH SO19 161 K7
Upfallow CHIN RG24 66 C1
Upham St BPWT SO32 310 C12
Uphill Rd FUFL SO22 288 B11
Upland La LISS GU33 308 A5
Upland Rd CBLY GU15 50 F1
Uplands Av NMIL/BTOS BH25 219 G8
Uplands Cl FERN BH22 205 J8
HASM GU27 118 D4
SHST GU47 43 K8
Uplands Crs FHAM/PORC PO16 11 G3
Uplands La ALTN GU34 293 L7
Uplands Rd CHAM PO6 169 J7
CHAR BH8 214 C6
FERN BH22 205 J8
FNM GU9 13 G1
FUFL SO22 122 E1
HAV PO9 157 J6
WVILLE PO7 154 B2
Uplands Wy PTSW SO17 147 G6
Uplyme Cl CFDH BH17 212 A6
Upmill Cl WEND SO18 148 B1
Upnor Cl RAND SP11 267 K1
Upper Arundel St PSEA PO1 21 H2
Upper Banister St WSHM SO15 160 F2
Upper Barn Copse ELGH SO50 141 H1
Upper Bere Wd WVILLE PO7 169 M2
Upper Bourne La RFNM GU10 78 E3
Upper Bourne V RFNM GU10 78 E3
Upper Broadmoor Rd
CWTH RG45 43 M3
Upper Brook Dr HLER SO31 179 L2
Upper Brook St WINC SO23 25 H5
Upper Brownhill Rd
ROWN SO16 145 M5
Upper Bugle St SHAM SO14 22 F5
Upper Charles St CBLY GU15 50 E2
Upper Chestnut Dr BSTK RG21 6 A8
Upper Chobham Rd FRIM GU16 51 J5
Upper Church La FNM GU9 12 F4
Upper Church Rd BPWT SO32 151 L5
Upper Common Rd
LYMN SO41 220 F5
Upper Cornaway La
FHAM/PORC PO16 167 H8
Upper Crabbick La
WVILLE PO7 154 C3
Upper Crescent Rd
NBAD SO52 137 M4
Upper Deacon Rd ITCH SO19 148 B6
Upper Dro AND SP10 95 L4
Upper Elms Rd ALDT GU11 2 E4
Upper Farm Rd DEAN RG23 91 K4
Upper Froyle Dr FLEETN GU51 58 F5
Upper Golf Links Rd
BDST BH18 211 H3
Upper Gordon Rd CBLY GU15 50 F3
CHCH/BSGR BH23 218 A7
Upper Grove Rd ALTN GU34 106 F6
Upper Hale Rd FNM GU9 76 F1
Upper Heyshott EPSF GU31 120 E6
Upper High St FUFL SO22 24 E4
Upper Hinton Rd BMTH BH1 8 F6
Upper House Ct WHAM PO17 152 A5
Upper Lamborough La
NARL SO24 304 A6
Upper Lanham La NARL SO24 292 B1
Upper Market St ELGH SO50 140 B1
Upper Mead Cl ELGH SO50 141 K2
Upper Moors Rd ELGH SO50 134 F4
Upper Mt HASM GU27 118 F3
LISS GU33 308 E9
Upper Mullin's La FAWY SO45 176 E5
Upper Neatham Mill La
ALTN GU34 107 J2
Upper New Rd HEND SO30 148 D3
Upper Northam Cl HEND SO30 149 G6
Upper Northam Dr
HEND SO30 148 E6
Upper Northam Rd
HEND SO30 149 H6
Upper Norwich Rd WCLF BH2 8 B6
Upper Old Park La FNM GU9 76 D3
Upper Old St
FHAM/STUB PO14 181 H8
Upper Park Rd CBLY GU15 50 F3
Upper Piece WVILLE PO7 155 G5
Upper Pinewood Rd
ASHV GU12 74 C5
Upper Rd BKME/WDN BH12 224 C2
Upper St Helens Rd
HEND SO30 149 H8
Upper St Michaels Gv
FHAM/STUB PO14 10 D8
Upper St Michael's Rd
ALDT GU11 3 G6
Upper School Dr
HASM GU27 117 M3
Upper Shaftesbury Av
PTSW SO17 147 H6
Upper Sherborne Rd
BSTK RG21 65 J5
Upper Shirley Av WSHM SO15 146 C7
Upper Soldridge Rd
ALTN GU34 292 H6
Upper South Vw FNM GU9 13 G2
Upper Spinney HLER SO31 179 J4
Upper Springfield
MFD/CHID GU8 260 H12
Upper Stanford Rd
CHOB/PIR GU24 63 M6
Upper St FLEETN GU51 59 H7
Upper Terrace Rd FARN GU14 61 G8
WCLF BH2 8 D6
Upper Toothill Rd ROWN SO16 137 L7
Upper Union St ALDT GU11 2 D3
Upper Union Ter ALDT GU11 2 E3
Upper Verran Rd CBLY GU15 50 F5
Upper Wardown EPSF GU31 120 F5
Upper Wy FNM GU9 12 D8
Upper Weston La ITCH SO19 162 A2
Upper Weybourne La FNM GU9 72 D8
Upper Whf FHAM/PORC PO16 11 J7
Upper Wield Dr FLEETN GU51 59 G4
Uppleby Rd BKME/WDN BH12 224 C3
Upron Field Cl KBH RG22 92 D5
Up St OVTN RG25 103 G3
OVTN RG25 103 L4
Upton Cl FARN GU14 61 K5
HAV PO9 170 D1
UPTN BH16 222 B1
Upton Ct UPTN BH16 222 C1
Upton Crs BSTK RG21 65 J5
ROWN SO16 145 J1
Upton Grey Cl FUFL SO22 122 D1
Upton Grey Rd ODIM RG29 68 A6
OVTN RG25 67 M7
Upton Heath Est UPTN BH16 222 D1
Upton La ROWN SO16 145 H3
Upton Rd CFDH BH17 222 F1
Upton Wy BDST BH18 210 F5
Upwey Av PLE BH15 222 E5
Urquhart Rd STHA RG19 35 K2
Usborne Cl LSOL/BMARY PO13 189 M5
Utrecht Ct CHCH/BSGR BH23 228 D1
Uxbridge Cl HLER SO31 163 M6

V

Vadne Gdns GPORT PO12 * 191 H2
Vaggs La LYMN SO41 219 L2
Vale Cl RFNM GU10 79 G4
Vale Dr WEND SO18 147 M7
Vale Gv GPORT PO12 191 G1
Valencia Cl CHCH/BSGR BH23 215 K4
Valencia Wy AND SP10 5 K3
Valentine Av ITCH SO19 162 C1
Valentine Cl FHAM PO15 181 J1
Valentine Ct WVILLE PO7 156 A8
Valerian Av FHAM PO15 180 F1
Valerian Cl ELGH SO50 141 J6
Valerian Rd HEND SO30 149 J6
Vale Rd ASHV GU12 74 A1
BMTH BH1 226 D4
CBLY GU15 50 C4
PSTN BH14 224 E4
RSAL SP5 332 F2
WINC SO23 25 L8
The Vale DEAN RG23 91 J3
FAWY SO45 176 F5
HLER SO31 180 B2
HORN PO8 321 L11
SSEA PO5 21 H9
Valetta Pk EMRTH PO10 171 L8
Valette Rd MOOR/WNTN BH9 214 A5
Vale View Dr THLE RG7 41 K3
Valeview Pk LYMN SO41 * 219 M1
Vale Wy WINC SO23 288 H7
Vale Wood Dr RFNM GU10 79 H4
Vale Wood La GSHT GU26 115 J4
Valewood Rd HASM GU27 118 C8
Valiant Gdns NEND PO2 184 D4
Valiant Wy CHCH/BSGR BH23 229 H1
FARN GU14 60 D8
Valley Cl CHCH/BSGR BH23 215 L5
FAWY SO45 354 G7
RSAL SP5 332 F2
RWIN SO21 134 F4
WVILLE PO7 169 J5
Valleydene FAWY SO45 176 F6
Valley Hl FUFL SO22 288 C11
Valley La CHCH/BSGR BH23 348 G8
FNM GU9 79 G1
Valley Md RAND SP11 95 L7
Valley Park Dr HORN PO8 321 M9
Valley Ri HLER SO31 163 L8
RAND SP11 96 A8
Valley Rd CHAR BH8 214 F5
CHFD SO53 139 J1
FRIM GU16 51 L8
FUFL SO22 288 B11
NWBY RG14 18 A9
TOTT SO40 158 F3
Valley Side LIPH GU30 116 B3
The Valley FUFL SO22 24 A9
Valley Vw BKME/WDN BH12 225 H1
SHST GU47 49 J1
Valley Wk BPWT SO32 311 J6
Valley Wy TADY RG26 44 E3
Vallis Cl PLE BH15 223 K7
Valmeade Cl HTWY RG27 56 D7
Valon Rd WHIT RG2 239 L7
Valroy Cl CBLY GU15 50 F2
Valsheba Dr FHAM/STUB PO14 189 H3
Vampire Wy FARN GU14 60 E8
Vanburgh Gdns KBH RG22 92 D5
Vanburgh Wy CHFD SO53 133 H7
Van Dyck Cl BSTK RG21 7 L8
Vanguard Hl FUFL SO22 288 C10
Vanguard Rd CHAR BH8 214 E7
GPORT PO12 183 J8
PLE BH15 223 J6
WEND SO18 148 A4
Vanners La KSCL RG20 32 D7
Vanstone Rd
LSOL/BMARY PO13 182 D8
Vantage Wy BKME/WDN BH12 212 B6
Vapery La CHOB/PIR GU24 63 K2
Vardy Cl ITCH SO19 162 D1
Varna Rd BOR GU35 113 G1
WSHM SO15 160 C3
Varndell Rd HTWY RG27 56 B7
Varney Cl FARN GU14 60 E3
Varos Cl GPORT PO12 191 G2
Vaudrey Cl WSHM SO15 146 C7
Vaughan Cl ITCH SO19 148 E7
Vaughan Rd FAWY SO45 176 C4
Vaughans ALTN GU34 107 G5
Vauxhall Wy PSF GU32 120 C6
Veal's La TOTT SO40 176 B1
Vear's La RWIN SO21 135 G4
Vecta Cl CHCH/BSGR BH23 229 J2
Vectis Cl ALTN GU34 293 M6
Vectis Rd GPORT PO12 190 E5
NMIL/BTOS BH25 230 D1
Vectis Wy CHAM PO6 184 F1
Velder Av ENEY PO4 193 H3
Vellan Ct ROWN SO16 145 J7
Velmead Cl FLEETS GU52 71 K1
Velmead Rd FLEETS GU52 71 J1
Velmore Rd CHFD SO53 139 H4
Velsheda Ct FAWY SO45 177 G3
Velvet Lawn Rd
NMIL/BTOS BH25 218 F4
Venator Pl WIMB BH21 207 J2
Venerable Rd
FHAM/STUB PO14 182 A3
Vengeance Rd
LSOL/BMARY PO13 189 L5
Venice Cl WVILLE PO7 156 A8
Venice Ct AND SP10 96 E1
Venison Ter STOK SO20 * 284 D9
Venning Av BWD BH11 212 E3
Venning Rd WHIT RG2 239 M8
Ventnor Rd ENEY PO4 21 M5
LSOL/BMARY PO13 182 B5
Ventnor Ter ASHV GU12 3 J5
Ventnor Wy
FHAM/PORC PO16 166 E7
Ventry Cl CCLF BH13 224 F4
Ventura Pl UPTN BH16 222 D2
Venture Ct HSEA PO3 * 185 G3
Venture Rd ROWN SO16 138 D7
Venture Sidings ENEY PO4 * 21 M4
Verbena Crs HORN PO8 156 B4
Verbena Wy HEND SO30 149 J6
Verdi Cl KBH RG22 92 F4
Verdon Av HLER SO31 178 E1
Verdun Wy AND SP10 96 B1
Verger Cl FHAM/STUB PO14 180 C1
Verge Wk ALDT GU11 2 F8
Verity Crs CFDH BH17 211 M8
Verity Sq AND SP10 96 E1
Vermont Cl ROWN SO16 146 F4
Vermont Woods EWKG RG40 42 A1
Vernalls Cl NBNE BH10 213 K2
Vernalls Ct NMIL/BTOS BH25 219 J3
Vernalls Gdns NBNE BH10 213 K3
Verner Cl BOR GU35 111 L8
Verne Rd VWD BH31 201 J3
The Verne FLEETS GU52 71 J3
Verney Cl BWD BH11 213 H5
Verney Rd BWD BH11 213 G5
Vernham Rd FUFL SO22 122 D2
Verno La CHCH/BSGR BH23 217 J6
Vernon Av ENEY PO4 193 G4
Vernon Cl GPORT PO12 14 D3
Vernon Crs WHIT RG2 238 B1
Vernon Hl BPWT SO32 143 J2
Vernon Ms ENEY PO4 * 193 G3
Vernon Rd GPORT PO12 14 D3
HSEA PO3 185 G6
Verona Av SBNE BH6 227 K3
Verona Rd CHFD SO53 139 L1
Veronica Cl KBH RG22 92 C5
Veronica Dr FLEETN GU51 70 F3
Verran Rd CBLY GU15 50 F6
Verulam Pl BMTH BH1 8 F5
Verulam Rd PLE BH15 223 M4
SHAM SO14 161 H1
Verwood Crs SBNE BH6 228 A4
Verwood Rd HAV PO9 171 H2
RGWD BH24 202 C3
WIMB BH21 200 C1
WIMB BH21 201 H7
Veryan FHAM PO15 10 A6
Vesey Cl FARN GU14 61 G3
Vespasian Gdns CHIN RG24 64 E4
Vespasian Rd AND SP10 84 D8
WEND SO18 161 K1
Vespasian Wy CHFD SO53 139 L2
Vesta Wy CHFD SO53 139 L1
Vestry Cl AND SP10 4 F5
Vetch Cl CHCH/BSGR BH23 217 H8
Vetch Flds HTWY RG27 56 E7
Viables La BSTK RG21 93 K3
Viables Rbt KBH RG22 93 J3
Vian Cl LSOL/BMARY PO13 182 C4
Vian Pl WINC SO23 289 J8
Vian Rd WVILLE PO7 169 K2
Vicarage Cl EWKG RG40 42 B2
FNM GU9 13 K9
Vicarage Ct WHIT RG2 * 238 D3
Vicarage Dr HEND SO30 149 H7
Vicarage Gdns FLEETS GU52 71 H4
GSHT GU26 115 J5
LYMN SO41 220 A6
Vicarage Hl ALTN GU34 106 F5
FNM GU9 13 K9
HTWY RG27 57 M3
Vicarage La BPWT SO32 150 C4
BPWT SO32 318 C6
FHAM/STUB PO14 189 J1
FNM GU9 12 F4
FNM GU9 13 K9
FNM GU9 77 G1
HASM GU27 117 M2
HTWY RG27 240 B11
LYMN SO41 220 A6
LYMN SO41 350 G11
NARL SO24 292 F12
NTHA RG18 28 E4
TOTT SO40 341 M3
WVILLE PO7 319 R9
YTLY GU46 48 E1
Vicarage Pk RSAL SP5 332 F2
Vicarage Rd ALTN GU34 106 E6
BLKW GU17 50 A4
MOOR/WNTN BH9 213 L7
PLE BH15 223 J3
RSAL SP5 333 J3
TOTT SO40 159 M7
VWD BH31 201 H2
YTLY GU46 48 E1
Vicarage Wy
CHCH/BSGR BH23 216 D6
Vice La ROMY SO51 334 E12
Viceroy Rd ITCH SO19 162 A1
Vickers Cl CHAR BH8 215 H6
Vickers Rd ASHV GU12 73 M3
Vickery Wy CHCH/BSGR BH23 216 D8
Victena Rd ELGH SO50 141 J2
Victoria Av CBLY GU15 50 C3
HISD PO11 194 F5
MOOR/WNTN BH9 213 L7
WVILLE PO7 169 H5
Victoria Cl HLER SO31 180 A3
WIMB BH21 210 D4
Victoria Ct AND SP10 5 G6
Victoria Crs BKME/WDN BH12 224 D2
Victoria Dr BLKW GU17 49 L4
Victoria Gdns FBDG SP6 196 F3
FERN BH22 209 K2
FLEETN GU51 * 59 H7
NWBY RG14 18 F2
RCWD BH24 203 J6
Victoria Gld HLER SO31 162 C7
Victoria Gv SSEA PO5 21 K7
Victoria Hill Rd FLEETN GU51 59 G7
Victoria Hl FLEETN GU51 * 59 H7
LYMN SO41 * 221 M4
WHAM PO17 165 L5
Victoria Pde FLEETN GU51 * 59 H7
Victoria Park Rd
MOOR/WNTN BH9 213 L7
Victoria Pl BMTH BH1 9 M1
GPORT PO12 * 14 F5
KBH RG22 * 64 D8
LYMN SO41 221 L6
RAND SP11 * 250 G9
WIMB BH21 207 H3
Victoria Rd ALDT GU11 2 F3
ALTN GU34 106 F4
BKME/WDN BH12 224 C3
BMTH BH1 9 M2
BPWT SO32 143 H4
CHCH/BSGR BH23 228 E3
ELGH SO50 134 B7
EMRTH PO10 171 L7
FARN GU14 61 H4
FBDG SP6 196 F3
FERN BH22 209 K2
FLEETN GU51 59 G7
FNM GU9 13 G4
HISD PO11 186 F6
HLER SO31 162 A6
ITCH SO19 161 K6
LYMN SO41 232 C4
PSEA PO1 191 M2
THLE RG7 39 M6
WIMB BH21 207 G3
WINC SO23 24 F3
WVILLE PO7 169 L1
Victoria Rd East ALTN GU34 107 G4
Victoria Rd North SSEA PO5 21 L4
Victoria Rd South SSEA PO5 21 J9
Victoria Sq
LSOL/BMARY PO13 189 L6
Victoria St BSTK RG21 6 E6
GPORT PO12 15 G3
PSEA PO1 192 C1
SHAM SO14 23 L2
Victoria Ter CHAM PO6 * 184 F1
Victoria Tr ALDT GU11 72 D1
Victoria Wy LIPH GU30 116 B4
Victor Pl THLE RG7 37 J2
Victor Rd HSEA PO3 192 F1
STHA RG19 35 L1
Victor St WSHM SO15 146 C8
Victor Wy FARN GU14 60 C8
Victory Av HORN PO8 156 A2
Victory Cl CHFD SO53 139 H3
WIMB BH21 205 K2
Victory Crs WSHM SO15 160 B1
Victory Gn NEND PO2 184 C6
Victory Rd FHAM/STUB PO14 189 K2
PSEA PO1 20 C3
WSHM SO15 160 B2
Victory Rbt BSTK RG21 6 D4
Victory Sq WSHM SO15 160 B2
Viewside Cl WIMB BH21 210 C3
Vigo La YTLY GU46 48 E3
Vigo Rd AND SP10 5 K4
Viking Cl FAWY SO45 354 H8
FHAM/STUB PO14 189 H1
ROWN SO16 145 L3
SBNE BH6 228 A4
The Vikings ROMY SO51 137 H1
Viking Wy AND SP10 84 D8
CHCH/BSGR BH23 229 G3
HORN PO8 321 L9
SBNE BH6 228 A4
Villa Gdns WVILLE PO7 155 L8
Village Cl FHAM/STUB PO14 189 J2
WHIT RG2 238 B2
Village Rd GPORT PO12 14 B9
Village St ALTN GU34 279 M7
PSF GU32 120 F3
STOK SO20 272 E8
The Village EWKG RG40 42 A5
Village Wy YTLY GU46 48 F1
Ville De Paris Rd
FHAM/STUB PO14 182 A3

Villette Cl
CHCH/BSGR BH23 216 A7
Villiers Rd FAWY SO45 176 F8
SSEA PO5 21 J9
WSHM SO15 160 C1
Villiers Wy NWBY RG14 33 J6
Vimoutiers Ct FBDG SP6 197 G3
Vince Cl BWD BH11 213 H3
Vincent Av ROWN SO16 146 C6
Vincent Cl NMIL/BTOS BH25 219 G6
Vincent Dr AND SP10 5 K6
Vincent Gv FHAM/PORC PO16 183 J1
Vincent Rd NMIL/BTOS BH25 218 F5
NTHA RG18 29 G8
WSHM SO15 146 C8
Vincent's Gv WSHM SO15 146 C8
Vincent's Wk SHAM SO14 23 G4
Vindomis Cl ALTN GU34 107 K1
Vine Bank WEND SO18 148 C4
Vine Cl ALDT GU11 73 G2
HLER SO31 179 K1
LTDN BH7 227 G1
RFNM GU10 78 E4
Vine Coppice WVILLE PO7 169 L4
Vine Farm Cl
BKME/WDN BH12 213 J8
Vine Farm Rd
BKME/WDN BH12 213 H8
Vinegar Hl LYMN SO41 232 D3
Vine Hl WIMB BH21 206 E3
Vine House Cl FRIM GU16 62 A5
Vineries Cl WIMB BH21 207 M2
The Vineries WIMB BH21 207 M2
Vine Rd ROWN SO16 146 A5
Vinery Gdns ROWN SO16 146 B6
Vinery Rd ROWN SO16 146 C6
Vineside LSOL/BMARY PO13 182 E7
The Vines WWKG RG41 239 Q5
Vine St ALDT GU11 2 E4
Vine Tree Cl TADY RG26 44 D5
Vine Wy RFNM GU10 78 E3
Vineyard Cl ITCH SO19 161 K5
The Vineyards NBAD SO52 138 A4
Viney Av ROMY SO51 131 H8
Viney Rd LYMN SO41 221 L7
Vinnells La PSF GU32 313 M1
Vinneys Cl CHCH/BSGR BH23 216 C6
Vinns La OVTN RG25 89 H5
Vinson Rd LISS GU33 308 G8
Vintney St FLEETN GU51 58 F5
Violet Av FHAM/STUB PO14 189 H2
Violet Cl CHFD SO53 139 G2
KBH RG22 92 C5
Violet Farm Cl WIMB BH21 206 D8
Violet Gv NTHA RG18 29 G7
Violet La NMIL/BTOS BH25 219 G4
TADY RG26 249 N6
Violet Rd ROWN SO16 147 G4
Virginia Cl BKME/WDN BH12 224 C1
Virginia Gdns FARN GU14 61 J6
Virginia Park Rd GPORT PO12 14 A1
Viscount Cl ASHV GU12 73 M3
Viscount Dr
CHCH/BSGR BH23 229 H2
Viscount Wk WIMB BH21 212 C3
Vita Rd NEND PO2 184 E5
Vitellius Gdns CHIN RG24 64 E4
Vitre Gdns LYMN SO41 221 L6
Vivaldi Cl KBH RG22 93 G5
Vivash Rd PSEA PO1 21 L3
Vivian Cl FLEETS GU52 71 K2
Vivian Rd BSTK RG21 65 L5
Vixen Cl FHAM/STUB PO14 189 H2
Vixen Wk NMIL/BTOS BH25 219 H3
Vockins Cl NTID SP9 264 E12
Vokes Cl ITCH SO19 148 B7
Vulcan Cl WSHM SO15 159 M2
Vulcan Rd WSHM SO15 159 M2
Vulcan Wy FARN GU14 60 C8
SHST GU47 49 J1
Vyne Cl ALTN GU34 106 F4
Vyne Meadow CHIN RG24 53 H8
Vyne Rd BSTK RG21 6 E2
CHIN RG24 53 H8
Vyse La SHAM SO14 * 22 F6

W

Wade Court Rd HAV PO9 17 G6
Wade La HAV PO9 17 G8
Wade Rd CHIN RG24 54 A8
Wadham Rd NEND PO2 184 D6
Wadhurst Gdns ITCH SO19 162 A4
Wadhurst Rd HEND SO30 149 J6
Wadmore Cl FAWY SO45 177 H4
Wadwick Bottom RAND SP11 86 B1
Waggoners Wy GSHT GU26 115 G5
Waggoners Wells Rd
GSHT GU26 115 G6
Wagner Cl KBH RG22 93 G4
Wagon La HTWY RG27 56 D6
Wagtail Dr NMIL/BTOS BH25 218 F6
Wagtail Rd HORN PO8 156 A2
Wagtail Wy FHAM/PORC PO16 166 F8
Wainscott Rd ENEY PO4 193 G6
Wainsford Cl LYMN SO41 * 221 H5
Wainsford Plantation
LYMN SO41 220 E8
Wainsford Rd LYMN SO41 220 E6
Wainwright Cl CHAM PO6 185 J2
Wait End Rd WVILLE PO7 169 L2
Wakefield Av
FHAM/PORC PO16 10 D1
NBNE BH10 213 L3
Wakefield Ct WEND SO18 148 A3
Wakefield Rd WEND SO18 148 A3
Wakeford Cl TADY RG26 44 E3
Wakeford Ct TADY RG26 * 44 E2
Wakefords Copse FLEETS GU52 71 K5
Wakefords Cnr FLEETS GU52 * 71 K4
Wakefords Pk FLEETS GU52 71 K5
Wakefords Wy HAV PO9 171 H2
Wakely Gdns BWD BH11 213 G3
Wakely Rd BWD BH11 213 H3
Walberton Av CHAM PO6 169 G8
Walburton Wy HORN PO8 321 M8
Walcheren Pl PLE BH15 222 C5
Walcott Av CHCH/BSGR BH23 215 M7
Waldegrave Cl ITCH SO19 161 K7
Waldegrave Pl NWBY RG14 * 18 E4
Walden Av WHIT RG2 239 J5
Walden Cots RGUW GU3 75 G5
Walden Gdns HORN PO8 156 B1
Walden Rd NEND PO2 184 C6
Walditch Gdns CFDH BH17 211 L6
Waldon Gdns WEND SO18 148 B2
Waldorf Hts BLKW GU17 49 M4
Waldren Cl PLE BH15 223 K6
Waleran Cl RSAL SP5 327 N2
Wales St WINC SO23 25 J5
Walford Cl WIMB BH21 207 J2
Walford Gdns WIMB BH21 207 H2
Walford Rd CHAM PO6 168 C8
Walhampton Hl LYMN SO41 221 M3
Walker Gdns HEND SO30 149 J4
Walker Pl LSOL/BMARY PO13 * 182 D7
Walker Rd NEND PO2 184 C6
Walkers Cl ELGH SO50 141 K2
Walkers La North FAWY SO45 354 H7
Walker's La South FAWY SO45 354 H9
Walker's Rdg CBLY GU15 51 G3
Walkford La NMIL/BTOS BH25 218 D5
Walkford Rd CHCH/BSGR BH23 218 C6
Walkford Wy CHCH/BSGR BH23 218 B7
Walking Field La PLE BH15 223 K6
The Walk FUFL SO22 * 122 E7
Walkwood Av LTDN BH7 215 H8
Wallace Gv THLE RG7 238 A4
Wallace La BROC SO42 353 J10
Wallace Rd BDST BH18 211 G5
ITCH SO19 161 M7
NEND PO2 184 F8
Wallace Wy ALDT GU11 2 C1
Walldown Rd BOR GU35 112 F4
The Walled Gdns ODIM RG29 * 257 Q5
Walled Meadow AND SP10 5 K6
Waller Dr NTHA RG18 28 A7
Wallington Ct
FHAM/STUB PO14 181 M6
Wallington Dr CHFD SO53 133 G8
Wallington Hl
FHAM/PORC PO16 11 J4
Wallington Orch
FHAM/PORC PO16 * 11 L2
Wallington Rd NEND PO2 184 F7
Wallington Shore Rd
FHAM/PORC PO16 11 K4
Wallingtons Rd HUNG RG17 30 F2
Wallington Wy
FHAM/PORC PO16 11 J4
Wallins Copse CHIN RG24 54 B6
Walliscott Rd BWD BH11 213 G7
Wallisdean Av
FHAM/STUB PO14 10 C8
HSEA PO3 193 H1
Wallisdown Rd
BKME/WDN BH12 212 D6
Wallis Dr TADY RG26 46 D6
Wallis Gdns WVILLE PO7 155 L7
Wallis Rd BSTK RG21 6 E8
NBNE BH10 213 H7
WVILLE PO7 155 L7
Wall La THLE RG7 45 J2
Wallop Dr KBH RG22 92 C6
Wallop Dro STOK SO20 283 R4
Wallop Rd STOK SO20 269 N8
Walmer Cl CWTH RG45 43 L3
ELGH SO50 134 A5
FRIM GU16 61 M1
Walmer Rd PSEA PO1 21 M3
Walnut Av WEND SO18 147 L3
Walnut Cl ALDT GU11 2 F7
ALTN GU34 106 F3
CHFD SO53 133 J6
NMIL/BTOS BH25 218 F5
ROWN SO16 145 M7
YTLY GU46 48 F4
Walnut Dr FHAM/STUB PO14 189 H2
Walnut Gv FUFL SO22 24 B3
ROWN SO16 145 M8
The Walnuts FLEETS GU52 70 F3
Walnut Tree Cl HISD PO11 194 F5
RWIN SO21 288 D4
Walnut Tree Dr EMRTH PO10 172 E3
Walnut Tree Rd AND SP10 4 E7
Wainwright Gdns HEND SO30 149 J1
Walpole Gdns HTWY RG27 57 M2
Walpole La HLER SO31 163 L5
Walpole Rd BMTH BH1 226 D3
FUFL SO22 122 C7
GPORT PO12 15 H4
Walrus Rd FARN GU14 60 D8
Walsall Rd HSEA PO3 193 G2
Walsford Rd WBNE BH4 225 J3
Walsingham Cl CHAM PO6 * 168 D7
Walsingham Dene LTDN BH7 214 F8
Walsingham Gdns WEND SO18 147 L5
Walters Cl NTHA RG18 28 E4
Waltham Cl BPWT SO32 318 G2
FHAM/PORC PO16 167 J6
SHST GU47 43 M7
Waltham Ct OVTN RG25 89 K4
Waltham Crs ROWN SO16 146 C4
Waltham La OVTN RG25 90 A8
Waltham Rd LTDN BH7 227 H1
OVTN RG25 89 K5
Waltham St SSEA PO5 20 F4
Walton Cl GPORT PO12 14 D5
WVILLE PO7 169 L3
Walton Ct FHAM PO15 165 K8
Walton Pl FUFL SO22 122 D7
Walton Rd CHAM PO6 185 J2
GPORT PO12 14 D5
ITCH SO19 148 D8
NBNE BH10 213 J6
PLE BH15 224 A2
Waltons Av FAWY SO45 354 F4
Walton Wy NWBY RG14 19 J2
Walworth Rd AND SP10 96 F2
RAND SP11 85 L8
RAND SP11 97 H2
Walworth Rbt AND SP10 96 F3
Wanborough Hl RGUW GU3 261 N2
Wandesford Pl GPORT PO12 183 G7
Wandle Cl ASHV GU12 74 A7
Wandsdyke Cl FRIM GU16 51 H8
Wangfield La BPWT SO32 150 C3
Wansbeck Cl CHFD SO53 139 H3
Wansey Gdns NWBY RG14 27 M7
Wanstead Cl RGWD BH24 203 K3
Wantage Rd SHST GU47 43 M8
Wapiti Wy FARN GU14 60 D8
Warbler Cl HORN PO8 156 A1
ROWN SO16 146 B2
UPTN BH16 210 B8
Warbleton Rd CHIN RG24 54 C5
Warblington Av HAV PO9 17 K5
Warblington Cl CHFD SO53 139 G5
TADY RG26 44 C5
Warblington Rd EMRTH PO10 187 L1
Warblington St PSEA PO1 20 D5
Warborne La LYMN SO41 351 R12
Warbrook Ct HAV PO9 171 H3
Warbrook La HTWY RG27 241 N4
Warburton Cl ITCH SO19 148 E8
Warburton Rd CFDH BH17 211 L8
ITCH SO19 148 D7
Ward Cl AND SP10 5 J7
Ward Crs EMRTH PO10 172 A3
Warden Cl HEND SO30 148 D3
Wardens Cl HISD PO11 194 F3
Wardle Rd ELGH SO50 134 D5
Ward Rd ENEY PO4 193 G6
Wardroom Rd NEND PO2 184 B7
Wareham Rd WIMB BH21 210 B5
Warehouse Rd STHA RG19 34 F7
Warfield Av WVILLE PO7 169 L1
Warfield Crs WVILLE PO7 169 L1
Wargrove Dr SHST GU47 43 M8
Warland Wy WIMB BH21 210 E1
Warlock Cl ITCH SO19 162 D1
Warmwell Cl CFDH BH17 211 M6
Warner Ct AND SP10 4 F5
Warner Ms HEND SO30 150 A5
Warnes La RGWD BH24 348 H2
Warnford Cl GPORT PO12 14 C5
Warnford Crs HAV PO9 170 D3
Warnford Rd BPWT SO32 319 J1
LTDN BH7 227 H1
Warren Av CHCH/BSGR BH23 228 F3
CHFD SO53 139 L3
ENEY PO4 193 H3
ROWN SO16 146 B7
Warren Cl BOR GU35 112 C2
CHFD SO53 139 L3
FLEETS GU52 71 K1
HISD PO11 194 C4
HTWY RG27 57 M3
RGWD BH24 202 F7
ROWN SO16 146 A6
SHST GU47 43 J8
Warren Cnr RFNM GU10 76 A1
Warren Crs ROWN SO16 146 A6
Warren Dr RAND SP11 270 H1
RGWD BH24 202 F7
Warren Edge Cl SBNE BH6 227 M5
Warren Edge Rd SBNE BH6 227 M5
Warren La BROC SO42 357 R4
EWKG RG40 239 R11
PSF GU32 307 N7
RGWD BH24 202 F7
RWIN SO21 302 E12
Warren Pk LYMN SO41 232 A2
Warren Pl TOTT SO40 144 C6
Warren Ri FRIM GU16 51 G5
Warren Rd LISS GU33 308 G5
LISS GU33 309 K2
NWBY RG14 33 K6
PSTN BH14 224 D4
WBNE BH4 225 H6
WINC SO23 25 M4
Warren Side EPSF GU31 323 M1
Warrens La RSAL SP5 327 J8
The Warren ALDT GU11 2 D4
FAWY SO45 354 D3
FNM GU9 2 A7
TADY RG26 44 A4
Warren Wk FERN BH22 209 H1
Warrington Ms ALDT GU11 2 A6
Warrior Cl CHFD SO53 139 H4
Warrys Cl FAWY SO45 177 G8
Warsash Cl HAV PO9 170 E2
Warsash Gv
LSOL/BMARY PO13 182 B6
Warsash Rd FHAM/STUB PO14 180 E3
HLER SO31 179 L3
Warspite Cl NEND PO2 184 D4
Warton Cl BROC SO42 353 J10
Warton Rd BSTK RG21 7 G2
Warwick Av NMIL/BTOS BH25 219 H5
Warwick Cl ALDT GU11 3 J7
CBLY GU15 51 K5
CHFD SO53 139 G4
LSOL/BMARY PO13 190 A4
WINC SO23 25 G1
Warwick Crs SSEA PO5 21 H5
Warwick Dr NWBY RG14 19 H8
Warwick Rd ASHV GU12 61 M7
DEAN RG23 64 F6
FARN GU14 60 D8
LTDN BH7 227 G3
PSTN BH14 224 C5
TOTT SO40 144 F8
WSHM SO15 146 D6
Warwick Wy WHAM PO17 * 152 A4
Wasdale Cl HORN PO8 321 L10
SHST GU47 43 M6
Wash Brook HTWY RG27 56 C6
Washbrook Rd CHAM PO6 168 D8
Washford La BOR GU35 111 H8
Washington Av BMTH BH1 226 D2
Washington Rd EMRTH PO10 171 M7
NEND PO2 184 D8
Wash Water KSCL RG20 246 D1
Wasing La THLE RG7 37 K6
Watchetts Dr CBLY GU15 50 E6
Watchetts Lake Cl CBLY GU15 50 F4
Watchetts Rd CBLY GU15 50 D5
Watchmoor Point CBLY GU15 * 50 D4
Watchmoor Rd CBLY GU15 50 C5
Watcombe Rd SBNE BH6 227 K3
Waterbeech Dr HEND SO30 149 J4
Waterberry Dr WVILLE PO7 155 J7
Watercress Meadow
NARL SO24 291 K12
Waterditch Rd
CHCH/BSGR BH23 216 F5
Water End La CHIN RG24 67 H1
Water End Park CHIN RG24 67 J1
Waterford Cl LYMN SO41 221 M5
PSTN BH14 224 A6
Waterford Gdns
CHCH/BSGR BH23 230 A1
Waterford La LYMN SO41 221 M5
Waterford Pl
CHCH/BSGR BH23 230 A1
Waterford Rd
CHCH/BSGR BH23 218 B8
NMIL/BTOS BH25 219 J5
Waterhouse La WSHM SO15 160 B2
Waterhouse Md SHST GU47 49 M1
Waterhouse Wy WSHM SO15 160 B1
Wateridge Rd BSTK RG21 65 L4
Water La FARN GU14 61 G1
FAWY SO45 176 E6
FNM GU9 77 K4
NARL SO24 292 A12
RAND SP11 96 B8
SBNE BH6 227 K1
STHA RG19 34 C5
TOTT SO40 144 D8
WINC SO23 25 J5
Waterlily Cl BSTK RG21 7 K5
Waterlock Gdns ENEY PO4 193 K4
Waterloo Av DEAN RG23 64 E5
Waterloo Cl CBLY GU15 51 K1
HORN PO8 155 K5
Waterloo Ct AND SP10 5 H6
Waterloo Pl CWTH RG45 * 43 K4
Waterloo Rd ASHV GU12 3 J5
CFDH BH17 211 J8
CWTH RG45 43 J4
GPORT PO12 191 J7
HAV PO9 16 F3
LYMN SO41 221 M4
MOOR/WNTN BH9 225 M1
WIMB BH21 210 B2
WSHM SO15 160 D2
Waterloo St SSEA PO5 21 H4
Waterloo Ter WSHM SO15 160 F2
Waterloo Wy RGWD BH24 203 J6
Watermain Rd RGWD BH24 346 G7
Waterman Cl BOR GU35 113 H2
Watermans La FAWY SO45 176 E7
The Watermeadows
AND SP10 96 B7
Watermead Rd CHAM PO6 185 L1
Watermill Ct THLE RG7 * 37 K2
Watermill Rd
CHCH/BSGR BH23 216 A8
Watermills Cl AND SP10 4 F9
Water Rede FLEETS GU52 71 G5
Water Ridges DEAN RG23 91 K4
Water's Edge HEND SO30 149 H6
Waters Edge Gdns
EMRTH PO10 171 M8
Watersedge Rd CHAM PO6 168 A8
Waters Gn BROC SO42 351 L2
Waters Green Ct BROC SO42 351 L2
Watership Dr RGWD BH24 203 M6
Waterside CHCH/BSGR BH23 228 F4
FAWY SO45 176 F3
Waterside Cl BOR GU35 111 G8
RGWD BH24 203 K3
Waterside Ct ALTN GU34 107 G4
FLEETN GU51 59 K5
Waterside Gdns
FHAM/PORC PO16 11 L5
Waterside La
FHAM/PORC PO16 183 L2
Waterside Ms FLEETN GU51 59 K5
Waterside Rd ROMY SO51 131 G7
Watersmeet
FHAM/PORC PO16 182 B2
The Waters WHAM PO17 165 L7
Waterston Cl CFDH BH17 211 K7
Water St WIMB BH21 336 F5
Water Tower Rd BDST BH18 211 J4
Water Wy BSTK RG21 7 K5
Waterworks Rd CHAM PO6 169 K8
PSF GU32 120 E3
RWIN SO21 124 C8
Watery La AND SP10 5 K2
CHCH/BSGR BH23 217 G7
FLEETS GU52 71 G5
KSCL RG20 31 M7
RCCH PO18 173 L1
Watkin Rd BOSC BH5 226 F4
HEND SO30 149 L3
Watley Cl ROWN SO16 145 K3
Watley La RWIN SO21 125 J7
RWIN SO21 135 K1
RWIN SO21 287 P12
Watling End KBH RG22 92 D5
Watson Acre AND SP10 4 C4
Watson Wk TOTT SO40 158 C1
Watson Wy DEAN RG23 64 F6
Watt Cl AND SP10 95 L3
Watton Cl CHAR BH8 215 G6
Watton La BPWT SO32 319 K2
Watton Rd FAWY SO45 354 E5
Watts Cl ROWN SO16 145 L6
Watts Common Rd ALDT GU11 72 E1
Watts Rd FARN GU14 60 F3
HEND SO30 149 J5
PSEA PO1 192 D1
Wavecrest Cl TOTT SO40 159 M5
Wavell Av CFDH BH17 211 G7
Wavell Cl KBH RG22 93 G2
Wavell Rd BWD BH11 213 H4
LSOL/BMARY PO13 182 D5
NTID SP9 264 D12
WEND SO18 148 A5
Wavell Wy FUFL SO22 122 C7
Wavendon Av
NMIL/BTOS BH25 218 E8
Waveney Cl
LSOL/BMARY PO13 189 M6
Waveney Gn ROWN SO16 145 L7
Waverley Av BSTK RG21 93 J2
FLEETN GU51 59 H5
HLER SO31 162 C6
Waverley Cl CBLY GU15 51 H4
FBDG SP6 197 H1
FNM GU9 * 13 J4
ODIM RG29 69 H5
ROMY SO51 131 H7
Waverley Ct HLER SO31 162 C7
Waverley Crs PLE BH15 223 K3
Waverley Dr ASHV GU12 74 A2
CBLY GU15 51 G3
RWIN SO21 288 E4
Waverley Gdns ASHV GU12 74 A2
Waverley Gv ENEY PO4 21 L9
Waverley La FNM GU9 13 K4
Waverley Rd CHAM PO6 169 J8
FARN GU14 61 K5
FBDG SP6 197 H1
NMIL/BTOS BH25 219 H6
SSEA PO5 21 L9
WSHM SO15 22 A1
The Waverleys NTHA RG18 28 F8
Wayfarer Cl ENEY PO4 * 193 J3
HLER SO31 179 M3
Wayfarers LSOL/BMARY PO13 190 D1
Wayfarer's Wk BPWT SO32 311 P8
BPWT SO32 318 H3
DEAN RG23 104 A1
EMRTH PO10 187 L1
HAV PO9 170 C6
KSCL RG20 244 H5
KSCL RG20 253 R2
NARL SO24 277 L8
OVTN RG25 91 G6
RAND SP11 245 M8
WVILLE PO7 154 F8
WVILLE PO7 169 H6
Wayground Rd WIMB BH21 206 E7
Waylands Pl HEND SO30 149 G8
Wayman Rd FARN GU14 50 A8
WIMB BH21 210 E2
Wayne Rd BKME/WDN BH12 224 B2
Waynflete Cl BPWT SO32 143 J4
Waynflete La FNM GU9 12 B4
Waynflete Pl FUFL SO22 24 A9
Ways End CBLY GU15 51 G4
Wayside HLER SO31 163 K4
Wayside Cl LYMN SO41 232 D3
Wayside Rd DEAN RG23 64 D7
RGWD BH24 346 E3
SBNE BH6 227 L4
Wayte St CHAM PO6 184 F1
Waytown Cl CFDH BH17 211 K7
Weald Cl HLER SO31 164 A8
Weale Ct BSTK RG21 6 E2
Weardale Rd CHFD SO53 139 K4
Weatherby Gdns HTWY RG27 57 M2
Weathermore La ALTN GU34 293 P6
Weaver Moss SHST GU47 49 K1
Weavers Cl AND SP10 5 J4
FERN BH22 205 G7
Weavers Down LIPH GU30 * 309 P1
Weavers Gdns RFNM GU10 78 D1
Weavers Gn HAV PO9 17 L1
Weavers Piece HTWY RG27 * 56 A3
Weavers Pl CHFD SO53 133 H8
Weavers Wk NWBY RG14 * 18 E3
Weavills Rd ELGH SO50 141 G2
Webb Cl CHIN RG24 54 A6
HISD PO11 195 G6
Webb La HISD PO11 195 G6
Webb Rd FHAM/PORC PO16 183 K2
Webbs Acre STHA RG19 35 M2
Webbs Cl RGWD BH24 205 M2
Webbs Farm Cl WHCH RG28 99 L1
Webbs Gn BPWT SO32 318 H9
Webburn Gdns WEND SO18 148 A1
Webster Rd FUFL SO22 122 B3
MOOR/WNTN BH9 214 A5
Wedderburn Av DEAN RG23 92 D7
Wedgewood Cl FAWY SO45 354 E4
Wedgewood Gdns
CHCH/BSGR BH23 348 E11
Wedgewood Wy HORN PO8 155 L5
Wedgwood Dr PSTN BH14 224 A6
Wedman's La HTWY RG27 56 B1
Wedmore Cl FUFL SO22 124 A1
Weeke Cl RSAL SP5 331 R1
Weeke Manor Cl FUFL SO22 24 A1
Weevil La GPORT PO12 15 J1
Weir Av FARN GU14 61 G5
Weir Cl FARN GU14 61 G5
Weir Rd FARN GU14 60 A6
HTWY RG27 57 K4
The Weirs WINC SO23 25 J7
The Weir WHCH RG28 99 L1
Welbeck Av PTSW SO17 147 H6
Welbeck Cl FARN GU14 60 F4
Welch Rd ENEY PO4 21 M9
GPORT PO12 191 G1
Welch Wy ROWN SO16 145 L3
Welchwood Cl HORN PO8 155 M2
Weldon Av BWD BH11 212 E3
Weldon Cl FLEETS GU52 71 K3
Welland Gdns WEND SO18 148 B2
Welland Gn ROWN SO16 145 L8
Welland Rd WIMB BH21 207 K4
Wellands Rd LYND SO43 345 L3
Wella Rd KBH RG22 93 H2
Wellbrooke Gdns CHFD SO53 139 H1
Wellburn Cl SHST GU47 49 K1
Well Cl CBLY GU15 50 D4
NMIL/BTOS BH25 218 F7
OVTN RG25 103 G3
Well Copse Cl HORN PO8 321 L11
Weller Dr CBLY GU15 50 E5
EWKG RG40 239 N10
Wellers Cl TOTT SO40 158 B1
Wellesley Av
CHCH/BSGR BH23 229 H1
Wellesley Cl ASHV GU12 73 M1
WVILLE PO7 169 L1
Wellesley Dr CWTH RG45 43 G3
Wellesley Gdn FNM GU9 77 G1
Wellesley Ga ASHV GU12 * 3 G4
Wellesley Rd ALDT GU11 72 D5
AND SP10 5 G9
FARN GU14 60 D8
RFNM GU10 262 H6
Welles Rd CHFD SO53 139 K2
Well House Cl FBDG SP6 330 H5
Well House La FUFL SO22 288 E11
HTWY RG27 240 H1
Wellhouse Rd ALTN GU34 279 R10
Wellington Av ALDT GU11 2 C2
BOR GU35 112 F2
CHCH/BSGR BH23 229 J1
FLEETN GU51 59 K6
WEND SO18 148 B5
Wellington Cl FAWY SO45 176 D7
HORN PO8 156 D2
NWBY RG14 27 L7
SHST GU47 43 L8
Wellington Ct HEND SO30 * 148 C2
Wellington Crs TADY RG26 249 P3
Wellington Gdns ALDT GU11 * 2 C4
Wellington Gv
FHAM/PORC PO16 183 J1
Wellingtonia Av EWKG RG40 42 D4
Wellington La FNM GU9 77 H1
Wellington Pk HEND SO30 149 G3
Wellington Pl ASHV GU12 73 M4
LYMN SO41 * 221 M4
Wellington Rd AND SP10 4 E3
CHAR BH8 9 G1
CWTH RG45 43 L4
PSTN BH14 224 C5
SHST GU47 43 K8
WEND SO18 147 K6
Wellington St ALDT GU11 2 F2
SSEA PO5 21 G4
Wellington Ter DEAN RG23 64 E5
SHST GU47 43 L8
Wellington Wy FARN GU14 72 D1
WVILLE PO7 169 L1
Well La ALTN GU34 258 F8
BPWT SO32 318 B5
FBDG SP6 338 A2
HASM GU27 118 D6
HLER SO31 179 G2
PLE BH15 223 J4
Wellmans Meadow KSCL RG20 248 C9
Well Meadow HAV PO9 170 E2
NWBY RG14 27 K7
Wellowbrook Cl CHFD SO53 139 G2
Wellow Cl HAV PO9 16 B1
WEND SO18 148 C5
Wellow Dro ROMY SO51 335 J1
Wellow Gdns
FHAM/STUB PO14 180 C2
Wellow Wood Rd ROMY SO51 128 D8
Well Rd RFNM GU10 259 N2
Wells Cots FNM GU9 78 E1
Wells La RGUW GU3 75 J4
Wellsmoor FHAM/STUB PO14 180 C1
Wells Pl ELGH SO50 140 A2
Wells's La WHCH RG28 87 K8
Well St KSCL RG20 247 J6
Wellswood Gdns HAV PO9 157 J5
Wellsworth La HAV PO9 157 J5
Welsh La THLE RG7 240 A2
Welshman's Rd THLE RG7 39 H7
Welton Ct BSTK RG21 6 C4
Wembley Gv CHAM PO6 185 H2
Wendan Rd NWBY RG14 18 D9
Wendover Cl NMIL/BTOS BH25 218 F7
Wendover Dr FRIM GU16 51 L5
Wendover Rd HAV PO9 16 C3
Wendys Crs FERN BH22 * 209 M5
Wenlock Wy STHA RG19 35 K2
Wensleydale Dr CBLY GU15 51 M3
Wensley Gdns EMRTH PO10 171 M5
Wentwood Gdns
NMIL/BTOS BH25 219 K6
Wentworth Av BOSC BH5 227 G4
Wentworth Cl ASHV GU12 74 A1
BOSC BH5 227 G5
CWTH RG45 43 H2
FNM GU9 77 K2
YTLY GU46 48 F3
Wentworth Ct NWBY RG14 19 G7
Wentworth Crs ASHV GU12 74 A2
DEAN RG23 92 C7
Wentworth Dr BDST BH18 211 G3
CHCH/BSGR BH23 227 M2
HORN PO8 156 B1
Wentworth Gdns ALTN GU34 106 E4
FAWY SO45 354 F6
ITCH SO19 162 B3
Wentworth Gra FUFL SO22 24 D8
Wentworth Gv FAWY SO45 354 F5
Wescott Wy BWD BH11 212 E4
Wesermarsch Rd HORN PO8 156 A4
Wesley Cl CHAR BH8 9 M1
ITCH SO19 148 D8
Wesley Gv HSEA PO3 184 F5
Wesley Rd PSTN BH14 224 C3
WIMB BH21 207 K3
WINC SO23 289 J9
Wessex Av NMIL/BTOS BH25 219 G6
ODIM RG29 68 F7
Wessex Cl BSTK RG21 6 C9

CHCH/BSGR BH23 229 J1
FAWY SO45 354 H7
LSOL/BMARY PO13 190 A2
Wessex Crs ODIM RG29 68 F7
Wessex Dr FUFL SO22 122 E2
ODIM RG29 68 F7
Wessex Est RGWD BH24 203 K4
Wessex Gdns AND SP10 4 F4
FHAM/PORC PO16 183 H1
ROMY SO51 137 H1
Wessex Ga CHAR BH8 226 C2
Wessex La WEND SO18 147 K4
Wessex Pl FNM GU9 13 H5
Wessex Rd HORN PO8 321 L9
PSTN BH14 224 A5
RGWD BH24 203 K4
Wessex Wy CHAR BH8 226 C2
RWIN SO21 135 G4
WBNE BH4 225 J4
WCLF BH2 8 C4
West Ashling Rd RCCH PO18 173 J3
West Av FNM GU9 77 H2
WIMB BH21 200 F8
West Bargate SHAM SO14 22 F4
West Battery Rd NEND PO2 184 B7
Westbeams Rd LYMN SO41 350 F10
Westborn Rd
FHAM/PORC PO16 11 H5
West Borough WIMB BH21 207 H3
Westbourne Ar WBNE BH4 * 225 H5
Westbourne Av EMRTH PO10 172 A4
FAWY SO45 354 E4
Westbourne Cl EMRTH PO10 172 A4
WBNE BH4 225 J5
Westbourne Crs PTSW SO17 146 F7
Westbourne Park Rd
WBNE BH4 225 H6
Westbourne Rd EMRTH PO10 172 A3
NEND PO2 184 F8
SHST GU47 50 A1
Westbourne Ter NWBY RG14 18 D1
Westbroke Gdns ROMY SO51 130 F7
West Brook Cl DEAN RG23 91 K4
Westbrook Cl AND SP10 5 H6
HLER SO31 164 A7
Westbrooke Cl HORN PO8 156 A2
Westbrooke Rd ALTN GU34 106 E5
Westbrook Gv WVILLE PO7 169 K3
Westbrook Hl MFD/CHID GU8 260 G12
Westbrook Rd
FHAM/PORC PO16 183 K2
Westbrook Wy WEND SO18 147 K4
Westburn ALTN GU34 258 G12
Westbury Av FLEETN GU51 59 M8
Westbury Cl CHAM PO6 168 B7
CHCH/BSGR BH23 217 G1
CHCH/BSGR BH23 217 K7
CWTH RG45 43 K2
FLEETN GU51 59 L8
NMIL/BTOS BH25 219 G8
Westbury Ct HEND SO30 149 J7
Westbury Gdns FLEETN GU51 59 M8
FNM GU9 77 J4
Westbury Rd
FHAM/PORC PO16 11 H5
RGWD BH24 203 K5
WSHM SO15 159 M1
Westbury Wy ASHV GU12 3 L2
West Butts St PLE BH15 223 H6
Westby Rd BOSC BH5 226 E4
Westcliff Cl LSOL/BMARY PO13 189 L5
West Cliff Gdns WCLF BH2 8 C8
Westcliff Ms ITCH SO19 161 K5
West Cliff Rd WBNE BH4 225 J6
WCLF BH2 8 D7
West Cl FNM GU9 77 H1
LYMN SO41 221 H6
SBNE BH6 * 228 A4
VWD BH31 200 F2
West Common FAWY SO45 354 F10
Westcot Rd FAWY SO45 354 D5
Westcroft Pde
NMIL/BTOS BH25 * 219 H6
Westcroft Pk BDST BH18 211 J4
Westcroft Rd GPORT PO12 14 A2
Westdeane Ct BSTK RG21 6 B6
Westdown Rd BWD BH11 213 G3
West Downs Cl
FHAM/PORC PO16 166 A4
West Dr ELGH SO50 134 D8
FERN BH22 * 346 B5
West End TADY RG26 52 F7
West End Cl FUFL SO22 24 D5
West End Gv FNM GU9 12 C4
West End La ALTN GU34 292 F4
HASM GU27 119 K4
RFNM GU10 109 L3
West End Rd HEND SO30 148 F8
THLE RG7 39 L7
WEND SO18 148 A4
Westend Rd ITCH SO19 148 A5
West End Ter FUFL SO22 24 D5
Westerdale STHA RG19 35 J1
Westerdale Dr FRIM GU16 51 K5
Westerham Cl CHAM PO6 168 E8
Westerham Rd CCLF BH13 225 H5
Westering ROMY SO51 131 J8
Westerley Cl HLER SO31 * 179 L3
Western Av AND SP10 5 G4
CCLF BH13 224 E6
EMRTH PO10 171 L8
NBNE BH10 213 K4
NMIL/BTOS BH25 218 D8
NWBY RG14 18 C1
WSHM SO15 159 M3
Western Cl NBNE BH10 213 K3
Western District Cut
WSHM SO15 160 D1
Western End NWBY RG14 18 A6
Western Esp SHAM SO14 22 D2
Western La ODIM RG29 68 F6
Western Pde EMRTH PO10 187 L1
ITCH SO19 161 L8
SSEA PO5 20 F7
Western Rd ALDT GU11 2 B4
AND SP10 5 G6
BOR GU35 110 E6
CCLF BH13 224 F8
CHAM PO6 184 E2
CHFD SO53 133 L7
FHAM/PORC PO16 11 G6
FUFL SO22 24 D4
HAV PO9 16 C3
HEND SO30 148 D3
LISS GU33 308 F8
LYMN SO41 221 K4
Western Wy FHAM/PORC PO16 10 F6
GPORT PO12 190 E5
KBH RG22 92 F2
West Farm MARL SN8 264 G3
Westfield Av FHAM/STUB PO14 10 D8
HISD PO11 194 E5
West Field Cl TADY RG26 44 D4
Westfield Cl ELGH SO50 141 J5
HLER SO31 178 E2
WIMB BH21 207 H3
Westfield Common
HLER SO31 178 D2
Westfield Crs CHFD SO53 139 J5
NTHA RG18 28 D8
Westfield Dr BPWT SO32 318 D10
Westfield Dro NARL SO24 303 N12
Westfield Gdns
CHCH/BSGR BH23 217 H7
Westfield La RFNM GU10 78 C2
West Field Rd WINC SO23 289 J8
Westfield Rd BSTK RG21 7 H9
CBLY GU15 50 D6
CHFD SO53 139 J5
ENEY PO4 193 G5
FUFL SO22 288 B11
GPORT PO12 14 B3
LYMN SO41 221 M6
NTHA RG18 28 C7
SBNE BH6 227 L4
TOTT SO40 144 F8
WSHM SO15 160 A1
Westfield Wy NWBY RG14 18 A6
West Flexford La RGUW GU3 75 L8
West Fryerne YTLY GU46 48 F1
Westgate FHAM/STUB PO14 189 J3
Westgate Pk WBNE BH4 225 H5
Westgate Rd NWBY RG14 18 A6
Westgate St SHAM SO14 22 F6
Westglade FARN GU14 60 D4
West Gn YTLY GU46 48 D1
West Green Rd HTWY RG27 57 H2
Westgrove FBDG SP6 197 G3
Westham Cl CFDH BH17 211 L5
West Ham Cl KBH RG22 64 E8
West Ham La KBH RG22 64 D8
West Haye Rd HISD PO11 195 K7
West Hayes LYMN SO41 221 M5
West Heath CHOB/PIR GU24 63 K4
Westheath Rd BDST BH18 211 H4
West Heath Rd FARN GU14 60 F4
West Hl FUFL SO22 * 24 D5
MFD/CHID GU8 263 Q1
West Hill Cl MFD/CHID GU8 263 Q1
West Hill Dr FAWY SO45 176 F3
FUFL SO22 24 C5
West Hill Gdns FLEETN GU51 58 F6
West Hill Pk FUFL SO22 24 B5
West Hill Pl WCLF BH2 8 C6
West Hill Rd WCLF BH2 8 C7
West Hill Rd North RWIN SO21 288 E3
West Hill Rd South RWIN SO21 288 E4
West Hoe La BPWT SO32 143 M4
West Horton La ELGH SO50 140 F3
West Howe Cl BWD BH11 213 G4
The West Hundreds
FLEETN GU51 58 F5
Westland NTHA RG18 28 D8
Westland Dr WVILLE PO7 169 L4
Westland Gdns GPORT PO12 14 C7
Westlands Ct
CHCH/BSGR BH23 348 C12
Westlands Gv
FHAM/PORC PO16 183 J1
Westlands Rd NWBY RG14 18 F9
West La HISD PO11 194 E4
LYMN SO41 220 E7
NBAD SO52 137 L3
Westley Cl FUFL SO22 24 A2
Westley Gv FHAM/STUB PO14 10 D7
Westley La RWIN SO21 287 N12
Westlyn Rd TADY RG26 44 E3
Westman Rd FUFL SO22 122 D2
West Marlands Rd SHAM SO14 22 F2
Westmead FARN GU14 61 H5
West Md FNM GU9 * 12 E3
Westmead Cl HISD PO11 194 D5
Westmead Dr NWBY RG14 33 M4
West Mills NWBY RG14 18 D4
West Mills Rd FBDG SP6 197 G3
West Mills Yd NWBY RG14 * 18 D4
Westminister Rd LYMN SO41 232 B4
Westminster Cl FLEETN GU51 59 J6
KBH RG22 92 D5
Westminster Gdns
FHAM/STUB PO14 180 C1
Westminster Ga FUFL SO22 122 B7
Westminster Rd CCLF BH13 225 H7
Westminster Rd East
CCLF BH13 225 H7
West Moors Rd FERN BH22 209 L1
WIMB BH21 200 F8
Westmorland Cl WWKG RG41 239 R2
Westmorland Dr CBLY GU15 51 K5
Westmorland Wy CHFD SO53 139 L3
Weston Av ENEY PO4 193 H4
Weston Cl ITCH SO19 161 M7
Weston Ct RAND SP11 84 D4
Weston Crs WEND SO18 148 C5
Weston Down Rd RWIN SO21 275 L7
Weston Dr BMTH BH1 9 K5
Weston Grove Rd ITCH SO19 161 K6
Weston La ITCH SO19 161 L8
PSF GU32 315 M8
RCCH PO18 173 K1
ROWN SO16 145 G4
RSAL SP5 282 F11
Weston Rd ELGH SO50 140 A1
EPSF GU31 120 E6
OVTN RG25 257 J5
WIMB BH21 207 M1
West Overcliff Dr WBNE BH4 225 J6
Westover La RGWD BH24 202 F6
Westover Rd BMTH BH1 8 F6
FLEETN GU51 59 K7
HSEA PO3 185 H8
LYMN SO41 232 D4
ROWN SO16 145 H8
West Pk RAND SP11 82 D6
West Park Dr FBDG SP6 330 D11
West Park La FBDG SP6 330 C11
West Park Rd WSHM SO15 22 E2
West Portway AND SP10 95 K2
West Quay Rd PLE BH15 223 H7
WSHM SO15 22 D3
Westray Cl BSTK RG21 7 J1
Westridge KSCL RG20 246 A8
West Rdg RFNM GU10 * 260 D3
Westridge Rd PTSW SO17 147 H7
West Ring RFNM GU10 260 D1
West Rd BOSC BH5 227 H4
CBLY GU15 50 F3
CHCH/BSGR BH23 348 C12
EMRTH PO10 171 L8
FARN GU14 50 C8
FAWY SO45 176 D7
FAWY SO45 177 K7
HEND SO30 148 F6
ITCH SO19 161 L6
LYMN SO41 232 A3
RWIN SO21 273 P5
SHAM SO14 23 G7
WHAM PO17 168 A2
West Rw WIMB BH21 207 H4
Westrow Gdns WSHM SO15 160 E1
Westrow Rd WSHM SO15 160 E1
Westside Cl KBH RG22 92 F1
Westside Vw WVILLE PO7 155 J7
West St AND SP10 5 G5
BPWT SO32 318 H7
EMRTH PO10 171 M8
FAWY SO45 176 F3
FBDG SP6 197 G3
FHAM/PORC PO16 10 F6
FHAM/STUB PO14 180 F4
FNM GU9 12 E4
HASM GU27 118 C6
HAV PO9 16 B4
KSCL RG20 246 G8
NARL SO24 291 M10
NWBY RG14 18 D3
ODIM RG29 68 E6
PLE BH15 223 H6
PSEA PO1 20 B6
RGWD BH24 203 G5
SHAM SO14 22 F5
TADY RG26 44 D4
WHAM PO17 167 L2
WIMB BH21 207 H4
WVILLE PO7 319 Q11
West Street Cl TADY RG26 44 C4
West Vw BOR GU35 * 112 D3
West View Dr STOK SO20 272 E9
Westview Gdns AND SP10 5 H7
West View Rd BOR GU35 114 C4
CHCH/BSGR BH23 228 E2
PLE BH15 223 J4
Westview Rd FUFL SO22 122 A2
Westward Rd HEND SO30 149 J4
West Wy AND SP10 96 F3
BDST BH18 210 F5
LYMN SO41 221 J6
MOOR/WNTN BH9 214 B6
Westway FHAM PO15 180 E1
West Way Cl
MOOR/WNTN BH9 214 B7
Westways CHAM PO6 169 M8
FHAM/STUB PO14 189 K2
Westways Cl ROWN SO16 145 K3
Westwood Av FERN BH22 209 J2
Westwood Cl EMRTH PO10 172 A3
Westwood Gdns CHFD SO53 133 L8
Westwood La RGUW GU3 75 G5
Westwood Pk
NMIL/BTOS BH25 * 218 E3
Westwood Rd HLER SO31 162 B5
LYND SO43 345 K2
NEND PO2 184 E4
NWBY RG14 19 H9
PTSW SO17 146 F8
Westwood Vw NARL SO24 304 A11
Wetherby Cl CFDH BH17 211 G6
Wetherby Gdns AND SP10 96 A2
FARN GU14 61 J8
TOTT SO40 144 C8
Wetherdown EPSF GU31 120 E6
Wey Bank ALTN GU34 108 E1
Weybank Cl FNM GU9 13 H2
Weybourne Rd FNM GU9 2 C8
Weybridge Cl HLER SO31 163 M6
Weybridge Md YTLY GU46 49 G1
Weybrook Ct TADY RG26 52 F8
Wey Cl ASHV GU12 74 A7
CBLY GU15 50 D3
Weycombe Rd HASM GU27 118 C4
Weydon Farm La FNM GU9 12 F7
Weydon Hill Cl FNM GU9 12 F7
Weydon Hill Rd FNM GU9 12 F7
Weydon La FNM GU9 12 B9
Weydon Mill La FNM GU9 12 E6
Weydown Rd HASM GU27 118 B5
Wey Hl HASM GU27 118 A6
Weyhill Cl FHAM/PORC PO16 167 J7
HAV PO9 170 D3
TADY RG26 44 B5
Weyhill Gdns RAND SP11 94 F2
Weyhill Rd AND SP10 4 E6
RAND SP11 94 F2
Weyland Cl LIPH GU30 116 C3
Wey Lodge Cl LIPH GU30 * 116 D4
Weyman's Av NBNE BH10 213 J2
Weymans Dr NBNE BH10 213 J2
Weymouth Av GPORT PO12 182 F8
Weymouth Rd NEND PO2 * 184 D7
PSTN BH14 224 C3
Weyside Pk ALTN GU34 * 107 H3
Weysprings HASM GU27 117 M1
Weysprings Cl BSTK RG21 7 J4
Weywood Cl FNM GU9 2 C9
Weywood La FNM GU9 2 B9
Whaddon Cha
FHAM/STUB PO14 189 H2
Whaddon Ct HAV PO9 170 C2
Whaddon La RWIN SO21 310 A8
Whale Island Wy NEND PO2 184 C7
Whalesmead Cl ELGH SO50 140 F3
Whalesmead Rd ELGH SO50 140 F3
Whaley Rd NEND PO2 184 B7
Wharf Cl BKME/WDN BH12 224 E2
Wharfdale Rd
BKME/WDN BH12 224 D2
WBNE BH4 225 J4
Wharfenden Wy FRIM GU16 61 M2
Wharf Hl WINC SO23 25 J8
Wharf Rd ASHV GU12 74 A4
FRIM GU16 61 M2
ITCH SO19 161 K5
NEND PO2 184 C8
NWBY RG14 18 F4
Wharfside THLE RG7 38 C1
Wharf St NWBY RG14 18 E4
The Wharf NWBY RG14 * 18 F4
Wharf Wy FRIM GU16 61 M2
Wharncliffe Gdns
CHCH/BSGR BH23 230 A1
Wharncliffe Rd BMTH BH1 226 D4
CHCH/BSGR BH23 230 A1
ITCH SO19 161 K5
Whartons La TOTT SO40 158 C4
Whatleigh Cl PLE BH15 223 J7
Wheat Cl CHFD SO53 138 F2
Wheatcroft Dr WEND SO18 148 B3
Wheatcroft Rd
LSOL/BMARY PO13 189 M6
Wheatear Dr EPSF GU31 121 G7
Wheatears Dr ROMY SO51 335 J5
Wheatfields Rd WHIT RG2 238 E3
Wheatland Cl FUFL SO22 122 D7
Wheatlands FHAM/STUB PO14 164 C8
Wheatlands Av HISD PO11 195 L7
Wheatlands Crs HISD PO11 195 L7
Wheatlands La NWBY RG14 33 H6
Wheatley La ALTN GU34 108 C5
Wheatley Rd ALDT GU11 2 D2
Wheaton Rd LTDN BH7 227 G3
Wheatsheaf Ct HEND SO30 149 H6
Wheatsheaf Dr HORN PO8 155 K5
Wheatsheaf La NWBY RG14 19 H1
Wheatstone Rd ENEY PO4 21 M7
Wheeler Cl GPORT PO12 191 H2
WHCH RG28 87 M8
Wheelers Green Wy STHA RG19 35 L2
Wheelers Hl HTWY RG27 56 E7
Wheelers La BWD BH11 212 D2
Wheelers Wk FAWY SO45 354 G8
Wheelers Yd RWIN SO21 * 274 C8
Wheelhouse Pk NBAD SO52 * 133 G7
Wheelwrights La GSHT GU26 115 G4
Whernside Cl ROWN SO16 145 M8
Wherwell Ct HAV PO9 171 H3
Whetstone Rd FARN GU14 60 D3
Whichers Cl HAV PO9 157 H8
Whichers Gate Rd HAV PO9 157 H8
Whimbrel Cl ENEY PO4 193 J3
Whinchat Cl FHAM PO15 165 J8
HTWY RG27 57 L1
ROWN SO16 146 B2
Whincroft Cl FERN BH22 209 L1
Whincroft Dr FERN BH22 209 L2
Whinfield Rd FAWY SO45 176 E7
Whin Holt FLEETS GU52 71 J2
Whins Cl CBLY GU15 50 D4
Whins Dr CBLY GU15 50 D4
Whinwhistle Rd ROMY SO51 335 M6
Whippingham Cl CHAM PO6 184 D1
Whistler Cl BSTK RG21 7 J8
Whistler Gv SHST GU47 49 M2
Whistler Rd ITCH SO19 162 C1
Whistlers Cl CHCH/BSGR BH23 348 D11
Whistlers La THLE RG7 45 H3
Whitaker Crs LYMN SO41 221 J5
Whitakers Cl NTHA RG18 28 D8
Whitby Av BDST BH18 211 G6
Whitby Cl CHCH/BSGR BH23 215 K4
FARN GU14 61 L7
Whitby Crs BDST BH18 211 G6
Whitby Rd LYMN SO41 232 B4
Whitchurch Av BDST BH18 211 J5
Whitchurch Cl ALDT GU11 260 B2
Whitchurch Ct ITCH SO19 161 M5
Whitchurch Rd FLEETN GU51 58 F5
Whitcombe Cl TOTT SO40 158 E1
Whitcombe Gdns HSEA PO3 192 F2
Whiteacres Cl GPORT PO12 14 E2
White Acres Rd FRIM GU16 61 M4
White Av LISS GU33 309 J2
White Barn Crs LYMN SO41 220 A5
Whitebeam Cl
FHAM/STUB PO14 10 A7
HORN PO8 156 C3
RWIN SO21 135 G4
WWKG RG41 239 R5
White Beam Ri HORN PO8 321 L7
Whitebeam Rd HEND SO30 149 K6
Whitebeams Gdns FARN GU14 60 C5
Whitebeam Wy NBAD SO52 138 A3
VWD BH31 201 K3
Whitechimney Rw
EMRTH PO10 172 B3
White City CWTH RG45 43 M3
Whitecliff Crs PSTN BH14 224 A6
Whitecliffe Av HSEA PO3 193 G1
Whitecliff Rd PSTN BH14 223 M6
White Cliff Rd PSTN BH14 224 A6
White Cl PLE BH15 224 A1
White Cloud Pk ENEY PO4 192 F5
White Cottage Cl FNM GU9 77 H2
Whitecroft FAWY SO45 * 177 G6
Whitecross Cl CFDH BH17 211 L5
Whitecross Gdns NEND PO2 184 F5
Whitedell La WHAM PO17 166 D4
White Dirt La HORN PO8 321 K10
Whitedown ALTN GU34 106 E6
Whitedown La ALTN GU34 106 D6
Whitedown Rd TADY RG26 249 R4
White Farm Cl NBNE BH10 213 K8
White Farm La MARL SN8 243 P3
Whitefield Rd FAWY SO45 354 E5
NMIL/BTOS BH25 219 G5
PSTN BH14 224 A6
White Gates BPWT SO32 142 B7
Whitehall CHCH/BSGR BH23 228 B3
Whitehall Dr WHIT RG2 239 L8
Whitehall Rd STOK SO20 286 C10
Whitehart Flds RGWD BH24 203 L4
White Hart La BSTK RG21 7 G6
FHAM/PORC PO16 183 H1
TADY RG26 52 A4
TOTT SO40 341 K4
White Hart Rd ELGH SO50 141 J3
GPORT PO12 14 F6
PSEA PO1 20 C6
Whitehaven
FHAM/PORC PO16 183 H1
HORN PO8 156 D2
Whitehayes Cl
CHCH/BSGR BH23 216 D6
Whitehayes Rd
CHCH/BSGR BH23 216 C7
Whitehead Cl CHIN RG24 66 B1
White Heather Ct FAWY SO45 177 G2
White Hl KSCL RG20 246 F10
KSCL RG20 247 P9
ODIM RG29 258 F6
RSAL SP5 296 A1
Whitehill Cl CBLY GU15 50 F1
Whitehill La NARL SO24 291 P12
Whitehill Rd BOR GU35 113 J3
Whitehorn Dr RSAL SP5 334 B8
White Horse Dr PLE BH15 223 J3
White Horse La EWKG RG40 239 Q11
WVILLE PO7 155 G2
Whitehouse Cl FARN GU14 61 H2
White House Cl KBH RG22 92 F2
Whitehouse Gdns PSF GU32 120 C4
White House Gdns
WSHM SO15 160 A2
YTLY GU46 48 E1
Whitehouse Rd WIMB BH21 207 K6
White House Wk FNM GU9 77 H1
White Knights
NMIL/BTOS BH25 230 F1
White Ladies Cl HAV PO9 17 G5
Whitelands CHCH/BSGR BH23 348 F9
Whitelands Rd NTHA RG18 28 E8
White La ASHV GU12 74 C7
OVTN RG25 67 M6
RFNM GU10 260 G1
RWIN SO21 125 G4
TADY RG26 255 J10
Whitelaw Rd WSHM SO15 160 B1
Whiteleaf La WVILLE PO7 319 Q5
Whitelegg Wy NBNE BH10 213 L3
Whiteley La FHAM PO15 164 F6
HLER SO31 164 C3
Whiteley Wy FHAM PO15 164 E5
White Lion Wk GPORT PO12 15 K3
White Lion Wy YTLY GU46 48 F1
White Lodge Gdns
FHAM/PORC PO16 165 L8
Whitemoor La TOTT SO40 335 Q12
Whitemoor Rd BROC SO42 350 H2
Whitenap Cl ROMY SO51 137 H2
Whitenap La ROMY SO51 137 J2
White Oak Wy RAND SP11 95 L8
White Post La RFNM GU10 78 E4
White Rd CBLY GU15 50 B2
ELGH SO50 134 D8
White Rose La FNM GU9 78 F1
Whitesbury Rd RSAL SP5 326 D3
Whites Cl HTWY RG27 56 B7
Whites Hl RWIN SO21 125 M8
Whiteshoot RSAL SP5 332 H4
STOK SO20 284 D9
Whiteshoot Hl RSAL SP5 332 G4
Whiteshute La WINC SO23 122 E8
Whites La FAWY SO45 355 K5
Whites Rd FARN GU14 61 L7
ITCH SO19 178 A7
Whitestone Cl ROWN SO16 145 M8
Whitestones KBH RG22 92 E6
White Swan Rd PSEA PO1 20 F3
Whitethorn Cl ASHV GU12 74 B7
Whitethorn Rd HISD PO11 195 H5
Whitewater Ri FAWY SO45 176 F6
HTWY RG27 56 E6
Whitewater Rd ODIM RG29 68 E4
White Wy RSAL SP5 296 A1
Whiteways WIMB BH21 207 L2
Whiteways Ms HLER SO31 179 K3
The White Wy BPWT SO32 312 C7
Whitewell Cl WHIT RG2 239 L6
Whitewood CHIN RG24 54 B5
Whitfield Cl HASM GU27 118 C3
Whitfield Pk RGWD BH24 202 D7
Whitfield Rd HASM GU27 118 C4
Whitgift Cl DEAN RG23 92 D7
Whithedwood Av WSHM SO15 146 D8
Whithers La BROC SO42 353 J10
Whitlet Cl FNM GU9 12 E5
Whitley Cl EMRTH PO10 172 B1
Whitley Rd HORN PO8 155 M2
YTLY GU46 48 F4
Whitley Wy FARN GU14 60 E7
NMIL/BTOS BH25 219 H3
Whitley Wood La WHIT RG2 238 C1
Whitley Wood Rd WHIT RG2 238 B2
Whitlock Ri RSAL SP5 324 E3
Whitmarsh La CHIN RG24 54 D5
Whitmead La RFNM GU10 260 C11
Whitmoor Vale Rd GSHT GU26 114 F1
Whitmore Cl SHST GU47 43 M8
Whitmore Gn FNM GU9 77 J2
Whitmore La WIMB BH21 200 B1
Whitmore V GSHT GU26 114 F2
Whitmore Vale Rd GSHT GU26 115 H4
Whitney Rd CHIN RG24 7 L1
Whitsbury Cl CHAR BH8 214 D6
Whitsbury Rd FBDG SP6 197 H2
HAV PO9 171 G3
Whitstable Rd CHAM PO6 168 E8
Whittington Cl FAWY SO45 176 F6
Whittington Ct EMRTH PO10 171 M8
Whittle Av FHAM PO15 164 C7
Whittle Cl ASHV GU12 73 M3
EWKG RG40 42 A1
SHST GU47 43 J7
Whittle Crs FARN GU14 60 F1
Whittle Rd AND SP10 95 K3
WIMB BH21 208 F1
Whittles Wy PLE BH15 223 H6
Whitwell HLER SO31 162 C5
Whitwell Rd ENEY PO4 192 E7
Whitworth Cl GPORT PO12 14 D4
Whitworth Crs WEND SO18 147 K8
Whitworth Rd GPORT PO12 14 D4
NEND PO2 184 F8
WEND SO18 147 K8
WHIT RG2 239 N9
Whynot La AND SP10 4 D5
Whyte Av ASHV GU12 3 L8
Whyte Cl FAWY SO45 354 D5
Whyteways ELGH SO50 139 M4
Wick Dr NMIL/BTOS BH25 218 E6
Wickers Cl WHIT RG2 238 E4
Wicket Hl RFNM GU10 78 E2
Wicket Rd NBNE BH10 213 J3
The Wicket FAWY SO45 176 F6
Wickfield Av CHCH/BSGR BH23 228 B2
Wickfield Cl CHCH/BSGR BH23 228 B2
Wickham Cl ALTN GU34 106 D6
FLEETS GU52 71 G3
TADY RG26 44 B4
Wickham Dr WIMB BH21 210 D4
Wickham Pl FLEETS GU52 71 G2
Wickham Rd BPWT SO32 318 G8
FHAM/PORC PO16 11 G1
FLEETS GU52 71 G2
WHAM PO17 166 B1
Wickham St PSEA PO1 20 C2
Wick Hill La EWKG RG40 42 C3
Wick La RSAL SP5 326 E12
SBNE BH6 228 B3
Wicklea Rd SBNE BH6 228 B4
Wicklow Cl KBH RG22 92 D1
Wicklow Dr CHFD SO53 139 G3
Wickmeads Rd SBNE BH6 228 A4
Wickor Cl EMRTH PO10 172 A4
Wickor Wy EMRTH PO10 171 M5
Wick Point Ms
CHCH/BSGR BH23 228 B3
Wicor Mill La
FHAM/PORC PO16 183 H2
Wicor Pth FHAM/PORC PO16 183 L2
Widbury Rd LYMN SO41 221 J6
Widden Cl LYMN SO41 350 F10
Widdicombe Av PSTN BH14 224 E6
Widecombe Dr FAWY SO45 176 E4
Wide La WEND SO18 147 L3
Wide Lane Cl BROC SO42 351 K3
Widgeon Cl GPORT PO12 191 H1
ROWN SO16 146 B2
Widgeons ALTN GU34 106 F3
Widget Cl BWD BH11 213 H6
Widlers La BPWT SO32 310 E10
Widley Ct FHAM/STUB PO14 181 M6
Widley Court Dr CHAM PO6 185 G1
Widley Gdns WVILLE PO7 169 K5
Widley Rd CHAM PO6 169 G8
NEND PO2 184 C6
Widley Wk CHAM PO6 168 F6
Widmore Rd KBH RG22 92 E2
Widworthy Dr BDST BH18 210 F3
Wield Cl HAV PO9 170 C4
Wield Rd ALTN GU34 278 F9
Wigan Crs HAV PO9 170 B6
Wigan Rd FARN GU14 60 D8
Wights Wk KBH RG22 92 D5
Wight Wk FERN BH22 209 L6
Wigmore Rd TADY RG26 249 R3
Wilberforce Cl FUFL SO22 122 C6
Wilberforce Rd GPORT PO12 191 J7
SSEA PO5 21 G6
Wild Arum Wy CHFD SO53 138 F3
Wild Briar EWKG RG40 42 B1
Wildburn Cl TOTT SO40 144 C6
Wild Cherry Wy CHFD SO53 139 G2
Wilde Cl TOTT SO40 158 D1
Wildern Cl HLER SO31 179 M1
Wildern Ct HEND SO30 149 H4
Wilderness Hts WEND SO18 148 C3
Wilderness Rd FRIM GU16 51 G6
Wildern La HEND SO30 149 H4
Wilders Cl FRIM GU16 50 F5
Wilderton Rd CCLF BH13 224 F5
Wilderton Rd West CCLF BH13 224 F4
Wildfell Cl CHCH/BSGR BH23 216 A7
Wild Herons HTWY RG27 56 E7
Wildmoor La HTWY RG27 54 E2
Wildown Gdns SBNE BH6 227 M5
Wildown Rd SBNE BH6 228 A5
Wild Ridings
FHAM/STUB PO14 181 H4
Wild Rose Crs HLER SO31 179 L2
Wildwood Dr TADY RG26 249 P3
Wildwood Gdns YTLY GU46 48 E4
Wilfred Rd BOSC BH5 226 F4
Wilfred Wy STHA RG19 35 M1
Wilkins Cl HORN PO8 321 K6
Wilkinson Dr CHAR BH8 215 G6

Wilks Cl ROWN SO16 145 J3
Willems Av ALDT GU11 2 C2
Willersley Cl CHAM PO6 168 C7
Willett Rd WIMB BH21 206 F6
Will Hall Cl ALTN GU34 106 D6
William Cl CHCH/BSGR BH23 218 A6
FHAM/STUB PO14 189 K3
STHA RG19 35 K2
William Farthing Cl ALDT GU11 2 E3
William Macleod Wy
ROWN SO16 146 A8
William Panter Ct ELGH SO50 140 A2
William Price Gdns
FHAM/PORC PO16 11 G3
William Rd LTDN BH7 226 F1
LYMN SO41 221 L3
Williams Cl FAWY SO45 354 F5
LSOL/BMARY PO13 190 D1
Williamson Cl HASM GU27 118 F3
RAND SP11 265 L10
Williams Rd HSEA PO3 185 H5
William St SHAM SO14 23 M1
Williams Wy FLEETN GU51 59 L7
William Wy ALTN GU34 107 G3
Willington Cl CBLY GU15 50 D2
Willis Av NBAD SO52 138 B4
Willis Cl NTHA RG18 28 D1
Willis La ALTN GU34 293 P7
Willis Rd GPORT PO12 15 H5
PSEA PO1 21 G2
ROWN SO16 147 K3
Willis Wy CFDH BH17 223 H2
Willis Waye WINC SO23 289 J11
Willoughby Cl ALTN GU34 106 E4
Willoughby Wy DEAN RG23 64 F6
Willow Av FBDG SP6 197 G2
Willow Cl BOR GU35 113 G1
FRIM GU16 61 L4
HAV PO9 17 G5
HEND SO30 148 E2
HEND SO30 149 K6
LIPH GU30 116 D5
NWBY RG14 18 D8
RGWD BH24 205 M4
UPTN BH16 222 D3
Willow Ct FRIM GU16 50 F7
ROWN SO16 146 A5
Willow Crs FARN GU14 61 H1
Willowdale Cl PSF GU32 315 K4
Willowdene Cl HAV PO9 170 B4
NMIL/BTOS BH25 219 J5
Willow Dr RGUW GU3 75 J7
RGWD BH24 203 J7
TOTT SO40 159 M8
WIMB BH21 208 C2
Willow Flds ASHV GU12 74 B7
Willowford YTLY GU46 48 F2
Willow Gdns EMRTH PO10 172 B2
LIPH GU30 116 D5
NBAD SO52 137 M3
Willow Gn RWIN SO21 135 G4
Willow Gv AND SP10 4 F7
ELGH SO50 141 K2
Willow Herb Cl HLER SO31 179 L2
Willow La BLKW GU17 49 M4
CHCH/BSGR BH23 348 F9
Willow Md CHAR BH8 214 D4
Willowmead Cl NWBY RG14 33 J7
Willow Ms NTID SP9 * 266 G1
Willow Pk ASHV GU12 73 M6
PSTN BH14 * 223 M5
Willow Pl GPORT PO12 14 F2
Willow Rd BPWT SO32 143 L5
KSCL RG20 247 P2
LISS GU33 308 F8
TADY RG26 44 B4
Willows End SHST GU47 43 K8
The Willows AND SP10 4 E8
CHFD SO53 * 139 J5
NMIL/BTOS BH25 219 H8
RFNM GU10 260 A4
WVILLE PO7 154 E4
Willow Tree Av HORN PO8 156 B6
Willow Tree Gdns
FHAM/STUB PO14 10 A7
Willow Tree Ri BWD BH11 213 H6
Willow Tree Wk ITCH SO19 162 B1
Willow Wk NMIL/BTOS BH25 231 H1
Willow Wy ASHV GU12 73 L8
CHCH/BSGR BH23 228 A3
DEAN RG23 64 F5
FERN BH22 209 K1
FNM GU9 77 H2
HTWY RG27 46 F7
SHST GU47 43 H7
STOK SO20 270 D8
Willow Wood Rd HISD PO11 195 G5
Wills Cl WIMB BH21 210 D4
Wills Rd PSTN BH14 224 F4
Wills Wy ROMY SO51 137 G2
Wilwood Cl CFDH BH17 211 L5
Wilmer Rd ELGH SO50 140 A2
Wilmington Cl WEND SO18 147 M5
Wilmot Cl ELGH SO50 134 E7
Wilmott Cl GPORT PO12 14 A3
Wilmott La GPORT PO12 14 A3
Wilmott Wy DEAN RG23 64 F6
Wilmot Wy CBLY GU15 51 H5
Wilmur Crs PLE BH15 223 L2
Wilsford Cl EARL RG6 238 E1
Wilsom Cl ALTN GU34 107 H5
Wilsom Rd ALTN GU34 107 H5
Wilson Gv SSEA PO5 21 K6
Wilson Rd ASHV GU12 3 M5
BMTH BH1 226 D3
FARN GU14 60 F5
NEND PO2 184 C6
PSTN BH14 224 C4
Wilsons Rd BOR GU35 114 B3
Wilson St SHAM SO14 23 L1
Wilton Av WSHM SO15 160 E2
Wilton Cl CHCH/BSGR BH23 215 K7
Wilton Ct FARN GU14 61 K5
Wilton Crs WSHM SO15 146 D7
Wilton Dr HORN PO8 156 A3
Wilton Gdns NMIL/BTOS BH25 218 F5
WSHM SO15 146 D7
Wilton Pl BSTK RG21 6 B5
SSEA PO5 21 H8
Wilton Rd CBLY GU15 50 D5
LTDN BH7 226 F3
WSHM SO15 146 D7
Wilton Ter SSEA PO5 * 21 J8
Wiltshire Av CWTH RG45 43 K2
Wiltshire Gdns
CHCH/BSGR BH23 348 B12
Wiltshire Rd
CHCH/BSGR BH23 348 B12
CHFD SO53 139 K5
Wiltshire St SSEA PO5 20 F6
Wilverley Av CHAR BH8 214 F6
HAV PO9 171 G4
Wilverley Pl FAWY SO45 354 G7
Wilverley Rd BROC SO42 351 K3
CHCH/BSGR BH23 217 G8
NMIL/BTOS BH25 349 P9
Wimbledon Park Rd SSEA PO5 21 K9
Wimborne Rd BWD BH11 212 F2
ENEY PO4 193 G4
MOOR/WNTN BH9 213 M8
NBNE BH10 213 M4
PLE BH15 223 J2
TWDS BH3 225 M1
WCLF BH2 8 F3
WIMB BH21 206 D8
WIMB BH21 207 H2
Wimborne Rd East
WIMB BH21 209 G2
Wimborne Rd West
WIMB BH21 208 B3
Wimborne St WIMB BH21 336 D7
Wimbushes EWKG RG40 239 R10
Wimpole St PSEA PO1 21 K1
Wimpson Gdns ROWN SO16 145 M7
Wimpson La ROWN SO16 145 M7
Wincanton Cl ALTN GU34 107 G6
Wincanton Rd WHIT RG2 238 C1
Wincanton Wy WVILLE PO7 156 B7
Winchcombe Cl FLEETN GU51 59 J7
Winchcombe Rd BSTK RG21 6 C6
CHAM PO6 168 B7
NWBY RG14 18 F5
Winchester By-Pass
WINC SO23 123 J1
Winchester Cl HLER SO31 162 B6
Winchester Ct
LSOL/BMARY PO13 * 190 D3
Winchester Gdns AND SP10 5 H9
Winchester Hl ROMY SO51 131 H8
RWIN SO21 274 C9
Winchester Rd ALTN GU34 106 E7
ALTN GU34 293 N5
AND SP10 5 J8
ASHV GU12 74 A5
BPWT SO32 142 D1
BPWT SO32 143 L8
BPWT SO32 149 L1
BPWT SO32 151 L4
BSTK RG21 6 B9
CHFD SO53 139 K2
DEAN RG23 92 A8
ELGH SO50 135 J8
KBH RG22 93 G2
KSCL RG20 254 C1
NARL SO24 291 J11
NEND PO2 184 E8
NMIL/BTOS BH25 219 J3
PSF GU32 120 B5
PSF GU32 314 F2
RAND SP11 96 C8
RAND SP11 272 B4
RFNM GU10 262 H5
ROMY SO51 136 F1
ROWN SO16 146 A7
RWIN SO21 275 P11
STOK SO20 272 F7
STOK SO20 299 R1
WHAM PO17 151 M7
WHCH RG28 99 L1
Winchester St AND SP10 5 J6
BSTK RG21 6 E6
FARN GU14 61 J8
HEND SO30 150 A4
OVTN RG25 89 K4
WHCH RG28 87 L8
WSHM SO15 160 F2
Winchester Wy BLKW GU17 49 L2
TOTT SO40 158 C1
Winchfield Cl ITCH SO19 162 A4
Winchfield Ct HTWY RG27 58 C7
Winchfield Crs HAV PO9 170 C4
Winchfield Gdns TADY RG26 44 B5
Wincombe Cl FERN BH22 209 K5
Wincombe Dr FERN BH22 209 K4
Windbury Rd ROWN SO16 145 L6
Windermere Av
FHAM/STUB PO14 181 K8
KBH RG22 92 C3
ROWN SO16 145 L6
Windermere Cl FARN GU14 60 E5
Windermere Ct ASHV GU12 * 73 M4
Windermere Gdns NARL SO24 291 M12
TOTT SO40 144 E8
Windermere Rd BOR GU35 110 F7
NEND PO2 184 F5
TWDS BH3 226 A2
WEND SO18 148 B3
Windermere Wy FNM GU9 76 E2
STHA RG19 35 G1
Windfield Dr ROMY SO51 131 H8
Windham Rd BMTH BH1 9 L2
Winding Wood Dr CBLY GU15 51 K4
Windmill Cl HORN PO8 321 L7
LYMN SO41 232 D3
RGWD BH24 202 F8
RSAL SP5 327 N2
Windmill Copse FAWY SO45 176 F7
Windmill Cnr THLE RG7 40 A2
Windmill Dr BOR GU35 114 B2
Windmill Fld WVILLE PO7 155 G4
Windmill Flds ALTN GU34 293 M5
Windmill Gv
FHAM/PORC PO16 183 H2
Windmill Hl ALTN GU34 107 G6
Windmill La HLER SO31 163 G2
RAND SP11 95 L8
RAND SP11 250 E9
RAND SP11 251 K5
RGWD BH24 202 F8
Windmill Rd ASHV GU12 3 J4
THLE RG7 40 A2
The Windmills ALTN GU34 * 106 F5
Windover Cl ITCH SO19 148 C6
Windrush Cl BSTK RG21 7 K5
Windrush Gdns WVILLE PO7 169 K1
Windrush Hts SHST GU47 43 K8
Windrush Rd ROWN SO16 145 L7
Windrush Wy FAWY SO45 177 G5
Windsor Cl ALTN GU34 106 D5
FARN GU14 61 H4
LYMN SO41 219 L4
RGWD BH24 202 B7
Windsor Ct ELGH SO50 134 D8
NWBY RG14 19 G4
Windsor Crs FNM GU9 76 F2
Windsor Gdns ASHV GU12 73 M7
KBH RG22 92 C6
Windsor Ga ELGH SO50 134 A6
Windsor La SSEA PO5 21 H5
Windsor Pk ALTN GU34 106 F6
Windsor Ride EWKG RG40 42 C1
Windsor Ri NWBY RG14 19 J9
Windsor Rd ALTN GU34 293 M4
AND SP10 4 F5
BOR GU35 111 H7
BOSC BH5 226 E4
CHAM PO6 184 F1
CHCH/BSGR BH23 215 L8
FARN GU14 60 D8
FARN GU14 61 K7
FHAM/PORC PO16 183 K1
GPORT PO12 14 D4
NARL SO24 291 L12
PSF GU32 120 D6
PSTN BH14 224 B5
WVILLE PO7 155 K6
Windsor Wk BOR GU35 111 H7
Windsor Wy ALDT GU11 3 H3
FBDG SP6 196 C6
FRIM GU16 51 H8
Windwhistle La RSAL SP5 327 R5
Windwhistle Wy RSAL SP5 327 P2
Winfield Wy EMRTH PO10 171 M4
Winfrith Crs BKME/WDN BH12 212 E8
Winfrith Wy ROWN SO16 145 K3
Wingate Ct ALDT GU11 2 D2
Wingate Dr ITCH SO19 148 B7
Wingate Rd
LSOL/BMARY PO13 182 F7
ODIM RG29 258 B5
TOTT SO40 144 D8
Wingfield Av
CHCH/BSGR BH23 217 K7
PLE BH15 223 K2
Wingfield Gdns FRIM GU16 51 M5
Wingfield St PSEA PO1 192 D1
Wingrove Rd TOTT SO40 158 C5
Wings Cl FNM GU9 76 F2
Wings Rd FNM GU9 76 F2
Winifred Cl ELGH SO50 141 J1
Winifred Rd PLE BH15 223 L3
WVILLE PO7 155 L8
Winkfield Rw HORN PO8 156 A3
Winklebury Wy DEAN RG23 64 D7
Winkle St SHAM SO14 22 F7
Winkton Cl CHCH/BSGR BH23 216 C5
HAV PO9 16 B1
Winkworth La THLE RG7 44 C2
Winnall Cl WINC SO23 25 M3
Winnall Manor Rd WINC SO23 25 M5
Winnall Valley Rd WINC SO23 25 L4
Winnards Cl FERN BH22 209 L6
Winnards Pk HLER SO31 179 K1
Winners Enclosure
ELGH SO50 * 141 K5
Winnham Dr
FHAM/PORC PO16 167 G8
Winnington FHAM PO15 165 K8
Winnipeg Cl LIPH GU30 116 C5
Winn Rd PTSW SO17 147 G8
Winscombe Av HORN PO8 156 A6
Winsford Av ELGH SO50 141 G3
Winsford Cl CHCH/BSGR BH23 217 K7
ELGH SO50 141 G3
Winsford Gdns ELGH SO50 141 G3
Winslade Rd FUFL SO22 288 C12
HAV PO9 170 D3
Winsley Av SBNE BH6 227 J4
Winslow Cl HISD PO11 195 K7
Winsor La TOTT SO40 341 P4
Winsor Rd TOTT SO40 159 G2
TOTT SO40 341 M5
Winspit Cl PLE BH15 222 E5
Winstanley Rd NEND PO2 184 C7
ROWN SO16 145 J3
Winston Av BKME/WDN BH12 225 H2
TADY RG26 44 D5
Winston Churchill Av SSEA PO5 21 H4
Winston Cl ELGH SO50 134 A8
FRIM GU16 61 M2
HISD PO11 194 E5
ROWN SO16 145 M6
THLE RG7 238 D6
Winstone Crs NBAD SO52 138 A5
Winston Gdns
BKME/WDN BH12 225 G2
Winston Ri ALTN GU34 293 M5
Winston Rd MOOR/WNTN BH9 214 A5
Winston Wk RFNM GU10 79 G2
Winston Wy RGWD BH24 203 K4
STHA RG19 28 B8
Winterbourne Rd CHAM PO6 167 M7
PLE BH15 223 K4
ROMY SO51 131 J7
Winterdyne Ms AND SP10 4 E6
Winterhayes Cl CFDH BH17 211 K5
Winterhill Rd CHAM PO6 168 D8
Winter Rd ENEY PO4 193 G5
Winters Cl FAWY SO45 354 F5
Winters Hl BPWT SO32 142 E4
Winterslow Dr HAV PO9 170 E2
Winters Rd BPWT SO32 318 A12
Winterthur Wy BSTK RG21 6 D4
Winterton Dr NWBY RG14 26 F7
Winton Cha AND SP10 96 F4
Winton Cl FUFL SO22 24 E1
LYMN SO41 221 M5
NTID SP9 266 F4
Winton Crs YTLY GU46 48 F3
Winton Hl STOK SO20 285 Q5
Winton Rd ALDT GU11 2 E5
FNM GU9 13 J1
NEND PO2 184 F6
PSF GU32 120 D6
Winton Sq BSTK RG21 6 E6
Winton St SHAM SO14 23 H2
Winton Wy NBNE BH10 213 K7
NMIL/BTOS BH25 219 H3
Wiremead La RAND SP11 94 C6
Wisbech Wy LYMN SO41 219 M5
Wisborough Rd SSEA PO5 21 K8
Wise's Firs THLE RG7 39 K1
Wishanger La BOR GU35 262 B10
Wishart Gdns
MOOR/WNTN BH9 214 B3
Wish Pl SSEA PO5 21 L8
Wisley Gdns FARN GU14 60 D6
Wisley Rd AND SP10 4 C7
Wistaria Ct AND SP10 4 B7
Wistaria La YTLY GU46 48 E3
Wisteria Dr BOR GU35 112 F2
VWD BH31 201 L4
Wisteria Gdns HAV PO9 171 H4
Witan Cl AND SP10 84 D8
Witan Ct WHCH RG28 87 K6
Witchampton Cl HAV PO9 * 171 G3
Witchampton Rd BDST BH18 210 F6
Witham Cl CHFD SO53 139 G2
Witherbed La FHAM PO15 164 E8
Witherington Rd RSAL SP5 327 K2
Withermoor Rd
MOOR/WNTN BH9 213 L8
Wither Ri DEAN RG23 91 J2
Witherslack Cl BOR GU35 114 B4
Withies Rd LSOL/BMARY PO13 182 D8
The Withies RSAL SP5 297 N3
Withingham Rd CCLF BH13 224 F5
Withybed La HUNG RG17 30 E2
Withybed Wy NTHA RG18 29 G7
Withy Cl ROMY SO51 130 F8
Witney Rd CFDH BH17 211 K7
Wittcomb Ter BOR GU35 * 112 E3
Wittensford La LYND SO43 340 G4
Wittering Rd HISD PO11 195 M6
ROWN SO16 145 M3
Wittmead Rd FRIM GU16 61 M4
Witton Hl NARL SO24 291 L12
Witt Rd ELGH SO50 141 J2
RSAL SP5 282 H10
Witts Hl WEND SO18 147 M7
Wivelrod Rd ALTN GU34 279 N12
Wiverley Cl LYMN SO41 221 H6
Woburn Av FARN GU14 61 K4
Woburn Cl ELGH SO50 134 A6
FRIM GU16 51 J7
Woburn Gdns KBH RG22 92 E1
Woburn Rd ROWN SO16 146 C3
Wode Cl HORN PO8 321 L9
Wodehouse Rd ITCH SO19 161 L4
Wokingham Rd CWTH RG45 43 G5
Woking Rd PSTN BH14 224 C4
The Wolds KBH RG22 92 D1
Wolfe Cl CHCH/BSGR BH23 228 E1
FUFL SO22 122 C7
Wolfe Rd ASHV GU12 3 K4
Wolfmere La LISS GU33 308 G2
Wolf's La ALTN GU34 106 E8
Wollaston Rd SBNE BH6 227 M5
Wollaton Rd FERN BH22 209 J5
Wollstonecraft Rd BOSC BH5 226 F5
Wolseley Rd ALDT GU11 2 F4
BKME/WDN BH12 224 D2
WSHM SO15 160 C1
Wolsey Wy LYMN SO41 232 D3
Wolsingham Wy STHA RG19 35 K2
Wolterton Rd
BKME/WDN BH12 225 G3
Wolverley Ct ROWN SO16 146 D6
Wolversdene Cl AND SP10 5 L7
Wolversdene Gdns AND SP10 5 M7
Wolversdene Rd AND SP10 5 K7
Wolverton La TADY RG26 249 K11
Wolverton Rd HAV PO9 170 E3
LTDN BH7 226 F3
SHAM SO14 * 23 K1
TADY RG26 249 J10
Wolverton Wy SHAM SO14 23 J1
Wolvesey Pl CHFD SO53 139 G4
Wolvesey Ter WINC SO23 25 J8
Wonderholme Pde
BWD BH11 * 213 H6
Wonston Cl RWIN SO21 274 D9
Wonston Ct HAV PO9 171 J2
Wonston La RWIN SO21 288 C1
Wonston Rd ROWN SO16 146 B4
Woodacre Gdns FERN BH22 209 L4
Woodavon Gdns NTHA RG18 28 F7
Wood Barn Rd FHAM PO15 181 K3
The Woodbarn FNM GU9 * 13 H5
Woodberry La EMRTH PO10 171 M1
HAV PO9 157 K7
Woodbind Wk HLER SO31 179 M2
Woodbine Cl SHST GU47 49 L1
Woodbine La KSCL RG20 246 H3
Woodbine Wy FNM GU9 2 B8
Woodbourne Cl FHAM PO15 181 K3
LISS GU33 308 G8
YTLY GU46 48 F2
Woodbridge Dr CBLY GU15 50 F1
Woodbridge Rd BLKW GU17 49 K3
Woodbury Av CHAR BH8 214 F6
HAV PO9 16 E7
PSF GU32 120 C4
Woodbury Cl
CHCH/BSGR BH23 215 L5
Woodbury Gv HORN PO8 155 M3
Woodbury Rd KBH RG22 92 D6
Wood Cl ITCH SO19 162 C1
KBH RG22 92 D6
Woodcock Cl NTID SP9 266 F2
Woodcock Ct THLE RG7 238 A5
Woodcock La LYMN SO41 220 A5
Woodcocks Crs LTDN BH7 227 G1
Woodcot Crs HAV PO9 171 G2
Woodcote Dr UPTN BH16 222 B2
Woodcote Gn FLEETN GU51 58 F8
Woodcote La BPWT SO32 310 G9
FHAM/STUB PO14 182 A6
Woodcote Rd MARL SN8 243 N1
PTSW SO17 147 J5
Woodcot Gdns FARN GU14 60 D4
Woodcott Ter ASHV GU12 3 L6
Woodcroft La HORN PO8 155 M3
Woodcut Rd RFNM GU10 78 D3
Wood End CHIN RG24 54 A5
CWTH RG45 43 H4
Woodend FARN GU14 61 K5
Woodend Rd FRIM GU16 62 C1
MOOR/WNTN BH9 225 L1
Wood End Rd RGWD BH24 342 A11
Wood End Wy CHFD SO53 139 G1
Wooden House La LYMN SO41 356 B2
Wooderson Cl ELGH SO50 141 G2
Woodfern FBDG SP6 197 M2
Woodfield BOR GU35 110 D3
Woodfield Av CHAM PO6 169 L7
Wood Field Cl ALTN GU34 * 281 N11
Woodfield Cl CHIN RG24 54 B5
Woodfield Dr FUFL SO22 122 B6
Woodfield Gdns
CHCH/BSGR BH23 217 K7
Woodfield Park Rd
EMRTH PO10 172 B5
Woodfield Ri CHIN RG24 54 B5
Woodfield Rd BWD BH11 213 G3
Woodford Cl RGWD BH24 203 K5
Woodford Rd BMTH BH1 9 L4
Woodgarston Dr KBH RG22 92 C6
Woodgason La HISD PO11 187 J7
Woodgate FLEETN GU51 59 L5
Wood Glade Cl TOTT SO40 159 M7
Woodgreen Av HAV PO9 16 B2
Woodgreen Dr BWD BH11 212 D4
Woodgreen Rd FUFL SO22 288 D12
Woodhall Wy FHAM PO15 10 B1
Woodhayes Av
CHCH/BSGR BH23 217 L6
Wood Hill La ODIM RG29 258 B4
Woodhouse La HEND SO30 149 L4
HORN PO8 157 G2
STHA RG19 249 J1
Woodhouse Rd HORN PO8 156 F1
Woodington Cl HAV PO9 171 G2
Woodington Rd ROMY SO51 335 N2
Woodlake Cl CFDH BH17 211 K7
Woodland Av BOSC BH5 227 G4
Woodland Cl ROMY SO51 335 M6
VWD BH31 201 G1
WEND SO18 148 D5
Woodland Crs FARN GU14 61 J2
Woodland Dr RFNM GU10 78 F2
RSAL SP5 282 F10
TADY RG26 46 D6
Woodland Dro RWIN SO21 135 G1
Woodland Ms HEND SO30 148 D3
Woodland Ri FLEETS GU52 71 G3
Woodlands CHIN RG24 54 C4
CWTH RG45 43 K5
FHAM/PORC PO16 11 M4
FLEETN GU51 59 H6
KSCL RG20 246 C5
OVTN RG25 89 J4
YTLY GU46 48 F5
Woodlands Av EMRTH PO10 171 L5
FNM GU9 2 C8
PLE BH15 222 F5
Woodlands Cl ASHV GU12 74 A3
CHCH/BSGR BH23 348 C12
CHFD SO53 133 K6
FARN GU14 50 A7
FAWY SO45 176 F7
HLER SO31 163 M6
LSOL/BMARY PO13 190 C2
Woodlands Ct FAWY SO45 176 E7
Woodlands Crs PLE BH15 222 F6
Woodlands Dr HLER SO31 162 D6
Woodlands Dro TOTT SO40 341 R9
Woodlands Gv WVILLE PO7 169 K3
Woodlands La HASM GU27 117 M1
HISD PO11 194 E3
LISS GU33 308 H10
Woodlands Rd BROC SO42 351 K5
CBLY GU15 50 D3
FARN GU14 60 D2
NMIL/BTOS BH25 230 E1
TADY RG26 249 P3
TOTT SO40 341 Q8
The Woodlands BOR GU35 112 F3
WINC SO23 289 J10
WWKG RG41 239 R4
Woodland St PSEA PO1 192 E2
Woodlands Wk FARN GU14 50 A7
Woodlands Wy AND SP10 5 L5
HAV PO9 170 F4
HLER SO31 162 F4
NBAD SO52 137 L4
NMIL/BTOS BH25 219 H2
RGWD BH24 202 B8
WSHM SO15 146 F8
Woodland Vw HLER SO31 162 F4
HORN PO8 155 M2
Woodland Wk BOSC BH5 227 G4
FERN BH22 209 M1
Woodland Wy
CHCH/BSGR BH23 217 L8
LYMN SO41 232 C4
Wood La BWD BH11 212 E2
FARN GU14 61 G5
FLEETN GU51 59 L7
HTWY RG27 67 L3
LYMN SO41 232 C4
NARL SO24 304 F7
RFNM GU10 260 G3
THLE RG7 41 L3
WHAM PO17 168 A1
WHIT RG2 239 M6
Woodlane Cl NARL SO24 304 F7
Woodlark Gdns EPSF GU31 121 G6
Wood Lawn Cl
NMIL/BTOS BH25 218 F8
Woodlea Cl FUFL SO22 122 E2
Woodlea Gdns HEND SO30 148 E3
Woodlea Gra RSAL SP5 327 N1
Woodlea Wy ROMY SO51 132 F6
Woodleaze Cl BDST BH18 211 H2
Woodleigh FLEETN GU51 59 J8
Woodleigh Cl HAV PO9 171 J5
Woodley Cl ROMY SO51 131 J6
Woodley Gdns LYMN SO41 221 K3
Woodley La ROMY SO51 131 G7
Woodley Rd GPORT PO12 15 G5
ITCH SO19 161 K5
Woodley Wy ROMY SO51 131 J6
Woodling Crs FBDG SP6 197 M2
Woodlinken Cl VWD BH31 201 L4
Woodlinken Dr VWD BH31 201 L3
Woodlinken Wy VWD BH31 201 L4
Wood Ldg TOTT SO40 144 B7
Woodman Cl RWIN SO21 301 P2
WHIT RG2 238 B2
Woodmancote La
EMRTH PO10 172 E2
Woodmancote Rd
ENEY PO4 193 G4
Woodman La RWIN SO21 301 Q1
Woodman's La THLE RG7 39 M1
Woodmere Cft KBH RG22 92 B5
Woodmill La WEND SO18 147 K5
Wood Moor EWKG RG40 42 B6
Woodmoor Cl TOTT SO40 160 A7
Woodpath SSEA PO5 21 H7
Woodpecker Cl BOR GU35 112 F2
HAV PO9 17 J4
KBH RG22 92 B4
RFNM GU10 71 K8
VWD BH31 201 H3
Woodpecker Copse
HLER SO31 180 B1
Woodpecker Dr CFDH BH17 210 E8
TOTT SO40 159 L7
Woodpeckers Dr FUFL SO22 122 C2
Woodpecker Wy ELGH SO50 139 K6
Wood Rdg NWBY RG14 33 L5
Wood Rd CBLY GU15 50 D7
FNM GU9 2 G1
GSHT GU26 115 K2
TOTT SO40 158 B6
Woodroffe Dr KBH RG22 92 E3
Woodrow WVILLE PO7 154 E4
Woodruff Cl
CHCH/BSGR BH23 217 J8
Woodrush Crs HLER SO31 179 L2
Woodsedge WVILLE PO7 170 A3
Woodside BLKW GU17 49 L5
CBLY GU15 50 B1
LSOL/BMARY PO13 182 B3
NTHA RG18 28 E3
NWBY RG14 33 K5
ROWN SO16 138 E6
Woodside Av ELGH SO50 139 M4
LYMN SO41 221 L7
Woodside Cl BOR GU35 112 F1
FERN BH22 209 L2
THLE RG7 29 L7
THLE RG7 40 A2
TOTT SO40 159 L7
Woodside Crs BOR GU35 112 F1
ROWN SO16 138 D6
Woodside Gdns CHIN RG24 54 B4
FLEETN GU51 59 L6
TOTT SO40 158 C6
Woodside La ALTN GU34 294 A4
LYMN SO41 221 L6
Woodside Pk BOR GU35 112 F1
Woodside Rd ALDT GU11 72 F1
BOSC BH5 227 H4
ELGH SO50 139 L4
FERN BH22 204 F4
FERN BH22 209 L2
FNM GU9 2 A9
NBAD SO52 137 M4
PSTN BH14 224 C5
PTSW SO17 147 H8
Woodside Wy HEND SO30 149 G7
WHIT RG2 238 D1
Woods La OVTN RG25 93 H5
Woodstock Av HORN PO8 156 A3
Woodstock Cl FHAM PO15 10 A5
HEND SO30 149 K7
Woodstock Dr PTSW SO17 147 G7
Woodstock La RGWD BH24 203 J5
Woodstock Md KBH RG22 92 D6
Woodstock Rd
CHCH/BSGR BH23 216 D6
GPORT PO12 15 G5
HAV PO9 170 C6
PSTN BH14 224 A6
Woodstocks FARN GU14 61 J2
Wood St ASHV GU12 74 A2
Woods View Rd
MOOR/WNTN BH9 213 K8
Woodthorpe Gdns HLER SO31 163 M6
Woodvale FHAM PO15 181 K2
Woodvale Gdns
NMIL/BTOS BH25 219 J4
Woodview Cl ROWN SO16 147 G2

Woodville Cl BLKW GU17 49 K3
Woodville Dr PSEA PO1 20 E6
Woodville Rd FAWY SO45 355 K5
HAV PO9 170 B6
Woodward Cl GPORT PO12 14 B5
Woodway CBLY GU15 50 D3
Woofferton Rd CHAM PO6 168 A7
Wooldridge Crs ODIM RG29 68 E8
Woolfield La ALTN GU34 306 F9
Woolford Cl FUFL SO22 122 C6
Woolfords La MFD/CHID GU8 263 N5
Woolford Wy DEAN RG23 64 F6
Wool Gv AND SP10 5 L6
Woolhampton Hl THLE RG7 37 J2
Woollards Rd ASHV GU12 74 A4
Woolley Sq AND SP10 96 E1
Woolmead Rd FNM GU9 13 G2
The Woolmead FNM GU9 13 G3
Woolmer Ct HAV PO9 171 H3
Woolmer Hill Rd HASM GU27 117 J1
Woolmer La LIPH GU30 114 C8
RGWD BH24 203 H2
Woolmer Rd LISS GU33 308 H1
Woolmer St EMRTH PO10 171 L4
Woolmer Wy BOR GU35 112 E2
Woolner Av CHAM PO6 169 G8
PSF GU32 120 D5
Wool Rd BKME/WDN BH12 212 B8
Wools Br RGWD BH24 205 L2
Woolslope Cl FERN BH22 205 G7
Woolslope Gdns FERN BH22 205 H7
Woolslope Rd FERN BH22 205 G7
Woolston Rd HAV PO9 170 C2
HLER SO31 162 B4
Woolton Lodge Gdns
KSCL RG20 246 B2
Woolven Cl PSTN BH14 224 A3
Woolwich Cl HLER SO31 162 F2
Wooteys Wy ALTN GU34 106 F3
Wootton Rd
LSOL/BMARY PO13 190 A4
Wootton HLER SO31 162 C5
Wootton Farm Rd
NMIL/BTOS BH25 349 N10
Wootton Gdns BMTH BH1 9 G5
Wootton Mt BMTH BH1 9 H5
Wootton Rough
NMIL/BTOS BH25 349 R12
Wootton St CHAM PO6 184 F1
Worbarrow Gdns
BKME/WDN BH12 212 C8
Worcester Av KBH RG22 92 D4
Worcester Cl FARN GU14 61 H1
SSEA PO5 21 H5
Worcester Ct
LSOL/BMARY PO13 * 190 C2
Worcester Pl ITCH SO19 162 B2
LYMN SO41 221 M6
Wordsworth Av CHAM PO6 167 L7
CHAR BH8 214 E7
YTLY GU46 48 D4
Wordsworth Cl BPWT SO32 143 L4
CHIN RG24 65 L4
FUFL SO22 24 B4
Wordsworth Pl HLER SO31 164 B3
Wordsworth Rd NTHA RG18 28 E8
ROWN SO16 146 C7
Worgret Rd PLE BH15 223 K1
Workhouse La PSF GU32 314 B7
Workman's La HLER SO31 179 L7
Workshop Rd WVILLE PO7 168 A6
Worldham Hl ALTN GU34 281 N11
Worley Wy FERN BH22 * 209 M5
Wormersley Rd STHA RG19 34 D5
Worrell Dr BKME/WDN BH12 212 C8
Worrell Sq AND SP10 * 96 E1
Worsam Ct KBH RG22 64 D8
Worsley Rd FRIM GU16 61 M1
SSEA PO5 21 H7
Worsley St ENEY PO4 193 G6
Worthing Av GPORT PO12 182 F8
Worthing Rd SSEA PO5 21 K9
Worthington Crs PSTN BH14 224 A5
Worthy Ct HAV PO9 * 171 H3
Worthy La WINC SO23 24 F3
Worthy Rd NMIL/BTOS BH25 219 G5
WINC SO23 25 G1
Worting Rd BSTK RG21 6 B6
DEAN RG23 64 A8
Wortley Rd
CHCH/BSGR BH23 230 A1
Wote St BSTK RG21 6 F6
Wouldham Cl RAND SP11 267 K1
Wraxhall Cl CFDH BH17 211 K7
Wraysbury Park Dr
EMRTH PO10 171 M4
Wrecclesham Hl RFNM GU10 78 C3
Wrecclesham Rd FNM GU9 12 A9
Wrekin Cl KBH RG22 92 D1
The Wrekin FARN GU14 61 L7
Wren Cl ALTN GU34 107 G3
CHCH/BSGR BH23 229 H3
FUFL SO22 122 D7
NMIL/BTOS BH25 218 F6
RGWD BH24 203 L6
YTLY GU46 * 48 D2
Wren Ct ASHV GU12 74 B5
Wren Crs BKME/WDN BH12 225 H3
Wren Gdns FBDG SP6 196 D6
Wren Rd ELGH SO50 139 L7
Wrenswood Cl WHIT RG2 238 B2
Wren Wy FARN GU14 60 F1
FHAM/PORC PO16 * 166 F8
Wrexham Gv HORN PO8 321 K9
Wright Cl FHAM PO15 164 F6
Wrights Cl RWIN SO21 288 D4
Wright's Hl ITCH SO19 162 A2
Wrights Wk HLER SO31 162 F3
Wrights Wy RWIN SO21 288 D4
Wroxham Rd
BKME/WDN BH12 224 F3
Wryneck Cl ROWN SO16 146 B2
Wulwyn Side CWTH RG45 43 J3
Wurford Dr STHA RG19 35 M1
Wyatts Cl WIMB BH21 210 D2
Wyatts La WIMB BH21 210 C2
Wyborn Cl HISD PO11 195 G6
Wychelm Rd WHIT RG2 238 E3
Wych La LSOL/BMARY PO13 182 B4
Wychwood Cl ASHV GU12 73 M6
WCLF BH2 8 D3
Wychwood Dr FAWY SO45 354 G9
WCLF BH2 8 E2
Wychwood Gv CHFD SO53 133 L8
Wyck La ALTN GU34 108 A6
ALTN GU34 281 N7
Wycliffe Rd MOOR/WNTN BH9 213 M8
WEND SO18 148 A3
Wycote Rd
LSOL/BMARY PO13 182 B4
Wye Ct AND SP10 5 M1
Wyeford Cl HAV PO9 171 H2
Wyelands Av WIMB BH21 208 D3
Wyke Av ASHV GU12 74 D5
Wykeham Cl CFDH BH17 211 L8
ROWN SO16 146 E4
Wykeham Ct ODIM RG29 68 F8
Wykeham Dr DEAN RG23 64 C8
Wykeham Fld WHAM PO17 152 A5
Wykeham Pk RWIN SO21 * 302 C5
Wykeham Pl FUFL SO22 122 D7
LYMN SO41 221 L5
Wykeham Rd FNM GU9 13 G1
HLER SO31 162 B6
NEND PO2 184 E7
Wyke La ASHV GU12 74 D5
Wykwood LIPH GU30 116 D4
Wylde Green La LISS GU33 308 G7
Wylds La PSF GU32 315 N8
Wyllie Rd NEND PO2 184 E4
Wylye Cl WEND SO18 148 B1
Wylye Rd NTID SP9 266 G1
Wymering Ct FARN GU14 61 K5
Wymering La CHAM PO6 168 E8
Wymering Manor Cl
CHAM PO6 * 168 E8
Wymering Rd NEND PO2 184 E8
Wyncombe Rd BOSC BH5 227 H3
Wyndcliffe Rd ENEY PO4 21 M7
Wyndham Cl
CHCH/BSGR BH23 218 B6
HORN PO8 156 B4
YTLY GU46 48 F1
Wyndham Ms PSEA PO1 * 20 D6
Wyndham Pl WSHM SO15 22 D1
Wyndham Rd AND SP10 4 D8
CHCH/BSGR BH23 218 B6
NWBY RG14 27 M7
PSTN BH14 224 B5
Wyndham St ASHV GU12 3 J4
Wynfields FRIM GU16 61 M5
Wynford Rd
MOOR/WNTN BH9 214 A4
PSTN BH14 224 C5
Wynne Cl BDST BH18 210 F4
Wynne Gdns FLEETS GU52 71 K3
Wynter Cl LTDN BH7 226 F1
Wynter Rd WEND SO18 148 B4
Wynton Wy FHAM PO15 181 J1
Wynyards Gap NBAD SO52 137 M4
Wyre Cl CHFD SO53 139 H2
Wyvern Cl ASHV GU12 * 73 M3
BKME/WDN BH12 224 D1
CHFD SO53 139 K2

Y

Yachtsman Cl HLER SO31 163 H4
Yaldhurst Ct HAV PO9 171 H2
Yaldhurst La LYMN SO41 221 H4
Yapton St PSEA PO1 21 G2
Yarborough Rd SSEA PO5 21 G7
Yardlea Cl HAV PO9 157 H7
Yardley Cl HSEA PO3 185 J4
Yardley Rd HEND SO30 149 H7
Yarmley La RSAL SP5 282 F10
Yarmouth Cl
BKME/WDN BH12 225 G3
Yarmouth Gdns WSHM SO15 146 B7
Yarmouth Rd
BKME/WDN BH12 224 F2
Yarnhams Cl ALTN GU34 293 M6
Yarrell Md LYMN SO41 221 H4
Yarrells Cl UPTN BH16 222 C2
Yarrells Dr UPTN BH16 222 B1
Yarrells La UPTN BH16 222 C2
Yarrow Cl CHCH/BSGR BH23 217 H8
NTHA RG18 28 F7
Yarrow Rd BKME/WDN BH12 212 A8
Yarrow Wy HLER SO31 179 L2
Yateley Cl HAV PO9 170 C3
Yateley Rd YTLY GU46 49 H1
Yatesbury Cl FNM GU9 12 A9
Yates Copse NTHA RG18 28 A7
Yaverland HLER SO31 162 C6
Yeatminster Rd CFDH BH17 211 M6
Yellowhammer Rd KBH RG22 92 B6
Yellowhammers ALTN GU34 106 F2
Yelverton Av FAWY SO45 177 G7
Yelverton Rd WCLF BH2 8 E5
Yeo Ct ENEY PO4 193 J5
Yeomans HTWY RG27 48 A1
Yeomans Cl FARN GU14 61 G3
RFNM GU10 73 M8
Yeomans Fld RCCH PO18 173 H5
Yeomans La KSCL RG20 247 J3
LIPH GU30 116 A4
Yeomans Pl BOR GU35 111 L7
Yeomans Rd CHAR BH8 214 E5
Yeomans Wy CBLY GU15 51 G3
CHAR BH8 214 F6
TOTT SO40 144 F8
Yeovil Cha WEND SO18 148 B4
Yeovil Cl FARN GU14 61 K7
Yeovilton Cl LYMN SO41 220 E7
Yerville Gdns LYMN SO41 219 M5
Yetminster Rd FARN GU14 61 K7
Yew Cl KSCL RG20 248 E10
Yew Ga NWBY RG14 27 H6
Yew La NMIL/BTOS BH25 219 J4
Yew Rd WEND SO18 148 A4
Yewside
LSOL/BMARY PO13 * 182 E7
The Yews HORN PO8 156 D1
Yew Tree Cl DEAN RG23 91 K4
ELGH SO50 141 J1
FARN GU14 * 60 C5
HEND SO30 149 H6
RAND SP11 271 Q3
RSAL SP5 282 F10
TADY RG26 46 C6
WIMB BH21 207 K3
Yewtree Cl FAWY SO45 177 G8
Yew Tree Ct HEND SO30 * 148 E3
Yew Tree Dr FHAM PO15 164 C4
Yew Tree Gdns WVILLE PO7 154 E4
Yew Tree La OVTN RG25 103 G3
RSAL SP5 297 P1
Yewtree La ROWN SO16 145 J5
Yew Tree Pl LISS GU33 308 G8
Yew Tree Rd HISD PO11 187 G8
Yew Tree Wk FRIM GU16 51 G7
Yockley Cl CBLY GU15 51 M5
Yoells Crs HORN PO8 155 M2
Yoells La HORN PO8 155 M2
Yokesford Hl ROMY SO51 130 E3
Yolland Cl FNM GU9 77 G1
Yonge Cl ELGH SO50 140 B1
York Av NMIL/BTOS BH25 219 H5
York Buildings SHAM SO14 23 G4
York Cl BDST BH18 211 G6
BOR GU35 112 F2
CHCH/BSGR BH23 227 M1
CHFD SO53 138 F4
ELGH SO50 141 K5
KBH RG22 92 D4
NWBY RG14 19 G6
PSF GU32 120 B6
SHAM SO14 161 J2
TOTT SO40 145 G8
York Crs ALDT GU11 2 D5
LSOL/BMARY PO13 190 A4
Yorkdale HLER SO31 179 J1
York Dro RSAL SP5 334 A8
WEND SO18 148 B5
Yorke St SSEA PO5 20 F5
Yorke Wy HLER SO31 178 E1
York Gdns FHAM/PORC PO16 183 K2
York La HTWY RG27 57 L3
York Ms ALTN GU34 107 G4
York Pl CBLY GU15 50 F1
LTDN BH7 227 G3
PSEA PO1 20 E1
York Rd ALDT GU11 2 D5
ASHV GU12 74 A5
BDST BH18 211 G5
BMTH BH1 9 K4
CBLY GU15 50 F1
ELGH SO50 140 A3
FARN GU14 60 F7
FNM GU9 13 H7
NWBY RG14 19 G6
WSHM SO15 160 C1
York Terrace La CBLY GU15 * 50 C3
Yorktown Rd SHST GU47 49 L1
York Wy SHST GU47 43 J8
Yorkwood LISS GU33 308 F8
Youlden Cl CBLY GU15 51 J3
Youlden Dr CBLY GU15 51 J3
Young Crs STHA RG19 19 M9
Youngs Dr ASHV GU12 73 M6
Youngs Paddock RSAL SP5 282 G10
Youngs Rd ALTN GU34 106 F4
BWD BH11 213 G3
Yves Ms SSEA PO5 * 21 J8

Z

Zamek Cl BWD BH11 213 G3
Zetland Rd CHAM PO6 185 K1
GPORT PO12 14 E3
Zeus La WVILLE PO7 169 M5
Zinnia Cl KBH RG22 92 C6
NBNE BH10 213 L6
WWKG RG41 239 R1
Zion Rd RAND SP11 269 K7
Zouch Av NTID SP9 266 E1
Zouch Cl NTID SP9 266 E1
Zouch Farm Rd NTID SP9 266 E1

Index - featured places

36 On the Quay Hotel
EMRTH PO10 171 M8
The AA-Fanum House
BSTK RG21 7 K3
Aaron Croham Hurst Hotel
WCLF BH2 8 B6
Abbey Business Park
FNM GU9 77 K8
Abbey Chiropractic Clinic
ROMY SO51 136 E1
Abbey House
WINC SO23 25 H6
Abbey Mill Business Park
GODL GU7 261 Q12
The Abbey School
FNM GU9 13 K6
Abbotsford Farm Business
Centre ALTN GU34 293 N5
Abbotswood School
TOTT SO40 158 D1
Abbotts Ann Primary School
RAND SP11 95 H8
ABC Cinema
BMTH BH1 8 F6
Abro Industrial Estate
ALDT GU11 73 K5
Acorn Business Centre
BKME/WDN BH12 212 B7
CHAM PO6 168 D8
Action Stations! Exhibition
PSEA PO1 20 C2
Ad Astra First School
CFDH BH17 211 M6
Addington Clinic
BWD BH11 213 H3
Admiral Lord Nelson School
HSEA PO3 185 H7
Adult Education Centre
CBLY GU15 50 D3
FNM GU9 12 E4
AFC Bournemouth
(Fitness First Stadium)
LTDN BH7 226 F2
AFC Newbury
NWBY RG14 19 G3
Airborne Forces Museum
ALDT GU11 73 G3
Airfield Industrial Estate
CHCH/BSGR BH23 228 F2
Albany Business Centre
WHAM PO17 166 B1
Albany Park Industrial Estate
FRIM GU16 50 D7
Alderbridge School
THLE RG7 38 C2
Alderbury Caravan &
Camping Park RSAL SP5 327 P4
Alderbury & West
Grimstead School
RSAL SP5 327 N1
Alder Hills Industrial Park
BKME/WDN BH12 224 F1
The Alderman Quilley School
ELGH SO50 139 M7
Aldermaston CE Primary
School THLE RG7 37 M5
Aldermoor Health Centre
ROWN SO16 146 C4
Alderney Community
Hospital BKME/WDN BH12 212 C7
Alderney Middle School
BKME/WDN BH12 212 D7
Aldershot & Farnham
County Court
ALDT GU11 3 G3
Aldershot Health Centre
ALDT GU11 2 D2
Aldershot Military Museum
ALDT GU11 73 J1
Aldershot Military Stadium
ALDT GU11 73 J2
Aldershot Outpatients
Department ALDT GU11 3 G1
Aldershot Town FC
ALDT GU11 3 J3
Aldro School
MFD/CHID GU8 261 N9
Aldworth Science College
KBH RG22 92 F2
Alexander Barracks
CHOB/PIR GU24 63 H2
Alexander House Business
Centre ALDT GU11 3 G3
Alice in Wonderland Park
CHCH/BSGR BH23 214 E1
Allenbourn Middle School
WIMB BH21 207 J2
All Hallows RC Comprehensive
School FNM GU9 2 C9
Allington Manor Business
Centre ELGH SO50 140 E5
Allington Manor School
ELGH SO50 140 F5
All Saints CE Infant School
RFNM GU10 263 J1
All Saints CE Junior School
FLEETN GU51 58 F8
All Saints CE Primary School
RSAL SP5 127 H5
RSAL SP5 296 C4
WINC SO23 25 K8
Alpha Business Park
SHAM SO14 161 H1
Alpine Snowsports Dry
Ski Slope ALDT GU11 73 J4
Alresford County Junior
School NARL SO24 291 M11
Alresford Golf Club
NARL SO24 303 Q1
Alton Business Centre
ALTN GU34 107 H5
Alton College
ALTN GU34 106 F3
Alton Community Centre
ALTN GU34 106 F5
Alton Community Hospital
ALTN GU34 106 D7
Alton Convent School
ALTN GU34 107 G2
Alton County Infant School
ALTN GU34 107 G4
Alton Golf Club ALTN GU34 280 E3
Alton Grange Hotel
ALTN GU34 107 H3
Alton Health Centre
ALTN GU34 107 G4
Alton House Hotel
ALTN GU34 107 G4
Alton Sports Centre
ALTN GU34 106 D7
Alton Town FC
ALTN GU34 107 H3
Alton Town RFC
ALTN GU34 107 H3
Alverstoke CE Junior School
GPORT PO12 14 C7
Alverstoke Infant School
GPORT PO12 14 C9
Ambassador Industrial
Estate CHCH/BSGR BH23 229 G2
Amery Hill Secondary School
ALTN GU34 106 F4
Amesbury School
GSHT GU26 115 L7
Amey Industrial Estate
PSF GU32 120 C6
AMF Bowling
ITCH SO19 148 A6
PSEA PO1 21 H2
Ampfield Par 3 Golf Club
ROMY SO51 132 C5
Ampfield Primary School
ROMY SO51 132 C4
Amport CE J & I School
RAND SP11 94 C7
Ampress Works Halt
LYMN SO41 221 K2
Anchor Business Centre
CHFD SO53 139 H2
Andover Athletics Club
AND SP10 95 L2
Andover CE Primary School
AND SP10 5 J6
Andover FC
AND SP10 95 L2
Andover Golf Club
AND SP10 5 H9
Andover Leisure Centre
AND SP10 5 H4
Andover Museum & The
Museum of the Iron Age
AND SP10 5 J4
Andover Road Retail Park
FUFL SO22 24 E3
Andrews Endowed CE
Primary School
ALTN GU34 107 J2
Annie Lawson School
NWBY RG14 18 B6
Ansells Farm Community
Centre FLEETN GU51 59 L4
Anstey County Junior School
ALTN GU34 106 F4
Anton County Infant School
AND SP10 5 G9
Anton Junior School
AND SP10 5 G9
Anton Trading Estate
AND SP10 5 G7
The Anvil Concert Hall
BSTK RG21 6 E4
Apollo Cinema
FHAM/PORC PO16 11 J6
Apollo Hotel
CHIN RG24 65 H4
Apple Industrial Estate
FHAM PO15 164 C7
Applemore College
FAWY SO45 176 C5
Applemore Recreation Centre
FAWY SO45 176 C5
Arborfield Newland &
Barkham CE Junior School
WHIT RG2 239 L5
Ardglen Industrial Estate
WHCH RG28 87 K7
Arena Leisure Centre
CBLY GU15 50 E2
Argyle Community Centre
SHAM SO14 23 H1
The Ark School
THLE RG7 38 F3
Arlington Hotel
BMTH BH1 8 F7
Army Apprentice College
WHIT RG2 239 M9
Army Golf Club
ALDT GU11 72 E2
Army Medical Services
Museum
FRIM GU16 62 B7
Army Training Regiment
CHOB/PIR GU24 63 J2
Arndale Court Hotel
PLE BH15 223 J5
The Arnewood School
NMIL/BTOS BH25 218 F6
Arnhem Barracks
ALDT GU11 73 G5
Arrow Industrial Estate
FARN GU14 60 F6
The Arts Institute of
Bournemouth
BKME/WDN BH12 213 J8
Arts Link Theatre Cinema
CBLY GU15 50 F2
Arundel Court J & I School
PSEA PO1 21 K1
Arundel Tower
SHAM SO14 22 F4
Ashburn Hotel
FBDG SP6 197 G3
Ashdown County Secondary
School CFDH BH17 211 L7
Ashdown Leisure Centre
CFDH BH17 211 M7
Ashford Hill Primary School
STHA RG19 249 J3
Ash Grange CP School
ASHV GU12 74 B6
Ashley Heath Industrial Estate
WIMB BH21 205 K1
Ashley Infant School
NMIL/BTOS BH25 219 K5
Ashley Junior School
NMIL/BTOS BH25 219 J5
Ash Manor School
ASHV GU12 73 M8
Ashurst Hospital
TOTT SO40 158 B7
Ash Vale Health Centre
ASHV GU12 74 B4
The Atherley School
ROWN SO16 145 H2
Audleys Wood Hotel
OVTN RG25 93 L4
Avenue Clinic
WSHM SO15 160 F2
The Avenue Shopping Centre
WCLF BH2 8 D5
Avington Park
RWIN SO21 290 A11
Avonbourne Girls School
LTDN BH7 227 G1
Avon Heath Country Park
RGWD BH24 346 G1
Avonlea School
RGWD BH24 203 K4
The Avonmouth Hotel
CHCH/BSGR BH23 229 G3
Avon Trading Park
CHCH/BSGR BH23 216 A8
Awbridge Primary School
ROMY SO51 129 K3
Baddesley Park Industrial
Estate NBAD SO52 138 B4
Baden Powell & St Peters
CE Middle School
PSTN BH14 224 B5
Badshot Lea Village Infant
School FNM GU9 77 L2
Balksbury Hill Industrial
Estate RAND SP11 96 A7
The Balksbury Junior School
AND SP10 4 B8
Ballard College
NMIL/BTOS BH25 219 G4
Balmer Lawn Hotel
BROC SO42 351 L1
Banister Infant School
WSHM SO15 160 F1
The Banks Medical Centre
TWDS BH3 225 L1
Bar End Industrial Estate
WINC SO23 123 H7
Barfield School
RFNM GU10 77 M5
Bargate Museum
SHAM SO14 22 F4
Bargate Shopping Centre
SHAM SO14 23 G4
Barncroft Infant School
HAV PO9 170 D4
Barncroft Junior School
HAV PO9 170 C4
Barratt Industrial Park
FHAM PO15 164 C7
Bartley CE Junior School
TOTT SO40 341 M5
Bartley Lodge Hotel
TOTT SO40 158 C5
TOTT SO40 341 K5
Bartley Wood Business Park
HTWY RG27 56 E8
Bartley Wood Business Park
(West) HTWY RG27 56 D8
Barton Industrial Estate
NARL SO24 278 D11
Barton-on-Sea Golf Club
NMIL/BTOS BH25 231 J1
Barton Peveril College
ELGH SO50 139 M7
Barton Stacey CE Primary
School RWIN SO21 273 Q4
Basing House
CHIN RG24 66 C2
Basingstoke Aquadrome
KBH RG22 64 E7
Basingstoke Business Centre
KBH RG22 93 G2
Basingstoke College of
Technology BSTK RG21 6 C5
Basingstoke County Court
BSTK RG21 7 H4
Basingstoke Crematorium
OVTN RG25 102 E5
Basingstoke Golf Club
DEAN RG23 92 B7
Basingstoke Leisure Park
KBH RG22 64 F7

Basingstoke Planet Ice KBH RG22 64 E7
Basingstoke RFC KBH RG22 92 D3
Basingstoke Sports Centre BSTK RG21 6 E4
Basingstoke Town FC KBH RG22 93 G2
Bassett Green Primary School ROWN SO16 147 H4
Baycroft School FHAM/STUB PO14 189 K2
Bay House School GPORT PO12 190 E6
Bay View Court Hotel BMTH BH1 9 L6
BBC South TV & Radio Solent WSHM SO15 22 E1
Beacon Hill County Primary School GSHT GU26 115 J2
Beacon Hill Touring Park UPTN BH16 210 B7
Bearwood College WWKG RG41 239 P1
Bearwood County Primary School WIMB BH21 212 C2
Bearwood Golf Club WWKG RG41 239 M1
Bearwood Medical Centre BWD BH11 212 D3
Beaucroft Foundation School WIMB BH21 207 L2
The Beaufort Hotel ENEY PO4 192 F6
Beaulieu Abbey BROC SO42 353 M6
Beaulieu Hotel BROC SO42 174 E7
Beaulieu:National Motor Museum BROC SO42 353 L6
Beaulieu Primary School BROC SO42 353 M7
Beaumont County Junior School ALDT GU11 2 B3
Beaver Industrial Estate CHCH/BSGR BH23 229 G2; LIPH GU30 116 C6
Bedales School PSF GU32 120 C2
Bedenham Primary School LSOL/BMARY PO13 182 C5
Beech Down Primary School KBH RG22 92 F4
Beechleas Hotel & Restaurant WIMB BH21 207 J4
Beechnut Industrial Estate ALDT GU11 3 H4
Beechwood Junior School WEND SO18 161 M1
The Beggarwood Surgery DEAN RG23 92 B7
Belbins Business Park ROMY SO51 131 G5
Belgrave Industrial Estate PTSW SO17 147 J6
Bellemoor Secondary School ROWN SO16 146 D6
Belle Vue Infant School ASHV GU12 3 M3
Bell Inn Hotel LYND SO43 340 E3
Belvedere Hotel BMTH BH1 9 G6
Benham Park KSCL RG20 26 C8
Benridge Business Park CFDH BH17 211 G8
Bentley Industrial Centre RFNM GU10 259 L12
Bentley Trimmings Business Park RFNM GU10 259 M11
Bentworth CE (Aided) Primary School ALTN GU34 279 L7
Berkeley Business Park WWKG RG41 239 Q5
Berkshire Business Centre STHA RG19 36 A2
Berrywood Business Village HEND SO30 149 H1
Berrywood Primary School HEND SO30 149 K3
Bethany CE Junior School BMTH BH1 226 D3
Bevois Town Primary School SHAM SO14 161 G1
Bicknell Special School LTDN BH7 227 G1
Bidbury J & I School HAV PO9 16 A2
Bilton Industrial Estate CHIN RG24 54 A7
Binsted CE Primary School ALTN GU34 281 R5
Binswood View Business Centre ALTN GU34 295 R4
Birchwood Medical Centre CFDH BH17 210 F8
Birdworld & Underwaterworld RFNM GU10 109 J1
Bishop Challoner RC School KBH RG22 92 E1
Bishop of Winchester Comprehensive School CHAR BH8 214 D7
Bishops Palace WINC SO23 25 H7
Bishop's Table Hotel FNM GU9 12 E3
Bishops Waltham Infant School BPWT SO32 143 K4
Bishop's Waltham Palace BPWT SO32 143 J5
Bishopswood Golf Club TADY RG26 249 R5
Bishopswood J & I Schools TADY RG26 44 B5
Bitterne CE (Controlled) Junior School ITCH SO19 161 M2
Bitterne CE Infant School ITCH SO19 161 M2
Bitterne Health Centre WEND SO18 148 A5
Bitterne Leisure Centre WEND SO18 148 A5
Bitterne Manor Primary School WEND SO18 161 K1
Bitterne Park Clinic WEND SO18 147 L8
Bitterne Park J & I School WEND SO18 147 K6
Bitterne Park Secondary School WEND SO18 147 L6
Blackbrook Business Park FHAM PO15 10 A5
Blackbushe Airport BLKW GU17 48 C6
Blackbushe Business Park YTLY GU46 48 E4
Blackfield Health Centre FAWY SO45 354 F6
Blackfield Infant School FAWY SO45 354 G7
Blackfield Junior School FAWY SO45 354 F7
Blackmoor Golf Club BOR GU35 112 C3
Blacknest Industrial Park ALTN GU34 108 E4
Blackwater & Hawley Leisure Centre BLKW GU17 49 M5
Blackwater Industrial Estate CBLY GU15 50 A3
Bleach's Yard Industrial Estate LIPH GU30 116 C6
The Boatyard Industrial Estate FHAM/PORC PO16 10 F7
Bohunt Community School LIPH GU30 116 B4
Bohunt Manor LIPH GU30 116 B5
Boldrewood Centre ROWN SO16 146 F5
Bone lane Industrial Area NWBY RG14 19 K3
Bordon Infant School BOR GU35 110 E8
Bordon Trading Estate BOR GU35 110 C7
Boscombe Dental Health Centre LTDN BH7 226 F3
Boscombe Manor Medical Centre BOSC BH5 226 F4
Boscombe Pier BOSC BH5 226 E6
Bosmere Junior School HAV PO9 16 E5
Botleigh Grange Hotel HEND SO30 149 K4
Botley CE Primary School HEND SO30 149 M5
Botley Park Hotel, Golf & Country Club BPWT SO32 149 M2
Boundary Oak School WHAM PO17 166 C3
Bourne Community College EMRTH PO10 172 C5
Bourne Hall Hotel WCLF BH2 8 D8
Bourne Mill Industrial Estate FNM GU9 13 L1
Bournemouth Aviation Museum CHCH/BSGR BH23 346 G12
Bournemouth Business Centre BMTH BH1 9 J4
Bournemouth College BMTH BH1 9 M4
Bournemouth Crematorium CHAR BH8 214 C7
Bournemouth Crown & County Courts LTDN BH7 215 H7
Bournemouth International Airport CHCH/BSGR BH23 346 F12
Bournemouth International Centre & Leisure Pool WCLF BH2 8 E8
Bournemouth Jewish Day School BMTH BH1 9 G5
Bournemouth Learning Support Centre NBNE BH10 213 J7
Bournemouth Magistrates Court BMTH BH1 9 H5
The Bournemouth Nuffield Hospital BMTH BH1 9 G1
Bournemouth Pier WCLF BH2 8 F8
Bournemouth & Poole College BMTH BH1 9 J5; PSTN BH14 223 M4
Bournemouth Sands Hotel WCLF BH2 8 C8
Bournemouth School CHAR BH8 214 C7
Bournemouth School for Girls CHAR BH8 214 C6
Bournemouth Sports Club CHCH/BSGR BH23 346 C11
Bournemouth University BKME/WDN BH12 213 J8; BMTH BH1 9 K5
The Bourne School RFNM GU10 79 H1
Bourne Tennis Club FNM GU9 13 H8
Bourne Valley Business Park BKME/WDN BH12 225 G3
Bowlplex KBH RG22 64 E7
Boyatt Shopping Centre ELGH SO50 139 M4
Boyatt Wood Industrial Estate ELGH SO50 139 M4
Bradbury Centre ROWN SO16 146 C4
Braishfield Primary School ROMY SO51 131 K2
Brambles Farm Industrial Estate WVILLE PO7 155 K8
Bramley CE J & I School TADY RG26 46 B4
Bramshaw Golf Club LYND SO43 340 E3
Branksome Cemetery BKME/WDN BH12 224 C1
Branksome Heath Middle School BKME/WDN BH12 224 C2
Bransgore CE Primary School CHCH/BSGR BH23 348 E12
Bratley Arch RGWD BH24 343 N1
Braxton Gardens LYMN SO41 220 E8
Breamore CE Primary School FBDG SP6 331 P8
Breamore House & Countryside Museum FBDG SP6 331 N5
Briar Park Business Centre CHCH/BSGR BH23 228 A1
Brickfield Trading Estate CHFD SO53 139 H3
Brick Kiln Industrial Estate TADY RG26 44 C3
Brickyards Industrial Estate PSF GU32 308 A11
Bridgemary Community School LSOL/BMARY PO13 182 C6
The Bridge Shopping Centre PSEA PO1 21 K2
Brighton Hill Community College KBH RG22 92 F3
Brighton Hill Retail Park KBH RG22 93 G2
Brimpton CE Primary School THLE RG7 36 F6
Bristow Infant School CBLY GU15 50 D6
British Gas Training Centre KBH RG22 93 G2
Broadbridge Business Centre RCCH PO18 173 M7
Broadlands House ROMY SO51 136 E3
Broadmarsh Business & Innovation Centre HAV PO9 170 C8
Broadmoor County Primary School CWTH RG45 43 M4
Broadstone Cemetery BDST BH18 211 J3
Broadstone (Dorset) Golf Club WIMB BH21 211 G2
Broadstone First School BDST BH18 211 H4
Broadstone Leisure Centre BDST BH18 211 G3
Broadstone Middle School BDST BH18 211 J3
Brockenhurst CE Primary School BROC SO42 351 K4
Brockenhurst College BROC SO42 351 L2
Brockhurst Infant School GPORT PO12 190 F1
Brockhurst Junior School GPORT PO12 191 G2
Brockhurst Medical Centre GPORT PO12 190 F1
Brokenford Business Centre TOTT SO40 158 F2
Brokenhurst Manor Golf Club BROC SO42 351 J6
Brookes Hill Industrial Estate TOTT SO40 144 B4
Brookfield Community School HLER SO31 163 L8
Brookfield Hotel EMRTH PO10 171 K7
Brookham School LIPH GU30 116 E6
Brook Park Estate WIMB BH21 207 L5
Brookside Business Centre THLE RG7 238 D10
The Brooks Shopping Centre WINC SO23 25 G5
The Brook Trading Estate ASHV GU12 73 L5
Brookvale Hall BSTK RG21 6 C5
Brookway Industrial Estate NWBY RG14 19 M5
Brookwood Industrial Estate ELGH SO50 140 A1
Broughton Primary School STOK SO20 284 D9
Browning Barracks ALDT GU11 73 G3
Brownsea Island (NT) CCLF BH13 236 D4
Brownsea Open Air Theatre CCLF BH13 236 E4
Broxhead Trading Estate BOR GU35 111 H6
Brune Park Community School LSOL/BMARY PO13 182 E8
Buckholme Towers School PSTN BH14 224 A5
Buckland Medical Centre NEND PO2 184 D8
Bucklebury CE Primary School THLE RG7 29 L6
Bucklers Hard Village & Maritime Museum BROC SO42 353 R12
Budds Lane Trading Estate ROMY SO51 130 D7
The Burgate School & Sixth Form Centre FBDG SP6 197 J1
Burghclere Primary School KSCL RG20 247 J6
Buriton Business Park EPSF GU31 315 N9
Buriton Primary School EPSF GU31 315 P11
Burley Court Hotel BMTH BH1 9 H6
Burley Golf Club RGWD BH24 349 K2
Burley Manor Hotel RGWD BH24 343 J12
Burley Primary School RGWD BH24 349 J1
Burnham Copse J & I Schools TADY RG26 44 A3
Burrfields Retail Park HSEA PO3 185 J7
Burridge Social & Sports Club HLER SO31 164 B2
Bursledon CE J & I School HLER SO31 163 G4
Bursledon Windmill Museum HLER SO31 163 G2
Burton CE Primary School CHCH/BSGR BH23 216 C5
Burton Medical Centre CHCH/BSGR BH23 216 D6
Buryfields Infant School ODIM RG29 69 G6
Bury Hill RAND SP11 95 M8
The Bush Hotel FNM GU9 13 G3
Business Aviation Centre ALDT GU11 72 F1
Busketts Lawn Hotel TOTT SO40 341 Q9
Butser Ancient Farm HORN PO8 321 Q7
The Butts CP School ALTN GU34 106 D6
Byngs Business Park WVILLE PO7 155 H6
Cabot Business Village CFDH BH17 211 H8
Cadogan Hotel WBNE BH4 8 A5
California Chalet & Touring Park EWKG RG40 239 R9
California Country Park EWKG RG40 239 Q9
Calleva THLE RG7 45 L2
Calleva Museum THLE RG7 45 H3
Calmore Industrial Estate TOTT SO40 144 E6
Calmore J & I School TOTT SO40 144 C7
Calmore Sports Club TOTT SO40 144 A6
Calshot Castle FAWY SO45 355 R7
Calshot Spit Lightship SHAM SO14 23 K7
Calthorpe Park School FLEETN GU51 58 E8
Camberley CC CBLY GU15 50 F5
Camberley County Infant School CBLY GU15 50 D3
Camberley Health Centre CBLY GU15 50 D5
Camberley Heath Golf Club CBLY GU15 51 J4
Camberley Magistrates Court CBLY GU15 50 F2
Camberley RFC CBLY GU15 50 E5
Camberley Town FC CBLY GU15 50 D5
Cameleon Theatre WSHM SO15 160 D2
Camelsdale County First School HASM GU27 117 M3
Camera Obscura WCLF BH2 8 E5
Campana Finishing School RFNM GU10 77 L7
Campbell Court Industrial Estate TADY RG26 46 C6
Camp Road Industrial Estate FARN GU14 61 J8
Cams Hall Estate Golf Club FHAM/PORC PO16 11 L9
Cams Hill School FHAM/PORC PO16 166 E8
Canada House Business Centre NMIL/BTOS BH25 219 J6
Candlesticks Inn RGWD BH24 203 H6
Canford Heath First School CFDH BH17 223 L1
Canford Heath Middle School CFDH BH17 223 K1
Canford Magna Golf Club BWD BH11 208 D8
Canford School WIMB BH21 208 A6
Cantell Secondary School ROWN SO16 147 G4
Careys Manor Hotel BROC SO42 351 L2
Carnival Hall BSTK RG21 6 E7
Carnegie Library PSEA PO1 21 L1
Carrington House Hotel BMTH BH1 226 D4
Carter Community Sports College PLE BH15 222 F6
Carvers Trading Estate RGWD BH24 203 J5
Carwarden House School FRIM GU16 51 J5
Cascades Shopping Centre PSEA PO1 21 G1
Castle County Primary School FHAM/PORC PO16 183 K1
Castle Court Preparatory School WIMB BH21 210 B1
Castledown School RAND SP11 265 J11
Castle Hill Infant School DEAN RG23 64 D7
Castle Industrial Park NWBY RG14 27 L7
Castlepoint Shopping Centre CHAR BH8 214 E6
The Castle Special School NWBY RG14 27 H6
Castle Trading Estate FHAM/PORC PO16 183 L1
Catchcold Tower SHAM SO14 22 F4
Cathedral Church of St Thomas of Canterbury PSEA PO1 20 C6
Cathedral Discovery Centre PSEA PO1 20 F1
Catherine Corbett Clinic HAV PO9 16 F4
Catherington CE Controlled Infant School HORN PO8 321 K11
Cedar School ROWN SO16 145 L4
Cedars School THLE RG7 38 A5
Cenotaph WSHM SO15 22 F1
Central Estate ALDT GU11 3 G4
Central Hall SHAM SO14 23 J4
Central Health Clinic WSHM SO15 23 G1
Central Industrial Estate HAV PO9 16 D5
Central Trading Estate SHAM SO14 23 K4
Centurion Industrial Park SHAM SO14 161 J1
Chalcroft Distribution Park HEND SO30 141 G7
Chalk Ridge Primary School KBH RG22 93 G3
Chalwyn Industrial Estate BKME/WDN BH12 224 A1
Chamberlayne Park School ITCH SO19 162 A3
Chandler's Ford Industrial Estate CHFD SO53 139 J3
Chandler's Ford Infant School CHFD SO53 139 K1
The Chantry Centre AND SP10 5 H5
Chapel of St Johns Hospital WINC SO23 25 H6
Charles Dickens' Birthplace Museum PSEA PO1 192 C1
Charles Dickens J & I School PSEA PO1 192 D2
Charles Kingsleys CE Primary School HTWY RG27 241 Q4
Charlton Hill Surgery AND SP10 4 D2
Charlton House School WEND SO18 161 L1
Charlton Sports & Leisure Centre AND SP10 95 L2
Charris Camping & Caravan Park WIMB BH21 206 E6
Chase Community Hospital BOR GU35 112 F2
Chaucer Business Centre WINC SO23 289 J12
Chawton Primary School ALTN GU34 294 D1
Cheam School STHA RG19 248 B4
The Chequers Hotel NWBY RG14 18 E2
Cherbourg Primary School ELGH SO50 140 A3
The Cheriton Brewhouse NARL SO24 303 Q7
Cheriton Primary School NARL SO24 303 Q6
Cherry Wood Primary School FARN GU14 61 G2
Chesil Theatre WINC SO23 25 J7
Chevron Business Park FAWY SO45 354 D2
Chewton Glen Hotel NMIL/BTOS BH25 218 C8
Chidham Parochial Primary School RCCH PO18 173 J8
Chilworth Golf Club NBAD SO52 138 B5
Chilworth Manor Hotel NBAD SO52 138 C7
Chineham Business Park CHIN RG24 54 A4
Chineham House CHIN RG24 65 M4
Chineham Park Primary School CHIN RG24 65 M4
Chineham Shopping Centre CHIN RG24 54 B7
Chine Hotel BOSC BH5 226 D5
Chinehurst Hotel WBNE BH4 225 J7
Christchurch Castle & Norman House CHCH/BSGR BH23 228 C2
Christchurch Hospital CHCH/BSGR BH23 215 M7
Christchurch J & I School CHCH/BSGR BH23 228 A1
Christchurch Medical Centre CHCH/BSGR BH23 228 E1; HAV PO9 171 J5
Christchurch Priory CHCH/BSGR BH23 228 C2
Christchurch Rowing Club CHCH/BSGR BH23 228 B3
Christchurch Ski & Leisure Centre CHCH/BSGR BH23 346 H9
Christ's Hospital WINC SO23 24 F7
Christ the King Catholic Primary School BWD BH11 213 G3
Church Cottage BSTK RG21 6 E5
Church Crookham Junior School FLEETS GU52 71 J4
Churchers College EPSF GU31 120 E5
Churchers College Junior Department PSF GU32 120 C6
Church Grange & Bramblys Grange Health Centre BSTK RG21 6 D6
Churchill Plaza BSTK RG21 6 F4
Churchill Yard Industrial Estate WVILLE PO7 155 L7
City Business Centre WINC SO23 25 G4
City Grove Trading Estate ELGH SO50 139 L4
City Industrial Park WSHM SO15 22 C4
City Museum & Records Office PSEA PO1 20 E5
The City of Portsmouth Boys School NEND PO2 184 E4
City of Portsmouth Girls School PSEA PO1 192 E1
City of Portsmouth Sports Club NEND PO2 184 D5
Civic Gateway BSTK RG21 6 F6
Civil Service Sports Ground HSEA PO3 185 G5; NBNE BH10 213 J1
Clanfield Junior School HORN PO8 321 K5
Clarence Pier & Amusement Centre PSEA PO1 20 D8
Clarendon J & I School NTID SP9 266 F2
Clatford CE J & I School RAND SP11 271 Q3
Clayfields Sports Centre FAWY SO45 176 D4
Clayton Barracks ALDT GU11 73 K4
The Clere School KSCL RG20 247 J5
Clewborough House School at Cheswycks FRIM GU16 62 B3
Cliddesden Primary School OVTN RG25 93 J7
Cliff Court Hotel WCLF BH2 8 B7
Cliffdale Primary School NEND PO2 184 F6
Cliffeside Hotel BMTH BH1 9 K6
Cloud Hotel BROC SO42 351 L2
The Club at Meyrick Park WCLF BH2 8 C3
Cluster Industrial Estate HSEA PO3 193 G3
The Coast Clinic FAWY SO45 355 K5
Cody Technology Park FARN GU14 60 C8
Cogdean Elms Industrial Estate WIMB BH21 206 E7
Cold Ash St Marks CE Primary School NTHA RG18 28 D3
Colden Common Primary School RWIN SO21 134 F3
Colehill First School WIMB BH21 208 B1
Coliseum Business Centre CBLY GU15 50 C5
College Park Infant School NEND PO2 184 F6
Collingbourne CE Primary School MARL SN8 264 G4
Collingwood Business Park FHAM/STUB PO14 182 A2
Colthrop Business Park STHA RG19 35 L1
Coltwood Business Centre ALDT GU11 3 G3
Combe Gibbet HUNG RG17 244 D3
Commercial Business Centre CHFD SO53 139 J2
Common Marsh STOK SO20 285 N7
Community Centre Cinema LYMN SO41 221 L4
Compton Acres Gardens PSTN BH14 224 E8

Compton CE Primary School *RWIN* SO21 124 D4
Compton Place Business Centre *CBLY* GU15 50 C4
Compton & Up Marden CE School *RCCH* PO18 323 K10
Concorde Club & Hotel *ELGH* SO50 139 L8
The Connaught Hotel *WCLF* BH2 8 C7
The Connaught School *ASHV* GU12 260 C1
Coombe Bissett CE Primary School *RSAL* SP5 325 M3
The Coombes Infants School *WHIT* RG2 239 M5
Copnor Bridge Business Centre *PSEA* PO1 192 F1
Copnor J & I School *HSEA* PO3 185 G7
Copythorne CE Infant School *TOTT* SO40 341 M2
Corfe Hills School *WIMB* BH21 210 F2
Corhampton Golf Club *BPWT* SO32 311 P10
BPWT SO32 312 A12
Corn Exchange *NWBY* RG14 18 E4
Corpus Christi Catholic Primary School *BOSC* BH5 226 F3
Corpus Christi RC (Aided) Primary School *NEND* PO2 184 D6
Corus Hotel *CWTH* RG45 43 J3
Cosham Health Centre *CHAM* PO6 184 F1
Costello Technical College *BSTK* RG21 7 H6
Cottage Grove Primary School *SSEA* PO5 21 H6
Courthill First School *PSTN* BH14 224 D4
Court Lane J & I School *CHAM* PO6 185 G1
Court Moor School *FLEETS* GU52 71 H2
Cove CC *FARN* GU14 60 E4
Cove Infant School *FARN* GU14 60 E2
Cove Junior School *FARN* GU14 60 E3
Cove Secondary School *FARN* GU14 60 E3
Cowplain Community School *WVILLE* PO7 155 L6
Coxlease School *LYND* SO43 345 K6
Coxmoor Farm Light Industrial Estate *RFNM* GU10 70 D6
Cracknore Industrial Park *TOTT* SO40 159 L7
TOTT SO40 160 B6
Cranborne First School *WIMB* BH21 336 F5
Cranborne Middle School *WIMB* BH21 336 F4
Cranbourne Secondary School *BSTK* RG21 6 B9
Craneswater Junior School *ENEY* PO4 21 M8
Crane Valley Golf Club *WIMB* BH21 200 D1
Crawley Ridge Primary School *CBLY* GU15 51 H2
The Crescent Primary School *ELGH* SO50 140 A1
The Crestwood College of Business & Enterprise *ELGH* SO50 139 M3
Cricklade College *AND* SP10 5 H4
Cricklade Theatre *AND* SP10 5 G4
Crofton Anne Dale J & I School *FHAM/STUB* PO14 189 J2
Crofton Hammond Infant School *FHAM/STUB* PO14 189 H2
Crofton School *FHAM/STUB* PO14 189 L2
Crondall Primary School *RFNM* GU10 259 P2
Crookham CE Infant School *FLEETS* GU52 71 H4
The Crookhorn Community School *WVILLE* PO7 169 M4
Cross Farm Infant School *FRIM* GU16 61 L2
Crow Arch Lane Industrial Estate *RGWD* BH24 203 K7
Crown Hotel *LYND* SO43 345 K3
Crowthorne Business Centre *CWTH* RG45 43 L1
Crowthorne CE Primary School *CWTH* RG45 43 K3
Cumberland Business Centre *SSEA* PO5 21 K3
Cumberland Hotel *BMTH* BH1 9 K6
Cumberland Infant School *ENEY* PO4 193 G5
Cupernham J & I School *ROMY* SO51 131 H7
Curdridge Primary School *BPWT* SO32 150 D3
Curtis Museum *ALTN* GU34 106 F5
Danebury Ring *STOK* SO20 270 G12
Daneshill East Industrial Estate *CHIN* RG24 7 L2
Daneshill House School *HTWY* RG27 47 M4
Daneshill Industrial Estate *CHIN* RG24 7 M1
Daneshill West Industrial Estate *CHIN* RG24 65 M4
Danesmead Community Centre *BSTK* RG21 65 L4
David Hart Business Centre *RSAL* SP5 327 J12
Dawkins Business Centre *PLE* BH15 222 D5
Days Inn *FLEETN* GU51 58 F4
D-Day Museum & Overlord Embroidery *SSEA* PO5 192 C7
Deacon Trading Estate *ELGH* SO50 140 C2
Deanery Campus *SHAM* SO14 23 J5
The Deanery *WINC* SO23 25 G7
Deane's Almhouses *BSTK* RG21 6 F7
Dean Farm Estate *WHAM* PO17 166 A3
Dean Farm Golf Club *BOR* GU35 110 D4
Deer Park Farm Industrial Estate *ELGH* SO50 141 L3
Delta Business Park *FHAM/PORC* PO16 182 B1
Denmark Road Medical Centre *MOOR/WNTN* BH9 213 M7
Denmead Health Centre *WVILLE* PO7 154 E3
Denmead Infant School *WVILLE* PO7 155 G4
Denmead Junior School *WVILLE* PO7 154 F4
Denvale Trading Park *NWBY* RG14 19 L5
Department of Social Services *BSTK* RG21 6 E6
Derry Down Health Clinic *RAND* SP11 86 C3
The Derwent Hospital *LTDN* BH7 215 H7
De Vere Grand Harbour Hotel *SHAM* SO14 22 E5
De Vere Royal Bath Hotel *BMTH* BH1 9 G7
Devonshire Infant School *ENEY* PO4 21 M5
Devon Towers Hotel *WCLF* BH2 8 D7
Dial House Hotel *CWTH* RG45 43 K3
Dibden Golf Centre *FAWY* SO45 176 C3
Dibles Park *HLER* SO31 179 L3
Ditcham Park School *EPSF* GU31 322 D4
Dockyard Apprentice Exhibition *PSEA* PO1 20 B2
Dogmersfield CE Primary School *HTWY* RG27 70 C1
The Dolphin Shopping Centre & Sports Centre *PLE* BH15 223 K6
Dolphin Swimming Pool *PLE* BH15 223 K6
The Donald Burrell Centre *CHIN* RG24 64 F4
Donnington Castle *NWBY* RG14 27 G5
Donnington Valley Golf Club *NWBY* RG14 27 H3
Donnington Valley Hotel *NWBY* RG14 27 H4
Dorset Heavy Horse Centre *WIMB* BH21 337 K10
Dorset Magistrates Court *PLE* BH15 223 K4
Dorset Medical Centre *SHAM* SO14 23 G2
Dorset Police Eastern Division HQ *FERN* BH22 204 D7
The Dorset Racquets & Health Club *CFDH* BH17 211 H8
Dove House School *BSTK* RG21 6 F1
Downe House School *NTHA* RG18 28 C1
Down Grange Athletics Track *KBH* RG22 92 D3
Down House *RSAL* SP5 327 P12
Downton CE Primary School *RSAL* SP5 327 J12
Downton Industrial Estate *RSAL* SP5 327 J12
Downton Secondary School *RSAL* SP5 332 A1
Drewitts Industrial Estate *BWD* BH11 212 E6
Droxford Junior School *BPWT* SO32 318 G3
Duck's Nest *FBDG* SP6 330 C3
Dudmoor Farm Golf Course *CHCH/BSGR* BH23 216 A4
Dudsbury Golf Club *FERN* BH22 209 J7
Dukes Mill *ROMY* SO51 136 E1
Dummer Golf Club *OVTN* RG25 104 A2
Dunces Arch *LYND* SO43 345 N2
Dunhurst (Bedales Junior School) *PSF* GU32 120 C3
Dunston Park Infant School *NTHA* RG18 28 F8
Dunwood Manor Golf Club *ROMY* SO51 129 K6
Durley CE Primary School *BPWT* SO32 142 A6
Durley Grange Hotel *WCLF* BH2 8 C6
Durley Hall Hotel *WBNE* BH4 8 A7
Durlston Court School *NMIL/BTOS* BH25 219 G8
Eagle House School *SHST* GU47 43 J6
East Anglia Hotel *WCLF* BH2 8 B5
East Berkshire Golf Club *CWTH* RG45 43 G3
East Cemetery *LTDN* BH7 226 F2
East Cliff Lift *BMTH* BH1 9 J7
Eastern Industrial Centre *CHAM* PO6 185 J2
Eastleigh College *ELGH* SO50 140 A2
Eastleigh College of FE *ELGH* SO50 139 M6
Eastleigh FC *ELGH* SO50 147 L1
Eastleigh Health Centre *ELGH* SO50 140 A1
Eastleigh Museum *ELGH* SO50 140 A2
Eastleigh RFC *ELGH* SO50 140 C1
Eastney Beam Engine House *ENEY* PO4 193 J5
Eastney Health Centre *ENEY* PO4 193 G5
Eastney Swimming Baths *ENEY* PO4 193 J6
Easton Lane Business Park *WINC* SO23 25 L4
Eastrop Community Centre *BSTK* RG21 7 K4
East Shore School *HSEA* PO3 193 H2
East Street Shopping Centre *SHAM* SO14 23 H4
Ebblake Industrial Estate *VWD* BH31 201 L4
The Eddie Read Swimming & Diving Complex *SHAM* SO14 22 E5
Edgebarrow School *CWTH* RG45 43 K5
Edgebarrow Sports Centre *CWTH* RG45 43 L5
Edgeborough School *RFNM* GU10 79 G5
The Edge Sports Centre *HASM* GU27 115 K8
Education Other Than At School (EOTAS) *GPORT* PO12 15 K8
Eelmoor Road Depot Trading Estate *FARN* GU14 61 G6
Eggars School *ALTN* GU34 107 H2
Eling Infant School *TOTT* SO40 159 G2
Elizabeth Barracks *CHOB/PIR* GU24 63 G2
Elizabeth House Hotel *WSHM* SO15 160 F1
Elliott Industrial Park *ASHV* GU12 73 L6
Elmers Court Hotel *LYMN* SO41 356 B9
Elm House Business Centre *MFD/CHID* GU8 261 K12
Elmhurst Business Park *GPORT* PO12 14 F4
Elmrise County Primary School *BWD* BH11 212 F4
Elson County Infant School *GPORT* PO12 183 G8
Elson County Junior School *GPORT* PO12 183 G8
Elstead Hotel *BMTH* BH1 9 L4
Elstree School *THLE* RG7 37 K1
Embley Park Industrial Estate *ROMY* SO51 335 Q1
Embley Park Junior School *ROMY* SO51 335 Q2
Embley Park School *ROMY* SO51 335 Q2
The Emmanuel CE VA Middle School *VWD* BH31 201 G3
Emsworth Museum *EMRTH* PO10 171 M8
Emsworth Primary School *EMRTH* PO10 171 L7
Enborne CE Primary School *KSCL* RG20 32 E6
Enterprise Industrial Estate *ASHV* GU12 73 M1
HORN PO8 321 L12
Enterprise Park *VWD* BH31 201 L4
The Epiphany CE Primary School *MOOR/WNTN* BH9 214 B4
Esseborne Manor Hotel *RAND* SP11 251 L6
Eversley CC *HTWY* RG27 42 B8
Exbury Gardens & Railway *FAWY* SO45 354 C11
Exbury House *FAWY* SO45 354 C11
Experimental Horticulture Station *LYMN* SO41 221 G8
Explosion! Museum of Naval Firepower *GPORT* PO12 191 K1
Express by Holiday Inn *HEND* SO30 148 E3
PLE BH15 223 K6
ROWN SO16 145 J5
Fairfax Industrial Estate *ASHV* GU12 73 L6
Fairfield Infant School *HAV* PO9 17 G4
Fairfields Arts Centre *BSTK* RG21 6 F7
Fairfields Primary School & Arts Centre *BSTK* RG21 6 F7
Fairisle Infant School *ROWN* SO16 145 L4
Fairisle Junior School *ROWN* SO16 145 L4
Fairlands Montessori School *BPWT* SO32 151 L5
Fair Oak Cemetery *ELGH* SO50 141 J3
Fair Oak Junior School *ELGH* SO50 141 J3
Fairway Business Centre *HSEA* PO3 185 J5
Falcon Business Park *EWKG* RG40 239 N10
Falcon Hotel *FARN* GU14 61 J7
Falkland Memorial *NWBY* RG14 33 K6
Falkland Primary School *NWBY* RG14 33 K6
Fareham College *FHAM/STUB* PO14 10 C6
The Fareham Gallery *FHAM/PORC* PO16 11 G6
Fareham Leisure Centre *FHAM/PORC* PO16 10 F4
Fareham Megabowl *FHAM/STUB* PO14 182 B3
Fareham Shopping Centre *FHAM/PORC* PO16 11 J5
Farleigh School *RAND* SP11 271 K4
Farley Hill Primary School *THLE* RG7 239 J11
Farley Mount *RWIN* SO21 301 L4
Farnborough Aerospace Centre *FARN* GU14 60 F8
Farnborough Airport *FARN* GU14 60 F7
Farnborough Business Centre *FARN* GU14 60 F6
Farnborough College of Technology *FARN* GU14 61 H8
FARN GU14 61 J6
Farnborough Gate Retail Park *FARN* GU14 61 J1
Farnborough Hill School *FARN* GU14 61 J3
Farnborough Recreation Centre *FARN* GU14 61 H5
Farnborough RFC *FARN* GU14 61 G2
Farnborough Town FC *FARN* GU14 50 C8
Farnham Business Centre *FNM* GU9 13 H2
Farnham Business Park *FNM* GU9 12 D7
Farnham Castle Keep *FNM* GU9 12 E1
Farnham College *FNM* GU9 13 H6
Farnham Golf Club *RFNM* GU10 260 B6
Farnham Health Centre *FNM* GU9 13 G2
Farnham Heath End School *FNM* GU9 77 J2
Farnham Hospital *FNM* GU9 13 L1
Farnham House Hotel *RFNM* GU10 76 A8
Farnham Museum *FNM* GU9 12 E4
Farnham Park Golf Club *FNM* GU9 76 F4
Farnham Retail Park *FNM* GU9 13 L1
Farnham Sports Centre *FNM* GU9 13 H3
Farnham Trading Estate *FNM* GU9 77 K4
Farringdon Industrial Centre *ALTN* GU34 294 C6
Farringdon Industrial Estate *ALTN* GU34 294 C6
Fawley Business Centre *FAWY* SO45 355 J5
Fawley Infant School *FAWY* SO45 355 J5
Fenwick Hospital *LYND* SO43 345 J2
Ferndown First School *FERN* BH22 209 J3
Ferndown Forest Golf Club *FERN* BH22 204 E7
Ferndown Golf Club *FERN* BH22 209 L4
Ferndown Industrial Estate *WIMB* BH21 208 F2
Ferndown Medical Centre *FERN* BH22 209 K3
Ferndown Middle School *FERN* BH22 209 J3
Ferndown Sports Centre *FERN* BH22 209 H2
Ferndown Upper School *FERN* BH22 209 H2
Ferneham Hall *FHAM/PORC* PO16 11 H5
Fernhill Primary School *FARN* GU14 50 B7
Fernhill Secondary School *FARN* GU14 50 B7
Fernhurst Junior School *ENEY* PO4 192 F4
Fernside Business Park *WIMB* BH21 209 G1
Festival Place Shopping Centre *BSTK* RG21 6 E5
The Fieldgate Centre *KSCL* RG20 248 C10
Field Studies Centre *MARL* SN8 242 G5
Fifehead Manor Hotel *STOK* SO20 269 R12
Finchampstead CE Primary School *EWKG* RG40 42 A5
Finchampstead Sports Club *EWKG* RG40 42 A5
Finkley Down Farm Park *RAND* SP11 97 G1
Finns Industrial Park *RFNM* GU10 70 D6
Fircroft Hotel *BOSC* BH5 226 E4
Fir Tree Primary School *NTHA* RG18 28 A8
Fish Farm *RSAL* SP5 327 K9
Fish Market *PSEA* PO1 20 C5
Flanders Industrial Park *HEND* SO30 149 H4
Fleet Business Park *FLEETS* GU52 71 K5
Fleet Community Hospital *FLEETN* GU51 59 G6
Fleet CC *FLEETN* GU51 59 G8
Fleet Infant School *FLEETS* GU52 71 K1
Fleetsbridge Business Centre *CFDH* BH17 223 H1
Fleetspoint Business Centre *PLE* BH15 223 H3
Fleet Town FC *FLEETN* GU51 59 G8
Fleming Park Golf Club *ELGH* SO50 139 L5
Fleming Park Leisure Centre *ELGH* SO50 139 L5
Flying Bull Primary School *NEND* PO2 184 D8
Focus 303 Business Centre *AND* SP10 96 F3
Folly Farm Touring Caravan Park *RWIN* SO21 287 L9
Folly Hill Infant School *FNM* GU9 76 E2
Fordingbridge Business Park *FBDG* SP6 196 E3
Fordingbridge Hospital *FBDG* SP6 197 H3
Fordingbridge J & I School *FBDG* SP6 197 H1
Forest Edge School *TOTT* SO40 158 E1
Forest Edge Touring Park *RGWD* BH24 205 M6
Forest Lodge Hotel *LYND* SO43 345 K2
Forest Park Hotel *BROC* SO42 351 J2
The Forest Shopping Centre *BOR* GU35 113 G1
Forres Sandle Manor School *FBDG* SP6 196 F2
Fort Brockhurst *LSOL/BMARY* PO13 182 F7
Fort Cumberland *ENEY* PO4 193 L5
Fort Fareham *FHAM/STUB* PO14 182 A2
Fort Fareham Industrial Estate *FHAM/STUB* PO14 182 A2
Fort Hill Community School *DEAN* RG23 64 E6
Fort Monckton *GPORT* PO12 191 J8
Fort Nelson *WHAM* PO17 167 H5
Fort Purbrook *CHAM* PO6 169 K7
Fort Southwick *WHAM* PO17 167 M6
Fort Wallington Industrial Estate *FHAM/PORC* PO16 11 L3
Fort Widley *CHAM* PO6 168 F6
Fosters Business Park *HTWY* RG27 67 M1
Foundry Lane Primary School *WSHM* SO15 160 B1
Four Lanes Infant & Community Junior School *CHIN* RG24 54 B5
Foxhills Infant School *TOTT* SO40 158 D4
Foxhills Junior School *TOTT* SO40 158 C4
Francis Avenue Industrial Estate *BWD* BH11 212 D5
Francis Baily Primary School *STHA* RG19 35 L1
Fratton Community Centre *PSEA* PO1 21 L1
Fratton Industrial Estate *ENEY* PO4 192 F3
Fred Woolley House (Hospital) *ELGH* SO50 139 H8
Freegrounds County J & I School *HEND* SO30 149 K6
Freemantle Business Centre *WSHM* SO15 160 C3
Freemantle CE (Controlled) Infant School *WSHM* SO15 160 C2
Frensham Common & Country Park *RFNM* GU10 262 E6
Frensham Pond Hotel *RFNM* GU10 262 C8
Frensham Pond Sailing Club *RFNM* GU10 262 C7
Friarsgate Medical Centre *WINC* SO23 25 H6
Friends Meeting House *WINC* SO23 25 H7
Frimley Business Park *FARN* GU14 50 D8
Frimley CE Junior School *FRIM* GU16 61 L1
Frimley Green Medical Centre *FRIM* GU16 61 M2
Frimley Hall Hotel *CBLY* GU15 51 H2
Frimley Park Hospital *FRIM* GU16 50 F6
Frobisher Industrial Centre *ROMY* SO51 130 E7
Frogmore Community School *BLKW* GU17 49 H3
Frogmore County Infant School *BLKW* GU17 49 K4
Frogmore Junior School *BLKW* GU17 49 K3
Front Lawn Junior School *HAV* PO9 170 F3
Froxfield Endowed Infant School *PSF* GU32 307 J10
Fryern J & I School *CHFD* SO53 139 L2
Funtington County Primary School *RCCH* PO18 173 M3
Furzeley Golf Club *WVILLE* PO7 154 F6
Furzey Gardens *LYND* SO43 340 E9
Futcher School *CHAM* PO6 169 J8
Garderobe Tower *SHAM* SO14 22 E5
Garrison Theatre *NTID* SP9 266 D2
Gaston's Wood Industrial Estate *CHIN* RG24 65 M3
Gatcombe Park Primary School *NEND* PO2 184 F4
George Gale & Co Ltd Brewery *HORN* PO8 156 D1
The George Hotel *ODIM* RG29 69 G5
George Street School Branch Clinic *PSEA* PO1 192 F1
Georgian House Hotel *HASM* GU27 118 D5
Giant's Grave *FBDG* SP6 331 J3
Gilbert White's House & The Oates Museum *ALTN* GU34 295 K8
Gillies Health Centre *KBH* RG22 92 F4
Glenfield Infant School *WEND* SO18 161 M1
Glenhurst School *HAV* PO9 17 G4
Glenmoor Girls School *NBNE* BH10 213 K7
Glenwood School *EMRTH* PO10 171 L7
Goal Farm Golf Club *CHOB/PIR* GU24 63 K2
Goldsmith Infant School *ENEY* PO4 21 M6
Gomer Infant School *GPORT* PO12 190 E5
Goodway Sea School *GPORT* PO12 183 H8
Gordleton Industrial Estate *LYMN* SO41 220 F3
Gordleton Industrial Park *LYMN* SO41 220 E3
Gore Road Industrial Estate *NMIL/BTOS* BH25 218 E6
Gorse Ride Junior School *EWKG* RG40 42 A1
Gosport Airfield *LSOL/BMARY* PO13 189 L3
Gosport Health Centre *GPORT* PO12 14 C5
Gosport Museum *GPORT* PO12 15 J4
Gosport & Stokes Bay Golf Club *GPORT* PO12 191 J7
Gosport War Memorial Hospital *GPORT* PO12 14 C5
The Grange Comprehensive School *CHCH/BSGR* BH23 228 E1
Grange Community Junior School *FARN* GU14 50 B8
Grange Farm Business Park *BPWT* SO32 151 J4
Grange J & I School *LSOL/BMARY* PO13 190 C1
Grange Road Business Centre *CHCH/BSGR* BH23 217 G8
The Grange *NARL* SO24 290 G3
Grateley Business Park *RAND* SP11 269 L5
Grateley Primary School *RAND* SP11 269 P4
Gravatom Business Centre *BPWT* SO32 143 H4
Grayshott CE Primary School *GSHT* GU26 115 H5
Grayshott Clinic *GSHT* GU26 115 H4
Grayswood CE Infant School *HASM* GU27 118 F2
Great Binfields Primary School *CHIN* RG24 54 B7

Greatbridge Business Park
ROMY SO51 ....130 D7
The Great Hall
WINC SO23 ....24 F5
Greatham Primary School
LISS GU33 ....308 F2
Greenfields Junior School
HTWY RG27 ....57 L3
Greenham Road Retail Park
NWBY RG14 ....18 F6
Greenhill Farm Camping &
Caravan Park *RSAL* SP5 ....334 D6
Green Pastures Farm
TOTT SO40 ....335 Q12
The Gregg School
WEND SO18 ....148 A1
Gresham Industrial Estate
ASHV GU12 ....73 L6
Grey House Preparatory
School *HTWY* RG27 ....57 M2
Greywell Shopping Centre
HAV PO9 ....170 F3
Griffin Industrial Park
TOTT SO40 ....144 D5
Grosvenor Casino
WSHM SO15 ....22 D4
Grosvenor Hotel
BMTH BH1 ....9 G6
Grovebell Industrial Estate
RFNM GU10 ....12 A9
Grove County Primary School
FRIM GU16 ....51 G6
Grove Farm Meadow Holiday
Caravan Park
CHCH/BSGR BH23 ......215 J7
Grove House Business Centre
CHIN RG24 ....54 B8
Groveley Business Centre
CHCH/BSGR BH23 ......228 E2
Grove Park Industrial Estate
ALTN GU34 ....107 H4
Grove Place Preparatory
School *ROWN* SO16 .....145 H2
The Guard Room
FUFL SO22 ....24 C5
Guildford Road
Industrial Estate *FNM* GU9 .13 K1
The Guildhall Gallery
WINC SO23 ....21 L7
Guillemont County Junior
School *FARN* GU14 ....60 C2
Gundrymoor Trading Estate
WIMB BH21 ....205 G3
Gunwharf Quays Retail &
Leisure Park
PSEA PO1 ....20 C4
Gurkha Museum *WINC* SO23 .24 E6
Hackwood House
OVTN RG25 ....93 M4
Hackwood Medical Centre
BSTK RG21 ....6 D5
Hale Primary School
FBDG SP6 ....332 E3
FNM GU9 ....76 F1
Halterworth Primary School
ROMY SO51 ....137 J1
Hamble Community Sports
College *HLER* SO31 ....162 E6
Hamble Court Business
Park *HLER* SO31 ....178 E1
Hambledon CC
WVILLE PO7 ....320 A7
Hambledon Infant School
WVILLE PO7 ....319 R9
Hamble Primary School
HLER SO31 ....162 E8
Hambrook Business Centre
RCCH PO18 ....173 H2
Hamilton Business Park
NMIL/BTOS BH25 ......218 A3
Hammond Industrial Estate
FHAM/STUB PO14 ......189 K3
Hammond Junior School
FHAM/STUB PO14 ......189 J2
Hampreston CE First School
WIMB BH21 ....208 E5
Hampshire Brewery
ROMY SO51 ....130 E8
Hampshire CCC
(The Rose Bowl)
HEND SO30 ....148 F3
The Hampshire Centrecourt
Hotel *CHIN* RG24 ....54 B7
The Hampshire Clinic
CHIN RG24 ....7 M2
Hampshire Golf Club
RAND SP11 ....271 R2
Hampshire International
Business Park *CHIN* RG24 .54 A4
Hampshire Records Office
WINC SO23 ....24 F4
Hampshire Tennis & Health
Club *HEND* SO30 ....148 F4
Hamptworth Golf & Country
Club *RSAL* SP5 ....333 Q4
Hamworthy Community
Clinic *PLE* BH15 ......222 E5
Hamworthy First School
PLE BH15 ....222 F7
Hamworthy Middle School
PLE BH15 ....222 F7
Handy Cross
RGWD BH24 ....342 H5
Hankley Common Golf Club
RFNM GU10 ....263 K3
Harbour Heights Hotel
CCLF BH13 ....237 K2
Harbour Lights Picture House
SHAM SO14 ....23 J8
Harbridge School
RGWD BH24 ....198 F4
The Hard Interchange
PSEA PO1 ....20 B3
Hardley School & Sixth Form
FAWY SO45 ....354 E3
Harefield Clinic
WEND SO18 ....148 A5
Harefield Infant School
WEND SO18 ....148 B4
Harefield Junior School
WEND SO18 ....148 B4
Harestock Primary School
FUFL SO22 ....122 D1
Harewood Forest Industrial
Estate *RAND* SP11 ....273 J1
Harlington Centre
FLEETN GU51 ....59 H4
Harrison Primary School
FHAM/PORC PO16 ......11 H4
Harrow Way Community
School *AND* SP10 ....4 A4
Harrow Wood Farm Caravan
Park *CHCH/BSGR* BH23 .348 E12
Hartley Park Farm Business
Centre *ALTN* GU34 ....295 K4
[H]artley Wintney CC
[H]TWY RG27 ....57 M2
[Hartl]ey Wintney Golf Club
[HTW]Y RG27 ....58 A1

Hart Plain Infant School
HORN PO8 ....155 L6
Hart Plain Junior School
WVILLE PO7 ....155 L6
Hart Shopping Centre
FLEETN GU51 ....59 H7
Hart Sports Centre
FLEETN GU51 ....58 E8
Haselworth County Primary
School *GPORT* PO12 .....14 F6
Haslemere Hall
HASM GU27 ....118 C5
Haslemere Hospital & Health
Centre *HASM* GU27 ....118 D5
Haslemere Museum
HASM GU27 ....118 D5
Haslemere Preparatory
School *HASM* GU27 ....118 D7
Hassocks Wood Industrial
Estate *CHIN* RG24 ......66 A1
Hatch Ride Primary School
CWTH RG45 ....43 K1
Hatch Warren Primary School
KBH RG22 ....92 E5
Hatch Warren Retail Park
KBH RG22 ....92 C6
Hatherden CE Primary School
RAND SP11 ....83 L3
Havant Arts Centre
HAV PO9 ....16 F5
Havant Business Centre
HAV PO9 ....16 B6
Havant Leisure Centre
HAV PO9 ....16 F2
Havant Museum
HAV PO9 ....17 G5
Havant Retail Park
HAV PO9 ....170 B7
Havant RFC
HAV PO9 ....16 B2
Havant Sixth Form College
HAV PO9 ....16 D1
Havant War Memorial Hospital
HAV PO9 ....16 D3
Havant & Waterlooville FC
HAV PO9 ....171 G3
Havelock Community Centre
SSEA PO5 ....21 L7
Haven Hotel
CCLF BH13 ....237 G5
The Hawk Conservancy
RAND SP11 ....94 C4
Hawley CP School
BLKW GU17 ....50 A5
Hawley Lane Industrial Estate
FARN GU14 ....50 D8
Hawley Place School
BLKW GU17 ....50 A7
The Hawthorns School
KBH RG22 ....92 E3
Hayeswood First School
WIMB BH21 ....208 A2
Hayling Billy Business Centre
HISD PO11 ....194 D4
Hayling Golf Club
HISD PO11 ....193 M4
HISD PO11 ....194 C5
Hayling Island Health Centre
HISD PO11 ....195 G5
The Hayling School
HISD PO11 ....195 G3
Haymarket Theatre
BSTK RG21 ....6 E6
Haymoor Middle School
CFDH BH17 ....211 L7
Hayward Business Centre
HAV PO9 ....171 H5
Hazel Wood Infant School
TOTT SO40 ....158 C1
Headlands Business Park
RGWD BH24 ....203 J2
RGWD BH24 ....203 L4
Headley Park Country Club
BOR GU35 ....111 K3
Health Club & Swimming Pool
STHA RG19 ....19 M6
Heatherlands First School
BKME/WDN BH12 ....224 D3
Heather Ridge County Infant
School *CBLY* GU15 ......51 M4
Heatherside Schools
FLEETS GU52 ....71 J1
Heatherview Medical Centre
BKME/WDN BH12 ....225 G1
Heathfield Junior School
ITCH SO19 ....162 C2
Heathfield School
FHAM/STUB PO14 ......181 J4
Heathlands Hotel
BMTH BH1 ....9 J6
Heathlands Primary School
BWD BH11 ....213 C5
Hedge End Business Centre
HEND SO30 ....149 H3
Hedge End Retail Park
HEND SO30 ....149 G5
Helix Business Park
CBLY GU15 ....50 D5
Henbury View First School
WIMB BH21 ....210 C2
Henry Beaufort School
FUFL SO22 ....288 E12
Henry Cort Community
School *FHAM* PO15 ....181 J1
Henry Tyndale School
FARN GU14 ....61 J2
Herbert Day Hospital
WBNE BH4 ....225 H6
Hermitage Hotel
BMTH BH1 ....8 F7
The Herne Farm Leisure
Centre *EPSF* GU31 ....120 E5
The Herne Junior School
EPSF GU31 ....120 E5
Heron Industrial Estate
THLE RG7 ....238 A8
The Herons Swimming &
Fitness Centre
HASM GU27 ....117 M2
Highbury College
CHAM PO6 ....185 G3
PSEA PO1 ....21 H2
Highbury College of
Technology *PSEA* PO1 .192 B2
Highbury Primary School
CHAM PO6 ....185 G2
Highclere Castle & Gardens
KSCL RG20 ....246 D10
Highcliffe Castle
CHCH/BSGR BH23 .....229 L1
Highcliffe Castle Golf Club
CHCH/BSGR BH23 .....229 L1
Highcliffe Junior School
CHCH/BSGR BH23 .....218 A7
Highcliffe Medical Centre
CHCH/BSGR BH23 .....217 M8
CHCH/BSGR BH23 .....229 H3
Highcliffe School
CHCH/BSGR BH23 .....217 K7

Highcliff Marriott Hotel
WCLF BH2 ....8 D8
Highcroft Industrial Estate
HORN PO8 ....321 L12
Highfield CE (Aided) Primary
School *PTSW* SO17 ....147 G5
Highfield School
LIPH GU30 ....116 E6
Highgrove Industrial Park
HSEA PO3 ....185 H5
Highlands Medical Centre
FHAM PO15 ....181 K2
Hightown Industrial Estate
RGWD BH24 ....203 K6
Hightown Primary School
ITCH SO19 ....148 E8
Hillbourne Community
First School *CFDH* BH17 .211 H6
Hillbourne Middle School
CFDH BH17 ....211 H6
Hill Farm Caravan Park
ROMY SO51 ....128 F5
Hill Head Preparatory School
FHAM/STUB PO14 ......189 H3
Hill House School
LYMN SO41 ....351 P11
Hill Park Clinic
FHAM PO15 ....10 B1
Hillside First School
VWD BH31 ....201 H1
Hillside Industrial Estate
HORN PO8 ....321 L12
Hillview Business Centre
NBNE BH10 ....213 L5
Hill View First School
NBNE BH10 ....213 L5
Hilsea Lines Business Park
HSEA PO3 ....185 G4
Hiitingbury County J & I
School *CHFD* SO53 ....133 J7
Hilton Hotel
BSTK RG21 ....7 K6
Hindhead Golf Club
GSHT GU26 ....115 H2
HM Prison
FUFL SO22 ....24 C5
PSEA PO1 ....192 F2
HMS Dolphin *GPORT* PO12 .15 L8
HMS Nelson *PSEA* PO1 ....20 E1
HMS Temeraire *PSEA* PO1 .20 E4
HMS Victory *PSEA* PO1 ....20 B1
HMS Warrior *PSEA* PO1 ....20 B3
Hoburne Bashley
NMIL/BTOS BH25 ......219 H1
Hockley Golf Club
RWIN SO21 ....125 G2
Hogs Back Brewery
RFNM GU10 ....260 D3
Hogwood Industrial Park
EWKG RG40 ....239 N10
Holbrook Primary School
LSOL/BMARY PO13 .....182 C5
Holbrook Recreation Centre
LSOL/BMARY PO13 .....182 C5
Holbury J & I School
FAWY SO45 ....354 E5
Holiday Inn *BSTK* RG21 ...93 L2
ELGH SO50 ....139 L5
FARN GU14 ....73 H1
FHAM PO15 ....180 E2
PSEA PO1 ....20 E7
WSHM SO15 ....22 E5
Hollybrook Cemetery
ROWN SO16 ....146 C5
Hollybrook Infant School
ROWN SO16 ....146 D5
Hollybrook Junior School
ROWN SO16 ....146 D5
Hollybush Industrial Park
ALDT GU11 ....73 L3
Holly Lodge Primary School
ASHV GU12 ....61 M8
Holmes Place Health Club
NBNE BH10 ....210 D1
Holy Cross Hospital
HASM GU27 ....117 M1
Holy Family RC (Aided) Primary
School *ROWN* SO16 ....145 J6
Holy Ghost Chapel Ruins
BSTK RG21 ....6 D5
Home Farm Business Centre
RSAL SP5 ....298 A7
Home Farm School
THLE RG7 ....37 K1
Homefield Preparatory School
CHCH/BSGR BH23 .....216 C3
Hones Yard Business Park
FNM GU9 ....13 J4
Hook Bowling Club
HTWY RG27 ....56 B7
Hook Community Centre
HTWY RG27 ....56 D7
Hook House Hotel
HTWY RG27 ....56 E6
Hook J & I School
HTWY RG27 ....56 D7
Hook with Warsash CE
Primary School *HLER* SO31 .179 K4
Hope Lodge School
WEND SO18 ....147 L8
The Hop Kiln
FNM GU9 ....12 F6
Hordle CE Primary School
LYMN SO41 ....220 A5
Hordle House School
LYMN SO41 ....231 M3
Hordle Walhampton School
LYMN SO41 ....356 A6
Horizon West Industrial
Estate *NWBY* RG14 ....19 M4
Horndean CE Junior School
HORN PO8 ....156 C1
Horndean FC
HORN PO8 ....156 C1
Horndean Health Centre
HORN PO8 ....156 D1
Horndean Infant School
HORN PO8 ....156 C1
Horndean Technology
College *HORN* PO8 ....156 B1
Horris Hill School
KSCL RG20 ....246 C1
Hoskins Place Industrial
Estate *CBLY* GU15 .....50 D5
Hospital of St Cross
WINC SO23 ....122 F4
Hotel Collingwood
WCLF BH2 ....8 D7
Hotel du Vin
WINC SO23 ....24 F6
Hotel Ibis
SSEA PO5 ....21 G4
WSHM SO15 ....22 D3
Hotel Miramar
BMTH BH1 ....9 H6
Hotel Piccadilly
BMTH BH1 ....9 H6
Houghton Lodge & Garden
STOK SO20 ....285 L9

Houndmills Industrial Estate
BSTK RG21 ....65 G6
Hounsdown Business Park
TOTT SO40 ....158 F4
Hounsdown Secondary
School *TOTT* SO40 ....158 F4
Household Waste Disposal
Centre *AND* SP10 ....5 J3
Hughes Business Centre
CHCH/BSGR BH23 .....229 G1
Hulbert Junior School
WVILLE PO7 ....169 M2
Hurlands Business Centre
FNM GU9 ....77 K4
Hurstbourne Tarrant CE
J & I School *RAND* SP11 .250 G10
Hurst Castle
LYMN SO41 ....233 K8
The Hurst Community College
TADY RG26 ....249 P3
Hurst Leisure Centre
TADY RG26 ....249 P3
Hurtmore Golf Club
GODL GU7 ....261 R9
Hyde Primary School
FBDG SP6 ....197 M7
Hythe Medical Centre
FAWY SO45 ....176 F6
Hythe Primary School
FAWY SO45 ....177 G4
Iford Bridge Golf Club
CHCH/BSGR BH23 .....215 K8
IMAX Cinema
BMTH BH1 ....8 F7
Indoor Bowls Centre
HAV PO9 ....16 E2
Indoor Tennis Centre
BSTK RG21 ....7 H8
PSEA PO1 ....20 E4
Inkpen Primary School
HUNG RG17 ....30 D7
Innkeeper's Lodge
FLEETN GU51 ....60 L4
FRIM GU16 ....51 G5
HAV PO9 ....157 H8
NEND PO2 ....184 F4
Intec Business Park
CHIN RG24 ....54 A8
Irish Centre
BSTK RG21 ....6 E7
Isle of Wight Car Ferry
Terminal *PSEA* PO1 ....20 B5
Itchen Abbas CP School
RWIN SO21 ....290 B10
Itchen College
ITCH SO19 ....148 A7
Itchen Valley Brewery
NARL SO24 ....291 L12
Itchen Valley Country Park
HEND SO30 ....140 C7
Jameson House
CHIN RG24 ....54 B7
Jane Austen's House
ALTN GU34 ....106 D8
WINC SO23 ....25 G7
Jellicoe Theatre
PSTN BH14 ....223 M3
The Jigsaw School
FARN GU14 ....61 L5
JML Trading Estate
WSHM SO15 ....22 C2
John Arlott Pavilion
BSTK RG21 ....7 H7
The John Hanson Secondary
School *AND* SP10 ....4 A6
John Hunt of Everest School
CHIN RG24 ....65 L3
John Neame Swimming Pool
PSTN BH14 ....224 B4
John Pounds Community
Centre *PSEA* PO1 ......20 D2
John Rankin Infant School
NWBY RG14 ....33 K4
John Rankin Junior School
NWBY RG14 ....33 K4
Jubilee Business Centre
WVILLE PO7 ....155 K8
Kanes Hill Primary School
ITCH SO19 ....148 E6
Keble Memorial Primary
School *RWIN* SO21 ....133 H2
Kempshott Infant School
KBH RG22 ....92 C4
Kempshott Junior School
KBH RG22 ....92 C4
Kemps Quay Industrial Park
WEND SO18 ....161 K1
Kemp Welch Leisure Centre
BKME/WDN BH12 ....212 D8
Kendall Court Business Park
CBLY GU15 ....50 B4
Kennet Leisure Centre
STHA RG19 ....35 L1
Kennet School
STHA RG19 ....35 L1
Kenwood Business Park
HAV PO9 ....17 J1
The Kerridge Industrial Estate
ALTN GU34 ....107 G4
Kimpton CE J & I School
RAND SP11 ....267 R7
King Alfreds Statue
WINC SO23 ....25 J6
King Edward VI School
WSHM SO15 ....146 E8
Kingfisher Court Industrial
Estate *NWBY* RG14 ....19 L4
King Richard Secondary
School *CHAM* PO6 ....167 M8
The Kings Centre
ALDT GU11 ....2 F2
Kingsclere CE Primary School
KSCL RG20 ....248 D10
Kingsclere Health Centre
KSCL RG20 ....248 C10
Kingsclere Park
KSCL RG20 ....248 C9
Kings Copse Primary School
HEND SO30 ....149 J7
Kings Court School
HORN PO8 ....321 J11
Kings Furlong Infant School
BSTK RG21 ....6 A8
Kings Furlong Junior School
BSTK RG21 ....6 A8
Kingsgrove Industrial Estate
FARN GU14 ....61 G5
Kings High School
NBNE BH10 ....213 J5
Kings International College
CBLY GU15 ....50 E6
Kingsland Centre
STHA RG19 ....35 K1
Kingsland Industrial Estate
CHIN RG24 ....54 A7
Kingsland Market
SHAM SO14 ....23 H3
Kingsleigh Primary School
NBNE BH10 ....213 J5

Kingsley Business Park
BOR GU35 ....110 E3
Kingsmead Shopping Centre
FARN GU14 ....61 H5
King's Park Athletics Centre
LTDN BH7 ....226 F2
Kings Park Community
Hospital *LTDN* BH7 ....226 F2
Kings Park Primary School
BMTH BH7 ....226 F2
The Kings Primary School
HEND SO30 ....148 D1
Kings Road Industrial Estate
HASM GU27 ....118 A6
The King's Royal Hussars
Regimental Museum
WINC SO23 ....24 E5
Kings School
BSTK RG21 ....6 C8
FUFL SO22 ....122 B6
The Kings School Senior
ELGH SO50 ....141 H4
Kings Somborne CE J & I
School *STOK* SO20 ....299 P2
Kings Theatre *SSEA* PO5 ..21 K7
Kingston Cemetery
PSEA PO1 ....192 F1
Kingston Great Common
National Nature Reserve
RGWD BH24 ....348 C2
Kingston Lacy House,
Garden & Park (NT)
WIMB BH21 ....206 B1
Kingstons Industrial Estate
ASHV GU12 ....73 L6
Kingsworthy Primary School
WINC SO23 ....289 J10
Kin Hon Clinic
SSEA PO5 ....20 F4
Kinson Cemetery
BWD BH11 ....213 H4
Kinson Pottery Industrial
Estate *PSTN* BH14 ....224 A2
Kinson Primary School
BWD BH11 ....213 H3
Kinson Road Medical Centre
NBNE BH10 ....213 J2
Kinson Swimming Pool
BWD BH11 ....213 H4
Kintbury St Marys CE Primary
School *HUNG* RG17 .....31 H2
Knighton Heath Golf Club
WIMB BH21 ....212 C5
Knighton Heath Industrial
Estate *BWD* BH11 ....212 E5
Knights Enham Junior School
AND SP10 ....96 C1
Knightwood Lodge
LYND SO43 ....345 M2
Knightwood Primary School
CHFD SO53 ....130 F1
Knoll Gardens & Nursery
WIMB BH21 ....208 F3
Knowl Hill School
CHOB/PIR GU24 ....63 L3
Ladle Hill (Unfinished Hill Fort)
WHCH RG28 ....253 K2
Lainston House Hotel
RWIN SO21 ....287 Q12
Lake Road Health Centre
PSEA PO1 ....192 G2
Lakeside Business Park
SHST GU47 ....49 J1
Lakeside Country Club
FRIM GU16 ....62 A2
Lakeside International Hotel
FRIM GU16 ....62 A2
Lakeside Primary School
FRIM GU16 ....51 H7
Lambs Farm Business Park
THLE RG7 ....238 A8
Lambs Lane Primary School
THLE RG7 ....238 A8
Landford CE Primary School
RSAL SP5 ....334 B4
Landport Community Centre
PSEA PO1 ....21 J1
Land Registry
PSEA PO1 ....20 F3
Langdown Infant School
FAWY SO45 ....177 H6
Langdown Junior School
FAWY SO45 ....177 H5
Langrish House Hotel
PSF GU32 ....314 C9
Langrish Primary School
PSF GU32 ....315 L5
Langside School
BKME/WDN BH12 ....213 C8
Langstone Infant School
HSEA PO3 ....193 G2
Langstone Junior School
HSEA PO3 ....193 G1
Langtry Manor Lovenest
of a King Hotel *BMTH* BH1 ..9 M4
Lankhills School
WINC SO23 ....24 F2
Lasham Airfield
ALTN GU34 ....279 P1
Laverstoke Mill (Engineering
Works) *WHCH* RG28 ....88 E6
Leckford Golf Club
STOK SO20 ....285 R2
Lee on Solent Health Centre
LSOL/BMARY PO13 ....189 L6
Lee-on-the-Solent Golf Club
LSOL/BMARY PO13 ....182 A8
Lee-on-the-Solent Infant
School *LSOL/BMARY* PO13 .189 M7
Lee-on-the-Solent Junior
School *LSOL/BMARY* PO13 .189 M7
Leesland CE Infant School
GPORT PO12 ....14 E4
Leesland CE Junior School
GPORT PO12 ....14 E4
Leigh House Hospital
CHFD SO53 ....133 H8
Lepe Country Park
FAWY SO45 ....235 K2
Le Poussin at Parkhill Hotel
LYND SO43 ....345 N5
Lido Sports Club
WINC SO23 ....25 G3
Lifeboat Museum
PLE BH15 ....223 J7
The Lighthouse
PLE BH15 ....223 K5
Lilliput CE First School
PSTN BH14 ....224 C8
Limington House School
KBH RG22 ....92 F1
Liners Industrial Estate
WSHM SO15 ....160 C2
Linsford Business Park
FRIM GU16 ....61 M5
Linwood School
TWDS BH3 ....226 A1
Lion & Lamb Yard Shopping
Centre *FNM* GU9 ......12 E2

Liphook CE Junior School *LIPH* GU30 ....116 A4
Liphook Infant School *LIPH* GU30 ....116 A4
Liss Business Centre *LISS* GU33 ....308 E7
Liss J & I School *LISS* GU33 ....308 G9
Littledown Leisure Centre *LTDN* BH7 ....215 G8
Littlegreen School *RCCH* PO18 ....323 J8
Local Education Office *HAV* PO9 ....17 G1
Lockerley CE J & I School *ROMY* SO51 ....298 C11
Locks Heath J & I School *HLER* SO31 ....180 A3
Lockyers Middle School *WIMB* SO21 ....206 D8
Loddon Business Centre *CHIN* RG24 ....7 M3
Loddon Centre *CHIN* RG24 ....54 A8
The Loddon School *HTWY* RG27 ....54 F3
London Road Industrial Estate *NWBY* RG14 ....19 G3
Longbridge Industrial Park *SHAM* SO14 ....23 L6
The Long Curtain (Old Town Defences) *PSEA* PO1 ....20 D7
Longdown Activity Farm *TOTT* SO40 ....158 D6
Longfleet CE Combined School *PLE* BH15 ....223 K4
Longford Castle *RSAL* SP5 ....327 J2
Long Meadow Industrial Estate *WIMB* BH21 ....205 H1
Longparish Primary School *RAND* SP11 ....98 D8
Longspee School *CFDH* BH17 ....223 K1
Long Sutton CE Primary School *ODIM* RG29 ....258 B5
Lordshill Health Centre *ROWN* SO16 ....145 M4
Lord Wandsworth College *ODIM* RG29 ....258 D6
Lord Wilson School *HLER* SO31 ....163 M8
Lower William Street Industrial Estate *SHAM* SO14 ....161 K2
Lucia Foster Welch College *SHAM* SO14 ....23 J6
Ludgershall Castle & Cross *RAND* SP11 ....265 L9
Ludgershall Castle Primary School *RAND* SP11 ....265 N10
Ludgershall Sports Club *RAND* SP11 ....265 L10
Ludlow Infant School *ITCH* SO19 ....161 L5
Ludlow Junior School *ITCH* SO19 ....161 L4
Ludshott Common (NT) *GSHT* GU26 ....114 E5
Lulworth Business Centre *TOTT* SO40 ....144 E6
Lydlynch Infant School *TOTT* SO40 ....158 E1
Lymington Barn Industrial Estate *ALTN* GU34 ....293 L5
Lymington Community Hospitals *LYMN* SO41 ....221 L4
Lymington Hospital *LYMN* SO41 ....221 K4
Lymington J & I School *LYMN* SO41 ....221 K4
Lymington RC Primary School *LYMN* SO41 ....221 M4
Lymington Recreation Centre *LYMN* SO41 ....221 J5
Lyndhurst Junior Foundation School *NEND* PO2 ....184 F7
Lyndhurst Park Hotel *LYND* SO43 ....345 L3
Lyndhurst School *CBLY* GU15 ....50 D3
Lyon Way Industrial Estate *FRIM* GU16 ....50 E7
Lysses House Hotel *FHAM/PORC* PO16 ....11 K4
Lythe Hill Hotel & Spa *HASM* GU27 ....119 H7
Lytton Lawn Touring Park *LYMN* SO41 ....232 E1
Magpies Sports Club *WIMB* BH21 ....201 J8
Mainline Business Centre *LISS* GU33 ....308 F8
Main Square Shopping Centre *CBLY* GU15 ....50 E2
The Malls Shopping Centre *BSTK* RG21 ....6 F4
Malmesbury Park CP School *CHAR* BH8 ....9 J1
Malvern Business Centre *ROWN* SO16 ....146 D6
Mannings Heath Retail Park *BKME/WDN* BH12 ....212 A8
Manor Farm Business Centre *RFNM* GU10 ....260 D3
Manor Farm Country Park *HLER* SO31 ....163 J1
Manor Field J & I School *KBH* RG22 ....93 G5
Manor Infant School *FAWY* SO45 ....354 E3
PSEA PO1 ....192 E1
Manor J & I School *FARN* GU14 ....60 F2
Manor Park Industrial Estate *ASHV* GU12 ....3 J4
Mansbridge Primary School *WEND* SO18 ....147 L4
Mansel Infant School *ROWN* SO16 ....145 J6
Mansel Junior School *ROWN* SO16 ....145 K6
Mansfield Business Park *ALTN* GU34 ....293 L4
Mansfield Hotel *WCLF* BH2 ....8 C8
Mansion House Hotel *PLE* BH15 ....223 H6
Maple Business Park *WIMB* BH21 ....208 F1
Maple Ridge School *BSTK* RG21 ....6 D1
Marchwood CE Infant School *TOTT* SO40 ....159 L8
Marchwood Industrial Park *TOTT* SO40 ....160 A5
Marchwood Junior School *TOTT* SO40 ....159 M7

Marchwood Priory Hospital *TOTT* SO40 ....176 A1
Market Quay *FHAM/PORC* PO16 ....11 H6
The Mark Way School *AND* SP10 ....5 M4
Marlands Shopping Centre *SHAM* SO14 ....22 F2
Marlborough County Infant School *ALDT* GU11 ....73 J1
Marnel J & I Schools *CHIN* RG24 ....65 L3
Marriott Meon Valley Hotel & Country Club *BPWT* SO32 ....151 K4
Marsham Court Hotel *BMTH* BH1 ....9 H7
Marsh Farm Business Centre *RFNM* GU10 ....70 F7
Marwell Hotel *RWIN* SO21 ....135 L5
Marwell Zoological Park *RWIN* SO21 ....135 M4
Marycourt School *GPORT* PO12 ....191 G7
Mary Hare Primary School *NWBY* RG14 ....34 E4
The Mary Hare School for the Deaf *NWBY* RG14 ....27 H1
Mary Rose Exhibition *PSEA* PO1 ....20 C5
Mary Rose Ship Hall *PSEA* PO1 ....20 B7
Mason Moore Primary School *ROWN* SO16 ....145 L8
Master Builders House Hotel *BROC* SO42 ....353 R11
Matbro Industrial Estate *RAND* SP11 ....272 H1
Mayfield Avenue Industrial Park *RAND* SP11 ....94 C2
Mayfield School *ALTN* GU34 ....107 H3
Mayfield Secondary School *NEND* PO2 ....184 E6
Mayflower Memorial *SHAM* SO14 ....22 F5
Mayflower Theatre *WSHM* SO15 ....21 D1
Mayhill Junior School *ODIM* RG29 ....69 G6
May's Bounty (Basingstoke & North Hants CC) *BSTK* RG21 ....6 E8
Maytree Nursery & Infant School *SHAM* SO14 ....161 H2
Mayville High School *SSEA* PO5 ....21 K9
Meadowlands Infant School *HORN* PO8 ....155 L3
Meadowlands Junior School *HORN* PO8 ....155 L3
The Meadow School *BOR* GU35 ....111 J8
The Meadows Hospital *HLER* SO31 ....163 M7
The Meadows (Superstores) *SHST* GU47 ....50 A3
Medina Primary School *CHAM* PO6 ....184 E4
Megabowl *BKME/WDN* BH12 ....212 B7
Mengham Infant School *HISD* PO11 ....195 G4
Mengham Junior School *HISD* PO11 ....195 G4
Menzies Anglo-Swiss Hotel *BMTH* BH1 ....9 J5
Menzies Carlton Hotel *BMTH* BH1 ....9 J7
Menzies East Cliff Court Hotel *BMTH* BH1 ....9 K6
Meoncross School *FHAM/STUB* PO14 ....181 K3
Meon Infant School *ENEY* PO4 ....193 H4
Meon Junior School *ENEY* PO4 ....193 H3
Meonstoke CE School *BPWT* SO32 ....312 E12
Meon Valley Police Station *BPWT* SO32 ....143 K4
Merdon Junior School *CHFD* SO53 ....139 K1
Meredith Infant School *NEND* PO2 ....184 E8
Meridian Shopping Centre *HAV* PO9 ....16 E4
Meridian TV Studios *SHAM* SO14 ....161 J2
Merley Court Touring Park *WIMB* BH21 ....207 H7
Merley First School *WIMB* BH21 ....207 K7
Merton J & I School *CHIN* RG24 ....65 J4
Micheldever Primary School *RWIN* SO21 ....275 N9
Middle Hill Health Clinic *ALDT* GU11 ....2 F1
Middle Park Medical Centre *HAV* PO9 ....170 C4
Middle Wallop Airfield *STOK* SO20 ....270 D10
Mid Hants Railway (Watercress Line) *ALTN* GU34 ....293 P4
NARL SO24 ....291 N11
NARL SO24 ....292 E10
Milestones Hampshire's Living History *KBH* RG22 ....65 G7
Milford CE Primary School *LYMN* SO41 ....232 E12
Military Cemetery *CHOB/PIR* GU24 ....63 M2
The Mill at Gordleton Hotel *LYMN* SO41 ....220 E3
Millbrook Clinic *ROWN* SO16 ....145 M8
Millbrook Community School *ROWN* SO16 ....145 L5
Millbrook Secondary School *ROWN* SO16 ....145 L5
Millbrook Trading Estate *WSHM* SO15 ....159 L1
Mill Chase Community School *BOR* GU35 ....113 H1
Mill House Business Centre *ITCH* SO19 ....161 L5
Mill House Hotel *THLE* RG7 ....238 D9
Mill Lane Industrial Estate *ALTN* GU34 ....107 H3
Mill Rythe J & I School *HISD* PO11 ....195 H2
Millstream Trading Estate *RGWD* BH24 ....203 J7
Milton Business Centre *NMIL/BTOS* BH25 ....218 E6
Miltoncross Secondary School *ENEY* PO4 ....193 G3

Milton Park J & I School *ENEY* PO4 ....193 H4
MLS College *BMTH* BH1 ....8 E5
MN War Memorial *SHAM* SO14 ....23 G5
Moniton Trading Estate *DEAN* RG23 ....64 D8
Monks Brook Industrial Park *CHFD* SO53 ....139 H3
Montacute Special School *CFDH* BH17 ....211 J6
Montagu Arms Hotel *BROC* SO42 ....353 M7
The Montague Hotel *WCLF* BH2 ....8 B7
Moordown Medical Centre *MOOR/WNTN* BH9 ....213 M5
Moorgreen Hospital SO30 ....148 F2
Moorhill House Hotel *RCWD* BH24 ....349 J3
Moorings Way Infant School *ENEY* PO4 ....193 J2
Moorlands College *CHCH/BSGR* BH23 ....216 B2
Moorlands Infant School *WEND* SO18 ....148 A3
Moors Valley Country Park *RCWD* BH24 ....202 A5
Moors Valley Golf Course *RCWD* BH24 ....201 M7
Moortown Lodge Hotel *RCWD* BH24 ....203 J7
More House School *RFNM* GU10 ....79 G6
Morelands Primary School *HORN* PO8 ....169 L6
Morgans Vale & Woodfalls CE Primary School *RSAL* SP5 ....332 F1
Mortimer St John's Infant School *THLE* RG7 ....40 A3
Mortimer St Marys CE Junior School *THLE* RG7 ....40 A3
Mortimers Farm Industrial Estate *ROMY* SO51 ....335 Q10
Mottisfont Club House *ROWN* SO51 ....298 G10
Mountbatten Business Centre *WSHM* SO15 ....22 B1
Mountbatten Business Park *CHAM* PO6 ....185 J2
Mountbatten Centre Athletics Track *NEND* PO2 ....184 D5
Mountbatten School *ROMY* SO51 ....137 J3
The Mount Hospital *ELGH* SO50 ....134 D7
Mount Pleasant Industrial Estate *SHAM* SO14 ....161 H1
Mount Pleasant Junior School *SHAM* SO14 ....161 H1
Mount Pleasant Touring Park *CHCH/BSGR* BH23 ....346 H9
Moyles Court School *RCWD* BH24 ....199 L6
Mrs Blands Infant School *THLE* RG7 ....39 M2
Mudeford Infant School *CHCH/BSGR* BH23 ....228 F2
Mudeford Junior School *CHCH/BSGR* BH23 ....228 F2
Murrell Green Business Park *HTWY* RG27 ....57 G6
Muscliff Primary School *MOOR/WNTN* BH9 ....214 C4
Museum of Archaeology *SHAM* SO14 ....23 G7
Museum of Army Flying *STOK* SO20 ....270 C9
Mylenroad Business Centre *AND* SP10 ....4 D4
Mytchett Primary School *FRIM* GU16 ....61 M4
Naked Man *BROC* SO42 ....349 R4
National Museum of Artillery *WHAM* PO17 ....167 H5
Natural History Museum & Butterfly House *ENEY* PO4 ....192 F7
Nelson Industrial Park *HEND* SO30 ....149 H3
Nest Business Park *HAV* PO9 ....171 H4
Nethercliffe Preparatory School *FUFL* SO22 ....24 D3
Netley Abbey *HLER* SO31 ....162 A6
Netley Abbey J & I School *HLER* SO31 ....162 B5
Netley Court School *HLER* SO31 ....162 A7
Netley Marsh CE Infant School *TOTT* SO40 ....158 A1
Neville Lovett Community School *FHAM/STUB* PO14 ....10 C8
Newbridge Junior School *NEND* PO2 ....192 F1
Newbury Business Park *NWBY* RG14 ....19 J2
Newbury Bus Station *NWBY* RG14 ....18 E5
Newbury College *NWBY* RG14 ....34 A5
Newbury Cricket & Hockey Club *NWBY* RG14 ....18 C5
Newbury & Crookham Golf Club *STHA* RG19 ....34 E5
Newbury Racecourse *STHA* RG19 ....19 K6
Newbury Retail Park *NWBY* RG14 ....34 B5
Newbury RFC *NWBY* RG14 ....33 M6
New College Swimming Pool *WSHM* SO15 ....160 F1
New Durley Dean Hotel *WCLF* BH2 ....8 B8
New Fields Business Park *CFDH* BH17 ....211 K8
New Forest Golf Club *LYND* SO43 ....345 N4
New Forest Museum & Visitor Centre *LYND* SO43 ....345 L4
The New Forest Otter, Owl & Wildlife Park *TOTT* SO40 ....158 E8
New Greenham Park *STHA* RG19 ....34 F7
New Greenham Park Leisure Centre *STHA* RG19 ....35 G7
New Hall Hospital *RSAL* SP5 ....326 H3
New Inn *HTWY* RG27 ....240 D7
Newlands CP School *YTLY* GU46 ....48 E3
The New Medical Centre *CHCH/BSGR* BH23 ....348 C11
New Milton J & I School *NMIL/BTOS* BH25 ....219 G7

New Milton Recreation Centre *NMIL/BTOS* BH25 ....218 F6
New Milton Sports Club *NMIL/BTOS* BH25 ....219 J5
New Park Manor Hotel *BROC* SO42 ....345 K11
Newport Junior School *ASHV* GU12 ....3 L5
New Scotland Hill Primary School *SHST* GU47 ....43 M6
New Street FC *RAND* SP11 ....83 M7
New Theatre Royal *PSEA* PO1 ....20 F3
The Newton Health Clinic *SHAM* SO14 ....161 G2
Newton Tony CE Primary School *AMSY* SP4 ....268 B7
Newtown Business Park *BKME/WDN* BH12 ....224 B1
Newtown Soberton Infant School *WHAM* PO17 ....153 H2
New Westcliff Hotel *WCLF* BH2 ....8 B7
The Nightingale Primary School *ELGH* SO50 ....139 K7
Noadswood Comprehensive School *FAWY* SO45 ....176 E6
Nomansland & Hamptworth CE Primary School *RSAL* SP5 ....333 R8
Norfolk Lodge Hotel *CCLF* BH13 ....237 K1
Norman Court Preparatory School *RSAL* SP5 ....297 M2
Norman Gate School *AND* SP10 ....5 M4
Northam Business Centre *SHAM* SO14 ....161 J2
Northam Community Centre *SHAM* SO14 ....23 L1
North Baddesley Infant School *NBAD* SO52 ....138 B4
North Baddesley Junior School *NBAD* SO52 ....138 B4
Northbrook Industrial Estate *ROWN* SO51 ....146 C6
North Cemetery *CHAR* BH8 ....214 C7
Northcroft Leisure Centre *NWBY* RG14 ....18 D3
Northern County J & I School *FHAM/PORC* PO16 ....167 J7
Northern Parade Clinic *NEND* PO2 ....184 E4
Northern Parade J School *NEND* PO2 ....184 D5
North Farnborough County Infant School *FARN* GU14 ....61 K3
North Hampshire Hospital *CHIN* RG24 ....65 G4
North Hampshire Maternity Hospital *CHIN* RG24 ....64 F4
North Hants Golf Club *FLEETN* GU51 ....59 J4
North Lodge Industrial Park *LIPH* GU30 ....116 D8
Northtown Trading Estate *ASHV* GU12 ....73 L7
North Waltham Business Centre *OVTN* RG25 ....103 K2
North Waltham Primary School *OVTN* RG25 ....103 K3
Norwood Primary School *ELGH* SO50 ....140 A1
Novotel *WSHM* SO15 ....22 C3
Nuffield Centre University of Portsmouth *PSEA* PO1 ....20 C4
Nuffield Industrial Estate *CFDH* BH17 ....211 K7
Nuffield Theatre *PTSW* SO17 ....147 G5
Nursling CE Primary School *ROWN* SO16 ....145 K3
Nursling Industrial Estate *ROWN* SO16 ....145 H4
Oakdale Middle School *PLE* BH15 ....223 J3
Oakdene Forest Park *FERN* BH22 ....346 B5
Oak Farm Community School *FARN* GU14 ....61 G2
Oakfield Primary School *TOTT* SO40 ....144 E7
Oakhurst First School *FERN* BH22 ....205 H6
Oaklands Catholic School *WVILLE* PO7 ....169 M3
Oaklands Community School *ROWN* SO16 ....145 L3
Oaklands County J & I School *CWTH* RG45 ....43 M3
Oaklands Swimming Pool *ROWN* SO16 ....145 M3
Oakley CE Junior School *DEAN* RG23 ....91 J3
Oakley County Infant School *DEAN* RG23 ....91 J3
Oakley Shopping Centre *WIMB* BH21 ....207 L7
Oak Lodge School *FAWY* SO45 ....176 C5
Oakmeadians RFC *WCLF* BH2 ....8 D2
Oak Meadow Early Years & Family Centre *FHAM* PO15 ....181 J1
Oakmead School College *BWD* BH11 ....212 F4
Oak Meadow Primary School *FHAM* PO15 ....181 J1
Oak Park Golf Club *RFNM* GU10 ....259 Q2
Oakridge West Community Centre *BSTK* RG21 ....65 J5
Oakwood Infant School *HTWY* RG27 ....57 M3
Oakwood Junior School *ROWN* SO16 ....146 B3
Oatlands House Health Clinic *ROWN* SO16 ....146 C6
Oceanarium *WCLF* BH2 ....8 F8
Ocean View Hotel *BMTH* BH1 ....9 L6
Odeon Cinema *BMTH* BH1 ....8 F1
CHAM PO6 ....184 F1
NEND PO2 ....184 D7
Odeon Leisure World *WSHM* SO15 ....22 D4
Odiham Airfield *ODIM* RG29 ....258 B1
Odiham Castle *ODIM* RG29 ....68 D4
Odiham Cottage Hospital *ODIM* RG29 ....69 G6
The Odiham Health Centre *ODIM* RG29 ....68 F5

Odstock Primary School *RSAL* SP5 ....326 D3
O Jays Industrial Park *HSEA* PO3 ....185 G6
Old Basing Infant School *CHIN* RG24 ....66 D2
Old Hambledonians CC *HORN* PO8 ....320 C3
Old House Hotel *WHAM* PO17 ....152 A5
Old Thorns Hotel, Golf & Country Club *LIPH* GU30 ....309 P1
Old Town First School *PLE* BH15 ....223 J4
Old Turnpike Business Park *FHAM/PORC* PO16 ....11 H3
Olivers Battery Primary School *FUFL* SO22 ....124 C1
The Omni Business Centre *ALTN* GU34 ....107 H5
Open Golf Centres *LTDN* BH7 ....215 J6
Orchard Infant School *FAWY* SO45 ....176 E6
Orchard Lea Infant School *FHAM* PO15 ....165 K8
Orchard Lea Junior School *FHAM* PO15 ....165 L8
Ordnance Survey Office *ROWN* SO16 ....145 M6
Oriel Business Park *ALTN* GU34 ....107 H4
Orion Business Centre *WEND* SO18 ....147 L3
Ormonde House Hotel *LYND* SO43 ....345 M3
The Osborn Clinic *FHAM/PORC* PO16 ....11 J5
Otterbourne CE Primary School *RWIN* SO21 ....134 B2
Our Lady & St Joseph Catholic Primary School *LYMN* SO41 ....221 G4
Our Ladys Preparatory School *CWTH* RG45 ....43 J3
Overton CE Primary School *OVTN* RG25 ....89 H3
Overton Community Centre *OVTN* RG25 ....89 J3
Owslebury CP School *RWIN* SO21 ....310 A4
Padnell Infant School *HORN* PO8 ....156 A5
Padnell Junior School *HORN* PO8 ....156 B5
Padworth College *THLE* RG7 ....38 E3
Palace House *BROC* SO42 ....353 M6
Palmers Road Industrial Estate *EMRTH* PO10 ....172 A5
Palmerston Business Park *FHAM/STUB* PO14 ....182 A1
Pamphill First School *WIMB* BH21 ....206 E2
Park Community School *HAV* PO9 ....170 C3
Park Crematorium *ASHV* GU12 ....260 B2
Park Farm Industrial Estate *FRIM* GU16 ....50 F2
Park Gate Business Centre *HLER* SO31 ....164 A6
Park Gate Primary School *HLER* SO31 ....164 B7
Park House Primary School *HAV* PO9 ....170 C3
Park House School *NWBY* RG14 ....33 L6
Parklands Business Park *WVILLE* PO7 ....154 F5
Parklands Hospital *CHIN* RG24 ....64 F3
Park Primary School *ALDT* GU11 ....3 J8
The Park School *CHAR* BH8 ....226 D2
Parkstone Cemetery *PSTN* BH14 ....224 B6
Parkstone Golf Club *PSTN* BH14 ....224 D6
Parkstone Grammar (Girls) School *CFDH* BH17 ....211 H7
Parkstone Health Centre *PSTN* BH14 ....224 C3
Park View Infant School *KBH* RG22 ....92 D2
Park View Junior School *KBH* RG22 ....92 D2
Parkway Retail Park *BMTH* BH1 ....9 K3
Parley First School *FERN* BH22 ....209 K5
Parley Golf Course *CHCH/BSGR* BH23 ....214 D1
Parley Sports Club *FERN* BH22 ....209 M7
Parsons Down Infant School *STHA* RG19 ....35 G1
Parsons Down Junior School *STHA* RG19 ....35 G1
Passfield Mill Business Park *LIPH* GU30 ....113 K3
Passford House Hotel *LYMN* SO41 ....351 L12
Paulsgrove Industrial Centre *CHAM* PO6 ....168 B8
Paulsgrove Primary School *CHAM* PO6 ....168 B8
Paultons Golf Centre *ROMY* SO51 ....335 Q10
Paultons Park *ROMY* SO51 ....335 P10
Pavilion Hotel *BMTH* BH1 ....9 H5
Pavilion Theatre *BMTH* BH1 ....8 F7
Peacock Trading Estate *ELGH* SO50 ....139 L4
Peel Common Infant School & Nursery *FHAM/STUB* PO14 ....182 A6
Peel Common Junior School *FHAM/STUB* PO14 ....182 A6
Pegham Industrial Park *FHAM* PO15 ....165 H6
Penhale Infant School *NEND* PO2 ....21 M2
Penn Hill Clinic *PSTN* BH14 ....224 E5
Pennington J & I School *LYMN* SO41 ....221 J5
Perins Community School *NARL* SO24 ....291 L11
Petersfield Business Park *PSF* GU32 ....120 B6
Petersfield Community Hospital *PSF* GU32 ....120 C6
Petersfield Golf Club *PSF* GU32 ....121 G1

Petersfield Golf Club (old course) EPSF GU31 120 E8
Petersfield Infant School PSF GU32 120 D6
Petersfield RFC EPSF GU31 121 H5
The Petersfield School PSF GU32 120 C7
Petersfield Swimming Pool EPSF GU31 120 E6
Petersfield Town FC EPSF GU31 120 E5
Petersgate Infant School HORN PO8 321 L8
Peter Symonds College FUFL SO22 24 E2
Philip Green Memorial School WIMB BH21 336 G1
The Phoenix Cinema ROWN SO16 146 F5
Phoenix Industrial Park ELGH SO50 140 C2
Pierreponte School RFNM GU10 79 J7
Pier Theatre WCLF BH2 8 F9
The Pilgrims School WINC SO23 25 H7
The Pilgrims Way Primary School FNM GU9 12 E7
Pine Ridge Golf Club FRIM GU16 51 M6
Pinewood Infant School FARN GU14 60 D1
Pipers Industrial Estate STHA RG19 35 M3
Pipers Wood Industrial Park WVILLE PO7 155 J8
Pirbright Camp CHOB/PIR GU24 63 H1
Pirbright Primary School CHOB/PIR GU24 63 L3
Pitmore School CHFD SO53 133 M8
The Plague Monument FUFL SO22 24 E5
Planet Ice-Gosport LSOL/BMARY PO13 182 E7
Plaza Theatre ROMY SO51 136 F1
Pokesdown Primary School BOSC BH5 227 H3
Polygon School WSHM SO15 160 E2
Polymonds Tower SHAM SO14 23 G4
The Pompey Centre (Retail Park) ENEY PO4 192 F3
Poole County Court Offices PLE BH15 223 M5
Poole Crematorium WIMB BH21 211 K3
Poole Freight Ferry Terminal PLE BH15 223 H8
Poole Grammar (Boys) School CFDH BH17 211 K6
Poole High School PLE BH15 223 J4
Poole Hospital NHS Trust PLE BH15 223 K5
Poole Passenger Ferry Terminal PLE BH15 223 H8
Poole Pottery PLE BH15 223 J7
Poole Stadium (Speedway Track & Football Stadium) PLE BH15 223 J4
Popham Airfield RWIN SO21 102 A7
Popham Beacons RWIN SO21 101 L8
Popley Fields Community Centre CHIN RG24 65 L2
Portcastrian RFC SBNE BH6 227 L2
Portchester Boys School LTDN BH7 227 G1
Portchester Castle FHAM/PORC PO16 183 L2
Portchester Community School FHAM/PORC PO16 183 J1
Portchester Crematorium FHAM/PORC PO16 167 H7
Portchester Health Centre FHAM/PORC PO16 167 K8
Portesbery School CBLY GU15 50 F2
Portfield School CHCH/BSGR BH23 346 B12
Portsdown Primary School CHAM PO6 168 F8
Portsea Clinic PSEA PO1 20 D3
Portsmouth College HSEA PO3 193 J1
Portsmouth Continental Ferry Port NEND PO2 184 C8
Portsmouth County Court PSEA PO1 21 G3
Portsmouth Crown Court PSEA PO1 21 G3
Portsmouth Deaf Association Centre PSEA PO1 21 K2
Portsmouth FC (Fratton Park) ENEY PO4 192 F3
Portsmouth Golf Club WVILLE PO7 169 L6
Portsmouth Grammar Junior School PSEA PO1 20 E5
Portsmouth Grammar School PSEA PO1 20 D5
Portsmouth High School SSEA PO5 21 G8
Portsmouth High School GDST SSEA PO5 20 F7
Portsmouth Marriott Hotel CHAM PO6 184 C1
Portsmouth Natural Health Centre SSEA PO5 20 F5
Portsmouth RFC HSEA PO3 185 G4
Portswood Primary School PTSW SO17 147 J6
Portuguese Fireplace LYND SO43 344 D4
Portway Industrial Estate AND SP10 95 L3
Portway Infant School AND SP10 95 L4
Portway Junior School AND SP10 95 L4
Potley Hill County Primary School BLKW GU17 49 J3
Potters Gate CE Primary School FNM GU9 12 D3
The Potters Heron Hotel ROMY SO51 132 E5
Potters Industrial Park FLEETS GU52 71 L3
Potters International Hotel ALDT GU11 72 F4
Poulner Junior School RGWD BH24 203 L2
Premier Business Centre FHAM/STUB PO14 182 B3
Premier Business Park FHAM/STUB PO14 10 A7
Premier Inn LTDN BH7 215 G7
Premier Lodge CFDH BH17 211 H8
OVTN RG25 103 H5
THLE RG7 36 D2
Preston Candover CE Primary School OVTN RG25 277 R4
Preston House OVTN RG25 277 R3
Preymead Industrial Estate FNM GU9 3 G9
Pride of the Valley Hotel RFNM GU10 262 H9
Priestlands School LYMN SO41 221 K6
Priest's House Museum & Garden WIMB BH21 207 J4
Prince Consort's Library ALDT GU11 72 F5
Princes Hall ALDT GU11 2 E2
Princes Mead School RWIN SO21 289 L10
Princes Mead Shopping Centre FARN GU14 61 H5
Princess Anne Hospital ROWN SO16 146 B5
Princess Marina College EWKG RG40 239 M7
Prior Heath Infant School CBLY GU15 51 J3
Priors Field School GODL GU7 261 R7
The Priory CE VA Primary School CHCH/BSGR BH23 228 B2
Priory College SSEA PO5 21 L4
Priory Industrial Park CHCH/BSGR BH23 229 H1
The Priory Primary School TADY RG26 52 D3
Prospect Business Centre NARL SO24 291 L12
Purbeck Pottery PLE BH15 223 H7
Purbrook CC WVILLE PO7 169 H4
Purbrook J & I School WVILLE PO7 169 K3
Purbrook Park School WVILLE PO7 169 K5
Puttenham CE Infant School RGUW GU3 261 M4
Puttenham Golf Club RGUW GU3 261 P4
The Pyramids Leisure Centre SSEA PO5 192 D7
The Quadrant Centre BMTH BH1 8 E6
Quality Hotel AND SP10 5 M7
BMTH BH1 9 H6
Quarley Hill RAND SP11 269 L3
Quayside Education Centre GPORT PO12 15 G1
Queen Alexandra Hospital CHAM PO6 168 F7
Queen Elizabeth Country Park EPSF GU31 321 Q1
Queen Elizabeths Leisure Centre WIMB BH21 206 F2
Queen Elizabeths School WIMB BH21 206 F2
Queen Marys College BSTK RG21 6 F9
Queen's Hotel BMTH BH1 9 J6
SSEA PO5 21 G8
Queens Inclosure Primary School WVILLE PO7 156 A7
Queen's Park Golf Club CHAR BH8 226 D1
Queens Park Infant School CHAR BH8 214 C7
Queens Park Junior School CHAR BH8 214 B7
Raceview Business Centre NWBY RG14 19 H5
Rachel Madocks School HORN PO8 155 L4
Railway Triangle Industrial Estate CHAM PO6 185 H2
Rake Business Park LISS GU33 309 L8
Rake CE First School LISS GU33 309 M7
Ranvilles Infant School FHAM/STUB PO14 181 J4
Ranvilles Junior School FHAM/STUB PO14 181 J4
Red Barn County Primary School FHAM/PORC PO16 167 H8
Redbridge Community School ROWN SO16 145 J8
Redbridge Primary School ROWN SO16 145 K8
Redfields Business Park FLEETS GU52 71 G6
Red Funnel Ferry Terminal SHAM SO14 22 E7
Red House Museum & Gardens CHCH/BSGR BH23 228 B3
Redlands Primary School FHAM/PORC PO16 10 F9
Red Lion Hotel BSTK RG21 6 F5
Red Lodge School ROWN SO16 146 E4
Redlynch CE Primary School RSAL SP5 332 H3
Red Shoot Brewery RGWD BH24 342 D1
Redwood Park Secondary School CHAM PO6 185 H2
Regency Park Hotel NTHA RG18 28 D6
The Regent Centre CHCH/BSGR BH23 228 B2
Regents Park Girls School ROWN SO16 146 A8
REME Museum EWKG RG40 239 N8
Rex Industrial Estate CHFD SO53 139 J3
Rhinefield House Hotel BROC SO42 344 D12
Richmond Court Business Centre CHAR BH8 226 B2
Riders J & I School HAV PO9 170 D3
Ridge House Pre-Preparatory School NTHA RG18 28 F4
Ridgemede Junior School BPWT SO32 143 K4
The Ridgeway Centre KBH RG22 92 D1
The Ridgeway Community School FNM GU9 13 H9
Ridgeway House School ITCH SO19 161 L3
Ringwood Brewery RGWD BH24 203 J6
Ringwood CE Infant School RGWD BH24 203 J5
Ringwood Junior School RGWD BH24 203 J6
Ringwood Recreation Centre RGWD BH24 203 J5
Ringwood Road Retail Park BWD BH11 212 E5
Ringwood Secondary School RGWD BH24 203 J5
Ringwood Trading Estate RGWD BH24 203 J6
Rivermead Industrial Estate STHA RG19 35 M3
Riverpark Industrial Estate NWBY RG14 19 J3
River Park Leisure Centre WINC SO23 25 H3
Riverside Business Park LYMN SO41 221 M4
Riverside Park HLER SO31 163 G7
Riverside Park Industrial Estate FNM GU9 13 J2
Riverside School WVILLE PO7 169 M5
Riverwey Industrial Park ALTN GU34 107 H4
The Riviera Hotel WBNE BH4 225 J7
RNLI Headquarters PLE BH15 223 H6
Robert Mays School ODIM RG29 68 E5
Robert Sandilands Primary School NWBY RG14 18 B1
Rockbourne Roman Villa FBDG SP6 330 F9
Rockley Park PLE BH15 222 C5
Rockley Viaduct PLE BH15 222 A5
Rogate CE Primary School EPSF GU31 317 M4
Romans Business Park FNM GU9 13 J1
Romans Country House Hotel THLE RG7 45 H4
Roman Way Primary School AND SP10 84 D8
Romsey Abbey CE (A) Primary School ROMY SO51 136 D1
Romsey CC ROMY SO51 136 F2
Romsey Golf Club ROWN SO16 145 J1
Romsey Hospital ROMY SO51 137 G1
Romsey Industrial Estate ROMY SO51 130 E7
Romsey Infant School ROMY SO51 136 F1
Romsey Junior School ROMY SO51 131 G8
Romsey RFC ROMY SO51 136 F2
The Romsey School ROMY SO51 130 E8
Romsey Sports Centre ROMY SO51 136 F2
Romsey Town FC ROMY SO51 136 F2
Rookesbury Park School WHAM PO17 152 D4
Rookwood School AND SP10 4 D6
Rosemary Medical Centre BKME/WDN BH12 224 B1
Rosewood School ROWN SO16 146 C4
Rossmore Community College BKME/WDN BH12 212 D8
Round Tower PSEA PO1 20 B6
Rowland's Castle Golf Club HAV PO9 157 H6
Rowledge CE (Controlled) Primary School RFNM GU10 109 K1
Rowner Health Centre LSOL/BMARY PO13 182 C8
Rowner Infant School LSOL/BMARY PO13 182 D7
Rowner Junior School LSOL/BMARY PO13 182 D7
Rowner Swimming Centre LSOL/BMARY PO13 190 C2
Rownhams House Industrial Estate ROWN SO16 145 L2
Rownhams St Johns Primary School ROWN SO16 145 L2
Royal Army Medical Corps ALDT GU11 73 K4
Royal Beach Hotel ENEY PO4 192 E7
Royal Bournemouth Hospital LTDN BH7 215 H7
Royal Exeter Hotel BMTH BH1 8 E7
Royal Hampshire County Hospital FUFL SO22 24 B6
Royal Hampshire Regiment Museum & Memorial Garden WINC SO23 24 E6
Royal Hospital Haslar GPORT PO12 15 K8
Royal Logistic Corps Museum FRIM GU16 51 M8
The Royal Marines Museum ENEY PO4 193 H6
Royal Military Academy CBLY GU15 50 B2
Royal Naval Museum PSEA PO1 20 A2
Royal Navy Memorial SSEA PO5 20 F9
Royal Navy Submarine Museum & HMS Alliance GPORT PO12 15 L7
Royal Pier SHAM SO14 22 F7
The Royal School for Girls HASM GU27 118 A2
Royal South Hants Hospital SHAM SO14 161 G2
Royal Victoria Country Park HLER SO31 162 C8
Royal Winchester Golf Club FUFL SO22 122 B5
RSPB Reserve CHAM PO6 185 L4
Rucstall Community Centre BSTK RG21 7 K8
Rucstall J & I School BSTK RG21 7 J8
Rufus Stone LYND SO43 340 E7
Rural Life Centre RFNM GU10 79 K5
Rushcombe First School WIMB BH21 210 D2
Rushington Business Park TOTT SO40 158 E3
Russell Cotes Art Gallery & Museum BMTH BH1 9 G7
Russell Court Hotel BMTH BH1 9 G6
Russell Hicks & Temple ROMY SO51 136 E1
Ryeish Green School THLE RG7 238 C4
St Albans CE Primary School HAV PO9 171 G5
St Albans Medical Centre CHAR BH8 214 B8
St Aldhelms CE Combined School BKME/WDN BH12 225 G2
St Andrews CE Infant School FNM GU9 12 F4
St Annes Catholic Primary School KBH RG22 92 F1
St Annes Convent RC Girls School WSHM SO15 160 F2
St Annes School LSOL/BMARY PO13 189 L5
St Anns Hospital CCLF BH13 237 K2
St Anthonys Catholic Primary School FHAM/STUB PO14 180 D3
St Barbe Museum & Visitor Centre LYMN SO41 221 L4
St Bartholomews Primary School HASM GU27 118 C4
St Bartholomews School NWBY RG14 18 B7
St Bede CE Primary School WINC SO23 25 H4
St Bedes Catholic Primary School CHIN RG24 65 J3
St Bernadettes County Primary School FARN GU14 61 G3
St Catherines RC Primary School WIMB BH21 208 A2
St Catherines Road Junior School ELGH SO50 134 A7
St Christophers Hospital FHAM/PORC PO16 11 J2
St Clements CE Infant School BMTH BH1 226 D3
St Denys Primary School PTSW SO17 147 J7
St Edmunds Catholic Secondary School PSEA PO1 21 J2
St Edmunds School GSHT GU26 115 K5
St Edwards Comprehensive School PLE BH15 223 M1
St Edwards School ROMY SO51 128 A7
St Faiths CE Primary School WINC SO23 122 F7
St Finians RC Primary School NTHA RG18 28 F4
St Francis Primary School CHFD SO53 139 G3
St Francis School FHAM/STUB PO14 181 J3
St Gabriels School KSCL RG20 34 B6
St George RC Boys School ELGH SO50 147 K2
St Georges Business Centre PSEA PO1 20 D4
St Georges CE Primary School PSEA PO1 20 C2
St Georges Hospital LYMN SO41 232 C4
St Georges Industrial Estate CBLY GU15 50 D5
ENEY PO4 193 G3
St Georges University School of Medicine WINC SO23 25 G5
St Ives First School RGWD BH24 202 C7
St Ives School HASM GU27 118 E4
St James CE First School FBDG SP6 196 C6
St James CE Primary School EMRTH PO10 171 M6
HEND SO30 148 F2
MFD/CHID GU8 263 Q1
St James CE VA Primary School LTDN BH7 227 H2
St James Hospital ENEY PO4 193 H3
St Johns Almshouses WINC SO23 25 J6
St Johns Cathedral PSEA PO1 192 A2
St Johns Catholic Primary School PSEA PO1 21 J2
St Johns CE First School WIMB BH21 207 K4
St Johns CE Infant School RFNM GU10 262 E11
St Johns CE Primary School BSTK RG21 6 D9
GPORT PO12 191 H1
St Johns College SSEA PO5 21 J7
St John's Cross RAND SP11 271 J2
St Johns Infant School SHAM SO14 22 F6
St Johns Primary School Rowlands Castle HAV PO9 157 H8
St Johns RC Cathedral PSEA PO1 20 F2
St John the Baptist CE Primary School BPWT SO32 151 L2
FHAM/STUB PO14 180 C2
St John the Baptist RC J & I School AND SP10 4 B6
St John the Evangelist Infant School NWBY RG14 18 D9
St John VA CE Primary School MOOR/WNTN BH9 213 M7
St Joseph RC Primary School NWBY RG14 19 H1
St Josephs Catholic Primary School ALDT GU11 2 F7
St Josephs Primary School CHCH/BSGR BH23 217 G8
St Josephs RC Combined School BKME/WDN BH12 224 E1
St Judes CE (Controlled) Primary School PSEA PO1 20 E6
St Judes Primary School FHAM/STUB PO14 10 B6
St Jude's Youth Centre SSEA PO5 20 F6
St Katharines CE VA Primary School SBNE BH6 228 B4
St Lawrence CE (Controlled) Primary School ALTN GU34 106 E4
St Leonards Community Hospital RGWD BH24 205 L7
St Lukes CE Primary School LYMN SO41 350 F10
St Lukes CE Secondary School SSEA PO5 21 H3
St Lukes CE VA Primary School MOOR/WNTN BH9 213 M8
St Marks CE Infant School CHCH/BSGR BH23 217 M7
St Marks CE Junior School WSHM SO15 160 D1
St Marks CE Primary School FARN GU14 61 K8
St Marks CE VA Primary School NBNE BH10 213 J7
St Marks Primary School KBH RG22 92 D6
St Martins East Woodhay CE Primary School KSCL RG20 245 N5
St Martins School TWDS BH3 225 M2
St Mary Bourne Primary School RAND SP11 86 B2
St Mary Extra Cemetery ITCH SO19 162 B2
St Mary Magdalen Almshouses WINC SO23 25 J7
St Marys Catholic Combined School PLE BH15 223 L3
St Marys CE Aided Infant School RFNM GU10 262 D5
St Marys CE (Controlled) Primary School SHAM SO14 23 J2
St Marys CE First School FERN BH22 204 F5
MFD/CHID GU8 261 Q10
St Marys CE Junior School CHIN RG24 66 D2
NTHA RG18 28 F7
St Mary's Church Centre BSTK RG21 7 G5
St Marys College WEND SO18 147 L8
St Marys County Primary School GPORT PO12 14 C2
St Marys Hospital HSEA PO3 192 F3
St Michael & All Angels Infant School LYND SO43 345 K3
St Michaels Abbey FARN GU14 61 J3
St Michaels CE Infant School ALDT GU11 3 H7
St Michaels CE Junior School ALDT GU11 3 J7
St Michaels CE Middle School WIMB BH21 207 L1
St Michaels CE Primary School SHST GU47 43 G8
St Michaels CE VC Primary School WCLF BH2 8 B6
St Michael's Hospice CHIN RG24 65 G3
St Michaels School KSCL RG20 246 H6
St Monica Infant School ITCH SO19 162 A1
St Monica Junior School ITCH SO19 162 A1
St Neots School HTWY RG27 241 M4
St Nicholas School FLEETS GU52 71 G6
St Nicolas CE Junior School NWBY RG14 18 D6
St Omer Barracks ALDT GU11 73 K4
St Patricks Catholic Primary School FARN GU14 61 K4
ITCH SO19 161 L5
St Pauls Catholic VA Primary School CHAM PO6 168 B8
St Pauls CE Infant School RFNM GU10 260 E1
St Peters Catholic Primary School WVILLE PO7 169 M3
St Peters CE (Aided) Primary School FNM GU9 78 D1
St Peters CE Junior School FARN GU14 61 J4
YTLY GU46 48 F2
St Peter's Church BMTH BH1 8 F6
St Peters CE Primary School RAND SP11 82 D5
St Peters RC Primary School FUFL SO22 122 B7
St Peters School LTDN BH7 215 H8
SBNE BH6 227 M4
St Polycarps Catholic Primary School FNM GU9 13 J5
St Swithuns RC (Aided) Primary School SSEA PO5 21 K9
St Swithuns School RWIN SO21 123 K4
St Swithun upon Kingsgate WINC SO23 25 G7
St Swithun Wells Primary School CHFD SO53 139 K3
St Thomas Clinic LYMN SO41 221 L5
St Thomas Infant School KSCL RG20 246 A4
St Thomas Mores RC Primary School HAV PO9 16 A1
St Vincent College GPORT PO12 14 F2
St Walburgas RC Primary School MOOR/WNTN BH9 214 B6
St Winifreds School PTSW SO17 147 G7
Salesian College FARN GU14 61 K7
Salisbury District Hospital RSAL SP5 326 E1
Salterns Harbourside Hotel PSTN BH14 224 B8
Salterns School TOTT SO40 145 G8
Salto Gym Club AND SP10 4 B1
Sammy Miller Motorcycle Museum NMIL/BTOS BH25 218 E3

Sampson Business Park CBLY GU15 50 D5
The Samuel Cody School ALDT GU11 73 H1
Sandbanks Business Centre CCLF BH13 237 G5
Sandbanks Hotel CCLF BH13 237 K3
Sandford Springs Golf Club TADY RG26 248 G10
Sandhurst School SHST GU47 43 M7
Sandhurst Sports Club SHST GU47 49 L1
Sandy Balls Holiday Centre FBDG SP6 197 M2
Sarisbury CE Junior School HLER SO31 163 L7
Sarisbury Infant School HLER SO31 163 L8
Sarum Road Hospital FUFL SO22 122 C5
Saxon Centre CHCH/BSGR BH23 228 B1
Saxon Shore Infant School CHAM PO6 167 L8
Saxon Square Shopping Centre CHCH/BSGR BH23 228 B2
Saxon Wood School DEAN RG23 64 D4
Scantabout Primary School CHFD SO53 139 M1
Screen Cinema WINC SO23 24 F7
Seacrest Hotel SSEA PO5 192 D7
Sea Life Centre SSEA PO5 192 C7
Seaview Business Centre BKME/WDN BH12 224 B2
Sea Vixen Industrial Estate CHCH/BSGR BH23 229 G1
Selborne Primary School ALTN GU34 295 K8
Shakespeare Business Centre ELGH SO50 134 B8
Shakespeare Infant School ELGH SO50 134 A8
Shamba Holiday Park RGWD BH24 205 L7
Shamblehurst Primary School HEND SO30 149 J4
Sharps Copse Primary School HAV PO9 171 H3
Shawcross Industrial Park HSEA PO3 185 G3
Shaw Cum Donnington Primary School NWBY RG14 27 J6
Shawfield Primary School ASHV GU12 74 A5
Sheet County Primary School PSF GU32 120 F3
Shelling School RGWD BH24 202 E6
Shelley Museum BOSC BH5 226 F4
Shepherds Down Special School RWIN SO21 124 C6
Sherborne St John CE Primary School CHIN RG24 53 G8
Sherbourne House School CHFD SO53 133 K8
Sherfield on Loddon CC HTWY RG27 46 F8
Shinfield Infant School WHIT RG2 238 E4
Shinfield Players Theatre & Arts Centre WHIT RG2 238 D1
Shinfield St Marys CE Junior School WHIT RG2 238 F4
Shipton Bellinger Primary School NTID SP9 266 D8
Shirley Business Park WSHM SO15 160 D2
The Shirley Health Centre WSHM SO15 160 C1
Shirley J & I School WSHM SO15 146 C7
Shirley Swimming Pool WSHM SO15 160 C1
Shirley Warren Primary School ROWN SO16 146 A6
Sholing J & I School ITCH SO19 148 A7
Sholing Technology College ITCH SO19 161 M4
Shottermill Infant School HASM GU27 117 M1
Sidings Industrial Estate HLER SO31 162 D7
Silchester CE Primary School THLE RG7 45 H3
Silk Mill WHCH RG28 87 L8
Silver Business Park CHCH/BSGR BH23 228 F1
Simcoe Clinic WSHM SO15 160 E1
Sinclair Primary School ROWN SO16 146 A3
The Sir Harold Hillier Gardens & Arboretum ROMY SO51 131 K4
Siskin Infant & Nursery School LSOL/BMARY PO13 190 D2
The Sixth Form College FARN GU14 61 H1
Skate Park SSEA PO5 192 C7
Smannell & Enham CE Primary School RAND SP11 84 F5
Snelsmore Common Country Park KSCL RG20 26 F2
Solent Business Centre WSHM SO15 160 B2
Solent Hotel & Spa FHAM PO15 164 D5
Solent Industrial Centre WSHM SO15 160 C1
Solent Industrial Estate HEND SO30 149 H3
Solent Infant School CHAM PO6 169 K8
Solent Junior School CHAM PO6 169 K8
Solent Peoples Theatre ITCH SO19 162 C1
Somerford Business Park CHCH/BSGR BH23 229 G1
Somerford Primary & Community School CHCH/BSGR BH23 228 E1
Somers Park Primary School SSEA PO5 21 J3
Somers Town Health Centre SSEA PO5 21 J4
Sopley Primary School CHCH/BSGR BH23 347 Q11
Southampton Cemetery WSHM SO15 146 E8
Southampton City Art Gallery WSHM SO15 22 F1
Southampton City College SHAM SO14 23 J4
Southampton FC (St Mary's Stadium) SHAM SO14 23 K2
Southampton General Hospital ROWN SO16 146 B5
Southampton Institute & Millais Gallery SHAM SO14 23 G2
Southampton International Airport ELGH SO50 147 M2
Southampton Magistrates Court WSHM SO15 161 G2
Southampton Maritime Museum SHAM SO14 22 F6
Southampton Municipal Golf Course ROWN SO16 146 E2
Southampton & New Forest Magistrates Courts WSHM SO15 22 D1
Southampton Oceanography Centre SHAM SO14 23 J9
Southampton Park Hotel WSHM SO15 22 E1
Southampton Sports Centre ROWN SO16 146 D4
Southampton Sports Club ROWN SO16 145 J6
South Baddesley Primary School LYMN SO41 356 D6
Southbourne County J & I School EMRTH PO10 172 E6
Southbourne Surgery SBNE BH6 227 J3
South Downs College WVILLE PO7 170 A5
Southdowns Country Hotel EPSF GU31 317 Q8
Southern Electric Museum CHCH/BSGR BH23 228 B1
South Farnborough County Junior School FARN GU14 61 K6
South Farnborough Infant School FARN GU14 61 K8
South Farnham Middle School FNM GU9 13 L5
Southfields Industrial Estate RCCH PO18 173 M8
South Ham Medical Centre KBH RG22 92 E1
South Hampshire Industrial Park TOTT SO40 144 D5
South Hants Country Club WHAM PO17 153 G7
Southlands School LYMN SO41 221 L1
South Lawn Hotel LYMN SO41 232 E1
Southlea Golf Club & Great Salterns Public Club HSEA PO3 185 H7
South Parade Pier ENEY PO4 192 E7
Southsea Castle SSEA PO5 192 C7
Southsea Community Centre SSEA PO5 20 F5
Southsea Hovercraft Terminal PSEA PO1 20 D9
Southsea Infant School SSEA PO5 21 L8
South View J & I School BSTK RG21 65 L5
Southwick Park Naval Recreation Centre WHAM PO17 168 A3
South Winchester Golf Club FUFL SO22 122 A8
South Wonston Primary School RWIN SO21 288 D4
Southwood Golf Club FARN GU14 60 E6
Sovereign Business Centre PLE BH15 223 H2
Sovereign Business Park CFDH BH17 223 H2
Sparsholt College RWIN SO21 287 L12
Sparsholt CE Primary School RWIN SO21 301 P1
Spectrum Sports Club SBNE BH6 227 J4
Speenhamland Primary School NWBY RG14 18 D1
Spinnaker Tower PSEA PO1 20 B4
Spinners Garden & Nursery LYMN SO41 351 Q11
Springdale First School BDST BH18 210 E4
Springfield School CHAM PO6 185 J1
Springhill Catholic Primary School WSHM SO15 160 E2
Springlake Country Club ASHV GU12 73 L4
Spurcroft Primary School STHA RG19 35 K2
Spurlings Industrial Estate WHAM PO17 11 M1
Square Tower PSEA PO1 20 B7
SS Shieldhall SHAM SO14 23 K8
Staff College CBLY GU15 50 E2
Staffwise Business Centre CHAM PO6 184 F2
Stag Business Park RGWD BH24 203 J7
Stakes Hill Infant School WVILLE PO7 169 M2
Stamshaw Infant School NEND PO2 184 D6
Stamshaw Junior School NEND PO2 184 C5
Stamshaw & Tipner Leisure Centre NEND PO2 184 C6
Stanbridge Earls School ROMY SO51 130 B5
Stanley Casino SHAM SO14 23 J6
Stanley Green First School PLE BH15 223 J2
Stanley Green Industrial Estate PLE BH15 223 H3
Stanmore Primary School FUFL SO22 122 E7
Stanton Industrial Estate WSHM SO15 160 A1
Stanton Road Industrial Estate WSHM SO15 160 A1
Stanwell House Hotel LYMN SO41 221 M5
Stapehill Abbey, Crafts & Garden WIMB BH21 208 E3
Station Industrial Estate FLEETN GU51 59 K5
Station Road Industrial Estate STHA RG19 35 M3
Station Theatre HISD PO11 194 D4
Staunton Country Park HAV PO9 156 E6
Staunton Park Community School HAV PO9 171 H1
Steep School PSF GU32 120 C2
Ster Century Cinema BSTK RG21 6 F5
Sterling Industrial Estate NWBY RG14 19 G5
Sterte Industrial Estate PLE BH15 223 H4
Stockbridge J & I School STOK SO20 285 Q5
Stockcross Primary School KSCL RG20 26 A6
Stoke Park Infant School ELGH SO50 140 E1
Stoke Park Junior School ELGH SO50 140 E2
Stoneham Golf Club ELGH SO50 147 H2
Stone Lane Industrial Estate WIMB BH21 207 G2
Stourfield Junior School SBNE BH6 227 K2
Stratfield Saye THLE RG7 47 K1
String of Horses Country House Hotel LYMN SO41 350 E10
Strouden Park Medical Centre CHAR BH8 214 E7
The Stroud School ROMY SO51 131 L8
Stubbs Industrial Estate ALDT GU11 73 L3
Studland Industrial Estate KSCL RG20 32 B8
Suncliff Hotel BMTH BH1 9 K6
Sun Court Hotel WCLF BH2 8 C7
Sundridge School HORN PO9 155 M6
Sun Hill Infant School NARL SO24 291 M12
Sun Valley Business Park WINC SO23 25 M3
Superbowl BMTH BH1 9 G5
Super Bowl WSHM SO15 159 M1
Surrey Heath Museum CBLY GU15 50 F2
Surrey Institute of Art & Design FNM GU9 12 E3
Swallowfield Park THLE RG7 238 E8
Swan Centre ELGH SO50 140 B2
Swan Hotel NARL SO24 291 M10
Swanmore Business Park BPWT SO32 143 M7
Swanmore CE Primary School BPWT SO32 318 B6
Swanmore College of Technology BPWT SO32 318 A7
Swanwick Business Park HLER SO31 163 K5
Swanwick Lodge HLER SO31 163 M5
Sway Manor Restaurant & Hotel LYMN SO41 350 F11
Sway Park Industrial Estate LYMN SO41 350 E10
Swaythling Clinic PTSW SO17 147 J5
Swaythling Primary School PTSW SO17 147 H5
Sylvan First School BKME/WDN BH12 224 B2
Tadley Community Primary School TADY RG26 44 C6
Tadley Swimming Pool TADY RG26 44 C5
Talavera Primary School ALDT GU11 2 F1
Talbot Combined School BKME/WDN BH12 213 H8
Talbot Heath School WBNE BH4 225 J3
Talbot House Preparatory School MOOR/WNTN BH9 213 L8
Talbot Medical Centre BWD BH11 213 G7
Talisman Business Centre HLER SO31 164 B6
The Tanneries Industrial Estate HAV PO9 16 D5
Tanners Brook J & I School WSHM SO15 159 M1
Taro Leisure Centre EPSF GU31 121 H6
Tatchbury Manor House TOTT SO40 341 R3
Tatchbury Mount Hospital TOTT SO40 144 A6
Tauntons College WSHM SO15 146 E7
Tavistock Infant School FLEETN GU51 58 F8
Tempus Business Centre BSTK RG21 6 A1
Tennis Centre HASM GU27 117 K1
Terminus Industrial Estate PSEA PO1 21 J3
Testbourne Community School WHCH RG28 99 M1
Test Valley Business Centre ROWN SO16 145 H6
Test Valley Business Park NBAD SO52 138 A2
Test Valley Golf Club OVTN RG25 101 K4
Test Valley School STOK SO20 285 M5
Testwood School TOTT SO40 144 F7
Thatcham Bowling Club NTHA RG18 28 F8
Thatcham Business Village STHA RG19 36 B2
Thatcham Town FC STHA RG19 35 M3
Theatre Royal WINC SO23 25 G4
Thomson House FARN GU14 61 J3
Thornden School CHFD SO53 133 M8
Thornford Park Track STHA RG19 35 L6
Thorngate Hall GPORT PO12 14 C5
Thorngrove School KSCL RG20 246 A5
Thornhill Clinic ITCH SO19 148 D6
Thornhill Primary School ITCH SO19 148 C7
Thornycroft Industrial Estate BSTK RG21 65 G8
Three Legged Cross First School WIMB BH21 201 G7
Thruxton Aerodrome & Motor Racing Circuit RAND SP11 267 P8
Thruxton Industrial Estate RAND SP11 267 P9
Tidworth Garrison Golf Club NTID SP9 266 C4
Tidworth Leisure Centre NTID SP9 266 F2
Tidworth Military Cemetery NTID SP9 264 E10
Tiptoe Primary School LYMN SO41 350 B12
Titanic Memorial WSHM SO15 22 F1
Titchfield Abbey FHAM PO15 181 G2
Titchfield Primary School FHAM/STUB PO14 180 F3
Tivoli Theatre WIMB BH21 207 H3
Tomlinscote School FRIM GU16 51 H6
Totton College
TOTT SO40 144 D8
TOTT SO40 158 E3
Totton Recreation Centre TOTT SO40 144 C8
Tower Hill Primary School FARN GU14 60 F5
Tower Industrial Estate ELGH SO50 140 C2
Tower Park BKME/WDN BH12 212 B7
Towngate Shopping Centre PLE BH15 223 J6
Townhill Infant School WEND SO18 148 A2
Townhill Junior School WEND SO18 148 A2
Townhill Park Health Clinic WEND SO18 148 A2
Town Quay SHAM SO14 22 F8
Townsend Primary School CHAR BH8 215 G6
Town Walls PSEA PO1 20 B6
Toynbee Further Education Centre CHFD SO53 139 K3
Travel Inn
ALDT GU11 2 B2
CHCH/BSGR BH23 217 G8
CHCH/BSGR BH23 227 M1
ELGH SO50 139 L5
FARN GU14 60 E5
FERN BH22 209 M1
FHAM PO15 164 C8
HAV PO9 170 B7
KBH RG22 64 F7
PLE BH15 223 H4
ROMY SO51 137 M8
ROWN SO16 145 K3
SHAM SO14 23 H2
SHST GU47 49 M1
Travelodge
ALTN GU34 293 K6
ELGH SO50 134 B6
EMRTH PO10 171 L6
KBH RG22 92 F3
KSCL RG20 246 G4
LIPH GU30 113 M7
LYND SO43 340 C8
NEND PO2 184 D8
RGWD BH24 346 E1
RWIN SO21 273 P2
RWIN SO21 274 C8
WSHM SO15 160 F1
Treadgolds Museum PSEA PO1 20 D2
Treloar College ALTN GU34 107 H1
Treloar School ALTN GU34 281 P2
Treloar Trust ALTN GU34 281 N2
Trilakes Country Park SHST GU47 49 H1
Trinidad First School BKME/WDN BH12 212 C8
Trinity Business Centre TOTT SO40 144 E6
Trinity CE VA First School VWD BH31 337 M12
Trinity Church Hall BSTK RG21 6 E6
Trinity Industrial Estate
WIMB BH21 207 L5
WSHM SO15 159 M1
Trinity School & Performing Arts College NWBY RG14 27 K7
Trojans Sports Club ELGH SO50 147 J1
Trosnant Primary & Infant School HAV PO9 170 E5
Trouville Hotel WCLF BH2 8 E7
Tudor House Museum SHAM SO14 22 F5
Tudor Merchants Hall SHAM SO14 22 F5
Tunworth House OVTN RG25 66 F8
Turbary Retail Park BWD BH11 212 D5
Turlin Moor Community First School UPTN BH16 222 C4
Turlin Moor Middle School UPTN BH16 222 C4
Turnpike Business Park FHAM/PORC PO16 11 H3
Turnpike Industrial Estate NWBY RG14 19 L1
Tweseldown Infant School FLEETS GU52 71 K4
Twin Oaks Medical Centre CHCH/BSGR BH23 348 D12
Two Riversmeet Leisure Centre CHCH/BSGR BH23 228 C2
Twyford St Mary's CE Primary School RWIN SO21 124 F6
Twyford School RWIN SO21 125 G6
Twynham School CHCH/BSGR BH23 228 A2
Tylney Hall Hotel HTWY RG27 55 M5
Tylney Park Golf Club HTWY RG27 55 M4
Tyrrells Ford Country House Hotel CHCH/BSGR BH23 347 M8
UCI Cinema
BKME/WDN BH12 212 A7
CHAM PO6 184 B2
Uddens Trading Estate WIMB BH21 208 E2
UGC Cinema SHAM SO14 23 J7
Ullswater Hotel WCLF BH2 8 B8
Unicorn Trading Estate HASM GU27 118 B5
United Services RFC PSEA PO1 20 E3
United Services Sports Ground PSEA PO1 20 D4
University College Winchester
FUFL SO22 24 B6
FUFL SO22 24 C7
University of Portsmouth
ENEY PO4 192 F6
HISD PO11 193 M4
PSEA PO1 20 D2
PSEA PO1 21 K3
SSEA PO5 20 F4
SSEA PO5 20 F7
SSEA PO5 21 H5
University of Southampton
PTSW SO17 146 F7
PTSW SO17 147 G5
WSHM SO15 160 F1
University of Southampton (Winchester School of Art) WINC SO23 25 J4
Upham CE Primary School BPWT SO32 310 E11
Uplands CP School SHST GU47 43 K8
Uplands Primary School FHAM/PORC PO16 10 E2
Uplands School PSTN BH14 224 C5
Upton Country Park UPTN BH16 222 E2
Upton Grey House OVTN RG25 257 J2
Upton Health Centre UPTN BH16 222 C1
Upton Infant School UPTN BH16 222 A1
Upton Junior School UPTN BH16 222 A1
Velmead Community Centre FLEETS GU52 70 F4
Venture Industrial Park
HSEA PO3 185 G3
LSOL/BMARY PO13 182 D5
Vermont School ROWN SO16 146 E4
Vernham Dean School RAND SP11 243 Q11
Verwood CE First School VWD BH31 201 G3
Verwood Industrial Estate VWD BH31 201 J2
Verwood Leisure Centre VWD BH31 201 H2
Viables Craft Centre KBH RG22 93 J3
Viables Industrial Estate KBH RG22 93 H4
Vicarage Farm Business Park ELGH SO50 135 J7
Vicarage Lane Clinic HASM GU27 117 M2
Vickers Business Centre CHIN RG24 65 G4
Victoria Cottage Hospital EMRTH PO10 171 M8
Victoria Park Swimming Centre PSEA PO1 20 F2
The Victoria School CCLF BH13 224 F4
Victoria Stadium PSEA PO1 20 E4
Victory Business Centre PSEA PO1 21 L3
Victory Retail Park PSEA PO1 192 C1
Victory Trading Estate HSEA PO3 185 H6
Vigo J & I School AND SP10 5 M3
The Vine School BPWT SO32 150 D4
The Vineyard at Stockcross KSCL RG20 26 C7
Vinyard & Winepress WVILLE PO7 319 R8
Vistarama Balloon BMTH BH1 8 E6
VUE Cinema
KBH RG22 64 F7
PSEA PO1 20 C4
The Vyne Community School BSTK RG21 6 E1
The Vyne (NT) TADY RG26 53 K6
Waite End Primary School WVILLE PO7 169 L2
Walbury Hill HUNG RG17 244 E4
Walford Mill Medical Centre WIMB BH21 207 H2
Wallisdean Infant School FHAM/STUB PO14 10 C7
Wallisdean Junior School FHAM/STUB PO14 10 C7
Wallop J & I School STOK SO20 270 B12
Walsh CE First & Middle School ASHV GU12 73 M7
Waltham Business Park BPWT SO32 318 A8
Walworth Road Industrial Estate AND SP10 96 F2
Warblington Secondary School HAV PO9 17 J4
War Memorial Hospital
AND SP10 4 D2
LYMN SO41 232 E4
Warren Avenue Industrial Estate HSEA PO3 193 H3
Warren Park Primary School HAV PO9 170 D1
Warrior Business Centre CHAM PO6 185 L1
The Watchetts Junior School CBLY GU15 50 E6
Waterford Lodge Hotel CHCH/BSGR BH23 229 H2

Waterfront Business Park
FLEETN GU51 ....59 K6
Waterfront Museum
PLE BH15 ....223 H7
Waterloo Industrial Estate
HEND S030 ....149 H3
Waterloo School
WVILLE PO7 ....169 L1
Waterlooville Golf Club
HORN PO8 ....156 B6
Waterlooville Health Centre
WVILLE PO7 ....155 K6
Watermill Theatre
KSCL RG20 ....26 E5
The Waterside Health Centre
FAWY S045 ....177 G6
Waterside Medical Centre
GPORT PO12 ....15 K3
Waterside School
NEND PO2 ....184 B5
Watersplash Hotel
BROC S042 ....351 K3
The Wavell Technology
College *ALDT* GU11 ....73 H1
Waverley Abbey CE School
RFNM GU10 ....260 A11
Waverley Abbey House
FNM GU9 ....77 M8
WEA Clovelly Centre
SHAM S014 ....161 G2
Webb Peploe House Surgery
LYMN S041 ....221 L5
Weeke CP School
FUFL S022 ....24 A1
Wellington Arms Hotel
HTWY RG27 ....47 K3
Wellington Business Park
CWTH RG45 ....43 G4
Wellington College
CWTH RG45 ....43 J4
Wellington Country Park
THLE RG7 ....240 D2
Wellingtonia Avenue
(Arboretum)
CWTH RG45 ....42 E4
Wellington Industrial Estate
THLE RG7 ....238 A7
Wellington Monument
HTWY RG27 ....240 B4
Wellington Shopping Centre
ALDT GU11 ....2 F3
Wellington Sports Centre
CWTH RG45 ....43 H4
Wellington Sports Club
ELGH S050 ....147 K1
Wellow Golf Club
ROMY S051 ....335 Q4
Wellow Primary School
ROMY S051 ....335 K5
Wentworth College
BOSC BH5 ....227 G4
Wessex Complementary
Medical Centre *SBNE* BH6 ....227 L3
Wessex Gate Retail Park
CFDH BH17 ....223 H2
Wessex Hotel
WCLF BH2 ....8 C7
The Wessex Hotel
WINC S023 ....25 G6
Wessex Nuffield Hospital
CHFD S053 ....133 M7
Wessex Road Surgery
PSTN BH14 ....224 A5
Wessex Super Bowl
BKME/WDN BH12 ....224 F4
HAV PO9 ....170 B7

West Berkshire Community
Hospital *NTHA* RG18 ....28 A8
West Berkshire Museum
NWBY RG14 ....18 E4
Westbourne County Primary
School *EMRTH* PO10 ....172 B2
Westbourne Medical Centre
WBNE BH4 ....225 J4
West Canford Heath Medical
Centre *CFDH* BH17 ....211 K7
West End Infant School
ROWN S016 ....2 D4
Western Community Hospital
ROWN S016 ....146 A7
Western Downland CE
Primary School *FBDG* SP6 ....330 F7
Western Primary School
ENEY PO4 ....24 B4
Westfield Hall Hotel
ENEY PO4 ....192 F6
Westfield Industrial
GPORT PO12 ....14 B4
Westfield Industrial Estate
HORN PO8 ....156 D1
Westfield Junior School
CHAM S031 ....167 L8
Westfields Primary School
YTLY GU46 ....48 D3
The Westgate School
FUFL S022 ....24 B3
The Westgate *WINC* S023 ....24 E5
West Hill Park School
FHAM/STUB PO14 ....180 E4
West Howe Clinic
BWD BH11 ....213 G5
West Howe Industrial Estate
BWD BH11 ....212 E5
Westlands Medical Centre
FHAM/PORC PO16 ....183 J1
West March Business Centre
AND SP10 ....5 K1
West Moors Middle School
FERN BH22 ....205 H7
Weston Park Boys School
ITCH S019 ....162 B3
Weston Park Infant School
ITCH S019 ....162 A3
Weston Park Junior School
ITCH S019 ....162 A3
Weston Shore Infant School
ITCH S019 ....161 M8
Westover Hall Hotel
LYMN S041 ....232 C4
Westover Primary School
HSEA PO3 ....185 G8
West Point Business Park
AND SP10 ....4 C5
West Portway Industrial
Estate *RAND* SP11 ....95 K3
West Quay Retail Park
SHAM S015 ....22 D3
West Quay Shopping Centre
SHAM S014 ....22 E3
West Tytherley Primary
School *RSAL* SP5 ....297 N4
Westwood Business Park
TOTT S040 ....144 F6
Weybourne County Infant
School *FNM* GU9 ....77 J2
Weybrook Park Golf Club
CHIN RG24 ....64 F3
Weydon County Secondary
School *FNM* GU9 ....12 B9
Weydown Industrial Estate
HASM GU27 ....118 C5

Weyford County Junior
School *BOR* GU35 ....111 H8
Weyford Primary School
BOR GU35 ....111 H8
Weyhill Business Park
RAND SP11 ....94 D2
Whaddon Business Park
RSAL SP5 ....327 P3
Wherwell J & I School
RAND SP11 ....272 F5
Whitchurch CE Primary
School *WHCH* RG28 ....87 M8
Whitchurch Medical Centre
WHCH RG28 ....87 K7
Whitedown Special School
ALTN GU34 ....106 D6
Whitehall Hotel
BMTH BH1 ....8 B3
White Hart Industrial Estate
BLKW GU17 ....50 A3
Whitehill Cemetery
BOR GU35 ....113 J1
The White Horse Hotel
ROMY S051 ....136 E1
Whitelands Park Primary
School *NTHA* RG18 ....28 E7
Whiteley Primary School
FHAM PO15 ....164 C5
Whitewater CE Primary
School *HTWY* RG27 ....56 A3
Whitley Ridge Country
House Hotel *BROC* S042 ....351 P2
Wick I Industrial Estate
NMIL/BTOS BH25 ....218 E6
Wick 2 Industrial Estate
NMIL/BTOS BH25 ....218 E6
Wickham CE Primary School
WHAM PO17 ....152 A4
Wickham Park Golf Club
WHAM PO17 ....151 L8
Wicor County Primary School
FHAM/PORC PO16 ....167 G8
Wildern Clinic
HEND S030 ....149 J5
Wildern Secondary School
HEND S030 ....149 L4
Wildground Infant School
FAWY S045 ....176 F7
Wildground Junior School
FAWY S045 ....176 F7
William Cobbett Junior School
FNM GU9 ....77 J2
William Gilpin CE Primary
School *LYMN* S041 ....351 R11
Williams Industrial Park
NMIL/BTOS BH25 ....218 E6
Willink Leisure Centre
THLE RG7 ....39 M2
Willink School
THLE RG7 ....39 M2
Willis Museum
BSTK RG21 ....6 F6
Willment Marine & Business
Park *ITCH* S019 ....161 K3
Wilverley Post
BROC S042 ....349 Q3
Wimbledon Park Sports
Centre *SSEA* PO5 ....21 K9
Wimborne First School
WIMB BH21 ....207 H3
Wimborne Hospital
WIMB BH21 ....207 G3
Wimborne Industrial Estate
WIMB BH21 ....207 J3
Wimborne J & I School
ENEY PO4 ....193 G4

Wimborne Market
WIMB BH21 ....207 K4
Wimborne Minster
WIMB BH21 ....207 H4
Wimborne RFC
WIMB BH21 ....207 L4
Wimborne St Giles CE
VA First School
WIMB BH21 ....336 A7
Wimborne Town FC
WIMB BH21 ....207 G3
Winchcombe J & I School
NWBY RG14 ....27 J7
Winchelsea Special School
BKME/WDN BH12 ....212 D7
Winchester Agricultural
Museum *WINC* S023 ....25 G3
Winchester Cathedral
WINC S023 ....25 G6
Winchester City FC
WINC S023 ....25 H2
Winchester City Mill (NT)
WINC S023 ....25 J6
Winchester City Museum
WINC S023 ....25 G6
Winchester College
WINC S023 ....25 G8
Winchester Lawn Tennis Club
FUFL S022 ....24 C1
Winchester RFC
WINC S023 ....25 J2
Winchester Road Industrial
Estate *KBH* RG22 ....93 H2
The Winchester Royal Hotel
WINC S023 ....25 G5
Winklebury Centre
DEAN RG23 ....64 C7
Winklebury J & I School
DEAN RG23 ....64 F6
Winklebury Medical Centre
DEAN RG23 ....64 E6
Winnall CP School
WINC S023 ....25 L5
Winnall Farm Industrial Estate
WINC S023 ....25 K4
Winnall Trading Estate
WINC S023 ....25 L3
Winter Gardens Theatre
WCLF BH2 ....8 D7
Winterslow CE Primary School
RSAL SP5 ....282 F10
Winton Primary School
MOOR/WNTN BH9 ....213 L6
Winton School
AND SP10 ....96 F4
NBNE BH10 ....213 K7
Wispers School *HASM* GU27 ....118 C3
Wolverdene School
AND SP10 ....5 K7
Wolvesey Castle
WINC S023 ....25 H7
Woodcote Primary School
FHAM/STUB PO14 ....182 B4
Woodhill Preparatory School
CHFD S053 ....139 K1
HEND S030 ....149 M5
Woodlands Business Village
BSTK RG21 ....7 J2
Woodlands Community School
WEND S018 ....148 C4
Woodlands Education Centre
HORN PO8 ....155 K4
The Woodlands Lodge Hotel
TOTT S040 ....341 P9
Woodlea Primary School
BOR GU35 ....112 F3

Woodside Business Park
WHIT RG2 ....238 B1
Wooldings Vineyard
WHCH RG28 ....88 B3
Woolmer Hill Athletics Track
HASM GU27 ....115 K8
Woolmer Hill Technology
College *HASM* GU27 ....117 K1
Woolsbridge Industrial Estate
WIMB BH21 ....205 K2
Woolsbridge Manor Farm
Caravan Park *WIMB* BH21 ....205 K2
Woolsbridge Small Business
Centre *WIMB* BH21 ....205 J2
Woolston Infant School
ITCH S019 ....161 L6
Woolton Hill Junior School
KSCL RG20 ....246 A4
Wootey Primary School
ALTN GU34 ....106 F2
Wordsworth House
ROWN S016 ....146 B6
Wordsworth Infant School
WSHM S015 ....146 B7
Works Industrial Estate
FBDG SP6 ....196 F3
Worting County Infant
School *DEAN* RG23 ....64 C8
Wyke CP School
RGUW GU3 ....74 F4
Wykeham Gallery
STOK S020 ....285 P5
Wykeham House School
FHAM/PORC PO16 ....11 K5
Wykeham Industrial Estate
WINC S023 ....25 L2
The Wykeham Industrial
Estate *WINC* S023 ....25 M1
WINC S023 ....123 J2
Wynford Farm Industrial
Estate *ROMY* S051 ....130 F4
Wyvern Technology College
ELGH S050 ....141 J3
Yarrells Preparatory School
UPTN BH16 ....222 B1
Yateley Common Country
Park *BLKW* GU17 ....49 H5
Yateley Health Centre
YTLY GU46 ....48 F2
Yateley Infant School
YTLY GU46 ....48 F2
Yateley Manor
Preparatory School
YTLY GU46 ....48 F2
Yateley School & Sixth
Form Centre *YTLY* GU46 ....48 E3
Yeoman Industrial Park
ROWN S016 ....145 H6
Yeomans Industrial Park
CHAR BH8 ....214 E5
York Town Industrial Estate
CBLY GU15 ....50 C3
Youngs Industrial Estate
THLE RG7 ....37 M8
Yys Business Park
BKME/WDN BH12 ....224 C1
Zouch Primary School
NTID SP9 ....264 D12

Acknowledgements

The Post Office is a registered trademark of Post Office Ltd. in the UK and other countries.

Schools address data provided by Education Direct.

Petrol station information supplied by Johnsons

One-way street data provided by © Tele Atlas N.V. Tele Atlas

Garden centre information provided by

Garden Centre Association   Britains best garden centres

Wyevale Garden Centres

The statement on the front cover of this atlas is sourced, selected and quoted
from a reader comment and feedback form received in 2004

AA Street by Street   QUESTIONNAIRE

Dear Atlas User
Your comments, opinions and recommendations are very important to us.
So please help us to improve our street atlases by taking a few minutes to
complete this simple questionnaire.

You do not need a stamp (unless posted outside the UK). If you do not want to remove this page from your street atlas, then photocopy it or write your answers on a plain sheet of paper.

Send to: The Editor, AA Street by Street, FREEPOST SCE 4598,
Basingstoke RG21 4GY

ABOUT THE ATLAS...

Which city/town/county did you buy?

Are there any features of the atlas or mapping that you find particularly useful?

Is there anything we could have done better?

Why did you choose an AA Street by Street atlas?

Did it meet your expectations?

Exceeded ☐   **Met all** ☐   **Met most** ☐   **Fell below** ☐

Please give your reasons

                                                                 continued overleaf

Where did you buy it?

For what purpose? (please tick all applicable)

To use in your own local area ☐   To use on business or at work ☐

Visiting a strange place ☐   In the car ☐   On foot ☐

Other (please state)

LOCAL KNOWLEDGE...

Local knowledge is invaluable. Whilst every attempt has been made to make the information contained in this atlas as accurate as possible, should you notice any inaccuracies, please detail them below (if necessary, use a blank piece of paper) or e-mail us at *streetbystreet@theAA.com*

ABOUT YOU...

Name (Mr/Mrs/Ms)

Address

Postcode

Daytime tel no   **Mobile tel no**

E-mail address

Please only give us your e-mail address and mobile phone number if you wish to hear from us about other products and services from the AA and partners by e-mail or text or mms.

Which age group are you in?

Under 25 ☐   25-34 ☐   35-44 ☐   45-54 ☐   55-64 ☐   65+ ☐

Are you an AA member?   YES ☐   NO ☐

Do you have Internet access?   YES ☐   NO ☐

Thank you for taking the time to complete this questionnaire. Please send it to us as soon as possible, and remember, you do not need a stamp (unless posted outside the UK).

MX